SUMMARY OF SELECTED FINANCIAL RATIOS

RATIO NAME	FORMULA	PAGE REFERENCE*
Liquidity Analysis		
Working capital	Current Assets − Current Liabilities	62, 632
Current ratio	$\dfrac{\text{Current Assets}}{\text{Current Liabilities}}$	**73–74**, 633, 647
Acid-test ratio (quick ratio)	$\dfrac{\text{Cash}+\text{Marketable Securities}+\text{Current Receivables}}{\text{Current Liabilities}}$	633, 647
Cash flow from operations to current liabilities ratio	$\dfrac{\text{Net Cash Provided by Operating Activities}}{\text{Average Current Liablities}}$	634, 647
Accounts receivable turnover ratio	$\dfrac{\text{Net Credit Sales}}{\text{Average Accounts Receivable}}$	**319–321**, 635, 647
Number of days' sales in receivables	$\dfrac{\text{Number of Days in the Period}}{\text{Accounts Receivable Turnover}}$	**321**, 635, 647
Inventory turnover ratio	$\dfrac{\text{Cost of Goods Sold}}{\text{Average Inventory}}$	**238–239**, 636, 647
Number of days' sales in inventory	$\dfrac{\text{Number of Days in the Period}}{\text{Inventory Turnover}}$	**239**, 636, 647
Cash-to-cash operating cycle	Number of Days' Sales in Inventory + Number of Days' Sales in Receivables	636, 647
Solvency Analysis		
Debt-to-equity ratio	$\dfrac{\text{Total Liabilities}}{\text{Total Stockholders' Equity}}$	473, **474–476**, 638, 647
Times interest earned ratio	$\dfrac{\text{Net Income}+\text{Interest Expense}+\text{Income Tax Expense}}{\text{Interest Expense}}$	473, **474–476**, 638, 647
Debt service coverage ratio	$\dfrac{\text{Cash Flow from Operations before Interest and Tax Payments}}{\text{Interest and Principal Payments}}$	639, 647
Cash flow from operations to capital expenditures ratio	$\dfrac{\text{Cash Flow from Operations}-\text{Total Dividends Paid}}{\text{Cash Paid for Acquisitions}}$	640, 647
Profitability Analysis		
Gross profit ratio	$\dfrac{\text{Gross Profit}}{\text{Net Sales}}$	**219–220**, 647
Profit margin ratio	$\dfrac{\text{Net Income}}{\text{Net Sales}}$	75, 647
Return on assets ratio	$\dfrac{\text{Net Income}+\text{Interest Expense, Net of Tax}}{\text{Average Total Assets}}$	641, 647
Return on sales ratio	$\dfrac{\text{Net Income}+\text{Interest Expense, Net of Tax}}{\text{Net Sales}}$	642, 647
Asset turnover ratio	$\dfrac{\text{Net Sales}}{\text{Average Total Assets}}$	642, 647
Return on common stockholders' equity ratio	$\dfrac{\text{Net Income}-\text{Preferred Dividends}}{\text{Average Common Stockholders' Equity}}$	643, 647
Earnings per share	$\dfrac{\text{Net Income}-\text{Preferred Dividends}}{\text{Weighted Average Number of Common Shares Outstanding}}$	644, 647
Price/earnings ratio	$\dfrac{\text{Current Market Price}}{\text{Earnings per Share}}$	645, 647
Dividend payout ratio	$\dfrac{\text{Common Dividends per Share}}{\text{Earnings per Share}}$	646, 647
Dividend yield ratio	$\dfrac{\text{Common Dividends per Share}}{\text{Market Price per Share}}$	646, 647
Cash flow adequacy	$\dfrac{\text{Cash Flow from Operating Activities}-\text{Capital Expenditures}}{\text{Average Amount of Debt Maturing over Next Five Years}}$	**583–585**, 589

*boldface = **Ratio Analysis Model**

Using Financial Accounting Information

THE ALTERNATIVE TO DEBITS AND CREDITS

Gary A. Porter
DRAKE UNIVERSITY

Curtis L. Norton
ARIZONA STATE UNIVERSITY

Australia • Brazil • Mexico • Singapore • United Kingdom • United States

**Using Financial Accounting Information:
The Alternative to Debits and Credits,
10th edition**

Gary A. Porter, Curtis L. Norton

Vice President, General Manager,
Social Science & Qualitative Business:
Erin Joyner

Executive Product Director: Mike Schenk

Product Director: Jason Fremder

Senior Product Manager: Matt Filimonov

Content Development Manager: Daniel Celenza

Content Developer: Jonathan Gross

Senior Digital Production Project Manager:
Sally Nieman

Executive Marketing Manager: Robin LeFevre

Senior Content Project Manager: Tim Bailey

Manufacturing Planner: Doug Wilke

Production Service: Cenveo Publisher Services

Senior Art Director: Michelle Kunkler

Cover and Internal Designer: Red Hanger Design

Cover Image: iStockPhoto.com/Piotr Krzeslak

Connection Design Image:
© Toria/Shutterstock.com

Intellectual Property

  Analyst: Brittani Morgan

  Project Manager: Betsy Hathaway

For product information and technology assistance, contact us at
Cengage Learning Customer & Sales Support, 1-800-354-9706
For permission to use material from this text or product,
submit all requests online at **www.cengage.com/permissions**
Further permissions questions can be emailed to
permissionrequest@cengage.com

Library of Congress Control Number: 2016954444
Student Edition ISBN: 978-1-337-27633-7
Loose-Leaf Edition ISBN: 978-1-337-27639-9

Cengage Learning
20 Channel Center Street
Boston, MA 02210
USA

Cengage Learning is a leading provider of customized learning solutions with employees residing in nearly 40 different countries and sales in more than 125 countries around the world. Find your local representative at **www.cengage.com**.

Cengage Learning products are represented in Canada by Nelson Education, Ltd.

To learn more about Cengage Learning Solutions, visit **www.cengage.com**

Purchase any of our products at your local college store or at our preferred online store **www.cengagebrain.com**

Printed in the United States of America
Print Number: 04   Print Year: 2018

To those who really "count"
Melissa
Kathy, Amy, Andrew

In memory of
Sophie

Brief Contents

Contents

Preface

Seeing the Forest for the Trees

Accounting is more than just recording business events. It is a powerful tool for investors, managers, and decision makers. It is a common and powerful tool in every business. This is even more true for the majority of business students who may never see a journal entry in their entire professional careers. *Using Financial Accounting Information*, 10e is written for these students—people who may not become accountants but still need to understand why accounting is important.

Connecting to the Big Picture

By demonstrating that accounting is an important decision-making tool, Porter/Norton's *Using Financial Accounting Information*, 10e helps students see the big picture and understand how accounting is more than recording a series of events. Students who understand why accounting is important are more motivated to learn and succeed.

This text uses a variety of methods to connect students to the big picture. First, a hallmark of this text has always been emphasizing why accounting is important through the use of financial statements and other data for real-world company examples, chapter openers, and end-of-chapter material, giving students the opportunity to use that data to apply what they're learning.

This emphasis is continued through the text's unique transaction model. Each transaction in the text and the solutions manual is notated using a two-part element that focuses on the relationships between accounts, their increases and decreases, and the resulting articulation of the financial statements.

This style provides instructors with maximum flexibility in teaching these key concepts.

1. "Identify and Analyze" This element shows how each transaction affects the income statement and the balance sheet, with key additional information in an active learning format. Students learn to Identify and Analyze:
   - The type of business activity—operating, investing, or financing.
   - The accounts affected by the transaction.
   - The financial statement(s) affected by the transaction—balance sheet, income statement, or both.
2. Transaction-Effects Equation This element shows how each transaction affects the accounting equation, the balance sheet, the income statement, and stockholders' equity.

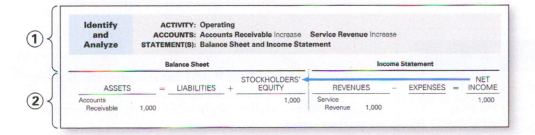

This integrated form of notation has benefits for both students and instructors:

- It provides a clear view of how transactions affect the balance sheet.
- Its separation of balance sheet and income statement sides differentiates these two equations and shows how the income statement elements are affected.

- Its arrow format better communicates the relationship between net income and stockholders' equity.
- When a transaction includes a contra account, this form explains clearly the effect of this account on the equation.

This model is extended into the end-of-chapter material and CengageNOWv2™. In CengageNOWv2, students are also expected to demonstrate that they understand the link between transactions and financial statements—consistent with the text.

Other features throughout the book help students make the connection and see the big picture:

- Focus on highly recognizable companies such as Chipotle, Panera Bread, Nike, and many others draws students into the chapter.

- Financial statements and notes from Chipotle and Panera Bread allow students to apply the accounting models they're learning to real financial data from two companies in the same industry.

The real-world flavor that demonstrates how accounting can be used to make decisions continues in the end-of-chapter activities. **Decision Cases** ask students to read and interpret financial statements:

DECISION CASES

Reading and Interpreting Financial Statements

Decision Case 4-1 Comparing Two Companies in the Same Industry: Chipotle and Panera Bread   **LO3**

Refer to the financial information for **Chipotle** and **Panera Bread** reproduced at the back of the book for the information needed to answer the following questions.

REAL WORLD

Required

1. Locate the note in each company's annual report included in its Form 10-K for the 2015 year in which it discusses revenue recognition. How does each company describe the point at which it recognizes revenue from customers? Are there any significant differences in the organizations' revenue recognition policies?
2. What dollar amount does Chipotle report for accounts receivable on its most recent balance sheet? What percent of the company's total current assets are comprised of accounts receivable? What is the dollar amount of Panera Bread's trade accounts receivable on its most recent balance sheet? What percent of total current assets is comprised of accounts receivable? For which company does its accounts receivable constitute a higher percentage of its total current assets?

- Each chapter highlights a focus company and real company information is used throughout the narrative and end-of-chapter activities to help students develop their analytical skills.

CONNECT TO THE REAL WORLD

NORDSTROM
READING THE BALANCE SHEET

4-1 The note from page 43 of Nordstrom's Form 10-K for the fiscal year ended January 30, 2016, explains that gift card liabilities are included in other current liabilities. The gift card liability is $327 million at the end of 2015 and $286 million at the end of 2014. Refer to Nordstrom's partial balance sheet shown in the chapter opener. What percentage of total current liabilities is made up of gift card liabilities at the end of 2015 and 2014?
(See answers on p. 205.)

- **Connect to the Real World** features ask students to read and interpret the financial statements of the chapter's focus company, applying what they have learned in the chapter.

- *NEW* **HOW WILL I USE ACCOUNTING?** feature **demonstrates relevance** by providing students with examples of how marketing, sales, and management professionals use accounting in their careers.

How Will I Use **ACCOUNTING?**

Inventory is the lifeblood of all businesses that sell products and chances are you will work for one of them at some time during your career. As a salesperson, you need to track inventory levels and know when to re-order merchandise. As a store manager, you need to evaluate the profitability of product lines and monitor how quickly inventory is turned over. Inventory matters to everyone in a business, not just the accountants.

- The Ratio Analysis Model guides students through formulating a question about a real company, and then calculating, comparing, and interpreting ratios. Students will identify relevant financial information, analyze that information, and make better business decisions based on what they uncover – powerfully demonstrating the relevance and importance of accounting.

A. The Ratio Analysis Model

1. Formulate the Question
How many times a year does the company turn over its accounts receivable?

2. Gather the Information from the Financial Statements
To calculate a company's accounts receivable turnover ratio, it is essential to know its net credit sales and the average balance in accounts receivable:

- Net credit sales: From the income statement
- Average accounts receivable: From the balance sheet at the end of the two most recent years

3. Calculate the Ratio

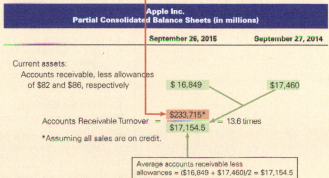

4. Compare the Ratio with Other Ratios
Ratios are of no use in a vacuum. It is necessary to compare them with prior years and with competitors.

ACCOUNTS RECEIVABLE TURNOVER RATIO			
Apple Inc.		Hewlett-Packard	
Year Ended September 26, 2015	Year Ended September 27, 2014	Year Ended October 31, 2015	Year Ended October 31, 2014
13.6 times	12.0 times	7.6 times**	7.5 times**

**Based on "Products and Services Revenues."

5. Interpret the Ratios

In fiscal year 2015, Apple Inc. turned over its accounts receivable an average of 13.6 times. This is faster than the turnover in the prior year, and the turnover for both years is quicker than the ratios for its competitor, Hewlett-Packard. An alternative way to look at a company's efficiency in managing its accounts receivable is to calculate the number of days, on average, that accounts receivables are outstanding. This measure is called **number of days' sales in receivables** and is calculated as follows for Apple Inc. in 2015, assuming 360 days in a year:

$$\text{Number of Days' Sales in Receivables} = \frac{\text{Number of Days in the Period}}{\text{Accounts Receivable Turnover Ratio}}$$

$$= \frac{360}{13.6}$$

$$= 26 \text{ days}$$

This measure tells us that it took Apple Inc. 26 days or less than a month on average to collect its accounts receivable.

The Business Decision Model moves a step beyond ratios by formulating a question as a user of financial information, gathering and analyzing the necessary information, making a decision, and then monitoring that decision. This framework, integrated throughout the text, provides students with models for honing their analysis and decision-making skills using real company information in a relevant, applicable context.

B. The Business Decision Model

1. Formulate the Question

If you were a banker, would you loan money to Apple Inc.?

2. Gather Information from the Financial Statements and Other Sources

This information will come from a variety of sources, not limited to but including:

- The balance sheet provides information about liquidity, the income statement regarding profitability, and the statement of cash flows on inflows and outflows of cash.
- The outlook for the computer industry, including consumer trends, foreign markets, labor issues, and other factors.
- The outlook for the economy in general.
- Alternative uses for the money.

3. Analyze the Information Gathered

- Compare Apple Inc.'s accounts receivable turnover ratio in (A) above with Hewlett-Packard as well as with industry averages.
- Look at trends over time in the accounts receivable turnover ratios.
- Look at trends in net income over time as an indication of the ability to control expenses other than cost of goods sold.
- Review projections for the economy and the industry.

4. Make the Decision

Taking into account all of the various sources of information, decide either to

- Loan money to Apple Inc. or
- Find an alternative use for the money

5. Monitor Your Decision

If you decide to make the loan, you will need to monitor it periodically. During the time the loan is outstanding, you will want to assess the company's continuing liquidity as well as other factors you considered before making the loan.

Built for Today's Students

In addition to helping students see the big picture and understand why accounting is important, Porter/Norton's *Using Financial Accounting Information*, 10e is built for today's students.

- **New to this edition, the unique modular organization** breaks the chapter into logical groupings of concepts, allowing students to absorb the chapter content in smaller sections for better retention.
- **Test Yourself reviews**, at the end of each module, provide students with an opportunity to check their understanding, answer questions, and work brief exercises to build confidence. Solutions to Test Yourself, located at the end of the chapter, allow students to check their answers.

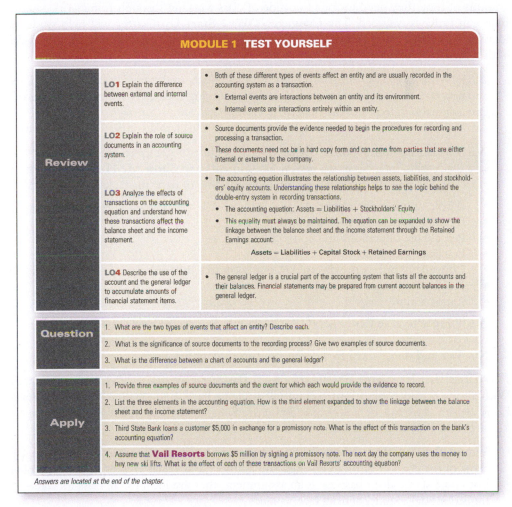

- **Study Tips** in the margins alert students to be on the lookout for certain things. This could be the similarities between two different concepts or a warning to watch out for a common pitfall.

CengageNOWv2. CengageNOWv2 for Porter/Norton's *Using Financial Accounting Information*, 10e helps elevate student thinking with unique content that addresses each stage of the learning process from motivation to mastery. This integrated solution provides tools and resources specifically developed to **motivate** students to learn, **apply accounting** concepts, and **achieve mastery** of course content.

In a recent survey of nearly 300 CengageNOW student users:

- Motivation: **77%** said that using CengageNOW made them more interested/engaged in the course.
- Application: **87%** said that CengageNOW made completing homework an effective learning process.
- Mastery: **72%** said CengageNOW helped them go beyond memorization and recall to reach higher levels of learning.
- **76%** said the use of CengageNOW helped them better understand why accounting matters and the importance of accounting in making critical business decisions.

STUDY TIP

Think of the Accumulated Depreciation account as an extension of the related asset account, in this case, the Store Fixtures account. Therefore, although the Store Fixtures account is not directly reduced for depreciation, an increase in its companion account, Accumulated Depreciation, has the effect of reducing the asset.

Motivation: Set Expectations and Prepare Students for the Course

CengageNOWv2 helps motivate students and get them ready to learn by reshaping their misconceptions about the introductory accounting course, and providing powerful tools to engage students.

CengageNOWv2 Start-Up Center. Students are often surprised by the amount of time they need to spend outside of class working through homework assignments in order to succeed. The **CengageNOWv2 Start-Up Center** will help students identify what they need to do and where they need to focus in order to be successful with a variety of brand new resources.

NEW **What Is Accounting?** Module ensures students understand course expectations and how to be successful in the introductory accounting course. This module consists of two assignable videos: *Introduction to Accounting* and *Success Strategies*. The Student Advice Videos offer advice from real students about what it takes to do well in the course.

NEW **Math Review Module**, designed to help students get up to speed with necessary math skills, includes **math review assignments** and **Show Me How** math review videos to ensure that students have an understanding of basic math skills, including:

- Whole number operations
- Decimal operations and rounding
- Percentage operations and conversion
- Fraction operations
- Converting numbers expressed in one form to a different form
- Positive and negative numbers
- Ratios and averages

NEW **How to Use CengageNOWv2 Module** focuses on learning accounting, not on a particular software system. Quickly familiarize your students with Cengage-NOWv2 and direct them to all of its built-in student resources.

Motivation: Engage Students and Better Prepare Them for Class.

With all the outside obligations accounting students have, finding time to read the textbook before class can be a struggle. Point students to the key concepts they need to know before they attend class.

Video: Tell Me More. Short Tell Me More lecture activities explain the core concepts of the chapter through an engaging auditory and visual presentation. Available both on a stand-alone basis or as an assignment, they are ideal for all class formats—flipped model, online, hybrid, face-to-face.

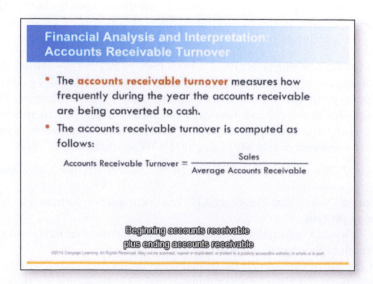

Students don't want to waste time going over concepts that they have already mastered. With the NEW Adaptive Study Plan, they can focus on learning new topics and fully understanding difficult concepts.

NEW Adaptive Study Plan in CengageNOWv2 is an assignable/gradable study center that adapts to each student's unique needs and provides a remediation pathway to keep students progressing. With the NEW Adaptive Study Plan, they can focus on learning new topics and fully understanding difficult concepts.

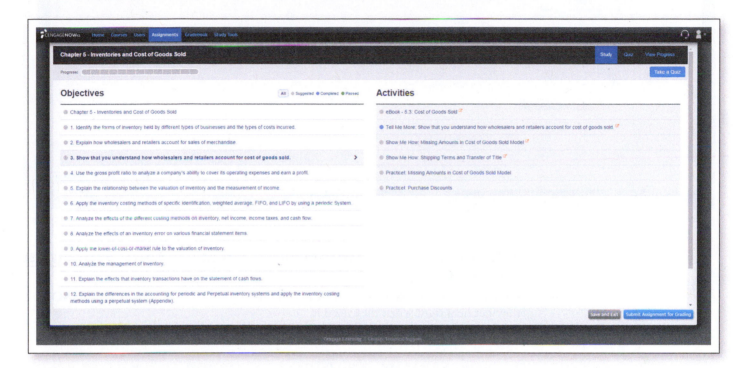

How Does It Work?

Step 1: Students take a chapter-level quiz consisting of random questions that cover both conceptual and procedural aspects of the chapter.

Step 2: Feedback is provided for each answer option explaining why the answer is right or wrong.

Step 3: Based on the quiz results, students are provided a remediation path that includes media assets and algorithmic practice problems to help them improve their understanding of the course material.

Instructors may use prerequisites that require students to achieve mastery in the Adaptive Study Plan before moving on to new material.

Using the Adaptive Study Plan, students may also review and check their knowledge with the new Practice! Activities. These items (generally one per learning objective) build application skills by allowing students to complete practice problems and "Try Another Version."

> "The new Adaptive Study Plan offers the benefit of customization coupled with remediation."
>
> – **Jennifer Schneider,**
> **professor at University of North Georgia**

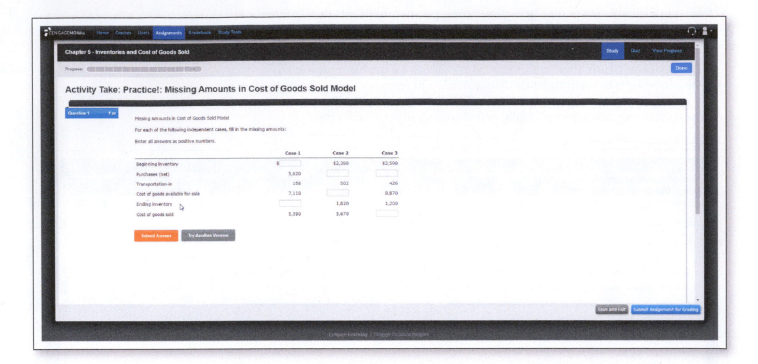

Application: Provide Help Right When Students Need It

Students often complete homework at odd times. And when they use CengageNOWv2, they get help right when they need it.

- **Check My Work Feedback** provides general guidance and hints as students work through homework assignments.
- *NEW* **Check My Work Feedback** in CengageNOWv2 now only reports on what students have actually attempted, which prevents them from "guessing" their way through assignments.

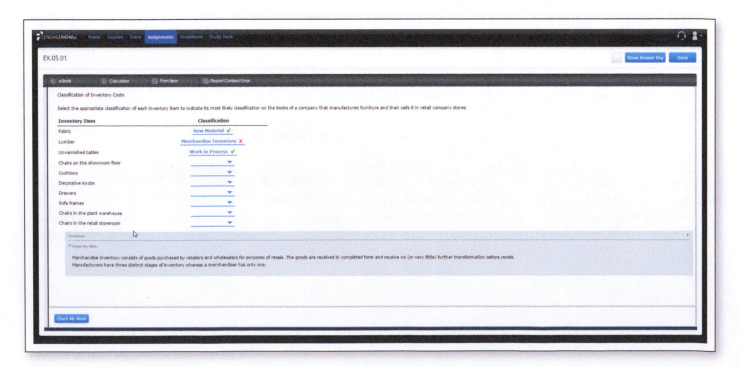

- **Post-Submission Feedback** is available after the assignment has been submitted and provides a detailed description of how to arrive at the solution.
- **Video: Show Me How**. Created for the most frequently assigned end-of-chapter items, NEW Show Me How problem demonstration videos provide a step-by-step model of a similar problem. Embedded tips and warnings help students avoid common mistakes and pitfalls.

Missing Amounts in Cost of Goods Sold Model

	Case 1	Case 2	Case 3
Beginning Inventory	$ 700	$2,500	$2,650
Purchases (net)	6,500	(c)	(e)
Transportation-in	300	550	450
Cost of goods available for sale	7,500	(d)	9,000
Ending inventory	(b)	2,000	1,500
Cost of goods sold	5,500	5,600	(f)

Case 1:

(a) Beginning Inventory = Cost of Goods Available for Sale – Cost of Goods Purchased

= $7,500 – $6,800

= $700

(b) Ending Inventory = Cost of Goods Available for Sale – Cost of Goods Sold

= Thus, by subtracting the cost of goods sold of $5,500

Mastery: Help Students Go Beyond Memorization to True Understanding.

Students often struggle to understand how concepts relate to one another. For most students, an introductory accounting course is their first exposure to both *business transactions* and the *accounting system*. While these concepts are already difficult to master individually, their combination and interdependency in the introductory accounting course often pose a challenge for students.

- **Mastery Problems**. New Mastery Problems enable you to assign problems and activities designed to test students' comprehension and mastery of difficult concepts. Can they apply what they have learned to a new problem set that offers a twist?
- **Decision Cases**. Decision Cases require students to read and interpret financial statements from real-world companies—applying learned concepts to real firms and real situations.

Enhanced Reporting Capabilities. CengageNOWv2's new Gradebook Analytics allow instructors unprecedented insight into classroom performance. This includes:

- classroom performance versus a variety of objectives, including Learning Objectives, AACSB, Bloom's, and more;
- classroom performance on specific items; and,
- classroom performance versus national scores.

Chapter-by-Chapter Changes

Chapter 1

- Introduced modular approach to chapter topics, including Test Yourself with Review, Question, and Apply at the end of each module.
- Introduced one of two new flagship companies, Chipotle Mexican Grill, Inc., as the focus company for Chapter 1.
- Revised Exhibits 1-1, 1-3, 1-7, and 1-8 to reflect new flagship company, Chipotle Mexican Grill, Inc.
- Introduced new feature: How Will I Use Accounting?
- Revised "Connect to the Real World" feature (Real World Practice in prior edition) to reflect new flagship company.
- Updated end-of-chapter material: E1-9, E1-16, P1-8, P1-9, P1-8A, and P1-9A.
- Revised DC1-1 and DC1-2 to reflect new flagship company, Chipotle Mexican Grill, Inc.
- Revised DC1-3 to reflect new flagship companies, Chipotle Mexican Grill, Inc., and Panera Bread Company.
- Added Answers to "Questions" and "Apply" at the end of the chapter for all modules.
- Added Answers to "Connect to the Real World" at the end of the chapter.

Chapter 2

- Introduced modular approach to chapter topics, including Test Yourself with Review, Question, and Apply at the end of each module.
- Introduced one of two new flagship companies, Panera Bread Company, as the focus company for Chapter 2.
- Introduced new feature: How Will I Use Accounting?
- Revised Exhibits 2-1, 2-2, and 2-3 to reflect new flagship company, Panera Bread Company.
- Revised "Connect to the Real World" feature (Real World Practice in prior edition) to reflect new flagship company.
- Revised Ratio Decision and Business Decision Models for the Current Ratio to reflect new flagship company.
- Revised Ratio Decision Model for the Profit Margin Ratio to reflect new flagship company.
- Revised Exercise 2-3 to reflect Regal Entertainment Group.
- Updated end-of-chapter material: P2-10 and P2-10A.
- Revised DC2-1 to reflect new flagship companies, Chipotle Mexican Grill, Inc., and Panera Bread Company.
- Revised DC2-2 to reflect new flagship company, Panera Bread Company.
- Added Answers to "Questions" and "Apply" at the end of the chapter for all modules.
- Added Answers to "Connect to the Real World" at the end of the chapter.

Chapter 3

- Introduced modular approach to chapter topics, including Test Yourself with Review, Question, and Apply at the end of each module.
- Introduced Vail Resorts, Inc., as the new focus company for Chapter 3.
- Revised "Connect to the Real World" feature (Real World Practice in prior edition) to reflect new focus company, Vail Resorts, Inc.
- Revised E3-8 and E3-17 to reflect new focus company, Vail Resorts, Inc.
- Revised DC3-1 to reflect new flagship companies, Chipotle Mexican Grill and Panera Bread Company.
- Revised DC3-2 to reflect new flagship company, Panera Bread Company.
- Updated end-of-chapter material: DC3-3.

- Added Answers to "Questions" and "Apply" at the end of the chapter for all modules.
- Added Answers to "Connect to the Real World" at the end of the chapter.

Chapter 4

- Introduced modular approach to chapter topics, including Test Yourself with Review, Question, and Apply at the end of each module.
- Updated the chapter opener with the most current information available and replaced the financial statements from Nordstrom as the focus company for Chapter 4.
- Introduced new feature: How Will I Use Accounting?
- Revised section on the revenue recognition principle to conform to new accounting standard.
- Updated "Connect to the Real World" (Real World Practice in prior edition) for new information for Nordstrom, Inc.
- Updated end-of-chapter material: DC4-2 and DC4-3.
- Revised DC4-1 to reflect new flagship companies, Chipotle Mexican Grill and Panera Bread Company.
- Added Answers to "Questions" and "Apply" at the end of the chapter for all modules.
- Added Answers to "Connect to the Real World" at the end of the chapter.

Chapter 5

- Introduced modular approach to chapter topics, including Test Yourself with Review, Question, and Apply at the end of each module.
- Updated the chapter opener with the most current information available and replaced the financial statements from Gap Inc. as the focus company for Chapter 5.
- Introduced new feature: How Will I Use Accounting?
- Revised Net Sales of Merchandise section to conform to new FASB standard on revenue recognition, "Revenue from Contracts with Customers."
- Revised coverage of purchase returns and allowances to conform to coverage of sales returns and allowances.
- Revised coverage of purchase discounts to illustrate the net method of recording.
- Updated Example 5-14 for Winnebago Industries' LIFO reserve.
- Revised Exhibit 5-9, substituting a partial statement of cash flows for Chipotle Mexican Grill, Inc.
- Updated "Connect to the Real World" (Real World Practice in prior edition) for new information for Gap Inc.
- Updated Ratio Model for the Gross Profit Ratio for new information available.
- Updated Ratio Model for the Inventory Turnover Ratio for new information available.
- Deleted Exercise requiring detailed analysis for purchase discounts, returns, and allowances.
- Updated end-of-chapter material: E5-15, P5-2, P5-5, P5-8, P5-14, P5-2A, P5-5A, P5-8A, P5-14A, DC5-2, and DC5-3.
- Revised DC5-1 to reflect new flagship companies, Chipotle Mexican Grill, Inc. and Panera Bread Company.
- Deleted Decision Case on sales returns and allowances.
- Revised DC5-9 to integrate the concept of ethics in accounting with the practice of modeling ethical decision making.
- Added Answers to "Questions" and "Apply" at the end of the chapter for all modules.
- Added Answers to "Connect to the Real World" at the end of the chapter.

Chapter 6

- Introduced modular approach to chapter topics, including Test Yourself with Review, Question, and Apply at the end of each module.
- Introduced Regal Entertainment Group as the new focus company for Chapter 6.

- Updated "Connect to the Real World" (Real World Practice in prior edition) for new flagship company, Panera Bread Company.
- Revised Exhibits 6-1, 6-3, and 6-4 to illustrate statements and reports for new focus company, Regal Entertainment Group.
- Revised DC6-1 to reflect new flagship companies, Chipotle Mexican Grill, Inc., and Panera Bread Company.
- Updated end-of-chapter material: DC6-2.
- Added Answers to "Questions" and "Apply" at the end of the chapter for all modules.
- Added Answers to "Connect to the Real World" at the end of the chapter.

Chapter 7

- Introduced modular approach to chapter topics, including Test Yourself with Review, Question, and Apply at the end of each module.
- Updated the chapter opener with the most current information available and replaced the financial statements from Apple Inc. as the focus company for Chapter 7.
- Introduced new feature: How Will I Use Accounting?
- Updated "Connect to the Real World" (Real World Practice in prior edition) for new information for Apple Inc.
- Updated Ratio Decision Model for the Accounts Receivable Turnover Ratio with new information available.
- Revised E7-5 to reflect Nike.
- Updated end-of-chapter material: P7-3, P7-3A, DC7-1, DC7-2, and DC7-3.
- Added Answers to "Questions" and "Apply" at the end of the chapter for all modules.
- Added Answers to "Connect to the Real World" at the end of the chapter.

Chapter 8

- Introduced modular approach to chapter topics, including Test Yourself with Review, Question, and Apply at the end of each module.
- Updated the chapter opener with the most current information available and replaced the financial statements from Nike as the focus company for Chapter 8.
- Introduced new feature: How Will I Use Accounting?
- Updated Ratio Decision Model with new information for Nike and Foot Locker.
- Updated end-of-chapter material: DC8-1 features Panera Bread Company, and DC8-2 reflects Panera Bread Company and Chipotle.
- Added Answers to "Questions" and "Apply" at the end of the chapter for all modules.
- Added Answers to "Connect to the Real World" at the end of the chapter.

Chapter 9

- Introduced modular approach to chapter topics, including Test Yourself with Review, Question, and Apply at the end of each module.
- Updated the chapter opener with the most current information available and replaced the financial statements from Starbucks as the focus company for Chapter 9.
- Introduced new feature: How Will I Use Accounting?
- Changed Exhibit 9-4 concerning contingent liabilities.
- Updated P9-2 for Burger King, P9-3 for Brinker, P9-2A for McDonald's, and P9-3A for Darden Restaurants.
- Changed DC9-1 to Panera Bread Company and Chipotle.
- Updated DC9-2 for Caribou Coffee, DC9-3 for Walmart, and DC9-4 for Hewlett-Packard.
- Added Answers to "Questions" and "Apply" at the end of the chapter for all modules.
- Added Answers to "Connect to the Real World" at the end of the chapter.

Chapter 10

- Introduced modular approach to chapter topics, including Test Yourself with Review, Question, and Apply at the end of each module.
- Updated the chapter opener with the most current information available and replaced the financial statements from Coca-Cola and Pepsi as the focus companies for Chapter 10.
- Updated Ratio Decision Model with new information for Coca-Cola and Pepsi.
- Eliminated references to extraordinary items because of FASB pronouncement.
- Updated P10-9 on Walgreens and P10-9A on Boeing.
- Retained the section on leasing but noted pending FASB pronouncement. This module can be skipped by instructors and it will not affect other portions of the chapter.
- DC10-1 features Panera Bread Company, and DC10-2 reflects Panera Bread Company and Chipotle. DC10-3 has been updated for Pepsi.
- Added Answers to "Questions" and "Apply" at the end of the chapter for all modules.
- Added Answers to "Connect to the Real World" at the end of the chapter.

Chapter 11

- Introduced modular approach to chapter topics, including Test Yourself with Review, Question, and Apply at the end of each module.
- Updated the chapter opener with the most current information available and replaced the financial statements from Southwest Airlines as the focus company for Chapter 11.
- Introduced new feature: How Will I Use Accounting?
- Updated end-of-chapter material: P11-7 for Southwest Airlines and P11-7A for Costco.
- DC11-1 features Panera Bread Company and Chipotle, and DC11-2 highlights Panera Bread Company.
- Made substantial changes to Interactive Problem to eliminate leasing as one of the alternatives. Problem is now more straigtforward.
- Added Answers to "Questions" and "Apply" at the end of the chapter for all modules.
- Added Answers to "Connect to the Real World" at the end of the chapter.

Chapter 12

- Introduced modular approach to chapter topics, including Test Yourself with Review, Question, and Apply at the end of each module.
- Updated the chapter opener with the most current information available and replaced the financial statements of the focus company for Chapter 12.
- Deleted exhibit detailing cash flow and net income differences for four companies.
- Updated "Connect to the Real World" (Real World Practice in prior edition) for new flagship company Chipotle Mexican Grill, Inc., and for new information for Walgreens Boots Alliance.
- Updated Ratio Decision Model for the Cash Flow Adequacy Ratio with new information available.
- Updated end-of-chapter material: E12-4, DC12-2, and DC12-3.
- Revised DC12-1 to reflect new flagship companies, Chipotle Mexican Grill, Inc., and Panera Bread Company.
- Added Answers to "Questions" and "Apply" at the end of the chapter for all modules.
- Added Answers to "Connect to the Real World" at the end of the chapter.

Chapter 13

- Introduced modular approach to chapter topics, including Test Yourself with Review, Question, and Apply at the end of each module.
- Updated the chapter opener with the most current information available and replaced the financial statements from lululemon athletica inc. as the focus company for Chapter 13.

- Updated Exhibit 13-1, with the most current information available for lululemon athletica inc.
- Updated "Connect to the Real World" (Real World Practice in prior edition) for new information for lululemon athletica inc. and for new flagship company Chipotle Mexican Grill, Inc.
- Deleted Appendix on Reporting and Analyzing Other Income Statement Items and end-of-chapter material to conform to new accounting standard to no longer allow recognition of extraordinary items on the income statement.
- Updated Review Problem for the most current information available for lululemon athletica inc.
- Updated end-of-chapter material: E13-5, E13-6, E13-7, E13-8, and E13-11.
- Revised DC13-1 and DC13-2 to reflect new flagship company, Chipotle Mexican Grill, Inc.
- Revised DC13-3 to reflect new flagship companies, Chipotle Mexican Grill, Inc., and Panera Bread Company.
- Revised DC13-4 to reflect new flagship company, Panera Bread Company.
- Added Answers to "Questions" and "Apply" at the end of the chapter for all modules.
- Added Answers to "Connect to the Real World" at the end of the chapter.

Additional Instructor and Student Supplements

Instructor's Manual

The Instructor's Manual contains detailed lecture outlines, lecture topics, and suggestions for classroom activities. The chapter activities in the Instructor's Manual have been analyzed and assigned the same set of objectives that are used in the Solutions Manual and the Test Bank (available on the Instructor Companion website).

Solutions Manual

The Solutions Manual, by the text authors, consists of solutions to all the end-of-chapter material keyed to learning objectives and using the transaction effects equation found in the text. (Available on the Instructor Companion website.)

Test Bank

The Test Bank contains a comprehensive set of test items to meet every assessment need from brief exercises to problems and decision cases. The Test Bank is offered in Cognero.

Cengage Learning Testing Powered by Cognero is a flexible, online system that allows instructors to:

- author, edit, and manage test bank content from multiple Cengage Learning solutions
- create multiple test versions in an instant
- deliver tests from your LMS, your classroom, or wherever you want

Excel® Templates

Selected problems in each chapter may be solved on a Microsoft Excel spreadsheet to increase awareness of basic software applications. Just download the Excel spreadsheets for homework items that are identified by icons in the text. (Excel templates are available on the Student Resources page of the product website. Password-protected Instructor solutions are available on the Instructor Companion website.)

PowerPoint® Slides

Student PowerPoint Slides, a smaller version of the Instructor PowerPoint Lectures, allow students to get ready for upcoming lectures, quizzes, homework, and exams with core material needed for chapter study. (Student PowerPoint Slides are available on the Student Resources page of the product website. More detailed, password-protected Instructor PowerPoint Slides are available on the Instructor Companion website.)

Student Web Resources

Chapter-by-chapter quizzes, topical discussions, updates on IFRS integration, and more are available. These items help reinforce and shed light on text topics. Discover more by logging into the text website. Visit www.cengagebrain.com.

Acknowledgments

Among those who have served as reviewers for this text are the following, to whom we are grateful for their insights:

Scott Ballantyne
Alvernia University
Cindy Bleasdale
Hilbert College
Bradley Boercker
Fletcher College, Lone Star College
Melba Boling
Virginia Highlands Community College
Bryan Bouchard
Southern New Hampshire University
Amy Bourne
Oregon State University
Scott Boylan
Washington and Lee University
Justin Breidenbach
Ohio Wesleyan University
Amy Browning
Ivy Tech Community College
Teresa Buckner
West Virginia Wesleyan College
Rachel Butts
Embry-Riddle Aeronautical University
Edward J. Bysiek
St. Bonaventure University
Allen Cherry
Loyola Marymount University
Cheryl Corke
Genesee Community College
Louann Cummings
The University of Findlay
Terena Dampier
Embry-Riddle Aeronautical University
Dana D'Angelo
Drexel University
Dori Danko
Grand Valley State University
Robert Derstine
West Chester University of Pennsylvania
Patricia Dorris-Crenny
Villanova University
Gerald Doyle, CPA
Mountwest Community & Technical College
James Emig
Villanova University
John A. Falk
DeSales University
Lucile Faurel
Arizona State University
Kenneth W. Gaines
East-West University

Carolyn Galantine
Pepperdine University
Andy Garcia
Bowling Green State University
Amy Giesler
Butler University
Joohyung Ha
University of San Francisco
Ben Johnson
University of Evansville
Benjamin W. Johnson
University of Evansville
Kailani Knutson
Porterville College
Christopher Kwak
De Anza College
Brandon Lanciloti
Freed-Harmon University
Greg Lauer
North Iowa Area Community College
Natasha Librizzi
Milwaukee Area Technical College
Anthony Masino
East Tennessee State University
Keith McBride
Northeast Alabama Community College
Allison McLeod
University of North Texas
Tammy McWherter
Mid-Continent University
Michael Meyer
University of Notre Dame
Jacqueline Michaud
Alvirne High School
Paul San Miguel
Western Michigan University
Don Minyard
University of Alabama
Jennifer Morton
Ivy Tech Community College
Rania Mousa
University of Evansville
Albert Nagy
John Carroll University
Ramesh Narasimhan
Montclair State University
Sy Pearlman
California State University Long Beach
Janice Pitera
SUNY-Broome

Wendy K. Potratz
University of Wisconsin Oshkosh
Cindy Powell
Southern Nazarene University
Robert Rusnacko
North Hennepin Community College
Monica Salomon
University of West Florida
Geeta Shankar
University of Dayton
Gregory Sinclair, CPA
San Francisco State University
Jere Smith, MBA, PhD (ABD)
Avila University
Ahmad Sohrabian
California State Polytechnic University, Pomona
Leslie "Andy" Speck
Embry-Riddle Aeronautical University
Jason Stanfield
Purdue University
George Starbuck
McMurry University
Ronald Strittmater
North Hennepin Community College
John Surdick
Xavier University
Steven Thoede
Texas State University, San Marcos
Robin Thomas
North Carolina State University
MaryBeth Tobin
Bridgewater State University
Greg Tondi
New Jersey City University
Melanie Torborg
Globe University/Minnesota School of Business
Jeannette Toth
University at Buffalo
Mark Ulrich
St. John's University
Dale Walker
Harding University; Heifer International Education Program
Roddrick West
Everest College, Dallas
Wendy Wilson
Texas Christian University
Bijan Zayer
DeVry University

Throughout previous editions, many other individuals have contributed helpful suggestions that have resulted in many positive changes. Although they are not cited here, we remain grateful for their assistance.

We also wish to thank Domenic Tavella, *Carlow University*. His help with supplements and verification aided us greatly. We are grateful to Cenveo Publisher Services for their invaluable production assistance. Finally, we are grateful to the editorial, marketing, media, and production staffs at Cengage Learning, primarily Matt Filimonov, Danny Celenza, Jonathan Gross, Andrea Meyer, Robin LeFevre, Sally Nieman, and Tim Bailey for their extensive help with the tenth edition and its supplements.

Gary A. Porter
Curtis L. Norton
September 2016

About the Authors

Gary A. Porter is currently a Distinguished Lecturer at Drake University. He earned Ph.D. and M.B.A. degrees from the University of Colorado and his B.S.B.A. from Drake University. As Professor of Accounting, Dr. Porter served as Department Chair and taught at numerous universities. He has published in the *Journal of Accounting Education, Journal of Accounting, Auditing & Finance,* and *Journal of Accountancy,* among others, and has conducted numerous workshops on the subjects of introductory accounting education and corporate financial reporting.

Dr. Porter's professional activities include experience as a staff accountant with Deloitte & Touche, a participant in KPMG Peat Marwick Foundation's Faculty Development program, and a leader in numerous bank training programs. He has won an Excellence in Teaching Award from the University of Colorado and Outstanding Professor Awards from both San Diego State University and the University of Montana. He served on the Illinois CPA Society's Innovations in Accounting Education Grants Committee, the steering committee of the Midwest region of the American Accounting Association, and the board of directors of the Chicago chapter of Financial Executives International.

Dr. Porter currently serves on the National Advisory Council for Drake University's College of Business and Public Administration. He is a member of the American Accounting Association and Financial Executives International.

Curtis L. Norton is currently a Clinical Professor at Arizona State University. He is also a Professor Emeritus at Northern Illinois University in Dekalb, Illinois, where he has taught since 1976. Dr. Norton received his Ph.D. from Arizona State University and an M.B.A. from the University of South Dakota. Dr. Norton earned the University Excellence in Teaching Award at NIU and has published in *The Accounting Review, The Journal of Accounting Education, CPA Journal,* and other journals. A member of the American Accounting Association and Financial Executives International, he also consults and conducts training for private and governmental authorities, banks, utilities, and others.

Using Financial Accounting Information

THE ALTERNATIVE TO DEBITS AND CREDITS

10e

Accounting as a Form of Communication

MODULES	LEARNING OBJECTIVES	WHY IS THIS CHAPTER IMPORTANT?
1 **The Nature of Business**	**LO1** Explain what business is about. **LO2** Distinguish among the forms of organization. **LO3** Describe the various types of business activities.	• You need to know what a business is. (See p. 4.) • You need to know what forms of organization carry on business activities. (See pp. 4–6.) • You need to know in what types of business activities those organizations engage. (See pp. 6–8.)
2 **Accounting and Financial Statements**	**LO4** Define accounting and identify the primary users of accounting information and their needs. **LO5** Explain the purpose of each of the financial statements and the relationships among them and prepare a set of simple statements.	• You need to know what net income is and how it is measured. (See p. 13.) • You need to know how revenue and net income relate to a company's assets. (See pp. 12–13.) • You need to know where the various items appear on a company's financial statements. (See pp. 12–15.)
3 **Conceptual Framework of Accounting**	**LO6** Identify and explain the primary assumptions made in preparing financial statements. **LO7** Identify the various groups involved in setting accounting standards and the role of auditors in determining whether the standards are followed. **LO8** Explain the critical role that ethics plays in providing useful financial information.	• You need to know who determines the rules for the preparation of financial statements. (See pp. 21–22.)

Area 52 Advertising Inc/Getty Images

CHIPOTLE MEXICAN GRILL, INC.

Why is learning financial accounting important? Why should you care about learning to read the financial statements of a company?

Simply put, the more you know about how successful companies work, the better are your chances of doing well in your chosen field. And to know why these companies are successful you need to be able to read their financial statements. Whatever you plan to do, your knowledge of business and accounting helps you compete whether you invest, work for a company, or go into business for yourself.

Consider one very successful company, **Chipotle Mexican Grill, Inc**. Maybe you are a frequent customer at one of its restaurants. The company got its start in 1993, when Steve Ells left his job as a chef and with a modest loan from his parents opened his first restaurant in a former ice cream shop in Denver. Over the next few years, additional restaurants were opened in the Denver area. In 1998 the entrepreneur brought in outside investors to help finance his grow-

ing chain. And, in 2006, Chipotle went public on the New York Stock Exchange.

With each of these decisions Steve Ells made was a calculated risk: quitting his job to go it alone, opening new restaurants, bringing in new investors, and going public. How can we know whether they were good decisions? The financial statements produced by an accounting system go a long way in assessing a company's performance. Look at the Revenue data shown below as they appeared in Chipotle's 2015 Form 10-K, the annual report filed with the Securities and Exchange Commission. You can see that Chipotle has grown to a chain of 2,010 restaurants generating revenue of over $4.5 billion!

As you study accounting, you will learn how to read financial statements and what they can tell you about a company's performance and the decisions they make—such as those made by a one-time chef who built one of the most successful restaurant chains in the country.

Revenue

	Year ended December 31,			% increase (decrease) 2015 over	% increase 2014 over
	2015	2014	2013	2014	2013
	(dollars in millions)				
Revenue	$4,501.2	$4,108.3	$3,214.6	9.6%	27.8%
Average restaurant sales	$ 2.424	$ 2.472	$ 2.169	(1.9%)	14.0%
Comparable restaurant sales increases	0.2%	16.8%	5.6%		
Number of restaurants as of the end of the period	2,010	1,783	1,595	12.7%	11.8%
Number of restaurants opened in the period, net of relocations	227	188	185		

Source: Chipotle Mexican Grill, Inc.: website and Form 10-K for the Fiscal Year Ended December 31, 2015.

MODULE 1 THE NATURE OF BUSINESS

Broadly defined, **business** consists of all activities necessary to provide the members of an economic system with goods and services. Certain business activities focus on providing goods or products such as ice cream, automobiles, and computers. Some of these companies produce or manufacture the products. Other companies are involved in the distribution of the products while others sell directly to the consumer, as does Chipotle in its restaurants. Other business activities, by their nature, are service-oriented. A broad range of service providers, such as **Walt Disney** and **United Airlines**, provide evidence of the growing importance of the service sector in the U.S. economy.

EXAMPLE 1-1 Identifying Types of Businesses

To appreciate the kinds of enterprises in our economy, consider the various types of companies that have a stake in the delivery of a shipment of cheese to Chipotle. First, a *supplier* of raw material, in this case, a dairy, must deliver the milk to make cheese to a *manufacturer* or producer. The producer uses the milk to make the cheese. At this stage, the producer sells the cheese to a *distributor* or *wholesaler*, who in turn sells the cheese to a restaurant such as Chipotle. Additionally, *service companies* are involved, such as the transportation companies that deliver the goods to the various companies in the process. Exhibit 1-1 summarizes the various types of businesses.

EXHIBIT 1-1 Types of Businesses

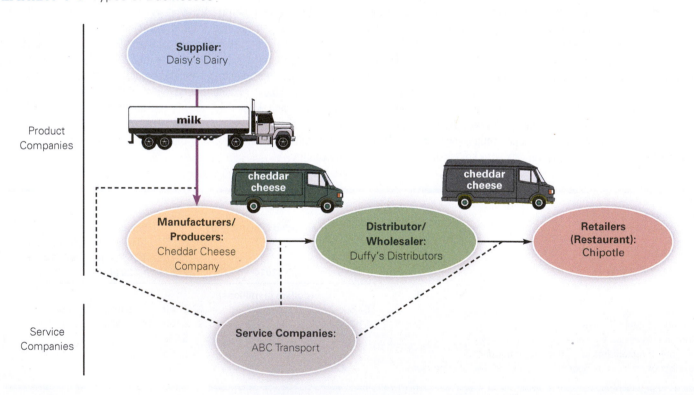

Forms of Organization

One convenient way to categorize the many different types of organizations in our society is to distinguish between those that are organized to earn money and those that exist for some other purpose. Although the lines can become blurred, *business entities* such as

Chipotle generally are organized to earn a profit, whereas *nonbusiness entities* generally exist to serve various segments of society. Both types are summarized in Exhibit 1-2.

EXHIBIT 1-2 Forms of Organization

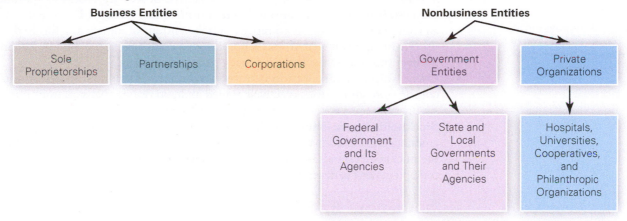

Business Entities

Business entities are organized to earn a profit. Legally, a profit-oriented company is one of three types: a sole proprietorship, a partnership, or a corporation.

Sole Proprietorships This form of organization is characterized by a single owner. Many small businesses are organized as **sole proprietorships**, often owned and operated by the same person. Because of the close relationship between the owner and the business, the affairs of the two must be kept separate. This is one example in accounting of the **economic entity concept**, which requires that a single, identifiable unit of organization be accounted for in all situations. For example, assume that Bernie Berg owns a neighborhood grocery store. In paying monthly bills such as utilities and supplies, Bernie must separate his personal costs from the costs associated with the grocery business. In turn, financial statements prepared for the business must not intermingle Bernie's personal affairs with the company affairs.

Unlike the distinction made for accounting purposes between an individual's personal and business affairs, the Internal Revenue Service (IRS) does not recognize the separate existence of a proprietorship from its owner. That is, a sole proprietorship is not a taxable entity; the business's profits are taxed on the individual's return.

Partnerships A **partnership** is a business owned by two or more individuals. Many small businesses begin as partnerships. When two or more partners start out, they need an agreement as to how much each will contribute to the business and how they will divide any profits. This agreement may be an oral understanding between the partners, or it may be a formalized written document.

Public accounting firms, law firms, and other types of service companies are often organized as partnerships. Like a sole proprietorship, a partnership is not a taxable entity. Individual partners pay taxes on their proportionate shares of the business's profits.

Corporations Although sole proprietorships and partnerships dominate in sheer number, corporations control a majority of the private resources in this country. A **corporation** is an entity organized under the laws of a particular state.

To start a corporation, articles of incorporation must be filed with the state. If the articles are approved by the state, a corporate charter is issued and the corporation can begin to issue stock. A **share of stock** is a certificate that acts as evidence of ownership in a corporation. Stocks of many corporations are traded on organized stock exchanges such as the New York Stock Exchange. Chipotle's stock is traded on the New York Stock Exchange.

Business entity
An organization operated to earn a profit.

Sole proprietorship
A form of organization with a single owner.

Economic entity concept
The assumption that a single, identifiable unit must be accounted for in all situations.

Partnership
A business owned by two or more individuals; the organization form often used by accounting firms and law firms.

Corporation
A form of entity organized under the laws of a particular state; ownership evidenced by shares of stock.

Share of stock
A certificate that acts as evidence of ownership in a corporation.

What are the advantages of running a business as a corporation?

- **A corporation has the ability to raise large amounts of money in a relatively brief period of time.** This is what prompted Chipotle to eventually "go public." To raise money, the company sold a specific type of security: stock. Corporations may also issue bonds. A **bond** is different from a share of stock because it represents a promise by the company to repay a certain amount of money at a future date. In other words, if you were to buy a bond from a company, you would be lending it money. Interest on the bond is usually paid semiannually.
- **Ownership in a corporation is transferred easily.** If you hold shares of stock in a corporation whose stock is actively traded and you decide that you want out, you simply call your broker and put in an order to sell.
- **Stockholders have limited liability.** Generally, a stockholder is liable only for the amount contributed to the business. That is, if a company goes out of business, the most the stockholder stands to lose is the amount invested. On the other hand, both proprietors and general partners usually can be held personally liable for the debts of the business.

Bond
A certificate that represents a corporation's promise to repay a certain amount of money and interest in the future.

Nonbusiness Entities

Most **nonbusiness entities** are organized to serve the needs of various segments of society. For example, a hospital provides health care to its patients. A municipal government is operated for the benefit of its citizens. A local school district meets the educational needs of the community's youth.

None of these entities has an identifiable owner. The lack of an identifiable owner and of the profit motive changes the type of accounting used by nonbusiness entities. This type, called *fund accounting,* is discussed in advanced accounting courses. Regardless of the lack of a profit motive in nonbusiness entities, they still need the information provided by an accounting system. For example, a local government needs detailed cost breakdowns in order to levy taxes. A hospital may want to borrow money and will need financial statements to present to the prospective lender.

Nonbusiness entity
An organization operated for some purpose other than to earn a profit.

Organizations and Social Responsibility

Although nonbusiness entities are organized specifically to serve members of society, U.S. business entities recognize the societal aspects of their overall mission and have established programs to meet these responsibilities. Some companies focus on local charities, while others donate to national or international causes.

The Nature of Business Activity

Corporations engage in many different types of activities. However, these activities can be categorized into one of three types: financing, investing, or operating.

LO3 Describe the various types of business activities.

Financing Activities

All businesses must start with financing. Steve Ells needed money in the 1990s to open his first Chipotle restaurant, so he went to his parents for a modest loan. The company needed additional financing later and thus made the decision in 2006 to sell stock to the public. Most companies not only sell stock to raise money but also borrow from various sources to finance their operations. These financing activities bring up two important accounting terms: *liabilities* and *capital stock.*

EXAMPLE 1-2 Distinguishing Between Liabilities and Capital Stock

A liability is an obligation of a business. When a company borrows money at a bank, the liability is called a *note payable.* When a company sells bonds, the obligation is termed *bonds payable.* Amounts owed to the government for taxes are called taxes *payable.* When Chipotle buys chicken and the supplier gives Chipotle 30 days to pay the amount owed, Chipotle's obligation is called *accounts payable.*

Liability
An obligation of a business.

Capital stock is the term used by accountants to indicate the dollar amount of stock sold to the public. Capital stock differs from liabilities in one very important respect. Those who buy stock in a corporation are not lending money to the business, as are those who buy bonds in the company or make a loan in some other form. One who buys stock in a company is called a **stockholder**, and that person is providing a permanent form of financing to the business. In other words, there is no due date when the stockholder must be repaid. Normally, the only way for a stockholder to get back his or her original investment from buying stock is to sell it to someone else. One who buys bonds in a company or in some other way makes a loan to it is called a **creditor**. A creditor does *not* provide a permanent form of financing to the business. That is, the creditor expects repayment of the amount loaned and, in many instances, payment of interest for the use of the money.

Capital stock
Indicates the owners' contributions to a corporation.

Stockholder
One of the owners of a corporation.
Alternate term: Shareholder.

Creditor
Someone to whom a company or person has a debt.
Alternate term: Lender.

Investing Activities

Once funds are generated from creditors and stockholders, money is available to invest in assets. **An asset is a future economic benefit to a business.** For example, cash is an asset to a company. To Chipotle, its restaurants are assets, as is its inventory of ingredients on hand for use in making menu items. However, not all assets are tangible in nature, as are buildings, equipment, and inventory.

Asset
A future economic benefit.

EXAMPLE 1-3 Identifying Assets

Assume that a company acquires a patent that will give it the exclusive right to produce a certain product. The right to the future economic benefits from the patent is an asset. In summary, an asset is a valuable resource to the company that controls it.

Notice the tie between assets and liabilities. Although there are some exceptions, most liabilities are settled by transferring assets. The asset most often used to settle a liability is cash.

Operating Activities

Once funds are obtained from financing activities and investments are made in productive assets, a business is ready to begin operations. Every business is organized with a purpose in mind. The purpose of some businesses, such as Chipotle, is to sell a *product*. Other companies provide *services*. Service-oriented businesses are becoming an increasingly important sector of the U.S. economy. Some of the largest corporations in this country, such as banks and airlines, sell services rather than products.

Revenue is the inflow of assets resulting from the sale of products and services. When a company makes a cash sale, the asset it receives is cash. When a sale is made on credit, the asset received is an account receivable. Revenue represents the dollar amount of sales of products and services for a specific period of time.

Revenue
An inflow of assets resulting from the sale of goods and services.

An **expense** is the outflow of assets resulting from the sale of goods and services. Expenses must be incurred to operate a business.

Expense
An outflow of assets resulting from the sale of goods and services.

- Chipotle must pay its employees salaries and wages.
- Suppliers must be paid for purchases of inventory, and the utility company has to be paid for heat and electricity.
- The government must be paid the taxes owed it.

Summary of Business Activities

Exhibit 1-3 summarizes the three types of activities conducted by a business. A company obtains money from various types of financing activities, uses the money raised to invest in productive assets, and then provides goods and services to its customers. Actual businesses have many different financing, investing, and operating activities going on at any one time.

EXHIBIT 1-3 A Model of Business Activities

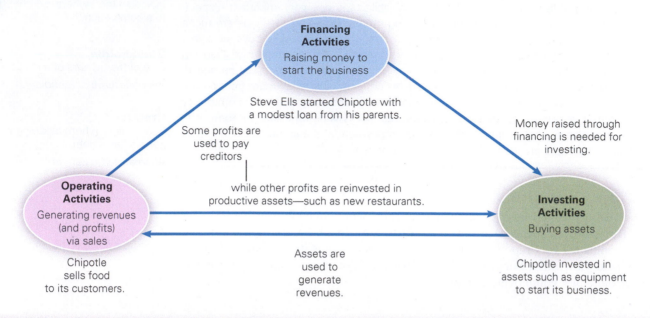

MODULE 1 TEST YOURSELF

Review		
	LO1 Explain what business is about.	• Business consists of all activities necessary to provide members of an economic system with goods and services. Suppliers, manufacturers, wholesalers, and retailers are examples of product companies.
	LO2 Distinguish among the forms of organization.	• Some entities are organized to earn a profit, while others are organized to serve various segments of society. • The three forms of business entities are sole proprietorships, partnerships, and corporations.
	LO3 Describe the various types of business activities.	• All business activities can be categorized as operating, investing, or financing activities. • Financing activities involve raising money from contributions made by the owners of a business as well as obtaining loans from outsiders. • Companies invest the amounts raised from financing activities in various types of assets, such as inventories, buildings, and equipment. • Once funds are obtained and investments are made in productive assets, a business can begin operations. Operating activities involve providing goods and services to customers.

Question	
	1. What is business about? What do all businesses have in common?
	2. What is an asset? Give three examples.
	3. What is a liability? How does the definition of *liability* relate to the definition of *asset*?
	4. Business entities are organized as one of three distinct forms. What are these three forms?

Apply	
	1. What does it mean when you own a share of stock in a company rather than one of its bonds?
	2. Consider your own situation in terms of assets and liabilities. Name three of your financial assets. Name three of your financial liabilities.
	3. What are the three distinct types of business activity in which companies engage? Assume that you start your own company to rent bicycles in the summer and skis in the winter. Give an example of at least one of each of the three types of business activities in which you would engage.

Answers are located at the end of the chapter.

MODULE 2 ACCOUNTING AND FINANCIAL STATEMENTS

Accounting is often referred to as the language of business. In fact, **accounting** is "the process of identifying, measuring, and communicating economic information to permit informed judgments and decisions by users of the information."[1] Each of the three activities in this definition—*identifying, measuring,* and *communicating*—requires the judgment of a trained professional. Note that the definition refers to the users of economic information and the decisions they make.

Users of Accounting Information and Their Needs

Internal users, primarily the managers of a company, are involved in the daily affairs of the business. All other groups are external users.

Internal Users The management of a company is in a position to obtain financial information in a way that best suits its needs. For example, if Chipotle's management wants to find out if the monthly payroll is more or less than the budgeted amount, a report can be generated to provide the answer. **Management accounting** is the branch of accounting concerned with providing internal users (management) with information to facilitate planning and control. The ability to produce management accounting reports is limited only by the extent of the data available and the cost involved in generating the information.

External Users External users, those not directly involved in the operations of a business, need information that differs from that needed by internal users. In addition, the ability of external users to obtain the information is more limited. Without day-to-day contact with the business's affairs, outsiders must rely on the information presented by the company's management.

Certain external users such as the IRS require that information be presented in a very specific manner, and they have the authority of the law to ensure that they get the required information. Stockholders and creditors must rely on *financial statements* for their information.[2] **Financial accounting** is the branch of accounting concerned with communication with outsiders through financial statements.

Stockholders and Potential Stockholders Both existing and potential stockholders need financial information about a business. If you currently own stock in Chipotle, you need information that will aid in your decision either to continue to hold the stock or to sell it. If you are considering buying stock, you need financial information that will help in choosing among competing alternative investments. What has been the recent performance of the company in the stock market? What were its profits for the most recent year? How do these profits compare with those of the prior year? Did the company pay any dividends? One source for much of this information is the company's financial statements.

Bondholders, Bankers, and Other Creditors Before buying a bond in a company, you need assurance that the company will be able to pay you the amount owed at maturity and the periodic interest payments. Financial statements can help you to decide whether to purchase a bond. Similarly, before lending money, a bank needs financial information that will help it determine the company's ability to repay both the amount of the loan and interest.

Government Agencies Numerous government agencies have information needs specified by law. For example, the IRS is empowered to collect a tax on income from both

LO4 Define accounting and identify the primary users of accounting information and their needs.

Accounting
The process of identifying, measuring, and communicating economic information to various users.

Management accounting
The branch of accounting concerned with providing management with information to facilitate planning and control.

Financial accounting
The branch of accounting concerned with the preparation of financial statements for outsider use.

---

[1] American Accounting Association, *A Statement of Basic Accounting Theory* (Evanston, Ill.: American Accounting Association, 1966), p. 1.

[2] Technically, stockholders are insiders because they own stock in the business. In most large corporations, however, it is not practical for stockholders to be involved in the daily affairs of the business. Thus, they are better categorized here as external users because they normally rely on general-purpose financial statements, as do creditors.

individuals and corporations. Every year, a company prepares a tax return to report to the IRS the amount of income it earned. Another government agency, the Securities and Exchange Commission (SEC), was created in the aftermath of the Great Depression. This regulatory agency sets the rules under which financial statements must be prepared for corporations that sell their stock to the public on organized stock exchanges. Companies operating in specialized industries submit financial reports to other regulatory agencies such as the Interstate Commerce Commission (ICC) and the Federal Trade Commission (FTC).

Increasingly, global companies must consider the reporting requirements in foreign countries where they operate. For example, a company might be listed on a stock exchange in the United States as well as in Tokyo or London. Additionally, companies often need to file tax returns in other countries.

Other External Users Many other individuals and groups rely on financial information. A supplier of raw material needs to know the creditworthiness of a company before selling it a product on credit. To promote its industry, a trade association must gather financial information on the various companies in the industry. Other important users are stockbrokers and financial analysts. They use financial reports in advising their clients on investment decisions. All of these users rely to a large extent on accounting information provided by management. Exhibit 1-4 summarizes the various users of financial information and the types of decisions they must make.

EXHIBIT 1-4 Users of Accounting Information

Categories of Users	Examples of Users	Common Decision	Relevant Question
Internal	Management	Should we add another restaurant to our chain?	How much will it cost to build the restaurant?
External	Stockholder	Should I buy shares of Chipotle's stock?	How much did the company earn last year?
	Banker	Should I lend money to Chipotle?	What debts or liabilities does the company have?
	Employee	Should I ask for a raise?	How much are the company's revenues, and how much is it paying out in salaries and wages? Is the compensation it is paying reasonable compared to its revenues?
	Supplier	Should I allow Chipotle to buy chicken from me and pay me later?	What is the current amount of the company's accounts payable?

Using Financial Accounting Information

You are considering whether you should buy stock in Chipotle. The Financial Decision Framework below can be used to help make such investment decisions.

Let's say you have been eagerly awaiting an earnings announcement from Chipotle. You have eaten at the company's restaurants for a few years but never gave much thought to the financial side of its business. Use the Financial Decision Framework to help you make the decision.

FINANCIAL DECISION FRAMEWORK

Use the following decision process to help you make an investment decision about Chipotle or any other public company.

1. Formulate the Question

I saved $1,000 from my summer job.

- Should I invest $1,000 in Chipotle stock?

2. Gather Information from the Financial Statements and Other Sources

The information needed will come from a variety of sources:

- My personal finances at the present time
- Alternative uses for the $1,000
- The outlook for the industry
- Publicly available information about Chipotle, including its financial statements

3. Analyze the Information Gathered

The information in the financial statements can be used to perform:

- Ratio analysis (looking at relationships among financial statement items)
- Horizontal analysis (looking at trends over time)
- Vertical analysis (comparing financial statement items in a single period)
- Comparisons with competitors
- Comparisons with industry averages

4. Make the Decision

Taking into account all of the various sources of information, you decide either to:

- Use the $1,000 for something else
- Invest the $1,000 in Chipotle

5. Monitor Your Decision

If you do decide to invest, you will want to monitor your investment periodically. Whether you made a good decision will be based on the answers to these two questions:

- Have I received any dividends on my shares?
- Has the price of the stock increased above what I paid for it?

A critical step in this framework is gathering information from the financial statements, the means by which an accountant communicates information about a company to those interested in it.

Financial Statements: How Accountants Communicate

The primary focus of this book is financial accounting. This branch of accounting is concerned with informing management and outsiders about a company through financial statements. We turn now to the composition of the four major statements: balance sheet, income statement, statement of retained earnings, and statement of cash flows.

LO5 Explain the purpose of each of the financial statements and the relationships among them and prepare a set of simple statements.

The Accounting Equation

The accounting equation is the foundation for the entire accounting system:

Assets = Liabilities + Owners' Equity

- The *left side* of the accounting equation refers to the *assets* of the company. Those items that are valuable economic resources and that will provide future benefit to the company should appear on the left side of the equation.
- The *right side* of the equation indicates who provided, or has a claim to, those assets. Some of the assets were provided by creditors, and they have a claim to them. For example, if a company has a delivery truck, the dealer that provided the truck to the company has a claim to the assets until the dealer is paid. The delivery truck would appear on the left side of the equation as an asset to the company; the company's *liability* to the dealer would appear on the right side of the equation. Other assets are provided by the owners of the business. Their claims to these assets are represented by the portion of the right side of the equation called **owners' equity**.

STUDY TIP

The accounting equation and the financial statements are at the heart of this course. Memorize the accounting equation and make sure you study this introduction to how the financial statements should look, how to read them, and what they say about a company.

Owners' equity
The owners' claims on the assets of an entity.

Stockholders' equity
The owners' equity in a corporation.
Alternate term: shareholders' equity.

The term *stockholders' equity*, or shareholders' equity, is used to refer to the owners' equity of a corporation. **Stockholders' equity is the difference between a corporation's assets and its obligations, or liabilities.** That is, after the amounts owed to bondholders, banks, suppliers, and other creditors are subtracted from the assets, the amount remaining is the stockholders' equity, the amount of interest or claim that the owners have on the assets of the business.

Stockholders' equity arises in two distinct ways.

1. It is created when a company issues stock to an investor. It represents the amounts contributed by the owners to the company.
2. As owners of shares in a corporation, stockholders have a claim on the assets of a business when it is profitable. **Retained earnings represents the owners' claims to the company's assets that result from its earnings that have not been paid out in dividends.** It is the earnings accumulated or retained by the company.

Retained earnings
The part of stockholders' equity that represents the income earned less dividends paid over the life of an entity.

The Balance Sheet

Balance sheet
The financial statement that summarizes the assets, liabilities, and owners' equity at a specific point in time.
Alternate term: Statement of financial position.

The **balance sheet** (sometimes called the *statement of financial position*) **is the financial statement that summarizes the assets, liabilities, and owners' equity of a company.** It is a snapshot of the business at a certain date. A balance sheet can be prepared on any day of the year, although it is most commonly prepared on the last day of a month, quarter, or year. At any point in time, the balance sheet must be "in balance." That is, assets must equal liabilities and owners' equity.

The financial statements for real companies can be quite complex. Therefore, before we attempt to read Chipotle's statements, we will start with a hypothetical company.

EXAMPLE 1-4 Preparing a Balance Sheet

Top of the World owns and operates a ski resort in the Rockies. The company's balance sheet on June 30, 2017, the end of its first year of business, is presented below. As you study the balance sheet, note the description for each item to help you understand it better.

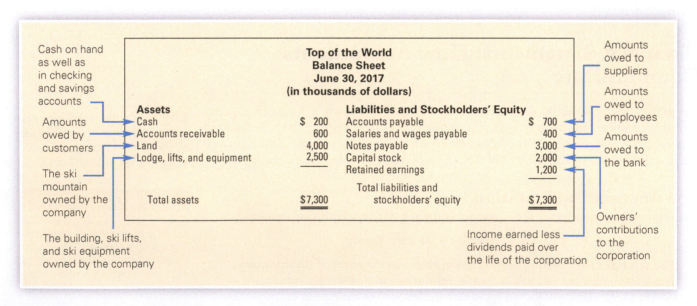

Two items should be noted in the heading of the statement. First, the company chose a date other than December 31, the calendar year-end, to finish its accounting, or fiscal, year. Although December 31 is the most common year-end, some companies choose a different year-end date. Often, this choice is based on when a company's peak selling season is over. For example, **Gap Inc.** ends its accounting year on the Saturday closest to January 31, after the busy holiday season. By June 30, Top of the World's ski season has ended and the company can devote its attention to preparing its financial statements. The second item to note in the heading of the statement is the last line: "in thousands of dollars." This means, for example, that rather than cash being $200, the amount is actually 1,000 × $200, or $200,000.

Exhibit 1-5 summarizes the relationship between the accounting equation and the items that appear on a balance sheet.

EXHIBIT 1-5 The Relationship Between the Accounting Equation and the Balance Sheet

Terminology Note: Exhibit 1-5 refers to Owners' Equity, while Example 1-4 refers to Stockholders' Equity. *Owners' equity* is the general term by which we refer to ownership. "Stockholders' equity" refers only to ownership of a corporation by shareholders. Because we emphasize corporations in this book, we will use the term *Stockholders' equity.*

Income statement
A statement that summarizes revenues and expenses.

Alternate term: Statement of income.

Net income
The excess of revenues over expenses.

Alternate term: Profits, earnings.

The Income Statement

An **income statement**, or statement of income, summarizes the revenues and expenses of a company for a period of time.

EXAMPLE 1-5 Preparing an Income Statement

An income statement for Top of the World for its first year in business is shown below. **Unlike the balance sheet, an income statement is a *flow* statement.** That is, it summarizes the flow of revenues and expenses for the year. The top portion of the income statement makes it clear that the ski company has two distinct types of revenues: those from selling lift tickets and those from renting ski equipment. For example, if you paid the company $50 for a one-day lift ticket and another $30 to rent equipment for the day, each of those amounts would be included in Top of the World's revenues for the year. The expenses reported on the income statement represent all of the various costs necessary to run a ski resort. For example, a significant cost for such an operation is payroll, as represented by salaries and wages on the income statement. Note that the amount reported for salaries and wages expense on the income statement is not the same amount that appeared as salaries and wages payable on the balance sheet. The expense of $2,000 on the income statement represents the total cost for the year, while the payable of $400 on the balance sheet is the amount owed to employees on June 30, 2017. Finally, note that the excess of revenues over expenses, or **net income**, appears as the bottom line on the income statement. A company's net income is sometimes referred to as its profits or earnings.

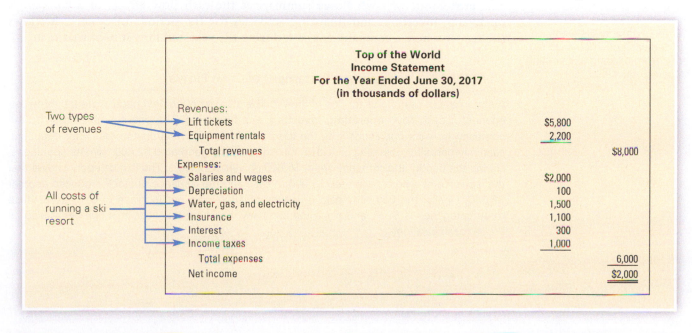

Top of the World Income Statement For the Year Ended June 30, 2017 (in thousands of dollars)		
Revenues:		
Lift tickets	$5,800	
Equipment rentals	2,200	
Total revenues		$8,000
Expenses:		
Salaries and wages	$2,000	
Depreciation	100	
Water, gas, and electricity	1,500	
Insurance	1,100	
Interest	300	
Income taxes	1,000	
Total expenses		6,000
Net income		$2,000

Two types of revenues

All costs of running a ski resort

Statement of retained earnings
The statement that summarizes the income earned and dividends paid over the life of a business.

Dividends
A distribution of the net income of a business to its stockholders.

The Statement of Retained Earnings

A **statement of retained earnings** explains the change in retained earnings for the period. As discussed earlier, Retained Earnings represents the accumulated earnings of a corporation less the amount paid in dividends to stockholders. **Dividends** are distributions of the net income of a business to its stockholders. Most companies that pay dividends do so four times a year. However, not all businesses pay cash dividends.

EXAMPLE 1-6 Preparing a Statement of Retained Earnings

A statement of retained earnings for Top of the World is shown below. Revenues minus expenses, or net income, is an increase in retained earnings, and dividends are a decrease in the balance. Why are dividends shown on a statement of retained earnings instead of on an income statement? Dividends are a distribution of the income of the business. They are not an expense and thus are not a component of net income.

Top of the World Statement of Retained Earnings For the Year Ended June 30, 2017 (in thousands of dollars)	
Retained earnings, beginning of the year	$ 0
Net income for the year	2,000
Dividends for the year	(800)
Retained earnings, end of the year	$1,200

Recall that stockholders' equity consists of two parts: capital stock and retained earnings. In lieu of a separate statement of retained earnings, many corporations prepare a comprehensive statement to explain the changes both in the various capital stock accounts and in retained earnings during the period. Chipotle for example, presents the more comprehensive statement.

The Statement of Cash Flows

Statement of cash flows
The financial statement that summarizes a company's cash receipts and cash payments during the period from operating, investing, and financing activities.

The **statement of cash flows** summarizes the cash flow effects of a company's operating, investing, and financing activities for the period. In essence, it shows the reader where a company got cash during the year and how it used that cash.

EXAMPLE 1-7 Preparing a Statement of Cash Flows

A statement of cash flows for Top of the World is shown on the next page. Note the three categories of cash flow: **operating, investing,** and **financing.** The one source of cash to the company from its operations was the cash it collected from its customers. After deducting cash payments for operating activities, the ski company generated $2,600 from its operations. During the period, the company spent $6,600 on various assets. The last category shows that the issuance of a note generated $3,000 of cash and the issuance of stock produced another $2,000. Finally, the company paid dividends of $800. The net increase in cash from these three categories is $200, and since the company was new this year, this number is also its ending cash balance.

Top of the World Statement of Cash Flows For the Year Ended June 30, 2017 (in thousands of dollars)		
Cash flows from operating activities:		
Cash collected from customers		$ 7,400
Cash payments for:		
Salaries and wages	$ 1,600	
Water, gas, and electricity	1,500	
Insurance	400	
Interest	300	
Income taxes	1,000	
Total cash payments		4,800
Net cash provided by operating activities		$ 2,600
Cash flows from investing activities:		
Purchase of land	$(4,000)	
Purchase of lodge, lifts, and equipment	(2,600)	
Net cash used by investing activities		(6,600)
Cash flows from financing activities:		
Proceeds from issuance of long-term note	$ 3,000	
Proceeds from issuance of capital stock	2,000	
Dividends declared and paid	(800)	
Net cash provided by financing activities		4,200
Net increase in cash		$ 200
Cash at beginning of year		0
Cash at end of year		$ 200

Relationships Among the Financial Statements

Note the natural progression in the items from one statement to another. Normally, a company starts the period with balances in each of the items on its balance sheet. Because Top of the World is a new company, Exhibit 1-6 shows zero balances on July 1, 2016, the beginning of its first year in business. The company's operations during the year resulted in net income of $2,000 as shown on the income statement at the top of the exhibit. The net income naturally flows ❶ onto the statement of retained earnings. Again, because the ski company is new, its beginning retained earnings balance is zero. After the distribution of $800 in cash dividends ❷, the ending retained earnings amounts to $1,200. The ending retained earnings number flows ❸ onto the ending balance sheet along with the other June 30, 2017, balance sheet items. Finally, the net increase in cash at the bottom of the statement of cash flows equals ❹ the amount shown on the June 30, 2017, balance sheet.

Looking at Financial Statements
for a Real Company: Chipotle

You would expect the financial statements of actual companies to be more complex than those for a hypothetical company such as Top of the World. Still, even this early in your study of accounting, there are certain fundamental points about all financial statements, real-world or otherwise, that you can appreciate.

Chipotle's Balance Sheet

Balance sheets for Chipotle at the end of two recent years are shown in Exhibit 1-7. For comparative purposes, the company reports its financial position at the end of the two most recent years. Also note that the amounts are in thousands of dollars.

EXHIBIT 1-6 Relationships Among the Financial Statements

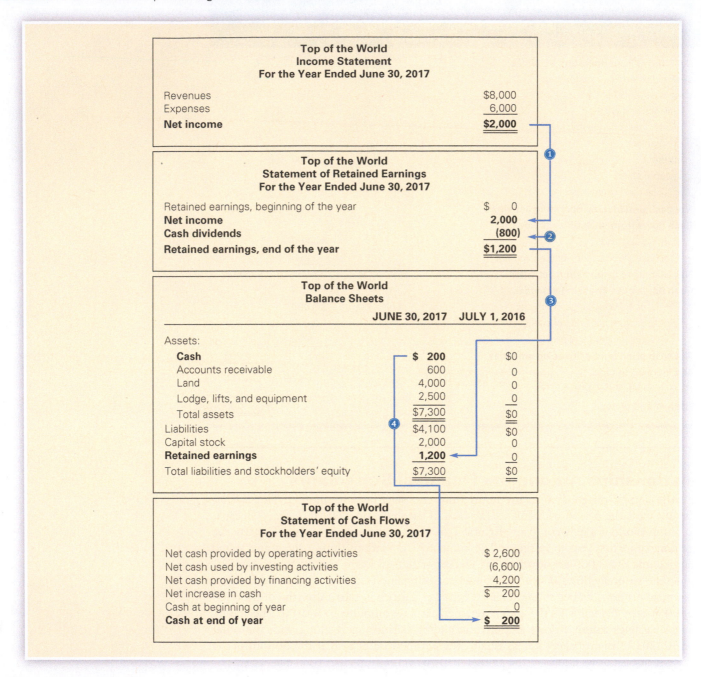

Top of the World Income Statement For the Year Ended June 30, 2017	
Revenues	$8,000
Expenses	6,000
Net income	**$2,000**

Top of the World Statement of Retained Earnings For the Year Ended June 30, 2017	
Retained earnings, beginning of the year	$ 0
Net income	**2,000**
Cash dividends	**(800)**
Retained earnings, end of the year	**$1,200**

Top of the World Balance Sheets	JUNE 30, 2017	JULY 1, 2016
Assets:		
Cash	**$ 200**	$0
Accounts receivable	600	0
Land	4,000	0
Lodge, lifts, and equipment	2,500	0
Total assets	$7,300	$0
Liabilities	$4,100	$0
Capital stock	2,000	0
Retained earnings	**1,200**	0
Total liabilities and stockholders' equity	$7,300	$0

Top of the World Statement of Cash Flows For the Year Ended June 30, 2017	
Net cash provided by operating activities	$ 2,600
Net cash used by investing activities	(6,600)
Net cash provided by financing activities	4,200
Net increase in cash	$ 200
Cash at beginning of year	0
Cash at end of year	**$ 200**

CHIPOTLE
READING THE BALANCE SHEET

1-1 State Chipotle's financial position at the end of 2015 in terms of the accounting equation. What amount of cash and cash equivalents does Chipotle have at the end of this year? What amount does Chipotle owe its suppliers at the end of this year? *(See answers on p. 48.)*

For example, this means that Chipotle had $2,725,066 × 1,000, or $2,725,066,000, or over $2.7 billion of total assets at the end of 2015. The total liabilities of $597,092 thousand at the end of 2015, when added to the total stockholders' equity of $2,127,974 thousand, equals $2,725,066 thousand, the same amount as the total assets.

A quick comparison of Chipotle's assets with those of Top of the World reveals one significant difference. Because the ski company is a service

EXHIBIT 1-7 Chipotle's Balance Sheet

Chipotle Mexican Grill, Inc. Consolidated Balance Sheet (in thousands, except per share data)		
	December 31,	
	2015	**2014**
		(as adjusted)
Assets		
Current assets:		
Cash and cash equivalents	$ 248,005	$ 419,465
Accounts receivable, net of allowance for doubtful accounts of $1,176 and $1,199 as of December 31, 2015 and December 31, 2014, respectively	38,283	34,839
Inventory	15,043	15,332
Prepaid expenses and other current assets	39,965	34,795
Income tax receivable	58,152	16,488
Investments	415,199	338,592
Total current assets	814,647	859,511
Leasehold improvements, property and equipment, net	1,217,220	1,106,984
Long term investments	622,939	496,106
Other assets	48,321	42,777
Goodwill	21,939	21,939
Total assets	$ 2,725,066	$2,527,317
Liabilities and shareholders' equity		
Current liabilities:		
Accounts payable	$ 85,709	$ 69,613
Accrued payroll and benefits	64,958	73,894
Accrued liabilities	129,275	102,203
Total current liabilities	279,942	245,710
Deferred rent	251,962	219,414
Deferred income tax liability	32,305	21,561
Other liabilities	32,883	28,263
Total liabilities	597,092	514,948
Shareholders' equity:		
Preferred stock, $0.01 par value, 600,000 shares authorized, no shares issued as of December 31, 2015 and December 31, 2014, respectively	—	—
Common stock $0.01 par value, 230,000 shares authorized, and 35,790 and 35,394 shares issued as of December 31, 2015 and December 31, 2014, respectively	358	354
Additional paid-in capital	1,172,628	1,038,932
Treasury stock, at cost, 5,206 and 4,367 common shares at December 31, 2015 and December 31, 2014, respectively	(1,234,612)	(748,759)
Accumulated other comprehensive income (loss)	(8,273)	(429)
Retained earnings	2,197,873	1,722,271
Total shareholders' equity	2,127,974	2,012,369
Total liabilities and shareholders' equity	$ 2,725,066	$2,527,317

See accompanying notes to consolidated financial statements.

Annotations:
- Restaurants and operating equipment are key assets for Chipotle.
- Total assets of over $2.7 billion.
- Shareholders' equity is the same as Stockholders' equity.
- Creditors' claims are about $597 million.
- Creditors' claims and shareholders' equity is the same amount as total assets.

CHIPOTLE
READING THE INCOME STATEMENT

1-2 Compute the percentage increase in Revenue and in Food, beverage and packaging costs from 2014 to 2015. Which of these two items on the income statement increased by the larger percentage? What does this mean to the management of Chipotle? *(See answers on p. 48.)*

company, it does not have an Inventory account on its balance sheet. As a product company, Chipotle does have an inventory account, although it is not large since the supply of fresh ingredients on hand at any one time is relatively small. Finally, note that Chipotle uses the term "shareholders' equity," which means the same as "stockholders' equity."

Chipotle's Income Statement

Comparative income statements for three recent years are shown in Exhibit 1-8.[3] Note the two largest items on the income statement: (1) Revenue and (2) Food, beverage, and packaging costs. Revenue for the most recent year amounted to $4,501,223 thousand, or

EXHIBIT 1-8 Chipotle's Income Statement

Chipotle Mexican Grill, Inc.
Consolidated Statement of Income and Comprehensive Income
(in thousands, except per share data)

	Year ended December 31,		
	2015	**2014**	**2013**
Revenue	$4,501,223	$4,108,269	$3,214,591
Restaurant operating costs (exclusive of depreciation and amortization shown separately below):			
Food, beverage and packaging	1,503,835	1,420,994	1,073,514
Labor	1,045,726	904,407	739,800
Occupancy	262,412	230,868	199,107
Other operating costs	514,963	434,244	347,401
General and administrative expenses	250,214	273,897	203,733
Depreciation and amortization	130,368	110,474	96,054
Pre-opening costs	16,922	15,609	15,511
Loss on disposal of assets	13,194	6,976	6,751
Total operating expenses	3,737,634	3,397,469	2,681,871
Income from operations	763,589	710,800	532,720
Interest and other income (expense), net	6,278	3,503	1,751
Income before income taxes	769,867	714,303	534,471
Provision for income taxes	(294,265)	(268,929)	(207,033)
Net income	$ 475,602	$ 445,374	$ 327,438
Other comprehensive income (loss), net of income taxes:			
Foreign currency translation adjustments	(6,322)	(2,049)	596
Unrealized loss on investments, net of income taxes of $946, $0, and $0	(1,522)	—	—
Other comprehensive income (loss), net of income taxes	(7,844)	(2,049)	596
Comprehensive income	$ 467,758	$ 443,325	$ 328,034
Earnings per share:			
Basic	$ 15.30	$ 14.35	$ 10.58
Diluted	$ 15.10	$ 14.13	$ 10.47
Weighted average common shares outstanding:			
Basic	31,092	31,038	30,957
Diluted	31,494	31,512	31,281

See accompanying notes to consolidated financial statements.

Revenue has grown steadily and topped $4.5 billion in 2015.

The cost to buy and package the food and beverages sold amounted to about $1.5 billion.

Net income for the year was about $475.6 million.

Source: Chipotle Mexican Grill, Inc.'s Form 10-K for the Fiscal Year Ended December 31, 2015.

[3] Chipotle prepares a combined statement of income and comprehensive income. Comprehensive income is covered in advanced accounting courses.

about $4.5 billion, and the cost for the food and beverages sold, including their packaging, was $1,503,835 thousand, or about $1.5 billion. Net income for the year amounted to $475,602 thousand, or about $475.6 million after taking into account all other expenses.

MODULE 2 TEST YOURSELF

Review

LO4 Define accounting and identify the primary users of accounting information and their needs.

- The primary users of financial statements depend on the economic information conveyed in those statements to make decisions. Primary users may be broadly classified as internal and external users.
- Internal users are usually managers of a company.
- External users include stockholders, investors, creditors, and government agencies.

LO5 Explain the purpose of each of the financial statements and the relationships among them and prepare a set of simple statements.

- Four major financial statements are covered in this chapter: balance sheet, income statement, statement of retained earnings, and statement of cash flows.
- The balance sheet is a snapshot of a company's financial position at the end of the period. It reflects the assets, liabilities, and stockholders' equity accounts.
- The income statement summarizes the financial activity for a period of time. Items of revenues, expenses, gains, and losses are reflected on the income statement.
- Ultimately, all net income (loss) and dividends are reflected in retained earnings on the balance sheet. The statement of retained earnings links the income statement to the balance sheet by showing how net income (loss) and dividends affect the Retained Earnings account.
- The statement of cash flows summarizes the cash flow effects of a company's operating, investing, and financing activities.

Question

1. What is accounting? Define it in terms understandable to someone without a business background.
2. What are the two distinct elements of owners' equity in a corporation? Define each element.
3. How should a balance sheet be dated: as of a particular day or for a particular period of time? Explain your answer.
4. How should an income statement be dated: as of a particular day or for a particular period of time? Explain your answer.

Apply

1. Think about Chipotle's business in balance sheet terms. Name three of Chipotle's assets. Name three of Chipotle's liabilities.
2. Place Chipotle's total assets, total liabilities, and total stockholders' equity in the form of the accounting equation.

Answers are located at the end of the chapter.

MODULE 3 CONCEPTUAL FRAMEWORK OF ACCOUNTING

The record-keeping aspect of accounting—what we normally think of as bookkeeping—is the routine part of the accountant's work and is only a small part of it. Most of the accountant's job requires a great deal of judgment in communicating relevant information to financial statement users.

Conceptual Framework for Accounting

The accounting profession has developed a *conceptual framework for accounting*. This framework is a foundation for the specific principles and standards needed by the profession. An important part of the conceptual framework is a set of assumptions accountants make in preparing financial statements.

LO6 Identify and explain the primary assumptions made in preparing financial statements.

STUDY TIP

The concepts in this section underlie everything you will learn throughout the course. You'll encounter them later in the context of specific topics.

Economic Entity Concept

The *economic entity concept* was discussed earlier in this chapter when we explored the different types of business entities. **This assumption requires that an identifiable, specific entity be the subject of a set of financial statements.** For example, even though some of Chipotle's employees are stockholders and therefore own part of the company, their personal affairs must be kept separate from the business affairs. When we look at a balance sheet for the company, we need assurance that it shows the financial position of that entity only and does not intermingle the personal assets and liabilities of the employees or any of the other stockholders.

How Will I Use ACCOUNTING?

Accounting is often called the "language of business." Regardless of your career path, you need to be able to speak that language.

Financial statements are how accountants communicate information about a business and you need to know what the statements are telling you.

Asset Valuation: Cost or Fair Value?

According to the **cost principle**, all assets are initially recorded at the cost to acquire them. For example, Chipotle would record in its Inventory account the amount paid to acquire its ingredients. Similarly, if Chipotle buys a parcel of land, the cost of this asset would be included in its Property account on the balance sheet.

Once assets have been recorded at their cost, an important accounting question still remains: how should these assets be *valued on* subsequent balance sheets? One approach is to continue to report assets at their original cost. Accountants use the term *historical cost* to refer to the original cost of an asset. Under current accounting standards, certain assets are valued at historical cost on all balance sheets until the company disposes of them. For example, the amount Chipotle paid to acquire land is verifiable by an independent observer and is considered more objective than some measure of what the asset *might be* worth today.

Cost principle
Assets are recorded at the cost to acquire them.

Alternate term: Original cost or historical cost.

But what if the value of an asset could be objectively determined? Would it be more useful to the reader of a balance sheet to know what the asset is worth today rather than what the company paid for it sometime in the past? As you will learn in later chapters, certain assets are valued on subsequent balance sheets at market value rather than historical cost. For example, assume that one company buys stock in another company. The amount that company would initially record as an asset is the amount it paid to buy the stock. However, it would value its investment at the amount for which it could *sell* the shares of stock on the date of the balance sheet.[4]

Going Concern

Accountants assume that the entity being accounted for is a **going concern**. That is, they assume that Chipotle is **not in the process of liquidation and that it will continue indefinitely into the future.** When we assume that a business is *not* a going concern, market value might be more relevant than historical cost as a basis for recognizing the assets. But if we are able to assume that a business will continue indefinitely, cost can be more easily justified as a basis for valuation.

Going concern
The assumption that an entity is not in the process of liquidation and that it will continue indefinitely.

The **monetary unit** used in preparing Chipotle's statements is the dollar. The dollar is used because it is the recognized medium of exchange in the United States. It provides a convenient yardstick to measure the business's position and earnings. However, the dollar, like the currencies of all other countries, is subject to instability. A dollar will not buy as much today as it did ten years ago.

Monetary unit
The yardstick used to measure amounts in financial statements; the dollar in the United States.

Inflation is evidenced by a general rise in the level of prices in an economy. Its effect on the measuring unit used in preparing financial statements is an important concern to the accounting profession. The financial statements of corporations are prepared under the assumption that the monetary unit is relatively stable. At various times in the past, this has been a reasonable assumption and at other times not so reasonable.

---

[4] The Financial Accounting Standards Board has created a system of classification using topic numbers to identify all accounting pronouncements. In this text, the codification topic and number are noted first followed by the reference to each original pronouncement. For example, *Fair Value Measurements and Disclosures*, ASC Topic 820 (formerly *Fair Value Measurements*, Statement of Financial Accounting Standards No. 157).

Time Period Assumption

Under the **time period** assumption, accountants assume that it is possible to prepare an income statement that accurately reflects net income or earnings for a specific time period. In the case of Chipotle, this time period is one year. It is somewhat artificial to measure the earnings of a business for a period of time indicated on a calendar, whether it be a month, a quarter, or a year. Of course, the most accurate point in time to measure the earnings of a business is at the end of its life. Accountants prepare periodic statements, however, because the users of the statements demand information about the entity on a regular basis.

Setting Accounting Standards

Management of a company is responsible for preparation of the financial statements. These financial statements must conform to **generally accepted accounting principles (GAAP)**. This term refers to the various methods, rules, practices, and other procedures that have evolved over time in response to the need for regulating the preparation of financial statements. GAAP have developed in response to changes in the business environment.

Who Determines the Rules for Financial Statements?

No one group is totally responsible for setting the standards or principles to be followed in preparing financial statements. The process is a joint effort among the following:

- The federal government, through the **Securities and Exchange Commission (SEC)**, has the ultimate authority to determine the rules for preparing financial statements by companies whose securities are sold to the general public. However, for the most part, the SEC has allowed the accounting profession to establish its own rules. Companies file various reports with the SEC, including the annual report containing the financial statements. The annual report filed with the SEC is called the *Form 10-K*.
- The **Financial Accounting Standards Board (FASB)** sets these accounting standards in the United States. Since its creation in the 1970s, this small, independent board has issued standards on a variety of topics as well as statements of financial accounting concepts. The standards deal with a variety of financial reporting issues, such as the proper accounting for lease arrangements and pension plans, and the concepts are used to guide the board in setting accounting standards.
- The **American Institute of Certified Public Accountants (AICPA)** is the professional organization of **Certified Public Accountants (CPAs)**. The CPA is the designation for an individual who has passed a uniform exam administered by the AICPA and met other requirements as determined by individual states. The AICPA advises the FASB and in the past was involved in setting the auditing standards to be followed by public accounting firms. However, the **Public Company Accounting Oversight Board (PCAOB)** was created by an act of Congress in 2002, and this body now has the authority to set the standards for conducting audits.
- Finally, if you are considering buying stock in a non-U.S. company like **Porsche**, the German-based car manufacturer, you'll want to be sure that the rules Porsche follows in preparing its statements are similar to those the FASB requires for U.S. companies. Unfortunately, accounting standards can differ considerably from one country to another. The **International Accounting Standards Board (IASB)** is the group responsible for developing worldwide accounting standards. Organizations from many different countries, including the FASB in this country, participate in the IASB's efforts to develop international reporting standards. The FASB currently has a project on its agenda to work with the IASB toward convergence of accounting standards. Appendix A at the end of the book describes in more detail the joint efforts of the two groups as well as some of the major differences in U.S. and international standards.

Earlier in this chapter, we saw that the cost principle requires that assets such as property and equipment be reported on the balance sheet at their historical cost, that is,

Time period
An artificial segment on the calendar used as the basis for preparing financial statements.

LO7 Identify the various groups involved in setting accounting standards and the role of auditors in determining whether the standards are followed.

Generally accepted accounting principles (GAAP)
The various methods, rules, practices, and other procedures that have evolved over time in response to the need to regulate the preparation of financial statements.

Securities and Exchange Commission (SEC)
The federal agency with ultimate authority to determine the rules for preparing statements for companies whose stock is sold to the public.

Financial Accounting Standards Board (FASB)
The group in the private sector with authority to set accounting standards.

American Institute of Certified Public Accountants (AICPA)
The professional organization of certified public accountants.

Certified Public Accountant (CPA)
The designation for an individual who has passed a uniform exam administered by the AICPA and has met other requirements as determined by individual states.

Public Company Accounting Oversight Board (PCAOB)
A five-member body created by an act of Congress in 2002 to set auditing standards.

International Accounting Standards Board (IASB)
The organization formed to develop worldwide accounting standards.

at the amount paid to acquire them. However, under international accounting standards, it is permissible to report certain types of assets on the balance sheet at their market value. With significant differences such as this between U.S. and international standards, it may be some time before all differences are eliminated.

In the meantime, U.S. standard setters continue to work closely with those in the international community. At one time, foreign companies that filed their financial statements with the SEC were required to adjust those statements to conform to U.S. accounting standards. As long as foreign companies follow IASB standards, they are no longer required to make these adjustments.

The Audit of Financial Statements

Auditing
The process of examining the financial statements and the underlying records of a company to render an opinion as to whether the statements are fairly presented.

Financial statements are prepared by a company's accountants and are the responsibility of the company's management. Because most stockholders are not actively involved in the daily affairs of the business, they must rely on someone else to ensure that management is fairly presenting the financial statements. **Auditing** is the process of examining the financial statements and underlying records of a company to render an opinion as to whether they are fairly presented. The primary objective of an audit is to assure stockholders and other users that the financial statements are fairly presented.

The external auditor performs various tests and procedures to be able to render an opinion. The next chapter will examine the auditors' report, which is essentially the auditors' opinion concerning the fairness of the presentation of the financial statements. Note that the auditors' report is an *opinion*, not a statement of fact. The firms that provide external audits for their clients are called *public accounting firms*. These firms range in size from those with a single owner to others with thousands of partners.

Introduction to Ethics in Accounting

LO8 Explain the critical role that ethics plays in providing useful financial information.

Rapidly changing markets, technological improvements, and business innovation all affect financial decisions. Decision makers consider information received from many sources, such as other investors in the marketplace, analysts' forecasts, and corporate officers and executives.

Why Should Accountants Be Concerned with Ethics?

In recent years, the news has been filled with reports of questionable accounting practices by some companies.

- **As a decision maker outside a company, you should be aware of the potential for ethical conflicts that arise within organizations.**
- **If you are a decision maker inside a company, you should stay alert for potential pressures on you or others to make choices that are not in the best interest of the company, its owners, and its employees as a whole.**

Companies may use aggressive accounting practices to misrepresent their earnings, and executives may misuse their companies' funds. You may encounter a corporate board of directors that undermines the goals of its own company or a public accounting firm that fails its auditing duty to watch for and disclose wrongdoing. You may also encounter circumstances when it appears as if GAAP may not have been used to resolve particular accounting issues because there are several conflicting rules, because no specific GAAP rules seem applicable, or because of fraud. As accountants analyze and attempt to solve the ethical dilemmas posed by certain financial transactions and complex business reporting decisions, they can turn to their profession's conceptual framework. According to the profession, the purpose of financial reporting is to provide information about a company that investors, lenders, and other creditors can use when deciding whether to provide resources to the entity.[5]

Is the Information Relevant and a Faithful Representation? When the accountant asks if the quality of the information that is disclosed is good or if it needs

---

[5] *Statement of Financial Accounting Concepts [SFAC] No. 8, Conceptual Framework for Financial Reporting*, Chapter 1, "The Objective of General Purpose Financial Reporting" (Norwalk, Conn.: Financial Accounting Standards Board, October 2010).

to be improved, the answer (which shapes all accounting decisions that follow) is this: **If the information is both relevant and a faithful representation, its quality is good.**[6]

Relevant information is information that is useful to the decision-making process. Relevant information may provide clear information about past financial events that is helpful for predicting the future. To be relevant, the information must also be timely; that is, it must be available at the time the decision is being made.

Accounting information should also be a faithful representation. This means that the information is complete, neutral, and free from error. *Neutrality* means the presentation of information is free from bias toward a particular result. Neutral information can be used by anyone, and it does not try to influence the decision in one direction.

Normally, the uncertainties of business transactions and reporting decisions must be resolved in accordance with GAAP, following the FASB statements. However, the appropriate application of accounting principles may not be easy to determine. You must be alert to pressures on the decision-making process that may be due to the self-interests of one or more of the decision makers. Bias, deception, and even fraud may distort the disclosed information.

Moral and Social Context of Ethical Behavior All decision makers should consider the moral and social implications of their decisions. How will the decisions affect others, such as shareholders, creditors, employees, suppliers, customers, and the local community? The process of determining the most ethical choice involves identifying the most significant facts of the situation. For financial reporting, this includes identifying who may be affected and how, the relevant GAAP principles, and a realistic appraisal of the possible consequences of the decision.

To assist your decision making for the cases and assignments throughout this book, we offer an ethical decision model, shown in Exhibit 1-9 and explained here.

Identification

1. Recognize the ethical dilemma. A dilemma occurs when this awareness is combined with the inability to clearly apply accounting principles to represent the situation accurately.

Analysis

2. Analyze the key elements in the situation by answering these questions in sequence:
   a. Who may benefit or be harmed?
   b. How are they likely to benefit or be harmed?
   c. What rights or claims may be violated?
   d. What specific interests are in conflict?
   e. What are my responsibilities and obligations?
3. Determine what alternative methods are available to report the transaction, situation, or event. Answer the following questions:
   a. Which of the alternatives is most relevant and a faithful representation? Timeliness should be considered; potential bias must be identified.
   b. Does the report accurately represent the situation it claims to describe?
   c. Is the information free from bias?

Resolution

4. Select the best or most ethical alternative, considering all of the circumstances and consequences.

Accountants and Ethical Judgments

Remember the primary goal of accounting: to provide useful information to aid in the decision-making process. As discussed, the work of the accountant in providing useful information is anything but routine and requires the accountant to make subjective judgments about what information to present and how to present it. The latitude given accountants in this respect is one of the major reasons accounting is a profession and its

---

[6] *Statement of Financial Accounting Concepts [SFAC] No. 8, Conceptual Framework for Financial Reporting*, Chapter 3, "Qualitative Characteristics of Useful Financial Information" (Norwalk, Conn.: Financial Accounting Standards Board, October 2010).

EXHIBIT 1-9 Ethics and Accounting: A Decision-Making Model

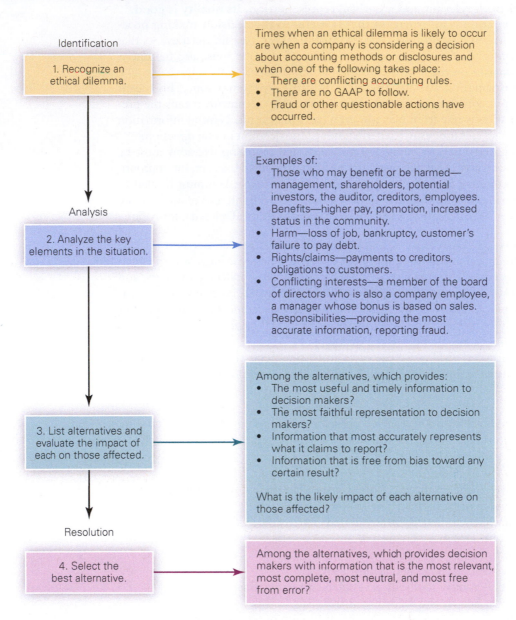

Identification

1. Recognize an ethical dilemma.

Times when an ethical dilemma is likely to occur are when a company is considering a decision about accounting methods or disclosures and when one of the following takes place:
• There are conflicting accounting rules.
• There are no GAAP to follow.
• Fraud or other questionable actions have occurred.

Analysis

2. Analyze the key elements in the situation.

Examples of:
• Those who may benefit or be harmed—management, shareholders, potential investors, the auditor, creditors, employees.
• Benefits—higher pay, promotion, increased status in the community.
• Harm—loss of job, bankruptcy, customer's failure to pay debt.
• Rights/claims—payments to creditors, obligations to customers.
• Conflicting interests—a member of the board of directors who is also a company employee, a manager whose bonus is based on sales.
• Responsibilities—providing the most accurate information, reporting fraud.

3. List alternatives and evaluate the impact of each on those affected.

Among the alternatives, which provides:
• The most useful and timely information to decision makers?
• The most faithful representation to decision makers?
• Information that most accurately represents what it claims to report?
• Information that is free from bias toward any certain result?

What is the likely impact of each alternative on those affected?

Resolution

4. Select the best alternative.

Among the alternatives, which provides decision makers with information that is the most relevant, most complete, most neutral, and most free from error?

members are considered professionals. Along with this designation as a professional, however, comes a serious responsibility. As we noted, financial statements are prepared for external parties who must rely on these statements to provide information on which to base important decisions.

At the end of each chapter are cases titled "Ethical Decision Making." The cases require you to evaluate difficult issues and make a decision. Judgment is needed in deciding which accounting method to select or how to report a certain item in the statements. As you are faced with these decisions, keep in mind the trust that various financial statement users place in the accountant.

The Changing Face of the Accounting Profession

Probably no time in the history of the accounting profession in the United States has seen more turmoil and change than the period since the start of the new millennium. Corporate scandals have led to some of the largest bankruptcies in the history of business. In addition to these scandals, the ongoing global economic crisis continues to present challenges for accountants.

Although the issues involved in these corporate scandals are complex, the accounting questions were often very basic. For example, the most fundamental accounting issue involved in the **Enron** case revolved around the entity concept that was explained earlier in this chapter. Specifically, should various entities under the control of Enron have been included in the company's financial statements? Similarly, the major question in the **WorldCom** case was whether certain costs should have been treated as expenses when incurred rather than accounted for as assets.

The scandals of the last few years have resulted in a major focus on nonaudit services such as tax planning and systems consulting provided by public accounting firms and the issue of auditor independence. For example, is it possible for an accounting firm to remain independent in rendering an opinion on a company's financial statements while simultaneously advising the company on other matters?

In 2002, Congress passed the **Sarbanes-Oxley Act**. This act was a direct response to the corporate scandals mentioned earlier and was an attempt to bring about major reforms in corporate accountability and stewardship. Among the most important provisions in the act are the following:

1. The establishment of the Public Company Accounting Oversight Board
2. A requirement that the external auditors report directly to the company's audit committee
3. A clause to prohibit public accounting firms that audit a company from providing any other services that could impair their ability to act independently in the course of their audit

Events of the last few years have placed accountants and the work they do in the spotlight. More than ever before, accountants realize the burden of responsibility they have to communicate openly and honestly with the public concerning the financial well-being of businesses.

Sarbanes-Oxley Act
An act of Congress in 2002 intended to bring reform to corporate accountability and stewardship in the wake of a number of major corporate scandals.

MODULE 3 TEST YOURSELF

Review

LO6 Identify and explain the primary assumptions made in preparing financial statements.

- The usefulness of accounting information is enhanced through the various assumptions set forth in the conceptual framework developed by the accounting profession. This conceptual framework is the foundation for the methods, rules, and practices that make up generally accepted accounting principles (GAAP).
- Important assumptions in the conceptual framework are as follows:
  - Economic entity concept
  - Cost principle
  - Going concern
  - Monetary unit
  - Time period

LO7 Identify the various groups involved in setting accounting standards and the role of auditors in determining whether the standards are followed.

- Financial statements are the responsibility of management. Various groups are involved in setting the standards that are used in preparing the statements. Although the SEC has the ultimate authority to determine the rules, the FASB currently sets the standards in the United States.
- The role of the external auditor is to perform various tests and procedures to render an opinion as to whether the financial statements of a company are fairly presented.

LO8 Explain the critical role that ethics plays in providing useful financial information.

- All decision makers must consider the moral and social implications of their decisions.
- Recent news of questionable accounting practices has placed increased scrutiny on the accounting profession. Professional judgment is often needed to arrive at appropriate decisions when some question arises about the application of GAAP.

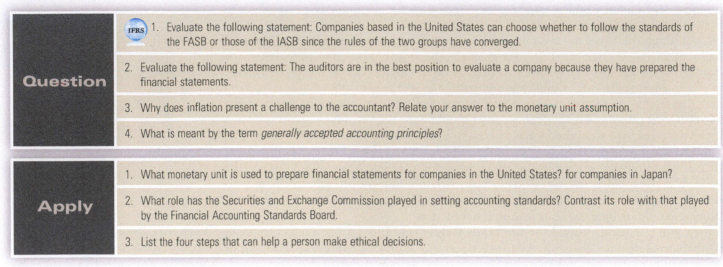

Question		
	IFRS 1.	Evaluate the following statement: Companies based in the United States can choose whether to follow the standards of the FASB or those of the IASB since the rules of the two groups have converged.
	2.	Evaluate the following statement: The auditors are in the best position to evaluate a company because they have prepared the financial statements.
	3.	Why does inflation present a challenge to the accountant? Relate your answer to the monetary unit assumption.
	4.	What is meant by the term *generally accepted accounting principles*?

Apply		
	1.	What monetary unit is used to prepare financial statements for companies in the United States? for companies in Japan?
	2.	What role has the Securities and Exchange Commission played in setting accounting standards? Contrast its role with that played by the Financial Accounting Standards Board.
	3.	List the four steps that can help a person make ethical decisions.

Answers are located at the end of the chapter.

KEY TERMS QUIZ

Note to the student: We conclude each chapter with a quiz on the key terms, which are shown in color in the chapter. Because of the large number of terms introduced in this chapter, there are two quizzes on key terms.

Read each definition below and write the number of the definition in the blank beside the appropriate term. The first one has been done for you. The quiz solutions appear at the end of the chapter. When reviewing terminology, come back to your completed key terms quiz. *Study tip:* Also check the glossary in the margin or at the end of the book.

Quiz 1: Introduction to Business

_____	Business	_____	Nonbusiness entity
_____	Business entity	_____	Liability
_____	Sole proprietorship	_____	Capital stock
_____	Economic entity concept	_____	Stockholder
_____	Partnership	_____	Creditor
_____	Corporation	___1___	Asset
_____	Share of stock	_____	Revenue
_____	Bond	_____	Expense

1. A future economic benefit.
2. A business owned by two or more individuals; the organization form often used by accounting firms and law firms.
3. An inflow of assets resulting from the sale of goods and services.
4. A form of entity organized under the laws of a particular state; ownership evidenced by shares of stock.
5. An organization operated for some purpose other than to earn a profit.
6. An outflow of assets resulting from the sale of goods and services.
7. An obligation of a business.
8. A certificate that acts as evidence of ownership in a corporation.
9. A certificate that represents a corporation's promise to repay a certain amount of money and interest in the future.
10. One of the owners of a corporation.
11. Someone to whom a company or person has a debt.

12. The assumption that a single, identifiable unit must be accounted for in all situations.
13. A form of organization with a single owner.
14. Indicates the owners' contributions to a corporation.
15. All of the activities necessary to provide the members of an economic system with goods and services.
16. An organization operated to earn a profit.

Quiz 2: Introduction to Accounting

_____ Accounting
_____ Management accounting
_____ Financial accounting
_____ Owners' equity
_____ Stockholders' equity
_____ Retained earnings
_____ Balance sheet
_____ Income statement
_____ Net income
_____ Statement of retained earnings
_____ Dividends
_____ Statement of cash flows
_____ Cost principle
_____ Going concern
_____ Monetary unit
_____ Time period

_____ Generally accepted accounting principles (GAAP)
_____ Securities and Exchange Commission (SEC)
_____ Financial Accounting Standards Board (FASB)
_____ American Institute of Certified Public Accountants (AICPA)
_____ Certified Public Accountant (CPA)
_____ Public Company Accounting Oversight Board (PCAOB)
_____ International Accounting Standards Board (IASB)
_____ Auditing
_____ Sarbanes-Oxley Act

1. A statement that summarizes revenues and expenses.
2. The statement that summarizes the income earned and dividends paid over the life of a business.
3. The owners' equity in a corporation.
4. The process of identifying, measuring, and communicating economic information to various users.
5. The branch of accounting concerned with the preparation of financial statements for outsider use.
6. The owners' claims on the assets of an entity.
7. The financial statement that summarizes the assets, liabilities, and owners' equity at a specific point in time.
8. The part of stockholders' equity that represents the income earned less dividends paid over the life of an entity.
9. The branch of accounting concerned with providing management with information to facilitate planning and control.
10. A distribution of the net income of a business to its stockholders.
11. The various methods, rules, practices, and other procedures that have evolved over time in response to the need to regulate the preparation of financial statements.
12. Assets are recorded at the cost to acquire them.
13. The federal agency with ultimate authority to determine the rules for preparing statements for companies whose stock is sold to the public.
14. The assumption that an entity is not in the process of liquidation and that it will continue indefinitely.
15. The group in the private sector with authority to set accounting standards.
16. The yardstick used to measure amounts in financial statements; the dollar in the United States.
17. The professional organization of certified public accountants.
18. An artificial segment on the calendar used as the basis for preparing financial statements.
19. The process of examining the financial statements and the underlying records of a company to render an opinion as to whether the statements are fairly presented.

20. The organization formed to develop worldwide accounting standards.
21. An act of Congress in 2002 intended to bring reform to corporate accountability and stewardship in the wake of a number of major corporate scandals.
22. The excess of revenues over expenses.
23. The designation for an individual who has passed a uniform exam administered by the AICPA and has met other requirements as determined by individual states.
24. A five-member body created by an act of Congress in 2002 to set auditing standards.
25. The financial statement that summarizes a company's cash receipts and cash payments during the period from operating, investing, and financing activities.

ALTERNATE TERMS

balance sheet statement of financial position
cost principle original cost or historical cost
creditor lender
income statement statement of income

net income profits, earnings
stockholder shareholder
stockholders' equity shareholders' equity

REVIEW PROBLEM & SOLUTION

Greenway Corporation is organized on June 1, 2017. The company will provide lawn-care and tree-trimming services on a contract basis. Following is an alphabetical list of the items that should appear on its income statement for the first month and on its balance sheet at the end of the first month. (You will need to determine on which statement each should appear.)

Accounts payable	$ 800	Lawn-care revenue	$1,500
Accounts receivable	500	Notes payable	6,000
Building	2,000	Retained earnings (beginning balance)	0
Capital stock	5,000	Salaries and wages expense	900
Cash	3,300	Tools	800
Gas, utilities, and other expenses	300	Tree-trimming revenue	500
Land	4,000	Truck	2,000

Required

1. Prepare an income statement for the month of June.
2. Prepare a balance sheet at June 30, 2017. *Note:* You will need to determine the balance in Retained Earnings at the end of the month.
3. The financial statements you have prepared are helpful, but in many ways, they are just a starting point. Assuming that this is your business, what additional questions do the financial statements raise that you need to consider?

Solution to Review Problem

1.

Greenway Corporation
Income Statement
For the Month Ended June 30, 2017

Revenues:		
Lawn care	$1,500	
Tree trimming	500	$2,000
Expenses:		
Salaries and wages	$ 900	
Gas, utilities, and other expenses	300	1,200
Net income		$ 800

2.

Greenway Corporation
Balance Sheet
June 30, 2017

Assets		Liabilities and Stockholders' Equity	
Cash	$ 3,300	Accounts payable	$ 800
Accounts receivable	500	Notes payable	6,000
Truck	2,000	Capital stock	5,000
Tools	800	Retained earnings	800
Building	2,000		
Land	4,000	Total liabilities and	
Total assets	$12,600	stockholders' equity	$12,600

3. Following are examples of questions that the financial statements raise:

- During June, 75% of the revenue was from lawn care and the other 25% was from tree trimming. Will this relationship hold in future months?
- Are the expenses representative of those that will be incurred in the future? Will any other expenses arise, such as advertising and income taxes?
- When can we expect to collect the accounts receivable? Is there a chance that not all will be collected?
- How soon will the accounts payable need to be paid?
- What is the interest rate on the note payable? When is interest paid? When is the note itself due?

EXERCISES

Exercise 1-1 Types of Business Activities   LO3

Braxton Corp. was organized on January 1 to operate a limousine service to and from the airport. For each of the following business activities, indicate whether it is a financing (F), investing (I), or operating (O) activity.

_____   1. Issued shares of stock to each of the four owners.

_____   2. Purchased two limousines.

_____   3. Paid first month's rent for use of garage.

_____   4. Obtained loan from local bank.

_____   5. Received cash from customer for trip to the airport.

_____   6. Paid driver first week's wages.

_____   7. Purchased 500-gallon fuel tank.

Exercise 1-2 Users of Accounting Information and Their Needs   LO4

Listed below are a number of the important users of accounting information. Following the list are descriptions of a major need of each of these various users. Fill in each blank with the one user group that is most likely to have the need described.

Company management   Banker

Stockholder   Supplier

Securities and Exchange Commission   Labor union

Internal Revenue Service

User Group   **Needs Information About**

_____   1. The profitability of each division in the company

_____   2. The prospects for future dividend payments

_____   3. The profitability of the company since the last contract with the workforce was signed

(Continued)

User Group	Needs Information About
_____	4. The financial status of a company issuing securities to the public for the first time
_____	5. The prospects that a company will be able to meet its interest payments on time
_____	6. The prospects that a company will be able to pay for its purchases on time
_____	7. The company's profitability based on the tax code

LO5
EXAMPLE 1-4

Exercise 1-3 The Accounting Equation

For each of the following independent cases, fill in the blank with the appropriate dollar amount.

	Assets	=	Liabilities	+	Owners' Equity
Case 1	$125,000		$ 75,000		$_____
Case 2	400,000		_____		100,000
Case 3	_____		320,000		95,000

LO5
EXAMPLE 1-4

Exercise 1-4 The Accounting Equation

Ginger Enterprises began the year with total assets of $500,000 and total liabilities of $250,000. Using this information and the accounting equation, answer each of the following independent questions.
1. What was the amount of Ginger's owners' equity at the beginning of the year?
2. If Ginger's total assets increased by $100,000 and its total liabilities increased by $77,000 during the year, what was the amount of Ginger's owners' equity at the end of the year?
3. If Ginger's total liabilities increased by $33,000 and its owners' equity decreased by $58,000 during the year, what was the amount of its total assets at the end of the year?
4. If Ginger's total assets doubled to $1,000,000 and its owners' equity remained the same during the year, what was the amount of its total liabilities at the end of the year?

LO5
EXAMPLE 1-4

Exercise 1-5 The Accounting Equation

Using the accounting equation, answer each of the following independent questions.
1. Burlin Company starts the year with $100,000 in assets and $80,000 in liabilities. Net income for the year is $25,000, and no dividends are paid. How much is owners' equity at the end of the year?
2. Chapman Inc. doubles the amount of its assets from the beginning to the end of the year. Liabilities at the end of the year amount to $40,000, and owners' equity is $20,000. What is the amount of Chapman's assets at the beginning of the year?
3. During the year, the liabilities of Dixon Enterprises triple in amount. Assets at the beginning of the year amount to $30,000, and owners' equity is $10,000. What is the amount of liabilities at the end of the year?

LO5
EXAMPLE 1-4

Exercise 1-6 Changes in Owners' Equity

The following amounts are available from the records of Coaches and Carriages Inc. at the end of the years indicated:

December 31	Total Assets	Total Liabilities
2015	$ 25,000	$ 12,000
2016	79,000	67,000
2017	184,000	137,000

Required

1. Compute the changes in Coaches and Carriages owners' equity during 2016 and 2017.
2. Compute the amount of Coaches and Carriages' net income (or loss) for 2016 assuming that no dividends were paid and the owners made no additional contributions during the year.

3. Compute the amount of Coaches and Carriages' net income (or loss) for 2017 assuming that dividends paid during the year amounted to $10,000 and no additional contributions were made by the owners.

Exercise 1-7 The Accounting Equation

LO5

For each of the following cases, fill in the blank with the appropriate dollar amount.

	Case 1	Case 2	Case 3	Case 4
Total assets, end of period	$40,000	$_____	$75,000	$50,000
Total liabilities, end of period	_____	15,000	25,000	10,000
Capital stock, end of period	10,000	5,000	20,000	15,000
Retained earnings, beginning of period	15,000	8,000	10,000	20,000
Net income for the period	8,000	7,000	_____	9,000
Dividends for the period	2,000	1,000	3,000	_____

Exercise 1-8 Classification of Financial Statement Items

LO5

EXAMPLE 1-3, 1-4, 1-5

Classify each of the following items according to (1) whether it belongs on the income statement (IS) or balance sheet (BS) and (2) whether it is a revenue (R), expense (E), asset (A), liability (L), or stockholders' equity (SE) item.

Item	Appears on the	Classified as
Example: Cash	BS	A
1. Salaries expense	_____	_____
2. Equipment	_____	_____
3. Accounts payable	_____	_____
4. Membership fees earned	_____	_____
5. Capital stock	_____	_____
6. Accounts receivable	_____	_____
7. Buildings	_____	_____
8. Advertising expense	_____	_____
9. Retained earnings	_____	_____

Exercise 1-9 Classification of Financial Statement Items

LO5

EXAMPLE 1-5

REAL WORLD

Regal Entertainment Group operates the largest chain of movie theaters in the U.S. Classify each of the following items found in the company's financial statements included in the Form 10-K for the year ended December 31, 2015, according to (1) whether it belongs on the income statement (IS) or balance sheet (BS) and (2) whether it is a revenue (R), expense (E), asset (A), liability (L), or stockholders' equity (SE) item.

Item	Appears on the	Classified as
Example: Cash and cash equivalents	BS	A
1. Trade and other receivables, net	_____	_____
2. Class A common stock	_____	_____
3. Inventories	_____	_____
4. Admissions	_____	_____
5. Cost of concessions	_____	_____
6. Equipment	_____	_____
7. Accounts payable	_____	_____
8. Retained earnings	_____	_____
9. Interest expense, net	_____	_____
10. Long-term debt, less current portion	_____	_____

LO5
EXAMPLE 1-4, 1-5, 1-6

Exercise 1-10 Net Income (or Loss) and Retained Earnings

The following information is available from the records of Prestige Landscape Design Inc. at the end of the year:

Accounts payable	$ 5,000	Landscaping revenues	$25,000
Accounts receivable	4,500	Office equipment	7,500
Capital stock	8,000	Rent expense	6,500
Cash	13,000	Retained earnings, beginning of year	8,500
Dividends paid during the year	3,000	Salary and wage expense	12,000

Required

Use the previous information to answer the following questions.

1. What is Prestige's net income for the year?
2. What is Prestige's Retained Earnings balance at the end of the year?
3. What is the total amount of Prestige's assets at the end of the year?
4. What is the total amount of Prestige's liabilities at the end of the year?
5. How much owners' equity does Prestige have at the end of the year?
6. What is Prestige's accounting equation at the end of the year?

LO5
EXAMPLE 1-6

Exercise 1-11 Statement of Retained Earnings

Ace Corporation has been in business for many years. Retained earnings on January 1, 2017, is $235,800. The following information is available for the first two months of 2017:

	January	February
Revenues	$83,000	$96,000
Expenses	89,000	82,000
Dividends paid	0	5,000

Required

Prepare a statement of retained earnings for the month ended February 28, 2017.

LO6

Exercise 1-12 Accounting Principles and Assumptions

The following basic accounting principles and assumptions were discussed in the chapter:

Economic entity
Monetary unit
Cost principle
Going concern
Time period

Fill in each of the blanks with the accounting principle or assumption that is relevant to the situation described.

_____ 1. Genesis Corporation is now in its 30th year of business. The founder of the company is planning to retire at the end of the year and turn the business over to his daughter.

_____ 2. Nordic Company purchased a 20-acre parcel of property on which to build a new factory. The company recorded the property on the records at the amount of cash given to acquire it.

_____ 3. Jim Bailey enters into an agreement to operate a new law firm in partnership with a friend. Each partner will make an initial cash investment of $10,000. Jim opens a checking account in the name of the partnership and transfers $10,000 from his personal account into the new account.

_____ 4. Multinational Corp. has a division in Japan. Prior to preparing the financial statements for the company and all of its foreign divisions, Multinational translates the financial statements of its Japanese division from yen to U.S. dollars.

_____ 5. Camden Company has always prepared financial statements annually, with a year-end of June 30. Because the company is going to sell its stock to the public for the first time, quarterly financial reports will also be required by the SEC.

Exercise 1-13 Organizations and Accounting LO7

Match each of the organizations listed below with the statement that most adequately describes the role of the group.

Securities and Exchange Commission
International Accounting Standards Board
Financial Accounting Standards Board
American Institute of Certified Public Accountants

_____ 1. The federal agency with ultimate authority to determine rules used for preparing financial statements for companies whose stock is sold to the public

_____ 2. The group in the private sector with authority to set accounting standards

_____ 3. The professional organization for certified public accountants

_____ 4. The organization formed to develop worldwide accounting standards

Exercise 1-14 Classification of Items on the Statement of Cash Flows LO5
EXAMPLE 1-7

Classify each of the following items according to the section on the statement of cash flows in which it should appear: operating (O), investing (I), or financing (F):

Item	Section
Example: Cash paid for insurance	O
1. Cash paid for land	____
2. Cash received from issuance of note	____
3. Cash paid for dividends	____
4. Cash received from issuance of capital stock	____
5. Cash collected from customers	____
6. Cash paid for income taxes	____

MULTI-CONCEPT EXERCISES

Exercise 1-15 Users of Accounting Information and the Financial Statements LO4 • 5

Following are a number of users of accounting information and examples of questions they need answered before making decisions. Fill in each blank to indicate whether the user is most likely to find the answer by looking at the income statement (IS), the balance sheet (BS), the statement of retained earnings (RE), or the statement of cash flows (SCF).

(Continued)

User	Question	Financial Statement
Stockholder	How did this year's sales compare to last year's?	_____
Banker	How much debt does the company already have on its books?	_____
Supplier	How much does the company currently owe to its suppliers?	_____
Stockholder	How much did the company pay in dividends this past year?	_____
Advertising account manager	How much did the company spend this past year to generate sales?	_____
Banker	What collateral or security can the company provide to ensure that any loan I make will be repaid?	_____

LO5 • 6 **Exercise 1-16 Chipotle's Land**

Refer to **Chipotle**'s balance sheet reproduced in the chapter.

REAL WORLD

Required

In which of the assets would you expect Chipotle's land to be included? What does this amount represent (i.e., cost, market value)? Why does Chipotle carry its land at one or the other values?

PROBLEMS

LO4 **Problem 1-1 You Won the Lottery**

You have won a lottery! You will receive $200,000, after taxes, each year for the next five years.

Required

Describe the process you will go through in determining how to invest your winnings. Consider at least two options and make a choice. You may consider the stock of a certain company, bonds, real estate investments, bank deposits, and so on. Be specific. What information do you need to make a final decision? How will your decision be affected by the fact that you will receive the winnings over a five-year period rather than in one lump sum? Would you prefer one payment? Explain.

LO4 **Problem 1-2 Users of Accounting Information and Their Needs**

Havre Company would like to buy a building and equipment to produce a new product line. Information about Havre is more useful to some people involved in the project than to others.

Required

Complete the following chart by identifying the information listed on the left with the user's need to know the information. Identify the information as one of the following:

a. *Need* to know
b. *Helpful* to know
c. *Not necessary* to know

Information	User of the Information		
	Management	Stockholders	Banker
1. Amount of current debt, repayment schedule, and interest rate	_____	_____	_____
2. Fair market value of the building	_____	_____	_____
3. Condition of the roof and heating and cooling, electrical, and plumbing systems	_____	_____	_____
4. Total cost of the building, improvements, and equipment to set up production	_____	_____	_____
5. Expected sales from the new product, variable production costs, and related selling costs	_____	_____	_____

Problem 1-3 Balance Sheet

LO5

The following items are available from records of Freescia Corporation at the end of the current year:

Accounts payable	$12,550	Notes payable	$50,000
Accounts receivable	23,920	Office equipment	12,000
Advertising expense	2,100	Retained earnings, end of year	37,590
Buildings	85,000	Salary and wage expense	8,230
Capital stock	25,000	Sales revenue	14,220
Cash	4,220		

Required

Prepare a balance sheet. *Hint:* Not all of the items listed should appear on a balance sheet. For each non-balance-sheet item, indicate where it should appear.

Problem 1-4 Corrected Balance Sheet

LO5

Dave is the president of Avon Consulting Inc. Avon began business at the beginning of the current year. The company's controller is out of the country on business. Dave needs a copy of the company's balance sheet for a meeting tomorrow and asks his assistant to obtain the required information from the company's records. She presents Dave with the following balance sheet. He asks you to review it for accuracy.

Avon Consulting Inc.
Balance Sheet
For the Current Year

Assets		Liabilities and Stockholders' Equity	
Accounts payable	$13,000	Accounts receivable	$16,000
Cash	21,000	Capital stock	20,000
Cash dividends paid	16,000	Net income for the year	72,000
Furniture and equipment	43,000	Supplies	9,000

Required

1. Prepare a corrected balance sheet.
2. Draft a memo explaining the major differences between the balance sheet Dave's assistant prepared and the one you prepared.

Problem 1-5 Income Statement, Statement of Retained Earnings, and Balance Sheet

LO5

The following list, in alphabetical order, shows the various items that regularly appear on the financial statements of Maple Park Theatres Corp. The amounts shown for balance sheet items are balances as of September 30, 2017 (with the exception of retained earnings, which is the balance on September 1, 2017), and the amounts shown for income statement items are balances for the month ended September 30, 2017.

Accounts payable	$17,600	Furniture and fixtures	$34,000
Accounts receivable	6,410	Land	26,000
Advertising expense	14,500	Notes payable	20,000
Buildings	60,000	Projection equipment	25,000
Capital stock	50,000	Rent expense—movies	50,600
Cash	15,230	Retained earnings	73,780
Concessions revenue	60,300	Salaries and wages expense	46,490
Cost of concessions sold	23,450	Ticket sales	95,100
Dividends paid during the month	8,400	Water, gas, and electricity	6,700

Required

1. Prepare an income statement for the month ended September 30, 2017.
2. Prepare a statement of retained earnings for the month ended September 30, 2017.

(Continued)

3. Prepare a balance sheet at September 30, 2017.
4. You have $1,000 to invest. On the basis of the statements you prepared, would you use it to buy stock in Maple Park? Explain. What other information would you want before making a final decision?

LO5   **Problem 1-6 Income Statement and Balance Sheet**

Green Bay Corporation began business in July 2017 as a commercial fishing operation and a passenger service between islands. Shares of stock were issued to the owners in exchange for cash. Boats were purchased by making a down payment in cash and signing a note payable for the balance. Fish are sold to local restaurants on open account, and customers are given 15 days to pay their account. Cash fares are collected for all passenger traffic. Rent for the dock facilities is paid at the beginning of each month. Salaries and wages are paid at the end of the month. The following amounts are from the records of Green Bay Corporation at the end of its first month of operations:

Accounts receivable	$18,500	Notes payable	$60,000
Boats	80,000	Passenger service revenue	12,560
Capital stock	40,000	Rent expense	4,000
Cash	7,730	Retained earnings	?
Dividends	5,400	Salary and wage expense	18,230
Fishing revenue	21,300		

Required

1. Prepare an income statement for the month ended July 31, 2017.
2. Prepare a balance sheet at July 31, 2017.
3. What information would you need about Notes Payable to fully assess Green Bay's long-term viability? Explain your answer.

LO5   **Problem 1-7 Corrected Financial Statements**

Hometown Cleaners Inc. operates a small dry-cleaning business. The company has always maintained a complete and accurate set of records. Unfortunately, the company's accountant left in a dispute with the president and took the 2017 financial statements with him. The following income statement and balance sheet were prepared by the company's president:

Hometown Cleaners Inc.
Income Statement
For the Year Ended December 31, 2017

Revenues:		
Accounts receivable	$15,200	
Cleaning revenue—cash sales	32,500	$47,700
Expenses:		
Dividends	$ 4,000	
Accounts payable	4,500	
Utilities	12,200	
Salaries and wages	17,100	37,800
Net income		$ 9,900

Hometown Cleaners Inc.
Balance Sheet
December 31, 2017

Assets		Liabilities and Stockholders' Equity	
Cash	$ 7,400	Cleaning revenue—	
Building and equipment	80,000	credit sales	$26,200
Notes payable	(50,000)	Capital stock	20,000
Land	40,000	Net income	9,900
		Retained earnings	21,300
Total assets	$ 77,400	Total liabilities and stockholders' equity	$77,400

The president is very disappointed with the net income for the year because it has averaged $25,000 over the last ten years. She has asked for your help in determining whether the reported net income accurately reflects the profitability of the company and whether the balance sheet is prepared correctly.

Required

1. Prepare a corrected income statement for the year ended December 31, 2017.
2. Prepare a statement of retained earnings for the year ended December 31, 2017. (The actual balance of Retained Earnings on January 1, 2017, was $42,700. Note that the December 31, 2017, Retained Earnings balance shown is incorrect. The president simply "plugged in" this amount to make the balance sheet balance.)
3. Prepare a corrected balance sheet at December 31, 2017.
4. Draft a memo to the president explaining the major differences between the income statement she prepared and the one you prepared.

Problem 1-8 Statement of Retained Earnings for The Coca-Cola Company

The Coca-Cola Company and Subsidiaries reported the following amounts in various statements included in its Form 10-K for the year ended December 31, 2015. (All amounts are stated in millions of dollars.)

Net income attributable to shareowners of The Coca-Cola Company for 2015	$ 7,351
Dividends in 2015	5,741
Reinvested earnings, December 31, 2014	63,408
Reinvested earnings, December 31, 2015	65,018

Required

1. Prepare a statement of retained earnings for The Coca-Cola Company for the year ended December 31, 2015.
2. The Coca-Cola Company does not actually present a statement of retained earnings in its annual report. Instead, it presents a broader statement of shareholders' equity. Describe the information that would be included on this statement that is not included on a statement of retained earnings.

Problem 1-9 Information Needs and Setting Accounting Standards

The Financial Accounting Standards Board requires companies to supplement their consolidated financial statements with disclosures about segments of their businesses. To comply with this standard, the notes to the financial statements included in **Time Warner Inc.**'s Form 10-K for the year ended December 31, 2015 provides various disclosures for the three segments in which it operates: Turner, Home Box Office, and Warner Bros.

Required

Which users of accounting information do you think the FASB had in mind when it set this standard? What types of disclosures do you think these users would find helpful?

MULTI-CONCEPT PROBLEM

Problem 1-10 Primary Assumptions Made in Preparing Financial Statements

Joe Hale opened a machine repair business in leased retail space, paying the first month's rent of $300 and a $1,000 security deposit with a check on his personal account. He took the tools, worth about $7,500, from his garage to the shop. He also bought some equipment to get started. The new equipment had a list price of $5,000, but Joe was able to purchase it on sale at Sears for only $4,200. He charged the new equipment on his personal Sears charge card. Joe's

(Continued)

first customer paid $400 for services rendered, so Joe opened a checking account for the company. He completed a second job, but the customer has not paid Joe the $2,500 for his work. At the end of the first month, Joe prepared the following balance sheet and income statement:

Joe's Machine Repair Shop
Balance Sheet
July 31, 2017

Cash	$ 400		
Equipment	5,000	Equity	$5,400
Total	$5,400	Total	$5,400

Joe's Machine Repair Shop
Income Statement
For the Month Ended July 31, 2017

Sales		$ 2,900
Rent	$ 300	
Tools	4,200	4,500
Net loss		$(1,600)

Joe believes that he should show a greater profit next month because he won't have large expenses for items such as tools.

Required

Identify the assumptions that Joe has violated and explain how each event should have been handled. Prepare a corrected balance sheet and income statement.

ALTERNATE PROBLEMS

LO4   Problem 1-1A   What to Do with a Million Dollars?

You have inherited $1 million!

Required

Describe the process you will go through in determining how to invest your inheritance. Consider at least two options and choose one. You may consider the stock of a certain company, bonds, real estate investments, bank deposits, and so on. Be specific. What information do you need to make a final decision? Where will you find the information you need? What additional information will you need to consider if you want to make a change in your investment?

LO4   Problem 1-2A   Users of Accounting Information and Their Needs

Billings Inc. would like to buy a franchise to provide a specialized service. Information about Billings is more useful to some people involved in the project than to others.

Required

Complete the following chart by identifying the information listed on the left with the user's need to know the information. Identify the information as one of the following:

a. *Need* to know
b. *Helpful* to know
c. *Not necessary* to know

Information	User of the Information		
	Manager	Stockholders	Franchisor
1. Expected revenue from the new service	_____	_____	_____
2. Cost of the franchise fee and recurring fees to be paid to the franchisor	_____	_____	_____
3. Cash available to Billings, the franchisee, to operate the business after the franchise is purchased	_____	_____	_____
4. Expected overhead costs of the service outlet	_____	_____	_____
5. Billings' required return on its investment	_____	_____	_____

Problem 1-3A Balance Sheet   LO5

The following items are available from the records of Victor Corporation at the end of the current year:

Accounts payable	$16,900	Delivery expense	$ 4,600
Accounts receivable	5,700	Notes payable	50,000
Buildings	35,000	Office equipment	12,000
Butter and cheese inventory	12,100	Retained earnings, end of year	26,300
Capital stock	25,000	Salary and wage expense	8,230
Cash	21,800	Sales revenue	14,220
Computerized mixers	25,800	Tools	5,800

Required

Prepare a balance sheet. *Hint:* Not all of the items listed should appear on a balance sheet. For each non-balance-sheet item, indicate where it should appear.

Problem 1-4A Corrected Balance Sheet   LO5

Pete is the president of Island Enterprises. Island Enterprises began business at the beginning of the current year. The company's controller is out of the country on business. Pete needs a copy of the company's balance sheet for a meeting tomorrow and asks his assistant to obtain the required information from the company's records. She presents Pete with the following balance sheet. He asks you to review it for accuracy.

Island Enterprises
Balance Sheet
For the Current Year

Assets		Liabilities and Stockholders' Equity	
Accounts payable	$ 29,600	Accounts receivable	$ 23,200
Building and equipment	177,300	Supplies	12,200
Cash	14,750	Capital stock	100,000
Cash dividends paid	16,000	Net income for the year	113,850

Required

1. Prepare a corrected balance sheet.
2. Draft a memo explaining the major differences between the balance sheet Pete's assistant prepared and the one you prepared.

Problem 1-5A Income Statement, Statement of Retained Earnings, and   LO5
Balance Sheet

The following list, in alphabetical order, shows the various items that regularly appear on the financial statements of Sterns Audio Book Rental Corp. The amounts shown for balance sheet items are balances as of December 31, 2017 (with the exception of retained earnings, which is the balance on January 1, 2017), and the amounts shown for income statement items are balances for the year ended December 31, 2017.

Accounts payable	$ 4,500	Notes payable	$ 10,000
Accounts receivable	300	Rental revenue	125,900
Advertising expense	14,500	Rent expense	60,000
Capital stock	50,000	Retained earnings	35,390
Cash	2,490	Salaries and wages expense	17,900
Display fixtures	45,000	Supplies inventory	70,000
Dividends paid during the year	12,000	Water, gas, and electricity	3,600

Required

1. Prepare an income statement for the year ended December 31, 2017.
2. Prepare a statement of retained earnings for the year ended December 31, 2017.
3. Prepare a balance sheet at December 31, 2017.
4. You have $1,000 to invest. On the basis of the statements you prepared, would you use it to buy stock in this company? Explain. What other information would you want before deciding?

LO5 **Problem 1-6A Income Statement and Balance Sheet**

Fort Worth Corporation began business in January 2017 as a commercial carpet-cleaning and drying service. Shares of stock were issued to the owners in exchange for cash. Equipment was purchased by making a down payment in cash and signing a note payable for the balance. Services are performed for local restaurants and office buildings on open account, and customers are given 15 days to pay their accounts. Rent for office and storage facilities is paid at the beginning of each month. Salaries and wages are paid at the end of the month. The following amounts are from the records of Fort Worth Corporation at the end of its first month of operations:

Accounts receivable	$24,750	Equipment	$62,000
Capital stock	80,000	Notes payable	30,000
Cash	51,650	Rent expense	3,600
Cleaning revenue	45,900	Retained earnings	?
Dividends	5,500	Salary and wage expense	8,400

Required

1. Prepare an income statement for the month ended January 31, 2017.
2. Prepare a balance sheet at January 31, 2017.
3. What information would you need about Notes Payable to fully assess Fort Worth's long-term viability? Explain your answer.

LO5 **Problem 1-7A Corrected Financial Statements**

Heidi's Bakery Inc. operates a small pastry business. The company has always maintained a complete and accurate set of records. Unfortunately, the company's accountant left in a dispute with the president and took the 2017 financial statements with her. The following balance sheet and income statement were prepared by the company's president:

Heidi's Bakery Inc.
Income Statement
For the Year Ended December 31, 2017

Revenues:		
Accounts receivable	$15,500	
Pastry revenue—cash sales	23,700	$39,200
Expenses:		
Dividends	$ 5,600	
Accounts payable	6,800	
Utilities	9,500	
Salaries and wages	18,200	40,100
Net loss		$ (900)

Heidi's Bakery Inc.
Balance Sheet
December 31, 2017

Assets		Liabilities and Stockholders' Equity	
Cash	$ 3,700	Pastry revenue—	
Building and equipment	60,000	credit sales	$22,100
Notes payable	(40,000)	Capital stock	30,000
Land	50,000	Net loss	(900)
		Retained earnings	22,500
Total assets	$ 73,700	Total liabilities and stockholders' equity	$73,700

The president is very disappointed with the net loss for the year because net income has averaged $21,000 over the last ten years. He has asked for your help in determining whether the reported net loss accurately reflects the profitability of the company and whether the balance sheet is prepared correctly.

Required

1. Prepare a corrected income statement for the year ended December 31, 2017.
2. Prepare a statement of retained earnings for the year ended December 31, 2017. (The actual amount of retained earnings on January 1, 2017, was $39,900. The December 31, 2017, Retained Earnings balance shown is incorrect. The president simply "plugged in" this amount to make the balance sheet balance.)
3. Prepare a corrected balance sheet at December 31, 2017.
4. Draft a memo to the president explaining the major differences between the income statement he prepared and the one you prepared.

Problem 1-8A Statement of Retained Earnings for Brunswick Corporation

LO5

REAL WORLD

Brunswick Corporation reported the following amounts in various statements included in its Form 10-K for the year ended December 31, 2015. (All amounts are stated in millions of dollars.)

Net earnings for 2015	$ 241.4
Cash dividends paid in 2015	48.3
Retained earnings, December 31, 2014	1,467.3
Retained earnings, December 31, 2015	1,660.4

Required

1. Prepare a statement of retained earnings for Brunswick Corporation for the year ended December 31, 2015.
2. Brunswick does not actually present a statement of retained earnings in its annual report. Instead, it presents a broader statement of shareholders' equity. Describe the information that would be included on this statement that is not included on a statement of retained earnings.

Problem 1-9A Information Needs and Setting Accounting Standards

LO4

REAL WORLD

The Financial Accounting Standards Board requires companies to supplement their consolidated financial statements with disclosures about segments of their businesses. To comply with this standard, the notes to the financial statements included in **Marriott International**'s Form 10-K for the fiscal year ended December 31, 2015 provides various disclosures for the three segments in which it operated at that time: North American Full-Service, North American Limited-Service, and International.

Required

Which users of accounting information do you think the FASB had in mind when it set this standard? What types of disclosures do you think these users would find helpful?

ALTERNATE MULTI-CONCEPT PROBLEM

LO5 • 6   **Problem 1-10A** **Primary Assumptions Made in Preparing Financial Statements**

Millie Abrams opened a ceramic studio in leased retail space, paying the first month's rent of $300 and a $1,000 security deposit with a check on her personal account. She took molds and paint, worth about $7,500, from her home to the studio. She also bought a new firing kiln to start the business. The new kiln had a list price of $5,000, but Millie was able to trade in her old kiln, worth $500 at the time of trade, on the new kiln. Therefore, she paid only $4,500 cash. She wrote a check on her personal account. Millie's first customers paid a total of $1,400 to attend classes for the next two months. Millie opened a checking account in the company's name with the $1,400. She has conducted classes for one month and has sold $3,000 of unfinished ceramic pieces called *greenware*. All greenware sales are cash. Millie incurred $1,000 of personal cost in making the greenware. At the end of the first month, Millie prepared the following balance sheet and income statement:

Millie's Ceramic Studio
Balance Sheet
July 31, 2017

Cash	$1,400		
Kiln	5,000	Equity	$6,400
Total	$6,400	Total	$6,400

Millie's Ceramic Studio
Income Statement
For the Month Ended July 31, 2017

Sales		$4,400
Rent	$300	
Supplies	600	900
Net income		$3,500

Millie needs to earn at least $3,000 each month for the business to be worth her time. She is pleased with the results.

Required

Identify the assumptions that Millie has violated and explain how each event should have been handled. Prepare a corrected balance sheet and income statement.

DECISION CASES

Reading and Interpreting Financial Statements

LO4 • 5   **Decision Case 1-1** **An Annual Report as Ready Reference**

REAL WORLD

Refer to the financial information for **Chipotle** reproduced at the back of the book and identify where each of the following users of accounting information would first look to answer their respective questions about Chipotle.

1. *Investors:* How much did the company earn for each share of stock that I own? Were any dividends paid, and how much was reinvested in the company?
2. *Potential investors:* What amount of earnings can I expect to see from Chipotle in the near future?
3. *Suppliers:* Should I extend credit to Chipotle? Does it have sufficient cash or cashlike assets to repay accounts payable?

4. *IRS:* How much does Chipotle owe for taxes?
5. *Bankers:* What is Chipotle's long-term debt? Should I make a new loan to the company?

Decision Case 1-2 Reading and Interpreting Chipotle's Financial Statements

LO5

REAL WORLD

Refer to the financial statements for **Chipotle** reproduced in the chapter and answer the following questions.

1. What was the company's net income for 2015?
2. State Chipotle's financial position on December 31, 2015, in terms of the accounting equation.
3. By what amount did Leasehold improvements, property and equipment, net, increase during 2015? Explain what would cause an increase in this item.

Decision Case 1-3 Comparing Two Companies in the Same Industry: Chipotle and Panera Bread

LO5

REAL WORLD

Refer to the financial information for **Chipotle** and **Panera Bread** reproduced at the back of the book and answer the following questions.

1. What was the total revenue for each company for the most recent year? By what percentage did each company's revenue increase or decrease from its total amount in the prior year?
2. What was each company's net income for the most recent year? By what percentage did each company's net income increase or decrease from its net income for the prior year?
3. What was the total asset balance for each company at the end of its most recent year? Among its assets, what was the largest asset each company reported on its year-end balance sheet?
4. Did either company pay its stockholders any dividends during the most recent year? Explain how you can tell.

Making Financial Decisions

Decision Case 1-4 An Investment Opportunity

LO4

You have saved enough money to pay for your college tuition for the next three years when a high-school friend comes to you with a deal. He is an artist who has spent most of the past two years drawing on the walls of old buildings. The buildings are about to be demolished, and your friend thinks you should buy the walls before the buildings are demolished and open a gallery featuring his work. Of course, you are levelheaded and would normally say no. Recently, however, your friend has been featured on several local radio and television shows and is talking to some national networks about doing a feature on a well-known news show. To set up the gallery would take all of your savings, but your friend thinks that you will be able to sell his artwork for ten times the cost of your investment. What information about the business do you need before deciding to invest your savings? What kind of profit split would you suggest to your friend?

Decision Case 1-5 Preparation of Projected Statements for a New Business

LO5

Upon graduation from MegaState University, you and your roommate decide to start your respective careers in accounting and salmon fishing in Remote, Alaska. Your career as a CPA in Remote is going well, as is your roommate's job as a commercial fisherman. After one year in Remote, he approaches you with a business opportunity.

As we are well aware, the winters are long up here and the locals need a way to stay fit. We each put up our first year's savings of $5,000 and file for articles of incorporation with the state of Alaska to do business as Remote Fitness World. In return for our investment of $5,000, we will each receive equal shares of capital stock in the corporation. Then we go to Corner National Bank and apply for a $10,000 loan. We take the total cash of $20,000 we have now raised and buy $20,000 of exercise equipment from a distributor. We hire a qualified instructor to offer a one-hour

(Continued)

group fitness class to be offered 15 times each week. We will pay the instructor $20 per hour for conducting the classes. We charge $10 for each class taken and sell monthly memberships for unlimited use of the facility for $50. Classes would be paid for on a cash basis, but we would give customers until the 10th of the following month to pay for a monthly membership. My most conservative estimate is that during the first month alone, the total number of classes signed up for will amount to 240 and we will sell 100 monthly memberships. As I see it, we will have only two expenses, the hourly wage for the instructor and rent for a vacant building of $1,000 per month, both payable during the month.

Required

1. Prepare a projected income statement for the first month of operations.
2. Prepare a balance sheet as it would appear at the end of the first month of operations.
3. Assume that the bank is willing to make the $10,000 loan. Would you be willing to join your roommate in this business? Explain your response. Also indicate any information other than what he has provided that you would like to have before making a final decision.

Ethical Decision Making

LO**4 • 5 • 8**   **Decision Case 1-6** **Identification of Errors in Financial Statements and Preparation of Revised Statements**

ETHICAL DECISION MODEL

Lakeside Slammers Inc. is a minor league baseball organization that has just completed its first season. You and three other investors organized the corporation; each put up $10,000 in cash for shares of capital stock. Because you live out of state, you have not been actively involved in the daily affairs of the club. However, you are thrilled to receive a dividend check for $10,000 at the end of the season—an amount equal to your original investment. Included with the check are the following financial statements, along with supporting explanations:

Lakeside Slammers Inc.
Income Statement
For the Year Ended December 31, 2017

Revenues:		
Single-game ticket revenue	$420,000	
Season ticket revenue	140,000	
Concessions revenue	280,000	
Advertising revenue	100,000	$940,000
Expenses:		
Cost of concessions sold	$110,000	
Salary expense—players	225,000	
Salary and wage expense—staff	150,000	
Rent expense	210,000	695,000
Net income		$245,000

Lakeside Slammers Inc.
Statement of Retained Earnings
For the Year Ended December 31, 2017

Beginning balance, January 1, 2017	$	0
Net income for 2017		245,000
Cash dividends paid in 2017		(40,000)
Ending balance, December 31, 2017		$205,000

Lakeside Slammers Inc.
Balance Sheet
December 31, 2017

Assets		Liabilities and Stockholders' Equity	
Cash	$ 5,000	Notes payable	$ 50,000
Accounts receivable:		Capital stock	40,000
Season tickets	140,000	Additional owners' capital	80,000
Advertisers	100,000	Parent club's equity	125,000
Auxiliary assets	80,000	Retained earnings	205,000
Equipment	50,000		
Player contracts	125,000	Total liabilities and	
Total assets	$500,000	stockholders' equity	$500,000

Additional information:

a. Single-game tickets sold for $4 per game. The team averaged 1,500 fans per game. With 70 home games × $4 per game × 1,500 fans, single-game ticket revenue amounted to $420,000.

b. No season tickets were sold during the first season. During the last three months of 2017, however, an aggressive sales campaign resulted in the sale of 500 season tickets for the 2018 season. Therefore, the controller (who is also one of the owners) chose to record an Account Receivable—Season Tickets and corresponding revenue for 500 tickets × $4 per game × 70 games, or $140,000.

c. Advertising revenue of $100,000 resulted from the sale of the 40 signs on the outfield wall at $2,500 each for the season. However, none of the advertisers have paid their bills yet (thus, an account receivable of $100,000 on the balance sheet) because the contract with Lakeside required payment only if the team averaged 2,000 fans per game during the 2017 season. The controller believes that the advertisers will be sympathetic to the difficulties of starting a new franchise and will be willing to overlook the slight deficiency in the attendance requirement.

d. Lakeside has a working agreement with one of the major league franchises. The minor league team is required to pay $5,000 *every year* to the major league team for each of the 25 players on its roster. The controller believes that each of the players is an asset to the organization and has therefore recorded $5,000 × 25, or $125,000, as an asset called Player Contracts. The item on the right side of the balance sheet entitled Parent Club's Equity is the amount owed to the major league team by February 1, 2018, as payment for the players for the 2017 season.

e. In addition to the cost described in item (d), Lakeside directly pays each of its 25 players a $9,000 salary for the season. This amount—$225,000—has already been paid for the 2017 season and is reported on the income statement.

f. The items on the balance sheet entitled Auxiliary Assets on the left side and Additional Owners' Capital on the right side represent the value of the controller's personal residence. She has a mortgage with the bank for the full value of the house.

g. The $50,000 note payable resulted from a loan that was taken out at the beginning of the year to finance the purchase of bats, balls, uniforms, lawn mowers, and other miscellaneous supplies needed to operate the team. (Equipment is reported as an asset for the same amount.) The loan, with interest, is due on April 15, 2018. Even though the team had a very successful first year, Lakeside is a little short of cash at the end of 2017 and has asked the bank for a three-month extension of the loan. The controller reasons, "By the due date of April 15, 2018, the cash due from the new season ticket holders will be available, things will be cleared up with the advertisers, and the loan can be easily repaid."

Required

Use the Ethical Decision Framework in Exhibit 1-9 to complete the following requirements:

1. **Recognize an ethical dilemma:** For each of the items of additional information in (a) through (g) above, identify any errors you think the controller has made in preparing

(Continued)

the financial statements. On the basis of your answers, prepare a revised income statement, statement of retained earnings, and balance sheet. What ethical dilemma(s) do you now face?

2. **Analyze the key elements in the situation:**

   a. Who may benefit or be harmed?
   b. How are they likely to benefit or be harmed?
   c. What rights or claims may be violated?
   d. What specific interests are in conflict?
   e. What are your responsibilities and obligations?

3. **List alternatives and evaluate the impact of each on those affected:** As one of the investors in this organization, what are your options in dealing with the ethical dilemma(s) you identified in (1) above? Which provides the other investors and the bank with information that is most relevant, most complete, most neutral, and most free from error?

4. **Select the best alternative:** Among the alternatives, which one would you select?

LO8 **Decision Case 1-7 Responsibility for Financial Statements and the Role of the Auditor**

Financial statements are the means by which accountants communicate to external users. Recent financial reporting scandals have focused attention on the accounting profession and its role in the preparation of these statements and the audits performed on the statements.

Required

1. Who is responsible for the preparation of the financial statements that are included in a company's annual report?
2. Who performs an audit of the financial statements referred to in part (1)?
3. Why is it important for those who are responsible for an audit of the financial statements to be independent of those who prepare the statements? Explain your answer.

Answers

MODULE 1 Answers to Questions

1. Business is concerned with all the activities necessary to provide the members of an economic system with goods and services. Some businesses are organized to earn a profit, whereas others are organized for some other purpose. Regardless, all businesses are organized to provide goods and/or services to their customers.

2. An asset is a future economic benefit to a business. Cash, accounts receivable, merchandise inventories, and property and equipment are all examples of assets.

3. A liability is an obligation of a business. Assets and liabilities are related in that most liabilities are satisfied by using assets, most often in the form of cash.

4. The three forms of business entities are sole proprietorships, partnerships, and corporations.

MODULE 1 Answers to Apply

1. When you own a share of stock in a corporation, you are part owner of that business. In contrast, if you own one of the corporation's bonds, you have made a loan to the company and you are one of its creditors.

2. Possible personal assets might include checking accounts, savings accounts, certificates of deposit, money market accounts, stocks, bonds, mutual funds, and amounts loaned to family and friends. Possible personal liabilities might include student loans, car loans, home mortgages, and amounts borrowed from family and friends.

MODULE 2 Answers to Questions

1. Accounting is a communication process. Its purpose is to provide economic information about an organization that will be useful to those who need to make decisions regarding that entity. For example, information provided by an accountant about an entity is useful to a banker in reaching a decision about whether to loan money to a business.

2. The two distinct elements of owners' equity in a corporation are contributed capital and retained earnings. Contributed capital, as represented by capital stock, is the original contribution to the company by the owners. Retained earnings represents the claims of the owners to the assets of the business. These claims result from the earnings of the company that have not been paid out in dividends.

3. The types of activities in which companies engage are financing, investing, and operating. To start a new business, such as renting bicycles and skis, requires initial financing, such as initial contributions by the owners and loans by a bank. Next, the business would need to invest in the assets it will rent—that is, bicycles and skis. Once investments in assets are made, the business would earn revenue by renting out bicycles and skis. The business would also incur various operating expenses, such as wages, advertising, and taxes.

3. A balance sheet should be dated as of a particular day. It is a statement of financial position and shows the assets, liabilities, and stockholders' equity of a business at a particular point in time. Unlike an income statement, it is not a flow statement and therefore is not dated for a particular period of time. Balance sheets are typically prepared to coincide with the end of an accounting period, such as the end of the month or the end of the year.

4. An income statement should be dated for a particular period of time: for example, for the month of June or for the year ended December 31, 2017. The income statement is a flow statement because it summarizes revenues and expenses for a period of time. Unlike a balance sheet, it is not an indication of position at any one particular point in time.

MODULE 2 Answers to Apply

1. Chipotle's assets are Cash and cash equivalents; Accounts receivable; Inventory; Prepaid expenses and other current assets; Income tax receivable; Investments; Leasehold improvements, property and equipment; Long term investments; Other assets; and Goodwill. Chipotle's liabilities are Accounts payable; Accrued payroll and benefits; Accrued liabilities; Deferred rent; Deferred income tax liability; and Other liabilities.

2.

$$\text{Assets} = \text{Liabilities} + \text{Stockholders' Equity}$$
$$\$2,725,066,000 = \$597,092,000 + \$2,127,974,000$$

MODULE 3 Answers to Questions

1. In the United States, the Securities and Exchange Commission (SEC) has ultimate authority for companies whose securities are sold to the general public. However, the SEC has relegated much of the standard setting to the private sector in the form of the Financial Accounting Standards Board (FASB). Standard setters in the United States continue to work closely with those in the international community. However, there are significant differences between U.S. and international standards; it may be some time before all differences are eliminated.

2. The auditors may be in an excellent position to evaluate a company, but not because they have prepared the financial statements. The preparation of the statements is the responsibility of management. The role of the auditor is to perform various tests and procedures as a basis for rendering an opinion on the fairness of the presentation of the statements.

3. Accountants make the assumption in preparing a set of financial statements that the dollar is a stable measuring unit. This assumption, called the monetary unit

(Continued)

assumption, may or may not be accurate, depending on the level of inflation in the economy. The higher the rate of inflation, the less reliable is the dollar as a measuring unit.

4. These are the methods, rules, practices, and other procedures that have evolved over time and that govern the preparation of financial statements. Two important

points are worth noting about GAAP. First, these principles are not static but rather change in response to changes in the ways companies conduct business. Second, there is not a single, identifiable source of GAAP. Both the private and public sectors have contributed to the development of generally accepted accounting principles.

MODULE 3 Answers to Apply

1. The dollar is the monetary unit used in the United States, and the yen is used in Japan.

2. Although the Securities and Exchange Commission has the ultimate authority to determine the rules in preparing financial statements, it has to a large extent allowed the accounting profession, through the Financial Accounting Standards Board, to establish its own rules. The SEC has at times taken an active role in the setting of accounting standards. It has stepped in when it has believed that the profession has not acted quickly enough or in the correct manner. Since its inception in

1934, the commission has been more involved in the enforcement of GAAP as a means of protecting the rights of investors than it has been in setting standards.

3. The four steps in the model presented in the chapter to help in making ethical decisions are:
   a. Recognize an ethical dilemma.
   b. Analyze the key elements in the situation.
   c. List alternatives and evaluate the impact of each on those affected.
   d. Select the best alternative.

Answers to Connect to the Real World

1-1 (p. 16)

Assets = Liabilities + Stockholders' Equity
$2,725,066,000 = $597,092,000 + $2,127,974,000

The amount of Chipotle's cash and cash equivalents at the end of 2015 is $248,005,000. The amount the company owes its suppliers is $85,709,000 as shown in the Accounts Payable account.

1-2 (p. 18)

Chipotle's revenue increased by ($4,501,223,000 – $4,108,269,000)/$4,108,269,000, or 9.6%. Food, beverage and packaging costs increased by ($1,503,835,000 – $1,420,994,000)/$1,420,994,000, or 5.8%. This means that management is successfully controlling product costs relative to the selling prices of those products.

Answers to Key Terms Quiz

Quiz 1: Introduction to Business

15	Business		5	Nonbusiness entity
16	Business entity		7	Liability
13	Sole proprietorship		14	Capital stock
12	Economic entity concept		10	Stockholder
2	Partnership		11	Creditor
4	Corporation		1	Asset
8	Share of stock		3	Revenue
9	Bond		6	Expense

Quiz 2: Introduction to Accounting

4	Accounting
9	Management accounting
5	Financial accounting
6	Owners' equity
3	Stockholders' equity
8	Retained earnings
7	Balance sheet
1	Income statement
22	Net income
2	Statement of retained earnings
10	Dividends
25	Statement of cash flows
12	Cost principle
14	Going concern
16	Monetary unit
18	Time period

11	Generally accepted accounting principles (GAAP)
13	Securities and Exchange Commission (SEC)
15	Financial Accounting Standards Board (FASB)
17	American Institute of Certified Public Accountants (AICPA)
23	Certified Public Accountant (CPA)
24	Public Company Accounting Oversight Board (PCAOB)
20	International Accounting Standards Board (IASB)
19	Auditing
21	Sarbanes-Oxley Act

2

Financial Statements and the Annual Report

MODULES	LEARNING OBJECTIVES		WHY IS THIS CHAPTER IMPORTANT?
1 **Financial Reporting Objectives and Characteristics of Useful Information**	**LO1**	Describe the objectives of financial reporting.	• You need to know what makes a set of financial statements understandable. (See p. 53.)
	LO2	Describe the qualitative characteristics of accounting information.	
2 **Classified Balance Sheets**	**LO3**	Explain the concept and purpose of a classified balance sheet and prepare the statement.	• You need to know how to distinguish a current asset from a long-term asset and a current liability from a long-term liability. (See pp. 58–60.)
	LO4	Use a classified balance sheet to analyze a company's financial position.	• You need to know how to use the numbers on a classified balance sheet to measure a company's liquidity. (See p. 62.)
3 **Income Statements, Statements of Retained Earnings, and Statements of Cash Flows**	**LO5**	Explain the difference between a single-step and a multiple-step income statement and prepare each type of income statement.	• You need to know how to use the numbers on an income statement to measure a company's profitability. (See pp. 66–67.)
	LO6	Use a multiple-step income statement to analyze a company's operations.	
	LO7	Identify the components of the statement of retained earnings and prepare the statement.	
	LO8	Identify the components of the statement of cash flows and prepare the statement.	• You need to know how information on a statement of cash flows can be used to analyze a company. (See pp. 68–69.)
4 **Reading and Using the Annual Report**	**LO9**	Read and use the financial statements and other elements in the annual report of a publicly held company.	• You need to know what useful nonfinancial information can be found in a company's annual report. (See pp. 76–78.)

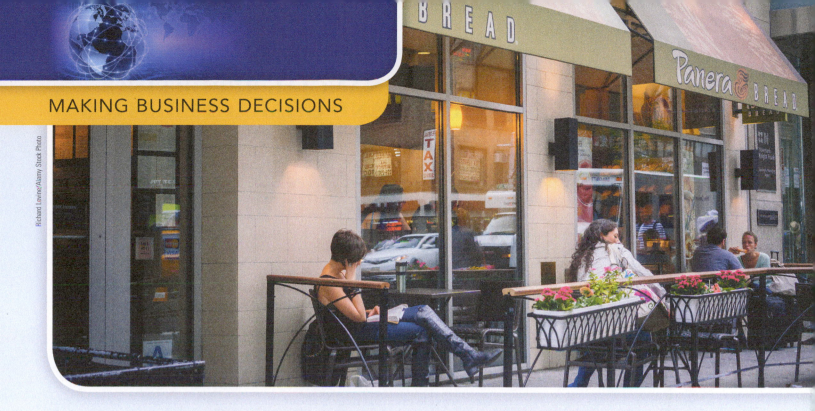

PANERA BREAD COMPANY

After learning about **Chipotle Mexican Grill, Inc.** in the last chapter, you are considering an investment in its stock. But before investing, you have decided to consider as an alternative one of the company's competitors in the industry, **Panera Bread Company**. Both companies compete for a growing share of the restaurant business, focused on providing customers the convenience of a fast-food dining experience combined with wholesome, fresh ingredients. At the end of 2015 there were 1,972 bakery-cafes in 46 states, the District of Columbia, and Ontario, Canada—very similar to the number of Chipotle locations.

Look at the Revenue data shown below as they appeared in Panera Bread's 2015 Form 10-K, the annual report filed with the Securities and Exchange Commission (SEC). Compare Panera Bread's revenue to that for Chipotle in Chapter 1. However, beyond the revenues generated by each company, you will need to look further before making a decision:

- What does an income statement tell you about each company's ability to control costs and earn a profit?
- What does a balance sheet tell you about each company's ability to pay its bills as they come due?
- What does a statement of cash flows reveal about each company's performance that an income statement does not?

Without understanding a company's financial statements, choosing a company to invest in is guesswork at best.

Revenues

The following table summarizes revenues for the periods indicated (dollars in thousands):

| | For the fiscal year ended | | | | |
	December 29, 2015	December 30, 2014	December 31, 2013	% Change in 2015	% Change in 2014
Bakery-cafe sales, net	$ 2,358,794	$2,230,370	$2,108,908	5.8%	5.8%
Franchise royalties and fees	138,563	123,686	112,641	12.0%	9.8%
Fresh dough and other product sales to franchisees	184,223	175,139	163,453	5.2%	7.1%
Total revenue	$ 2,681,580	$2,529,195	$2,385,002	6.0%	6.0%
System-wide average weekly net sales	$ 48,357	$ 47,655	$ 47,403	1.5%	0.5%

Source: Panera Bread Company: website and Form 10-K for the year ended December 29, 2015.

MODULE 1 FINANCIAL REPORTING OBJECTIVES AND CHARACTERISTICS OF USEFUL INFORMATION

LO1 Describe the objectives of financial reporting.

A variety of external users need information to make sound business decisions, including stockholders, bondholders, bankers, and other types of creditors such as suppliers. The balance sheet, the income statement, and the statement of cash flows, along with the supporting notes and other information found in an annual report, are the key sources of information that external users need to make sound business decisions. These statements are not intended to tell the reader the value of a company, but they should provide information that will allow the users to make their own estimates.

How Will I Use ACCOUNTING?

If you plan to run your own business someday, you need to be able to read a balance sheet—to know your equity in the business, the difference between your assets and liabilities.

Even if you don't own a business, the same principle applies to your personal financial condition.

- The *balance sheet* shows what obligations will be due in the near future and what assets will be available to satisfy them.
- The *income statement* shows the revenues and expenses for a period of time.
- The *statement of cash flows* shows where cash came from and how it was used during the period.
- The *notes* provide essential details about the company's accounting policies and other key factors that affect its financial condition and performance.

In preparing financial statements, accountants consider:

- The objectives of financial reporting.
- The characteristics that make accounting information useful.
- The most useful way to display the information found in the balance sheet, the income statement, and the statement of cash flows.

Financial information users are the main reason financial statements are prepared. After all, it is the investors, creditors, and other groups and individuals outside and inside the company who must make economic decisions based on these statements. Therefore, as you learned in Chapter 1, financial statements must be based on agreed-upon assumptions such as time period, going concern, and other GAAP. Moreover, when the accountants for companies such as **Panera Bread** prepare their financial statements, they must keep in mind financial reporting objectives that are focused on providing the most understandable and useful information possible. **Financial reporting has one overall objective and a set of related objectives, all of them concerned with how the information may be most useful to the readers.**

The overall objective of financial reporting is to provide financial information to permit external users of the information to make informed decisions on whether to provide resources to the company.[1] Users include both the management of a company (internal users) and others not involved in the daily operations of the business (external users). External users, such as investors and creditors, usually do not have access to the detailed records of the business or the benefit of daily involvement in the company's affairs. They make decisions based on *general-purpose financial statements* prepared by management.

You can now see how closely the objective of financial reporting is tied to decision making. **The purpose of financial reporting is to help the users reach their decisions in an informed manner.** What types of information do these users need? How does the information they need relate to what is reported on financial statements? To answer these questions, consider the following:

- **Investors and Creditors Need Information about Prospective Cash Receipts**
  INVESTOR: If I buy stock in this company, how much cash will I receive:
  - In dividends?
  - From the sale of the stock?

---

[1] *Statement of Financial Accounting Concepts [SFAC] No. 8, Conceptual Framework for Financial Reporting*, Chapter 1, "The Objective of General Purpose Financial Reporting" (Norwalk, Conn.: Financial Accounting Standards Board, October 2010).

BANKER: If I lend money to this company, how much cash will I receive:
- In interest on the loan?
- When and if the loan is repaid?

- **The Company Needs Information about Its Own Prospective Cash Flows**
  Investors, bankers, and other users ultimately care about their cash receipts, but this depends to some extent on the company's skills in managing its *own* cash flows.
- **The Company Also Needs Information about Its Resources and Claims to Those Resources**
  A company's cash flows are inherently tied to the information on the:
  - Balance sheet (assets, liabilities, and owners' equity).
  - Income statement (revenues and expenses).
  - Statement of cash flows (operating, investing, and financing activities).

EXAMPLE 2-1   Using Financial Reporting Objectives to Make Investment Decisions

Assume that you are trying to decide whether to buy stock in Panera Bread. Even though the financial reporting objectives may seem abstract, think about how they can be used to help make a decision.

Financial Reporting Objectives	Potential Investor's Questions
1. Provide information for decision making.	Based on the financial information, should I buy shares of stock in Panera Bread?
2. Reflect prospective cash receipts to investors and creditors.	How much cash, if any, will I receive in dividends each year and how much from the sale of the stock of Panera Bread in the future?
3. Reflect prospective cash flows to an enterprise.	After paying its suppliers and employees and meeting all of its obligations, how much cash will Panera Bread take in during the time I own the stock?
4. Reflect resources and claims to resources.	How much has Panera Bread invested in new restaurants and equipment?

What Makes Accounting Information Useful? Qualitative Characteristics

Since accounting information must be useful for decision making, what makes it useful? This section focuses on the qualities that accountants strive for in their financial reporting and on some challenges they face in making reporting judgments. It also reveals what users of financial information expect from financial statements.

Quantitative considerations such as tuition costs certainly were a concern when you chose your current school. In addition, you made subjective judgments about your college's *qualitative* characteristics. Similarly, certain qualities make accounting information useful.

LO2 Describe the qualitative characteristics of accounting information.

Understandability

For anything to be useful, it must be understandable.

Understandability of financial information varies considerably depending on the user's background. For example, should financial statements be prepared so that they are understandable by anyone with a college education? Or should it be assumed that all users have completed at least one accounting course? Is a background in business necessary for a good understanding of financial reports, regardless of one's formal training? There are no simple answers to these questions. However, financial information should be comprehensible to *those who are willing to spend the time to understand it*.

Understandability alone is certainly not enough to render information useful. According to the FASB, two fundamental characteristics make accounting information useful. The information must be **relevant**, and it must be a **faithful representation**.[2]

Understandability
The quality of accounting information that makes it comprehensible to those willing to spend the necessary time.

---

[2] *Statement of Financial Accounting Concepts [SFAC] No. 8, Conceptual Framework for Financial Reporting*, Chapter 3, "Qualitative Characteristics of Useful Accounting Information" (Norwalk, Conn.: Financial Accounting Standards Board, October 2010).

Relevance

To be useful, information must be relevant.

Relevance
The capacity of information to make a difference in a decision.

Relevance is the capacity of information to make a difference in a decision. Sometimes, information may have **predictive value**. For example, assume that you are a banker evaluating the financial statements of a company seeking a loan. The financial statements point to a strong, profitable company. However, today's news revealed that the company has been named in a multimillion-dollar lawsuit. This information would be relevant to your talks with the company. Disclosure of the lawsuit in the financial statements would help you *predict* whether it would be wise to make a loan to the company.

In other cases, information may have **confirming value**. For example, assume you invest in a company because you think it may enter new Asian markets in the near future. Disclosure in the statements that the company acquired a Chinese subsidiary would *confirm* you made the right decision to invest in the company.

Faithful Representation

Faithful representation
The quality of information that makes it complete, neutral, and free from error.

According to the FASB, information is a **faithful representation** when it is **complete**, **neutral**, and **free from error**. Information is neutral when it is not slanted to make a company's position look any better or worse than the actual circumstances would dictate—such as when the probable losses from a major lawsuit are disclosed accurately in the notes to the financial statements, with all potential effects on the company.

Comparability and Consistency

Comparability allows comparisons to be made *between or among companies.*

Comparability
For accounting information, the quality that allows a user to analyze two or more companies and look for similarities and differences.

Depreciation
The process of allocating the cost of a long-term tangible asset over its useful life.

GAAP allow a certain amount of freedom in choosing among alternative treatments for certain transactions. For example, companies may choose from several methods of accounting for the depreciation of certain long-term assets. **Depreciation** is the *process of allocating* the cost of a long-term tangible asset, such as a building or equipment, over its useful life. Each method may affect the value of the assets differently. How does this freedom of choice affect investors' ability to compare companies?

Assume that you are considering buying stock in one of three companies. Their annual reports indicate that one company uses the "accelerated" depreciation method and the other two companies use the "straight-line" depreciation method. (We'll learn about these methods in Chapter 8.) Does this lack of a common depreciation method make it impossible to compare the performance of the three companies?

Obviously, comparing these companies would be easier and more meaningful if all three used the same depreciation method. However, comparisons are not impossible just because companies use different methods. Certainly, the more uniform statements are in terms of the principles used to prepare them, the more comparable they will be.

To render statements of companies using different methods more meaningful, *disclosure* assumes a very important role. For example, as we will see later in this chapter, the first note in the annual report of a publicly traded company is the disclosure of its accounting policies. Disclosure of accounting policies allows the reader to make a subjective adjustment to the statements of one or more of the companies and thus to compensate for the different depreciation method being used.

Consistency
For accounting information, the quality that allows a user to compare two or more accounting periods for a single company.

Consistency means that financial statements can be compared *within a single company from one accounting period to the next.* Consistency is closely related to comparability. Both involve the relationship between two numbers—comparability between numbers of different companies (usually for the same period) and comparability between the numbers of a single company for different periods. However, whereas financial statements are comparable when they can be compared between one company and another, statements are consistent when they can be compared within a single company from one accounting period to the next.

Occasionally, companies decide to change their accounting method. Will it be possible to compare a company's earnings in a period in which it switches methods with its earnings in prior years? When a company makes an accounting change, accounting standards require various disclosures to help the reader evaluate the impact of the change.

Materiality

For accounting information to be useful, it must be relevant to a decision.

Materiality is closely related to relevance and deals with the size of an error in accounting information. The issue is whether the error is large enough to affect the judgment of someone relying on the information. Suppose a company pays cash for two separate purchases: a $5 pencil sharpener and a $50,000 computer. Each expenditure results in the acquisition of an asset that should be depreciated over its useful life. However, what if the company decides to account for the $5 paid for the pencil sharpener as an expense of the period rather than depreciate it over the life of the pencil sharpener? *Will this error in any way affect the judgment of someone relying on the financial statements?* Because such a slight error will *not* affect any decisions, minor expenditures of this nature are considered *immaterial* and are accounted for as an expense of the period.

The *threshold* for determining materiality varies from one company to the next depending largely on the company's size. Many companies establish policies that *any* expenditure under a certain dollar amount should be accounted for as an expense of the period. The threshold might be $50 for the corner grocery store but $1,000 for a large corporation. Finally, the amount of a transaction may be immaterial by company standards but still be considered significant by financial statement users. For example, a transaction involving illegal or unethical behavior by a company officer would be of concern, regardless of the dollar amounts involved.

> **Materiality**
> The magnitude of an accounting information omission or misstatement that will affect the judgment of someone relying on the information.

Conservatism

Conservatism is the practice of using the least optimistic estimate when two estimates of amounts are about equally likely. The practice of conservatism is reserved for those situations in which there is *uncertainty* about how to account for a particular item or transaction.

Various accounting rules are based on the concept of conservatism. For example, inventory held for resale is reported on the balance sheet at *the lower-of-cost-or-market value*. This rule requires a company to compare the cost of its inventory with the market price, or current cost to replace that inventory, and to report the lower of the two amounts on the balance sheet at year-end. Chapter 5 will more fully explore the lower-of-cost-or-market rule as it pertains to inventory.

> **Conservatism**
> The practice of using the least optimistic estimate when two estimates of amounts are about equally likely.

EXAMPLE 2-2 Summarizing the Characteristics That Make Information Useful

The various qualities that make information useful in making decisions can be summarized by asking a series of questions as follows:

Characteristic	Why Important?
Understandability	Must understand information to use it
Relevance	Must be information that could affect a decision
Faithful representation	Must be information that is complete, neutral, and free from error
Comparability	Must be able to compare with other companies
Consistency	Must be able to compare with prior years
Materiality	Must be an amount large enough to affect a decision
Conservatism	If any doubt, use the least optimistic estimate

An International Perspective on Qualitative Characteristics

Chapter 1 introduced the IASB and its efforts to improve the development of accounting standards around the world. This international body worked with the FASB in this country to develop a conceptual framework for accounting. The result is that the objectives and qualitative characteristics of financial reporting as described in this chapter are the same for both groups.

MODULE 1 TEST YOURSELF

Review

LO1 Describe the objectives of financial reporting.

- The objective of financial reporting is to convey useful and timely information to parties for making economic decisions.
  - Decision makers include investors, creditors, and other individuals or groups inside and outside the firm.
- These decision makers need information to evaluate cash flows, resources of the company, and claims to those resources.

LO2 Describe the qualitative characteristics of accounting information.

- Qualitative characteristics make accounting information useful to financial statements users and include:
  - Understandability—pertains to those willing to spend time to understand the information.
  - Relevance—the capacity of information to make a difference in a decision.
  - Faithful representation—information that investors can depend on must be complete, neutral, and free from error.
  - Comparability and consistency—GAAP provide guidelines that standardize accounting practices and make information comparable from one company to another or from one period to the next for the same company.
  - Conservatism—where uncertainty about how to account for economic activity exists, accounting choices that result in the least optimistic amount should be employed.

Question

1. How would you evaluate the following statement: The cash flows to a company are irrelevant to an investor; all the investor cares about is the potential for receiving dividends on the investment.
2. What does *relevance* mean with regard to the use of accounting information?
3. What is the difference between comparability and consistency as they relate to the use of accounting information?
4. How does the concept of materiality relate to the size of a company?

Apply

1. State the overriding objective of financial reporting. Are financial statements intended to report the value of the reporting entity? Explain your answer.
2. What two fundamental characteristics make accounting information useful? What other qualities enhance the usefulness of financial information?

Answers are located at the end of the chapter.

MODULE 2 CLASSIFIED BALANCE SHEETS

LO3 Explain the concept and purpose of a classified balance sheet and prepare the statement.

Now that we have learned about the conceptual framework of accounting, we turn to the outputs of the system: the financial statements. First, we will use a hypothetical company, Dixon Sporting Goods, to consider the significance of a *classified balance sheet*. We will then examine the *income statement*, the *statement of retained earnings*, and the *statement of cash flows* for this company. The chapter concludes with a brief look at the financial statements of Panera Bread and at the other elements in an annual report.

Understanding the Operating Cycle

For a company that sells a product, the **operating cycle** begins when cash is invested in inventory and ends when cash is collected by the enterprise from its customers. Determining the operating cycle is a key skill in understanding any business.

Operating cycle
The period of time between the purchase of inventory and the collection of any receivable from the sale of the inventory.

EXAMPLE 2-3 Determining the Operating Cycle

Consider the typical operating cycle for a bike shop. On August 1, the shop buys a bike from the manufacturer for $400. At this point, the shop has merely substituted one asset, cash, for another, inventory. On August 20, the shop sells the bike to a customer for $500. If the customer pays cash for the bike, the bike shop will have completed its cash-to-cash operating cycle in a total of 20 days, as shown below.

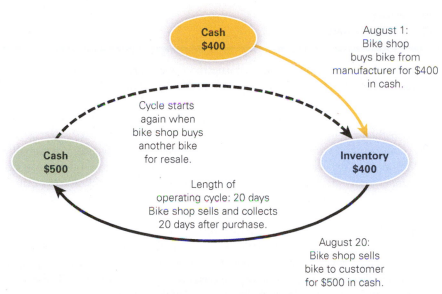

The shop's operating cycle is extended if it sells the same bike to a customer on August 20 and allows the customer to pay for it in 30 days. Instead of an operating cycle of 20 days, a total of 50 days has passed between the use of cash to buy the bike from the manufacturer and the collection of cash from the customer, as shown below:

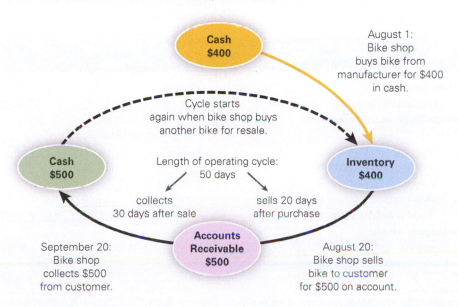

Current Assets

Current asset
An asset that is expected to be realized in cash or sold or consumed during the operating cycle or within one year if the cycle is shorter than one year.

The basic distinction on a classified balance sheet is between current and noncurrent items. **Current assets** are "cash and other assets that are reasonably expected to be realized in cash or sold or consumed during the normal operating cycle of a business or within one year if the operating cycle is shorter than one year."[3]

The Current Assets section of Dixon Sporting Goods' balance sheet appears as follows:

Dixon Sporting Goods Partial Balance Sheet	
Current assets	
Cash	$ 5,000
Marketable securities	11,000
Accounts receivable	23,000
Merchandise inventory	73,500
Prepaid insurance	4,800
Store supplies	700
Total current assets	$118,000

Most businesses have an operating cycle shorter than one year. For example, the bike shop's cycle in the second half of Example 2-3 was assumed to be 50 days. Therefore, for most companies, the cutoff for current classification is one year. We will use the one-year cutoff for current classification in the remainder of this chapter. Thus, on Dixon's balance sheet, cash, accounts receivable, and inventory are classified as current assets because they *are* cash or will be *realized* in (converted to) cash (accounts receivable) or will be *sold* (inventory) within one year.

In addition to cash, accounts receivable, and inventory, the two other most common types of current assets are marketable securities and prepaid expenses. Excess cash is often invested in the stocks and bonds of other companies as well as in various government instruments. If the investments are made for the short term, they are classified as current and are typically called *short-term investments* or *marketable securities*. (Alternatively, some investments are made for the purpose of exercising influence over another company and thus are made for the long term. These investments are classified as noncurrent assets.) Various prepayments, such as office supplies, rent, and insurance, are classified as *prepaid expenses*. These assets qualify as current assets because they are usually *consumed* within one year.

Noncurrent Assets

Any asset not meeting the definition of a current asset is classified as *long term* or *noncurrent*. Three common categories of long-term assets are investments; property, plant, and equipment; and intangibles. For Dixon, these are as follows:

Dixon Sporting Goods Partial Balance Sheet			
Investments			
Land held for future office site			$150,000
Property, plant, and equipment			
Land		$100,000	
Buildings	$150,000		
Accumulated depreciation	60,000	90,000	
Store furniture and fixtures	$ 42,000		
Accumulated depreciation	12,600	29,400	
Total property, plant, and equipment			219,400
Intangible assets			
Franchise agreement			55,000

---

[3] Accounting Principles Board, *Statement of the Accounting Principles Board, No. 4,* "Basic Concepts and Accounting Principles Underlying Financial Statements of Business Enterprises" (New York: American Institute of Certified Public Accountants, 1970), par. 198.

Investments Securities not expected to be sold within the next year are classified as *investments*. In many cases, the investment is in the common stock of another company. Sometimes, companies invest in another company to exercise some influence over it or to control its operations. Other assets classified as investments are land held for future use and buildings and equipment not currently used in operations. Dixon classifies as an investment some land it holds for a future office site. A special fund held for the retirement of debt or for the construction of new facilities is also an investment.

Property, Plant, and Equipment This category consists of the various *tangible, productive assets* used in the operation of a business. Land, buildings, equipment, machinery, furniture and fixtures, trucks, and tools are all examples of assets held for use in the *operation* of a business rather than for *resale*. The distinction between inventory and equipment, for instance, depends on the company's *intent* in acquiring the asset. For example, **IBM** classifies a computer system as inventory because IBM's intent is to offer it for resale. This same computer in the hands of a law firm would be classified as equipment because the firm's intent is to use it in the long-term operation of the business.

The relative size of property, plant, and equipment depends largely on a company's business. Consider **Carnival Corporation**, a cruise company with over $39 billion in total assets at the end of its 2015 fiscal year. Carnival's property and equipment, including its ships, make up a very large portion of the company's total assets. In fact, this category accounted for over 81% of total assets. On the other hand, property and equipment represented less than 9% of the total assets of **Microsoft** on June 30, 2015. Regardless of the relative size of property, plant, and equipment, all assets in this category are subject to depreciation except land. A separate accumulated depreciation account is used to account for the depreciation recorded on each of these assets over its life. Depreciation is explained more fully in Chapter 8.

Intangibles Intangible assets are similar to property, plant, and equipment in that they provide benefits to the firm over the long term. The distinction, however, is in the *form* of the asset. *Intangible assets lack physical substance.* Trademarks, copyrights, franchise rights, patents, and goodwill are examples of intangible assets.

The cost principle governs the accounting for intangibles, just as it does for tangible assets. For example, the amount paid to an inventor for the patent rights to a new project is recorded as an intangible asset. Similarly, the amount paid to purchase a franchise for a fast-food restaurant is recorded as an intangible asset. With a few exceptions, intangibles are written off to expense over their useful lives. This process for intangible assets is called *amortization*. Amortization is explained more fully in Chapter 8.

Current Liabilities

A **current liability** is an obligation that will be satisfied within the next operating cycle or within one year if the cycle (as is normally the case) is shorter than one year. The classification of a note payable on the balance sheet depends on its maturity date. If the note will be paid within the next year, it is classified as current; otherwise, it is classified as a long-term liability. Accounts payable, wages payable, and income taxes payable are all short-term or current liabilities, as on Dixon's balance sheet:

Current liability
An obligation that will be satisfied within the next operating cycle or within one year if the cycle is shorter than one year.

Dixon Sporting Goods Partial Balance Sheet		
Current liabilities		
Accounts payable	$15,700	
Salaries and wages payable	9,500	
Income taxes payable	7,200	
Interest payable	2,500	
Bank loan payable	25,000	
Total current liabilities		$59,900

Most liabilities are satisfied by the payment of cash. However, certain liabilities are eliminated from the balance sheet when the company performs services. The liability Subscriptions Received in Advance, which would appear on the balance sheet of a magazine publisher, is satisfied by delivery of the magazine to the customers. It is also possible to satisfy one liability by substituting another in its place. A supplier might ask a customer to sign a written promissory note to replace an existing account payable if the customer is unable to pay at the present time.

Long-Term Liabilities

Any obligation that will not be paid or otherwise satisfied within the next year or the operating cycle, whichever is longer, is classified as a long-term liability, or long-term debt. Notes payable and bonds payable, both promises to pay money in the future, are two common forms of long-term debt. Some bonds have a life as long as 25 or 30 years. Dixon's notes payable for $120,000 is classified as a long-term liability because it is not due in the next year:

Dixon Sporting Goods Partial Balance Sheet	
Long-term debt	
Notes payable, due December 31, 2027	$120,000

Stockholders' Equity

Recall that stockholders' equity represents the owners' claims on the assets of the business that arise from two sources: *contributed capital* and *earned capital*. The Stockholders' Equity section of Dixon's balance sheet reports the following:

Dixon Sporting Goods Partial Balance Sheet		
Contributed capital		
Capital stock, $10 par, 5,000 shares issued and outstanding	$ 50,000	
Paid-in capital in excess of par value	25,000	
Total contributed capital	$ 75,000	
Retained earnings	287,500	
Total stockholders' equity		$362,500

Capital stock indicates the owners' investment in the business. *Retained earnings* represents the accumulated earnings, or net income, of the business since its inception less all dividends paid during that time.

Most companies have a single class of capital stock called *common stock*. This is the most basic form of ownership in a business. *Preferred stock* is a form of capital stock that carries with it certain preferences and has priority over common stock. For example, the company must pay dividends on preferred stock before it makes any distribution of dividends on common stock. In the event of liquidation, preferred stockholders have priority over common stockholders in the distribution of the entity's assets.

Capital stock may appear as two separate items on the balance sheet: *Par Value* and *Paid-In Capital in Excess of Par Value*. The total of these two items is the amount that has been paid by the owners for the stock. We will take a closer look at these items in Chapter 11.

EXAMPLE 2-4 Preparing a Classified Balance Sheet

A classified balance sheet can be prepared using each of the categories presented in the previous section:

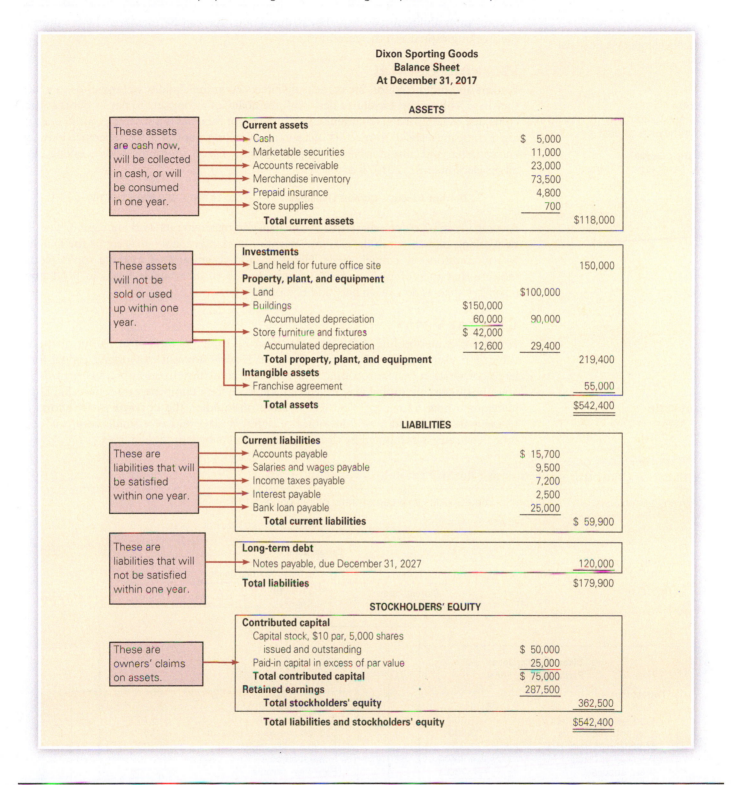

Dixon Sporting Goods
Balance Sheet
At December 31, 2017

ASSETS

These assets are cash now, will be collected in cash, or will be consumed in one year.

Current assets		
Cash		$ 5,000
Marketable securities		11,000
Accounts receivable		23,000
Merchandise inventory		73,500
Prepaid insurance		4,800
Store supplies		700
Total current assets		$118,000

These assets will not be sold or used up within one year.

Investments			
Land held for future office site			150,000
Property, plant, and equipment			
Land		$100,000	
Buildings	$150,000		
Accumulated depreciation	60,000	90,000	
Store furniture and fixtures	$ 42,000		
Accumulated depreciation	12,600	29,400	
Total property, plant, and equipment			219,400
Intangible assets			
Franchise agreement			55,000
Total assets			$542,400

LIABILITIES

These are liabilities that will be satisfied within one year.

Current liabilities		
Accounts payable		$ 15,700
Salaries and wages payable		9,500
Income taxes payable		7,200
Interest payable		2,500
Bank loan payable		25,000
Total current liabilities		$ 59,900

These are liabilities that will not be satisfied within one year.

Long-term debt		
Notes payable, due December 31, 2027		120,000
Total liabilities		$179,900

STOCKHOLDERS' EQUITY

These are owners' claims on assets.

Contributed capital		
Capital stock, $10 par, 5,000 shares		
issued and outstanding		$ 50,000
Paid-in capital in excess of par value		25,000
Total contributed capital		$ 75,000
Retained earnings		287,500
Total stockholders' equity		362,500
Total liabilities and stockholders' equity		$542,400

Using a Classified Balance Sheet: Introduction to Ratios

LO4 Use a classified balance sheet to analyze a company's financial position.

A company's ability to pay its debts as they come due can be measured by computing the working capital and the current ratio.

Working Capital

Liquidity
The ability of a company to pay its debts as they come due.

Working capital
Current assets minus current liabilities.

Bankers and other creditors are particularly interested in the liquidity of businesses to which they have lent money. **Liquidity** deals with the ability of a company to pay its debts as they come due. A comparison of current assets and current liabilities is a starting point in evaluating a company's ability to meet its obligations. **Working capital** is the difference between current assets and current liabilities at a point in time. Dixon Sporting Goods' working capital on December 31, 2017, is as follows:

Current Assets − Current Liabilities   **$118,000 − $59,900 = $58,100**

A company must continually strive for a balance in managing its working capital. Too little working capital—or in the extreme, negative working capital—may signal the inability to pay creditors on a timely basis. However, a large amount of working capital could indicate that the company is not investing enough of its available funds in productive resources such as new machinery and equipment.

Current Ratio

Current ratio
Current assets divided by current liabilities.

Because it is an absolute dollar amount, working capital is limited in its informational value. For example, $1 million may be an inadequate amount of working capital for a large corporation but far too much for a smaller company. In addition, a certain dollar amount of working capital may have been adequate for a company earlier in its life but is inadequate now. However, a related measure of liquidity, the **current ratio**, allows us to compare the liquidity of companies of different sizes and of a single company over time. The ratio is computed by dividing current assets by current liabilities.

EXAMPLE 2-5 Computing the Current Ratio

The following formula shows that Dixon Sporting Goods has a current ratio of just under 2 to 1:

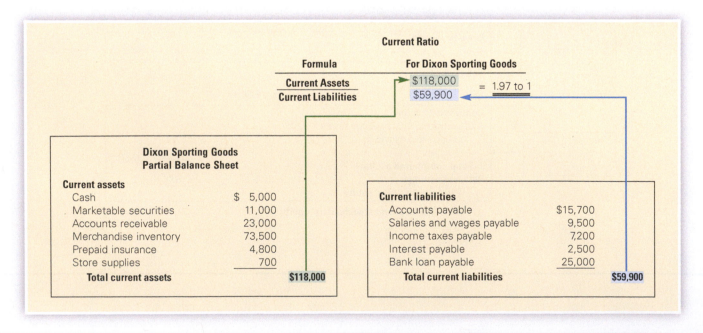

Current Ratio

Formula	For Dixon Sporting Goods
$\dfrac{\text{Current Assets}}{\text{Current Liabilities}}$	$\dfrac{\$118,000}{\$59,900}$ = 1.97 to 1

Dixon Sporting Goods
Partial Balance Sheet

Current assets		Current liabilities	
Cash	$ 5,000	Accounts payable	$15,700
Marketable securities	11,000	Salaries and wages payable	9,500
Accounts receivable	23,000	Income taxes payable	7,200
Merchandise inventory	73,500	Interest payable	2,500
Prepaid insurance	4,800	Bank loan payable	25,000
Store supplies	700		
Total current assets	**$118,000**	**Total current liabilities**	**$59,900**

In general, the higher the current ratio, the more liquid the company. Some analysts use a rule of thumb of 2 to 1 for the current ratio as a sign of short-term financial health. Companies in certain industries have operated quite efficiently with a current ratio of less than 2 to 1, whereas a ratio much higher than that is necessary to survive in other industries. It is not uncommon for companies with large amounts of inventory to maintain current ratios higher than 3 to 1. On the other hand, companies in the telephone communication business routinely have current ratios from well under 1 to 1. **AT&T**'s current ratio at the end of 2015 was only 0.75 to 1.

Unfortunately, neither the amount of working capital nor the current ratio tells us anything about the *composition* of current assets and current liabilities. For example, assume that two companies have total current assets equal to $100,000. Company A has cash of $10,000, accounts receivable of $50,000, and inventory of $40,000. Company B also has cash of $10,000 but accounts receivable of $20,000 and inventory of $70,000.

All other things being equal, Company A is more liquid than Company B because more of its total current assets are in receivables than inventory. Receivables are only one step away from being cash, whereas inventory must be sold and then the receivable collected. Dixon's inventory of $73,500 makes up a large portion of its total current assets of $118,000. Examining the *relative* size of the various current assets for a company may reveal certain strengths and weaknesses not evident in the current ratio.

In addition to the composition of the current assets, the *frequency* with which they are "turned over" is important. For instance, how long does it take to sell an item of inventory? How long is required to collect an account receivable? Many companies could not exist with the current ratio of 0.52 reported by **Delta Air Lines** at the end of 2015. An airline, however, which does not have large amounts in inventories or accounts receivable, can operate with a lower current ratio.

MODULE 2 TEST YOURSELF

Review		
	LO3 Explain the concept and purpose of a classified balance sheet and prepare the statement.	• The classified balance sheet classifies items of assets, liabilities, and stockholders' equity in a way that makes them useful to users of this financial statement. • Assets and liabilities are classified according to the length of time they will serve the company or require its resources. • Current assets or liabilities are those whose expected lives are one year or one operating cycle, whichever is longer. Noncurrent assets or liabilities are expected to last beyond this period of time. • Assets and liabilities are further subclassified into categories that describe the nature of these assets and liabilities; for example, "Property, Plant, and Equipment."
	LO4 Use a classified balance sheet to analyze a company's financial position.	• Balance sheet classifications allow users to analyze a company's financial position. • Liquidity relates to the ability of a company to pay its obligations as they come due. • Working capital and the current ratio are two measures of liquidity.

Question	
	1. How does the concept of the operating cycle relate to the definition of a current asset?
	2. How would you evaluate the following statement: A note payable with an original maturity of five years will be classified on the balance sheet as a long-term liability until it matures.
	3. How do the two basic forms of owners' equity for a corporation—capital stock and retained earnings—differ?
	4. What are the limitations of working capital as a measure of the liquidity of a business as opposed to the current ratio?

Apply

1. Indicate whether each of the following assets is a current asset (CA) or a noncurrent asset (NCA).

    _____ Accounts receivable
    _____ Land
    _____ Inventories
    _____ Cash
    _____ Furniture and fixtures
    _____ Office supplies
    _____ Buildings

2. A company reported current assets of $80,000 and current liabilities of $60,000. Compute the amount of working capital and the current ratio.

3. Big has current assets of $500,000 and current liabilities of $400,000. Small reports current assets of $80,000 and current liabilities of $20,000. Which company is more liquid? Why?

Answers are located at the end of the chapter.

MODULE 3 INCOME STATEMENTS, STATEMENTS OF RETAINED EARNINGS, AND STATEMENTS OF CASH FLOWS

LO5 Explain the difference between a single-step and a multiple-step income statement and prepare each type of income statement.

The income statement summarizes the results of operations of an entity for a *period of time*. All companies prepare income statements at least once a year. Companies that must report to the SEC prepare financial statements, including an income statement, every three months. Monthly income statements are usually prepared for internal use by management.

What Appears on the Income Statement?

In general, the income statement reports the excess of revenue over expense—that is, the *net income* (or in the event of an excess of expense over revenue, the net loss) of the period. It is common to use the term *profits* or *earnings* as a synonym for *net income*.

As discussed in Chapter 1, *revenue* is the inflow of assets resulting from the sale of products and services. Revenue is the dollar amount of sales of products and services for a period of time. An *expense* is the outflow of assets resulting from the sale of goods and services for a period of time. Wages and salaries, utilities, and taxes are examples of expenses.

Certain special types of revenues, called *gains*, are sometimes reported on the income statement, as are certain special types of expenses, called *losses*. For example, assume that Sanders Company holds a parcel of land for a future building site. It paid $50,000 for the land ten years ago. The state pays Sanders $60,000 for the property to use in a new highway project. Sanders has a special type of revenue from the condemnation of its property. It will have a *gain* of $10,000: the excess of the cash received from the state, $60,000, over the cost of the land, $50,000.

Format of the Income Statement

Corporations use one of two formats to prepare the income statement: single-step or multiple-step form. Both forms are generally accepted, although more companies use the multiple-step form.

Single-step income statement
An income statement in which all expenses are added together and subtracted from all revenues.

Single-Step Format for the Income Statement In a **single-step income statement**, all expenses and losses are added together and then deducted *in a single step* from all revenues and gains to arrive at net income. No attempt is made to classify revenues or expenses or to associate any of the expenses with any of the revenues. The primary advantage of the single-step form is its simplicity.

EXAMPLE 2-6 Preparing a Single-Step Income Statement

A single-step format for the income statement of Dixon Sporting Goods is presented below.

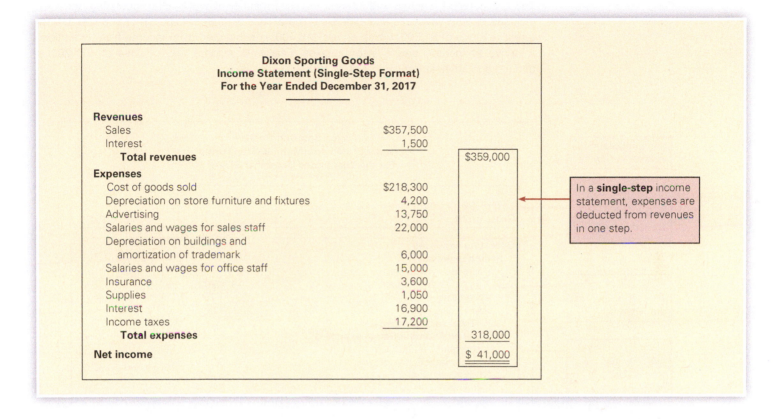

Dixon Sporting Goods
Income Statement (Single-Step Format)
For the Year Ended December 31, 2017

Revenues		
Sales	$357,500	
Interest	1,500	
Total revenues		$359,000
Expenses		
Cost of goods sold	$218,300	
Depreciation on store furniture and fixtures	4,200	
Advertising	13,750	
Salaries and wages for sales staff	22,000	
Depreciation on buildings and amortization of trademark	6,000	
Salaries and wages for office staff	15,000	
Insurance	3,600	
Supplies	1,050	
Interest	16,900	
Income taxes	17,200	
Total expenses		318,000
Net income		$ 41,000

In a **single-step** income statement, expenses are deducted from revenues in one step.

Multiple-Step Format for the Income Statement The purpose of the **multiple-step income statement** is to subdivide the income statement into specific sections and provide the reader with important subtotals.

Multiple-step income statement
An income statement that shows classifications of revenues and expenses as well as important subtotals.

EXAMPLE 2-7 Preparing a Multiple-Step Income Statement

The multiple-step format is illustrated for Dixon Sporting Goods below. The multiple-step income statement for Dixon (shown on the next page) indicates three important subtotals.

First, ❶ cost of goods sold is deducted from sales to arrive at **gross profit**:

Gross profit
Sales less cost of goods sold.

Gross Profit = Sales − Cost of Goods Sold	
Sales	$357,500
Cost of goods sold	218,300
Gross profit	$139,200

Cost of goods sold is the cost of the units of inventory sold during the year. It is logical to associate cost of goods sold with the sales revenue for the year because the latter represents the *selling price* of the inventory sold during the period.

The second important subtotal on Dixon's income statement is ❷ *income from operations* of $73,600. This is found by subtracting *total operating expenses* of $65,600 from the gross profit of $139,200. Operating expenses are further subdivided between *selling expenses* and *general and administrative expenses*. Note that two depreciation amounts are included in operating expenses. Depreciation on store furniture and fixtures is classified as a selling expense because the store is where sales take place. On the other hand, the buildings are offices for the administrative staff; thus, depreciation on the buildings is classified as a general and administrative expense.

The third important subtotal on the income statement is ❸ *income before income taxes* of $58,200. Interest revenue and interest expense, neither of which is an operating item, are included in *other revenues and expenses*. The excess of interest expense of $16,900 over interest revenue of $1,500, which equals $15,400, is subtracted from income from operations to arrive at income before income taxes. Finally, ❹ *income tax expense* of $17,200 is deducted to arrive at *net income* of $41,000.

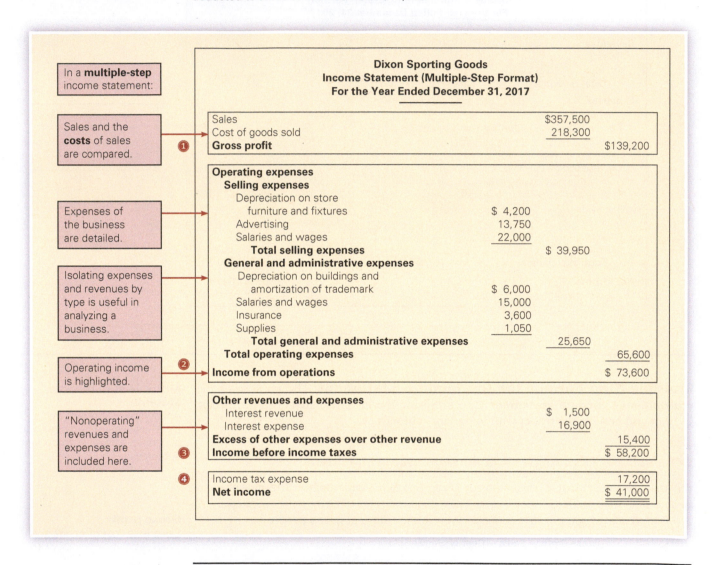

In a **multiple-step** income statement:		

Dixon Sporting Goods
Income Statement (Multiple-Step Format)
For the Year Ended December 31, 2017

Sales and the costs of sales are compared. ❶	Sales	$357,500	
	Cost of goods sold	218,300	
	Gross profit		$139,200
Expenses of the business are detailed.	**Operating expenses**		
	Selling expenses		
	Depreciation on store furniture and fixtures	$ 4,200	
	Advertising	13,750	
	Salaries and wages	22,000	
	Total selling expenses	$ 39,950	
Isolating expenses and revenues by type is useful in analyzing a business.	**General and administrative expenses**		
	Depreciation on buildings and amortization of trademark	$ 6,000	
	Salaries and wages	15,000	
	Insurance	3,600	
	Supplies	1,050	
	Total general and administrative expenses	25,650	
	Total operating expenses		65,600
Operating income is highlighted. ❷	**Income from operations**		$ 73,600
"Nonoperating" revenues and expenses are included here. ❸	**Other revenues and expenses**		
	Interest revenue	$ 1,500	
	Interest expense	16,900	
	Excess of other expenses over other revenue		15,400
	Income before income taxes		$ 58,200
❹	Income tax expense		17,200
	Net income		$ 41,000

Using an Income Statement

LO6 Use a multiple-step income statement to analyze a company's operations.

Profit margin
Net income divided by sales.

Alternate term: Return on sales.

An important use of the income statement is to evaluate the *profitability* of a business. A company's **profit margin** is the ratio of its net income to its sales or revenues. Some analysts refer to a company's profit margin as its *return on sales*. If the profit margin is high, this generally means that the company is generating revenue but that it is also controlling its costs.

EXAMPLE 2-8 Computing the Profit Margin

We compute Dixon Sporting Goods' profit margin by dividing net income by total sales as follows:

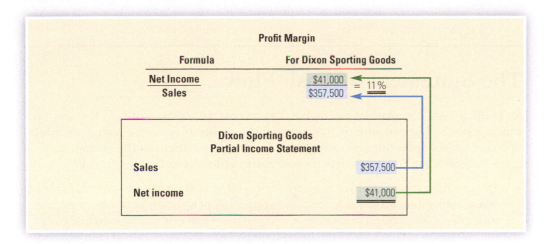

A profit margin of 11% means that for every dollar of sales, Dixon has $0.11 in net income.

Keep two key factors in mind when evaluating any financial statement ratio.

- **How does this year's ratio differ from ratios of prior years?** A decrease in the profit margin may indicate that the company is having trouble controlling certain costs.
- **How does the ratio compare with industry norms?** In some industries, the profit margin is considerably lower than in others, such as in mass merchandising. (Although **Wal-Mart**'s profit margin was only 3.1% for the year ended January 31, 2016, its consolidated net income amounted to over $15 billion.) It is helpful to compare key ratios such as the profit margin with an industry average or with the same ratio for a close competitor of the company.

The Statement of Retained Earnings

The purpose of a statement of stockholders' equity is to explain the changes in the components of owners' equity during the period. Retained earnings and capital stock are the two primary components of stockholders' equity. If during the period no changes occur in a company's capital stock, the company may choose to present a statement of retained earnings instead of a statement of stockholders' equity.

LO7 Identify the components of the statement of retained earnings and prepare the statement.

EXAMPLE 2-9 Preparing a Statement of Retained Earnings

A statement of retained earnings for Dixon Sporting Goods is shown below.

Dixon Sporting Goods Statement of Retained Earnings For the Year Ended December 31, 2017	
Retained earnings, January 1, 2017	$271,500
Net income for 2017	41,000
Dividends declared and paid in 2017	(25,000)
Retained earnings, December 31, 2017	$287,500

Dixon's net income of $41,000, as detailed on the income statement, is an *addition* to retained earnings. Note that the dividends declared and paid of $25,000 do not appear on the income statement because they are a payout, or *distribution,* of net income to stockholders rather than one of the expenses deducted to arrive at net income. Accordingly, they appear as a direct deduction on the statement of retained earnings. The beginning balance in retained earnings is carried forward from last year's statement of retained earnings.

The Statement of Cash Flows

LO8 Identify the components of the statement of cash flows and prepare the statement.

All publicly held corporations are required to present a statement of cash flows in their annual reports. **The purpose of the statement is to summarize the cash-flow effects of a company's operating, investing, and financing activities for the period.** Each of these categories can result in a net inflow or a net outflow of cash.

- Dixon's **operating activities** generated $56,100 of cash during the period, as shown below. Operating activities concern the acquisition of sporting goods from distributors and the subsequent sale of those goods. Dixon had one major source of cash, the collection of $362,500 from its customers. Dixon's largest use of cash was the $217,200 it paid for inventory. Chapter 12 discusses the statement of cash flows in detail and the preparation of this section of the statement.

Dixon Sporting Goods Partial Statement of Cash Flows		
CASH FLOWS FROM OPERATING ACTIVITIES		
Cash collected from customers	$362,500	
Cash collected in interest	1,500	
Total cash collections		$364,000
Cash payments for:		
Inventory	$217,200	
Salaries and wages	38,500	
Interest	16,900	
Store supplies	850	
Insurance	4,800	
Advertising	13,750	
Income taxes	15,900	
Total cash payments		307,900
Net cash provided by operating activities		$ 56,100

- **Investing activities** involve the acquisition and sale of long-term or noncurrent assets such as long-term investments; property, plant, and equipment; and intangible assets. Dixon spent $150,000 for land for a future office site.

Dixon Sporting Goods Partial Statement of Cash Flows	
CASH FLOWS FROM INVESTING ACTIVITIES	
Purchase of land for future office site	$(150,000)

- **Financing activities** result from the issuance and repayment, or retirement, of long-term liabilities and capital stock and the payment of dividends. Dixon had two financing activities: dividends of $25,000 required the use of cash, and the issuance of a long-term note generated cash of $120,000.

Dixon Sporting Goods Partial Statement of Cash Flows		
CASH FLOWS FROM FINANCING ACTIVITIES		
Dividends declared and paid	$ (25,000)	
Proceeds from issuance of long-term note	120,000	
Net cash provided by financing activities		$95,000

EXAMPLE 2-10 Preparing a Statement of Cash Flows

The complete cash flow statement for Dixon Sporting Goods is given below. The balance of cash on the bottom of the statement of $5,000 must agree with the balance for cash shown on the balance sheet in Example 2-4.

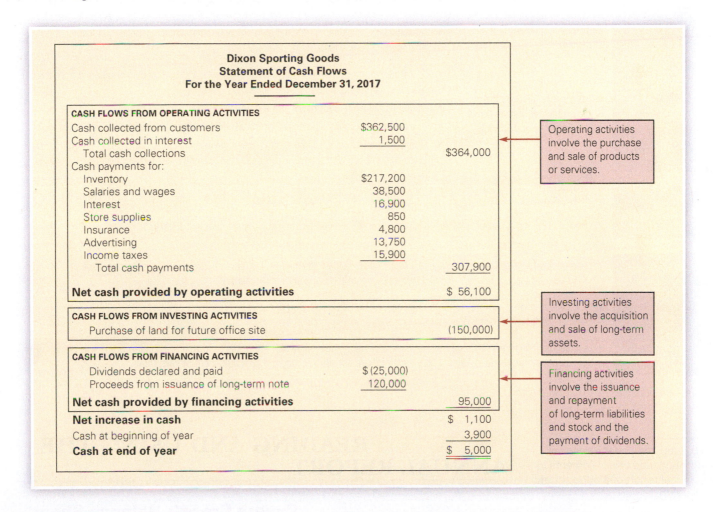

Dixon Sporting Goods Statement of Cash Flows For the Year Ended December 31, 2017			
CASH FLOWS FROM OPERATING ACTIVITIES			
Cash collected from customers	$362,500		
Cash collected in interest	1,500		
Total cash collections		$364,000	Operating activities involve the purchase and sale of products or services.
Cash payments for:			
Inventory	$217,200		
Salaries and wages	38,500		
Interest	16,900		
Store supplies	850		
Insurance	4,800		
Advertising	13,750		
Income taxes	15,900		
Total cash payments		307,900	
Net cash provided by operating activities		$ 56,100	
CASH FLOWS FROM INVESTING ACTIVITIES			
Purchase of land for future office site		(150,000)	Investing activities involve the acquisition and sale of long-term assets.
CASH FLOWS FROM FINANCING ACTIVITIES			
Dividends declared and paid	$ (25,000)		
Proceeds from issuance of long-term note	120,000		Financing activities involve the issuance and repayment of long-term liabilities and stock and the payment of dividends.
Net cash provided by financing activities		95,000	
Net increase in cash		$ 1,100	
Cash at beginning of year		3,900	
Cash at end of year		$ 5,000	

MODULE 3 TEST YOURSELF

Review	**LO5** Explain the difference between a single-step and a multiple-step income statement and prepare each type of income statement.	• The multiple-step income statement classifies revenues and expenses in a manner that makes the statement more useful than the simple single-step income statement. Important subtotals are presented in the multiple-step income statement, including the following:
		  • Gross profit
		  • Income from operations
		  • Income before income taxes

	LO6 Use a multiple-step income statement to analyze a company's operations.	• The multiple-step income statement can be used to evaluate different aspects of a company's profitability. • Profit margin is one useful ratio used to evaluate the relative profitability.
	LO7 Identify the components of the statement of retained earnings and prepare the statement.	• The statement of retained earnings provides a link between the income statement and the balance sheet. • It explains the changes in retained earnings during the period, of which net income (loss) is an important component.
	LO8 Identify the components of the statement of cash flows and prepare the statement.	• The statement of cash flows classifies cash inflows and outflows as originating from three activities: operating, investing, and financing. • Operating activities are related to the primary purpose of a business. • Investing activities are those generally involved with the acquisition and sale of noncurrent assets. • Financing activities are related to the acquisition and repayment of capital that ultimately funds the operations of a business; for example, issuing stock or borrowing.
Question	1. What is the major weakness of the single-step form for the income statement?	
	2. How does a statement of retained earnings act as a link between an income statement and a balance sheet?	
Apply	1. A company reported sales of $100,000; cost of goods sold of $60,000; selling, general, and administrative expenses of $15,000; and income tax expense of $10,000. Compute the company's profit margin.	
	2. A company started the year with retained earnings of $200,000. During the year, it reported net income of $80,000 and paid dividends of $50,000. Compute the company's ending retained earnings.	
	3. A company borrowed $100,000 from its bank and the next day used $80,000 of the cash from the loan to buy a new piece of equipment for its plant. Explain how each of those activities is reported on a statement of cash flows.	

Answers are located at the end of the chapter.

LO9 Read and use the financial statements and other elements in the annual report of a publicly held company.

MODULE 4 READING AND USING THE ANNUAL REPORT

PANERA BREAD
READING THE BALANCE SHEET

2-1 What was the amount of working capital at December 29, 2015? at December 30, 2014? *(See answers on p. 98.)*

Panera Bread's Balance Sheet

Balance sheets for Panera Bread are shown in Exhibit 2-1. Panera Bread releases *consolidated financial statements*, which reflect the position and results of all operations that are controlled by a single entity. Like most other large corporations, Panera Bread owns other companies. Often, these companies are legally separate and are called *subsidiaries*. How a company accounts for its investment in a subsidiary is covered in advanced accounting courses.

EXHIBIT 2-1 Comparative Balance Sheets for Panera Bread Company

Panera Bread Company
Consolidated Balance Sheets
(in thousands, except share and per share information)

	December 29, 2015	December 30, 2014
Assets		
Current assets:		
Cash and cash equivalents	$ 241,886	$ 196,493
Trade accounts receivable, net	38,211	36,584
Other accounts receivable	77,575	70,069
Inventories	22,482	22,811
Prepaid expenses and other	59,457	51,588
Deferred income taxes	34,479	28,621
Assets held for sale	28,699	—
Total current assets	502,789	406,166
Property and equipment, net	776,248	787,294
Other assets:		
Goodwill	121,791	120,778
Other intangible assets, net	63,877	70,940
Deposits and other	10,613	5,508
Total other assets	196,281	197,226
Total assets	$ 1,475,318	$1,390,686
Liabilities, Redeemable Noncontrolling Interest, and Stockholders' Equity		
Current liabilities:		
Accounts payable	$ 19,805	$ 19,511
Accrued expenses	359,464	333,201
Current portion of long-term debt	17,229	—
Liabilities associated with assets held for sale	2,945	—
Total current liabilities	399,443	352,712
Long-term debt	388,971	99,784
Deferred rent	62,610	67,390
Deferred income taxes	70,447	76,589
Other long-term liabilities	52,566	58,027
Total liabilities	974,037	654,502
Commitments and contingencies (Note 14)		
Redeemable noncontrolling interest	3,981	—
Stockholders' equity:		
Common stock, $.0001 par value per share:		
Class A, 112,500,000 shares authorized; 30,836,669 shares issued and 23,346,188 shares outstanding at December 29, 2015 and 30,703,472 shares issued and 25,442,728 shares outstanding at December 30, 2014	3	3
Class B, 10,000,000 shares authorized; 1,381,730 shares issued and outstanding at December 29, 2015 and 1,381,865 shares issued and outstanding at December 30, 2014	—	—
Treasury stock, carried at cost; 7,490,481 shares at December 29, 2015 and 5,260,744 shares at December 30, 2014	(1,111,586)	(706,073)
Preferred stock, $.0001 par value per share; 2,000,000 shares authorized and no shares issued or outstanding at December 29, 2015 and December 30, 2014	—	—
Additional paid-in capital	235,393	214,437
Accumulated other comprehensive income (loss)	(5,029)	(1,360)
Retained earnings	1,378,519	1,229,177
Total stockholders' equity	497,300	736,184
Total liabilities, redeemable noncontrolling interest, and stockholders' equity	$ 1,475,318	$1,390,686

The accompanying notes are an integral part of the consolidated financial statements.

> Companies can place the most recent year-end either before or after the prior year's year-end. Panera Bread places the latest year on the left, which is the most common technique. Check the dates in the headings before you start to read a set of comparative balance sheets.

Source: Panera Bread Company, Form 10-K for the year ended December 29, 2015.

PANERA BREAD
READING THE INCOME STATEMENT

2-2 Compute the percentage decrease in Panera Bread's net income over the three years. That is, by what percent did it decrease from 2013 to 2015? Compare this to the percentage increase in total revenues. What does a comparison of the two tell you? *(See answers on p. 98.)*

Panera Bread presents comparative balance sheets to indicate its financial position at the end of each of the last two years. As a minimum standard, the SEC requires that the annual report include balance sheets as of the two most recent year-ends and income statements for each of the three most recent years. Note that all amounts on the balance sheet are stated in thousands of dollars. This type of rounding is common and is justified under the materiality concept. Knowing the exact dollar amount of each asset would not change an investor's decision.

Panera Bread's Income Statement

Multiple-step income statements for Panera Bread for a three-year period are presented in Exhibit 2-2. Note that unlike Dixon Sporting Goods, Panera Bread does not report cost of goods sold, but rather a line item called "Cost of food and paper products." The inclusion of three years allows the reader to note certain general trends during this period. For example, note the increase in total revenues from the first year, 2013, to the third year, 2015, calculated as:

Increase in total revenues from 2013 to 2015:
Total revenues in 2013

$$\frac{\$2,681,580 - \$2,385,002}{\$2,385,002} = \frac{\$296,578}{\$2,385,002} = 12.4\%$$

EXHIBIT 2-2 Comparative Income Statements for Panera Bread Company

Panera Bread Company
Consolidated Statements of Income
(in thousands, except per share information)

Panera Bread includes items of other comprehensive income at the bottom of its statement. Those items are covered in advanced accounting courses.

	For the fiscal year ended		
	December 29, 2015	December 30, 2014	December 31, 2013
Revenues:			
Bakery-cafe sales, net	$2,358,794	$2,230,370	$2,108,908
Franchise royalties and fees	138,563	123,686	112,641
Fresh dough and other product sales to franchisees	184,223	175,139	163,453
Total revenues	$2,681,580	$2,529,195	$2,385,002
Costs and expenses:			
Bakery-cafe expenses:			
Cost of food and paper products	$ 715,502	$ 669,860	$ 625,622
Labor	754,646	685,576	625,457
Occupancy	169,998	159,794	148,816
Other operating expenses	334,635	314,879	295,539
Total bakery-cafe expenses	1,974,781	1,830,109	1,695,434
Fresh dough and other product cost of sales to franchisees	160,706	152,267	142,160
Depreciation and amortization	135,398	124,109	106,523
General and administrative expenses	142,904	138,060	123,335
Pre-opening expenses	9,089	8,707	7,794
Refranchising loss	17,108	—	—
Total costs and expenses	2,439,986	2,253,252	2,075,246
Operating profit	241,594	275,943	309,756
Interest expense	3,830	1,824	1,053
Other (income) expense, net	1,192	(3,175)	(4,017)
Income before income taxes	236,572	277,294	312,720
Income taxes	87,247	98,001	116,551
Net income	$ 149,325	$ 179,293	$ 196,169
Less: Net loss attributable to noncontrolling interest	(17)	—	—
Net income attributable to Panera Bread Company	$ 149,342	$ 179,293	$ 196,169

Noncontrolling interest is covered in advanced accounting courses. Use the line above for all computations involving "Net income"

(Continued)

	For the fiscal year ended		
	December 29, 2015	December 30, 2014	December 31, 2013
Earnings per common share:			
Basic	$ 5.81	$ 6.67	$ 6.85
Diluted	$ 5.79	$ 6.64	$ 6.81
Weighted average shares of common and common equivalent shares outstanding:			
Basic	25,685	26,881	28,629
Diluted	25,788	26,999	28,794

The accompanying notes are an integral part of the consolidated financial statements.

Source: Panera Bread Company, Form 10-K for the year ended December 29, 2015.

MAKING BUSINESS DECISIONS
PANERA BREAD

The Current Ratio

A banker must be able to assess a company's liquidity before loaning it money. *Liquidity* is the ability of a company to pay its debts as they come due. Use the following models to help you in your role as a banker to decide whether to loan money to Panera Bread:

A. The Ratio Analysis Model

1. Formulate the Question
How liquid is Panera Bread?

2. Gather the Information from the Financial Statements
The **current ratio** measures liquidity. To calculate a company's current ratio, it is essential to know its current assets and current liabilities. Current assets are the most liquid of all assets. Current liabilities are the debts that will be paid the soonest.

Current assets: From the balance sheet
Current liabilities: From the balance sheet

3. Calculate the Ratio

$$\text{Current Ratio} = \frac{\text{Current Assets}}{\text{Current Liabilities}}$$

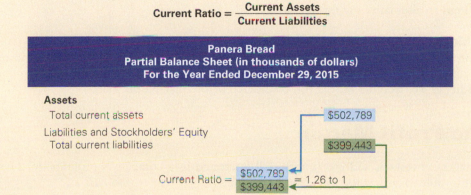

Panera Bread
Partial Balance Sheet (in thousands of dollars)
For the Year Ended December 29, 2015

Assets
Total current assets $502,789

Liabilities and Stockholders' Equity
Total current liabilities $399,443

$$\text{Current Ratio} = \frac{\$502,789}{\$399,443} = 1.26 \text{ to } 1$$

4. Compare the Ratio with Other Ratios

Ratios are of no use in a vacuum. It is necessary to compare them with prior years and with competitors.

	CURRENT RATIO		
Panera Bread		**Chipotle**	
12/29/15	**12/30/14**	**12/31/15**	**12/31/14**
1.26 to 1	1.15 to 1	2.91 to 1	3.50 to 1

5. Interpret the Ratios

In general, the higher the current ratio, the more liquid the company. Panera Bread's current ratio was 1.15 at the end of 2014 and slightly higher at the end of 2015. Conversely, Chipotle's current ratios of 3.50 at the end of 2014 and 2.91 at the end of 2015 are much higher than Panera's. Chipotle has a large amount of investments classifed as current assets, resulting in a higher current ratio.

B. The Business Decision Model

1. Formulate the Question

If you were a banker, would you be willing to loan money to Panera Bread?

2. Gather Information from the Financial Statements and Other Sources

This information will come from a variety of sources, not limited to but including:

- The balance sheet, which provides information about liquidity, the income statement regarding profitability, and the statement of cash flows on inflows and outflows of cash.
- The outlook for the restaurant industry (consumer preferences for dining out, labor issues, supply and cost of ingredients, etc.).
- The outlook for the economy during the time the loan would be outstanding. Is inflation projected to increase or decrease during this time?
- Projections for interest rates for similar loans during the term of the loan.
- Alternative uses for the bank's money.

3. Analyze the Information Gathered

- Compare Panera Bread's current ratio computed in A. above with Chipotle's as well as with industry averages.
- Look at trends over time in the current ratios.
- Review projections for economic outlook and interest rates.

4. Make the Decision

Taking into account all of the various sources of information, decide either to

- Loan money to Panera Bread or
- Find an alternative use for the money

5. Monitor Your Decision

If you decide to make the loan, you will need to monitor the loan periodically. During the time the loan is outstanding, you will want to assess the company's continuing liquidity as well as other factors you considered before making the loan.

The Profit Margin

Managers, investors, and creditors are all interested in a company's profitability. They must be able to answer the following question:

How profitable has the company been in recent years?

Use the following models in your role as an investor to decide whether to buy stock in Panera Bread.

A. The Ratio Analysis Model

1. Formulate the Question
How profitable is Panera Bread?

2. Gather the Information from the Financial Statements
The **profit margin** is a measure of a company's profitability. To calculate the ratio, it is essential to know a company's:

Net income: From the income statement
Net sales or revenues: From the income statement

3. Calculate the Ratio

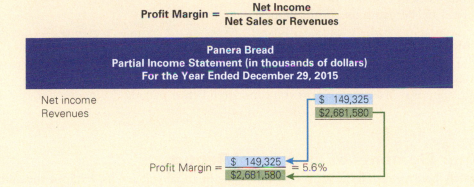

$$\text{Profit Margin} = \frac{\text{Net Income}}{\text{Net Sales or Revenues}}$$

Panera Bread
Partial Income Statement (in thousands of dollars)
For the Year Ended December 29, 2015

Net income $ 149,325
Revenues $2,681,580

$$\text{Profit Margin} = \frac{\$\ 149,325}{\$2,681,580} = 5.6\%$$

4. Compare the Ratio with Other Ratios
Ratios are of no use in a vacuum. It is necessary to compare them with prior years and with competitors.

PROFIT MARGIN			
Panera Bread		Chipotle	
December 29, 2015	December 30, 2014	December 31, 2015	December 31, 2014
5.6%	7.1%	10.6%	10.8%

5. Interpret the Ratios
A high profit margin indicates that the company is controlling its expenses. This is because revenues minus expenses equals net income; if the ratio of net income to revenue is high, the company is not only generating revenue but also minimizing expenses.

Both companies' profit margins indicate that the companies are able to control their expenses while increasing their revenues. However, Chipotle's profit margin in the most recent year is nearly double that of Panera. Panera Bread's profit margin decreased by 1.5% over the two-year period, while Chipotle's remained fairly constant.

B. The Business Decision Model

1. Formulate the Question
If you were an investor, would you buy stock in Panera Bread?

2. Gather Information from the Financial Statements and Other Sources
This information will come from a variety of sources, not limited to but including:

- The balance sheet, which provides information about liquidity, the income statement regarding profitability, and the statement of cash flows on inflows and outflows of cash.
- The outlook for the restaurant industry (consumer preferences for dining out, labor issues, supply and cost of ingredients, etc.).
- The outlook for the economy over the time you expect to hold the stock. Is inflation projected to increase or decrease during this time?
- Alternative uses for your money.

3. Analyze the Information Gathered
- Compare Panera Bread's profit margin computed in (A) above with Chipotle's as well as with industry averages.
- Look at trends over time in the profit margins.
- Review projections for economic outlook.

4. Make the Decision
Taking into account all of the various sources of information, decide either to

- Buy stock in Panera Bread or
- Find an alternative use for the money.

5. Monitor Your Decision
If you decide to buy the stock, you will need to monitor your investment periodically. During the time you own the stock, you will want to assess the company's continuing profitability as well as other factors you considered before making the investment.

Other Elements of an Annual Report

Privately held companies tend to distribute only financial statements, without the additional information normally included in the annual reports of public companies. For the annual reports of public companies, however, certain basic elements are considered standard:

- A letter to the stockholders from either the president or the chair of the board of directors appears in the first few pages of most annual reports.
- A section describing the company's products and markets is usually included.
- The financial report or review, which consists of the financial statements accompanied by notes to explain various items on the statements, is included.

Report of Independent Accountants (Auditors' Report) As Exhibit 2-3 shows, Panera Bread is audited by **PricewaterhouseCoopers LLP**, one of the largest international accounting firms in the world. Two key phrases should be noted in the first sentence of the first paragraph of the independent accountants' report (also called the **auditors' report**): *in our opinion* and *present fairly*. The report also indicates that responsibility for the statements rests with Panera Bread and that the auditors' job is to *express an opinion* on the statements based on certain tests. It would be impossible for an auditing firm to spend the time or money to retrace and verify every single transaction that Panera Bread entered into during the year. Instead, the auditing firm performs various tests of the accounting records to be able to assure itself that the statements are free of *material misstatement*. Auditors do not "certify" the total accuracy of a set of financial statements, but render an opinion as to the reasonableness of those statements.

The Ethical Responsibility of Management and the Auditors A company's management and its auditors must protect the interests of stockholders. In large corporations, the stockholders are normally removed from the daily affairs of the

Auditors' report
The opinion rendered by a public accounting firm concerning the fairness of the presentation of the financial statements.

Alternate term: Report of independent accountants.

EXHIBIT 2-3 Report of Independent Accountants for Panera Bread Company

---

Report of Independent Registered Public Accounting Firm

To Board of Directors and Stockholders of Panera Bread Company:

In our opinion, the accompanying consolidated balance sheets and the related consolidated statements of income, comprehensive income, of changes in equity and redeemable noncontrolling interest, and of cash flows present fairly, in all material respects, the financial position of Panera Bread Company and its subsidiaries at December 29, 2015 and December 30, 2014, and the results of their operations and their cash flows for each of the three years in the period ended December 29, 2015 in conformity with accounting principles generally accepted in the United States of America. In addition, in our opinion, the financial statement schedule listed in the accompanying index appearing under Item 15(a)(2) presents fairly, in all material respects, the information set forth therein when read in conjunction with the related consolidated financial statements. Also in our opinion, the Company maintained, in all material respects, effective internal control over financial reporting as of December 29, 2015, based on criteria established in *Internal Control - Integrated Framework (2013)* issued by the Committee of Sponsoring Organizations of the Treadway Commission (COSO). The Company's management is responsible for these financial statements and financial statement schedule, for maintaining effective internal control over financial reporting and for its assessment of the effectiveness of internal control over financial reporting, included in Management's Report on Internal Control over Financial Reporting under Item 9A. Our responsibility is to express opinions on these financial statements, on the financial statement schedule, and on the Company's internal control over financial reporting based on our integrated audits. We conducted our audits in accordance with the standards of the Public Company Accounting Oversight Board (United States). Those standards require that we plan and perform the audits to obtain reasonable assurance about whether the financial statements are free of material misstatement and whether effective internal control over financial reporting was maintained in all material respects. Our audits of the financial statements included examining, on a test basis, evidence supporting the amounts and disclosures in the financial statements, assessing the accounting principles used and significant estimates made by management, and evaluating the overall financial statement presentation. Our audit of internal control over financial reporting included obtaining an understanding of internal control over financial reporting, assessing the risk that a material weakness exists, and testing and evaluating the design and operating effectiveness of internal control based on the assessed risk. Our audits also included performing such other procedures as we considered necessary in the circumstances. We believe that our audits provide a reasonable basis for our opinions.

A company's internal control over financial reporting is a process designed to provide reasonable assurance regarding the reliability of financial reporting and the preparation of financial statements for external purposes in accordance with generally accepted accounting principles. A company's internal control over financial reporting includes those policies and procedures that (i) pertain to the maintenance of records that, in reasonable detail, accurately and fairly reflect the transactions and dispositions of the assets of the company; (ii) provide reasonable assurance that transactions are recorded as necessary to permit preparation of financial statements in accordance with generally accepted accounting principles, and that receipts and expenditures of the company are being made only in accordance with authorizations of management and directors of the company; and (iii) provide reasonable assurance regarding prevention or timely detection of unauthorized acquisition, use, or disposition of the company's assets that could have a material effect on the financial statements.

Because of its inherent limitations, internal control over financial reporting may not prevent or detect misstatements. Also, projections of any evaluation of effectiveness to future periods are subject to the risk that controls may become inadequate because of changes in conditions, or that the degree of compliance with the policies or procedures may deteriorate.

/s/ PricewaterhouseCoopers LLP
St. Louis, Missouri
February 18, 2016

Source: Panera Bread Company, Form 10-K for the year ended December 29, 2015.

business. A professional management team must run the business, and a periodic independent audit must be performed on the company's records. Stockholders need assurances that the business is being operated effectively and efficiently and that the financial statements are a fair representation of the company's operations and financial position. The management and the auditors have a very important ethical responsibility to stockholders.

Management Discussion and Analysis

Preceding the financial statements is a section of Panera Bread's annual report titled "Management's Discussion and Analysis of Consolidated Financial Condition and Results of Operations." This report gives management the opportunity to discuss the financial statements and also provides insights concerning future trends in the business. Consider the following excerpt from this section of Panera Bread's report under the heading "Impact of Inflation":

Our profitability depends in part on our ability to anticipate and react to changes in food, supply, labor, occupancy, and other costs. In the past, we have been able to recover a significant portion of inflationary costs and commodity price increases, including price increases in fuel, proteins, dairy, wheat, tuna, and cream cheese among others, through increased menu prices. There have been, and there may be in the future, delays in implementing such menu price increases, and competitive pressures may limit our ability to recover such cost increases in their entirety. Historically, the effects of inflation on our consolidated results of operations have not been materially adverse. However, inherent volatility experienced in certain commodity markets, such as those for wheat, proteins, including chicken raised without antibiotics, and fuel may have an adverse effect on us in the future. The extent of the impact will depend on our ability and timing to increase food prices.[4]

Notes to Consolidated Financial Statements

The sentence *The accompanying notes are an integral part of the consolidated financial statements* appears at the bottom of each of Panera Bread's financial statements. These comments, or *notes*, are necessary to satisfy the need for *full disclosure* of all facts relevant to a company's results and financial position. Note 2 is a summary of *significant accounting policies*. Panera Bread describes its policy for recognizing revenue as follows:

The Company records revenues from bakery-cafe sales upon delivery of the related food and other products to the customer. Revenues from fresh dough and other product sales to franchisees are recorded upon delivery to the franchisees. Sales of soup and other branded products outside of the Company's bakery-cafes are recognized upon delivery to customers.[5]

The accounting standards followed in preparing the statements, as well as the appearance of the annual report itself, differ in other countries. As has been noted elsewhere, although many corporations operate internationally, accounting principles are not yet standardized.

MODULE 4 TEST YOURSELF

Review	**LO9** Read and use the financial statements and other elements in the annual report of a publicly held company.	• The classified balance sheet and multiple-step income statement are more complex than simpler versions of these financial statements and yield more useful information to decision makers. • Annual reports contain more information than just the financial statements. This information can be used alone or in conjunction with the financial statements to gain a more complete financial picture of a company. • Management's Discussion and Analysis provides explanatory comments about certain results reflected in the financial statements and sometimes forward-looking commentary. • The Report of Independent Accountants is provided by the company's auditor, whose job is to express an opinion on whether the financial statements fairly represent the accounting treatment of a company's economic activity for the year. • Notes to the Consolidated Financial Statements are generally supplementary disclosures required by GAAP that help explain detail behind the accounting treatment of certain items in the financial statements.
Question		1. In auditing the financial statements of a company, does the auditor *certify* that the statements are totally accurate without errors of any size or variety? Explain. 2. What is the second note that accompanies Panera Bread's financial statements in its Form 10-K? What is its purpose?
Apply		List three examples of the types of information that normally appear in a company's annual report?

Answers are located at the end of the chapter.

---

[4] Panera Bread Company, Form 10-K for the year ended December 29, 2015, p. 38.
[5] Panera Bread Company, Form 10-K for the year ended December 29, 2015, p. 51.

RATIO REVIEW

$$\text{Current Ratio} = \frac{\text{Current Assets (balance sheet)}}{\text{Current Liabilities (balance sheet)}}$$

$$\text{Profit Margin} = \frac{\text{Net Income (income statement)}}{\text{Net Sales or Revenues (income statement)}}$$

KEY TERMS QUIZ

Read each definition below and write the number of the definition in the blank beside the appropriate term. The quiz solutions appear at the end of the chapter.

_____	Understandability	_____	Current liability
_____	Relevance	_____	Liquidity
_____	Faithful representation	_____	Working capital
_____	Comparability	_____	Current ratio
_____	Depreciation	_____	Single-step income statement
_____	Consistency	_____	Multiple-step income statement
_____	Materiality	_____	Gross profit
_____	Conservatism	_____	Profit margin
_____	Operating cycle	_____	Auditors' report
_____	Current asset		

1. An income statement in which all expenses are added together and subtracted from all revenues.
2. The magnitude of an accounting information omission or misstatement that will affect the judgment of someone relying on the information.
3. The capacity of information to make a difference in a decision.
4. An income statement that shows classifications of revenues and expenses as well as important subtotals.
5. The practice of using the least optimistic estimate when two estimates of amounts are about equally likely.
6. The quality of accounting information that makes it comprehensible to those willing to spend the necessary time.
7. Current assets divided by current liabilities.
8. The quality of information that makes it complete, neutral, and free from error.
9. An obligation that will be satisfied within the next operating cycle or within one year if the cycle is shorter than one year.
10. Current assets minus current liabilities.
11. Net income divided by sales.
12. For accounting information, the quality that allows a user to analyze two or more companies and look for similarities and differences.
13. An asset that is expected to be realized in cash or sold or consumed during the operating cycle or within one year if the cycle is shorter than one year.
14. The ability of a company to pay its debts as they come due.
15. For accounting information, the quality that allows a user to compare two or more accounting periods for a single company.
16. The process of allocating the cost of a long-term tangible asset over its useful life.
17. The period of time between the purchase of inventory and the collection of any receivable from the sale of the inventory.
18. Sales less cost of goods sold.
19. The opinion rendered by a public accounting firm concerning the fairness of the presentation of the financial statements.

ALTERNATE TERMS

auditors' report report of independent accountants

long-term assets noncurrent assets

long-term liability long-term debt

net income profits or earnings

profit margin return on sales

REVIEW PROBLEM & SOLUTION

The following review problem will give you the opportunity to apply what you have learned by preparing both an income statement and a balance sheet.

The following items, listed in alphabetical order, are taken from the records of Grizzly Inc., a chain of outdoor recreational stores in the Northwest. Use the items to prepare two statements. First, prepare an income statement for the year ended December 31, 2017. The income statement should be in multiple-step form. Second, prepare a classified balance sheet at December 31, 2017. All amounts are in thousands of dollars.

Accounts payable	$ 6,500	Income tax expense	$ 13,000
Accounts receivable	8,200	Insurance expense	2,000
Accumulated depreciation—buildings	25,000	Interest expense	12,000
Accumulated depreciation—furniture and fixtures	15,000	Interest payable	1,000
		Interest revenue	2,000
Advertising expense	3,100	Land	100,000
Buildings	80,000	Long-term notes payable, due December 31, 2025	120,000
Capital stock, $1 par, 10,000 shares issued and outstanding	10,000	Merchandise inventories	6,000
Cash	2,400	Office supplies	900
Commissions expense	8,600	Paid-in capital in excess of par value	40,000
Cost of goods sold	110,000	Prepaid rent	3,000
Depreciation on buildings	2,500	Rent expense for salespeople's autos	9,000
Depreciation on furniture and fixtures	1,200	Retained earnings	48,800
Furniture and fixtures	68,000	Salaries and wages for office staff	11,000
Income taxes payable	2,200	Sales revenue	190,000

Solution to Review Problem

1. Multiple-step income statement:

Grizzly Inc.
Income Statement
For the Year Ended December 31, 2017
(In thousands of dollars)

Sales revenue		$190,000	
Cost of goods sold		110,000	
Gross profit			$80,000
Operating expenses:			
Selling expenses:			
Advertising expense	$ 3,100		
Depreciation on furniture and fixtures	1,200		
Rent expense for salespeople's autos	9,000		
Commissions expense	8,600		
Total selling expenses		$ 21,900	
General and administrative expenses:			
Depreciation on buildings	$ 2,500		
Insurance expense	2,000		
Salaries and wages for office staff	11,000		
Total general and administrative expenses		15,500	

Total operating expenses			37,400
Income from operations			$42,600
Other revenues and expenses:			
Interest revenue		$ 2,000	
Interest expense		12,000	
Excess of other expense over other revenue			10,000
Income before income taxes			$32,600
Income tax expense			13,000
Net income			$19,600

2. Classified balance sheet:

Grizzly Inc.
Balance Sheet
At December 31, 2017
(In thousands of dollars)

Assets

Current assets:			
Cash		$ 2,400	
Accounts receivable		8,200	
Merchandise inventories		6,000	
Office supplies		900	
Prepaid rent		3,000	
Total current assets			$ 20,500
Property, plant, and equipment:			
Land		$100,000	
Buildings	$ 80,000		
Accumulated depreciation	(25,000)	55,000	
Furniture and fixtures	$ 68,000		
Accumulated depreciation	(15,000)	53,000	
Total property, plant, and equipment			208,000
Total assets			$228,500

Liabilities

Current liabilities:			
Accounts payable		$ 6,500	
Income taxes payable		2,200	
Interest payable		1,000	
Total current liabilities			$ 9,700
Long-term notes payable, due December 31, 2025			120,000
Total liabilities			$129,700

Stockholders' Equity

Contributed capital:			
Capital stock, $1 par, 10,000 shares			
issued and outstanding		$ 10,000	
Paid-in capital in excess of par value		40,000	
Total contributed capital		$ 50,000	
Retained earnings		48,800	
Total stockholders' equity			98,800
Total liabilities and stockholders' equity			$228,500

EXERCISES

Exercise 2-1 Characteristics of Useful Accounting Information

LO2
EXAMPLE 2-2

Fill in the blank with the qualitative characteristic for each of the following descriptions.

_____ 1. The information to include in reports should take into account whether an omission or misstatement could influence a user's decision

_____ 2. Information that has the capacity to make a difference in a decision

_____ 3. Information that is complete, neutral, and free from error

    _____ 4. Information that allows for comparisons to be made for two or more accounting periods for a single company

    _____ 5. Information that is meaningful to those who are willing to learn to use it properly

    _____ 6. Information that allows for comparisons to be made between or among companies

LO3

EXAMPLE 2-3

Exercise 2-2 The Operating Cycle

Two Wheeler Cycle Shop buys all of its bikes from one manufacturer, Baxter Bikes. On average, bikes are on hand for 45 days before Two Wheeler sells them. The company sells some bikes for cash but also extends credit to its customers for 30 days.

Required

1. On average, what is the minimum length of Two Wheeler's operating cycle? the maximum length?
2. Explain why the operating cycle for Baxter, the manufacturer of the bikes, would normally be longer than that of Two Wheeler, the retailer.

LO3

EXAMPLE 2-4

REAL WORLD

Exercise 2-3 Classification of Financial Statement Items

Regal Entertainment Group operates the largest chain of movie theaters in the U.S. Classify each of the following items found on the company's balance sheet included in the Form 10-K for the fiscal year ended December 31, 2015 as a current asset (CA), noncurrent asset (NCA), current liability (CL), long-term liability (LTL), or stockholders' equity (SE) item.

_____ 1. Trade and other receivables, net
_____ 2. Class A common stock
_____ 3. Land
_____ 4. Inventories
_____ 5. Interest payable
_____ 6. Equipment
_____ 7. Accounts payable
_____ 8. Retained earnings
_____ 9. Cash and cash equivalents
_____ 10. Long-term debt, less current portion

LO4

EXAMPLE 2-5

Exercise 2-4 Current Ratio

Baldwin Corp. reported the following current accounts at the end of two recent years:

	December 31, 2017	December 31, 2016
Cash	$ 3,000	$ 6,000
Accounts receivable	15,000	10,000
Inventory	12,000	8,000
Accounts payable	12,000	7,000
Wages payable	2,000	1,000
Notes payable	6,000	4,000

Required

1. Compute Baldwin's current ratio at the end of each of the two years.
2. How has Baldwin's liquidity changed at the end of 2017 compared to the end of 2016?
3. Comment on the relative composition of Baldwin's current assets at the end of 2017 compared to the end of 2016.

LO3

EXAMPLE 2-3, 2-4

Exercise 2-5 Classification of Assets and Liabilities

Indicate the appropriate classification of each of the following as a current asset (CA), noncurrent asset (NCA), current liability (CL), or long-term liability (LTL).

_____ 1. Inventory
_____ 2. Accounts payable
_____ 3. Cash
_____ 4. Patents
_____ 5. Notes payable, due in six months
_____ 6. Taxes payable
_____ 7. Prepaid rent (for the next nine months)
_____ 8. Bonds payable, due in ten years
_____ 9. Machinery

Exercise 2-6 Selling Expenses and General and Administrative Expenses

LO5
EXAMPLE 2-7

Operating expenses are subdivided between selling expenses and general and administrative expenses when a multiple-step income statement is prepared. Identify each of the following items as a selling expense (S) or general and administrative expense (G&A).

_____ 1. Advertising expense
_____ 2. Depreciation expense—store furniture and fixtures
_____ 3. Office rent expense
_____ 4. Office salaries expense
_____ 5. Store rent expense
_____ 6. Store salaries expense
_____ 7. Insurance expense
_____ 8. Supplies expense
_____ 9. Utilities expense

Exercise 2-7 Missing Income Statement Amounts

LO5
EXAMPLE 2-7

For each of the following cases, fill in the blank with the appropriate dollar amount.

	Sara's Coffee Shop	Amy's Deli	Jane's Bagels
Net sales	$ 35,000	$_____	$ 78,000
Cost of goods sold	_____	45,000	_____
Gross profit	7,000	18,000	_____
Selling expenses	3,000	_____	9,000
General and administrative expenses	1,500	2,800	_____
Total operating expenses	_____	8,800	13,600
Net income	$ 2,500	$ 9,200	$ 25,400

Exercise 2-8 Income Statement Ratio

LO6
EXAMPLE 2-8

The income statement of Holly Enterprises shows operating revenues of $134,800, selling expenses of $38,310, general and administrative expenses of $36,990, interest expense of $580, and income tax expense of $13,920. Holly's stockholders' equity was $280,000 at the beginning of the year and $320,000 at the end of the year. The company has 20,000 shares of stock outstanding at the end of the year.

Required

Compute Holly's profit margin. What other information would you need in order to comment on whether this ratio is favorable?

Exercise 2-9 Statement of Retained Earnings

LO7
EXAMPLE 2-9

Landon Corporation was organized on January 2, 2015, with the investment of $100,000 by each of its two stockholders. Net income for its first year of business was $85,200. Net income increased during 2016 to $125,320 and to $145,480 during 2017. Landon paid $20,000 in dividends to each of the two stockholders in each of the three years.

Required

Prepare a statement of retained earnings for the year ended December 31, 2017.

LO8

EXAMPLE 2-10

Exercise 2-10 Components of the Statement of Cash Flows

Identify each of the following items as operating (O), investing (I), financing (F), or not on the statement of cash flows (N).

_____ 1. Paid for supplies
_____ 2. Collected cash from customers
_____ 3. Purchased land (held for resale)
_____ 4. Purchased land (for construction of new building)
_____ 5. Paid dividend
_____ 6. Issued stock
_____ 7. Purchased computers (for use in the business)
_____ 8. Sold old equipment

LO9

Exercise 2-11 Basic Elements of Financial Reports

Most financial reports contain the following list of basic elements. For each element, identify the person(s) who prepared the element and describe the information a user would expect to find in each element. Some information is verifiable; other information is subjectively chosen by management. Comment on the verifiability of information in each element.

1. Management discussion and analysis
2. Product/markets of company
3. Financial statements
4. Notes to financial statements
5. Independent accountants' report

MULTI-CONCEPT EXERCISES

LO3 • 5 • 7

EXAMPLE 2-4, 2-7, 2-9

Exercise 2-12 Financial Statement Classification

Potential stockholders and lenders are interested in a company's financial statements. Identify the statement—balance sheet (BS), income statement (IS), or retained earnings statement (RE)—on which each of the following items would appear.

_____ 1. Accounts payable
_____ 2. Accounts receivable
_____ 3. Advertising expense
_____ 4. Bad debt expense
_____ 5. Bonds payable
_____ 6. Buildings
_____ 7. Cash
_____ 8. Common stock
_____ 9. Depreciation expense
_____ 10. Dividends

_____ 11. Land held for future expansion
_____ 12. Loan payable
_____ 13. Office supplies
_____ 14. Patent
_____ 15. Patent amortization expense
_____ 16. Prepaid insurance
_____ 17. Retained earnings
_____ 18. Sales
_____ 19. Utilities expense
_____ 20. Wages payable

LO5 • 6

EXAMPLE 2-6, 2-7

Exercise 2-13 Single- and Multiple-Step Income Statement

Some headings and/or items are used on either the single- or multiple-step income statement. Some are used on both. Identify each of the following items as single-step (S), multiple-step (M), both formats (B), or not used on either income statement (N).

_____ 1. Sales
_____ 2. Cost of goods sold
_____ 3. Selling expenses
_____ 4. Total revenues
_____ 5. Utilities expense
_____ 6. Administrative expense

_____ 7. Net income
_____ 8. Supplies on hand
_____ 9. Accumulated depreciation
_____ 10. Income before income taxes
_____ 11. Gross profit

Exercise 2-14 Multiple-Step Income Statement

LO5 • 6
EXAMPLE 2-7, 2-8

Gaynor Corporation's partial income statement is as follows:

Sales	$1,200,000
Cost of sales	450,000
Selling expenses	60,800
General and administrative expenses	75,000

Required

Determine the profit margin. Would you invest in Gaynor Corporation? Explain your answer.

PROBLEMS

Problem 2-1 Materiality

LO2

Joseph Knapp, a newly hired accountant wanting to impress his boss, stayed late one night to analyze the office supplies expense. He determined the cost by month for the previous 12 months of each of the following: computer paper, copy paper, fax paper, pencils and pens, notepads, postage, stationery, and miscellaneous items.

Required

1. What did Joseph think his boss would learn from this information? What action might be taken as a result of knowing it?
2. Would this information be more relevant if Joseph worked for a hardware store or for a real estate company? Discuss.

Problem 2-2 Costs and Expenses

LO2

The following costs are incurred by a retailer:
1. Display fixtures in a retail store
2. Advertising
3. Merchandise for sale
4. Incorporation (i.e., legal costs, stock issue costs)
5. Cost of a franchise
6. Office supplies
7. Wages and salaries
8. Computer software
9. Computer hardware

Required

For each cost, explain whether all of the cost or only a portion of the cost would appear as an expense on the income statement for the period in which the cost was incurred. If not all of the cost would appear on the income statement for that period, explain why not.

Problem 2-3 Classified Balance Sheet

LO3

The following balance sheet items, listed in alphabetical order, are available from the records of Ruth Corporation at December 31, 2017:

Accounts payable	$ 18,255	Income taxes payable	$ 6,200
Accounts receivable	23,450	Interest payable	1,500
Accumulated depreciation—		Inventory	45,730
automobiles	22,500	Land	250,000
Accumulated depreciation—		Long-term investments	85,000
buildings	40,000	Notes payable, due June 30, 2018	10,000
Automobiles	112,500	Office supplies	2,340
Bonds payable, due December 31,		Paid-in capital in excess of par value	50,000
2021	160,000	Patents	40,000
Buildings	200,000	Prepaid rent	1,500
Capital stock, $10 par value	150,000	Retained earnings	311,095
Cash	13,230	Salaries and wages payable	4,200

Required

1. Prepare in good form a classified balance sheet as of December 31, 2017.
2. Compute Ruth's current ratio.
3. On the basis of your answer to (2), does Ruth appear to be liquid? What other information do you need to fully answer that question?

LO4   Problem 2-4 Financial Statement Ratios

The following items, in alphabetical order, are available from the records of Walker Corporation as of December 31, 2017 and 2016:

	December 31, 2017	December 31, 2016
Accounts payable	$ 8,400	$ 5,200
Accounts receivable	27,830	35,770
Cash	20,200	19,450
Cleaning supplies	450	700
Interest payable	0	1,200
Inventory	24,600	26,200
Marketable securities	6,250	5,020
Note payable, due in six months	0	12,000
Prepaid rent	3,600	4,800
Taxes payable	1,450	1,230
Wages payable	1,200	1,600

Required

1. Calculate the following as of December 31, 2017, and December 31, 2016:

    a. Working capital
    b. Current ratio

2. On the basis of your answers to (1), comment on the company's relative liquidity at the beginning and end of the year. Explain the change in the company's liquidity from the beginning to the end of 2017.

LO4   Problem 2-5 Working Capital and Current Ratio

The balance sheet of Stevenson Inc. includes the following items:

Cash	$23,000	Accounts payable	$ 54,900
Accounts receivable	13,000	Salaries payable	1,200
Inventory	45,000	Capital stock	100,000
Prepaid insurance	800	Retained earnings	5,700
Land	80,000		

Required

1. Determine the current ratio and working capital.
2. Beyond the information provided in your answers to (1), what does the composition of the current assets tell you about Stevenson's liquidity?
3. What other information do you need to fully assess Stevenson's liquidity?

LO5   Problem 2-6 Single-Step Income Statement

The following income statement items, arranged in alphabetical order, are taken from the records of Shaw Corporation for the current year:

Advertising expense	$ 1,500	Interest expense	$ 1,400
Commissions expense	2,415	Interest revenue	1,340
Cost of goods sold	29,200	Rent revenue	6,700
Depreciation expense—office building	2,900	Salaries and wages expense—office	12,560
Income tax expense	1,540	Sales revenue	48,300
Insurance expense— salesperson's auto	2,250	Supplies expense—office	890

Required

1. Prepare a single-step income statement for the current year.
2. What weaknesses do you see in this form for the income statement?

Problem 2-7 Multiple-Step Income Statement and Profit Margin   LO5

Refer to the list of income statement items in Problem 2-6. Assume that Shaw Corporation classifies all operating expenses into two categories: (1) selling and (2) general and administrative.

Required

1. Prepare a multiple-step income statement for the current year.
2. What advantages do you see in this form for the income statement?
3. Compute Shaw's profit margin.
4. Comment on Shaw's profitability. What other factors need to be taken into account to assess Shaw's profitability?

Problem 2-8 Statement of Cash Flows   LO8

Colorado Corporation was organized at the beginning of the year, with the investment of $250,000 in cash by its stockholders. The company immediately purchased an office building for $300,000, paying $210,000 in cash and signing a three-year promissory note for the balance. Colorado signed a five-year, $60,000 promissory note at a local bank during the year and received cash in the same amount. During its first year, Colorado collected $93,970 from its customers. It paid $65,600 for inventory, $20,400 in salaries and wages, and another $3,100 in taxes. Colorado paid $5,600 in cash dividends.

Required

1. Prepare a statement of cash flows for the year.
2. What does this statement tell you that an income statement does not?

Problem 2-9 Basic Elements of Financial Reports   LO9

Comparative income statements for Grammar Inc. are as follows:

	2017	2016
Sales	$1,000,000	$500,000
Cost of sales	500,000	300,000
Gross profit	$ 500,000	$200,000
Operating expenses	120,000	100,000
Operating income	$ 380,000	$100,000
Loss on sale of subsidiary	(400,000)	—
Net income (loss)	$ (20,000)	$100,000

Required

The president and management believe that the company performed better in 2017 than it did in 2016. Write the president's letter to be included in the 2017 annual report. Explain why the company is financially sound and why shareholders should not be alarmed by the $20,000 loss in a year when operating revenues increased significantly.

MULTI-CONCEPT PROBLEMS

Problem 2-10 Making Business Decisions: Loaning Money to The Coca-Cola Company   LO2 • 4

As chief lending officer for a bank, you need to decide whether to make a loan to **The Coca-Cola Company**. The current items, listed in alphabetical order, are taken from the consolidated balance sheets of The Coca-Cola Company and its competitor **PepsiCo** at the end of 2015 and 2014

RATIO ANALYSIS

BUSINESS DECISION MODEL

(Continued)

REAL WORLD

(included in the companies' Form 10-Ks for the year ended December 31, 2015 for Coca-Cola and December 26, 2015 for PepsiCo; all amounts are in millions of dollars):

The Coca-Cola Company	12/31/15	12/31/14
Accounts payable and accrued expenses	$ 9,660	$ 9,234
Accrued income taxes	331	400
Assets held for sale	3,900	679
Cash and cash equivalents	7,309	8,958
Current maturities of long-term debt	2,677	3,552
Inventories	2,902	3,100
Loans and notes payable	13,129	19,130
Liabilities held for sale	1,133	58
Marketable securities	4,269	3,665
Prepaid expenses and other assets	2,752	3,066
Short-term investments	8,322	9,052
Trade accounts receivable, less allowances of $352 and $331, respectively	3,941	4,466

PepsiCo	12/26/15	12/27/14
Accounts and notes receivable, net	$ 6,437	$ 6,651
Accounts payable and other current liabilities	13,507	13,016
Cash and cash equivalents	9,096	6,134
Inventories	2,720	3,143
Prepaid expenses and other current assets	1,865	2,143
Short-term investments	2,913	2,592
Short-term obligations	4,071	5,076

Required

Part A. The Ratio Analysis Model

A banker must be able to assess a company's liquidity before loaning it money. Liquidity is the ability of a company to pay its debts as they come due. Replicate the five steps in the Ratio Analysis Model on pages 73–74 to analyze the current ratios for The Coca-Cola Company and PepsiCo:

1. Formulate the Question
2. Gather the Information from the Financial Statements
3. Calculate the Ratio
4. Compare the Ratio with Other Ratios
5. Interpret the Ratios

Part B. The Business Decision Model

A banker must consider a variety of factors, including financial ratios, before making a loan. Replicate the five steps in the Business Decision Model on page 74 to decide whether to make a loan to The Coca-Cola Company:

1. Formulate the Question
2. Gather Information from the Financial Statements and Other Sources
3. Analyze the Information Gathered
4. Make the Decision
5. Monitor Your Decision

LO2 • 5   **Problem 2-11 Comparability and Consistency in Income Statements**

The following income statements were provided by Gleeson Company, a retailer:

2017 Income Statement		2016 Income Statement	
Sales	$1,700,000	Sales	$1,500,000
Cost of sales	520,000	Cost of sales	$ 450,000
Gross profit	$1,180,000	Sales salaries	398,000
Selling expense	$ 702,000	Advertising	175,000
Administrative expense	95,000	Office supplies	54,000

2017 Income Statement			2016 Income Statement	
Total selling and administrative expense	$ 797,000		Depreciation—building	40,000
			Delivery expense	20,000
			Total expenses	$1,137,000
Net income	$ 383,000		Net income	$ 363,000

Required

1. Identify each income statement as either single- or multiple-step format.
2. Convert the 2016 income statement to the same format as the 2017 income statement.

Problem 2-12 Cash Flow

LO1 • 4 • 8

Franklin Co., a specialty retailer, has a history of paying quarterly dividends of $0.50 per share. Management is trying to determine whether the company will have adequate cash on December 31, 2018, to pay a dividend if one is declared by the board of directors. The following additional information is available:

- All sales are on account, and accounts receivable are collected one month after the sale. Sales volume has been increasing 5% each month.
- All purchases of merchandise are on account, and accounts payable are paid one month after the purchase. Cost of sales is 40% of the sales price. Inventory levels are maintained at $75,000.
- Operating expenses in addition to the mortgage are paid in cash. They amount to $3,000 per month and are paid as they are incurred.

Franklin Co.
Balance Sheet
September 30, 2018

Cash	$ 5,000	Accounts payable	$ 5,000
Accounts receivable	12,500	Mortgage note**	150,000
Inventory	75,000	Common stock—$1 par	50,000
Note receivable*	10,000	Retained earnings	66,500
Building/Land	169,000	Total liabilities and	
Total assets	$271,500	stockholders' equity	$271,500

*Note receivable represents a one-year, 5% interest-bearing note due November 1, 2018.
**Mortgage note is a 30-year, 7% note due in monthly installments of $1,200.

Required

Determine the cash that Franklin will have available to pay a dividend on December 31, 2018. Round all amounts to the nearest dollar. What can Franklin's management do to increase the cash available? Should management recommend that the board of directors declare a dividend? Explain.

ALTERNATE PROBLEMS

Problem 2-1A Materiality

LO2

Jane Erving, a newly hired accountant wanting to impress her boss, stayed late one night to analyze the long-distance calls by area code and time of day placed. She determined the monthly cost for the previous 12 months by hour and area code called.

Required

1. What did Jane think her boss would learn from this information? What action might be taken as a result of knowing it?
2. Would this information be more relevant if Jane worked for a hardware store or for a real estate company? Discuss.

LO2 Problem 2-2A Costs and Expenses

The following costs are incurred by a retailer:
1. Point-of-sale systems in a retail store
2. An ad in the yellow pages
3. An inventory-control computer software system
4. Shipping merchandise for resale to chain outlets

Required

For each cost, explain whether all of the cost or only a portion of the cost would appear as an expense on the income statement for the period in which the cost was incurred. If not all of the cost would appear on the income statement for that period, explain why not.

LO3 Problem 2-3A Classified Balance Sheet

The following balance sheet items, listed in alphabetical order, are available from the records of Singer Company at December 31, 2017:

Accounts payable	$ 34,280	Interest payable	$ 2,200
Accounts receivable	26,700	Land	250,000
Accumulated depreciation—buildings	40,000	Marketable securities	15,000
Accumulated depreciation—equipment	12,500	Merchandise inventory	112,900
Bonds payable, due December 31,		Notes payable, due April 15, 2018	6,500
2023	250,000	Office supplies	400
Buildings	150,000	Paid-in capital in excess of par value	75,000
Capital stock, $1 par value	200,000	Patents	45,000
Cash	60,790	Prepaid rent	3,600
Equipment	84,500	Retained earnings	113,510
Income taxes payable	7,500	Salaries payable	7,400

Required

1. Prepare a classified balance sheet as of December 31, 2017.
2. Compute Singer's current ratio.
3. On the basis of your answer to (2), does Singer appear to be liquid? What other information do you need to fully answer that question?

LO4 Problem 2-4A Financial Statement Ratios

The following items, in alphabetical order, are available from the records of Quinn Corporation as of December 31, 2017 and 2016:

	December 31, 2017	December 31, 2016
Accounts payable	$10,500	$ 6,500
Accounts receivable	16,500	26,000
Cash	12,750	11,800
Interest receivable	200	0
Note receivable, due 12/31/2019	12,000	12,000
Office supplies	900	1,100
Prepaid insurance	400	250
Salaries payable	1,800	800
Taxes payable	10,000	5,800

Required

1. Calculate the following as of December 31, 2017, and December 31, 2016:
   a. Working capital
   b. Current ratio

2. On the basis of your answers to (1), comment on the company's relative liquidity at the beginning and end of the year. Explain the change in the company's liquidity from the beginning to the end of 2017.

Problem 2-5A Working Capital and Current Ratio
LO4

The balance sheet of Kapinski Inc. includes the following items:

Cash	$23,000	Accounts payable	$ 84,900
Accounts receivable	43,000	Salaries payable	3,200
Inventory	75,000	Capital stock	100,000
Prepaid insurance	2,800	Retained earnings	35,700
Land	80,000		

Required

1. Determine the current ratio and working capital.
2. Kapinski appears to have a positive current ratio and a large net working capital. Why would it have trouble paying bills as they come due?
3. Suggest three things that Kapinski can do to help pay its bills on time.

Problem 2-6A Single-Step Income Statement
LO5

The following income statement items, arranged in alphabetical order, are taken from the records of Corbin Enterprises for the current year:

Advertising expense	$ 9,000	Rent expense—office	$ 26,400
Cost of goods sold	150,000	Rent expense—salesperson's car	18,000
Depreciation expense—computer	4,500	Sales revenue	350,000
Dividend revenue	2,700	Supplies expense—office	1,300
Income tax expense	30,700	Utilities expense	6,750
Interest expense	1,900	Wages expense—office	45,600

Required

1. Prepare a single-step income statement for the current year.
2. What weaknesses do you see in this form for the income statement?

Problem 2-7A Multiple-Step Income Statement and Profit Margin
LO5

Refer to the list of income statement items in Problem 2-6A. Assume that Corbin Enterprises classifies all operating expenses into two categories: (1) selling and (2) general and administrative.

Required

1. Prepare a multiple-step income statement for the current year.
2. What advantages do you see in this form for the income statement?
3. Compute Corbin's profit margin.
4. Comment on Corbin's profitability. What other factors need to be taken into account to assess Corbin's profitability?

Problem 2-8A Statement of Cash Flows
LO8

Wisconsin Corporation was organized at the beginning of the year with the investment of $400,000 in cash by its stockholders. The company immediately purchased a manufacturing facility for $300,000, paying $150,000 in cash and signing a five-year promissory note for the balance. Wisconsin signed another five-year note at the bank for $50,000 during the year and received cash in the same amount. During its first year, Wisconsin collected $310,000 from its customers. It paid $185,000 for inventory, $30,100 in salaries and wages, and another $40,000 in taxes. Wisconsin paid $4,000 in cash dividends.

Required

1. Prepare a statement of cash flows for the year.
2. What does this statement tell you that an income statement does not?

LO9   Problem 2-9A Basic Elements of Financial Reports

Comparative income statements for Thesaurus Inc. are as follows:

	2017	2016
Operating revenues	$500,000	$200,000
Operating expenses	120,000	100,000
Operating income	$380,000	$100,000
Gain on the sale of subsidiary	—	400,000
Net income	$380,000	$500,000

Required

The president and management believe that the company performed better in 2017 than it did in 2016. Write the president's letter to be included in the 2017 annual report. Explain why the company is financially sound and why shareholders should not be alarmed by the reduction in income in a year when operating revenues increased significantly.

ALTERNATE MULTI-CONCEPT PROBLEMS

RATIO ANALYSIS
BUSINESS DECISION MODEL

REAL WORLD

LO2 • 4   Problem 2-10A Making Business Decisions: Loaning Money to Starwood Hotels & Resorts Worldwide, Inc.

As chief lending officer for a bank, you need to decide whether to make a loan to **Starwood Hotels & Resorts Worldwide, Inc.** The current items, listed in alphabetical order, are taken from the consolidated balance sheets of Starwood Hotels & Resorts Worldwide, Inc., and its competitor **Hyatt Hotels Corporation and Subsidiaries** at the end of 2015 and 2014 (included in the companies' Form 10-Ks for the years ended December 31, 2015; all amounts are in millions of dollars):

Starwood Hotels & Resorts Worldwide, Inc.	12/31/15	12/31/14
Accounts payable	$ 98	$ 101
Accounts receivable, net of allowance for doubtful accounts of $78 and $63	690	661
Accrued expenses	1,354	1,307
Accrued salaries, wages and benefits	400	416
Accrued taxes and other	303	256
Cash and cash equivalents	1,048	935
Current maturities of long-term securitized vacation ownership debt	48	73
Deferred income taxes*	—	199
Inventories	319	236
Prepaid expenses and other	152	159
Restricted cash	54	84
Securitized vacation ownership notes receivable, net of allowance for doubtful accounts of $2 and $4	32	47
Short-term borrowings and current maturities of long-term debt	33	297

*This item is reported as an asset.

Hyatt Hotels Corporation and Subsidiaries	12/31/15	12/31/14
Accounts payable	$141	$130
Accrued compensation and benefits	122	120
Accrued expenses and other current liabilities	516	468
Assets held for sale	—	63
Cash and cash equivalents	457	685
Current maturities of long-term debt	328	9
Deferred tax assets	—	26
Inventories	12	17
Prepaids and other assets	152	108

Liabilities held for sale	—	3
Prepaid income taxes	63	47
Receivables, net of allowances of $15 and $13 at December 31, 2015 and 2014, respectively	298	274
Restricted cash	96	359
Short-term investments	46	130

Required

Part A. The Ratio Analysis Model

A banker must be able to assess a company's liquidity before loaning it money. Liquidity is the ability of a company to pay its debts as they come due. Replicate the five steps in the Ratio Analysis Model on pages 73–74 to analyze the current ratios for Starwood Hotels & Resorts Worldwide, Inc., and Hyatt Hotels Corporation and Subsidiaries:

1. Formulate the Question
2. Gather the Information from the Financial Statements
3. Calculate the Ratio
4. Compare the Ratio with Other Ratios
5. Interpret the Ratios

Part B. The Business Decision Model

A banker must consider a variety of factors, including financial ratios, before making a loan. Replicate the five steps in the Business Decision Model on page 74 to decide whether to make a loan to Starwood Hotels & Resorts Worldwide, Inc.:

1. Formulate the Question
2. Gather Information from the Financial Statements and Other Sources
3. Analyze the Information Gathered
4. Make the Decision
5. Monitor Your Decision

Problem 2-11A Comparability and Consistency in Income Statements   LO2 • 5

The following income statements were provided by Chisholm Company, a wholesale food distributor:

	2017	2016
Sales	$1,700,000	$1,500,000
Cost of sales	$ 612,000	$ 450,000
Sales salaries	427,000	398,000
Delivery expense	180,000	175,000
Office supplies	55,000	54,000
Depreciation—truck	40,000	40,000
Computer line expense	23,000	20,000
Total expenses	$1,337,000	$1,137,000
Net income	$ 363,000	$ 363,000

Required

1. Identify each income statement as either single- or multiple-step format.
2. Restate each item in the income statements as a percentage of sales. Why did net income remain unchanged when sales increased in 2017?

Problem 2-12A Cash Flow   LO1 • 4 • 8

Roosevelt Inc., a consulting service, has a history of paying annual dividends of $1 per share. Management is trying to determine whether the company will have adequate cash on December 31, 2018, to pay a dividend if one is declared by the board of directors. The following additional information is available:

- All sales are on account, and accounts receivable are collected one month after the sale. Sales volume has been decreasing 5% each month.
- Operating expenses are paid in cash in the month incurred. Average monthly expenses are $10,000 (excluding the biweekly payroll).

(Continued)

- Biweekly payroll is $4,500, and it will be paid December 15 and December 31.
- Unearned revenue is expected to be earned in December. This amount was taken into consideration in the expected sales volume.

Roosevelt Inc.
Balance Sheet
December 1, 2018

Cash	$ 15,000	Unearned revenue	$ 2,000
Accounts receivable	40,000	Note payable*	30,000
Computer equipment	120,000	Common stock—$2 par	50,000
		Retained earnings	93,000
		Total liabilities and	
Total assets	$175,000	stockholders' equity	$175,000

*The note payable plus 3% interest for six months is due January 15, 2019.

Required

Determine the cash that Roosevelt will have available to pay a dividend on December 31, 2018. Round all amounts to the nearest dollar. Should management recommend that the board of directors declare a dividend? Explain.

DECISION CASES

Reading and Interpreting Financial Statements

LO4   **Decision Case 2-1 Comparing Two Companies in the Same Industry: Chipotle and Panera Bread**

REAL WORLD

Refer to the financial information for **Chipotle** and **Panera Bread** reproduced at the back of the book for the information needed to answer the following questions.

Required

1. Compute each company's working capital at the end of the two most recent years. Also, for each company, compute the change in working capital during the most recent year.
2. Compute each company's current ratio at the end of the two most recent years. Compute the percentage change in the ratio during the most recent year.
3. How do the two companies differ in terms of the accounts that made up their current assets at the end of the most recent year? What is the largest current asset each company reports on the balance sheet at the end of the most recent year?
4. On the basis of your answers to (2) and (3), comment on each company's liquidity.

LO4   **Decision Case 2-2 Reading Panera Bread's Balance Sheet**

REAL WORLD

Refer to **Panera Bread**'s balance sheet reproduced at the back of the book to answer the following questions.

Required

1. Which is the largest of Panera Bread's current assets on December 29, 2015? What percentage of total current assets does it represent? Is it favorable or unfavorable that this is such a significant asset? Explain your answer.
2. Which is the smallest of Panera Bread's current assets on December 29, 2015? What percentage of total current assets does it represent? Explain why this asset would be relatively small for a company such as Panera Bread.

Making Financial Decisions

Decision Case 2-3 Analysis of Cash Flow for a Small Business   LO8

Charles, a financial consultant, has been self-employed for two years. His list of clients has grown, and he is earning a reputation as a shrewd investor. Charles rents a small office, uses the pool secretarial services, and has purchased a car that he is depreciating over three years. The following income statements cover Charles's first two years of business:

	Year 1	Year 2
Commissions revenue	$ 25,000	$65,000
Rent	$ 12,000	$12,000
Secretarial services	3,000	9,000
Car expenses, gas, insurance	6,000	6,500
Depreciation	15,000	15,000
Net income	$(11,000)	$22,500

Charles believes that he should earn more than $11,500 for working very hard for two years. He is thinking about going to work for an investment firm where he can earn $40,000 per year. What would you advise Charles to do?

Decision Case 2-4 Factors Involved in an Investment Decision   LO9

As an investor, you are considering purchasing stock in a chain of theaters. The annual reports of several companies are available for comparison.

Required

Prepare an outline of the steps you would follow to make your comparison. Start by listing the first section that you would read in the financial reports. What would you expect to find there? Why did you choose that section to read first? Continue with the other sections of the financial report.

Ethical Decision Making

Decision Case 2-5 The Expenditure Approval Process   LO2

Roberto is the plant superintendent of a small manufacturing company that is owned by a large corporation. The corporation has a policy that any expenditure over $1,000 must be approved by the chief financial officer in the corporate headquarters. The approval process takes a minimum of three weeks. Roberto would like to order a new labeling machine that is expected to reduce costs and pay for itself in six months. The machine costs $2,200, but Roberto can buy the sales rep's demo for $1,800. Roberto has asked the sales rep to send two separate bills for $900 each.

What would you do if you were the sales rep? Do you agree or disagree with Roberto's actions? What do you think about the corporate policy?

Decision Case 2-6 Susan Applies for a Loan   LO4 • 6

Susan Spiffy, owner of Spiffy Cleaners, a drive-through dry cleaners, would like to expand her business from its current location to a chain of cleaners. Revenues at the one location have been increasing an average of 8% each quarter. Profits have been increasing accordingly. Susan is conservative in spending and is a very hard worker. She has an appointment with a banker to apply for a loan to expand the business. To prepare for the appointment, she instructs you, as chief financial officer and payroll clerk, to copy the quarterly income statements for the past two years but not to include a balance sheet. Susan already has a substantial loan from another bank. In fact, she has very little of her own money invested in the business.

ETHICAL DECISION MODEL

Required

Use the Ethical Decision Framework in Exhibit 1-9 to complete the following requirements:
1. **Recognize an ethical dilemma:** What ethical dilemma(s) do you face?

2. **Analyze the key elements in the situation:**
   a. Who may benefit if you follow Susan's instructions? Who may be harmed?
   b. How are they likely to benefit or be harmed?
   c. What rights or claims may be violated?
   d. What specific interests are in conflict?
   e. What are your responsibilities and obligations?

3. **List alternatives and evaluate the impact of each on those affected:** As chief financial officer, what are your options in dealing with the ethical dilemma(s) you identified in (1) above? If the bank does not receive the balance sheet, will it have all the relevant information needed to make a decision on a loan? Why or why not? Will the information provided by your company be neutral?

4. **Select the best alternative:** Among the alternatives, which one would you select?

Answers

MODULE 1 Answers to Questions

1. The primary concern to an investor is the future cash to be received from the investment. However, this does not mean that the cash flows of the company that has been invested in are not relevant. A relationship exists between the cash flows to the investor and those to the company. For example, a company that does not consistently generate sufficient cash flows from its operations will not be able to pay cash dividends to the investors over a sustained time.

2. Relevance is the capacity of accounting information to make a difference in a financial decision. For example, an income statement is relevant when the use of it has at least the potential to make a difference in an investment decision.

3. Comparability is the quality of information that allows for comparisons to be made between two or more companies, whereas consistency is the quality that allows for comparisons to be made within a single entity from one accounting period to the next.

4. The concept of materiality is closely related to the size of a company. For example, assume that a company must decide whether a $500 expenditure that will benefit future periods should be expensed immediately or capitalized (i.e., recorded as an asset). The decision cannot be made without considering the amount in relation to the size of the company. An amount that is immaterial for a large multinational corporation may be material for a smaller business.

MODULE 1 Answers to Apply

1. The overriding objective of financial reporting is to provide financial information to permit users of the information to make informed decisions. Financial statements do not report the value of the reporting entity, but should provide useful information to allow users to make estimates of the value of the entity.

2. The two fundamental qualities that make accounting information useful are relevance and faithful representation. Financial information is enhanced when it is understandable, comparable, and consistent.

MODULE 2 Answers to Questions

1. A current asset is an asset that a company expects to realize in cash, sell, or consume during its normal operating cycle. Therefore, accounts receivable, inventory, and supplies all meet this definition and are classified as current assets. By their nature, the benefits from each of these assets will be realized during the normal operating cycle of the business.

2. The note payable will be classified on the balance sheet as long term until one year from its maturity date. At that time, it should be reclassified from long term to current because it will be paid within the next year. Any liability that will mature within one year of the date of the balance sheet should be classified as current, regardless of the original term of the loan (five years in this case).

3. Capital stock and retained earnings represent claims of the stockholders on the assets of the business, but differ in the source of those claims. Capital stock represents the claims of the stockholders that arise from their contributions of cash and other assets to the business. Retained earnings represent the accumulated earnings, or net income, of the business since its inception less all dividends declared during that time.

4. Using working capital as a measure of liquidity does not allow someone to compare the relative liquidity of two companies of different sizes. Even within a single company, it may be difficult to compare the relative liquidity of the company over time if the company has grown. The current ratio (current assets divided by current liabilities) overcomes these deficiencies by focusing attention on the relative size of the current assets and current liabilities.

MODULE 2 Answers to Apply

1.
   Accounts receivable—CA   Furniture and fixtures—NCA
   Land—NCA   Office supplies—CA
   Inventories—CA   Buildings—NCA
   Cash—CA

2. Working Capital = Current Assets − Current Liabilities

   Working Capital = $80,000 − $60,000 = $20,000

   Current Ratio = Current Assets/Current Liabilities

   Current Ratio = $80,000/$60,000 = 1.33 to 1

3. On the surface, Small appears to be more liquid. Its current ratio of $80,000/$20,000, or 4 to 1, is significantly higher than Big's current ratio of $500,000/$400,000, or 1.25 to 1.

MODULE 3 Answers to Questions

1. The single-step form does not highlight the relationships between key items on the statement. For example, the relationship between sales revenue and the cost of the products sold is very important for a product-oriented company. The difference between the two amounts is called gross profit and would appear on a multiple-step statement but not on the single-step form.

2. A statement of retained earnings shows the beginning balance in the account, the addition (deduction) to the account for the net income (loss) of the period, and any deduction from the account for dividends. The beginning balance in Retained Earnings is taken from the balance sheet at the end of the prior period. The income statement indicates the net income for the period. The ending balance in Retained Earnings appears on the balance sheet at the end of the period.

MODULE 3 Answers to Apply

1. Profit Margin = Net Income/Sales = ($100,000 − $60,000 − $15,000 − $10,000)/$100,000 = $15,000/$100,000 = 15%

2. Ending retained earnings = $200,000 + $80,000 − $50,000 = $230,000

3. The amount borrowed from the bank, $100,000, would be reported on the statement of cash flows as an inflow from financing activities. The amount used to buy a new piece of equipment, $80,000, would be shown on the statement of cash flows as an outflow from investing activities.

MODULE 4 Answers to Questions

1. An audit of a set of financial statements does not ensure that the statements contain no errors. Because of the sheer number of transactions entered into during a period of time, it would be impossible for an auditor to check every single transaction to determine that it was correctly recorded. Instead, through various types of tests, the auditor renders an opinion as to whether the statements are free of material misstatement.

2. The second note is the summary of significant accounting policies. The purpose of this note is to summarize all of the company's important accounting policies, such as those relating to the method of depreciating assets and the policy for recognizing revenue.

MODULE 4 Answers to Apply

In addition to the financial statements, an annual report usually includes the following items: a letter to the stockholders from either the president or the chair of the board of directors, a section describing the company's products/services and markets, the auditors' report, management discussion and analysis, and notes to the financial statements.

Answers to Connect to the Real World

2-1 (p. 70)

The amount of working capital at December 29, 2015, was $502,789 thousand − $399,443 thousand = $103,346 thousand. On December 30, 2014, the working capital amounted to $406,166 thousand − $352,712 thousand = $53,454 thousand.

2-2 (p. 72)

Net income decreased over the three years from $196,169 thousand in 2013 to $149,325 thousand in 2015, a decrease of $46,844 thousand. This represents a percentage decrease of $46,844/$196,169, or 23.9%. During this same time period, total revenues increased from $2,385,002 thousand to $2,681,580 thousand, an increase of $296,578 thousand. This represents a percentage increase of $296,578/ $2,385,002, or 12.4%. Thus, total revenues increased at a rate of over 12% while net income decreased by nearly 24%. This is an indication that the company needs to find ways to control its costs.

Answers to Key Terms Quiz

6	Understandability		9	Current liability
3	Relevance		14	Liquidity
8	Faithful representation		10	Working capital
12	Comparability		7	Current ratio
16	Depreciation		1	Single-step income statement
15	Consistency		4	Multiple-step income statement
2	Materiality		18	Gross profit
5	Conservatism		11	Profit margin
17	Operating cycle		19	Auditors' report
13	Current asset			

3

Processing Accounting Information

MODULES	LEARNING OBJECTIVES	WHY IS THIS CHAPTER IMPORTANT?
1 **Transactions, the Accounting Equation, and Ledger Accounts**	**LO1** Explain the difference between external and internal events. **LO2** Explain the role of source documents in an accounting system. **LO3** Analyze the effects of transactions on the accounting equation and understand how these transactions affect the balance sheet and the income statement. **LO4** Describe the use of the account and the general ledger to accumulate amounts of financial statement items.	• You need to know what source documents are used as the necessary evidence to record transactions. (See p. 102.) • You need to know how transactions affect the accounting equation and the financial statements. (See pp. 102–107.) • You need to know how ledger accounts facilitate the preparation of financial statements. (See pp. 107–110.)
2 **Debits and Credits (Appendix)**	**LO5** Explain the rules of debits and credits (Appendix).	• You need to know about the double-entry system of accounting and its role in the recording process. (See pp. 111–116.)
3 **Journal Entries and Trial Balances (Appendix)**	**LO6** Explain the purposes of a journal and the posting process (Appendix). **LO7** Explain the purpose of a trial balance (Appendix).	• You need to know some of the tools that accountants use to effectively and efficiently process the information that appears on financial statements. (See pp. 117–120.)

© Capture Light/Shutterstock.com

VAIL RESORTS, INC.

In these difficult economic times, all companies face challenges in generating revenues. This is certainly true of those that rely on consumer discretionary spending. The vacation and outdoor recreation business is a prime example. How do companies convince people to take ski vacations and, at the same time, hold down their own costs in this tough economy? As one of the largest mountain resort companies in the world, this is the challenge facing **Vail Resorts, Inc.**

The company's income statement appears below, beginning with revenue broken down into its Mountain, Lodging, and Real Estate operations. But, as you know by now in your study of accounting,

revenues are only one side of the equation in determining a company's profitability. Profit, or net income, is the result of deducting expenses from revenues.

So far, we have not yet given any thought to how the numbers on an income statement (or on any of the other statements) got where they did. After all, before the information on the statements can be used for decision making, someone must decide how to record the various transactions that underlie the amounts reported. How does Vail Resorts record the sale of a lift ticket? How does it record the payment of wages to the lift ticket operator? These are the sorts of questions we turn to now.

Vail Resorts, Inc.
Consolidated Statements of Operations
(In thousands, except per share amounts)

	Year Ended July 31,		
	2015	**2014**	**2013**
Net revenue:			
Mountain	$1,104,029	$ 963,573	$ 867,514
Lodging	254,553	242,287	210,974
Real Estate	41,342	48,786	42,309
Total net revenue	1,399,924	1,254,646	1,120,797
Segment operating expense (exclusive of depreciation and amortization shown separately below):			
Mountain	777,147	712,785	639,706
Lodging	232,877	225,563	198,813
Real Estate	48,408	55,826	58,090
Total segment operating expense	1,058,432	994,174	896,609
Other operating (expense) income:			
Depreciation and amortization	(149,123)	(140,601)	(132,688)
Gain on sale of real property	151	—	6,675
Gain on litigation settlement (Note 5)	16,400	—	—
Change in fair value of contingent consideration (Note 9)	3,650	(1,400)	—
Loss on disposal of fixed assets and other, net	(2,057)	(1,208)	(1,222)
Income from operations	210,513	117,263	96,953
Mountain equity investment income, net	822	1,262	891
Investment income, net	246	375	351
Interest expense	(51,241)	(63,997)	(38,966)
Loss on extinguishment of debt (Note 4)	(11,012)	(10,831)	—
Income before provision for income taxes	149,328	44,072	59,229
Provision for income taxes (Note 10)	(34,718)	(15,866)	(21,619)
Net income	$ 114,610	$ 28,206	$ 37,610
Net loss attributable to noncontrolling interests	144	272	133
Net income attributable to Vail Resorts, Inc.	$ 114,754	$ 28,478	$ 37,743
Per share amounts (Note 3):			
Basic net income per share attributable to Vail Resorts, Inc.	$ 3.16	$ 0.79	$ 1.05
Diluted net income per share attributable to Vail Resorts, Inc.	$ 3.07	$ 0.77	$ 1.03
Cash dividends declared per share	$ 2.0750	$ 1.2450	$ 0.7900

The accompanying Notes are an integral part of these consolidated financial statements.

Vail Resorts generates revenue from three sources.

Operating expenses are reported for the same three segments.

Investments in ski areas and lodging result in large amounts of depreciation.

MODULE 1 TRANSACTIONS AND THE ACCOUNTING EQUATION

LO1 Explain the difference between external and internal events.

Event
A happening of consequence to an entity.

External event
An event involving interaction between an entity and its environment.

Internal event
An event occurring entirely within an entity.

Transaction
Any event that is recognized in a set of financial statements.

Many different types of economic events affect an entity during the year. A sale is made to a customer. Supplies are purchased from a vendor. A loan is taken out at a bank. A fire destroys a warehouse. In short, "An **event** is a happening of consequence to an entity."[1]

External and Internal Events

Two types of events affect an entity: internal and external.

- An **external event** "involves interaction between the entity and its environment."[2] For example, the *payment* of wages to an employee is an external event, as is a *sale* to a customer.
- An **internal event** occurs entirely within the entity. The use of a piece of equipment is an internal event.

We will use the term **transaction** to refer to any event, external or internal, that is recognized in a set of financial statements.[3]

What is necessary to recognize an event in the records? Are all economic events recognized as transactions by the accountant? The answers to those questions involve the concept of *measurement*. An event must be measured to be recognized. Certain events are relatively easy to measure: the payroll for the week, the amount of equipment destroyed by an earthquake, or the sales for the day. Not all events that affect an entity can be measured *reliably*, however. For example, how does a manufacturer of breakfast cereal measure the effect of a drought on the price of wheat? A company hires a new chief executive. How can it reliably measure the value of the new officer to the company? Having no definitive answer to the measurement problem is a continuing challenge to the accounting profession.

CONNECT TO THE REAL WORLD

VAIL RESORTS
READING THE FINANCIAL STATEMENTS

3-1 Is the acquisition of a new ski lift an internal or external event? The company subsequently recognizes the use of the lift by recording depreciation. Is this an internal or external event? *(See answers on p. 147.)*

The Role of Source Documents in Recording Transactions

LO2 Explain the role of source documents in an accounting system.

Source document
A piece of paper that is used as evidence to record a transaction.

A **source document** provides the evidence needed in an accounting system to record a transaction. Source documents take many different forms. An invoice received from a supplier is the source document for a purchase of inventory on credit. A cash register tape is the source document used by a retailer to recognize a cash sale. The payroll department sends the accountant the time cards for the week as the necessary documentation to record wages.

Not all recognizable events are supported by a standard source document. For certain events, some form of documentation must be generated. For example, no standard source document exists to recognize the financial consequences from a fire or the settlement of a lawsuit. Documentation is just as important for those types of events as it is for standard, recurring transactions.

[1] *Statement of Financial Accounting Concepts (SFAC) No. 3,* "Elements of Financial Statements of Business Enterprises" (Stamford, Conn.: Financial Accounting Standards Board, 1982), par. 65.
[2] *SFAC No. 3.*
[3] Technically, a *transaction* is defined by the FASB as a special kind of external event in which the entity exchanges something of value with an outsider. Because the term *transaction* is used in practice to refer to any event that is recognized in the statements, we will use this broader definition.

Analyzing the Effects of Transactions on the Accounting Equation

Economic events are the basis for recording transactions in an accounting system. For every transaction, it is essential to analyze its effect on the accounting equation:

LO3 Analyze the effects of transactions on the accounting equation and understand how these transactions affect the balance sheet and the income statement.

Assets = Liabilities + Stockholders' Equity

We will now consider a series of transactions for a hypothetical corporation, Glengarry Health Club. The transactions are for January 2017, the first month of operations for the new business.

EXAMPLE 3-1 Analyzing the Effects of Transactions on the Accounting Equation

(1) Issuance of capital stock. The company is started when Karen Bradley and Kathy Drake file articles of incorporation with the state to obtain a charter. Each invests $50,000 in the business. In return, each receives 5,000 shares of capital stock. Thus, each of them owns 50% of the outstanding stock of the company and has a claim to 50% of its assets. The effect of this transaction on the accounting equation is to increase both assets and stockholders' equity:

Transaction Number	Assets					=	Liabilities		+	Stockholders' Equity	
	Cash	Accounts Receivable	Equipment	Building	Land		Accounts Payable	Notes Payable		Capital Stock	Retained Earnings
1	$100,000									$100,000	
Totals			$100,000							$100,000	

Each side of the accounting equation increases by $100,000. Cash is increased, and because the owners contributed this amount, their claim to the assets is increased in the form of Capital Stock.

(2) Acquisition of property in exchange for a note. The company buys a piece of property for $200,000. The seller agrees to accept a five-year promissory note. The note is given by the health club to the seller and is a written promise to repay the principal amount of the loan at the end of five years. To the company, the promissory note is a liability. The property consists of land valued at $50,000 and a newly constructed building valued at $150,000. The effect of this transaction on the accounting equation is to increase both assets and liabilities by $200,000:

Transaction Number	Assets					=	Liabilities		+	Stockholders' Equity	
	Cash	Accounts Receivable	Equipment	Building	Land		Accounts Payable	Notes Payable		Capital Stock	Retained Earnings
Bal.	$100,000									$100,000	
2				$150,000	$50,000			$200,000			
Bal.	$100,000			$150,000	$50,000			$200,000		$100,000	
Totals			$300,000							$300,000	

(3) Acquisition of equipment on an open account. Karen and Kathy contact an equipment supplier and buy $20,000 of exercise equipment: treadmills, barbells, and stationary bicycles. The supplier agrees to accept payment in full in 30 days. The health club has acquired an asset and incurred a liability:

Transaction Number	Assets					=	Liabilities		+	Stockholders' Equity	
	Cash	Accounts Receivable	Equipment	Building	Land		Accounts Payable	Notes Payable		Capital Stock	Retained Earnings
Bal.	$100,000			$150,000	$50,000			$200,000		$100,000	
3			$20,000				$20,000				
Bal.	$100,000		$20,000	$150,000	$50,000		$20,000	$200,000		$100,000	
Totals			$320,000							$320,000	

(4) Sale of monthly memberships on account. The owners open their doors for business. During January, they sell 300 monthly club memberships for $50 each, or a total of $15,000. The members have until the 10th of the following month to pay. Glengarry does not have cash from the new members; instead, it has a promise from each member to pay cash in the future. This promise from a customer to pay an amount owed is an asset called an *account receivable*. The other side of this transaction is an increase in the stockholders' equity (specifically, Retained Earnings) in the business. In other words, the assets have increased by $15,000 without any increase in a liability or any decrease in another asset. The increase in stockholders' equity indicates that the owners' residual interest in the assets of the business has increased by this amount. This inflow of assets resulting from the sale of goods and services by a business is called *revenue*. The change in the accounting equation is as follows:

Transaction Number	Cash	Accounts Receivable	Equipment	Building	Land		Accounts Payable	Notes Payable	Capital Stock	Retained Earnings
			Assets			=	Liabilities	+	Stockholders' Equity	
Bal.	$100,000		$20,000	$150,000	$50,000		$20,000	$200,000	$100,000	
4		$15,000								$15,000
Bal.	$100,000	$15,000	$20,000	$150,000	$50,000		$20,000	$200,000	$100,000	$15,000
Totals			$335,000						$335,000	

(5) Sale of court time for cash. In addition to memberships, Glengarry sells court time. Court fees are paid at the time of use and amount to $5,000 for the first month:

Transaction Number	Cash	Accounts Receivable	Equipment	Building	Land		Accounts Payable	Notes Payable	Capital Stock	Retained Earnings
			Assets			=	Liabilities	+	Stockholders' Equity	
Bal.	$100,000	$15,000	$20,000	$150,000	$50,000		$20,000	$200,000	$100,000	$15,000
5	5,000									5,000
Bal.	$105,000	$15,000	$20,000	$150,000	$50,000		$20,000	$200,000	$100,000	$20,000
Totals			$340,000						$340,000	

The only difference between this transaction and that of (4) is that cash is received rather than a promise to pay at a later date. Both transactions result in an increase in an asset and an increase in the owners' claim to the assets. In both cases, there is an inflow of assets in the form of Accounts Receivable or Cash. Thus, in both cases, the company should record revenue.

(6) Payment of wages and salaries. The wages and salaries for the first month amount to $10,000. The payment of this amount results in a decrease in Cash and a decrease in the owners' claim on the assets, that is, a decrease in Retained Earnings. This outflow of assets resulting from the sale of goods or services is called an *expense*. The effect of this transaction is to decrease both sides of the accounting equation:

Transaction Number	Cash	Accounts Receivable	Equipment	Building	Land		Accounts Payable	Notes Payable	Capital Stock	Retained Earnings
			Assets			=	Liabilities	+	Stockholders' Equity	
Bal.	$105,000	$15,000	$20,000	$150,000	$50,000		$20,000	$200,000	$100,000	$20,000
6	−10,000									−10,000
Bal.	$ 95,000	$15,000	$20,000	$150,000	$50,000		$20,000	$200,000	$100,000	$10,000
Totals			$330,000						$330,000	

(7) Payment of utilities. The cost of utilities for the first month is $3,000. Glengarry pays this amount in cash. Both the utilities and the salaries and wages are expenses, and they have the same effect on the accounting equation. Cash is decreased, accompanied by a corresponding decrease in the owners' claim on the assets of the business:

Transaction Number	Cash	Accounts Receivable	Equipment	Building	Land		Accounts Payable	Notes Payable	Capital Stock	Retained Earnings
			Assets			=	Liabilities	+	Stockholders' Equity	
Bal.	$95,000	$15,000	$20,000	$150,000	$50,000		$20,000	$200,000	$100,000	$10,000
7	−3,000									−3,000
Bal.	$92,000	$15,000	$20,000	$150,000	$50,000		$20,000	$200,000	$100,000	$ 7,000
Totals			$327,000						$327,000	

(8) Collection of accounts receivable. Even though the January monthly memberships are not due until the 10th of the following month, some of the members pay their bills by the end of January. The amount received from members in payment of their accounts is $4,000. The effect of the collection of an open account is to increase Cash and decrease Accounts Receivable:

Transaction Number	Assets					=	Liabilities		+	Stockholders' Equity	
	Cash	Accounts Receivable	Equipment	Building	Land		Accounts Payable	Notes Payable		Capital Stock	Retained Earnings
Bal.	$92,000	$15,000	$20,000	$150,000	$50,000		$20,000	$200,000		$100,000	$7,000
8	4,000	−4,000									
Bal.	$96,000	$11,000	$20,000	$150,000	$50,000		$20,000	$200,000		$100,000	$7,000
Totals			$327,000							$327,000	

This is the first transaction we have seen that affects only one side of the accounting equation. In fact, the company simply traded assets: Accounts Receivable for Cash. Thus, the totals for the accounting equation remain at $327,000. Also, note that Retained Earnings is not affected by this transaction because revenue was recognized earlier, in **(4)**, when Accounts Receivable was increased.

(9) Payment of dividends. At the end of the month, Karen and Kathy, acting on behalf of Glengarry Health Club, decide to pay a dividend of $1,000 on the shares of stock that each of them owns, or $2,000 in total. The effect of this dividend is to decrease both Cash and Retained Earnings. That is, the company is returning cash to the owners based on the profitable operations of the business. The transaction not only reduces Cash but also decreases the owners' claims on the assets. Dividends are not an expense, but rather a direct reduction of Retained Earnings. The effect on the accounting equation is as follows:

Transaction Number	Assets					=	Liabilities		+	Stockholders' Equity	
	Cash	Accounts Receivable	Equipment	Building	Land		Accounts Payable	Notes Payable		Capital Stock	Retained Earnings
Bal.	$96,000	$11,000	$20,000	$150,000	$50,000		$20,000	$200,000		$100,000	$7,000
9	−2,000										−2,000
Bal.	$94,000	$11,000	$20,000	$150,000	$50,000		$20,000	$200,000		$100,000	$5,000
Totals			$325,000							$325,000	

The Cost Principle

An important principle governs the accounting for both the exercise equipment in **(3)** and the building and land in **(2)**. The *cost principle* requires that we record an asset at the cost to acquire it and continue to show this amount on all balance sheets until we dispose of the asset. With a few exceptions, an asset is not carried at its market value, but at its original cost. *Why not show the land on future balance sheets at its market value?* Although this might seem more appropriate in certain instances, the subjectivity inherent in determining market values is a major reason behind the practice of carrying assets at their historical cost. The cost of an asset can be verified by an independent observer and is more *objective* than market value.

Exhibit 3-1 summarizes the effect of each transaction on the individual items increased or decreased by each transaction. Note the *dual* effect of each transaction—at least two items were involved in each transaction. For example, the initial investment by the owners resulted in an increase in an asset and an increase in Capital Stock. The payment of the utility bill caused a decrease in an asset and a decrease in Retained Earnings.

You can now see the central idea behind the accounting equation:

- **Even though individual transactions may change the amount and composition of the assets and liabilities, the *equation* must always balance *for* each transaction and the *balance sheet* must balance *after* each transaction.**

Balance Sheet and Income Statement for Glengarry Health Club

A balance sheet for Glengarry Health Club appears in Exhibit 3-2. All of the information needed to prepare this statement is available in Exhibit 3-1. The balances at the bottom of this exhibit are entered on the balance sheet, with assets on the left side and liabilities and stockholders' equity on the right side.

EXHIBIT 3-1 Glengarry Health Club Transactions for the Month of January

Trans. No.	Cash	Accounts Receivable	Equipment	Building	Land	=	Accounts Payable	Notes Payable	+	Capital Stock	Retained Earnings
						Assets	**Liabilities**		**Stockholders' Equity**		
1	$100,000									$100,000	
2				$150,000	$50,000			$200,000			
Bal.	$100,000			$150,000	$50,000			$200,000		$100,000	
3			$20,000				$20,000				
Bal.	$100,000		$20,000	$150,000	$50,000		$20,000	$200,000		$100,000	
4		$15,000									$ 15,000
Bal.	$100,000	$15,000	$20,000	$150,000	$50,000		$20,000	$200,000		$100,000	$ 15,000
5	5,000										5,000
Bal.	$105,000	$15,000	$20,000	$150,000	$50,000		$20,000	$200,000		$100,000	$ 20,000
6	−10,000										−10,000
Bal.	$ 95,000	$15,000	$20,000	$150,000	$50,000		$20,000	$200,000		$100,000	$ 10,000
7	−3,000										−3,000
Bal.	$ 92,000	$15,000	$20,000	$150,000	$50,000		$20,000	$200,000		$100,000	$ 7,000
8	4,000	−4,000									
Bal.	$ 96,000	$11,000	$20,000	$150,000	$50,000		$20,000	$200,000		$100,000	$ 7,000
9	−2,000										−2,000
	$ 94,000	$11,000	$20,000	$150,000	$50,000		$20,000	$200,000		$100,000	$ 5,000

Total assets: $325,000   Total liabilities and stockholders' equity: $325,000

EXHIBIT 3-2 Balance Sheet for Glengarry Health Club

Glengarry Health Club
Balance Sheet
January 31, 2017

Assets		Liabilities and Stockholders' Equity	
Cash	$ 94,000	Accounts payable	$ 20,000
Accounts receivable	11,000	Notes payable	200,000
Equipment	20,000	Capital stock	100,000
Building	150,000	Retained earnings	5,000
Land	50,000	Total liabilities and	
Total assets	$325,000	stockholders' equity	$325,000

An income statement for Glengarry is shown in Exhibit 3-3. An income statement summarizes the revenues and expenses of a company for a period of time. In the example, the statement is for the month of January, as indicated on the third line of the heading of the statement. Glengarry has revenues from two sources: (1) memberships and (2) court fees. Two types of expenses were incurred: (1) salaries and wages and (2) utilities. The difference between the total revenues of $20,000 and the total expenses of $13,000 is the net income of $7,000. **Dividends do not appear on the income statement. They are a *distribution* of net income of the period, not a *determinant* of net income as are expenses.**

We have seen how transactions are analyzed and how they affect the accounting equation and ultimately the financial statements. While the approach we took in analyzing the nine transactions of the Glengarry Health Club was manageable, can you imagine using this type of analysis for a company with *thousands* of transactions in any one month? We now turn to various *tools* that the accountant uses to process a large volume of transactions effectively and efficiently.

EXHIBIT 3-3 Income Statement for Glengarry Health Club

Glengarry Health Club Income Statement For the Month Ended January 31, 2017		
Revenues:		
Memberships	$15,000	
Court fees	5,000	$20,000
Expenses:		
Wages and salaries	$10,000	
Utilities	3,000	13,000
Net income		$ 7,000

What Is an Account?

An account is the basic unit for recording transactions. It is the record used to accumulate monetary amounts for each asset, liability, and component of stockholders' equity, such as Capital Stock, Retained Earnings, and Dividends. Each revenue and expense has its own account. In the Glengarry Health Club example, nine accounts were used: Cash, Accounts Receivable, Equipment, Building, Land, Accounts Payable, Notes Payable, Capital Stock, and Retained Earnings. (Recall that revenues, expenses, and dividends were recorded directly in the Retained Earnings account. Later in the chapter, we will see that each revenue and expense usually is recorded in a separate account.) In the real world, a company might have hundreds, even thousands, of individual accounts.

No two entities have exactly the same set of accounts. To a certain extent, the accounts used by a company depend on its business. For example, a manufacturer normally has three inventory accounts: Raw Materials, Work in Process, and Finished Goods. A retailer uses just one account for inventory, Merchandise Inventory. A service business has no need for an inventory account.

LO4 Describe the use of the account and the general ledger to accumulate amounts of financial statement items.

Account
A record used to accumulate amounts for each individual asset, liability, revenue, expense, and component of stockholders' equity.

Chart of Accounts

A **chart of accounts** is a numerical list of all of the accounts an entity uses. The numbering system is a convenient way to identify accounts. For example, all asset accounts might be numbered from 100 to 199; liability accounts, from 200 to 299; equity accounts, from 300 to 399; revenues, from 400 to 499; and expenses, from 500 to 599. A chart of accounts for a hypothetical company, Widescreen Theaters Corporation, is shown in Exhibit 3-4. Note the division of account numbers within each of the financial statement categories. Within the asset category, the various cash accounts are numbered from 100 to 109; receivables, from 110 to 119; etc. Not all of the numbers are assigned. For example, only three of the available nine numbers are currently utilized for cash accounts. This allows the company to add accounts as needed.

CONNECT TO THE REAL WORLD

VAIL RESORTS
READING THE INCOME STATEMENT

3-2 What are the company's three segments for reporting revenue and operating expense? What is the dollar amount of revenue and operating expense for the largest of these segments? *(See answers on p. 147.)*

Chart of accounts
A numerical list of all accounts used by a company.

The General Ledger

In a manual accounting system, a separate card or sheet is used to record the activity in each account. A **general ledger** is simply the file or book that contains the accounts.[4] For example, the general ledger for Widescreen Theaters Corporation might consist of a file of cards in a cabinet, with a card for each of the accounts listed in the chart of accounts.

General ledger
A book, a file, a hard drive, or another device containing all of the accounts.

Alternate term: Set of accounts.

[4] In addition to a general ledger, many companies maintain subsidiary ledgers. For example, an accounts receivable subsidiary ledger contains a separate account for each customer. The use of a subsidiary ledger for Accounts Receivable is discussed further in Chapter 7.

EXHIBIT 3-4 Chart of Accounts for a Theater

100–199:	ASSETS		300–399:	STOCKHOLDERS' EQUITY
100–109:	Cash		301:	Preferred Stock
101:	Cash, Checking, Second National Bank		302:	Common Stock
102:	Cash, Savings, Third State Bank		303:	Retained Earnings
103:	Cash, Change, or Petty Cash Fund (coin and currency)		400–499:	REVENUES
			401:	Tickets
110–119:	Receivables		402:	Video Rentals
111:	Accounts Receivable		403:	Concessions
112:	Due from Employees		404:	Interest
113:	Notes Receivable		500–599:	EXPENSES
120–129:	Prepaid Assets		500–509:	Rentals
121:	Cleaning Supplies		501:	Films
122:	Prepaid Insurance		502:	Videos
130–139:	Property, Plant, and Equipment		510–519:	Concessions
131:	Land		511:	Candy
132:	Theater Buildings		512:	Soda
133:	Projection Equipment		513:	Popcorn
134:	Furniture and Fixtures		520–529:	Wages and Salaries
200–299:	LIABILITIES		521:	Hourly Employees
200–209:	Short-Term Liabilities		522:	Salaries
201:	Accounts Payable		530–539:	Utilities
202:	Wages and Salaries Payable		531:	Heat
203:	Taxes Payable		532:	Electric
203.1:	Income Taxes Payable		533:	Water
203.2:	Sales Taxes Payable		540–549:	Advertising
203.3:	Unemployment Taxes Payable		541:	Newspaper
204:	Short-Term Notes Payable		542:	Radio
204.1:	Six-Month Note Payable to First State Bank		550–559:	Taxes
			551:	Income Taxes
210–219:	Long-Term Liabilities		552:	Unemployment Taxes
211:	Bonds Payable, due in 2022			

In today's business world, most companies have an automated accounting system. The computer is ideally suited for the job of processing vast amounts of data rapidly. **All of the tools discussed in this chapter are as applicable to computerized systems as they are to manual systems.** For example, the ledger in an automated system might be contained on a computer file server rather than stored in a file cabinet. Throughout the book, a manual system will be used to explain the various tools, such as ledger accounts. The reason is that it is easier to illustrate and visualize the tools in a manual system.

Identify and Analyze

In this chapter, we analyzed the effects of the transactions of Glengarry Health Club on the accounting equation. Because the accounting equation is the basis for financial statements, the ability to analyze transactions in terms of their effect on the equation is an essential skill to master. In the appendix to this chapter, tools used by the accountant to effectively and efficiently process large volumes of transactions during the period are examined. One of the key tools used by the accountant is a system of debits and credits.

The emphasis throughout this book is on the use of financial statements to make decisions, as opposed to the tools used by accountants to process information. Therefore, in future chapters, our emphasis will not be on the accountant's

various tools, such as debits and credits, but on the effects of the transactions on the accounting equation and financial statements.

For every transaction, three questions must be answered:

1. What type of **activity** did the transaction reflect? All transactions are the result of an operating, financing, or investing activity of the company.
2. What **accounts** are affected by the transaction, and are they increased or decreased? Every transaction involves at least two accounts.
3. Which **financial statements** are affected by the transaction? All transactions affect either just the balance sheet or both the balance sheet and the income statement.

Recall transaction 4, Glengarry Health Club's sale of monthly memberships on account, discussed on page 104 and summarized in Exhibit 3-1:

		Assets				=	Liabilities		+	Stockholder's Equity	
Transaction Number	Cash	Accounts Receivable	Equipment	Building	Land		Accounts Payable	Notes Payable		Capital Stock	Retained Earnings
4		$15,000									$15,000

Each of the three questions would be answered for this transaction as follows:

1. The sale of memberships on account is an **operating** activity.
2. Two accounts are affected by this transaction: Both **Accounts Receivable** and revenue, specifically **Membership Revenue** are increased.
3. The sale of memberships affects both the **balance sheet** (Accounts Receivable) and the **income statement** (specifically, Membership Revenue).

In future chapters, we will start by answering each of these questions for all transactions and then we will use a variation of the format in Exhibit 3-1:

	Balance Sheet				Income Statement		
ASSETS	=	LIABILITIES	+	STOCKHOLDERS' EQUITY	REVENUES	− EXPENSES =	NET INCOME
Accounts Receivable 15,000				15,000	Membership Revenue 15,000		15,000

Note two important changes in this version of the equation. First, rather than having a separate column for each individual financial statement item (Cash, Accounts Receivable, and so on), the items are simply listed under the appropriate categories. For example, transaction 4 results in an increase in Accounts Receivable, which is shown in the assets category. Second, in this **expanded version** of the accounting equation, the income statement is viewed as an extension of the balance sheet. Membership Revenue is recorded in the Revenues column and then extended to the final column as an increase in net income. Because net income increases Retained Earnings, and Retained Earnings is part of Stockholders' Equity, an arrow is drawn to illustrate the flow of net income into stockholders' equity.

To illustrate how this new element will appear in future chapters, recall transaction 6 for Glengarry in which $10,000 was paid in wages and salaries:

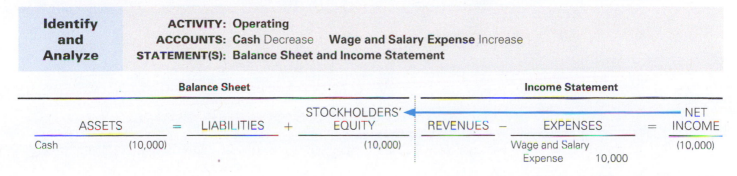

Identify and Analyze	**ACTIVITY: Operating**
	ACCOUNTS: Cash Decrease **Wage and Salary Expense** Increase
	STATEMENT(S): Balance Sheet and Income Statement

	Balance Sheet				Income Statement		
ASSETS	=	LIABILITIES	+	STOCKHOLDERS' EQUITY	REVENUES −	EXPENSES	= NET INCOME
Cash (10,000)				(10,000)		Wage and Salary Expense 10,000	(10,000)

Because the asset account Cash decreased, the amount of decrease is in brackets. The increase in Wage and Salary Expense is shown without brackets in the Expenses column. But because an expense reduces net income on the income statement, the amount is bracketed in the Net Income column. Finally, because a decrease in net income reduces Retained Earnings and thus stockholders' equity, the amount is bracketed in the Stockholders' Equity column to indicate a decrease.

Exhibit 3-5 summarizes how the new element "Identify and Analyze" will be used in Chapters 4–13.

EXHIBIT 3-5 Introducing the Identify and Analyze Transaction Format

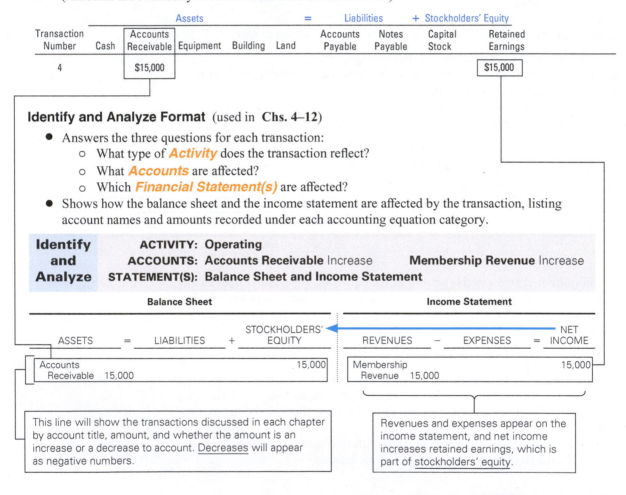

Example: Transaction 4, p. 104 : Sale of monthly memberships on account:

Transaction Analysis Format (used in **Ch. 3**)

- Shows how transactions are analyzed in account names (**Cash, Accounts Receivable**, etc., as shown below) and accounting equation categories (**Assets, Liabilities, Stockholders' Equity**). (Amounts are eventually reflected in the financial statements.)

| | | Assets | | | | = | Liabilities | | + Stockholders' Equity | |
Transaction Number	Cash	Accounts Receivable	Equipment	Building	Land		Accounts Payable	Notes Payable	Capital Stock	Retained Earnings
4		$15,000								$15,000

Identify and Analyze Format (used in **Chs. 4–12**)

- Answers the three questions for each transaction:
  - What type of *Activity* does the transaction reflect?
  - What *Accounts* are affected?
  - Which *Financial Statement(s)* are affected?
- Shows how the balance sheet and the income statement are affected by the transaction, listing account names and amounts recorded under each accounting equation category.

Identify and Analyze	ACTIVITY: Operating		
	ACCOUNTS: Accounts Receivable Increase		Membership Revenue Increase
	STATEMENT(S): Balance Sheet and Income Statement		

Balance Sheet   **Income Statement**

ASSETS	=	LIABILITIES	+	STOCKHOLDERS' EQUITY		REVENUES	–	EXPENSES	=	NET INCOME
Accounts Receivable 15,000				15,000		Membership Revenue 15,000				15,000

This line will show the transactions discussed in each chapter by account title, amount, and whether the amount is an increase or a decrease to account. Decreases will appear as negative numbers.

Revenues and expenses appear on the income statement, and net income increases retained earnings, which is part of stockholders' equity.

Review		
LO1 Explain the difference between external and internal events.	• Both of these different types of events affect an entity and are usually recorded in the accounting system as a transaction. • External events are interactions between an entity and its environment. • Internal events are interactions entirely within an entity.	
LO2 Explain the role of source documents in an accounting system.	• Source documents provide the evidence needed to begin the procedures for recording and processing a transaction. • These documents need not be in hard copy form and can come from parties that are either internal or external to the company.	
LO3 Analyze the effects of transactions on the accounting equation and understand how these transactions affect the balance sheet and the income statement.	• The accounting equation illustrates the relationship between assets, liabilities, and stockholders' equity accounts. Understanding these relationships helps to see the logic behind the double-entry system in recording transactions. • The accounting equation: Assets = Liabilities + Stockholders' Equity • This equality must always be maintained. The equation can be expanded to show the linkage between the balance sheet and the income statement through the Retained Earnings account: **Assets = Liabilities + Capital Stock + Retained Earnings**	
LO4 Describe the use of the account and the general ledger to accumulate amounts of financial statement items.	• The general ledger is a crucial part of the accounting system that lists all the accounts and their balances. Financial statements may be prepared from current account balances in the general ledger.	

Question

1. What are the two types of events that affect an entity? Describe each.
2. What is the significance of source documents to the recording process? Give two examples of source documents.
3. What is the difference between a chart of accounts and the general ledger?

Apply

1. Provide three examples of source documents and the event for which each would provide the evidence to record.
2. List the three elements in the accounting equation. How is the third element expanded to show the linkage between the balance sheet and the income statement?
3. Third State Bank loans a customer $5,000 in exchange for a promissory note. What is the effect of this transaction on the bank's accounting equation?
4. Assume that **Vail Resorts** borrows $5 million by signing a promissory note. The next day the company uses the money to buy new ski lifts. What is the effect of each of these transactions on Vail Resorts' accounting equation?

Answers are located at the end of the chapter.

MODULE 2 DEBITS AND CREDITS

Accounting Tools: The Double-Entry System

APPENDIX

The origin of the double-entry system of accounting can be traced to Venice, Italy, in 1494. In that year, Fra Luca Pacioli, a Franciscan monk, wrote a mathematical treatise. Included in his book was the concept of debits and credits that is still used almost universally today.

The T Account

The most popular format for writing out a general ledger account will be illustrated later in the chapter. However, the format often used to analyze transactions—the format for showing amounts coming into and leaving an account—is called the *T account*, so named because it resembles the capital letter T. The name of the account appears across the horizontal line. One side is used to show increases to that account; the other side, decreases. But as you will see, the same side is not used for increases for every account. As a matter of convention, the *left* side of an *asset* account is used to record *increases*; the *right* side, to record *decreases*.

EXAMPLE 3-2 Using a T Account

To illustrate a T account, we will look at the Cash account for Glengarry Health Club. The transactions recorded in the account can be traced to Exhibit 3-1.

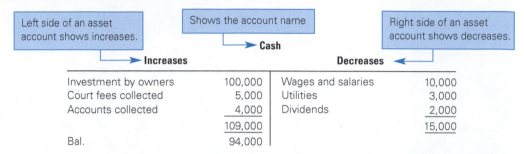

The amounts $109,000 and $15,000 are called *footings*. They represent the totals of the amounts on each side of the account. Neither these amounts nor the balance of $94,000 represents transactions. They are simply shown to indicate the totals and the balance in the account.

Debits and Credits

LO5 Explain the rules of debits and credits (Appendix).

Debit
An entry on the left side of an account.

Credit
An entry on the right side of an account.

Rather than refer to the left or right side of an account, accountants use specific labels for each side. The *left* side of any account is the **debit** side, and the *right* side of any account is the **credit** side.

We will also use the terms *debit* and *credit* as verbs. If we *debit* the Cash account, we enter an amount on the left side. Similarly, if we want to enter an amount on the right side of an account, we *credit* the account. To *charge* an account has the same meaning as to *debit* it. No such synonym exists for the act of crediting an account.

Debit and *credit* are *locational* terms. They simply refer to the left or right side of a T account. They do *not* represent increases or decreases. When one type of account is increased (for example, the Cash account), the increase is on the left, or *debit*, side. When certain other types of accounts are increased, however, the entry will be on the right, or *credit*, side.

As you would expect from your understanding of the accounting equation, the conventions for using T accounts for assets and liabilities are opposite. Assets are future economic benefits, and liabilities are obligations to transfer economic benefits in the future. If an asset is *increased* with a *debit*, how do you think a liability would be increased? Because assets and liabilities are opposites, if an asset is increased with a debit, a liability is increased with a credit. Thus, the right side, or credit side, of a liability account is used to record an increase. Like liabilities, stockholders' equity accounts are on the opposite side of the accounting equation from assets. Thus, like a liability, a stockholders' equity account is increased with a credit. We can summarize the logic of debits and credits, increases and decreases, and the accounting equation in the following way:

STUDY TIP

Once you know the rule to increase an asset with a debit, the rules for the other increases and decreases follow logically. For example, because a liability is the opposite of an asset, it is increased with a credit. And it follows logically that it would be decreased with a debit.

Assets		=	Liabilities		+	Stockholders' Equity	
Debits	Credits		Debits	Credits		Debits	Credits
Increases	Decreases		Decreases	Increases		Decreases	Increases
+	−		−	+		−	+

Debits Aren't Bad, and Credits Aren't Good

Students often approach their first encounter with debits and credits with preconceived notions. The use of the terms *debit* and *credit* in everyday language leads to many of these notions: Joe is a real credit to his team. Nancy should be credited with saving Mary's career. They both appear to be positive statements. You must resist the temptation to associate the term *credit* with something good or positive and the term *debit* with something bad or negative. In accounting, debit means one thing: an entry made on the left side of an account. A credit means an entry made on the right side of an account.

Debits and Credits for Revenues, Expenses, and Dividends

Revenues   In the Glengarry Health Club example, revenues recognized in (4) and (5) were an increase in Accounts Receivable and Retained Earnings. These transactions resulted in an increase in the owners' claim on the assets of the business. Rather than being recorded directly in Retained Earnings, however, each revenue item is maintained in a separate account. The following logic is used to arrive at the rules for increasing and decreasing revenues:[5]

1. Retained Earnings is increased with a credit.
2. Revenue is an increase in Retained Earnings.
3. Revenue is increased with a credit.
4. Because revenue is increased with a credit, it is decreased with a debit.

Expenses   The same logic is applied to the expenses recognized in (6) and (7). The rules for increasing and decreasing expense accounts are as follows:

1. Retained Earnings is decreased with a debit.
2. Expense is a decrease in Retained Earnings.
3. Expense is increased with a debit.
4. Because expense is increased with a debit, it is decreased with a credit.

Dividends   Recall that the dividend in (9) reduced cash. But dividends also reduce the owners' claim on the assets of the business. Earlier, we recognized this decrease in the owners' claim as a reduction of Retained Earnings. As we do for revenue and expense accounts, we will use a separate Dividends account.

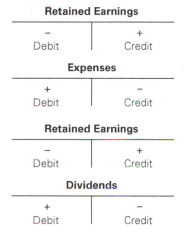

1. Retained Earnings is decreased with a debit.
2. Dividends are a decrease in Retained Earnings.
3. Dividends are increased with a debit.
4. Because dividends are increased with a debit, they are decreased with a credit.

Summary of the Rules for Increasing and Decreasing Accounts

Using the accounting equation, the rules for increasing and decreasing the various types of accounts can be summarized as follows:

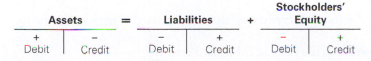

Normal Account Balances

Each account has a "normal" balance. For example, assets normally have debit balances. Would it be possible for an asset such as Cash to have a credit balance? Assume that a company has a checking account with a bank. A credit balance in the account would

---

[5] We normally think of revenues and expenses as being increased, not decreased. Because we will need to decrease them as part of the closing procedure, it is important to know how to reduce as well as increase these accounts.

indicate that the decreases in the account, from checks written and other bank charges, were more than the deposits into the account. If this were the case, however, the company would no longer have an asset, Cash, but instead would have a liability to the bank.

EXAMPLE 3-3 Determining Normal Account Balances

The normal balances for the accounts we have looked at are as follows:

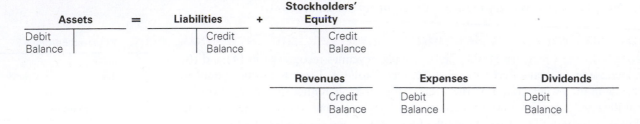

Debits and Credits Applied to Transactions

Recall the first transaction recorded by Glengarry Health Club: the owners invested $100,000 cash in the business. The transaction resulted in an increase in the Cash account and an increase in the Capital Stock account. Applying the rules of debits and credits, we would *debit* the Cash account for $100,000 and *credit* the Capital Stock account for the same amount.[6]

Cash		Capital Stock	
(1) 100,000			100,000 (1)

Double-entry system
A system of accounting in which every transaction is recorded with equal debits and credits, and the accounting equation is kept in balance.

In the **double-entry system** of accounting, every transaction is recorded so that the equality of debits and credits is maintained, and the accounting equation is kept in balance.

> Every transaction is entered in at least two accounts on opposite sides of T accounts. Glengarry's first transaction resulted in an increase in an asset account and an increase in a stockholders' equity account. For every transaction, the debit side must equal the credit side. The debit of $100,000 to the Cash account equals the credit of $100,000 to the Capital Stock account.

It naturally follows that if the debit side must equal the credit side for every transaction, at any time, the total of all debits recorded must equal the total of all credits recorded. Thus, the fundamental accounting equation remains in balance.

Transactions for Glengarry Health Club

Three distinct steps are involved in recording a transaction in the accounts:

1. *Analyze* **the transaction**. That is, decide what accounts are increased or decreased and by how much.
2. *Recall* **the rules of debits and credits** as they apply to the transaction being analyzed.
3. *Record* **the transaction** using the rules of debits and credits.

As we will see later in the chapter, transactions are first recorded in journal entries and then transferred to accounts. However, for purposes of analysis, we will show transactions recorded in T accounts in this section, using Glengarry's eight remaining transactions for the month. Refer to Exhibit 3-1 for a summary of the transactions.

---

[6] We will use the number of each transaction as it was labeled earlier in the chapter to identify the transaction. In practice, a formal ledger account is used and transactions are entered according to their date.

EXAMPLE 3-4 Analyzing and Recording Transactions Using Debits and Credits

(2) **Acquisition of property in exchange for a note.** A building and land are exchanged for a promissory note.

    Analyze: Two asset accounts are increased: Building and Land. The liability account Notes Payable is also increased.

    Recall: An asset is increased with a debit, and a liability is increased with a credit.

    Record:

Building	Notes Payable
(2) 150,000	200,000 (2)

Land	
(2) 50,000	

(3) **Acquisition of equipment on an open account.** Exercise equipment is purchased from a supplier on open account. The purchase price is $20,000.

    Analyze: An asset account, Equipment, is increased. A liability account, Accounts Payable, is also increased. Thus, the transaction is identical to the last transaction in that an asset is increased, and a liability is increased.

    Recall: An asset is increased with a debit, and a liability is increased with a credit.

    Record:

Equipment	Accounts Payable
(3) 20,000	20,000 (3)

(4) **Sale of monthly memberships on account.** Three hundred club memberships are sold for $50 each. The members have until the 10th of the following month to pay.

    Analyze: The asset account Accounts Receivable is increased by $15,000. This amount is an asset because the company has the right to collect it in the future. The owners' claim to the assets is increased by the same amount. Recall, however, that we do not record these claims—revenues—directly in a stockholders' equity account, but instead use a separate revenue account. We will call the account Membership Revenue.

    Recall: An asset is increased with a debit. Stockholders' equity is increased with a credit. Because revenue is an increase in stockholders' equity, it is increased with a credit.

    Record:

Accounts Receivable	Membership Revenue
(4) 15,000	15,000 (4)

(5) **Sale of court time for cash.** Court fees are paid at the time of use and amount to $5,000 for the first month.

    Analyze: The asset account Cash is increased by $5,000. The stockholders' claim to the assets is increased by the same amount. The account used to record the increase in the stockholders' claim is Court Fee Revenue.

    Recall: An asset is increased with a debit. Stockholders' equity is increased with a credit. Because revenue is an increase in stockholders' equity, it is increased with a credit.

    Record:

Cash	Court Fee Revenue
(1) 100,000	5,000 (5)
(5) 5,000	

(6) **Payment of wages and salaries.** Wages and salaries amount to $10,000, and they are paid in cash.

    Analyze: The asset account Cash is decreased by $10,000. At the same time, the owners' claim to the assets is decreased by this amount. However, rather than record a decrease directly to Retained Earnings, we set up an expense account, Wage and Salary Expense.

    Recall: An asset is decreased with a credit. Stockholders' equity is decreased with a debit. Because expense is a decrease in stockholders' equity, it is increased with a debit.

    Record:

Cash		Wage and Salary Expense
(1) 100,000	10,000 (6)	(6) 10,000
(5) 5,000		

(7) **Payment of utilities.** The utility bill of $3,000 for the first month is paid in cash.

    Analyze: The asset account Cash is decreased by $3,000. At the same time, the owners' claim to the assets is decreased by this amount. However, rather than record a decrease directly to Retained Earnings, we set up an expense account, Utilities Expense.

    Recall: An asset is decreased with a credit. Stockholders' equity is decreased with a debit. Because expense is a decrease in stockholders' equity, it is increased with a debit.

    Record:

Cash		Utilities Expense
(1) 100,000	10,000 (6)	(7) 3,000
(5) 5,000	3,000 (7)	

(8) **Collection of accounts receivable.** Cash of $4,000 is collected from members for their January dues.

Analyze: Cash is increased by the amount collected from the members. Another asset, Accounts Receivable, is decreased by the same amount. Glengarry has simply traded one asset for another.

Recall: An asset is increased with a debit and decreased with a credit. Thus, one asset is debited, and another is credited.

Record:

Cash			Accounts Receivable	
(1) 100,000	10,000 (6)		(4) 15,000	**4,000 (8)**
(5) 5,000	3,000 (7)			
(8) 4,000				

(9) **Payment of dividends.** Dividends of $2,000 are distributed to the owners.

Analyze: The asset account Cash is decreased by $2,000. At the same time, the owners' claim to the assets is decreased by this amount. Earlier in the chapter, we decreased Retained Earnings for dividends paid to the owners. Now we will use a separate account, Dividends, to record these distributions.

Recall: An asset is decreased with a credit. Retained earnings is decreased with a debit. Because dividends are a decrease in retained earnings, they are increased with a debit.

Record:

Cash			Dividends	
(1) 100,000	10,000 (6)		**(9) 2,000**	
(5) 5,000	3,000 (7)			
(8) 4,000	**2,000 (9)**			

MODULE 2 TEST YOURSELF

Review	**LO5** Explain the rules of debits and credits.	• T accounts are a convenient way to analyze the activity in any particular account. One side of the account is used to record increases; the other side, decreases.
		• Debits and credits represent the left and right sides of a T account, respectively. They take on meaning only when associated with the recording of transactions involving asset, liability, and equity accounts.
		  • In general, debits increase asset accounts and credits increase liability and equity accounts.
		  • The double-entry system requires that total debits equal total credits for any transaction recorded in the accounting system.

Question	1. What do accountants mean when they refer to the double-entry system of accounting?
	2. A friend comes to you with the following plight: "I'm confused. An asset is something positive, and it is increased with a debit. However, an expense is something negative, and it is also increased with a debit. I don't get it." How can you "straighten out" your friend?
	3. The payment of dividends reduces cash. If the Cash account is reduced with a credit, why is the Dividends account debited when dividends are paid?
	4. If Cash is increased with a debit, why does the bank credit your account when you make a deposit?

Answers are located at the end of the chapter.

MODULE 3 JOURNAL ENTRIES AND TRIAL BALANCES

The Journal: The Firm's Chronological Record of Transactions

To focus attention on analysis in the previous section, each of Glengarry Health Club's nine transactions was entered directly in the ledger accounts. By looking at the Cash account, we see that it increased by $5,000 in (5). But what was the other side of this transaction? That is, what account was credited? To have a record of *each entry*, transactions are recorded first in a journal. A **journal** is a chronological record of each transaction entered into by a business. Because a journal lists transactions in the order in which they took place, it is called the *book of original entry*. Transactions are recorded first in a journal and then are posted to the ledger accounts. **Posting** is the process of transferring a journal entry to the ledger accounts:

Note that posting does not result in any change in the amounts recorded. It is simply a process of re-sorting the transactions from a chronological order to a topical arrangement.

Journalizing is the process of recording entries in a journal. A standard format is normally used for recording journal entries.

EXAMPLE 3-5 Recording Transactions in Journal Entry Form

Consider the original investment [see (1), Issuance of capital stock, on page 103] by the owners of Glengarry Health Club. The format of the journal entry is as follows:

		Debit	Credit
Jan. xx	Cash	100,000	
	Capital Stock		100,000
	To record the issuance of 10,000 shares of stock for cash.		

Each journal entry contains a date with columns for the amounts debited and credited. Accounts credited are indented to distinguish them from accounts debited. A brief explanation normally appears on the line below the entry.

LO6 Explain the purposes of a journal and the posting process (Appendix).

Journal
A chronological record of transactions.

Alternate term: Book of original entry.

Posting
The process of transferring amounts from a journal to the ledger accounts.

Journalizing
The act of recording journal entries.

The remaining eight transactions for Glengarry Health Club would appear in journal entry form as follows:

		Debit	Credit
Jan. xx	Building	150,000	
	Land	50,000	
	Notes Payable		200,000
	To record acquisition of property in exchange for note.		
Jan. xx	Equipment	20,000	
	Accounts Payable		20,000
	To record acquisition of equipment on open account.		
Jan. xx	Accounts Receivable	15,000	
	Membership Revenue		15,000
	To record sale of monthly memberships on account.		
Jan. xx	Cash	5,000	
	Court Fee Revenue		5,000
	To record sale of court time for cash.		
Jan. xx	Wage and Salary Expense	10,000	
	Cash		10,000
	To record payment of wages and salaries.		
Jan. xx	Utilities Expense	3,000	
	Cash		3,000
	To record payment of utilities.		
Jan. xx	Cash	4,000	
	Accounts Receivable		4,000
	To record collection of accounts receivable.		
Jan. xx	Dividends	2,000	
	Cash		2,000
	To record payment of dividends.		

General journal
The journal used in place of a specialized journal.

Transactions are normally recorded in a **general journal**. Specialized journals may be used to record repetitive transactions. For example, a cash receipts journal may be used to record all transactions in which cash is received. Special journals accomplish the same purpose as a general journal, but they save time in recording similar transactions. This chapter will use a general journal to record all transactions.

An excerpt from Glengarry Health Club's general journal appears in the top portion of Example 3-6 on the next page. One column needs further explanation. *Post. Ref.* is an abbreviation for *Posting Reference*. As part of the posting process, which is explained later in this section, the debit and credit amounts are posted to the appropriate accounts and this column is filled in with the number assigned to the account.

The frequency of posting differs among companies, partly based on the degree to which their accounting system is automated. For example, in some computerized systems, amounts are posted to the ledger accounts at the time an entry is recorded in the journal. In a manual system, posting is normally done periodically; for example, daily, weekly, or monthly. Regardless of when it is performed, the posting process simply reorganizes the transactions by account.

Journal entries and ledger accounts are *tools* used by the accountant. The end result, a set of financial statements, is the most important part of the process. Journalizing provides a chronological record of each transaction. So why not just prepare financial statements directly from the journal entries? In the simple example of Glengarry Health Club, it would be possible to prepare the statements directly from the journal entries. In real-world situations, however, the number of transactions in any given period is so large that it would be virtually impossible to bypass the accounts. Accounts provide a convenient summary of the activity as well as the balance for a specific financial statement item.

EXAMPLE 3-6 Posting from the Journal to the Ledger

The posting process for Glengarry Health Club is illustrated below for the health club's fifth transaction, in which cash is collected for court fees. Rather than a T-account format for the general ledger accounts, the *running balance form* is illustrated. A separate column indicates the balance in the ledger account after each transaction. The use of the explanation column in a ledger account is optional. Because an explanation of the entry in the account can be found by referring to the journal, this column is often left blank.

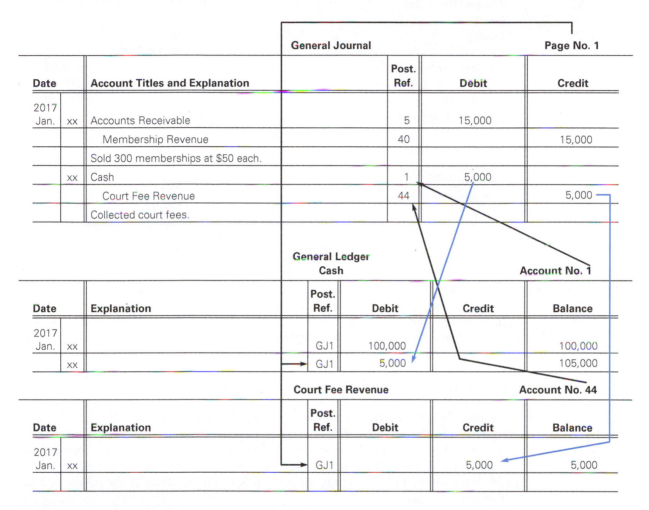

Note the cross-referencing between the journal and the ledger. As amounts are entered in the ledger accounts, the Posting Reference column is filled in with the page number of the journal. For example, GJ1 indicates page 1 from the general journal. At the same time, the Posting Reference column of the journal is filled in with the appropriate account number.

The Trial Balance

Accountants use one other tool to facilitate the preparation of a set of financial statements. A **trial balance** is a list of each account and its balance at a specific point in time. The trial balance is *not* a financial statement but merely a convenient device to prove the equality of the debit and credit balances in the accounts. It can be as informal as an adding machine tape with the account titles penciled in next to the debit and credit amounts.

LO7 Explain the purpose of a trial balance (Appendix).

Trial balance
A list of each account and its balance; used to prove equality of debits and credits.

EXAMPLE 3-7 Preparing a Trial Balance

A trial balance for Glengarry Health Club as of January 31, 2017, is shown on the next page. The balance in each account was determined by adding the increases and subtracting the decreases for the account for the transactions detailed earlier.

Glengarry Health Club Trial Balance January 31, 2017		
Account Titles	**Debits**	**Credits**
Cash	$ 94,000	
Accounts Receivable	11,000	
Equipment	20,000	
Building	150,000	
Land	50,000	
Accounts Payable		$ 20,000
Notes Payable		200,000
Capital Stock		100,000
Membership Revenue		15,000
Court Fee Revenue		5,000
Wage and Salary Expense	10,000	
Utilities Expense	3,000	
Dividends	2,000	
Totals	$340,000	$340,000

STUDY TIP

Remember from p. 114 that every account has a normal balance, either debit or credit. Note the normal balance for each account on this trial balance.

Certain types of errors are detectable from a trial balance. For example, if the balance of an account is incorrectly computed, the total of the debits and credits in the trial balance will not equal. If a debit is posted to an account as a credit, or vice versa, the trial balance will be out of balance. The omission of part of a journal entry in the posting process will also be detected by the preparation of a trial balance.

Do not attribute more significance to a trial balance, however, than is warranted. It does provide a convenient summary of account balances for preparing financial statements. It also assures us that the balances of all of the debit accounts equal the balances of all of the credit accounts. But an equality of debits and credits does not necessarily mean that the *correct* accounts were debited and credited in an entry. For example, the entry to record the purchase of land by signing a promissory note *should* result in a debit to Land and a credit to Notes Payable. If the accountant incorrectly debited Cash instead of Land, the trial balance would still show an equality of debits and credits. A trial balance can be prepared at any time; it is usually prepared before the release of a set of financial statements.

MODULE 3   TEST YOURSELF

Review		
	LO6 Explain the purposes of a journal and the posting process.	• A journal documents the details of transactions by date. Entries are made to a journal every time a transaction occurs. • Similar transactions that occur regularly may be recorded in special journals. • Ultimately, information is posted from the journal to the ledger for each individual account.
	LO7 Explain the purpose of a trial balance.	• At the end of a period, a trial balance may be prepared that lists all of the accounts in the general ledger along with their debit or credit balances. • The purpose of the trial balance is to see whether total debits equal total credits. This provides some assurance that the accounting equation was adhered to in the processing of transactions but is no guarantee that transactions have been recorded properly.

Question	1. Your friend presents the following criticism of the accounting system: "Accounting involves so much duplication of effort. First, entries are recorded in a journal; then the same information is recorded in a ledger. No wonder accountants work such long hours!" Do you agree with this criticism? Explain.
	2. What is the benefit of using a cross-referencing system between a ledger and a journal?
	3. What is the purpose of a trial balance?
Apply	1. Prepare in good form the journal entry to record each of the following transactions on the books of ABC. *Show me how* January 10: ABC is incorporated by issuing $50,000 of common stock to each of the three owners. January 12: ABC borrows $100,000 at the local bank. January 15: ABC pays $200,000 cash to buy ten acres of land.
	2. For each of the following errors, indicate with a *Y* for yes or an *N* for no whether it would be detected by preparation of a trial balance. _____ a. Cash is debited instead of Accounts Receivable for a sale on account. _____ b. A sale on account for $500 is recorded with a debit to Accounts Receivable for $500 and a credit to Sales for $5,000. _____ c. A cash sale is recorded by debiting Cash and Sales for the same amount.

Answers are located at the end of the chapter.

KEY TERMS QUIZ

Note: A separate quiz is available for the terms in the appendix to this chapter.

Read each definition below and write the number of the definition in the blank beside the appropriate term. The quiz solutions appear at the end of the chapter.

Quiz 1: Processing Accounting Information

_____ Event   _____ Source document
_____ External event   _____ Account
_____ Internal event   _____ Chart of accounts
_____ Transaction   _____ General ledger

1. A numerical list of all the accounts used by a company.
2. A happening of consequence to an entity.
3. An event occurring entirely within an entity.
4. A piece of paper, such as a sales invoice, that is used as the evidence to record a transaction.
5. An event involving interaction between an entity and its environment.
6. The record used to accumulate monetary amounts for each individual asset, liability, revenue, expense, and component of owners' equity.
7. A book, file, hard drive, or other device containing all of a company's accounts.
8. Any event, external or internal, that is recognized in a set of financial statements.

Quiz 2: Appendix

_____ Debit   _____ Posting
_____ Credit   _____ Journalizing
_____ Double-entry system   _____ General journal
_____ Journal   _____ Trial balance

1. A list of each account and its balance at a specific point in time; used to prove the equality of debits and credits.
2. An entry on the right side of an account.
3. The act of recording journal entries.
4. An entry on the left side of an account.
5. The process of transferring amounts from a journal to the appropriate ledger accounts.
6. A chronological record of transactions, also known as the *book of original entry*.
7. The journal used in place of a specialized journal.
8. A system of accounting in which every transaction is recorded with equal debits and credits and the accounting equation is kept in balance.

ALTERNATE TERMS

credit side of an account right side of an account

debit an account charge an account

debit side of an account left side of an account

general ledger set of accounts

journal book of original entry

journalizing an entry recording an entry

posting an account transferring an amount from the journal to the ledger

REVIEW PROBLEM & SOLUTION

The following transactions are entered into by Sparkle Car Wash during its first month of operations:

a. Articles of incorporation are filed with the state, and 20,000 shares of capital stock are issued. Cash of $40,000 is received from the new owners for the shares.
b. A five-year promissory note is signed at the local bank. The cash received from the loan is $120,000.
c. An existing car wash is purchased for $150,000 in cash. The values assigned to the land, building, and equipment are $25,000, $75,000, and $50,000, respectively.
d. Cleaning supplies are purchased on account for $2,500 from a distributor. None of the supplies are used in the first month.
e. During the first month, $1,500 is paid to the distributor for the cleaning supplies. The remaining $1,000 will be paid next month.
f. Gross receipts from car washes during the first month of operations amount to $7,000.
g. Wages and salaries paid in the first month amount to $2,000.
h. The utility bill of $800 for the month is paid.
i. A total of $1,000 in dividends is paid to the owners.

Required

1. Prepare a table to summarize the preceding transactions as they affect the accounting equation. Use the format in Exhibit 3-1. Identify each transaction by letter.
2. Prepare an income statement for the month.
3. Prepare a balance sheet at the end of the month.

Solution to Review Problem

1.

Sparkle Car Wash
Transactions for the Month

Trans. No.	Assets					=	Liabilities		+ Stockholders' Equity	
	Cash	Cleaning Supplies	Land	Building	Equipment		Accounts Payable	Notes Payable	Capital Stock	Retained Earnings
a.	$ 40,000								$40,000	
b.	120,000							$120,000		
Bal.	$160,000							$120,000	$40,000	
c.	−150,000		$25,000	$75,000	$50,000					
Bal.	$ 10,000		$25,000	$75,000	$50,000			$120,000	$40,000	
d.		$2,500					$2,500			
Bal.	$ 10,000	$2,500	$25,000	$75,000	$50,000		$2,500	$120,000	$40,000	
e.	−1,500						−1,500			
Bal.	$ 8,500	$2,500	$25,000	$75,000	$50,000		$1,000	$120,000	$40,000	
f.	7,000									$7,000
Bal.	$ 15,500	$2,500	$25,000	$75,000	$50,000		$1,000	$120,000	$40,000	$7,000
g.	−2,000									−2,000
Bal.	$ 13,500	$2,500	$25,000	$75,000	$50,000		$1,000	$120,000	$40,000	$5,000
h.	−800									−800
Bal.	$ 12,700	$2,500	$25,000	$75,000	$50,000		$1,000	$120,000	$40,000	$4,200
i.	−1,000									−1,000
Bal.	$ 11,700	$2,500	$25,000	$75,000	$50,000		$1,000	$120,000	$40,000	$3,200

Total assets: $164,200   Total liablities and stockholders' equity: $164,200

2.

Sparkle Car Wash
Income Statement
For the Month Ended XX/XX/XX

Car wash revenue		$7,000
Expenses:		
Wages and salaries	$2,000	
Utilities	800	2,800
Net income		$4,200

3.

Sparkle Car Wash
Balance Sheet
XX/XX/XX

Assets		Liabilities and Stockholders' Equity	
Cash	$ 11,700	Accounts payable	$ 1,000
Cleaning supplies	2,500	Notes payable	120,000
Land	25,000	Capital stock	40,000
Building	75,000	Retained earnings	3,200
Equipment	50,000	Total liabilities and stockholders'	
Total assets	$164,200	equity	$164,200

EXERCISES

LO1   Exercise 3-1 Types of Events

For each of the following events, identify whether it is an external event that would be recorded as a transaction (E), an internal event that would be recorded as a transaction (I), or not recorded (NR).

_____   1. A vendor for a company's supplies is paid an amount owed on account.
_____   2. A customer pays its open account.
_____   3. A new chief executive officer is hired.
_____   4. The biweekly payroll is paid.
_____   5. Depreciation on equipment is recognized.
_____   6. A new advertising agency is hired to develop a series of newspaper ads for the company.
_____   7. The advertising bill for the first month is paid.
_____   8. The accountant determines the federal income taxes owed based on the income for the period.

LO2   Exercise 3-2 Source Documents Matched with Transactions

Following are a list of source documents and a list of transactions. Indicate by letter next to each transaction the source document that would serve as evidence for the recording of the transaction.

Source Documents

a. Purchase invoice
b. Sales invoice
c. Cash register tape
d. Time cards
e. Promissory note

f. Stock certificates
g. Monthly statement from utility company
h. No standard source document would normally be available.

Transactions

_____   1. Utilities expense for the month is recorded.
_____   2. A cash settlement is received from a pending lawsuit.
_____   3. Owners contribute cash to start a new corporation.
_____   4. The biweekly payroll is paid.
_____   5. Services are provided in exchange for cash.
_____   6. Equipment is acquired on a 30-day open account.
_____   7. Service is provided to a customer.
_____   8. A building is acquired by signing an agreement to repay a stated amount plus interest in six months.

LO3   Exercise 3-3 The Effect of Transactions on the Accounting Equation

EXAMPLE 3-1

For each of the following transactions, indicate whether it increases (I), decreases (D), or has no effect (NE) on the total dollar amount of each of the elements of the accounting equation.

Transactions	Assets	= Liabilities	+ Stockholders' Equity
Example: Common stock is issued in exchange for cash.	I	NE	I
1. Equipment is purchased for cash.			
2. Services are provided to customers on account.			
3. Services are provided to customers in exchange for cash.			
4. An account payable is paid off.			
5. Cash is collected on an account receivable.			
6. Buildings are purchased in exchange for a three-year note payable.			
7. Advertising bill for the month is paid.			
8. Dividends are paid to stockholders.			
9. Land is acquired by issuing shares of stock to the owner of the land.			

Exercise 3-4 Types of Transactions

LO3
EXAMPLE 3-1

There are three elements to the accounting equation: assets, liabilities, and stockholders' equity. Although other possibilities exist, five types of transactions are described here. For *each* of these five types, write descriptions of two transactions that illustrate the type of transaction.

Type of Transaction	Assets =	Liabilities + Stockholders' Equity
1.	Increase	Increase
2.	Increase	Increase
3.	Decrease	Decrease
4.	Decrease	Decrease
5.	Increase	
	Decrease	

Exercise 3-5 Analyzing Transactions

LO3
EXAMPLE 3-1

Prepare a table to summarize the following transactions as they affect the accounting equation. Use the format in Exhibit 3-1.

1. Services provided on account of $1,530
2. Purchases of supplies on account for $1,365
3. Services provided for cash of $750
4. Purchase of equipment for cash of $4,240
5. Issuance of a promissory note for $2,500
6. Collections on account for $890
7. Sale of capital stock in exchange for a parcel of land; the land is appraised at $50,000
8. Payment of $4,000 in salaries and wages
9. Payment of open account in the amount of $500

Exercise 3-6 Balance Sheet Accounts and Their Use

LO4

Choose from the following list of account titles the one that most accurately fits the description of that account or is an example of that account. An account title may be used more than once or not at all.

Cash   Accounts Receivable   Notes Receivable
Prepaid Asset   Land   Buildings
Investments   Accounts Payable   Notes Payable
Taxes Payable   Retained Earnings   Common Stock
Preferred Stock

_____ 1. A written obligation to repay a fixed amount, with interest, at some time in the future

_____ 2. Twenty acres of land held for speculation

_____ 3. An amount owed by a customer

_____ 4. Corporate income taxes owed to the federal government

_____ 5. Ownership in a company that allows the owner to receive dividends before common shareholders receive any distributions

_____ 6. Five acres of land used as the site for a factory

_____ 7. Amounts owed on an open account to a vendor, due in 90 days

_____ 8. A checking account at a bank

_____ 9. A warehouse used to store equipment

_____ 10. Claims by the owners on the undistributed net income of a business

_____ 11. Rent paid on an office building in advance of use of the facility

LO5 Exercise 3-7 Normal Account Balances (Appendix)

EXAMPLE 3-3

Each account has a normal balance. For the following list of accounts, indicate whether the normal balance of each is a debit or a credit.

Account	Normal Balance
1. Cash	_____
2. Prepaid Insurance	_____
3. Retained Earnings	_____
4. Bonds Payable	_____
5. Investments	_____
6. Capital Stock	_____
7. Advertising Fees Revenue	_____
8. Wages and Salaries Expense	_____
9. Wages and Salaries Payable	_____
10. Office Supplies	_____
11. Dividends	_____

LO5 Exercise 3-8 Normal Account Balances for Vail Resorts (Appendix)

EXAMPLE 3-3

REAL WORLD

Each account has a normal balance. Classify each of the following items found on **Vail Resorts'** 2015 financial statements included in the Form 10-K for the year ended July 31, 2015, according to (1) whether it is a revenue (R), expense (E), asset (A), liability (L), or stockholders' equity (SE) item and (2) whether it has a normal balance of a debit (D) or a credit (C).

Item	Classified as	Normal Balance
Example: Cash and cash equivalents	A	D
1. Trade receivables, net of allowances	_____	_____
2. Segment operating expense—Lodging	_____	_____
3. Common stock	_____	_____
4. Income taxes payable	_____	_____
5. Net revenue—Mountain	_____	_____
6. Interest expense	_____	_____
7. Property, plant and equipment, net	_____	_____
8. Accounts payable and accrued liabilities	_____	_____
9. Retained earnings	_____	_____
10. Long-term debt	_____	_____

LO5 Exercise 3-9 Debits and Credits (Appendix)

EXAMPLE 3-4, 3-5

Show me how

The new bookkeeper for Darby Corporation is getting ready to mail the daily cash receipts to the bank for deposit. Because his previous job was at a bank, he is aware that the bank "credits" an account for all deposits and "debits" an account for all checks written. Therefore, he makes the following entry before sending the daily receipts to the bank:

June 5	Accounts Receivable	10,000	
	Sales Revenue	2,450	
	Cash		12,450
	To record cash received on June 5: $10,000 collections on account and $2,450 in cash sales.		

Required

Explain why that entry is wrong and prepare the correct journal entry. Why does the bank refer to cash received from a customer as a *credit* to that customer's account?

LO7 Exercise 3-10 Trial Balance (Appendix)

EXAMPLE 3-7

Show me how

The following list of accounts was taken from the general ledger of Spencer Corporation on December 31. The bookkeeper thought it would be helpful if the accounts were arranged in alphabetical order. Each account contains the balance that is normal for that type of account; for example, Cash normally has a debit balance. Prepare a trial balance as of this date with the accounts arranged in the following order: (1) assets, (2) liabilities, (3) stockholders' equity, (4) revenues, (5) expenses, and (6) dividends.

Account	Balance	Account	Balance
Accounts Payable	$ 7,650	Heat, Light, and Water Expense	$ 1,400
Accounts Receivable	5,325	Income Tax Expense	1,700
Automobiles	9,200	Income Taxes Payable	2,500
Buildings	150,000	Interest Revenue	1,300
Capital Stock	100,000	Land	50,000
Cash	10,500	Notes Payable	90,000
Commissions Expense	2,600	Office Salaries Expense	6,000
Commissions Revenue	12,750	Office Supplies	500
Dividends	2,000	Retained Earnings	110,025
Equipment	85,000		

MULTI-CONCEPT EXERCISES

Exercise 3-11 Determining an Ending Account Balance (Appendix)

LO3 • 4 • 5

EXAMPLE 3-2, 3-4

Jessie's Accounting Services was organized on June 1. The company received a contribution of $1,000 from each of the two principal owners. During the month, Jessie's Accounting Services provided services for cash of $1,400 and services on account for $450, received $250 from customers in payment of their accounts, purchased supplies on account for $600 and equipment on account for $1,350, received a utility bill for $250 that will not be paid until July, and paid the full amount due on the equipment. Use a T account to determine the company's Cash balance on June 30.

Exercise 3-12 Reconstructing a Beginning Account Balance (Appendix)

LO3 • 4 • 5

EXAMPLE 3-2, 3-4

During the month, services performed for customers on account amounted to $7,500 and collections from customers in payment of their accounts totaled $6,000. At the end of the month, the Accounts Receivable account had a balance of $2,500. What was the Accounts Receivable balance at the beginning of the month?

Exercise 3-13 Journal Entries Recorded Directly in T Accounts (Appendix)

LO3 • 4 • 5

EXAMPLE 3-2, 3-4

Record each of the following transactions directly in T accounts using the numbers preceding the transactions to identify them in the accounts. Each account needs a separate T account.
1. Received contribution of $6,500 from each of the three principal owners of We-Go Delivery Service in exchange for shares of stock.
2. Purchased office supplies for cash of $130.
3. Purchased a van for $15,000 on an open account. The company has 25 days to pay for the van.
4. Provided delivery services to residential customers for cash of $125.
5. Billed a local business $200 for delivery services. The customer is to pay the bill within 15 days.
6. Paid the amount due on the van.
7. Received the amount due from the local business billed in (5).

Exercise 3-14 Trial Balance (Appendix)

LO4 • 7

EXAMPLE 3-7

Refer to the transactions recorded directly in T accounts for We-Go Delivery Service in Exercise 3-13. Assume that all of the transactions took place during December. Prepare a trial balance at December 31.

Exercise 3-15 Journal Entries (Appendix)

LO3 • 5 • 6

EXAMPLE 3-4, 3-5

Prepare the journal entry to record each of the following independent transactions. (Use the number of the transaction in lieu of a date for identification purposes.)
1. Services provided on account of $1,530
2. Purchases of supplies on account for $1,365

(Continued)

3. Services provided for cash of $750
4. Purchase of equipment for cash of $4,240
5. Issuance of a promissory note for $2,500
6. Collections on account for $890
7. Sale of capital stock in exchange for a parcel of land; the land is appraised at $50,000
8. Payment of $4,000 in salaries and wages
9. Payment of open account in the amount of $500

LO3 • 5 • 6   Exercise 3-16 Journal Entries (Appendix)
EXAMPLE 3-4, 3-5

Following is a list of transactions entered into during the first month of operations of Gardener Corporation, a new landscape service. Prepare in journal form the entry to record each transaction.

April 1:	Articles of incorporation are filed with the state, and 100,000 shares of common stock are issued for $100,000 in cash.
April 4:	A six-month promissory note is signed at the bank. Interest at 9% per annum will be repaid in six months along with the principal amount of the loan of $50,000.
April 8:	Land and a storage shed are acquired for a lump sum of $80,000. On the basis of an appraisal, 25% of the value is assigned to the land and the remainder to the building.
April 10:	Mowing equipment is purchased from a supplier at a total cost of $25,000. A down payment of $10,000 is made, with the remainder due by the end of the month.
April 18:	Customers are billed for services provided during the first half of the month. The total amount billed of $5,500 is due within ten days.
April 27:	The remaining balance due on the mowing equipment is paid to the supplier.
April 28:	The total amount of $5,500 due from customers is received.
April 30:	Customers are billed for services provided during the second half of the month. The total amount billed is $9,850.
April 30:	Salaries and wages of $4,650 for the month of April are paid.

LO3 • 5 • 6   Exercise 3-17 Journal Entries for Vail Resorts (Appendix)
EXAMPLE 3-4, 3-5

REAL WORLD

Refer to the income statement for **Vail Resorts** shown in the chapter opener. Using the account titles reported there, prepare the journal entry for each of the following hypothetical transactions. Assume that all transactions include either a debit or a credit to Cash.
1. Fuel for the motors in the ski lifts is purchased for $1,000.
2. A skier purchases a lift ticket for $80.
3. Salaries and wages for hotel staff of $4,000 are paid.
4. A guest pays $150 for one night's lodging.

LO5 • 6   Exercise 3-18 The Process of Posting Journal Entries to General Ledger Accounts (Appendix)
EXAMPLE 3-6

On June 1, Campbell Corporation purchased ten acres of land in exchange for a promissory note in the amount of $50,000. Using the formats shown in Example 3-6, prepare the journal entry to record this transaction in a general journal and post it to the appropriate general ledger accounts. The entry will be recorded on page 7 of the general journal. Use whatever account numbers you like in the general ledger. Assume that none of the accounts to be debited or credited currently contain a balance.

   If at a later date, you wanted to review this transaction, would you examine the general ledger or the general journal? Explain your answer.

PROBLEMS

LO1   Problem 3-1 Events to Be Recorded in Accounts

The following events take place at Dillon's Delivery Service:
1. Supplies are ordered from vendors who will deliver the supplies within the week.
2. Vendors deliver supplies on account, payment due in 30 days.

3. Customers' deliveries are made, and the customers are billed.
4. Trash is taken to dumpsters, and the floors are cleaned.
5. Cash is received from customers billed in (3).
6. Cash is deposited in the bank night depository.
7. Employees are paid weekly paychecks.
8. Vendors noted in (2) are paid for the supplies delivered.

Required

Identify each event as internal (I) or external (E) and indicate whether each event would or would not be recorded in the *accounts* of the company. For each event that is to be recorded, identify the names of at least two accounts that would be affected.

Problem 3-2 Transaction Analysis and Financial Statements   LO3

Just Rolling Along Inc. was organized on May 1 by two college students who recognized an opportunity to make money while spending their days at a beach along Lake Michigan. The two entrepreneurs plan to rent bicycles and in-line skates to weekend visitors to the lakefront. The following transactions occurred during the first month of operations:

May 1: Received contribution of $9,000 from each of the two principal owners of the new business in exchange for shares of stock.

May 1: Purchased ten bicycles for $300 each on an open account. The company has 30 days to pay for the bicycles.

May 5: Registered as a vendor with the city and paid the $15 monthly fee.

May 9: Purchased 20 pairs of in-line skates at $125 per pair, 20 helmets at $50 each, and 20 sets of protective gear (knee and elbow pads and wrist guards) at $45 per set for cash.

May 10: Purchased $100 in miscellaneous supplies on account. The company has 30 days to pay for the supplies.

May 15: Paid $125 bill from local radio station for advertising for the last two weeks of May.

May 17: Customers rented in-line skates and bicycles for cash of $1,800.

May 24: Billed the local park district $1,200 for in-line skating lessons provided to neighborhood children. The park district is to pay one-half of the bill within five working days and the rest within 30 days.

May 29: Received 50% of the amount billed to the park district.

May 30: Customers rented in-line skates and bicycles for cash of $3,000.

May 30: Paid wages of $160 to a friend who helped over the weekend.

May 31: Paid the balance due on the bicycles.

Required

1. Prepare a table to summarize the preceding transactions as they affect the accounting equation. Use the format in Exhibit 3-1. Identify each transaction with the date.
2. Prepare an income statement for the month of May.
3. Prepare a classified balance sheet at May 31.
4. Why do you think the two college students decided to incorporate their business rather than operate it as a partnership?

Problem 3-3 Transaction Analysis and Financial Statements   LO3

Expert Consulting Services Inc. was organized on March 1 by two former college roommates. The corporation provides computer consulting services to small businesses. The following transactions occurred during the first month of operations:

March 2: Received contributions of $20,000 from each of the two principal owners of the new business in exchange for shares of stock.

March 7: Signed a two-year promissory note at the bank and received cash of $15,000. Interest, along with the $15,000, will be repaid at the end of the two years.

(Continued)

March 12:   Purchased $700 in miscellaneous supplies on account. The company has 30 days to pay for the supplies.

March 19:   Billed a client $4,000 for services rendered by Expert in helping to install a new computer system. The client is to pay 25% of the bill upon its receipt and the remaining balance within 30 days.

March 20:   Paid $1,300 bill from the local newspaper for advertising for the month of March.

March 22:   Received 25% of the amount billed to the client on March 19.

March 26:   Received cash of $2,800 for services provided in assisting a client in selecting software for its computer.

March 29:   Purchased a computer system for $8,000 in cash.

March 30:   Paid $3,300 of salaries and wages for March.

March 31:   Received and paid $1,400 in gas, electric, and water bills.

Required

1. Prepare a table to summarize the preceding transactions as they affect the accounting equation. Use the format in Exhibit 3-1. Identify each transaction with the date.
2. Prepare an income statement for the month of March.
3. Prepare a classified balance sheet at March 31.
4. From reading the balance sheet you prepared in part (3), what events would you expect to take place in April? Explain your answer.

LO3   **Problem 3-4 Transactions Reconstructed from Financial Statements**

The following financial statements are available for Elm Corporation for its first month of operations:

Elm Corporation
Income Statement
For the Month of June

Service revenue		$93,600
Expenses:		
Rent	$ 9,000	
Salaries and wages	27,900	
Utilities	13,800	50,700
Net income		$42,900

Elm Corporation
Balance Sheet
June 30

Assets		Liabilities and Stockholders' Equity	
Cash	$ 22,800	Accounts payable	$ 18,000
Accounts receivable	21,600	Notes payable	90,000
Equipment	18,000	Capital stock	30,000
Building	90,000	Retained earnings	38,400
Land	24,000	Total liabilities and	
Total assets	$176,400	stockholders' equity	$176,400

Required

Using the format illustrated in Exhibit 3-1, prepare a table to summarize the transactions entered into by Elm Corporation during its first month of business. State any assumptions you believe are necessary in reconstructing the transactions.

MULTI-CONCEPT PROBLEMS

Problem 3-5 Identification of Events with Source Documents   LO1 • 2

Many events are linked to a source document. The following is a list of events that occurred in an entity:

a. Paid a one-year insurance policy.
b. Paid employee payroll.
c. Provided services to a customer on account.
d. Identified supplies in the storeroom destroyed by fire.
e. Received payment of bills from customers.
f. Purchased land for future expansion.
g. Calculated taxes due.
h. Entered into a car lease agreement and paid the tax, title, and license.

Required

For each item (a) through (h), indicate whether the event should or should not be recorded in the entity's accounts. For each item that should be recorded in the entity's books:

1. Identify one or more source documents that are generated from the event.
2. Identify which source document would be used to record an event when it produces more than one source document.
3. For each document, identify the information that is most useful in recording the event in the accounts.

Problem 3-6 Transaction Analysis and Financial Statements   LO1 • 3

Blue Jay Delivery Service is incorporated on January 2 and enters into the following transactions during its first month of operations:

January 2:   Filed articles of incorporation with the state and issued 100,000 shares of capital stock. Cash of $100,000 is received from the new owners for the shares.

January 3:   Purchased a warehouse and land for $80,000 in cash. An appraiser values the land at $20,000 and the warehouse at $60,000.

January 4:   Signed a three-year promissory note at Third State Bank in the amount of $50,000.

January 6:   Purchased five new delivery trucks for a total of $45,000 in cash.

January 31:   Performed services on account that amounted to $15,900 during the month. Cash amounting to $7,490 was received from customers on account during the month.

January 31:   Established an open account at a local service station at the beginning of the month. Purchases of gas and oil during January amounted to $3,230. Blue Jay has until the 10th of the following month to pay its bill.

Required

1. Prepare a table to summarize the preceding transactions as they affect the accounting equation. Ignore depreciation expense and interest expense. Use the format in Exhibit 3-1.
2. Prepare an income statement for the month of January.
3. Prepare a classified balance sheet at January 31.
4. Assume that you are considering buying stock in this company. Beginning with the transaction to record the purchase of the property on January 3, list any additional information you would like to have about each of the transactions during the remainder of the month.

LO 1 • 3   Problem 3-7 Transaction Analysis and Financial Statements

Neveranerror Inc. was organized on June 2 by a group of accountants to provide accounting and tax services to small businesses. The following transactions occurred during the first month of business:

June 2:	Received contributions of $10,000 from each of the three owners of the business in exchange for shares of stock.
June 5:	Purchased a computer system for $12,000. The agreement with the vendor requires a down payment of $2,500 with the balance due in 60 days.
June 8:	Signed a two-year promissory note at the bank and received cash of $20,000.
June 15:	Billed $12,350 to clients for the first half of June. Clients are billed twice a month for services performed during the month, and the bills are payable within ten days.
June 17:	Paid a $900 bill from the local newspaper for advertising for the month of June.
June 23:	Received the amounts billed to clients for services performed during the first half of the month.
June 28:	Received and paid gas, electric, and water bills. The total amount is $2,700.
June 29:	Received the landlord's bill for $2,200 for rent on the office space that Neveranerror leases. The bill is payable by the 10th of the following month.
June 30:	Paid salaries and wages for June. The total amount is $5,670.
June 30:	Billed $18,400 to clients for the second half of June.
June 30:	Declared and paid dividends in the amount of $6,000.

Required

1. Prepare a table to summarize the preceding transactions as they affect the accounting equation. Ignore depreciation expense and interest expense. Use the format in Table 3-1.
2. Prepare the following financial statements:

   a. Income statement for the month of June
   b. Statement of retained earnings for the month of June
   c. Classified balance sheet at June 30

3. Assume that you have just graduated from college and have been approached to join this company as an accountant. From your reading of the financial statements for the first month, would you consider joining the company? Explain your answer. Limit your answer to financial considerations only.

LO3 • 5   Problem 3-8 Accounts Used to Record Transactions (Appendix)

A list of accounts, with an identifying number for each, is provided. Following the list of accounts is a series of transactions entered into by a company during its first year of operations.

Required

For each transaction, indicate the account or accounts that should be debited and credited.

1. Cash	7. Accounts Payable	13. Wage and Salaries Expense
2. Accounts Receivable	8. Income Taxes Payable	14. Selling Expense
3. Office Supplies	9. Notes Payable	15. Utilities Expense
4. Buildings	10. Capital Stock	16. Income Tax Expense
5. Automobiles	11. Retained Earnings	
6. Land	12. Service Revenue	

	Accounts	
Transactions	**Debited**	**Credited**
Example: Purchased land and building in exchange for a three-year promissory note.	4,6	9
a. Issued capital stock for cash.		
b. Purchased ten automobiles; paid part in cash and signed a 60-day note for the balance.		

Transactions	Accounts	
	Debited	**Credited**
c. Purchased land in exchange for a note due in six months.	_____	_____
d. Purchased office supplies; agreed to pay total bill by the 10th of the following month.	_____	_____
e. Billed clients for services performed during the month and gave them until the 15th of the following month to pay.	_____	_____
f. Received cash on account from clients for services rendered to them in past months.	_____	_____
g. Paid employees salaries and wages earned during the month.	_____	_____
h. Paid newspaper for company ads appearing during the month.	_____	_____
i. Received monthly gas and electric bill from the utility company; payment is due anytime within the first ten days of the following month.	_____	_____
j. Computed amount of taxes due based on the income of the period; amount will be paid in the following month.	_____	_____

Problem 3-9 Transaction Analysis and Journal Entries Recorded Directly in T Accounts (Appendix)

LO3 • 4 • 5

Four brothers organized Beverly Entertainment Enterprises on October 1. The following transactions occurred during the first month of operations:

October 1: Received contributions of $10,000 from each of the four principal owners of the new business in exchange for shares of stock.

October 2: Purchased the Ace Theater for $125,000. The seller agreed to accept a down payment of $12,500 and a seven-year promissory note for the balance. The Ace property consists of land valued at $35,000, and a building valued at $90,000.

October 3: Purchased new seats for the theater at a cost of $5,000, paying $2,500 down and agreeing to pay the remainder in 60 days.

October 12: Purchased candy, popcorn, cups, and napkins for $3,700 on an open account. The company has 30 days to pay for the concession supplies.

October 13: Sold tickets for the opening-night movie for cash of $1,800 and took in $2,400 at the concession stand.

October 17: Rented out the theater to a local community group for $1,500. The community group is to pay one-half of the bill within five working days and has 30 days to pay the remainder.

October 23: Received 50% of the amount billed to the community group.

October 24: Sold movie tickets for cash of $2,000 and took in $2,800 at the concession stand.

October 26: The four brothers, acting on behalf of Beverly Entertainment, paid a dividend of $750 on the shares of stock owned by each of them, or $3,000 in total.

October 27: Paid $500 for utilities.

October 30: Paid wages and salaries of $2,400 total to the ushers, projectionist, concession stand workers, and maintenance crew.

October 31: Sold movie tickets for cash of $1,800 and took in $2,500 at the concession stand.

Required

1. Prepare a table to summarize the preceding transactions as they affect the accounting equation. Ignore depreciation expense and interest expense. Use the format in Exhibit 3-1. Identify each transaction with a date.
2. Record each transaction directly in T accounts using the dates preceding the transactions to identify them in the accounts. Each account involved in the problem needs a separate T account.

Problem 3-10 Trial Balance and Financial Statements (Appendix)

LO4 • 7

Refer to the table for Beverly Entertainment Enterprises in part (1) of Problem 3-9.

(Continued)

Required

1. Prepare a trial balance at October 31.
2. Prepare an income statement for the month of October.
3. Prepare a statement of retained earnings for the month of October.
4. Prepare a classified balance sheet at October 31.

LO3 • 5 • 6   **Problem 3-11 Journal Entries (Appendix)**

Atkins Advertising Agency began business on January 2. The transactions entered into by Atkins during its first month of operations are as follows:

a. Acquired its articles of incorporation from the state and issued 100,000 shares of capital stock in exchange for $200,000 in cash.
b. Purchased an office building for $150,000 in cash. The building is valued at $110,000, and the remainder of the value is assigned to the land.
c. Signed a three-year promissory note at the bank for $125,000.
d. Purchased office equipment at a cost of $50,000, paying $10,000 down and agreeing to pay the remainder in ten days.
e. Paid wages and salaries of $13,000 for the first half of the month. Office employees are paid twice a month.
f. Paid the balance due on the office equipment.
g. Sold $24,000 of advertising during the first month. Customers have until the 15th of the following month to pay their bills.
h. Paid wages and salaries of $15,000 for the second half of the month.
i. Recorded $3,500 in commissions earned by the salespeople during the month. They will be paid on the fifth of the following month.

Required

Prepare in journal form the entry to record each transaction.

LO3 • 4 • 5   **Problem 3-12 Journal Entries Recorded Directly in T Accounts (Appendix)**

Refer to the transactions for Atkins Advertising Agency in Problem 3-11.

Required

1. Record each transaction directly in T accounts using the letters preceding the transactions to identify them in the accounts. Each account involved in the problem needs a separate T account.
2. Prepare a trial balance at January 31.

LO3 • 5 • 7   **Problem 3-13 The Detection of Errors in a Trial Balance and Preparation of a Corrected Trial Balance (Appendix)**

Malcolm Inc. was incorporated on January 1 with the issuance of capital stock in return for $90,000 of cash contributed by the owners. The only other transaction entered into prior to beginning operations was the issuance of a $75,300 note payable in exchange for building and equipment. The following trial balance was prepared at the end of the first month by the bookkeeper for Malcolm Inc.:

Malcolm Inc.
Trial Balance
January 31

Account Titles	Debits	Credits
Cash	$ 9,980	
Accounts Receivable	8,640	
Land	80,000	
Building	50,000	
Equipment	23,500	
Notes Payable		$ 75,300
Capital Stock		90,000
Service Revenue		50,340

Account Titles	Debits	Credits
Wage and Salary Expense	23,700	
Advertising Expense	4,600	
Utilities Expense	8,420	
Dividends		5,000
Totals	$208,840	$220,640

Required

1. Identify the *two* errors in the trial balance. Ignore depreciation expense and interest expense.
2. Prepare a corrected trial balance.

Problem 3-14 Journal Entries, Trial Balance, and Financial Statements (Appendix)   LO 3 • 5 • 6 • 7

Refer to the transactions for Blue Jay Delivery Service in Problem 3-6.

Required

1. Prepare journal entries on the books of Blue Jay to record the transactions entered into during the month. Ignore depreciation expense and interest expense.
2. Prepare a trial balance at January 31.
3. Prepare an income statement for the month of January.
4. Prepare a classified balance sheet at January 31.
5. Assume that you are considering buying stock in the company. Beginning with the transaction to record the purchase of the property on January 3, list any additional information you would like to have about each of the transactions during the remainder of the month.

Problem 3-15 Journal Entries, Trial Balance, and Financial Statements (Appendix)   LO 3 • 5 • 6 • 7

Refer to the transactions for Neveranerror Inc. in Problem 3-7.

Required

1. Prepare journal entries on the books of Neveranerror to record the transactions entered into during the month. Ignore depreciation expense and interest expense.
2. Prepare a trial balance at June 30.
3. Prepare the following financial statements:

   a. Income statement for the month of June.
   b. Statement of retained earnings for the month of June.
   c. Classified balance sheet at June 30.

4. Assume that you have just graduated from college and have been approached to join the company as an accountant. From your reading of the financial statements for the first month, would you consider joining the company? Explain your answer. Limit your answer to financial considerations only.

ALTERNATE PROBLEMS

Problem 3-1A Events to Be Recorded in Accounts   LO1

The following events take place at Anaconda Accountants Inc.:

1. Supplies are ordered from vendors, who will deliver the supplies within the week.
2. Vendors deliver supplies on account, payment due in 30 days.
3. New computer system is ordered.
4. Old computer system is sold for cash.
5. Services are rendered to customers on account. The invoices are mailed and due in 30 days.
6. Cash received from customer payments is deposited in the bank night depository.

(Continued)

7. Employees are paid weekly paychecks.
8. Vendors noted in (2) are paid for the supplies delivered.

Required

Identify each event as internal (I) or external (E) and indicate whether each event would or would not be recorded in the *accounts* of the company. For each event that is to be recorded, identify the names of at least two accounts that would be affected.

LO3   Problem 3-2A Transaction Analysis and Financial Statements

Beachway Enterprises was organized on June 1 by two college students who recognized an opportunity to make money while spending their days at a beach in Florida. The two entrepreneurs plan to rent beach umbrellas. The following transactions occurred during the first month of operations:

June 1:	Received contributions of $2,000 from each of the two principal owners of the new business in exchange for shares of stock.
June 1:	Purchased 25 beach umbrellas for $250 each on account. The company has 30 days to pay for the beach umbrellas.
June 5:	Registered as a vendor with the city and paid the $35 monthly fee.
June 10:	Purchased $50 in miscellaneous supplies on an open account. The company has 30 days to pay for the supplies.
June 15:	Paid $70 bill from a local radio station for advertising for the last two weeks of June.
June 17:	Customers rented beach umbrellas for cash of $1,000.
June 24:	Billed a local hotel $2,000 for beach umbrellas provided for use during a convention being held at the hotel. The hotel is to pay one-half of the bill in five days and the rest within 30 days.
June 29:	Received 50% of the amount billed to the hotel.
June 30:	Customers rented beach umbrellas for cash of $1,500.
June 30:	Paid wages of $90 to a friend who helped over the weekend.
June 30:	Paid the balance due on the beach umbrellas.

Required

1. Prepare a table to summarize the preceding transactions as they affect the accounting equation. Use the format in Exhibit 3-1. Identify each transaction with a date.
2. Prepare an income statement for the month of June.
3. Prepare a classified balance sheet at June 30.

LO3   Problem 3-3A Transaction Analysis and Financial Statements

Dynamic Services Inc. was organized on March 1 by two former college roommates. The corporation will provide computer tax services to small businesses. The following transactions occurred during the first month of operations:

March 2:	Received contributions of $10,000 from each of the two principal owners in exchange for shares of stock.
March 7:	Signed a two-year promissory note at the bank and received cash of $7,500. Interest, along with the $7,500, will be repaid at the end of the two years.
March 12:	Purchased miscellaneous supplies on account for $350, payment due in 30 days.
March 19:	Billed a client $2,000 for tax preparation services. According to an agreement between the two companies, the client is to pay 25% of the bill upon its receipt and the remaining balance within 30 days.
March 20:	Paid a $650 bill from the local newspaper for advertising for the month of March.
March 22:	Received 25% of the amount billed the client on March 19.
March 26:	Received cash of $1,400 for services provided in assisting a client in preparing its tax return.
March 29:	Purchased a computer system for $4,000 in cash.

March 30: Paid $1,650 in salaries and wages for March.

March 31: Received and paid $700 of gas, electric, and water bills.

Required

1. Prepare a table to summarize the preceding transactions as they affect the accounting equation. Use the format in Exhibit 3-1. Identify each transaction with the date.
2. Prepare an income statement for the month of March.
3. Prepare a classified balance sheet at March 31.
4. From reading the balance sheet you prepared in part (3), what events would you expect to take place in April? Explain your answer.

Problem 3-4A Transactions Reconstructed from Financial Statements   LO3

The following financial statements are available for Oak Corporation for its first month of operations:

Oak Corporation
Income Statement
For the Month of July

Service revenue		$75,400
Expenses:		
Rent	$ 6,000	
Salaries and wages	24,600	
Utilities	12,700	43,300
Net income		$32,100

Oak Corporation
Balance Sheet
July 31

Assets		Liabilities and Stockholders' Equity	
Cash	$ 13,700	Wages payable	$ 6,000
Accounts receivable	25,700	Notes payable	50,000
Equipment	32,000	Deferred service revenue	4,500
Furniture	14,700	Capital stock	30,000
Land	24,000	Retained earnings	19,600
		Total liabilities and	
Total assets	$110,100	stockholders' equity	$110,100

Required

Describe as many transactions as you can that were entered into by Oak Corporation during the first month of business.

ALTERNATE MULTI-CONCEPT PROBLEMS

Problem 3-5A Identification of Events with Source Documents   LO1 • 2

Many events are linked to a source document. The following is a list of events that occurred in an entity:

a. Paid a security deposit and six months' rent on a building.
b. Hired three employees and agreed to pay them $400 per week.
c. Provided services to a customer for cash.
d. Reported a fire that destroyed a billboard that is on the entity's property and that is owned and maintained by another entity.
e. Received payment of bills from customers.
f. Purchased stock in another entity to gain some control over it.
g. Signed a note at the bank and received cash.
h. Contracted with a cleaning service to maintain the interior of the building in good repair. No money is paid at this time.

(Continued)

Required

For each item (a) through (h), indicate whether the event should or should not be recorded in the entity's accounts. For each item that should be recorded in the entity's books:

1. Identify one or more source documents that are generated from the event.
2. Identify which source document would be used to record an event when it produces more than one source document.
3. For each document, identify the information that is most useful in recording the event in the accounts.

LO 1 • 3 Problem 3-6A Transaction Analysis

Overnight Delivery Inc. is incorporated on February 1 and enters into the following transactions during its first month of operations:

February 15: Received $8,000 cash from customer accounts.

February 26: Provided $16,800 of services on account during the month.

February 27: Received a $3,400 bill from the local service station for gas and oil used during February.

February 28: Paid $400 for wages earned by employees for the month.

February 28: Paid $3,230 for February advertising.

February 28: Declared and paid $2,000 cash dividends to stockholders.

Required

1. Prepare a table to summarize the preceding transactions as they affect the accounting equation. Use the format in Exhibit 3-1.
2. Explain why you agree or disagree with the following: The transactions on February 28 all represent expenses for the month of February because cash was paid. The transaction on February 27 does not represent an expense in February because cash has not yet been paid.

LO 1 • 3 Problem 3-7A Transaction Analysis and a Balance Sheet

Krittersbegone Inc. was organized on July 1 by a group of technicians to provide termite inspections and treatment to homeowners and small businesses. The following transactions occurred during the first month of business:

July 2: Received contributions of $3,000 from each of the six owners in exchange for shares of stock.

July 3: Paid $1,000 rent for the month of July.

July 5: Purchased flashlights, tools, spray equipment, and ladders for $18,000, with a down payment of $5,000 and the balance due in 30 days.

July 17: Paid a $200 bill for the distribution of door-to-door advertising.

July 28: Paid August rent and July utilities to the landlord in the amounts of $1,000 and $450, respectively.

July 30: Received $8,000 in cash from homeowners for services performed during the month. In addition, billed $7,500 to other customers for services performed during the month. Billings are due in 30 days.

July 30: Paid commissions of $9,500 to the technicians for July.

Required

1. Prepare a table to summarize the preceding transactions as they affect the accounting equation. Ignore depreciation expense. Use the format in Exhibit 3-1.
2. Prepare a classified balance sheet dated July 31. From the balance sheet, what cash inflow and what cash outflow can you predict in the month of August? Who would be interested in the cash flow information? Why?

Problem 3-8A Accounts Used to Record Transactions (Appendix)   LO3 • 5

A list of accounts, with an identifying number for each, is provided. Following the list of accounts is a series of transactions entered into by a company during its first year of operations.

Required

For each transaction, indicate the account or accounts that should be debited and credited.

1. Cash	6. Land	11. Retained Earnings
2. Accounts Receivable	7. Accounts Payable	12. Service Revenue
3. Prepaid Insurance	8. Income Taxes Payable	13. Wage and Salary Expense
4. Office Supplies	9. Notes Payable	14. Utilities Expense
5. Automobiles	10. Capital Stock	15. Income Tax Expense

	Accounts	
Transactions	Debited	Credited
Example: Purchased office supplies for cash.	4	1
a. Issued capital stock for cash.		
b. Purchased an automobile and signed a 60-day note for the total amount.		
c. Acquired land in exchange for capital stock.		
d. Received cash from clients for services performed during the month.		
e. Paid employees salaries and wages earned during the month.		
f. Purchased flyers and signs from a printer, payment due in ten days.		
g. Paid for the flyers and signs purchased in (f).		
h. Received monthly telephone bill; payment is due within ten days of receipt.		
i. Paid for a six-month liability insurance policy.		
j. Paid monthly telephone bill.		
k. Computed amount of taxes due based on the income of the period and paid the amount.		

Problem 3-9A Transaction Analysis and Journal Entries Recorded Directly in T Accounts   LO3 • 4 • 5

Three friends organized Rapid City Roller Rink on October 1. The following transactions occurred during the first month of operations:

October 1:   Received contribution of $22,000 from each of the three principal owners of the new business in exchange for shares of stock.

October 2:   Purchased land valued at $15,000 and a building valued at $75,000. The seller agreed to accept a down payment of $9,000 and a five-year promissory note for the balance.

October 3:   Purchased new tables and chairs for the lounge at the roller rink at a cost of $25,000, paying $5,000 down and agreeing to pay for the remainder in 60 days.

October 9:   Purchased 100 pairs of roller skates for cash at $35 per pair.

October 12: Purchased food and drinks for $2,500 on an open account. The company has 30 days to pay for the concession supplies.

October 13: Sold tickets for cash of $400 and took in $750 at the concession stand.

October 17: Rented out the roller rink to a local community group for $750. The community group is to pay one-half of the bill within five working days and has 30 days to pay the remainder.

October 23: Received 50% of the amount billed to the community group.

October 24: Sold tickets for cash of $500 and took in $1,200 at the concession stand.

October 26: The three friends, acting on behalf of Rapid City Roller Rink, paid a dividend of $250 on the shares of stock owned by each of them, or $750 in total.

October 27: Paid $1,275 for utilities.

October 30: Paid wages and salaries of $2,250.

October 31: Sold tickets for cash of $700 and took in $1,300 at the concession stand.

(Continued)

Required

1. Prepare a table to summarize the preceding transactions as they affect the accounting equation. Ignore depreciation expense and interest expense. Use the format in Exhibit 3-1. Identify each transaction with a date.
2. Record each transaction directly in T accounts using the dates preceding the transactions to identify them in the accounts. Each account involved in the problem needs a separate T account.

LO4 • 7   Problem 3-10A Trial Balance and Financial Statements (Appendix)

Refer to the table for Rapid City Roller Rink in part (1) of Problem 3-9A.

Required

1. Prepare a trial balance at October 31.
2. Prepare an income statement for the month of October.
3. Prepare a statement of retained earnings for the month of October.
4. Prepare a classified balance sheet at October 31.

LO3 • 5 • 6   Problem 3-11A Journal Entries (Appendix)

Castle Consulting Agency began business in February. The transactions entered into by Castle during its first month of operations are as follows:

a. Acquired articles of incorporation from the state and issued 10,000 shares of capital stock in exchange for $150,000 in cash.
b. Paid monthly rent of $400.
c. Signed a five-year promissory note for $100,000 at the bank.
d. Purchased software to be used on future jobs. The software costs $950 and is expected to be used on five to eight jobs over the next two years.
e. Billed customers $12,500 for work performed during the month.
f. Paid office personnel $3,000 for the month of February.
g. Received a utility bill of $100. The total amount is due in 30 days.

Required

Prepare in journal form, the entry to record each transaction.

LO3 • 4 • 5 • 7   Problem 3-12A Journal Entries Recorded Directly in T Accounts

Refer to the transactions for Castle Consulting Agency in Problem 3-11A.

Required

1. Record each transaction directly in T accounts using the letters preceding the transactions to identify them in the accounts. Each account involved in the problem needs a separate T account.
2. Prepare a trial balance at February 28.

LO3 • 4 • 5 • 7   Problem 3-13A Entries Prepared from a Trial Balance and Proof of the Cash Balance (Appendix)

Russell Company was incorporated on January 1 with the issuance of capital stock in return for $120,000 of cash contributed by the owners. The only other transaction entered into prior to beginning operations was the issuance of a $50,000 note payable in exchange for equipment and fixtures. The following trial balance was prepared at the end of the first month by the bookkeeper for Russell Company:

Russell Company
Trial Balance
January 31

Account Titles	Debits	Credits
Cash	$?	
Accounts Receivable	30,500	
Equipment and Fixtures	50,000	

Account Titles	Debits	Credits
Wages Payable		$ 10,000
Notes Payable		50,000
Capital Stock		120,000
Service Revenue		60,500
Wage and Salary Expense	24,600	
Advertising Expense	12,500	
Rent Expense	5,200	

Required

1. Determine the balance in the Cash account.
2. Identify all of the transactions that affected the Cash account during the month. Use a T account to prove what the balance in Cash will be after all transactions are recorded.

Problem 3-14A Journal Entries (Appendix)   LO 3 • 5 • 6

Refer to the transactions for Overnight Delivery Inc. in Problem 3-6A.

Required

1. Prepare journal entries on the books of Overnight to record the transactions entered into during February.
2. Explain why you agree or disagree with following: The transactions on February 28 all represent expenses for the month of February because cash was paid. The transaction on February 27 does not represent an expense because cash has not yet been paid.

Problem 3-15A Journal Entries and a Balance Sheet (Appendix)   LO 3 • 5 • 6

Refer to the transactions for Krittersbegone in Problem 3-7A.

Required

1. Prepare journal entries on the books of Krittersbegone to record the transactions entered into during the month. Ignore depreciation expense.
2. Prepare a classified balance sheet dated July 31. From the balance sheet, what cash inflow and what cash outflow can you predict in the month of August? Who would be interested in the cash flow information? Why?

DECISION CASES

Reading and Interpreting Financial Statements

Decision Case 3-1 Comparing Two Companies in the Same Industry: LO4
Chipotle and Panera Bread

Refer to the income statements for **Chipotle** and **Panera Bread** reproduced at the back of the book.

REAL WORLD

Required

1. Which is the largest expense for each company in the most recent year? What is its dollar amount? Explain why this might be the largest expense given the nature of each company's business.
2. One of the accounts on each company's income statement is "General and administrative expenses." For each of the two most recent years, compute the ratio of this expense to Total revenues for each company. Did this ratio increase or decrease from one year to the next for each company? Which company has the lower ratio in each of the two years?
3. Compute the ratio of income tax expense (Chipotle uses the term "Provision for income taxes") to income before income taxes for the two most recent years for each company. Did this ratio increase or decrease from one year to the next for each company? Which company has the lower ratio for each of the two years?

REAL WORLD

LO3   **Decision Case 3-2** **Reading and Interpreting Panera Bread's Statement of Cash Flows**

Refer to **Panera Bread**'s statement of cash flows for the year ended December 29, 2015, as reproduced at the end of the book.

Required

1. What amount did the company spend on additions to property and equipment during the year? Determine the effect on the accounting equation of these additions.
2. What amount did the company receive from the issuance of long-term debt during the year? Determine the effect on the accounting equation from the issuance of this long-term debt.

REAL WORLD

LO1 • 3   **Decision Case 3-3** **Reading and Interpreting Carnival Corporation's Balance Sheet**

Carnival Corporation is the largest cruise company in the world. The following item appears in the current liabilities section of it's balance sheet included in the Form 10-K for the year ended November 30, 2015:

Customer deposits $3,272 million

In addition, Note 2 to the financial statements includes the following:

Revenue and Expense Recognition
Guest cruise deposits represent unearned revenues and are initially included in customer deposit liabilities when received. Customer deposits are subsequently recognized as cruise revenues, together with revenues from onboard and other activities, and all associated direct costs and expenses of a voyage are recognized as cruise costs and expenses, upon completion of voyages with durations of ten nights or less and on a pro rata basis for voyages in excess of ten nights....

Required

1. What economic event caused Carnival to incur this liability? Was it an external or internal event?
2. Describe the effect on the accounting equation from the transaction to record the customer deposits.
3. Assume that one customer makes a deposit of $1,000 on a future cruise. Determine the effect on the accounting equation from this transaction.
4. What economic event will cause Carnival to reduce its customer deposits liability? Is this an external or internal event?

Making Financial Decisions

LO2 • 3   **Decision Case 3-4** **Cash Flow versus Net Income**

Shelia Young started a real estate business at the beginning of January. After approval by the state for a charter to incorporate, she issued 1,000 shares of stock to herself and deposited $20,000 in a bank account under the name Young Properties. Because business was booming, she spent all of her time during the first month selling properties rather than keeping financial records.

At the end of January, Shelia comes to you with the following plight:

I put $20,000 in to start this business at the beginning of the month. My January 31 bank statement shows a balance of $17,000. After all of my efforts, it appears as if I'm "in the hole" already! On the other hand, that seems impossible—we sold five properties for clients during the month. The total sales value of these properties was $600,000, and I received a commission of 5% on each sale. Granted, one of the five sellers still owes me an $8,000 commission, but the other four have been collected in full. Three of the sales, totaling $400,000, were actually made by my assistants. I pay them 4% of the sales value of a property. Sure, I have a few office expenses for my car, utilities, and a secretary, but that's about it. How can I have possibly lost $3,000 this month?

You agree to help Shelia figure out how she did this month. The bank statement is helpful. The total deposits during the month amount to $22,000. Shelia explains that this amount represents the commissions on the four sales collected so far. The canceled checks reveal the following expenditures:

Check No.	Payee—Memo at Bottom of Check	Amount
101	Stevens Office Supply	$ 2,000
102	Why Walk, Let's Talk Motor Co.—new car	3,000
103	City of Westbrook—heat and lights	500
104	Alice Hill—secretary	2,200
105	Ace Property Management—office rent for month	1,200
106	Jerry Hayes (sales assistant)	10,000
107	Joan Harper (sales assistant)	6,000
108	Don's Fillitup—gas and oil for car	100

According to Shelia, the $2,000 check to Stevens Office Supply represents the down payment on a word processor and a copier for the office. The remaining balance of $3,000 must be paid to Stevens by February 15. Similarly, the $3,000 check is the down payment on a car for the business. A $12,000 note was given to the car dealer and is due along with interest in one year.

Required

1. Prepare an income statement for the month of January for Young Properties.
2. Prepare a statement of cash flows for the month of January for Young Properties.
3. Draft a memo to Shelia Young explaining as simply and clearly as possible why she *did*, in fact, have a profitable first month in business but experienced a decrease in her Cash account. Support your explanation with any necessary figures.
4. The down payments on the car and the office equipment are reflected on the statement of cash flows. They are assets that will benefit the business for a number of years. Do you think that any of the cost associated with the acquisition of these assets should be recognized in some way on the income statement? Explain your answer.

Decision Case 3-5 Loan Request (Appendix)

LO3 • 5 • 7

Simon Fraser started a landscaping and lawn-care business in April by investing $20,000 cash in the business in exchange for capital stock. Because his business is in the Midwest, the season begins in April and concludes in September. He prepared the following trial balance (with accounts in alphabetical order) at the end of the first season in business:

Fraser Landscaping
Trial Balance
September 30

	Debits	Credits
Accounts Payable	—	$13,000
Accounts Receivable	$23,000	
Capital Stock		20,000
Cash	1,200	
Gas and Oil Expense	15,700	
Insurance Expense	2,500	
Landscaping Revenue		33,400
Lawn Care Revenue		24,000
Mowing Equipment	5,000	
Rent Expense	6,000	
Salaries Expense	22,000	
Truck	15,000	
Totals	$90,400	$90,400

Simon is pleased with his first year in business. "I paid myself a salary of $22,000 during the year and still have $1,200 in the bank. Sure, I have a few bills outstanding, but my accounts receivable will more than cover those." In fact, Simon is so happy with the first year that he has come to you in your role as a lending officer at the local bank to ask for a $20,000 loan to allow him to add another truck and mowing equipment for the second season.

(Continued)

Required

1. From your reading of the trial balance, what do you believe Simon did with the $20,000 in cash he originally contributed to the business? Determine the effect on the accounting equation of the transaction that you think took place.
2. Prepare an income statement for the six months ended September 30.
3. The mowing equipment and truck are assets that will benefit the business for a number of years. Do you think that any of the costs associated with the purchase of these assets should have been recognized as expenses in the first year? How would this have affected the income statement?
4. Prepare a classified balance sheet as of September 30. As a banker, what two items on the balance sheet concern you the most? Explain your answer.
5. As a banker, would you loan Simon $20,000 to expand his business during the second year? Draft a memo to respond to Simon's request for the loan, indicating whether you will make the loan.

Ethical Decision Making

LO1 • 3   **Decision Case 3-6**   **Revenue Recognition**

You are controller for an architectural firm whose accounting year ends on December 31. As part of the management team, you receive a year-end bonus directly related to the firm's earnings for the year. One of your duties is to review the transactions recorded by the bookkeepers. A new bookkeeper recorded the receipt of $10,000 in cash as an increase in cash and an increase in service revenue. The $10,000 is a deposit and the bookkeeper explains to you that the firm plans to provide the services to the client in March of the following year.

Required

1. Did the bookkeeper correctly record the client's deposit? Explain your answer.
2. What would you do as controller for the firm? Do you have a responsibility to do anything to correct the books? Explain your answer.

LO3 • 5 • 6   **Decision Case 3-7**   **Delay in the Posting of a Journal Entry (Appendix)**

ETHICAL DECISION MODEL

As assistant controller for a small consulting firm, you are responsible for recording and posting the daily cash receipts and disbursements to the ledger accounts. After you have posted the entries, your boss, the controller, prepares a trial balance and the financial statements. You make the following entries on June 30:

June 30	Cash	1,430	
	Accounts Receivable	1,950	
	Service Revenue		3,380
	To record daily cash sales and sales on account.		
June 30	Advertising Expense	12,500	
	Utilities Expense	22,600	
	Rent Expense	24,000	
	Salary and Wage Expense	17,400	
	Cash		76,500
	To record daily cash disbursements.		

The daily cash disbursements are much larger on June 30 than on any other day because many of the company's major bills are paid on the last day of the month. After you have recorded these two transactions and *before* you have posted them to the ledger accounts, your boss comes to you with the following request:

> As you are aware, the first half of the year has been a tough one for the consulting industry and for our business in particular. With first-half bonuses based on net income, I am wondering whether you or I will get a bonus this time around. However, I have a suggestion that should allow us to receive something for our hard work and at the same time not hurt anyone. Go ahead and post the June 30 cash receipts to the ledger, but don't bother to post that day's cash disbursements. Even though the treasurer writes the

checks on the last day of the month and you normally journalize the transaction on the same day, it is silly to bother posting the entry to the ledger since it takes at least a week for the checks to clear the bank.

Required

Use the Ethical Decision Framework in Exhibit 1-9 to complete the following requirements:

1. **Recognize an ethical dilemma:** Explain why the controller's request will result in an increase in net income. On the basis of your answer, what ethical dilemma(s) do you now face?

2. **Analyze the key elements in the situation:**

    a. Do you agree with the controller that the omission of the journal entry on June 30 "will not hurt anyone"? Who may benefit from the omission of the entry? Who may be harmed?

    b. How are they likely to benefit or be harmed?

    c. What rights or claims may be violated?

    d. What specific interests are in conflict?

    e. What are your responsibilities and obligations?

3. **List alternatives and evaluate the impact of each on those affected:** As assistant controller, what are your options in dealing with the ethical dilemma(s) you identified in (1) above? Which provides stockholders and other outsiders with information that is most relevant, most complete, most neutral, and most free from error?

4. **Select the best alternative:** Among the alternatives, which one would you select? Explain why.

Answers

MODULE 1 Answers to Questions

1. Both external and internal events affect an entity. An external event involves interaction with someone outside of the entity. For example, the purchase of land is an external event. An internal event takes place entirely within the entity. The transfer of raw materials into production is an internal event.

2. Source documents are the basis for recording transactions. They provide the evidence, or documentation, needed to recognize an event for accounting purposes. Purchase invoices, time cards, and cash register tapes are all examples of source documents.

3. A chart of accounts is simply a numerical listing of all the accounts. The general ledger is the actual file or book that contains all the accounts.

MODULE 1 Answers to Apply

1. Purchase invoice: acquisition of goods or services from a supplier

    Sales invoice: sale of goods or services to a customer

    Cash register tape: cash sale of goods or services to a customer

    Time cards: payment of periodic payroll

    Promissory note: borrowing money in return for promise to repay in the future with interest

2. The three elements in the accounting equation are assets, liabilities, and stockholders' equity. Stockholders'

equity consists of capital stock and retained earnings. Net income, as reported on the income statement, is an addition to retained earnings, which appears on the balance sheet. This connection between net income and retained earnings provides a link between the income statement and the balance sheet.

3. The bank's assets in the form of a note receivable increase $5,000 and its assets in the form of cash decrease $5,000.

4. If the company borrows $5 million, assets in the form of cash increase $5 million and liabilities in the form of a note payable increase $5 million. If the company uses the money to buy new ski lifts, assets in the form of property, plant and equipment increase $5 million and assets in the form of cash decrease $5 million.

MODULE 2 Answers to Questions

1. The term double-entry system of accounting means that every transaction is entered in at least two accounts on opposite sides of T accounts. In this system, every transaction is recorded in such a way that the equality of debits and credits is maintained, and in the process, the accounting equation is kept in balance.

2. Assets are positive in that they represent future economic benefits. It is merely a matter of convention that an asset is increased with a debit. An expense is negative in the sense that it reduces net income, which in turn reduces retained earnings, one of the two elements of owners' equity. Because owners' equity is on the opposite side of the accounting equation from assets, it is increased with a credit. Therefore, any item that reduces owners' equity, like an expense, is itself increased with a debit.

3. There are two sides to every transaction. The two sides of the transaction when a dividend is paid are the decrease in cash and the decrease in retained earnings. Assets are increased with debits and decreased with credits. Cash is an asset and is therefore decreased with a credit. Retained Earnings is on the opposite side of the accounting equation from assets and is therefore increased with a credit. Retained Earnings is decreased with a debit. Because dividends are a decrease in retained earnings, they are increased with a debit.

4. When you deposit money in your account, the bank has a liability. The entry on the bank's books consists of a debit to Cash and a credit to some type of liability account, such as Customers' Deposits. Therefore, when you make a deposit, the bank "credits" your account; that is, it increases its liability.

MODULE 2 Answers to Apply

1. Prepaid Insurance: BS
   Sales Revenue: IS
   Income Taxes Payable: BS
   Accounts Receivable: BS
   Utilities Expense: IS
   Furniture and Fixtures: BS
   Retained Earnings: BS

2. Accounts Payable: credit
   Office Supplies: debit
   Interest Revenue: credit
   Income Tax Expense: debit
   Income Tax Payable: credit
   Cash: debit
   Common Stock: credit
   Land: debit

MODULE 3 Answers to Questions

1. A business actually saves time by first recording transactions in a journal and then posting them to the ledger. Because of the sheer volume of transactions, it would be impractical to prepare financial statements directly from the journal. The journal serves as a book of original entry; the ledger accounts are the basis for preparing a trial balance, which in turn is used to prepare the financial statements.

2. At the time of posting, the Posting Reference column of the account in the ledger is filled in with the page number of the journal entry. At the same time, the account number is placed in the Posting Reference column of the journal. This cross-referencing system used in posting allows the accountant to trace an entry made in the journal to the account it was posted to, or, conversely, to trace from an account back to the entry in the journal.

3. A trial balance proves the equality of debits and credits. It does not prove that the correct accounts were debited and credited or that the correct amounts were necessarily recorded. It simply ensures that the balance of all of the debits in the ledger accounts is equal to the balance of all the credits at any point in time.

MODULE 3 Answers to Apply

1.

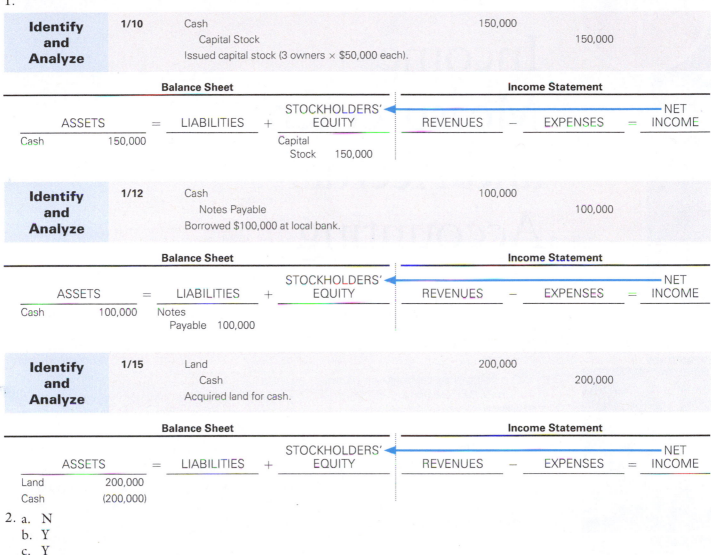

Identify and Analyze	1/10	Cash		150,000	
		Capital Stock			150,000
		Issued capital stock (3 owners × $50,000 each).			

	Balance Sheet					Income Statement				
ASSETS		=	LIABILITIES	+	STOCKHOLDERS' EQUITY	REVENUES	−	EXPENSES	=	NET INCOME
Cash	150,000				Capital Stock 150,000					

Identify and Analyze	1/12	Cash		100,000	
		Notes Payable			100,000
		Borrowed $100,000 at local bank.			

	Balance Sheet					Income Statement				
ASSETS		=	LIABILITIES	+	STOCKHOLDERS' EQUITY	REVENUES	−	EXPENSES	=	NET INCOME
Cash	100,000		Notes Payable 100,000							

Identify and Analyze	1/15	Land		200,000	
		Cash			200,000
		Acquired land for cash.			

	Balance Sheet					Income Statement				
ASSETS		=	LIABILITIES	+	STOCKHOLDERS' EQUITY	REVENUES	−	EXPENSES	=	NET INCOME
Land	200,000									
Cash	(200,000)									

2. a. N
   b. Y
   c. Y

Answers to Connect to the Real World

3-1 (p. 102)

The acquisition of a new ski lift is an external event for Vail Resorts. Depreciation of the lift is an internal event.

3-2 (p. 107)

The three segments of Vail Resorts' business are Mountain, Lodging, and Real Estate. The largest of these is Mountain, with net revenue of $1,104,029,000 and operating expense of $777,147,000.

Answers to Key Terms Quiz

Quiz 1: Processing Accounting Information

2	Event
5	External event
3	Internal event
8	Transaction
4	Source document
6	Account
1	Chart of accounts
7	General ledger

Quiz 2: Appendix

4	Debit
2	Credit
8	Double-entry system
6	Journal
5	Posting
3	Journalizing
7	General journal
1	Trial balance

4

Income Measurement and Accrual Accounting

MODULES	LEARNING OBJECTIVES	WHY IS THIS CHAPTER IMPORTANT?
1 Accrual Accounting Principles	**LO1** Explain the significance of recognition and measurement in the preparation and use of financial statements. **LO2** Explain the differences between the cash and accrual bases of accounting. **LO3** Describe the revenue recognition principle and explain its application in various situations. **LO4** Describe the matching principle and the various methods for recognizing expenses.	• You need to know what information the accrual basis of accounting provides to users of the statements that a cash basis does not. (See pp. 152–154.) • You need to know what the revenue recognition principle is and why it is important. (See p. 155.) • You need to know what is meant by the matching principle and how it is applied. (See pp. 155–157.)
2 Adjustments	**LO5** Identify the four major types of adjustments and analyze their effects on the financial statements.	• You need to know the various types of adjustments companies make and how they are recorded in an accounting system. (See pp. 158–166.)
3 The Accounting Cycle (Appendix)	**LO6** Explain the steps in the accounting cycle and the significance of each step.	• You need to know the steps in the accounting cycle that lead up to a set of financial statements. (See pp. 172–174.)

NORDSTROM, INC.

From a single shoe store in Seattle, Washington, in 1901, **Nordstrom, Inc.**, has grown to become one of the most highly respected fashion retailers in the country. With its reputation for superior customer service, sales climbed to a record $14.1 billion in fiscal year 2015.

If you are thinking of buying stock in Nordstrom, you need to be able to read and interpret its financial statements. And you cannot do this unless you understand the accrual system of accounting. A glimpse at Nordstrom's partial balance sheet shown here will help you begin to understand the important differences between the cash and accrual bases of accounting (we will focus on each of the four shaded acounts).

Accounts receivable arise when Nordstrom sells on credit, either when a customer uses the company's private label card or some other

card. **Accrued revenues**, such as accounts receivable, appear on the balance sheet when a company has recorded revenue but will only receive cash at a later date. Similarly, there are times when Nordstrom will record expense but only pay cash at a later date. Accrued salaries, wages, and related benefits reported under the current liabilities are examples of **accrued expenses**.

Alternatively, Nordstrom may receive cash prior to making a sale. This happens when someone buys a gift card. Nordstrom includes in its other current liabilities the amount of gift cards that have not yet been redeemed. This liability is an example of **deferred revenue**. Finally, Nordstrom sometimes pays cash prior to actually incurring an expense. **Prepaid expenses** represent amounts the retailer has paid in advance for items such as supplies. The company will record the expense as the supplies are used.

Nordstrom, Inc. Consolidated Balance Sheets (Partial)		
(in millions)	January 30, 2016	January 31, 2015
Assets		
Current assets:		
Cash and cash equivalents	$ 595	$ 827
Accounts receivable, net	196	2,306
Merchandise inventories	1,945	1,733
Current deferred tax assets, net	—	256
Prepaid expenses and other	278	102
Total current assets	3,014	5,224
Liabilities and Shareholders' Equity		
Current liabilities:		
Accounts payable	$1,324	$1,328
Accrued salaries, wages and related benefits	416	416
Other current liabilities	1,161	1,048
Current portion of long-term debt	10	8
Total current liabilities	2,911	2,800

The accompanying Notes to Consolidated Financial Statements are an integral part of these financial statements.

Source: Nordstrom Inc. Form 10-K for the fiscal year ended January 30, 2016.

MODULE 1 ACCRUAL ACCOUNTING PRINCIPLES

LO1 Explain the significance of recognition and measurement in the preparation and use of financial statements.

To successfully communicate information to the users of financial statements, accountants and managers must answer two questions:

1. **What economic events should be communicated, or *recognized*, in the statements?**
2. **How should the effects of these events be *measured* in the statements?**

The dual concepts of recognition and measurement are crucial to the success of accounting as a form of communication.

Recognition

Recognition

The process of recording an item in the financial statements as an asset, a liability, a revenue, an expense, or the like.

"Recognition is the process of formally recording or incorporating an item into the financial statements of an entity as an asset, a liability, a revenue, an expense, or the like. Recognition includes depiction of an item in both words and numbers, with the amount included in the totals of the financial statements."[1] We see in this definition the central idea behind general-purpose financial statements. They are a form of communication between the entity and external users. Stockholders, bankers, and other creditors have limited access to relevant information about a company. They depend on the periodic financial statements that management issues to provide the necessary information to make decisions. Acting on behalf of management, accountants have a moral and ethical responsibility to provide users with financial information that will be useful in making their decisions. The process by which the accountant depicts, or describes, the effects of economic events on the entity is called *recognition*.

Assets, liabilities, revenues, and expenses depicted in financial statements are representations. Simply stated, the accountant cannot show a stockholder or another user the company's assets, such as cash and buildings. What the user sees in a set of financial statements is a depiction of the real thing. That is, the accountant describes, with words and numbers, the various items in a set of financial statements. As society and the business environment have become more complex, the accounting profession has searched for ways to improve financial statements as a means of communicating with statement users.

Measurement

Accountants depict a financial statement item in both words and numbers. The accountant must *quantify* the effects of economic events on the entity. It is not enough to decide that an event is important and thus warrants recognition in the financial statements. To be able to recognize an event, the statement preparer must measure the event's financial effects on the company.

Measurement of an item in financial statements requires that two choices be made:

1. The accountant must decide on the *attribute* to be measured.
2. A scale of measurement, or *unit of measure*, must be chosen.

Choice 1: The Attribute to Be Measured
Assume that a company holds a parcel of real estate as an investment. What attribute—that is, *characteristic*—of the property should be used to measure and thus recognize it as an asset on the balance sheet? The cost of the asset at the time it is acquired is the most logical choice. *Cost* is the amount of cash or its equivalent paid to acquire the asset. But how do we report the property on a balance sheet a year from now?

Historical cost

The amount paid for an asset and used as a basis for recognizing it on the balance sheet and carrying it on later balance sheets.

• The simplest approach is to show the property on the balance sheet at its original or **historical cost**. The use of historical cost is not only simple but also an amount that can be agreed upon. Assume that two accountants are asked to independently measure the cost of the asset. After examining the sales contract for the land, they should arrive at the same amount.

---

[1] *Statement of Financial Accounting Concepts No. 5,* "Recognition and Measurement in Financial Statements of Business Enterprises" (Stamford, Conn.: Financial Accounting Standards Board, December 1984), par. 6.

- An alternative to historical cost as the attribute to be measured is **current value**. Current value is the amount of cash or its equivalent that could be received currently from the sale of the asset. For the company's piece of property, current value is the *estimated* selling price of the land, reduced by any commissions or other fees involved in making the sale. But the amount is only an estimate, not an actual amount.

Current value
The amount of cash or its equivalent that could be received by selling an asset currently.

The choice between current value and historical cost as the attribute to be measured is a good example of the trade-offs that must sometimes be made. As indicated earlier, historical cost is an amount that can be agreed upon. But is it as relevant to the needs of the decision makers as current value? Put yourself in the position of a banker trying to decide whether to lend money to the company. In evaluating the company's assets as collateral for the loan, is it more relevant to your decision to know what the firm paid for a piece of land 20 years ago or what it could be sold for today? But what *could* the property be sold for today? Two accountants might not arrive at the same current value for the land. Whereas value or selling price may be more relevant to your decision on the loan, differing opinions on an asset's current value make use of this attribute more difficult.

Because of its objective nature, historical cost is the attribute used to measure many of the assets recognized on the balance sheet. However, certain other attributes, such as current value, have increased in popularity in recent years. Other chapters of the book will discuss some of the alternatives to historical cost.

Choice 2: The Unit of Measure Regardless of the attribute of an item to be measured, it is still necessary to choose a yardstick, or unit of measure. The yardstick currently used is units of money. *Money* is something accepted as a medium of exchange or as a means of payment. The unit of money in the United States is the dollar. In Japan, the medium of exchange is the yen; and in Great Britain, it is the pound.

The use of the dollar as a unit of measure for financial transactions is widely accepted. The *stability* of the dollar as a yardstick is subject to considerable debate, however. Assume that you are thinking about buying a certain parcel of land. As part of your decision process, you measure the dimensions of the property and determine that the lot is 80 feet wide and 120 feet deep. Thus, the unit of measure used to determine the lot's size is the square foot. The company that owns the land offers to sell it for $10,000. Although the offer sounds attractive, you decide against the purchase today.

You return in one year to take a second look at the lot. You measure the lot again and, not surprisingly, find the width still to be 80 feet and the depth 120 feet. The owner is still willing to sell the lot for $10,000. This may appear to be the same price as last year. But the *purchasing power* of the unit of measure, the dollar, may have changed since last year. Even though the foot is a stable measuring unit, the dollar often is not. A *decline* in the purchasing power of the dollar is evidenced by *inflation*, or a continuing *rise* in the general level of prices in an economy. For example, rather than paying $10,000 last year to buy the lot, you could have spent the $10,000 on other goods or services. However, a year later the same $10,000 may not buy the same amount of goods and services.

In the past, the accounting profession has experimented with financial statements adjusted for the changing value of the dollar. As inflation has declined in recent years in the United States, the debate over the use of the dollar as a stable measuring unit has somewhat subsided.[2] It is still important to recognize the inherent weakness in the use of a measuring unit that is subject to change, however.

Summary of Recognition and Measurement in Financial Statements

The purpose of financial statements is to communicate various types of economic information about a company. The job of the accountant is to decide which information should be recognized in the financial statements and how the effects of that information

---

[2] The rate of inflation in some countries, most noticeably those in South America, has far exceeded the rate in the United States. Companies operating in some of these countries with hyperinflationary economies are required to make adjustments to their statements.

on the entity should be measured. Exhibit 4-1 summarizes the role of recognition and measurement in the preparation of financial statements.

EXHIBIT 4-1 Recognition and Measurement in Financial Statements

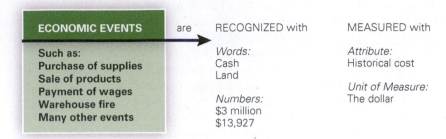

The Accrual Basis of Accounting

LO2 Explain the differences between the cash and accrual bases of accounting.

The accrual basis of accounting is the foundation for the measurement of income in our modern system of accounting. The best way to understand the accrual basis is to compare it with the simpler cash approach.

Comparing the Cash and Accrual Bases of Accounting

The cash and accrual bases of accounting differ with respect to the *timing* of the recognition of revenues and expenses.

EXAMPLE 4-1 Comparing the Cash and Accrual Bases of Accounting

Assume that on July 24, Barbara White, a salesperson for Spiffy House Painters, contracts with a homeowner to repaint a house for $1,000. A large crew comes in and paints the house the next day, July 25. The customer has 30 days to pay and does, in fact, pay Spiffy on August 25. When should Spiffy recognize the $1,000 as revenue—as soon as the contract is signed on July 24; on July 25, when the work is done; or on August 25, when the customer pays the bill?

When Is Revenue Recognized?

Cash basis
A system of accounting in which revenues are recognized when cash is received and expenses are recognized when cash is paid.

- In an income statement prepared on a **cash basis**, revenues are recognized when cash is *received*. Thus, on a cash basis, the $1,000 would not be recognized as revenue until the cash is collected, on August 25.

- In an income statement prepared on an **accrual basis**, revenue is recognized when the company has *satisfied its performance obligation*.[3] For example, Spiffy paints the house on July 25, so this is the date it has performed its obligation and is the point at which $1,000 of revenue should be recognized.

Accrual basis

A system of accounting in which revenues are recognized when a performance obligation is satisfied and expenses are recognized when incurred.

Under the accrual basis, cash has not yet been received on July 25, but another account, Accounts Receivable, is recognized as an asset. This asset represents the right to receive cash in the future. The effect on the accounting equation when the job is completed can be identified and analyzed as follows:

Identify and Analyze

ACTIVITY: Operating
ACCOUNTS: Accounts Receivable Increase   Service Revenue Increase
STATEMENT(S): Balance Sheet and Income Statement

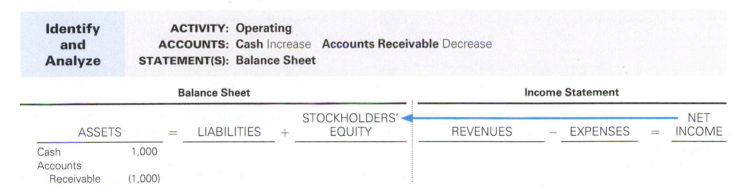

Balance Sheet				Income Statement				
ASSETS	=	LIABILITIES	+	STOCKHOLDERS' EQUITY	REVENUES	–	EXPENSES	= NET INCOME
Accounts Receivable 1,000				1,000	Service Revenue 1,000			1,000

At the time cash is collected, accounts receivable is reduced and cash is increased. The effect of the transaction can be identified and analyzed as follows:

Identify and Analyze

ACTIVITY: Operating
ACCOUNTS: Cash Increase   Accounts Receivable Decrease
STATEMENT(S): Balance Sheet

Balance Sheet				Income Statement				
ASSETS	=	LIABILITIES	+	STOCKHOLDERS' EQUITY	REVENUES	–	EXPENSES	= NET INCOME
Cash 1,000								
Accounts Receivable (1,000)								

Assume that Barbara White is paid a 10% commission for all contracts and is paid on the 15th of the month following the month a house is painted. Thus, for this job, she will receive a $100 commission check on August 15. When should Spiffy recognize her commission of $100 as an expense? On July 24, when White gets the homeowner to sign a contract? When the work is completed, on July 25? Or on August 15, when she receives the commission check? Again, on a cash basis, commission expense would be recognized on August 15, when cash is *paid* to the salesperson. But on an accrual basis, expenses are recognized when they are *incurred*. In Example 4-1 the commission expense is incurred when the house is painted, on July 25.

Exhibit 4-2 summarizes the essential differences between recognition of revenues and expenses on a cash basis and recognition on an accrual basis.

STUDY TIP

Think of "incurred" in this example to mean that Spiffy is responsible or liable for paying the commission, since the house has been painted.

---

[3] *Revenue from Contracts with Customers*, ASC Topic 606, Financial Accounting Standards Board, May 2014, Norwalk, CT.

EXHIBIT 4-2 Comparing the Cash and Accrual Bases of Accounting

	Cash Basis	Accrual Basis
Revenue is recognized	**When Received**	**When Performance Obligation Satisfied**
Expense is recognized	**When Paid**	**When Incurred**

What the Income Statement and the Statement of Cash Flows Reveal

Most business entities use the accrual basis of accounting. Thus, the income statement reflects the accrual basis. However, stockholders and creditors are also interested in information concerning the cash flows of an entity. The purpose of a statement of cash flows is to provide this information.

Each of these two financial statements serves a useful purpose:

- The income statement reflects the revenues and expenses on an accrual basis, regardless of when cash is received or paid.
- The statement of cash flows tells the reader about the actual cash inflows and outflows during a period of time.

EXAMPLE 4-2 Comparing the Income Statement and the Statement of Cash Flows

Recall the example of Glengarry Health Club in Chapter 3. The club's revenue is from two sources—memberships and court fees. Both forms of revenue are shown in the income statement below. Recall, however, that members have 30 days to pay and that at the end of the first month of operation, only $4,000 of the membership fees of $15,000 had been collected.

Now consider the partial statement of cash flows for the first month of operation, shown below the income statement. Because we want to compare the income statement to the statement of cash flows, only the Operating Activities section of the statement is shown below. (The Investing and Financing Activities sections have been omitted from the statement.) Why is net income for the month a *positive* $7,000 but cash from operating activities is a *negative* $4,000? Of the membership revenue of $15,000 reflected on the income statement, only $4,000 was collected in cash. Glengarry has accounts receivable for the other $11,000. Thus, cash from operating activities, as reflected on a statement of cash flows, is $11,000 *less* than net income of $7,000, or a negative $4,000.

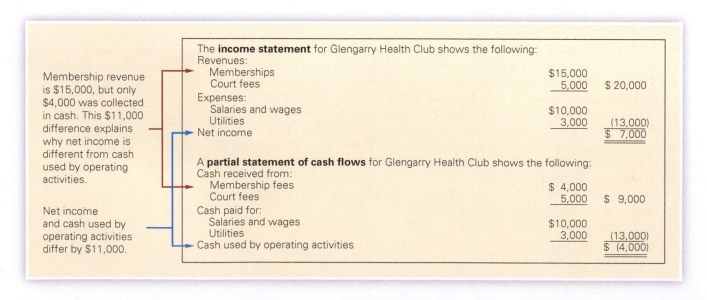

Membership revenue is $15,000, but only $4,000 was collected in cash. This $11,000 difference explains why net income is different from cash used by operating activities.

Net income and cash used by operating activities differ by $11,000.

The **income statement** for Glengarry Health Club shows the following:

Revenues:		
Memberships	$15,000	
Court fees	5,000	$ 20,000
Expenses:		
Salaries and wages	$10,000	
Utilities	3,000	(13,000)
Net income		$ 7,000

A **partial statement of cash flows** for Glengarry Health Club shows the following:

Cash received from:		
Membership fees	$ 4,000	
Court fees	5,000	$ 9,000
Cash paid for:		
Salaries and wages	$10,000	
Utilities	3,000	(13,000)
Cash used by operating activities		$ (4,000)

Accrual Accounting and Time Periods

The *time period assumption* was introduced in Chapter 1. We assume that it is possible to prepare an income statement that fairly reflects the earnings of a business for a specific period of time, such as a month or a year. However, it is somewhat artificial to divide the operations of a business into periods of time. The conflict arises because earning income is a process that takes place over a period of time rather than at any one point in time.

Consider an alternative to our present system of reporting the operations of a business on a periodic basis. A new business begins operations with an investment of $50,000. The business operates for ten years, during which time no records are kept other than a checkbook for the cash on deposit at the bank. At the end of the ten years, the owners decide to go their separate ways and convert all of their assets to cash. They divide among them the balance of $80,000 in the bank account. What is the profit of the business for the ten-year period? The answer is $30,000, the difference between the $50,000 original cash contributed and the $80,000 cash available at liquidation.

We could be very precise in measuring the income of a business if it were not necessary to artificially divide operations according to a calendar. Stockholders, bankers, and other interested parties cannot wait until a business liquidates to make decisions, however. They need information on a periodic basis. Thus, the justification for the accrual basis of accounting lies in the needs of financial statement users for periodic information on the financial position and the profitability of the entity.

The Revenue Recognition Principle

"**Revenues** are inflows or other enhancements of assets of an entity or settlements of its liabilities (or a combination of both) from delivering or producing goods, rendering services, or other activities that constitute the entity's ongoing major or central operations."[4] Two points should be noted about this formal definition of revenues. First, an asset is not always involved when revenue is recognized. The recognition of revenue may result from the settlement of a liability rather than from the acquisition of an asset. Second, entities generate revenue in different ways: some companies produce goods, others distribute or deliver the goods to users, and still others provide some type of service.

Under the **revenue recognition principle** (as recently revised by the FASB in *Revenues from Contracts with Customers*), revenues are recognized when a *performance obligation is satisfied*. This is normally interpreted to mean at the time the product or service is delivered to the customer. For example, **Chipotle's** obligation to perform is satisfied when it delivers a burrito to a customer. **Vail Resorts** satisfies its obligation to perform when it transports a skier up and down the mountain for a day.

In some cases, revenue is recognized continuously over time. In these cases, a product or service is not delivered at a specific point in time; instead, the earnings process takes place with the passage of time. Interest, for example, is the cost associated with the use of someone else's money for a period of time. When should a bank recognize the interest from granting a 90-day loan? Even though the interest may not be received until the loan is repaid, interest adds up every day the loan is outstanding. Later in the chapter, we will look at the process for recognizing interest not yet received. The same procedure is used to recognize revenue from rent that has not yet been collected.

Expense Recognition and the Matching Principle

Consider the following costs:

- A new office building is constructed.
- Supplies are purchased.

LO3 Describe the revenue recognition principle and explain its application in various situations.

Revenues
Inflows of assets or settlements of liabilities from delivering or producing goods, rendering services, or conducting other activities.

Revenue recognition principle
Revenues are recognized when a performance obligation is satisfied.

LO4 Describe the matching principle and the various methods for recognizing expenses.

---

[4] *Statement of Financial Accounting Concepts No. 6,* "Elements of Financial Statements" (Stamford, Conn.: Financial Accounting Standards Board, December 1985), par. 78.

- Employees perform services.
- The electric meter is read.

In each of those situations, there is a cost, regardless of when cash is paid. Conceptually, **anytime a cost is incurred, an asset is acquired**. However, according to the definition in Chapter 1, an asset represents a future economic benefit. An asset ceases being an asset and becomes an expense when the economic benefits from having incurred the cost have expired. Assets are unexpired costs, and expenses are expired costs.

At what point do costs expire and become expenses? The expense recognition principle requires that expenses be recognized in different ways depending on the nature of the cost. The ideal approach to recognizing expenses is to match them with revenues. Under the **matching principle**, the accountant attempts to associate revenues of a period with the costs necessary to generate those revenues. For certain types of expenses, a direct form of matching is possible; for others, it is necessary to associate costs with a particular period. The classic example of direct matching is cost of goods sold expense with sales revenue. Cost of goods sold is the cost of the inventory associated with a particular sale. A cost is incurred and an asset is recorded when the inventory is purchased. The asset, inventory, becomes an expense when it is sold.

An indirect form of matching is used to recognize the benefits associated with certain types of costs, most noticeably long-term assets such as buildings and equipment. These costs benefit many periods, but it is not usually possible to match them directly with the specific sale of a product. Instead, they are matched with the periods during which they will provide benefits. For example, an office building may be useful to a company for 30 years. *Depreciation* is the process of allocating the cost of a tangible long-term asset to its useful life. Depreciation Expense is the account used to recognize this type of expense.

The benefits associated with the incurrence of certain other costs are treated as expiring simultaneously with the acquisition of the costs. The justification for this treatment is that no future benefits from the incurrence of the cost are discernible. This is true of most selling and administrative costs. For example, the costs of heat and light in a building benefit only the current period and therefore are recognized as expenses as soon as the costs are incurred. Likewise, income taxes incurred during the period do not benefit any period other than the current period; thus, they are written off as an expense in the period incurred.

Matching principle
The association of revenue of a period with all of the costs necessary to generate that revenue.

STUDY TIP

Another example of a cost that can be matched directly with revenue is commissions. The commission paid to a salesperson can be matched directly with the sale.

EXAMPLE 4-3 Comparing Three Methods for Matching Costs with Revenue

The relationships among costs, assets, and expenses are depicted below.

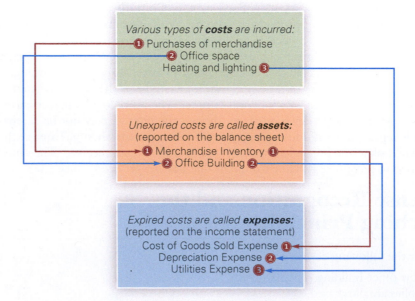

❶ Costs incurred for purchases of merchandise result in an asset, Merchandise Inventory, and are eventually matched with revenue at the time the product is sold.

❷ Costs incurred for office space result in an asset, Office Building, which is recognized as Depreciation Expense over the useful life of the building.

❸ The cost of heating and lighting benefits only the current period and thus is recognized immediately as Utilities Expense.

According to the FASB, **expenses** are "outflows or other using up of assets or incurrences of liabilities (or a combination of both) from delivering or producing goods, rendering services, or carrying out other activities that constitute the entity's ongoing major or central operations."[5] The key point to note about expenses is that they come about in two different ways:

- From the use of an asset
- From the recognition of a liability

For instance, when a retailer sells a product, the asset sacrificed is Inventory. Cost of Goods Sold is the expense account that is increased when the Inventory account is decreased. As you will see in the next section, the incurrence of an expense also may result in a liability.

Expenses
Outflows of assets or incurrences of liabilities resulting from delivering goods, rendering services, or carrying out other activities.

MODULE 1   TEST YOURSELF

Review		
	LO1 Explain the significance of recognition and measurement in the preparation and use of financial statements.	• Determining which economic events should be recognized and how they should be measured is critical for accounting information to be useful. • Recognition drives how and when the effects of economic events are described in the financial statements. • Measurement involves deciding on the attribute of an economic event that must be measured and the appropriate unit of measure.
	LO2 Explain the differences between the cash and accrual bases of accounting.	• Cash and accrual bases are two alternatives used to account for transactions or economic events. They differ in the timing of when revenues and expenses are recognized. • Under the accrual method, which is the focus of this text, revenues are recognized when a performance obligation is satisfied and expenses are recognized when incurred. • By contrast, under the cash method, revenues are recognized when cash is received and expenses are recognized when cash is paid.
	LO3 Describe the revenue recognition principle and explain its application in various situations.	• Revenues are inflows of assets (or reductions of liabilities), generally from providing goods or services to customers. • Revenues are recognized when a performance obligation is satisfied.
	LO4 Describe the matching principle and the various methods for recognizing expenses.	• The matching principle attempts to associate expenses with the time periods in which the expenditures help generate revenues. • This principle is particularly important with expenditures for items that last for more than one accounting period. An example is the depreciation of a building.

[5] SFAC No. 6, par. 80.

Question	1. What is the meaning of the following statement? The choice between historical cost and current value is a good example of the trade-offs in accounting that must sometimes be made.
	2. A realtor earns a 10% commission on the sale of a $150,000 home. The realtor lists the home on June 5, the sale occurs on June 12, and the seller pays the realtor the $15,000 commission on July 8. When should the realtor recognize revenue from the sale assuming (a) the cash basis of accounting and (b) the accrual basis of accounting?
	3. Is it necessary for an asset to be acquired when revenue is recognized? Explain your answer.
	4. A friend says to you: "I just don't get it. Assets cost money. Expenses reduce income. There must be some relationship among assets, costs, and expenses—I'm just not sure what it is!" What is the relationship? Can you give an example of it?

Apply	1. Give the two possible attributes to be measured when an item is to be included in financial statements? What unit of money is used to measure items in the United States?
	2. For the following situations, indicate the date on which revenue would be recognized, assuming the accrual basis of accounting. _____ a. On June 10, a customer orders a product over the phone. The product is shipped to the customer on June 14, and the customer pays the amount owed on July 10. _____ b. On March 15, a law firm agrees to draft a legal document for a client. The document is completed and delivered to the client on April 5, and the client pays the amount owed on May 2. _____ c. A homeowner signs a contract on August 6 to have a company install a central air conditioning system. The work is completed on August 30, and the homeowner pays the amount owed on September 25.
	3. Explain whether a company must have an inflow of an asset to be able to recognize revenue. Give two examples of situations in which revenue is recognized continuously over a period of time.
	4. Assume that a company purchases merchandise for resale on December 20, 2017. The merchandise is still on hand on December 31, the company's year-end. On January 12, 2018, the merchandise is sold to a customer. Explain how the merchandise will be treated on any of the financial statements at year-end. In which year will revenue from the sale be recorded? In which year will cost of goods sold expense be recorded?

Answers are located at the end of the chapter.

MODULE 2 ADJUSTMENTS

LO5 Identify the four major types of adjustments and analyze their effects on the financial statements.

Adjusting entries
Journal entries made at the end of a period by a company using the accrual basis of accounting.

The accrual basis of accounting necessitates a number of adjustments at the end of a period. **Adjusting entries** are the journal entries the accountant makes at the end of a period for a company on the accrual basis of accounting. Adjusting entries are not needed if a cash basis is used. The very nature of the accrual basis results in the need for adjusting entries. The frequency of the adjustment process depends on how often financial statements are prepared. Most businesses make adjustments at month-end.

Recall from Chapter 3 that the emphasis throughout this book is on the *use* of financial statements rather than their preparation. Thus, rather than focus on the adjusting entries that accountants make, we will concern ourselves with the effect of these adjustments on the accounting equation.

Types of Adjustments

Why are there four basic categories of adjustments? The answer lies in the distinction between the cash and the accrual bases of accounting:

- On a cash basis, no differences exist in the timing of revenue and the receipt of cash. The same holds true for expenses.
- On an accrual basis, *revenue* can be recognized before or after cash is received. *Expenses* can be incurred before or after cash is paid. Each of these four distinct situations requires a different type of adjustment at the end of the period.

(1) Cash Paid Before Expense Is Incurred (Deferred Expense)

Assets are often acquired before their actual use in the business. Insurance policies typically are prepaid, as is rent. Office supplies are purchased in advance of their use, as are all types of property and equipment. Recall that unexpired costs are assets. As the costs expire and the benefits are used up, the asset must be written off and replaced with an expense.

EXAMPLE 4-4 Adjusting a Deferred Expense Account

Assume that on September 1, **Nordstrom** prepays $2,400 for an insurance policy for the next 12 months. The effect of the transaction can be identified and analyzed as follows:

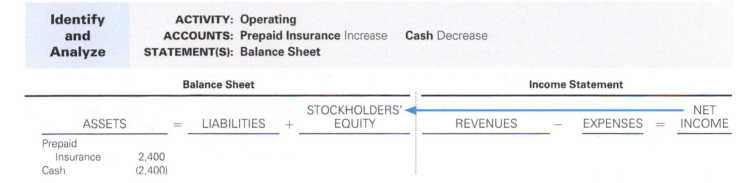

Identify and Analyze	**ACTIVITY: Operating**
	ACCOUNTS: Prepaid Insurance Increase **Cash** Decrease
	STATEMENT(S): Balance Sheet

Balance Sheet

ASSETS	=	LIABILITIES	+	STOCKHOLDERS' EQUITY
Prepaid Insurance 2,400				
Cash (2,400)				

Income Statement

REVENUES	−	EXPENSES	=	NET INCOME

An asset account, Prepaid Insurance, is recorded because the company will receive benefits over the next 12 months. Because the insurance is for a 12-month period, $200 of benefits from the asset expires at the end of each month. The adjustment at the end of September to record this expiration accomplishes two purposes: (1) it recognizes the reduction in the asset Prepaid Insurance, and (2) it recognizes the expense associated with using up the benefits for one month. On September 30, the accountant makes an adjustment to recognize the expense and reduce the asset. The effect of the adjustment can be identified and analyzed as follows:

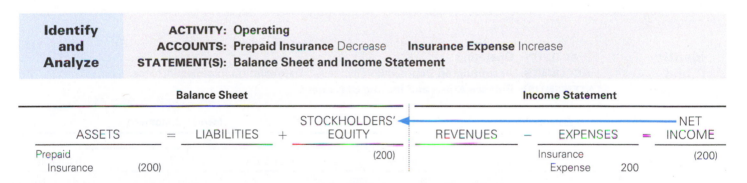

Identify and Analyze	**ACTIVITY: Operating**
	ACCOUNTS: Prepaid Insurance Decrease **Insurance Expense** Increase
	STATEMENT(S): Balance Sheet and Income Statement

Balance Sheet

ASSETS	=	LIABILITIES	+	STOCKHOLDERS' EQUITY
Prepaid Insurance (200)				(200)

Income Statement

REVENUES	−	EXPENSES	=	NET INCOME
		Insurance Expense 200		(200)

The balance in Prepaid Insurance represents the unexpired benefits from the prepayment of insurance for the remaining 11 months: $200 × 11 = $2,200. The Insurance Expense account reflects the expiration of benefits during the month of September.

Recall that depreciation is the process of allocating the cost of a long-term tangible asset over its estimated useful life. The accountant does not attempt to measure the decline in *value* of the asset, but tries to allocate the cost of the asset over its useful life. Thus, the deferred expense adjustment for depreciation (shown in Example 4-5 below) is similar to the one made for insurance expense in Example 4-4 above.

EXAMPLE 4-5 Recording Depreciation

Assume that on January 1, Nordstrom buys new store fixtures, for which it pays $5,000. The effect of the transaction can be identified and analyzed as follows:

Identify and Analyze	ACTIVITY: Investing ACCOUNTS: Store Fixtures Increase Cash Decrease STATEMENT(S): Balance Sheet

Balance Sheet						Income Statement				
ASSETS		=	LIABILITIES	+	STOCKHOLDERS' EQUITY	REVENUES	–	EXPENSES	=	NET INCOME
Store Fixtures	5,000									
Cash	(5,000)									

Two estimates must be made in depreciating the fixtures:

1. The useful life of the asset
2. The estimated salvage value of the fixtures, which is the amount a company expects to receive when it sells the asset at the end of its estimated useful life.

According to a note on page 45 of Nordstrom's Form 10-K for the year ended January 30, 2016, the company uses an estimated useful life for its store fixtures and equipment of 3 to 15 years. Although it is not stated, assume that Nordstrom uses an estimated useful life of five years and an estimated salvage value of $500 at the end of that time for these particular fixtures. Thus, the *depreciable cost* of the fixtures is $5,000 – $500, or $4,500. To allocate this cost over the asset's life, we will use the approach that Nordstrom uses, called the **straight-line method**. This method assigns an equal amount of depreciation to each period. The monthly depreciation is found by dividing the depreciable cost of $4,500 over the estimated useful life of 60 months (5 years = 60 months), which equals $75 per month.

Straight-line method
The assignment of an equal amount of depreciation to each period.

The adjustment to recognize depreciation is conceptually the same as the adjustment to write off Prepaid Insurance. That is, the asset account is reduced and an expense is recognized. However, accountants normally use a contra account to reduce the total amount of long-term tangible assets by the amount of depreciation. A **contra account** has a balance that is opposite the balance in its related account. For example, Accumulated Depreciation is used to record the decrease in a long-term asset for depreciation. The effect of the adjustment can be identified and analyzed as follows:

Contra account
An account with a balance that is opposite that of a related account.

Identify and Analyze	ACTIVITY: Operating ACCOUNTS: Accumulated Depreciation Increase Depreciation Expense Increase STATEMENT(S): Balance Sheet and Income Statement

Balance Sheet						Income Statement				
ASSETS		=	LIABILITIES	+	STOCKHOLDERS' EQUITY	REVENUES	–	EXPENSES	=	NET INCOME
Accumulated Depreciation*	(75)				(75)			Depreciation Expense 75		(75)

*The Accumulated Depreciation account has increased. It is shown as a decrease in the equation above because it is a contra account and causes total assets to decrease.

STUDY TIP

Think of the Accumulated Depreciation account as an extension of the related asset account, in this case, the Store Fixtures account. Therefore, although the Store Fixtures account is not directly reduced for depreciation, an increase in its companion account, Accumulated Depreciation, has the effect of reducing the asset.

Why do companies use a contra account for depreciation rather than simply reduce the long-term asset directly? If the asset account were reduced each time depreciation was recorded, its original cost would not be readily determinable from the accounting records. One of the most important reasons for knowing the historical cost is for computing depreciation for tax purposes.

On a balance sheet prepared on January 31, the contra account is shown as a reduction in the carrying value of the store fixtures:

Store Fixtures	$5,000	
Accumulated Depreciation	75	4,925

(2) Cash Received Before Revenue Is Recognized (Deferred Revenue)

Example 4-6 below shows that one company's asset is another company's liability.

EXAMPLE 4-6 Adjusting a Deferred Revenue Account

In Example 4-4 involving the purchase of an insurance policy, the insurance company received the cash paid by Nordstrom. The insurance company has a liability because it has taken cash from Nordstrom but has not yet performed the service to recognize the revenue. The revenue will be recognized with the passage of time. The effect of the transaction to the insurance company can be identified and analyzed as follows:

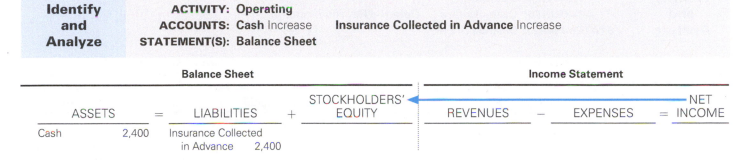

Identify and Analyze	**ACTIVITY: Operating**	
	ACCOUNTS: Cash Increase	**Insurance Collected in Advance** Increase
	STATEMENT(S): Balance Sheet	

Balance Sheet						Income Statement					
ASSETS	=	LIABILITIES	+	STOCKHOLDERS' EQUITY		REVENUES	−	EXPENSES	=	NET INCOME
Cash 2,400		Insurance Collected in Advance 2,400								

The account Insurance Collected in Advance is a liability. The insurance company is obligated to provide Nordstrom protection for the next 12 months. With the passage of time, the liability is satisfied. The adjustment at the end of each month accomplishes two purposes: it recognizes (1) the reduction in the liability and (2) the revenue each month. The effect of the adjustment can be identified and analyzed as follows:

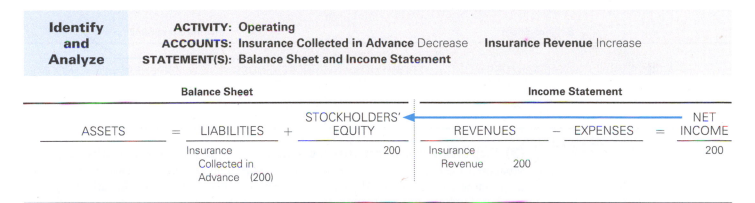

Identify and Analyze	**ACTIVITY: Operating**	
	ACCOUNTS: Insurance Collected in Advance Decrease	**Insurance Revenue** Increase
	STATEMENT(S): Balance Sheet and Income Statement	

Balance Sheet						Income Statement					
ASSETS	=	LIABILITIES	+	STOCKHOLDERS' EQUITY		REVENUES	−	EXPENSES	=	NET INCOME
		Insurance Collected in Advance (200)		200		Insurance Revenue 200				200

As another example of deferred revenue, consider the following sentence from a note in Nordstrom's Form 10-K for the fiscal year ended January 30, 2016 (page 43): "We recognize revenue from the sale of gift cards when the gift card is redeemed by the customer, or we recognize breakage income when the likelihood of redemption, based on historical experience, is deemed to be remote." Example 4-7 shows this process.

CONNECT TO THE REAL WORLD

NORDSTROM
READING THE BALANCE SHEET

4-1 The note from page 43 of Nordstrom's Form 10-K for the fiscal year ended January 30, 2016, explains that gift card liabilities are included in other current liabilities. The gift card liability is $327 million at the end of 2015 and $286 million at the end of 2014. Refer to Nordstrom's partial balance sheet shown in the chapter opener. What percentage of total current liabilities is made up of gift card liabilities at the end of 2015 and 2014? *(See answers on p. 205.)*

EXAMPLE 4-7 Adjusting a Gift Card Deferred Revenue Account

Assume that on March 1, a friend gives you a $100 Nordstrom gift card. At the time the friend buys the card, Nordstrom has an increase in cash of $100 but has yet to perform its obligation, that is, to deliver a product to you as the holder of the gift card. As the above note explains, Nordstrom does not recognize any revenue until you redeem the card. This will be the point at which Nordstrom gives you merchandise and records revenue. Until the card is redeemed, Nordstrom has a liability; that is, it is obligated to deliver merchandise in the future. That liability is mentioned in the same note on page 43 of Nordstrom's Form 10-K for the year ended January 30, 2016 (amounts are in millions of dollars): "We had outstanding gift card liabilities of $327 and $286 at the end of 2015 and 2014, which are included in other current liabilities."

The effect of Nordstrom's receipt of $100 from your friend can be identified and analyzed as follows:

Identify and Analyze	ACTIVITY: Operating
	ACCOUNTS: Cash Increase Deferred Revenue Increase
	STATEMENT(S): Balance Sheet

Balance Sheet					Income Statement			
ASSETS	=	LIABILITIES	+	STOCKHOLDERS' EQUITY	REVENUES	−	EXPENSES	= NET INCOME
Cash 100		Deferred Revenue 100						

Like Insurance Collected in Advance in Example 4-6, Deferred Revenue is a liability. If you redeem your card at a Nordstrom store on March 31, the effect of the adjustment on Nordstrom's books on this date can be identified and analyzed as follows:

Identify and Analyze	ACTIVITY: Operating
	ACCOUNTS: Deferred Revenue Decrease Sales Revenue Increase
	STATEMENT(S): Balance Sheet and Income Statement

Balance Sheet					Income Statement			
ASSETS	=	LIABILITIES	+	STOCKHOLDERS' EQUITY	REVENUES	−	EXPENSES	= NET INCOME
		Deferred Revenue (100)		100	Sales Revenue 100			100

(3) Expense Incurred Before Cash Is Paid (Accrued Liability) This situation is the opposite of (1). That is, cash is paid after an expense is actually incurred rather than before its incurrence. Many normal operating costs, such as payroll, various types of taxes, and utilities, fit this situation. Refer to Nordstrom's partial balance sheet in the chapter opener. The second line under current liabilities represents the company's accrued liabilities for salaries, wages, and related benefits, amounting to $416 million on January 30, 2016.

EXAMPLE 4-8 Recording an Accrued Liability for Wages

Assume that at one of its stores, Nordstrom pays a total of $280,000 in wages on every other Friday. Assume that the last payday was Friday, May 31. The next two paydays will be Friday, June 14, and Friday, June 28. The effect of the transaction on each of these paydays can be identified and analyzed as follows:

Identify and Analyze	ACTIVITY: Operating
	ACCOUNTS: Cash Decrease Wages Expense Increase
	STATEMENT(S): Balance Sheet and Income Statement

Balance Sheet					Income Statement			
ASSETS	=	LIABILITIES	+	STOCKHOLDERS' EQUITY	REVENUES	−	EXPENSES	= NET INCOME
Cash (280,000)				(280,000)			Wages Expense 280,000	(280,000)

On a balance sheet prepared as of June 30, a liability must be recognized. Even though the next payment is not until July 12, Nordstrom owes employees wages for the last two days of June and must recognize an expense for the wages earned by employees for those two days. We will assume that the store is open seven days a week and that the daily cost is 1/14th of the biweekly amount of $280,000, or $20,000. In addition to recognizing a liability on June 30, Nordstrom must adjust the records to reflect an expense associated with the cost of the wages for the last two days of the month. The effect of the adjustment can be identified and analyzed as follows:

| Identify and Analyze | **ACTIVITY:** Operating
ACCOUNTS: Wages Payable Increase   Wages Expense Increase
STATEMENT(S): Balance Sheet and Income Statement |

Balance Sheet			Income Statement		
ASSETS =	LIABILITIES +	STOCKHOLDERS' EQUITY	REVENUES −	EXPENSES	= NET INCOME
	Wages Payable 40,000	(40,000)		Wages Expense 40,000	(40,000)

What adjustment will be made on the next payday, July 12? Nordstrom will need to eliminate the liability of $40,000 for the last two days of wages recorded on June 30 because the amount has now been paid. An additional $240,000 of expense has been incurred for the $20,000 cost per day associated with the first 12 days in July. Finally, cash is reduced by $280,000, which represents the biweekly payroll. The effect of the transaction can be identified and analyzed as follows:

CONNECT TO THE REAL WORLD

NORDSTROM
READING THE BALANCE SHEET

4-2 Refer to Nordstrom's balance sheet shown in the chapter opener. What is the amount of Accrued Salaries, Wages and Related Benefits at the end of each of the two years shown? Compute the ratio of this liability to total current liabilities at the end of each of the two years. (*See answers on p. 205.*)

| Identify and Analyze | **ACTIVITY:** Operating
ACCOUNTS: Cash Decrease   Wages Payable Decrease
Wages Expense Increase
STATEMENT(S): Balance Sheet and Income Statement |

Balance Sheet			Income Statement		
ASSETS =	LIABILITIES +	STOCKHOLDERS' EQUITY	REVENUES −	EXPENSES	= NET INCOME
Cash (280,000)	Wages Payable (40,000)	(240,000)		Wages Expense 240,000	(240,000)

The following time line illustrates the amount of expense incurred in each of the two months, June and July, for the biweekly payroll:

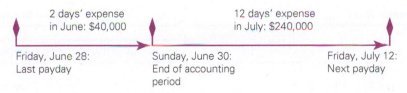

2 days' expense in June: $40,000		12 days' expense in July: $240,000
Friday, June 28: Last payday	Sunday, June 30: End of accounting period	Friday, July 12: Next payday

Another typical expense incurred before the payment of cash is interest. In many cases, the interest on a short-term loan is repaid with the amount of the loan, called the *principal* (see Example 4-9).

EXAMPLE 4-9 Recording an Accrued Liability for Interest

Assume that Granger Company takes out a 9%, 90-day, $20,000 loan with its bank on March 1. Granger will repay the principal and interest on May 30. On March 1, both an asset and a liability, Notes Payable, are increased. The effect of the transaction can be identified and analyzed as follows:

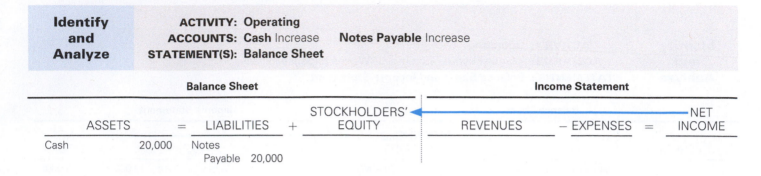

Identify and Analyze	**ACTIVITY:** Operating
	ACCOUNTS: Cash Increase **Notes Payable** Increase
	STATEMENT(S): Balance Sheet

Balance Sheet   **Income Statement**

ASSETS	=	LIABILITIES	+	STOCKHOLDERS' EQUITY		REVENUES	− EXPENSES	=	NET INCOME
Cash 20,000		Notes Payable 20,000							

The basic formula for computing interest follows:

$$I = P \times R \times T$$

where I = The dollar amount of interest

P = The principal amount of the loan

R = The annual rate of interest as a percentage

T = Time in years (often stated as a fraction of a year)

The total interest on Granger's loan is as follows:

$20,000 × 0.09 × 3/12 = $450

Therefore, the amount of interest that must be recognized as expense at the end of March is one-third of $450 because one month of a total of three has passed. Alternatively, the formula for finding the total interest on the loan can be modified to compute the interest for one month.[6]

$20,000 × 0.09 × 1/12 = $150

On March 31 and April 30, the accountant records adjustments to recognize interest both as an expense and an obligation. The effect of the adjustment on March 31 can be identified and analyzed as follows:

Identify and Analyze	**ACTIVITY:** Operating
	ACCOUNTS: **Interest Payable** Increase **Interest Expense** Increase
	STATEMENT(S): Balance Sheet and Income Statement

Balance Sheet   **Income Statement**

ASSETS	=	LIABILITIES	+	STOCKHOLDERS' EQUITY		REVENUES	− EXPENSES	=	NET INCOME
		Interest Payable 150		(150)			Interest Expense 150		(150)

---

[6] In practice, interest is calculated on the basis of days rather than months. For example, the interest for March would be $20,000 × 0.09 × 30/365, or $147.95, to reflect 30 days in the month out of a total of 365 days in the year. The reason the number of days in March is 30 rather than 31 is because in computing interest, **businesses normally count the day a note matures but not the day it is signed.** To simplify the calculations, we will use months, even though the result is slightly inaccurate.

The effect of the adjustment at the end of April is the same as the one at the end of March:

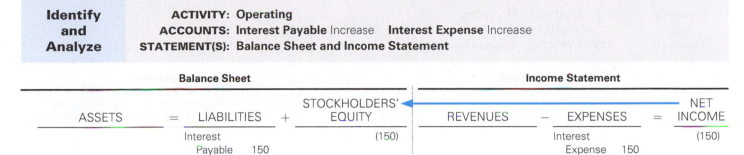

The adjustment on Granger's books on May 30 when it repays the principal and interest can be identified and analyzed as follows:

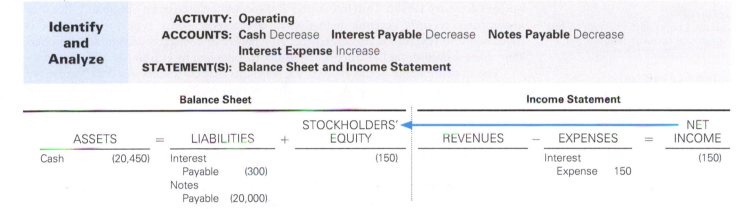

The reduction in Interest Payable eliminates the liability recorded at the end of March and April. The recognition of $150 in Interest Expense is the cost associated with the month of May.[7] The reduction in Cash represents the $20,000 of principal and the total interest of $450 for three months.

(4) Revenue Recognized Before Cash Is Received (Accrued Asset)

Revenue is sometimes recognized before the receipt of cash. Rent and interest are recognized with the passage of time and require an adjustment if cash has not yet been received.

EXAMPLE 4-10 Recording an Accrued Asset

Assume that Grand Management Company rents warehouse space to a number of tenants. Most of its contracts call for prepayment of rent for six months at a time. Its agreement with one tenant, however, allows the tenant to pay Grand $2,500 in monthly rent anytime within the first ten days of the following month. The effect of the adjustment on April 30, the end of the first month of the agreement, can be identified and analyzed as follows:

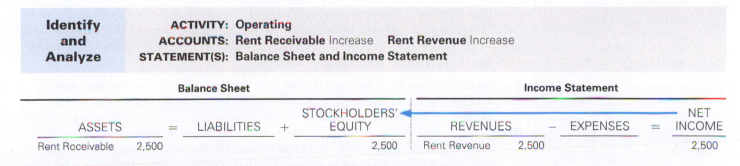

[7] This assumes that Granger did not make a separate adjustment prior to this to recognize interest expense for the month of May. If a separate adjustment had been made, Interest Payable would be reduced by $450.

The effect of the transaction when the tenant pays its rent on May 7 can be identified and analyzed as follows:

Identify and Analyze	**ACTIVITY:** Operating
	ACCOUNTS: Cash Increase **Rent Receivable** Decrease
	STATEMENT(S): Balance Sheet

Balance Sheet				Income Statement				
ASSETS	=	LIABILITIES	+	STOCKHOLDERS' EQUITY	REVENUES	−	EXPENSES	= NET INCOME
Cash 2,500								
Rent Receivable (2,500)								

Deferral

Cash has been paid or received but expense or revenue has not yet been recognized.

Deferred expense

An asset resulting from the payment of cash before the incurrence of expense.

Alternate term: Prepaid expense

Deferred revenue

A liability resulting from the receipt of cash before the recognition of revenue.

Accrual

Cash has not yet been paid or received but expense has been incurred or revenue recognized.

Accrued liability

A liability resulting from the recognition of an expense before the payment of cash.

Accrued asset

An asset resulting from the recognition of a revenue before the receipt of cash.

STUDY TIP

Now that you have seen examples of all four types of adjusting entries, think about a key difference between deferrals (the first two categories) and accruals (the last two categories). When you make adjustments involving deferrals, you must consider any existing balance in a deferred balance sheet account. Conversely, there is no existing account when an accrual is made.

Although the example of rent was used to illustrate this category, the membership revenue of Glengarry Health Club in Chapter 3 also could be used as an example. **Whenever a company records revenue before cash is received, some type of receivable is increased and revenue is also increased.** In Chapter 3, Glengarry recognized membership revenue even though members had until the following month to pay their dues.

The same principle would apply to any amounts that customers owed to Nordstrom at the end of a period. As shown in the chapter opener, Nordstrom reported Accounts Receivable, net of $196 million on January 30, 2016.

Accruals and Deferrals

The term **deferral** is used to refer to a situation in which cash has been paid or received but the expense or revenue has been deferred to a later time. A **deferred expense** indicates that cash has been paid but the recognition of expense has been deferred. Because a deferred expense represents a *future benefit* to a company, it is an asset. An alternative name for deferred expense is *prepaid expense*. Prepaid insurance and office supplies are deferred expenses. An adjustment is made periodically to record the portion of the deferred expense that has expired. A **deferred revenue** means that cash has been received but the recognition of any revenue has been deferred until a later time. Because a deferred revenue represents an *obligation* to a company, it is a liability. Rent collected in advance is deferred revenue. The periodic adjustment recognizes the portion of the deferred revenue that is recognized in that period.

The term **accrual** is used to refer to a situation in which no cash has been paid or received yet but it is necessary to recognize, or accrue, an expense or a revenue. An **accrued liability** is recognized at the end of the period in cases in which an expense has been incurred but cash has not yet been paid. Wages payable and interest payable are examples of accrued liabilities. An **accrued asset** is recorded when revenue has been recognized but cash has not yet been collected. Rent receivable is an accrued asset.

Summary of Adjustments

The four types of adjustments are summarized in Exhibit 4-3. Common examples of each are shown, along with the structure of the adjustments associated with the four categories. Finally, the following generalizations should help you gain a better understanding of adjustments and how they are used:

1. **An adjustment is an internal transaction. It does not involve another entity.**
2. **Because it is an internal transaction, an adjustment does not involve an increase or a decrease in Cash.**
3. **At least one balance sheet account and one income statement account are involved in an adjustment. It is the nature of the adjustment process that an asset or a liability account is adjusted with a corresponding change in a revenue or an expense account.**

EXHIBIT 4-3 Accruals and Deferrals

Type	Situation	Examples	Transaction during Period	Adjustment at End of Period
Deferred expense	Cash paid before expense is incurred	Insurance policy	Increase Asset	Increase Expense
		Supplies		
		Rent	Decrease Cash	Decrease Asset
		Buildings, equipment		
Deferred revenue	Cash received before revenue is recognized	Deposits, rent	Increase Cash	Decrease Liability
		Subscriptions	Increase Liability	Increase Revenue
		Gift certificates		
Accrued liability	Expense incurred before cash is paid	Salaries, wages	No Transaction	Increase Expense
		Interest		Increase Liability
		Taxes		
		Rent		
Accrued asset	Revenue recognized before cash is received	Interest	No Transaction	Increase Asset
		Rent		Increase Revenue

Comprehensive Example of Adjustments

We will now consider a comprehensive example involving the transactions for the first month of operations and the end-of-period adjustments for a hypothetical business, Duffy Transit Company. A list of accounts and their balances is shown for Duffy Transit at January 31, the end of the first month of business (prior to making any adjustments):

Assets	
Cash	$ 50,000
Prepaid Insurance	48,000
Land	20,000
Buildings—Garage	160,000
Equipment—Buses	300,000
Liabilities	
Discount Tickets Sold in Advance	25,000
Notes Payable	150,000
Stockholders' Equity	
Capital Stock	400,000
Revenues	
Daily Ticket Revenue	30,000
Expenses	
Gas, Oil, and Maintenance Expense	12,000
Wage and Salary Expense	10,000
Dividends	5,000

Duffy wants to prepare a balance sheet at the end of January and an income statement for its first month of operations. Use of the accrual basis necessitates a number of adjustments to update certain asset and liability accounts and to recognize the correct amounts for the various revenues and expenses.

EXAMPLE 4-11 Using a List of Accounts to Prepare Adjustments

1. At the beginning of January, Duffy issued an 18-month, 12%, $150,000 promissory note for cash. Although interest will not be repaid until the loan's maturity date, Duffy must accrue interest for the first month. The calculation of interest for one month is $150,000 × 0.12 × 1/12. The effect of the adjustment can be identified and analyzed as follows:

| Identify and Analyze | ACTIVITY: Operating
ACCOUNTS: Interest Payable Increase   Interest Expense Increase
STATEMENT(S): Balance Sheet and Income Statement |

Balance Sheet   **Income Statement**

ASSETS	=	LIABILITIES	+	STOCKHOLDERS' EQUITY	REVENUES	−	EXPENSES	=	NET INCOME
		Interest Payable 1,500		(1,500)			Interest Expense 1,500		(1,500)

2. Wage and salary expense of $10,000 reflects the amount paid to employees during January. At the end of the month, Duffy owes employees an additional $2,800 in salaries and wages. The effect of the adjustment can be identified and analyzed as follows:

| Identify and Analyze | ACTIVITY: Operating
ACCOUNTS: Wages and Salaries Payable Increase   Wage and Salary Expense Increase
STATEMENT(S): Balance Sheet and Income Statement |

Balance Sheet   **Income Statement**

ASSETS	=	LIABILITIES	+	STOCKHOLDERS' EQUITY	REVENUES	−	EXPENSES	=	NET INCOME
		Wages and Salaries Payable 2,800		(2,800)			Wage and Salary Expense 2,800		(2,800)

3. At the beginning of January, at a cost of $160,000, Duffy acquired a garage to house the buses. Land is not subject to depreciation. The cost of the land acquired in connection with the purchase of the building will remain on the books until the property is sold. The garage has an estimated useful life of 20 years and an estimated salvage value of $16,000 at the end of its life. The monthly depreciation is found by dividing the depreciable cost of $144,000 by the useful life of 240 months:

$$\frac{\$160,000 - \$16,000}{20 \text{ years} \times 12 \text{ months}} = \frac{\$144,000}{240 \text{ months}} = \underline{\$600} \text{ per month}$$

The effect of the adjustment to record the depreciation on the garage for January for a full month can be identified and analyzed as follows:

| Identify and Analyze | ACTIVITY: Operating
ACCOUNTS: Accumulated Depreciation—Garage Increase   Depreciation Expense—Garage Increase
STATEMENT(S): Balance Sheet and Income Statement |

Balance Sheet   **Income Statement**

ASSETS	=	LIABILITIES	+	STOCKHOLDERS' EQUITY	REVENUES	−	EXPENSES	=	NET INCOME
Accumulated Depreciation— Garage* (600)				(600)			Depreciation Expense— Garage 600		(600)

*The Accumulated Depreciation account has increased. It is shown as a decrease in the equation above because it is a contra account and causes total assets to decrease.

4. Duffy purchased ten buses for $30,000 each at the beginning of January. The buses have an estimated useful life of five years, at which time the company plans to sell them for $6,000 each. The monthly depreciation on the ten buses is as follows:

$$10 \times \frac{\$30,000 - \$6,000}{5 \text{ years} \times 12 \text{ months}} = 10 \times \frac{\$24,000}{60 \text{ months}} = \underline{\$4,000} \text{ per month}$$

The effect of the adjustment to allocate the cost to expense for the first month can be identified and analyzed as follows:

Identify and Analyze	**ACTIVITY: Operating**
	ACCOUNTS: Accumulated Depreciation—Buses Increase **Depreciation Expense—Buses** Increase
	STATEMENT(S): Balance Sheet and Income Statement

Balance Sheet					Income Statement				
ASSETS	=	LIABILITIES	+	STOCKHOLDERS' EQUITY	REVENUES	−	EXPENSES	=	NET INCOME
				(4,000)					(4,000)
Accumulated Depreciation— Buses* (4,000)							Depreciation Expense— Buses 4,000		

*The Accumulated Depreciation account has increased. It is shown as a decrease in the equation above because it is a contra account and causes total assets to decrease.

5. An insurance policy was purchased for $48,000 on January 1. The policy provides property and liability protection for a 24-month period. Thus, the monthly cost is $48,000/24 = $2,000. The effect of the adjustment to allocate the cost to expense for the first month can be identified and analyzed as follows:

Identify and Analyze	**ACTIVITY: Operating**
	ACCOUNTS: Prepaid Insurance Decrease **Insurance Expense** Increase
	STATEMENT(S): Balance Sheet and Income Statement

Balance Sheet					Income Statement				
ASSETS	=	LIABILITIES	+	STOCKHOLDERS' EQUITY	REVENUES	−	EXPENSES	=	NET INCOME
				(2,000)					(2,000)
Prepaid Insurance (2,000)							Insurance Expense 2,000		

6. In addition to selling tickets on the bus, Duffy sells discount tickets at the terminal. The tickets are good for a ride anytime within 12 months of purchase. Thus, as these tickets are sold, Duffy increases Cash as well as a liability account, Discount Tickets Sold in Advance. The sale of $25,000 worth of these tickets was recorded during January. At the end of the first month, Duffy counts the number of tickets that has been redeemed. Because $20,400 worth of tickets has been turned in, this is the amount by which the company reduces its liability and recognizes revenue for the month. The effect of the adjustment can be identified and analyzed as follows:

Identify and Analyze	**ACTIVITY: Operating**
	ACCOUNTS: Discount Tickets Sold in Advance Decrease **Discount Ticket Revenue** Increase
	STATEMENT(S): Balance Sheet and Income Statement

Balance Sheet					Income Statement				
ASSETS	=	LIABILITIES	+	STOCKHOLDERS' EQUITY	REVENUES	−	EXPENSES	=	NET INCOME
		Discount Tickets Sold in Advance (20,400)		20,400	Discount Ticket Revenue 20,400				20,400

7. Duffy does not need all of the space in its garage and rents a section of it to another company for $2,500 per month. The tenant has until the 10th day of the following month to pay its rent. The effect of the adjustment on Duffy's books on the last day of the month can be identified and analyzed as follows:

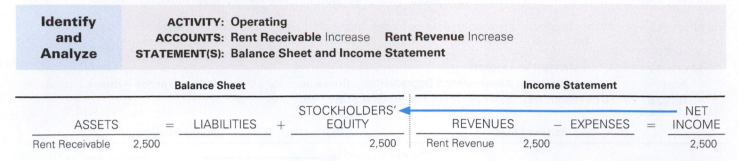

Identify and Analyze

ACTIVITY: Operating
ACCOUNTS: Rent Receivable Increase   **Rent Revenue** Increase
STATEMENT(S): Balance Sheet and Income Statement

Balance Sheet					Income Statement				
ASSETS	=	LIABILITIES	+	STOCKHOLDERS' EQUITY	REVENUES	–	EXPENSES	=	NET INCOME
Rent Receivable 2,500				2,500	Rent Revenue 2,500				2,500

8. Because Duffy is preparing an income statement for the month of January, it must estimate its taxes for the month. We will assume a corporate tax rate of 34% on income before tax. The computation of income tax expense is as follows. (The amounts shown for the revenues and expenses reflect the effect of the adjustments.)

Revenues:		
Daily ticket revenue	$30,000	
Discount ticket revenue	20,400	
Rent revenue	2,500	$ 52,900
Expenses:		
Gas, oil, and maintenance expense	$12,000	
Wage and salary expense	12,800	
Depreciation expense	4,600	
Insurance expense	2,000	
Interest expense	1,500	32,900
Net income before tax		$ 20 000
Corporate tax rate		× 0.34
Income tax expense		$ 6,800

Based on this estimate of taxes, the effect of the final adjustment Duffy makes can be identified and analyzed as follows:

Identify and Analyze

ACTIVITY: Operating
ACCOUNTS: Income Tax Payable Increase   **Income Tax Expense** Increase
STATEMENT(S): Balance Sheet and Income Statement

Balance Sheet					Income Statement				
ASSETS	=	LIABILITIES	+	STOCKHOLDERS' EQUITY	REVENUES	–	EXPENSES	=	NET INCOME
		Income Tax Payable 6,800		(6,800)			Income Tax Expense 6,800		(6,800)

Income Statement and Balance Sheet for Duffy Transit

Now that the adjustments have been made, financial statements can be prepared. An income statement for January and a balance sheet as of January 31 are shown in Exhibit 4-4. Each of the account balances on the statements was determined by taking the balances in the list of accounts on page 167 and adding or subtracting as appropriate the necessary adjustments. Note the balance in Retained Earnings of $8,200. This amount was found by taking the net income of $13,200 and deducting the dividends of $5,000.

EXHIBIT 4-4 Financial Statements for Duffy Transit Company

Duffy Transit Company
Income Statement
For the month of January

Revenues:		
Daily ticket revenue	$30,000	
Discount ticket revenue	20,400	
Rent revenue	2,500	$52,900
Expenses:		
Gas, oil, and maintenance	$12,000	
Wages and salaries	12,800	
Depreciation—garage	600	
Depreciation—buses	4,000	
Insurance	2,000	
Interest	1,500	
Income taxes	6,800	39,700
Net income		$13,200

Duffy Transit Company
Balance Sheet
January 31

Assets			Liabilities and Stockholders' Equity	
Cash		$ 50,000	Discount tickets sold in advance	$ 4,600
Rent receivable		2,500	Notes payable	150,000
Prepaid insurance		46,000	Interest payable	1,500
Land		20,000	Wages and salaries payable	2,800
Buildings—garage	$160,000		Income tax payable	6,800
Accumulated depreciation	600	159,400	Capital stock	400,000
Equipment—buses	$300,000		Retained earnings	8,200
Accumulated depreciation	4,000	296,000		
Total assets		$573,900	Total liabilities and stockholders' equity	$573,900

Ethical Considerations for a Company on the Accrual Basis

Adjustments are *internal* transactions in that they do not involve an exchange with an outside entity. Because adjustments do not involve another company, accountants may at times feel pressure from others within the organization either to speed or delay the recognition of certain adjustments.

A decision-making model was presented on page 24 in Chapter 1 to help you make the best choices when confronted with ethical dilemmas in accounting. Step 1 in the model required the recognition of an ethical concern. One of the instances in which a dilemma is possible is when some questionable action has occurred. Consider the following two examples for a landscaping company that is concerned about its net income. A number of jobs are in progress, but because of inclement weather, none of them are very far along.

1. Management wants to show stockholders that it has increased its revenue for a period, so it asks the accountant to recognize all of the revenue from a job in progress even though no significant work has been done on the job.
2. Management wants to avoid showing the full extent of its costs to a key investor, so it asks the accountant to delay the recognition of various short-term accrued liabilities (and, of course, the accompanying expenses) until the beginning of the new year.

Although the accountant's decision may seem difficult, the "correct" response to each of those requests may seem obvious: no revenue on the one job should be recognized, and all accrued liabilities should be expensed at year-end. **The accountant must remember that his or her primary responsibility in preparing financial statements is to portray the affairs of the company accurately to the various outside users.** Bankers, stockholders, and others rely on the accountant to serve their best interests.

MODULE 2 TEST YOURSELF

Review	**LO5** Identify the four major types of adjustments and analyze their effects on the financial statements.	• Adjustments are made at the end of an accounting period to update revenue or expense accounts in accordance with the revenue recognition and matching principles.
		• There are four basic categories of adjustments:
		  • Adjustments where cash is paid before expenses are incurred—deferred expenses.
		  • Adjustments where cash is received before revenues are recognized—deferred revenues.
		  • Adjustments where expenses are incurred before cash is paid—accrued liabilities.
		  • Adjustments where revenues are recognized before cash is received—accrued assets.

Question	1. Give an example of each of the four basic types of adjustments.

Apply

1. For the following situations, indicate the types of accounts affected in a year-end adjustment. Use the following legend:
   IA = Increase in Asset; DA = Decrease in Asset; IL = Increase in Liability; DL = Decrease in Liability; IR = Increase in Revenue; IE = Increase in Expense.

Accounts Affected		Situation
_____	_____	a. A company owes employees for wages earned but not yet paid.
_____	_____	b. Rent is recognized for the month, and the tenant is given until the 10th of the following month to pay.
_____	_____	c. A portion of an insurance policy paid for in advance has expired.
_____	_____	d. A gift card is redeemed by its recipient.

2. ABC Corp. purchases a 24-month fire insurance policy on January 1, for $5,400. Identify and analyze the effect of the adjustment on January 31.

3. DEF Corp. purchases a new car on March 1, for $25,000. The estimated useful life of the car is four years with an estimated salvage value of $1,000. Identify and analyze the effect of the adjustment on March 31.

4. On April 1, GHI Corp. took out a 12%, 120-day, $10,000 loan at its bank. Identify and analyze the effect of the adjustment on April 30.

Answers are located at the end of the chapter.

LO6 Explain the steps in the accounting cycle and the significance of each step.

Accounting cycle
A series of steps performed each period and culminating with the preparation of a set of financial statements.

MODULE 3 THE ACCOUNTING CYCLE

The accountant for a business follows a series of steps each period. The objective is always the same: **collect the necessary information to prepare a set of financial statements**. Together these steps make up the **accounting cycle**. The name comes from the fact that the steps are repeated each period.

The steps in the accounting cycle are shown in Exhibit 4-5. Note that Step 1 involves not only *collecting* information but also *analyzing* it. Transaction analysis is probably the most challenging of all of the steps in the accounting cycle. It requires the ability to think logically about an event and its effect on the financial position of the entity. Once the transaction is analyzed, it is recorded in the journal, as indicated by the second step in the exhibit. The first two steps in the cycle take place continuously.

Transactions are posted to the accounts on a periodic basis. The frequency of posting to the accounts depends on two factors: the type of accounting system used by a company and the volume of transactions. In a manual system, transactions might be posted daily, weekly, or even monthly depending on the amount of activity. In an automated accounting system, posting is likely done automatically by the computer each time a transaction is recorded.

The Use of a Work Sheet

Step 4 in Exhibit 4-5 calls for the preparation of a work sheet. The use of a **work sheet** allows the accountant to gather and organize the information required to adjust the accounts without actually recording and posting the adjustments to the accounts. Recording adjustments and posting them to the accounts can be done after the financial statements are prepared. **The work sheet is optional and is not a financial statement.**

If a work sheet is not used, Step 6, recording and posting adjustments, comes before Step 5, preparing the financial statements.

Work sheet
A device used at the end of the period to gather the information needed to prepare financial statements without actually recording and posting adjustments.

EXHIBIT 4-5 Steps in the Accounting Cycle

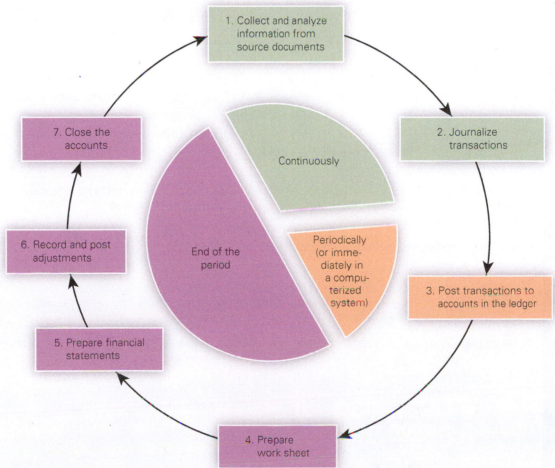

The Closing Process

Step 7 in Exhibit 4-5 is the closing process. For purposes of closing the books, accountants categorize accounts into two types:

1. Balance sheet accounts are called **real accounts** because they are *permanent* in nature. Real accounts are never closed and the balance in each of them is carried over from one period to the next.

2. Revenue, expense, and dividend accounts are *temporary* or **nominal accounts**. The balances in the income statement accounts and the Dividends account are closed and *not* carried forward from one accounting period to the next.

Closing entries serve two important purposes: (1) to return the balances in all temporary or nominal accounts to zero to start the next accounting period and (2) to transfer the net income (or net loss) and the dividends of the period to the Retained Earnings account.

Interim Financial Statements

Statements prepared monthly, quarterly, or at other intervals less than a year in duration are called **interim statements**. Many companies prepare monthly financial statements for their own internal use. Similarly, corporations whose shares are publicly traded on one of the stock exchanges are required to file quarterly financial statements with the SEC.

Suppose a company prepares monthly financial statements for internal use and completes the accounting cycle in its entirety only once a year. In this case, a work sheet is prepared each month as the basis for interim financial statements. Formal adjusting and closing of the books is done only at the end of each year. The adjustments that appear on the monthly work sheet are not posted to the accounts. They are entered on the work sheet simply as a basis for preparing the monthly financial statements.

Real accounts
The name given to balance sheet accounts because they are permanent and are not closed at the end of the period.
Alternate term: Permanent account

Nominal accounts
The name given to revenue, expense, and dividend accounts because they are temporary and are closed at the end of the period.
Alternate term: Temporary account

Closing entries
Journal entries made at the end of the period to return the balance in all nominal accounts to zero and transfer the net income or loss and the dividends to Retained Earnings.

Interim statements
Financial statements prepared monthly, quarterly, or at other intervals less than a year in duration.

MODULE 3 TEST YOURSELF

Review	**LO6** Explain the steps in the accounting cycle and the significance of each step.	• The accounting cycle involves seven steps that are repeated each period. (See Exhibit 4-5.) • Collecting and analyzing data and journalizing transactions occur on a continuous basis. • Periodically, transactions are posted to accounts in the ledger. • At the end of the period, a work sheet is prepared, financial statements are prepared, adjustments are recorded and posted, and accounts are closed.

Question

1. Which of the following steps in the accounting cycle requires the most thought and judgment by the accountant: (a) posting adjustments and closing the accounts, or (b) analyzing and recording transactions? Explain your answer.

2. What two purposes are served in making closing entries?

Apply

1. Recall the steps in the accounting cycle shown in Exhibit 4-5. Assume that a company does not prepare a work sheet. Which of the two remaining steps in the accounting cycle are performed in a different order than they would be if a work sheet were prepared? Explain your answer.

2. For the following accounts, indicate whether each would be (Yes) or would not be (No) closed at the end of the accounting period.

_____ a. Prepaid Insurance
_____ b. Supplies Expense
_____ c. Capital Stock
_____ d. Sales Revenue
_____ e. Depreciation Expense
_____ f. Accumulated Depreciation
_____ g. Cash
_____ h. Income Tax Expense

Answers are located at the end of the chapter.

ACCOUNTS HIGHLIGHTED

Account Titles	Where It Appears	In What Section	Page Number
Prepaid Insurance	Balance Sheet	Current Assets	159
Accumulated Depreciation	Balance Sheet	Noncurrent Assets (contra)	160
Deferred Revenue	Balance Sheet	Current Liabilities*	162
Wages Payable	Balance Sheet	Current Liabilities	163
Interest Payable	Balance Sheet	Current Liabilities	164
Rent Receivable	Balance Sheet	Current Assets	165

*If any part of deferred revenue will not be recognized within the next year, it should be classified as a noncurrent liability.

KEY TERMS QUIZ

Read each definition below and write the number of the definition in the blank beside the appropriate term. The quiz solutions appear at the end of the chapter.

_____ Recognition	_____ Deferral
_____ Historical cost	_____ Deferred expense
_____ Current value	_____ Deferred revenue
_____ Cash basis	_____ Accrual
_____ Accrual basis	_____ Accrued liability
_____ Revenues	_____ Accrued asset
_____ Revenue recognition principle	_____ Accounting cycle
_____ Matching principle	_____ Work sheet
_____ Expenses	_____ Real accounts
_____ Adjusting entries	_____ Nominal accounts
_____ Straight-line method	_____ Closing entries
_____ Contra account	_____ Interim statements

1. A device used at the end of the period to gather the information needed to prepare financial statements without actually recording and posting adjustments.
2. Inflows of assets or settlements of liabilities from delivering or producing goods, rendering services, or conducting other activities.
3. Journal entries made at the end of a period by a company using the accrual basis of accounting.
4. Journal entries made at the end of the period to return the balance in all nominal accounts to zero and transfer the net income or loss and the dividends to Retained Earnings.
5. A liability resulting from the receipt of cash before the recognition of revenue.
6. The name given to balance sheet accounts because they are permanent and are not closed at the end of the period.
7. An asset resulting from the recognition of a revenue before the receipt of cash.
8. The amount of cash or its equivalent that could be received by selling an asset currently.
9. The assignment of an equal amount of depreciation to each period.
10. Cash has been paid or received but expense or revenue has not yet been recognized.

11. A system of accounting in which revenues are recognized when a performance obligation is satisfied and expenses are recognized when incurred.
12. Cash has not yet been paid or received but expense has been incurred or revenue recognized.
13. Financial statements prepared monthly, quarterly, or at other intervals less than a year in duration.
14. Revenues are recognized in the income statement when a performance obligation is satisfied.
15. The process of recording an item in the financial statements as an asset, a liability, a revenue, an expense, or the like.
16. An asset resulting from the payment of cash before the incurrence of expense.
17. The name given to revenue, expense, and dividend accounts because they are temporary and are closed at the end of the period.
18. A system of accounting in which revenues are recognized when cash is received and expenses are recognized when cash is paid.
19. A liability resulting from the recognition of an expense before the payment of cash.
20. The association of revenue of a period with all of the costs necessary to generate that revenue.
21. An account with a balance that is opposite that of a related account.
22. The amount paid for an asset and used as a basis for recognizing it on the balance sheet and carrying it on later balance sheets.
23. Outflows of assets or incurrences of liabilities resulting from delivering goods, rendering services, or carrying out other activities.
24. A series of steps performed each period and culminating with the preparation of a set of financial statements.

ALTERNATE TERMS

asset unexpired cost
deferred expense prepaid expense
expense expired cost

historical cost original cost
nominal account temporary account
real account permanent account

REVIEW PROBLEM & SOLUTION

A list of accounts for Northern Airlines at January 31 is shown. It reflects the recurring transactions for the month of January, but it does not reflect any month-end adjustments.

Cash	$ 75,000
Parts Inventory	45,000
Land	80,000
Buildings—Hangars	250,000
Accumulated Depreciation—Hangars	24,000
Equipment—Aircraft	650,000
Accumulated Depreciation—Aircraft	120,000
Tickets Sold in Advance	85,000
Capital Stock	500,000
Retained Earnings	368,000
Ticket Revenue	52,000
Maintenance Expense	19,000
Wage and Salary Expense	30,000

The following additional information is available:

a. Airplane parts needed for repairs and maintenance are purchased regularly, and the amounts paid are added to the asset account Parts Inventory. At the end of each month, the inventory is counted. At the end of January, the amount of parts on hand is $36,100. *Hint:* What adjustment is needed to reduce the asset account to its proper carrying value? Any expense involved should be included in Maintenance Expense.

b. The estimated useful life of the hangar is 20 years with an estimated salvage value of $10,000 at the end of its life. The original cost of the hangar was $250,000.

c. The estimated useful life of the aircraft is ten years with an estimated salvage value of $50,000. The original cost of the aircraft was $650,000.

d. As tickets are sold in advance, the amounts are added to Cash and to the liability account Tickets Sold in Advance. A count of the redeemed tickets reveals that $47,000 worth of tickets were used during January.

e. Wages and salaries owed but unpaid to employees at the end of January total $7,600.

f. Northern rents excess hangar space to other companies. The amount owed but unpaid to Northern at the end of January is $2,500.

g. Assume a corporate income tax rate of 34%.

Required

1. For each of the preceding items of additional information, identify and analyze the effect of the adjustment.

2. Prepare an income statement for January and a balance sheet at January 31.

Solution to Review Problem

1.

a.

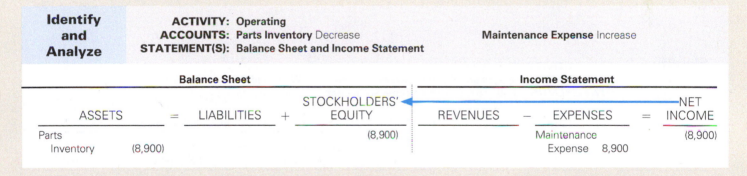

b.

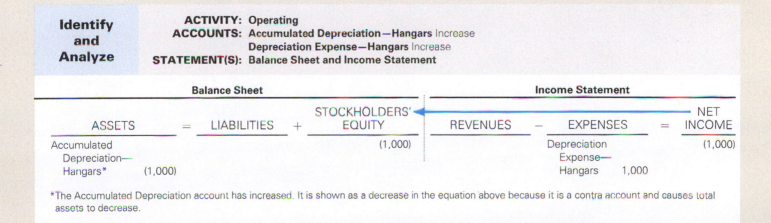

c.

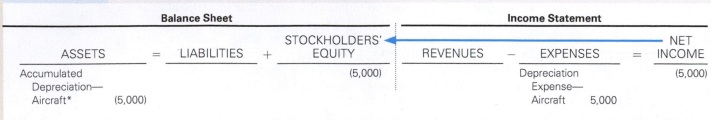

| **Identify and Analyze** | **ACTIVITY:** Operating
ACCOUNTS: Accumulated Depreciation—Aircraft Increase
Depreciation Expense—Aircraft Increase
STATEMENT(S): Balance Sheet and Income Statement |

Balance Sheet			Income Statement			
ASSETS	=	LIABILITIES	+	STOCKHOLDERS' EQUITY	REVENUES	−	EXPENSES	=	NET INCOME

Balance Sheet		Income Statement	
ASSETS = LIABILITIES +	STOCKHOLDERS' EQUITY	REVENUES − EXPENSES =	NET INCOME
Accumulated Depreciation— Aircraft* (5,000)	(5,000)	Depreciation Expense— Aircraft 5,000	(5,000)

*The Accumulated Depreciation account has increased. It is shown as a decrease in the equation above because it is a contra account and causes total assets to decrease.

d.

| **Identify and Analyze** | **ACTIVITY:** Operating
ACCOUNTS: Tickets Sold in Advance Decrease **Ticket Revenue** Increase
STATEMENT(S): Balance Sheet and Income Statement |

Balance Sheet		Income Statement	
ASSETS = LIABILITIES +	STOCKHOLDERS' EQUITY	REVENUES − EXPENSES =	NET INCOME
Tickets Sold in Advance (47,000)	47,000	Ticket Revenue 47,000	47,000

e.

| **Identify and Analyze** | **ACTIVITY:** Operating
ACCOUNTS: Wages and Salaries Payable Increase   Wage and Salary Expense Increase
STATEMENT(S): Balance Sheet and Income Statement |

Balance Sheet		Income Statement	
ASSETS = LIABILITIES +	STOCKHOLDERS' EQUITY	REVENUES − EXPENSES =	NET INCOME
Wages and Salaries Payable 7,600	(7,600)	Wage and Salary Expense 7,600	(7,600)

f.

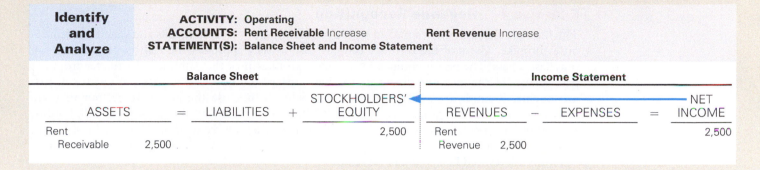

Identify and Analyze	**ACTIVITY:** Operating **ACCOUNTS:** Rent Receivable Increase — Rent Revenue Increase **STATEMENT(S):** Balance Sheet and Income Statement

Balance Sheet

ASSETS	=	LIABILITIES	+	STOCKHOLDERS' EQUITY
Rent Receivable 2,500				2,500

Income Statement

REVENUES	–	EXPENSES	=	NET INCOME
Rent Revenue 2,500				2,500

g.

Identify and Analyze	**ACTIVITY:** Operating **ACCOUNTS:** Income Tax Payable Increase — Income Tax Expense Increase **STATEMENT(S):** Balance Sheet and Income Statement

Balance Sheet

ASSETS	=	LIABILITIES	+	STOCKHOLDERS' EQUITY
		Income Tax Payable 10,200		(10,200)

Income Statement

REVENUES	–	EXPENSES	=	NET INCOME
		Income Tax Expense 10,200		(10,200)

2. Financial Statements:

Northern Airlines
Income Statement
For the Month of January

Revenues:		
Ticket revenue	$99,000	
Rent revenue	2,500	$101,500
Expenses:		
Maintenance	$27,900	
Wages and salaries	37,600	
Depreciation—hangars	1,000	
Depreciation—aircraft	5,000	
Income taxes	10,200	81,700
Net income		$ 19,800

Northern Airlines
Balance Sheet
January 31

Assets			Liabilities and Stockholders' Equity	
Cash		$ 75,000	Tickets sold in advance	$ 38,000
Rent receivable		2,500	Wages and salaries payable	7,600
Parts inventory		36,100	Income tax payable	10,200
Land		80,000	Capital stock	500,000
Buildings—Hangars	$250,000		Retained earnings	387,800
Accumulated depreciation	25,000	225,000		
Aircraft	$650,000			
Accumulated depreciation	125,000	525,000		
Total assets		$943,600	Total liabilities and stockholders' equity	$943,600

EXERCISES

LO3 **Exercise 4-1 Revenue Recognition**

The highway department contracted with a private company to collect tolls and maintain facilities on a turnpike. Users of the turnpike can pay cash as they approach the toll booth, or they can purchase a pass. The pass is equipped with an electronic sensor that subtracts the toll fee from the pass balance as the motorist slowly approaches a special toll booth. The passes are issued in $10 increments. Refunds are available to motorists who do not use the pass balance, but they are issued very infrequently. Last year, $3,000,000 was collected at the traditional toll booths, $2,000,000 of passes were issued, and $1,700,000 of passes were used at the special toll booth. How much should the company recognize as revenue for the year? Explain how the revenue recognition rule should be applied in this case.

LO2 **Exercise 4-2 Comparing the Income Statement and the Statement**
EXAMPLE 4-1, 4-2 **of Cash Flows**

On January 1, Campus Internet Connection opened for business across the street from Upper Eastern University. The company charges students a monthly fee of $20 and $1 for each hour they are online. During January, 500 students signed up for the service, and each will have until the fifth of the following month to pay the monthly fee. By the end of January, 200 students had paid the monthly fee. Student usage, payable at the time connected, was 3,000 hours during January. Assume that Campus uses the accrual basis of accounting.

Required

1. Prepare the Revenues section of Campus's income statement for the month of January.
2. Prepare the Cash Receipts section of Campus's statement of cash flows for the month of January.
3. In addition to the Cash account, what other account will appear on Campus's balance sheet at the end of January? What amount will be in this account?

LO4 **Exercise 4-3 The Matching Principle**
EXAMPLE 4-3

Three methods of matching costs with revenue were described in the chapter: (a) directly match a specific form of revenue with a cost incurred in generating that revenue, (b) indirectly match a cost with the periods during which it will provide benefits or revenue, and (c) immediately recognize a cost incurred as an expense because no future benefits are expected. For each of the following costs, indicate how it is normally recognized as expense by indicating either (a), (b), or (c). If you think that more than one answer is possible for any of the situations, explain why.

1. New office copier
2. Monthly bill from the utility company for electricity
3. Office supplies
4. Biweekly payroll for office employees
5. Commissions earned by salespeople
6. Interest incurred on a six-month loan from the bank
7. Cost of inventory sold during the current period
8. Taxes owed on income of the current period
9. Cost of three-year insurance policy

LO5 **Exercise 4-4 Accruals and Deferrals**
EXAMPLE 4-4, 4-5, 4-7,
4-8, 4-10

For the following situations, indicate whether each involves a deferred expense (DE), a deferred revenue (DR), an accrued liability (AL), or an accrued asset (AA).

Example: <u>DE</u> Office supplies purchased in advance of their use

_____ 1. Wages earned by employees but not yet paid
_____ 2. Cash collected from subscriptions in advance of publishing a magazine
_____ 3. Interest on a customer loan for which principal and interest have not yet been collected
_____ 4. One year's premium on life insurance policy paid in advance

_____	5. Office building purchased for cash
_____	6. Rent collected in advance from a tenant
_____	7. State income taxes owed at the end of the year
_____	8. Rent owed by a tenant but not yet collected

Exercise 4-5 Office Supplies

LO5
EXAMPLE 4-4

Somerville Corp. purchases office supplies once a month and prepares monthly financial statements. The asset account Office Supplies on Hand has a balance of $1,450 on May 1. Purchases of supplies during May amount to $1,100. Supplies on hand at May 31 amount to $920. Identify and analyze the effect of the adjustment on May 31. What will be the effect on net income for May if this adjustment is *not* recorded?

Exercise 4-6 Prepaid Rent—Quarterly Adjustments

LO5
EXAMPLE 4-4

On September 1, Northhampton Industries signed a six-month lease for office space, which is effective September 1. Northhampton agreed to prepay the rent and mailed a check for $12,000 to the landlord on September 1. Assume that Northhampton prepares adjustments only four times a year: on March 31, June 30, September 30, and December 31.

Required

1. Compute the rental cost for each full month.
2. Identify and analyze the transaction for the payment of rent on September 1.
3. Identify and analyze the adjustment on September 30.
4. Assume that the accountant prepares the adjustment on September 30 but forgets to record an adjustment on December 31. Will net income for the year be understated or overstated? by what amount?

Exercise 4-7 Working Backward: Prepaid Insurance

LO5
EXAMPLE 4-4

On December 31, 2017, Baxter Company reported $8,000 in prepaid insurance on its balance sheet. The insurer requires Baxter to pay the annual premium of $24,000 in advance.

Required

1. How much will Baxter recognize each month in insurance expense?
2. On what date does Baxter renew its insurance policy? Explain your answer.

Exercise 4-8 Depreciation

LO5
EXAMPLE 4-5, 4-11

On July 1, 2017, Dexter Corp. buys a computer system for $260,000 in cash. Assume that the computer is expected to have a four-year life and an estimated salvage value of $20,000 at the end of that time.

Required

1. Identify and analyze the transaction to record the purchase of the computer on July 1, 2017.
2. Compute the depreciable cost of the computer.
3. Using the straight-line method, compute the monthly depreciation.
4. Identify and analyze the adjustment to record depreciation at the end of July 2017.
5. Compute the computer's carrying value that will be shown on Dexter's balance sheet prepared on December 31, 2017.

Exercise 4-9 Working Backward: Depreciation

LO5
EXAMPLE 4-5

Polk Corp. purchased new store fixtures for $55,000 on January 31, 2015. Polk depreciates assets using the straight-line method and estimated a salvage value for the machine of $5,000. On its December 31, 2017, balance sheet, Polk reported the following:

Property, plant, and equipment:		
Store fixtures	$55,000	
Accumulated depreciation	15,000	$40,000

(Continued)

Required

1. What is the yearly amount of depreciation expense for the store fixtures?
2. What is the estimated useful life in years for the store fixtures? Explain your answer.

LO5
EXAMPLE 4-4

Exercise 4-10 Prepaid Insurance—Annual Adjustments

On April 1, 2017, Briggs Corp. purchases a 24-month property insurance policy for $72,000. The policy is effective immediately. Assume that Briggs prepares adjustments only once a year, on December 31.

Required

1. Compute the monthly cost of the insurance policy.
2. Identify and analyze the transaction to record the purchase of the policy on April 1, 2017.
3. Identify and analyze the adjustment on December 31, 2017.
4. Assume that the accountant forgets to record an adjustment on December 31, 2017. Will net income for the year ended December 31, 2017, be understated or overstated? Explain your answer.

LO5
EXAMPLE 4-7

Exercise 4-11 Subscriptions

Horse Country Living publishes a monthly magazine for which a 12-month subscription costs $30. All subscriptions require payment of the full $30 in advance. On August 1, the balance in the Subscriptions Received in Advance account was $40,500. During the month of August, the company sold 900 yearly subscriptions. After the adjustment at the end of August, the balance in the Subscriptions Received in Advance account is $60,000.

Required

1. Identify and analyze the transaction to record the sale of the 900 yearly subscriptions during the month of August.
2. Identify and analyze the adjustment on August 31.
3. Assume that the accountant made the correct entry during August to record the sale of the 900 subscriptions but forgot to make the adjustment on August 31. Would net income for August be overstated or understated? Explain your answer.

LO5
EXAMPLE 4-6

Exercise 4-12 Customer Deposits

Wolfe & Wolfe collected $9,000 from a customer on April 1 and agreed to provide legal services during the next three months. Wolfe & Wolfe expects to provide an equal amount of services each month.

Required

1. Identify and analyze the transaction for the receipt of the customer deposit on April 1.
2. Identify and analyze the adjustment on April 30.
3. What will be the effect on net income for April if the adjustment in (2) is not recorded?

LO5
EXAMPLE 4-7

Exercise 4-13 Concert Tickets Sold in Advance

Rock N Roll produces an outdoor concert festival that runs from June 28, 2017, through July 1, 2017. Concertgoers pay $80 for a four-day pass to the festival, and all 10,000 tickets are sold out by the May 1, 2017, deadline to buy tickets. Assume that Rock N Roll prepares adjustments at the end of each month.

Required

1. Identify and analyze the transaction on May 1, 2017, assuming that all 10,000 tickets are sold on this date.
2. Identify and analyze the adjustment on June 30, 2017.
3. Identify and analyze the adjustment on July 31, 2017.

Exercise 4-14 Working Backward: Gift Card Liability

LO5
EXAMPLE 4-7

Dexter Department Stores reported the following on its year-end balance sheets:

	December 31, 2017	December 31, 2016
Current Liabilities:		
Gift card liability	$25,750	$22,640

During 2017, gift cards redeemed at the stores amounted to $33,750.

Required

How much did Dexter receive during 2017 from the sale of gift cards? Explain your answer.

Exercise 4-15 Wages Payable

LO5
EXAMPLE 4-8, 4-11

Denton Corporation employs 50 workers in its plant. Each employee is paid $10 per hour and works seven hours per day, Monday through Friday. Employees are paid every Friday. The last payday was Friday, September 19.

Required

1. Compute the dollar amount of the weekly payroll.
2. Identify and analyze the transaction on Friday, September 26, for the payment of the weekly payroll.
3. Denton prepares monthly financial statements. Identify and analyze the adjustment on Tuesday, September 30, the last day of the month.
4. Identify and analyze the transaction on Friday, October 3, for the payment of the weekly payroll.
5. Will net income for the month of September be understated or overstated if Denton doesn't bother with an adjustment on September 30? Explain your answer.

Exercise 4-16 Interest Payable

LO5
EXAMPLE 4-9, 4-11

Billings Company takes out a 12%, 90-day, $100,000 loan with First National Bank on March 1, 2017.

Required

1. Identify and analyze the transaction to take out the loan on March 1, 2017.
2. Identify and analyze the adjustments for the months of March and April 2017.
3. Identify and analyze the transaction on May 30, 2017, when Billings repays the principal and interest to First National.

Exercise 4-17 Working Backward: Interest Payable

LO5
EXAMPLE 4-9

On July 1, 2017, Rogers Corp. took out a 60-day, $100,000 loan at the bank. On July 31, 2017, Rogers made the following adjustment:

Identify and Analyze	ACTIVITY: Operating
	ACCOUNTS: Interest Payable Increase Interest Expense Increase
	STATEMENT(S): Balance Sheet and Income Statement

Balance Sheet				Income Statement				
ASSETS	=	LIABILITIES	+	STOCKHOLDERS' EQUITY	REVENUES	−	EXPENSES	= NET INCOME
		Interest Payable 500		(500)			Interest Expense 500	(500)

Required

1. What is the interest rate on the loan? Explain your answer.
2. Identify and analyze the transaction on Rogers Corp.'s books on August 31, 2017, when the company repays the principal and interest on the loan.

LO5
EXAMPLE 4-9

Exercise 4-18 Interest Payable—Quarterly Adjustments

Glendive takes out a 12%, 90-day, $100,000 loan with Second State Bank on March 1, 2017. Assume that Glendive prepares adjustments only four times a year: on March 31, June 30, September 30, and December 31.

Required

1. Identify and analyze the transaction to take out the loan on March 1, 2017.
2. Identify and analyze the adjustment on March 31, 2017.
3. Identify and analyze the transaction on May 30, 2017, when Glendive repays the principal and interest to Second State Bank.

LO5
EXAMPLE 4-8

Exercise 4-19 Property Taxes Payable—Annual Adjustments

Lexington Builders owns property in Kaneland County. Lexington's 2016 property taxes amounted to $50,000. Kaneland County will send out the 2017 property tax bills to property owners during April 2018. Taxes must be paid by June 1, 2018. Assume that Lexington prepares adjustments only once a year, on December 31, and that property taxes for 2017 are expected to increase by 5% over those for 2016.

Required

1. Identify and analyze the adjustment to record the property taxes payable on December 31, 2017.
2. Identify and analyze the transaction to record the payment of the 2017 property taxes on June 1, 2018.

LO5
EXAMPLE 4-10

Exercise 4-20 Interest Receivable

On June 1, 2017, MicroTel Enterprises lends $60,000 to MaxiDriver Inc. The loan will be repaid in 60 days with interest at 10%.

Required

1. Identify and analyze the transaction on MicroTel's books on June 1, 2017.
2. Identify and analyze the adjustment on MicroTel's books on June 30, 2017.
3. Identify and analyze the adjustment on MicroTel's books on July 31, 2017, when MaxiDriver repays the principal and interest.

LO5
EXAMPLE 4-10

Exercise 4-21 Rent Receivable

Hudson Corp. has extra space in its warehouse and agrees to rent it out to Stillwater Company at the rate of $2,000 per month. The space was made available to Stillwater beginning on September 1. Under the terms of the agreement, Stillwater pays the month's rent on the fifth day after the end of the month. Assume that Hudson prepares adjustments at the end of each month.

Required

1. How much revenue should Hudson record in September? How much revenue should Hudson record in October?
2. Identify and analyze the transactions, including any adjustments, on Hudson's books during the month of October.

LO5
EXAMPLE 4-10

Exercise 4-22 Working Backward: Rent Receivable

Randy's Rentals reported the following on its year-end balance sheets:

	December 31, 2017	December 31, 2016
Current Assets:		
Rent receivable	$55,000	$35,800

Randy's rents space to a number of tenants, all of whom pay their monthly rent on the 10th of the following month. Randy's reported rent revenue for 2017 of $64,200.

Required

How much cash did Randy's collect from its tenants during 2017? Explain your answer.

Exercise 4-23 The Effect of Ignoring Adjustments on Net Income

LO5
EXAMPLE 4-4, 4-5, 4-6, 4-8, 4-9, 4-10

For each of the following independent situations, determine whether the effect of ignoring the required adjustment will result in an understatement (U), will result in an overstatement (O), or will have no effect (NE) on net income for the period.

Situation	Effect on Net Income
Example: Taxes owed but not yet paid are ignored.	O
1. A company fails to record depreciation on equipment.	_____
2. Sales made during the last week of the period are not recorded.	_____
3. A company neglects to record the expired portion of a prepaid insurance policy. (Its cost was originally recorded in an asset account.)	_____
4. Interest due but not yet paid on a long-term note payable is ignored.	_____
5. Commissions earned by salespeople but not payable until the 10th of the following month are ignored.	_____
6. A landlord receives cash on the date a lease is signed for the rent for the first six months and records Deferred Rent Revenue. The landlord fails to make any adjustment at the end of the first month.	_____

Exercise 4-24 The Effect of Adjustments on the Accounting Equation

LO5
EXAMPLE 4-4, 4-5, 4-6, 4-8, 4-9, 4-10

Determine whether recording each of the following adjustments will increase (I), decrease (D), or have no effect (NE) on each of the three elements of the accounting equation.

	Assets	= Liabilities	+ Stock. Equity
Example: Wages earned during the period but not yet paid are accrued.	NE	I	D
1. Prepaid insurance is reduced for the portion of the policy that has expired during the period.	_____	_____	_____
2. Interest incurred during the period but not yet paid is accrued.	_____	_____	_____
3. Depreciation for the period is recorded.	_____	_____	_____
4. Revenue is recorded for a portion of the liability for amounts collected in advance from customers.	_____	_____	_____
5. Rent revenue is recorded for amounts owed by a tenant but not yet received.	_____	_____	_____
6. Income taxes owed but not yet paid are accrued.	_____	_____	_____

Exercise 4-25 The Accounting Cycle

LO6

The steps in the accounting cycle are listed in random order. Fill in the blank next to each step to indicate its order in the cycle. The first step in the cycle is filled in as an example.

Order	Procedure
_____	Prepare a work sheet.
_____	Close the accounts.
1	Collect and analyze information from source documents.
_____	Prepare financial statements.
_____	Post transactions to accounts in the ledger.
_____	Record and post adjustments.
_____	Journalize daily transactions.

MULTI-CONCEPT EXERCISES

Exercise 4-26 Revenue Recognition, Cash and Accrual Bases

LO1 • 2 • 3
EXAMPLE 4-1, 4-2

Hathaway Health Club sold three-year memberships at a reduced rate during its opening promotion. It sold 1,000 three-year nonrefundable memberships for $366 each. The club expects to sell

(Continued)

100 additional three-year memberships for $900 each over each of the next two years. Membership fees are paid when clients sign up. The club's bookkeeper has prepared the following income statement for the first year of business and projected income statements for Years 2 and 3.

Cash-basis income statements:

	Year 1	Year 2	Year 3
Sales	$366,000	$90,000	$90,000
Equipment*	$100,000	$ 0	$ 0
Salaries and wages	50,000	50,000	50,000
Advertising	5,000	5,000	5,000
Rent and utilities	36,000	36,000	36,000
Net income (loss)	$175,000	$ (1,000)	$ (1,000)

*Equipment was purchased at the beginning of Year 1 for $100,000 and is expected to last for three years and then to be worth $1,000.

Required

1. Convert the income statements for each of the three years to the accrual basis.
2. Describe how the revenue recognition principle applies. Do you believe that the cash-basis or the accrual-basis income statements are more useful to management? to investors? Why?

LO4 • 5 **Exercise 4-27 Depreciation Expense**

EXAMPLE 4-5

During 2017, Carter Company acquired three assets with the following costs, estimated useful lives, and estimated salvage values:

Date	Asset	Cost	Estimated Useful Life	Estimated Salvage Value
March 28	Truck	$ 18,000	5 years	$ 3,000
June 22	Computer	55,000	10 years	5,000
October 3	Building	250,000	30 years	10,000

The company uses the straight-line method to depreciate all assets and computes depreciation to the nearest month. For example, the computer system will be depreciated for six months in 2017.

Required

1. Compute the depreciation expense that Carter will record on each of the three assets for 2017.
2. Comment on the following statement: Accountants could save time and money by simply expensing the cost of long-term assets when they are purchased. In addition, this would be more accurate because depreciation requires estimates of useful life and salvage value.

LO4 • 5 **Exercise 4-28 Accrual of Interest on a Loan**

EXAMPLE 4-9

On July 1, Paxson Corporation takes out a 12%, two-month, $50,000 loan at Friendly National Bank. Principal and interest are to be repaid on August 31.

Required

1. Identify and analyze the transactions or adjustments for July 1 to record the borrowing, for July 31 to record the accrual of interest, and for August 31 to record repayment of the principal and interest.
2. Evaluate the following statement: It would be much easier not to bother with an adjustment on July 31 and simply record interest expense on August 31 when the loan is repaid.

PROBLEMS

Problem 4-1 Adjustments

LO5

Kretz Corporation prepares monthly financial statements and therefore adjusts its accounts at the end of every month. The following information is available for March 2017:

a. Kretz Corporation takes out a 90-day, 8%, $15,000 note on March 1, 2017, with interest and principal to be paid at maturity.

b. The asset account Office Supplies on Hand has a balance of $1,280 on March 1, 2017. During March, Kretz adds $750 to the account for purchases during the period. A count of the supplies on hand at the end of March indicates a balance of $1,370.

c. The company purchased office equipment last year for $62,600. The equipment has an estimated useful life of six years and an estimated salvage value of $5,000.

d. The company's plant operates seven days per week with a daily payroll of $950. Wage earners are paid every Sunday. The last day of the month is Friday, March 31.

e. The company rented an idle warehouse to a neighboring business on February 1, 2017, at a rate of $2,500 per month. On this date, Kretz Corporation recorded Rent Collected in Advance for six months' rent received in advance.

f. On March 1, 2017, Kretz Corporation recorded a liability account, Customer Deposits, for $4,800. This sum represents an amount that a customer paid in advance and that Kretz will earn evenly over a four-month period.

g. Based on its income for the month, Kretz Corporation estimates that federal income taxes for March amount to $3,900.

Required

1. For each of the preceding situations, identify and analyze the adjustments to be recorded on March 31, 2017.

2. Assume that Kretz reports income of $23,000 before any of the adjustments. What net income will Kretz report for March?

Problem 4-2 Annual Adjustments

LO5

Palmer Industries prepares annual financial statements and adjusts its accounts only at the end of the year. The following information is available for the year ended December 31, 2017:

a. Palmer purchased computer equipment two years ago for $15,000. The equipment has an estimated useful life of five years and an estimated salvage value of $250.

b. The Office Supplies account had a balance of $3,600 on January 1, 2017. During 2017, Palmer added $17,600 to the account for purchases of office supplies during the year. A count of the supplies on hand at the end of December 2017 indicates a balance of $1,850.

c. On August 1, 2017, Palmer created a liability account, Customer Deposits, for $24,000. This sum represents an amount that a customer paid in advance and that will be recognized evenly by Palmer over a six-month period.

d. Palmer rented some office space on November 1, 2017, at a rate of $2,700 per month. On that date, Palmer recorded Prepaid Rent for three months' rent paid in advance.

e. Palmer took out a 120-day, 9%, $200,000 note on November 1, 2017, with interest and principal to be paid at maturity.

f. Palmer operates five days per week with an average daily payroll of $500. Palmer pays its employees every Thursday. December 31, 2017, is a Sunday.

Required

1. For each of the preceding situations, identify and analyze the adjustment to be recorded on December 31, 2017.

2. Assume that Palmer's accountant forgets to record the adjustments on December 31, 2017. Will net income for the year be understated or overstated? by what amount? (Ignore the effect of income taxes.)

LO5   Problem 4-3 Recurring Transactions and Adjustments

Following are Butler Realty Corporation's accounts, identified by number. The company has been in the real estate business for ten years and prepares financial statements monthly. Following the list of accounts is a series of transactions entered into by Butler. For each transaction, enter the number(s) of the account(s) affected.

Accounts

1. Cash	11. Notes Payable
2. Accounts Receivable	12. Capital Stock, $10 par
3. Prepaid Rent	13. Paid-In Capital in Excess of Par
4. Office Supplies	14. Commissions Revenue
5. Automobiles	15. Office Supply Expense
6. Accumulated Depreciation	16. Rent Expense
7. Land	17. Salaries and Wages Expense
8. Accounts Payable	18. Depreciation Expense
9. Salaries and Wages Payable	19. Interest Expense
10. Income Tax Payable	20. Income Tax Expense

Transaction

a. Example: Issued additional shares of stock to owners at amount in excess of par.   <u>1, 12, 13</u>

b. Purchased automobiles for cash.   _____

c. Purchased land; made cash down payment and signed a promissory note for the balance.   _____

d. Paid cash to landlord for rent for next 12 months.   _____

e. Purchased office supplies on account.   _____

f. Collected cash for commissions from clients for properties sold during the month.   _____

g. Collected cash for commissions from clients for properties sold the prior month.   _____

h. During the month, sold properties for which cash for commissions will be collected from clients next month.   _____

i. Paid for office supplies purchased on account in an earlier month.   _____

j. Recorded an adjustment to recognize wages and salaries incurred but not yet paid.   _____

k. Recorded an adjustment for office supplies used during the month.   _____

l. Recorded an adjustment for the portion of prepaid rent that expired during the month.   _____

m. Made required month-end payment on note taken out in (c); payment is part principal and part interest.   _____

n. Recorded an adjustment for monthly depreciation on the autos.   _____

o. Recorded an adjustment for income taxes.   _____

LO5   Problem 4-4 Use of Account Balances as a Basis for Annual Adjustments

The following account balances are taken from the records of Chauncey Company at December 31, 2017. The Prepaid Insurance account represents the cost of a three-year policy purchased on August 1, 2017. The Rent Collected in Advance account represents the cash received from a tenant on June 1, 2017, for 12 months' rent beginning on that date. The Note Receivable represents a nine-month promissory note received from a customer on September 1, 2017. Principal and interest at an annual rate of 9% will be received on June 1, 2018.

Prepaid Insurance	$ 7,200
Rent Collected in Advance	6,000
Note Receivable	50,000

Required

1. Identify and analyze the three necessary adjustments on the books of Chauncey on December 31, 2017. Assume that Chauncey prepares adjustments only once a year, on December 31.
2. Assume that adjustments are made at the end of each month rather than only at the end of the year. What would be the balance in Prepaid Insurance *before* the December adjustment was made? Explain your answer.

Problem 4-5 Use of Account Balances as a Basis for Adjustments   LO5

Bob Reynolds operates a real estate business. A list of accounts on April 30, 2017, *before* any adjustments are recorded, appears as follows:

Cash	$15,700
Prepaid Insurance	450
Office Supplies	250
Office Equipment	50,000
Accumulated Depreciation—Office Equipment	5,000
Automobile	12,000
Accumulated Depreciation—Auto	1,400
Accounts Payable	6,500
Deferred Commissions	9,500
Notes Payable	2,000
Capital Stock	10,000
Retained Earnings	40,000
Dividends	2,500
Commissions Revenue	17,650
Utilities Expense	2,300
Salaries Expense	7,400
Advertising Expense	1,450

Other Data

a. The monthly insurance cost is $50.

b. Office supplies on hand on April 30, 2017, amount to $180.

c. The office equipment was purchased on April 1, 2016. On that date, it had an estimated useful life of ten years.

d. On September 1, 2016, the automobile was purchased; it had an estimated useful life of five years.

e. A deposit is received in advance of providing any services for first-time customers. Amounts received in advance are recorded initially in the account Deferred Commissions. Based on services provided to these first-time customers, the balance in this account at the end of April should be $5,000.

f. Repeat customers are allowed to pay for services one month after the date of the sale of their property. Services rendered during the month but not yet collected or billed to these customers amount to $1,500.

g. Interest owed on the note payable but not yet paid amounts to $20.

h. Salaries owed but unpaid to employees at the end of the month amount to $2,500.

Required

1. For each of the items of other data (a) through (h), identify and analyze the adjustment necessary on April 30, 2017.
2. Compute the net increase or decrease in net income for the month from the recognition of the adjustments in (1). (Ignore income taxes.)
3. Note the balance in Accumulated Depreciation—Office Equipment of $5,000. Explain why the account contains a balance of $5,000 on April 30, 2017.

LO5 **Problem 4-6 Reconstruction of Adjustments from Account Balances**

Taggart Corp. records adjustments each month before preparing monthly financial statements. The following selected account balances on May 31, 2017 and June 30, 2017, reflect month-end adjustments:

Account Title	May 31, 2017	June 30, 2017
Prepaid Insurance	$3,600	$3,450
Equipment	9,600	9,600
Accumulated Depreciation	1,280	1,360
Notes Payable	9,600	9,600
Interest Payable	2,304	2,448

Required

1. The company purchased a 36-month insurance policy on June 1, 2016. Identify and analyze the adjustment necessary for insurance on June 30, 2017.
2. What was the original cost of the insurance policy? Explain your answer.
3. The equipment was purchased on February 1, 2016, for $9,600. Taggart uses straight-line depreciation and estimates that the equipment will have no salvage value. Identify and analyze the adjustment necessary for depreciation on June 30, 2017.
4. What is the equipment's estimated useful life in months? Explain your answer.
5. Taggart signed a two-year note payable on February 1, 2016, for the purchase of the equipment. Interest on the note accrues on a monthly basis and will be paid at maturity along with the principal amount of $9,600. Identify and analyze the adjustment necessary for interest on June 30, 2017.
6. What is the monthly interest rate on the loan? Explain your answer.

LO5 **Problem 4-7 Use of Account Balances as a Basis for Adjustments**

Four Star Video has been in the video rental business for five years. The following is a list of accounts for Four Star Video at May 31, 2017. It reflects the recurring transactions for the month of May but does not reflect any month-end adjustments.

Cash	$ 4,000
Prepaid Rent	6,600
Video Inventory	25,600
Display Stands	8,900
Accumulated Depreciation	5,180
Accounts Payable	3,260
Customer Subscriptions	4,450
Capital Stock	5,000
Retained Earnings	22,170
Rental Revenue	9,200
Wage and Salary Expense	2,320
Utilities Expense	1,240
Advertising Expense	600

The following additional information is available:

a. Four Star rents a store in a shopping mall and prepays the annual rent of $7,200 on April 1 of each year.
b. The asset account Video Inventory represents the cost of videos purchased from suppliers. When a new title is purchased from a supplier, its cost is added to this account. When a title has served its useful life and can no longer be rented (even at a reduced price), it is removed from the inventory in the store. Based on the monthly count, the cost of titles on hand at the end of May is $23,140.
c. The display stands have an estimated useful life of five years and an estimated salvage value of $500.

d. Wages and salaries owed but unpaid to employees at the end of May amount to $1,450.
e. In addition to individual rentals, Four Star operates a popular discount subscription program. Cus-
    tomers pay an annual fee of $120 for an unlimited number of rentals. Based on the $10 per month
    fee on each of these subscriptions, the amount recognized for the month of May is $2,440.
f. Four Star accrues income taxes using an estimated tax rate equal to 30% of the income for the
    month.

Required

1. For each of the items of additional information, (a) through (f), identify and analyze the nec-
    essary adjustment on May 31, 2017.
2. On the basis of the information you have, does Four Star appear to be a profitable business?
    Explain your answer.

MULTI-CONCEPT PROBLEMS

Problem 4-8 Revenue and Expense Recognition   LO3 • 4

Two years ago, Darlene Darby opened a delivery service. Darby reports the following accounts
on her income statement:

Sales	$69,000
Advertising Expense	3,500
Salaries Expense	39,000
Rent Expense	10,000

These amounts represent two years of revenue and expenses. Darby asks you how she can tell
how much of the income is from the first year of business and how much is from the second year.
She provides the following additional data:

a. Sales in the second year are double those of the first year.
b. Advertising expense is for a $500 opening promotion and weekly ads in the newspaper.
c. Salaries represent one employee for the first nine months and two employees for the remain-
    der of the time. Each is paid the same salary. No raises have been granted.
d. Rent has not changed since the business opened.

Required

Prepare income statements for Years 1 and 2.

Problem 4-9 Monthly Transactions, Adjustments,   LO5 • 6
and Financial Statements

Moonlight Bay Inn is incorporated on January 2, 2017, by its three owners, each of whom contributes $20,000 in cash in exchange for shares of stock in the business. In addition to the sale of
stock, the following transactions are entered into during the month of January:

January 2: A Victorian inn is purchased for $50,000 in cash. An appraisal performed on this
            date indicates that the land is worth $15,000, and the remaining balance of the
            purchase price is attributable to the house. The owners estimate that the house will
            have an estimated useful life of 25 years and an estimated salvage value of $5,000.

January 3: A two-year, 12%, $30,000 promissory note was signed at Second State Bank.
            Interest and principal will be repaid on the maturity date of January 3, 2019.

January 4: New furniture for the inn is purchased at a cost of $15,000 in cash. The furniture
            has an estimated useful life of ten years and no salvage value.

January 5: A 24-month property insurance policy is purchased for $6,000 in cash.

January 6: An advertisement for the inn is placed in the local newspaper. Moonlight Bay pays
            $450 cash for the ad, which will run in the paper throughout January.

(Continued)

January 7:	Cleaning supplies are purchased on account for $950. The bill is payable within 30 days.
January 15:	Wages of $4,230 for the first half of the month are paid in cash.
January 16:	A guest mails the business $980 in cash as a deposit for a room to be rented for two weeks. The guest plans to stay at the inn during the last week of January and the first week of February.
January 31:	Cash receipts from rentals of rooms for the month amount to $8,300.
January 31:	Cash receipts from operation of the restaurant for the month amount to $6,600.
January 31:	Each stockholder is paid $200 in cash dividends.

Required

1. Identify and analyze each of the preceding transactions.
2. Prepare a list of accounts and their balances for Moonlight Bay at January 31, 2017. Reflect the recurring transactions for the month of January but not the necessary month-end adjustments.
3. Identify and analyze the necessary adjustments for each of the following:

    a. Depreciation of the house
    b. Depreciation of the furniture
    c. Interest on the promissory note
    d. Recognition of the expired portion of the insurance
    e. Recognition of a portion of the guest's deposit
    f. Wages earned during the second half of January amount to $5,120 and will be paid on February 3.
    g. Cleaning supplies on hand on January 31 amount to $230.
    h. A gas and electric bill that is received from the city amounts to $740 and is payable by February 5.
    i. Income taxes are to be accrued at a rate of 30% of income before taxes.

4. Prepare in good form the following financial statements:

    a. Income statement for the month ended January 31, 2017
    b. Statement of retained earnings for the month ended January 31, 2017
    c. Balance sheet at January 31, 2017

5. Assume that you are the loan officer at Second State Bank. (Refer to the transaction on January 3.) What are your reactions to Moonlight's first month of operations? Are you comfortable with the loan you made? Explain your answer.

ALTERNATE PROBLEMS

LO5   Problem 4-1A   Adjustments

Flood Relief Inc. prepares monthly financial statements and therefore adjusts its accounts at the end of every month. The following information is available for June 2017:

a. Flood received a $10,000, 4%, two-year note receivable from a customer for services rendered. The principal and interest are due on June 1, 2019. Flood expects to be able to collect the note and interest in full at that time.
b. Office supplies totaling $5,600 were purchased during the month. The asset account Supplies is increased whenever a purchase is made. A count in the storeroom on June 30, 2017, indicates that supplies on hand amount to $507. The supplies on hand at the beginning of the month total $475.
c. The company purchased machines last year for $170,000. The machines are expected to be used for four years and have an estimated salvage value of $2,000.
d. On June 1, the company paid $4,650 for rent for June, July, and August and increased the asset Prepaid Rent. It did not have a balance on June 1.
e. The company operates seven days per week with a weekly payroll of $7,000. Wage earners are paid every Sunday. The last day of the month is Friday, June 30.

f. Based on its income for the month, Flood estimates that federal income taxes for June amount to $2,900.

Required

1. For each of the preceding situations, prepare in general journal form the appropriate adjusting entry to be recorded on June 30, 2017.
2. Assume that Flood Relief reports income of $35,000 before any of the adjustments. What net income will Flood Relief report for June?

Problem 4-2A Annual Adjustments   LO5

Ogonquit Enterprises prepares annual financial statements and adjusts its accounts only at the end of the year. The following information is available for the year ended December 31, 2017:

a. Ogonquit purchased office furniture last year for $25,000. The furniture has an estimated useful life of seven years and an estimated salvage value of $4,000.
b. The Supplies account had a balance of $1,200 on January 1, 2017. During 2017, Ogonquit added $12,900 to the account for purchases of supplies during the year. A count of the supplies on hand at the end of December 2017 indicates a balance of $900.
c. On July 1, 2017, Ogonquit created a liability account, Customer Deposits, for $8,800. This sum represents an amount that a customer paid in advance and that will be recognized evenly by Ogonquit over an eight-month period.
d. Ogonquit rented some warehouse space on September 1, 2017, at a rate of $4,000 per month. On that date, Ogonquit recorded Prepaid Rent for six months' rent paid in advance.
e. Ogonquit took out a 90-day, 6%, $30,000 note on November 1, 2017, with interest and principal to be paid at maturity.
f. Ogonquit operates five days per week with an average weekly payroll of $4,150. Ogonquit pays its employees every Thursday. December 31, 2017, is a Sunday.

Required

1. For each of the preceding situations, identify and analyze the adjustment necessary on December 31, 2017.
2. Assume that Ogonquit's accountant forgets to record the adjustments on December 31, 2017. Will net income for the year be understated or overstated? by what amount? (Ignore the effect of income taxes.)

Problem 4-3A Recurring Transactions and Adjustments   LO5

Following are the accounts of Dominique Inc., an interior decorator. The company has been in the decorating business for ten years and prepares quarterly financial statements. Following the list of accounts is a series of transactions entered into by Dominique. For each transaction, enter the number(s) of the account(s) affected.

Accounts

1. Cash	11. Capital Stock, $1 par
2. Accounts Receivable	12. Paid-In Capital in Excess of Par
3. Prepaid Rent	13. Consulting Revenue
4. Office Supplies	14. Office Supply Expense
5. Office Equipment	15. Rent Expense
6. Accumulated Depreciation	16. Salaries and Wages Expense
7. Accounts Payable	17. Depreciation Expense
8. Salaries and Wages Payable	18. Interest Expense
9. Income Tax Payable	19. Income Tax Expense
10. Interim Financing Notes Payable	

a. Example: Issued additional shares of stock to owners; shares issued at greater than par.   1, 11, 12

b. Purchased office equipment for cash.   _____

c. Collected open accounts receivable from customer.   _____

(Continued)

d. Purchased office supplies on account.   _____

e. Paid office rent for the next six months.   _____

f. Paid interest on an interim financing note.   _____

g. Paid salaries and wages.   _____

h. Purchased office equipment; made a down payment in cash and signed an interim
   financing note.   _____

i. Provided services on account.   _____

j. Recorded depreciation on equipment.   _____

k. Recorded income taxes due next month.   _____

l. Recorded the used office supplies.   _____

m. Recorded the used portion of prepaid rent.   _____

LO5 Problem 4-4A Use of Account Balances as a Basis for Annual Adjustments

The following account balances are taken from the records of Laugherty Inc. at December 31, 2017. The Supplies account represents the cost of supplies on hand at the beginning of the year plus all purchases. A physical count on December 31, 2017, shows only $1,520 of supplies on hand. The Deferred Revenue account represents the cash received from a customer on May 1, 2017, for 12 months of service beginning on that date. The Note Payable represents a six-month promissory note signed with a supplier on September 1, 2017. Principal and interest at an annual rate of 10% will be paid on March 1, 2018.

Supplies	$ 5,790
Deferred Revenue	1,800
Note Payable	60,000

Required

1. Identify and analyze the adjustments necessary on the books of Laugherty on December 31, 2017. Assume that Laugherty prepares adjustments only once a year, on December 31.

2. Assume that adjustments are made at the end of each month rather than only at the end of the year. What would be the balance in Deferred Revenue *before* the December adjustment was made? Explain your answer.

LO5 Problem 4-5A Use of Account Balances as a Basis for Adjustments

Lori Matlock operates a graphic arts business. A list of accounts on June 30, 2017, *before* recording any adjustments, appears as follows:

Cash	$ 7,000
Prepaid Rent	18,000
Supplies	15,210
Office Equipment	46,120
Accumulated Depreciation—Equipment	4,000
Accounts Payable	1,800
Notes Payable	2,000
Capital Stock	50,000
Retained Earnings	24,350
Dividends	8,400
Revenue	46,850
Utilities Expense	2,850
Salaries Expense	19,420
Advertising Expense	12,000

Other Data

a. The monthly rent is $600.

b. Supplies on hand on June 30, 2017, amount to $1,290.

c. The office equipment was purchased on June 1, 2016. On that date, it had an estimated useful life of ten years and a salvage value of $6,120.

d. Interest owed on the note payable but not yet paid amounts to $50.

e. Salaries of $620 are owed but unpaid to employees at the end of the month.

Required

1. For each of the items of other data, (a) through (e), identify and analyze the necessary adjustment at June 30, 2017.
2. Note the balance in Accumulated Depreciation—Equipment of $4,000. Explain why the account contains a balance of $4,000 on June 30, 2017.

Problem 4-6A Reconstruction of Adjustments from Account Balances   LO5

Zola Corporation records adjustments each month before preparing monthly financial statements. The following selected account balances reflect the month-end adjustments.

Account Title	May 31, 2017	June 30, 2017
Prepaid Rent	$4,000	$3,000
Equipment	9,600	9,600
Accumulated Depreciation	800	900
Notes Payable	9,600	9,600
Interest Payable	768	864

Required

1. The company paid for a six-month lease on April 1, 2017. Identify and analyze the adjustment for rent on June 30, 2017.
2. What amount was prepaid on April 1, 2017? Explain your answer.
3. The equipment was purchased on September 30, 2016, for $9,600. Zola uses straight-line depreciation and estimates that the equipment will have no salvage value. Identify and analyze the adjustment for depreciation on June 30, 2017.
4. What is the equipment's estimated useful life in months? Explain your answer.
5. Zola signed a two-year note on September 30, 2016, for the purchase of the equipment. Interest on the note accrues on a monthly basis and will be paid at maturity along with the principal amount of $9,600. Identify and analyze the adjustment for interest expense on June 30, 2017.
6. What is the monthly interest rate on the loan? Explain your answer.

Problem 4-7A Use of Account Balances as a Basis for Adjustments   LO5

Lewis and Associates has been in the termite inspection and treatment business for five years. The following is a list of accounts for Lewis on June 30, 2017. It reflects the recurring transactions for the month of June but does not reflect any month-end adjustments:

Cash	$ 6,200
Accounts Receivable	10,400
Prepaid Rent	4,400
Chemical Inventory	9,400
Equipment	18,200
Accumulated Depreciation	1,050
Accounts Payable	1,180
Capital Stock	5,000
Retained Earnings	25,370
Treatment Revenue	40,600
Wages and Salary Expense	22,500
Utilities Expense	1,240
Advertising Expense	860

(Continued)

The following additional information is available:

a. Lewis rents a warehouse with office space and prepays the annual rent of $4,800 on May 1 of each year.

b. The asset account Equipment represents the cost of treatment equipment, which has an estimated useful life of ten years and an estimated salvage value of $200.

c. Chemical inventory on hand equals $1,300.

d. Wages and salaries owed but unpaid to employees at the end of the month amount to $1,080.

e. Lewis accrues income taxes using an estimated tax rate equal to 30% of the income for the month.

Required

1. For each of the items of additional information, (a) through (e), identify and analyze the necessary adjustment on June 30, 2017.

2. On the basis of the information you have, does Lewis appear to be a profitable business? Explain your answer.

ALTERNATE MULTI-CONCEPT PROBLEMS

LO3 • 4   Problem 4-8A   Revenue and Expense Recognition

Two years ago, Sue Stern opened an audio book rental shop. Sue reports the following accounts on her income statement:

Sales	$84,000
Advertising Expense	10,500
Salaries Expense	12,000
Depreciation on CDs	5,000
Rent Expense	18,000

These amounts represent two years of revenue and expenses. Sue asks you how she can tell how much of the income is from the first year and how much is from the second year of business. She provides the following additional data:

a. Sales in the second year are triple those of the first year.

b. Advertising expense is for a $1,500 opening promotion and weekly ads in the newspaper.

c. Salaries represent one employee who was hired eight months ago. No raises have been granted.

d. Rent has not changed since the shop opened.

Required

Prepare income statements for Years 1 and 2.

LO5 • 6   Problem 4-9A   Adjustments and Financial Statements

The following account balances are available for Tenfour Trucking Company on January 31, 2017:

Cash	$ 27,340
Accounts Receivable	41,500
Prepaid Insurance	18,000
Warehouse	40,000
Accumulated Depreciation—Warehouse	21,600
Truck Fleet	240,000
Accumulated Depreciation—Truck Fleet	112,500
Land	20,000
Accounts Payable	32,880
Notes Payable	50,000
Interest Payable	4,500

Customer Deposits	6,000
Capital Stock	100,000
Retained Earnings	40,470
Freight Revenue	165,670
Gas and Oil Expense	57,330
Maintenance Expense	26,400
Wage and Salary Expense	43,050
Dividends	20,000

Required

1. Identify and analyze the necessary adjustments at January 31, 2017, for each of the following:

   a. Prepaid insurance represents the cost of a 24-month policy purchased on January 1, 2017.

   b. The warehouse has an estimated useful life of 20 years and an estimated salvage value of $4,000.

   c. The truck fleet has an estimated useful life of six years and an estimated salvage value of $15,000.

   d. The promissory note was signed on January 1, 2016. Interest at an annual rate of 9% and the principal of $50,000 are due on December 31, 2017.

   e. The customer deposits represent amounts paid in advance by new customers. A total of $4,500 of the balance in Customer Deposits was recognized during January 2017.

   f. Wages and salaries earned by employees at the end of January but not yet paid amount to $8,200.

   g. Income taxes are accrued at a rate of 30% at the end of each month.

2. Prepare in good form the following financial statements:

   a. Income statement for the month ended January 31, 2017
   b. Statement of retained earnings for the month ended January 31, 2017
   c. Balance sheet at January 31, 2017

3. Compute Tenfour's current ratio. What does this ratio tell you about the company's liquidity?
4. Compute Tenfour's profit margin. What does this ratio tell you about the company's profitability?

DECISION CASES

Reading and Interpreting Financial Statements

Decision Case 4-1 Comparing Two Companies in the Same Industry: Chipotle and Panera Bread

LO3

REAL WORLD

Refer to the financial information for **Chipotle** and **Panera Bread** reproduced at the back of the book for the information needed to answer the following questions.

Required

1. Locate the note in each company's annual report included in its Form 10-K for the 2015 year in which it discusses revenue recognition. How does each company describe the point at which it recognizes revenue from customers? Are there any significant differences in the organizations' revenue recognition policies?

2. What dollar amount does Chipotle report for accounts receivable on its most recent balance sheet? What percent of the company's total current assets are comprised of accounts receivable? What is the dollar amount of Panera Bread's trade accounts receivable on its most recent balance sheet? What percent of total current assets is comprised of accounts receivable? For which company does its accounts receivable constitute a higher percentage of its total current assets?

LO3

REAL WORLD

Decision Case 4-2 Reading and Interpreting Nordstrom's Notes—Revenue Recognition

The following excerpt is taken from Note 1 on page 41 of **Nordstrom**'s Form 10-K for the fiscal year ended January 30, 2016:

Net Sales

We recognize revenue net of estimated returns and excluding sales taxes. Revenue from sales to customers shipped directly from our stores, website and catalog, which includes shipping revenue when applicable, is recognized upon estimated receipt by the customer. We estimate customer merchandise returns based on historical return patterns and reduce sales and cost of sales accordingly.

The following excerpt on page 43 is from the same note:

Gift Cards

We recognize revenue from the sale of gift cards when the gift card is redeemed by the customer, or we recognize breakage income when the likelihood of redemption, based on historical experience, is deemed to be remote.

Required

1. According to the note, when does Nordstrom recognize revenue from sales to customers shipped directly from its stores, its website and catalog sales? Why would the way in which revenue is recognized from these three types of sales differ from sales in its retail stores?
2. According to the note, how does Nordstrom recognize revenue associated with its gift cards? Assume that you buy a gift card for a friend. Identify and analyze the transaction Nordstrom records at the time you buy the card. Identify and analyze the adjustment Nordstrom records when your friend redeems the card.

LO3

REAL WORLD

Decision Case 4-3 Reading and Interpreting Sears Holdings Corporation's Notes—Revenue Recognition

The following excerpt is taken from page 66 of the **Sears Holdings Corporation** (parent company of Kmart and Sears) 10-K for the fiscal year ended January 30, 2016: "Revenues from the sale of service contracts and the related direct acquisition costs are deferred and amortized over the lives of the associated contracts, while the associated service costs are expensed as incurred."

Required

1. Assume that you buy a wide-screen television from Sears for $2,500, including a $180 service contract that will cover three years. Why does Sears recognize the revenue associated with the service contract over its life even though cash is received at the time of the sale?
2. How much revenue will Sears recognize from your purchase of the television and the service contract in Years 1, 2, and 3? (Assume a straight-line approach.) What corresponding account can you look for in the financial statements to determine the amount of service contract revenue that will be recognized in the future?

Making Financial Decisions

LO2 • 3 • 4

Decision Case 4-4 The Use of Net Income and Cash Flow to Evaluate a Company

After you have gained five years of experience with a large CPA firm, one of your clients, Duke Inc., asks you to take over as chief financial officer for the business. Duke advises its clients on the purchase of software products and assists them in installing the programs on their computer systems. Because the business is relatively new (it began servicing clients in January 2017), its accounting records are somewhat limited. In fact, the only statement available is the following income statement for the first year:

Duke Inc.
Statement of Income
For the Year Ended December 31, 2017

Revenues		$1,250,000
Expenses:		
Salaries and wages	$480,000	
Supplies	65,000	
Utilities	30,000	
Rent	120,000	
Depreciation	345,000	
Interest	138,000	
Total expenses		1,178,000
Net income		$ 72,000

Based on its relatively modest profit margin of 5.76% (net income of $72,000 divided by revenues of $1,250,000), you are concerned about joining the new business. To alleviate your concerns, the president of the company is able to give you the following additional information:

a. Clients are given 90 days to pay their bills for consulting services provided by Duke. On December 31, 2017, $230,000 of the revenues is yet to be collected in cash.

b. Employees are paid on a monthly basis. Salaries and wages of $480,000 include the December payroll of $40,000, which will be paid on January 5, 2018.

c. The company purchased $100,000 of operating supplies when it began operations in January. The balance of supplies on hand at December 31 amounts to $35,000.

d. Office space is rented in a downtown high-rise building at a monthly cost of $10,000. When the company moved into the office in January, it prepaid its rent for the next 18 months beginning January 1, 2017.

e. On January 1, 2017, Duke purchased a computer system and related accessories at a cost of $1,725,000. The estimated useful life of the system is five years.

f. The computer system was purchased by signing a three-year, 8% note payable for $1,725,000 on the date of purchase. The principal amount of the note and interest for the three years are due on January 1, 2020.

Required

1. Based on the income statement and the additional information given, prepare a statement of cash flows for Duke for 2017. (*Hint:* Simply list all of the cash inflows and outflows that relate to operations.)

2. On the basis of the income statement given and the statement of cash flows prepared in part (1), do you think it would be a wise decision to join the company as its chief financial officer? Include in your response any additional questions that you believe are appropriate to ask before joining the company.

Decision Case 4-5 Depreciation   LO4

Jensen Inc., a graphic arts studio, is considering the purchase of computer equipment and software for a total cost of $18,000. Jensen can pay for the equipment and software over three years at the rate of $6,000 per year. The equipment is expected to last 10 to 20 years, but because of changing technology, Jensen believes it may need to replace the system in as soon as three to five years. A three-year lease of similar equipment and software is available for $6,000 per year. Jensen's accountant has asked you to recommend whether the company should purchase or lease the equipment and software and to suggest the length of time over which to depreciate the software and equipment if the company makes the purchase.

Required

Ignoring the effect of taxes, would you recommend the purchase or the lease? Why or why not? Referring to the definition of *depreciation*, what appropriate useful life should be used for the equipment and software?

Ethical Decision Making

ETHICAL DECISION MODEL

LO2 • 3 • 4 • 5   **Decision Case 4-6** **Revenue Recognition and the Matching Principle**

Listum & Sellum Inc. is a medium-sized midwestern real estate company. It was founded five years ago by its two principal stockholders, Willie Listum and Dewey Sellum. Willie is president of the company, and Dewey is vice president of sales. Listum & Sellum has enjoyed tremendous growth since its inception by aggressively seeking out listings for residential real estate and paying a generous commission to the selling agent.

The company receives a 6% commission for selling a client's property and gives two-thirds of this, or 4% of the selling price, to the selling agent. For example, if a house sells for $100,000, Listum & Sellum receives $6,000 and pays $4,000 of this to the selling agent. At the time of the sale, the company records increases in Accounts Receivable and Sales Revenue of $6,000 each. The accounts receivable is normally collected within 30 days. Also at the time of sale, the company records increases in Commissions Expense and Commissions Payable of $4,000 each. Sales agents are paid by the 15th of the month following the month of the sale. In addition to the commissions expense, Listum & Sellum's other two major expenses are advertising of listings in local newspapers and depreciation of the company's fleet of Cadillacs. (Dewey believes that all of the sales agents should drive Cadillacs.) The newspaper ads will run for one month, and the company has until the 10th of the following month to pay that month's bill. The automobiles are depreciated over four years. (Dewey doesn't believe that any salesperson should drive a car that is more than four years old.)

Due to a downturn in the economy in the Midwest, sales have been sluggish for the first 11 months of the current year, which ends on June 30. Willie is very disturbed by the slow sales this particular year because a large note payable to the local bank is due in July and the company plans to ask the bank to renew the note for another three years. Dewey seems less concerned by the unfortunate timing of the recession and has some suggestions as to how he and Willie can "paint the rosiest possible picture for the banker" when they go for the loan extension in July. In fact, Dewey has some very specific recommendations for you as to how to account for transactions during June, the last month in the fiscal year.

You are the controller for Listum & Sellum and have been treated very well by Willie and Dewey since joining the company two years ago. In fact, Dewey insists that you drive the top-of-the-line Cadillac. Following are his suggestions:

First, for any sales made in June, we can record the 6% commission revenue immediately but delay recording the 4% commission expense until July, when the sales agent is paid. We record the sales at the same time we always have, the sales agents get paid when they always have, the bank sees how profitable we have been, we get our loan, and everybody is happy!

Second, since we won't be paying our advertising bills for the month of June until July 10, we can wait until then to record the expense. The timing seems perfect since we are meeting with the bank for the loan extension on July 8.

Third, since we will be depreciating the fleet of "Caddys" for the year ending June 30, how about changing the estimated useful life on them to eight years instead of four years? We won't say anything to the sales agents; no need to rile them up about having to drive their cars for eight years. Anyhow, the change to eight years would just be for accounting purposes. In fact, we could even switch back to four years for accounting purposes next year. Likewise, the changes in recognizing commission expense and advertising expense don't need to be permanent either; these are just slight bookkeeping changes to help us get over the hump!

Required

Use the Ethical Decision Framework in Exhibit 1-9 to complete the following requirements:

1. **Recognize an ethical dilemma:** Explain why each of the three proposed changes in accounting will result in an increase in net income for the year ending June 30. Identify any concerns you have with each of these proposed changes in accounting from the perspective of GAAP. What ethical dilemma(s) do you now face?

2. **Analyze the key elements in the situation:**
   a. Who may benefit or be harmed?
   b. How are they likely to benefit or be harmed?
   c. What rights or claims may be violated?
   d. What specific interests are in conflict?
   e. What are your responsibilities and obligations?

3. **List alternatives and evaluate the impact of each on those affected:** As the controller, what are your options in dealing with the ethical dilemma(s) you identified in (1) above? Which provides the other investors and the bank with information that is most relevant, most complete, most neutral, and most free from error?

4. **Select the best alternative:** Among the alternatives, which one would you select? Explain your decision in the form of a memo written to the two owners.

Decision Case 4-7 Advice to a Potential Investor   LO4

Century Company was organized 15 months ago as a management consulting firm. At that time, the owners invested a total of $50,000 cash in exchange for stock. Century purchased equipment for $35,000 cash and supplies to be used in the business. The equipment is expected to last seven years with no salvage value. Supplies are purchased on account and paid for in the month after the purchase. Century normally has about $1,000 of supplies on hand. Its client base has increased so dramatically that the president and chief financial officer have approached an investor to provide additional cash for expansion. The balance sheet and income statement for the first year of business are as follows:

Century Company
Balance Sheet
December 31, 2017

Assets		Liabilities and Stockholders' Equity	
Cash	$10,100	Accounts payable	$ 2,300
Accounts receivable	1,200	Common stock	50,000
Supplies	16,500	Retained earnings	10,500
Equipment	35,000		
Total	$62,800	Total	$62,800

Century Company
Income Statement
For the Year Ended December 31, 2017

Revenues		$82,500
Wages and salaries	$60,000	
Utilities	12,000	72,000
Net income		$10,500

Required

The investor has asked you to look at these financial statements and give an opinion about Century's future profitability. Are the statements prepared in accordance with GAAP? Why or why not? Based on these two statements, what would you advise? What additional information would you need to give an educated opinion?

INTEGRATIVE PROBLEM

Completing Financial Statements, Computing Ratios, Comparing Accrual versus Cash Income, and Evaluating the Company's Cash Needs

Mountain Home Health Inc. provides home nursing services in the Great Smoky Mountains of Tennessee. When contacted by a client or referred by a physician, nurses visit the patient and discuss needed services with the physician.

Mountain Home Health earns revenue from patient services. Most of the revenue comes from billing insurance companies, the state of Tennessee, or the Medicare program. Amounts billed are recorded in the Billings Receivable account. Insurance companies, the state government, and the federal government do not fully fund all procedures. For example, the state of Tennessee pays an average 78% of billed amounts. Mountain Home Health has already removed the uncollectible amounts from the Billings Receivable account and reports it and Medical Services Revenue at the net amount. Services provided but not yet recorded totaled $16,000, net of allowances for uncollectible amounts. The firm earns a minor portion of its total revenue directly from patients in the form of cash.

Employee salaries, medical supplies, depreciation, and gasoline are the major expenses. Employees are paid every Friday for work performed during the Saturday-to-Friday pay period. Salaries amount to $800 per day. In 2017, December 31 falls on a Sunday. Medical supplies (average use of $1,500 per week) are purchased periodically to support healthcare coverage. The inventory of supplies on hand on December 31 amounted to $8,653.

The firm owns five automobiles (all purchased at the same time) that average 50,000 miles per year and are replaced every three years. They typically have no residual value. The building has an expected life of 20 years with no residual value. Straight-line depreciation is used on all of the firm's assets. Gasoline costs, which are a cash expenditure, average $375 per day. The firm purchases a three-year extended warranty contract to cover maintenance costs. The contract costs $9,000. (Assume equal use each year.)

On December 29, 2017, Mountain Home Health declared a dividend of $10,000, payable on January 15, 2018. The firm makes annual mortgage payments of principal and interest each June 30. The interest rate on the mortgage is 6%.

The following account balances are available for Mountain Home Health on December 31, 2017:

Cash	$ 77,400
Billings Receivable (net)	151,000
Medical Supplies	73,000
Extended Warranty	3,000
Automobiles	90,000
Accumulated Depreciation—Automobiles	60,000
Building	200,000
Accumulated Depreciation—Building	50,000
Accounts Payable	22,000
Dividend Payable	10,000
Mortgage Payable	100,000
Capital Stock	100,000
Additional Paid-In Capital	50,000
Retained Earnings	99,900
Medical Services Revenue	550,000
Salary and Wages Expense	288,000
Gasoline Expense	137,500
Utilities Expense	12,000
Dividends	10,000

Required

1. Identify and analyze the necessary adjustments on December 31, 2017.
2. Prepare an income statement and a statement of retained earnings for Mountain Home Health for the year ended December 31, 2017.
3. Prepare a balance sheet for Mountain Home Health as of December 31, 2017.
4. Compute the following as of December 31, 2017: (a) working capital and (b) current ratio.
5. Which of the adjustments could cause a difference between cash- and accrual-based income?
6. Mary Francis, controller of Mountain Home, became concerned about the company's cash flow after talking to a local bank loan officer. The firm tries to maintain a seven-week supply of cash to meet the demands of payroll, medical supply purchases, and gasoline. Determine the amount of cash Mountain Home needs to meet the seven-week supply.

Answers

MODULE 1 Answers to Questions

1. As an example, in deciding whether or not an asset that a company pledges as collateral for a loan is sufficient, a banker may be most interested in the current value of the asset. The accountant, however, may be reluctant to present the current value of the asset on the balance sheet because of the difficulty in measuring the value of the asset. Because of its objective nature, historical cost is the attribute used to measure many of the assets recognized on the balance sheet.

2. The realtor will recognize revenue from the sale of the home on July 8 if the cash basis is used because this is the date cash is received. Revenue will be recognized on June 12 if the accrual basis is used because this is the date the sale takes place and the realtor has performed his or her obligation.

3. No, the recognition of revenue is not always the result of the acquisition of an asset. For instance, assume that a publisher sells a magazine subscription and collects cash from the customer in advance. At the time cash is collected, the publisher incurs a liability. As each month's magazine is mailed to the customer, a portion of the liability is satisfied and revenue is recognized.

4. A company incurs a cost when it acquires an asset. For example, assume that a retailer buys office supplies for $100 on October 21. On this date, it has incurred a cost of $100 to acquire an asset, namely office supplies. The asset will be removed from the records and an expense recognized, namely office supplies expense, when the supplies are used up.

MODULE 1 Answers to Apply

1. The two possible attributes are historical cost and current value. The simplest approach is to show an item such as an asset at its original cost, thus the designation historical cost. An alternative to historical cost as the attribute to be measured is current value. Current value is the amount of cash or its equivalent that could be received currently from the sale of the asset. Current value is not as simple and often not as easy to get agree-

ment upon. The dollar is the unit of money used in the United States to measure items.

2. a. June 14
   b. April 5
   c. August 30

3. It is not necessary for there to be an inflow of an asset in order to recognize revenue. For example, revenue can be recognized when a company provides a service

for which it had earlier received a deposit. The deposit represents a liability, and it is satisfied when the service is provided. Revenue is recognized continuously over a period of time for both rent and interest.

4. The merchandise will be reported on the December 31, 2017, balance sheet as a current asset. Revenue from the sale, along with cost of goods sold expense, will be recorded in 2018, the year in which the merchandise is sold.

MODULE 2 Answers to Questions

1. a. To recognize the expired portion of a prepaid expense. For example, an adjustment is needed at the end of each month to recognize insurance expense for the portion of an insurance policy that has expired during the period.

b. To recognize a portion of a deferred revenue or liability. For example, a publisher has to make an adjustment at the end of each period to recognize the expired portion of a subscription.

c. To recognize expense at the end of the period before cash is paid. For example, an adjustment is made at the end of the year to recognize income tax expense, even though the taxes will not be paid until early in the following year.

d. To recognize revenue at the end of the period before cash is received. For example, a landlord will need to make an adjustment at the end of the month for the rent owed by a tenant but not payable until some time during the following month.

MODULE 2 Answers to Apply

1.

	Accounts Affected	
a.	IE	IL
b.	IA	IR
c.	IE	DA
d.	DL*	IR*

*This is how the company which issued the gift card will record the adjustment when the card is redeemed.

2.

| Identify and Analyze | ACTIVITY: Operating
ACCOUNTS: Prepaid Insurance Decrease   Insurance Expense Increase
STATEMENT(S): Balance Sheet and Income Statement |

Balance Sheet | **Income Statement**

ASSETS	=	LIABILITIES	+	STOCKHOLDERS' EQUITY		REVENUES	−	EXPENSES	=	NET INCOME
Prepaid Insurance (225)				(225)				Insurance Expense 225		(225)

3.

| Identify and Analyze | ACTIVITY: Operating
ACCOUNTS: Accumulated Depreciation-Car Increase   Depreciation Expense Increase
STATEMENT(S): Balance Sheet and Income Statement |

Balance Sheet | **Income Statement**

ASSETS	=	LIABILITIES	+	STOCKHOLDERS' EQUITY		REVENUES	−	EXPENSES	=	NET INCOME
Accumulated Depreciation—Car* (500)				(500)				Depreciation Expense 500		(500)

*The Accumulated Depreciation-Car account has increased. It is shown as a decrease in the equation above because it is a contra account and causes total assets to decrease.

4.

Identify and Analyze	ACTIVITY: Operating
	ACCOUNTS: Interest Payable Increase Interest Expense Increase
	STATEMENT(S): Balance Sheet and Income Statement

Balance Sheet — Income Statement

ASSETS = LIABILITIES + STOCKHOLDERS' EQUITY   REVENUES − EXPENSES = NET INCOME

Interest Payable 100   (100)   Interest Expense 100   (100)

MODULE 3 Answers to Questions

1. The posting of adjustments and closing the accounts are purely mechanical in nature. In fact, these steps are normally performed by the computer. On the other hand, the analysis of transactions requires analytical skill. The accountant must consider all the available evidence and make a determination as to which accounts are affected and what amounts to use in recording a transaction. As is the case with posting, the actual recording of the transaction can be performed by the computer.

2. Closing the accounts is done at the end of an accounting period. It has two important purposes: (1) to return the balance in all temporary or nominal accounts (revenues, expenses, and dividends) to zero to start the next accounting period and (2) to transfer the net income (or net loss) and the dividends of the period to Retained Earnings.

MODULE 3 Answers to Apply

1. If a work sheet is not prepared, financial statements would only be prepared after recording and posting adjustments.

2.
   a. No
   b. Yes
   c. No
   d. Yes
   e. Yes
   f. No
   g. No
   h. Yes

Answers to Connect to the Real World

4-1 (p. 161)

At the end of the 2015 fiscal year, gift card liabilities accounted for $327 million/$2,911 million, or 11.2%, of total current liabilities. At the end of 2014, the percentage was $286 million/$2,800 million, or 10.2%.

4-2 (p. 163)

Accrued Salaries, Wages and Related Benefits amount to $416 million and represent $416 million/$2,911 million, or 14.3%, of total current liabilities at the end of the 2015 fiscal year. Accrued Salaries, Wages and Related Benefits amount to $416 million, which represented $416 million/$2,800 million, or 14.9%, of total current liabilities at the end of 2014.

Answers to Key Terms Quiz

15	Recognition		10	Deferral
22	Historical cost		16	Deferred expense
8	Current value		5	Deferred revenue
18	Cash basis		12	Accrual
11	Accrual basis		19	Accrued liability
2	Revenues		7	Accrued asset
14	Revenue recognition principle		24	Accounting cycle
20	Matching principle		1	Work sheet
23	Expenses		6	Real accounts
3	Adjusting entries		17	Nominal accounts
9	Straight-line method		4	Closing entries
21	Contra account		13	Interim statements

Inventories and Cost of Goods Sold

MODULES	LEARNING OBJECTIVES	WHY IS THIS CHAPTER IMPORTANT?
1 Sales, Cost of Goods Sold, and Gross Profit	**LO1** Identify the forms of inventory held by different types of businesses and the types of costs incurred. **LO2** Explain how wholesalers and retailers account for sales of merchandise. **LO3** Show that you understand how wholesalers and retailers account for cost of goods sold. **LO4** Use the gross profit ratio to analyze a company's ability to cover its operating expenses and earn a profit.	• You need to know how a company keeps track of the cost of its inventory. (See pp. 214–215.) • You need to know how the relationship between the company's sales and the cost of those sales can be used to assess the company's performance. (See pp. 218–220.)
2 Inventory Costing Methods	**LO5** Explain the relationship between the valuation of inventory and the measurement of income. **LO6** Apply the inventory costing methods of specific identification, weighted average, FIFO, and LIFO by using a periodic system. **LO7** Analyze the effects of the different costing methods on inventory, net income, income taxes, and cash flow.	• You need to know how inventory methods assign costs to the products sold. (See pp. 222–227.)
3 Other Inventory Issues	**LO8** Analyze the effects of an inventory error on various financial statement items. **LO9** Apply the lower-of-cost-or-market rule to the valuation of inventory.	• You need to know how inventory errors affect the financial statements. (See pp. 232–235.) • You need to know how to apply the lower-of-cost-or-market rule to value inventory. (See pp. 235–237.)
4 Inventory Management and Cash Flow Issues	**LO10** Analyze the management of inventory. **LO11** Explain the effects that inventory transactions have on the statement of cash flows.	• You need to know how the relationship between sales on the income statement and inventory on the balance sheet can be used to assess how well a company is managing its inventory. (See pp. 237–239.) • You need to know how inventory transactions affect cash flows. (See pp. 240–241.)
5 Inventory Costing Methods with a Perpetual System (Appendix)	**LO12** Explain the differences in the accounting for periodic and perpetual inventory systems and apply the inventory costing methods using a perpetual system (Appendix).	• You need to know how to apply the inventory costing methods with a perpetual system (Appendix). (See pp. 242–244.)

© Northfoto/Shutterstock.com

GAP INC.

Gap Inc. had its humble beginning when Doris and Don Fisher opened their first store in San Francisco in 1969. From that single store, the company now has global operations that generated revenues of about $16 billion in each of the last three years. It counts among its brands some of the most recognizable in the world of apparel: Gap®, Banana Republic®, Old Navy®, and Athleta®.

As a retailer, Gap Inc. measures success in terms of what it earns from buying and selling jeans and other apparel. The statements of income shown below provide an accounting of the company's success in this regard. As is evident from the income statements, the cost that a retailer pays for the merchandise that it sells is the most important

factor in determining whether the company is profitable. For Gap Inc., "Cost of goods sold and occupancy expenses" topped $10 billion in each of the last two years. One of the biggest challenges a retailer faces is controlling the cost of its inventory while at the same time ensuring the quality of its merchandise.

Besides being important for retailers to control the cost of what they sell, it is also imperative that they minimize the amount of stock they carry at any one time while at the same time making sure they have enough merchandise to meet customers' demands. The significance of inventory as an asset to Gap Inc. is indicated by the partial balance sheet shown below.

The Gap, Inc.
Consolidated Statements of Income

($ and shares in millions except per share amounts)	Fiscal Year		
	2015	**2014**	**2013**
Net sales	$15,797	$16,435	$16,148
Cost of goods sold and occupancy expenses	10,077	10,146	9,855
Gross profit	5,720	6,289	6,293
Operating expenses	4,196	4,206	4,144
Operating income	1,524	2,083	2,149
Interest expense	59	75	61
Interest income	(6)	(5)	(5)
Income before income taxes	1,471	2,013	2,093
Income taxes	551	751	813
Net income	$ 920	$ 1,262	$ 1,280
Weighted-average number of shares—basic	411	435	461
Weighted-average number of shares—diluted	413	440	467
Earnings per share—basic	$ 2.24	$ 2.90	$ 2.78
Earnings per share—diluted	$ 2.23	$ 2.87	$ 2.74

> **Net Sales decreased 3.9% from 2014 to 2015**

> **The cost of the products sold decreased 0.7%**

See Accompanying Notes to Consolidated Financial Statements

The Gap, Inc.
Consolidated Balance Sheets (Partial)

($ and shares in millions except par value)	January 30, 2016	January 31, 2015
ASSETS		
Current assets:		
Cash and cash equivalents	$1,370	$1,515
Merchandise inventory	1,873	1,889
Other current assets	742	913
Total current assets	3,985	4,317

> **The company's inventory on hand remained relatively stable over the two-year period.**

See Accompanying Notes to Consolidated Financial Statements

Source: Gap Inc. website and Form 10-K for fiscal year ended January 30, 2016.

MODULE 1 SALES, COST OF GOODS SOLD, AND GROSS PROFIT

LO1 Identify the forms of inventory held by different types of businesses and the types of costs incurred.

Companies that sell inventory can be categorized into two types:

- **Retailers and wholesalers purchase inventory in finished form and hold it for resale.** For example, as a retailer, **Gap Inc.** buys clothes directly from other companies and then offers them for sale to consumers.
- **Manufacturers transform raw materials into a finished product prior to sale.** A good example of a manufacturing company is **Ford Motor Company**. It buys all of the various materials that are needed to make cars and trucks and then sells the finished product to its customers.

How Will I Use ACCOUNTING?

Inventory is the lifeblood of all businesses that sell products and chances are you will work for one of them at some time during your career. As a salesperson, you need to track inventory levels and know when to re-order merchandise. As a store manager, you need to evaluate the profitability of product lines and monitor how quickly inventory is turned over. Inventory matters to everyone in a business, not just the accountants.

Whether a company is a wholesaler, retailer, or manufacturer, its inventory is an asset that is held for *resale* in the normal course of business. The distinction between inventory and an operating asset is the *intent* of the owner. For example, some of the cars that Ford owns are operating assets such as those driven by company executives. Many more of the cars **Ford** owns are inventory, however, because the company makes them and intends to sell them. This chapter is concerned with the proper valuation of inventory and the related effect on cost of goods sold.

Three Types of Inventory Costs and Three Forms of Inventory

Merchandise Inventory
The account wholesalers and retailers use to report inventory held for resale.

It is important to distinguish between the *types* of inventory costs incurred and the *form* the inventory takes. Wholesalers and retailers incur a single type of cost, the *purchase price,* of the inventory they sell. On the balance sheet, they use a single account for inventory, titled **Merchandise Inventory**. Wholesalers and retailers buy merchandise in finished form and offer it for resale without transforming the product in any way. Merchandise companies typically have a relatively large dollar amount in inventory. For example, on its January 30, 2016, balance sheet, Gap Inc. reported merchandise inventory of $1,873 million and total assets of $7,473 million. It is not unusual for inventories to account for half the total assets of a merchandise company.

Three Types of Manufacturing Costs Three distinct *types* of costs are incurred by a *manufacturer*—direct materials, direct labor, and manufacturing overhead. Each is explained here.

Raw materials
The inventory of a manufacturer before the addition of any direct labor or manufacturing overhead.

Alternate term: Direct materials.

1. *Direct materials*, also called **raw materials**, are the ingredients used in making a product. The costs of direct materials used in making a pair of shoes include the *costs* of fabric, plastic, and rubber.
2. *Direct labor* consists of the amounts paid to workers to manufacture the product. The hourly wage paid to an assembly line worker is a primary ingredient in the cost to make the shoes.
3. *Manufacturing overhead* includes all other costs that are related to the manufacturing process but cannot be directly matched to specific units of output. Depreciation of a factory building and the salary of a supervisor are two examples of overhead costs. Accountants have developed various techniques to assign, or allocate, these manufacturing overhead costs to specific products.

Three Forms of Inventory The inventory of a manufacturer takes three distinct *forms.*

1. Direct materials or raw materials enter a production process in which they are transformed into a finished product by the addition of direct labor and manufacturing overhead.

2. At any time, including the end of an accounting period, some of the materials have entered the process and some labor costs have been incurred but the product is not finished. The cost of unfinished products is appropriately called **work in process** or *work in progress*.

3. Inventory that has completed the production process and is available for sale is called **finished goods**. Finished goods are the equivalent of merchandise inventory for a retailer or wholesaler in that both represent the inventory of goods held for sale.

Work in process
The cost of unfinished products in a manufacturing company.

Alternate term: Work in progress.

Finished goods
A manufacturer's inventory that is complete and ready for sale.

Many manufacturers disclose the dollar amounts of the various forms of inventory in their annual report. For example, consider the following excerpt from Note 7 of **Caterpillar Inc.**'s 2015 Form 10-K:

(millions of dollars)	December 31, 2015
Raw materials	$2,467
Work-in-process	1,857
Finished goods	5,122
Supplies	254
Total inventories	$9,700

As a company that makes construction machinery and other related products, Caterpillar has over one-half of its inventory in finished products.

Exhibit 5-1 summarizes the relationships between the types of costs incurred and the forms of inventory for different types of businesses.

EXHIBIT 5-1 Relationships between Types of Businesses and Inventory Costs

Type of Company	Activities	Assets on Balance Sheet	Income Statement When Inventory Is Sold
Retailer/ Wholesaler	Buys finished products ⟶	Merchandise inventory ⟶	Cost of goods sold
Manufacturer	Buys raw materials and then adds: ⟶	Raw materials	
	Direct labor ⟶	Work in process	
	Overhead ⟶	Finished goods ⟶	Cost of goods sold

Net Sales of Merchandise

A *condensed* multiple-step income statement for Daisy's Running Depot is presented in Exhibit 5-2. Daisy's ends its fiscal year on December 31. However, retailers often choose a date toward the end of January because the busy holiday shopping season is over and time can be devoted to closing the records and preparing financial statements. For example, Gap Inc. ends its fiscal year on the Saturday closest to the end of January.

We will concentrate on the first two items on Daisy's statement: net sales and cost of goods sold. The major difference between this income statement and one for a service company is the inclusion of cost of goods sold. Because a service company does not sell a product, it does not report cost of goods sold. On the income statement of a merchandising company, cost of goods sold is deducted from net sales to arrive at **gross profit**, or gross margin.

Merchandising companies make sales for cash or on credit, allowing the customer to pay at a later date. **Sales revenue**, or sales, represents the inflow of assets, either cash or accounts receivable, from the sale of a product during the period. Accounting standards require companies to **estimate the amount they expect to receive from a sale**.[1] Two

LO2 Explain how wholesalers and retailers account for sales of merchandise.

Gross profit
Net sales less cost of goods sold.
Alternate term: Gross margin.

Sales revenue
A representation of the inflow of assets from the sale of a product.
Alternate term: Sales.

---
[1] *Revenue from Contracts with Customers*, ASC Topic 606, Financial Accounting Standards Board, May 2014, Norwalk, CT.

EXHIBIT 5-2 Condensed Income Statement for a Merchandiser

Daisy's Running Depot Income Statement For the Year Ended December 31, 2017	
Net sales	$100,000
Cost of goods sold	60,000
Gross profit	$ 40,000
Selling and administrative expenses	29,300
Net income before tax	$ 10,700
Income tax expense	4,280
Net income	$ 6,420

Net sales
Sales revenue less sales returns and allowances and sales discounts.

deductions are made from sales revenue to arrive at **net sales**: for sales returns and allowances and for sales discounts.

Sales Returns and Allowances

Most companies have standard policies that allow the customer to *return* merchandise within a stipulated period of time. **Nordstrom**, the Seattle-based retailer, has a very liberal policy regarding returns. That policy has, in large measure, fueled its growth. A company's policy might be that a customer who is not completely satisfied can return the merchandise anytime within 30 days of purchase for a full refund. Alternatively, the customer may be given an *allowance* for spoiled or damaged merchandise—that is, the customer keeps the merchandise but receives a credit for a certain amount in the account balance. If the customer has already paid for the merchandise, either a cash refund is given or the credit amount is applied to future purchases.

Recall that sales are to be recorded at the estimated amount a company expects to receive. However, at the time a sale is made it would be impossible to know the amount of any returns and allowances. Also, in some instances a return might not be made until a later accounting period. Therefore, under the accrual accounting concept, an adjusting entry is needed at the end of the period for the *estimated* amount of returns and allowances from sales made during the period.

Credit Terms and Sales Discounts

Special notation is normally used to indicate a firm's policy for granting credit. For example, credit terms of n/30 mean that the net amount of the selling price (i.e., the amount determined after deducting any returns or allowances) is due within 30 days of the date of the invoice. Net, 10 EOM means that the net amount is due anytime within ten days after the end of the month in which the sale took place.

Another common element of the credit terms offered to customers is sales discounts, a reduction from the selling price given for early payment. Assume that Daisy's makes a sale for $1,000 with credit terms of 1/10, n/30. This means that the customer can deduct 1% from the selling price if the bill is paid within ten days of the date of the invoice. Normally, the discount period begins the day *after* the invoice date. If the customer does not pay within the first ten days, the full invoice amount is due within 30 days. The following example illustrates whether it would be advantageous for the customer to pay within the discount period.

EXAMPLE 5-1 Determining Whether to Take a Discount

Assume a $1,000 sale with a 1% discount for payment within the first ten days with the full amount due within 30 days.

If a customer pays at the end of ten days, the amount paid is: $1,000 − 0.01($1,000) = $990.

The customer saves $10 ($1,000 − $990) by paying 20 days early.

The customer's rate of return for paying early is calculated as follows:

Number of periods of 20 days in a year: 360/20 = 18

Equivalent savings in a year: 18 × $10 = $180

Rate of return: $180/$990 = 18.2%

The customer should pay in the first ten days unless another investment can be found offering a return in excess of 18.2%.

This analysis indicates that Daisy's customer is likely to take advantage of the discount for early payment. At the time of the sale Daisy would record an increase in Accounts Receivable and Sales Revenue for $990, the *estimated* amount it expects to receive from the customer.

Cost of Goods Sold

The Cost of Goods Sold Model

The Cost of Goods Sold section of the income statement for Daisy's is shown in Exhibit 5-3. The recognition of cost of goods sold as an expense is an excellent example of the *matching principle*. Sales revenue represents the *inflow* of assets, in the form of cash and accounts receivable, from the sale of products during the period. Likewise, cost of goods sold represents the *outflow* of an asset, inventory, from the sale of those same products. The company needs to match the revenue of the period with the cost of the goods sold.

It may be helpful in understanding cost of goods sold to realize what it is not. *Cost of goods sold is not necessarily equal to the cost of purchases of merchandise during the period.* Except in the case of a new business, a merchandiser starts the year with a certain stock of inventory on hand, called *beginning inventory*. For Daisy's, beginning inventory is the cost of merchandise on hand on January 1, 2017. During the year, Daisy's purchases merchandise. When the cost of goods purchased is added to beginning inventory, the result is **cost of goods available for sale**.

As shown in Exhibit 5-4, think of cost of goods available for sale as a "pool" of costs to be distributed between what was sold and what was not sold. The result of subtracting from the pool the cost of what did not sell, the *ending inventory*, is the amount that did sell, the **cost of goods sold**.

LO3 Show that you understand how wholesalers and retailers account for cost of goods sold.

Cost of goods available for sale
Beginning inventory plus cost of goods purchased.

Cost of goods sold
Cost of goods available for sale minus ending inventory.

EXHIBIT 5-3 Cost of Goods Sold Section of the Income Statement

Daisy's Running Depot Partial Income Statement For the Year Ended December 31, 2017			
Cost of goods sold:			
Inventory, January 1, 2017		$ 15,000	What is on hand to start the period
Net purchases	$59,500		
Transportation-in	3,500		
Cost of goods purchased		63,000	What was acquired for resale during the period
Cost of goods available for sale		$ 78,000	The "pool" of costs to be distributed
Inventory, December 31, 2017		(18,000)	What was not sold during the period and therefore is on hand to start the next period
Cost of goods sold		$60,000	What was sold during the period

EXHIBIT 5-4 The Cost of Goods Sold Model

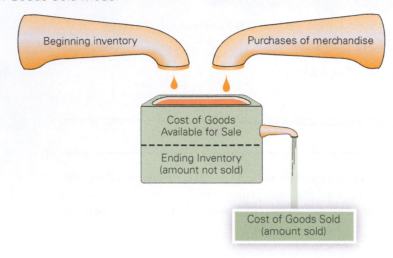

EXAMPLE 5-2 Calculating Cost of Goods Sold

The amounts shown below are taken from the Cost of Goods Sold section of Daisy's income statement as shown in Exhibit 5-3.

Description	Item	Amount	
Merchandise on hand to start the period	Beginning inventory	$ 15,000	
Acquisitions of merchandise during the period	+ Cost of goods purchased	63,000	A $3,000 excess of ending inventory over beginning inventory means that the company bought $3,000 more than it sold ($63,000 bought versus $60,000 sold).
Pool of merchandise available for sale during the period	= Cost of goods available for sale	$ 78,000	
Merchandise on hand at end of period	− Ending inventory	(18,000)	
Expense recognized on the income statement	= Cost of goods sold	$ 60,000	

Notice that ending inventory exceeds beginning inventory by $3,000. That means that the cost of goods purchased exceeds cost of goods sold by that same amount. Indeed, a key point for stockholders, bankers, and other users is whether inventory is building up, that is, whether a company is not selling as much inventory during the period as it is buying. A buildup may indicate that the company's products are becoming less desirable or that prices are becoming uncompetitive.

Perpetual system
A system in which the Inventory account is increased at the time of each purchase and decreased at the time of each sale.

Periodic system
A system in which the Inventory account is updated only at the end of the period.

Inventory Systems: Perpetual and Periodic

All businesses use one of two distinct approaches to account for inventory. With the **perpetual system**, the Inventory account is updated perpetually after each sale or purchase of merchandise. Conversely, with the **periodic system**, the Inventory account is updated only at the end of the period, when the cost of goods sold is also determined.

EXAMPLE 5-3 Recording Cost of Goods Sold in a Perpetual System

Assume that Daisy's sells a pair of running shoes that costs the company $70. In addition to the entry to record the sale, Daisy's would also record an adjustment that can be identified and analyzed as follows:

Identify and Analyze	**ACTIVITY:** Operating
	ACCOUNTS: Inventory Decrease **Cost of Goods Sold** Increase
	STATEMENT(S): Balance Sheet and Income Statement

Balance Sheet					Income Statement				
ASSETS	=	LIABILITIES	+	STOCKHOLDERS' EQUITY	REVENUES	−	EXPENSES	=	NET INCOME
Inventory (70)				(70)			Cost of Goods Sold 70		(70)

Thus, at any point during the period, the Inventory account is up to date. It has been increased for the cost of purchases during the period and reduced for the cost of the sales.

Depending on the volume of inventory transactions, a perpetual system can be extremely costly to maintain. Historically, businesses with a relatively small volume of sales at a high unit price have used perpetual systems. For example, dealers in automobiles, furniture, appliances, and jewelry normally use a perpetual system. Each purchase of a unit of merchandise, such as an automobile, can be easily identified and an increase recorded in the Inventory account. When an auto is sold, the dealer can determine the cost of the particular car sold by looking at a perpetual inventory record.

To a certain extent, the ability of mass merchandisers to maintain perpetual inventory records has improved with the advent of point-of-sale terminals. When a scanner at the grocery checkout reads the bar code on a can of corn, the grocer's computer receives a message that the corn has been sold. In some companies, however, an update of the inventory record is in units only and is used as a means to determine when a product needs to be reordered. The company still relies on a periodic system to maintain the *dollar* amount of inventory. The remainder of this chapter discusses the periodic system. The perpetual system is discussed in more detail in the appendix to this chapter.

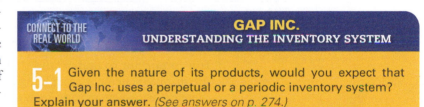

CONNECT TO THE REAL WORLD

GAP INC.
UNDERSTANDING THE INVENTORY SYSTEM

5-1 Given the nature of its products, would you expect that Gap Inc. uses a perpetual or a periodic inventory system? Explain your answer. *(See answers on p. 274.)*

Beginning and Ending Inventories in a Periodic System

In a periodic system, the Inventory account throughout the year contains the amount of merchandise on hand at the beginning of the year. The account is adjusted only at the end of the year. A company using the periodic system must physically count the units of inventory on hand at the end of the period. The number of units of each product is then multiplied by the cost per unit to determine the dollar amount of ending inventory. This ending inventory is the next period's beginning inventory. In Exhibit 5-3, for example, Daisy's ending inventory of $18,000 is the beginning inventory on January 1, 2018.

In summary, the ending inventory in a periodic system is determined by counting the merchandise, not by looking at the Inventory account at the end of the period. The periodic system results in a trade-off. Use of the periodic system reduces record keeping, but at the expense of a certain degree of control. Losses of merchandise due to theft, breakage, spoilage, or other reasons may go undetected in a periodic system because management may assume that all merchandise not on hand at the end of the year was sold. In contrast, with a perpetual inventory system, a count of inventory at the end of the period serves as a control device. For example, if the Inventory account shows a balance of $45,000 at the end of the year but only $42,000 of merchandise is counted, management is able to investigate the discrepancy.

In addition to the loss of control, the use of a periodic system presents a dilemma when a company wants to prepare *interim* financial statements (these statements were introduced in Chapter 4). Because most companies that use a periodic system find it cost prohibitive to count the entire inventory more than once a year, they use estimation techniques to determine inventory for monthly or quarterly statements.

Cost of Goods Purchased

Transportation-In
An adjunct account used to record freight costs paid by the buyer.
Alternate term: Freight-In.

Daisy's net purchases as shown in Exhibit 5-3 amounted to $59,500. Two amounts are deducted from the purchases of the period to arrive at *net* purchases: purchase returns and allowances and purchase discounts. The exhibit also shows that Daisy's incurred costs of $3,500 to ship the goods to its place of business. This cost is called **transportation-in**, or freight-in. It is added to net purchases of $59,500 to arrive at the cost of goods purchased of $63,000.

Purchases
An account used in a periodic inventory system to record acquisitions of merchandise.

Purchases **Purchases** is the temporary account used in a periodic inventory system to record acquisitions of merchandise.

EXAMPLE 5-4 Recording Purchases in a Periodic System

Assume that Daisy's buys shoes on account from **Nike** at a cost of $4,000. The effect of this transaction is to increase liabilities and increase cost of goods sold, which is an expense. The effect of the transaction can be identified and analyzed as follows:

Identify and Analyze	ACTIVITY: Operating
	ACCOUNTS: Accounts Payable Increase Purchases Increase
	STATEMENT(S): Balance Sheet and Income Statement

Balance Sheet					Income Statement			
ASSETS	=	LIABILITIES	+	STOCKHOLDERS' EQUITY	REVENUES	−	EXPENSES	= NET INCOME
		Accounts Payable 4,000		(4,000)			Purchases 4,000	(4,000)

It is important to understand that Purchases is *not* an asset account. It is included in the income statement as an integral part of the calculation of cost of goods sold and is therefore shown as an increase in expenses and thus a reduction in net income and stockholders' equity in the accounting equation.

Purchase Discounts Discounts were discussed earlier in the chapter from the seller's viewpoint. Merchandising companies often purchase inventory on terms that allow for a cash discount for early payment, such as 2/10, n/30. To the buyer, a cash discount is called a *purchase discount* and results in a reduction of the cost to purchase merchandise. Management must monitor the amount of purchase discounts taken as well as those opportunities missed by not taking advantage of the discounts for early payment.

EXAMPLE 5-5 Recording Purchase Discounts in a Periodic System

Assume Daisy's purchases merchandise on March 13 for $500, with credit terms of 1/10, n/30. Because Daisy's is likely to take advantage of the discount for early payment, we will record the purchase at the net amount, that is the *estimated* amount it expects to pay: $500 − ($500 × 0.01), or $495. The effect of the transaction can be identified and analyzed as follows:

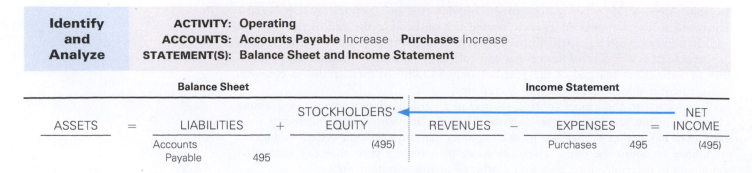

Identify and Analyze	ACTIVITY: Operating
	ACCOUNTS: Accounts Payable Increase Purchases Increase
	STATEMENT(S): Balance Sheet and Income Statement

Balance Sheet					Income Statement			
ASSETS	=	LIABILITIES	+	STOCKHOLDERS' EQUITY	REVENUES	−	EXPENSES	= NET INCOME
		Accounts Payable 495		(495)			Purchases 495	(495)

If the company does not pay within the discount period, an adjustment will need to be made for the additional $5 cost to purchase the merchandise, representing the missed opportunity by not paying early. However, assume that the company does pay its account on March 23, within the discount period. The effect of the transaction can be identified and analyzed as follows:

Identify and Analyze	ACTIVITY: Operating ACCOUNTS: Cash Decrease Accounts Payable Decrease STATEMENT(S): Balance Sheet

Balance Sheet						Income Statement			
ASSETS	=	LIABILITIES	+	STOCKHOLDERS' EQUITY		REVENUES	−	EXPENSES	= NET INCOME
Cash (495)		Accounts Payable (495)							

Purchase Returns and Allowances

Returns and allowances were discussed earlier in the chapter from the seller's point of view. From the buyer's standpoint, purchase returns and allowances are reductions in the cost to purchase merchandise. They have the same effect on purchases as purchase discounts. And like purchase discounts, management must continually monitor the amount of returns and allowances. For example, a large number of returns during the period relative to the amount purchased may signal that the purchasing department is not buying from reputable sources.

Shipping Terms and Transportation Costs

The *cost principle* governs the recording of all assets. All costs necessary to prepare an asset for its intended use should be included in its cost. For example, any sales tax paid and merchandise transportation costs incurred by the buyer should be included in the cost of the merchandise.

The buyer does not always pay to ship the merchandise. This depends on the terms of shipment. Goods are normally shipped either **FOB destination point** or **FOB shipping point**; *FOB* stands for "free on board." When merchandise is shipped FOB destination point, it is the responsibility of the seller to deliver the products to the buyer. Thus, the seller either delivers the product to the customer or pays a trucking firm, the railroad, or another carrier to transport it. Alternatively, the agreement between the buyer and the seller may provide for the goods to be shipped FOB shipping point. In this case, the merchandise is the responsibility of the buyer as soon as it leaves the seller's premises. When the terms of shipment are FOB shipping point, the buyer incurs transportation costs.

FOB destination point
Terms that require the seller to pay for the cost of shipping the merchandise to the buyer.

FOB shipping point
Terms that require the buyer to pay for the shipping costs.

EXAMPLE 5-6   Recording Transportation-In in a Periodic System

Assume that on delivery of a shipment of goods, Daisy's pays an invoice for $300 from Rocky Mountain Railroad. The terms of shipment are FOB shipping point. The effect of the transaction can be identified and analyzed as follows:

Identify and Analyze	ACTIVITY: Operating ACCOUNTS: Cash Decrease Transportation-In Increase STATEMENT(S): Balance Sheet and Income Statement

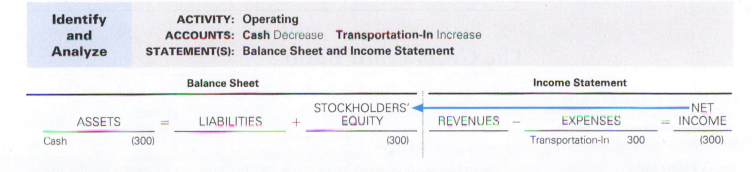

Balance Sheet						Income Statement			
ASSETS	=	LIABILITIES	+	STOCKHOLDERS' EQUITY		REVENUES	−	EXPENSES	= NET INCOME
Cash (300)				(300)				Transportation-In 300	(300)

As shown in Exhibit 5-3, transportation-in is added to net purchases, which increases the cost of goods purchased (in the Expenses column of the equation here).

The total of net purchases and transportation-in is called the *cost of goods purchased.* Transportation-In will be closed at the end of the period.

When the goods are shipped FOB (free on board) destination point, the seller is responsible for the cost of delivering the merchandise to the buyer. This cost, sometimes called *transportation-out,* is not an addition to the cost of purchases of the seller; instead, it is one of the costs necessary to *sell* the merchandise. Transportation-out is classified as a *selling expense* on the income statement.

Shipping Terms and Transfer of Title to Inventory   Terms of shipment take on additional significance at the end of an accounting period. For example, if Daisy's purchases merchandise that is in transit at the end of the year, to whom does the inventory belong? The answer depends on the terms of shipment. If goods are shipped FOB destination point, they remain the legal property of the seller until they reach their destination. Alternatively, legal title to goods shipped FOB shipping point passes to the buyer as soon as the seller turns the goods over to the carrier.

EXAMPLE 5-7 Determining the Effect of Shipping Terms on Purchases and Sales

Assume that on December 28, 2017, Nike ships running shoes to Daisy's Running Depot. The trucking company delivers the merchandise to Daisy's on January 2, 2018. Daisy's fiscal year-end is December 31. The effect of shipping terms on purchases and sales can be summarized as follows:

Company		If Merchandise Is Shipped FOB	
		Destination Point	Shipping Point
Nike	Pay freight costs?	Yes	No
(seller)	Record sale in 2017?	No	Yes
	Include inventory on balance sheet at December 31, 2017?	Yes	No
Daisy's	Pay freight costs?	No	Yes
(buyer)	Record purchase in 2017?	No	Yes
	Include inventory on balance sheet at December 31, 2017?	No	Yes

Nike, the seller of the goods, pays the transportation charges only if the terms are FOB destination point. However, Nike records a sale for goods in transit at year-end only if the terms of shipment are FOB shipping point. If Nike does not record a sale because the goods are shipped FOB destination point, the inventory appears on its December 31 balance sheet. Daisy's, the buyer, pays freight costs only if the goods are shipped FOB shipping point. Only in this situation does Daisy's record a purchase of the merchandise and include it as an asset on its December 31 balance sheet.

The Gross Profit Ratio

LO4 Use the gross profit ratio to analyze a company's ability to cover its operating expenses and earn a profit.

Gross profit ratio
Gross profit divided by net sales.

The first three lines on Daisy's income statement in Exhibit 5-2 are as follows:

Net sales	$100,000
Cost of goods sold	60,000
Gross profit	$ 40,000

The relationship between gross profit and net sales—as measured by the **gross profit ratio**—is one of the most important measures used by managers, investors, and creditors to assess the performance of a company.

$$\frac{\text{Gross Profit}}{\text{Net Sales}} \qquad \frac{\$40,000}{\$100,000} = 40\%$$

A 40% gross profit ratio says that for every dollar of sales, Daisy's has a gross profit of 40 cents. After deducting 60 cents for the cost of the product, the company has 40 cents to cover its operating costs and to earn a profit. We will now apply the Ratio Analysis Model to analyze this ratio for Gap Inc.

MAKING BUSINESS DECISIONS
GAP INC.

The Gross Profit Ratio

An investor must be able to assess a company's profitability before buying its stock. One measure of profitability is the gross profit ratio. Use the following models to help you in your role as an investor to decide whether to buy stock in Gap Inc.

A. The Ratio Analysis Model

1. Formulate the Question

How much of the sales revenue is used for the cost of the products, and thus, how much remains to cover other expenses and to earn net income?

2. Gather the Information from the Financial Statements

To calculate a company's gross profit ratio, it is essential to know its net sales and cost of goods sold:

Net sales: From the income statement
Cost of goods sold: From the income statement

3. Calculate the Ratio

$$\text{Gross Profit Ratio} = \frac{\text{Gross Profit}}{\text{Net Sales}}$$

Gap Inc. Partial Consolidated Statements of Income (in millions)			
	Fiscal Year		
	2015	2014	2013
Net sales	$15,797	$16,435	$16,148
Cost of goods sold and occupancy expenses	10,077	10,146	9,855
Gross profit	5,720	6,289	6,293

$$\text{Gross Profit Ratio} = \frac{\$5,720}{\$15,797} = 36.2\%$$

4. Compare the Ratio with Other Ratios

Ratios are of no use in a vacuum. It is necessary to compare them with prior years and with competitors.

GROSS PROFIT RATIO			
Gap Inc.		**American Eagle Outfitters, Inc.**	
Year Ended January 30, 2016	**Year Ended January 31, 2015**	**Year Ended January 30, 2016**	**Year Ended January 31, 2015**
36.2%	38.3%	37.0%	35.2%

5. Interpret the Ratios.

For every dollar of sales, Gap Inc. has 36.2 cents available after deducting the cost of its products. The ratio was higher in the previous year. The ratio for one of Gap's competitors, American Eagle Outfitters, is very similar for the most recent year.

B. The Business Decision Model

1. Formulate the Question.

If you were an investor, would you buy stock in Gap Inc.?

2. Gather Information from the Financial Statements and Other Sources

This information will come from a variety of sources, not limited to but including:

- The balance sheet provides information about liquidity, the income statement regarding profitability, and the statement of cash flows on inflows and outflows of cash.
- The outlook for the apparel industry, including consumer trends, foreign markets, labor issues, and other factors.
- The outlook for the economy in general.
- Alternative uses for the money.

3. Analyze the Information Gathered.

- Compare Gap Inc.'s gross profit ratio in (A) above with American Eagle Outfitters as well as with industry averages.
- Look at trends over time in the gross profit ratios.
- Look at trends in net income over time as an indication of the ability to control expenses other than cost of goods sold.
- Review projections for the economy and the industry.

4. Make the Decision.

Taking into account all of the various sources of information, decide either to:

- Buy stock in Gap Inc. or
- Find an alternative use for the money.

5. Monitor Your Decision.

If you decide to buy the stock, you will need to monitor your investment periodically. During the time you hold the stock, you will want to assess the company's continuing profitability as well as other factors you considered before making the investment.

MODULE 1 TEST YOURSELF

Review

LO1 Identify the forms of inventory held by different types of businesses and the types of costs incurred.

- Inventory is a current asset held for resale in the normal course of business. The nature of inventory held depends on whether a business is a reseller of goods (wholesaler or retailer) or a manufacturer.
  - Resellers incur a single cost to purchase inventory held for sale.
  - Manufacturers incur costs that can be classified as raw materials, direct labor, and manufacturing overhead.

LO2 Explain how wholesalers and retailers account for sales of merchandise.

- Net sales represents sales less deductions for discounts and merchandise returned (returns and allowances) and is a key figure on the income statement.
  - Sales discounts are given to customers who pay their bills promptly.
  - Returns and allowances have the same effect on sales that sales discounts do; that is, they reduce sales.

LO3 Show that you understand how wholesalers and retailers account for cost of goods sold.

- The cost of goods sold represents goods sold, as opposed to the inventory purchased during the year. Cost of goods sold is matched with the sales of the period.
  - The cost of goods sold in any one period is equal to: Beginning inventory + Purchases − Ending inventory.
  - Under the perpetual method, the Inventory account is updated after each sale or purchase of merchandise.
  - In contrast, under the periodic method, the Inventory account is updated only at the end of the period.
- The cost of goods purchased includes any costs necessary to acquire the goods less any purchase discounts, returns, and allowances.
  - Transportation-in is the cost to ship goods to a company and is typically classified as part of cost of goods purchased.

LO4 Use the gross profit ratio to analyze a company's ability to cover its operating expenses and earn a profit.

- The gross profit ratio is the relationship between gross profit and net sales. Managers, investors, and creditors use this important ratio to measure one aspect of profitability.
  - The ratio is calculated as follows: $\dfrac{\text{Gross Profit}}{\text{Net Sales}}$

Question

1. What are three distinct types of costs that manufacturers incur? Describe each of them.

2. What is the difference between a periodic inventory system and a perpetual inventory system?

3. Why are shipping terms such as FOB shipping point or FOB destination point important in deciding ownership of inventory at the end of the year?

4. How is a company's gross profit determined? What does the gross profit ratio tell you about a company's performance during the year?

Apply

1. The following amounts are taken from White Wholesalers' records. (All amounts are for 2017.)

Inventory, January 1	$14,200
Inventory, December 31	10,300
Purchases (net)	81,500
Transportation-in	4,500

Prepare the Cost of Goods Sold section of White's 2017 income statement.

2. For each of the following items, indicate whether it increases (I) or decreases (D) cost of goods sold.
   - _____ Purchases
   - _____ Beginning inventory
   - _____ Transportation-in
   - _____ Ending inventory

3. Dexter Inc. recorded net sales of $50,000 during the period, and its cost of goods sold amounted to $30,000. Compute the company's gross profit ratio.

Answers are located at the end of the chapter.

MODULE 2 INVENTORY COSTING METHODS

LO5 Explain the relationship between the valuation of inventory and the measurement of income.

One of the most fundamental concepts in accounting is the relationship between *asset valuation* and the *measurement of income*. Recall a point made in Chapter 4:

Assets are unexpired costs, and expenses are expired costs.

Thus, **the value assigned to an asset such as inventory on the balance sheet determines the amount eventually recognized as an expense on the income statement.** An error in assigning the proper amount to inventory on the balance sheet will affect the amount recognized as cost of goods sold on the income statement. You can understand the relationship between inventory as an asset and cost of goods sold by recalling the Cost of Goods Sold section of the income statement. Assume the following amounts:

Beginning inventory	$ 500
Purchases	1,200
Cost of goods available for sale	$1,700
Ending inventory	(600)
Cost of goods sold	$1,100

The amount assigned to ending inventory is deducted from cost of goods available for sale to determine cost of goods sold. **If the ending inventory amount is incorrect, cost of goods sold will be wrong; thus, the net income of the period will be in error as well.** (Inventory errors will be discussed later in the chapter.)

Inventory Costs: What Should Be Included?

All assets, including inventory, are initially recorded at cost. Cost is defined as "the price paid or consideration given to acquire an asset. As applied to inventories, cost means in principle the sum of the applicable expenditures and charges directly or indirectly incurred in bringing an article to its existing condition and location."[2]

Note the reference to the existing *condition* and *location*. This means that certain costs may also be included in the "price paid." Here are examples:

- Any **freight costs** incurred by the buyer in shipping inventory to its place of business should be included in the cost of the inventory.
- The **cost of insurance** taken out during the time that inventory is in transit should be added to the cost of the inventory.
- The **cost of storing inventory** before it is ready to be sold should be included in the cost of the inventory.
- Various types of **taxes paid,** such as excise and sales taxes, are other examples of costs necessary to put the inventory into a position to be able to sell it.

However, it is often difficult to allocate many of these incidental costs among the various items of inventory purchased. For example, consider a $500 freight bill that a supermarket paid on a merchandise shipment that included 100 different items of inventory. To address the difficulty of assigning this type of cost to different products, many companies have a policy by which such costs are charged to expense of the period when they are immaterial in amount. Thus, shipments of merchandise are recorded at the net invoice price, that is, after taking any cash discounts for early payment. It is a practical solution to a difficult allocation problem. Once again, the company must apply the cost/benefit test to accounting information.

---

[2] *Inventory*, ASC Topic 330 (formerly *Inventory Pricing*, Accounting Research Bulletin No. 43).

Inventory Costing Methods with a Periodic System

To this point, we have assumed that the cost to purchase an item of inventory is constant. For most merchandisers, however, the unit cost of inventory changes frequently.

LO6 Apply the inventory costing methods of specific identification, weighted average, FIFO, and LIFO by using a periodic system.

EXAMPLE 5-8 Assigning Costs to Units Sold and Units on Hand

Everett Company purchases merchandise twice during the first year of business. The dates, number of units purchased, and costs are as follows:

> February 4   200 units purchased at $1.00 per unit = $200
> October 13   200 units purchased at $1.50 per unit = $300

Everett sells 200 units during the first year. Individual sales of the units take place relatively evenly throughout the year. The question is, *which* 200 units did the company sell—the $1.00 units, the $1.50 units, or some combination of each? The answer determines not only the value assigned to the 200 units of ending inventory but also the amount allocated to the cost of goods sold for the 200 units sold.

One possible method of assigning amounts to the ending inventory and the cost of goods sold is to specifically identify which 200 units were sold and which 200 units are on hand. This method is feasible for a few types of businesses in which units can be identified by serial numbers, but it is totally impractical in most situations. As an alternative to specific identification, we could make an assumption as to which units were sold and which are on hand. Three different answers are possible, as follows:

1. 200 units sold at $1.00 each   = $200 cost of goods sold
   and 200 units on hand at $1.50 each   = $300 ending inventory
   or
2. 200 units sold at $1.50 each   = $300 cost of goods sold
   and 200 units on hand at $1.00 each   = $200 ending inventory
   or
3. 200 units sold at $1.25 each   = $250 cost of goods sold
   and 200 units on hand at $1.25 each   = $250 ending inventory

The third alternative assumes an *average cost* for the 200 units on hand and the 200 units sold. The average cost is the cost of the two purchases of $200 and $300, or $500, divided by the 400 units available to sell, or $1.25 per unit.

If we are concerned with the actual physical flow of the units of inventory, all three methods illustrated may be incorrect. The only approach that will yield a "correct" answer in terms of the actual flow of *units* of inventory is the specific identification method. In the absence of a specific identification approach, it is impossible to say which particular units were actually sold. In fact, there may have been sales from each of the two purchases; that is, some of the $1.00 units may have been sold and some of the $1.50 units may have been sold. To solve the problem of assigning costs to identical units, accountants have developed inventory costing assumptions or methods. Each of these methods makes a specific assumption about the flow of costs rather than the physical flow of units. The only approach that uses the actual flow of the units in assigning costs is the specific identification method.

To look at specific identification as well as three alternative approaches to valuing inventory, assume the following set of data for Russell Company for Examples 5-9, 5-10, 5-11, 5-12, and 5-13.

	Units	Unit Cost	Total Cost
Beginning inventory			
January 1	500	$10	$ 5,000*
Purchases			
January 20	300	11	$ 3,300
April 8	400	12	4,800
September 5	200	13	2,600
December 12	100	14	1,400
Total purchases	1,000		$12,100
Available for sale	1,500		$17,100
Units sold	900		?
Units in ending inventory	600		?

*Beginning inventory of $5,000 is carried over as the ending inventory from the prior period. It is highly unlikely that each of the four methods we will illustrate would result in the same dollar amount of inventory at any point in time. It is helpful when first learning the methods, however, to assume the same amount of beginning inventory.

The question marks indicate the dilemma. What portion of the cost of goods available for sale of $17,100 should be assigned to the 900 units sold? What portion should be assigned to the 600 units remaining in ending inventory? The purpose of an inventory costing method is to provide a reasonable answer to those two questions.

Specific Identification Method

In certain situations, it may be possible to specifically identify which units are sold and which units are on hand. As shown in the illustration below, the unique characteristics of each automobile allow a dealer to specifically identify which one has been sold. Similarly, an appliance dealer with 15 refrigerators on hand at the end of the year can identify the unit cost of each by matching a tag number with the purchase records.

EXAMPLE 5-9 Determining Ending Inventory and Cost of Goods Sold Using Specific Identification

Specific identification method
An inventory costing method that relies on matching unit costs with the actual units sold.

To illustrate the **specific identification method**, assume that Russell Company is able to identify the specific units in inventory at the end of the year and their costs as follows:

Units on Hand

Date Purchased	Units	Cost	Total Cost
January 20	100	$11	$1,100
April 8	300	12	3,600
September 5	200	13	2,600
Ending inventory	600		$7,300

One of two techniques can be used to find cost of goods sold. Ending inventory can be deducted from the cost of goods available for sale as follows:

Cost of goods available for sale	$17,100
Ending inventory	7,300
Equals: Cost of goods sold	$ 9,800

Or cost of goods sold can be calculated independently by matching the units sold with their respective unit costs. By eliminating the units in ending inventory from the original acquisition schedule, the units sold and their costs are determined as follows:

Units Sold

Date Purchased	Units	Cost	Total Cost
Beginning inventory	500	$10	$5,000
January 20	200	11	2,200
April 8	100	12	1,200
December 12	100	14	1,400
Cost of goods sold	900		$9,800

One problem with the specific identification method is that it allows management to manipulate income. For example, assume that a company is not having a particularly good year. Management may be tempted to boost net income by selectively selling units with the lowest possible unit cost to keep cost of goods sold down and net income up.

Specific Identification

Cars on the Lot:

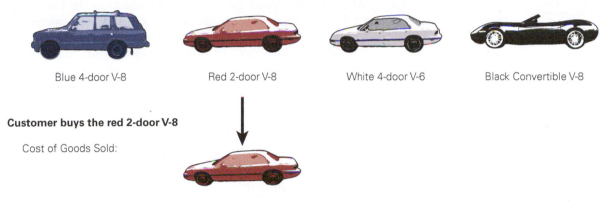

Blue 4-door V-8   Red 2-door V-8   White 4-door V-6   Black Convertible V-8

Customer buys the red 2-door V-8

Cost of Goods Sold:

Red 2-door V-8

Weighted Average Cost Method

The **weighted average cost method** is a relatively easy approach to costing inventory. It assigns the same unit cost to all units available for sale during the period.

EXAMPLE 5-10 Determining Ending Inventory and Cost of Goods Sold Using Weighted Average

> **Weighted average cost method**
> An inventory costing method that assigns the same unit cost to all units available for sale during the period.

The weighted average cost for Russell Company is calculated as follows:

$$\frac{\text{Cost of Goods Available for Sale}}{\text{Units Available for Sale}} = \text{Weighted Average Cost}$$

$$\frac{\$17,100}{1,500} = \$11.40$$

Ending inventory is found by multiplying the weighted average unit cost by the number of units on hand.

Weighted Average Cost		Number of Units in Ending Inventory		Ending Inventory
$11.40	×	600	=	$6,840

Cost of goods sold can be calculated in one of two ways.

Cost of goods available for sale	$17,100
Ending inventory	6,840
Cost of goods sold	$10,260

or

Weighted Average Cost		Number of Units Sold		Cost of Goods Sold
$11.40	×	900	=	$10,260

Note that the computation of the weighted average cost is based on the cost of all units available for sale during the period, not just the beginning inventory or purchases. Also, note that the method is called the weighted average cost method. As the name indicates, each of the individual unit costs is multiplied by the number of units acquired at each price. The simple arithmetic average of the unit costs for the beginning inventory and the four purchases is ($10 + $11 + $12 + $13 + $14)/5 = $12. The weighted average cost is slightly less than $12 ($11.40), however, because more units were acquired at the lower prices than at the higher prices.

First-In, First-Out Method (FIFO)

FIFO method
An inventory costing method that assigns the most recent costs to ending inventory.

The **FIFO method** assumes that the first units in, or purchased, are the first units out, or sold. The first units sold during the period are assumed to come from the beginning inventory. After the beginning inventory is sold, the next units sold are assumed to come from the first purchase during the period, and so on. Thus, ending inventory consists of the most recent purchases of the period. In many businesses, such as a grocery store, this cost-flow assumption is a fairly accurate reflection of the physical flow of products.

EXAMPLE 5-11 Determining Ending Inventory and Cost of Goods Sold Using FIFO

To calculate Russell Company's ending inventory using FIFO, we start with the most recent inventory acquired and work backward as follows:

Units on Hand

Date Purchased	Units	Cost	Total Cost
December 12	100	$14	$1,400
September 5	200	13	2,600
April 8	300	12	3,600
Ending inventory	600		$7,600

Cost of goods sold can then be found as follows:

Cost of goods available for sale	$17,100
Ending inventory	7,600
Cost of goods sold	$ 9,500

Or because the FIFO method assumes that the first units purchased are the first ones sold, cost of goods sold can be calculated by starting with the beginning inventory and working forward as follows:

Units Sold

Date Purchased	Units	Cost	Total Cost
Beginning inventory	500	$10	$5,000
January 20	300	11	3,300
April 8	100	12	1,200
Units sold	900	Cost of goods sold	$9,500

Last-In, First-Out Method (LIFO)

The **LIFO method** assumes that the last units in, or purchased, are the first units out, or sold. The first units sold during the period are assumed to come from the latest purchase made during the period, and so on. Although this situation is not as common as a FIFO physical flow, a stockpiling operation, such as in a rock quarry, operates on this basis.

LIFO method
An inventory costing method that assigns the most recent costs to cost of goods sold.

EXAMPLE 5-12 Determining Ending Inventory and Cost of Goods Sold Using LIFO

To calculate Russell Company's ending inventory using LIFO, we start with the beginning inventory and work forward.

Units on Hand

Date Purchased	Units	Cost	Total Cost
Beginning inventory	500	$10	$5,000
January 20	100	11	1,100
Ending inventory	600		$6,100

Cost of goods sold can then be found as follows:

Cost of goods available for sale	$17,100
Ending inventory	6,100
Cost of goods sold	$11,000

Or because the LIFO method assumes that the last units purchased are the first ones sold, cost of goods sold can be calculated by starting with the most recent inventory acquired and working backward.

Units Sold

Date Purchased	Units	Cost	Total Cost
December 12	100	$14	$ 1,400
September 5	200	13	2,600
April 8	400	12	4,800
January 20	200	11	2,200
Units sold	900	Cost of goods sold	$11,000

STUDY TIP

There may be cases, such as this illustration of LIFO, in which it is easier to determine ending inventory and then deduct it from cost of goods available for sale to find cost of goods sold. This approach is easier in this example because there are fewer layers in ending inventory than in cost of goods sold. In other cases, it may be quicker to determine cost of goods sold first and then plug in ending inventory.

Selecting an Inventory Costing Method

The primary determinant in selecting an inventory costing method should be the ability of the method to accurately reflect the net income of the period. Accountants have raised a number of arguments, however, to justify the use of one method over the others.

LO7 Analyze the effects of the different costing methods on inventory, net income, income taxes, and cash flow.

Costing Methods and Cash Flow

Comparative income statements for the three methods used in Examples 5-10, 5-11, and 5-12 are presented in Exhibit 5-5. Note that the weighted average method normally yields results between LIFO and FIFO. The major advantage of using the weighted average method is its simplicity.

The original data on page 224 involved a situation in which prices were rising throughout the period: beginning inventory cost $10 per unit, and the last purchase during the year was at $14. With LIFO, the most recent costs are assigned to cost of goods sold; with FIFO, the older costs are assigned to expense. Thus, in a period of rising prices, the assignment of the higher prices to cost of goods sold under LIFO results in a lower gross profit under LIFO than under FIFO ($7,000 for LIFO and $8,500 for FIFO).

EXHIBIT 5-5 Income Statements for the Inventory Costing Methods

	Weighted Average	FIFO	LIFO
Sales revenue—$20 each	$18,000	$18,000	$18,000
Beginning inventory	$ 5,000	$ 5,000	$ 5,000
Purchases	12,100	12,100	12,100
Cost of goods available for sale	$17,100	$17,100	$17,100
Ending inventory	**6,840**	**7,600**	**6,100**
Cost of goods sold	**$10,260**	**$ 9,500**	**$11,000**
Gross profit	**$ 7,740**	**$ 8,500**	**$ 7,000**
Operating expenses	2,000	2,000	2,000
Net income before tax	**$ 5,740**	**$ 6,500**	**$ 5,000**
Income tax expense (40%)	**2,296**	**2,600**	**2,000**
Net income	**$ 3,444**	**$ 3,900**	**$ 3,000**

NOTE: Figures that differ among the three methods are in bold.

EXAMPLE 5-13 Computing Taxes Saved by Using LIFO Instead of FIFO

The lower gross profit under LIFO results in lower income before tax, which in turn leads to lower taxes. If we assume a 40% tax rate, income tax expense under LIFO is only $2,000, compared with $2,600 under FIFO, a savings of $600 in taxes. Another way to look at the taxes saved by using LIFO is to focus on the difference in the expense under each method, as follows:

LIFO cost of goods sold	$11,000
− FIFO cost of goods sold	9,500
Additional expense from use of LIFO	$ 1,500
× Tax rate	0.40
Tax savings from the use of LIFO	$ 600

To summarize, during a period of rising prices, the two methods result in the following:

Item	LIFO	Relative to	FIFO
Cost of goods sold	Higher		Lower
Gross profit	Lower		Higher
Income before taxes	Lower		Higher
Taxes	Lower		Higher

The tax savings available from the use of LIFO during a period of rising prices is largely responsible for its popularity. Keep in mind, however, that the cash saved from a lower tax bill with LIFO is only a temporary savings, called a *tax deferral*. At some point in the life of the business, the inventory that is carried at the older, lower-priced amounts will be sold. This will result in a tax bill higher than that under FIFO. Yet even a tax deferral is beneficial; given the opportunity, it is better to pay less tax today and more in the future because today's tax savings can be invested.

LIFO Liquidation

LIFO liquidation
The result of selling more units than are purchased during the period, which can have negative tax consequences if a company is using LIFO.

When LIFO is used, the costs of the oldest units remain in inventory, and if prices are rising, the costs of these units will be lower than the costs of more recent purchases. Now assume that the company sells more units than it buys during the period. In a LIFO liquidation, some of the units assumed to be sold come from the older layers, with a relatively low unit cost. This situation, called a **LIFO liquidation**, presents a dilemma for the company.

A partial or complete liquidation of the older, lower-priced units will result in a low cost of goods sold figure and a correspondingly high gross profit for the period. In turn, the company faces a large tax bill because of the relatively high gross profit. In fact, a liquidation causes the tax advantages of using LIFO to reverse on the company, which is faced with paying off some of the taxes that were deferred in earlier periods. Should a company facing this situation buy inventory at the end of the year to avoid the consequences of a liquidation? That is a difficult question to answer and depends on many factors, including the company's cash position. The accountant must at least be aware of the potential for a large tax bill if a liquidation occurs.

Of course, a LIFO liquidation also benefits—and may even distort—reported earnings if the liquidation is large enough. For this reason and the tax problem, many companies are reluctant to liquidate their LIFO inventory. The problem often festers, and companies find themselves with inventory costed at decade-old price levels.

The LIFO Conformity Rule

Would it be possible for a company to have the best of both worlds? That is, could it use FIFO to report its income to stockholders, thus maximizing the amount of net income reported to this group, and use LIFO to report to the IRS, minimizing its taxable income and the amount paid to the government? Unfortunately, the IRS says that if a company chooses LIFO for reporting cost of goods sold on its tax return, it must also use LIFO on its books, that is, in preparing its income statement. This is called the **LIFO conformity rule**. Note that the rule applies only to the use of LIFO on the tax return. A company is free to use different methods in preparing its tax return and its income statement as long as the method used for the tax return is *not* LIFO.

LIFO conformity rule
The IRS requirement that when LIFO is used on a tax return, it must also be used in reporting income to stockholders.

The LIFO Reserve: Estimating LIFO's Effect on Income and on Taxes Paid for Winnebago Industries

An investor can determine the approximate tax savings to a company that decides to use LIFO.

EXAMPLE 5-14 Computing Taxes Saved by Using LIFO Instead of FIFO for Winnebago Industries

Consider Note 3 from the Form 10-K for the year ended August 29, 2015 for **Winnebago Industries**, the RV maker.

Note 3: Inventories
Inventories consist of the following:

(In thousands)	August 29, 2015	August 30, 2014
Finished goods	$ 12,179	$ 28,029
Work-in-process	66,602	49,919
Raw materials	65,928	66,200
Total	144,709	144,148
LIFO reserve	(32,544)	(31,300)
Total inventories	$112,165	$112,848

The above value of inventories, before reduction for the LIFO reserve, approximates replacement cost at the respective dates. Of the $144.7 million inventory at August 29, 2015, $135.3 million is valued on a LIFO basis and the Towables inventory of $8.4 million is valued on a FIFO basis. Of the $144.1 million inventory at August 30, 2014, $137.7 million is valued on a LIFO basis and the Towables inventory of $6.4 million is valued on a FIFO basis.

During Fiscal 2015 and Fiscal 2014 we recorded an increase to LIFO reserves of $1.2 million and $1.5 million based on increases in inflation.

The following steps explain the logic for using the information in the inventory note to estimate LIFO's effect on income and on taxes:

1. The excess of the value of a company's inventory stated at FIFO over the value stated at LIFO is called the **LIFO reserve**. The cumulative excess of the value of Winnebago

LIFO reserve
The excess of the value of a company's inventory stated at FIFO over the value stated at LIFO.

Industries' inventory on a FIFO basis over the value on a LIFO basis is $32,544,000 at the end of 2015.

2. Because Winnebago Industries reports inventory at a lower value on its balance sheet using LIFO, it will report a higher cost of goods sold amount on the income statement. Thus, the LIFO reserve not only represents the excess of the inventory balance on a FIFO basis over that on a LIFO basis but also represents the cumulative amount by which cost of goods sold on a LIFO basis exceeds cost of goods sold on a FIFO basis.

3. The increase in Winnebago Industries' LIFO reserve in 2015 was $1,244,000 ($32,544,000 − $31,300,000). This means that the increase in cost of goods sold for 2015 from using LIFO instead of FIFO was also this amount. Thus, income before tax for 2015 was $1,244,000 lower because the company used LIFO.

4. If we assume a corporate tax rate of 35%, the tax savings from using LIFO amounted to $1,244,000 × 0.35, or $435,400.

Costing Methods and Inventory Profits

Replacement cost
The current cost of a unit of inventory.

FIFO, LIFO, and weighted average are all cost-based methods to value inventory. An alternative to assigning any of the historical costs incurred during the year to ending inventory and cost of goods sold is to use **replacement cost** to value each of these. Use of a replacement cost of $15 results in the following:

Ending inventory = 600 units × $15 per unit = $ 9,000
Cost of goods sold = 900 units × $15 per unit = $13,500

Inventory profit
The portion of the gross profit that results from holding inventory during a period of rising prices.

A replacement cost approach is not acceptable under the profession's current standards, but many believe that it provides more relevant information to users. Many accountants argue that the use of historical cost in valuing inventory leads to what is called **inventory profit**, particularly when FIFO is used in a period of rising prices. The cost of goods sold in Example 5-11 was only $9,500 on a FIFO basis, compared with $13,500 when the replacement cost of $15 per unit was used. The $4,000 difference between the two cost of goods sold figures is a profit from holding the inventory during a period of rising prices and is called *inventory profit*.

EXAMPLE 5-15 Reconciling the Difference Between Gross Profit on a FIFO Basis and on a Replacement Cost Basis

Assume that the units in Example 5-11 are sold for $20 each. The following analysis reconciles the difference between gross profit on a FIFO basis and on a replacement cost basis:

Sales revenue (900 units × $20)		$18,000
Cost of goods sold—FIFO basis		9,500
Gross profit—FIFO basis		$ 8,500
Cost of goods sold—replacement cost basis	$13,500	
Cost of goods sold—FIFO basis	9,500	
Profit from holding inventory during a period of inflation		4,000
Gross profit on a replacement cost basis		$ 4,500

Those who argue in favor of a replacement cost approach would report only $4,500 of gross profit. They believe that the additional $4,000 of profit reported on a FIFO basis is simply due to holding the inventory during a period of rising prices. According to this viewpoint, if the 900 units sold during the period are to be replaced, the use of replacement cost in calculating cost of goods sold results in a better measure of gross profit than if it is calculated using FIFO.

Because LIFO assigns the cost of the most recent purchases to cost of goods sold, it most nearly approximates the results with a replacement cost system. The other side of the argument, however, is that whereas LIFO results in the best approximation of replacement cost of goods sold on the income statement, FIFO most nearly approximates replacement cost of the inventory on the balance sheet. A comparison of the amounts from the running example verifies this:

	Ending Inventory	Cost of Goods Sold
FIFO	$7,600	$ 9,500
LIFO	6,100	11,000
Replacement cost	9,000	13,500

Changing Inventory Methods

The purpose of each of the inventory costing methods is to match costs with revenues. If a company believes that a different method will result in a better matching than that being provided by the method currently being used, the company should change methods. A company must be able to justify a change in methods, however. Taking advantage of the tax breaks offered by LIFO is *not* a valid justification for a change in methods.

Inventory Valuation in Other Countries

The acceptable methods of valuing inventory differ considerably around the world. Although FIFO is the most popular method in the United States, LIFO continues to be widely used, as is the average cost method. Many countries prohibit the use of LIFO for tax or financial reporting purposes. Additionally, the IASB strictly prohibits the use of LIFO by companies that follow its standards. As GAAP in the United States come closer to converging with the international standards, it is still uncertain whether LIFO will survive as an acceptable inventory valuation method.

MODULE 2   TEST YOURSELF

Review	**LO5** Explain the relationship between the valuation of inventory and the measurement of income.	• Inventory costs ultimately become the cost of goods sold reflected in the income statement. • Since inventory is not expensed as the cost of goods sold until merchandise is sold, determining which costs belong in inventory affects the timing of when these expenses are reflected in net income.

	LO6 Apply the inventory costing methods of specific identification, weighted average, FIFO, and LIFO by using a periodic system.	• The purchase price of inventory items may change frequently, and several alternatives are available to assign costs to the goods sold and those that remain in ending inventory.
		  • Specific identification assigns the actual costs of acquisition to items of inventory. In some circumstances, it is not practical to do this.
		  • Three other methods involve making assumptions about the cost of inventory.
		    • Weighted average assigns the same unit cost to all units available for sale during the period.
		    • The FIFO method assumes that the first units purchased are the first units sold.
		    • The LIFO method assumes that the last units purchased are the first units sold.

	LO7 Analyze the effects of the different costing methods on inventory, net income, income taxes, and cash flow.	• The ability to measure net income accurately for a period should be the driving force behind selecting an inventory costing method.
		  • Inventory costing methods impact the cost of goods sold and, therefore, net income.
		  • When a company uses LIFO for tax purposes, it must use it for financial reporting purposes as well.

Question

1. What is the relationship between the valuation of inventory as an asset on the balance sheet and the measurement of income?

2. What is the significance of the adjective *weighted* in the weighted average cost method? Use an example to illustrate your answer.

3. Which inventory costing method should a company use if it wants to minimize taxes? Does your response depend on whether prices are rising or falling? Explain your answers.

4. What does the term *LIFO liquidation* mean? How can it lead to poor buying habits?

Apply

1. Baxter operates a chain of electronics stores and buys its products from a number of manufacturers around the world. Give at least three examples of costs that Baxter might incur that should be added to the purchase price of its inventory.

2. Busby Corp. began the year with 75 units of inventory that it paid $2 each to acquire. During the year, it purchased an additional 100 units for $3 each. Busby sold 150 units during the year.
   a.   Compute cost of goods sold and ending inventory assuming Busby uses FIFO.
   b.   Compute cost of goods sold and ending inventory assuming Busby uses LIFO.

3. Belden started the year with 1,000 units of inventory with a unit cost of $5. During the year, it bought 3,000 units at a cost of $6 per unit. A year-end count revealed 500 units on hand.
   Compute ending inventory assuming:
   a.   FIFO
   b.   LIFO

4. A company currently uses the LIFO method to value its inventory. For each of the following items, indicate whether it would be higher (H) or lower (L) if the company changed to the FIFO method. Assume a period of rising prices.
   a.   _____ Cost of goods sold
   b.   _____ Gross profit
   c.   _____ Income before taxes
   d.   _____ Income taxes
   e.   _____ Cash outflow

Answers are located at the end of the chapter.

MODULE 3 OTHER INVENTORY ISSUES

LO8 Analyze the effects of an inventory error on various financial statement items.

Earlier in the chapter, we considered the inherent tie between the valuation of assets, such as inventory, and the measurement of income, such as cost of goods sold. The importance of inventory valuation to the measurement of income can be illustrated by considering inventory errors. Many different types of inventory errors exist. Some errors are mathematical, such as adding a column total incorrectly. Other errors relate specifically to the physical count of inventory at year-end, or arise from cutoff problems at year-end. For example, merchandise in transit at the end of the year belongs to the buyer when it is shipped FOB shipping point. Because the shipment has not arrived at the end of the year, however, it cannot be included in the physical count. Unless some type of control is in place, the amount in transit may be erroneously omitted from the valuation of inventory at year-end.

Inventory Errors

To demonstrate the effect of an inventory error on the income statement, assume that the correct amount of ending inventory is $250,000, but the amount recorded is $300,000. This error resulted because two different teams were assigned to count inventory in the same warehouse on December 31, 2017.

EXAMPLE 5-16 Analyzing the Effect of an Inventory Error on Net Income

The overstatement of ending inventory in 2017 leads to an understatement of the 2017 cost of goods sold expense. Because cost of goods sold is understated, gross profit for the year is overstated. Thus, net income in 2017 is overstated by the same amount of the overstatement of gross profit,[3] as shown in the following analysis:

	2017			2018		
	Reported	Corrected	Effect of Error	Reported	Corrected	Effect of Error
Sales	$1,000*	$1,000		$1,500	$1,500	
Cost of goods sold:						
Beginning inventory	$ 200	$ 200		$ 300	$ 250	$50 OS
Purchases	700	700		1,100	1,100	
Cost of goods available for sale	$ 900	$ 900		$1,400	$1,350	50 OS
Ending inventory	(300)	(250)	$50 OS†	(350)	(350)	
Cost of goods sold	$ 600	$ 650	50 US‡	$1,050	$1,000	50 OS
Gross profit	$ 400	$ 350	50 OS	$ 450	$ 500	50 US
Operating expenses	(100)	(100)		(120)	(120)	
Net income	$ 300	$ 250	50 OS	$ 330	$ 380	50 US

NOTE: Figures that differ as a result of the error are in bold.

*All amounts are in thousands of dollars.

†OS = Overstatement

‡US = Understatement

The most important conclusion from the analysis is that an overstatement of ending inventory leads to a corresponding overstatement of net income.

Unfortunately, the effect of a misstatement of the year-end inventory is not limited to the net income for that year. The error also affects the income statement for the following year, as indicated in the two "2018" columns. This counterbalancing error happens because the ending inventory of one period is the beginning inventory of the following period. The overstatement of the 2018 beginning inventory leads to an overstatement of cost of goods available for sale. Because cost of goods available for sale is overstated, cost of goods sold is also overstated. The overstatement of cost of goods sold expense results in an understatement of gross profit and thus an understatement of net income.

EXAMPLE 5-17 Analyzing the Effect of an Inventory Error on Retained Earnings

Assume that retained earnings at the beginning of 2017 is correctly stated at $300,000. The counterbalancing nature of the error is seen by analyzing retained earnings. For 2017, the analysis would indicate the following (OS = overstated and US = understated):

	2017 Reported	2017 Corrected	Effect of Error
Beginning retained earnings	$300,000	$300,000	Correct
Net income	300,000	250,000	$50,000 OS
Ending retained earnings	$600,000	$550,000	$50,000 OS

An analysis for 2018 would show the following:

	2018 Reported	2018 Corrected	Effect of Error
Beginning retained earnings	$600,000	$550,000	$50,000 OS
Net income	330,000	380,000	$50,000 US
Ending retained earnings	$930,000	$930,000	Correct

Even though retained earnings is overstated at the end of the first year, it is correctly stated at the end of the second year. This is the nature of a counterbalancing error.

[3] An overstatement of gross profit also results in an overstatement of income tax expense. Thus, because tax expense is overstated, the overstatement of net income is not as large as the overstatement of gross profit. For now, we will ignore the effect of taxes.

EXAMPLE 5-18 Analyzing the Effect of an Inventory Error on the Balance Sheet

The only accounts on the balance sheet affected by the error are Inventory and Retained Earnings. The overstatement of the 2017 ending inventory results in an overstatement of total assets at the end of the first year. Similarly, as the earlier analysis indicates, the overstatement of 2017 net income leads to an overstatement of retained earnings by the same amount. Because the error is counterbalancing, the 2018 year-end balance sheet is correct. That is, ending inventory is not affected by the error; thus, the amount for total assets at the end of 2018 is also correct. The effect of the error on retained earnings is limited to the first year because of the counterbalancing nature of the error.

	2017		**2018**	
	Reported	**Corrected**	**Reported**	**Corrected**
Inventory	$ **300***	$ **250**	$ 350	$ 350
All other assets	1,700	1,700	2,080	2,080
Total assets	**$2,000**	**$1,950**	$ 2,430	$ 2,430
Total liabilities	$ 400	$ 400	$ 500	$ 500
Capital stock	1,000	1,000	1,000	1,000
Retained earnings	**600**	**550**	930	930
Total liabilities and stockholders' equity	**$2,000**	**$1,950**	$ 2,430	$ 2,430

NOTE: Figures that differ as a result of the error are in bold.

*All amounts are in thousands of dollars.

STUDY TIP

Note the logic behind the notion that an overstatement of ending inventory leads to overstatements of total assets and retained earnings at the end of the year. This is logical because a balance sheet must balance; that is, the left side must equal the right side. If the left side (inventory) is overstated, the right side (retained earnings) will also be overstated.

The effects of inventory errors on various financial statement items are summarized in Exhibit 5-6. The analysis focused on the effects of an overstatement of inventory. The effects of an understatement are just the opposite and are summarized in the bottom portion of the exhibit.

Part of the auditor's job is to perform the necessary tests to obtain reasonable assurance that inventory has not been overstated or understated. If there is an error and inventory is wrong, however, both the balance sheet and the income statement will be distorted. For example, if ending inventory is overstated, inflating total assets, cost of goods sold will be understated, boosting profits. Thus, such an error overstates the financial health of the

EXHIBIT 5-6 Summary of the Effects of Inventory Errors

	Effect of Overstatement of Ending Inventory on	
	Current Year	**Following Year**
Cost of goods sold	Understated	Overstated
Gross profit	Overstated	Understated
Net income	Overstated	Understated
Retained earnings, end of year	Overstated	Correctly stated
Total assets, end of year	Overstated	Correctly stated

	Effect of Understatement of Ending Inventory on	
	Current Year	**Following Year**
Cost of goods sold	Overstated	Understated
Gross profit	Understated	Overstated
Net income	Understated	Overstated
Retained earnings, end of year	Understated	Correctly stated
Total assets, end of year	Understated	Correctly stated

organization in two ways. A lender or an investor must make a decision based on the current year's statement and cannot wait until the next accounting cycle, when this error is reversed. This is one reason that investors and creditors insist on audited financial statements.

Valuing Inventory at Lower of Cost or Market

One of the components sold by an electronics firm has become obsolete. It is likely that the retailer will have to sell the merchandise for less than the normal selling price. In this situation, a departure from the cost basis of accounting may be necessary because the market value of the inventory may be less than its cost to the company. The departure is called the **lower-of-cost-or-market (LCM) rule**.

At the end of each accounting period, the original cost, as determined using one of the costing methods such as FIFO, is compared with the market price of the inventory. If market is less than cost, the inventory is written down to the lower amount. For example, if cost is $100,000 and market value is $85,000, the accountant makes an adjustment that can be identified and analyzed as follows:

LO9 Apply the lower-of-cost-or-market rule to the valuation of inventory.

Lower-of-cost-or-market (LCM) rule
A conservative inventory valuation approach that is an attempt to anticipate declines in the value of inventory before its actual sale.

Identify and Analyze	**ACTIVITY: Operating** **ACCOUNTS: Inventory** Decrease **Loss on Decline in Value of Inventory** Increase **STATEMENT(S): Balance Sheet and Income Statement**

Balance Sheet				Income Statement			
ASSETS	=	LIABILITIES	+	STOCKHOLDERS' EQUITY	REVENUES	−	EXPENSES	=	NET INCOME
Inventory (15,000)				(15,000)			Loss on Decline in Value of Inventory 15,000		(15,000)

Note that the adjustment reduces inventory and net income. The reduction in net income is the result of reporting the Loss on Decline in Value of Inventory on the income statement as an item of Other Expense.

Why Replacement Cost Is Used as a Measure of Market

A better name for the lower-of-cost-or-market rule would be the lower-of-cost-or-replacement-cost rule because accountants define *market* as "replacement cost."[4] To understand why replacement cost is used as a basis to compare with original cost, assume that Daisy's Running Depot pays $75 for a pair of running shoes and normally sells them for $100. Thus, the normal markup on selling price is $25/$100, or 25%, as indicated in the Before Price Change column in Exhibit 5-7. Now assume that this style of running shoes becomes less popular. The retailer finds that because of the style change, the cost to replace the pair of running shoes is now only $60. The retailer realizes that if the shoes are to be sold at all, they will have to be offered at a reduced price. The selling price is dropped from $100 to $80. If the retailer now buys a pair of shoes for $60 and sells them for $80, the gross profit will be $20 and the gross profit percentage will be maintained at 25%, as indicated in the right-hand column of Exhibit 5-7.

To compare the results with and without the use of the LCM rule, assume that the retailer has ten pairs of the running shoes in inventory on December 31, 2017. In addition, assume that all ten pairs are sold in January 2018 at the reduced price

---

[4] Technically, the use of replacement cost as a measure of market value is subject to two constraints. First, market cannot be more than the net realizable value of the inventory. Second, inventory should not be recorded at less than net realizable value less a normal profit margin. The rationale for these two constraints is covered in intermediate accounting texts. For our purposes, we assume that replacement cost falls between the two constraints.

of $80 each. If the lower-of-cost-or-market rule is not used, the results for the years will be as follows:

LCM Rule Not Used	2017	2018	Total
Sales revenue ($80 per unit)	$0	$ 800	$ 800
Cost of goods sold (original cost of $75 per unit)	0	(750)	(750)
Gross profit	$0	$ 50	$ 50

EXHIBIT 5-7 Gross Profit Percentage Before and After Price Change

	Before Price Change	After Price Change
Selling price	$100	$80
Cost	75	60
Gross profit	$ 25	$20
Gross profit percentage	25%	25%

If the LCM rule is not applied, the gross profit is distorted. Instead of the normal 25%, a gross profit percentage of $50/$800, or 6.25%, is reported in 2018 when the ten pairs of shoes are sold. If the LCM rule is applied, however, the results for the two years are as follows:

LCM Rule Used	2017	2018	Total
Sales revenue ($80 per unit)	$ 0	$ 800	$ 800
Cost of goods sold			
(replacement cost of $60 per unit)	0	(600)	(600)
Loss on decline in value of inventory:			
10 units × ($75 − $60)	(150)	0	(150)
Gross profit	$(150)	$ 200	$ 50

The use of the LCM rule serves two important functions: (1) to report the loss in value of the inventory, $15 per pair of running shoes, or $150 total, in the year the loss occurs; and (2) to report in the year the shoes are actually sold the normal gross profit of $200/$800, or 25%, which is not affected by a change in the selling price.

The write-down of the shoes violates the historical cost principle, which says that assets should be carried on the balance sheet at their original cost. However, the departure from the cost basis is normally justified on the basis of conservatism. This concept is invoked by accountants when there is uncertainty. For example, in the preceding scenario, the future selling price of a pair of shoes is uncertain because of style changes.

Application of the LCM Rule

Three different interpretations of the LCM rule are possible.

1. The lower of total cost or total market value for the **entire inventory** could be reported.
2. The lower of cost or market value for **each individual product or item** could be reported.
3. The lower of cost or market value for **groups of items** could be reported.

A company is free to choose any one of these approaches in applying the lower-of-cost-or-market rule. The approach chosen to apply the rule should be used consistently from one period to the next.

The item-by-item approach (Number 2) is the most popular of the three approaches for two reasons. First, it produces the most conservative result. The reason is that with either a group-by-group or a total approach, increases in the values of some items of inventory offset declines in the values of other items. The item-by-item approach, however, ignores increases in value and recognizes all declines in value. Second, the item-by-item approach is the method required for tax purposes, although unlike LIFO, it is not required for book purposes merely because it is used for tax computations.

Lower-of-Cost-or-Market under International Standards

Both U.S. GAAP and international financial reporting standards (IFRS) require the use of the lower-of-cost-or-market rule to value inventories. However, these sets of standards differ in two respects. The first difference is the result of how market value is defined. U.S. GAAP define market value as *replacement cost,* subject to a maximum and a minimum amount. In contract, IFRS uses *net realizable value* with no upper or lower limits imposed. The second difference relates to what happens in future periods after inventory has been written down to a lower market value. Under U.S. standards, this new amount becomes the basis for any future adjustments. However, under IFRS, write-downs of inventory can be reversed in later periods. This means that a gain is recognized when the value of the inventory goes back up.

MODULE 3   TEST YOURSELF

Review

LO8 Analyze the effects of an inventory error on various financial statement items.

- The link between the balance sheet and the income statement can be seen through the effect of errors in inventory valuation.
  - Overstatement of ending inventory results in an understatement of the cost of goods sold and therefore an overstatement of net income.
  - The effects of errors in inventory may offset themselves over time. These are known as counterbalancing errors.

LO9 Apply the lower-of-cost-or-market rule to the valuation of inventory.

- The principle of conservatism in accounting may warrant a departure from historical cost. This departure is known as the lower-of-cost-or-market rule (LCM).
  - Under LCM, the historical cost of inventory is compared with its replacement cost. If the replacement cost is lower, the Inventory account is reduced and a loss is recognized.

Question

1. Delevan Corp. uses a periodic inventory system and is counting its year-end inventory. Due to a lack of communication, two different teams count the same section of the warehouse. What effect will this error have on net income?

2. What is the rationale for valuing inventory at the lower of cost or market?

3. Why is it likely that the result from applying the lower-of-cost-or-market rule using a total approach (i.e., by comparing total cost to total market value) and the result from applying the rule on an item-by-item basis will differ?

Apply

1. Due to a clerical error, a company overstated by $50,000 the amount of inventory on hand at the end of the year. Will net income for the year be overstated or understated? Identify the two accounts on the year-end balance sheet that will be in error and indicate whether they will be understated or overstated.

2. Glendive reports its inventory on a FIFO basis and has inventory with a cost of $78,000 on December 31. The cost to replace the inventory on this date would be only $71,000. Identify and analyze the necessary adjustment on December 31.

Answers are located at the end of the chapter.

MODULE 4 INVENTORY MANAGEMENT AND CASH FLOW ISSUES

Inventory is the lifeblood of a company that sells a product. Gap Inc. must strike a balance between maintaining a sufficient variety of products to meet customers' needs and incurring the high cost of carrying inventory. The cost of storage and the lost income from the money tied up in inventory make inventory very expensive to keep on hand. Thus, the more quickly a company can sell—that is, turn over—its inventory, the better.

LO10 Analyze the management of inventory.

Inventory turnover ratio
A measure of the number of times inventory is sold during the period.

Using data from Exhibit 5-3, the **inventory turnover ratio** for Daisy's Running Depot is calculated as follows:

$$\frac{\text{Cost of Goods Sold}}{\text{Average Inventory}} = \frac{\$60,000}{(\$15,000 + \$18,000)/2} = \frac{\$60,000}{\$16,500} = 3.6 \text{ times}$$

MAKING BUSINESS DECISIONS
GAP INC.

Analyzing the Management of Inventory

An investor must be able to assess how well a company manages its inventory. The quicker inventory can be sold, the sooner the money will be available to buy more products or to use for other purposes. Use the following models to help you in your role as an investor to decide whether to buy stock in Gap Inc.

A. The Ratio Analysis Model

1. Formulate the Question
How many times a year does the company turn over its inventory?

2. Gather the Information from the Financial Statements
To calculate a company's inventory turnover ratio, it is essential to know its cost of goods sold and the average balance in inventory:

Cost of goods sold: From the income statement
Average inventory: From the balance sheet at the end of the two most recent years

3. Calculate the Ratio

$$\text{Inventory Turnover Ratio} = \frac{\text{Cost of Goods Sold}}{\text{Average Inventory}}$$

Gap Inc.
Partial Consolidated Statements of Income (in millions)

| | Fiscal Year | | |
	2015	2014	2013
Net sales	$15,797	$16,435	$16,148
Cost of goods sold and occupancy expenses	10,077	10,146	9,855

Gap Inc.
Partial Consolidated Balance Sheets (in millions)

	January 30, 2016	January 31, 2015
Assets		
Current assets:		
Merchandise inventory	$1,873	$1,889

Average merchandise inventory = ($1,873 + $1,889)/2 = **$1,881**

$$\text{Inventory Turnover} = \frac{\$10,077}{\$1,881} = 5.4 \text{ times}$$

4. Compare the Ratio with Other Ratios

Ratios are of no use in a vacuum. It is necessary to compare them with prior years and with competitors.

INVENTORY TURNOVER RATIO			
Gap Inc.		American Eagle Outfitters, Inc.	
Year Ended January 30, 2016	Year Ended January 31, 2015	Year Ended January 30, 2016	Year Ended January 31, 2015
5.4 times	5.3 times	7.6 times	7.5 times

5. Interpret the Ratios

In fiscal year 2015, Gap Inc. turned over its inventory an average of 5.4 times. This is nearly the same as the turnover in the prior year, but less often than the turnover for its competitor, American Eagle Outfitters, Inc. An alternative way to look at a company's efficiency in managing its inventory is to calculate the number of days, on average, that inventory is on hand before it is sold. This measure is called **number of days' sales in inventory** and is calculated as follows for Gap Inc. in 2015, assuming 360 days in a year:

$$\text{Number of Day's Sales in Inventory} = \frac{\text{Number of Days in the Period}}{\text{Inventory Turnover Ratio}}$$

$$= \frac{360}{5.4}$$

$$= 67 \text{ days}$$

Number of days' sales in inventory
A measure of how long it takes to sell inventory.

This measure tells us that it took Gap Inc. 67 days, or about two months, on average to sell its inventory.

B. The Business Decision Model

1. Formulate the Question

If you were an investor, would you buy stock in Gap Inc.?

2. Gather Information from the Financial Statements and Other Sources

This information will come from a variety of sources, not limited to but including:

- The balance sheet provides information about liquidity, the income statement regarding profitability, and the statement of cash flows on inflows and outflows of cash.
- The outlook for the apparel industry, including consumer trends, foreign markets, labor issues, and other factors.
- The outlook for the economy in general.
- Alternative uses for the money.

3. Analyze the Information Gathered

- Compare Gap Inc.'s inventory turnover ratio in (A) above with American Eagle Outfitters as well as with industry averages.
- Look at trends over time in the inventory turnover ratios.
- Look at trends in net income over time as an indication of the ability to control expenses other than cost of goods sold.
- Review projections for the economy and the industry.

4. Make the Decision

Taking into account all of the various sources of information, decide either to

- Buy stock in Gap Inc., or
- Find an alternative use for the money.

5. Monitor Your Decision

If you decide to buy the stock, you will need to monitor your investment periodically. During the time you hold the stock, you will want to assess the company's continuing profitability as well as other factors you considered before making the investment.

How Inventories Affect the Cash Flows Statement

The effects on the income statement and the statement of cash flows from inventory-related transactions differ significantly. This chapter has focused on how the purchase and sale of inventory are reported on the income statement. We found that the cost of the inventory sold during the period is deducted on the income statement as cost of goods sold.

The appropriate reporting on a statement of cash flows for inventory transactions depends on whether the direct or indirect method is used. If the direct method is used to prepare the Operating Activities category of the statement, the amount of cash paid to suppliers of inventory is shown as a deduction in this section of the statement.

If the more popular indirect method is used, it is necessary to make adjustments to net income for the changes in two accounts: Inventory and Accounts Payable. These adjustments are summarized in Exhibit 5-8. An increase in inventory is deducted because it indicates that the company is building up its stock of inventory and thus expending cash. A decrease in inventory is added to net income. An increase in accounts payable is added because it indicates that during the period, the company increased the amount it owes suppliers and therefore conserved its cash. A decrease in accounts payable is deducted because the company actually reduced the amount owed suppliers during the period.

EXHIBIT 5-8 Inventories and the Statement of Cash Flows

Item	Cash Flow Statement	
	Operating Activities	
	Net income	**XXX**
Increase in inventory ⟶		–
Decrease in inventory ⟶		+
Increase in accounts payable ⟶		+
Decrease in accounts payable ⟶		–
	Investing Activities	
	Financing Activities	

The Operating Activities category of the statement of cash flows for **Chipotle** is presented in Exhibit 5-9. The decrease in inventory is added because the decrease in this asset conserves the company's cash. An increase in accounts payable also conserves Chipotle's cash. Thus, the increase in this item in 2015 is added to net income.

EXHIBIT 5-9 Partial Consolidated Statement of Cash Flows for Chipotle

Chipotle Mexican Grill, Inc. Consolidated Statement of Cash Flows (in thousands)			
	Year ended December 31		
	2015	**2014**	**2013**
Operating activities			
Net income	$475,602	$445,374	$327,438
Adjustments to reconcile net income to net cash provided by operating activities:			
Depreciation and amortization	130,368	110,474	96,054
Deferred income tax (benefit) provision	11,666	(20,671)	2,103
Loss on disposal of assets	13,194	6,976	6,751
Bad debt allowance	(23)	9	19
Stock-based compensation expense	57,911	96,440	63,657
Excess tax benefit on stock-based compensation	(74,442)	(21,667)	(38,379)
Other	582	104	507

(Continued)

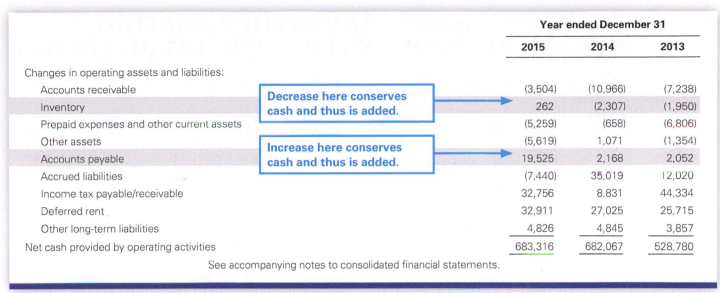

| | Year ended December 31 | | |
	2015	2014	2013
Changes in operating assets and liabilities:			
Accounts receivable	(3,504)	(10,966)	(7,238)
Inventory	262	(2,307)	(1,950)
Prepaid expenses and other current assets	(5,259)	(658)	(6,806)
Other assets	(5,619)	1,071	(1,354)
Accounts payable	19,525	2,168	2,052
Accrued liabilities	(7,440)	35,019	12,020
Income tax payable/receivable	32,756	8,831	44,334
Deferred rent	32,911	27,025	25,715
Other long-term liabilities	4,826	4,845	3,857
Net cash provided by operating activities	683,316	682,067	528,780

Decrease here conserves cash and thus is added.

Increase here conserves cash and thus is added.

See accompanying notes to consolidated financial statements.

Source: Chipotle Mexican Grill Inc.'s Form 10-K for the fiscal year ended December 31, 2015.

MODULE 4 TEST YOURSELF

Review

LO10 Analyze the management of inventory.

- Inventory turnover is a measure of how efficiently inventory is managed. The ratio measures how quickly inventory is sold and is calculated as follows:

$$\frac{\text{Cost of Goods Sold}}{\text{Average Inventory}}$$

The higher the ratio, the less time inventory resides in storage (i.e., the more quickly it turns over).

- The average length of time that it takes to sell inventory can be derived from the inventory turnover ratio:

$$\text{Number of Days' Sales in Inventory} = \frac{\text{Number of Days in the Period}}{\text{Inventory Turnover Ratio}}$$

LO11 Explain the effects that inventory transactions have on the statement of cash flows.

- Under the indirect method of calculating cash flows from operating activities, both the changes in the Inventory account and the Accounts Payable account must be taken into consideration.

Question

1. Ralston Corp.'s cost of goods sold has remained steady over the last two years. During this same time period, however, its inventory has increased considerably. What does this information tell you about the company's inventory turnover? Explain your answer.

2. Why is an increase in Accounts Payable added to net income when the indirect method is used to prepare the statement of cash flows?

Apply

1. Sidney began the year with $130,000 in merchandise inventory and ended the year with $190,000. Sales and cost of goods sold for the year were $900,000 and $640,000, respectively.
   a. Compute Sidney's inventory turnover ratio.
   b. Compute the number of days' sales in inventory.

2. Two companies each recorded $10 million in cost of goods sold for the year. Company A had average inventory of $100,000 on hand during the year. Company B's average inventory was $1 million. One company is a car dealer, and the other is a wholesaler of fresh fruits and vegetables. Which company sells cars, and which company sells fruits and vegetables? Explain your answer.

3. Grogan's inventory increased by $50,000 during the year, and its accounts payable increased by $35,000. Indicate how each of those changes would be reflected on a statement of cash flows prepared using the indirect method.

Answers are located at the end of the chapter.

APPENDIX

MODULE 5 INVENTORY COSTING METHODS WITH A PERPETUAL SYSTEM

This appendix will show how the inventory costing methods are applied when a company maintains a perpetual inventory system. It is important to understand the difference between inventory *costing systems* and inventory *methods*. The perpetual and periodic inventory systems differ in terms of how often the Inventory account is updated. However, when a company sells identical units of product and the cost to purchase each unit is subject to change, the company also must choose an inventory costing method such as FIFO, LIFO, or weighted average.

Earlier, the chapter provided illustrations of the various costing methods with a periodic system. The same data are now used to illustrate how the methods differ when a perpetual system is used (if specific identification is used, the results will be the same regardless of whether a periodic or perpetual system is used). To compare the periodic and perpetual systems for FIFO, LIFO, and weighted average, we must add the date of each of the sales. The original data as well as the number of units sold on the various dates are summarized as follows:

Date	Purchases	Sales	Balance
Beginning inventory			500 units @ $10
January 20	300 units @ $11		800 units
February 18		450 units	350 units
April 8	400 units @ $12		750 units
June 19		300 units	450 units
September 5	200 units @ $13		650 units
October 20		150 units	500 units
December 12	100 units @ $14		600 units

FIFO Costing with a Perpetual System

Example 5-19, shown below, illustrates the FIFO method on a perpetual basis. With a perpetual system, FIFO is applied at the time of each sale. For example, in Example 5-19 the 450 units assumed to be sold on February 18 are taken from the beginning inventory of 500 units with a unit cost of $10. Thus, the inventory or balance after this sale as shown in the last three columns is 50 units at $10 and 300 units at $11, for a total of $3,800. The purchase on April 8 of 400 units at $12 is added to the running balance. On a FIFO basis, the sale of 300 units on June 19 comes from the remainder of the beginning inventory of 50 units and another 250 units from the first purchase at $11 on January 20. The balance after this sale is 50 units at $11 and 400 units at $12. Note that the ending inventory of $7,600 is the same amount calculated for FIFO periodic earlier in the chapter:

FIFO periodic (Example 5-11)	$7,600
FIFO perpetual (Example 5-19)	$7,600

EXAMPLE 5-19 Determining Ending Inventory Using FIFO with a Perpetual System

Date	Purchases Units	Unit Cost	Total Cost	Sales Units	Unit Cost	Total Cost	Balance Units	Unit Cost	Balance
1/1							500	$10	$5,000
1/20	300	$11	$3,300				500	10	
							300	11	8,300
2/18				450	$10	$4,500	50	10	
							300	11	3,800
4/8	400	12	4,800				50	10	
							300	11	
							400	12	8,600

(Continued)

Date	Purchases Units	Unit Cost	Total Cost	Sales Units	Unit Cost	Total Cost	Balance Units	Unit Cost	Balance
6/19				50	10	500	50	11	
				250	11	2,750	400	12	5,350
9/5	200	13	2,600				50	11	
							400	12	
							200	13	7,950
10/20				50	11	550	300	12	
				100	12	1,200	200	13	6,200
12/12	100	14	1,400				300	12	
							200	13	
							100	14	7,600

LIFO Costing with a Perpetual System

A LIFO cost flow with the use of a perpetual system is illustrated in Example 5-20. First, the 450 units assumed to be sold on February 18 consist of the most recent units acquired, 300 units at $11, and 150 units from the beginning inventory at $10. Thus, the balance after this sale is simply the remaining 350 units from the beginning inventory priced at $10. The purchase on April 8 results in a balance of 350 units at $10 and 400 units at $12.

When LIFO is applied on a perpetual basis, a gap is created. Units acquired at the earliest price of $10 and units acquired at the most recent price of $12 are on hand, but none of those at the middle price of $11 remain. This situation arises because LIFO is applied every time a sale is made rather than only at the end of the year. Because of this difference, the amount of ending inventory differs depending on which system is used:

LIFO periodic (Example 5-12) $6,100
LIFO perpetual (Example 5-20) $6,750

EXAMPLE 5-20 Determining Ending Inventory Using LIFO with a Perpetual System

Date	Purchases Units	Unit Cost	Total Cost	Sales Units	Unit Cost	Total Cost	Balance Units	Unit Cost	Balance
1/1							500	$10	$5,000
1/20	300	$11	$3,300				500	10	
							300	11	8,300
2/18				300	$11	$3,300			
				150	10	1,500	350	10	3,500
4/8	400	12	4,800				350	10	
							400	12	8,300
6/19				300	12	3,600	350	10	
							100	12	4,700
9/5	200	13	2,600				350	10	
							100	12	
							200	13	7,300
10/20				150	13	1,950	350	10	
							100	12	
							50	13	5,350
12/12	100	14	1,400				350	10	
							100	12	
							50	13	
							100	14	6,750

Moving Average with a Perpetual System

Moving average
The name given to an average cost method when a weighted average cost assumption is used with a perpetual inventory system.

When a weighted average cost assumption is applied with a perpetual system, it is sometimes called a **moving average**. As indicated in Example 5-21, each time a purchase is made, a new weighted average cost must be computed, thus the name *moving average*. For example, the goods available for sale after the January 20 purchase consist of 500 units at $10 and 300 units at $11, which results in an average cost of $10.38. This is the unit cost applied to the 450 units sold on February 18. The 400 units purchased on April 8 require the computation of a new unit cost, as indicated in the second footnote in Example 5-21. Thus, the ending inventory with an average cost flow differs depending on whether a periodic or a perpetual system is used:

Weighted average periodic (Example 5-10)	$6,840
Moving average perpetual (Example 5-21)	$7,290

EXAMPLE 5-21 Determining Ending Inventory Using Moving Average with a Perpetual System

	Purchases			Sales			Balance		
Date	Units	Unit Cost	Total Cost	Units	Unit Cost	Total Cost	Units	Unit Cost	Balance
1/1							500	$10.00	$5,000
1/20	300	$11	$3,300				800	10.38*	8,304
2/18				450	$10.38	$4,671	350	10.38	3,633
4/8	400	12	4,800				750	11.24†	8,430
6/19				300	11.24	3,372	450	11.24	5,058
9/5	200	13	2,600				650	11.78‡	7,657
10/20				150	11.78	1,767	500	11.78	5,890
12/12	100	14	1,400				600	12.15§	7,290

The moving average prices per unit are calculated as follows:
*($5,000 + $3,300)/800 units = $10.38 (rounded to nearest cent)
†($3,633 + $4,800)/750 units = $11.24
‡($5,058 + $2,600)/650 units = $11.78
§($5,890 + $1,400)/600 units = $12.15

MODULE 5   TEST YOURSELF

Review	**LO12** Explain the differences in the accounting for periodic and perpetual inventory systems and apply the inventory costing methods using a perpetual system.	• The three inventory costing methods—FIFO, LIFO, and weighted average—may be used in combination with a perpetual inventory system. • The inventory costing method is applied after each sale of merchandise to update the Inventory account. • The results from using LIFO differ depending on whether a periodic or perpetual system is used. The same is true with weighted average, which is called moving average in a perpetual system.
Question		1. Why is the weighted average cost method called a moving average when a company uses a perpetual inventory system?
		2. Will the dollar amount assigned to inventory differ when a company uses the LIFO method depending on whether a periodic or perpetual inventory system is used? Explain your answer.
Apply		Long Corp. began the year with 100 units of inventory, each with a unit cost of $5. The company purchased 20 units for $6 each on June 16, sold 65 units for $15 each on August 19, and purchased another 25 units for $7 each on December 2. Calculate the value of Long's inventory on December 31 assuming it uses a perpetual inventory system and the LIFO method.

Answers are located at the end of the chapter.

RATIO REVIEW

Gross Profit Ratio = $\dfrac{\text{Gross Profit (Income Statement)}}{\text{Net Sales (Income Statement)}}$

Inventory Turnover Ratio = $\dfrac{\text{Cost of Goods Sold (Income Statement)}}{\text{Average Inventory*(Balance Sheet)}}$

Average inventory can be estimated using the following calculation:

$\dfrac{\textbf{Beginning Inventory} + \textbf{Ending Inventory}}{2}$

Number of Days' Sales in Inventory = $\dfrac{\text{Number of Days in the Period**}}{\text{Inventory Turnover Ratio}}$

**Usually assume 360 days unless some other number is a better estimate of the number of days in the period.*

ACCOUNTS HIGHLIGHTED

Account Titles	Where It Appears	In What Section	Page Number
Merchandise Inventory	Balance Sheet	Current Assets	210
Sales Revenue	Income Statement	Sales	211
Cost of Goods Sold	Income Statement	Expenses	213
Purchases	Income Statement	Cost of Goods Sold	216
Transportation-In	Income Statement	Added to Purchases	216
Transportation-Out	Income Statement	Selling Expense	218
Loss on Decline in Value of Inventory	Income Statement	Other Expenses	235

KEY TERMS QUIZ

Because of the large number of terms introduced in this chapter, there are two quizzes on key terms. Read each definition below and write the number of the definition in the blank beside the appropriate term. The quiz solutions appear at the end of the chapter.

Quiz 1: Merchandise Accounting

_____ Merchandise Inventory		_____ Cost of goods sold
_____ Raw materials		_____ Perpetual system
_____ Work in process		_____ Periodic system
_____ Finished goods		_____ Transportation-In
_____ Gross profit		_____ Purchases
_____ Net sales		_____ FOB destination point
_____ Sales revenue		_____ FOB shipping point
_____ Cost of goods available for sale		_____ Gross profit ratio

1. An adjunct account used to record freight costs paid by the buyer.
2. A system in which the Inventory account is increased at the time of each purchase and decreased at the time of each sale.
3. Terms that require the seller to pay for the cost of shipping the merchandise to the buyer.
4. Terms that require the buyer to pay for the shipping costs.
5. A system in which the Inventory account is updated only at the end of the period.
6. Beginning inventory plus cost of goods purchased.
7. An account used in a periodic inventory system to record acquisitions of merchandise.
8. Sales revenue less sales returns and allowances and sales discounts.
9. Cost of goods available for sale minus ending inventory.
10. Gross profit divided by net sales.
11. Net sales less cost of goods sold.

12. The cost of unfinished products in a manufacturing company.
13. The account wholesalers and retailers use to report inventory held for sale.
14. The inventory of a manufacturer before the addition of any direct labor or manufacturing overhead.
15. A manufacturer's inventory that is complete and ready for sale.
16. A representation of the inflow of assets from the sale of a product.

Quiz 2: Inventory Valuation

_____ Specific identification method	_____ Replacement cost
_____ Weighted average cost method	_____ Inventory profit
_____ FIFO method	_____ Lower-of-cost-or-market (LCM)
_____ LIFO method	rule
_____ LIFO liquidation	_____ Inventory turnover ratio
_____ LIFO conformity rule	_____ Number of days' sales in inventory
_____ LIFO reserve	_____ Moving average (Appendix)

1. The name given to an average cost method when a weighted average cost assumption is used with a perpetual inventory system.
2. An inventory costing method that assigns the same unit cost to all units available for sale during the period.
3. A conservative inventory valuation approach that is an attempt to anticipate declines in the value of inventory before its actual sale.
4. An inventory costing method that assigns the most recent costs to ending inventory.
5. The current cost of a unit of inventory.
6. An inventory costing method that assigns the most recent costs to cost of goods sold.
7. A measure of how long it takes to sell inventory.
8. The IRS requirement that when LIFO is used on a tax return, it must also be used in reporting income to stockholders.
9. An inventory costing method that relies on matching unit costs with the actual units sold.
10. The portion of the gross profit that results from holding inventory during a period of rising prices.
11. The result of selling more units than are purchased during the period, which can have negative tax consequences if a company is using LIFO.
12. The excess of the value of a company's inventory stated at FIFO over the value stated at LIFO.
13. A measure of the number of times inventory is sold during the period.

ALTERNATE TERMS

gross profit gross margin
merchandiser wholesaler, retailer
raw materials direct materials

sales revenue sales
transportation-in freight-in
work in process work in progress

REVIEW PROBLEM & SOLUTION

Stewart Distributing Company sells a single product for $2 per unit and uses a periodic inventory system. The following data are available for the year:

Date	Transaction	Number of Units	Unit Cost	Total
1/1	Beginning inventory	500	$1.00	$500.00
2/5	Purchase	350	1.10	385.00
4/12	Sale	(550)		
7/17	Sale	(200)		
9/23	Purchase	400	1.30	520.00
11/5	Sale	(300)		

Required

1. Compute cost of goods sold assuming the use of the weighted average costing method.
2. Compute the dollar amount of ending inventory assuming the FIFO costing method.
3. Compute gross profit assuming the LIFO costing method.
4. Assume a 40% tax rate. Compute the amount of taxes saved if Stewart uses the LIFO method rather than the FIFO method.

Solution to Review Problem

1. Cost of goods sold, weighted average cost method:

Cost of goods available for sale	
$500 + $385 + $520 =	$ 1,405
Divided by:	
Units available for sale:	
500 + 350 + 400 =	÷ 1,250 units
Weighted average cost	$ 1.124 per unit
× Number of units sold:	
550 + 200 + 300 =	× 1,050 units
Cost of goods sold	$ 1,180.20

2. Ending inventory, FIFO cost method:

Units available for sale	1,250
–Units sold	– 1,050
= Units in ending inventory	200
× Most recent purchase price of	× $ 1.30
= Ending inventory	$ 260

3. Gross profit, LIFO cost method:

Sales revenue: 1,050 units × $2 each	$ 2,100
Cost of goods sold	
400 units × $1.30 = $520	
350 units × $1.10 = $385	
300 units × $1.00 = $300	– 1,205
Gross profit	$ 895

4. Taxes saved from using LIFO instead of FIFO:

LIFO Cost of goods sold		$ 1,205
– FIFO Cost of goods sold:		
Cost of goods available for sale	$ 1,405	
Ending inventory from part (2)	– 260	
Cost of goods sold		– 1,145
Additional expense from use of LIFO		$ 60
× Tax rate		× 0.40
Tax savings from the use of LIFO		$ 24

EXERCISES

Exercise 5-1 Classification of Inventory Costs   LO1

Put an *X* in the appropriate column next to the inventory item to indicate its most likely classification on the books of a company that manufactures furniture and then sells it in retail company stores.

(Continued)

Inventory Item	Classification			
	Raw Material	Work in Process	Finished Goods	Merchandise Inventory
Fabric				
Lumber				
Unvarnished tables				
Chairs on the showroom floor				
Cushions				
Decorative knobs				
Drawers				
Sofa frames				
Chairs in the plant warehouse				
Chairs in the retail storeroom				

LO1

Exercise 5-2 Inventoriable Costs

During the first month of operations, ABC Company incurred the following costs in ordering and receiving merchandise for resale. No inventory was sold.

List price, $100, 200 units purchased

Volume discount, 10% off list price

Paid freight costs, $56

Insurance cost while goods were in transit, $32

Long-distance phone charge to place orders, $4.35

Purchasing department salary, $1,000

Supplies used to label goods at retail price, $9.75

Interest paid to supplier, $46

Required

What amount do you recommend the company record as merchandise inventory on its balance sheet? Explain your answer. For any items not to be included in inventory, indicate their appropriate treatment in the financial statements.

LO3

EXAMPLE 5-3

Exercise 5-3 Perpetual and Periodic Inventory Systems

Following is a partial list of account balances for two different merchandising companies. The amounts in the accounts represent the balances at the end of the year *before* any adjustments are made or the books are closed.

Company A		Company B	
Sales Revenue	$50,000	Sales Revenue	$85,000
Merchandise Inventory	12,000	Merchandise Inventory	9,000
Cost of Goods Sold	38,000	Purchases	41,000
		Transportation-in	5,000

Required

1. Identify which inventory system, perpetual or periodic, each of the two companies uses. Explain how you know which system each company uses by looking at the types of accounts on its books.
2. How much inventory should Company A have on hand at the end of the year? What is its cost of goods sold for the year?
3. Explain why you cannot determine Company B's cost of goods sold for the year from the information available.

LO3

Exercise 5-4 Perpetual and Periodic Inventory Systems

From the following list, identify whether the merchandisers described would most likely use a perpetual or a periodic inventory system.

_____ Appliance store

_____ Car dealership

_____ Drugstore

_____ Furniture store

_____ Grocery store

_____ Hardware store

_____ Jewelry store

How might changes in technology affect the ability of merchandisers to use perpetual inventory systems?

Exercise 5-5 Missing Amounts in Cost of Goods Sold Model

LO3

For each of the following independent cases, fill in the missing amounts.

	Case 1	Case 2	Case 3
Beginning inventory	$ (a)	$2,350	$1,890
Purchases (net)	5,560	(c)	(e)
Transportation-in	150	500	420
Cost of goods available for sale	7,110	(d)	8,790
Ending inventory	(b)	1,750	1,200
Cost of goods sold	5,220	5,570	(f)

Exercise 5-6 Purchase Discounts

LO3

EXAMPLE 5-1, 5-4, 5-5

Identify and analyze each of the following transactions of Buckeye Corporation. (All purchases on credit are made with terms of 1/10, n/30, and Buckeye uses the periodic system of inventory.)

July   3:   Purchased merchandise on credit from Wildcat Corp. for $3,500.

July   12:   Paid amount owed to Wildcat Corp.

Exercise 5-7 Shipping Terms and Transfer of Title

LO3

EXAMPLE 5-7

On December 23, 2017, Miller Wholesalers ships merchandise to Michael Retailers with terms of FOB destination point. The merchandise arrives at Michael's warehouse on January 3, 2018.

Required

1.   Identify who pays to ship the merchandise.
2.   Determine whether the inventory should be included as an asset on Michael's December 31, 2017, balance sheet. Should the sale be included on Miller's 2017 income statement? Explain.
3.   Explain how your answers to part (2) would have been different if the terms of shipment had been FOB shipping point.

Exercise 5-8 Transfer of Title to Inventory

LO3

EXAMPLE 5-7

Identify whether the transactions described should be recorded by Cameron Companies during December 2017 (fill in the blank with a D) or January 2018 (fill in the blank with a J).

Purchases of merchandise that are in transit from vendors to Cameron Companies on December 31, 2017.

_____   Shipped FOB shipping point
_____   Shipped FOB destination point

Sales of merchandise that are in transit to customers of Cameron Companies on December 31, 2017.

_____   Shipped FOB shipping point
_____   Shipped FOB destination point

Exercise 5-9 Working Backward: Gross Profit Ratio

LO4

Acme's gross profit ratio increased by 20% over the prior year. Net sales and cost of goods sold for the prior year were $120,000 and $90,000, respectively. Cost of goods sold for the current year is $140,000.

Required

Determine the amount of Acme's sales for the current year.

LO5   Exercise 5-10 Inventory and Income Manipulation

The president of SOS Inc. is concerned that the net income at year-end will not reach the expected figure. When the sales manager receives a large order on the last day of the fiscal year, the president tells the accountant to record the sale but to ignore any inventory adjustment because the physical inventory has already been taken. How will this affect the current year's net income? next year's income? What would you do if you were the accountant? Would your answer differ if your company followed IFRS rather than U.S. GAAP? Assume that SOS uses a periodic inventory system.

LO6   Exercise 5-11 Inventory Costing Methods

EXAMPLE 5-9, 5-10, 5-11, 5-12

VanderMeer Inc. reported the following information for the month of February:

Inventory, February 1	65 units @ $20
Purchases:	
February 7	50 units @ $22
February 18	60 units @ $23
February 27	45 units @ $24

During February, VanderMeer sold 140 units. The company uses a periodic inventory system.

Required

What is the value of ending inventory and cost of goods sold for February under the following assumptions:

1. Of the 140 units sold, 55 cost $20, 35 cost $22, 45 cost $23, and 5 cost $24.
2. FIFO
3. LIFO
4. Weighted average

LO7   Exercise 5-12 Evaluation of Inventory Costing Methods

EXAMPLE 5-15

Write the letter of the method that is most applicable to each statement.

a. Specific identification
b. Average cost
c. First-in, first-out (FIFO)
d. Last-in, first-out (LIFO)

_____   1. Is the most realistic ending inventory
_____   2. Results in cost of goods sold being closest to current product costs
_____   3. Results in highest income during periods of inflation
_____   4. Results in highest ending inventory during periods of inflation
_____   5. Smooths out costs during periods of inflation
_____   6. Is not practical for most businesses
_____   7. Puts more weight on the cost of the larger number of units purchased
_____   8. Is an assumption that most closely reflects the physical flow of goods for most businesses
_____   9. Is not an acceptable method under IFRS

LO8   Exercise 5-13 Inventory Errors

EXAMPLE 5-16, 5-17, 5-18

For each of the following independent situations, fill in the blanks to indicate the effect of the error on each of the various financial statement items. Indicate an understatement (U), an overstatement (O), or no effect (NE). Assume that each of the companies uses a periodic inventory system.

Error	Balance Sheet		Income Statement	
	Inventory	Retained Earnings	Cost of Goods Sold	Net Income
1. Goods in transit at year-end are not included in the physical count; they were shipped FOB shipping point.	_____	_____	_____	_____
2. One section of a warehouse is counted twice during the year-end count of inventory.	_____	_____	_____	_____
3. During the count at year-end, the inventory sheets for one of the stores of a discount retailer are lost.	_____	_____	_____	_____

Exercise 5-14 Transfer of Title to Inventory

LO3

EXAMPLE 5-7

For each of the following transactions, indicate which company should include the inventory on its December 31, 2017, balance sheet:

1. Michelson Supplies Inc. shipped merchandise to PJ Sales on December 28, 2017, terms FOB destination. The merchandise arrives at PJ's on January 4, 2018.
2. Quarton Inc. shipped merchandise to Filbrandt on December 27, 2017, FOB destination. Filbrandt received the merchandise on December 31, 2017.
3. James Bros. Inc. shipped merchandise to Randall Company on December 27, 2017, FOB shipping point. Randall Company received the merchandise on January 3, 2018.
4. Hinz Company shipped merchandise to Barner Inc. on December 24, 2017, FOB shipping point. The merchandise arrived at Barner on December 29, 2017.

Exercise 5-15 Inventory Turnover for Nordstrom

LO10

The following amounts are available from the 2015 financial statements in the Form 10-K for **Nordstrom, Inc.**, the fashion retailer. (All amounts are in millions of dollars and January 30, 2016, is the end of the company's 2015 fiscal year.)

REAL WORLD

Cost of sales and related buying and occupancy costs	$9,168
Merchandise inventories, January 30, 2016	1,945
Merchandise inventories, January 31, 2015	1,733

Required

1. Compute Nordstrom's inventory turnover ratio for 2015.
2. What is the average length of time it takes to sell an item of inventory? Explain your answer.
3. Do you think the average length of time it took Nordstrom to sell inventory in 2015 is reasonable? What other information do you need to fully answer that question?

Exercise 5-16 Working Backward: Inventory Turnover

LO10

It takes Bradley Retailers 90 days on average to sell its inventory. The company began the year with $17,000 in inventory. Sales and cost of goods sold for the year amounted to $95,000 and $60,000, respectively.

Required

Assuming 360 days in a year, determine the amount of Bradley's ending inventory.

Exercise 5-17 Impact of Transactions Involving Inventories on Statement of Cash Flows

LO11

From the following list, identify whether the change in the account balance during the year is added to (A) or deducted from (D) net income when the indirect method is used to determine cash flows from operating activities.

_____ Increase in accounts payable
_____ Decrease in accounts payable

_____ Increase in inventories
_____ Decrease in inventories

LO11   Exercise 5-18 Effects of Transactions Involving Inventories on the Statement of Cash Flows—Direct Method

Masthead Company's comparative balance sheets included inventory of $180,400 at December 31, 2016, and $241,200 at December 31, 2017. Masthead's comparative balance sheets also included accounts payable of $85,400 at December 31, 2016, and $78,400 at December 31, 2017. Masthead's accounts payable balances are composed solely of amounts due to suppliers for purchases of inventory on account. Cost of goods sold, as reported by Masthead on its 2017 income statement, amounted to $1,200,000.

Required

What is the amount of cash payments for inventory that Masthead will report in the Operating Activities category of its 2017 statement of cash flows assuming that the direct method is used?

LO11   Exercise 5-19 Effects of Transactions Involving Inventories on the Statement of Cash Flows—Indirect Method

Refer to all of the facts in Exercise 5-18.

Required

Assume instead that Masthead uses the indirect method to prepare its statement of cash flows. Indicate how each item will be reflected as an adjustment to net income in the Operating Activities category of the statement of cash flows.

MULTI-CONCEPT EXERCISES

LO2 • 3   Exercise 5-20 Income Statement for a Merchandiser

EXAMPLE 5-2

Fill in the missing amounts in the following income statement for Carpenters Department Store Inc.

Net sales			$122,040
Cost of goods sold:			
Beginning inventory		$ 23,400	
Net purchases	$ (a)		
Transportation-in	6,550		
Cost of goods purchased		81,150	
Cost of goods available for sale		$104,550	
Ending inventory		(c)	
Cost of goods sold			(b)
Gross profit			$ 38,600
Operating expenses			(d)
Income before tax			$ 26,300
Income tax expense			10,300
Net income			$ (e)

LO2 • 3   Exercise 5-21 Partial Income Statement—Periodic System

LaPine Company has the following account balances as of December 31, 2017:

Inventory, January 1	$ 4,000
Net sales	78,300
Transportation-in	1,000
Inventory, December 31	3,800
Net purchases	28,800

Required

Prepare a partial income statement for LaPine Company for 2017 through gross profit. Calculate LaPine's gross profit ratio for 2017.

Exercise 5-22 Cost of Goods Sold, FIFO, and LIFO

LO3 • 6
EXAMPLE 5-2, 5-11, 5-12

Kramer began operations early in 2017 and made the following purchases:

February 5	200	$5
June 10	500	6
October 4	300	7

Kramer used the FIFO method to value its inventory and reported cost of goods sold expense for the year of $4,000.

Required

Determine the cost of goods sold expense assuming Kramer had used the LIFO method instead of the FIFO method.

Exercise 5-23 Weighted Average Cost Method and Gross Profit Ratio

LO4 • 6
EXAMPLE 5-10

Martin Corp. began the year with 2,000 units of inventory that had been purchased for $6 per unit. During the year, 5,000 units were purchased for $8 each and 8,000 units for $10 each. Martin sold 9,000 units during the year for $15 each. The company uses the weighted average cost method.

Required

1. Compute cost of goods sold expense.
2. Compute the gross profit ratio.

Exercise 5-24 Inventory Costing Methods—Periodic System

LO6 • 7
EXAMPLE 5-10, 5-11,
5-12, 5-13, 5-14

The following information is available concerning the inventory of Carter Inc.:

	Units	Unit Cost
Beginning inventory	200	$10
Purchases:		
March 5	300	11
June 12	400	12
August 23	250	13
October 2	150	15

During the year, Carter sold 1,000 units. It uses a periodic inventory system.

Required

1. Calculate ending inventory and cost of goods sold for each of the following three methods:
   a. Weighted average
   b. FIFO
   c. LIFO
2. Assume an estimated tax rate of 30%. How much more or less (indicate which) will Carter pay in taxes by using FIFO instead of LIFO? Explain your answer.
3. Assume that Carter prepares its financial statements in accordance with IFRS. Which costing method should it use to pay the least amount of taxes? Explain your answer.

Exercise 5-25 Lower-of-Cost-or-Market Rule

LO5 • 9

Awards Etc. carries an inventory of trophies and ribbons for local sports teams and school clubs. The cost of trophies has dropped in the past year, which pleases the company except for the fact that it has on hand considerable inventory that was purchased at the higher prices. The president is not pleased with the lower profit margin the company is earning. "The lower profit margin will continue until we sell all of this old inventory," he grumbled to the new staff accountant. "Not really," replied the accountant. "Let's write down the inventory to the replacement cost this year, and then next year our profit margin will be in line with the competition."

(Continued)

Required

Explain why the inventory can be carried at an amount less than its cost. Which accounts will be affected by the write-down? What will be the effect on income in the current year and future years?

LO3 • 11
EXAMPLE 5-2

Exercise 5-26 Working Backward: Cost of Goods Sold and the Statement of Cash Flows

Texas Corp.'s statement of cash flows reported an addition of $6,000 for the change in the Inventory account during the year. Cost of goods sold expense on the income statement amounted to $50,000.

Required

Determine the amount of purchases during the year.

LO7 • 12
EXAMPLE 5-19, 5-20, 5-21

Exercise 5-27 Inventory Costing Methods—Perpetual System (Appendix)

The following information is available concerning Stillwater Inc.:

	Units	Unit Cost
Beginning inventory	200	$10
Purchases:		
March 5	300	11
June 12	400	12
August 23	250	13
October 2	150	15

Stillwater, which uses a perpetual system, sold 1,000 units for $22 each during the year. Sales occurred on the following dates:

	Units
February 12	150
April 30	200
July 7	200
September 6	300
December 3	150

Required

1. Calculate ending inventory and cost of goods sold for each of the following three methods:
   a. Moving average
   b. FIFO
   c. LIFO
2. For each of the three methods, compare the results with those of Carter in Exercise 5-25. Which method gives a different answer depending on whether a company uses a periodic or a perpetual inventory system?
3. Assume the use of the perpetual system and an estimated tax rate of 30%. How much more or less (indicate which) will Stillwater pay in taxes by using LIFO instead of FIFO? Explain your answer.

PROBLEMS

LO1

Problem 5-1 Inventory Costs in Various Businesses

Businesses incur various costs in selling goods and services. Each business must decide which costs are expenses of the period and which should be included in the cost of the inventory. The following table lists various types of businesses along with certain types of costs they incur:

Business	Types of Costs	Accounting Treatment		
		Expense of the Period	Inventory Cost	Other Treatment
Retail shoe store	Shoes for sale			
	Shoe boxes			
	Advertising signs			
Grocery store	Canned goods on the shelves			
	Produce			
	Cleaning supplies			
	Cash registers			
Frame shop	Wooden frame supplies			
	Nails			
	Glass			
Walk-in print shop	Paper			
	Copy machines			
	Toner cartridges			
Restaurant	Frozen food			
	China and silverware			
	Prepared food			
	Spices			

Required

Fill in the table to indicate the correct accounting for each type of cost by placing an X in the appropriate column. For any costs that receive other treatment, explain what the appropriate treatment is for accounting purposes.

Problem 5-2 Making Business Decisions: Analyzing Wal-Mart's Gross Profit Ratio

LO4

You are considering an investment in the common stock of **Wal-Mart**. The following information is from the consolidated statements of income of Wal-Mart Stores, Inc. and Subsidiaries for the years ended January 31, 2016 and 2015 and the consolidated statements of operations for its competitor **Target Corporation** for the years ended January 30, 2016, and January 31, 2015 (included in the companies' Form 10-Ks, amounts in millions of dollars):

RATIO ANALYSIS
BUSINESS DECISION MODEL

	Wal-Mart		Target	
(in millions)	Year Ended January 31, 2016	Year Ended January 31, 2015	Year Ended January 30, 2016	Year Ended January 31, 2015
Sales*	$478,614	$482,229	$73,785	$72,618
Cost of sales	360,984	365,086	51,997	51,278

REAL WORLD

*Described as net sales by Wal-Mart.

Required

Part A. The Ratio Analysis Model

An investor must assess a company's profitability before buying its stock. The gross profit ratio tells us how many cents on every dollar are available to cover expenses other than cost of goods sold and to earn a profit. Replicate the five steps in the Ratio Analysis Model on pages 219–220 to analyze the gross profit ratios for Wal-Mart and Target:

1. Formulate the Question
2. Gather the Information from the Financial Statements
3. Calculate the Ratio
4. Compare the Ratio with Other Ratios
5. Interpret the Ratios

(Continued)

Part B. The Business Decision Model
An investor must consider a variety of factors, including financial ratios, before buying stock. Replicate the five steps in the Business Decision Model on page 220 to decide whether to buy stock in Wal-Mart.
1. Formulate the Question
2. Gather Information from the Financial Statements and Other Sources
3. Analyze the Information Gathered
4. Make the Decision
5. Monitor Your Decision

LO7   Problem 5-3 Evaluation of Inventory Costing Methods

Users of financial statements rely on the information available to them to decide whether to invest in a company or lend it money. As an investor, you are comparing three companies in the same industry. The cost to purchase inventory is rising in the industry. Assume that all expenses incurred by the three companies are the same except for cost of goods sold. The companies use the following methods to value ending inventory:

Company A—weighted average cost
Company B—first-in, first-out (FIFO)
Company C—last-in, first-out (LIFO)

Required

1. Which of the three companies will report the highest net income? Explain your answer.
2. Which of the three companies will pay the least in income taxes? Explain your answer.
3. Which method of inventory costing do you believe is superior to the others in providing information to potential investors? Explain.
4. Explain how your answers to parts (1), (2), and (3) would change if the costs to purchase inventory had been falling instead of rising.

LO8   Problem 5-4 Inventory Error

The following highly condensed income statements and balance sheets are available for Budget Stores for a two-year period. (All amounts are stated in thousands of dollars.)

Income Statements	2017	2016
Revenues	$20,000	$15,000
Cost of goods sold	13,000	10,000
Gross profit	$ 7,000	$ 5,000
Operating expenses	3,000	2,000
Net income	$ 4,000	$ 3,000

Balance Sheets	December 31, 2017	December 31, 2016
Cash	$ 1,700	$ 1,500
Inventory	4,200	3,500
Other current assets	2,500	2,000
Long-term assets	15,000	14,000
Total assets	$23,400	$21,000
Liabilities	$ 8,500	$ 7,000
Capital stock	5,000	5,000
Retained earnings	9,900	9,000
Total liabilities and stockholders' equity	$23,400	$21,000

Before releasing the 2017 annual report, Budget's controller learns that the inventory of one of the stores (amounting to $600,000) was inadvertently omitted from the count on December 31, 2016. The inventory of the store was correctly included in the December 31, 2017, count.

Required

1. Prepare revised income statements and balance sheets for Budget Stores for each of the two years. Ignore the effect of income taxes.
2. If Budget did not prepare revised statements before releasing the 2017 annual report, what would be the amount of overstatement or understatement of net income for the two-year period? What would be the overstatement or understatement of retained earnings at December 31, 2017, if revised statements were not prepared?
3. Given your answers in part (2), does it matter if Budget bothers to restate the financial statements of the two years to rectify the error? Explain your answer.

Problem 5-5 Making Business Decisions: Analyzing Apple's Inventory Turnover Ratio

LO10

You are considering an investment in the common stock of **Apple Inc**. The following information is from the financial statements included in Form 10-K for fiscal years 2015 and 2014 (in millions of dollars):

RATIO ANALYSIS
BUSINESS DECISION MODEL

Cost of sales for the year ended:	
September 26, 2015	$140,089
September 27, 2014	112,258
Inventories:	
September 26, 2015	2,349
September 27, 2014	2,111
September 28, 2013	1,764

REAL WORLD

The following information is from the financial statements included in Form 10-K for fiscal years 2015 and 2014 for **Hewlett-Packard Company** (in millions of dollars):

Cost of products for the year ended:	
October 31, 2015	$53,081
October 31, 2014	56,469
Inventory:	
October 31, 2015	6,485
October 31, 2014	6,415
October 31, 2013	6,046

Required

Part A. The Ratio Analysis Model

An investor must assess how well a company is managing its inventory before buying its stock. The inventory turnover ratio tells us how many times in a year a company sells its inventory. Replicate the five steps in the Ratio Analysis Model on pages 238–239 to analyze the inventory turnover ratios for Apple Inc. and Hewlett-Packard:

1. Formulate the Question
2. Gather the Information from the Financial Statements
3. Calculate the Ratio
4. Compare the Ratio with Other Ratios
5. Interpret the Ratios

Part B. The Business Decision Model

An investor must consider a variety of factors, including financial ratios, before buying stock. Replicate the five steps in the Business Decision Model on page 239 to decide whether to buy stock in Apple Inc.

1. Formulate the Question
2. Gather Information from the Financial Statements and Other Sources
3. Analyze the Information Gathered
4. Make the Decision
5. Monitor Your Decision

LO11 **Problem 5-6 Effects of Changes in Inventory and Accounts Payable Balances on Statement of Cash Flows**

Copeland Antiques reported a net loss of $33,200 for the year ended December 31, 2017. The following items were included on Copeland's balance sheets at December 31, 2017 and 2016:

	12/31/17	12/31/16
Cash	$ 65,300	$ 46,100
Trade accounts payable	123,900	93,700
Inventories	192,600	214,800

Copeland uses the indirect method to prepare its statement of cash flows. Copeland does not have any other current assets or current liabilities and did not enter into any investing or financing activities during 2017.

Required

1. Prepare Copeland's 2017 statement of cash flows.
2. Draft a brief memo to the president explaining why cash increased during such an unprofitable year.

MULTI-CONCEPT PROBLEMS

LO2 • 3 • 11 **Problem 5-7 Purchases and Sales of Merchandise, Cash Flows**

Two Wheeler, a bike shop, opened for business on April 1. It uses a periodic inventory system. The following transactions occurred during the first month of business:

April 1: Purchased five units from Duhan Co. for $500 total, with terms 3/10, n/30, FOB destination.

April 10: Paid for the April 1 purchase.

April 15: Sold one unit for $200 cash.

April 18: Purchased ten units from Clinton Inc. for $900 total, with terms 3/10, n/30, FOB destination.

April 25: Sold three units for $200 each, cash.

April 28: Paid for the April 18 purchase.

Required

1. Identify and analyze each of the preceding transactions of Two Wheeler.
2. Determine net income for the month of April. Two Wheeler incurred and paid $100 for rent and $50 for miscellaneous expenses during April. Ending inventory is $967. (Ignore income taxes.)
3. Assuming that these are the only transactions during April (including rent and miscellaneous expenses), compute net cash flow from operating activities.
4. Explain why cash outflow is so much larger than expenses on the income statement.

LO2 • 3 • 4 **Problem 5-8 Gap Inc.'s Sales, Cost of Goods Sold, and Gross Profit**

REAL WORLD

The consolidated balance sheets of **Gap Inc.** included merchandise inventory in the amount of $1,873,000,000 as of January 30, 2016 (the end of fiscal year 2015) and $1,889,000,000 as of January 31, 2015 (the end of fiscal year 2014). Net sales were $15,797,000,000 and $16,435,000,000 for fiscal years 2015 and 2014, respectively. Cost of goods sold and occupancy expenses were $10,077,000,000 and $10,146,000,000 for fiscal years 2015 and 2014, respectively. All amounts are from Gap Inc.'s 2015 Form 10-K.

Required

1. Unlike most other merchandisers, Gap Inc. doesn't include accounts receivable on its balance sheet. Why doesn't Gap Inc.'s balance sheet include this account?
2. Identify and analyze the transaction to record sales during the year ended January 30, 2016.

3. Gap Inc. sets forth net sales but not gross sales on its income statement. What type(s) of deduction(s) would be made from gross sales to arrive at the amount of net sales reported?
4. Reconstruct the Cost of Goods Sold section of Gap Inc.'s 2015 income statement.
5. Calculate the gross profit ratios for Gap Inc. for 2015 and 2014 and comment on any change noted. Is the company's performance improving? Explain. What factors might have caused the change in the gross profit ratio?

Problem 5-9 Financial Statements   LO2 • 3

A list of accounts for Maple Inc. at December 31, 2017, follows:

Accounts Receivable	$ 2,359	Land	$20,000
Advertising Expense	4,510	Net purchases	39,400
Buildings and Equipment, Net	55,550	Retained Earnings, January 1, 2017	32,550
Capital Stock	50,000	Salaries Expense	25,600
Cash	590	Salaries Payable	650
Depreciation Expense	2,300	Net sales	83,584
Dividends	6,000	Transportation-In	375
Income Tax Expense	3,200	Utilities Expense	3,600
Income Tax Payable	3,200		
Interest Receivable	100		
Inventory:			
January 1, 2017	6,400		
December 31, 2017	7,500		

Required

1. Determine cost of goods sold for 2017.
2. Determine net income for 2017.
3. Prepare a balance sheet dated December 31, 2017.

Problem 5-10 Comparison of Inventory Costing Methods—Periodic System   LO5 • 6 • 7

Bitten Company's inventory records show 600 units on hand on October 1 with a unit cost of $5 each. The following transactions occurred during the month of October:

Date	Unit Purchases	Unit Sales
October 4		500 @ $10.00
8	800 @ $5.40	
9		700 @ $10.00
18	700 @ $5.76	
20		800 @ $11.00
29	800 @ $5.90	

All expenses other than cost of goods sold amount to $3,000 for the month. The company uses an estimated tax rate of 30% to accrue monthly income taxes.

Required

1. Prepare a chart comparing cost of goods sold and ending inventory using the periodic system and the following costing methods:

	Cost of Goods Sold	Ending Inventory	Total
Weighted average			
FIFO			
LIFO			

2. What does the Total column represent?
3. Prepare income statements for each of the three methods.
4. Will the company pay more or less tax if it uses FIFO rather than LIFO? How much more or less?

LO5 • 7 • 12

Show me how

Problem 5-11 Comparison of Inventory Costing Methods—Perpetual System (Appendix)

Repeat Problem 5-10 using the perpetual system.

LO5 • 6 • 7

Problem 5-12 Inventory Costing Methods—Periodic System

Oxendine Company's inventory records for the month of November reveal the following:

Show me how

Inventory, November 1	200 units @ $18.00
November 4, purchase	250 units @ $18.50
November 7, sale	300 units @ $42.00
November 13, purchase	220 units @ $18.90
November 18, purchase	150 units @ $19.00
November 22, sale	380 units @ $42.50
November 24, purchase	200 units @ $19.20
November 28, sale	110 units @ $43.00

Selling and administrative expenses for the month were $10,800. Depreciation expense was $4,000. Oxendine's tax rate is 35%.

Required

IFRS

1. Calculate the cost of goods sold and ending inventory under each of the following three methods assuming a periodic inventory system: (a) FIFO, (b) LIFO, and (c) weighted average.
2. Calculate the gross profit and net income under each costing assumption.
3. Under which costing method will Oxendine pay the least taxes? Explain your answer.
4. Assume that Oxendine prepares its financial statements in accordance with IFRS. Which costing method should the company use to pay the least amount of taxes? Explain your answer.

LO5 • 6 • 7

Problem 5-13 Inventory Costing Methods—Periodic System

Following is an inventory acquisition schedule for Weaver Corp. for 2017:

	Units	Unit Cost
Beginning inventory	5,000	$10
Purchase:		
February 4	3,000	9
April 12	4,000	8
September 10	2,000	7
December 5	1,000	6

During the year, Weaver sold 12,500 units at $12 each. All expenses except cost of goods sold and taxes amounted to $20,000. The tax rate is 30%.

Required

1. Compute cost of goods sold and ending inventory under each of the following three methods assuming a periodic inventory system: (a) weighted average, (b) FIFO, and (c) LIFO.
2. Prepare income statements under each of the three methods.
3. Which method do you recommend so that Weaver pays the least amount of taxes during 2017? Explain your answer.
4. Weaver anticipates that unit costs for inventory will increase throughout 2018. Will Weaver be able to switch from the method you recommended that it use in 2017 to another method to take advantage of the increase in prices for tax purposes? Explain your answer.

LO1 • 7 • 9

Problem 5-14 Interpreting Gannett Co.'s Inventory Accounting Policy

REAL WORLD

The 2015 Form 10-K of **Gannett Co., Inc.** (publisher of *USA Today* and many other newspapers) includes the following in the note that summarizes its accounting policies:

Inventories Inventories, consisting principally of newsprint, printing ink and plate material for our publishing operations, are valued at the lower of cost (first-in, first-out) or market.

Required

1. What *types* of inventory cost does Gannett carry? What about newspapers? Are newspapers considered inventory?
2. Which method does Gannett use to value its inventory?

ALTERNATE PROBLEMS

Problem 5-1A Inventory Costs in Various Businesses

LO1

Sound Traxs Inc. sells and rents DVDs to retail customers. The accountant is aware that at the end of the year, she must account for inventory, but is unsure what DVDs are considered inventory and how to value them. DVDs purchased by the company are placed on the shelf for rental. Every three weeks, the company performs a detailed analysis of the rental income from each DVD and decides whether to keep it as a rental or to offer it for sale in the resale section of the store. Resale DVDs sell for $10 each regardless of the price Sound Traxs paid for the tape.

Required

1. How should Sound Traxs account for each of the two types of DVDs—rentals and resales—on its balance sheet?
2. How would you suggest Sound Traxs account for the DVDs as they are transferred from one department to another?

Problem 5-2A Making Business Decisions: Analyzing Coca-Cola's Gross Profit Ratio

LO4

You are considering an investment in the common stock of **Coca-Cola**. The following information is from the consolidated statements of income of The Coca-Cola Company and Subsidiaries for the years ended December 31, 2015 and 2014 and for its competitor **PepsiCo, Inc. and Subsidiaries** for the years ended December 26, 2015 and December 27, 2014 (included in the companies' Form 10-Ks, in millions of dollars):

RATIO ANALYSIS
BUSINESS DECISION MODEL

REAL WORLD

	Coca-Cola		PepsiCo	
(in millions)	Year Ended December 31, 2015	Year Ended December 31, 2014	Year Ended December 26, 2015	Year Ended December 27, 2014
Sales*	$44,294	$45,998	$63,056	$66,683
Cost of goods sold**	17,482	17,889	28,384	30,884

*Described as "Net operating revenues" by Coca-Cola and "Net revenue" by PepsiCo.
**Described as "Cost of sales" by PepsiCo.

Required

Part A. The Ratio Analysis Model

An investor must assess a company's profitability before buying its stock. The gross profit ratio tells us how many cents on every dollar are available to cover expenses other than cost of goods sold and to earn a profit. Replicate the five steps in the Ratio Analysis Model on pages 219–220 to analyze the gross profit ratios for Coca-Cola and PepsiCo:

1. Formulate the Question
2. Gather the Information from the Financial Statements
3. Calculate the Ratio
4. Compare the Ratio with Other Ratios
5. Interpret the Ratios

(Continued)

Part B. The Business Decision Model

An investor must consider a variety of factors, including financial ratios, before buying stock. Replicate the five steps in the Business Decision Model on page 220 to decide whether to buy stock in Coca-Cola.

1. Formulate the Question
2. Gather Information from the Financial Statements and Other Sources
3. Analyze the Information Gathered
4. Make the Decision
5. Monitor Your Decision

LO7 Problem 5-3A Evaluation of Inventory Costing Methods

Three large mass merchandisers use the following methods to value ending inventory:

Company X—weighted average cost

Company Y—first-in, first-out (FIFO)

Company Z—last-in, first-out (LIFO)

The cost of inventory has steadily increased over the past ten years of the product life. Recently, however, prices have started to decline slightly due to foreign competition.

Required

1. Will the effect on net income of the decline in cost of goods sold be the same for all three companies? Explain your answer.
2. Company Z would like to change its inventory costing method from LIFO to FIFO. Write an acceptable note for its annual report to justify the change.

LO8 Problem 5-4A Inventory Error

The following condensed income statements and balance sheets are available for Planter Stores for a two-year period. (All amounts are stated in thousands of dollars.)

Income Statements	2017	2016
Revenues	$35,982	$26,890
Cost of goods sold	12,594	9,912
Gross profit	$23,388	$16,978
Operating expenses	13,488	10,578
Net income	$ 9,900	$ 6,400

Balance Sheets	December 31, 2017	December 31, 2016
Cash	$ 9,400	$ 4,100
Inventory	4,500	5,400
Other current assets	1,600	1,250
Long-term assets, net	24,500	24,600
Total assets	$40,000	$35,350
Current liabilities	$ 9,380	$10,600
Capital stock	18,000	18,000
Retained earnings	12,620	6,750
Total liabilities and stockholders' equity	$40,000	$35,350

Before releasing the 2017 annual report, Planter's controller learns that the inventory of one of the stores (amounting to $500,000) was counted twice in the December 31, 2016, inventory. The inventory was correctly counted in the December 31, 2017, inventory.

Required

1. Prepare revised income statements and balance sheets for Planter Stores for each of the two years. Ignore the effect of income taxes.

2. Compute the current ratio at December 31, 2016, before the statements are revised and compute the current ratio at the same date after the statements are revised. If Planter applied for a loan in early 2017 and the lender required a current ratio of at least 1 to 1, would the error have affected the loan? Explain your answer.
3. If Planter did not prepare revised statements before releasing the 2017 annual report, what would be the amount of overstatement or understatement of net income for the two-year period? What would be the overstatement or understatement of retained earnings at December 31, 2017, if revised statements were not prepared?
4. Given your answers to parts (2) and (3), does it matter if Planter bothers to restate the financial statements of the two years to correct the error? Explain your answer.

Problem 5-5A Making Business Decisions: Analyzing Wal-Mart's Inventory Turnover Ratio

LO10

RATIO ANALYSIS
BUSINESS DECISION MODEL

You are considering an investment in the common stock of **Wal-Mart**. The following information is from the financial statements of Wal-Mart Stores, Inc. and Subsidiaries included in Form 10-K for fiscal years 2016 and 2015 (in millions of dollars):

Cost of sales for the year ended:	
January 31, 2016	$360,984
January 31, 2015	365,086
Inventories:	
January 31, 2016	44,469
January 31, 2015	45,141
January 31, 2014	44,858

REAL WORLD

The following information is from the financial statements included in Form 10-K for fiscal years 2015 and 2014 for **Target Corporation** (in millions of dollars):

Cost of sales for the year ended:	
January 30, 2016	$51,997
January 31, 2015	51,278
Inventory:	
January 30, 2016	8,601
January 31, 2015	8,282
February 1, 2014	8,278

Required

Part A. The Ratio Analysis Model

An investor must assess how well a company is managing its inventory before buying its stock. The inventory turnover ratio tells us how many times in a year a company sells its inventory. Replicate the five steps in the Ratio Analysis Model on pages 238–239 to analyze the inventory turnover ratios for Wal-Mart and Target:

1. Formulate the Question
2. Gather the Information from the Financial Statements
3. Calculate the Ratio
4. Compare the Ratio with Other Ratios
5. Interpret the Ratios

Part B. The Business Decision Model

An investor must consider a variety of factors, including financial ratios, before buying stock. Replicate the five steps in the Business Decision Model on page 239 to decide whether to buy stock in Wal-Mart.

1. Formulate the Question
2. Gather Information from the Financial Statements and Other Sources
3. Analyze the Information Gathered
4. Make the Decision
5. Monitor Your Decision

LO11   **Problem 5-6A** **Effects of Changes in Inventory and Accounts Payable Balances on Statement of Cash Flows**

Carpetland City reported net income of $78,500 for the year ended December 31, 2017. The following items were included on Carpetland's balance sheet at December 31, 2017 and 2016:

	12/31/17	12/31/16
Cash	$ 14,400	$26,300
Trade accounts payable	23,900	93,700
Inventories	105,500	84,900

Carpetland uses the indirect method to prepare its statement of cash flows. Carpetland does not have any other current assets or current liabilities and did not enter into any investing or financing activities during 2017.

Required

1. Prepare Carpetland's 2017 statement of cash flows.
2. Draft a brief memo to the president to explain why cash decreased during a profitable year.

ALTERNATE MULTI-CONCEPT PROBLEMS

LO2 • 3 • 11   **Problem 5-7A** **Purchases and Sales of Merchandise, Cash Flows**

Chestnut Corp., a ski shop, opened for business on October 1. It uses a periodic inventory system. The following transactions occurred during the first month of business:

October 1:   Purchased three units from Elm Inc. for $250 total, terms 2/10, n/30, FOB destination.

October 10:   Paid for the October 1 purchase.

October 15:   Sold one unit for $200 cash.

October 18:   Purchased ten units from Wausau Company for $800 total, with terms 2/10, n/30, FOB destination.

October 25:   Sold three units for $200 each, cash.

October 27:   Paid for the October 18 purchase.

Required

1. Identify and analyze each of the preceding transactions of Chestnut.
2. Determine the number of units on hand on October 31.
3. If Chestnut started the month with $2,000, determine its balance in cash at the end of the month assuming that these are the only transactions that occurred during October. Why has the cash balance decreased when the company reported net income?

LO2 • 3 • 4   **Problem 5-8A** **Walgreens Boots Alliance's Sales, Cost of Goods Sold, and Gross Profit**

The following information was summarized from the consolidated balance sheets of **Walgreens Boots Alliance, Inc. and Subsidiaries** (the company created with the combination of Walgreens and Boots Alliance) as of August 31, 2015 and 2014 and the consolidated statements of earnings for the years ended August 31, 2015 and 2014. All amounts are from Walgreens Boots Alliance's 2015 Form 10-K.

REAL WORLD

(in millions)	2015	2014
Accounts receivable, net	$ 6,849	$ 3,218
Cost of sales	76,520	54,823
Inventories	8,678	6,076
Net sales	103,444	76,392

Required

1. Identify and analyze the transaction related to the collection of accounts receivable and sales during 2015. Assume that all of the company's sales are on account.

2. Walgreens Boots Alliance sets forth net sales but not gross sales on its income statement. What type(s) of deduction(s) would be made from gross sales to arrive at the amount of net sales reported?
3. Reconstruct the Cost of Goods Sold section of Walgreens Boots Alliance's 2015 income statement.
4. Calculate the gross profit ratios for Walgreens Boots Alliance for 2015 and 2014 and comment on the change noted, if any. Is the company's performance improving? What factors might have caused the change in the gross profit ratio?

Problem 5-9A Financial Statements

LO2 • 3

A list of accounts for Lloyd Inc. at December 31, 2017, follows:

Accounts Receivable	$56,359	Net purchases	$ 61,608
Advertising Expense	12,900	Retained Earnings, January 1, 2017	28,252
Capital Stock	50,000	Salaries Payable	650
Cash	22,340	Net sales	111,760
Dividends	6,000	Transportation-In	375
Income Tax Expense	1,450	Utilities Expense	1,800
Income Tax Payable	1,450	Wages and Salaries Expense	23,000
Inventory:		Wages Payable	120
January 1, 2017	6,400		
December 31, 2017	5,900		

Required

1. Determine cost of goods sold for 2017.
2. Determine net income for 2017.
3. Prepare a balance sheet dated December 31, 2017.

Problem 5-10A Comparison of Inventory Costing Methods—Periodic System

LO5 • 6 • 7

Stellar Inc.'s inventory records show 300 units on hand on November 1 with a unit cost of $4 each. The following transactions occurred during the month of November:

Date	Unit Purchases	Unit Sales
November 4		200 @ $9.00
8	500 @ $4.50	
9		500 @ $9.00
18	700 @ $4.75	
20		400 @ $9.50
29	600 @ $5.00	

All expenses other than cost of goods sold amount to $2,000 for the month. The company uses an estimated tax rate of 25% to accrue monthly income taxes.

Required

1. Prepare a chart comparing cost of goods sold and ending inventory using the periodic system and the following costing methods:

	Cost of Goods Sold	Ending Inventory	Total
Weighted average			
FIFO			
LIFO			

2. What does the Total column represent?
3. Prepare income statements for each of the three methods.
4. Will the company pay more or less tax if it uses FIFO rather than LIFO? How much more or less?

LO5 • 7 • 12   **Problem 5-11A Comparison of Inventory Costing Methods—Perpetual System (Appendix)**

Repeat Problem 5-10A using the perpetual system.

LO5 • 6 • 7   **Problem 5-12A Inventory Costing Methods—Periodic System**

Story Company's inventory records for the month of November reveal the following:

Inventory, November 1	300 units @ $27.00
November 4, purchase	375 units @ $26.50
November 7, sale	450 units @ $63.00
November 13, purchase	330 units @ $26.00
November 18, purchase	225 units @ $25.40
November 22, sale	570 units @ $63.75
November 24, purchase	300 units @ $25.00
November 28, sale	165 units @ $64.50

Selling and administrative expenses for the month were $16,200. Depreciation expense was $6,000. Story's tax rate is 35%.

Required

1. Calculate the cost of goods sold and ending inventory under each of the following three methods assuming a periodic inventory system: (a) FIFO, (b) LIFO, and (c) weighted average.
2. Calculate the gross profit and net income under each costing assumption.
3. Under which costing method will Story pay the least taxes? Explain your answer.

LO5 • 6 • 7   **Problem 5-13A Inventory Costing Methods—Periodic System**

Following is an inventory acquisition schedule for Fees Corp. for 2017:

	Units	Unit Cost
Beginning inventory	4,000	$20
Purchases:		
February 4	2,000	18
April 12	3,000	16
September 10	1,000	14
December 5	2,500	12

During the year, Fees sold 11,000 units at $30 each. All expenses except cost of goods sold and taxes amounted to $60,000. The tax rate is 30%.

Required

1. Compute cost of goods sold and ending inventory under each of the following three methods assuming a periodic inventory system: (a) weighted average, (b) FIFO, and (c) LIFO.
2. Prepare income statements under each of the three methods.
3. Which method do you recommend so that Fees pays the least amount of taxes during 2017? Explain your answer.
4. Fees anticipates that unit costs for inventory will increase throughout 2018. Will Fees be able to switch from the method you recommended that it use in 2017 to another method to take advantage of the increase in prices for tax purposes? Explain your answer.

LO1 • 7 • 8   **Problem 5-14A Interpreting The New York Times Company's Financial Statements**

REAL WORLD

The 2015 Form 10-K of **The New York Times Company** includes the following in the note that summarizes its significant accounting policies:

Inventories

Inventories are stated at the lower of cost or current market value. Inventory cost is generally based on the last-in, first-out ("LIFO") method for newsprint and the first-in, first-out ("FIFO") method for other inventories.

Required

1. What *types* of inventory costs does The New York Times Company carry? What about newspapers? Are newspapers considered inventory?
2. Why would the company choose more than one method to value its inventory?

DECISION CASES

Reading and Interpreting Financial Statements

Decision Case 5-1 Comparing Two Companies in the Same Industry: Chipotle and Panera Bread

LO1 • 3

REAL WORLD

Refer to the financial information for **Chipotle** and **Panera Bread** reproduced at the end of this book and answer the following questions:

Required

1. What is the dollar amount of inventories that each company reports on its balance sheet at the end of the most recent year? What percentage of total assets do inventories represent for each company? What does this tell you about the nature of their business?
2. Refer to Note 1 in Chipotle's annual report. What inventory valuation method does the company use?
3. Refer to Note 2 in Panera Bread's annual report. What inventory valuation method does the company use?
4. How do both companies deal with situations in which the market value of inventory is less than its cost?
5. Given the nature of their businesses, which inventory system, periodic or perpetual, would you expect both Chipotle and Panera Bread to use? Explain your answer.

Decision Case 5-2 Reading and Interpreting Walgreens Boots Alliance's Inventory Note

LO6 • 7

REAL WORLD

Walgreens Boots Alliance, Inc. and Subsidiaries' (the company created with the combination of Walgreens and Boots Alliance) Form 10-K includes the following in the note that summarizes its accounting policies:

Inventory

The Company's Retail Pharmacy USA segment inventory is accounted for using the last-in-first-out ("LIFO") method. At August 31, 2015 and August 31, 2014, Retail Pharmacy USA segment inventories would have been greater by $2.5 billion and $2.3 billion, respectively, if they had been valued on a lower of first-in-first-out ("FIFO") cost or market basis.

Required

1. What inventory costing method does Walgreens Boots Alliance use for its Retail Pharmacy USA segment? Explain why you think the company uses this method.
2. What is the amount of the LIFO reserve at the end of each of the two years?
3. Explain the meaning of the increase or decrease in the LIFO reserve during 2015. What does this tell you about inventory costs for the company? Are they rising or falling? Explain your answer.

LO6 • 9   Decision Case 5-3 Reading and Interpreting Gap Inc.'s Inventory Note

REAL WORLD

The 2015 Form 10-K for **Gap Inc.** includes the following information in the note that summarizes its accounting policies:

Merchandise Inventory

We value inventory at the lower of cost or market, with cost determined using the weighted-average cost method. We record an adjustment when future estimated selling price is less than cost. We review our inventory levels in order to identify slow-moving merchandise and broken assortments (items no longer in stock in a sufficient range of sizes or colors) and use promotions and markdowns to clear merchandise. In addition, we estimate and accrue shortage for the period between the last physical count and the balance sheet date.

Required

1. What inventory costing method does Gap Inc. use? Explain why you think Gap uses this method.
2. Gap Inc. values its inventory at the lower of cost or market. How does the company define *market*? What factors does it take into account in deciding whether to write down its inventory?

Making Financial Decisions

LO2 • 3 • 4   Decision Case 5-4 Gross Profit for a Merchandiser

Emblems For You sells specialty sweatshirts. The purchase price is $10 per unit plus 10% tax and a shipping cost of 50¢ per unit. When the units arrive, they must be labeled, at an additional cost of 75¢ per unit. Emblems purchased, received, and labeled 1,500 units, of which 750 units were sold during the month for $20 each. The controller has prepared the following income statement:

Sales	$15,000
Cost of sales ($11 × 750)	8,250
Gross profit	$ 6,750
Shipping expense	750
Labeling expense	1,125
Net income	$ 4,875

Emblems is aware that a gross profit of 40% is standard for the industry. The marketing manager believes that Emblems should lower the price because the gross profit is higher than the industry average.

Required

1. Calculate Emblems' gross profit ratio.
2. Explain why Emblems should or should not lower its selling price.

LO2 • 3 • 4   Decision Case 5-5 Pricing Decision

Caroline's Candy Corner sells gourmet chocolates. The company buys chocolates in bulk for $5 per pound plus 5% sales tax. Credit terms are 2/10, n/25, and the company always pays promptly to take advantage of the discount. The chocolates are shipped to Caroline FOB shipping point. Shipping costs are $0.05 per pound. When the chocolates arrive at the shop, Caroline's Candy repackages them into one-pound boxes labeled with the store name. Boxes cost $0.70 each. The company pays its employees an hourly wage of $5.25 plus a commission of $0.10 per pound.

Required

1. What is the cost per one-pound box of chocolates?
2. What price must Caroline's Candy charge in order to have a 40% gross profit?
3. Do you believe this is a sufficient gross profit for this kind of business? Explain. What other costs might the company still incur?

Decision Case 5-6 Use of a Perpetual Inventory System

LO3

Darrell Keith is starting a new business. He plans to keep a tight control over it. Therefore, he wants to know *exactly* how much gross profit he earns on each unit that he sells. Darrell sets up an elaborate numbering system to identify each item as it is purchased and to match the item with a sales price. Each unit is assigned a number as follows:

0000-000-00-000

a. The first four numbers represent the month and day an item was received.
b. The second set of numbers is the last three numbers of the purchase order that authorized the purchase of the item.
c. The third set of numbers is the two-number department code assigned to different types of products.
d. The last three numbers are a chronological code assigned to units as they are received during a given day.

Required

1. Write a short memo to Darrell explaining the benefits and costs involved in a perpetual inventory system in conjunction with his quest to know exactly how much he will earn on each unit.
2. Comment on Darrell's inventory system assuming that he is selling (a) automobiles or (b) trees, shrubs, and plants.

Decision Case 5-7 Inventory Costing Methods

LO6 • 7

You are the controller for Georgetown Company. At the end of its first year of operations, the company is experiencing cash flow problems. The following information has been accumulated during the year:

Purchases	
January	1,000 units @ $8
March	1,200 units @ 8
October	1,500 units @ 9

During the year, Georgetown sold 3,000 units at $15 each. The expected tax rate is 35%. The president doesn't understand how to report inventory in the financial statements because no record of the cost of the units sold was kept as each sale was made.

Required

1. What inventory system must Georgetown use?
2. Determine the number of units on hand at the end of the year.
3. Explain cost-flow assumptions to the president and the method you recommend. Prepare income statements to justify your position, comparing your recommended method with at least one other method.

Decision Case 5-8 Inventory Errors

LO8

You are the controller of a rapidly growing mass merchandiser. The company uses a periodic inventory system. As the company has grown and accounting systems have developed, errors have occurred in both the physical count of inventory and the valuation of inventory on the balance sheet. You have been able to identify the following errors as of December 2017:

- In 2015, one of the retail sections was omitted from the physical count of inventory. The error resulted in inventory being understated on December 31, 2015, by approximately $28,700.
- In 2015, one section of the warehouse was counted twice. The error resulted in inventory being overstated on December 31, 2015, by approximately $45,600.

(Continued)

- In 2016, the replacement cost of some inventory was less than the FIFO value used on the balance sheet. The inventory would have been $6,000 less on the balance sheet dated December 31, 2016.

Required

What, if anything, should you do to correct each of these errors? Explain your answers.

Ethical Decision Making

LO7   Decision Case 5-9 Selection of an Inventory Method

As controller of a widely held public company, you are concerned with making the best decisions for the stockholders. At the end of its first year of operations, you are faced with the choice of method to value inventory. Specific identification is out of the question because the company sells a large quantity of diversified products. You are trying to decide between FIFO and LIFO. Inventory costs have increased 33% over the year, and therefore, you think LIFO will most accurately match these most recent costs with the revenues of the period. The chief executive officer has instructed you to do whatever it takes in all areas to report the highest income possible.

ETHICAL DECISION MODEL

Required

Use the Ethical Decision Framework in Exhibit 1-9 to complete the following requirements:
1. **Recognize an ethical dilemma:** What ethical dilemma(s) do you face?
2. **Analyze the key elements in the situation:**

    a. Who may benefit if you follow the chief executive officer's instructions? Who may be harmed?
    b. How are they likely to benefit or be harmed?
    c. What rights or claims may be violated?
    d. What specific interests are in conflict?
    e. What are your responsibilities and obligations?

3. **List alternatives and evaluate the impact of each on those affected:** As controller, what are your options in dealing with the ethical dilemma(s) you identified in (1) above?
4. **Select the best alternative:** Among the alternatives, which one would you select?

LO9   Decision Case 5-10 Write-Down of Obsolete Inventory

As a newly hired staff accountant, you are assigned the responsibility of physically counting inventory at the end of the year. The inventory count proceeds in a timely fashion. The inventory is outdated, however. You suggest that the inventory cannot be sold for the cost at which it is carried and that the inventory should be written down to a much lower level. The controller replies that experience has taught her how the market changes and she knows that the units in the warehouse will be more marketable again. The company plans to keep the goods until they are back in style.

Required

1. What effect will writing off the inventory have on the current year's income?
2. What effect does not writing off the inventory have on the year-end balance sheet?
3. What factors should you consider in deciding whether to persist in your argument that the inventory should be written down?
4. If you fail to write down the inventory, do outside readers of the statements have information that is a faithful representation? Explain your answer.
5. Assume that the company prepares its financial statements in accordance with IFRS. Is it necessary that the inventory be written down?

IFRS

Answers

MODULE 1 Answers to Questions

1. The three distinct types of costs incurred by a manufacturer are direct materials, direct labor, and manufacturing overhead. Direct, or raw, materials are the ingredients used in making a product. Direct labor consists of the amounts paid to factory workers to manufacture the product. Manufacturing overhead includes all the other costs that are related to the manufacturing process but cannot be directly matched to specific units of output.

2. The two inventory systems differ with respect to how often the Inventory account is updated. Under the perpetual system, the Merchandise Inventory account is updated each time a sale or purchase is made. With the periodic system, the Inventory account is updated only at the end of the period. A temporary account, called Purchases, is used to keep track of the acquisitions of inventory during the period. The periodic method relies on a count of the inventory on hand at the end of the period to determine the amount to assign to ending inventory on the balance sheet and to cost of goods sold expense on the income statement.

3. For inventory in transit at the end of the year, the terms of shipment dictate whether the buyer should record the purchase of the inventory. FOB shipping point means that the goods belong to the buyer as soon as they are shipped, and the purchases should be recorded at this point in time. Alternatively, FOB destination point means that the goods do not belong to the buyer until they are received and therefore should not be recorded if they are in transit at year-end.

4. Gross profit is computed by deducting cost of goods sold from net sales. The gross profit ratio indicates how well the company controlled its product costs during the year. For example, a 30% gross profit ratio indicates that for every dollar of net sales, the company has a gross profit of 30 cents. That is, after deducting 70 cents on every dollar for the cost of the inventory that is sold, the company has 30 cents to cover its operating costs and earn a profit.

MODULE 1 Answers to Apply

1.

White Wholesalers
Partial Income Statement
For the Year Ended December 31, 2017

Inventory, January 1, 2017		$ 14,200
Net purchases	$81,500	
Transportation-in	4,500	
Cost of goods purchased		86,000
Cost of goods available for sale		$100,200
Inventory, December 31, 2017		(10,300)
Cost of goods sold		$ 89,900

2.   Purchases: I

Beginning inventory: I

Transportation-in: I

Ending inventory: D

3.   Gross profit ratio: ($50,000 − $30,000)/$50,000 = 40%

MODULE 2 Answers to Questions

1.   According to the cost of goods sold model, beginning inventory plus purchases minus ending inventory equals cost of goods sold. Therefore, the amount assigned to inventory on the balance sheet has a direct effect on the measurement of cost of goods sold on the income statement. Any errors in valuing inventory will flow through to cost of goods sold and thus have an impact on the measurement of net income.

2.   The weighted average cost method assigns more weight to unit costs at which more units were purchased. For example, assume that beginning inventory consists of 100 units with a unit cost of $10 per unit. Assume that during the period, 100 units were purchased at $15 per unit and 200 units were purchased at $20 per unit. The arithmetic average unit cost for the period would be ($10 + $15 + $20)/3 = $15. However, the weighted average unit cost would be [100($10) + 100($15) + 200($20)]/400 units, or $16.25. The acquisition of twice as many units at $20 as opposed to those purchased at $10 and $15 drives the weighted average up to $16.25.

3.   In a period of rising prices, the use of LIFO will result in a lower tax bill. Because the most recent purchases are charged to cost of goods sold under LIFO, in a period of rising prices, these units will be higher-priced. Thus, the result will be lower gross margin as well as lower net income before tax. Lower net income will result in a lower amount of tax to pay. If prices are declining during the period, FIFO will result in a lower tax bill.

4.   A LIFO liquidation occurs when a company using the LIFO inventory method sells more units during the period than it purchases. A liquidation of some or all of the older, relatively lower-priced units (assuming rising prices) will result in a low cost of goods sold amount and a correspondingly higher gross margin. If the company sells the lower-priced units, its net income will improve, but higher taxes will have to be paid. To avoid facing this situation, a company might buy inventory at the end of the year to avoid these consequences of a liquidation. Unfortunately, the somewhat forced purchase of inventory to avoid the liquidation may not be in the best interests of the company.

MODULE 2 Answers to Apply

1.   Examples of costs that should be added to the purchase price of inventory are freight costs on purchases, insurance during the time inventory is in transit, storage costs before inventory is ready to be sold, and various taxes such as excise and sales taxes.

2. a.   Cost of goods sold: (75 × $2) + (75 × $3) = $375
Ending inventory: 25 × $3 = $75
   b.   Cost of goods sold: (100 × $3) + (50 × $2) = $400
Ending inventory: 25 × $2 = $50

3. a.   FIFO: 500 × $6 = $3,000
   b.   LIFO: 500 × $5 = $2,500
4. a.   Cost of goods sold: L
   b.   Gross profit: H
   c.   Income before taxes: H
   d.   Income taxes: H
   e.   Cash outflow: H

MODULE 3 Answers to Questions

1.   Ending inventory will be overstated. According to the cost of goods sold model, ending inventory is subtracted from cost of goods available to sell to arrive at cost of goods sold expense. Therefore, an overstatement of ending inventory will lead to an understatement of cost of goods sold expense. An understatement of an expense results in an overstatement of net income for the period.

2.   The lower-of-cost-or-market rule is invoked when the utility of inventory is less than its cost to the company. It is a departure from the historical cost principle and is justified on the basis of conservatism. The rule is a reaction to uncertainty by anticipating a decline in the value of inventory and writing down the asset before it is sold.

3. Application of the lower-of-cost-or-market rule on a total basis, compared with an item-by-item basis, will usually yield a different result. The reason is that with the total approach, increases in market value above cost are allowed to offset decreases in value. Alternatively, when the item-by-item approach is used, any increases in value are essentially ignored and it is the declines in value for each item that are recognized.

MODULE 3 Answers to Apply

1. If ending inventory is overstated by $50,000, then cost of goods sold will be understated by $50,000 and gross profit will overstated by $50,000. Net income will be overstated, resulting in an overstatement of retained earnings on the balance sheet. Inventory on the balance sheet will also be overstated. This ignores the effect of taxes.

2.

Identify and Analyze	**ACTIVITY:** Operating **ACCOUNTS:** Inventory Decrease Loss on Decline in Value of Inventory Increase **STATEMENT(S):** Balance Sheet and Income Statement

Balance Sheet						Income Statement		
ASSETS	=	LIABILITIES	+	STOCKHOLDERS' EQUITY		REVENUES −	EXPENSES =	NET INCOME
Inventory (7,000)				(7,000)			Loss on Decline in Value of Inventory 7,000	(7,000)

MODULE 4 Answers to Questions

1. Inventory turnover equals cost of goods sold divided by average inventory. If the cost of goods sold remains constant while the denominator (average inventory) increases, inventory turnover will decrease. This indicates that inventory is staying on the shelf for a longer time. The company should probably evaluate the salability of its inventory.

2. An increase in accounts payable is an indication that during the period a company increased the amount it owes suppliers and therefore conserved its cash. Therefore, the increase in the account is added on the statement of cash flows.

MODULE 4 Answers to Apply

1. a. $\text{Inventory Turnover Ratio} = \dfrac{\text{Cost of Goods Sold}}{\text{Average Inventory}}$

$= \dfrac{\$640,000}{(\$130,000 + \$190,000)/2}$

$= \dfrac{\$640,000}{\$160,000} = 4 \text{ times}$

b. $\text{Number of Days' Sales in Inventory} = \dfrac{\text{Number of Days in the Period}}{\text{Inventory Turnover Ratio}}$

$= \dfrac{360}{4} = 90 \text{ days}$

2. Company A's inventory turnover is $10,000,000/ $100,000, or 100 times. Company B's turnover is $10,000,000/$1,000,000, or 10 times. Company A with the much higher turnover is the wholesaler of fresh fruits and vegetables. Company B is the car dealer because its inventory would not turn over nearly as often given the nature of its products.

3. The increase in inventory would be deducted from net income on the statement of cash flows prepared using the indirect method since the buildup of inventory required cash outflow. The increase in accounts payable conserves cash and is therefore added to net income.

MODULE 5 Answers to Questions

1. When a perpetual inventory system is used, the dollar amount of inventory is calculated after each sale. Thus, when it is used in conjunction with the weighted average cost method, a new average cost is calculated after each sale. The weighted average changes each time a sale is made; therefore, the unit cost is called a *moving average*.

2. When LIFO is applied on a perpetual basis, a gap is created. This situation arises because LIFO is applied every time a sale is made rather than only at the end of the period. Therefore, the amount assigned to inventory will be different than it would be if LIFO was applied only at the end of the period, that is using a periodic system.

MODULE 5 Answers to Apply

Date	Units	Unit Cost	Balance
1/1	100	$5	$500
6/16 Purchase	20	$6	120
			$620
8/19 Sale	(65)		
Balance	55	$5	$275
12/2 Purchase	25	$7	175
12/31			$450

Answers to Connect to the Real World

5-1 (p. 215)

Because annual reports do not disclose the inventory system used, it is not possible to say for certain whether Gap Inc. uses a perpetual or a periodic system. However, it is possible that the company uses a perpetual system given the ability to maintain computerized records.

5-2 (p. 236)

Gap Inc. sells a wide variety of apparel and accessories. The nature of this business requires the company to continually monitor its inventory for products that can no longer be sold, due to changes in style, consumer preferences, and other factors. If market is less than cost, the company should write down the inventory to reflect market value. The company uses the weighted-average method for determining cost.

Answers to Key Terms Quiz

Quiz 1: Merchandise Accounting

13	Merchandise Inventory		9	Cost of goods sold
14	Raw materials		2	Perpetual system
12	Work in process		5	Periodic system
15	Finished goods		1	Transportation-In
11	Gross profit		7	Purchases
8	Net sales		3	FOB destination point
16	Sales revenue		4	FOB shipping point
6	Cost of goods available for sale		10	Gross profit ratio

Quiz 2: Inventory Valuation

9	Specific identification method	5	Replacement cost
2	Weighted average cost method	10	Inventory profit
4	FIFO method	3	Lower-of-cost-or-market (LCM) rule
6	LIFO method	13	Inventory turnover ratio
11	LIFO liquidation	7	Number of days' sales in inventory
8	LIFO conformity rule	1	Moving average (Appendix)
12	LIFO reserve		

Cash and Internal Control

MODULES	LEARNING OBJECTIVES	WHY IS THIS CHAPTER IMPORTANT?
1 **Accounting and Controlling for Cash**	**LO1** Identify and describe the various forms of cash reported on a balance sheet. **LO2** Describe the various techniques that companies use to control cash.	• You need to know what is included in cash and cash equivalents. (See p. 278.) • You need to know the techniques that companies use to control cash. (See pp. 278–283.)
2 **Internal Control**	**LO3** Explain the importance of internal control to a business and the significance of the Sarbanes-Oxley Act of 2002. **LO4** Describe the basic internal control procedures. **LO5** Describe the various documents used in recording purchases and their role in controlling cash disbursements.	• You need to know why a company must maintain an effective internal control system and what basic procedures help make a system effective. (See pp. 284–288.) • You need to know how the use of business documents can add to the effectiveness of an internal control system. (See pp. 287–296.)

REGAL ENTERTAINMENT GROUP

Regal Entertainment Group is the largest movie theatre company in the United States, with revenues topping $3.1 billion in 2015. At the end of that year, it operated 572 theatres in 42 states, as well as in Guam, Saipan, American Samoa, and the District of Columbia. Approximately 217 million attendees filled Regal's seats in its theatres during the 2015 fiscal year!

Regal Entertainment relies on a steady flow of cash to run smoothly. Cash is needed to pay its distributors for films, to buy concessions, and to expand its ever-growing chain of theatres. Cash flows into the theatres continuously in the form of concession and ticket revenues. It is no wonder that 50% of the company's total current assets are in the form of cash and cash equivalents, as shown here.

Because cash is such a liquid asset, control over it is crucial to a company's long-term success. This chapter looks at the accounting for cash and cash equivalents and at the ways companies maintain effective control over all valuable assets, including cash.

Regal Entertainment Group Consolidated Balance Sheets (Partial) (in millions, except share data)		
	December 31, 2015	**January 1, 2015**
Assets		
Current assets:		
Cash and cash equivalents	$219.6	$147.1
Trade and other receivables, net	149.6	126.0
Income tax receivable	3.5	9.6
Inventories	22.4	17.8
Prepaid expenses and other current assets	20.9	21.7
Assets held for sale	1.0	—
Deferred income tax asset	21.2	19.2
Total current assets	438.2	341.4

> Regal added over $72 million to its cash and cash equivalents during the year

> Cash and cash equivalents account for 50% of total current assets

See accompanying notes to consolidated financial statements.

Source: Regal Entertainment Group, Form 10-K for the fiscal year ended December 31, 2015.

MODULE 1 ACCOUNTING AND CONTROLLING FOR CASH

LO1 Identify and describe the various forms of cash reported on a balance sheet.

Cash takes many forms. Coin and currency on hand and cash on deposit in the form of checking and savings accounts are the most obvious forms of cash. Also included in cash are checks, including undeposited checks from customers as well as cashier checks and certified checks. **The key to the classification of an amount as cash is that it be *readily available to pay debts.*** Technically, a bank has the legal right to demand that a customer notify it before making withdrawals from savings accounts, or time deposits, as they are often called. Because this right is rarely exercised, however, savings accounts are normally classified as cash. In contrast, a certificate of deposit has a specific maturity date and carries a penalty for early withdrawal and therefore is not included in cash.

CONNECT TO THE REAL WORLD

PANERA BREAD
READING THE STATEMENT OF CASH FLOWS

6-1 Refer to the company's statement of cash flows, for 2015 as included in Appendix C. Did its cash and cash equivalents increase or decrease during the most recent year? Summarize the changes in cash and cash equivalents for the year using the framework shown in Exhibit 6-1 on the next page. *(See answers on p. 308.)*

EXAMPLE 6-1 Determining the Amount of Cash and Cash Equivalents

Given the following items, what amount should be reported on the balance sheet as Cash and cash equivalents?

Cashier's check	$ 2,000
Certificate of deposit due in nine months	10,000
Checking account	4,500
Coin and currency on hand	1,500
Employee IOU	3,000
Money market account	12,000
Postage stamps	500
Savings account	8,000
Undeposited customer checks	850

Cash and cash equivalents would be reported as $28,850 ($2,000 + $4,500 + $1,500 + $12,000 + $8,000 + $850).

Cash Equivalents and the Statement of Cash Flows

The first item on **Regal Entertainment**'s balance sheet in the chapter opener is Cash and cash equivalents. Examples of items normally classified as cash equivalents are commercial paper issued by corporations, Treasury bills issued by the federal government, and money market funds offered by financial institutions. According to U.S. GAAP, classification as a **cash equivalent** is limited to those investments that are readily convertible to known amounts of cash and that have an original maturity to the investor of three months or less. According to that definition, a six-month bank certificate of deposit would *not* be classified as a cash equivalent. The IFRS definition of cash equivalents is very similar to that used by U.S. GAAP.

Cash equivalent
An investment that is readily convertible to a known amount of cash and has an original maturity to the investor of three months or less.

IFRS

A summary of the major categories appearing on Regal Entertainment's statement of cash flows is shown in Exhibit 6-1. Note the direct tie between this statement and the balance sheet. When the net increase in cash and cash equivalents of $72.5 million is added to the beginning balance in cash and cash equivalents of $147.1 million, the result is the ending balance of $219.6 million. Recall that this is the same balance in cash and cash equivalents as shown on the partial balance sheet in the chapter opener.

Control Over Cash

LO2 Describe the various techniques that companies use to control cash.

Because cash is universally accepted as a medium of exchange, control over it is critical to the smooth functioning of any business, no matter how large or small.

EXHIBIT 6-1 Cash and Cash Equivalents on the Balance Sheet and the Statement of Cash Flows for Regal Entertainment

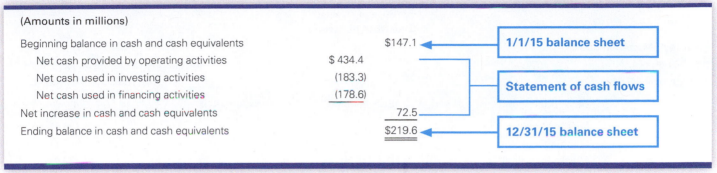

(Amounts in millions)

Beginning balance in cash and cash equivalents		$147.1
Net cash provided by operating activities	$ 434.4	
Net cash used in investing activities	(183.3)	
Net cash used in financing activities	(178.6)	
Net increase in cash and cash equivalents		72.5
Ending balance in cash and cash equivalents		$219.6

1/1/15 balance sheet
Statement of cash flows
12/31/15 balance sheet

Source: Regal Entertainment Group, Form 10-K for the fiscal year ended December 31, 2015.

Cash Management

In addition to the need to guard against theft and other abuses related to the physical custody of cash, management of this asset is also important. Regal Entertainment must constantly be sure that it has neither too little nor too much cash on hand. The need to have enough cash on hand is obvious: suppliers, employees, taxing agencies, banks, and all other creditors must be paid on time. It is equally important that a company not maintain cash on hand and on deposit in checking accounts beyond the minimal amount necessary to support ongoing operations since cash is essentially a nonearning asset. The potential return from investing idle cash in various forms of marketable securities dictates that companies carefully monitor cash on hand at all times.

An important tool in cash management, the cash flows statement, is discussed in detail in Chapter 12. Cash budgets, which are also critical to cash management, are discussed in management accounting and business finance texts. Companies often use two other cash control features: bank reconciliations and petty cash funds. Before turning to those control devices, we need to review the basic features of a bank statement.

Reading a Bank Statement

Two fundamental principles of internal control are applicable to cash:

1. All cash receipts should be deposited intact daily.
2. All cash payments should be made by check.

Checking accounts at banks are critical in this regard. These accounts allow a company to carefully monitor and control cash receipts and cash payments. Control is aided further by the monthly **bank statement**. This statement provides a detailed list of all activity for a particular account during the month. The example of a typical bank statement shown in Exhibit 6-2 indicates the activity in one of the cash accounts maintained by Mickey's Marathon Sports at Mt. Etna State Bank.

It is important to understand the route a check takes after it is written. Assume that Mickey's writes a check on its account at Mt. Etna State Bank. Mickey's mails the check to one of its suppliers, Keese Corp., which deposits the check in its account at Second City Bank. At this point, Second City presents the check to Mt. Etna for payment, and Mt. Etna reduces the balance in Mickey's account accordingly. The canceled check has now "cleared" the banking system.

The following types of items appear on Mickey's bank statement:

Canceled checks—Mickey's checks that cleared the bank during the month of June are listed with the corresponding check number and the date paid. Some of these checks may have been written by Mickey's in a previous month but were not presented for payment to the bank until June. Also, during June Mickey's may have written some checks that do not yet appear on the bank statement because they have not been presented for payment. A check written by a company but not yet presented to the bank for payment is called an **outstanding check**.

Bank statement
A detailed list, provided by the bank, of all activity for a particular account during the month.

Outstanding check
A check written by a company but not yet presented to the bank for payment.

EXHIBIT 6-2 Bank Statement

Mt. Etna State Bank
Chicago, Illinois
Statement of Account

Mickey's Marathon Sports
502 Dodge St.
Chicago, IL 66666

For the Month Ending June 30, 2017
Account   0371-22-514

Date	Description	Subtractions	Additions	Balance
6-01	Previous balance			3,236.41
6-01	Check 497	723.40		2,513.01
6-02	Check 495	125.60		2,387.41
6-06	Check 491	500.00		1,887.41
6-07	Deposit		1,423.16	3,310.57
6-10	Check 494	185.16		3,125.41
6-13	NSF check	245.72		2,879.69
6-15	Deposit		755.50	3,635.19
6-18	Check 499	623.17		3,012.02
6-20	Check 492	125.00		2,887.02
6-22	Deposit		1,875.62	4,762.64
6-23	Service charge	20.00		4,742.64
6-24	Check 493	875.75		3,866.89
6-24	Check 503	402.10		3,464.79
6-26	Customer note, interest		550.00	4,014.79
6-26	Service fee on note	16.50		3,998.29
6-27	Check 500	1,235.40		2,762.89
6-28	Deposit		947.50	3,710.39
6-30	Check 498	417.25		3,293.14
6-30	Interest earned		15.45	3,308.59
6-30	Statement Totals	5,495.05	5,567.23	

Deposit in transit
A deposit recorded on the books but not yet reflected on the bank statement.

Deposits—Most companies deposit all checks, coins, and currency on a daily basis; this is in keeping with an internal control principle that all cash receipts should be deposited in their entirety. For the sake of brevity, we have limited to four the number of deposits that Mickey's made during the month. Mickey's also may have made a deposit on the last day or two of the month, and this deposit may not yet be reflected on the bank statement. This type of deposit is called a **deposit in transit**.

NSF check—NSF stands for "not sufficient funds." The NSF check listed on the bank statement on June 13 is a customer's check that Mickey's recorded on its books, deposited, and thus included in its Cash account. When Mt. Etna State Bank learned that the customer did not have sufficient funds on hand in its bank account to cover the check, the bank deducted the amount from Mickey's account. Mickey's needs to contact its customer to collect the amount due. Ideally, the customer will issue a new check once it has sufficient funds in its accounts.

Service charge—The most common bank service charges are monthly activity fees and fees charged for new checks, for the rental of a lockbox in which to store valuable company documents, and for the collection of customer notes by the bank.

Customer note and interest—It is often convenient to have customers pay amounts owed to a company directly to that company's bank. The bank simply acts as a collection agency for the company.

Interest earned—Most checking accounts pay interest on the average daily balance in the account. Rates paid on checking accounts are usually significantly less than could be earned on most other forms of investment.

The Bank Reconciliation

A **bank reconciliation** should be prepared for each individual bank account as soon as the bank statement is received. Ideally, the reconciliation should be performed or thoroughly reviewed by someone independent of custody, record-keeping, and authorization responsibilities relating to cash. As the name implies, the purpose of a bank reconciliation is to *reconcile,* or resolve, any differences between the bank's recorded balance and the balance that appears on the company's books. Differences between the two amounts are investigated, and necessary adjustments are made. The following steps are used in preparing a bank reconciliation:

1. Trace deposits listed on the bank statement to the books. Any deposits recorded on the books but not yet shown on the bank statement are deposits in transit. **Prepare a list of the deposits in transit.**
2. Arrange the canceled checks in numerical order and trace each of them to the books. Any checks recorded on the books but not yet listed on the bank statement are outstanding. **Prepare a list of the outstanding checks.**
3. List all items, other than deposits, shown as additions on the bank statement, such as interest paid by the bank and amounts collected by the bank from one of the company's customers. When the bank pays interest or collects an amount owed to a company, the bank increases its liability to the company on its own books. These items are called **credit memoranda**. **Prepare a list of credit memoranda.**
4. List all amounts, other than canceled checks, shown as subtractions on the bank statement, such as any NSF checks and service charges. When a company deposits money in a bank, a liability is created on the books of the bank. This liability is reduced for items such as NSF checks and service charges. These items are called **debit memoranda**. **Prepare a list of debit memoranda.**
5. **Identify any errors** made by the bank or by the company in recording cash transactions.

Companies use a number of different formats in preparing bank reconciliations. For example, some companies take the balance shown on the bank statement and reconcile this amount to the balance shown on the books. Another approach, which will be illustrated for Mickey's, involves reconciling the bank balance and the book balance to an adjusted balance, rather than one to the other. The advantage of this second approach is that it yields the correct balance and makes it easy for the company to make any necessary adjustments to its books.

Bank reconciliation
A form used by the accountant to reconcile or resolve any differences between the balance shown on the bank statement for a particular account with the balance shown in the accounting records.

Credit memoranda
Additions on a bank statement for such items as interest paid on the account and notes collected by the bank for the customer.

Debit memoranda
Deductions on a bank statement for items such as NSF checks and various service charges.

EXAMPLE 6-2 Preparing a Bank Reconciliation

A bank reconciliation for Mickey's Marathon Sports is shown below.

Mickey's Marathon Sports Bank Reconciliation June 30, 2017		
Balance per bank statement, June 30		$3,308.59
Add: Deposit in transit		642.30
Deduct: Outstanding checks:		
No. 496	$ 79.89	
No. 501	213.20	
No. 502	424.75	(717.84)
Adjusted balance, June 30		$3,233.05
Balance per books, June 30		$2,895.82
Add: Customer note collected	$500.00	
Interest on customer note	50.00	
Interest earned during June	15.45	
Error in recording check 498	54.00	619.45
Deduct: NSF check	$245.72	
Collection fee on note	16.50	
Service charge for lockbox	20.00	(282.22)
Adjusted balance, June 30		$3,233.05

The following are explanations for the various items on the reconciliation.

1. The balance per bank statement of $3,308.59 is taken from the June statement as shown in Exhibit 6-2.

2. Mickey's records showed a deposit for $642.30 made on June 30 that is not reflected on the bank statement. The deposit in transit is listed as an addition to the bank statement balance.

3. The accounting records indicate three checks written but not yet reflected on the bank statement. The three outstanding checks are as follows:

496	$ 79.89
501	$213.20
502	$424.75

    Outstanding checks are the opposite of deposits in transit and therefore are deducted from the bank statement balance.

4. The adjusted balance of $3,233.05 is found by adding the deposit in transit and deducting the outstanding checks from the bank statement balance.

5. The $2,895.82 book balance on June 30 is taken from the company's records as of that date.

6. According to the bank statement, $550 was added to the account on June 26 for the collection of a note with interest. We assume that the repayment of the note accounted for $500 of this amount and that the other $50 was for interest. The bank statement notifies Mickey's that the note with interest has been collected. Therefore, Mickey's must add $550 to the book balance.

7. An entry on June 30 on the bank statement shows an increase of $15.45 for interest earned on the bank account during June. This amount is added to the book balance.

8. A review of the canceled checks returned with the bank statement detected an error that Mickey's made. The company records indicated that check 498 was recorded incorrectly as $471.25; the check was actually written for $417.25 and reflected as such on the bank statement. This error, referred to as a *transposition error,* resulted from transposing the 7 and the 1 in recording the check in the books. The error is the difference between the amount of $471.25 recorded and the amount of $417.25 that should have been recorded, or $54.00. Because Mickey's recorded the cash payment at too large an amount, $54.00 must be added back to the book balance.

9. In addition to canceled checks, three other deductions appear on the bank statement. Each of these must be deducted from the book balance:
    a. A customer's NSF check for $245.72 (see June 13 entry on bank statement)
    b. A $16.50 fee charged by the bank to collect the customer's note discussed in (6) (see June 26 entry on bank statement)
    c. A service fee of $20.00 charged by the bank for rental of a lockbox (see June 23 entry on bank statement)

10. The additions of $619.45 and deductions of $282.22 resulted in an adjusted cash balance of $3,233.05. Note that this adjusted balance agrees with the adjusted bank statement balance on the bank reconciliation [see (4)]. Thus, all differences between the two balances have been explained.

The Need for Adjustments to the Records

After it completes the bank reconciliation, Mickey's must prepare a number of adjustments to its records. In fact, all of the information for these adjustments will be from one section of the bank reconciliation. Are the additions and deductions made to the bank balance or the ones made to the book balance the basis for the adjustments? The additions and deductions to the Cash account *on the books* should be the basis for the adjustments because these are items that Mickey's was unaware of before receiving the bank statement. Conversely, the additions and deductions to the bank's balance (i.e., the deposits in transit and the outstanding checks) are items that Mickey's has already recorded on its books.

Establishing a Petty Cash Fund

Most businesses make an exception to the rule that all disbursements should be made by check. For minor expenditures, they use a **petty cash fund**, which consists of coin and currency kept on hand to make minor disbursements. The necessary steps in setting up and maintaining a petty cash fund are as follows:

1. A check is written for a lump-sum amount, such as $100 or $500. The check is cashed, and the coin and currency are entrusted to a petty cash custodian.

2. A journal entry is made to record the establishment of the fund.

3. Upon presentation of the necessary documentation, employees receive minor disbursements from the fund. In essence, cash is traded from the fund in exchange for a receipt.

4. Periodically, the fund is replenished by writing and cashing a check in the amount necessary to bring the fund back to its original balance.

5. At the time the fund is replenished, an adjustment is made to record its replenishment and to recognize the various expenses incurred.

The use of this fund is normally warranted on the basis of cost versus benefits. That is, the benefits in time saved in making minor disbursements from cash are thought to outweigh the cost associated with the risk of loss from decreased control over cash disbursements. The fund also serves a practical purpose for certain expenditures, such as taxi fares and postage, that often must be paid in cash.

Petty cash fund
Money kept on hand for making minor disbursements in coin and currency rather than by writing checks.

MODULE 1 TEST YOURSELF

Review	**LO1** Identify and describe the various forms of cash reported on a balance sheet.	• Cash can take many forms; however, the key attribute is that the asset is readily available to pay debts. • Cash equivalents are investments that are readily convertible to a known amount of cash. *Readily* means three months or less.
	LO2 Describe the various techniques that companies use to control cash.	• The liquidity of cash makes controls over it very important to have in place. • Cash management means managing the need to have enough cash on hand to ensure cash flow needs but not so much that excess funds earn little return and may be vulnerable to misappropriation. • Bank reconciliations use third-party documents (bank statements) to reconcile differences between the amount in the bank and on the books. Done by an independent party, bank reconciliations are effective control procedures. • Petty cash funds are an effective way to minimize access to large cash accounts to pay for relatively small expenditures.
Question	1. Why does the purchase of an item classified as a cash equivalent *not* appear on the statement of cash flows as an investing activity?	
	2. Different formats for bank reconciliations are possible. What is the format for a bank reconciliation in which a service charge for a lockbox is *added* to the balance per the bank statement? Explain your answer.	

Apply

1. For the following items, indicate whether each should be included (I) or excluded (E) from the line item titled Cash and cash equivalents on the balance sheet.

_____ a. Certificate of deposit maturing in 60 days
_____ b. Checking account
_____ c. Certificate of deposit maturing in six months
_____ d. Savings account
_____ e. Shares of GM stock
_____ f. Petty cash
_____ g. Corporate bonds maturing in 30 days
_____ h. Certified check

2. Using Y for yes and N for no, indicate whether each of the following items should or should not be included with cash and cash equivalents on the balance sheet.

_____ Cash in a checking account
_____ Coin and currency in a cash register drawer
_____ A six-month certificate of deposit
_____ Postage stamps
_____ An amount owed by an employee for a travel advance
_____ A three-month Treasury bill
_____ Cash in a money market account

3. Indicate whether each of the following items is an adjustment to the balance per books (BK) or to the balance per bank statement (BS) on a reconciliation that adjusts the bank balance and the bank statement to the correct balance.

_____ Customer's NSF check
_____ Service charge for a lockbox
_____ Outstanding checks
_____ Interest earned on an account for the month
_____ Check written on the account but recorded on the books at the wrong amount
_____ Deposits in transit

Answers are located at the end of the chapter.

MODULE 2 INTERNAL CONTROL

LO3 Explain the importance of internal control to a business and the significance of the Sarbanes-Oxley Act of 2002.

Internal control system
Policies and procedures necessary to ensure the safeguarding of an entity's assets, the reliability of its accounting records, and the accomplishment of overall company objectives.

An employee of a large auto parts warehouse routinely takes spare parts home for personal use. A payroll clerk writes and signs two checks for an employee and then splits the amount of the second check with the worker. Through human error, an invoice is paid for merchandise never received from the supplier. These cases all point to a deficiency in a company's internal control system. An **internal control system** consists of the policies and procedures necessary to ensure the safeguarding of an entity's assets, the reliability of its accounting records, and the accomplishment of its overall objectives.

Three assets are especially critical to the operation of merchandising companies: cash, accounts receivable, and inventory. Activities related to those three assets compose the operating cycle of a business. Cash is used to buy inventory; the inventory is eventually sold; and assuming a sale on credit, the account receivable from the customer is collected. After looking at the government's response to huge lapses in internal control by major U.S. companies, we turn to the ways in which a company attempts to *control* the assets at its disposal.

The Sarbanes-Oxley Act of 2002

Sarbanes-Oxley Act
An act of Congress in 2002 intended to bring reform to corporate accountability and stewardship in the wake of a number of major corporate scandals.

As briefly described in Chapter 1, the **Sarbanes-Oxley Act** of 2002 (or SOX) was a direct response to the numerous corporate scandals that surfaced in the first few years of the new millennium. High-profile cases involving questionable accounting practices by companies such as **Enron** and **WorldCom** caused the federal government to step in and attempt to restore the public's confidence in the financial reporting system. SOX's various provisions are far-reaching, including provisions designed to ensure the independence of a company's auditors. For example, external auditors can no longer provide bookkeeping, human resource, information system design, and brokerage services for clients that they audit.

Another major part of SOX, Section 404, deals with a company's internal control system. Section 404 requires the annual report to include an **internal control report** in which management is required to:

1. State its responsibility to establish and maintain an adequate internal control structure and procedures for financial reporting.
2. Assess the effectiveness of its internal control structure and procedures for financial reporting.

Regal Entertainment's Report on Internal Control over Financial Reporting is shown in Exhibit 6-3. The first paragraph states management's responsibility for its system of internal control, and the second paragraph indicates that management believes internal control over financial reporting is effective.

Another important provision in SOX is that a company's outside auditors must issue a report on their assessment of the company's internal control. The statement in the last paragraph in Exhibit 6-3 calls attention to this report. **KPMG** is Regal Entertainment's independent auditor, and its report is shown in Exhibit 6-4. Note the reference in the second paragraph to the **Public Company Accounting Oversight Board (PCAOB)**. The PCAOB is the five-member body created by SOX that was given authority to set auditing standards in the United States. The last sentence in KPMG's report also contains the important statement that, in its opinion, Regal Entertainment has maintained effective internal control over financial reporting.

The top of the independent auditors' report in Exhibit 6-4 states that it is directed to the board of directors and stockholders of Regal Entertainment. The **board of directors** usually consists of key officers of the corporation as well as a number of directors whom it does not directly employ. Another key provision in SOX requires that the audit committee be made up entirely of outside directors. The **audit committee** is a subset of the board of directors that provides direct contact between stockholders and the independent accounting firm.

Stockholders and others affected by the scandals thought that top management of these organizations should have taken more responsibility for the accuracy of the information presented in the financial statements. SOX places this responsibility directly in the hands of the CEO (chief executive officer) and the CFO (chief financial officer). Now, the CEO and the CFO must certify that the information in the financial statements fairly presents the financial condition and results of operations of the company.

Internal control report
A report required by Section 404 of the Sarbanes-Oxley Act to be included in a company's annual report in which management assesses the effectiveness of the internal control structure.

Public Company Accounting Oversight Board (PCAOB)
The five-member body created by the Sarbanes-Oxley Act that was given the authority to set auditing standards in the United States.

Board of directors
A group composed of key officers of a corporation and outside members responsible for general oversight of the affairs of the entity.

Audit committee
A board of directors subset that acts as a direct contact between the stockholders and the independent accounting firm.

EXHIBIT 6-3 Management Report on Internal Control—Regal Entertainment

Management's Report on Internal Control over Financial Reporting

The Board of Directors
Regal Entertainment Group:

Management states its responsibility for the internal control system. → Management is responsible for establishing and maintaining adequate internal control over financial reporting as such term is defined in Rules 13a-15(f) and 15d-15(f) under the Securities Exchange Act of 1934, as amended.

Management assesses the effectiveness of the internal control system. → Management, including our principal executive officer and principal financial officer, conducted an evaluation of the effectiveness of such controls as of December 31, 2015. This assessment was based on criteria for effective internal control over financial reporting described in the *Internal Control-Integrated Framework* (2013) by the Committee of Sponsoring Organizations of the Treadway Commission (COSO). Based on this assessment, our management believes that the Company's internal control over financial reporting is effective as of December 31, 2015.

Auditors have issued a report on management's assessment. → KPMG LLP, independent registered public accounting firm of the Company's consolidated financial statements, has issued an audit report on the effectiveness of the Company's internal control over financial reporting as of December 31, 2015, as stated in their report which is included herein.

Source: Regal Entertainment Group, Form 10-K for the fiscal year ended December 31, 2015.

EXHIBIT 6-4 Auditors' Report—Regal Entertainment

Report of Independent Registered Public Accounting Firm

The Board of Directors and Stockholders
Regal Entertainment Group:

We have audited the accompanying consolidated balance sheets of Regal Entertainment Group and subsidiaries as of December 31, 2015 and January 1, 2015, and the related consolidated statements of income, comprehensive income, deficit, and cash flows for each of the years in the three-year period ended December 31, 2015. We also have audited Regal Entertainment Group's internal control over financial reporting as of December 31, 2015, based on criteria established in *Internal Control - Integrated Framework* (2013) issued by the Committee of Sponsoring Organizations of the Treadway Commission (COSO). Regal Entertainment Group's management is responsible for these consolidated financial statements, for maintaining effective internal control over financial reporting, and for its assessment of the effectiveness of internal control over financial reporting, included in the accompanying Management's Report on Internal Control over Financial Reporting. Our responsibility is to express an opinion on these consolidated financial statements and an opinion on the Company's internal control over financial reporting based on our audits.

We conducted our audits in accordance with the standards of the Public Company Accounting Oversight Board (United States). Those standards require that we plan and perform the audits to obtain reasonable assurance about whether the financial statements are free of material misstatement and whether effective internal control over financial reporting was maintained in all material respects. Our audits of the consolidated financial statements included examining, on a test basis, evidence supporting the amounts and disclosures in the financial statements, assessing the accounting principles used and significant estimates made by management, and evaluating the overall financial statement presentation. Our audit of internal control over financial reporting included obtaining an understanding of internal control over financial reporting, assessing the risk that a material weakness exists, and testing and evaluating the design and operating effectiveness of internal control based on the assessed risk. Our audits also included performing such other procedures as we considered necessary in the circumstances. We believe that our audits provide a reasonable basis for our opinions.

> **Audit followed the standards of the Public Company Accounting Oversight Board.**

A company's internal control over financial reporting is a process designed to provide reasonable assurance regarding the reliability of financial reporting and the preparation of financial statements for external purposes in accordance with generally accepted accounting principles. A company's internal control over financial reporting includes those policies and procedures that (1) pertain to the maintenance of records that, in reasonable detail, accurately and fairly reflect the transactions and dispositions of the assets of the company; (2) provide reasonable assurance that transactions are recorded as necessary to permit preparation of financial statements in accordance with generally accepted accounting principles, and that receipts and expenditures of the company are being made only in accordance with authorizations of management and directors of the company; and (3) provide reasonable assurance regarding prevention or timely detection of unauthorized acquisition, use, or disposition of the company's assets that could have a material effect on the financial statements.

Because of its inherent limitations, internal control over financial reporting may not prevent or detect misstatements. Also, projections of any evaluation of effectiveness to future periods are subject to the risk that controls may become inadequate because of changes in conditions, or that the degree of compliance with the policies or procedures may deteriorate.

In our opinion, the consolidated financial statements referred to above present fairly, in all material respects, the financial position of Regal Entertainment Group and subsidiaries as of December 31, 2015 and January 1, 2015, and the results of its operations and its cash flows for each of the years in the three-year period ended December 31, 2015, in conformity with U.S. generally accepted accounting principles. Also in our opinion, Regal Entertainment Group maintained, in all material respects, effective internal control over financial reporting as of December 31, 2015, based on criteria established in *Internal Control-Integrated Framework* (2013) issued by the Committee of Sponsoring Organizations of the Treadway Commission (COSO).

> **Auditors' opinion**

/s/ KPMG LLP
Knoxville, Tennessee
February 29, 2016

Source: Regal Entertainment Group, Form 10-K for the fiscal year ended December 31, 2015.

The Control Environment

Management's operating style will have a major impact on the effectiveness of various policies. An *autocratic* style, in which a few key officers tightly control operations, will result in an environment different from that of a *decentralized* organization, in which departments have more freedom to make decisions. Personnel policies and practices form another factor in the internal control of a business. An appropriate system for hiring competent employees and firing incompetent ones is crucial to an efficient operation. After all, no internal control system will work very well if employees who are dishonest or poorly trained are on the payroll. On the other hand, too few people doing too many tasks defeats the purpose of an internal control system. Finally, the effectiveness of internal control in a business is influenced by the board of directors, particularly its audit committee.

The Accounting System

Internal controls are important to all businesses, regardless of the degree of automation of the accounting system. An **accounting system** consists of all of the methods and records used to report an entity's transactions accurately and to maintain accountability for its assets and liabilities. An integral part of all accounting systems is the use of a journal to record transactions. However, refinements may be made to the basic components of the system. For example, most companies use specialized journals to record recurring transactions, such as sales of merchandise on credit.

An accounting system can be completely manual, fully computerized, or as is often the case, a mixture of the two. It must be capable of handling the volume and complexity of transactions entered into by a business.

Accounting system
Methods and records used to accurately report an entity's transactions and to maintain accountability for its assets and liabilities.

Internal Control Procedures

Management establishes policies and procedures on a number of different levels to ensure that corporate objectives will be met. Some procedures are formalized in writing, while others may not be written. Certain **administrative controls** within a company are more concerned with the efficient operation of the business and adherence to managerial policies than with the accurate reporting of financial information. For example, a company policy that requires all prospective employees to be interviewed by the personnel department is an administrative control. Other **accounting controls** primarily concern safeguarding assets and ensuring the reliability of the financial statements. Some of the most important internal control procedures are as follows:

LO4 Describe the basic internal control procedures.

Administrative controls
Procedures concerned with efficient operation of the business and adherence to managerial policies.

Accounting controls
Procedures concerned with safeguarding the assets or the reliability of the financial statements.

- Proper authorizations
- Segregation of duties
- Independent verification
- Safeguarding of assets and records
- Independent review and appraisal
- Design and use of business documents

Proper Authorizations Management grants specific departments the authority to perform various activities. Along with the *authority* comes *responsibility*. Most large organizations give the authority to hire new employees to the personnel department. Management authorizes the purchasing department to order goods and services for the company and the credit department to establish specific policies for granting credit to customers. By specifically authorizing certain individuals to carry out specific tasks for the business, management is able to hold those same people accountable for the outcome of their actions.

The authorizations for some transactions are general in nature; others are specific. For example, a cashier authorizes the sale of a book in a bookstore by ringing up the transaction (a general authorization). However, the bookstore manager's approval may be required before a book can be returned (a specific authorization).

Segregation of Duties *What might happen if one employee is given the authority to prepare checks and to sign them? What might happen if a single employee is allowed to order inventory and receive it from the shipper? Or what if the cashier at a checkout stand* *records the daily receipts in the journal?* If the employee in each of these situations is honest and never makes mistakes, nothing bad will happen. However, if the employee is dishonest or makes errors, the company can experience losses. Without segregation of duties, an employee is able not only to perpetrate a fraud but also to conceal it. A good system of internal control requires that the *physical custody* of assets be separated from the *accounting* for those same assets.

Like most internal control principles, the concept of segregation of duties is an ideal that is not always attainable. Many smaller businesses do not have adequate personnel to achieve complete segregation of key functions. In certain instances, these businesses need to rely on the direct involvement of the owners and on independent verification.

Independent Verification Independent verification means the work of one department should act as a check on the work of another. For example, the physical count of the inventory in a perpetual inventory system provides such a check. The accounting department maintains the general ledger card for inventory and updates it as sales and purchases are made. The physical count of the inventory by an independent department acts as the check on the work of the accounting department.

Or consider the bank reconciliation shown earlier in the chapter. The reconciliation of a company's bank account with the bank statement by someone not responsible for either the physical custody of cash or the cash records acts as an independent check on the work of these parties.

Safeguarding of Assets and Records Adequate safeguards must be in place to protect assets and the accounting records from losses of various kinds. Cash registers, safes, and lockboxes are important safeguards for cash. Secured storage areas with limited access are essential for the safekeeping of inventory. Protection of the accounting records against misuse is equally important. Access to a computerized accounting record should be limited to those employees authorized to prepare journal entries. This can be done with the use of a personal identification number and a password to access the system.

Independent Review and Appraisal A well-designed system of internal control provides for periodic review and appraisal of the accounting system as well as the people operating it. The group primarily responsible for review and appraisal of the system is the **internal audit staff**. Most large corporations have a full-time staff of internal auditors. They provide management with periodic reports on the effectiveness of the control system and the efficiency of operations.

The primary concern of the independent public accountants (or external auditors) is whether the financial statements have been presented fairly. Internal auditors focus more on the efficiency with which the organization is run. They are responsible for periodically reviewing both accounting and administrative controls. The internal audit staff also helps to ensure that the company's policies and procedures are followed.

Internal audit staff
The department responsible for monitoring and evaluating the internal control system.

Design and Use of Business Documents *Business documents* are the crucial link between economic transactions entered into by an entity and the accounting record of those events. They are often called *source documents* and may be generated by computer or completed manually. The source document for the recognition of the expense of an employee's wages is the time card. The source documents for a sale include the sales order, the sales invoice, and the related shipping document. Business documents must be designed to capture all relevant information about an economic event and to ensure that related transactions are properly classified.

Business documents must be properly controlled. For example, a key feature for documents is a *sequential numbering system* just like you have for your personal checks. This system results in a complete accounting for all documents in the series and negates the opportunity for an employee to misdirect one. Another key feature of well-designed business documents is the use of *multiple copies.* The various departments involved in a particular activity, such as sales or purchasing, are kept informed of the status of outstanding orders through the use of copies of documents.

Limitations on Internal Control

No system of internal control is totally foolproof. An entity's size affects the degree of control that it can obtain. In general, large organizations are able to devote a substantial amount of resources to safeguarding assets and records. Because the installation and maintenance of controls can be costly, an internal audit staff is a luxury that many small businesses cannot afford. The mere segregation of duties can result in added costs if two employees must be involved in a task previously performed by only one.

CONNECT TO THE REAL WORLD

PANERA BREAD
READING THE MANAGEMENT'S REPORT

6-2 Refer to page C-39 in Appendix C for Management's Report on Internal Control over Financial Reporting for Panera Bread. Where does management discuss limitations on internal control? Why are there risks in making any projections about the effectiveness of controls in the future? *(See answers on p. 308.)*

Segregation of duties can be effective in preventing collusion, but no system of internal control can ensure that it will not happen. It does no good to have one employee count the cash at the end of the day and another to record it if the two act in concert to steal from the company. Rotation of duties can help lessen the likelihood of such problems. An employee is less likely to collude with someone to steal if the assignment is a temporary one. Another control feature, a system of authorizations, is meaningless if management continually overrides or fails to support it.

Human errors can weaken a system of internal control. Misunderstood instructions, carelessness, fatigue, and distraction can all lead to errors. A well-designed internal control system should result in the best possible people being hired to perform the various tasks.

Computerized Business Documents and Internal Control

In addition to separating the custodianship of cash from its recording in the accounts, two other fundamental principles apply to its control. **First, all cash receipts should be deposited intact in the bank on a daily basis.** *Intact* means that no disbursements should be made from the cash received from customers. Second, **all cash disbursements should be made by check.** Using sequentially numbered checks results in a clear record of all disbursements. The only exception to this rule is the use of a petty cash fund to make cash disbursements for minor expenditures such as postage stamps and repairs.

LO5 Describe the various documents used in recording purchases and their role in controlling cash disbursements.

Control Over Cash Receipts

Most merchandisers receive checks and currency from customers in two ways: (1) cash received over the counter from cash sales and (2) cash received in the mail from credit sales. Each type of cash receipt poses its own control problems.

Cash Received Over the Counter
Several control mechanisms are used to handle these cash receipts.

- First, cash registers allow the customer to see the display, which deters the salesclerk from ringing up a sale for less than the amount received from the customer and pocketing the difference.
- A locked-in cash register tape is another control feature. At various times during the day, an employee other than the clerk unlocks the register, removes the tape, and forwards it to the accounting department. At the end of the shift, the salesclerk remits the coin and currency from the register to a central cashier. Any difference between the amount of cash remitted to the cashier and the amount on the tape submitted to the accounting department is investigated.
- Finally, prenumbered customer receipts, prepared in duplicate, are a useful control mechanism. The customer is given a copy, and the salesclerk retains another. The salesclerk is accountable for all numbers in a specific series of receipts and must be able to explain any differences between the amount of cash remitted to the cashier and the amount collected per the receipts.

Cash Received in the Mail Most customers send checks rather than currency through the mail. Any form of cash received in the mail from customers should be applied to their account balances. The customer wants assurance that the account is appropriately reduced for the amount of the payment. The company must be assured that all cash received is deposited in the bank and that the account receivable is reduced accordingly.

To achieve a reasonable degree of control, two employees should be present when the mail is opened.[1]

1. The first employee opens the mail in the presence of the second employee, counts the money received, and prepares a control list of the amount received on that particular day.
2. The second employee takes the original list and the cash to the cashier, who makes the bank deposit.
3. One copy of the list is forwarded to the accounting department to be used as the basis for recording the increase in Cash and the decrease in Accounts Receivable.
4. The other copy is retained by one of the two people who opens the mail.
5. A comparison of the list to the bank deposit slip is a timely way to detect receipts that do not make it to the bank.
6. Because the two employees acting in concert could circumvent the control process, rotation of duties is important.

Monthly customer statements act as an additional control device for customer payments received in the mail. Assume that the two employees responsible for opening the mail and remitting checks to the cashier decide to pocket a check received from a customer. Because the check is not remitted to the cashier, the accounting department will not be notified to reduce the customer's account for the payment. The monthly statement, however, should alert the customer to the problem. At this point, the customer should ask the company to investigate the discrepancy. As evidence of its payment on account, the customer will be able to point to a canceled check—which was cashed by the unscrupulous employees.

The use of customer statements as a control device will be effective only if the employees responsible for the custody of cash received through the mail, for record keeping, and for authorization of adjustments to customers' accounts are not allowed to prepare and mail statements to customers. Employees allowed to do so are in a position to alter customers' statements.

Cash Discrepancies Discrepancies occur occasionally due to theft by dishonest employees and to human error. For example, if a salesclerk intentionally or unintentionally gives the wrong amount of change, the amount remitted to the cashier will not agree with the cash register tape. Any material differences should be investigated.

Of particular significance are *recurring* differences between the amount remitted by any one cashier and the amount on the cash register tape.

The Role of Computerized Business Documents in Controlling Cash Disbursements

A company makes cash payments to purchase merchandise and supplies, to pay operating expenditures, and to cover payroll expenses. We will concentrate on the disbursement of cash to purchase goods for resale, focusing particularly on the role of business documents in the process. Suppliers must be paid on time so that companies can continue to make goods available for resale to customers.

The following example begins with a requisition for merchandise by Mickey's Marathon Sports, continues through the receipt of the goods, and concludes with the eventual payment to the supplier. The entire process is summarized in Exhibit 6-5.

Purchase Requisition The shoe department at Mickey's Marathon Sports reviews its stock weekly to determine if any items need replenishing. On the basis of its

---

[1] In some companies, this control procedure may be omitted because of the cost of having two employees present when the mail is opened.

EXHIBIT 6-5 Document Flow for the Purchasing Function

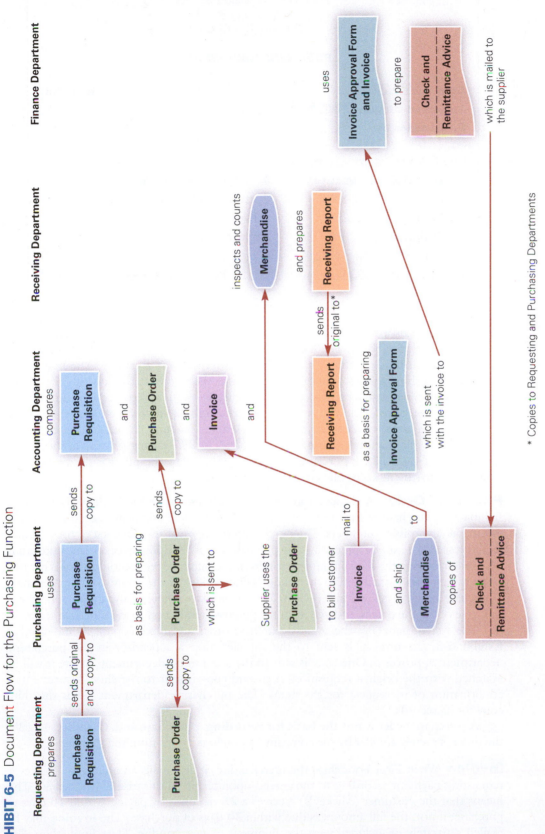

EXHIBIT 6-6 Purchase Requisition

```
┌──────────────────────────────────────────────────────────────┐
│                    Mickey's Marathon Sports                     │
│                        502 Dodge St.                            │
│                      Chicago, IL 66666                          │
│                                                                 │
│                    PURCHASE REQUISITION                         │
│                                                                 │
│   Date    5/28/17                              PR 75638         │
│   Preferred vendor   Fleet Foot                                 │
│   Date needed by     6/5/17                                     │
│                                                                 │
│   The following items are requested for   weekly dept. order    │
│                                                                 │
│       Item No.      Quantity      Description/Vendor No.        │
│       314627        24 PR         Sprinter/5265                 │
│       323515        12 PR         Blazer/7512                   │
│       323682        6 PR          Enduros/1580                  │
│                                                                 │
│   Requested by   Joe Smith      Department  Shoe department     │
└──────────────────────────────────────────────────────────────┘
```

Purchase requisition form
A form a department uses to initiate a request to order merchandise.

needs, the supervisor of the shoe department fills out the **purchase requisition form** shown in Exhibit 6-6 above. The form indicates the supplier or vendor, Fleet Foot.

The purchasing department makes the final decision on a vendor. The purchasing department is thus held accountable for acquiring the goods at the lowest price, given certain standards for merchandise quality. Mickey's assigns a separate item number to each of the thousands of individual items of merchandise it stocks. Note that the requisition also indicates the vendor's number for each item. The unit of measure for each item is indicated in the quantity column. For example, "24 PR" means 24 pairs of shoes. The original and a copy of the purchase requisition are sent to the purchasing department. The shoe department keeps one copy for its records.

Purchase order
A form sent by the purchasing department to the supplier.

Purchase Order A computer-generated **purchase order** for Mickey's is shown in Exhibit 6-7. Purchase orders are usually prenumbered, and a company should periodically investigate any missing numbers. The purchasing department uses its copy of the purchase requisition as a basis for preparing the purchase order. An employee in the purchasing department keys in the relevant information from the purchase requisition and adds the unit cost for each item gathered from the vendor's price guide. The software program generates a purchase order, as shown in Exhibit 6-7. You should trace all of the information for at least one of the three items ordered from the purchase requisition to the purchase order.

The system generates the original purchase order and three copies. As indicated in Exhibit 6-5, the original is sent to the supplier after a supervisor in the purchasing department approves it. One copy is sent to the accounting department, where it will be matched with the original requisition. A second copy is sent to the shoe department as confirmation of its request for the items. The purchasing department keeps the third copy for its records.

A purchase order is not the basis for recording a purchase and a liability. Legally, the order is merely an offer by the company to purchase goods from the supplier.

Invoice
A form sent by the seller to the buyer as evidence of a sale.

Alternate terms: Purchase invoice, Sales invoice.

Invoice When Fleet Foot ships the merchandise, it also mails an invoice to Mickey's, requesting payment according to the agreed-upon terms, in this case 2/10, net 30. This means that the customer (Mickey's) receives a 2% discount by paying within 10 days of purchase; if not, the full amount is due within 30 days of purchase. The **invoice** may be mailed separately or included with the shipment of merchandise. Fleet Foot, the seller, calls this document a *sales invoice*; it is the basis for recording a sale and an account

EXHIBIT 6-7 Computer-Generated Purchase Order

```
                          Mickey's Marathon Sports
                              502 Dodge St.
                            Chicago, IL 66666

                             PURCHASE ORDER

TO:                                                    PO 54296

Fleet Foot
590 West St.
Milwaukee, WI 77777

Date 5/30/17    Ship by    Best Express    Instructions  FOB destination point
Terms 2/10, net 30                         Date required 6/5/17


Item No.  Quantity  Description/Vendor No.      Unit price      Amount
314627    24 PR     Sprinter/5265               $60.50       $1,452.00
323515    12 PR     Blazer/7512                  53.70          644.40
323682     6 PR     Enduros/1580                 75.40          452.40
                                                             $2,548.80


Approved by   Mary Jones
```

receivable. Mickey's, the buyer, calls the same document a *purchase invoice*, which is the basis for recording a purchase and an account payable. The invoice that Fleet Foot sent to Mickey's accounting department is shown in Exhibit 6-8.

Receiving Report The accounting department receives the invoice for the three items ordered. Within a few days before or after the receipt of the invoice, the merchandise arrives at Mickey's warehouse. As soon as the items are unpacked, the receiving

EXHIBIT 6-8 Invoice

```
                                                    NO. 427953

                              Fleet Foot
                             590 West St.
                           Milwaukee, WI 77777

                               INVOICE

Sold to  Mickey's Marathon Sports    Date        6/2/17
         502 Dodge St.               Order No.   54296
         Chicago, IL 66666           Shipped via  Best Express
Ship to  Same                        Date shipped 6/2/17
Terms    2/10, net 30                Ship terms   FOB destination


Quantity  Description/No.          Price          Amount
24 PR     Sprinter/5265            $60.50       $1,452.00
12 PR     Blazer/7512               53.70          644.40
 6 PR     Enduros/1580              75.40          452.40
                                                $2,548.80
```

EXHIBIT 6-9 Computer-Generated Receiving Report

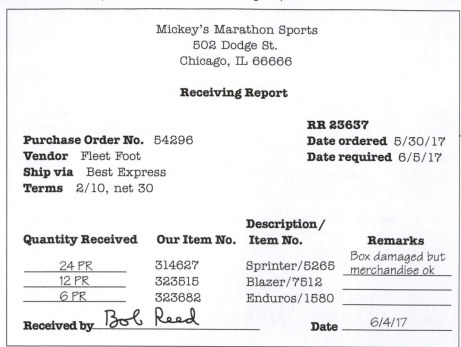

department inspects and counts them. The same software used to generate the purchase order also generates a receiving report, as shown in Exhibit 6-9.

Mickey's uses a **blind receiving report**. The column for the quantity received is left blank and is filled in by the receiving department. Rather than simply being able to indicate that the number ordered was received, an employee must count the pairs of shoes to determine that the number ordered is actually received.

The accounting system generates an original receiving report and three copies. The receiving department keeps one copy for its records and sends the original to the accounting department. One copy is sent to the purchasing department to be matched with the purchase order, and the other copy is sent to the shoe department as verification that the items it originally requested have been received.

Invoice Approval Form Mickey's accounting department has copies of the purchase requisition from the shoe department, the purchase order from the purchasing department, the invoice from the supplier, and the receiving report from the warehouse. The accounting department uses an **invoice approval form** to document the accuracy of the information on each of these other forms. The invoice approval form for Mickey's Marathon Sports is shown in Exhibit 6-10. Some businesses do not use a separate invoice approval form, but simply note approval directly on the invoice.

The invoice is compared to the purchase requisition to ensure that the company is billed for goods that it requested. A comparison of the invoice with the purchase order ensures that the goods were in fact ordered. Finally, the receiving report is compared with the invoice to verify that all goods for which the company is being billed were received. An accounting department employee must also verify the mathematical accuracy of the amounts that appear on the invoice. The date the invoice must be paid to take advantage of the discount is noted so that the finance department will be sure to send the check by this date. At this point, the accounting department prepares the journal entry to increase the inventory and accounts payable accounts. The invoice approval form and the invoice are then sent to the finance department. Some businesses call the invoice approval form a voucher, which is used for all expenditures, not just for purchases of merchandise.

Check with Remittance Advice Mickey's finance department is responsible for issuing checks. This results from the need to segregate custody of cash (the signed check) from record keeping (the updating of the ledger). Upon receipt of the invoice

Blind receiving report
A form used by the receiving department to account for the quantity and condition of merchandise received from a supplier.

Invoice approval form
A form the accounting department uses before making payment to document the accuracy of all information about a purchase.
Alternate term: Voucher.

EXHIBIT 6-10 Invoice Approval Form

Mickey's Marathon Sports
502 Dodge St.
Chicago, IL 66666

Invoice Approval Form

	No.	**Check**
Purchase Requisition	PR 75638	✔
Purchase Order	PO 54296	✔
Receiving Report	RR 23637	✔

Invoice:

No.	427953
Date	6/2/17
Price	✔
Extensions	✔
Footings	✔

Last Day to Pay for Discount   6/2/17

Approved for Payment by   _Alice Johnson_

approval form from the accounting department, a clerk in the finance department processes a check with a remittance advice attached, as shown in Exhibit 6-11.[2] Before the check is signed, the documents referred to on the invoice approval form are reviewed and

EXHIBIT 6-11 Check with Remittance Advice

3690

Mickey's Marathon Sports
502 Dodge St.
Chicago, IL 66666   June 12   2017

PAY TO THE
ORDER OF _____Fleet Foot_____ $2,497.82

Two thousand four hundred ninety seven and 82/100   DOLLARS

Second National Bank

Chicago, IL

3690 035932 9321   _John B. Martin_

Purchase Order No.	Invoice No.	Invoice Date	Description	Amount
PO 54296	427953	6/2/17	24 PR Sprinter	$1,452.00
			12 PR Blazer	644.40
			6 PR Enduros	452.40
			Total	$2,548.80
			2% discount	(50.98)
			Net remitted	$2,497.82

---

[2] In some companies, an employee in the accounting department prepares checks and sends them to the finance department for review and signature. Most companies use computer-generated checks rather than manually typed ones.

canceled to prevent reuse. The clerk then forwards the check to one of the company officers authorized to sign checks. According to one of Mickey's internal control policies, only the treasurer and the assistant treasurer are authorized to sign checks. Both officers must sign check amounts above a specified dollar limit. To maintain separation of duties, the finance department should mail the check. The remittance advice informs the supplier as to the nature of the payment.

MODULE 2 TEST YOURSELF

Review		
	LO3 Explain the importance of internal control to a business and the significance of the Sarbanes-Oxley Act of 2002.	• The Sarbanes-Oxley Act of 2002 required publicly traded companies to improve the documentation and functioning of their internal controls. • Management must now render an opinion on the efficiency of the company's internal control system. A strong control environment is a must for companies. • Auditors also must increase their documentation and understanding of the internal controls of their clients. • Significant amounts of resources have been devoted to comply with the provisions of Sarbanes-Oxley.
	LO4 Describe the basic internal control procedures.	• Control procedures are actions that company personnel take to make sure that policies set forth by management are followed. • Important accounting controls are concerned with safeguarding assets and producing accurate and timely financial statements. They include: • Proper authorizations—only certain personnel may authorize transactions. • Segregation of duties—physical custody of assets must not be combined with the ability to account for those assets. • Independent verification—for example, an inventory count. • Safeguarding of assets and records—both must be adequately protected. • Independent review and appraisal—done primarily by internal audit. • Design and use of business documents—source document control.
	LO5 Describe the various documents used in recording purchases and their role in controlling cash disbursements.	• The documents used to record purchase transactions are instrumental in controlling both cash and inventory. • The document flow diagram in Exhibit 6-5 provides an excellent summary of documents in the purchasing process. Some of the key documents are as follows: • Purchase order • Receiving report • Vendor invoice • Check

Question	
	1. What circumstances led to the passage of the Sarbanes-Oxley Act in 2002?
	2. An order clerk fills out a purchase requisition for an expensive item of inventory and the receiving report when the merchandise arrives. The clerk takes the inventory home, then sends the invoice to the accounting department so that the supplier will be paid. What basic internal control procedure could have prevented this misuse of company assets?
	3. What two basic procedures are essential to an effective system of internal control over cash?
	4. What is the purpose of comparing a purchase invoice with a purchase order? of comparing a receiving report with a purchase invoice?

1. Provide answers to each of the following questions.
    a. Who is responsible for establishing and maintaining an adequate internal control structure for a company?
    b. Who provides an independent opinion as to whether management has maintained effective internal control over financial reporting?
    c. To whom should the independent auditors' report be directed?
    d. Which committee of the board of directors provides direct contact between stockholders and the independent accounting firm?

Apply

2. List the internal control procedures discussed in the text.

3. Number each of the following documents to indicate the order in which each document would be used.
    _____ Purchase order
    _____ Invoice approval form
    _____ Check and remittance advice
    _____ Purchase requisition
    _____ Invoice
    _____ Receiving report

Answers are located at the end of the chapter.

ACCOUNTS HIGHLIGHTED

Account Titles	Where It Appears	In What Section	Page Number
Cash and Cash Equivalents	Balance Sheet	Current Assets	278
Petty Cash Fund	Balance Sheet	Current Assets	283

KEY TERMS QUIZ

Read each definition below and write the number of the definition in the blank beside the appropriate term. The quiz solutions appear at the end of the chapter.

_____ Cash equivalent
_____ Bank statement
_____ Outstanding check
_____ Deposit in transit
_____ Bank reconciliation
_____ Credit memoranda
_____ Debit memoranda
_____ Petty cash fund
_____ Internal control system
_____ Sarbanes-Oxley Act
_____ Internal control report
_____ Public Company Accounting Oversight Board (PCAOB)

_____ Board of directors
_____ Audit committee
_____ Accounting system
_____ Administrative controls
_____ Accounting controls
_____ Internal audit staff
_____ Purchase requisition form
_____ Purchase order
_____ Invoice
_____ Blind receiving report
_____ Invoice approval form

1. A form sent by the seller to the buyer as evidence of a sale.
2. A group composed of key officers of a corporation and outside members responsible for general oversight of the affairs of the entity.
3. Policies and procedures necessary to ensure the safeguarding of an entity's assets, the reliability of its accounting records, and the accomplishment of overall company objectives.

4. Procedures concerned with safeguarding the assets or the reliability of the financial statements.
5. A form a department uses to initiate a request to order merchandise.
6. A form the accounting department uses before making payment to document the accuracy of all information about a purchase.
7. A form used by the accountant to reconcile or resolve any differences between the balance shown on the bank statement for a particular account with the balance shown in the accounting records.
8. An investment that is readily convertible to a known amount of cash and has an original maturity to the investor of three months or less.
9. Deductions on a bank statement for items such as NSF checks and various service charges.
10. A check written by a company but not yet presented to the bank for payment.
11. A detailed list, provided by the bank, of all activity for a particular account during the month.
12. A report required by Section 404 of the Sarbanes-Oxley Act to be included in a company's annual report in which management assesses the effectiveness of the internal control structure.
13. A deposit recorded on the books but not yet reflected on the bank statement.
14. Methods and records used to accurately report an entity's transactions and to maintain accountability for its assets and liabilities.
15. Additions on a bank statement for such items as interest paid on the account and notes collected by the bank for the customer.
16. A board of directors subset that acts as a direct contact between the stockholders and the independent accounting firm.
17. Money kept on hand for making minor disbursements in coin and currency rather than by writing checks.
18. The five-member body created by the Sarbanes-Oxley Act that was given the authority to set auditing standards in the United States.
19. A form used by the receiving department to account for the quantity and condition of merchandise received from a supplier.
20. Procedures concerned with efficient operation of the business and adherence to managerial policies.
21. A form sent by the purchasing department to the supplier.
22. An act of Congress in 2002 intended to bring reform to corporate accountability and stewardship in the wake of a number of major corporate scandals.
23. The department responsible for monitoring and evaluating the internal control system.

ALTERNATE TERMS

invoice purchase invoice, sales invoice   **invoice approval form** voucher

REVIEW PROBLEM & SOLUTION

The following information is available for McCarthy Corp. on June 30:

a. The balance in cash as reported on the June 30 bank statement is $5,654.98.
b. McCarthy made a deposit of $865 on June 30 that is not included on the bank statement.
c. A comparison between the canceled checks returned with the bank statement and McCarthy's records indicated that two checks had not yet been returned to the bank for payment. The amounts of the two checks were $236.77 and $116.80.
d. The Cash account on the company's books reported a balance on June 30 of $4,165.66.
e. McCarthy rents some excess storage space in one of its warehouses, and the tenant pays its monthly rent directly to the bank for deposit in McCarthy's account. The bank statement indicates that a deposit of $1,500 was made during the month of June.
f. Interest earned on the checking account and added to McCarthy's account during June was $11.75.

g. Bank service charges were $15 for the month of June as reported on the bank statement.

h. A comparison between the checks returned with the bank statement and the company's records revealed that a check written by the company in the amount of $56 was recorded by the company erroneously as a check for $560.

Required

Prepare a bank reconciliation for the month of June in good form.

Solution to Review Problem

McCarthy Corp.
Bank Reconciliation
June 30

Balance per bank statement, June 30		$5,654.98
Add: Deposit in transit		865.00
Deduct: Outstanding checks:	$ 236.77	
	116.80	(353.57)
Adjusted balance, June 30		$6,166.41
Balance per books, June 30		$4,165.66
Add: Tenant's rent collected by bank	$1,500.00	
Interest earned on checking account	11.75	
Error in recording check	504.00	2,015.75
Deduct: Bank service charges		(15.00)
Adjusted balance, June 30		$6,166.41

EXERCISES

Exercise 6-1 Cash Equivalents

LO1
EXAMPLE 6-1

Systematic Enterprises invested its excess cash in the following instruments during December 2017:

Certificate of deposit, due January 31, 2020	$ 75,000
Certificate of deposit, due March 30, 2018	150,000
Commercial paper, original maturity date February 28, 2018	125,000
Deposit into a money market fund	25,000
Investment in stock	65,000
90-day Treasury bills	100,000
Treasury note, due December 1, 2047	500,000

Show me how

Required

Determine the amount of cash equivalents that should be combined with cash on the company's balance sheet at December 31, 2017, and for purposes of preparing a statement of cash flows for the year ended December 31, 2017.

Exercise 6-2 Cash and Cash Equivalents and the Statement of Cash Flows

LO1

Bedford Corp. began the year with $15,000 in cash and another $8,500 in cash equivalents. During the year, operations generated $140,000 in cash. Net cash used in investing activities during the year was $210,000, and the company raised a net amount of $180,000 from financing activities.

Required

Determine the year-end balance in cash and cash equivalents.

LO2

EXAMPLE 6-2

Exercise 6-3 Items on a Bank Reconciliation

Assume that a company is preparing a bank reconciliation for the month of June. It reconciles the bank balance and the book balance to the correct balance. For each of the following items, indicate whether the item is an addition to the bank balance (A-Bank), an addition to the book balance (A-Book), a deduction from the bank balance (D-Bank), a deduction from the book balance (D-Book), or would not appear on the June reconciliation (NA). Also, write ADJ next to your answer for any items that will require an adjustment on the company's books.

_____ 1. Check written in June but not yet returned to the bank for payment
_____ 2. Customer's NSF check
_____ 3. Customer's check written in the amount of $54 but recorded on the books in the amount of $45*
_____ 4. Service charge for new checks
_____ 5. Principal and interest on a customer's note collected for the company by the bank
_____ 6. Customer's check deposited on June 30 but not reflected on the bank statement
_____ 7. Check written on the company's account, paid by the bank, and returned with the bank statement
_____ 8. Check written on the company's account for $123 but recorded on the books as $132*
_____ 9. Interest on the checking account for the month of June

*Answer in terms of the adjustment needed to correct for the error.

LO2

EXAMPLE 6-2

Exercise 6-4 Working Backward: Bank Reconciliation

Dexter Company's bank reconciliation shows an adjusted cash balance of $3,254.33. The following items also appear on the reconciliation:

NSF check	$110.50
Deposit in transit	332.10
Interest earned	65.42
Outstanding checks	560.55
Bank service charges	30.00

Required

1. Determine the balance on the bank statement prior to adjustment.
2. Determine the balance on the books prior to adjustment.

LO4

Exercise 6-5 Internal Control

The university drama club is planning a raffle. The president overheard you talking about internal control to another accounting student, so she asked you to set up some guidelines to "make sure" that all money collected for the raffle is accounted for by the club.

Required

1. Describe guidelines that the club should follow to achieve an acceptable level of internal control.
2. Comment on the president's request that she "be sure" all money is collected and recorded.

LO4

Exercise 6-6 Segregation of Duties

The following tasks are performed by three employees, each of whom is capable of performing all of the tasks. Do not be concerned with the time required to perform the tasks, but with the need to provide for segregation of duties. Assign the duties by using a check mark to indicate which employee should perform each task. You can assign any one of the tasks to any of the employees.

Task	Employee		
	Mary	Sue	John
Prepare invoices			
Mail invoices			
Pick up mail from post office			
Open mail, separate checks			
List checks on deposit slip in triplicate			
Post payment to customer's account			
Deposit checks			
Prepare monthly schedule of accounts receivable			
Reconcile bank statements			

MULTI-CONCEPT EXERCISE

Exercise 6-7   Composition of Cash

LO1 • 2

EXAMPLE 6-1, 6-2

Using Y for yes and N for no, indicate whether each of the following items should be included in cash and cash equivalents on the balance sheet. If an item should not be included in cash and cash equivalents, indicate where it should appear on the balance sheet.

_____   1. Checking account at Third County Bank

_____   2. Petty cash fund

_____   3. Coin and currency

_____   4. Postage stamps

_____   5. An IOU from an employee

_____   6. Savings account at Ft. Worth Savings & Loan

_____   7. A six-month CD

_____   8. Undeposited customer checks

_____   9. A customer's check returned by the bank and marked NSF

_____   10. Sixty-day U.S. Treasury bills

_____   11. A cashier's check

PROBLEMS

Problem 6-1   Bank Reconciliation

LO2

The following information is available to assist you in preparing a bank reconciliation for Calico Corners on May 31:

a. The balance on the May 31 bank statement is $8,432.11.

b. Not included on the bank statement is a $1,250 deposit made by Calico Corners late on May 31.

c. A comparison between the canceled checks returned with the bank statement and the company records indicated that the following checks are outstanding at May 31:

No. 123	$ 23.40
No. 127	145.00
No. 128	210.80
No. 130	67.32

d. The Cash account on the company's books shows a balance of $9,965.34.

e. The bank acts as a collection agency for interest earned on some municipal bonds held by Calico Corners. The May bank statement indicates interest of $465.00 earned during the month.

f. Interest earned on the checking account and added to Calico Corners' account during May was $54.60. Miscellaneous bank service charges amounted to $50.00.

g. A customer's NSF check in the amount of $166.00 was returned with the May bank statement.

h. A comparison between the deposits listed on the bank statement and the company's books revealed that a customer's check in the amount of $123.45 was recorded on the books during May but was never added to the company's account. The bank erroneously added the check to the account of Calico Closet, which has an account at the same bank.

(*Continued*)

i. The comparison of deposits per the bank statement with those per the books revealed that another customer's check in the amount of $101.10 was correctly added to the company's account. In recording the check on the company's books, however, the accountant erroneously increased the Cash account by $1,011.00.

Required

1. Prepare a bank reconciliation in good form.
2. A friend says to you: "I don't know why companies bother to prepare bank reconciliations—it seems a waste of time. Why don't they just do like I do and adjust the Cash account for any difference between what the bank shows as a balance and what shows up in the books?" Explain to your friend why a bank reconciliation should be prepared as soon as a bank statement is received.

LO4 **Problem 6-2 Internal Control Procedures**

You are opening a summer business, a chain of three drive-through snow-cone stands. You have hired other college students to work and have purchased a cash register with locked-in tapes. You retain one key, and the other is available to the lead person on each shift.

Required

1. Write a list of the procedures for all employees to follow when ringing up sales and giving change.
2. Write a list of the procedures for the lead person to follow in closing out at the end of the day. Be specific so that employees will have few if any questions.
3. What is your main concern in the design of internal control for the snow-cone stands? How did you address that concern? Be specific.

LO5 **Problem 6-3 The Design of Internal Control Documents**

Motel $49.99 has purchased a large warehouse to store all supplies used by housekeeping departments in the company's expanding chain of motels. In the past, each motel bought supplies from local distributors and paid for the supplies from cash receipts.

Required

1. Name some potential problems with the old system.
2. Design a purchase requisition form and a receiving report to be used by the housekeeping departments and the warehouse. Indicate how many copies of each form should be used and who should receive each copy.

MULTI-CONCEPT PROBLEMS

LO1 • 2 **Problem 6-4 Cash and Liquid Assets on the Balance Sheet**

The following current assets are listed in a company's general ledger. The accountant wants to place the items in order of liquidity on the balance sheet.

Accounts Receivable
Certificates of Deposit (six months)
Investment in Stock
Prepaid Rent
Money Market Fund
Petty Cash Fund

Required

Rank the accounts in terms of liquidity. Identify items to be included in the total of cash and cash equivalents and explain why the items not included are not as liquid. Explain how these items should be classified.

Problem 6-5 Internal Control

LO3 • 4

At Morris Mart Inc., all sales are on account. Mary Morris-Manning is responsible for mailing invoices to customers, recording the amount billed, opening mail, and recording the payment. Mary is very devoted to the family business and never takes off more than one or two days for a long weekend. The customers know Mary and sometimes send personal notes with their payments. Another clerk handles all aspects of accounts payable. Mary's brother, who is president of Morris Mart, has hired an accountant to help with expansion.

Required

1. List some problems with the current accounts receivable system.
2. What suggestions would you make to improve internal control?
3. How would you explain to Mary that she personally is not the problem?

ALTERNATE PROBLEMS

Problem 6-1A Bank Reconciliation

LO2

The following information is available to assist you in preparing a bank reconciliation for Karen's Catering on March 31:

a. The balance on the March 31 bank statement is $6,506.10.
b. Not included on the bank statement is a $423 deposit made by Karen's late on March 31.
c. A comparison between the canceled checks listed on the bank statement and the company records indicated that the following checks are outstanding at March 31:

No. 112	$ 42.92
No. 117	307.00
No. 120	10.58
No. 122	75.67

d. The bank acts as a collection agency for checks returned for insufficient funds. The March bank statement indicates that one such check in the amount of $45.00 was collected and deposited and a collection fee of $4.50 was charged.
e. Interest earned on the checking account and added to Karen's account during March was $4.30. Miscellaneous bank service charges amounted to $22.
f. A comparison between the deposits listed on the bank statement and the company's books revealed that a customer's check in the amount of $1,250 appears on the bank statement in March but was never added to the customer's account on the company's books.
g. The comparison of checks cleared per the bank statement with those per the books revealed that the wrong amount was charged to the company's account for a check. The amount of the check was $990. The proof machine encoded the check in the amount of $909, the amount charged against the company's account.

Required

1. Determine the balance on the books before any adjustments as well as the corrected balance to be reported on the balance sheet.
2. What would you recommend Karen's do as a result of the bank error in (g)? Why?

Problem 6-2A Internal Control Procedures

LO4

The loan department in a bank is subject to regulation. Internal auditors work for the bank to ensure that the loan department complies with requirements. The internal auditors must verify that each car loan file has a note signed by the maker, verification of insurance, and a title issued by the state that names the bank as co-owner.

(Continued)

Required

1. Explain why the bank and the regulatory agency are concerned with these documents.
2. Describe the internal control procedures that should be in place to ensure that these documents are obtained and safeguarded.

LO5   **Problem 6-3A The Design of Internal Control Documents**

Tiger's Group is a newly formed company that produces and sells children's movies about an imaginary character. The movies are in such great demand that they are shipped to retail outlets as soon as they are produced. The company must pay a royalty to several actors for each movie that it sells to retail outlets.

Required

1. Describe some internal control features that should be in place to ensure that all royalties are paid to the actors.
2. Design the shipping form that Tiger's Group should use for the movies. Make sure you include authorizations and indicate the number of copies and the routing of the copies.

ALTERNATE MULTI-CONCEPT PROBLEMS

LO1 • 2   **Problem 6-4A Cash and Liquid Assets on the Balance Sheet**

The following current assets are listed in a company's general ledger:

	December 31, 2017	December 31, 2016
Accounts Receivable	$12,300	$10,000
Certificates of Deposit (three months)	10,000	10,000
Marketable Securities	4,500	4,000
Petty Cash Fund	1,200	1,500
Money Market Fund	25,800	28,000
Cash in Checking Account	6,000	6,000

Required

1. Which items are cash equivalents?
2. Explain where items that are not cash equivalents should be classified on the balance sheet.
3. What are the amount and the direction of change in cash and cash equivalents for 2017? Is the company as liquid at the end of 2017 as it was at the end of 2016? Explain your answer.

LO3 • 4   **Problem 6-5A Internal Control**

Abbott Inc. is expanding and needs to hire more personnel in the accounting office. Barbara Barker, the chief accounting clerk, knew that her cousin Cheryl was looking for a job. Barbara and Cheryl are also roommates. Barbara offered Cheryl a job as her assistant. Barbara will be responsible for Cheryl's performance reviews and training.

Required

1. List some problems with the proposed personnel situations in the accounting department.
2. Explain why accountants are concerned with the hiring of personnel. What suggestions would you make to improve internal control at Abbott?
3. How would you explain to Barbara and Cheryl that they personally are not the problem?

DECISION CASES

Reading and Interpreting Financial Statements

Decision Case 6-1 Comparing Two Companies in the Same Industry: Chipotle and Panera Bread

Refer to the financial information for **Chipotle** and **Panera Bread** reproduced at the back of this book.

Required

1. What is the balance in Cash and cash equivalents on the balance sheet of each company at the end of the most recent year? What is the amount of increase or decrease in this balance from the end of the prior year?
2. On what other statement in each company's annual report does the increase or decrease in Cash and cash equivalents appear? Explain why it appears on this statement.
3. According to the notes to their financial statements, how does each company define "Cash and cash equivalents"? Are there any differences in their definitions?

Decision Case 6-2 Reading and Interpreting IBM's Report of Management

IBM's Form 10-K for the year ended December 31, 2015, includes the following section from its Report of Management found on page 74:

Management Responsibility for Financial Information
Responsibility for the integrity and objectivity of the financial information presented in this Annual Report rests with IBM management. The accompanying financial statements have been prepared in accordance with accounting principles generally accepted in the United States of America, applying certain estimates and judgments as required.

IBM maintains an effective internal control structure. It consists, in part, of organizational arrangements with clearly defined lines of responsibility and delegation of authority, and comprehensive systems and control procedures. An important element of the control environment is an ongoing internal audit program. Our system also contains self-monitoring mechanisms, and actions are taken to correct deficiencies as they are identified.

To assure the effective administration of internal controls, we carefully select and train our employees, develop and disseminate written policies and procedures, provide appropriate communication channels and foster an environment conducive to the effective functioning of controls. We believe that it is essential for the company to conduct its business affairs in accordance with the highest ethical standards, as set forth in the IBM Business Conduct Guidelines. These guidelines, translated into numerous languages, are distributed to employees throughout the world, and reemphasized through internal programs to assure that they are understood and followed.

The Audit Committee of the Board of Directors is composed solely of independent, non-management directors, and is responsible for recommending to the Board the independent registered public accounting firm to be retained for the coming year, subject to stockholder ratification. The Audit Committee meets periodically and privately with the independent registered public accounting firm, with the company's internal auditors, as well as with IBM management, to review accounting, auditing, internal control structure and financial reporting matters.

Required

1. Describe the main components of IBM's internal control structure.
2. What is the composition of IBM's Audit Committee? Describe its role.

Making Financial Decisions

Decision Case 6-3 Liquidity

R Montague and J Capulet distribute films to movie theatres. Following are the current assets for each distributor at the end of the year. (All amounts are in millions of dollars.)

(Continued)

	R Montague	J Capulet
Cash	$10	$ 5
Six-month certificates of deposit	9	0
Short-term investments in stock	0	6
Accounts receivable	15	23
Allowance for doubtful accounts	(1)	(1)
Total current assets	$33	$33

Required

As a loan officer for First National Bank of Verona Heights, assume that both companies have come to you asking for a $10 million six-month loan. If you could lend money to only one of the two, which one would it be? Justify your answer by writing a brief memo to the president of the bank.

Ethical Decision Making

ETHICAL DECISION MODEL

LO1 • 2   Decision Case 6-4 Using a Bank Reconciliation to Determine Cash Balance

You have just forwarded to your boss the monthly bank reconciliation you prepared for the company. One of the reconciling items is a customer's NSF check in the amount of $10,000. As part of your responsibility as controller, you have drafted an adjustment to reduce Cash and increase Accounts Receivable for the amount of the check. Your boss comes to you and indicates that based on his personal relationship with the customer, he knows "they are good for the money" and that you should revise the reconciliation to treat the NSF check as an outstanding check and also remove the adjustment you prepared.

Required

Use the Ethical Decision Framework in Exhibit 1-9 to complete the following requirements:
1. **Recognize an ethical dilemma:** What ethical dilemma(s) do you face?
2. **Analyze the key elements in the situation:**

   a. Who may benefit if you follow your boss's recommendation? Who may be harmed?
   b. How are they likely to benefit or be harmed?
   c. What rights or claims may be violated?
   d. What specific interests are in conflict?
   e. What are your responsibilities and obligations?

3. **List alternatives and evaluate the impact of each on those affected:** As controller, what are your options in dealing with the ethical dilemma(s) you identified in (1) above? If you follow your boss's recommendation, will users have all the relevant information needed to make decisions? Why or why not?
4. **Select the best alternative:** Among the alternatives, which one would you select?

LO3 • 4   Decision Case 6-5 Cash Receipts in a Bookstore

You were recently hired by a large retail bookstore chain. Your training involved spending a week at the largest and most profitable store in the district. The store manager assigned the head cashier to train you on the cash register and closing procedures required by the company's home office. In the process, the head cashier instructed you to keep an envelope for cash over and short that would include cash or IOUs equal to the net amount of overages or shortages in the cash drawer. "It is impossible to balance exactly, so just put extra cash in this envelope and use the cash when you are short." You studied accounting for one semester in college and remembered your professor saying that "all deposits should be made intact daily."

Required

Draft a memo to the store manager detailing any problems you see with the current system. This memo should address the issue of the accuracy of the cash receipts number. It should also answer the following question: Does this method provide information to the company that would enable someone to detect whether theft has occurred during the particular day in question? Your memo should suggest an alternative method of internal control for cash receipts.

Answers

MODULE 1 Answers to Questions

1. A cash equivalent is convertible to a known amount of cash. Therefore, the purchase of a cash equivalent is not considered a significant investing activity to be reported on the statement of cash flows. Cash equivalents are included with cash on the balance sheet, and thus the company is merely trading one cash item for another when it writes a check and uses the proceeds to invest in a cash equivalent.

2. When the balance per the bank statement and the balance per the books are reconciled to the correct balance, a service charge is deducted from the balance on the books. However, if it is added to the balance per the bank, it is because the company is reconciling the balance on the bank statement to the balance on the books. The bank has deducted the charge from the balance it shows. Because the company has not yet deducted this amount, a reconciliation of the bank balance to the book balance requires that the charge be added back.

MODULE 1 Answers to Apply

1. a. I b. I c. E d. I e. E f. I g. E h. I
2. Y, Y, N, N, N, Y, Y

3. BK, BK, BS, BK, BK, BS

MODULE 2 Answers to Questions

1. The Sarbanes-Oxley Act was passed in the wake of a number of high-profile cases involving questionable accounting practices. Congress decided that action by the federal government was needed to protect the interests of various parties that rely on corporate financial statements in making decisions.

2. This misuse of corporate assets could have been prevented by having a procedure in place for segregation of duties. A single employee should not be allowed to order merchandise, receive it, and approve payment for it.

3. First, all cash receipts should be deposited intact in a bank on a daily basis. That is, no disbursements should be made from any amounts received prior to their deposit in the bank. Second, all cash disbursements should be made by check. The use of serially numbered checks results in a clear record of all payments.

4. A purchase invoice is compared with a purchase order to ensure that the goods were in fact ordered. The comparison of a receiving report with an invoice ensures that all goods that a company is being billed for were in fact received.

MODULE 2 Answers to Apply

1. a. Management is responsible for establishing and maintaining an adequate internal control structure.
   b. The independent auditor provides an opinion as to whether management has maintained effective internal control over financial reporting.
   c. The independent auditors' report should be directed to the board of directors and the stockholders.
   d. The audit committee provides direct contact between stockholders and the independent accounting firm.

2. a. Proper authorizations
   b. Segregation of duties
   c. Independent verification
   d. Safeguarding of assets and records
   e. Independent review and appraisal
   f. Design and use of business documents

3. 2, 5, 6, 1, 3, 4

Answers to Connect to the Real World

6-1 (p. 278)

Panera Bread's Cash and cash equivalents increased during the year. The changes can be summarized as follows (dollars in thousands):

Beginning balance in cash and cash equivalents		$196,493
Net cash provided by operating activities	$ 318,045	
Net cash used in investing activities	(165,415)	
Net cash used in financing activities	(107,237)	
Net increase in cash and cash equivalents		45,393
Ending balance in cash and cash equivalents		$241,886

6-2 (p. 289)

The management of Panera Bread discusses limitations on internal control in the second paragraph of its annual report on internal control over financial reporting. The report explains that risks are present in making projections about the effectiveness of controls in the future because of changes in conditions, or because the degree of compliance with the various policies and procedures may deteriorate.

Answers to Key Terms Quiz

8	Cash equivalent
11	Bank statement
10	Outstanding check
13	Deposit in transit
7	Bank reconciliation
15	Credit memoranda
9	Debit memoranda
17	Petty cash fund
3	Internal control system
22	Sarbanes-Oxley Act
12	Internal control report
18	Public Company Accounting Oversight Board (PCAOB)

2	Board of directors
16	Audit committee
14	Accounting system
20	Administrative controls
4	Accounting controls
23	Internal audit staff
5	Purchase requisition form
21	Purchase order
1	Invoice
19	Blind receiving report
6	Invoice approval form

Receivables and Investments

MODULES	LEARNING OBJECTIVES	WHY IS THIS CHAPTER IMPORTANT?
1 **Accounting for Accounts Receivable**	**LO1** Explain how to account for accounts receivable, including bad debts. **LO2** Explain how information about sales and receivables can be combined to evaluate how efficient a company is in collecting its receivables.	• You need to know how a company reports accounts receivable on its balance sheet. (See pp. 312–313.) • You need to know the purpose of subtracting an allowance from the balance of accounts receivable. (See pp. 313–315.) • You need to know how you can use the relationship between sales on the income statement and accounts receivable on the balance sheet to assess a company's performance. (See pp. 319–321.)
2 **Accounting for Notes Receivable**	**LO3** Explain how to account for interest-bearing notes receivable. **LO4** Explain various techniques that companies use to accelerate the inflow of cash from sales.	• You need to know how a company reports notes receivable on its balance sheet. (See pp. 322–324.)
3 **Accounting for Investments**	**LO5** Explain the accounting for and disclosure of various types of investments that companies make.	• You need to know what types of investments companies make. (See p. 330.) • You need to know how companies report short-term investments on their balance sheets. (See p. 332.) • You need to know how companies earn income from these investments. (See pp. 328–332.)
4 **How Liquid Assets Affect the Statement of Cash Flows**	**LO6** Explain the effects of transactions involving liquid assets on the statement of cash flows.	• You need to know how receivables and investments affect cash flows. (See pp. 333–334.)

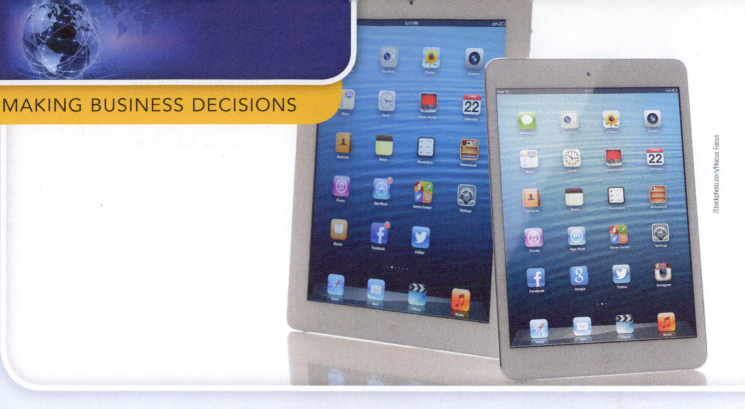

APPLE INC.

iPhones, iPads, iTunes, and iPods—these brand names have set **Apple Inc.** apart in the highly competitive tech world. For 40 years, the California-based company has been at the forefront in developing products that have revolutionized the way we work and play. The company that Steve Jobs made famous has seen sales skyrocket over this stretch, topping $233 billion in fiscal 2015.

Apple makes many of its sales—whether laptops, tablets, or phones—on credit. The resulting receivables must be collected to add cash to its balance sheet. As you know from personal experience, idle cash does not earn a very good return and so Apple invests its idle cash in various marketable securities. It should come as no surprise that the three largest current assets on Apple's recent partial balance sheet, shown here, are its cash and cash equivalents, marketable securities, and accounts receivable.

Consolidated Balance Sheets
(In millions, except number of shares which are reflected in thousands and par value)

Assets	September 26, 2015	September 27, 2014
Current assets:		
Cash and cash equivalents	$21,120	$13,844
Short-term marketable securities	20,481	11,233
Accounts receivable, less allowances of $82 and $86, respectively	16,849	17,460
Inventories	2,349	2,111
Deferred tax assets	5,546	4,318
Vendor non-trade receivables	13,494	9,759
Other current assets	9,539	9,806
Total current assets	89,378	68,531

Apple's three most important liquid assets

See accompanying Notes to Consolidated Financial Statements.

Source: Apple Inc., Form 10-K. For the Fiscal Year Ended September 26, 2015.

MODULE 1 ACCOUNTING FOR ACCOUNTS RECEIVABLE

LO1 Explain how to account for accounts receivable, including bad debts.

Account receivable
A receivable arising from the sale of goods or services with a verbal promise to pay.

The most common type of receivables is **accounts receivable**, which arise from the sale of goods or services to customers with a verbal promise to pay within a specified period of time. Accounts receivable do not bear interest. **Apple** or any other company prefers to make all sales for cash, because selling on credit causes two problems: it slows down the inflow of cash to the company, and it raises the possibility that the customer may not pay its bill on time or possibly ever. To remain competitive, however, Apple and most other businesses must sell their products and services on credit.

The Use of a Subsidiary Ledger

Assume that Apple sells $25,000 of hardware to a school. The sale results in the recognition of an asset and revenue. The transaction can be identified and analyzed as follows:

Identify and Analyze	
ACTIVITY: Operating	
ACCOUNTS: Accounts Receivable Increase Sales Revenue Increase	
STATEMENT(S): Balance Sheet and Income Statement	

Balance Sheet				Income Statement			
ASSETS	=	LIABILITIES	+	STOCKHOLDERS' EQUITY	REVENUES	− EXPENSES =	NET INCOME
Accounts Receivable 25,000				25,000	Sales Revenue 25,000		25,000

How Will I Use ACCOUNTING?

If you start up your own company it is very likely you will extend credit to your customers. Financial statements are the starting point in evaluating the credit-worthiness of a potential customer. They tell you about the company's liquidity, its profitability and how it uses its cash. Granting credit always involves some degree of risk, but only after reading the financials are you able to make an informed decision.

It is important for control purposes that Apple keep a record of each sale and include that amount on a periodic statement or bill sent to the customer. What if a company has a hundred or a thousand different customers? The mechanism that companies use to track the balance owed by each customer is called a **subsidiary ledger**.

A subsidiary ledger contains the necessary detail on items that collectively make up a single general ledger account, called the **control account**. This detail is shown in the following example for accounts receivable:

Subsidiary ledger
The detail for a number of individual items that collectively make up a single general ledger account.

Control account
The general ledger account that is supported by a subsidiary ledger.

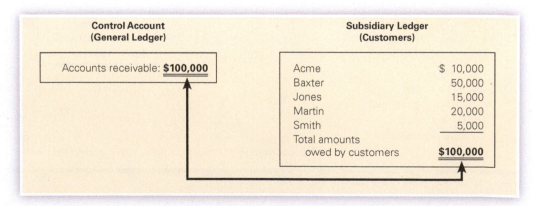

Control Account (General Ledger)	Subsidiary Ledger (Customers)	
Accounts receivable: **$100,000**	Acme	$ 10,000
	Baxter	50,000
	Jones	15,000
	Martin	20,000
	Smith	5,000
	Total amounts owed by customers	**$100,000**

In theory, any one of the accounts in the general ledger could be supported by a subsidiary ledger. In addition to Accounts Receivable, two other common accounts supported by subsidiary ledgers are Plant and Equipment and Accounts Payable. An accounts payable subsidiary ledger contains a separate account for each of the suppliers or vendors from which a company purchases inventory. A plant and equipment subsidiary ledger consists of individual accounts, along with their balances, for each of the various long-term tangible assets the company owns.

A subsidiary ledger does not take the place of the control account in the general ledger. Instead, at any point in time, the balances of the accounts that make up the subsidiary ledger should total to the single balance in the related control account. The remainder of this chapter will illustrate the use of only the control account. However, whenever a specific customer's account is increased or decreased, the name of the customer will be noted next to the control account.

The Valuation of Accounts Receivable

Apple's 2015 Form 10-K revealed the following receivables on the balance sheet:

(amounts in millions)	September 26, 2015	September 27, 2014
Accounts receivable, less allowances of $82 and $86, respectively	$16,849	$17,460

Apple does not sell its products under the assumption that any particular customer will not pay its bill. In fact, the credit department of a business is responsible for performing a credit check on all potential customers before granting them credit. Apple's management knows, however, that not all customers will be able to pay their accounts when due.

The reduction in Apple's receivables for an allowance is how most companies deal with bad debts in their accounting records. Bad debts are unpaid customer accounts that are uncollectible. Some companies describe the allowance as the allowance for doubtful accounts or the allowance for uncollectible accounts. Using the end of 2015 as an example, Apple believes that the net recoverable amount of its receivables is $16,849 million even though the gross amount of receivables is $82 million higher than this amount. The company has reduced the gross receivables for an amount it believes is necessary to reflect the asset on the books at the net recoverable amount or **net realizable value**.

CONNECT TO THE REAL WORLD

APPLE
READING THE BALANCE SHEET

7-1 Refer to Apple's partial balance sheet as presented in the chapter opener. By what amount did accounts receivable increase or decrease during 2015? How significant are accounts receivable to the amount of total current assets at the end of 2015? *(See answers on p. 354.)*

Net realizable value
The amount a company expects to collect on an account receivable.

Two Methods to Account for Bad Debts

EXAMPLE 7-1 **Using the Direct Write-Off Method for Bad Debts**

Assume that Roberts Corp. makes a $500 sale to Dexter Inc. on November 10, 2017, with credit terms of 2/10, n/60.[1] The effect of the transaction can be identified and analyzed as follows:

Identify and Analyze	**ACTIVITY:** Operating
	ACCOUNTS: Accounts Receivable—Dexter Increase Sales Revenue Increase
	STATEMENT(S): Balance Sheet and Income Statement

Balance Sheet					Income Statement				
ASSETS	=	LIABILITIES	+	STOCKHOLDERS' EQUITY	REVENUES	−	EXPENSES	=	NET INCOME
Accounts Receivable—Dexter 500				500	Sales Revenue 500				500

Assume further that Dexter is unable to pay within 60 days. After pursuing the account for four months into 2018, the credit department of Roberts informs the accounting department

---

[1] Credit terms were explained in Chapter 5.

that it has given up on collecting the $500 from Dexter and advises that the account be written off. To do so, the accounting department makes an adjustment. The effect of the adjustment can be identified and analyzed as follows:

Identify and Analyze	ACTIVITY: Operating
	ACCOUNTS: Accounts Receivable—Dexter Decrease Bad Debts Expense Increase
	STATEMENT(S): Balance Sheet and Income Statement

Balance Sheet			Income Statement			
ASSETS	= LIABILITIES	+ STOCKHOLDERS' EQUITY	REVENUES	− EXPENSES	=	NET INCOME
Accounts Receivable—Dexter (500)		(500)		Bad Debts Expense 500		(500)

Direct write-off method
The recognition of bad debts expense at the point an account is written off as uncollectible.

This approach to accounting for bad debts, called the **direct write-off method**, has some deficiencies.

- *What about Roberts' balance sheet at the end of 2017?* By ignoring the possibility that not all of its outstanding accounts receivable will be collected, Roberts is overstating the value of this asset at December 31, 2017.
- *What about the income statement for 2017?* By ignoring the possibility of bad debts on sales made during 2017, Roberts has violated the matching principle. This principle requires that all costs associated with making sales in a period be matched with the sales of that period. Roberts has overstated net income for 2017 by ignoring bad debts as expense. The problem is one of timing: even though any one particular account may not prove to be uncollectible until a later period (e.g., the Dexter account), the cost associated with making sales on credit (bad debts) should be recognized in the period of sale.

Allowance method
A method of estimating bad debts on the basis of either the net credit sales of the period or the accounts receivable at the end of the period.

Accountants use the **allowance method** to overcome the deficiencies of the direct write-off method. They estimate the amount of bad debts before these debts actually occur.

EXAMPLE 7-2 Using the Allowance Method for Bad Debts

Assume that Roberts' total sales during 2017 amount to $600,000 and that at the end of the year, the outstanding accounts receivable total $250,000. Also, assume that Roberts estimates that 1% of the sales of the period, or $6,000, will prove to be uncollectible. Under the allowance method, Roberts makes an adjustment at the end of 2017. The effect of the adjustment can be identified and analyzed as follows:

Identify and Analyze	ACTIVITY: Operating
	ACCOUNTS: Allowance for Doubtful Accounts Increase Bad Debts Expense Increase
	STATEMENT(S): Balance Sheet and Income Statement

Balance Sheet			Income Statement			
ASSETS	= LIABILITIES	+ STOCKHOLDERS' EQUITY	REVENUES	− EXPENSES	=	NET INCOME
Allowance for Doubtful Accounts* (6,000)		(6,000)		Bad Debts Expense 6,000		(6,000)

*The Allowance for Doubtful Accounts account has increased. It is shown as a decrease in the equation above because it is a contra account and causes total assets to decrease.

Bad Debts Expense recognizes the cost associated with the reduction in value of Accounts Receivable. The cost is charged to the income statement in the form of Bad Debts Expense. A contra-asset account is used to reduce the asset to its net realizable value. This is accomplished by crediting an allowance account, **Allowance for Doubtful Accounts**.

Roberts presents accounts receivable on its December 31, 2017, balance sheet as follows:

Accounts receivable	$250,000
Allowance for doubtful accounts	6,000
Net accounts receivable	$244,000

Allowance for doubtful accounts
A contra-asset account used to reduce accounts receivable to its net realizable value.

Alternate term: Allowance for uncollectible accounts.

Assume, as we did earlier, that Dexter's $500 account is written off on May 1, 2018. Under the allowance method, the following entry is recorded:

Identify and Analyze	**ACTIVITY: Operating** **ACCOUNTS: Allowance for Doubtful Accounts** Decrease **Accounts Receivable—Dexter** Decrease **STATEMENT(S): Balance Sheet**

Balance Sheet					Income Statement				
ASSETS	=	LIABILITIES	+	STOCKHOLDERS' EQUITY	REVENUES	−	EXPENSES	=	NET INCOME
Allowance for Doubtful Accounts* 500									
Accounts Receivable— Dexter (500)									

*The Allowance for Doubtful Accounts account has decreased. It is shown as an increase in the equation above because it is a contra account and causes total assets to increase.

To summarize, whether the direct write-off method or the allowance method is used, the adjustment to write off a specific customer's account reduces Accounts Receivable. It is the other side of the adjustment that differs between the two methods:

- Under the direct write-off method, an *expense* is increased.
- Under the allowance method, the *allowance* account is reduced.

Two Approaches to the Allowance Method of Accounting for Bad Debts

Because the allowance method results in a better matching, accounting standards require it rather than the direct write-off method unless bad debts are immaterial in amount. Accountants use one of two variations of the allowance method to estimate bad debts. One approach emphasizes matching bad debts expense with revenue on the income statement and bases bad debts on a percentage of the sales of the period. This was the method illustrated earlier for Roberts Corp. The other approach emphasizes the net realizable amount (value) of accounts receivable on the balance sheet and bases bad debts on a percentage of the accounts receivable balance at the end of the period.

Percentage of Net Credit Sales Approach If a company has been in business for enough years, it may be able to use the past relationship between bad debts and net credit sales to predict bad debt amounts. *Net* means that credit sales have been adjusted for sales discounts and returns and allowances.

> **STUDY TIP**
>
> Note the similarities between the Allowance for Doubtful Accounts contra account and another contra account, Accumulated Depreciation. Both are used to reduce an asset account to a lower carrying or book value.

EXAMPLE 7-3 Using the Percentage of Net Credit Sales Approach

Assume that the accounting records for Bosco Corp. reveal the following:

Year	Net Credit Sales	Bad Debts
2012	$1,250,000	$ 26,400
2013	1,340,000	29,350
2014	1,200,000	23,100
2015	1,650,000	32,150
2016	2,120,000	42,700
	$7,560,000	$153,700

Although the exact percentage varied slightly over the five-year period, the average percentage of bad debts to net credit sales is very close to 2% ($153,700/$7,560,000 = 0.02033). Bosco needs to determine whether this estimate is realistic for the current period. For example, are current economic conditions considerably different from those in prior years? Has the company made sales to any new customers with significantly different credit terms? If the answers to these types of questions are yes, Bosco should consider adjusting the 2% experience rate to estimate future bad debts. Assuming that it uses the 2% rate and that its net credit sales during 2017 are $2,340,000, Bosco makes an adjustment of 0.02 × $2,340,000, or $46,800 that can be identified and analyzed as follows:

Identify and Analyze	**ACTIVITY:** Operating **ACCOUNTS:** Allowance for Doubtful Accounts Increase **Bad Debts Expense** Increase **STATEMENT(S):** Balance Sheet and Income Statement

Balance Sheet			Income Statement			
ASSETS	= LIABILITIES +	STOCKHOLDERS' EQUITY	REVENUES −	EXPENSES	=	NET INCOME
Allowance for Doubtful Accounts* (46,800)		(46,800)		Bad Debts Expense 46,800		(46,800)

*The Allowance for Doubtful Accounts account has increased. It is shown as a decrease in the equation above because it is a contra account and causes total assets to decrease.

Thus, Bosco matches bad debts expense of $46,800 with sales revenue of $2,340,000.

Percentage of Accounts Receivable Approach
Some companies believe that they can more accurately estimate bad debts by relating them to the balance in the Accounts Receivable account at the end of the period rather than to the sales of the period.

EXAMPLE 7-4 Using the Percentage of Accounts Receivable Approach

Assume that the records for Cougar Corp. reveal the following:

Year	Balance in Accounts Receivable, December 31	Bad Debts
2012	$ 650,000	$ 5,250
2013	785,000	6,230
2014	854,000	6,950
2015	824,000	6,450
2016	925,000	7,450
	$4,038,000	$32,330

The ratio of bad debts to the ending balance in Accounts Receivable over the past five years is $32,330/$4,038,000, or approximately 0.008 (0.8%). Assuming balances in Accounts Receivable and Allowance for Doubtful Accounts on December 31, 2017, of $865,000 and $2,100, respectively, Cougar makes an adjustment that can be identified and analyzed as follows:

Identify and Analyze	**ACTIVITY: Operating**
	ACCOUNTS: Allowance for Doubtful Accounts Increase **Bad Debts Expense** Increase
	STATEMENT(S): Balance Sheet and Income Statement

Balance Sheet					Income Statement			
ASSETS	=	LIABILITIES	+	STOCKHOLDERS' EQUITY	REVENUES	−	EXPENSES	= NET INCOME
Allowance for Doubtful Accounts* (4,820)				(4,820)			Bad Debts Expense 4,820**	(4,820)

*The Allowance for Doubtful Accounts account has increased. It is shown as a decrease in the equation above because it is a contra account and causes total assets to decrease.

**Balance required in allowance account after adjustment ($865,000 × 0.8%)	$6,920
Balance in allowance account before adjustment	2,100
Amount of adjustment	$4,820

The adjustment of $4,820 results in a balance in Allowance for Doubtful Accounts of $6,920, which is 0.8% of the Accounts Receivable balance of $865,000. The net realizable value of Accounts Receivable is determined as follows:

Accounts receivable	$865,000
Allowance for doubtful accounts	6,920
Net realizable value	$858,080

Note the one major difference between this approach and the percentage of sales approach:

- Under the percentage of net credit sales approach, the balance in the allowance account is ignored and the bad debts expense is simply a percentage of the sales of the period.
- Under the percentage of accounts receivable approach, however, the balance in the allowance account must be considered.

Aging of Accounts Receivable Some companies use a refinement of the percentage of accounts receivable approach to estimate bad debts. This variation considers the length of time that the receivables have been outstanding. The older an account receivable is, the less likely it is to be collected. An **aging schedule** categorizes the various accounts by length of time outstanding. A partial aging schedule is shown in Exhibit 7-1. We assume that the company's policy is to allow 30 days for payment of an outstanding account. After that time, the account is past due. An alphabetical list of customers appears in the first column, with the balance in each account shown in the appropriate column to the right. The dotted lines after A. Matt's account indicate that many more accounts appear in the records; only a few have been included to show the format of the schedule.

Aging schedule
A form used to categorize the various individual accounts receivable according to the length of time each has been outstanding.

CONNECT TO THE REAL WORLD

APPLE
READING THE BALANCE SHEET

7-2 Refer to the excerpt from Apple's balance sheet in the chapter opener. Compute for each of the two year-ends the amount of accounts receivable before deducting the balance in the allowance account. Did this amount increase or decrease during 2015? Did the allowance account increase or decrease during 2015? What would cause the allowance account to increase or decrease in any one year? (See answers on p. 354.)

EXHIBIT 7-1 Aging Schedule

Customer	Current	Number of Days Past Due			
		1–30	31–60	61–90	Over 90
L. Ash	$ 4,400				
B. Budd	3,200				
C Cox		$ 6,500			
E. Fudd					$6,300
G. Hoff			$ 900		
A. Matt	5,500				
....					
....					
....					
T. West		3,100			
M. Young				$ 4,200	
Totals*	$85,600	$31,200	$24,500	$18,000	$9,200

*Only a few of the customer accounts are illustrated; thus, the column totals are higher than the amounts for the accounts illustrated.

EXAMPLE 7-5 Using an Aging Schedule to Estimate Bad Debts

The totals on the aging schedule are used as the basis for estimating bad debts, as shown below.

Category	Amount	Estimated Percent Uncollectible	Estimated Amount Uncollectible
Current	$ 85,600	1%	$ 856
Past due:			
1–30 days	31,200	4%	1,248
31–60 days	24,500	10%	2,450
61–90 days	18,000	30%	5,400
Over 90 days	9,200	50%	4,600
Totals	$168,500		$14,554

The estimated percentage of uncollectibles increases as the period of time the accounts have been outstanding lengthens. If we assume that Allowance for Doubtful Accounts has a balance of $1,230 before adjustment, an adjustment is made that can be identified and analyzed as follows:

Identify and Analyze	**ACTIVITY:** Operating **ACCOUNTS:** Allowance for Doubtful Accounts Increase Bad Debts Expense Increase **STATEMENT(S):** Balance Sheet and Income Statement

Balance Sheet				Income Statement			
ASSETS	=	LIABILITIES	+	STOCKHOLDERS' EQUITY	REVENUES −	EXPENSES	= NET INCOME
Allowance for Doubtful Accounts* (13,324)				(13,324)		Bad Debts Expense 13,324**	(13,324)

*The Allowance for Doubtful Accounts account has increased. It is shown as a decrease in the equation above because it is a contra account and causes total assets to decrease.

**Balance required in allowance account after adjustment $14,554
    Balance in allowance account before adjustment   1,230
    Amount of adjustment $13,324

The net realizable value of accounts receivable would be determined as follows:

Accounts receivable	$168,500
Less: Allowance for doubtful accounts	14,554
Net realizable value	$153,946

The Accounts Receivable Turnover Ratio

Managers, investors, and creditors are keenly interested in how well a company manages its accounts receivable. One simple measure is to compare a company's sales to its accounts receivable. The result is the **accounts receivable turnover ratio**:

$$\text{Accounts Receivable Turnover} = \frac{\text{Net Credit Sales}}{\text{Average Accounts Receivable}}$$

LO2 Explain how information about sales and receivables can be combined to evaluate how efficient a company is in collecting its receivables.

Accounts receivable turnover ratio
A measure of the number of times accounts receivable is collected during the period.

EXAMPLE 7-6 Computing the Accounts Receivable Turnover Ratio

Assume that a company has sales on credit of $10 million and an average accounts receivable of $1 million. This means it turns over its accounts receivable $10 million/$1 million, or ten times per year. If we assume 360 days in a year, that is once every 360/10, or 36 days. An observer would compare that figure with historical figures to see if the company is experiencing slower or faster collections. A comparison also could be made to other companies in the same industry. If receivables are turning over too slowly, the company's credit department may not be operating effectively; therefore, the company is missing opportunities with the cash that isn't available. On the other hand, a turnover rate that is too fast might mean that the company's credit policies are too stringent and that sales are being lost as a result.

MAKING BUSINESS DECISIONS
APPLE

Analyzing the Accounts Receivable Rate of Collection

Managers, investors, and creditors must be able to assess how well a company manages its accounts receivable. Each dollar of sales on credit produces a dollar of accounts receivable. And the quicker each dollar of receivables can be collected, the sooner the money will be available for other purposes. Use the following models to help you in your role as a banker to decide whether to lend money to Apple Inc.

A. The Ratio Analysis Model

1. Formulate the Question

How many times a year does the company turn over its accounts receivable?

2. Gather the Information from the Financial Statements

To calculate a company's accounts receivable turnover ratio, it is essential to know its net credit sales and the average balance in accounts receivable:

- Net credit sales: From the income statement
- Average accounts receivable: From the balance sheet at the end of the two most recent years

3. Calculate the Ratio

$$\text{Accounts Receivable Turnover} = \frac{\text{Net Credit Sales}}{\text{Average Accounts Receivable}}$$

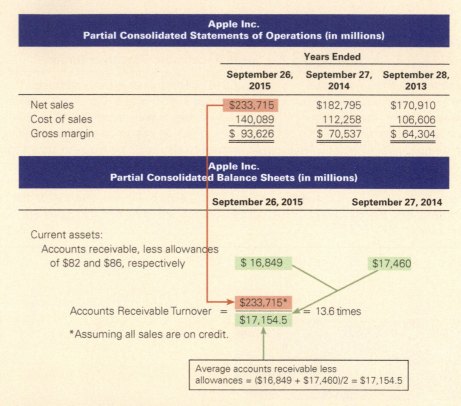

Apple Inc. **Partial Consolidated Statements of Operations (in millions)**			
	Years Ended		
	September 26, 2015	**September 27, 2014**	**September 28, 2013**
Net sales	$233,715	$182,795	$170,910
Cost of sales	140,089	112,258	106,606
Gross margin	$ 93,626	$ 70,537	$ 64,304

Apple Inc. **Partial Consolidated Balance Sheets (in millions)**		
	September 26, 2015	**September 27, 2014**
Current assets:		
Accounts receivable, less allowances of $82 and $86, respectively	$ 16,849	$17,460

$$\text{Accounts Receivable Turnover} = \frac{\$233,715^*}{\$17,154.5} = 13.6 \text{ times}$$

*Assuming all sales are on credit.

Average accounts receivable less allowances = ($16,849 + $17,460)/2 = $17,154.5

4. Compare the Ratio with Other Ratios

Ratios are of no use in a vacuum. It is necessary to compare them with prior years and with competitors.

ACCOUNTS RECEIVABLE TURNOVER RATIO			
Apple Inc.		**Hewlett-Packard**	
Year Ended September 26, 2015	**Year Ended September 27, 2014**	**Year Ended October 31, 2015**	**Year Ended October 31, 2014**
13.6 times	12.0 times	7.6 times**	7.5 times**

**Based on "Products and Services Revenues."

5. Interpret the Ratios

In fiscal year 2015, Apple Inc. turned over its accounts receivable an average of 13.6 times. This is faster than the turnover in the prior year, and the turnover for both years is quicker than the ratios for its competitor, Hewlett-Packard. An alternative way to look at a company's efficiency in managing its accounts receivable is to calculate the number of days, on average, that accounts receivables are outstanding. This measure is called **number of days' sales in receivables** and is calculated as follows for Apple Inc. in 2015, assuming 360 days in a year:

Number of days' sales in receivables
A measure of how long it takes to collect receivables.

$$\text{Number of Days' Sales in Receivables} = \frac{\text{Number of Days in the Period}}{\text{Accounts Receivable Turnover Ratio}}$$

$$= \frac{360}{13.6}$$

$$= 26 \text{ days}$$

This measure tells us that it took Apple Inc. 26 days or less than a month on average to collect its accounts receivable.

B. The Business Decision Model

1. Formulate the Question

If you were a banker, would you loan money to Apple Inc.?

2. Gather Information from the Financial Statements and Other Sources

This information will come from a variety of sources, not limited to but including:

- The balance sheet provides information about liquidity, the income statement regarding profitability, and the statement of cash flows on inflows and outflows of cash.
- The outlook for the computer industry, including consumer trends, foreign markets, labor issues, and other factors.
- The outlook for the economy in general.
- Alternative uses for the money.

3. Analyze the Information Gathered

- Compare Apple Inc.'s accounts receivable turnover ratio in (A) above with Hewlett-Packard as well as with industry averages.
- Look at trends over time in the accounts receivable turnover ratios.
- Look at trends in net income over time as an indication of the ability to control expenses other than cost of goods sold.
- Review projections for the economy and the industry.

4. Make the Decision

Taking into account all of the various sources of information, decide either to

- Loan money to Apple Inc. or
- Find an alternative use for the money

5. Monitor Your Decision

If you decide to make the loan, you will need to monitor it periodically. During the time the loan is outstanding, you will want to assess the company's continuing liquidity as well as other factors you considered before making the loan.

MODULE 1 TEST YOURSELF

Review	**LO1** Explain how to account for accounts receivable, including bad debts.	• Accounts receivable arise from sales on credit. Companies with many customers may keep detailed records of accounts receivable in a separate subsidiary ledger.
		 • Because not all customers pay their outstanding bills, an estimate of the accounts receivable less any doubtful accounts must be presented on the balance sheet.
		 • Bad debts are estimated under the allowance method by one of two approaches:
		  • Percentage of net credit sales
		  • Percentage of accounts receivable

	LO2 Explain how information about sales and receivables can be combined to evaluate how efficient a company is in collecting its receivables.	• Information about net credit sales and the average accounts receivable balance may be combined to calculate the accounts receivable turnover to see how well a company is managing its collections on account.

Question	1. Why do accountants prefer the allowance method of accounting for bad debts?
	2. When bad debts are estimated, why is the balance in the Allowance for Doubtful Accounts considered when the percentage of receivables approach is used, but not when the percentage of sales approach is used?
	3. When computing the accounts receivable turnover ratio, why is the average of accounts receivable for the period used in the denominator of the ratio?

Apply	1. Badger recorded $500,000 of net sales for the year of which 2% is estimated to be uncollectible. Identify and analyze the adjustment required at the end of the year to record bad debts.

	2. Brown Corp. ended the year with balances in Accounts Receivable of $60,000 and in Allowance for Doubtful Accounts of $800 (balance before adjustment). Net sales for the year amounted to $200,000. Identify and analyze the effect of the adjustment at the end of the year assuming the following:
	  a. Estimated percentage of net sales uncollectible is 1%.
	  b. Estimated percentage of year-end accounts receivable uncollectible is 4%.

	3. Hawkeye recorded sales of $240,000 for the year. Accounts receivable amounted to $40,000 at the beginning of the year and $20,000 at the end of the year. Compute the company's accounts receivable turnover for the year.

Answers are located at the end of the chapter.

LO3 Explain how to account for interest-bearing notes receivable.

Promissory note
A written promise to repay a definite sum of money on demand or at a fixed or determinable date in the future.

Maker
The party that agrees to repay the money for a promissory note at some future date.

Payee
The party that will receive the money from a promissory note at some future date.

MODULE 2 ACCOUNTING FOR NOTES RECEIVABLE

A **promissory note** is a written promise to repay a definite sum of money on demand or at a fixed or determinable date in the future. The party that agrees to repay money is the **maker** of the note, and the party that receives money in the future is the **payee**. A company that holds a promissory note received from another company has an asset, called a **note receivable**. The company that makes or gives a promissory note to another company has a liability, a **note payable**. Over the life of the note, the maker incurs interest expense on its note payable and the payee earns interest revenue on its note receivable. The following summarizes this relationship:

Party	Recognizes on Balances Sheet	Recognizes on Income Statement
Maker	Note payable	Interest expense
Payee	Note receivable	Interest revenue

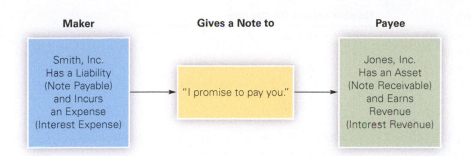

Maker	Gives a Note to	Payee
Smith, Inc. Has a Liability (Note Payable) and Incurs an Expense (Interest Expense)	"I promise to pay you."	Jones, Inc. Has an Asset (Note Receivable) and Earns Revenue (Interest Revenue)

Note receivable
An asset resulting from the acceptance of a promissory note from another company.

Note payable
A liability resulting from the signing of a promissory note.

Promissory notes are used for a variety of purposes. Banks normally require a company to sign a promissory note to borrow money. Promissory notes are often used in the sale of consumer durables with relatively high purchase prices, such as appliances and automobiles. At times, a promissory note is issued to replace an existing overdue account receivable.

Important Terms Connected with Promissory Notes

It is important to understand the following terms when dealing with promissory notes:

Principal—the amount of cash received, or the fair value of the products or services received, by the maker when a promissory note is issued.

Maturity date—the date the promissory note is due.

Term—the length of time a note is outstanding, that is, the period of time between the date it is issued and the date it matures.

Maturity value—the amount of cash the maker is to pay the payee on the maturity date of the note.

Interest—the difference between the principal amount of the note and its maturity value.

Key terms for promissory notes
These terms, with their definitions in the text, are important for your understanding.

EXAMPLE 7-7 Accounting for a Note Receivable

Assume that on December 13, 2017, High Tec sells a computer to Baker Corp. at an invoice price of $15,000. Because Baker is short of cash, it gives High Tec a 90-day, 12% promissory note. The total amount of interest due on the maturity date is determined as follows:

$$\$15{,}000 \times 0.12 \times 90/360 = \underline{\$450}$$

The effect of the receipt of the note by High Tec can be identified and analyzed as follows:

Identify and Analyze	ACTIVITY: Operating ACCOUNTS: Notes Receivable Increase Sales Revenue Increase STATEMENT(S): Balance Sheet and Income Statement

Balance Sheet						Income Statement					
ASSETS	=	LIABILITIES	+	STOCKHOLDERS' EQUITY		REVENUES		−	EXPENSES	=	NET INCOME
Notes Receivable 15,000					15,000	Sales Revenue	15,000				15,000

If we assume that December 31 is the end of High Tec's accounting year, an adjustment is needed to recognize interest earned but not yet received. It is required when a company uses the accrual basis of accounting. How many days of interest have been earned during December? In computing interest, it is normal practice to count the day a note matures but not the day it is signed. Thus, in the example, interest would be earned for 18 days (December 14 to December 31) during 2017 and for 72 days in 2018:

Month	Number of Days Outstanding
December 2017	18 days
January 2018	31 days
February 2018	28 days
March 2018	13 days (matures on March 13, 2018)
Total days	90 days

The amount of interest earned during 2017 is $15,000 \times 0.12 \times 18/360$, or $90. An adjustment is made on December 31 to record interest earned during 2017. The effect of the adjustment can be identified and analyzed as follows:

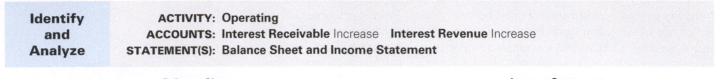

Identify and Analyze

ACTIVITY: Operating
ACCOUNTS: Interest Receivable Increase   **Interest Revenue** Increase
STATEMENT(S): Balance Sheet and Income Statement

Balance Sheet					Income Statement			
ASSETS	=	LIABILITIES	+	STOCKHOLDERS' EQUITY	REVENUES	−	EXPENSES =	NET INCOME
Interest Receivable 90				90	Interest Revenue 90			90

On March 13, 2018, High Tec collects the principal amount of the note and interest from Baker. The effect of the transaction can be identified and analyzed as follows:

Identify and Analyze

ACTIVITY: Operating
ACCOUNTS: Cash Increase   **Notes Receivable** Decrease
            Interest Receivable Decrease   **Interest Revenue** Increase
STATEMENT(S): Balance Sheet and Income Statement

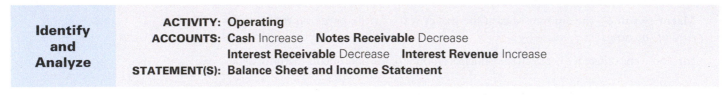

Balance Sheet					Income Statement			
ASSETS	=	LIABILITIES	+	STOCKHOLDERS' EQUITY	REVENUES	−	EXPENSES =	NET INCOME
Cash 15,450				360	Interest Revenue 360			360
Notes Receivable (15,000)								
Interest Receivable (90)								

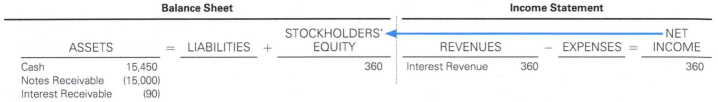

This adjustment removes the amount of $15,000 originally recorded in the Notes Receivable account. It also increases Interest Revenue for the interest earned during the 72 days in 2018 that the note was outstanding. The calculation of interest earned during 2018 is as follows:

$$\$15,000 \times 0.12 \times 72/360 = \$360$$

The adjustment decreases Interest Receivable by $90 to remove this account from the records now that the note has been collected. Finally, it increases Cash by $15,450, which represents the principal amount of the note, $15,000, plus interest of $450 for 90 days.

Accelerating the Inflow of Cash from Sales

LO4 Explain various techniques that companies use to accelerate the inflow of cash from sales.

Earlier in the chapter, we pointed out that credit sales slow down the inflow of cash to the company and create the potential for bad debts. To remain competitive, most businesses find it necessary to grant credit to customers. Companies have found it possible, however, to circumvent the problems inherent in credit sales.

Credit Card Sales

Most retail establishments as well as many service businesses accept one or more major credit cards. Among the most common cards are MasterCard®, VISA®, and American Express®. Most merchants find that they must honor at least one or more of these credit cards to remain competitive. In return for a fee, the merchant passes the responsibility for collection on to the credit card company. Thus, the credit card issuer assumes the risk of nonpayment. The basic relationships among the three parties—the customer, the merchant, and the credit company—are illustrated in Exhibit 7-2.

EXHIBIT 7-2 Basic Relationships Among Parties with Credit Card Sales

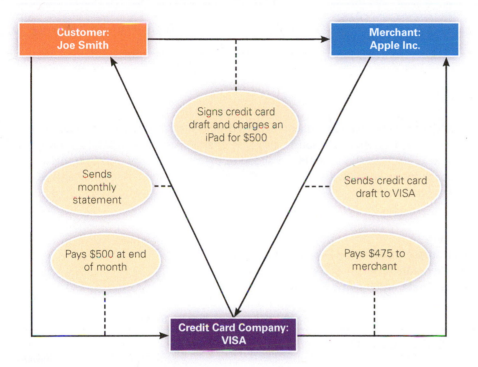

EXAMPLE 7-8 Accounting for Credit Card Sales

Assume that Joe Smith buys an iPad in an Apple store and charges the $500 cost to his VISA card. When Joe is presented with the bill, he is asked to sign the salesperson's iPhone and then a copy of the receipt is emailed to Joe. The store uses the receipt as the basis for recording its sales of the day and sends a copy to VISA for payment. VISA uses the receipt it gets for two purposes: to reimburse Apple $475 (keeping $25, or 5% of the original sale, as a collection fee) and to include Joe Smith's $500 purchase on the monthly bill it mails him.

Assume that total credit card sales on June 5 amount to $8,000. The effect of the transaction can be identified and analyzed as follows:

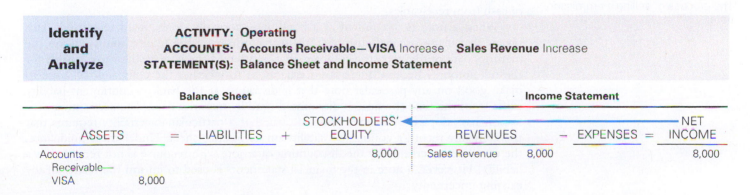

Identify and Analyze	**ACTIVITY:** Operating
	ACCOUNTS: Accounts Receivable—VISA Increase Sales Revenue Increase
	STATEMENT(S): Balance Sheet and Income Statement

Balance Sheet					Income Statement			
ASSETS	=	LIABILITIES	+	STOCKHOLDERS' EQUITY	REVENUES	−	EXPENSES =	NET INCOME
Accounts Receivable— VISA 8,000				8,000	Sales Revenue 8,000			8,000

Assume that Apple remits the credit card receipts to VISA once a week and that the total sales for the week ending June 11 amount to $50,000. Further assume that on June 13, VISA pays the amount due to Apple after deducting a 5% collection fee. The effect of the transaction can be identified and analyzed as follows:

Identify and Analyze	ACTIVITY: Operating
	ACCOUNTS: Cash Increase Accounts Receivable—VISA Decrease
	Collection Fee Expense Increase
	STATEMENT(S): Balance Sheet and Income Statement

Balance Sheet				Income Statement			
ASSETS	=	LIABILITIES +	STOCKHOLDERS' EQUITY	REVENUES	−	EXPENSES	= NET INCOME
Cash 47,500			(2,500)			Collection Fee Expense 2,500	(2,500)
Accounts Receivable— VISA (50,000)							

Some credit cards, such as MasterCard and VISA, allow a merchant to present receipts directly for deposit in a bank account, in much the same way the merchant deposits checks, coins, and currency. Obviously, this type of arrangement is even more advantageous for the merchant because the funds are available as soon as the receipts are added to the bank account. Assume that on July 9, Apple presents VISA credit card receipts to its bank for payment in the amount of $20,000 and that the collection charge is 4%. The effect of the collection can be identified and analyzed as follows:

Identify and Analyze	ACTIVITY: Operating
	ACCOUNTS: Cash Increase Collection Fee Expense Increase
	Sales Revenue Increase
	STATEMENT(S): Balance Sheet and Income Statement

Balance Sheet				Income Statement			
ASSETS	=	LIABILITIES +	STOCKHOLDERS' EQUITY	REVENUES	−	EXPENSES	= NET INCOME
Cash 19,200			19,200	Sales Revenue 20,000		Collection Fee Expense 800	19,200

Discounting Notes Receivable

Promissory notes are negotiable, which means that they can be endorsed and given to someone else for collection. In other words, a company can sign the back of a note (just as it would a check), sell it to a bank, and receive cash before the note's maturity date. This process, called **discounting**, is another way for companies to speed the collection of cash from receivables.

Discounting
The process of selling a promissory note.

When a note is discounted at a bank, it is normally done "with recourse." This means that if the original customer fails to pay the bank the total amount due on the maturity date of the note, the company that transferred the note to the bank is liable for the full amount. Because there is uncertainty as to whether the company will have to make good on any particular note that it discounts at the bank, a contingent liability exists from the time the note is discounted until its maturity date. The accounting profession has adopted guidelines to decide whether a particular uncertainty requires that the company record a contingent liability on its balance sheet. Under these guidelines, the contingency created by the discounting of a note with recourse is not recorded as a liability. However, a note in the financial statements is used to inform the reader of the existing uncertainty.

MODULE 2 TEST YOURSELF

Review	**LO3** Explain how to account for interest-bearing notes receivable.	• Notes receivable ultimately result in the receipt of both interest and principal to the holder of the notes. • Because interest receipts may not coincide with the end of the period, adjustments may need to be made to accrue interest receivable and interest revenue.
	LO4 Explain various techniques that companies use to accelerate the inflow of cash from sales.	• To be competitive, companies must make sales on credit to customers. • One way to avoid bad debts associated with extending credit directly to the customer and to accelerate cash collections from sales is to accept credit cards for payment of goods and services.

Question	1. What is the distinction between an account receivable and a note receivable?
	2. Why does the discounting of a note receivable with recourse result in a contingent liability? Should the liability be reported on the balance sheet? Explain.

Apply	1. On November 1, 2017, Gopher received a $50,000, 6%, 90-day promissory note. Identify and analyze the adjustment required on December 31, the end of the company's fiscal year.	
	2. On July 20, Wolverine presents credit card receipts to its bank in the amount of $10,000; the collection charge is 4%. Identify and analyze the transaction on Wolverine's books on July 20, the date of deposit.	

Answers are located at the end of the chapter.

MODULE 3 ACCOUNTING FOR INVESTMENTS

Some corporations have excess cash during certain times of the year and invest this idle cash in various highly liquid financial instruments such as certificates of deposit and money market funds. Chapter 6 pointed out that these investments are included with cash and are called cash equivalents when they have an original maturity to the investor of three months or less. Otherwise, they are accounted for as short-term investments.

Some companies invest in the stocks and bonds of other corporations as well as bonds issued by various government agencies. Securities issued by corporations as a form of ownership in the business, such as common stock and preferred stock, are called **equity securities**. Because these securities are a form of ownership, they do not have a maturity date. As we will see later, investments in equity securities can be classified as either current or long term depending on the company's intent. Alternatively, securities issued by corporations and governmental bodies as a form of borrowing are called **debt securities** and often take the form of bonds. The term of a bond can be relatively short, such as five years, or much longer, such as 20 or 30 years. Regardless of the term, classification as a current or noncurrent asset by the investor depends on whether it plans to sell or redeem the debt securities within the next year.

LO5 Explain the accounting for and disclosure of various types of investments that companies make.

Equity securities
Securities issued by corporations as a form of ownership in the business.
Alternate term: Stocks.

Debt securities
Securities issued by corporations and governmental bodies as a form of borrowing.
Alternate term: Bonds.

Investments in Highly Liquid Financial Instruments

The seasonal nature of most businesses leads to a potential cash shortage during certain times of the year and an excess of cash during other times. Companies typically deal with cash shortages by borrowing on a short-term basis either from a bank in the form of notes or from other entities in the form of commercial paper. The maturities of the bank notes or the commercial paper generally range from 30 days to six months. These same companies use various financial instruments as a way to invest excess cash during other times of the year. The most common type of highly liquid financial instrument is a certificate of deposit (CD).

EXAMPLE 7-9 Accounting for an Investment in a Certificate of Deposit

On October 2, 2017, Creston Corp. invests $100,000 of excess cash in a 120-day CD. The CD matures on January 30, 2018, at which time Creston receives the $100,000 and interest at an annual rate of 6%. The effect of the transaction to record the purchase of the CD can be identified and analyzed as follows:

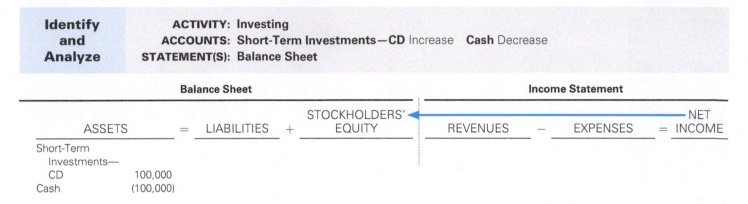

Identify and Analyze	ACTIVITY: Investing
	ACCOUNTS: Short-Term Investments—CD Increase Cash Decrease
	STATEMENT(S): Balance Sheet

Balance Sheet			Income Statement		
ASSETS = LIABILITIES + STOCKHOLDERS' EQUITY			REVENUES − EXPENSES = NET INCOME		
Short-Term Investments— CD 100,000					
Cash (100,000)					

December 31 is the end of Creston's fiscal year, so an adjustment is needed on this date to record interest earned during 2017 even though no cash will be received until the CD matures in 2018. The effect of the adjustment can be identified and analyzed as follows:

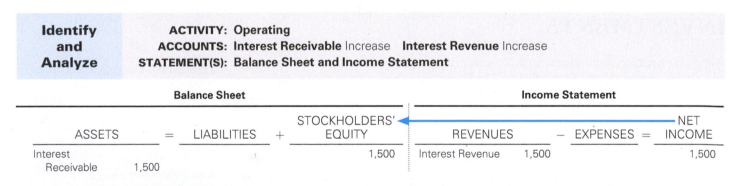

Identify and Analyze	ACTIVITY: Operating
	ACCOUNTS: Interest Receivable Increase Interest Revenue Increase
	STATEMENT(S): Balance Sheet and Income Statement

Balance Sheet			Income Statement		
ASSETS = LIABILITIES + STOCKHOLDERS' EQUITY			REVENUES − EXPENSES = NET INCOME		
Interest Receivable 1,500		1,500	Interest Revenue 1,500		1,500

The basic formula to compute interest is as follows:

$$\text{Interest (I)} = \text{Principal (P)} \times \text{Interest Rate (R)} \times \text{Time (T)}$$

Because interest rates are normally stated on an annual basis, time is interpreted to mean the fraction of a year that the investment is outstanding. The amount of interest is based on the principal or amount invested ($100,000) times the rate of interest (6%) times the fraction of a year the CD was outstanding in 2016 (29 days in October + 30 days in November + 31 days in December = 90 days). To simplify interest calculations, it is easiest to assume 360 days in a year. With the availability of computers to do the work, however, most businesses now use 365 days in a year to calculate interest. Throughout this book, we assume 360 days in a year to allow us to focus on concepts rather than detailed calculations. Thus, in this example, the fraction of a year that the CD is outstanding during 2017 is 90/360.

The effect of the receipt of the principal amount of the CD of $100,000 and interest for 120 days can be identified and analyzed as follows:

Identify and Analyze	**ACTIVITY:** Investing and Operating **ACCOUNTS:** Cash Increase Short-Term Investments—CD Decrease Interest Receivable Decrease Interest Revenue Increase **STATEMENT(S):** Balance Sheet and Income Statement

Balance Sheet						Income Statement				
ASSETS		=	LIABILITIES	+	STOCKHOLDERS' EQUITY	REVENUES		−	EXPENSES =	NET INCOME
Cash	102,000				500	Interest Revenue	500			500
Short-Term Investments—										
CD	(100,000)									
Interest Receivable	(1,500)									

This results in the removal of both the CD and the interest receivable from the records and recognizes $500 in interest earned during the first 30 days of 2018: $100,000 × 0.06 × 30/360 = $500. Exhibit 7-3 below summarizes the calculation of interest in each of the two accounting periods.

Investments in Stocks and Bonds

Corporations frequently invest in the debt securities (bonds) and equity securities of other businesses. The company that invests is the *investor*, and the company whose stocks or bonds are purchased is the *investee*.

No Significant Influence In some cases, companies may invest excess funds in stocks and bonds over the short run. In other cases, stocks and bonds are purchased as a way to invest cash over the long run. Often, these types of investments are made in anticipation of a need for cash at some distant point in the future. For example, a company may invest today in a combination of stocks and bonds because it will need cash ten years from now to build a new plant. The investor may be interested primarily in periodic income in the form of interest and dividends, in appreciation in the value of the securities, or in some combination of the two.

EXHIBIT 7-3 Interest Calculation

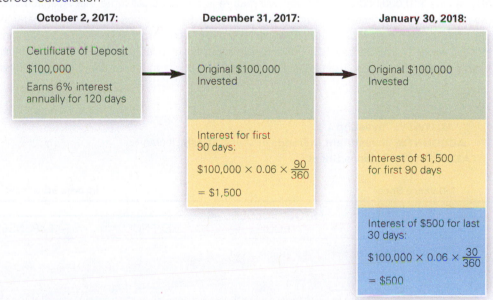

Significant Influence Sometimes a company buys a relatively large percentage of the common stock of the investee in order to secure significant influence over this company's policies. For example, a company might buy 30% of the common stock of a supplier of its raw materials to ensure a steady source of inventory. When an investor is able to secure influence over the investee, the equity method of accounting is used. According to current accounting standards, this method is appropriate when an investor owns at least 20% of the common stock of the investee.

Control A corporation may buy stock in another company with the purpose of obtaining control over the other entity. Normally, this requires an investment in excess of 50% of the common stock of the investee. When an investor owns more than half the stock of another company, accountants normally prepare a set of consolidated financial statements. This involves combining the financial statements of the individual entities into a single set of statements. An investor with an interest of more than 50% in another company is called the *parent*, and the investee in these situations is called the *subsidiary*.

The following chart summarizes the accounting by an investor for investments in the common stock of another company:

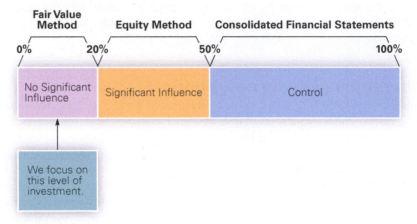

The remainder of this section will discuss how companies account for investments that do not give them significant influence over the other company.[2]

EXAMPLE 7-10   Accounting for an Investment in Bonds

On January 1, 2017, ABC issues $10,000,000 of bonds that will mature in ten years. Assume that Atlantic buys $100,000 of these bonds at face value, which is the amount that will be repaid to the investor when the bonds mature. In many instances, bonds are purchased at an amount more or less than face value. However, the discussion here will be limited to the simpler case in which bonds are purchased for face value. The bonds pay 10% interest semiannually on June 30 and December 31. Atlantic will receive 5% of $100,000, or $5,000, on each of those dates. The transaction on Atlantic's books to record the purchase can be identified and analyzed as follows:

Identify and Analyze	ACTIVITY: **Investing**
	ACCOUNTS: **Investment in Bonds** Increase **Cash** Decrease
	STATEMENT(S): **Balance Sheet**

Balance Sheet				Income Statement			
ASSETS	=	LIABILITIES	+	STOCKHOLDERS' EQUITY	REVENUES	− EXPENSES	= NET INCOME
Investment in Bonds 100,000							
Cash (100,000)							

[2] Accounting for investments in which there is significant influence or control is covered in advanced accounting textbooks.

On June 30, Atlantic must record the receipt of semiannual interest. The transaction on this date can be identified and analyzed as follows:

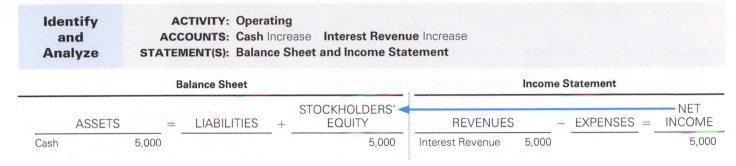

		ACTIVITY: Operating
Identify and Analyze		**ACCOUNTS:** Cash Increase Interest Revenue Increase
		STATEMENT(S): Balance Sheet and Income Statement

Balance Sheet					Income Statement			
ASSETS	=	LIABILITIES	+	STOCKHOLDERS' EQUITY	REVENUES	−	EXPENSES =	NET INCOME
Cash 5,000				5,000	Interest Revenue 5,000			5,000

Income was recognized when interest was received. If interest is not received at the end of an accounting period, a company should accrue interest earned but not yet received.

Before the maturity date, Atlantic needs cash and decides to sell the bonds. Any difference between the proceeds received from the sale of the bonds and the amount paid for the bonds is recognized as either a gain or a loss. On July 1, 2017, Atlantic sells all of its ABC bonds at 99. The amount of cash received is 0.99 × $100,000, or $99,000. The effect of the sale of the bonds can be identified and analyzed as follows:

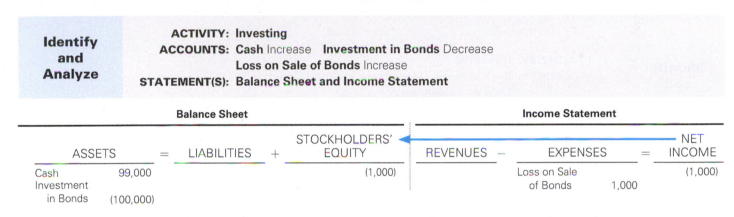

		ACTIVITY: Investing
Identify and Analyze		**ACCOUNTS:** Cash Increase Investment in Bonds Decrease
		Loss on Sale of Bonds Increase
		STATEMENT(S): Balance Sheet and Income Statement

Balance Sheet					Income Statement			
ASSETS	=	LIABILITIES	+	STOCKHOLDERS' EQUITY	REVENUES −		EXPENSES	= NET INCOME
Cash 99,000				(1,000)			Loss on Sale of Bonds 1,000	(1,000)
Investment in Bonds (100,000)								

The $1,000 loss on the sale of the bonds is the excess of the amount paid for the purchase of the bonds of $100,000 over the cash proceeds from the sale of $99,000. The loss is reported in the Other Income and Expenses section on the 2017 income statement.

EXAMPLE 7-11 Accounting for an Investment in Stock

All investments in stock are recorded initially at cost, including any brokerage fees, commissions, or other fees paid to acquire the shares. On February 1, 2017, Dexter Corp. pays $50,000 for shares of Stuart common stock and another $1,000 in commissions. The effect of the purchase of the stock can be identified and analyzed as follows:

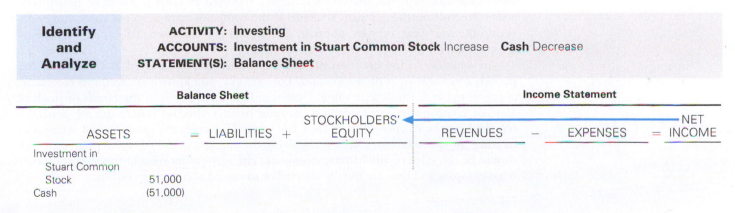

		ACTIVITY: Investing
Identify and Analyze		**ACCOUNTS:** Investment in Stuart Common Stock Increase Cash Decrease
		STATEMENT(S): Balance Sheet

Balance Sheet					Income Statement			
ASSETS	=	LIABILITIES +		STOCKHOLDERS' EQUITY	REVENUES	−	EXPENSES	= INCOME
Investment in Stuart Common Stock 51,000								
Cash (51,000)								

Many companies attempt to pay dividends every year as a signal of overall financial strength and profitability.[3] On March 31, 2017, Dexter received dividends of $500 from Stuart. The dividends received are recognized as income in a transaction that can be identified and analyzed as follows:

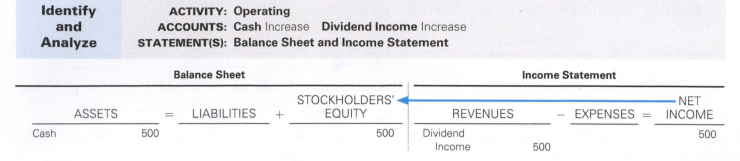

Identify and Analyze	**ACTIVITY:** Operating							
	ACCOUNTS: Cash Increase **Dividend Income** Increase							
	STATEMENT(S): Balance Sheet and Income Statement							

Balance Sheet				Income Statement			
ASSETS	=	LIABILITIES	+	STOCKHOLDERS' EQUITY	REVENUES	−	EXPENSES = NET INCOME
Cash 500				500	Dividend Income 500		500

Unlike interest on a bond or note, dividends do not accrue over time. In fact, a company has no legal obligation to pay dividends until its board of directors declares them. Up to that point, the investor has no guarantee that dividends will ever be paid.

Dexter sells the Stuart stock on May 20, 2017, for $53,000. In this case, Dexter recognizes a gain for the excess of the cash proceeds, $53,000, over the amount recorded on the books, $51,000. The effect of the sale of the stock can be identified and analyzed as follows:

Identify and Analyze	**ACTIVITY:** Investing
	ACCOUNTS: Cash Increase **Investment in Stuart Common Stock** Decrease
	Gain on Sale of Stock Increase
	STATEMENT(S): Balance Sheet and Income Statement

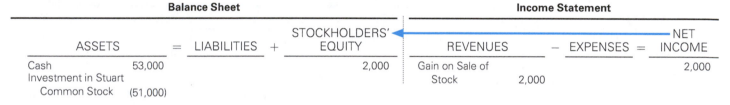

Balance Sheet				Income Statement			
ASSETS	=	LIABILITIES	+	STOCKHOLDERS' EQUITY	REVENUES	−	EXPENSES = NET INCOME
Cash 53,000				2,000	Gain on Sale of Stock 2,000		2,000
Investment in Stuart Common Stock (51,000)							

The gain is classified on the income statement as other income.

Valuing and Reporting Investments on the Financial Statements

Investments in other companies' bonds and stocks are reported on a company's balance sheet as assets. Whether the investments are reported as current assets or noncurrent assets depends on the company's intent. If the company intends to sell the investments within the next year, they are normally classified as current assets. All other investments are classified on the balance sheet as noncurrent.

In addition to the question of where investments are reported at the end of the period, another issue is their valuation. For example, you know that accounts receivable are reported at net realizable value. How should an investment in the bonds or stock of another company be reported on a year-end balance sheet? Investments are generally reported on the balance sheet at their fair value. However, the question still remains as to when any gains or losses from recognizing the changes in the fair value of investments should be recorded on the income statement. The accounting rules in this area are somewhat complex and thus are usually covered in advanced accounting courses.

---

[3] IBM's most recent dividend continued a string of consecutive quarterly dividends that started in 1916.

MODULE 3 TEST YOURSELF

Review	**LO5** Explain the accounting for and disclosure of various types of investments that companies make.	• Typically, excess cash expected to last for short periods of time is invested in highly liquid financial instruments such as CDs.
		• Sometimes cash is invested in securities of other corporations:
		  • Equity securities—securities issued by corporations as a form of ownership in the business.
		  • Debt securities—securities issued by corporations as a form of borrowing.
		• At times, a company may want to purchase a relatively large portion of another firm's stock to acquire influence over that firm.

Question	1. On December 31, Stockton Inc. invests idle cash in two different certificates of deposit. The first is an 8%, 90-day CD, and the second has an interest rate of 9% and matures in 120 days. How is each of these CDs classified on the December 31 balance sheet?	
	2. Stanzel Corp. purchased 1,000 shares of Canby Company common stock. What will determine whether the shares are classified as current assets or noncurrent assets?	

Apply	1. Indicate whether each of the following events will result in an increase (I), will result in a decrease (D), or will have no effect (NE) on net income for the period.
	  a. Stock held as an investment is sold for more than its carrying value.
	  b. Interest is recognized on bonds held as an investment.
	  c. Stock held as an investment is sold for less than its carrying value.
	  d. Bonds held as an investment are redeemed on their maturity date at face value.
	  e. Stock is purchased and a commission is paid to a broker.	

	2. On March 5, Spartan sold stock in another company for $12,300. Spartan bought the stock on February 14 for $10,100. Identify and analyze the transaction on Spartan's books on March 5.	

Answers are located at the end of the chapter.

MODULE 4 HOW LIQUID ASSETS AFFECT THE STATEMENT OF CASH FLOWS

As was discussed in Chapter 6, cash equivalents are combined with cash on the balance sheet. These items are very near maturity and do not present any significant risk of collectibility. Because of this, any purchases or redemptions of cash equivalents are not considered significant activities to be reported on a statement of cash flows.

LO6 Explain the effects of transactions involving liquid assets on the statement of cash flows.

The purchase and sale of investments are considered significant activities and therefore are reported on the statement of cash flows. Cash flows from purchases, sales, and maturities of investments are usually classified as investing activities. The following excerpt from Apple's 2015 statement of cash flows in its Form 10-K illustrates the reporting for these activities (all amounts in millions of dollars):

	Years ended		
Investing Activities	**September 26, 2015**	**September 27, 2014**	**September 28, 2013**
Purchases of marketable securities	$(166,402)	$(217,128)	$(148,489)
Proceeds from maturities of marketable securities	14,538	18,810	20,317
Proceeds from sales of marketable securities	107,447	189,301	104,130

EXHIBIT 7-4 How Investments and Receivables Affect the Statement of Cash Flows

The collection of accounts receivable and notes receivable generates cash for a business and affects the Operating Activities section of the statement of cash flows. Most companies use the indirect method of reporting cash flows and begin the statement of cash flows with the net income of the period. Net income includes the sales revenue for the period. Therefore, a decrease in accounts receivable or notes receivable during the period indicates that the company collected more cash than it recorded in sales revenue. Thus, a decrease in accounts receivable or notes receivable must be added back to net income because more cash was collected than is reflected in the sales revenue number.

Alternatively, an increase in accounts receivable or notes receivable indicates that the company recorded more sales revenue than cash collected during the period. Therefore, an increase in accounts receivable or notes receivable requires a deduction from the net income of the period to arrive at cash flow from operating activities. The following excerpt from Apple's 2015 statement of cash flows in its Form 10-K illustrates how it reports the change in accounts receivable on its statement of cash flows (all amounts in millions of dollars). A decrease in accounts receivable in the most recent year is added back to net income:

	Years ended		
Operating Activities	**September 26, 2015**	**September 27, 2014**	**September 28, 2013**
Changes in operating assets and liabilities:			
Accounts receivable, net	$611	$(4,232)	$(2,172)

These adjustments as well as the cash flows from buying and selling investments are summarized in Exhibit 7-4.[4]

MODULE 4　TEST YOURSELF

Review	**LO6** Explain the effects of transactions involving liquid assets on the statement of cash flows.	• Changes in cash equivalents are not shown on the statement. • Cash flows related to the purchase and sale of investments are classified as Investing Activities in the statement of cash flows. • Under the indirect method, increases in accounts and notes receivable are deducted and decreases in these accounts are added back in the Operating Activities section of the statement.

---

[4] A complete discussion of the statement of cash flows, including the reporting of investments, will be presented in Chapter 12.

Question	1. How are purchases of investments classified and reported on the statement of cash flows?
	2. In what section of the statement of cash flows are changes in accounts receivable reported when the indirect method is used to prepare the statement?

Apply	Wildcat started the year with $25,000 in accounts receivable and ended the year with $40,000 in the account. Describe how information regarding the company's accounts receivable should be reflected on its statement of cash flows, assuming the use of the indirect method.

Answers are located at the end of the chapter.

RATIO REVIEW

Accounts Receivable Turnover = $\dfrac{\text{Net Credit Sales (Income Statement)}}{\text{Average Accounts Receivable* (Balance Sheet)}}$

*Average accounts receivable can be estimated using the following calculation:

$$\dfrac{\text{Beginning Accounts Receivable + Ending Accounts Receivable}}{2}$$

Number of Days' Sales in Receivables = $\dfrac{\text{Number of Days in the Period**}}{\text{Accounts Receivable Turnover Ratio}}$

**Usually assume 360 days unless some other number is a better estimate of the number of days in the period.

ACCOUNTS HIGHLIGHTED

Account Titles	Where It Appears	In What Section	Page Number
Accounts Receivable	Balance Sheet	Current Assets	312
Allowance for Doubtful Accounts	Balance Sheet	Current Assets	314
Bad Debts Expense	Income Statement	Operating Expenses	314
Notes Receivable	Balance Sheet	Current or Noncurrent Assets	323
Interest Receivable	Balance Sheet	Current Assets	324
Interest Revenue	Income Statement	Other Income	324
Short-Term Investments	Balance Sheet	Current Assets	328

KEY TERMS QUIZ

Read each definition below and write the number of the definition in the blank beside the appropriate term. The quiz solutions appear at the end of the chapter.

_____ Account receivable
_____ Subsidiary ledger
_____ Control account
_____ Net realizable value
_____ Direct write-off method
_____ Allowance method

_____ Allowance for doubtful accounts
_____ Aging schedule
_____ Accounts receivable turnover ratio
_____ Number of days' sales in receivables
_____ Promissory note
_____ Maker

(Continued)

_____ Payee   _____ Maturity value
_____ Note receivable   _____ Interest
_____ Note payable   _____ Discounting
_____ Principal   _____ Equity securities
_____ Maturity date   _____ Debt securities
_____ Term

1. Securities issued by corporations as a form of ownership in the business.
2. Securities issued by corporations and governmental bodies as a form of borrowing.
3. A method of estimating bad debts on the basis of either the net credit sales of the period or the accounts receivable at the end of the period.
4. The party that will receive the money from a promissory note at some future date.
5. A written promise to repay a definite sum of money on demand or at a fixed or determinable date in the future.
6. A liability resulting from the signing of a promissory note.
7. An asset resulting from the acceptance of a promissory note from another company.
8. The process of selling a promissory note.
9. The party that agrees to repay the money for a promissory note at some future date.
10. A form used to categorize the various individual accounts receivable according to the length of time each has been outstanding.
11. The detail for a number of individual items that collectively make up a single general ledger account.
12. The recognition of bad debts expense at the point an account is written off as uncollectible.
13. The general ledger account that is supported by a subsidiary ledger.
14. The difference between the principal amount of the note and its maturity value.
15. The amount of cash received, or the fair value of the products or services received, by the maker when a promissory note is issued.
16. The amount of cash the maker is to pay the payee on the maturity date of the note.
17. The length of time a note is outstanding, that is, the period of time between the date it is issued and the date it matures.
18. The date the promissory note is due.
19. A contra-asset account used to reduce accounts receivable to its net realizable value.
20. A receivable arising from the sale of goods or services with a verbal promise to pay.
21. A measure of how long it takes to collect receivables.
22. A measure of the number of times accounts receivable is collected during the period.
23. The amount a company expects to collect on an account receivable.

ALTERNATE TERMS

allowance for doubtful accounts allowance for uncollectible accounts
debt securities bonds

equity securities stocks
net realizable value net recoverable amount

REVIEW PROBLEM & SOLUTION

The following items pertain to the Current Assets section of the balance sheet for Jackson Corp. at the end of its accounting year, December 31, 2017. Each item must be considered and any necessary adjustment recognized. Additionally, the accountant for Jackson wants to develop the Current Assets section of the balance sheet as of the end of 2017.

a. Cash and cash equivalents amount to $19,375.
b. A 9%, 120-day certificate of deposit was purchased on December 1, 2017, for $10,000.
c. Gross accounts receivable at December 31, 2017, amount to $44,000. Before adjustment, the balance in Allowance for Doubtful Accounts is $340. Based on past experience, the

accountant estimates that 3% of the gross accounts receivable outstanding at December 31, 2017, will prove to be uncollectible.

d. A customer's 12%, 90-day promissory note in the amount of $6,000 is held at the end of the year. The note has been held for 45 days during 2017.

Required

1. Identify and analyze the year-end adjustments needed in (b), (c), and (d).
2. Prepare the Current Assets section of Jackson's balance sheet as of December 31, 2017. In addition to the information in the preceding items, the balances in Inventory and Prepaid Insurance on this date are $65,000 and $4,800, respectively.

Solution to Review Problem

1. The following adjustments are needed at December 31, 2017:

b. Jackson needs an adjustment to record interest earned on the certificate of deposit. The CD has been outstanding for 30 days during 2017; therefore, the amount of interest earned is calculated as follows:

$$\$10,000 \times 0.09 \times 30/360 = \$75$$

The adjustment can be identified and analyzed as follows:

Identify and Analyze	**ACTIVITY:** Operating **ACCOUNTS:** Interest Receivable Increase Interest Revenue Increase **STATEMENT(S):** Balance Sheet and Income Statement

Balance Sheet				Income Statement			
ASSETS	=	LIABILITIES	+	STOCKHOLDERS' EQUITY	REVENUES	−	EXPENSES = NET INCOME
Interest Receivable 75				75	Interest Revenue 75		75

c. Based on gross accounts receivable of $44,000 at year-end and an estimate that 3% of this amount will be uncollectible, the balance in Allowance for Doubtful Accounts should be $1,320 ($44,000 × 3%). Given a current balance of $340, an adjustment for $980 ($1,320 − $340) is needed to bring the balance to the desired amount of $1,320. The adjustment can be identified and analyzed as follows:

Identify and Analyze	**ACTIVITY:** Operating **ACCOUNTS:** Allowance for Doubtful Accounts Increase Bad Debts Expense Increase **STATEMENT(S):** Balance Sheet and Income Statement

Balance Sheet				Income Statement			
ASSETS	=	LIABILITIES	+	STOCKHOLDERS' EQUITY	REVENUES	−	EXPENSES = NET INCOME
Allowance for Doubtful Accounts* (980)				(980)			Bad Debts Expense 980 (980)

*The Allowance for Doubtful Accounts account has increased. It is shown as a decrease in the equation above because it is a contra account and causes total assets to decrease.

d. An adjustment is needed to accrue interest on the promissory note ($6,000 × 0.12 × 45/360 = $90). The effect of the adjustment can be identified and analyzed as follows:

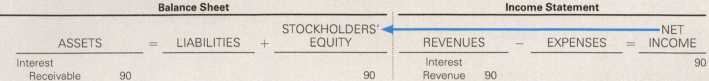

Identify and Analyze	ACTIVITY: Operating ACCOUNTS: Interest Receivable Increase Interest Revenue Increase STATEMENT(S): Balance Sheet and Income Statement

Balance Sheet					Income Statement				
ASSETS	=	LIABILITIES	+	STOCKHOLDERS' EQUITY	REVENUES	−	EXPENSES	=	NET INCOME
Interest Receivable 90				90	Interest Revenue 90				90

2. The Current Assets section of Jackson's balance sheet appears as follows:

Jackson Corp.
Partial Balance Sheet
December 31, 2017

Current assets:		
Cash and cash equivalents		$ 19,375
Certificate of deposit		10,000
Accounts receivable	$44,000	
Allowance for doubtful accounts	1,320	42,680
Notes receivable		6,000
Interest receivable		165*
Inventory		65,000
Prepaid insurance		4,800
Total current assets		$148,020

*$75 from CD and $90 from promissory note.

EXERCISES

LO1
EXAMPLE 7-1, 7-2, 7-3

Exercise 7-1 Comparison of the Direct Write-Off and Allowance Methods of Accounting for Bad Debts

In its first year of business, Rideaway Bikes has net income of $145,000, exclusive of any adjustment for bad debts expense. The president of the company has asked you to calculate net income under each of two alternatives of accounting for bad debts: the direct write-off method and the allowance method. The president would like to use the method that will result in the higher net income. So far, no adjustments have been made to write off uncollectible accounts or to estimate bad debts. The relevant data are as follows:

Write-offs of uncollectible accounts during the year	$10,500
Net credit sales	$650,000
Estimated percentage of net credit sales that will be uncollectible	2%

Required

Compute net income under each of the two alternatives. Does Rideaway have a choice as to which method to use? If so, should it base its choice on which method will result in the higher net income? (Ignore income taxes.) Explain.

Exercise 7-2 Allowance Method of Accounting for Bad Debts—Comparison of the Two Approaches

LO1
EXAMPLE 7-2, 7-3, 7-4

Kandel Company had the following data available for 2017 (before making any adjustments):

Accounts receivable, 12/31/17	$320,100
Allowance for doubtful accounts	2,600
Net credit sales, 2017	834,000

Required

1. Identify and analyze the adjustment to recognize bad debts under the following assumptions: (a) bad debts expense is expected to be 2% of net credit sales for the year and (b) Kandel expects it will not be able to collect 6% of the balance in accounts receivable at year-end.
2. Assume instead that the balance in the allowance account is a negative $2,600. How will this affect your answers to part (1)?

Exercise 7-3 Working Backward: Allowance for Doubtful Accounts

LO1
EXAMPLE 7-2

Olson Corp. reported the following in the Current Assets section of its December 31, 2017, balance sheet:

	12/31/17	12/31/16
Accounts receivable, net of allowances of $5,000 and $3,000, respectively	$54,000	$48,000

During 2017, Olson recorded $80,000 of sales on credit and wrote off $4,000 of uncollectible accounts.

Required

1. Determine the amount of cash collected during 2017 from sales on credit.
2. Determine the amount of bad debts expense for 2017.

Exercise 7-4 Using an Aging Schedule to Account for Bad Debts

LO1
EXAMPLE 7-5

Carter Company sells on credit with terms of n/30. For the $500,000 of accounts at the end of the year that are not overdue, there is a 90% probability of collection. For the $200,000 of accounts that are less than a month past due, Carter estimates the likelihood of collection going down to 70%. The probability of collecting the $100,000 of accounts more than a month past due is estimated to be 25%.

Required

1. Prepare an aging schedule to estimate the amount of uncollectible accounts.
2. On the basis of the schedule in part (1), identify and analyze the adjustment needed to estimate bad debts. Assume that the balance in Allowance for Doubtful Accounts is $20,000.

Exercise 7-5 Accounts Receivable Turnover for Nike

LO2
EXAMPLE 7-6

The financial statements included in the 2015 Form 10-K of **Nike** reported the following amounts (in millions of dollars):

Revenues, for the year ended May 31, 2015	$30,601
Accounts receivable, net, May 31, 2015	3,358
Accounts receivable, net, May 31, 2014	3,434

REAL WORLD

Required

1. Compute Nike's accounts receivable turnover ratio for the year ended May 31, 2015. (Assume that all sales are on credit.)
2. What is the average collection period in days for an account receivable? Explain your answer.
3. Give some examples of the types of customers you would expect Nike to have. Do you think the average collection period for sales to these customers is reasonable? What other information do you need to fully answer that question?

LO2

EXAMPLE 7-6

Exercise 7-6 Working Backward: Accounts Receivable Turnover

It takes Carlson Corp. 30 days on average to collect its accounts receivable. The company began the year with $10,500 in accounts receivable. Sales on credit for the year amounted to $150,000.

Required

Assuming 360 days in a year, determine the amount of Carlson's accounts receivable at the end of the year.

LO3

EXAMPLE 7-7

Exercise 7-7 Notes Receivable

On September 1, 2017, Dougherty Corp. accepted a six-month, 7%, $45,000 interest-bearing note from Rozelle Company in payment of an account receivable. Dougherty's year-end is December 31. Rozelle paid the note and interest on the due date.

Required

1. Who is the maker and who is the payee of the note?
2. What is the maturity date of the note?
3. Identify and analyze the effect of the transactions or adjustments to be recorded on each of the following dates:

   a. September 1, 2017
   b. December 31, 2017
   c. March 1, 2018

Exercise 7-8 Working Backward: Notes Receivable

LO3

EXAMPLE 7-7

On December 1, 2017, Roper Corp. accepted a two-month, $24,000 interest-bearing note from a customer in payment of an account receivable. On December 31, 2017, Roper made an adjustment with the following effect on the accounting equation:

Identify and Analyze	
	ACTIVITY: Operating
	ACCOUNTS: Interest Receivable Increase Interest Revenue Increase
	STATEMENT(S): Balance Sheet and Income Statement

Balance Sheet				Income Statement		
ASSETS	=	LIABILITIES	+	STOCKHOLDERS' EQUITY	REVENUES	− EXPENSES = NET INCOME
Interest Receivable 200				200	Interest Revenue 200	200

Required

1. What is the interest rate on the note? Explain your answer.
2. Identify and analyze the transaction recorded on January 31, 2018, when the company collects the principal and interest on the note.

LO4

EXAMPLE 7-8

Exercise 7-9 Credit Card Sales

Darlene's Diner accepts American Express® credit cards from its customers. Darlene's is closed on Sundays and on that day records the weekly sales and remits the credit card receipts to American Express. For the week ending on Sunday, June 12, cash sales totaled $2,430 and credit card sales amounted to $3,500. On June 15, Darlene's received $3,360 from American Express as payment for the credit card receipts. Identify and analyze the transactions on June 12 and June 15. As a percentage, what collection fee is American Express charging Darlene's?

LO5

EXAMPLE 7-9

Exercise 7-10 Certificate of Deposit

On May 31, 2017, Elmer Corp. purchased a 120-day, 9% certificate of deposit for $50,000. The CD was redeemed on September 28, 2017. Identify and analyze the transactions or adjustments on Elmer's books to account for:

a. The purchase of the CD.

b. The accrual of interest adjustment for interest earned through June 30, the end of the company's fiscal year.

c. The redemption of the CD.

Assume 360 days in a year.

Exercise 7-11   Classification of Cash Equivalents and Investments on a Balance Sheet   LO5

Classify each of the following items as a cash equivalent (CE), a short-term investment (STI), or a long-term investment (LTI).

1. A 120-day certificate of deposit.
2. Three hundred shares of MG common stock. The company plans on selling the stock in six months.
3. A six-month U.S. Treasury bill.
4. A 60-day certificate of deposit.
5. Maple Co. bonds maturing in 15 years. The company intends to hold the bonds until maturity.
6. Commercial paper issued by ABC Corp., maturing in four months.
7. Five hundred shares of Copper common stock. The company plans to sell the stock in 60 days to help pay for a note due at that time at the bank.
8. Two hundred shares of EG preferred stock. The company intends to hold the stock for ten years and then sell it to help finance construction of a new factory.
9. Ten-year U.S. Treasury bonds. The company plans to sell the bonds on the open market in six months.
10. A 90-day U.S. Treasury bill.

Exercise 7-12   Purchase and Sale of Bonds   LO5

EXAMPLE 7-10

Starship Enterprises enters into the following transactions during 2017 and 2018:

2017

Jan. 1:   Purchased $100,000 face value of Northern Lights Inc. bonds at face value.

            The newly issued bonds have an interest rate of 8% paid semiannually on June 30 and December 31. The bonds mature in five years.

June 30:   Received interest on the Northern Lights Inc. bonds.

Dec. 31:   Received interest on the Northern Lights Inc. bonds.

2018

Jan. 1:   Sold the Northern Lights Inc. bonds for $102,000.

Required

1. Identify and analyze all transactions on Starship's records to account for its investment in the Northern Lights bonds.
2. Why was Starship able to sell its Northern Lights bonds for $102,000?

Exercise 7-13   Investment in Stock   LO5

EXAMPLE 7-11

On October 1, 2017, Chicago Corp. purchases 1,000 shares of the preferred stock of Denver Corp. for $40 per share. Chicago pays another $1,000 in commissions. On October 20, 2017, Denver declares and pays a dividend of $1 per share. Chicago sells the stock on November 5, 2017, at a price of $45 per share.

Required

Identify and analyze all transactions on Chicago's books in connection with its investment, beginning with the purchase of the preferred stock on October 1, 2017; the dividend received on October 20, 2017; and the sale on November 5, 2017.

LO5

EXAMPLE 7-11

Exercise 7-14 Investment in Stock

On August 15, 2017, Cubs Corp. purchases 5,000 shares of common stock in Sox Inc. at a market price of $15 per share. In addition, Cubs pays brokerage fees of $1,000. On October 20, 2017, Cubs sells the Sox stock for $10 per share.

Required

Identify and analyze all transactions on Cubs's books in connection with the investment beginning with the purchase of the common stock on August 15, 2017, and the sale on October 20, 2017.

LO5

EXAMPLE 7-11

Exercise 7-15 Working Backward: Investment in Stock

On its December 31, 2017, income statement, Durango reported a loss on sale of stock of $4,500. The loss resulted from the sale of 2,000 shares of ABC Corp. stock that Durango purchased during 2017 at $25 per share, excluding $500 in commissions to buy the shares.

Required

Determine the amount of cash Durango received from the sale of the ABC stock.

LO6

Exercise 7-16 Impact of Transactions Involving Receivables on Statement of Cash Flows

From the following list, identify whether the change in the account balance during the year would be added to or deducted from net income when the indirect method is used to determine cash flows from operating activities:

> Increase in accounts receivable
> Decrease in accounts receivable
> Increase in notes receivable
> Decrease in notes receivable

LO6

Exercise 7-17 Working Backward: Accounts Receivable and the Statement of Cash Flows

Troy Corp.'s statement of cash flows reported an addition of $2,000 for the change in the Accounts Receivable account during the year. Sales on account for the year amounted to $24,500.

Required

Determine the cash collected on accounts receivable for the year.

LO6

Exercise 7-18 Cash Collections—Direct Method

Emily Enterprises' comparative balance sheets included accounts receivable of $224,600 at December 31, 2016, and $205,700 at December 31, 2017. Sales reported on Emily's 2017 income statement amounted to $2,250,000. What is the amount of cash collections that Emily will report in the Operating Activities category of its 2017 statement of cash flows assuming that the direct method is used?

MULTI-CONCEPT EXERCISE

LO1 • 5 • 6

Exercise 7-19 Impact of Transactions Involving Cash, Investments, and Receivables on Statement of Cash Flows

From the following list, identify each item as operating (O), investing (I), financing (F), or not separately reported on the statement of cash flows (N). Assume that the indirect method is used to determine the cash flows from operating activities.

> Purchase of cash equivalents
> Redemption of cash equivalents
> Purchase of investments
> Sale of investments
> Write-off of customer account (under the allowance method)

PROBLEMS

Problem 7-1 Allowance Method for Accounting for Bad Debts

LO1

At the beginning of 2017, EZ Tech Company's Accounts Receivable balance was $140,000, and the balance in Allowance for Doubtful Accounts was $2,350. EZ Tech's sales in 2017 were $1,050,000, 80% of which were on credit. Collections on account during the year were $670,000. The company wrote off $4,000 of uncollectible accounts during the year.

Required

1. Identify and analyze the transactions related to the sale, collections, and write-offs of accounts receivable during 2017.
2. Identify and analyze the adjustments to recognize bad debts assuming that (a) bad debts expense is 3% of credit sales and (b) amounts expected to be uncollectible are 6% of the year-end accounts receivable.
3. What is the net realizable value of accounts receivable on December 31, 2017, under each assumption in part (2)?
4. What effect does the recognition of bad debts expense have on the net realizable value? What effect does the write-off of accounts have on the net realizable value?

Problem 7-2 Using an Aging Schedule to Account for Bad Debts

LO1

Sparkle Jewels distributes fine stones. It sells on credit to retail jewelry stores and extends terms that require the stores to pay in 60 days. For accounts that are not overdue, Sparkle has found that there is a 95% probability of collection. For accounts up to one month past due, the likelihood of collection decreases to 80%. If accounts are between one and two months past due, the probability of collection is 60%, and if an account is over two months past due, Sparkle Jewels estimates only a 40% chance of collecting the receivable.

On December 31, 2017, the balance in Allowance for Doubtful Accounts is $12,300. The amounts of gross receivables by age on this date are as follows:

Category	Amount
Current	$200,000
Past due:	
Less than one month	45,000
One to two months	25,000
Over two months	1,000

Required

1. Prepare a schedule to estimate the amount of uncollectible accounts at December 31, 2017.
2. On the basis of the schedule in part (1), identify and analyze the adjustment on December 31, 2017, to estimate bad debts.
3. Show how accounts receivable would be presented on the December 31, 2017, balance sheet.

Problem 7-3 Making Business Decisions: Analyzing The Coca-Cola Company's Accounts Receivable Turnover Ratio

LO2

RATIO ANALYSIS
BUSINESS DECISION MODEL

You are considering making a loan to **The Coca-Cola Company**. The following information is from the financial statements included in Form 10-K for fiscal years 2014 and 2013 (in millions of dollars):

Net operating revenues for the year ended:	
December 31, 2014	$45,998
December 31, 2013	46,854
Trade accounts receivable, less allowances of $331, 61, and 53, respectively:	
December 31, 2014	4,466
December 31, 2013	4,873
December 31, 2012	4,759

REAL WORLD

(Continued)

The following information is from the financial statements included in Form 10-K for fiscal years 2014 and 2013 for **PepsiCo, Inc.** (in millions of dollars):

Net revenue for the year ended:	
December 27, 2014	$66,683
December 28, 2013	66,415
Accounts and notes receivable, net:	
December 27, 2014	6,651
December 28, 2013	6,954
December 29, 2012	7,041

Required

Part A. The Ratio Analysis Model

A lender must assess how well a company is managing its accounts receivable before making a loan. The accounts receivable turnover ratio tells us how many times in a year a company collects its receivables. Replicate the five steps in the Ratio Analysis Model on pages 320–321 to analyze the accounts receivable turnover ratios for The Coca-Cola Company and PepsiCo:

1. Formulate the Question
2. Gather the Information from the Financial Statements
3. Calculate the Ratio
4. Compare the Ratio with Other Ratios
5. Interpret the Ratios

Part B. The Business Decision Model

A lender must consider a variety of factors, including financial ratios, before making a loan. Replicate the five steps in the Business Decision Model on page 321 to decide whether to loan money to The Coca-Cola Company:

1. Formulate the Question
2. Gather Information from the Financial Statements and Other Sources
3. Analyze the Information Gathered
4. Make the Decision
5. Monitor Your Decision

LO4 Problem 7-4 Credit Card Sales

Gas stations sometimes sell gasoline at a lower price to customers who pay cash than to customers who use a credit card. A local gas station owner pays 2% of the sales price to the credit card company when customers pay with a credit card. The owner pays $2.00 per gallon of gasoline and must earn at least $0.99 per gallon of gross margin to stay competitive.

Required

1. Determine the price the owner must charge credit card customers to maintain the station's gross margin.
2. How much discount could the owner offer to cash customers and still maintain the same gross margin?

LO5 Problem 7-5 Investments in Bonds and Stock

Swartz Inc. enters into the following transactions during 2017:

July 1:   Paid $10,000 to acquire on the open market $10,000 face value of Gallatin bonds. The bonds have a stated annual interest rate of 6% with interest paid semiannually on June 30 and December 31. The bonds mature in 5½ years.

Oct. 23:   Purchased 600 shares of Eagle Rock common stock at $20 per share.

Nov. 21:   Purchased 200 shares of Montana preferred stock at $30 per share.

Dec. 10:   Received dividends of $1.50 per share on the Eagle Rock stock and $2.00 per share on the Montana stock.

Dec. 28:   Sold 400 shares of Eagle Rock common stock at $25 per share.

Dec. 31:   Received interest from the Gallatin bonds.

Required

Identify and analyze all transactions on Swartz's records to account for its investments during 2017.

Problem 7-6 Investments in Stock

LO5

Atlas Superstores occasionally finds itself with excess cash to invest and consequently entered into the following transactions during 2017:

Jan. 15:	Purchased 200 shares of Bassett common stock at $50 per share, plus $500 in commissions.
May 23:	Received dividends of $2 per share on the Bassett stock.
June 1:	Purchased 100 shares of Boxer stock at $74 per share, plus $300 in commissions.
Oct. 20:	Sold all of the Bassett stock at $42 per share, less commissions of $400.
Dec. 15:	Received notification from Boxer that a $1.50-per-share dividend had been declared. The checks will be mailed to stockholders on January 10, 2018.

Required

Identify and analyze all transactions on the books of Atlas Superstores during 2017, including any necessary adjustment on December 15 when the dividend was declared.

Problem 7-7 Effects of Changes in Receivable Balances on Statement of Cash Flows

LO6

Stegner Inc. reported net income of $130,000 for the year ended December 31, 2017. The following items were included on Stegner's balance sheets at December 31, 2017 and 2016:

	12/31/17	12/31/16
Cash	$105,000	$110,000
Accounts receivable	223,000	83,000
Notes receivable	95,000	100,000

Stegner uses the indirect method to prepare its statement of cash flows. Stegner does not have any other current assets or current liabilities and did not enter into any investing or financing activities during 2017.

Required

1. Prepare Stegner's 2017 statement of cash flows.
2. Draft a brief memo to the owner to explain why cash decreased during a profitable year.

MULTI-CONCEPT PROBLEM

Problem 7-8 Accounts and Notes Receivable

LO1 • 3

Lenox Corp. sold merchandise for $5,000 to M. Baxter on May 15, 2017, with payment due in 30 days. Subsequent to this, Baxter experienced cash-flow problems and was unable to pay its debt. On August 10, 2017, Lenox stopped trying to collect the outstanding receivable from Baxter and wrote off the account as uncollectible. On December 1, 2017, Baxter sent Lenox a check for $1,000 and offered to sign a two-month, 9%, $4,000 promissory note to satisfy the remaining obligation. Baxter paid the entire amount due Lenox, with interest, on January 31, 2018. Lenox ends its accounting year on December 31 each year and uses the allowance method to account for bad debts.

Required

1. Identify and analyze all transactions or adjustments on the books of Lenox Corp. from May 15, 2017, to January 31, 2018.
2. Why would Baxter bother to send Lenox a check for $1,000 on December 1 and agree to sign a note for the balance, given that such a long period of time had passed since the original purchase?

ALTERNATE PROBLEMS

LO1 **Problem 7-1A Allowance Method for Accounting for Bad Debts**

At the beginning of 2017, Miyazaki Company's Accounts Receivable balance was $105,000, and the balance in Allowance for Doubtful Accounts was $1,950. Miyazaki's sales in 2017 were $787,500, 80% of which were on credit. Collections on account during the year were $502,500. The company wrote off $3,000 of uncollectible accounts during the year.

Required

1. Identify and analyze the transactions related to the sales, collections, and write-offs of accounts receivable during 2017.
2. Identify and analyze the adjustments to recognize bad debts assuming that (a) bad debts expense is 3% of credit sales and (b) amounts expected to be uncollectible are 6% of the year-end accounts receivable.
3. What is the net realizable value of accounts receivable on December 31, 2017, under each assumption in part (2)?
4. What effect does the recognition of bad debts expense have on the net realizable value? What effect does the write-off of accounts have on the net realizable value?

LO1 **Problem 7-2A Using an Aging Schedule to Account for Bad Debts**

Rough Stuff is a distributor of large rocks. It sells on credit to commercial landscaping companies and extends terms that require customers to pay in 60 days. For accounts that are not overdue, Rough Stuff has found that there is a 90% probability of collection. For accounts up to one month past due, the likelihood of collection decreases to 75%. If accounts are between one and two months past due, the probability of collection is 65%, and if an account is over two months past due, Rough Stuff estimates only a 25% chance of collecting the receivable.

On December 31, 2017, the balance in Allowance for Doubtful Accounts is $34,590. The amounts of gross receivables, by age, on this date are as follows:

Category	Amount
Current	$200,000
Past due:	
Less than one month	60,300
One to two months	35,000
Over two months	45,000

Required

1. Prepare a schedule to estimate the amount of uncollectible accounts at December 31, 2017.
2. Rough Stuff knows that $40,000 of the $45,000 amount that is more than two months overdue is due from one customer that is in severe financial trouble. It is rumored that the customer will be filing for bankruptcy in the near future. As controller for Rough Stuff, how would you handle this situation?
3. Show how accounts receivable would be presented on the December 31, 2017, balance sheet.

LO2 **Problem 7-3A Making Business Decisions: Analyzing The Hershey Company's Accounts Receivable Turnover Ratio**

RATIO ANALYSIS
BUSINESS DECISION MODEL

REAL WORLD

You are considering making a loan to **The Hershey Company**. The following information is from the financial statements included in Form 10-K for fiscal years 2014 and 2013 (in thousands of dollars):

Net sales for the year ended:	
December 31, 2014	$7,421,768
December 31, 2013	7,146,079
Accounts receivable—trade, net:	
December 31, 2014	596,940
December 31, 2013	477,912
December 31, 2012	461,383

The following information is from the financial statements included in Form 10-K for fiscal years 2014 and 2013 for **Tootsie Roll Industries, Inc.** (in thousands of dollars):

Net product sales for the year ended:	
December 31, 2014	$539,895
December 31, 2013	539,627
Accounts receivable trade, less allowances of $1,968, $2,042, and $2,142 respectively:	
December 31, 2014	43,253
December 31, 2013	40,721
December 31, 2012	42,108

Required

Part A. The Ratio Analysis Model

A lender must assess how well a company is managing its accounts receivable before making a loan. The accounts receivable turnover ratio tells us how many times in a year a company collects its receivables. Replicate the five steps in the Ratio Analysis Model on pages 320–321 to analyze the accounts receivable turnover ratios for The Hershey Company and Tootsie Roll Industries, Inc.:

1. Formulate the Question
2. Gather the Information from the Financial Statements
3. Calculate the Ratio
4. Compare the Ratio with Other Ratios
5. Interpret the Ratios

Part B. The Business Decision Model

A lender must consider a variety of factors, including financial ratios, before making a loan. Replicate the five steps in the Business Decision Model on page 321 to decide whether to loan money to The Hershey Company:

1. Formulate the Question
2. Gather Information from the Financial Statements and Other Sources
3. Analyze the Information Gathered
4. Make the Decision
5. Monitor Your Decision

Problem 7-4A Credit Card Sales

LO4

A local fast-food store is considering accepting major credit cards in its outlets. Current annual sales are $800,000 per outlet. The company can purchase the equipment needed to handle credit cards and have an additional phone line installed in each outlet for approximately $800 per outlet. The equipment will be an expense in the year it is installed. The employee training time is minimal. The credit card company will charge a fee equal to 1.5% of sales for the use of credit cards. The company is unable to determine by how much, if any, sales will increase and whether cash customers will use a credit card rather than cash. No other fast-food stores in the local area accept credit cards for sales payment.

Required

1. Assuming that only 5% of existing cash customers will use a credit card, what increase in sales is necessary to pay for the credit card equipment in the first year?
2. What other factors might the company consider in addition to an increase in sales dollars?

Problem 7-5A Investments in Bonds and Stock

LO5

Vermont Corp. enters into the following transactions during 2017:

July 1:	Paid $10,000 to acquire on the open market $10,000 face value of Maine bonds. The bonds have a stated annual interest rate of 8% with interest paid semiannually on June 30 and December 31. The remaining life of the bonds on the date of purchase is 3½ years.
Oct. 23:	Purchased 1,000 shares of Virginia common stock at $15 per share.
Nov. 21:	Purchased 600 shares of Carolina preferred stock at $8 per share.
Dec. 10:	Received dividends of $0.50 per share on the Virginia stock and $1.00 per share on the Carolina stock.

(Continued)

Dec. 28:   Sold 700 shares of Virginia common stock at $19 per share.

Dec. 31:   Received interest from the Maine bonds.

Required

Identify and analyze all transactions on Vermont's records to account for its investments during 2017.

LO5   Problem 7-6A Investments in Stock

Trendy Supercenter occasionally finds itself with excess cash to invest and consequently entered into the following transactions during 2017:

Jan. 15:   Purchased 100 shares of BMI common stock at $130 per share, plus $250 in commissions.

May 23:   Received dividends of $1 per share on the BMI stock.

June 1:   Purchased 200 shares of MG stock at $60 per share, plus $300 in commissions.

Oct. 20:   Sold all of the BMI stock at $140 per share, less commissions of $400.

Dec. 15:   Received notification from MG that a $0.75-per-share dividend had been declared. The checks will be mailed to stockholders on January 10, 2018.

Required

Identify and analyze all transactions on the books of Trendy Supercenter during 2017, including any necessary adjustment on December 15 when the dividend was declared.

LO6   Problem 7-7A Effects of Changes in Receivable Balances on Statement of Cash Flows

St. Charles Antique Market reported a net loss of $6,000 for the year ended December 31, 2017. The following items were included on St. Charles Antique Market's balance sheets at December 31, 2017 and 2016:

	12/31/17	12/31/16
Cash	$ 36,300	$ 3,100
Accounts receivable	79,000	126,000
Notes receivable	112,600	104,800

St. Charles Antique Market uses the indirect method to prepare its statement of cash flows. It does not have any other current assets or current liabilities and did not enter into any investing or financing activities during 2017.

Required

1. Prepare St. Charles Antique Market's 2017 statement of cash flows.
2. Draft a brief memo to the owner to explain why cash increased during such an unprofitable year.

ALTERNATE MULTI-CONCEPT PROBLEM

LO1 • 3   Problem 7-8A Accounts and Notes Receivable

Tuscon Inc. sold merchandise for $6,000 to P. Paxton on July 31, 2017, with payment due in 30 days. Subsequent to this, Paxton experienced cash-flow problems and was unable to pay its debt. On December 24, 2017, Tuscon stopped trying to collect the outstanding receivable from Paxton and wrote off the account as uncollectible. On January 15, 2018, Paxton sent Tuscon a check for $1,500 and offered to sign a two-month, 8%, $4,500 promissory note to satisfy the remaining obligation. Paxton paid the entire amount due Tuscon, with interest, on March 15, 2018. Tuscon ends its accounting year on December 31 each year.

Required

1. Identify and analyze all transactions or adjustments on the books of Tuscon Inc. from July 31, 2017, to March 15, 2018.
2. Why would Paxton bother to send Tuscon a check for $1,500 on January 15 and agree to sign a note for the balance, given that such a long period of time had passed since the original purchase?

DECISION CASES

Reading and Interpreting Financial Statements

Decision Case 7-1 Reading 3M Company's Balance Sheet: Accounts Receivable

LO1

The following current asset appears on the balance sheet in **3M Company**'s Form 10-K for the year ended December 31, 2014 (amounts in millions of dollars):

	12/31/14	12/31/13
Accounts receivable—net of allowances of $94 and $104	$4,238	$4,253

Required

1. What is the balance in 3M Company's Allowance for Doubtful Accounts at the end of 2014 and 2013?
2. What is the net realizable value of 3M Company's accounts receivable at the end of each of these two years?
3. What caused increases in the allowance account during 2014? What caused decreases? Explain what a net decrease in the account for the year means.

Decision Case 7-2 Reading Apple Inc.'s Statement of Cash Flows

LO1 • 6

The following items appeared in the Investing Activities section of **Apple Inc.**'s statement of cash flows included in Form 10-K for the year ended September 26, 2015. (All amounts are in millions of dollars.)

	2015	2014	2013
Purchases of marketable securities	$(166,402)	$(217,128)	$(148,489)
Proceeds from maturities of marketable securities	14,538	18,810	20,317
Proceeds from sales of marketable securities	107,447	189,301	104,130

Required

1. What amount did Apple spend in 2015 to purchase marketable securities? How does this amount compare to the amounts spent in the two prior years?
2. What amount did Apple receive from marketable securities that matured in 2015? How does this amount compare to the amounts received in the two prior years?
3. The third line in the preceding excerpt reports proceeds from sales, rather than maturities, of marketable securities. Why would certain types of marketable securities mature while others would be sold?

Decision Case 7-3 Comparing Two Companies in the Same Industry: Under Armour and Columbia Sportswear

LO2

The following information is available from the financial statements included in Form 10-K for fiscal years 2014 and 2013 for **Under Armour, Inc.** and **Columbia Sportswear Company** (in thousands of dollars):

	Under Armour, Inc.	Columbia Sportswear Company
Net revenues (Net sales for Columbia Sportswear) for the year ended December 31, 2014	$3,084,370	$2,100,590
Accounts receivable, net:		
December 31, 2014	279,835	344,390
December 31, 2013	209,952	306,878

(Continued)

Required

1. Calculate the accounts receivable turnover ratios for both companies for the most recent year. Assume all sales are on credit.
2. Calculate the average length of time it takes each company to collect its accounts receivable.
3. Compare the two companies on the basis of your calculations in parts (1) and (2).

Making Financial Decisions

LO1 • 5   Decision Case 7-4 Liquidity

Oak and Maple both provide computer consulting services to their clients. The following are the current assets for each company at the end of the year. (All amounts are in millions of dollars.)

	Oak	Maple
Cash	$10	$ 5
Six-month certificates of deposit	9	0
Short-term investments in stock	0	6
Accounts receivable	15	23
Allowance for doubtful accounts	(1)	(1)
Total current assets	$33	$33

Required

As a loan officer for First National Bank of Verona Heights, assume that both companies have come to you asking for a $10 million, six-month loan. If you could lend money to only one of the two, which one would it be? Justify your answer by writing a brief memo to the president of the bank.

Ethical Decision Making

LO4   Decision Case 7-5 Notes Receivable

ETHICAL DECISION MODEL

Patterson Company is a large diversified business with a unit that sells commercial real estate. As a company, Patterson has been profitable in recent years with the exception of the real estate business, where economic conditions have resulted in weak sales. The vice president of the real estate division is aware of the poor performance of his group and needs to find ways to "show a profit."

During the current year, the division is successful in selling a 100-acre tract of land for a new shopping center. The original cost of the property to Patterson was $4 million. The buyer has agreed to sign a $10 million note with payments of $2 million due at the end of each of the next five years. The property was appraised late last year at a market value of $7.5 million. The vice president has come to you, the controller, asking that you record a sale for $10 million with a corresponding increase in Notes Receivable for $10 million.

Required

Use the Ethical Decision Framework in Exhibit 1-9 to complete the following requirements:

1. **Recognize an ethical dilemma:** What ethical dilemma(s) do you face?
2. **Analyze the key elements in the situation:**
    a. Who may benefit if you follow the vice president's request? Who may be harmed?
    b. How are they likely to benefit or be harmed?
    c. What rights or claims may be violated?
    d. What specific interests are in conflict?
    e. What are your responsibilities and obligations?
3. **List alternatives and evaluate the impact of each on those affected:** As controller, what are your options in dealing with the ethical dilemma(s) you identified in (1) above? If the sale of the real estate is recorded as the vice president requests, will users have the reliable information needed to make decisions? Why or why not?
4. **Select the best alternative:** Among the alternatives, which one would you select?

Answers

MODULE 1 Answers to Questions

1. The allowance method of accounting for bad debts tries to match one of the costs associated with granting credit, i.e., uncollectible accounts, with the revenue of the period. Under the matching principle, an estimate of bad debts is made on the basis of either the sales of the period or the accounts receivable at the end of the period. The allowance method properly matches the revenue for the period against an expense for the same period.

2. When bad debts expense is estimated by using the percentage of receivables approach, the balance already in the allowance account must be considered. For example, if the estimate of the accounts receivable that will prove to be uncollectible is $20,000 and the allowance account has a balance of $3,000 before adjustment, only $17,000 has to be added to it. Under the percentage of sales approach, however, the emphasis is on Bad Debts Expense. The balance in the allowance account before adjustment is ignored.

3. The numerator of the ratio is net credit sales for the entire period, so an average of accounts receivable for that period is used in the denominator.

MODULE 1 Answers to Apply

1.

Identify and Analyze	ACTIVITY: Operating ACCOUNTS: Allowance for Doubtful Accounts Increase Bad Debts Expense Increase STATEMENT(S): Balance Sheet and Income Statement

Balance Sheet					Income Statement				
ASSETS	=	LIABILITIES	+	STOCKHOLDERS' EQUITY	REVENUES	−	EXPENSES	=	NET INCOME
Allowance for Doubtful Accounts* (10,000)				(10,000)			Bad Debts Expense 10,000**		(10,000)

*The Allowance for Doubtful Accounts account has increased. It is shown as a decrease in the equation above because it is a contra account and causes total assets to decrease.

**2% × $500,000.

2. a.

Identify and Analyze	ACTIVITY: Operating
	ACCOUNTS: Allowance for Doubtful Accounts Increase Bad Debts Expense Increase
	STATEMENT(S): Balance Sheet and Income Statement

Balance Sheet					Income Statement			
ASSETS	=	LIABILITIES	+	STOCKHOLDERS' EQUITY	REVENUES	−	EXPENSES	= NET INCOME
Allowance for Doubtful Accounts* (2,000)				(2,000)			Bad Debts Expense 2,000**	(2,000)

*The Allowance for Doubtful Accounts account has increased. It is shown as a decrease in the equation above because it is a contra account and causes total assets to decrease.
**1% × $200,000.

b.

Identify and Analyze	ACTIVITY: Operating
	ACCOUNTS: Allowance for Doubtful Accounts Increase Bad Debts Expense Increase
	STATEMENT(S): Balance Sheet and Income Statement

Balance Sheet					Income Statement			
ASSETS	=	LIABILITIES	+	STOCKHOLDERS' EQUITY	REVENUES	−	EXPENSES	= NET INCOME
Allowance for Doubtful Accounts* (1,600)				(1,600)			Bad Debts Expense 1,600**	(1,600)

*The Allowance for Doubtful Accounts account has increased. It is shown as a decrease in the equation above because it is a contra account and causes total assets to decrease.
**(4% × $60,000) − $800.

3. Accounts Receivable Turnover = Net Credit Sales/Average Accounts Receivable

   Accounts Receivable Turnover = $240,000/[($40,000 + $20,000)/2]

   Accounts Receivable Turnover = $240,000/$30,000 = 8 times

MODULE 2 Answers to Questions

1. A note receivable arises from a written promise by someone to pay a specific amount of money in the future with interest. An account receivable arises from granting a customer an open line of credit and does not normally include interest.

2. When a note receivable is discounted with recourse, it means that if the customer fails to pay the bank the total amount due on the maturity date, the company that sold the note to the bank is liable to the bank for the full amount. Therefore, during the time a discounted note is outstanding, the seller of the note is contingently liable. Accounting standards do not require the seller to recognize the contingency as a liability, but a note is required to alert the statement reader of the uncertainty.

MODULE 2 Answers to Apply

1.

Identify and Analyze	**ACTIVITY:** Operating
	ACCOUNTS: Interest Receivable Increase Interest Revenue Increase
	STATEMENT(S): Balance Sheet and Income Statement

Balance Sheet					Income Statement				
ASSETS	=	LIABILITIES	+	STOCKHOLDERS' EQUITY	REVENUES	–	EXPENSES	=	NET INCOME
Interest				500	Interest				500
Receivable 500					Revenue 500*				

*$50,000 × 6% × 60/360.

2.

Identify and Analyze	**ACTIVITY:** Operating
	ACCOUNTS: Cash Increase Collection Fee Expense Increase
	Sales Revenue Increase
	STATEMENT(S): Balance Sheet and Income Statement

Balance Sheet					Income Statement				
ASSETS	=	LIABILITIES	+	STOCKHOLDERS' EQUITY	REVENUES	–	EXPENSES	=	NET INCOME
Cash 9,600				9,600	Sales		Collection Fee		9,600
					Revenue** 10,000		Expense 400*		

*4% × $10,000 = $400.
**Accounts Receivable if sale was already recorded.

MODULE 3 Answers to Questions

1. The first CD should be classified as a cash equivalent because it has an original maturity of three months or less. The second CD is classified as a short-term investment. It is a current asset because it will be converted into cash within the next year, even though its original maturity of more than three months disqualifies it from classification as a cash equivalent.

2. The intent of the company determines the proper classification. If Stanzel purchases the Canby Company shares with the intent of selling them in the near term, they should be classified as current assets. Otherwise, the shares should be classified as noncurrent assets.

MODULE 3 Answers to Apply

1. a. I b. I c. D d. NE e. NE

2.

Identify and Analyze	**ACTIVITY:** Investing
	ACCOUNTS: Cash Increase Investment in Spartan Stock Decrease
	Gain on Sale of Stock Increase
	STATEMENT(S): Balance Sheet and Income Statement

Balance Sheet					Income Statement				
ASSETS	=	LIABILITIES	+	STOCKHOLDERS' EQUITY	REVENUES	–	EXPENSES	=	NET INCOME
Cash 12,300				2,200	Gain on Sale				2,200
Investment in Stock (10,100)					of Stock 2,200				

MODULE 4 Answers to Questions

1. Purchases of investments are classified on the statement of cash flows as Investing Activities and reported as an outflow of cash on the statement.

2. Changes in accounts receivable are reported in the Operating Activities section of the statement.

MODULE 4 Answers to Apply

The increase of $40,000 – $25,000, or $15,000, in accounts receivable should be deducted from net income under the indirect method of preparing the statement of cash flows. Sales increase net income. An increase in accounts receivable is an indication that sales exceeded cash collections; therefore, to arrive at cash from operations, a deduction is needed.

Answers to Connect to the Real World

7-1 (p. 313)

According to Apple's balance sheet, accounts receivable decreased by $16,849 – $17,460, or $611 million, during the 2015 fiscal year. Accounts receivable make up $16,849/$89,378, or 18.85%, of the total current assets at the end of the 2015 fiscal year.

7-2 (p. 317)

The amount of accounts receivable before deducting the balance in the allowance account is $16,849 + $82, or

$16,931 million, at the end of the 2015 fiscal year. This amount at the end of 2014 is $17,460 + $86, or $17,546 million. The gross amount of accounts receivable decreased during 2015 by $16,931 – $17,546, or $615 million. The allowance account decreased by $82 – $86, or $4 million, during 2015. Changes in the allowance during the year are a result of adding additional amounts to it for the estimated bad debts and reducing the account for customers' accounts written off.

Answers to Key Terms Quiz

20	Account receivable		4	Payee
11	Subsidiary ledger		7	Note receivable
13	Control account		6	Note payable
23	Net realizable value		15	Principal
12	Direct write-off method		18	Maturity date
3	Allowance method		17	Term
19	Allowance for doubtful accounts		16	Maturity value
10	Aging schedule		14	Interest
22	Accounts receivable turnover ratio		8	Discounting
21	Number of days' sales in receivables		1	Equity securities
5	Promissory note		2	Debt securities
9	Maker			

8

Operating Assets: Property, Plant, and Equipment, and Intangibles

MODULES	LEARNING OBJECTIVES	WHY IS THIS CHAPTER IMPORTANT?
1 **Acquisition of Operating Assets**	**LO1** Understand balance sheet disclosures for operating assets. **LO2** Determine the acquisition cost of an operating asset. **LO3** Explain how to calculate the acquisition cost of assets purchased for a lump sum. **LO4** Describe the impact of capitalizing interest as part of the acquisition cost of an asset.	• You need to know how operating assets appear on the balance sheet and how a company accounts for the acquisition of assets. (See pp. 358–360.)
2 **Depreciation and Disposal of Operating Assets**	**LO5** Compare depreciation methods and understand the factors affecting the choice of method. **LO6** Understand the impact of a change in the estimate of the asset life or residual value. **LO7** Determine which expenditures should be capitalized as asset costs and which should be treated as expenses. **LO8** Analyze the effect of the disposal of an asset at a gain or loss.	• You need to know how a company can record depreciation of operating assets and the factors that affect the choice of depreciation method. (See pp. 361–365.) • You need to know how a company accounts for repairs of the asset and how to analyze the effect of disposal of an asset at a gain or loss. (See pp. 366–370.)
3 **Intangible Assets**	**LO9** Understand the balance sheet presentation of intangible assets. **LO10** Understand the proper amortization of intangible assets.	• You need to understand the importance of intangible assets on the balance sheet. (See pp. 372–374.)
4 **Cash Flow and Analysis Issues**	**LO11** Explain the impact that long-term assets have on the statement of cash flows. **LO12** Understand how investors can analyze a company's operating assets.	• You need to know what impact operating assets can have on the cash flows of the company and how investors can analyze a company's operating assets. (See pp. 376–377.)

NIKE

Nike is the largest seller of athletic footwear, apparel, equipment, and accessories in the world. Reaching this position of dominance requires a large investment in property, plant, and equipment. At May 31, 2015, the company's balance sheet indicates more than $3.0 billion of property, plant, and equipment. The company's decisions to continually invest in new plant and equipment are vital to its future. Investors and others who read Nike's financial statements must analyze its tangible assets to gauge its ability to generate future profits.

But Nike's intangible assets are equally important. The Nike brand name and company logo are some of the most recognizable in the world. In fact, Nike believes its NIKE® and Swoosh Design® trademarks are among its most valuable assets and has registered them in over 100 countries. In addition, the company owns many other trademarks, including the Converse®, Chuck Taylor®, All Star®, and One

Star® lines of athletic footwear. Nike also has valuable licenses and patents on its revolutionary footwear production method known as "Air" technology. A portion of Nike's growth has come from acquiring other sports-related companies. A large portion of the purchase in such Nike acquisitions represents the intangible asset of goodwill. These acquisitions have strengthened Nike's already dominant position in the athletic footwear, apparel, and equipment industry.

Accountants have had to consider carefully the accounting for all long-lived assets, but especially for intangible assets. Investors must be able to read Nike's financial statements and understand how these assets influence the value of the company. The stock price should accurately reflect the value of those assets and the company's ability to use the assets wisely.

The accompanying partial balance sheet presents Nike's property, plant, and equipment and its intangible assets.

Nike, Inc. Consolidated Balance Sheets		
	May 31,	
(In millions)	2015	2014
Assets		
Current assets:		
Cash and equivalents	$ 3,852	$ 2,220
Short-term investments	2,072	2,922
Accounts receivable, net	3,358	3,434
Inventories	4,337	3,947
Deferred income taxes	389	355
Prepaid expenses and other current assets	1,968	818
Total current assets	15,976	13,696
Property, plant and equipment, net	3,011	2,834
Identifiable intangible assets, net	281	282
Goodwill	131	131
Deferred income taxes and other assets	2,201	1,651
Total assets	**$21,600**	**$18,594**

Source: Nike, Inc., Form 10-k for fiscal year ended May 31, 2015.

MODULE 1 ACQUISITION OF OPERATING ASSETS

LO1 Understand balance sheet disclosures for operating assets.

Operating assets constitute the major productive assets of many companies. They are absolutely essential to a company's long-term future, because they are used to produce the goods or services the company sells to customers. The dollar amount invested in operating assets may be very large, as is the case with most manufacturing companies. On the other hand, operating assets on the balance sheet may be insignificant to a company's value, as is the case with a computer software firm and many of the so-called Internet firms. Users of financial statements must assess the operating assets to make important decisions. For example, lenders are interested in the value of the operating assets as collateral when they make lending decisions. Investors must evaluate whether the operating assets indicate long-term potential and can provide a return to the stockholders.

The terms used to describe the operating assets and the balance sheet presentation of those assets vary somewhat by company. Some firms refer to this category of assets as *fixed* or *plant assets*. **Nike, Inc.**'s balance sheet uses one line item for *property, plant, and equipment* and presents the details in the notes.

The May 31, 2015, notes of Nike, Inc., present property, plant, and equipment shown below (in millions). Note that the acquisition costs of the land, buildings, machinery and equipment, leasehold improvements, and construction in process are stated and that the amount of accumulated depreciation is deducted to determine the net amount. The accumulated depreciation is related to the last four assets since land is not depreciable.

Note 3 — Property, Plant and Equipment

Property, plant and equipment, net included the following:

(In millions)	As of May 31, 2015	As of May 31, 2014
Land	$ 273	$ 270
Buildings	1,250	1,261
Machinery, equipment and internal-use software	3,329	3,376
Leasehold improvements	1,150	1,066
Construction in process	350	247
Total property, plant and equipment, gross	6,352	6,220
Less accumulated depreciation	3,341	3,386
Total property, plant and equipment, net	$3,011	$2,834

Source: Nike, Inc., Form 10-k for fiscal year ended May 31, 2015.

Acquisition of Property, Plant, and Equipment

LO2 Determine the acquisition cost of an operating asset.

Acquisition cost
The amount that includes all of the cost normally necessary to acquire an asset and prepare it for its intended use.

Alternate term: Historical cost and original cost.

Assets classified as property, plant, and equipment are initially recorded at acquisition cost (also referred to as *historical cost* or *original cost*). **Acquisition cost** should include all of the costs that are normal and necessary to acquire the asset and prepare it for its intended use, such as

- Purchase price
- Taxes paid at time of purchase (for example, sales tax)
- Transportation charges
- Installation costs

An accountant must exercise careful judgment to determine which costs are "normal" and "necessary." Acquisition cost should not include expenditures unrelated to the acquisition (e.g., repair costs if an asset is damaged during installation) or costs incurred after the asset was installed and use begun.

Group Purchase Quite often, a firm purchases several assets as a group and pays a lump-sum amount. This is most common when a company purchases land and a building situated on it and pays a lump-sum amount for both. It is important to measure the acquisition cost of the land and the building separately, because land is not a depreciable asset. The purchase price should be allocated between land and building on the basis of the proportion of the *fair market value* of each.

LO3 Explain how to calculate the acquisition cost of assets purchased for a lump sum.

EXAMPLE 8-1 Determining Cost When a Group of Assets Is Purchased

Assume that on January 1, ExerCo purchased a building and the land on which it is situated for $100,000. The accountant established the assets' fair market value on January 1 as follows:

Land	$ 30,000
Building	90,000
Total	$120,000

Based on the estimated market values, the purchase price should be allocated as follows:

To land $100,000 \times $30,000/$120,000 = $25,000
To building $100,000 \times $90,000/$120,000 = $75,000

The effect of the transaction can be identified and analyzed as follows:

Identify and Analyze	**ACTIVITY: Investing** **ACCOUNTS: Land** Increase **Building** Increase **Cash** Decrease **STATEMENT[S]: Balance Sheet**

Balance Sheet						Income Statement			
ASSETS	=	LIABILITIES	+	STOCKHOLDERS' EQUITY		REVENUES	−	EXPENSES	= NET INCOME
Land 25,000									
Building 75,000									
Cash (100,000)									

Market value is best established by an independent appraisal of the property. If such appraisal is not possible, the accountant must rely on the market value of other similar assets, on the value of the assets in tax records, or on other available evidence.

Capitalization of Interest Generally, the interest on borrowed money should be treated as an expense of the period. If a company buys an asset and borrows money to finance the purchase, the interest on the borrowed money is not considered part of the asset's cost. Financial statements generally treat investing and financing as separate decisions. Purchase of an asset, an investing activity, is treated as a business decision that is separate from the decision concerning the financing of the asset. Therefore, interest is treated as a period cost and should appear on the income statement as interest expense in the period incurred.

    There is one exception to this general guideline, however. If a company constructs an asset over a period of time and borrows money to finance the construction, the interest incurred during the construction period is not treated as interest expense. Instead, the interest must be included as part of the acquisition cost of the asset. This is referred to as **capitalization of interest**. The amount of interest that is capitalized (treated as an asset) is based on the *average accumulated expenditures.* The average accumulated expenditure is used

LO4 Describe the impact of capitalizing interest as part of the acquisition cost of an asset.

Capitalization of interest
Interest on constructed assets is added to the asset account.

STUDY TIP

Land improvements represent a depreciable asset with a limited life. Land itself is not depreciable.

because this number represents an average amount of money tied up in the project over a year. If it takes $400,000 to construct a building, the interest should not be figured on the full $400,000 because there were times during the year when less than the full amount was being used.

When the cost of building an asset is $400,000 and the amount of interest to be capitalized is $10,000, the acquisition cost of the asset is $410,000. The asset should appear on the balance sheet at that amount. Depreciation of the asset should be based on $410,000 less any residual value.

Land improvements
Costs that are related to land but that have a limited life.

Land Improvements The acquisition cost of land should be kept in a separate account because land has an unlimited life and is not subject to depreciation. Other costs associated with land should be recorded in an account such as Land Improvements. For example, the costs of paving a parking lot are properly treated as **land improvements**, which have a limited life. Some landscaping costs also have a limited life. Therefore, the acquisition costs of land improvements should be depreciated over their useful lives.

MODULE 1 TEST YOURSELF

Review		
	LO1 Understand balance sheet disclosures for operating assets.	• Operating assets are the major productive assets of many companies, and investors must be able to evaluate the long-term potential of these assets for a return on their investments. • Operating assets may be classified as either tangible or intangible assets. • Tangible assets are referred to as property, plant, and equipment (or fixed assets). • Intangible assets include goodwill, patents, copyrights, and various types of intellectual property.
	LO2 Determine the acquisition cost of an operating asset.	• Assets classified as property, plant, and equipment (or fixed assets) are initially recorded at the cost to acquire the assets, also referred to as *historical cost* or *original cost.* • Acquisition costs include those costs that are normal and necessary to acquire the asset and prepare it for its intended use. Generally, acquisition costs include purchase price, taxes paid at time of purchase, transportation charges, and installation costs.
	LO3 Explain how to calculate the acquisition cost of assets purchased for a lump sum.	• If more than one asset is purchased for a single sum of money, the acquisition costs must be allocated between the assets. • In these cases, the purchase price should be allocated between the assets acquired based on the proportion of the fair market value each asset represents of the total purchase price.
	LO4 Describe the impact of capitalizing interest as part of the acquisition cost of an asset.	• Generally, the interest on borrowed money used to acquire assets should not be capitalized; instead, it should be treated as an expense of the period.

Question	
	1. What are several examples of operating assets? Why are operating assets essential to a company's long-term future?
	2. What is the meaning of the term *acquisition cost of operating assets*? Give some examples of costs that should be included in the acquisition cost.
	3. When assets are purchased as a group, how should the acquisition cost of the individual assets be determined?
	4. Under what circumstances should interest be capitalized as part of the cost of an asset?

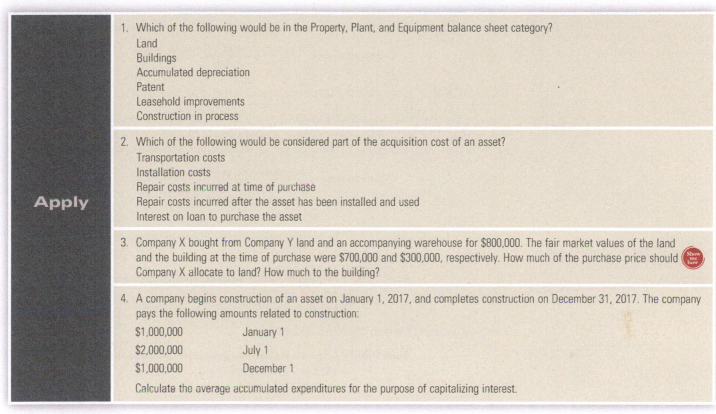

Apply

1. Which of the following would be in the Property, Plant, and Equipment balance sheet category?
   Land
   Buildings
   Accumulated depreciation
   Patent
   Leasehold improvements
   Construction in process

2. Which of the following would be considered part of the acquisition cost of an asset?
   Transportation costs
   Installation costs
   Repair costs incurred at time of purchase
   Repair costs incurred after the asset has been installed and used
   Interest on loan to purchase the asset

3. Company X bought from Company Y land and an accompanying warehouse for $800,000. The fair market values of the land and the building at the time of purchase were $700,000 and $300,000, respectively. How much of the purchase price should Company X allocate to land? How much to the building?

4. A company begins construction of an asset on January 1, 2017, and completes construction on December 31, 2017. The company pays the following amounts related to construction:

$1,000,000	January 1
$2,000,000	July 1
$1,000,000	December 1

   Calculate the average accumulated expenditures for the purpose of capitalizing interest.

Answers are located at the end of the chapter.

MODULE 2 DEPRECIATION AND DISPOSAL OF OPERATING ASSETS

All property, plant, and equipment, except land, have a limited life and decline in usefulness over time. The accrual accounting process requires a proper *matching* of expenses and revenue to measure income accurately. Therefore, the accountant must estimate the decline in usefulness of operating assets and allocate the acquisition cost in a manner consistent with the decline in usefulness. This allocation is the process generally referred to as **depreciation**.

An asset's decline in usefulness is related to:

- Physical deterioration from usage or from the passage of time
- Obsolescence factors such as changes in technology
- The company's repair and maintenance policies

Because the decline in an asset's usefulness is related to a variety of factors, several depreciation methods have been developed. A company should use a depreciation method that allocates the original cost of the asset to the periods benefited and that allows the company to accurately match the expense to the revenue generated by the asset. We will present three methods of depreciation: *straight line*, *units of production*, and *double declining balance*.

All depreciation methods are based on the asset's original acquisition cost. In addition, all methods require an estimate of two additional factors: the asset's *life* and its *residual value*. The residual value (also referred to as *salvage value*) should represent the amount that could be obtained from selling or disposing of the asset at the end of its useful life. Often, this amount may be small or even zero.

LO5 Compare depreciation methods and understand the factors affecting the choice of method.

Depreciation
The allocation of the original cost of an asset to the periods benefited by its use.

CONNECT TO THE REAL WORLD

NIKE
READING THE BALANCE SHEET

8-1 What amount did Nike present for operating assets for 2015? Why did the company not show depreciation on the balance sheet? *(See answers on p. 401.)*

Straight-line method
A method by which the same dollar amount of depreciation is recorded in each year of asset use.

Straight-Line Method The **straight-line method** of depreciation allocates the cost of the asset evenly over time. This method calculates the annual depreciation as follows:

$$\text{Depreciation} = \frac{\text{Acquisition Cost} - \text{Residual Value}}{\text{Life}}$$

EXAMPLE 8-2 Computing Depreciation Using the Straight-Line Method

Assume that on January 1, 2017, ExerCo, a manufacturer of exercise equipment, purchased a machine for $20,000. The machine's estimated life would be five years, and its residual value at the end of 2020 would be $2,000. The annual depreciation should be calculated as follows:

$$\text{Depreciation} = \frac{\text{Acquisition Cost} - \text{Residual Value}}{\text{Life}}$$
$$= (\$20,000 - \$2,000)/5$$
$$= \$3,600$$

Book value
The original cost of an asset minus the amount of accumulated depreciation.

An asset's **book value** is defined as its acquisition cost minus its total amount of accumulated depreciation. Thus, the book value of the machine in this example is $16,400 at the end of 2016.

$$\text{Book Value} = \text{Acquisition Cost} - \text{Accumulated Depreciation}$$
$$= \$20,000 - \$3,600$$
$$= \$16,400$$

The book value at the end of 2017 is $12,800.

$$\text{Book Value} = \text{Acquisition Cost} - \text{Accumulated Depreciation}$$
$$= \$20,000 - (2 \times \$3,600)$$
$$= \$12,800$$

The most attractive feature of the straight-line method is its simplicity. It is the most popular method for presenting depreciation in the annual report to stockholders.

Units-of-Production Method In some cases, the decline in an asset's usefulness is directly related to wear and tear as a result of the number of units it produces. In those cases, depreciation should be calculated by the **units-of-production method**. With this method, the asset's life is expressed in terms of the number of units that the asset can produce. The depreciation *per unit* can be calculated as follows:

Units-of-production method
Depreciation is determined as a function of the number of units the asset produces.

$$\text{Depreciation per Unit} = \frac{\text{Acquisition Cost} - \text{Residual Value}}{\text{Total Number of Units in Asset's Life}}$$

The annual depreciation for a given year can be calculated based on the number of units produced during that year, as follows:

$$\text{Annual Depreciation} = \text{Depreciation per Unit} \times \text{Units Produced in Current Year}$$

EXAMPLE 8-3 Computing Depreciation Using the Units-of-Production Method

Assume that ExerCo in Example 8-2 wanted to use the units-of-production method for 2017. ExerCo has estimated that the total number of units that will be produced during the asset's five-year life is 18,000. During 2017, ExerCo produced 4,000 units. The depreciation per unit for ExerCo's machine can be calculated as follows:

$$\text{Depreciation per Unit} = (\text{Acquisition Cost} - \text{Residual Value})/\text{Life in Units}$$
$$= (\$20,000 - \$2,000)/18,000$$
$$= \$1 \text{ per Unit}$$

The amount of depreciation that should be recorded as an expense for 2017 is $4,000.

$$\text{Annual Depreciation} = \text{Depreciation per Unit} \times \text{Units Produced in 2017}$$
$$= \$1 \text{ per Unit} \times 4,000 \text{ Units}$$
$$= \$4,000$$

In Example 8-2, depreciation will be recorded until the asset produces 18,000 units. The machine cannot be depreciated below its residual value of $2,000.

The units-of-production method is most appropriate when the accountant is able to estimate the total number of units that will be produced over the asset's life. For example, if a factory machine is used to produce a particular item, the life of the asset may be expressed in terms of the number of units produced. Further, the units produced must be related to particular time periods so that depreciation expense can be matched accurately with the related revenue. A variation of the units-of-production method can be used when the life of the asset is expensed in other factors, such as miles driven or hours of use.

Accelerated Depreciation Methods In some cases, more cost should be allocated to the early years of an asset's use and less to the later years. For those assets, an accelerated depreciation method is appropriate. The term **accelerated depreciation** refers to several depreciation methods by which a higher amount of depreciation is recorded in the early years than in later years.

One form of accelerated depreciation is the **double-declining-balance method**. Under this method, depreciation is calculated at double the straight-line rate but on a declining amount.

Accelerated depreciation
A higher amount of depreciation is recorded in the early years and a lower amount in the later years.

Double-declining-balance method
Depreciation is recorded at twice the straight-line rate, but the balance is reduced each period.

EXAMPLE 8-4 Computing Depreciation Using the Double-Declining-Balance Method

Assume that ExerCo wants to depreciate its asset using the double-declining-balance method. The first step is to calculate the straight-line rate as a percentage. The straight-line rate for the ExerCo asset with a five-year life is as follows:

100% / 5 Years = 20%

The second step is to double the straight-line rate, as follows:

2 × 20% = 40%

This rate will be applied in all years to the asset's book value at the beginning of each year. As depreciation is recorded, the book value declines. Thus, a constant rate is applied to a declining amount. This constant rate is applied to the full cost or initial book value, not to cost minus residual value as in the other methods. However, the machine cannot be depreciated below its residual value.

The amount of depreciation for 2017 would be calculated as follows:

Depreciation = Beginning Book Value × Rate
= $20,000 × 40%
= $8,000

The amount of depreciation for 2018 would be calculated as follows:

Depreciation = Beginning Book Value × Rate
= ($20,000 − $8,000) × 40%
= $4,800

The complete depreciation schedule for ExerCo for all five years of the machine's life would be as follows:

Year	Rate	Book Value at Beginning of Year	Depreciation	Book Value at End of Year
2017	40%	$20,000	$ 8,000	$12,000
2018	40	12,000	4,800	7,200
2019	40	7,200	2,880	4,320
2020	40	4,320	1,728	2,592
2021	40	2,592	592	2,000
Total			$18,000	

The depreciation for 2021 cannot be calculated as $2,592 × 40% because this would result in an accumulated depreciation amount of more than $18,000. The total amount of depreciation recorded in Years 1 through 4 is $17,408. The accountant should record only $592 depreciation ($18,000 − $17,408) in 2021 so that the remaining value of the machine is $2,000 at the end of 2021.

The double-declining-balance method of depreciation is most appropriate for assets subject to a rapid decline in usefulness as a result of technical or obsolescence factors. Double-declining-balance depreciation is not widely used for financial statement purposes but may be appropriate for certain assets. As discussed earlier, most companies use straight-line depreciation for financial statement purposes because it generally produces the highest net income, especially in growing companies that have a stable or expanding base of assets.

Comparison of Depreciation Methods Exhibit 8-1 presents a comparison of the depreciation and book values of the ExerCo asset for 2017–2021 using the straight-line and double-declining-balance methods. (We have excluded the units-of-production method.) Note that both methods result in a depreciation total of $18,000 over the five-year period. The amount of depreciation per year depends, however, on the method of depreciation chosen.

Nonaccountants often misunderstand the accountant's concept of depreciation. Accountants do not consider depreciation to be a process of *valuing* the asset. That is, depreciation does not describe the increase or decrease in the market value of the asset. Accountants consider depreciation to be a process of *cost allocation*. The purpose is to allocate the original acquisition cost to the periods benefited by the asset. The depreciation method chosen should be based on the decline in the asset's usefulness. A company can choose a different depreciation method for each individual fixed asset or for each class or category of fixed assets.

Depreciation and Income Taxes Depreciation is deducted for income tax purposes. Sometimes depreciation is referred to as a *tax shield* because it reduces (as do other expenses) the amount of income tax that would otherwise have to be paid. When depreciating an asset for tax purposes, a company should generally choose a depreciation method that reduces the present value of its tax burden to the lowest possible amount over the life of the asset. Normally, this is best accomplished with an accelerated depreciation method, which allows a company to save more income tax in the early years of the asset. This happens because the higher depreciation charges reduce taxable income more than the straight-line method does. The method allowed for tax purposes is referred to as the Modified Accelerated Cost Recovery System (MACRS). As a form of accelerated depreciation, it results in a larger amount of depreciation in the asset's early years and a smaller amount in later years.

Choice of Depreciation Method The choice of depreciation method can have a significant impact on the bottom line. If two companies are essentially identical in every other respect, a different depreciation method for fixed assets can make one

EXHIBIT 8-1 Comparison of Depreciation and Book Values of Straight-Line and Double-Declining-Balance Methods

Year	Straight-Line		Double-Declining-Balance	
	Depreciation	Book Value	Depreciation	Book Value
2017	$ 3,600	$16,400	$ 8,000	$12,000
2018	3,600	12,800	4,800	7,200
2019	3,600	9,200	2,880	4,320
2020	3,600	5,600	1,728	2,592
2021	3,600	2,000	592	2,000
Totals	$18,000		$18,000	

EXHIBIT 8-2 Management's Choice of Depreciation Method

Factor	Likely Choice
Simplicity ⟶	The straight-line method is easiest to compute and record.
Reporting to stockholders ⟶	Usually, firms want to maximize net income in reporting to stockholders and will use the straight-line method.
Comparability ⟶	Usually, firms use the same depreciation method as other firms in the same industry or line of business.
Management bonus plans ⟶	If management is paid a bonus based on net income, it will likely use the straight-line method.
Technological competitiveness ⟶	If technology is changing rapidly, a firm should consider an accelerated method of depreciation.
Reporting to the Internal Revenue Service ⟶	Firms usually use an accelerated method of depreciation to minimize taxable income in reporting to the IRS.

company look more profitable than the other. Or a company that uses accelerated depreciation for one year can find that its otherwise declining earnings are no longer declining if it switches to straight-line depreciation. Investors should pay some attention to depreciation methods when comparing companies. Exhibit 8-2 presents the factors that affect the choice of depreciation method. Usually, the most important factor is whether depreciation is calculated for presentation on the financial statements to stockholders or whether it is calculated for income tax purposes.

When depreciation is calculated for financial statement purposes, a company generally wants to present the most favorable impression (the highest income) possible. More than 90% of large companies use the straight-line method for financial statement purposes.

If management's objective is to minimize the company's income tax liability, the company will generally not choose the straight-line method for tax purposes. As discussed in the preceding section, accelerated depreciation allows the company to save more on income taxes because depreciation is a tax shield.

It is not unusual for a company to use *two* **depreciation methods** for the same asset, one for financial reporting purposes and another for tax purposes. This may seem somewhat confusing, but it is the direct result of the differing goals of financial and tax accounting.

Change in Depreciation Estimate
An asset's acquisition cost is known at the time it is purchased, but its life and residual value must be estimated. These estimates are then used as the basis for depreciating it. Occasionally, an estimate of the asset's life or residual value must be altered after the depreciation process has begun. This type of accounting change is referred to as a **change in estimate**.

A change in estimate should be recorded *prospectively*, meaning that the depreciation recorded in prior years is not corrected or restated. Instead, the new estimate should affect the current year and future years.

LO6 Understand the impact of a change in the estimate of the asset life or residual value.

Change in estimate
A change in the life of the asset or in its residual value.

EXAMPLE 8-5 Calculating a Change in Depreciation Estimate

ExerCo purchased a machine on January 1, 2017, for $20,000. ExerCo estimated that the machine's life would be five years and its residual value at the end of five years would be $2,000. ExerCo has depreciated the machine using the straight-line method for two years. At the beginning of 2019, ExerCo believes that the total machine life will be seven years, or another five years beyond the two years the machine has been used. Thus, depreciation must be adjusted to reflect the new estimate of the asset's life.

ExerCo should depreciate the remaining depreciable amount during 2019 through 2023. The amount to be depreciated over that time period should be calculated as follows:

Acquisition cost, January 1, 2017	$20,000
Accumulated depreciation (2 years at $3,600 per year)	7,200
Book value, January 1, 2019	$12,800
Residual value	2,000
Remaining depreciable amount	$10,800

The remaining depreciable amount should be recorded as depreciation over the remaining life of the machine. The depreciation amount for 2019 and the following four years would be $2,160:

Depreciation = Remaining Depreciable Amount/Remaining Life

= $10,800/5 Years

= $2,160

In Example 8-5, the effect of the transaction can be identified and analyzed as follows:

Identify and Analyze	
ACTIVITY:	**Operating**
ACCOUNTS:	**Depreciation Expense** Increase
	Accumulated Depreciation Increase
STATEMENT[S]:	**Balance Sheet and Income Statement**

Balance Sheet					Income Statement				
ASSETS	=	LIABILITIES	+	STOCKHOLDERS' EQUITY	REVENUES	−	EXPENSES	=	NET INCOME
Accumulated Depreciation* (2,160)				(2,160)			Depreciation Expense 2,160		(2,160)

*The Accumulated Depreciation account has increased. It is shown as a decrease in the equation above because it is a contra account and causes total assets to decrease.

If the change in estimate is a material amount, the company should disclose in the footnotes to the 2019 financial statements that depreciation has changed as a result of a change in estimate. The company's auditors have to be very careful that management's decision to change its estimate of the depreciable life of the asset is not an attempt to manipulate earnings. Particularly in capital-intensive manufacturing concerns, lengthening the useful life of equipment can have a material impact on earnings.

A change in estimate of an asset's residual value is treated in a manner that is similar to a change in an asset's life. There should be no attempt to correct or restate the income statements of past periods that were based on the original estimate. Instead, the accountant should use the new estimate of residual value to calculate depreciation for the current and future years.

Capital versus Revenue Expenditures

LO7 Determine which expenditures should be capitalized as asset costs and which should be treated as expenses.

Accountants often must decide whether certain expenditures related to operating assets should be treated as an addition to the cost of the asset or as an expense. One of the most common examples involving this decision concerns repairs to an asset. Should the repairs constitute capital expenditures or revenue expenditures?

- **A capital expenditure** is a cost that is added to the acquisition cost of an asset.
- **A revenue expenditure** is not treated as part of the cost of the asset, but as an expense on the income statement.

Thus, the company must decide whether to treat an item as an asset (balance sheet) and depreciate its cost over its life or to treat it as an expense (income statement) of a single period.

The distinction between capital and revenue expenditures is a matter of judgment. Generally, the following guidelines should be followed:

- When an expenditure *increases the life of the asset or its productivity*, it should be treated as a capital expenditure and added to the asset account.
- When an expenditure *simply maintains an asset in its normal operating condition*, however, it should be treated as an expense.

The *materiality* of the expenditure must also be considered. Most companies establish a policy of treating an expenditure that is smaller than a specified amount as a revenue expenditure (an expense on the income statement).

A company must not improperly capitalize a material expenditure that should have been written off right away. Analysts trying to assess the value of a company closely monitor its capitalization policies. When a company is capitalizing rather than expensing certain items to artificially boost earnings, that revelation can be very damaging to the stock price.

Expenditures related to operating assets may be classified in several categories. For each type of expenditure, its treatment as capital or revenue should be as follows:

Category	Example	Asset or Expense
Normal maintenance	Repaint	Expense
Minor repair	Replace spark plugs	Expense
Major repair	Replace a vehicle's engine	Asset if life or productivity is enhanced
Addition	Add a wing to a building	Asset

An item treated as a capital expenditure affects the amount of depreciation that should be recorded over the asset's remaining life. We will use an example involving ExerCo to illustrate. Assume again that ExerCo purchased a machine on January 1, 2016, for $20,000. ExerCo estimated that its residual value at the end of five years would be $2,000 and has depreciated the machine $3,600 per year for 2016 and 2017, using the straight-line method.

$$\text{Depreciation} = (\text{Acquisition Cost} - \text{Residual Value})/\text{Life}$$
$$= (\$20,000 - \$2,000)/5$$
$$= \$3,600$$

EXAMPLE 8-6 Capitalizing Costs of a Major Repair

At the beginning of 2019, ExerCo made a $3,000 overhaul to the machine, extending its life by three years. Because the expenditure qualifies as a capital expenditure, the cost of overhauling the machine should be added to the asset account.

Beginning in 2019, the company should record depreciation of $2,300 per year, computed as follows:

Original cost, January 1, 2017	$20,000
Accumulated depreciation (2 years × $3,600)	(7,200)
Book value, January 1, 2019	$12,800
Major overhaul	3,000
Residual value	(2,000)
Remaining depreciable amount	$13,800

$$\text{Depreciation} = \text{Remaining Depreciable Amount}/\text{Remaining Life}$$
$$= \$13,800/6 \text{ Years}$$
$$= \$2,300$$

Capital expenditure
A cost that improves the asset and is added to the asset account.
Alternate term: Item treated as asset.

Revenue expenditure
A cost that keeps an asset in its normal operating condition and is treated as an expense.
Alternate term: Item treated as an expense of the period.

The effect of the transaction for the overhaul in Example 8-6 is as follows:

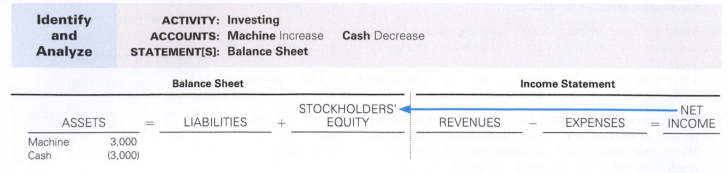

The effect of the transaction to record depreciation for 2019 can be identified and analyzed as follows:

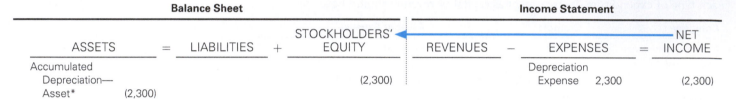

*The Accumulated Depreciation account has increased. It is shown as a decrease in the equation above because it is a contra account and causes total assets to decrease.

Environmental Aspects of Operating Assets

As the government's environmental regulations have increased, businesses have been required to expend more money complying with them. A common example involves costs to comply with federal requirements to clean up contaminated soil surrounding plant facilities. In some cases, the costs are high and may exceed the value of the property. Should such costs be considered an expense and recorded entirely in one accounting period, or should they be treated as a capital expenditure and added to the cost of the asset? If there is a legal obligation to clean up the property or restore it to its original condition, companies are required to record the cost of asset retirement obligations as part of the asset's cost. For example, if a company owns a factory and has made a binding promise to restore to its original condition the property used by the factory, the costs of restoring the property must be added to the asset account. Of course, it is sometimes difficult to determine whether a legal obligation exists. However, companies should at least conduct a thorough investigation to determine the potential environmental considerations that may affect the value of operating assets and to ponder carefully the accounting implications of new environmental regulations.

Disposal of Property, Plant, and Equipment

LO8 Analyze the effect of the disposal of an asset at a gain or loss.

An asset may be disposed of in several different ways. One common method is to sell the asset for cash. Sale of an asset involves two important considerations. First, depreciation must be recorded up to the date of sale. If the sale does not occur at the fiscal year-end, usually December 31, depreciation must be recorded for a partial period from the beginning of the year to the date of sale. Second, the gain or loss on the sale must be calculated and recorded.

Gain on Sale of Assets Assume that ExerCo purchased a machine on January 1, 2017, for $20,000, estimating its life to be five years and the residual value to be $2,000. ExerCo used the straight-line method of depreciation. ExerCo sold the machine on July 1, 2019. Depreciation for the six-month period from January 1 to July 1, 2019, is $1,800 ($3,600 per year × 1/2 year = $1,800). The effect of the transaction can be identified and analyzed as follows:

Identify and Analyze		
ACTIVITY:	**Operating**	
ACCOUNTS:	**Depreciation Expense** Increase	
	Accumulated Depreciation—Machine Increase	
STATEMENT[S]:	**Balance Sheet and Income Statement**	

Balance Sheet					Income Statement		
ASSETS	=	LIABILITIES	+	STOCKHOLDERS' EQUITY	REVENUES −	EXPENSES	= NET INCOME
Accumulated Depreciation— Machine* (1,800)				(1,800)		Depreciation Expense 1,800	(1,800)

*The Accumulated Depreciation account has increased. It is shown as a decrease in the equation above because it is a contra account and causes total assets to decrease.

EXAMPLE 8-7 Calculating the Gain on Sale of an Asset

ExerCo sold the asset on July 1, 2019, for $12,400. The gain can be calculated as follows:

Asset cost	$20,000
Accumulated depreciation	9,000
Book value	$11,000
Sales price	12,400
Gain on sale of asset	$ 1,400

After the July 1 entry, the balance of the Accumulated Depreciation—Machine account is $9,000, which reflects depreciation for the 2½ years from the date of purchase to the date of sale. The effect of the transaction for the sale can be identified and analyzed as follows:

Identify and Analyze		
ACTIVITY:	**Investing**	
ACCOUNTS:	**Accumulated Depreciation—Machine** Decrease **Cash** Increase	
	Machine Decrease **Gain on Sale of Asset** Increase	
STATEMENT[S]:	**Balance Sheet and Income Statement**	

Balance Sheet					Income Statement		
ASSETS	=	LIABILITIES	+	STOCKHOLDERS' EQUITY	REVENUES −	EXPENSES	= NET INCOME
Accumulated Depreciation— Machine* 9,000				1,400	Gain on Sale of Asset 1,400		1,400
Cash 12,400							
Machine (20,000)							

*The Accumulated Depreciation account has decreased. It is shown as an increase in the equation above because it is a contra account and causes total assets to increase.

When an asset is sold, all accounts related to it must be removed. In the preceding entry, the Machine account is reduced (credited) to eliminate the account and the Accumulated Depreciation—Machine account is reduced (debited) to eliminate it. The

Gain on Sale of Asset
The excess of the selling price over the asset's book value.

Gain on Sale of Asset indicates the amount by which the sales price of the machine *exceeds* the book value. **The Gain on Sale of Asset account** is an income statement account. Therefore, it should appear in the Other Income/Expense category of the statement because it does not result from the company's ongoing or central activity.

Loss on Sale of Assets The calculation of a loss on the sale of an asset is similar to that of a gain. Depreciation must be recorded to the date of sale, July 1.

The effect of the transaction for the sale can be identified and analyzed as follows:

Identify and Analyze	
ACTIVITY:	Investing
ACCOUNTS:	Accumulated Depreciation—Machine Decrease Cash Increase
	Loss on Sale of Asset Increase Machine Decrease
STATEMENT[S]:	Balance Sheet and Income Statement

Balance Sheet					Income Statement			
ASSETS	=	LIABILITIES	+	STOCKHOLDERS' EQUITY	REVENUES	−	EXPENSES	= NET INCOME
Accumulated				(1,000)			Loss on Sale	
Depreciation—							of Asset 1,000	(1,000)
Machine* 9,000								
Cash 10,000								
Machine (20,000)								

*The Accumulated Depreciation account has decreased. It is shown as an increase in the equation above because it is a contra account and causes total assets to increase.

EXAMPLE 8-8 Calculating the Loss on Sale of an Asset

Assume that ExerCo sold the asset on July 1, 2019, for $10,000. The loss could be calculated as follows:

Asset cost	$20,000
Accumulated depreciation	9,000
Book value	$11,000
Sales price	10,000
Loss on sale of asset	$ 1,000

Loss on Sale of Asset
The amount by which selling price is less than book value.

The **Loss on Sale of Asset** indicates the amount by which the asset's sales price is less than its book value. The Loss on Sale of Asset account is an income statement account and should appear in the Other Income/Expense category of the income statement.

IFRS and Property, Plant, and Equipment

Generally, the Financial Accounting Standards Board's (FASB) standards concerning property, plant, and equipment are similar to the international accounting standards, and conversion to those standards should not impose great difficulties for U.S. companies. There are important differences, however. First, when depreciation is calculated, the international standards require that estimates of residual value and the life of the asset be reviewed at least annually and revised if necessary. If the estimate is revised, it should be treated as a change in estimate as we have described in this chapter. The FASB standards do not have a specific rule that requires residual value and asset life to be reviewed annually, so this is an instance where the international standards are more explicit than U.S. standards. The international standards also indicate that companies should determine the components of an asset and depreciate each component separately. For example, if a company buys a building, some parts of the building may be depreciated using one estimate of useful life and other parts may use a different estimate of useful life.

Another difference involves the valuation of property, plant, and equipment. The FASB generally requires operating assets to be recorded at acquisition cost, less depreciation, and the assets' values are not changed to reflect their fair market values, or selling prices. International accounting standards allow but do not require companies to revalue their property, plant, and equipment to reflect fair market values. This gives firms additional flexibility in portraying their assets, but may also cause difficulties in comparing one company with another.

MODULE 2 TEST YOURSELF

Review

LO5 Compare depreciation methods and understand the factors affecting the choice of method.

- Several depreciation methods are available, including straight-line, units-of-production, and accelerated depreciation methods.
- In theory, the depreciation method that best allocates the original cost of the asset to the periods benefited by the use of the asset should be chosen.

LO6 Understand the impact of a change in the estimate of the asset life or residual value.

- Occasionally, an estimate of the asset's life or residual value must be modified after the depreciation process has begun. This is an example of an accounting change that is referred to as a change in estimate.

LO7 Determine which expenditures should be capitalized as asset costs and which should be treated as expenses.

- Capital expenditures are added to the acquisition cost of an asset and are depreciated over time.
- Revenue expenditures are not treated as part of the cost of the asset, but as an expense on the income statement in the period incurred.

LO8 Analyze the effect of the disposal of an asset at a gain or loss.

- The gain or loss on an asset is the difference between the sales (or exchange) price and the book value of the asset, where book value is the acquisition cost less any accumulated depreciation on the asset.

Question

1. What factors should influence the choice of depreciation method? Must a company choose just one method of depreciation for all assets?

2. Why do many companies use one method to calculate depreciation for the income statement developed for stockholders and another method for income tax purposes?

3. What should a company do if it finds that the original estimate of the life of an asset or the residual value of the asset must be changed?

4. How is the gain or loss on the sale of an operating asset calculated? Where would the Gain on Sale of Asset account appear on the financial statements?

Apply

1. A company uses the double-declining-balance method of depreciation. The company purchases an asset for $40,000, which is expected to have a ten-year life and a $4,000 residual value.
   a. What depreciation rate will be applied each year?
   b. What amount will be charged for depreciation in the first and second years?
   c. What amount will be treated as depreciation over the ten-year life?

2. A company purchased an asset on January 1, 2015, for $10,000. The asset was expected to have a ten-year life and a $1,000 salvage value. The company uses the straight-line method of depreciation. On January 1, 2017, the company determines that the asset will last only five more years.
   Calculate the amount of depreciation for 2017.

3. A company purchased an asset on January 1, 2015, for $10,000. The asset was expected to have a ten-year life and a $1,000 salvage value. The company uses the straight-line method of depreciation. On January 1, 2017, the company made a major repair to the asset of $5,000, extending its life. The asset is expected to last ten years from January 1, 2017.
   Calculate the amount of depreciation for 2017.

4. A machine with a cost of $100,000 and accumulated depreciation of $80,000 was sold at a loss of $6,000. What amount of cash was received from the sale?

Answers are located at the end of the chapter.

MODULE 3 INTANGIBLE ASSETS

LO9 Understand the balance sheet presentation of intangible assets.

Intangible assets
Assets with no physical properties.

Intangible assets are long-term assets with no physical properties. Intangibles are recorded as assets, because they provide future economic benefits to the company. For example, a pharmaceutical company's most important asset may be its patent for a particular drug or process. Likewise, the company that publishes this textbook may consider the copyrights to textbooks to be among its most important revenue-producing assets.

The balance sheet does not include all of the items that may produce future benefit to the company. A company's employees, its management team, its location, or the intellectual capital of a few key researchers may well provide important future benefits and value. They are not recorded on the balance sheet, however, because they do not meet the accountant's definition of *assets* and cannot be easily identified or measured.

Balance Sheet Presentation

Intangible assets are long-term assets and should be shown separately from property, plant, and equipment. Exhibit 8-3 lists the most common intangible assets. Nike's balance sheet presents two lines for intangible assets: Identifiable Intangible Assets and Goodwill. Exhibit 8-4 presents the note that indicates that Nike's intangible assets consist primarily of trademarks and goodwill.

Goodwill represents the amount of the purchase price paid in excess of the market value of the individual net assets when a business is purchased. Goodwill is recorded only when a business is purchased. Customer loyalty or a good management team may represent goodwill, but neither meets the accountants' criteria to be recorded as an asset on a firm's financial statements.

How Will I Use ACCOUNTING?

If you are a financial analyst, you will need to analyze all of the company's assets, including goodwill.

A large balance can hint a company's history of overpaying for acquisitions or being highly acquisitive in general. Additionally, a large amount of goodwill can also be an indication that a company may later have to declare that some of these assets are impaired.

Goodwill
The excess of the purchase price to acquire a business over the value of the individual net assets acquired.

Alternate term: Purchase price in excess of the market value of the assets.

Acquisition Cost of Intangible Assets

As was the case with property, plant, and equipment, the acquisition cost of an intangible asset includes all of the costs to acquire the asset and prepare it for its intended use. This should include all necessary costs, such as legal costs incurred at the time of acquisition. Acquisition cost also should include those costs that are incurred after acquisition and that are necessary to the existence of the asset. For example, if a firm must pay legal fees to protect a patent from infringement, the costs should be considered part of the acquisition cost and should be included in the Patent account.

Research and development costs
Costs incurred in the discovery of new knowledge.

Research and Development Costs You should also be aware of one item that is similar to intangible assets but is *not* on the balance sheet. **Research and development costs** are expenditures incurred in the discovery of new knowledge and the translation of research into a design or plan for a new product or service or in a significant improvement to an existing product or service. Firms that engage in research and development do so because they believe such activities provide future benefit to the company. In fact, many firms have become leaders in an industry by engaging in research and development and the

EXHIBIT 8-3 Most Common Intangible Assets

Intangible Asset	Description
Patent	Right to use, manufacture, or sell a product; granted by the U.S. Patent Office. Patents have a legal life of 20 years.
Copyright	Right to reproduce or sell a published work. Copyrights are granted for 70 years plus the life of the creator.
Trademark	A symbol or name that allows a product or service to be identified; provides legal protection for 20 years in addition to an indefinite number of renewal periods.
Goodwill	The excess of the purchase price to acquire a business over the value of the individual net assets acquired.

EXHIBIT 8-4 The Nike, Inc., Consolidated Assets Section and Intangibles Notes

NOTE 4 — Identifiable Intangible Assets and Goodwill

Identifiable intangible assets, net consists of indefinite-lived trademarks, which are not subject to amortization, and acquired trademarks and other intangible assets, which are subject to amortization. At May 31, 2015 and 2014, indefinite-lived trademarks were $281 million and $282 million, respectively. Acquired trademarks and other intangible assets at May 31, 2015 and 2014 were $17 million and $39 million, respectively, and were fully amortized at the end of both periods. *Goodwill* was $131 million at May 31, 2015 and 2014 of which $65 million and $64 million were included in the Converse segment in the respective periods. The remaining amounts were included in Global Brand Divisions for segment reporting purposes. There were no accumulated impairment balances for goodwill as of either period end.

discovery of new products or technology. It is often very difficult, however, to identify the amount of future benefits of research and development and to associate those benefits with specific time periods. Because of the difficulty in predicting future benefits, the FASB has ruled that firms are not allowed to treat research and development costs as assets; all such expenditures must be treated as expenses in the period incurred. Financial statement users need to be aware of those "hidden assets" when analyzing the balance sheets of companies that must expense research and development costs.

It is important to distinguish between patent costs and research and development costs. Patent costs include legal and filing fees necessary to acquire a patent. Such costs are capitalized as an intangible asset, Patent. However, the Patent account should not include the costs of research and development of a new product.

Amortization of Intangibles

Amortization is very similar to depreciation of property, plant, and equipment. Amortization involves allocating the acquisition cost of an intangible asset to the periods benefited by the use of the asset. Most companies use the straight-line method of amortization.

LO10 Understand the proper amortization of intangible assets.

Intangibles with Finite Life If an intangible asset has a finite life, amortization must be recognized. A finite life exists when an intangible asset is legally valid for only a certain length of time. For example, a patent is granted for a time period of 20 years and gives the patent holder the legal right to exclusive use of the patented design or invention. A copyright is likewise granted for a specified legal life. A finite life also exists when there is no legal life but company management knows for certain that it will be able to use the intangible asset for only a specified period of time. For example, a company may have purchased the right to use a list of names and addresses of customers for a two-year time period.

Amortization should be recorded over the legal life or the useful life, whichever is shorter. For example, patents may have a legal life of 20 years, but many are not useful for that long because new products and technology make the patent obsolete. The patent should be amortized over the number of years in which the firm receives benefits, which may be a period shorter than the legal life.

EXAMPLE 8-9 Calculating the Amortization of Intangibles

Assume that Nike developed a patent for a new shoe product on January 1, 2017. The costs involved with patent approval were $10,000, and the company wants to record amortization on the straight-line basis over a five-year life with no residual value. In this case, the useful life of the patent is less than the legal life. Nike should record amortization over the useful life as $10,000/5 years = $2,000.

The effect of the amortization for 2017 is as follows:

Identify and Analyze	ACTIVITY: Operating ACCOUNTS: Patent Amortization Expense Increase Accumulated Amortization—Patent Increase STATEMENT[S]: Balance Sheet and Income Statement

Balance Sheet					Income Statement				
ASSETS	=	LIABILITIES	+	STOCKHOLDERS' EQUITY	REVENUES	−	EXPENSES	=	NET INCOME
Accumulated Amortization—Patent* (2,000)				(2,000)			Patent Amortization Expense 2,000		(2,000)

*The Accumulated Amortization account has increased. It is shown as a decrease in the equation above because it is a contra account and causes total assets to decrease.

Rather than use an accumulated amortization account, some companies decrease the intangible asset account directly. In that case, the effect of the amortization can be identified and analyzed as follows:

Identify and Analyze	ACTIVITY: Operating ACCOUNTS: Patent Amortization Expense Increase Patent Decrease STATEMENT[S]: Balance Sheet and Income Statement

Balance Sheet					Income Statement				
ASSETS	=	LIABILITIES	+	STOCKHOLDERS' EQUITY	REVENUES	−	EXPENSES	=	NET INCOME
Patent (2,000)				(2,000)			Patent Amortization Expense 2,000		(2,000)

No matter which of the two preceding entries is used, the asset should be reported on the balance sheet at acquisition cost ($10,000) less accumulated amortization ($2,000), or $8,000, as of December 31, 2017.

Intangibles with Indefinite Life If an intangible asset has an indefinite life, amortization should not be recognized. For example, a television or radio station may have paid to acquire a broadcast license. A broadcast license is usually for a certain time period but can be renewed at the end of that time period. In that case, the life of the asset is indefinite and amortization of the intangible asset representing the broadcast rights should not be recognized. A second example would be a trademark. For many companies, such as Nike and **The Coca-Cola Company**, a trademark is a valuable asset that provides name recognition and enhances sales. A trademark is granted for a certain time period but can be renewed at the end of that period, so the life may be quite indefinite. If the life of an intangible asset represented by trademarks is indefinite, amortization should not be recorded. Note in Exhibit 8-4 that Nike has considered some trademarks to have an indefinite life and has not amortized them. Others have been amortized because they have a limited life.

Goodwill and Impairments Goodwill is an important intangible asset on the balance sheet of many companies. At one time, accounting rules had required companies to record amortization of goodwill over a time period not to exceed 40 years. However, the current stance of the FASB is that goodwill should be treated as an intangible asset with an *indefinite* life and that companies should no longer record amortization expense related to goodwill.

While companies should not record amortization of intangible assets that have an indefinite life, they are required each year to determine whether the asset has been *impaired*. A discussion of asset impairment is beyond the scope of this text, but generally, it means that a loss should be recorded when the value of the asset has declined. For example, some trademarks, such as **Xerox** and **Polaroid**, that were quite powerful in the past have declined in value over time. When an impairment of the asset is recognized, the loss is recorded in the time period that the value declines rather than the date the asset is sold.

Assume that Nike learns on January 1, 2018, when accumulated amortization is $2,000 (or the book value of the patent is $8,000), that a competing company has developed a new product that renders Nike's patent worthless. Nike has a loss of $8,000 and should record an entry to write off the asset. The effect of the transaction can be identified and analyzed as follows:

Identify and Analyze	**ACTIVITY:** Operating and Investing **ACCOUNTS:** Loss on Patent Increase Accumulated Amortization—Patent Decrease Patent Decrease **STATEMENT[S]:** Balance Sheet and Income Statement

Balance Sheet					Income Statement			
ASSETS	=	LIABILITIES	+	STOCKHOLDERS' EQUITY	REVENUES	−	EXPENSES	= NET INCOME

Accumulated
  Amortization—
  Patent*   2,000
Patent   (10,000)
				(8,000)			Loss on Patent 8,000	(8,000)

*The Accumulated Amortization account has decreased. It is shown as an increase in the equation above because it is a contra account and causes total assets to increase.

IFRS and Intangible Assets

The international standards are more flexible than the FASB standards in allowing the use of fair market values for intangible assets. However, such values can only be used for those assets where an "active market" exists and it is possible to determine fair value.

The treatment of research and development costs also differs. FASB standards require all research and development costs to be treated as an expense. The international standards make a distinction between research costs and development costs. All research costs must be treated as an expense, but development costs can be capitalized as an asset if certain criteria are met.

These differences between U.S. and international standards will likely be addressed and eliminated as U.S. companies move to adopt the international standards.

MODULE 3 TEST YOURSELF

Review	**LO9** Understand the balance sheet presentation of intangible assets.	• Intangible assets are long-term assets that should be shown separately from property, plant, and equipment on the balance sheet.
	LO10 Understand the proper amortization of intangible assets.	• The amortization of intangibles is a process similar to that of depreciating capital assets. • If an intangible asset has a finite useful life, amortization expense must be taken on the asset over the legal life or useful life, whichever is shorter.

Question	1. Give several examples of intangible assets. In what balance sheet category should intangible assets appear?
	2. Define the term *goodwill*. Give an example of a transaction that would result in the recording of goodwill on the balance sheet.
	3. When an intangible asset is amortized, should the asset's amortization occur over its legal life or its useful life? Give an example in which the legal life exceeds the useful life.
	4. Suppose that an intangible asset is being amortized over a ten-year time period but a competitor has just introduced a new product that will have a serious negative impact on the asset's value. Should the company continue to amortize the intangible asset over the ten-year life?

Apply	1. Which of the following would be considered intangible assets on the balance sheet? Which intangibles should be amortized? Patents Copyrights Research and development Goodwill The company's advantageous location Broadcast rights
	2. A company develops a patent on January 1, 2015, and the costs involved with patent approval are $12,000. The legal life of the patent is 20 years, but the company projects that it will provide useful benefits for only 12 years. At January 1, 2018, the company discovers that a competitor will introduce a new product, making this patent useless in five years. How much amortization should be recorded in 2015, 2016, and 2017?

Answers are located at the end of the chapter.

MODULE 4 CASH FLOW AND ANALYSIS ISSUES

LO11 Explain the impact that long-term assets have on the statement of cash flows.

Exhibit 8-5 illustrates the items discussed in this chapter and their effect on the statement of cash flows.

The acquisition of a long-term asset is an investing activity and should be reflected in the Investing Activities category of the statement of cash flows. The acquisition should appear as a deduction, or negative item, in that section because it requires the use of cash to purchase the asset. This applies whether the long-term asset is property, plant, and equipment or an intangible asset.

The depreciation or amortization of a long-term asset is not a cash item. It was referred to earlier as a noncash charge to earnings. Nevertheless, it must be presented on the statement of cash flows (if the indirect method is used for the statement). The reason

EXHIBIT 8-5 Long-Term Assets and the Statement of Cash Flows

Item	Cash-Flow Statement	
	Operating Activities	
	Net Income	XXX
Depreciation and amortization	⟶	+
Gain on sale of asset	⟶	−
Loss on sale of asset	⟶	+
	Investing Activities	
Purchase of asset	⟶	−
Sale of asset	⟶	+
	Financing Activities	

is that it was deducted from earnings in calculating the net income figure. Therefore, it must be eliminated or "added back" if the net income amount is used to indicate the amount of cash generated from operations. **Thus, depreciation and amortization should be presented in the Operating Activities category of the statement of cash flows as an addition to net income.**

The sale or disposition of long-term assets is an investing activity. When an asset is sold, the amount of cash received should be reflected as an addition in the Investing Activities category of the statement of cash flows. If the asset was sold at a gain or loss, however, one additional aspect should be reflected. Because the gain or loss was reflected on the income statement, it should be eliminated from the net income amount presented in the Operating Activities category (if the indirect method is used). A sale of an asset is not an activity related to normal ongoing operations, and all amounts involved with the sale should be removed from the Operating Activities category.

Exhibit 8-6 indicates the Operating and Investing categories of the 2015 statement of cash flows of Nike, Inc. The company had a net income of $3,273 million during 2015. Note that the company generated a positive cash flow from operating activities of $4,680 million. One of the reasons was that depreciation of $606 million and amortization of $43 million affected the income statement but did not involve a cash outflow and therefore are added back on the statement of cash flows. Also note that the Investing Activities category indicates major outlays of cash for new property, plant, and

EXHIBIT 8-6 Nike, Inc.'s Consolidated Partial Statement of Cash Flows

NIKE, Inc. Consolidated Statements of Cash Flows	
(In millions)	Year Ended May 31, 2015
Cash provided by operations:	
Net income	$ 3,273
Income charges (credits) not affecting cash:	
Depreciation	606
Deferred income taxes	(113)
Stock-based compensation (Note 11)	191
Amortization and other	43
Net foreign currency adjustments	424
Net gain on divestitures	—
Changes in certain working capital components and other assets and liabilities:	
(Increase) decrease in accounts receivable	(216)
(Increase) in inventories	(621)
(Increase) in prepaid expenses and other current assets	(144)
Increase in accounts payable, accrued liabilities and income taxes payable	1,237
Cash provided by operations	4,680
Cash used by investing activities:	
Purchases of short-term investments	(4,936)
Maturities of short-term investments	3,655
Sales of short-term investments	2,216
Investments in reverse repurchase agreements	(150)
Additions to property, plant and equipment	(963)
Disposals of property, plant and equipment	3
Proceeds from divestitures	—
(Increase) in other assets, net of other liabilities	—
Cash used by investing activities	(175)

Source: Nike, Inc., Form 10-k for fiscal year ended May 31, 2015.

equipment of $963 million. These cash outflows are indications of Nike's need for cash that must be generated from its operating activities.

Analyzing Long-Term Assets for Average Life and Asset Turnover

LO12 Understand how investors can analyze a company's operating assets.

Because long-term assets constitute the major productive assets of most companies, the age and composition of these assets should be analyzed. Analysis of the age of the assets can be accomplished fairly easily for those companies that use the straight-line method of depreciation. A rough measure of the average life of the assets can be calculated as follows:

$$\text{Average Life} = \frac{\text{Property, Plant, and Equipment}}{\text{Depreciation Expense}}$$

The average age of the assets can be calculated as follows:

$$\text{Average Age} = \frac{\text{Accumulated Depreciation}}{\text{Depreciation Expense}}$$

The Assets category of the balance sheet is also important in analyzing a company's profitability. The asset turnover is a measure of the assets' productivity and is measured as follows:

$$\text{Asset Turnover} = \frac{\text{Net Sales}}{\text{Average Total Assets}}$$

This ratio is a measure of how many dollars of assets are necessary for every dollar of sales. That is, the ratio is a measure of how productive the assets are in generating sales. If a company is using its assets efficiently, each dollar of assets will create a high amount of sales. A company with less productive assets will generate fewer sales from its dollar of assets. Technically, a ratio is based on average total assets, but long-term assets often constitute the largest portion of a company's total assets.

MAKING BUSINESS DECISIONS
NIKE

Analyzing Operating Assets

Investors and lenders who read financial statements must determine the age, composition, and productivity of operating assets.

A. The Ratio Analysis Model

1. Formulate the Question
What is the average life of the assets?
What is the average age of the assets?
How productive are the assets in producing revenue for the company? This is referred to as *asset turnover*.

2. Gather the Information from the Financial Statements
To calculate a company's average life of assets and average age of assets, it is essential to know its total operating assets and accumulated depreciation from the balance sheet and depreciation expense from the income statement or statement of cash flows.

To calculate a company's asset turnover, it is essential to know a company's total sales from the income statement and its average total assets from the balance sheet.

3. Calculate the Ratio for Nike, Inc.

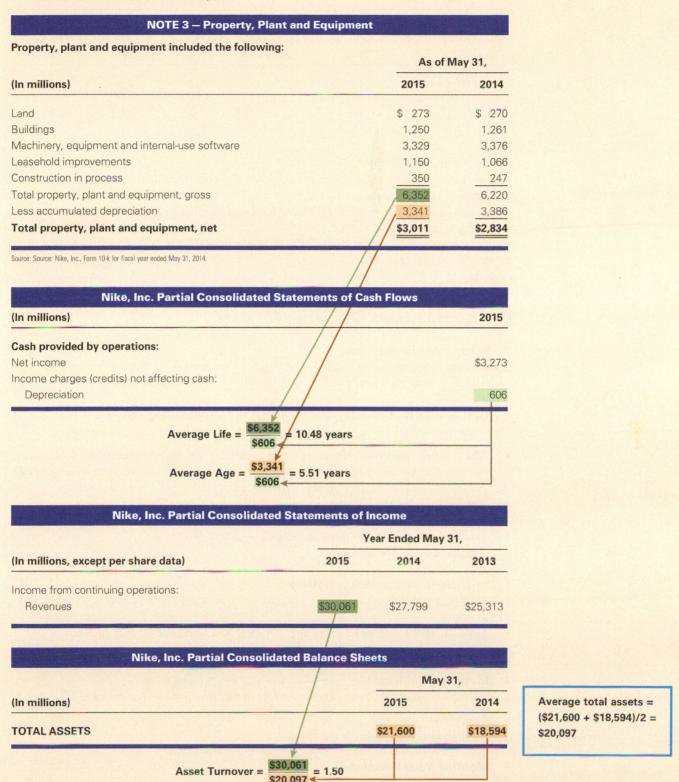

NOTE 3 — Property, Plant and Equipment

Property, plant and equipment included the following:

(In millions)	As of May 31, 2015	2014
Land	$ 273	$ 270
Buildings	1,250	1,261
Machinery, equipment and internal-use software	3,329	3,376
Leasehold improvements	1,150	1,066
Construction in process	350	247
Total property, plant and equipment, gross	6,352	6,220
Less accumulated depreciation	3,341	3,386
Total property, plant and equipment, net	$3,011	$2,834

Source: Source: Nike, Inc., Form 10-k for fiscal year ended May 31, 2014.

Nike, Inc. Partial Consolidated Statements of Cash Flows

(In millions)	2015
Cash provided by operations:	
Net income	$3,273
Income charges (credits) not affecting cash:	
Depreciation	606

$$\text{Average Life} = \frac{\$6,352}{\$606} = 10.48 \text{ years}$$

$$\text{Average Age} = \frac{\$3,341}{\$606} = 5.51 \text{ years}$$

Nike, Inc. Partial Consolidated Statements of Income

(In millions, except per share data)	Year Ended May 31, 2015	2014	2013
Income from continuing operations:			
Revenues	$30,061	$27,799	$25,313

Nike, Inc. Partial Consolidated Balance Sheets

(In millions)	May 31, 2015	2014
TOTAL ASSETS	$21,600	$18,594

Average total assets =
($21,600 + $18,594)/2 =
$20,097

$$\text{Asset Turnover} = \frac{\$30,061}{\$20,097} = 1.50$$

4. Compare the Ratio with Others

Nike's age, composition, and productivity of operating assets should be compared with those of prior years and to those of companies in the same industry.

	Nike, Inc.			Foot Locker	
	Year Ended 2015	Year Ended 2014	Year Ended 2013	Year Ended 2015	Year Ended 2014
Average life of assets	10.48	12.01	12.56	6.88	7.13
Average age of assets	5.51	6.54	6.96	4.36	4.67
Asset turnover	1.50	1.54	1.56	2.02	1.90

5. Interpret the Ratios

The average life and age of Nike's assets have been consistent from year to year and are in line with other companies in the industry. The asset turnover ratio is a measure of how many dollars of assets are necessary for every dollar of sales. If a company uses its assets efficiently, each dollar of assets will create a high amount of sales. Nike's asset turnover ratio indicates that each dollar of assets in 2015 produced $1.50 of sales. It is an indication that the assets are productive and will be able to provide sales in future periods.

B. The Business Decision Model

1. Formulate the Question

If you were a lender, would you be willing to lend money to Nike, Inc., and use the operating assets as collateral for the loan?

2. Gather Information from the Financial Statements and Other Sources

This information will come from a variety of sources, not limited to but including:

- The balance sheet provides information about the age and composition of the assets, the income statement regarding profitability and depreciation, and the statement of cash flows on inflows and outflows of cash.
- The outlook for the industry, including consumer trends, foreign markets, labor issues, and other factors.
- The outlook for the economy in general.
- Alternative uses for the money.

3. Analyze the Information Gathered

- Compare Nike, Inc.'s ratios in (A) above with Foot Locker's as well as with industry averages.
- Look at trends over time in the age, composition, and productivity of assets.
- Review projections for the economy and the industry.

4. Make the Decision

Taking into account all of the various sources of information, decide either to

- Lend money to Nike, Inc., or
- Find an alternative use for the money

5. Monitor Your Decision

If you decide to lend the money, you will need to monitor your investment periodically. During the time of the loan, you will want to assess the company's operating assets as well as other factors you considered before making the investment.

MODULE 4 TEST YOURSELF

Review	**LO11** Explain the impact that long-term assets have on the statement of cash flows.	• Long-term assets impact the statement of cash flows when they are acquired, depreciated, and sold. • Cash used to acquire long-term assets or cash received on the sale of long-term assets is reflected in the Investing Activities section of the statement of cash flows. • Depreciation and amortization are noncash expenses recorded on the accrual income statement. Accordingly, net income on a cash basis must be arrived at by adding depreciation and amortization back to accrual net income.
	LO12 Understand how investors can analyze a company's operating assets.	• Investors are interested in how productive a company's operating assets are. • The Ratios are a valuable tool that can be used to examine the productivity of operating assets with the asset turnover ratio.

Apply	1. In which category of the statement of cash flows (indirect method) should the following items appear? Depreciation of an operating asset Gain on the sale of an asset Amortization of an intangible Loss on the sale of an asset Amount paid to purchase an asset Amount received upon sale of an asset
	2. At December 31, 2017, a company has the following amounts on its financial statements: Property, plant, and equipment $10,000 Accumulated depreciation 5,000 Total assets at January 1, 2017 30,000 Total assets at December 31, 2017 40,000 Net sales 62,000 Depreciation expense 1,000 Calculate the following ratios: Average life of the assets Average age of the assets Asset turnover

Answers are located at the end of the chapter.

RATIO REVIEW

$$\text{Average Life} = \frac{\text{Property, Plant, and Equipment}}{\text{Depreciation Expense}}$$

$$\text{Average Age} = \frac{\text{Accumulated Depreciation}}{\text{Depreciation Expenses}}$$

$$\text{Asset Turnover} = \frac{\text{Net Sales}}{\text{Average Total Assets}}$$

ACCOUNTS HIGHLIGHTED

Account Title	Appears on the	In the Section of	Page Number
Land	Balance Sheet	Operating Assets	358
Buildings	Balance Sheet	Operating Assets	358
Machinery	Balance Sheet	Operating Assets	358
Accumulated Depreciation (a contra account)	Balance Sheet	Operating Assets	366
Depreciation Expense	Income Statement	Operating Expenses	369
Gain on Sale of Asset	Income Statement	Other Income	370
Loss on Sale of Asset	Income Statement	Other Expense	370
Copyright	Balance Sheet	Intangible Assets	372
Trademark	Balance Sheet	Intangible Assets	372
Amortization Expense	Income Statement	Operating Expenses	373
Accumulated Amortization (a contra account)	Balance Sheet	Intangible Assets	373
Goodwill	Balance Sheet	Intangible Assets	374

KEY TERMS QUIZ

Read each definition below and write the number of the definition in the blank beside the appropriate term. The quiz solutions appear at the end of the chapter.

_____ Acquisition cost   _____ Change in estimate
_____ Capitalization of interest _____ Capital expenditure
_____ Land improvements   _____ Revenue expenditure
_____ Depreciation   _____ Gain on Sale of Asset
_____ Straight-line method   _____ Loss on Sale of Asset
_____ Book value   _____ Intangible assets
_____ Units-of-production method _____ Goodwill
_____ Accelerated depreciation   _____ Research and development costs
_____ Double-declining-balance method

1. The amount that includes all of the cost normally necessary to acquire an asset and prepare it for its intended use.
2. Costs that are related to land but that have a limited life.
3. A method by which the same dollar amount of depreciation is recorded in each year of asset use.
4. Depreciation is determined as a function of the number of units the asset produces.
5. Interest on constructed assets is added to the asset account.
6. A change in the life of the asset or in its residual value.
7. The allocation of the original cost of an asset to the periods benefited by its use.
8. A cost that improves the asset and is added to the asset account.
9. The original cost of an asset minus the amount of accumulated depreciation.
10. A cost that keeps an asset in its normal operating condition and is treated as an expense.
11. The excess of the selling price over the asset's book value.
12. The amount by which selling price is less than book value.
13. A higher amount of depreciation is recorded in the early years and a lower amount in the later years.
14. Assets with no physical properties.
15. Depreciation is recorded at twice the straight-line rate, but the balance is reduced each period.
16. The excess of the purchase price to acquire a business over the value of the individual net assets acquired.
17. Costs incurred in the discovery of new knowledge.

ALTERNATE TERMS

accumulated depreciation allowance for depreciation

acquisition cost historical cost and original cost

capitalize expenditure item treated as asset

construction in progress construction in process

goodwill purchase price in excess of the market value of the assets

hidden assets unrecorded or off-balance-sheet assets

property, plant, and equipment fixed assets

prospective current and future years

residual value salvage value

revenue expenditure item treated as an expense of the period

REVIEW PROBLEM & SOLUTION

The accountant for Becker Company wants to develop a balance sheet as of December 31, 2017. A review of the asset records has revealed the following information:

a. Asset A was purchased on July 1, 2015, for $40,000 and has been depreciated on the straight-line basis using an estimated life of six years and a residual value of $4,000.

b. Asset B was purchased on January 1, 2016, for $66,000. The straight-line method has been used for depreciation purposes. Originally, the estimated life of the asset was projected to be six years with a residual value of $6,000; however, at the beginning of 2017, the accountant learned that the remaining life of the asset was only three years with a residual value of $2,000.

c. Asset C was purchased on January 1, 2016, for $50,000. The double-declining-balance method has been used for depreciation purposes, with a four-year life and a residual value estimate of $5,000.

Required

1. Assume that these assets represent pieces of equipment. Calculate the acquisition cost, accumulated depreciation, and book value of each asset as of December 31, 2017.
2. How would the assets appear on the balance sheet on December 31, 2017?
3. Assume that Becker Company sold Asset B on January 2, 2018, for $25,000. Calculate the amount of the resulting gain or loss and indicate the effect on the accounting equation for the sale. Where would the gain or loss appear on the income statement?

Solution to Review Problem

1.

Asset A

2015	Depreciation	($40,000 − $4,000)/6 × 1/2 Year	=	$ 3,000
2016		($40,000 − $4,000)/6	=	6,000
2017		($40,000 − $4,000)/6	=	6,000
	Accumulated Depreciation			$15,000

Asset B

2016	Depreciation	($66,000 − $6,000)/6	=	$10,000
2017		($66,000 − $10,000 − $2,000)/3	=	18,000
	Accumulated Depreciation			$28,000

Note the impact of the change in estimate on 2015 depreciation.

Asset C

2016	Depreciation	$50,000 × 25% × 2	=	$25,000
2017		($50,000 − $25,000) × (25% × 2)	=	12,500
	Accumulated Depreciation			$37,500

(Continued)

Becker Company
Summary of Asset Cost and Accumulated Depreciation
As of December 31, 2017

Asset	Acquisition Cost	Accumulated Depreciation	Book Value
A	$ 40,000	$15,000	$25,000
B	66,000	28,000	38,000
C	50,000	37,500	12,500
Totals	$156,000	$80,500	$75,500

2. The assets would appear in the Long-Term Assets category of the balance sheet as follows:

Equipment	$156,000
Accumulated depreciation	80,500
Equipment (net)	$ 75,500

3.

Asset B book value	$38,000
Selling price	25,000
Loss on sale of asset	$13,000

The effect of the transaction for the sale is as follows:

Identify and Analyze	ACTIVITY: Investing
	ACCOUNTS: Accumulated Depreciation—Machine Decrease Cash Increase
	Loss on Sale of Asset Increase Asset B Decrease
	STATEMENT[S]: Balance Sheet and Income Statement

Balance Sheet				Income Statement			
ASSETS	=	LIABILITIES	+	STOCKHOLDERS' EQUITY	REVENUES −	EXPENSES	= NET INCOME
Accumulated Depreciation— Machine*	28,000			(13,000)		Loss on Sale of Asset 13,000	(13,000)
Cash	25,000						
Asset B	(66,000)						

*The Accumulated Depreciation account has decreased. It is shown as an increase in the equation above because it is a contra account and causes total assets to increase.

The Loss on Sale of Asset account should appear in the Other Income/Other Expense category of the income statement. It is similar to an expense but is not the company's major activity.

EXERCISES

LO2   Exercise 8-1   Acquisition Cost

On January 1, 2017, Ruby Company purchased a piece of equipment with a list price of $60,000. The following amounts were related to the equipment purchase:

- Terms of the purchase were 2/10, net 30. Ruby paid for the purchase on January 8.
- Freight costs of $1,000 were incurred.
- A state agency required that a pollution control device be installed on the equipment at a cost of $2,500.
- During installation, the equipment was damaged and repair costs of $4,000 were incurred.

- Architect's fees of $6,000 were paid to redesign the work space to accommodate the new equipment.
- Ruby purchased liability insurance to cover possible damage to the asset. The three-year policy cost $8,000.
- Ruby financed the purchase with a bank loan. Interest of $3,000 was paid on the loan during 2016.

Required

Determine the acquisition cost of the equipment.

Exercise 8-2 Lump-Sum Purchase

LO3

EXAMPLE 8-1

To add to his growing chain of grocery stores, on January 1, 2017, Danny Marks bought a grocery store of a small competitor for $520,000. An appraiser, hired to assess the acquired assets' values, determined that the land, building, and equipment had market values of $200,000, $150,000, and $250,000, respectively.

Required

1. What is the acquisition cost of each asset? Identify and analyze the effect of the acquisition.
2. Danny plans to depreciate the operating assets on a straight-line basis for 20 years. Determine the amount of depreciation expense for 2017 on these newly acquired assets. You can assume zero residual value for all assets.
3. How would the assets appear on the balance sheet as of December 31, 2017?

Exercise 8-3 Straight-Line and Units-of-Production Methods

LO5

EXAMPLE 8-2, 8-3

Assume that Sample Company purchased factory equipment on January 1, 2017, for $60,000. The equipment has an estimated life of five years and an estimated residual value of $6,000. Sample's accountant is considering whether to use the straight-line or the units-of-production method to depreciate the asset. Because the company is beginning a new production process, the equipment will be used to produce 10,000 units in 2017, but production subsequent to 2017 will increase by 10,000 units each year.

Required

Calculate the depreciation expense, accumulated depreciation, and book value of the equipment under both methods for each of the five years of its life. Would the units-of-production method yield reasonable results in this situation? Explain.

Exercise 8-4 Accelerated Depreciation

LO5

EXAMPLE 8-4

Koffman's Warehouse purchased a forklift on January 1, 2017, for $6,000. The forklift is expected to last for five years and have a residual value of $600. Koffman's uses the double-declining-balance method for depreciation. Round amounts to the nearest dollar.

Required

1. Calculate the depreciation expense, accumulated depreciation, and book value for each year of the forklift's life.
2. Identify and analyze the effect of the depreciation for 2017.
3. Refer to Exhibit 8-2. What factors may have influenced Koffman to use the double-declining-balance method?

Exercise 8-5 Change in Estimate

LO6

EXAMPLE 8-5

Assume that Bloomer Company purchased a new machine on January 1, 2017, for $80,000. The machine has an estimated useful life of nine years and a residual value of $8,000. Bloomer has chosen to use the straight-line method of depreciation. On January 1, 2019, Bloomer discovered that the machine would not be useful beyond December 31, 2022, and estimated its value at that time to be $2,000.

(Continued)

Required

1. Calculate the depreciation expense, accumulated depreciation, and book value of the asset for each year 2017 to 2022.
2. Was the depreciation recorded wrong in 2017 and 2018? If so, why was it not corrected?

LO8 Exercise 8-6 Asset Disposal

Assume that Gonzalez Company purchased an asset on January 1, 2015, for $60,000. The asset had an estimated life of six years and an estimated residual value of $6,000. The company used the straight-line method to depreciate the asset. On July 1, 2017, the asset was sold for $40,000.

Required

1. Identify and analyze the effect of the transaction for depreciation for 2017. Identify and analyze the effect of the sale of the asset.
2. How should the gain or loss on the sale of the asset be presented on the income statement?

LO8 Exercise 8-7 Asset Disposal

EXAMPLE 8-7, 8-8

Refer to Exercise 8-6. Assume that Gonzalez Company sold the asset on July 1, 2017, and received $15,000 cash and a note for an additional $15,000.

Required

1. Identify and analyze the effect of the transaction for depreciation for 2017. Identify and analyze the effect of the sale of the asset.
2. How should the gain or loss on the sale of the asset be presented on the income statement?

LO10 Exercise 8-8 Amortization of Intangibles

EXAMPLE 8-9

For each of the following intangible assets, indicate the amount of amortization expense that should be recorded for the year 2017 and the amount of accumulated amortization on the balance sheet as of December 31, 2017.

	Trademark	Patent	Copyright
Cost	$40,000	$50,000	$80,000
Date of purchase	1/1/10	1/1/12	1/1/15
Useful life	indefinite	10 yrs.	20 yrs.
Legal life	undefined	20 yrs.	50 yrs.
Method	SL*	SL	SL

*Represents the straight-line method.

LO11 Exercise 8-9 Impact of Transactions Involving Operating Assets on Statement of Cash Flows

From the following list, identify each item as operating (O), investing (I), financing (F), or not separately reported on the statement of cash flows (N).

_____ Purchase of land
_____ Proceeds from sale of land
_____ Gain on sale of land
_____ Purchase of equipment
_____ Depreciation expense
_____ Proceeds from sale of equipment
_____ Loss on sale of equipment

LO11 Exercise 8-10 Impact of Transactions Involving Intangible Assets on Statement of Cash Flows

From the following list, identify each item as operating (O), investing (I), financing (F), or not separately reported on the statement of cash flows (N).

_____ Cost incurred to acquire copyright
_____ Proceeds from sale of patent
_____ Gain on sale of patent
_____ Research and development costs
_____ Amortization of patent

MULTI-CONCEPT EXERCISES

Exercise 8-11 Capital versus Revenue Expenditures

LO1 • 7
EXAMPLE 8-6

On January 1, 2015, Jose Company purchased a building for $200,000 and a delivery truck for $20,000. The following expenditures have been incurred during 2017:

- The building was painted at a cost of $5,000.
- To prevent leaking, new windows were installed in the building at a cost of $10,000.
- To improve production, a new conveyor system was installed at a cost of $40,000.
- The delivery truck was repainted with a new company logo at a cost of $1,000.
- To allow better handling of large loads, a hydraulic lift system was installed on the truck at a cost of $5,000.
- The truck's engine was overhauled at a cost of $4,000.

Required

1. Determine which of those costs should be capitalized. Also, identify and analyze the effect of the capitalized costs. Assume that all costs were incurred on January 1, 2017.
2. Determine the amount of depreciation for the year 2017. The company uses the straight-line method and depreciates the building over 25 years and the truck over six years. Assume zero residual value for all assets.
3. How would the assets appear on the balance sheet of December 31, 2017?

Exercise 8-12 Capitalization of Interest and Depreciation

LO4 • 5
EXAMPLE 8-2

During 2017, Mercator Company borrowed $80,000 from a local bank. In addition, Mercator used $120,000 of cash to construct a new corporate office building. Based on average accumulated expenditures, the amount of interest capitalized during 2017 was $8,000. Construction was completed, and the building was occupied on January 1, 2018.

Required

1. Determine the acquisition cost of the new building.
2. The building has an estimated useful life of 20 years and a $5,000 salvage value. Assuming that Mercator uses the straight-line basis to depreciate its operating assets, determine the amount of depreciation expense for 2017 and 2018.

Exercise 8-13 Research and Development and Patents

LO9 • 10

Erin Company incurred the following costs during 2017 and 2018:

a. Research and development costing $20,000 was conducted on a new product to sell in future years. A product was successfully developed, and a patent for it was granted during 2017. Erin is unsure of the period benefited by the research, but believes the product will result in increased sales over the next five years.
b. Legal costs and application fees of $10,000 for the 20-year patent were incurred on January 1, 2017.
c. A patent infringement suit was successfully defended at a cost of $8,000. Assume that all costs were incurred on January 1, 2018.

Required

Determine how the costs in (a) and (b) should be presented on Erin's financial statements as of December 31, 2017. Also determine the amount of amortization of intangible assets that Erin should record in 2017 and 2018.

PROBLEMS

LO3 Problem 8-1 Lump-Sum Purchase of Assets and Subsequent Events

Carter Development Company purchased, for cash, a large tract of land that was immediately platted and deeded into the following smaller sections:

> Section 1, retail development with highway frontage
> Section 2, multifamily apartment development
> Section 3, single-family homes in the largest section

Based on recent sales of similar property, the fair market values of the three sections are as follows:

> Section 1, $630,000
> Section 2, $378,000
> Section 3, $252,000

Required

1. What value is assigned to each section of land if the tract was purchased for (a) $1,260,000, (b) $1,560,000, and (c) $1,000,000?
2. How does the purchase of the tract affect the balance sheet?
3. Why would Carter be concerned with the value assigned to each section? Would Carter be more concerned with the values assigned if instead of purchasing three sections of land, it purchased land with buildings? Explain.

LO5 Problem 8-2 Depreciation as a Tax Shield

The term *tax shield* refers to the amount of income tax saved by deducting depreciation for income tax purposes. Assume that Supreme Company is considering the purchase of an asset as of January 1, 2017. The cost of the asset with a five-year life and zero residual value is $100,000. The company will use the straight-line method of depreciation.

Supreme's income for tax purposes before recording depreciation on the asset will be $50,000 per year for the next five years. The corporation is currently in the 35% tax bracket.

Required

Calculate the amount of income tax that Supreme must pay each year if the asset is not purchased. Calculate the amount of income tax that Supreme must pay each year if the asset is purchased. What is the amount of the depreciation tax shield?

LO5 Problem 8-3 Book versus Tax Depreciation

Griffith Delivery Service purchased a delivery truck for $33,600. The truck has an estimated useful life of six years and no salvage value. For purposes of preparing financial statements, Griffith is planning to use straight-line depreciation. For tax purposes, Griffith follows MACRS. Depreciation expense using MACRS is $6,720 in Year 1, $10,750 in Year 2, $6,450 in Year 3, $3,870 in each of Years 4 and 5, and $1,940 in Year 6.

Required

1. What is the difference between straight-line and MACRS depreciation expense for each of the six years?
2. Griffith's president has asked why you use one method for the books and another for tax calculations. "Can you do this? Is it legal? Don't we take the same total depreciation either way?" he asked. Write a brief memo answering his questions and explaining the benefits of using two methods for depreciation.

LO11 Problem 8-4 Depreciation and Cash Flow

O'hare Company's only asset as of January 1, 2017, was a limousine. During 2017, only the following three transactions occurred:

Services of $100,000 were provided on account.
All accounts receivable were collected.
Depreciation on the limousine was $15,000.

Required

1. Develop an income statement for O'hare for 2017.
2. Determine the amount of the net cash inflow for O'hare for 2017.
3. Explain why O'hare's net income does not equal net cash inflow.
4. If O'hare developed a cash flow statement for 2017 using the indirect method, what amount would appear in the category titled Cash Flow from Operating Activities?

Problem 8-5 Reconstruct Net Book Values Using Statement of Cash Flows

LO11

Centralia Stores Inc. had property, plant, and equipment, net of accumulated depreciation, of $4,459,000 and intangible assets, net of accumulated amortization, of $673,000 at December 31, 2017. The company's 2016 statement of cash flows, prepared using the indirect method, included the following items:

a. The Cash Flows from Operating Activities section included three additions to net income:
    (1) Depreciation expense of $672,000
    (2) Amortization expense of $33,000
    (3) Loss on the sale of equipment of $35,000
b. The Cash Flows from Operating Activities section also included a subtraction from net income for the gain on the sale of a copyright of $55,000.
c. The Cash Flows from Investing Activities section included outflows for the purchase of a building of $292,000 and $15,000 for the payment of legal fees to protect a patent from infringement.
d. The Cash Flows from Investing Activities section also included inflows from the sale of equipment of $315,000 and the sale of a copyright of $75,000.

Required

1. Determine the book values of the assets that were sold during 2017.
2. Reconstruct the amount of property, plant, and equipment, net of accumulated depreciation, that was reported on the company's balance sheet at December 31, 2016.
3. Reconstruct the amount of intangibles, net of accumulated amortization, that was reported on the company's balance sheet at December 31, 2016.

MULTI-CONCEPT PROBLEMS

Problem 8-6 Cost of Assets, Subsequent Book Values, and Balance Sheet Presentation

LO1 • 3 • 5 • 7 • 8

The following events took place at Pete's Painting Company during 2017:

a. On January 1, Pete bought a used truck for $14,000. He added a tool chest and side racks for ladders for $4,800. The truck is expected to last four years and then be sold for $800. Pete uses straight-line depreciation.
b. On January 1, he purchased several items at an auction for $2,400. These items had fair market values as follows:

10 cases of paint trays and roller covers	$ 200
Storage cabinets	600
Ladders and scaffolding	2,400

Pete will use all of the paint trays and roller covers this year. The storage cabinets are expected to last nine years; the ladders and scaffolding, four years.

c. On February 1, Pete paid the city $1,500 for a three-year license to operate the business.
d. On September 1, Pete sold an old truck for $4,800 that had cost $12,000 when it was purchased on September 1, 2012. It was expected to last eight years and have a salvage value of $800. Pete used the straight line method of depreciation.

(Continued)

Required

1. For each situation, explain the value assigned to the asset when it is purchased [or for (d), the book value when sold].
2. Determine the amount of depreciation or other expense to be recorded for each asset for 2017.
3. How would these assets appear on the balance sheet as of December 31, 2017?

LO2 • 5   ## Problem 8-7 Cost of Assets and the Effect on Depreciation

Early in its first year of business, Toner Company, a fitness and training center, purchased new workout equipment. The acquisition included the following costs:

Purchase price	$150,000
Tax	15,000
Transportation	4,000
Setup*	25,000
Painting*	3,000

*The equipment was adjusted to Toner's specific needs
and painted to match the other equipment in the gym.

The bookkeeper recorded an asset, Equipment, $165,000 (purchase price and tax). The remaining costs were expensed for the year. Toner used straight-line depreciation. The equipment was expected to last ten years with zero salvage value.

Required

1. How much depreciation did Toner report on its income statement related to this equipment in Year 1? What is the correct amount of depreciation to report in Year 1?
2. Income is $100,000 before costs related to the equipment are reported. How much income will Toner report in Year 1? What amount of income should it report? You can ignore income tax.
3. Using the equipment as an example, explain the difference between a cost and an expense.

LO5 • 7 • 8   ## Problem 8-8 Capital Expenditures, Depreciation, and Disposal

Merton Company purchased a building on January 1, 2016, at a cost of $364,000. Merton estimated that its life would be 25 years and its residual value would be $14,000.

On January 1, 2017, the company made several expenditures related to the building. The entire building was painted and floors were refinished at a cost of $21,000. A federal agency required Merton to install additional pollution control devices in the building at a cost of $42,000. With the new devices, Merton believed it was possible to extend the life of the building by six years.

In 2018, Merton altered its corporate strategy dramatically. The company sold the building on April 1, 2018, for $392,000 in cash and relocated all operations to another state.

Required

1. Determine the depreciation that should be on the income statement for 2016 and 2017.
2. Explain why the cost of the pollution control equipment was not expensed in 2017. What conditions would have allowed Merton to expense the equipment? If Merton has a choice, would it prefer to expense or capitalize the equipment?
3. What amount of gain or loss did Merton record when it sold the building? What amount of gain or loss would have been reported if the pollution control equipment had been expensed in 2017?

LO6 • 10   ## Problem 8-9 Amortization of Intangible, Revision of Rate

During 2012, Reynosa Inc.'s research and development department developed a new manufacturing process. Research and development costs were $85,000. The process was patented on October 1, 2012. Legal costs to acquire the patent were $11,900. Reynosa decided to expense the patent over a 20-year time period. Reynosa's fiscal year ends on September 30.

On October 1, 2017, Reynosa's competition announced that it had obtained a patent on a new process that would make Reynosa's patent completely worthless.

Required

1. How should Reynosa record the $85,000 and $11,900 costs?
2. How much amortization expense should Reynosa report in each year through the year ended September 30, 2017?
3. What amount of loss should Reynosa report in the year ended September 30, 2018?

Problem 8-10 Purchase and Disposal of Operating Asset and Effects on Statement of Cash Flows

LO8 • 11

On January 1, 2017, Castlewood Company purchased machinery for its production line for $104,000. Using an estimated useful life of eight years and a residual value of $8,000, the annual straight-line depreciation of the machinery was calculated to be $12,000. Castlewood used the machinery during 2017 and 2018, but then decided to automate its production process. On December 31, 2018, Castlewood sold the machinery at a loss of $5,000 and purchased new, fully automated machinery for $205,000.

Required

1. How would the previous transactions be presented on Castlewood's statements of cash flows for the years ended December 31, 2017 and 2018?
2. Why would Castlewood sell at a loss machinery that had a remaining useful life of six years and purchase new machinery with a cost almost twice that of the old?

Problem 8-11 Amortization of Intangibles and Effects on Statement of Cash Flows

LO9 • 10 • 11

Tableleaf Inc. purchased a patent a number of years ago. The patent is being amortized on a straight-line basis over its estimated useful life. The company's comparative balance sheets as of December 31, 2017 and 2016, included the following line item:

	12/31/17	12/31/16
Patent, less accumulated amortization of $119,000 (2017) and $102,000 (2016)	$170,000	$187,000

Required

1. How much amortization expense was recorded during 2017?
2. What was the patent's acquisition cost? When was it acquired? What is its estimated useful life? How was the acquisition of the patent reported on that year's statement of cash flows?
3. Assume that Tableleaf uses the indirect method to prepare its statement of cash flows. How is the amortization of the patent reported annually on the statement of cash flows?
4. How would the sale of the patent on January 1, 2017, for $200,000 be reported on the 2017 statement of cash flows?

ALTERNATE PROBLEMS

Problem 8-1A Lump-Sum Purchase of Assets and Subsequent Events

LO3

Dixon Manufacturing purchased, for cash, three large pieces of equipment. Based on recent sales of similar equipment, the fair market values are as follows:

Piece 1	$200,000
Piece 2	$200,000
Piece 3	$440,000

Required

1. What value is assigned to each piece of equipment if the equipment was purchased for (a) $480,000, (b) $680,000, and (c) $800,000?
2. How does the purchase of the equipment affect total assets?

LO5   Problem 8-2A Depreciation as a Tax Shield

The term *tax shield* refers to the amount of income tax saved by deducting depreciation for income tax purposes. Assume that Rummy Company is considering the purchase of an asset as of January 1, 2017. The cost of the asset with a five-year life and zero residual value is $60,000. The company will use the double-declining-balance method of depreciation.

Rummy's income for tax purposes before recording depreciation on the asset will be $62,000 per year for the next five years. The corporation is currently in the 30% tax bracket.

Required

Calculate the amount of income tax that Rummy must pay each year if (a) the asset is not purchased and (b) the asset is purchased. What is the amount of tax shield over the life of the asset? What is the amount of tax shield for Rummy if it uses the straight-line method over the life of the asset? Why would Rummy choose to use the accelerated method?

LO5   Problem 8-3A Book versus Tax Depreciation

Payton Delivery Service purchased a delivery truck for $28,200. The truck will have a useful life of six years and zero salvage value. For the purposes of preparing financial statements, Payton is planning to use straight-line depreciation. For tax purposes, Payton follows MACRS. Depreciation expense using MACRS is $5,650 in Year 1, $9,025 in Year 2, $5,400 in Year 3, $3,250 in each of Years 4 and 5, and $1,625 in Year 6.

Required

1. What is the difference between straight-line and MACRS depreciation expense for each of the six years?
2. Payton's president has asked why you use one method for the books and another for tax calculations. "Can you do this? Is it legal? Don't we take the same total depreciation either way?" he asked. Write a brief memo answering his questions and explaining the benefits of using two methods for depreciation.

LO11   Problem 8-4A Amortization and Cash Flow

Book Company's only asset as of January 1, 2017, was a copyright. During 2017, only the following three transactions occurred:

·   Royalties earned from copyright use, $500,000 in cash
     Cash paid for advertising and salaries, $62,500
     Amortization, $50,000

Required

1. What amount of income will Book report in 2017?
2. What is the amount of cash on hand at December 31, 2017?
3. Explain how the cash balance increased from zero at the beginning of the year to its year-end balance. Why does the increase in cash not equal the income?

LO11   Problem 8-5A Reconstruct Net Book Values Using Statement of Cash Flows

E-Gen Enterprises Inc. had property, plant, and equipment, net of accumulated depreciation, of $1,555,000 and intangible assets, net of accumulated amortization, of $34,000 at December 31, 2017. The company's 2017 statement of cash flows, prepared using the indirect method, included the following items:

a. The Cash Flows from Operating Activities section included three additions to net income:
    (1) Depreciation expense of $205,000
    (2) Amortization expense of $3,000
    (3) Loss on the sale of land of $17,000
b. The Cash Flows from Operating Activities section also included a subtraction from net income for the gain on the sale of a trademark of $7,000.

c. The Cash Flows from Investing Activities section included outflows for the purchase of equipment of $277,000 and $6,000 for the payment of legal fees to protect a copyright from infringement.

d. The Cash Flows from Investing Activities section also included inflows from the sale of land of $187,000 and the sale of a trademark of $121,000.

Required

1. Determine the book values of the assets that were sold during 2017.
2. Reconstruct the amount of property, plant, and equipment, net of accumulated depreciation, that was reported on the company's balance sheet at December 31, 2016.
3. Reconstruct the amount of intangibles, net of accumulated amortization, that was reported on the company's balance sheet at December 31, 2016.

ALTERNATE MULTI-CONCEPT PROBLEMS

Problem 8-6A Cost of Assets, Subsequent Book Values, and Balance Sheet Presentation

LO1 • 5 • 8 • 9 • 10

The following events took place at Tasty-Toppins Inc., a pizza shop that specializes in home delivery, during 2017:

a. January 1, purchased a truck for $16,000 and added a cab and an oven at a cost of $10,900. The truck is expected to last five years and be sold for $300 at the end of that time. The company uses straight-line depreciation for its trucks.

b. January 1, purchased equipment for $2,700 from a competitor who was retiring. The equipment is expected to last three years with zero salvage value. The company uses the double-declining-balance method to depreciate its equipment.

c. April 1, sold a truck for $1,500. The truck had been purchased for $8,000 exactly five years earlier, had an expected salvage value of $1,000, and was depreciated over an eight-year life using the straight-line method.

d. July 1, purchased a $14,000 patent for a unique baking process to produce a new product. The patent is valid for 15 more years; however, the company expects to produce and market the product for only four years. The patent's value at the end of the four years will be zero.

Required

For each situation, explain the amount of depreciation or amortization recorded for each asset in the current year and the book value of each asset at the end of the year. For (c), indicate the accumulated depreciation and book value at the time of sale.

Problem 8-7A Cost of Assets and the Effect on Depreciation

LO2 • 5

Early in its first year of business, Key Inc., a locksmith and security consultant, purchased new equipment. The acquisition included the following costs:

Purchase price	$168,000
Tax	16,500
Transportation	4,400
Setup*	1,100
Operating cost for first year	26,400

*The equipment was adjusted to Key's specific needs.

The bookkeeper recorded the asset Equipment at $216,400. Key used straight-line depreciation. The equipment was expected to last ten years with zero residual value.

Required

1. Was $216,400 the proper amount to record for the acquisition cost? If not, explain how each expenditure should be recorded.

(Continued)

2. How much depreciation did Key report on its income statement related to this equipment in Year 1? How much should have been reported?
3. If Key's income before the costs associated with the equipment is $55,000, what amount of income did Key report? What amount should it have reported? You can ignore income tax.
4. Explain how Key should determine the amount to capitalize when recording an asset. What is the effect of Key's error on the income statement and balance sheet?

LO7 • 8   Problem 8-8A Capital Expenditures, Depreciation, and Disposal

Wagner Company purchased a retail shopping center on January 1, 2016, at a cost of $612,000. Wagner estimated that its life would be 25 years and its residual value would be $12,000.

On January 1, 2017, the company made several expenditures related to the building. The entire building was painted and floors were refinished at a cost of $115,200. A local zoning agency required Wagner to install additional fire protection equipment, including sprinklers and built-in alarms, at a cost of $87,600. With the new protection, Wagner believed it was possible to increase the residual value of the building to $30,000.

In 2018, Wagner altered its corporate strategy dramatically. The company sold the retail shopping center on January 1, 2018, for $360,000 cash.

Required

1. Determine the depreciation that should be on the income statement for 2016 and 2017.
2. Explain why the cost of the fire protection equipment was not expensed in 2016. What conditions would have allowed Wagner to expense it? If Wagner has a choice, would it prefer to expense or capitalize the equipment?
3. What amount of gain or loss did Wagner record when it sold the building? What amount of gain or loss would have been reported if the fire protection equipment had been expensed in 2017?

LO6 • 10   Problem 8-9A Amortization of Intangible, Revision of Rate

During 2012, Maciel Inc.'s research and development department developed a new manufacturing process. Research and development costs were $350,000. The process was patented on October 1, 2012. Legal costs to acquire the patent were $23,800. Maciel decided to expense the patent over a 20-year time period using the straight-line method. Maciel's fiscal year ends on September 30.

On October 1, 2017, Maciel's competition announced that it had obtained a patent on a new process that would make Maciel's patent completely worthless.

Required

1. How should Maciel record the $350,000 and $23,800 costs?
2. How much amortization expense should Maciel report in each year through the year ended September 30, 2017?
3. What amount of loss should Maciel report in the year ended September 30, 2018?

LO8 • 11   Problem 8-10A Purchase and Disposal of Operating Asset and Effects on Statement of Cash Flows

On January 1, 2017, Mansfield Inc. purchased a medium-sized delivery truck for $45,000. Using an estimated useful life of five years and a residual value of $5,000, the annual straight-line depreciation of the trucks was calculated to be $8,000. Mansfield used the truck during 2017 and 2018, but then decided to purchase a larger delivery truck. On December 31, 2018, Mansfield sold the delivery truck at a loss of $12,000 and purchased a new, larger delivery truck for $80,000.

Required

1. How would the previous transactions be presented on Mansfield's statements of cash flows for the years ended December 31, 2017 and 2018?
2. Why would Mansfield sell at a loss a truck that had a remaining useful life of three years and purchase a new truck with a cost almost twice that of the old?

Problem 8-11A Amortization of Intangibles and Effects on Statement of Cash Flows

LO9 • 10 • 11

Quickster Inc. acquired a patent a number of years ago. The patent is being amortized on a straight-line basis over its estimated useful life. The company's comparative balance sheets as of December 31, 2017 and 2016, included the following line item:

	12/31/17	12/31/16
Patent, less accumulated amortization of $1,661,000 (2017) and $1,510,000 (2016)	$1,357,000	$1,508,000

Required

1. How much amortization expense was recorded during 2017?
2. What was the patent's acquisition cost? When was it acquired? What is its estimated useful life? How was the acquisition of the patent reported on that year's statement of cash flows?
3. Assume that Quickster uses the indirect method to prepare its statement of cash flows. How is the amortization of the patent reported annually on the statement of cash flows?
4. How would the sale of the patent on January 1, 2018, for $1,700,000 be reported on the 2018 statement of cash flows?

DECISION CASES

Reading and Interpreting Financial Statements

Decision Case 8-1 Panera Bread Company

LO1 • 9

Refer to the financial statements and notes for **Panera Bread Company** included at the back of the book.

REAL WORLD

Required

1. What items does the company list in the Property and Equipment category?
2. What method is used to depreciate the operating assets?
3. What is the estimated useful life of the operating assets?
4. What are the accumulated depreciation and book values of property and equipment for the most recent fiscal year?
5. Were any assets purchased or sold during the most recent fiscal year? Explain.

Decision Case 8-2 Making Business Decisions: Comparing Two Companies in the Same Industry: Chipotle and Panera Bread

LO1 • 9

Investors and lenders who read financial statements must determine the age, composition, and productivity of operating assets.

Refer to the financial information at the back of the book for **Chipotle** and **Panera Bread**.

RATIO ANALYSIS

BUSINESS DECISION MODEL

Required

Part A. The Ratio Analysis Model

For each company, determine:

Replicate the five steps in the Ratio Analysis Model on page 378 to perform the analysis.

1. Formulate the Question
2. Gather the Information from the Financial Statements
3. Calculate the Ratio
4. Compare the Ratio with Other Ratios
5. Interpret the Ratios

REAL WORLD

(Continued)

Part B. The Business Decision Model

1. Formulate the Question
2. Gather Information from the Financial Statements and Other Sources
3. Analyze the Information Gathered
4. Make the Decision
5. Monitor Your Decision

Making Financial Decisions

LO1 • 5   Decision Case 8-3 Comparing Companies

Assume that you are a financial analyst attempting to compare the financial results of two companies. The 2017 income statement of Straight Company is as follows:

Sales		$720,000
Cost of goods sold		360,000
Gross profit		$360,000
Administrative costs	$ 96,000	
Depreciation expense	120,000	216,000
Income before tax		$144,000
Tax expense (40%)		57,600
Net income		$ 86,400

Straight Company depreciates all operating assets using the straight-line method for tax purposes and for the annual report provided to stockholders. All operating assets were purchased on the same date, and all assets had an estimated life of five years when purchased. Straight Company's balance sheet reveals that on December 31, 2017, the balance of the Accumulated Depreciation account was $240,000.

You want to compare the annual report of Straight Company to that of Accelerated Company. Both companies are in the same industry, and both have the same assets, sales, and expenses except that Accelerated uses the double-declining-balance method for depreciation for income tax purposes and for the annual report provided to stockholders.

Required

Develop Accelerated Company's 2017 income statement. As a financial analyst interested in investing in one of the companies, do you find Straight or Accelerated to be more attractive? Because depreciation is a "noncash" expense, should you be indifferent in deciding between the two companies? Explain your answer.

LO5   Decision Case 8-4 Depreciation Alternatives

Medsupply Inc. produces supplies used in hospitals and nursing homes. Its sales, production, and costs to produce are expected to remain constant over the next five years. The corporate income tax rate is expected to increase over the next three years. The current rate, 15%, is expected to increase to 20% next year, then to 25%, continuing at that rate indefinitely.

Medsupply is considering the purchase of new equipment that is expected to last five years and to cost $150,000 with zero salvage value. As the controller, you are aware that the company can use one method of depreciation for accounting purposes and another method for tax purposes. You are trying to decide between the straight-line and the double-declining-balance methods.

Required

Recommend which method to use for accounting purposes and which to use for tax purposes. Be able to justify your answer on both a numerical and a theoretical basis. How does a noncash adjustment to income, such as depreciation, affect cash flow?

Ethical Decision Making

Decision Case 8-5 Valuing Assets

LO3

ETHICAL DECISION MODEL

Denver Company recently hired Terry Davis as an accountant. He was given responsibility for all accounting functions related to fixed asset accounting. Tammy Sharp, Terry's boss, asked him to review all transactions involving the current year's acquisition of fixed assets and to take necessary action to ensure that acquired assets were recorded at proper values. Terry is satisfied that all transactions are proper except for an April 15 purchase of an office building and the land on which it is situated. The purchase price of the acquisition was $200,000. However, Denver Company has not reported the land and building separately. Terry hired an appraiser to determine the market values of the land and the building. The appraiser reported that his best estimates of the values were $150,000 for the building and $70,000 for the land. When Terry proposed that these values be used to determine the acquisition cost of the assets, Tammy disagreed. She told Terry to request another appraisal of the property and asked him to stress to the appraiser that the land component of the acquisition could not be depreciated for tax purposes. The second appraiser estimated that the values were $180,000 for the building and $40,000 for the land. Terry and Tammy agreed that the second appraisal should be used to determine the acquisition cost of the assets.

Required

Use the Ethical Decision Framework in Exhibit 1-9 to complete the following requirements:
1. **Recognize an ethical dilemma:** What ethical dilemma(s) do you face?
2. **Analyze the key elements in the situation:**

   a. Who may benefit from using the second appraisal? Who may be harmed?

   b. How are they likely to benefit or be harmed?

   c. What rights or claims may be violated?

   d. What specific interests are in conflict?

   e. What are your responsibilities and obligations?

3. **List alternatives and evaluate the impact of each on those affected:** What are your options in dealing with the ethical dilemma(s) you identified in (1) above?
4. **Select the best alternative:** Among the alternatives, which one would you select?

Decision Case 8-6 Depreciation Estimates

LO5

Langsom's Mfg. is planning for a new project. Usually, Langsom's depreciates long-term equipment for ten years. The equipment for this project is specialized and will have no further use at the end of the project in three years. The manager of the project wants to depreciate the equipment over the usual ten years and plans on writing off the remaining book value at the end of Year 3 as a loss. You believe that the equipment should be depreciated over the three-year life.

Required

Which method do you think is conceptually better? What should you do if the manager insists on depreciating the equipment over ten years?

INTEGRATIVE PROBLEM

Correct an income statement and statement of cash flows and assess the impact of a change in inventory method; compute the effect of a bad debt recognition.

The following income statement, statement of cash flows, and additional information are available for PEK Company:

(Continued)

PEK Company
Income Statement
For the Year Ended December 31, 2017

Sales revenue		$1,250,000
Cost of goods sold		636,500
Gross profit		$ 613,500
Depreciation on plant equipment	$58,400	
Depreciation on buildings	12,000	
Interest expense	33,800	
Other expenses	83,800	188,000
Income before taxes		$ 425,500
Income tax expense (30% rate)		127,650
Net income		$ 297,850

PEK Company
Statement of Cash Flows
For the Year Ended December 31, 2017

Cash flows from operating activities:	
Net income	$297,850
Adjustments to reconcile net income to net cash provided by operating activities (includes depreciation expense)	83,200
Net cash provided by operating activities	$381,050
Cash flows from financing activities:	
Dividends	(35,000)
Net increase in cash	$346,050

Additional information:

a. Beginning inventory and purchases for the one product the company sells are as follows:

	Units	Unit Cost
Beginning inventory	50,000	$2.00
Purchases:		
February 5	25,000	2.10
March 10	30,000	2.20
April 15	40,000	2.50
June 16	75,000	3.00
September 5	60,000	3.10
October 3	40,000	3.25

b. During the year, the company sold 250,000 units at $5 each.

c. PEK uses the periodic FIFO method to value its inventory and the straight-line method to depreciate all of its long-term assets.

d. During the year-end audit, it was discovered that a January 3, 2017, transaction for the lump-sum purchase of a mixing machine and a boiler was not recorded. The fair market values of the mixing machine and the boiler were $200,000 and $100,000, respectively. Each asset has an estimated useful life of ten years with no residual value expected. The purchase of the assets was financed by issuing a $270,000 five-year promissory note directly to the seller. Interest of 8% is paid annually on December 31.

Required

1. Prepare a revised income statement and a revised statement of cash flows to take into account the omission of the entry to record the purchase of the two assets. (*Hint:* You will need to take into account any change in income taxes as a result of changes in any income statement items. Assume that income taxes are paid on December 31 of each year.)

2. Assume the same facts as in part (1), except that the company is considering the use of an accelerated method rather than the straight-line method for the assets purchased on

January 3, 2017. All other assets would continue to be depreciated on a straight-line basis. Prepare a revised income statement and a revised statement of cash flows assuming that the company decides to use the accelerated method for these two assets rather than the straight-line method, resulting in depreciation of $49,091 for 2017.

Treat the answers in parts (3) and (4) as independent of the other parts.

3. Assume that PEK decides to use the LIFO method rather than the FIFO method to value its inventory and recognize cost of goods sold for 2017. Compute the effect (amount of increase or decrease) this would have on cost of goods sold, income tax expense, and net income.

4. Assume that PEK failed to record an estimate of bad debts for 2017. (Bad debt expense is normally included in "other expenses.") Before any adjustment, the balance in Allowance for Doubtful Accounts is $8,200. The credit manager estimates that 3% of the $800,000 of sales on account will prove to be uncollectible. Based on this information, compute the effect (amount of increase or decrease) of recognition of the bad debt estimate on other expenses, income tax expense, and net income.

Answers

MODULE 1 Answers to Questions

1. Operating assets include property, plant, and equipment, and intangibles. Examples of assets considered operating assets are buildings, equipment, land, land improvements, patents, copyrights, and goodwill. Operating assets are important to the long-term future of the company because they are the assets used to produce a product or service sold to customers.

2. The acquisition cost of an operating asset includes all the costs normally necessary to acquire the asset and prepare it for its intended use. Acquisition costs include the purchase price, freight costs, installation costs, taxes paid at the time of purchase, and repairs made to prepare the asset for use.

3. The acquisition cost of assets purchased as a group should be determined by allocating the purchase price on the basis of the proportion of the fair market value to the total fair market value.

4. If a company constructs an asset over a period of time and borrows money to finance the construction, the interest incurred during the construction period is not treated as interest expense. Instead, the interest must be included as part of the acquisition cost of the asset.

MODULE 1 Answers to Apply

1. All of these accounts would be in the Property, Plant, and Equipment category except for Patent, which would be in the Intangibles category.

2. Transportation costs—yes
   Installation costs—yes

   Repair costs incurred at time of purchase—yes, if it was known at the time of purchase that the item needed repair
   Repair costs incurred after the asset has been installed and used—no
   Interest on loan to purchase the asset—no

(Continued)

3.		
Land		$ 700,000
Building		300,000
Total		$1,000,000

Land: $800,000 × ($700,000/$1,000,000) = $560,000
Building: $800,000 × ($300,000/$1,000,000) = $240,000

4.		
$1,000,000 × 12/12		$1,000,000
$2,000,000 × 6/12		1,000,000
$1,000,000 × 1/12		83,333
Average accumulated expenditures		$2,083,333

MODULE 2 Answers to Questions

1. A company should use a depreciation method that allocates the original cost of the asset to the periods benefited and that allows the company to accurately match the expense to the revenue generated by the asset. However, the company is not required to use the same method for all depreciable assets

2. The purpose in recording depreciation for financial reporting purposes is to allocate the original cost of the asset to the periods benefited in a manner that matches the decline in usefulness of the asset. The purpose in recording depreciation for tax purposes is to minimize the amount of income tax that must be paid.

3. The remaining depreciable amount should be recorded over the remaining life of the asset, using the revised estimate or estimates of residual value and asset life.

4. The gain or loss should be calculated as the difference between the selling price and the book value of the asset as of the date of sale. The account Gain on Sale of Asset or Loss on Sale of Asset should appear on the income statement in the Other Income/Expense category.

MODULE 2 Answers to Apply

1. a. Straight-line rate of $1/10 \times 2 = 20\%$

   b. First-year depreciation: $\$40,000 \times 20\% = \$8,000$
   Second-year depreciation: $(\$40,000 - \$8,000) \times 20\% = \$6,400$

   c. The maximum amount that can be treated as depreciation over ten years is $36,000. ($40,000 − $4,000 residual value = $36,000).

2. Depreciation for 2015 and 2016:

   $(\$10,000 - \$1,000)/10$ years $= \$900$ per year $\times 2$ years $= \$1,800$

   Depreciation for 2017:

Remaining depreciable amount	$8,200 − $1,000 =	$ 7,200
Divided by remaining life		÷5 years
Depreciation		$ 1,440

3.

Original cost, January 1, 2015	$10,000
Accumulated depreciation (2 years at $900 per year)	(1,800)
Book value, January 1, 2017	$ 8,200
Major overhaul	5,000
Residual value	(1,000)
Remaining depreciable amount	$12,200

Depreciation = Remaining Depreciable Amount/Remaining Life
Depreciation per Year = $12,200/10 years
= $1,220

4. Loss = Book Value − Sales Price
$6,000 = $20,000 − X

Solving for X indicates sales price, and cash received was $14,000.

MODULE 3 Answers to Questions

1. Patents, copyrights, trademarks, and goodwill are examples of intangible assets. Some companies have a separate category on the balance sheet titled Intangibles for such assets. Other companies include intangibles in a category titled Long-Term Assets or in the Other Assets category of the balance sheet.

2. Goodwill represents the difference between the acquisition price paid to acquire a business and the total of the fair market values of the identifiable net assets acquired. Goodwill can be recorded as an asset only when one company acquires another.

3. Amortization should occur over the shorter of the legal life or useful life. For example, a patent has a legal life of 20 years. But if the invention under patent will be useful over only ten years, then the patent should be amortized over the shorter ten-year period.

4. If an intangible becomes worthless, the asset should be written off as an expense in the period when the decline in value occurs. If the intangible continues to have value but will provide benefit over a period shorter than was originally estimated, the event should be treated as a change in estimate.

MODULE 3 Answers to Apply

1. Patents—intangible asset and amortized*
   Copyrights—intangible asset and amortized*
   Research and development—not an intangible asset
   Goodwill—intangible asset and not amortized
   The company's advantageous location—not an intangible asset that is recognized on the balance sheet
   Broadcast rights—intangible asset and may be amortized if it has a finite life*

   *Since these intangibles have a limited life, they should be amortized.

2. Amortization for 2015 and 2016: $12,000/12 years
   = $1,000 per year
   Amortization for 2017: $10,000*/5 years = $2,000
   *In 2017 patent = $12,000 − $2,000 = $10,000

MODULE 4 Answers to Apply

1. Depreciation of an operating asset—Operating category
   Gain on the sale of an asset—Operating category
   Amortization of an intangible—Operating category
   Loss on the sale of an asset—Operating category
   Amount paid to purchase an asset—Investing category
   Amount received upon sale of an asset—Investing category

2.
Average Life of the Assets =	Property, Plant, and Equipment/Depreciation Expense
=	$10,000/$1,000 = 10 years
Average Age of the Assets =	Accumulated Depreciation/Depreciation Expense
=	$5,000/$1,000 = 5 years
Asset Turnover =	Sales/Average Total Assets
Average Total Assets =	($30,000 + $40,000)/2 = $35,000
Asset Turnover =	$62,000/$35,000 = 1.77

Answers to Connect to the Real World

8-1 (p. 361)

Nike had property, plant, and equipment, net of depreciation, of $3,011 million as of May 31, 2015. The company does not show the amount of accumulated depreciation on the balance sheet, but that amount is disclosed in the notes to the financial statements. The amount of depreciation expense for the current year is not shown on the balance sheet. It is shown on the income statement.

Answers to Key Terms Quiz

1	Acquisition cost		6	Change in estimate
5	Capitalization of interest		8	Capital expenditure
2	Land improvements		10	Revenue expenditure
7	Depreciation		11	Gain on Sale of Asset
3	Straight-line method		12	Loss on Sale of Asset
9	Book value		14	Intangible assets
4	Units-of-production method		16	Goodwill
13	Accelerated depreciation		17	Research and development costs
15	Double-declining-balance method			

9

Current Liabilities, Contingencies, and the Time Value of Money

MODULES	LEARNING OBJECTIVES	WHY IS THIS CHAPTER IMPORTANT?
1 Current Liabilities	**LO1** Identify the components of the Current Liability category of the balance sheet. **LO2** Examine how accruals affect the Current Liability category.	• You need to know how current liabilities appear on the balance sheet and how a company accounts for the accrual of current liabilities. (See pp. 404–409.)
2 Cash Flow Effects	**LO3** Explain how changes in current liabilities affect the statement of cash flows.	• You need to know what impact current liabilities have on the cash flows of the company. (See pp. 410–411.)
3 Contingent Liabilities	**LO4** Determine when contingent liabilities should be presented on the balance sheet or disclosed in notes and how to calculate their amounts.	• You need to know when contingent liabilities should be presented on the balance sheet or disclosed in the notes. (See pp. 411–414.)
4 Time Value of Money	**LO5** Explain the difference between simple and compound interest. **LO6** Calculate amounts using the future value and present value concepts. **LO7** Apply the compound interest concepts to some common accounting situations.	• You need to know how to do interest rate calculations using the time value of money concepts. (See pp. 415–422.)

STARBUCKS CORPORATION

When you think of coffee, **Starbucks Corporation** may come to mind. The company's objective is to establish itself as one of the most recognized and respected brands in the world. It took only a few years for the company to be well on its way to achieving that goal. The company offers brewed coffees, espresso beverages, cold blended beverages, various complementary food items, coffee-related accessories and equipment, a selection of premium teas, and a line of compact discs through its retail stores.

Starbucks' balance sheet reveals that it must monitor liquidity carefully. A significant portion of the company's assets are current assets because most of its sales involve cash, credit card, and debit card.

Starbucks also has a significant amount of current liabilities. The company realizes the importance of maintaining its current liabilities at a level that will allow them to be paid when they are due. In short, the company's long-term profitability goals are directly linked to its ability to effectively manage its current liabilities and liquidity.

The accompanying partial balance sheet presents Starbucks Corporation's current assets and liabilities.

The financial statements of Starbucks, and other companies, will aid in your understanding of the important concepts related to current and contingent liabilities.

STARBUCKS CORPORATION CONSOLIDATED BALANCE SHEETS (in millions, except per share data)		
	Sep 27, 2015	Sep 28, 2014
Assets		
Current assets:		
Cash and cash equivalents	$ 1,530.1	$ 1,708.4
Short-term investments	81.3	135.4
Accounts receivable, net	719.0	631.0
Inventories	1,306.4	1,090.9
Prepaid expenses and other current assets	334.2	285.6
Deferred income taxes, net	381.7	317.4
Total current assets	4,352.7	4,168.7
Long-term investments	312.5	318.4
Equity and cost investments	352.0	514.9
Property, plant and equipment, net	4,088.3	3,519.0
Deferred income taxes, net	828.9	903.3
Other long-term assets	415.9	198.9
Other intangible assets	520.4	273.5
Goodwill	1,575.4	856.2
Total Assets	$12,446.1	$10,752.9
Liabilities and Equity		
Current liabilities:		
Accounts payable	$ 684.2	$ 533.7
Accrued liabilities	1,760.7	1,514.4
Insurance reserves	224.8	196.1
Stored value card liability	983.8	794.5
Total current liabilities	3,653.5	3,038.7

Source: Starbucks, Inc., Form 10-K, For the Fiscal Year Ended September 27, 2015.

MODULE 1 CURRENT LIABILITIES

LO1 Identify the components of the Current Liability category of the balance sheet.

Current liability
Accounts that will be satisfied within one year or the current operating cycle.

Alternate term: Short-term liability.

The balance sheet generally presents two categories of liabilities: current and long term. A **current liability** is an obligation that will be satisfied within one year. The face amount is generally used for all current liabilities because the time period involved is short enough that it is not necessary to record or calculate an interest factor.

Some companies list the accounts in the Current Liability category in the order of payment due date. That is, the account that requires payment first is listed first, the account requiring payment next is listed second, etc. This allows users of the statement to assess the cash-flow implications of each account. Starbucks presents the Accounts Payable account as the first current liability and that account likely requires payment first.

CONNECT TO THE REAL WORLD

STARBUCKS
READING THE BALANCE SHEET

9-1 Refer to Starbucks' September 27, 2015, balance sheet in the chapter opener. What accounts are listed as current liabilities? How much did Accounts Payable change from 2014 to 2015? *(See answers on p. 453.)*

The current liability classification is important because it is closely tied to the concept of *liquidity*. Management of a firm must be prepared to pay current liabilities within a short time period. Therefore, management must have access to liquid assets, cash, or other assets that can be converted to cash in amounts sufficient to pay the current liabilities. Firms that do not have sufficient resources to pay their current liabilities are often said to have a liquidity problem.

A handy ratio to help creditors or potential creditors determine a company's liquidity is the current ratio—the ratio of current assets to current liabilities. A current ratio of 2 to 1 is usually a comfortable margin. If the firm has a large amount of inventory, it is sometimes useful to exclude inventory (prepayments are also excluded) when computing the ratio. That provides the "quick" ratio. Usually, a quick ratio of at least 1.5 to 1 would be preferred so that the company could pay its bills on time. Of course, the guidelines given for the current ratio 2 to 1 and the quick ratio 1.5 to 1 are only rules of thumb. The actual current and quick ratios of companies vary widely and depend on the company, the management policies, and the type of industry. Exhibit 9-1 presents the current and quick ratios for Starbucks and two of its competitors. The ratios vary from company to company, yet all are solid companies without liquidity problems. Note especially that the current ratio for Starbucks is less than 2 to 1 because of the nature of its business and because of the efficient use of its current assets.

Accounting for current liabilities is an area in which U.S. accounting standards are similar to those of most other countries. Nearly all countries encourage firms to provide a breakdown of liabilities into current and long term to allow users to evaluate liquidity.

Accounts Payable

Accounts payable
Amounts owed for inventory, goods, or services acquired in the normal course of business.

Accounts payable represent amounts owed for the purchase of inventory, goods, or services acquired in the normal course of business. Accounts payable usually do not require the payment of interest, but terms may be given to encourage early payment. For example, terms may be stated as 2/10, n/30, which means that a 2% discount is available if payment occurs within the first ten days and that if payment is not made within ten days, the full amount must be paid within 30 days.

EXHIBIT 9-1 Current and Quick Ratios of Selected Companies for 2015

Company	Industry	Current Ratio	Quick Ratio
Starbucks	Food	1.19	0.64
Coffee Holding Company	Food	3.18	1.47
Keurig Green Mountain	Food	2.52	1.10

Timely payment of accounts payable is an important aspect of cash-flow management. Generally, it is to the company's benefit to take advantage of available discounts. If your supplier is going to give you a 2% discount for paying on Day 10 instead of Day 30, that means you are earning 2% on your money over 20/360 of a year. If you took the 2% discount throughout the year, you would be getting a 36% annual return on your money, since there are 18 periods of 20 days each in a year. Therefore, the accounts payable system must be established in a manner that alerts management to take advantage of discounts offered.

Notes Payable

How is a note payable different from an account payable? The most important difference is that an account payable is not a formal contractual arrangement, whereas a **note payable** is represented by a formal agreement or note signed by the parties to the transaction. Notes payable may arise from dealing with a supplier or from acquiring a cash loan from a bank or creditor. Those notes that are expected to be paid within one year of the balance sheet date should be classified as current liabilities.

Notes payable
Amounts owed that are represented by a formal contract.

The accounting for notes payable depends on whether the interest is paid on the note's due date or is deducted before the borrower receives the loan proceeds. With the first type of note, the terms stipulate that the borrower receives a short-term loan and agrees to repay the principal and interest at the note's due date.

How Will I Use **ACCOUNTING?**

If you are a broker in a real estate firm, you will need to understand current liabilities.

If your company needs a bank loan, the bank will analyze your liabilities carefully to see if you can pay back the loan.

EXAMPLE 9-1 Recording the Interest on Notes Payable

Assume that Hot Coffee Inc. receives a one-year loan from First National Bank on January 1. The face amount of the note of $1,000 must be repaid on December 31 along with interest at the rate of 12%. Hot Coffee could identify and analyze the effect of the loan as follows:

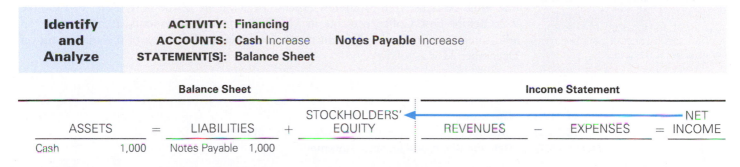

The company could identify and analyze the effect of the repayment as follows:

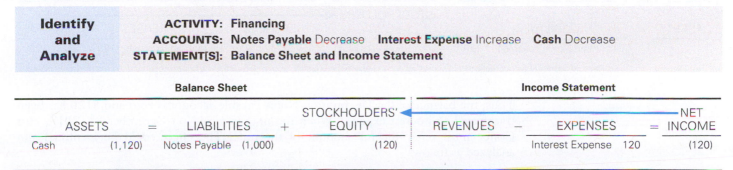

Banks also use another form of note, one in which the interest is deducted in advance. This is sometimes referred to as *discounting a note.*

EXAMPLE 9-2 Discounting a Note

Suppose that on January 1, 2017, First National Bank granted to Hot Coffee a $1,000 loan, due on December 31, 2017, but deducted the interest in advance and gave Hot Coffee the remaining amount of $880 ($1,000 face amount of the note less interest of $120). On January 1, Hot Coffee could identify and analyze the effect of the loan as follows:

Identify and Analyze	**ACTIVITY:** Financing		
	ACCOUNTS: Cash Increase	**Discount on Notes Payable** Increase	**Notes Payable** Increase
	STATEMENT[S]: Balance Sheet		

Balance Sheet				Income Statement			
ASSETS	=	LIABILITIES	+	STOCKHOLDERS' EQUITY ←	REVENUES	− EXPENSES	= NET INCOME
Cash 880		Notes Payable 1,000					
		Discount on Notes Payable* (120)					

*The Discount on Notes Payables account has increased. It is shown as a decrease in the equation above because it is contra account and causes total liabilities to decrease.

Discount on notes payable
A contra-liability that represents interest deducted from a loan in advance.

The **Discount on Notes Payable** account should be treated as a reduction of Notes Payable. If a balance sheet was developed immediately after the January 1 loan, the note would appear in the Current Liability category as follows:

Notes payable	$1,000
Discount on notes payable	120
Net liability	$ 880

STUDY TIP

Discount on Notes Payable is a contra-liability account and will have a debit balance.

The original balance in the Discount on Notes Payable account represents interest that must be transferred to interest expense over the life of the note. Refer to Example 9-2. Before Hot Coffee presents its year-end financial statements, it must make an adjustment to transfer the discount to interest expense. The effect of the adjustment on December 31 is as follows:

Identify and Analyze	**ACTIVITY:** Operating	
	ACCOUNTS: Interest Expense Increase	**Discount on Notes Payable** Decrease
	STATEMENT[S]: Balance Sheet and Income Statement	

Balance Sheet				Income Statement			
ASSETS	=	LIABILITIES	+	STOCKHOLDERS' EQUITY ←	REVENUES	− EXPENSES	= NET INCOME
		Discount on Notes Payable* 120		(120)		Interest Expense 120	(120)

*The Discount on Notes Payable account has decreased. It is shown as an increase in the equation above because it is a contra account and causes total liabilities to increase.

Thus, the balance of the Discount on Notes Payable account is zero and $120 has been transferred to interest expense. When the note is repaid on December 31, 2017, Hot Coffee must repay the full amount of the note. The effect could be identified and analyzed as follows:

Identify and Analyze	**ACTIVITY: Financing**
	ACCOUNTS: Notes Payable Decrease **Cash** Decrease
	STATEMENT[S]: Balance Sheet

Balance Sheet					Income Statement		
ASSETS	=	LIABILITIES	+	STOCKHOLDERS' EQUITY	REVENUES –	EXPENSES	= INCOME → NET
Cash (1,000)		Notes Payable (1,000)					

In the previous two examples, the stated interest rate on each note was 12%. The dollar amount of interest incurred in each case was $120. However, the interest *rate* on a discounted note, the second example, is always higher than it appears. Hot Coffee received the use of only $880, yet it was required to repay $1,000. Therefore, the interest rate incurred on the note was actually $120/$880, or approximately 13.6%.

Current Maturities of Long-Term Debt

Some companies may have an account that is titled Current Portion of Long-Term Debt. On other companies' balance sheets, this item may appear as **Current Maturities of Long-Term Debt**. This account should appear when a firm has a long-term liability and must make periodic payments.

Current maturities of long-term debt
The portion of a long-term liability that will be paid within one year.

Alternate term: Long-term debt, current portion.

EXAMPLE 9-3 Recording Current Maturities of Long-Term Debt

Assume that on January 1, 2017, your firm obtained a $10,000 loan from the bank. The terms of the loan require you to make payments in the amount of $1,000 per year for ten years payable each January 1 beginning January 1, 2018. On December 31, 2017, an entry should be made to classify a portion of the balance as a current liability. The effect could be identified and analyzed as follows:

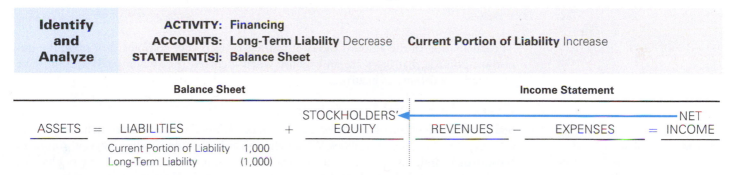

Identify and Analyze	**ACTIVITY: Financing**
	ACCOUNTS: Long-Term Liability Decrease **Current Portion of Liability** Increase
	STATEMENT[S]: Balance Sheet

Balance Sheet				Income Statement		
ASSETS =	LIABILITIES	+	STOCKHOLDERS' EQUITY	REVENUES –	EXPENSES	= INCOME → NET
	Current Portion of Liability 1,000					
	Long-Term Liability (1,000)					

The December 31, 2017, balance sheet should indicate that the liability for the note payable is classified into two portions: a $1,000 current liability that must be repaid within one year and a $9,000 long-term liability.

Refer to the information in Example 9-3. On January 1, 2018, the company must pay $1,000. The effect could be identified and analyzed as follows:

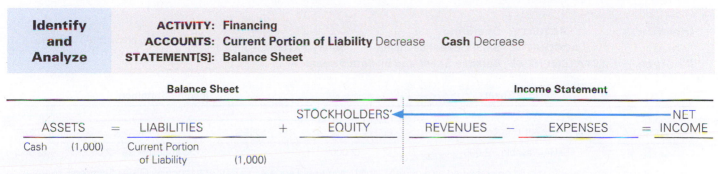

Identify and Analyze	**ACTIVITY: Financing**
	ACCOUNTS: Current Portion of Liability Decrease **Cash** Decrease
	STATEMENT[S]: Balance Sheet

Balance Sheet				Income Statement		
ASSETS =	LIABILITIES	+	STOCKHOLDERS' EQUITY	REVENUES –	EXPENSES	= INCOME → NET
Cash (1,000)	Current Portion of Liability (1,000)					

On December 31, 2018, the company should again record the current portion of the liability. Therefore, the 2018 year-end balance sheet should indicate that the liability is classified into two portions: a $1,000 current liability and an $8,000 long-term liability. The process should be repeated each year until the bank loan has been fully paid. When an investor or a creditor reads a balance sheet, he or she wants to distinguish between debt that is long term and debt that is short term. Therefore, it is important to segregate the portion of the debt that becomes due within one year.

The balance sheet account labeled Current Portion of Long-Term Debt should include only the amount of principal to be paid. The amount of interest that has been incurred but is unpaid should be listed separately in an account such as Interest Payable.

Taxes Payable

LO2 Examine how accruals affect the Current Liability category.

Corporations pay a variety of taxes, including federal and state income taxes, property taxes, and other taxes. Taxes are an expense of the business and should be accrued in the same manner as any other business expense. A company that ends its accounting year on December 31 is not required to calculate the amount of tax owed to the government until the following March 15 or April 15, depending on the type of business. Therefore, the business must make an accounting entry, usually as one of the year-end adjusting entries, to record the amount of tax that has been incurred but is unpaid. Normally, the effect could be identified and analyzed as follows:

Identify and Analyze	
ACTIVITY:	Operating
ACCOUNTS:	Tax Expense Increase Taxes Payable Increase
STATEMENT[S]:	Balance Sheet and Income Statement

Balance Sheet			Income Statement		
ASSETS	= LIABILITIES	+ STOCKHOLDERS' EQUITY	REVENUES	− EXPENSES	= NET INCOME
	Taxes Payable XXX	(XXX)		Tax Expense XXX	(XXX)

The calculation of the amount of tax a business owes is very complex. For now, the important point is that taxes are an expense when incurred (not when paid) and must be recorded as a liability as incurred.

Other Accrued Liabilities

Accrued liability
A liability that has been incurred but has not yet been paid.

Starbucks' 2015 balance sheet listed an amount of $1,269.3 million as current liability under the category of Accrued Liabilities. What items might be included in this category? **Accrued liabilities** include any amount that has been incurred due to the passage of time but has not been paid as of the balance sheet date. A common example is salary or wages payable.

EXAMPLE 9-4 Recording Accrued Liabilities

Suppose that your firm has a payroll of $1,000 per day Monday through Friday and that employees are paid at the close of work each Friday. Also, suppose that December 31 is the end of your accounting year and that it falls on a Tuesday. The effect of the adjusting entry for salaries could be identified and analyzed as follows:

Identify and Analyze	
ACTIVITY:	Operating
ACCOUNTS:	Salary Expense Increase Salary Payable Increase
STATEMENT[S]:	Balance Sheet and Income Statement

Balance Sheet			Income Statement		
ASSETS	= LIABILITIES	+ STOCKHOLDERS' EQUITY	REVENUES	− EXPENSES	= NET INCOME
	Salary Payable 2,000	(2,000)		Salary Expense 2,000	(2,000)

The amount of the salary payable would be classified as a current liability and could appear in a category such as Other Accrued Expenses.

Interest is another item that often must be accrued at year-end. Assume that you received a one-year loan of $10,000 on December 1. The loan carries a 12% interest rate. On December 31, an accounting entry must be made to record interest even though the money may not actually be due. The effect could be identified and analyzed as follows:

Identify and Analyze	**ACTIVITY:** Operating **ACCOUNTS:** Interest Expense Increase Interest Payable Increase **STATEMENT[S]:** Balance Sheet and Income Statement

Balance Sheet			Income Statement		
ASSETS	= LIABILITIES	+ STOCKHOLDERS' EQUITY	REVENUES	− EXPENSES	= NET INCOME
	Interest Payable 100	(100)		Interest Expense 100	(100)

The Interest Payable account should be classified as a current liability, assuming that it is to be paid within one year of the December 31 date.

IFRS and Current Liabilities

The accounting for current liabilities in U.S. and international standards is generally similar, but there are a few important differences. In this chapter, we have presented classified balance sheets with liabilities classified as either current or long term. Interestingly, U.S. standards do not require a classified balance sheet, and financial statements of some U.S. companies may list liabilities in order by size or by order of liquidity.

International accounting standards require companies to present classified balance sheets with liabilities classified as either current or long term. An unclassified balance sheet based on the order of liquidity is acceptable only when it provides more reliable information.

MODULE 1 TEST YOURSELF

Review	**LO1** Identify the components of the Current Liability category of the balance sheet.	• Current liabilities are obligations of a company that generally must be satisfied within one year. Some companies list them in the balance sheet in order of the account that requires payment first. • Current liability accounts include Accounts Payable, Notes Payable, Current Portion of Long-Term Debt, Taxes Payable, and Accrued Liabilities.
	LO2 Examine how accruals affect the Current Liability category.	• Accrued liabilities result from expenses that are incurred but have not yet been paid. • Common accrued liabilities include taxes payable, salaries payable, and interest payable.

Question	1. What is the definition of *current liabilities*? Why is it important to distinguish between current and long-term liabilities?
	2. Is the account Discount on Notes Payable an income statement or a balance sheet account?
	3. A firm's year ends on December 31. Its tax is computed and submitted to the U.S. Treasury on March 15 of the following year. When should the taxes be reported as a liability?

Apply	1. A company has the following current assets: Cash, $10,000; Accounts Receivable, $70,000; and Inventory, $20,000. The company also has current liabilities of $40,000. Calculate the company's current ratio and quick ratio.
	2. You receive an invoice from a supplier for $5,000 on January 1 with terms 3/15, n/30. If you pay between January 1 and January 16, how much must you pay? If you pay after January 16, how much must you pay?

Answers are located at the end of the chapter.

MODULE 2 CASH FLOW EFFECTS

LO3 Explain how changes in current liabilities affect the statement of cash flows.

It is important to understand the impact that current liabilities have on a company's cash flows. Exhibit 9-2 illustrates the placement of current liabilities on the statement of cash flows (using the indirect method) and their effect. Most current liabilities are directly related to a firm's ongoing operations. Therefore, the change in the balance of each current liability account should be reflected in the Operating Activities category of the statement of cash flows. A decrease in a current liability account indicates that cash has been used to pay the liability and should appear as a deduction on the cash-flow statement. An increase in a current liability account indicates a recognized expense that has not yet been paid.

EXHIBIT 9-2 Current Liabilities on the Statement of Cash Flows

Item	Cash-Flow Statement Operating Activities	
Net Income		xxx
Increase in current liability	⟶	+
Decrease in current liability	⟶	−
	Investing Activities	
	Financing Activities	
Increase in notes payable	⟶	+
Decrease in notes payable	⟶	−

A partial statement of cash flows of Starbucks Corporation is presented in Exhibit 9-3. In 2015, the company has a positive amount of $137.7 million for Accounts Payable on

EXHIBIT 9-3 Starbucks Corporation Partial Consolidated Statement of Cash Flows (In millions)

STARBUCKS CORPORATION
CONSOLIDATED STATEMENTS OF CASH FLOWS
(in millions)

Fiscal Year Ended	Sep 27, 2015	Sep 28, 2014	Sep 29, 2013
Operating Activities:			
Net earnings including noncontrolling interests	$2,759.3	$ 2,067.7	$ 8.8
Adjustments to reconcile net earnings to net cash provided by operating activities:			
Depreciation and amortization	933.8	748.4	655.6
Litigation charge	—	—	2,784.1
Deferred income taxes, net	21.2	10.2	(1,045.9)
Income earned from equity method investees	(190.2)	(182.7)	(171.8)
Distributions received from equity method investees	148.2	139.2	115.6
Gain resulting from acquisition/sale of equity in joint ventures and certain retail operations	(394.3)	(70.2)	(80.1)
Loss on extinguishment of debt	61.1	—	—
Stock-based compensation	209.8	183.2	142.3
Excess tax benefit on share-based awards	(132.4)	(114.4)	(258.1)
Other	53.8	36.2	23.0
Cash provided/(used) by changes in operating assets and liabilities:			
Accounts receivable	(82.8)	(79.7)	(68.3)
Inventories	(207.9)	14.3	152.5
Accounts payable	137.7	60.4	88.7
Accrued litigation charge	—	(2,763.9)	—
Income taxes payable, net	87.6	309.8	298.4
Accrued liabilities and insurance reserves	124.4	103.9	47.3
Stored value card liability	170.3	140.8	139.9
Prepaid expenses, other current assets and other long-term assets	49.5	4.6	76.3
Net cash provided by operating activities	3,749.1	607.8	2,908.3

Source: Starbucks, Inc., Form 10-K, For the Fiscal Year Ended September 27, 2015.

the statement of cash flows and a positive amount of $87.6 million for Income Taxes Payable and a positive amount of $124.4 for Accrued Liabilities and Insurance Reserves. This is an indication that those accounts increased, resulting in an increase in cash.

Almost all current liabilities appear in the Operating Activities category of the statement of cash flows, but there are exceptions. If a current liability is not directly related to operating activities, it should not appear in the Operating Activities category. For example, if Starbucks uses some notes payable as a means of financing, distinct from operating activities, those borrowings and repayments are reflected in the Financing Activities rather than the Operating Activities category.

MODULE 2 TEST YOURSELF

Review	LO3 Explain how changes in current liabilities affect the statement of cash flows.	• Most current liabilities are directly related to the ongoing operations of a company. • Decreases in current liabilities indicate that cash has been used to satisfy obligations and are cash outflows not represented by some expenses on the income statement. • Increases in current liabilities indicate that some expenses on the income statement have not been paid in cash and are not cash outflows represented by some expenses on the income statement.
Question		If a company has current liabilities that have increased during the year, how will they appear on the statement of cash flows? In what category? Will they appear as positive or negative amounts?
Apply		A company has the following current liabilities at the beginning of the period: Accounts Payable, $30,000; Taxes Payable, $10,000. At the end of the period, the balances of the account are as follows: Accounts Payable, $20,000; Taxes Payable, $15,000. What amounts will appear in the cash-flow statement? In what category of the statement will they appear?

Answers are located at the end of the chapter.

MODULE 3 CONTINGENT LIABILITIES

Accountants must exercise a great deal of expertise and judgment in deciding what to record and in determining the amount to record. This is certainly true regarding contingent liabilities. A **contingent liability** is an obligation that involves an existing condition for which the outcome is not known with certainty and depends on some event that will occur in the future. The actual amount of the liability must be estimated because we cannot clearly predict the future. **The important accounting issues are whether contingent liabilities should be recorded and, if so, in what amounts.**

This judgment call is normally resolved through discussions between a company's management and its outside auditors. Management would rather not disclose contingent liabilities until they come due because investors and creditors judge management based on the company's earnings, and the recording of a contingent liability must be accompanied by a charge to (reduction in) earnings. Auditors, on the other hand, want to see as much information as possible because they essentially represent the interests of investors and creditors who want to know as much as possible.

LO4 Determine when contingent liabilities should be presented on the balance sheet or disclosed in notes and how to calculate their amounts.

Contingent liability
An existing condition for which the outcome is not known but depends on some future event.

Alternate term: Contingent loss.

Contingent Liabilities That Are Recorded

A contingent liability should be accrued and presented on the balance sheet if it is probable and if the amount can be reasonably estimated. But when is an event *probable*, and what does *reasonably estimated* mean? The terms must be defined based on the facts of each situation. A financial statement user would want the company to err on the side of full disclosure. On the other hand, the company should not be required to disclose every remote possibility.

Product Warranties and Guarantees: Common Contingent Liabilities That Are Recorded

A common contingent liability that firms must present as a liability involves product warranties and guarantees. Many firms sell products for which they provide the customer a warranty against potential defects. If a product becomes defective within the warranty period, the selling firm ensures that it will repair or replace the item.

At the end of each period, the selling firm must estimate how many of the products sold in the current year will become defective in the future and the cost of repair or replacement. This type of contingent liability is often referred to as an **estimated liability** to emphasize that the costs are not known at year-end and must be estimated.

Estimated liability
A contingent liability that is accrued and reflected on the balance sheet.

EXAMPLE 9-5 Recording a Liability for Warranties

Assume that Quickkey Computer sells a computer product for $5,000 with a one-year warranty in case the product must be repaired. Assume that in 2017, Quickkey sold 100 computers for a total sales revenue of $500,000. At the end of 2017, Quickkey must record an estimate of the warranty costs that will occur on 2017 sales. Using an analysis of past warranty records, Quickkey estimates that repairs will average 2% of total sales. The effect of the recording of warranty costs at the end of 2017 could be identified and analyzed as follows:

Identify and Analyze	ACTIVITY: Operating ACCOUNTS: Warranty Expense Increase Estimated Liability Increase STATEMENT[S]: Balance Sheet and Income Statement

Balance Sheet				Income Statement				
ASSETS	=	LIABILITIES	+	STOCKHOLDERS' EQUITY	REVENUES	−	EXPENSES	= NET INCOME
		Estimated Liability 10,000		(10,000)			Warranty Expense 10,000	(10,000)

The amount of warranty costs that a company presents as an expense is of interest to investors and potential creditors. If the expense as a percentage of sales begins to rise, a logical conclusion is that the product is becoming less reliable.

Warranties are an excellent example of the matching principle. In Example 9-5, the warranty costs related to 2017 sales were estimated and recorded in 2017. This was done to match the 2017 sales with the expenses related to those sales. When actual repairs of the computers occur in 2018, they do not result in an expense. The repair costs incurred in 2018 should be treated as a reduction in the liability that had been estimated previously. The ending balance of the Estimated Liability account can be calculated as:

Beginning Balance + Estimated Warranty Costs Recorded − Actual Repair Costs Incurred = Ending Balance

A company must analyze past warranty records carefully and incorporate any changes in customer buying habits, usage, technological changes, and other changes. Still, even with careful analysis, the actual amount of the expense is not likely to equal the estimated amount. Generally, firms do not change the amount of the expense recorded in past periods for such differences. They may adjust the amount recorded in future periods, however.

Premiums or Coupons: Other Contingent Liabilities That Are Recorded Another example of a contingent liability is premium or coupon offers that accompany many products. Cereal boxes often allow customers to purchase a toy or game at a reduced price if the purchase is accompanied by cereal box tops or proof of purchase. The offer given to cereal customers represents a contingent liability. At the end of each year, the cereal company must estimate the number of premium offers that will be redeemed and the cost involved and must report a contingent liability for that amount.

Some Lawsuits and Legal Claims Are Contingent Liabilities That Must Be Recorded Legal claims that have been filed against a firm are also examples of contingent liabilities. Lawsuits and legal claims represent a contingent liability because an event has occurred but the outcome of that event, the resolution of the lawsuit, is not known. The defendant must make a judgment about the lawsuit's outcome to decide whether the item should be recorded on the balance sheet or disclosed in the notes. When the legal claim's outcome is likely to be unfavorable, a contingent liability should be recorded on the balance sheet. Exhibit 9-4 contains footnote disclosure of Burger King Corporation. Burger King was involved in a lawsuit that began in 2008 and continued through 2011. It appears that the company is facing an unfavorable outcome. In such cases, the company must decide when the liability should be recorded.

As you might imagine, firms are not eager to record contingent lawsuits as liabilities because the amount of loss is often difficult to estimate. Also, some may view the accountant's decision as an admission of guilt when a lawsuit is recorded as a liability before the courts have finalized a decision. Accountants often must consult with lawyers

EXHIBIT 9-4 Note Disclosure of Contingencies for Burger King Corporation

On September 10, 2008, a class action lawsuit was filed against the Company in the United States District Court for the Northern District of California. The complaint alleged that all 96 Burger King restaurants in California leased by the Company and operated by franchisees violate accessibility requirements under federal and state law. In September 2009, the court issued a decision on the plaintiffs' motion for class certification. In its decision, the court limited the class action to the 10 restaurants visited by the named plaintiffs, with a separate class of plaintiffs for each of the 10 restaurants and 10 separate trials. In March 2010, the Company agreed to settle the lawsuit with respect to the 10 restaurants and, in July 2010, the court gave final approval to the settlement. In February 2011, a class action lawsuit was filed with respect to the other 86 restaurants. The plaintiffs sought injunctive relief, statutory damages, attorneys' fees and costs. In January 2012, BKC agreed to settle the lawsuit. The parties are finalizing the terms of the proposed settlement which will be submitted to the court for approval.

Source: Burger King Corporation, Form 10-K, For the Fiscal Year Ended December 31, 2011.

or other legal experts to determine the probability of the loss of a lawsuit. In cases involving contingencies, the accountant must make an independent judgment based on the facts and not be swayed by the desires of other parties.

Contingent Liabilities That Are Disclosed

Any contingent liability that is probable and that can be reasonably estimated must be reported as a liability. We now must consider contingent liabilities that do not meet the probable criterion or cannot be reasonably estimated. In either case, **a contingent liability must be disclosed in the financial statement notes but not reported on the balance sheet if the contingent liability is at least reasonably possible.** Most lawsuits are not recorded as liabilities because the risk of loss is not considered probable or the amount of the loss cannot be reasonably estimated. If a company does not record a lawsuit as a liability, it still must consider whether the lawsuit should be disclosed in the notes to the financial statements. When the risk of loss is at least *reasonably possible*, the company should provide note disclosure. This is the course of action taken for most contingent liabilities involving lawsuits. Readers of the financial statements and analysts must read the notes carefully to determine the impact of such contingent liabilities.

The amount and the timing of the cash outlays associated with contingent liabilities are especially difficult to determine. Lawsuits, for example, may extend several years into the future, and the dollar amount of possible loss may be subject to great uncertainty.

Contingent Liabilities versus Contingent Assets

Contingent asset
An existing condition for which the outcome is not known but by which the company stands to gain.

Alternate term: Contingent gain.

Contingent liabilities that are probable and can be reasonably estimated must be presented on the balance sheet before the outcome of the future events is known. This accounting rule applies only to contingent losses or liabilities. It does not apply to contingencies by which the firm may gain. Generally, contingent gains or **contingent assets** are not reported until the gain actually occurs. **That is, contingent liabilities may be accrued but contingent assets are not accrued.** Remember that accounting is a discipline based on a conservative set of principles. It is prudent and conservative to delay the recording of a gain until an asset is actually received but to record contingent liabilities in advance.

Even though the contingent assets are not reported, the information still may be important to investors. Investment analysts try to place a value on contingent assets that they believe will result in future benefits. By buying stock of a company that has unrecorded assets (or advising their clients to do so), analysts hope to make money when those assets become a reality.

IFRS and Contingencies

There are very important differences between U.S. and international standards regarding contingencies. In international standards, the term *contingent liability* is used only for those items that are not recorded on the balance sheet but are disclosed in the notes that accompany the statements. International standards use the term *provision* for those items that must be recorded on the balance sheet. As in U.S. standards, an item should be recorded if the loss or outflow is probable and can be reasonably estimated. But the meaning of the term *probable* is somewhat different. In international standards, *probable* means the loss or outflow is "more likely than not" to occur. This is a lower threshold than in U.S. standards and may cause more items to be recorded as liabilities. Also, international standards require the amount recorded as a liability to be "discounted" or recorded as a present value amount, while U.S. standards do not have a similar requirement.

MODULE 4 TIME VALUE OF MONEY

This section will discuss the impact that interest has on decision making because of the time value of money. The **time value of money** concept means that people prefer a payment at the present time rather than in the future because of the interest factor. If an amount is received at the present time, it can be invested and the resulting accumulation will be larger than if the same amount is received in the future. Thus, there is a *time value* to cash receipts and payments.

Exhibit 9-5 indicates some of the personal and accounting decisions affected by the time value of money concept. In your personal life, you make decisions based on the

LO5 Explain the difference between simple and compound interest.

Time value of money
An immediate amount should be preferred over an amount in the future.

EXHIBIT 9-5 Importance of the Time Value of Money

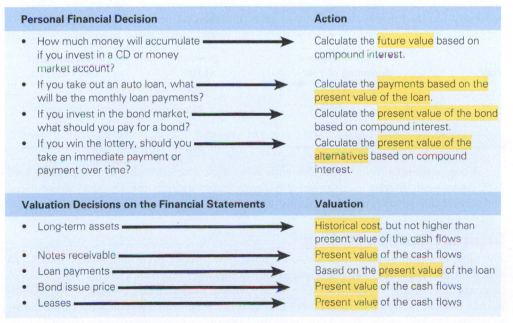

Personal Financial Decision	Action
• How much money will accumulate if you invest in a CD or money market account?	Calculate the future value based on compound interest.
• If you take out an auto loan, what will be the monthly loan payments?	Calculate the payments based on the present value of the loan.
• If you invest in the bond market, what should you pay for a bond?	Calculate the present value of the bond based on compound interest.
• If you win the lottery, should you take an immediate payment or payment over time?	Calculate the present value of the alternatives based on compound interest.

Valuation Decisions on the Financial Statements	Valuation
• Long-term assets	Historical cost, but not higher than present value of the cash flows
• Notes receivable	Present value of the cash flows
• Loan payments	Based on the present value of the loan
• Bond issue price	Present value of the cash flows
• Leases	Present value of the cash flows

time value of money concept nearly every day. When you invest money, you are interested in how much will be accumulated and you must determine the *future value* based on the amount of interest that will be compounded. When you borrow money, you must determine the amount of the loan payments. The amount of the loan payment is based on the *present value* of the loan, another time value of money concept.

Time value of money is also important because of its implications for accounting valuations. Chapter 10 explains that the issue price of a bond is based on the present value of the cash flows that the bond will produce. The valuation of the bond and the recording of the bond on the balance sheet are based on this concept. Further, the amount that is considered interest expense on the financial statements is also based on time value of money concepts. The bottom portion of Exhibit 9-5 indicates that the valuations of many other accounts, including Notes Receivable and Leases, are based on compound interest calculations.

Simple Interest

Simple interest
Interest is calculated on the principal amount only.

Simple interest is interest earned on the principal amount. If the amount of principal is unchanged from year to year, the interest per year will remain the same. Interest can be calculated using the following formula:

$$I = P \times R \times T$$

where

I = Dollar amount of interest per year
P = Principal
R = Interest rate as a percentage
T = Time in years

For example, assume that a firm has signed a two-year note payable for $3,000. Interest and principal are to be paid at the due date with simple interest at the rate of 10% per year. The amount of interest on the note would be $600, calculated as $3,000 × 0.10 × 2. The firm would be required to pay $3,600 on the due date: $3,000 principal and $600 interest.

Compound Interest

Compound interest
Interest calculated on the principal plus previous amounts of interest.

Alternate term: Interest on interest.

Compound interest means that interest is calculated on the principal plus previous amounts of accumulated interest. Thus, interest is compounded, or there is interest on interest.

EXAMPLE 9-6 Calculating Compound Interest

Assume a $3,000 note payable for which interest and principal are due in two years with interest compounded annually at 10% per year. Interest would be calculated as follows:

Year	Principal Amount at Beginning of Year	Interest at 10%	Accumulated at Year-End
1	$3,000	$300	$3,300
2	3,300	330	3,630

We would be required to pay $3,630 at the end of two years, $3,000 principal and $630 interest.

A comparison of the note payable with 10% simple interest with the note payable with 10% compound interest in Example 9-6 clearly indicates that the amount accumulated with compound interest is a higher amount because of the interest-on-interest feature.

Interest Compounding

LO6 Calculate amounts using the future value and present value concepts.

For most accounting problems, we will assume that interest is compounded annually. In actual business practice, compounding usually occurs over much shorter intervals. This can be confusing because the interest rate is often stated as an annual rate even though it is compounded over a shorter period. If compounding is not done annually, you must adjust the interest rate by dividing the annual rate by the number of compounding periods per year.

EXAMPLE 9-7 Compounding Interest Semiannually

Assume that the note payable from the previous example carried a 10% interest rate compounded semiannually for two years. The 10% annual rate should be converted to 5% per period for four semiannual periods. The amount of interest would be compounded, as in the previous example, but for four periods instead of two. The compounding process is as follows:

Period	Principal Amount at Beginning of Year	Interest at 5% per Period	Accumulated at End of Period
1	$3,000	$150	$3,150
2	3,150	158	3,308
3	3,308	165	3,473
4	3,473	174	3,647

Example 9-7 illustrates that compounding more frequently results in a larger amount accumulated. In fact, many banks and financial institutions now compound interest on savings accounts on a daily basis.

In the remainder of this section, we will assume that compound interest is applicable. The following four compound interest calculations must be understood:

Future value of a single amount
Present value of a single amount
Future value of an annuity
Present value of an annuity

Present Value and Future Value: Single Amounts

Future Value of a Single Amount

A future amount or future value is the amount of interest plus principal that will be accumulated at a future time. The future amount is always larger than the principal amount (payment) because of the interest that accumulates. In some cases, we will use time diagrams to illustrate the relationships. A time diagram to illustrate a future value would be of the following form:

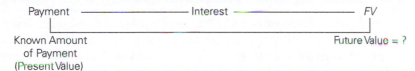

The formula to calculate the **future value of a single amount** is as follows:

$$FV = p(1 + i)^n$$

where

FV = Future value to be calculated
p = Present value or principal amount
i = Interest rate
n = Number of periods of compounding

Future value of a single amount
Amount accumulated at a future time from a single payment or investment.

EXAMPLE 9-8 Calculating Future Values with Formula

Your three-year-old son Robert inherits $50,000 in cash and securities from his grandfather. If the funds are left in the bank and in the stock market and receive an annual return of 10%, how much will be available in 15 years when Robert starts college?

Solution:

$$FV = \$50,000(1 + 0.10)^{15}$$
$$= \$50,000(4.17725)$$
$$= \$208,863 \text{ (rounded to the nearest dollar)}$$

Consider a $2,000 note payable that carries interest at the rate of 10% compounded annually. The note is due in two years, and the principal and interest must be paid at that time. The amount that must be paid in two years is the future value. The future value can be calculated in the manner used in the previous examples:

Year	Principal Amount at Beginning of Year	Interest at 10%	Accumulated at Year-End
1	$2,000	$200	$2,200
2	2,200	220	2,420

The future value can also be calculated by using the following formula:

$$FV = \$2,000(1 + 0.10)^2$$
$$= \$2,000(1.21000)$$
$$= \$2,420$$

Instead of a formula, other methods can be used to calculate future value. Tables can be constructed to assist in the calculations. Table 9-1 on page 423 indicates the future value of $1 at various interest rates for various time periods. To find the future value of a two-year note at 10% compounded annually, you read across the line for two periods and down the 10% column, which gives you an interest rate factor of 1.21000. Because the table has been constructed for future values of $1, we would determine the future value of $2,000 as follows:

$$FV = \$2,000 \times 1.21000$$
$$= \$2,420$$

A second method is to use the built-in functions of a computerized spreadsheet. The appendix to this chapter will illustrate how to use a common spreadsheet, Microsoft® Excel®, to perform the same calculations. **The numbers produced by each method may differ by a few dollars because of rounding differences.**

Remember that compounding does not always occur annually. How does this affect the calculation of future value amounts?

EXAMPLE 9-9 Calculating Future Values with Quarterly Compounding

Suppose we want to find the future value of a $2,000 note payable due in two years. The note payable requires interest to be compounded quarterly at the rate of 12% per year. To calculate the future value, we must adjust the interest rate to a quarterly basis by dividing the 12% rate by the number of compounding periods per year, which in the case of quarterly compounding is four:

12%/4 quarters = 3% per quarter

Also, the number of compounding periods is eight—four per year times two years.

The future value of the note can be found in two ways. First, we can insert the proper values into the future value formula:

$$FV = \$2,000(1 + 0.03)^8$$
$$= \$2,000(1.26677)$$
$$= \$2,534 \text{ (rounded to the nearest dollar)}$$

We can arrive at the same future value amount with the use of Table 9-1. Refer to the interest factor in the table indicated for eight periods and 3%. The future value would be calculated as follows:

$$FV = \$2,000 \text{ (interest factor)}$$
$$= \$2,000(1.26677)$$
$$= \$2,534$$

Present Value of a Single Amount

In many situations, we want to determine the present amount that is equivalent to an amount at a future time. This is the present value concept. The **present value of a single amount** represents the value today of a single amount to be received or paid at a future time. This can be portrayed in a time diagram as follows:

The time diagram portrays discount rather than interest because we often speak of "discounting" the future payment back to the present time.

EXAMPLE 9-10 Calculating Present Value of a Single Amount

Suppose you know that you will receive $2,000 in two years. If you had the money now, you could invest it at 10% compounded annually. What is the present value of the $2,000? In other words, what amount must be invested today at 10% compounded annually to have $2,000 accumulated in two years?

The formula used to calculate present value is as follows:

$$PV = \text{Future Value} \times (1 + i)^{-n}$$

where

$$PV = \text{Present value amount in dollars}$$
$$\text{Future value} = \text{Amount to be received in the future}$$
$$i = \text{Interest rate or discount rate}$$
$$n = \text{Number of periods}$$

We can use the present value formula to solve for the present value of the $2,000 note as follows:

$$PV = \$2,000 \times (1 + 0.10)^{-2}$$
$$= \$2,000 \times (0.82645)$$
$$= \$1,653 \text{ (rounded to the nearest dollar)}$$

Tables have also been developed to determine the present value of $1 at various interest rates and number of periods. Table 9-2 on page 424 presents the present value or discount factors for an amount of $1 to be received at a future time. To use the table for Example 9-10, you must read across the line for two periods and down the 10% column to the discount factor of 0.82645. The present value of $2,000 would be calculated as follows:

$$PV = \$2,000 \text{ (discount factor)}$$
$$= \$2,000(0.82645)$$
$$= \$1,653 \text{ (rounded to the nearest dollar)}$$

The example illustrates that the present value amount is always less than the future payment. This happens because of the discount factor. In other words, if we had a smaller amount at the present (the present value), we could invest it and earn interest that would accumulate to an amount equal to the larger amount (the future payment). Also, study of the present value and future value formulas indicates that each is the reciprocal of the other. When we want to calculate a present value amount, we normally use Table 9-2 and multiply a discount factor times the payment. However, we could also use Table 9-1 and divide by the interest factor. Thus, the present value of the $2,000 to be received in the future could also be calculated as follows:

$$PV = \$2,000/1.21000$$
$$= \$1,653 \text{ (rounded to the nearest dollar)}$$

Present value of a single amount
The amount at a present time that is equivalent to a payment or an investment at a future time.

STUDY TIP

When interest rates *increase*, present values *decrease*. This is called an *inverse relationship*.

Present Value and Future Value of an Annuity

Future Value of an Annuity

Annuity
A series of payments of equal amounts.

Annuity means a series of payments of equal amounts. Suppose you are to receive $3,000 per year at the end of each of the next four years. Also, assume that each payment could be invested at an interest rate of 10% compounded annually. How much would be accumulated in principal and interest by the end of the fourth year? This is an example of an annuity of payments of equal amounts. A time diagram would portray the payments as follows:

$3,000		$3,000		$3,000		$3,000
	Interest		Interest		Interest	

$$FV = ?$$

Because we are interested in calculating the future value, we could use the future value of $1 concept and calculate the future value of each $3,000 payment using Table 9-1 as follows:

$3,000 × 1.33100 Interest for 3 Periods	$ 3,993
3,000 × 1.21000 Interest for 2 Periods	3,630
3,000 × 1.10000 Interest for 1 Period	3,300
3,000 × 1.00000 Interest for 0 Periods	3,000
Total Future Value	$13,923

Note that four payments would be received but that only three of them would draw interest because the payments are received at the end of each period.

Future value of an annuity
The amount accumulated in the future when a series of payments is invested and accrues interest.

Alternate term: Amount of an annuity.

Fortunately, there is an easier method to calculate the **future value of an annuity**. Table 9-3 on page 425 has been constructed to indicate the future value of a series of payments of $1 per period at various interest rates and number of periods. The table can be used for the previous example by reading across the four-period line and down the 10% column to a table factor of 4.64100. The future value of an annuity of $3,000 per year can be calculated as follows:

$$FV = \$3,000(\text{table factor})$$
$$= \$3,000(4.64100)$$
$$= \$13,923$$

EXAMPLE 9-11 Calculating Future Value of an Annuity

Your cousin had a baby girl two weeks ago and is already thinking about sending her to college. When the girl is 15, how much money would be in her college account if your cousin deposited $2,000 into it on each of her 15 birthdays? The interest rate is 10%. The future value could be calculated as follows.

$$FV = \$2,000(\text{table factor})$$
$$= \$2,000(31.77248)$$
$$= \$63,545 \text{ (rounded to the nearest dollar)}$$

What if the scenario was modified so that $1,000 was deposited semiannually and the interest rate was 10% compounded semiannually (or 5% per period) for 15 years? Table 9-3 could be used by reading across the line for 30 periods and down the column for 5% to obtain a table factor of 66.43885. The future value would be calculated as follows:

$$FV = \$1,000(\text{table factor})$$
$$= \$1,000(66.43885)$$
$$= \$66,439 \text{ (rounded to the nearest dollar)}$$

Comparing the two scenarios illustrates once again that more frequent compounding results in larger accumulated amounts.

Present Value of an Annuity

Many accounting applications of the time value of money concept concern situations for which we want to know the present value of a series of payments that will occur in the future. This involves calculating the present value of an annuity. An annuity is a series of payments of equal amounts.

Suppose you will receive an annuity of $4,000 per year for four years, with the first received one year from today. The amounts received can be invested at a rate of 10% compounded annually. What amount would you need at the present time to have an amount equivalent to the series of payments and interest in the future? To answer that question, you must calculate the **present value of an annuity**. A time diagram of the series of payments would appear as follows:

Present value of an annuity
The amount at a present time that is equivalent to a series of payments and interest in the future.

	$4,000	$4,000	$4,000	$4,000
Discount	Discount	Discount	Discount	

PV = ?

Because you are interested in calculating the present value, you could refer to the present value of $1 concept and discount each of the $4,000 payments individually using table factors from Table 9-2 as follows:

$4,000 × 0.68301 Factor for 4 Periods	$ 2,732
4,000 × 0.75131 Factor for 3 Periods	3,005
4,000 × 0.82645 Factor for 2 Periods	3,306
4,000 × 0.90909 Factor for 1 Period	3,636
Total Present Value	$12,679

Tables have been constructed to ease the computational burden. Table 9-4 on page 426 provides table factors to calculate the present value of an annuity of $1 per year at various interest rates and number of periods. The previous example can be solved by reading across the four-year line and down the 10% column to obtain a table factor of 3.16987. The present value would then be calculated as follows:

PV = $4,000(table factor)
= $4,000(3.16987)
= $12,679 (rounded to the nearest dollar)

EXAMPLE 9-12 Calculating Present Value of an Annuity

You just won the lottery. You can take your $1 million in a lump sum today, or you can receive $100,000 per year over the next 12 years. Assuming a 5% interest rate, which would you prefer, ignoring tax considerations? The present value of the series of payments can be calculated as follows:
Solution:

PV = $100,000(table factor)
= $100,000(8.86325)
= $886,325

Because the present value of the payments over 12 years is less than the $1 million immediate payment, you should take the immediate payment.

Solving for Unknowns

In some cases, the present value or future value amounts will be known but the interest rate or the number of payments must be calculated. The formulas presented thus far can be used for such calculations.

LO7 Apply the compound interest concepts to some common accounting situations.

EXAMPLE 9-13   Solving for an Interest Rate

Assume that you have just purchased an automobile for $14,419 and must decide how to pay for it. Your local bank has graciously granted you a five-year loan. Because you are a good credit risk, the bank will allow you to make annual payments on the loan at the end of each year. The amount of the loan payments, which include principal and interest, is $4,000 per year. You are concerned that your total payments will be $20,000 ($4,000 per year for five years) and want to calculate the interest rate that is being charged on the loan.

Because the market or present value of the car, as well as the loan, is $14,419, a time diagram of the example would appear as follows:

$4,000	$4,000	$4,000	$4,000	$4,000
Discount	Discount	Discount	Discount	Discount

$PV = \$14,419$

The interest rate we must solve for represents the discount rate that was applied to the $4,000 payments to result in a present value of $14,419. Therefore, the applicable formula is the following:

$$PV = \$4,000(\text{table factor})$$

In this case, *PV* is known, so the formula can be rearranged as follows:

$$
\begin{aligned}
\textbf{Table factor} &= \textbf{PV/\$4,000} \\
&= \$14,419/\$4,000 \\
&= 3.605
\end{aligned}
$$

You need to use Table 9-4 to find the interest rate. You must read across the five-year line until you find a table factor that is near the value of 3.605. In this case, that table factor of 3.60478 is found in the 12% column. Therefore, the rate of interest being paid on the auto loan is approximately 12%.

EXAMPLE 9-14   Solving for the Number of Years

Assume that you want to accumulate $12,000 as a down payment on a home. You believe that you can save $1,000 per semiannual period, and your bank will pay interest of 8% per year, or 4% per semiannual period. How long will it take you to accumulate the desired amount?

The accumulated amount of $12,000 represents the future value of an annuity of $1,000 per semiannual period. Therefore, we can use the interest factors of Table 9-3 to assist in the solution. The applicable formula in this case is the following:

$$FV = \$1,000(\text{table factor})$$

The future value is known to be $12,000, and we must solve for the interest factor or table factor. Therefore, we can rearrange the formula as follows:

$$
\begin{aligned}
\textbf{Table factor} &= \textbf{FV/\$1,000} \\
&= \$12,000/\$1,000 \\
&= 12.00
\end{aligned}
$$

You need to use Table 9-3 and the 4% column to find a table value that is near 12.00. The closest table value you find is 12.00611. That table value corresponds to ten periods. Therefore, if $1,000 is deposited per semiannual period and the money is invested at 4% per semiannual period, it will take ten semiannual periods (five years) to accumulate $12,000.

TABLE 9-1 Future Value of $1

(N) Periods	2%	3%	4%	5%	6%	7%	8%	10%	12%	15%
1	1.02000	1.03000	1.04000	1.05000	1.06000	1.07000	1.08000	1.10000	1.12000	1.15000
2	1.04040	1.06090	1.08160	1.10250	1.12360	1.14490	1.16640	1.21000	1.25440	1.32250
3	1.06121	1.09273	1.12486	1.15763	1.19102	1.22504	1.25971	1.33100	1.40493	1.52088
4	1.08243	1.12551	1.16986	1.21551	1.26248	1.31080	1.36049	1.46410	1.57352	1.74901
5	1.10408	1.15927	1.21665	1.27628	1.33823	1.40255	1.46933	1.61051	1.76234	2.01136
6	1.12616	1.19405	1.26532	1.34010	1.41852	1.50073	1.58687	1.77156	1.97382	2.31306
7	1.14869	1.22987	1.31593	1.40710	1.50363	1.60578	1.71382	1.94872	2.21068	2.66002
8	1.17166	1.26677	1.36857	1.47746	1.59385	1.71819	1.85093	2.14359	2.47596	3.05902
9	1.19509	1.30477	1.42331	1.55133	1.68948	1.83846	1.99900	2.35795	2.77308	3.51788
10	1.21899	1.34392	1.48024	1.62889	1.79085	1.96715	2.15892	2.59374	3.10585	4.04556
11	1.24337	1.38423	1.53945	1.71034	1.89830	2.10485	2.33164	2.85312	3.47855	4.65239
12	1.26824	1.42576	1.60103	1.79586	2.01220	2.25219	2.51817	3.13843	3.89598	5.35025
13	1.29361	1.46853	1.66507	1.88565	2.13293	2.40985	2.71962	3.45227	4.36349	6.15279
14	1.31948	1.51259	1.73168	1.97993	2.26090	2.57853	2.93719	3.79750	4.88711	7.07571
15	1.34587	1.55797	1.80094	2.07893	2.39656	2.75903	3.17217	4.17725	5.47357	8.13706
16	1.37279	1.60471	1.87298	2.18287	2.54035	2.95216	3.42594	4.59497	6.13039	9.35762
17	1.40024	1.65285	1.94790	2.29202	2.69277	3.15882	3.70002	5.05447	6.86604	10.76126
18	1.42825	1.70243	2.02582	2.40662	2.85434	3.37993	3.99602	5.55992	7.68997	12.37545
19	1.45681	1.75351	2.10685	2.52695	3.02560	3.61653	4.31570	6.11591	8.61276	14.23177
20	1.48595	1.80611	2.19112	2.65330	3.20714	3.86968	4.66096	6.72750	9.64629	16.36654
22	1.54598	1.91610	2.36992	2.92526	3.60354	4.43040	5.43654	8.14027	12.10031	21.64475
24	1.60844	2.03279	2.56330	3.22510	4.04893	5.07237	6.34118	9.84973	15.17863	28.62518
26	1.67342	2.15659	2.77247	3.55567	4.54938	5.80735	7.39635	11.91818	19.04007	37.85680
28	1.74102	2.28793	2.99870	3.92013	5.11169	6.64884	8.62711	14.42099	23.88387	50.06561
30	1.81136	2.42726	3.24340	4.32194	5.74349	7.61226	10.06266	17.44940	29.95992	66.21177

TABLE 9-2 Present Value of $1

(N) Periods	2%	3%	4%	5%	6%	7%	8%	10%	12%	15%
1	.98039	.97087	.96154	.95238	.94340	.93458	.92593	.90909	.89286	.86957
2	.96117	.94260	.92456	.90703	.89000	.87344	.85734	.82645	.79719	.75614
3	.94232	.91514	.88900	.86384	.83962	.81630	.79383	.75131	.71178	.65752
4	.92385	.88849	.85480	.82270	.79209	.76290	.73503	.68301	.63552	.57175
5	.90573	.86261	.82193	.78353	.74726	.71299	.68058	.62092	.56743	.49718
6	.88797	.83748	.79031	.74622	.70496	.66634	.63017	.56447	.50663	.43233
7	.87056	.81309	.75992	.71068	.66506	.62275	.58349	.51316	.45235	.37594
8	.85349	.78941	.73069	.67684	.62741	.58201	.54027	.46651	.40388	.32690
9	.83676	.76642	.70259	.64461	.59190	.54393	.50025	.42410	.36061	.28426
10	.82035	.74409	.67556	.61391	.55839	.50835	.46319	.38554	.32197	.24718
11	.80426	.72242	.64958	.58468	.52679	.47509	.42888	.35049	.28748	.21494
12	.78849	.70138	.62480	.55684	.49697	.44401	.39711	.31863	.25668	.18691
13	.77303	.68095	.60057	.53032	.46884	.41496	.36770	.28966	.22917	.16253
14	.75788	.66112	.57748	.50507	.44230	.38782	.34046	.26333	.20462	.14133
15	.74301	.64186	.55526	.48102	.41727	.36245	.31524	.23939	.18270	.12289
16	.72845	.62317	.53391	.45811	.39365	.33873	.29189	.21763	.16312	.10686
17	.71416	.60502	.51337	.43630	.37136	.31657	.27027	.19784	.14564	.09293
18	.70016	.58739	.49363	.41552	.35034	.29586	.25025	.17986	.13004	.08081
19	.68643	.57029	.47464	.39573	.33051	.27651	.23171	.16351	.11611	.07027
20	.67297	.55368	.45639	.37689	.31180	.25842	.21455	.14864	.10367	.06110
22	.64684	.52189	.42196	.34185	.27751	.22571	.18394	.12285	.08264	.04620
24	.62172	.49193	.39012	.31007	.24698	.19715	.15770	.10153	.06588	.03493
26	.59758	.46369	.36069	.28124	.21981	.17220	.13520	.08391	.05252	.02642
28	.57437	.43708	.33348	.25509	.19583	.15040	.11591	.06934	.04187	.01997
30	.55207	.41199	.30832	.23138	.17411	.13137	.09938	.05731	.03338	.01510

TABLE 9-3 Future Value of Annuity of $1

(N) Periods	2%	3%	4%	5%	6%	7%	8%	10%	12%	15%
1	1.00000	1.00000	1.00000	1.00000	1.00000	1.00000	1.00000	1.00000	1.00000	1.00000
2	2.02000	2.03000	2.04000	2.05000	2.06000	2.07000	2.08000	2.10000	2.12000	2.15000
3	3.06040	3.09090	3.12160	3.15250	3.18360	3.21490	3.24640	3.31000	3.37440	3.47250
4	4.12161	4.18363	4.24646	4.31013	4.37462	4.43994	4.50611	4.64100	4.77933	4.99338
5	5.20404	5.30914	5.41632	5.52563	5.63709	5.75074	5.86660	6.10510	6.35285	6.74238
6	6.30812	6.46841	6.63298	6.80191	6.97532	7.15329	7.33593	7.71561	8.11519	8.75374
7	7.43428	7.66246	7.89829	8.14201	8.39384	8.65402	8.92280	9.48717	10.08901	11.06680
8	8.58297	8.89234	9.21423	9.54911	9.89747	10.25980	10.63663	11.43589	12.29969	13.72682
9	9.75463	10.15911	10.58280	11.02656	11.49132	11.97799	12.48756	13.57948	14.77566	16.78584
10	10.94972	11.46388	12.00611	12.57789	13.18079	13.81645	14.48656	15.93742	17.54874	20.30372
11	12.16872	12.80780	13.48635	14.20679	14.97164	15.78360	16.64549	18.53117	20.65458	24.34928
12	13.41209	14.19203	15.02581	15.91713	16.86994	17.88845	18.97713	21.38428	24.13313	29.00167
13	14.68033	15.61779	16.62684	17.71298	18.88214	20.14064	21.49530	24.52271	28.02911	34.35192
14	15.97394	17.08632	18.29191	19.59863	21.01507	22.55049	24.21492	27.97498	32.39260	40.50471
15	17.29342	18.59891	20.02359	21.57856	23.27597	25.12902	27.15211	31.77248	37.27971	47.58041
16	18.63929	20.15688	21.82453	23.65749	25.67253	27.88805	30.32428	35.94973	42.75328	55.71747
17	20.01207	21.76159	23.69751	25.84037	28.21288	30.84022	33.75023	40.54470	48.88367	65.07509
18	21.41231	23.41444	25.64541	28.13238	30.90565	33.99903	37.45024	45.59917	55.74971	75.83636
19	22.84056	25.11687	27.67123	30.53900	33.75999	37.37896	41.44626	51.15909	63.43968	88.21181
20	24.29737	26.87037	29.77808	33.06595	36.78559	40.99549	45.76196	57.27500	72.05244	102.44358
22	27.29898	30.53678	34.24797	38.50521	43.39229	49.00574	55.45676	71.40275	92.50258	137.63164
24	30.42186	34.42647	39.08260	44.50200	50.81558	58.17667	66.76476	88.49733	118.15524	184.16784
26	33.67091	38.55304	44.31174	51.11345	59.15638	68.67647	79.95442	109.18177	150.33393	245.71197
28	37.05121	42.93092	49.96758	58.40258	68.52811	80.69769	95.33883	134.20994	190.69889	327.10408
30	40.56808	47.57542	56.08494	66.43885	79.05819	94.46079	113.28321	164.49402	241.33268	434.74515

TABLE 9-4 Present Value of Annuity of $1

(N) Periods	2%	3%	4%	5%	6%	7%	8%	10%	12%	15%
1	.98039	.97087	.96154	.95238	.94340	.93458	.92593	.90909	.89286	.86957
2	1.94156	1.91347	1.88609	1.85941	1.83339	1.80802	1.78326	1.73554	1.69005	1.62571
3	2.88388	2.82861	2.77509	2.72325	2.67301	2.62432	2.57710	2.48685	2.40183	2.28323
4	3.80773	3.71710	3.62990	3.54595	3.46511	3.38721	3.31213	3.16987	3.03735	2.85498
5	4.71346	4.57971	4.45182	4.32948	4.21236	4.10020	3.99271	3.79076	3.60478	3.35216
6	5.60143	5.41719	5.24214	5.07569	4.91732	4.76654	4.62288	4.35526	4.11141	3.78448
7	6.47199	6.23028	6.00205	5.78637	5.58238	5.38929	5.20637	4.86842	4.56376	4.16042
8	7.32548	7.01969	6.73274	6.46321	6.20979	5.97130	5.74664	5.33493	4.96764	4.48732
9	8.16224	7.78611	7.43533	7.10782	6.80169	6.51523	6.24689	5.75902	5.32825	4.77158
10	8.98259	8.53020	8.11090	7.72173	7.36009	7.02358	6.71008	6.14457	5.65022	5.01877
11	9.78685	9.25262	8.76048	8.30641	7.88687	7.49867	7.13896	6.49506	5.93770	5.23371
12	10.57534	9.95400	9.38507	8.86325	8.38384	7.94269	7.53608	6.81369	6.19437	5.42062
13	11.34837	10.63496	9.98565	9.39357	8.85268	8.35765	7.90378	7.10336	6.42355	5.58315
14	12.10625	11.29607	10.56312	9.89864	9.29498	8.74547	8.24424	7.36669	6.62817	5.72448
15	12.84926	11.93794	11.11839	10.37966	9.71225	9.10791	8.55948	7.60608	6.81086	5.84737
16	13.57771	12.56110	11.65230	10.83777	10.10590	9.44665	8.85137	7.82371	6.97399	5.95423
17	14.29187	13.16612	12.16567	11.27407	10.47726	9.76322	9.12164	8.02155	7.11963	6.04716
18	14.99203	13.75351	12.65930	11.68959	10.82760	10.05909	9.37189	8.20141	7.24967	6.12797
19	15.67846	14.32380	13.13394	12.08532	11.15812	10.33560	9.60360	8.36492	7.36578	6.19823
20	16.35143	14.87747	13.59033	12.46221	11.46992	10.59401	9.81815	8.51356	7.46944	6.25933
22	17.65805	15.93692	14.45112	13.16300	12.04158	11.06124	10.20074	8.77154	7.64465	6.35866
24	18.91393	16.93554	15.24696	13.79864	12.55036	11.46933	10.52876	8.98474	7.78432	6.43377
26	20.12104	17.87684	15.98277	14.37519	13.00317	11.82578	10.80998	9.16095	7.89566	6.49056
28	21.28127	18.76411	16.66306	14.89813	13.40616	12.13711	11.05108	9.30657	7.98442	6.53351
30	22.39646	19.60044	17.29203	15.37245	13.76483	12.40904	11.25778	9.42691	8.05518	6.56598

MODULE 4 TEST YOURSELF

Review

LO5 Explain the difference between simple and compound interest.
- Simple interest is earned only on the principal amount, whereas compound interest is earned on the principal plus previous amounts of accumulated interest.

LO6 Calculate amounts using the future value and present value concepts.
- Present and future value calculations are made for four different scenarios:
  - Future value of a single amount
  - Present value of a single amount
  - Future value of an annuity
  - Present value of an annuity

LO7 Apply the compound interest concepts to some common accounting situations.
- Often, all of the variables necessary to calculate amounts related to present and future value concepts will be available except for one unknown amount that can be solved for.
- Financial calculators allow for these situations and easily solve for unknown values such as present or future value, payments, and interest rate.

Question

1. What is the meaning of the terms *present value* and *future value*? How can you determine whether to calculate the present value or the future value of an amount?
2. What is the meaning of the word *annuity*? Can the present value of an annuity be calculated as a series of single amounts? If so, how?
3. Assume that you know the total dollar amount of a loan and the amount of the monthly payments. How can you determine the interest rate as a percentage of the loan?

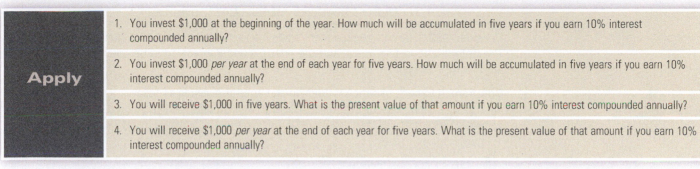

1. You invest $1,000 at the beginning of the year. How much will be accumulated in five years if you earn 10% interest compounded annually?

2. You invest $1,000 *per year* at the end of each year for five years. How much will be accumulated in five years if you earn 10% interest compounded annually?

3. You will receive $1,000 in five years. What is the present value of that amount if you earn 10% interest compounded annually?

4. You will receive $1,000 *per year* at the end of each year for five years. What is the present value of that amount if you earn 10% interest compounded annually?

Answers are located at the end of the chapter.

Accounting Tools: Using Excel® for Problems Involving Interest Calculations

APPENDIX

The purpose of this appendix is to illustrate how the functions built in to the Excel® spreadsheet can be used to calculate future value and present value amounts. The use of Excel® will be illustrated with the same examples that are used in this chapter.

To view the Excel® functions, click on the PASTE function of the Excel® toolbar (the paste function is on the top of the Excel® toolbar and is noted by the symbol *fx*); then choose the FINANCIAL option. Several different calculations are available. We will illustrate two of them: FV and PV.

EXAMPLE 9-15 Using Excel® for Future Values

Your three-year-old son Robert inherits $50,000 in cash and securities from his grandfather. If the funds are left in the bank and in the stock market and receive an annual return of 10%, how much will be available in 15 years when Robert starts college?

Solution: In Excel®, use the FV function and enter the values as follows:

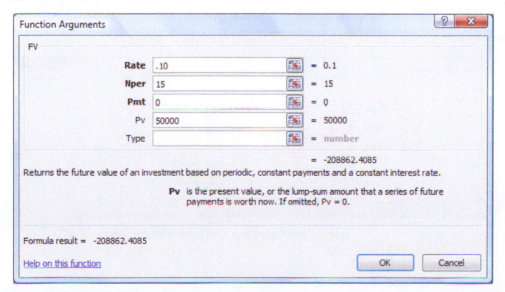

Note that the future value of $208,862 is slightly different from that given in the body of the text because of rounding when using the table factors.

EXAMPLE 9-16 Using Excel® for Annual Compounding

Consider a $2,000 note payable that carries interest at the rate of 10% compounded annually. The note is due in two years, and the principal and interest must be paid at that time. What amount must be paid in two years?

Solution: In Excel®, use the FV function and enter the values as follows:

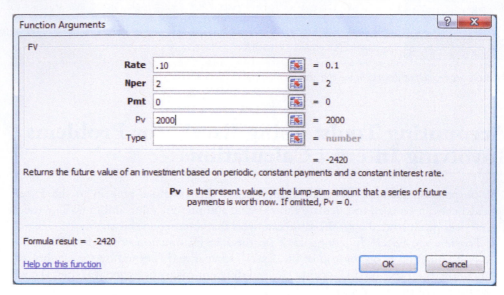

The future value is $2,420.

EXAMPLE 9-17 Using Excel® for Quarterly Compounding

Suppose we want to find the future value of a $2,000 note payable due in two years. The note payable requires interest to be compounded quarterly at the rate of 12% per year. What future amount must be paid in two years?

Solution: In Excel®, use the FV function and enter the values as follows:

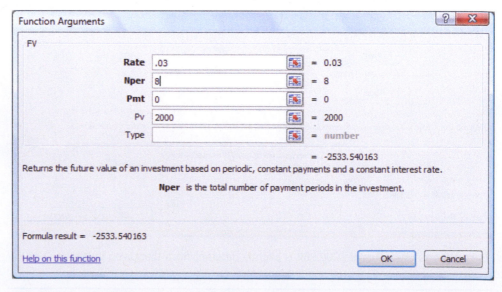

The future value is $2,534 (rounded to the nearest dollar).

EXAMPLE 9-18 Using Excel® for Present Values

Suppose you know that you will receive $2,000 in two years. If you had the money now, you could invest it at 10% compounded annually. What is the present value of the $2,000?

Solution: Since this problem requires the calculation of a present value, the PV function of Excel® should be chosen and used as follows:

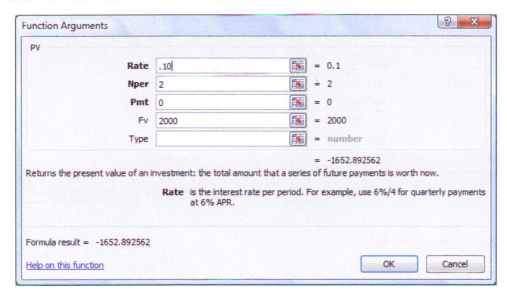

The present value is $1,653 (rounded to the nearest dollar).

EXAMPLE 9-19 Using Excel® for Future Value of an Annuity

Suppose you are to receive $3,000 per year at the end of each of the next four years. Also, assume that each payment could be invested at an interest rate of 10% compounded annually. How much would be accumulated in principal and interest by the end of the fourth year?

Solution: This problem involves the calculation of the future value of an annuity; you should use the FV function of Excel® as follows:

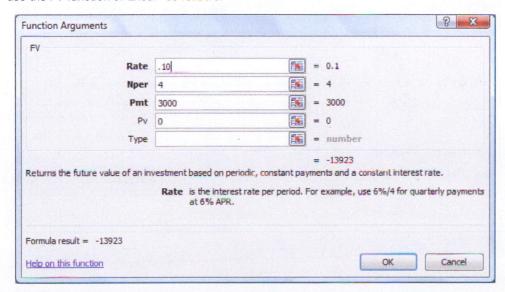

The future value of the series of payments is $13,923. Note that the payments are simply entered as the Pmt variable in the spreadsheet.

EXAMPLE 9-20 Using Excel® for Semiannual Compounding Annuities

Your cousin had a baby girl two weeks ago and is already thinking about sending her to college. When the girl is 15, how much money would be in her college account if your cousin deposited $2,000 into it on each of her 15 birthdays? The interest rate is 10%.

Solution: Use the Excel® FV function as follows:

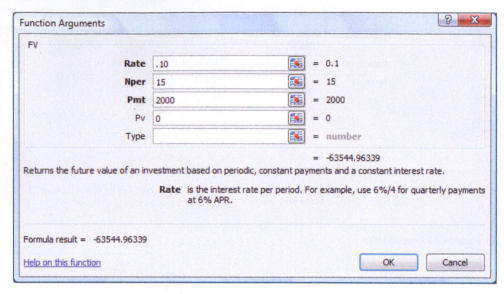

The future value amount is $63,545 (rounded to the nearest dollar).

What if the scenario was modified so that $1,000 was deposited semiannually and the interest rate was 10% compounded semiannually (or 5% per period) for 15 years?

Solution: Because the compounding is semiannual, use the FV function of Excel® as follows:

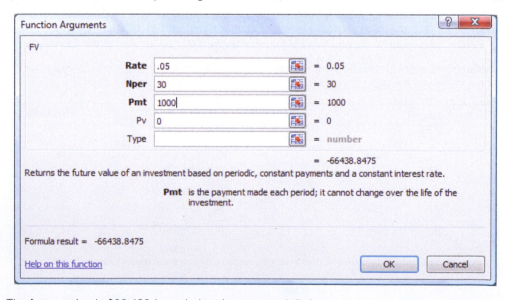

The future value is $66,439 (rounded to the nearest dollar).

EXAMPLE 9-21 Using Excel® for Present Value of an Annuity

You just won the lottery. You can take your $1 million in a lump sum today, or you can receive $100,000 per year over the next 12 years. Assuming a 5% interest rate, which would you prefer, ignoring tax considerations?

Solution: Use the PV function of Excel® as follows:

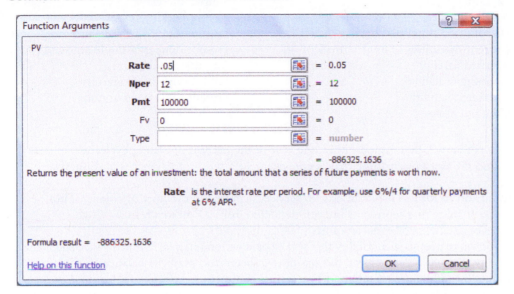

Because the present value of the payments over 12 years is $886,325 (rounded to the nearest dollar) and is less than the $1 million available immediately, you should choose the immediate payment.

RATIO REVIEW

Working Capital* = **Current Assets** − **Current Liabilities**

Current Ratio = **Current Assets/Current Liabilities**

Quick Ratio = **Quick Assets**** /Current Liabilities**

* *Working capital is defined and discussed in Chapter 2.*

** *Quick assets are those assets that can be converted into cash quickly. They may be measured differently by different companies but generally are measured as Total Current Assets − Inventory − Prepaid Expenses.*

ACCOUNTS HIGHLIGHTED

Account Titles	Where It Appears	In What Section	Page Number
Accounts Payable	Balance Sheet	Current Liabilities	404
Notes Payable	Balance Sheet	Current Liabilities	405
Current Maturities of Long-Term Debt	Balance Sheet	Current Liabilities	407
Taxes Payable	Balance Sheet	Current Liabilities	408
Accrued Liabilities	Balance Sheet	Current Liabilities	408
Contingent Liabilities	Balance Sheet	Current Liabilities or Long-Term (depending upon when it will be paid)	411

KEY TERMS QUIZ

Read each definition below and write the number of the definition in the blank beside the appropriate term. The quiz solutions appear at the end of the chapter.

_____ Current liability	_____ Time value of money
_____ Accounts payable	_____ Simple interest
_____ Notes payable	_____ Compound interest
_____ Discount on notes payable	_____ Future value of a single amount
_____ Current maturities of long-term debt	_____ Present value of a single amount
_____ Accrued liability	_____ Annuity
_____ Contingent liability	_____ Future value of an annuity
_____ Estimated liability	_____ Present value of an annuity
_____ Contingent asset	

1. Accounts that will be satisfied within one year or the current operating cycle.
2. The amount at a present time that is equivalent to a series of payments and interest in the future.
3. Amounts owed for inventory, goods, or services acquired in the normal course of business.
4. A contra-liability that represents interest deducted from a loan in advance.
5. A series of payments of equal amounts.
6. The portion of a long-term liability that will be paid within one year of the balance sheet date.
7. A liability that has been incurred but has not yet been paid as of the balance sheet date.
8. Amounts owed that are represented by a formal contract.
9. An existing condition for which the outcome is not known but depends on some future event.
10. Interest is calculated on the principal amount only.
11. A contingent liability that is accrued and reflected on the balance sheet.
12. An existing condition for which the outcome is not known but by which the company stands to gain.
13. Interest calculated on the principal plus previous amounts of interest.
14. An immediate amount should be preferred over an amount in the future.
15. Amount accumulated at a future time from a single payment or investment.
16. The amount accumulated in the future when a series of payments is invested and accrues interest.
17. The amount at a present time that is equivalent to a payment or an investment at a future time.

ALTERNATE TERMS

accrued interest interest payable

compound interest interest on interest

contingent asset contingent gain

contingent liability contingent loss

current liability short-term liability

current maturities of long-term debt long-term debt, current portion

discounting a note interest in advance

future value of an annuity amount of an annuity

income tax liability income tax payable

warranties guarantees

REVIEW PROBLEM & SOLUTION

Part A

The accountant for Lunn Express wants to develop a balance sheet as of December 31, 2017. The following items pertain to the Liability category and must be considered to determine the items that should be reported in the Current Liabilities section of the balance sheet. You may assume that Lunn began business on January 1, 2017; therefore, the beginning balance of all accounts was zero.

a. During 2017, Lunn purchased $100,000 of inventory on account from suppliers. By year-end, $40,000 of the balance had been eliminated as a result of payments. All items were purchased on terms of 2/10, n/30. Lunn uses the gross method of recording payables.

b. On April 1, 2017, Lunn borrowed $10,000 on a one-year note payable from Philips Bank. Terms of the loan indicate that Lunn must repay the principal and 12% interest at the due date of the note.

c. On October 1, 2017, Lunn also borrowed $8,000 from Dove Bank on a one-year note payable. Dove Bank deducted 10% interest in advance and gave to Lunn the net amount. At the due date, Lunn must repay the principal of $8,000.

d. On January 1, 2017, Lunn borrowed $20,000 from Owens Bank by signing a ten-year note payable. Terms of the note indicate that Lunn must make annual payments of principal each January 1 beginning in 2018 and must pay interest each January 1 in the amount of 8% of the outstanding balance of the loan.

e. The accountant for Lunn has completed an income statement for 2017 that indicates that income before taxes was $10,000. Lunn must pay tax at the rate of 40% and must remit the tax to the Internal Revenue Service by April 15, 2018.

f. As of December 31, 2017, Lunn owes its employees salaries of $3,000 for work performed in 2017. The employees will be paid on the first payday of 2018.

g. During 2017, two lawsuits were filed against Lunn. In the first lawsuit, a customer sued for damages because of an injury that occurred on Lunn's premises. Lunn's legal counsel advised that it is probable that the lawsuit will be settled in 2018 at an amount of $7,000. The second lawsuit involves a patent infringement suit of $14,000 filed against Lunn by a competitor. The legal counsel has advised that Lunn may be at fault but that a loss does not appear probable at this time.

Part B

a. What amount will be accumulated by January 1, 2021, if $5,000 is invested on January 1, 2017, at 10% interest compounded semiannually?

b. Assume that $5,000 is to be received on January 1, 2021. What amount at January 1, 2017, is equivalent to the $5,000 that is to be received in 2021? Assume that interest is compounded annually at 10%.

c. What amount will be accumulated by January 1, 2021, if $5,000 is invested each semiannual period for eight periods beginning June 30, 2017, and ending December 31, 2020? Interest will accumulate at 10% compounded semiannually.

d. Assume that $5,000 is to be received each semiannual period for eight periods beginning on June 30, 2017. What amount at January 1, 2021, is equivalent to the future series of payments? Assume that interest will accrue at 10% compounded semiannually.

e. Assume that a new bank has begun a promotional campaign to attract savings accounts. The bank advertisement indicates that customers who invest $1,000 will double their money in ten years. Assuming annual compounding of interest, what rate of interest is the bank offering?

Required

1. Consider all items in Part A. Develop the Current Liabilities section of Lunn's balance sheet as of December 31, 2017. To make investment decisions about this company, what additional data would you need? You do not need to consider the notes that accompany the balance sheet.

2. Answer the five questions in Part B.

Solutions to Review Problem Part A

1. The accountant's decisions for items (a) through (g) of Part A should be as follows:

   a. The balance of the Accounts Payable account should be $60,000. The payables should be reported at the gross amount, and discounts would not be reported until the time of payment.

   b. The note payable to Philips Bank of $10,000 should be included as a current liability. Also, interest payable of $900 ($10,000 × 12% × 9/12) should be considered a current liability.

c. The note payable to Dove Bank should be considered a current liability and listed at $8,000 minus the contra account Discount on Notes Payable of $600 ($8,000× 10% × 9/12 remaining).

d. The debt to Owens Bank should be split between current liability and long-term liability with the current portion shown as $2,000. Also, interest payable of $1,600 ($20,000 × 8% × 1 year) should be considered a current liability.

e. Income taxes payable of $4,000 ($10,000 × 40%) is a current liability.

f. Salaries payable of $3,000 represent a current liability.

g. The lawsuit involving the customer must be reported as a current liability of $7,000 because the possibility of loss is probable. The second lawsuit should not be reported but should be disclosed as a note to the balance sheet.

Lunn Express
Partial Balance Sheet
As of December 31, 2017

Current Liabilities		
Accounts payable		$60,000
Interest payable ($900 + $1,600)		2,500
Salaries payable		3,000
Taxes payable		4,000
Note payable to Philips Bank		10,000
Note payable to Dove Bank	$8,000	
Discount on notes payable	600	7,400
Current maturity of long-term debt		2,000
Contingent liability for pending lawsuit		7,000
Total Current Liabilities		$95,900

Other data necessary to make an investment decision might include current assets and total assets as of December 31, 2017. If current assets are significantly larger than current liabilities, you can be assured that the company is capable of paying its short-term debt. The dollar amount of current assets and liabilities must be evaluated with regard to the size of the company. The larger the company, the less significant $95,900 in current liabilities would be.

Solutions to Review Problem Part B

a. **FV = $5,000(table factor)**   using Table 9-1
    = **$5,000(1.47746)**   where $i = 5\%$, $n = 8$
    = **$7,387 (rounded to the nearest dollar)**

b. **PV = $5,000(table factor)**   using Table 9-2
    = **$5,000(0.68301)**   where $i = 10\%$, $n = 4$
    = **$3,415 (rounded to the nearest dollar)**

c. **FV annuity = $5,000(table factor)**   using Table 9-3
    = **$5,000(9.54911)**   where $i = 5\%$, $n = 8$
    = **$47,746 (rounded to the nearest dollar)**

d. **PV annuity = $5,000(table factor)**   using Table 9-4
    = **$5,000(6.46321)**   where $i = 5\%$, $n = 8$
    = **$32,316 (rounded to the nearest dollar)**

e. **FV = $1,000(table factor)**   using Table 9-1

Because the future value is known to be $2,000, the formula can be written as

       $2,000 = $1,000(table factor)

and rearranged as

       Table factor = $2,000/$1,000 = 2.0.

In Table 9-1, the table factor of 2.0 and ten years corresponds with an interest rate of between 7% and 8%.

EXERCISES

Exercise 9-1 Current Liabilities   LO1

The following items are accounts on Smith's balance sheet of December 31, 2017:

Taxes Payable	Estimated Warranty Payable in 2018
Accounts Receivable	Retained Earnings
Notes Payable, 9%, due in 90 days	Trademark
Investment in Bonds	Mortgage Payable ($10,000 due every
Capital Stock	year until 2030)
Accounts Payable	

Required

Identify which of the accounts should be classified as a current liability on Smith's balance sheet. For each item that is not a current liability, indicate the category of the balance sheet in which it would be classified. Assume the company has the following balance sheet categories: current asset; property, plant, and equipment; long-term investment; intangible asset; current liability; long-term liability; and stockholders' equity.

Exercise 9-2 Current Liabilities   LO1

The following items represent liabilities on a firm's balance sheet:

a. An amount of money owed to a supplier based on the terms 2/20, n/40, for which no note was executed.
b. An amount of money owed to a creditor on a note due April 30, 2018.
c. An amount of money owed to a creditor on a note due August 15, 2019.
d. An amount of money owed to employees for work performed during the last week in December.
e. An amount of money owed to a bank for the use of borrowed funds due on March 1, 2018.
f. An amount of money owed to a creditor as an annual installment payment on a ten-year note.
g. An amount of money owed to the federal government based on the company's annual income.

Required

1. For each item, state whether it should be classified as a current liability on the December 31, 2017, balance sheet. Assume that the operating cycle is shorter than one year. If the item should not be classified as a current liability, indicate where on the balance sheet it should be presented.
2. For each item identified as a current liability in part (1), state the account title that is normally used to report the item on the balance sheet.
3. Why would an investor or a creditor be interested in whether an item is a current or a long-term liability?

Exercise 9-3 Current Liabilities Section   LO1

Jackie Company had the following accounts and balances on December 31, 2017:

Income Taxes Payable	$61,250	Notes Payable, 10%, due June 2, 2018	$ 1,000
Allowance for Doubtful Accounts	17,800	Accounts Receivable	67,500
Accounts Payable	24,400	Discount on Notes Payable	150
Interest Receivable	5,000	Current Maturities of Long-Term Debt	6,900
Unearned Revenue	4,320	Interest Payable	3,010
Wages Payable	6,000		

Required

Prepare the Current Liabilities section of Jackie Company's balance sheet as of December 31, 2017.

LO2

Exercise 9-4 Transaction Analysis

EXAMPLE 9-1, 9-4

Polly's Cards & Gifts Shop had the following transactions during the year:

a. Polly's purchased inventory on account from a supplier for $8,000. Assume that Polly's uses a periodic inventory system.
b. On May 1, land was purchased for $44,500. A 20% down payment was made, and an 18-month, 8% note was signed for the remainder.
c. Polly's returned $450 worth of inventory purchased in (a), which was found broken when the inventory was received.
d. Polly's paid the balance due on the purchase of inventory.
e. On June 1, Polly signed a one-year, $15,000 note to First State Bank and received $13,800.
f. Polly's sold 200 gift certificates for $25 each for cash. Sales of gift certificates are recorded as a liability. At year-end, 35% of the gift certificates had been redeemed.
g. Sales for the year were $120,000, of which 90% were for cash. State sales tax of 6% applied to all sales must be remitted to the state by January 31.

Required

1. Identify and analyze the effect of transactions a–g.
2. Assume that Polly's accounting year ends on December 31. Identify and analyze the effect of any year-end adjustments.
3. What is the total of the current liabilities at the end of the year?

LO2

Exercise 9-5 Current Liabilities and Ratios

Several accounts that appeared on Kruse's 2017 balance sheet are as follows:

Accounts Payable	$ 55,000	Equipment	$950,000
Marketable Securities	40,000	Taxes Payable	15,000
Accounts Receivable	180,000	Retained Earnings	250,000
Notes Payable, 12%, due in 60 days	20,000	Inventory	85,000
Capital Stock	1,150,000	Allowance for Doubtful Accounts	20,000
Salaries Payable	10,000	Land	600,000
Cash	15,000		

Required

1. Prepare the Current Liabilities section of Kruse's 2017 balance sheet.
2. Compute Kruse's working capital.
3. Compute Kruse's current ratio. What does this ratio indicate about Kruse's condition?

LO2

Exercise 9-6 Discounts

Each of the following situations involves the use of discounts:
1. How much discount may Seals Inc. take in each of the following transactions? What was the annualized interest rate?

   a. Seals purchases inventory costing $450, terms 2/10, n/40.
   b. Seals purchases new office furniture costing $1,500, terms 1/10, n/30.

2. Calculate the discount rate that Croft Co. received in each of these transactions.

   a. Croft purchased office supplies costing $200 and paid within the discount period with a check for $196.
   b. Croft purchased merchandise for $2,800. It paid within the discount period with a check for $2,674.

LO2

Exercise 9-7 Notes Payable and Interest

EXAMPLE 9-1, 9-4

On July 1, 2017, Jo's Flower Shop borrowed $25,000 from the bank. Jo's signed a ten-month, 8% promissory note for the entire amount. Jo's uses a calendar year-end.

Required

1. Identify and analyze the effect of the issuance of the promissory note.
2. Identify and analyze the effect of any adjustments needed at year-end.
3. Identify and analyze the effect of the payment of principal and interest.

Exercise 9-8   Non-Interest-Bearing Notes Payable

LO2

EXAMPLE 9-2

On October 1, 2017, Ratkowski Inc. borrowed $18,000 from Second National Bank by issuing a 12-month note. The bank discounted the note at 9%.

Required

1. Identify and analyze the effect of the issuance of the note.
2. Identify and analyze the effect of the accrual of interest on December 31, 2017.
3. Identify and analyze the effect of the payment of the note on October 1, 2018.
4. What effective rate of interest did Ratkowski pay?

Exercise 9-9   Impact of Transactions Involving Current Liabilities on Statement of Cash Flows

LO3

From the following list, identify whether the change in the account balance during the year would be reported as an operating (O), an investing (I), or a financing (F) activity or not separately reported on the statement of cash flows (N). Assume that the indirect method is used to determine the cash flows from operating activities.

_____	Accounts payable	_____	Other accrued liabilities
_____	Current maturities of	_____	Salaries and wages payable
	long-term debt	_____	Taxes payable
_____	Notes payable		

Exercise 9-10   Impact of Transactions Involving Contingent Liabilities on Statement of Cash Flows

LO3

From the following list, identify whether the change in the account balance during the year would be reported as an operating (O), an investing (I), or a financing (F) activity or not separately reported on the statement of cash flows (N). Assume that the indirect method is used to determine the cash flows from operating activities.

_____ Estimated liability for warranties
_____ Estimated liability for product premiums
_____ Estimated liability for probable loss relating to litigation

Exercise 9-11   Warranties

LO4

EXAMPLE 9-5

Clean Corporation manufactures and sells dishwashers. Clean provides all customers with a two-year warranty guaranteeing to repair, free of charge, any defects reported during this time period. During the year, it sold 100,000 dishwashers for $325 each. Analysis of past warranty records indicates that 12% of all sales will be returned for repair within the warranty period. Clean expects to incur expenditures of $14 to repair each dishwasher. The account Estimated Liability for Warranties had a balance of $120,000 on January 1. Clean incurred $150,000 in actual expenditures during the year.

Required

Identify and analyze the effect of the events related to the warranty transactions during the year. Determine the adjusted ending balance in the Estimated Liability for Warranties account.

Exercise 9-12   Simple versus Compound Interest

LO5

EXAMPLE 9-6, 9-7

For each of the following notes, calculate the simple interest due at the end of the term.

(Continued)

Note	Face Value (Principal)	Rate	Term
1	$20,000	4%	6 years
2	20,000	6%	4 years
3	20,000	8%	3 years

Now assume that the interest on the notes is compounded annually. Calculate the amount of interest due at the end of the term for each note.

Finally, assume that the interest on the notes is compounded semiannually. Calculate the amount of interest due at the end of the term for each note.

What conclusion can you draw from a comparison of your results of each of the three scenarios?

LO6
EXAMPLE 9-10

Exercise 9-13 Present Value and Future Value

Brian Inc. estimates that it will need $150,000 in ten years to expand its manufacturing facilities. A bank has agreed to pay Brian 5% interest compounded annually if the company deposits the entire amount now needed to accumulate $150,000 in ten years. How much money does Brian need to deposit?

LO6
EXAMPLE 9-9

Exercise 9-14 Effect of Compounding Period

Kern Company deposited $1,000 in the bank on January 1, 2017, earning 8% interest. Kern Company withdraws the deposit plus accumulated interest on January 1, 2019. Compute the amount of money Kern withdraws from the bank assuming that interest is compounded (a) annually, (b) semiannually, and (c) quarterly.

LO6
EXAMPLE 9-9, 9-10

Exercise 9-15 Present Value and Future Value

The following situations involve time value of money calculations:
1. A deposit of $7,000 is made on January 1, 2017. The deposit will earn interest at a rate of 8%. How much will be accumulated on January 1, 2022, assuming that interest is compounded (a) annually, (b) semiannually, and (c) quarterly?
2. A deposit is made on January 1, 2017, to earn interest at an annual rate of 8%. The deposit will accumulate to $15,000 by January 1, 2022. How much money was originally deposited assuming that interest is compounded (a) annually, (b) semiannually, and (c) quarterly?

LO6
EXAMPLE 9-9, 9-10

Exercise 9-16 Present Value and Future Value

The following situations require the application of the time value of money:
1. On January 1, 2017, $16,000 is deposited. Assuming an 8% interest rate, calculate the amount accumulated on January 1, 2022, if interest is compounded (a) annually, (b) semiannually, and (c) quarterly.
2. Assume that a deposit made on January 1, 2017, earns 8% interest. The deposit plus interest accumulated to $20,000 on January 1, 2022. How much was invested on January 1, 2017, if interest was compounded (a) annually, (b) semiannually, and (c) quarterly?

LO6
EXAMPLE 9-11

Exercise 9-17 Annuity

Steve Jones has decided to start saving for his son's college education by depositing $2,000 at the end of every year for 15 years. A bank has agreed to pay interest at the rate of 4% compounded annually. How much will Steve have in the bank immediately after his 15th deposit?

LO7
EXAMPLE 9-13

Exercise 9-18 Calculation of Years

Kelly Seaver has decided to start saving for her daughter's college education. Kelly wants to accumulate $32,000. The bank will pay interest at the rate of 4% compounded annually. If Kelly plans to make payments of $1,600 at the end of each year, how long will it take her to accumulate $32,000?

LO7
EXAMPLE 9-8

Exercise 9-19 Value of Payments

Upon graduation from college, Susana Lopez signed an agreement to buy a used car. Her annual payments, which are due at the end of each year for two years, are $1,480. The car dealer used a 12% rate compounded annually to determine the amount of the payments.

Required

1. What should Susana consider the value of the car to be?
2. If she had wanted to make quarterly payments, what would her payments have been based on the value of the car as determined in part (1)? How much less interest would she have paid if she had been making quarterly payments instead of annual payments? What would have happened to the payment amount and the interest if she had asked for monthly payments?

MULTI-CONCEPT EXERCISES

Exercise 9-20 Comparison of Alternatives

LO6 • 7
EXAMPLE 9-10, 9-12

Jane Bauer has won the lottery and has the following four options for receiving her winnings:
1. Receive $100,000 at the beginning of the current year
2. Receive $108,000 at the end of the year
3. Receive $20,000 at the end of each year for eight years
4. Receive $10,000 at the end of each year for 30 years

Jane can invest her winnings at an interest rate of 8% compounded annually at a major bank. Which of the payment options should Jane choose?

Exercise 9-21 Two Situations

LO6 • 7
EXAMPLE 9-13

The following situations involve the application of the time value of money concepts:
1. Sampson Company just purchased a piece of equipment with a value of $53,300. Sampson financed this purchase with a loan from the bank and must make annual loan payments of $13,000 at the end of each year for the next five years. Interest is compounded annually on the loan. What is the interest rate on the bank loan?
2. Simon Company needs to accumulate $200,000 to repay bonds due in six years. Simon estimates it can save $13,300 at the end of each semiannual period at a local bank offering an annual interest rate of 8% compounded semiannually. Will Simon have enough money saved at the end of six years to repay the bonds?

PROBLEMS

Problem 9-1 Notes and Interest

LO2

Glencoe Inc. operates with a June 30 year-end. During 2017, the following transactions occurred:

a. January 1: Signed a one-year, 10% loan for $25,000. Interest and principal are to be paid at maturity.
b. January 10: Signed a line of credit with Little Local Bank to establish a $400,000 line of credit. Interest of 9% will be charged on all borrowed funds.
c. February 1: Issued a $20,000 non-interest-bearing, six-month note to pay for a new machine. Interest on the note, at 12%, was deducted in advance.
d. March 1: Borrowed $150,000 on the line of credit.
e. June 1: Repaid $100,000 on the line of credit plus accrued interest.
f. June 30: Made all necessary adjusting entries.
g. August 1: Repaid the non-interest-bearing note.
h. September 1: Borrowed $200,000 on the line of credit.
i. November 1: Issued a three-month, 8%, $12,000 note in payment of an overdue open account.
j. December 31: Repaid the one-year loan [from transaction (a)] plus accrued interest.

Required

1. Identify and analyze the effect of these transactions.
2. As of December 31, which notes are outstanding? How much interest is due on each?

LO3 **Problem 9-2 Effects of Yum! Brands Current Liabilities on Its Statement of Cash Flows**

The following items are classified as current liabilities on **Yum! Brands**' balance sheets as of December 27, 2014, and December 28, 2013:

Consolidated Balance Sheets
YUM! Brands, Inc. and Subsidiaries
December 27, 2014 and December 28, 2013
(in millions)

	2014	2013
Current Liabilities		
Accounts payable and other current liabilities	$1,972	$1,929
Income taxes payable	77	169
Short-term borrowings	267	71
Advertising cooperative liabilities	95	96
Total Current Liabilities	$2,411	$2,265

Source: Yum! Brands, Inc., 2014 Form 10-K.

Required

1. Yum! Brands uses the indirect method to prepare its statement of cash flows. Prepare the Operating Activities section of the cash-flow statement, which indicates how each item will be reflected as an adjustment to net income. If you did not include any of the preceding items, explain why.
2. How would you decide if Yum! Brands has the ability to pay these liabilities as they become due?

LO3 **Problem 9-3 Effects of Brinker International's Current Liabilities on Its Statement of Cash Flows**

Brinker International operates Chili's, Macaroni Grill, and other restaurant chains. The following items are classified as current liabilities on Brinker International's balance sheets as of 2015 and 2014:

Brinker International, Inc.
Consolidated Balance Sheets
(In thousands, except share and per share amounts)

	2015	2014
Current Liabilities:		
Current installments of long-term debt	$ 3,439	$ 27,884
Accounts payable	92,947	102,931
Gift card liability	114,726	104,378
Accrued payroll	82,915	77,585
Other accrued liabilities	111,197	146,054
Income taxes payable	13,251	7,278
Total current liabilities	$418,475	$466,110

Required

1. Brinker uses the indirect method to prepare its statement of cash flows. Prepare the Operating Activities section of the cash-flow statement, which indicates how each item will be reflected as an adjustment to net income.
2. Explain why an increase in a current liability account such as Accounts Payable appears as a positive amount on the statement of cash flows.

Problem 9-4 Warranties   LO4

Clearview Company manufactures and sells high-quality television sets. The most popular line sells for $1,000 each and is accompanied by a three-year warranty to repair, free of charge, any defective unit. Average costs to repair each defective unit will be $90 for replacement parts and $60 for labor. Clearview estimates that warranty costs of $12,600 will be incurred during 2017. The company actually sold 600 television sets and incurred replacement part costs of $3,600 and labor costs of $5,400 during the year. The adjusted 2017 ending balance in the Estimated Liability for Warranties account is $10,200.

Required

1. How many defective units from this year's sales does Clearview Company estimate will be returned for repair?
2. What percentage of sales does Clearview Company estimate will be returned for repair?
3. What steps should Clearview take if actual warranty costs incurred during 2018 are significantly higher than the estimated liability recorded at the end of 2017?

Problem 9-5 Warranties   LO4

Bombeck Company sells a product for $1,500. When the customer buys it, Bombeck provides a one-year warranty. Bombeck sold 120 products during 2017. Based on analysis of past warranty records, Bombeck estimates that repairs will average 3% of total sales.

Required

1. Prepare the journal entry to record the estimated liability.
2. Assume that during 2017, products under warranty must be repaired using repair parts from inventory costing $4,950. Prepare the journal entry to record the repair of products.

Problem 9-6 Comparison of Simple and Compound Interest   LO5

On June 30, 2017, Rolf Inc. borrowed $25,000 from its bank, signing an 8%, two-year note.

Required

1. Assuming that the bank charges simple interest on the note, prepare the journal entry Rolf will record on each of the following dates:

   December 31, 2017
   December 31, 2018
   June 30, 2019

2. Assume instead that the bank charges 8% on the note, which is compounded semiannually. Identify and analyze the effect on the dates in part (1).
3. How much additional interest expense will Rolf have in part (2) than in part (1)?

Problem 9-7 Investment with Varying Interest Rate   LO6

Shari Thompson invested $1,000 in a financial institution on January 1, 2017. She leaves her investment in the institution until December 31, 2021. How much money does Shari accumulate if she earns interest, compounded annually, at the following rates?

2017	4%
2018	5
2019	6
2020	7
2021	8

Problem 9-8 Comparison of Alternatives   LO6

On January 1, 2017, Chen Yu's Office Supply Store plans to remodel the store and install new display cases. Chen has the following options of payment. Chen's interest rate is 8%.

a. Pay $180,000 on January 1, 2017.
b. Pay $196,200 on January 1, 2018.

(Continued)

   c. Pay $220,500 on January 1, 2019.

   d. Make four annual payments of $55,000 beginning on December 31, 2017.

Required

Which option should he choose? (*Hint:* Calculate the present value of each option as of January 1, 2017.)

MULTI-CONCEPT PROBLEMS

LO2 • 5 **Problem 9-9** **Interest in Advance versus Interest Paid When Loan Is Due**

On July 1, 2017, Leach Company needs exactly $103,200 in cash to pay an existing obligation. Leach has decided to borrow from State Bank, which charges 14% interest on loans. The loan will be due in one year. Leach is unsure, however, whether to ask the bank for (a) an interest-bearing loan with interest and principal payable at the end of the year or (b) a loan due in one year but with interest deducted in advance.

Required

1. What will be the face value of the note assuming that:

   a. Interest is paid when the loan is due?

   b. Interest is deducted in advance?

2. Calculate the effective interest rate on the note assuming that:

   a. Interest is paid when the loan is due.

   b. Interest is deducted in advance.

3. Assume that Leach negotiates and signs the one-year note with the bank on July 1, 2017. Also, assume that Leach's accounting year ends December 31. Identify and analyze the effect of the issuance of the note and the interest on the note assuming that:

   a. Interest is paid when the loan is due.

   b. Interest is deducted in advance.

4. Prepare the appropriate balance sheet presentation for July 1, 2017, immediately after the note has been issued assuming that:

   a. Interest is paid when the loan is due.

   b. Interest is deducted in advance.

LO1 • 4 **Problem 9-10** **Contingent Liabilities**

Several independent items are listed for which the outcome of events is unknown at year-end.

   a. A company offers a two-year warranty on sales of new computers. It believes that 4% of the computers will require repairs.

   b. A company is involved in a trademark infringement suit. The company's legal experts believe that an award of $500,000 in the company's favor will be made.

   c. A company is involved in an environmental cleanup lawsuit. The company's legal counsel believes that the outcome may be unfavorable but has not been able to estimate the costs of the possible loss.

   d. A soap manufacturer has included a coupon offer in the Sunday newspaper supplements. The manufacturer estimates that 25% of the 50¢ coupons will be redeemed.

   e. A company has been sued by the federal government for price fixing. The company's legal counsel believes that there will be an unfavorable verdict and has made an estimate of the probable loss.

Required

1. Identify which of the items (a) through (e) should be recorded at year-end.

2. Identify which of the items (a) through (e) should not be recorded but should be disclosed in the year-end financial statements.

Problem 9-11 Time Value of Money Concept   LO6 • 7

The following situations involve the application of the time value of money concept:

1. Janelle Carter deposited $9,750 in the bank on January 1, 2000, at an interest rate of 12% compounded annually. How much has accumulated in the account by January 1, 2017?
2. Mike Smith deposited $21,600 in the bank on January 1, 2007. On January 2, 2017, this deposit has accumulated to $42,486. Interest is compounded annually on the account. What rate of interest did Mike earn on the deposit?
3. Lee Spony made a deposit in the bank on January 1, 2010. The bank pays interest at the rate of 8% compounded annually. On January 1, 2017, the deposit has accumulated to $15,000. How much money did Lee originally deposit on January1, 2010?
4. Nancy Holmes deposited $5,800 in the bank on January 1 a few years ago. The bank pays an interest rate of 10% compounded annually, and the deposit is now worth $15,026. How many years has the deposit been invested?

Problem 9-12 Comparison of Alternatives   LO6 • 7

Brian Imhoff's grandparents want to give him some money when he graduates from high school. They have offered Brian three choices as follows:

a. Receive $15,000 immediately. Assume that interest is compounded annually.
b. Receive $2,250 at the end of each six months for four years. Brian will receive the first check in six months.
c. Receive $4,350 at the end of each year for four years. Assume that interest is compounded annually.

Required

Brian wants to have money for a new car when he graduates from college in four years. Assuming an interest rate of 8%, what option should he choose to have the most money in four years?

ALTERNATE PROBLEMS

Problem 9-1A Notes and Interest   LO2

McLaughlin Inc. operates with a June 30 year-end. During 2017, the following transactions occurred:

a. January 1: Signed a one-year, 10% loan for $35,000. Interest and principal are to be paid at maturity.
b. January 10: Signed a line of credit with Little Local Bank to establish a $560,000 line of credit. Interest of 9% will be charged on all borrowed funds.
c. February 1: Issued a $28,000 non-interest-bearing, six-month note to pay for a new machine. Interest on the note, at 12%, was deducted in advance.
d. March 1: Borrowed $210,000 on the line of credit.
e. June 1: Repaid $140,000 on the line of credit plus accrued interest.
f. June 30: Made all necessary adjusting entries.
g. August 1: Repaid the non-interest-bearing note.
h. September 1: Borrowed $280,000 on the line of credit.
i. November 1: Issued a three-month, 8%, $16,800 note in payment of an overdue open account.
j. December 31: Repaid the one-year loan [from transaction (a)] plus accrued interest.

Required

1. Identify and analyze the effect of these transactions.
2. As of December 31, which notes are outstanding? How much interest is due on each?

Problem 9-2A Effects of McDonald's Current Liabilities on Its Statement of Cash Flows   LO3

The following items are classified as current liabilities on **McDonald's** consolidated statements of financial condition (or balance sheet) at December 31 (in millions):

REAL WORLD

(Continued)

Consolidated Balance Sheet
In millions, except per share data

	December 31	
	2014	2013
Current liabilities		
Accounts payable	$ 860.1	$1,086.0
Income taxes	166.8	215.5
Other taxes	330.0	383.1
Accrued interest	233.7	221.6
Accrued payroll and other liabilities	1,157.3	1,263.8
Total current liabilities	$2,747.9	$3,170.0

Required

1. McDonald's uses the indirect method to prepare its statement of cash flows. Prepare the Operating Activities section of the cash-flow statement, which indicates how each item will be reflected as an adjustment to net income. If you did not include any of the preceding items, explain why.
2. How would you decide if McDonald's has the ability to pay these liabilities as they become due?

LO3 Problem 9-3A Effects of Darden Restaurants' Changes in Current Assets and Liabilities on Its Statement of Cash Flows

The following items are included in the Current Liabilities category on the consolidated balance sheet of **Darden Restaurants** at May 31, 2015 and May 25, 2014:

REAL WORLD

Darden Restaurants, Inc.
Consolidated Balance Sheets
(In millions)

	May 31, 2015	May 25, 2014
Current liabilities:		
Accounts payable	$ 198.8	$ 233.1
Short-term debt	—	207.6
Accrued payroll	141.1	125.7
Accrued income taxes	12.6	—
Other accrued taxes	51.5	64.5
Unearned revenues	328.6	299.7
Current portion of long-term debt	15.0	15.0
Other current liabilities	449.1	457.4
Liabilities associated with assets held for sale	—	215.5
Total current liabilities	$1,196.7	$1,618.5

Required

1. Darden Restaurants uses the indirect method to prepare its statement of cash flows. Prepare the Operating Activities section of the cash-flow statement, which indicates how each item will be reflected as an adjustment to net income.
2. If you did not include any of the preceding items in your answer to part (1), explain how these items would be reported on the statement of cash flows.

LO4 Problem 9-4A Warranties

Sound Company manufactures and sells high-quality stereos. The most popular line sells for $2,000 each and is accompanied by a three-year warranty to repair, free of charge, any defective unit. Average costs to repair each defective unit will be $180 for replacement parts and $120 for labor. Sound estimates that warranty costs of $25,200 will be incurred during 2017. The company actually sold 600 sets and incurred replacement part costs of $7,200 and labor costs of $10,800 during the year. The adjusted 2017 ending balance in the Estimated Liability for Warranties account is $20,400.

Required

1. How many defective units from this year's sales does Sound Company estimate will be returned for repair?
2. What percentage of sales does Sound Company estimate will be returned for repair?

Problem 9-5A Warranties   LO4

Beck Company sells a product for $3,200. When the customer buys it, Beck provides a one-year warranty. Beck sold 120 products during 2017. Based on analysis of past warranty records, Beck estimates that repairs will average 4% of total sales.

Required

1. Prepare the journal entry to record the estimated liability.
2. Assume that during 2017, products under warranty must be repaired using repair parts from inventory costing $10,200. Prepare the journal entry to record the repair of products.
3. Assume that the balance of the Estimated Liability for Warranties account as of the beginning of 2017 was $1,100. Calculate the balance of the account as of the end of 2017.

Problem 9-6A Comparison of Simple and Compound Interest   LO5

On June 30, 2017, Rolloff Inc. borrowed $25,000 from its bank, signing a 6% note. Principal and interest are due at the end of two years.

Required

1. Assuming that the note earns simple interest for the bank, calculate the amount of interest accrued on each of the following dates:

   December 31, 2017
   December 31, 2018
   June 30, 2019

2. Assume instead that the note earns 6% for the bank but is compounded semiannually. Calculate the amount of interest accrued on the same dates as in part (1).
3. How much additional interest expense will Rolloff have to pay with semiannual interest?

Problem 9-7A Investment with Varying Interest Rate   LO6

Trena Thompson invested $2,000 in a financial institution on January 1, 2017. She leaves her investment in the institution until December 31, 2021. How much money does Trena accumulate if she earns interest, compounded annually, at the following rates?

2017	4%
2018	5
2019	6
2020	7
2021	8

Problem 9-8A Comparison of Alternatives   LO6

On January 1, 2017, Chen Yu's Office Supply Store plans to remodel the store and install new display cases. Chen has the following options of payment. Chen's interest rate is 8%.

a. Pay $270,000 on January 1, 2017.
b. Pay $294,300 on January 1, 2018.
c. Pay $334,750 on January 1, 2019.
d. Make four annual payments of $82,500 beginning on December 31, 2017.

Required

Which option should he choose? (*Hint:* Calculate the present value of each option as of January 1, 2017.)

ALTERNATE MULTI-CONCEPT PROBLEMS

LO2 • 5   Problem 9-9A Interest in Advance versus Interest Paid When Loan Is Due

On July 1, 2017, Moton Company needs exactly $206,400 in cash to pay an existing obligation. Moton has decided to borrow from State Bank, which charges 14% interest on loans. The loan will be due in one year. Moton is unsure, however, whether to ask the bank for (a) an interest-bearing loan with interest and principal payable at the end of the year or (b) a non-interest-bearing loan due in one year but with interest deducted in advance.

Required

1.   What will be the face value of the note assuming that:

   a. Interest is paid when the loan is due?
   b. Interest is deducted in advance?

2.   Calculate the effective interest rate on the note assuming that:

   a. Interest is paid when the loan is due.
   b. Interest is deducted in advance.

3.   Assume that Moton negotiates and signs the one-year note with the bank on July 1, 2017. Also, assume that Moton's accounting year ends December 31. Identify and analyze the effect of the issuance of the note and the interest on the note assuming that:

   a. Interest is paid when the loan is due.
   b. Interest is deducted in advance.

4.   Prepare the appropriate balance sheet presentation for July 1, 2017, immediately after the note has been issued assuming that:

   a. Interest is paid when the loan is due.
   b. Interest is deducted in advance.

LO1 • 4   Problem 9-10A Contingent Liabilities

Several independent items are listed for which the outcome of events is unknown at year-end.

   a. A company has been sued by the federal government for price fixing. The company's legal counsel believes that there will be an unfavorable verdict and has made an estimate of the probable loss.
   b. A company is involved in an environmental cleanup lawsuit. The company's legal counsel believes that the outcome may be unfavorable but has not been able to estimate the costs of the possible loss.
   c. A company is involved in a trademark infringement suit. The company's legal experts believe that an award of $750,000 in the company's favor will be made.
   d. A company offers a three-year warranty on sales of new computers. It believes that 6% of the computers will require repairs.
   e. A snack food manufacturer has included a coupon offer in the Sunday newspaper supplements. The manufacturer estimates that 30% of the 40¢ coupons will be redeemed.

Required

1.   Identify which of the items (a) through (e) should be recorded at year-end.
2.   Identify which of the items (a) through (e) should not be recorded but should be disclosed in the year-end financial statements.

LO6 • 7   Problem 9-11A Time Value of Money Concept

The following situations involve the application of the time value of money concept:

1.   Jan Cain deposited $19,500 in the bank on January 1, 2000, at an interest rate of 12% compounded annually. How much has accumulated in the account by January 1, 2017?
2.   Mark Schultz deposited $43,200 in the bank on January 1, 2007. On January 2, 2017, this deposit has accumulated to $84,974. Interest is compounded annually on the account. What rate of interest did Mark earn on the deposit?

3. Les Hinckle made a deposit in the bank on January 1, 2010. The bank pays interest at the rate of 8% compounded annually. On January 1, 2017, the deposit has accumulated to $30,000. How much money did Les originally deposit on January 1, 2010?

4. Val Hooper deposited $11,600 in the bank on January 1 a few years ago. The bank pays an interest rate of 10% compounded annually, and the deposit is now worth $30,052. For how many years has the deposit been invested?

Problem 9-12A Comparison of Alternatives   LO6 • 7

Darlene Page's grandparents want to give her some money when she graduates from high school. They have offered Darlene the following three choices:

a. Receive $16,000 immediately. Assume that interest is compounded annually.
b. Receive $2,400 at the end of each six months for four years. Darlene will receive the first check in six months.
c. Receive $4,640 at the end of each year for four years. Assume that interest is compounded annually.

Required

Darlene wants to have money for a new car when she graduates from college in four years. Assuming an interest rate of 8%, what option should she choose to have the most money in four years?

DECISION CASES

Reading and Interpreting Financial Statements

Decision Case 9-1 Comparing Two Companies: Panera Bread's and Chipotle's Current Liabilities   LO1 • 2

Refer to **Panera Bread**'s and **Chipotle**'s financial statements reprinted at the back of the book. Using the companies' balance sheets and accompanying notes, write a response to the following questions:

REAL WORLD

Required

1. Determine Panera Bread's and Chipotle's current ratio for fiscal years 2015 and 2014. What do the ratios indicate about the liquidity of the company?
2. How do the current liabilities of the two companies compare?
3. Refer to the companies' notes. Do the companies have any contingent liabilities for lawsuits or litigation? If so, how were these contingent liabilities treated on the financial statements?

Decision Case 9-2 Keurig Green Mountain's Current Liabilities   LO4

Following is the current assets and current liabilities portion of the balance sheet of **Keurig Green Mountain** for the years ended September 26, 2015 and September 27, 2014:

REAL WORLD

(Dollars in thousands)	September 26, 2015	September 27, 2014
Assets		
Current assets:		
Cash and cash equivalents	$ 59,334	$ 761,214
Restricted cash and cash equivalents	30,460	378
Short-term investment	—	100,000
Receivables, less uncollectible accounts and return allowances of $35,459 and $66,120 at September 26, 2015 and September 27, 2014, respectively	517,936	621,451
Inventories	691,980	835,167
Income taxes receivable	51,786	—

(Continued)

(Dollars in thousands)	September 26, 2015	September 27, 2014
Other current assets	95,526	69,272
Deferred income taxes, net	70,181	58,038
Total current assets	$1,517,203	$2,445,520
Current liabilities:		
Current portion of long-term debt	$ 279	$ 19,077
Current portion of capital lease and financing obligations	3,271	2,226
Accounts payable	298,609	411,107
Accrued expenses	226,519	305,677
Income tax payable	1,085	53,586
Dividend payable	44,048	40,580
Deferred income taxes, net	264	340
Other current liabilities	28,049	10,395
Total current liabilities	$ 602,124	$ 842,988

Source: Keurig Green Mountain, Inc Form 10-K for year ended September 26, 2015.

Required

Determine the company's current ratio for each fiscal year. What do the ratios indicate about the liquidity of the company? What were the major causes for any changes in liquidity?

LO3 • 4   **Decision Case 9-3**   **Walmart's Contingent Liabilities**

REAL WORLD

The following excerpts are from the footnotes that accompany **Walmart**'s financial statements of January 31, 2015.

Wage-and-Hour Class Action: The Company is a defendant in *Braun/Hummel v. Wal-Mart Stores, Inc.*, a class-action lawsuit commenced in March 2002 in the Court of Common Pleas in Philadelphia, Pennsylvania. The plaintiffs allege that the Company failed to pay class members for all hours worked and prevented class members from taking their full meal and rest breaks. On October 13, 2006, a jury awarded back-pay damages to the plaintiffs of approximately $78 million on their claims for off-the-clock work and missed rest breaks. The jury found in favor of the Company on the plaintiffs' meal-period claims. On November 14, 2007, the trial judge entered a final judgment in the approximate amount of $188 million, which included the jury's back-pay award plus statutory penalties, prejudgment interest and attorneys' fees. By operation of law, post-judgment interest accrues on the judgment amount at the rate of six percent per annum from the date of entry of the judgment, which was November 14, 2007, until the judgment is paid, unless the judgment is set aside on appeal. On December 7, 2007, the Company filed its Notice of Appeal. On June 10, 2011, the Pennsylvania Superior Court of Appeals issued an opinion upholding the trial court's certification of the class, the jury's back pay award, and the awards of statutory penalties and prejudgment interest, but reversing the award of attorneys' fees. On September 9, 2011, the Company filed a Petition for Allowance of Appeal with the Pennsylvania Supreme Court. On July 2, 2012, the Pennsylvania Supreme Court granted the Company's Petition. On December 15, 2014, the Pennsylvania Supreme Court issued its opinion affirming the Superior Court of Appeals' decision. At that time, the Company recorded expenses of $249 million for the judgment amount and post-judgment interest incurred to date. The Company will continue to accrue for the post-judgment interest until final resolution. However, the Company continues to believe it has substantial factual and legal defenses to the claims at issue and, on March 13, 2015, the Company filed a petition for writ of certiorari with the U.S. Supreme Court.

Source: Walmart, Inc., Form 10-K, For the Fiscal Year Ended January 31, 2015.

Required

Regarding the contingency note, at what point should an accrual of a contingent liability occur? What is the effect on the financial statements of an accrual?

Decision Case 9-4 Hewlett-Packard's Contingent Liability

LO4

REAL WORLD

Following are excerpts from the notes that accompanied the financial statements of **Hewlett-Packard** for the year ended October 31, 2015.

HEWLETT PACKARD ENTERPRISE COMPANY AND SUBSIDIARIES

Note 17: Litigation and Contingencies

In re HP Securities Litigation consists of two consolidated putative class actions filed on November 26 and 30, 2012 in the United States District Court for the Northern District of California alleging, among other things, that from August 19, 2011 to November 20, 2012, the defendants violated Sections 10(b) and 20(a) of the Exchange Act by concealing material information and making false statements related to HP Inc.'s acquisition of Autonomy and the financial performance of HP Inc.'s enterprise services business. On June 9, 2015, HP Inc. entered into a settlement agreement with the lead plaintiff in the consolidated securities class action. Under the terms of the settlement, HP Inc., through its insurers, will contribute $100 million to a settlement fund that will be used to compensate persons who purchased HP Inc.'s shares during the period from August 19, 2011 through November 20, 2012. On July 17, 2015, the court granted preliminary approval to the settlement. On November 13, 2015, the court granted final approval to the settlement.

Environmental The Company's operations and products are or may in the future become subject to various federal, state, local and foreign laws and regulations concerning environmental protection, including laws addressing the discharge of pollutants into the air and water, the management hazardous substances and wastes, the clean-up of contaminated sites, the substances and materials used in the Company's products, the energy consumption of products, services and operations and the operational or financial responsibility for recycling, treatment and disposal of those products. The amount and timing of costs to comply with environmental laws are difficult to predict.

In particular, the Company may become a party to, or otherwise involved in, proceedings brought by U.S. or state environmental agencies under the Comprehensive Environmental Response, Compensation and Liability Act ("CERCLA"), known as "Superfund," or other federal, state or foreign laws and regulations addressing the clean-up of contaminated sites, and may become a party to, or otherwise involved in, proceedings brought by private parties for contribution towards clean-up costs.

Source: Hewlett Packard, Form 10-K, For the Fiscal Year Ended October 31, 2015.

Required

1. Based on the excerpt, how did the company treat the contingency on its financial statements for the year ended October 31, 2015? What criteria were likely used to lead to that treatment?
2. What was the effect on the financial statements of the company's treatment of the contingency?

Making Financial Decisions

Decision Case 9-5 Current Ratio Loan Provision

LO1 • 2

Assume that you are the controller of a small, growing sporting-goods company. The prospects for your firm in the future are quite good, but like many other firms, it has been experiencing some cash-flow difficulties because all available funds have been used to purchase inventory and to finance start-up costs associated with a new business. At the beginning of the current year, your local bank advanced a loan to your company. Included in the loan is the following provision:

> The company is obligated to pay interest payments each month for the next five years. Principal is due and must be paid at the end of Year 5. The company is further obligated to maintain a current assets to current liabilities ratio of 2 to 1 as indicated on quarterly statements to be submitted to the bank. If the company fails to meet any loan provisions, all amounts of interest and principal are due immediately upon notification by the bank.

You, as controller, have just gathered the following information as of the end of the first month of the current quarter:

(Continued)

Current liabilities:

Accounts payable	$400,000
Taxes payable	100,000
Accrued expenses	50,000
Total current liabilities	$550,000

You are concerned about the loan provision that requires a 2 to 1 ratio of current assets to current liabilities.

Required

1. Indicate what actions could be taken during the next two months to meet the loan provision. Which of the available actions should be recommended?
2. Could management take short-term actions to make the company's liquidity appear to be better? What are the long-run implications of such actions?

LO7   **Decision Case 9-6**   **Alternative Payment Options**

Kathy Clark owns a small company that makes ice machines for restaurants and food-service facilities. Kathy knows a great deal about producing ice machines but is less familiar with the best terms to extend to her customers. One customer is opening a new business and has asked Kathy to consider one of the following options that he can use to pay for his new $20,000 ice machine.

a. Term 1: 10% down, the remainder paid at the end of the year plus 8% simple interest
b. Term 2: 10% down, and $1,800 each quarter for 3 years
c. Term 3: $0 down, but $21,600 due at the end of the year

Required

Make a recommendation to Kathy. She believes that 8% is a fair return on her money at this time. Should she accept option (a), (b), or (c) or take the $20,000 cash at the time of the sale? Justify your recommendation with calculations. What factors other than the actual amount of cash received from the sale should you consider?

Ethical Decision Making

LO4   **Decision Case 9-7**   **Warranty Cost Estimate**

John Walton is an accountant for ABC Auto Dealers, a large auto dealership in a metropolitan area. ABC sells both new and used cars. New cars are sold with a five-year warranty, the cost of which is carried by the manufacturer. For several years, however, ABC has offered a two-year warranty on used cars. The cost of the warranty is an expense to ABC, and John has been asked by his boss, Mr. Sawyer, to review warranty costs and recommend the amount to accrue on the year-end financial statements.

For the past several years, ABC has recorded as warranty expense 5% of used car sales. John analyzed past repair records and found that repairs, although fluctuating somewhat from year to year, have averaged near the 5% level. John is convinced, however, that 5% is inadequate for the coming year. He bases his judgment on industry reports of increased repair costs and on the fact that several cars that were recently sold on warranty have experienced very high repair costs. John believes that the current year repair accrual will be at least 10%. He discussed the higher expense amount with Mr. Sawyer, who is the controller of ABC.

Mr. Sawyer was not happy with John's decision concerning warranty expense. He reminded John of the need to control expenses during the recent sales downturn. He also reminded John that ABC was seeking a large loan from the bank and that its loan officers might not be happy with recent operating results, especially if ABC began to accrue larger amounts for future estimated amounts such as warranties. Finally, Mr. Sawyer reminded John that most of the employees of ABC, including Mr. Sawyer, were members of the company's profit-sharing plan and would not be happy with the reduced share of profits. Mr. Sawyer thanked John for his judgment concerning warranty cost but told him that the accrual for the current year would remain at 5%.

John left the meeting with Mr. Sawyer feeling somewhat frustrated. He was convinced that his judgment concerning the warranty costs was correct. He knew that the owner of ABC would be visiting the office next week and wondered whether he should discuss the matter with him at that time. John also had met one of the loan officers from the bank several times and considered calling her to discuss his concern about the warranty expense amount on the year-end statements.

Required

Discuss the courses of action available to John. What should John do concerning his judgment of warranty costs?

Decision Case 9-8 Retainer Fees as Sales

LO4

ETHICAL DECISION MODEL

Bunch o' Balloons markets balloon arrangements to companies that want to thank clients and employees. Bunch o' Balloons has a unique style that has put it in high demand. Consequently, Bunch o' Balloons has asked clients to establish an account. Clients are asked to pay a retainer fee equal to about three months of purchases. The fee will be used to cover the cost of arrangements delivered and will be reevaluated at the end of each month. At the end of the current month, Bunch o' Balloons has $43,900 of retainer fees in its possession. The controller is eager to show this amount as sales because "it represents certain sales for the company."

Required

Use the Ethical Decision Framework in Exhibit 1-9 to complete the following requirements:
1. **Recognize an ethical dilemma:** What ethical dilemma(s) do you face?
2. **Analyze the key elements in the situation:**
   a. Who may benefit from using the second appraisal? Who may be harmed?
   b. How are they likely to benefit or be harmed?
   c. What rights or claims may be violated?
   d. What specific interests are in conflict?
   e. What are your responsibilities and obligations?
3. **List alternatives and evaluate the impact of each on those affected:** What are your options in dealing with the ethical dilemma(s) you identified in (1) above
4. **Select the best alternative:** Among the alternatives, which one would you select?

Answers

MODULE 1 Answers to Questions

1. Current liabilities are obligations which will be satisfied within one year. Current liabilities are important to determine a firm's liquidity, i.e., its ability to pay for those items due within a short time period.

2. The account Discount on Notes Payable is a balance sheet account. It should be classified as a contra liability.

3. Income tax is an item that should be accrued as a liability as of year-end. If the firm's year-end is December 31, then the amount should appear as a current liability on the balance sheet dated December 31.

MODULE 1 Answers to Apply

1. Current Ratio: Current Assets/Current Liabilities
   Cash ($10,000) + Accounts Receivable ($70,000) +
   Inventory ($20,000) = $100,000
   $100,000/$40,000 = 2.5 Current Ratio
   Quick Ratio: Quick Assets/Current Liabilities
   Cash ($10,000) + Accounts Receivable ($70,000) =
   $80,000
   $80,000/$40,000 = 2.0 Quick Ratio

2. If you pay within 15 days, you receive a 3% discount
   and must pay $4,850.*
   If you pay after 15 days, you must pay $5,000.
   $5,000 − ($5,000 × 3%) = $5,000 − $150 =
   $4,850*

MODULE 2 Answers to Questions

Increases in current liabilities will be reflected on the statement of cash flows as positive amounts because the liabilities have not been paid. Generally, the current liabilities will appear in the operating category of the cash flow statement.

MODULE 2 Answers to Apply

The amounts appearing in the cash-flow statement should be in the Operating Activities category of the statement. The amounts shown should be the *changes* in the balances of the accounts.

Accounts Payable decreased by $10,000 and should appear as a decrease in the cash-flow statement.

Taxes Payable increased by $5,000 and should appear as an increase in the cash-flow statement.

MODULE 3 Answers to Questions

1. A contingent liability involves an existing condition where the outcome of that condition is not known with certainty and is dependent on some event that will occur in the future. Contingent liabilities are accounted for differently than contingent assets because of the principle of conservatism. Generally, contingent gains or contingent assets are not reported until the gain actually occurs. That is, contingent liabilities may be accrued, but contingent assets are not accrued.

2. The lawsuit should be described in as much detail as possible in the notes to the financial statements. The nature of the lawsuit and the expected resolution should be described. If the dollar amount can be estimated, it should be disclosed. If it cannot be estimated, it may be possible to determine and disclose a range of values that represents the potential loss to the firm.

MODULE 3 Answers to Apply

A contingent liability must be recorded as a liability on the balance sheet if the likelihood of loss is probable, and the amount can be reasonably estimated. It must be disclosed in the footnotes if the likelihood of loss is at least reasonably possible.

A contingent asset is treated more conservatively. It normally is not recorded as an asset on the balance sheet until the asset is received.

MODULE 4 Answers to Questions

1. A future value represents the amount that will be accumulated at a future time if a known amount is invested for a given time at a given interest rate. The present value represents the value today of an amount to be received or paid at a future time. You can determine whether or not to calculate a present value or future value based on the timing of the known and unknown quantities.

2. The word annuity means a series of payments of the same amount. The present value of an annuity could be calculated as a series of single amounts, but not with a single calculation. Tables have been developed to calculate the present value of an annuity based on one calculation.

3. The interest rate of the loan could be calculated by dividing the total dollar amount of the loan by the dollar amount of the monthly payments. The result is a number that represents an interest factor or table value in the table for the present value of an annuity. Find the table value that corresponds to the number of years of the loan, and then read across that row to find the interest rate.

MODULE 4 Answers to Apply

1. **FV = $1,000(table factor)**
   = $1,000(1.61051)   using Table 9-1
   = $1,611 (rounded to the nearest dollar)   where i = 10%, n = 5

2. **FV = $1,000(table factor)**
   = $1,000(6.10510)   using Table 9-3
   = $6,105 (rounded to the nearest dollar)   where i = 10%, n = 5

3. **PV = $1,000(table factor)**
   = $1,000(0.62092)   using Table 9-2
   = $621 (rounded to the nearest dollar)   where i = 10%, n = 5

4. **PV = $1,000(table factor)**
   = $1,000(3.79076)   using Table 9-4
   = $3,791 (rounded to the nearest dollar)   where i = 10%, n= 5

Answers to Connect to the Real World

9-1 (p. 404)

The balance sheet indicates the following are included as current liabilities:

Accounts payable

Insurance reserves
Stored value card liability

Accounts Payable increased from $533.7 million to $684.2 million during 2014 to 2015.

Answers to Key Terms Quiz

1	Current liability
3	Accounts payable
8	Notes payable
4	Discount on notes payable
6	Current maturities of long-term debt
7	Accrued liability
9	Contingent liability
11	Estimated liability
12	Contingent asset

14	Time value of money
10	Simple interest
13	Compound interest
15	Future value of a single amount
17	Present value of a single amount
5	Annuity
16	Future value of an annuity
2	Present value of an annuity

Long-Term Liabilities

MODULES	LEARNING OBJECTIVES	WHY IS THIS CHAPTER IMPORTANT?
1 **Long-Term Liabilities Including Bonds Payable**	**LO1** Identify the components of the Long-Term Liability category of the balance sheet. **LO2** Define the important characteristics of bonds payable. **LO3** Determine the issue price of a bond using compound interest techniques. **LO4** Show that you understand the effect on the balance sheet of the issuance of bonds.	• You need to know how long-term liabilities appear on the balance sheet and how a company accounts for the issuance of bonds payable. (See pp. 456–462.)
2 **Bond Amortization and Bond Retirement**	**LO5** Find the amortization of premium or discount using the effective interest method. **LO6** Find the gain or loss on retirement of bonds.	• You need to understand how a company amortizes the premium or discount on bonds payable and how it accounts for the retirement of bonds. (See pp. 463–468.)
3 **Liability for Leases**	**LO7** Determine whether a lease agreement must be reported as a liability on the balance sheet.	• You need to understand the importance of financial arrangements such as leases as a means of financing a company. (See pp. 469–473.)
4 **Analysis of Long-Term Liabilities and Cash Flow Issues**	**LO8** Explain how investors use ratios to evaluate long-term liabilities. **LO9** Explain the effects that transactions involving long-term liabilities have on the statement of cash flows.	• You need to know how investors use ratios to evaluate long-term liabilities and how long-term liabilities affect a company's cash flows. (See pp. 473–477.)
5 **Deferred Tax (Appendix)**	**LO10** Explain deferred taxes and calculate the deferred tax liability.	• You need to be able to explain the liability for deferred taxes. (Appendix) (See pp. 478–480.)

COCA-COLA

Coca-Cola® is truly a global corporation with more than 500 brands in almost 200 countries. While it began many years ago in the United States, now more than 70% of **The Coca-Cola Company**'s income comes from business outside the United States.

To meet long-term growth objectives, Coca-Cola must make significant investments to support its products. The process also involves investment to develop new global brands and to acquire local or global brands when appropriate. In addition, the company makes significant marketing investments to encourage consumer loyalty. Coca-Cola has developed relationships with many sports organizations, including the **NBA** and **NASCAR**, to enhance consumer awareness and promote sales of its products. Outside the United States, there is a strong push to sell in many other markets, including India, Brazil, Africa, and Europe.

To expand profitably, Coca-Cola requires more money than it generates in profits. Therefore, it uses a common financing tool: *long-term debt*. The company monitors interest rate conditions carefully and in 2015 retired nearly $38 billion in long-term debt and replaced it with $40 billion in other debt. Because it is a global company, Coca-Cola has access to key financial markets around the world, which allows it to borrow at the lowest possible rates. While most of its loans are in U.S. dollars, management continually adjusts the composition of the debt to accommodate shifting interest rates and currency exchange rates to minimize the overall cost.

The accompanying balance sheet presents the Liabilities and Shareowners' Equity portion of the balance sheet for The Coca-Cola Company and its subsidiaries.

The Coca-Cola Company and Subsidiaries Consolidated Balance Sheets		
December 31,	**2015**	**2014**
LIABILITIES AND EQUITY		
CURRENT LIABILITIES		
Accounts payable and accrued expenses	$ 9,660	$ 9,234
Loans and notes payable	13,129	19,130
Current maturities of long-term debt	2,677	3,552
Accrued income taxes	331	400
Liabilities held for sale	1,133	58
TOTAL CURRENT LIABILITIES	26,930	32,374
LONG-TERM DEBT	28,407	19,063
OTHER LIABILITIES	4,301	4,389
DEFERRED INCOME TAXES	4,691	5,636
THE COCA-COLA COMPANY SHAREOWNERS' EQUITY		
Common stock, $0.25 par value; Authorized—11,200 shares; Issued—7,040 and 7,040 shares, respectively	1,760	1,760
Capital surplus	14,016	13,154
Reinvested earnings	65,018	63,408
Accumulated other comprehensive income (loss)	(10,174)	(5,777)
Treasury stock, at cost—2,716 and 2,674 shares, respectively	(45,066)	(42,225)
EQUITY ATTRIBUTABLE TO SHAREOWNERS OF THE COCA-COLA COMPANY	25,554	30,320
EQUITY ATTRIBUTABLE TO NONCONTROLLING INTERESTS	210	241
TOTAL EQUITY	25,764	30,561
TOTAL LIABILITIES AND EQUITY	$ 90,093	$ 92,023

Source: The Coca-Cola Company, Form 10-K, For the Fiscal Year Ended December 31, 2015.

MODULE 1 LONG-TERM LIABILITIES INCLUDING BONDS PAYABLE

LO1 Identify the components of the Long-Term Liability category of the balance sheet.

Long-term liability
An obligation that will not be satisfied within one year or the current operating cycle.

In general, **long-term liabilities** are obligations that will not be satisfied within one year. Essentially, all liabilities that are not classified as current liabilities are classified as long term. We will concentrate on the long-term liabilities of bonds or notes, leases, and deferred taxes. For example, the Noncurrent Liabilities section of **PepsiCo, Inc.**'s balance sheet is highlighted in Exhibit 10-1. PepsiCo has acquired financing through a combination of long-term debt, stock issuance, and internal growth or retained earnings. Exhibit 10-1 indicates that long-term debt is one portion of the **Long-Term Liability** category of the balance sheet. But the balance sheet also reveals two other items that must be considered part of the Long-Term Liability category: deferred income taxes and other liabilities. We will concentrate on these long-term liabilities:

- Bonds or notes
- Leases
- Deferred taxes

EXHIBIT 10-1 PepsiCo's Balance Sheet

PepsiCo, Inc. and Subsidiaries December 26, 2015 and December 27, 2014		
	2015	**2014**
LIABILITIES AND EQUITY		
Current Liabilities		
Short-term obligations	$ 4,071	$ 5,076
Accounts payable and other current liabilities	13,507	13,016
Total Current Liabilities	17,578	18,092
Long-Term Debt Obligations	29,213	23,821
Other Liabilities	5,887	5,744
Deferred Income Taxes	4,959	5,304
Total Liabilities	57,637	52,961
Commitments and contingencies		
Preferred Stock, no par value	41	41
Repurchased Preferred Stock	(186)	(181)
PepsiCo Common Shareholders' Equity		
Common stock, par value 1⅔ ¢ per share (authorized 3,600 shares, issued, net of repurchased common stock at par value: 1,448 and 1,488 shares, respectively)	24	25
Capital in excess of par value	4,076	4,115
Retained earnings	50,472	49,092
Accumulated other comprehensive loss	(13,319)	(10,669)
Repurchased common stock, in excess of par value (418 and 378 shares, respectively)	(29,185)	(24,985)
Total PepsiCo Common Shareholders' Equity	12,068	17,578
Noncontrolling interests	107	110
Total Equity	12,030	17,548
Total Liabilities and Equity	$ 69,667	$ 70,509

Source: PepsiCo, Inc., Form 10-K, For the Fiscal Year Ended December 26, 2015.

Bonds Payable: Characteristics

A bond is a security or financial instrument that allows firms to borrow money and repay the loan over a long period of time. The bonds are sold, or *issued*, to investors who want a return on their investment. The *borrower* (issuing firm) promises to pay interest on specified dates, usually annually or semiannually. The borrower also promises to repay the principal on a specified date, the *due date* or maturity date.

A bond certificate, illustrated in Exhibit 10-2, is issued at the time of purchase and indicates the terms of the bond. Unlike the bond in the exhibit, bonds are issued usually in denominations of $1,000. The denomination of the bond is usually referred to as the **face value** or par value. This is the amount that the firm must pay at the maturity date of the bond.

Firms issue bonds in very large amounts, often in millions in a single issue. After bonds are issued, they may be traded on a bond exchange in the same way that stocks are sold on the stock exchanges. Therefore, bonds are not always held until maturity by the initial investor, but may change hands several times before their eventual due date. Because bond maturities are as long as 30 years, the market for bonds already issued is a critical factor in a company's ability to raise money. Investors in bonds may want to sell them if interest rates paid by competing investments become more attractive or if the issuer becomes less creditworthy. Buyers of these bonds may be betting that interest rates will reverse course or that the company will get back on its feet.

Following are some important features that often appear in the bond certificate.

LO2 Define the important characteristics of bonds payable.

Face value
The principal amount of the bond as stated on the bond certificate.
Alternate term: Par value.

How Will I Use ACCOUNTING?

If you are a financial advisor or bond fund manager, you will use accounting every day to analyze the creditworthiness, price, and yield of bonds. The most successful managers determine risk on a continual basis using their accounting and finance expertise.

Risk analysis is an art, not a science.

EXHIBIT 10-2 Bond Certificate

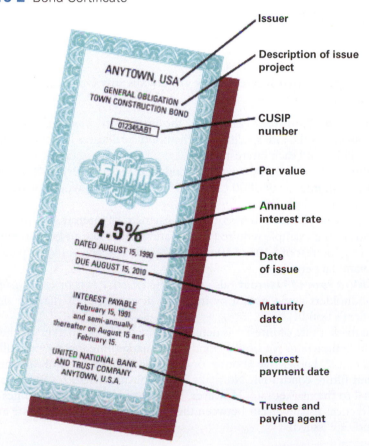

Debenture bonds
Bonds that are not backed by specific collateral.

Serial bonds
Bonds that do not all have the same due date; a portion of the bonds comes due each time period.

Callable bonds
Bonds that may be redeemed or retired before their specified due date.

Collateral The bond certificate should indicate the *collateral* of the loan. Collateral represents the assets that back the bonds in case the issuer cannot make the interest and principal payments and must default on the loan. **Debenture bonds** are not backed by specific collateral of the issuing company. Rather, the investor must examine the general creditworthiness of the issuer. If a bond is a *secured bond*, the certificate indicates specific assets that serve as collateral in case of default.

Due Date The bond certificate specifies the date that the bond principal must be repaid. Normally, bonds are *term bonds*, meaning that the entire principal amount is due on a single date. Alternatively, bonds may be issued as **serial bonds**, meaning that not all of the principal is due on the same date. For example, a firm may issue serial bonds that have a portion of the principal due each year for the next ten years. Issuing firms may prefer serial bonds because a firm does not need to accumulate the entire amount for principal repayment at one time.

Other Features Some bonds are issued as convertible or callable bonds. *Convertible bonds* can be converted into common stock at a future time. This feature allows the investor to buy a security that pays a fixed interest rate but that can be converted at a future date into an equity security (stock) if the issuing firm is growing and profitable. The conversion feature is also advantageous to the issuing firm because convertible bonds normally carry a lower rate of interest.

Callable bonds may be retired before their specified due date. *Callable* generally refers to the issuer's right to retire the bonds. If the buyer or investor has the right to retire the bonds, they are referred to as *redeemable bonds*. Usually, callable bonds stipulate the price to be paid at redemption; this price is referred to as the *redemption price* or the *reacquisition price*.

Issuance of Bonds

LO3 Determine the issue price of a bond using compound interest techniques.

Face rate of interest
The rate of interest on the bond certificate.

Alternate term: Stated rate, nominal rate, contract rate, coupon rate.

Market rate of interest
The rate that investors could obtain by investing in other bonds that are similar to the issuing firm's bonds.

Alternate term: Effective rate, bond yield.

> **STUDY TIP**
>
> Calculating the issue price of a bond always involves a calculation of the present value of the cash flows.

Factors Affecting Bond Price

With bonds payable, two interest rates are always involved: the face rate and the market rate.

1. The **face rate of interest** (also called the *stated rate, nominal rate, contract rate,* or *coupon rate)* is the rate specified on the bond certificate. It is the amount of interest that will be paid each interest period.
   - For example, if $10,000 worth of bonds was issued with an 8% *annual* face rate of interest, interest of $800 ($10,000 $\times$ 8% $\times$ 1 year) would be paid at the end of each annual period.
   - Alternatively, bonds often require the payment of interest semiannually. If the bonds in the example required the 8% annual face rate to be paid *semiannually* (at 4%), interest of $400 ($10,000 $\times$ 8% $\times$ 1/2 year) would be paid each semiannual period.

2. The **market rate of interest** (also called the *effective rate* or *bond yield*) is the rate that bondholders could obtain by investing in other bonds that are similar to the issuing firm's bonds.
   - The market rate of interest is determined by the bond market on the basis of many transactions for similar bonds. The market rate incorporates all of the "market's" knowledge about economic conditions and all of its expectations about future conditions. Normally, issuing firms try to set a face rate that is equal to the market rate. However, because the market rate changes daily, small differences usually occur between the face rate and the market rate at the time bonds are issued.

In addition to the number of interest payments and the maturity length of the bond, both the face rate and the market rate of interest must be known to calculate the issue price of a bond. The **bond issue price** equals the *present value* of the two types of cash flows that the bond will produce for the investor:

1. Interest receipts
2. Repayment of principal (face value)

The interest receipts constitute an annuity of payments each interest period over the life of the bonds. The repayment of principal (face value) is a one-time receipt that occurs at the end of the term of the bonds. The present value of the interest receipts (using Table 9-4 on page 426) plus the present value of the principal amount (using Table 9-2 on page 424) equals the issue price of the bond.

Bond issue price
The present value of the annuity of interest payments plus the present value of the principal.

EXAMPLE 10-1 Calculating Bond Issuance at a Discount

Suppose that on January 1, 2017, Discount Firm wants to issue bonds with a face value of $10,000. The face, or coupon, rate of interest has been set at 8%. The bonds will pay interest annually, and the principal amount is due in four years. Also, suppose that the market rate of interest for other similar bonds is currently 10%. Because the market rate of interest exceeds the coupon rate, investors will not be willing to pay $10,000. We want to calculate the amount that will be obtained from the issuance of Discount Firm's bonds.

Discount's bond will produce two sets of cash flows for the investor:

1. An annual interest payment of $800 ($10,000 × 8%) per year for four years.
2. Repayment of the principal of $10,000 at the end of the fourth year.

To calculate the issue price, we must calculate the present value of the two sets of cash flows. A time diagram portrays the cash flows as follows:

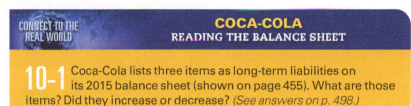

CONNECT TO THE REAL WORLD

COCA-COLA
READING THE BALANCE SHEET

10-1 Coca-Cola lists three items as long-term liabilities on its 2015 balance sheet (shown on page 455). What are those items? Did they increase or decrease? *(See answers on p. 498.)*

We can calculate the issue price by using the compound interest tables found in Chapter 9, as follows:

$800 × 3.16987 (factor from Table 9-4 for 4 periods, 10%)	$2,536
$10,000 × 0.68301 (factor from Table 9-2 for 4 periods, 10%)	6,830
Issue price	$9,366

The factors used to calculate the present value represent four periods and 10% interest.

> The issue price of a bond is always calculated using the market rate of interest. The face rate of interest determines the amount of the interest payments, but the market rate determines the present value of the payments and the present value of the principal (and therefore the issue price).

The example of Discount Firm reveals that the bonds with a $10,000 face value amount would be issued for $9,366. The bond markets and the financial press often state the issue price as a percentage of the face amount. The percentage for Discount's bonds can be calculated as ($9,366/$10,000) × 100, or 93.66%.

EXHIBIT 10-3 Listing of Bonds on the Bond Market

Bonds	Cur Yld	Vol	Close	Net Chg
IBM 6³/₈ 27	6.5	280	98³/₄	−¼
IBM 7¼ 28	7.1	68	101½	+¼

Exhibit 10-3 illustrates how bonds are actually listed in the reporting of the bond markets. The exhibit lists two types of **IBM** bonds that were traded on a particular day. The portion immediately after the company name (e.g., 6³/₈ 27) indicates that the face rate of interest is 6³/₈% and the due date of the bonds is the year 2027. The next column, (e.g., 6.5) indicates that the bond investor who purchased the bonds on that day will receive a yield of 6.5%. The column labeled "Vol" indicates the number of bonds, in thousands that were bought and sold during the day. The column labeled "Close" indicates the market price of the bonds at the end of the day. For example, the first issue of IBM bonds closed at 98³/₄%, which means that the price was 98³/₄% of the face value of the bonds. These bonds are trading at a discount because the face rate (6³/₈%) is less than the market rate of 6.5%. The bonds in the second issue (7¼%) have a face rate of 7¼%; will become due in the year 2028; and closed at 101½, or at a premium. The Net Chg column indicates the change in the bond price that occurred for the day's trading.

Premium or Discount on Bonds

LO4 Show that you understand the effect on the balance sheet of the issuance of bonds.

Premium
The excess of the issue price over the face value of the bonds.

Discount
The excess of the face value of bonds over the issue price.

Premium or **discount** represents the difference between the face value and the issue price of a bond. The relationship is stated as follows:

$$\text{Premium} = \text{Issue Price} - \text{Face Value}$$
$$\text{Discount} = \text{Face Value} - \text{Issue Price}$$

In other words, when issue price exceeds face value, the bonds have sold at a premium and when the face value exceeds the issue price, the bonds have sold at a discount.

We will continue with the Discount Firm in Example 10-1 to illustrate the accounting for bonds sold at a discount. Discount Firm's bonds sold at a discount calculated as follows:

$$\text{Discount} = \$10,000 - \$9,366$$
$$= \$634$$

Discount Firm would identify and analyze the effect of the issuance of the bonds as follows:

Identify and Analyze	
ACTIVITY:	Financing
ACCOUNTS:	Cash Increase Discount on Bonds Payable Increase Bonds Payable Increase
STATEMENT[S]:	Balance Sheet

Balance Sheet					Income Statement			
ASSETS	=	LIABILITIES	+	STOCKHOLDERS' EQUITY	REVENUES	−	EXPENSES	= NET INCOME
Cash 9,366		Bonds Payable 10,000 Discount on Bonds Payable* (634)						

*The Discount on Bonds Payable account has increased. It is shown as a decrease in the equation above because it is a contra account and causes total liabilities to decrease.

The Discount on Bonds Payable account is shown as a contra liability on the balance sheet as a deduction from Bonds Payable. If Discount Firm prepared a balance sheet immediately after the bond issuance, the following would appear in the Long-Term Liabilities category of the balance sheet:

Long-term liabilities:
Bonds payable	$10,000
Discount on bonds payable	634
	$ 9,366

Now we will examine the opposite situation, when the face rate exceeds the market rate.

EXAMPLE 10-2 Calculating Bond Issuance at a Premium

Suppose that on January 1, 2017, Premium Firm wants to issue the same bonds as in Example 10-1: $10,000 face value bonds with an 8% face rate of interest and with interest paid annually each year for four years. Assume, however, that the market rate of interest is 6% for similar bonds. The issue price is calculated as the present value of the annuity of interest payments plus the present value of the principal at the market rate of interest. The calculations are as follows:

$800 × 3.46511 (factor from Table 9-4 for 4 periods, 6%)	$ 2,772
$10,000 × 0.79209 (factor from Table 9-2 for 4 periods, 6%)	7,921
Issue price	$10,693

We have calculated that the bonds would be issued for $10,693. The amount of the premium is calculated as follows:

$$\text{Premium} = \$10,693 - \$10,000$$
$$= \$693$$

Premium Firm could identify and analyze the effect of the issuance of the bonds as follows:

Identify and Analyze	ACTIVITY: **Financing**
	ACCOUNTS: **Cash** Increase **Premium on Bonds Payable** Increase **Bonds Payable** Increase
	STATEMENT[S]: **Balance Sheet**

Balance Sheet				Income Statement		
ASSETS	=	LIABILITIES	+	STOCKHOLDERS' EQUITY	REVENUES – EXPENSES	= NET INCOME
Cash 10,693		Bonds Payable 10,000				
		Premium on				
		Bonds Payable 693				

The account Premium on Bonds Payable is an addition to the Bonds Payable account. If Premium Firm presented a balance sheet immediately after the bond issuance, the Long-Term Liabilities category of the balance sheet would appear as follows:

Long-term liabilities:
Bonds payable	$10,000
Premium on bonds payable	693
	$10,693

Note two important points from Discount Firm in Example 10-1 and Premium Firm in Example 10-2:

STUDY TIP

When interest rates increase, present values decrease. This is called an inverse relationship.

- **You should be able to determine whether a bond will sell at a premium or a discount by the relationship that exists between the face rate and the market rate of interest.** *Premium* and *discount* do not mean "good" and "bad," respectively. Premium or discount arises solely because of the difference that exists between the face rate and the market rate of interest for a bond issue. The same relationship always exists, so the following statements hold true:

  > **If Market Rate = Face Rate, THEN bonds are issued at face value amount.**
  > **If Market Rate > Face Rate, THEN bonds are issued at a discount.**
  > **If Market Rate < Face Rate, THEN bonds are issued at a premium.**

- **The relationship between interest rates and bond prices is always inverse.** The bonds of the two firms in Examples 10-1 and 10-2 are identical in all respects except for the market rate of interest. When the market rate was 10%, the bond issue price was $9,366 (Example 10-1). When the market rate was 6%, the bond issue price increased to $10,693 (Example 10-2). These examples illustrate that as interest rates decrease, prices on the bond markets increase and that as interest rates increase, bond prices decrease.

MODULE 1 TEST YOURSELF

Review		
	LO1 Identify the components of the Long-Term Liability category of the balance sheet.	• Generally, long-term liabilities are obligations of a company that will not be satisfied within one year. On the balance sheet, they are listed after current liabilities.
	LO2 Define the important characteristics of bonds payable.	• Important characteristics of bonds payable include par value, due date, interest rate, an indication of whether the bonds are convertible or callable, and any property collateralizing the bonds.
	LO3 Determine the issue price of a bond using compound interest techniques.	• Bonds are issued at a price that reflects the market rate of interest on the day the bond is purchased. The actual issue price of a bond represents the present value of all future cash flows related to the bond.
	LO4 Show that you understand the effect on the balance sheet of the issuance of bonds.	• Bonds are recorded on the balance sheet at an amount that takes into account the premium or discount associated with bonds on the date they are issued.

Question	
	1. Which interest rate, the face rate or the market rate, should be used when calculating the issue price of a bond? Why?
	2. What is the tax advantage that companies experience when bonds are issued instead of stock?
	3. Does the issuance of bonds at a premium indicate that the face rate is higher or lower than the market rate of interest?

Apply

1. A bond payable is dated January 1, 2017, and is issued on that date. The face value of the bond is $100,000, and the face rate of interest is 8%. The bond pays interest semiannually. The bond will mature in five years.

   a. What will be the issue price of the bond if the market rate of interest is 6% at the time of issuance?

   b. What will be the issue price of the bond if the market rate of interest is 8% at the time of issuance?

   c. What will be the issue price of the bond if the market rate of interest is 10% at the time of issuance?

2. A bond with a face value of $10,000 is issued at a discount of $800 on January 1, 2017. The face rate of interest on the bond is 7%.

   a. Was the market rate at the time of issuance greater than 7% or less than 7%?

   b. If a balance sheet is presented on January 1, 2017, how will the bonds appear on the balance sheet?

   c. If a balance sheet is presented on December 31, 2017, will the amount for the bonds be higher or lower than on January 1, 2017?

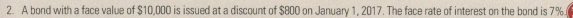

Answers are located at the end of the chapter.

MODULE 2 BOND AMORTIZATION AND BOND RETIREMENT

The amount of interest expense that should be reflected on a firm's income statement for bonds payable is the true, or effective, interest. The effective interest should reflect the face rate of interest as well as interest that results from issuing the bond at a premium or discount. To reflect that interest component, the amount initially recorded in the Premium on Bonds Payable or the Discount on Bonds Payable account must be amortized, or spread over the life of the bond.

Amortization refers to the process of transferring an amount from the discount or premium account to interest expense each time period to adjust interest expense. One commonly used method of amortization is the effective interest method.

To illustrate amortization of a discount, the issue price of the bond in Example 10-1 could be calculated as $9,366, resulting in a contra-liability balance of $634 in the Discount on Bonds Payable account. But what does the initial balance of the Discount account really represent? The discount should be thought of as additional interest that Discount Firm must pay over and above the 8% face rate. Remember that Discount received only $9,366 but must repay the full principal of $10,000 at the bond due date. For that reason, the $634 discount is an additional interest cost that must be reflected as interest expense by the process of amortization.

Effective Interest Method: Impact on Expense

The **effective interest method of amortization** amortizes discount or premium in a manner that produces a constant effective interest rate from period to period, but the dollar amount of interest expense will vary from period to period. The interest rate is referred to as the *effective interest rate* and is equal to the market rate of interest at the time the bonds are issued. The effective interest rate is represented by the following:

Effective Rate = Annual Interest Expense/Carrying Value

The **carrying value** of bonds is represented by the following:

Carrying Value = Face Value − Unamortized Discount

The carrying value of the bonds for Discount Firm in Example 10-1 as of the date of issuance of January 1, 2017, could be calculated as follows:

$10,000 − $634 = $9,366

In those situations in which there is a premium instead of a discount, carrying value is represented by the following:

Carrying Value = Face Value + Unamortized Premium

The carrying value of the bonds for Premium Firm in Example 10-2 as of the date of issuance of January 1, 2017, could be calculated as follows:

$10,000 + $693 = $10,693

As illustrated in Exhibit 10-4, the effective interest method of amortization for Discount Firm in Example 10-1 is based on several important concepts. The relationships can be stated in equation form as follows:

Cash Interest (in Column 1) = Bond Face Value × Face Rate
Interest Expense (in Column 2) = Carrying Value × Effective Rate
Discount Amortized (in Column 3) = Interest Expense − Cash Interest

LO5 Find the amortization of premium or discount using the effective interest method.

Effective interest method of amortization
The process of transferring a portion of the premium or discount to interest expense; this method results in a constant effective interest rate.

Alternate term: Interest method.

Carrying value
The face value of a bond plus the amount of unamortized premium or minus the amount of unamortized discount.

Alternate term: Book value.

EXHIBIT 10-4 Discount Amortization: Effective Interest Method of Amortization

Date	Column 1 Cash Interest	Column 2 Interest Expense	Column 3 Discount Amortized	Column 4 Carrying Value
	8%	10%	Col. 2 − Col. 1	
1/1/2017	—	—	—	$ 9,366
12/31/2017	$800	$937	$137	9,503
12/31/2018	800	950	150	9,653
12/31/2019	800	965	165	9,818
12/31/2020	800	982	182	10,000

Column 1 indicates that the cash interest to be paid is $800 ($10,000 × 8%). Column 2 indicates the annual interest expense at the effective rate of interest. The interest expense is calculated by multiplying the carrying value as of the beginning of the period by the market rate of interest. In 2017, the interest expense is $937 ($9,366 × 10%). Note that the amount of interest expense changes each year because the carrying value changes as discount is amortized. The amount of discount amortized each year in Column 3 is the difference between the cash interest in Column 1 and the interest expense in Column 2. Also, note that the amount of discount amortized changes in each of the four years. Finally, the carrying value in Column 4 is the previous year's carrying value plus the discount amortized in Column 3. When bonds are issued at a discount, the carrying value starts at an amount less than face value and increases each period until it reaches the face value amount.

EXAMPLE 10-3   Recording Amortization of Discount

Exhibit 10-4 is the basis for determining the effect of amortization on the firm's financial statements. The effect of the payment of interest and amortization of discount is as follows:

Identify and Analyze	**ACTIVITY:** Operating **ACCOUNTS:** Interest Expense Increase **Discount on Bonds Payable** Decrease **Cash** Decrease **STATEMENT[S]:** Balance Sheet and Income Statement

Balance Sheet					Income Statement			
ASSETS	=	LIABILITIES	+	STOCKHOLDERS' EQUITY	REVENUES −	EXPENSES	=	NET INCOME
Cash (800)		Discount on Bonds Payable* 137		(937)		Interest Expense 937		(937)

*The Discount on Bonds Payable account has decreased. It is shown as an increase in the equation above because it is a contra account and causes total liabilities to increase.

The balance of the Discount on Bonds Payable account as of December 31, 2017, would be calculated as follows:

Beginning balance, January 1, 2017	$634
Amount amortized	137
Ending balance, December 31, 2017	$497

In Example 10-3, the December 31, 2017, balance represents the amount *unamortized*, or the amount that will be amortized in future time periods. On the balance sheet presented as of December 31, 2017, the unamortized portion of the discount appears as the balance of the Discount on Bonds Payable account as follows:

Long-term liabilities	
Bonds payable	$10,000
Discount on bonds payable	497
	$ 9,503

The process of amortization would continue for four years, until the balance of the Discount on Bonds Payable account has been reduced to zero. By the end of 2020, all of the balance of the Discount on Bonds Payable account will have been transferred to the Interest Expense account and represents an increase in interest expense each period.

The amortization of a premium has an impact opposite that of the amortization of a discount. In Example 10-2, recall that on January 1, 2017, Premium Firm issued $10,000 face value bonds with a face rate of interest of 8%. At the time the bonds were issued, the market rate was 6%, resulting in an issue price of $10,693 and a balance in the Premium on Bonds Payable account of $693.

The amortization table in Exhibit 10-5 illustrates effective interest amortization of the bond premium for Premium Firm. As the exhibit illustrates, the following relationships still hold true:

> **Cash Interest (in Column 1) = Bond Face Value × Face Rate**
> **Interest Expense (in Column 2) = Carrying Value × Effective Rate**

Column 1 indicates that the cash interest to be paid is $800 ($10,000 × 8%). Column 2 indicates the annual interest expense at the effective rate. In 2017, the interest expense is $642 ($10,693 × 6%). Note, however, two differences between Exhibits 10-4 and 10-5. In the amortization of a premium, the cash interest in Column 1 exceeds the interest expense in Column 2. Therefore, the premium amortized is defined as follows:

> **Premium Amortized (in Column 3) = Cash Interest − Interest Expense**

Also, note that the carrying value in Column 4 starts at an amount higher than the face value of $10,000 ($10,693) and is amortized downward until it reaches face value. Therefore, the carrying value at the end of each year is the carrying value at the beginning of the period minus the premium amortized for that year. For example, the carrying value in Exhibit 10-5 at the end of 2017 ($10,535) was calculated by subtracting the premium amortized for 2017 ($158 in Column 3) from the carrying value at the beginning of 2017 ($10,693).

STUDY TIP

Amortization of a discount increases interest expense. Amortization of a premium reduces interest expense.

EXHIBIT 10-5 Premium Amortization: Effective Interest Method of Amortization

Date	Column 1 Cash Interest	Column 2 Interest Expense	Column 3 Premium Amortized	Column 4 Carrying Value
	8%	6%	Col. 1 − Col. 2	
1/1/2017	—	—	—	$10,693
12/31/2017	$800	$642	$158	10,535
12/31/2018	800	632	168	10,367
12/31/2019	800	622	178	10,189
12/31/2020	800	611	189	10,000

EXAMPLE 10-4 Recording Amortization of a Premium

Exhibit 10-5 is the basis for determining the effect of amortization of a premium on the firm's financial statements. Premium Firm could identify and analyze the effect of the payment of interest and amortization of premium as follows:

Identify and Analyze	ACTIVITY: Operating ACCOUNTS: Interest Expense Increase Premium on Bonds Payable Decrease Cash Decrease STATEMENT[S]: Balance Sheet and Income Statement

Balance Sheet				Income Statement			
ASSETS	=	LIABILITIES	+	STOCKHOLDERS' EQUITY	REVENUES	− EXPENSES	= NET INCOME
Cash (800)		Premium on Bonds Payable (158)		(642)		Interest Expense 642	(642)

The balance of the Premium on Bonds Payable account as of December 31, 2017, would be calculated as follows:

Beginning balance, January 1, 2017	$693
Amount amortized	158
Ending balance, December 31, 2017	$535

In Example 10-4, the December 31, 2017, balance represents the amount *unamortized*, or the amount that will be amortized in future time periods. On the balance sheet presented as of December 31, 2017, the unamortized portion of the premium appears as the balance of the Premium on Bonds Payable account as follows:

Long-term liabilities:	
Bonds payable	$10,000
Premium on bonds payable	535
	$10,535

The process of amortization would continue for four years, until the balance of the Premium on Bonds Payable account has been reduced to zero. By the end of 2020, all of the balance of the Premium on Bonds Payable account will have been transferred to the Interest Expense account and represents a reduction of interest expense each period.

Redemption of Bonds

LO6 Find the gain or loss on retirement of bonds.

The term *redemption* refers to retirement of bonds by repayment of the principal. When bonds are retired on their due date, the accounting entry is not difficult. Refer again to Discount Firm from Examples 10-1 and 10-3. If Discount Firm retires its bonds on the due date of December 31, 2020, it must repay the principal of $10,000 and Cash is reduced by $10,000. No gain or loss is incurred because the carrying value of the bond at that point is $10,000.

Retired Early at a Gain or a Loss

A firm may want to retire bonds before their due date for several reasons. A firm may simply have excess cash and determine that the best use of those funds is to repay outstanding bond obligations. Bonds also may be retired early because of changing interest rate conditions. If interest rates in the economy decline, firms may find it advantageous to retire bonds that have been issued at higher rates. Of course, what is advantageous to the issuer is not necessarily so for the investor. Early retirement of callable bonds is always a possibility that must be anticipated. Large institutional investors expect such a development and merely reinvest the money elsewhere. Many individual investors are more seriously inconvenienced when a bond issue is called.

Bond terms generally specify that if bonds are retired before their due date, they are not retired at the face value amount, but at a call price or redemption price indicated on the bond certificate. Also, the amount of unamortized premium or discount on the bonds must be considered when bonds are retired early. The retirement results in a **gain or loss on redemption** that must be calculated as follows:

Gain or loss on redemption
The difference between the carrying value and the redemption price at the time bonds are redeemed.

$$\text{Gain} = \text{Carrying Value} - \text{Redemption Price}$$
$$\text{Loss} = \text{Redemption Price} - \text{Carrying Value}$$

If the carrying value is higher than the redemption price, the issuing firm must record a gain. If the carrying value is lower than the redemption price, the issuing firm must record a loss.

EXAMPLE 10-5 Calculating a Gain on Bond Redemption

Refer to Premium Firm from Example 10-4. Assume that on December 31, 2017, Premium Firm wants to retire its bonds due in 2020. Assume, as in the previous section, that the bonds were issued at a premium of $692 at the beginning of 2017. Premium Firm has used the effective interest method of amortization and has recorded the interest and amortization entries for the year. (See page 466.) This has resulted in a balance of $535 in the Premium on Bonds Payable account as of December 31, 2017. Also, assume that Premium Firm's bond certificates indicate that the bonds may be retired early at a call price of 102 (meaning 102% of face value). Thus, the redemption price is 102% of $10,000, or $10,200.

Premium Firm's retirement of bonds would result in a gain. The gain can be calculated using two steps:

1. **Calculate the carrying value of the bonds as of the date they are retired.** The carrying value of Premium Firm's bonds at that date is calculated as follows:

$$\text{Carrying Value} = \text{Face Value} + \text{Unamortized Premium}$$
$$= \$10,000 + \$535$$
$$= \$10,535$$

Note that the carrying value calculated is the same amount indicated for December 31, 2017, in Column 4 of the effective interest amortization table of Exhibit 10-5.

2. **Calculate the gain:**

$$\text{Gain} = \text{Carrying Value} - \text{Redemption Price}$$
$$= \$10,535 - (\$10,000 \times 1.02)$$
$$= \$10,535 - \$10,200$$
$$= \$335$$

When bonds are retired, the balance of the Bonds Payable account and the remaining balance of the Premium on Bonds Payable account must be eliminated from the balance sheet.

EXAMPLE 10-6 Calculating a Loss on Bond Redemption

Refer to Premium Firm from Example 10-4. Assume that Premium Firm retires bonds at December 31, 2017, as in the previous section. However, assume that the call price for the bonds is 107 (or 107% of face value).

Again, the calculations can be performed in two steps:

1. **Calculate the carrying value:**

$$\text{Carrying Value} = \text{Face Value} + \text{Unamortized Premium}$$
$$= \$10,000 + \$535$$
$$= \$10,535$$

2. **Compare the carrying value with the redemption price to calculate the amount of the loss:**

$$\text{Loss} = \text{Redemption Price} - \text{Carrying Value}$$
$$= (\$10,000 \times 1.07) - \$10,535$$
$$= \$10,700 - \$10,535$$
$$= \$165$$

In Example 10-6, a loss of \$165 means that Premium Firm paid more to retire the bonds than the amount at which the bonds were recorded on the balance sheet.

Financial Statement Presentation of Gain or Loss

The accounts Gain on Bond Redemption and Loss on Bond Redemption are income statement accounts. A gain on bond redemption increases Premium Firm's income; a loss decreases its income. While gains and losses should be treated as part of the company's operating income, some statement users may consider them as "one-time" events and choose to exclude them when predicting a company's future income. For that reason, it is helpful if companies present their gains and losses separately on the income statement so that readers can determine whether such amounts will affect future periods.

MODULE 2 TEST YOURSELF

Review	**LO5** Find the amortization of premium or discount using the effective interest method.	• The premium or discount on bonds must be amortized over the life of the bond to accurately reflect the interest expense. • The effective interest method amortizes discounts or premiums in a way that produces a constant interest rate from one period to the next.
	LO6 Find the gain or loss on retirement of bonds.	• Bonds are retired for various reasons, and if they are retired before their due date, the amount is different from the face value. Unamortized bond premiums or discounts may result in a gain or loss. • When the redemption price is less than the carrying value, a gain results. When the redemption price is greater than the carrying value, a loss results.

Question	1. How does the effective interest method of amortization result in a constant rate of interest?
	2. Does amortization of a premium increase or decrease the bond carrying value? Does amortization of a discount increase or decrease the bond carrying value?
	3. Is there always a gain or loss when bonds are redeemed? How is the gain or loss calculated?

Apply	1. Bonds payable are dated January 1, 2017, and are issued on that date. The face value of the bonds is \$100,000, and the face rate of interest is 8%. The bonds pay interest semiannually. The bonds will mature in five years. The market rate of interest at the time of issuance was 6%.
	a. Using the effective interest amortization method, what amount should be amortized for the first six-month period? What amount of interest expense should be reported for the first six-month period?
	b. Using the effective interest amortization method, what amount should be amortized for the period from July 1 to December 31, 2017? What amount of interest expense should be reported for the period from July 1 to December 31, 2017?
	2. Refer to the previous exercise. Assume that the bonds are redeemed on December 31, 2017, at 102.
	a. Calculate the gain or loss on bond redemption.
	b. Identify and analyze the effect of the bond redemption.

Answers are located at the end of the chapter.

MODULE 3 LIABILITY FOR LEASES

Leases are a major source of financing for many companies. Another liability, deferred taxes, is introduced in the appendix at the end of this chapter. In some cases, these liabilities are required to be reported on the financial statements and are important components of the Long-Term Liabilities section of the balance sheet. In other cases, the items are not required to be presented in the financial statements and can be discerned only by a careful reading of the notes to the financial statements.

LO7 Determine whether a lease agreement must be reported as a liability on the balance sheet.

Leases

A *lease*, a contractual arrangement between two parties, allows one party, the *lessee*, the right to use an asset in exchange for making payments to its owner, the *lessor*. A common example of a lease arrangement is the rental of an apartment. The tenant is the lessee, and the landlord is the lessor.

Lease agreements are a form of financing. In some cases, it is more advantageous to lease an asset than to borrow money to purchase it. The lessee can conserve cash because a lease does not require a large initial cash outlay. Lease arrangements are popular because of their flexibility. The terms of a lease can be structured in many ways to meet the needs of the lessee and lessor. This results in difficult accounting questions:

1. *Should the right to use property be reported as an asset by the lessee?*
2. *Should the obligation to make payments be reported as a liability by the lessee?*
3. *Should all leases be accounted for in the same manner regardless of the terms of the lease agreement?*

The answers are that not all lease agreements should be accounted for in the same manner. The accountant must examine the terms of the lease agreement and compare those terms with an established set of criteria.[1]

Lease Criteria
From the viewpoint of the lessee, there are two types of lease agreements: operating and capital. In an **operating lease**, the lessee acquires the right to use an asset for a limited period of time. The lessee is *not* required to record the right to use the property as an asset or to record the obligation for payments as a liability. Therefore, the lessee is able to attain a form of *off-balance-sheet financing*. That is, the lessee has attained the right to use property but has not recorded that right, or the accompanying obligation, on the balance sheet. By escaping the balance sheet, the lease does not add to debt or impair the debt-to-equity ratio that investors usually calculate. Management has a responsibility to make sure that such off-balance-sheet financing is not, in fact, a long-term obligation.

Operating lease
A lease that does not meet any of the four criteria and is not recorded as an asset by the lessee.

In the second type of lease agreement, a **capital lease** (also called a finance lease), the lessee has acquired sufficient rights of ownership and control of the property to be considered its owner. The lease is called a *capital lease* or *finance lease* because it is capitalized (recorded) on the balance sheet by the lessee.

Capital lease
A lease that is recorded as an asset by the lessee.

A lease should be considered a capital lease or finance lease by the lessee when certain criteria are met.

If the criteria are met, the lease agreement is accounted for as an operating lease. In some cases, firms may take elaborate measures to evade or manipulate the criteria that would require lease capitalization. The accountant should determine what is full and fair disclosure based on an unbiased evaluation of the substance of the transaction.

Operating Leases
You have already accounted for operating leases in previous chapters when recording rent expense and prepaid rent. A rental agreement for a limited time period is also a lease agreement.

---

[1] *Leasing*, ASC Topic 840.25 (formerly *Statement of Financial Accounting Standards No. 13*, "Accounting for Leases"). The FASB has issued a new leasing standard. Those rules are effective in 2019 for public companies and 2020 for non-public companies. You can refer to those revised standards at that time.

EXAMPLE 10-7 Recording an Operating Lease

Suppose that Lessee Firm wants to lease a car for a new salesperson. A lease agreement is signed with Lessor Dealer on January 1, 2017, to lease a car for the year for $4,000, payable on December 31, 2017. Typically, a car lease does not transfer title at the end of the term, does not include a bargain-purchase price, and does not last for more than 75% of the car's life. In addition, the present value of the lease payments is not 90% of the car's value. Because the lease does not meet any of the specified criteria, it should be presented as an operating lease. Lessee Firm would simply record lease expense (or rent expense) of $4,000 for the year.

Although operating leases are not recorded on the balance sheet by the lessee, the FASB requires note disclosure of the amount of future lease obligations for leases that are considered operating leases. Exhibit 10-6 provides a portion of the note from **Target**'s annual report of January 31, 2015, contained in the Form 10-K. Target has used operating leases as an important source of financing and has significant off-balance-sheet commitments in future periods as a result. An investor might want to add this off-balance-sheet item to the debt on the balance sheet to get a conservative view of the company's obligations.

Capital Leases Capital leases are presented as assets and liabilities by the lessee because they meet certain lease criteria.

EXAMPLE 10-8 Calculating the Amount to Capitalize for a Lease

Suppose that Lessee Firm in Example 10-7 wanted to lease a car for a longer period of time. Assume that on January 1, 2017, Lessee signs a lease agreement with Lessor Dealer. The terms of the agreement specify that Lessee will make annual lease payments of $4,000 per year for five years, payable each December 31. Also, assume that the lease specifies that at the end of the lease agreement, the title to the car is transferred to Lessee Firm.

The lease should be treated as a capital lease by Lessee because it meets at least one of the four criteria. (It meets the first criteria concerning transfer of title.) A capital lease must be recorded at its present value by Lessee as an asset and as an obligation. As of January 1, 2017, we must calculate the present value of the annual payments. If we assume an interest rate of 8%, the present value of the payments is $15,972 (rounded) ($4,000 × an annuity factor of 3.99271 from Table 9-4 on page 426).

> **STUDY TIP**
>
> It is called a capital lease because the lease is capital or put on the books of the lessee as an asset.

EXHIBIT 10-6 Target's Note Disclosure of Leases, January 31, 2015

Target Corp. January 31, 2015		
Future Minimum Lease Payments (millions)	**Operating Leases**	**Capital Leases**
2015	$ 186	$ 123
2016	178	94
2017	170	58
2018	165	55
2019	154	54
After 2019	2,974	1,019
Total future minimum lease payments	$3,827	$1,403

Source: Target, Form 10-K, For the Fiscal Year Ended January 31, 2015.

The contractual arrangement between Lessee Firm and Lessor Dealer is called a lease agreement, but clearly the agreement is much different than a year-to-year lease arrangement. Essentially, Lessee Firm has acquired the right to use the asset for its entire life and does not need to return it to Lessor Dealer. Lessee has actually purchased the asset, with payments made over time.

For Example 10-8, the first entry is made on the basis of the present value. The effect of the lease could be identified and analyzed as follows:

Identify and Analyze	**ACTIVITY:** Investing and Financing **ACCOUNTS:** Leased Asset Increase Lease Obligation Increase **STATEMENT[S]:** Balance Sheet

Balance Sheet					Income Statement			
ASSETS	=	LIABILITIES	+	STOCKHOLDERS' EQUITY	REVENUES	−	EXPENSES	= NET INCOME
Leased Asset 15,972		Lease Obligation 15,972						

The Leased Asset account is a long-term asset similar to plant and equipment and represents Lessee's right to use and retain the asset. Because the leased asset represents depreciable property, depreciation (or amortization) must be reported for each of the five years of asset use as follows. On December 31, 2017, Lessee records depreciation of $3,194 ($15,972/5 years), assuming that the straight-line method is adopted. The effect of the depreciation is as follows.

Identify and Analyze	**ACTIVITY:** Operating **ACCOUNTS:** Depreciation Expense Increase Accumulated Depreciation—Leased Assets Increase **STATEMENT[S]:** Balance Sheet and Income Statement

Balance Sheet					Income Statement			
ASSETS	=	LIABILITIES	+	STOCKHOLDERS' EQUITY	REVENUES	−	EXPENSES	= NET INCOME
Accumulated Depreciation— Leased Assets* (3,194)				(3,194)			Depreciation Expense 3,194	(3,194)

*The Accumulated Depreciation—Leased Assets account has increased. It is shown as a decrease in the equation above because it is a contra account and causes total assets to decrease.

On December 31, Lessee Firm also must make a payment of $4,000 to Lessor Dealer. A portion of each payment represents interest on the obligation (loan), and the remainder represents a reduction of the principal amount. An effective interest table can be established using the same concepts used to amortize a premium or discount on bonds payable.

Exhibit 10-7 illustrates the effective interest method applied to Lessee Firm in Example 10-8. Note that the table begins with an obligation amount equal to the present value of the payments of $15,972. Each payment is separated into principal and interest amounts so that the amount of the loan obligation at the end of the lease agreement equals zero. The amortization table is the basis for the amounts that are reflected on the financial statement. Exhibit 10-7 indicates that the $4,000 payment in

EXHIBIT 10-7 Lease Amortization: Effective Interest Method of Amortization

Date	Column 1 Lease Payment	Column 2 Interest Expense	Column 3 Reduction of Obligation	Column 4 Lease Obligation
		8%	Col. 1 − Col. 2	
1/1/2017	—	—	—	$15,972
12/31/2017	$4,000	$1,278	$2,722	13,250
12/31/2018	4,000	1,060	2,940	10,310
12/31/2019	4,000	825	3,175	7,135
12/31/2020	4,000	571	3,429	3,706
12/31/2021	4,000	294	3,706	0

2017 should be considered as interest of $1,278 (8% of $15,972) and reduction of principal of $2,722. On December 31, 2017, the effect of the annual lease payment is as follows:

Identify and Analyze	**ACTIVITY:** Operating
	ACCOUNTS: Interest Expense Increase **Lease Obligation** Decrease **Cash** Decrease
	STATEMENT[S]: Balance Sheet and Income Statement

Balance Sheet					Income Statement			
ASSETS	=	LIABILITIES	+	STOCKHOLDERS' EQUITY	REVENUES	−	EXPENSES	= NET INCOME
Cash (4,000)		Lease Obligation (2,722)		(1,278)			Interest Expense 1,278	(1,278)

For a capital lease, Lessee Firm must record both an asset and a liability. The asset is reduced by the process of depreciation. The liability is reduced by reductions of principal using the effective interest method. According to Exhibit 10-7, the total lease obligation as of December 31, 2017, is $13,250. This amount must be separated into Current and Long-Term categories. The portion of the liability that will be paid within one year of the balance sheet should be considered a current liability. Exhibit 10-7 indicates that the liability will be reduced by $2,940 in 2018 and that amount should be considered a current liability. The remaining amount of the liability, $10,310 ($13,250 − $2,940), should be considered long-term. On the balance sheet as of December 31, 2017, Lessee Firm reports the following balances related to the lease obligation:

Assets:		
Leased assets	$15,972	
Accumulated depreciation	3,194	
		$12,778
Current liabilities:		
Lease obligation		$ 2,940
Long-term liabilities:		
Lease obligation		$10,310

Notice that the depreciated asset does not equal the present value of the lease obligation. This is not unusual. For example, an automobile may be completely depreciated but still have payments due on it.

IFRS and Leasing

The accounting for leases is an excellent example of the differences in how U.S. and IFRS accounting standards are applied. Earlier in the text, we indicated that U.S. standards are often "rule-based" and international standards are "principles-based." In the United States, the criteria to determine whether a lease contract should be considered a capital lease are applied in a rather rigid way. If a lease meets certain criteria, it must be accounted for as a capital lease. If it does not meet the criteria, even by a small margin, then it is considered an operating lease. The international accounting standards provide lease criteria that are similar to the U.S. standards. However, the criteria are used as "guidelines" rather than rigid rules. Therefore, there is much more flexibility in applying the lease standards when using the international standards.

MODULE 3 TEST YOURSELF

Review	**LO7** Determine whether a lease agreement must be reported as a liability on the balance sheet.	• Leases can be classified as two types: operating leases and capital leases. Capital leases imply more rights of ownership. The accounting for these two types of leases is as follows: • Under an operating lease, the lessee does not record the right to use the leased asset or any related obligation to make lease payments on the balance sheet. • Under a capital lease, the lessee records the right to use the property and the lease payments that are obligated to be paid on the balance sheet.
Question	What are the reasons that not all leases are accounted for in the same manner? Do you think it would be possible to develop a new accounting rule that would treat all leases in the same manner? Explain.	

Apply	You have signed an agreement to lease a car for four years and will make annual payments of $4,000 at the end of each year. (Assume that the lease meets the criteria for a capital lease.)
	  a. Calculate the present value of the lease payments assuming an 8% interest rate.
	  b. Identify and analyze the effect of the signing of the lease.
	  c. When the first lease payment is made, what portion of the payment will be considered interest?	

Answers are located at the end of the chapter.

MODULE 4 ANALYSIS OF LONG-TERM LIABILITIES AND CASH FLOW ISSUES

Long-term liabilities are a component of the "capital structure" of the company and are included in the calculation of the debt-to-equity ratio:

LO8 Explain how investors use ratios to evaluate long-term liabilities.

$$\text{Debt-to-Equity Ratio} = \frac{\textbf{Total Liabilities}}{\textbf{Total Stockholders' Equity}}$$

Most investors would prefer to see equity rather than debt on the balance sheet. Debt and its interest charges make up a fixed obligation that must be repaid in a finite period of time. In contrast, equity never has to be repaid and the dividends that are declared on it are optional. Stock investors view debt as a claim against the company that must be satisfied before they get a return on their money.

Another ratio used to measure the degree of debt obligation is the times interest earned ratio:

$$\text{Times Interest Earned Ratio} = \frac{\textbf{Income Before Interest and Tax}}{\textbf{Interest Expense}}$$

Lenders want to be sure that borrowers can pay the interest and repay the principal on a loan. This ratio reflects the degree to which a company can make its debt payment.

MAKING BUSINESS DECISIONS
PEPSICO

A. The Ratio Analysis Model

1. Formulate the Question
The use of debt is a good management strategy, but sometimes a company may have too much debt. The important questions to ask are:

What is the amount of debt in relation to the total equity of the company?

Will the company be able to meet its obligations related to the debt? That is, when an interest payment comes due, will the company have the ability to make the payment?

2. Gather the Information from the Financial Statements
For those questions to be addressed, information from the balance sheet and the income statement needs to be collected and analyzed.

- Total debt and total equity: From the balance sheet
- Income before interest and tax: From the income statement
- Interest expense from the income statement

3. Calculate the Ratios for PepsiCo, Inc.

$$\text{Debt-to-Equity Ratio} = \frac{\text{Total Liabilities}}{\text{Total Stockholders' Equity}}$$

PepsiCo, Inc. and Subsidiaries, Partial Consolidated Balance Sheet December 26, 2015 and December 27, 2014		
(In millions except per share amounts)	2015	2014
Total Liabilities	57,492	52,961
...		
Total Common Shareholders' Equity	12,068	17,578

$$\text{Debt-to-Equity Ratio} = \frac{\$57,492}{\$12,068} = 4.76$$

$$\text{Times Interest Earned Ratio} = \frac{\text{Income Before Interest and Tax}}{\text{Interest Expense}}$$

PepsiCo, Inc. and Subsidiaries, Partial Consolidated Statement of Income, Fiscal years ended December 26, 2015 and December 27, 2014		
(In millions except per share amounts)	2015	2014
Net Revenue	$63,056	$66,683
Cost of sales	28,384	30,884
Gross profit	34,672	35,799
Selling, general and administrative expenses	24,885	26,126
Venezuela impairment charge	1,359	0
Amortization of intangible assets	75	92
Operating Profit	8,353	9,581
Interest expense	(970)	(909)
Interest income and other	59	85
Income Before Income Taxes	7,442	8,757

> Since the ratio concerns income before interest and income tax, you must add the amount of interest, $970, to $7,442 to get $8,412.

$$\text{Times Interest Earned Ratio} = \frac{\$8,412}{\$970} = 8.67$$

4. Compare the Ratio with Others

PepsiCo's debt-to-equity ratio and times interest earned ratio should be compared to those of prior years and to those of companies in the same industry.

	PepsiCo		Coca-Cola	
	2015	2014	2015	2014
Debt-to-equity ratio	4.76	3.01	2.52	2.03
Times interest earned ratio	8.67	10.63	12.22	20.31

5. Interpret the Results

PepsiCo and Coca-Cola are strong companies with a very safe balance of debt to equity. Both companies had a debt-to-equity ratio that increased from 2015 to 2014. This is probably the result of the low interest rates that existed during the year. Both companies have a small amount of interest obligations compared to their income available to meet those obligations. PepsiCo has 8.67 times more income than its interest expense for 2015, while Coca-Cola has 12.22. These ratios indicate that the creditors for both companies are confident that each company will be able to meet its interest obligations on its long-term debt.

B. The Business Decision Model

1. Formulate the Question

If you were a lender, would you be willing to lend money to PepsiCo, Inc., based on its use of debt?

2. Gather Information from the Financial Statements and Other Sources

This information will come from a variety of sources, not limited to but including:

- The balance sheet provides information about the amount of debt and equity, the income statement regarding interest, and the statement of cash flows on inflows and outflows of cash.
- The outlook for the industry, including consumer trends, foreign markets, labor issues, and other factors.
- The outlook for the economy in general.
- Alternative uses for the money.

3. Analyze the Information Gathered
- Compare PepsiCo's ratios in (A) above with Coca-Cola's as well as with industry averages.
- Look at trends over time in the use of debt by the companies.
- Review projections for the economy and the industry.

4. Make the Decision
Taking into account all of the various sources of information, decide either to

- Lend money to PepsiCo or
- Find an alternative use for the money

5. Monitor Your Decision
If you decide to lend money to the company, you will need to monitor your investment periodically. During the time of the investment, you will want to assess the company's debt levels as well as other factors you considered before making the investment.

How Long-Term Liabilities Affect the Statement of Cash Flows

LO9 Explain the effects that transactions involving long-term liabilities have on the statement of cash flows.

Exhibit 10-8 indicates the impact that long-term liabilities have on a company's cash flow and their placement on the cash flow statement. Most long-term liabilities are related to a firm's financing activities. Therefore, the change in the balance of each long-term liability account should be reflected in the Financing Activities category of the statement of cash flows. The decrease in a long-term liability account indicates that cash has been used to pay the liability. Therefore, in the statement of cash flows, a decrease in a long-term liability account should appear as a subtraction, or reduction. The increase in a long-term liability account indicates that the firm has obtained additional cash via a long-term obligation. Therefore, an increase in a long-term liability account should appear on the statement of cash flows as an addition.

The statement of cash flows of The Coca-Cola Company is presented in Exhibit 10-9 on page 477. Note that the Financing Activities category contains two items related to long-term liabilities. In 2015, long-term debt was issued for $40,434 million and is an addition to cash. This indicates that Coca-Cola increased its cash position by borrowings. Second, the payment of debt is listed as a deduction of $37,738 million. This indicates that Coca-Cola paid long-term liabilities, resulting in a reduction of cash.

EXHIBIT 10-8 Long-Term Liabilities on the Statement of Cash Flows

Item	Statement of Cash Flows	
	Operating Activities	
Net Income		xxx
Increase in current liability	⟶	+
Decrease in current liability	⟶	–
	Investing Activities	
	Financing Activities	
Increase in long-term payable	⟶	+
Decrease in long-term payable	⟶	–

EXHIBIT 10-9 The Coca-Cola Company and Subsidiaries' 2015 Consolidated Statements of Cash Flows

Year Ended December 31,	2015	2014	2013
(In millions)			
OPERATING ACTIVITIES			
Consolidated net income	$ 7,366	$ 7,124	$ 8,626
Depreciation and amortization	1,970	1,976	1,977
Stock-based compensation expense	236	209	227
Deferred income taxes	73	(40)	648
Equity (income) loss — net of dividends	(122)	(371)	(201)
Foreign currency adjustments	(137)	415	168
Significant (gains) losses on sales of assets — net	(374)	831	(670)
Other operating charges	929	761	465
Other items	744	149	234
Net change in operating assets and liabilities	(157)	(439)	(932)
Net cash provided by operating activities	10,528	10,615	10,542
INVESTING ACTIVITIES			
Purchases of investments	(15,831)	(17,800)	(14,782)
Proceeds from disposals of investments	14,079	12,986	12,791
Acquisitions of businesses, equity method investments and nonmarketable securities	(2,491)	(389)	(353)
Proceeds from disposals of businesses, equity method investments and nonmarketable securities	565	148	872
Purchases of property, plant and equipment	(2,553)	(2,406)	(2,550)
Proceeds from disposals of property, plant and equipment	85	223	111
Other investing activities	(40)	(268)	(303)
Net cash provided by (used in) investing activities	(6,186)	(7,506)	(4,214)
FINANCING ACTIVITIES			
Issuances of debt	40,434	41,674	43,425
Payments of debt	(37,738)	(36,962)	(38,714)
Issuances of stock	1,245	1,532	1,328
Purchases of stock for treasury	(3,564)	(4,162)	(4,832)
Dividends	(5,741)	(5,350)	(4,969)
Other financing activities	251	(363)	17
Net cash provided by (used in) financing activities	(5,113)	(3,631)	(3,745)
EFFECT OF EXCHANGE RATE CHANGES ON CASH AND CASH EQUIVALENTS	(878)	(934)	(611)
CASH AND CASH EQUIVALENTS			
Net increase (decrease) during the year	(1,649)	(1,456)	1,972
Balance at beginning of year	8,958	10,414	8,442
Balance at end of year	$ 7,309	$ 8,958	$ 10,414

Source: The Coca-Cola Company, Form 10-K, For the Fiscal Year Ended December 31, 2015.

Although most long-term liabilities are reflected in the Financing Activities category of the statement of cash flows, the Deferred Tax account (discussed in the appendix at the end of this chapter) is reflected in the Operating Activities category. This presentation is necessary because the Deferred Tax account is related to an operating item, income tax expense. For example, in Exhibit 10-9, Coca-Cola listed an addition of $73 million in the Operating Activities category of the 2015 statement of cash flows. This indicates that $73 million more was recorded as expense than was paid out in cash. Therefore, the amount is a positive amount in the Operating Activities category.

MODULE 4 TEST YOURSELF

Review	**LO8** Explain how investors use ratios to evaluate long-term liabilities.	• Investors use the debt-to-equity ratio and the times interest earned ratio as measures of a company's abilities to meet its long-term obligations.
	LO9 Explain the effects that transactions involving long-term liabilities have on the statement of cash flows.	• Cash flows related to long-term liabilities are generally related to a firm's financing activities.

Question	In what category of the statement of cash flows should the following items be shown? Should they appear as a positive or negative amount on the statement of cash flows? Increase in long-term liabilities Decrease in long-term liabilities Interest expense Depreciation expense on leased assets Increase in deferred tax

Apply	Will Able Corporation's balance sheet showed the following amounts: Current Liabilities, $10,000; Bonds Payable, $3,000; Lease Obligations, $4,000; and Notes Payable, $600. Total stockholders' equity was $12,000. The debt-to-equity ratio is: a. 0.63. b. 0.83. c. 1.42. d. 1.47.

Answers are located at the end of the chapter.

APPENDIX

MODULE 5 DEFERRED TAX

LO10 Explain deferred taxes and calculate the deferred tax liability.

Deferred tax
The account used to reconcile the difference between the amount recorded as income tax expense and the amount that is payable as income tax.

Permanent difference
A difference that affects the tax records but not the accounting records, or vice versa.

The financial statements of most major firms include an item titled Deferred Income Taxes or Deferred Tax. (See PepsiCo's deferred taxes in Exhibit 10-1 on page 456 and Coca-Cola's in the chapter opening on page 455.) In most cases, the account appears in the Long-Term Liabilities section of the balance sheet, and the dollar amount may be large.

Deferred tax is an amount that reconciles the differences between the accounting done for purposes of financial reporting to stockholders ("book" purposes) and the accounting done for tax purposes. U.S. firms are allowed to use accounting methods for financial reporting that differ from those used for tax calculations. The reason is that the IRS defines income and expense differently than does the FASB. As a result, companies tend to use accounting methods that minimize income for tax purposes but maximize income in the annual report to stockholders. This is not true in some foreign countries where financial accounting and tax accounting are more closely aligned. Firms in those countries do not report deferred tax because the difference between methods is not significant.

When differences between financial and tax reporting do occur, the differences can be classified into two types: permanent and temporary. **Permanent differences** occur when an item is included in the tax calculation and is never included for book purposes—or vice versa, when an item is included for book purposes but not for tax purposes. For example, the tax laws allow taxpayers to exclude interest on certain investments, usually state and municipal bonds, from their income. When a corporation buys these tax-exempt bonds, it does not have to declare the interest as income for tax purposes. When the corporation develops its income statement for stockholders (book purposes), however, the interest is included and appears in the Interest Income account.

Therefore, tax-exempt interest represents a permanent difference between tax and book calculations.

Temporary differences occur when an item affects both book and tax calculations but not in the same time period. A difference caused by depreciation methods is the most common type of temporary difference. In previous chapters, you learned that depreciation may be calculated using a straight-line method or an accelerated method such as the double-declining-balance method. Most firms do not use the same depreciation method for book and tax purposes, however. Generally, straight-line depreciation is used for book purposes and an accelerated method is used for tax purposes because accelerated depreciation lowers taxable income—at least in early years—and therefore reduces the tax due. The IRS's *Modified Accelerated Cost Recovery System (MACRS)* is similar to other accelerated depreciation methods in that it allows the firm to take larger depreciation deductions for tax purposes in the early years of the asset and smaller deductions in the later years. Over the life of the depreciable asset, the total depreciation using straight-line is equal to that using MACRS. Therefore, this difference is an example of a temporary difference between book and tax reporting.

The Deferred Tax account is used to reconcile the differences between the accounting for book purposes and for tax purposes. It is important to distinguish between permanent and temporary differences because the FASB has ruled that not all differences should affect the Deferred Tax account. The Deferred Tax account should reflect temporary differences but not items that are permanent differences between book accounting and tax reporting.[2]

> **Temporary difference**
> A difference that affects both book and tax records but not in the same time period.
>
> *Alternate term: Timing difference.*

EXAMPLE 10-9 Calculation and Reporting Deferred Tax

Assume that Startup Firm begins business on January 1, 2017. During 2017, the firm has sales of $6,000 and has no expenses other than depreciation and income tax at the rate of 40%. Startup has depreciation on only one asset. That asset was purchased on January 1, 2017, for $10,000 and has a four-year life. Startup has decided to use the straight-line depreciation method for financial reporting purposes. Startup's accountants have chosen to use MACRS for tax purposes, however, resulting in $4,000 depreciation in 2017 and a decline of $1,000 per year thereafter.

The depreciation amounts for each of the four years for Startup's asset are as follows:

Year	Tax Depreciation	Book Depreciation	Difference
2017	$ 4,000	$ 2,500	$ 1,500
2018	3,000	2,500	500
2019	2,000	2,500	(500)
2020	1,000	2,500	(1,500)
Totals	$10,000	$10,000	$ 0

Startup's tax calculation for 2017 is based on the accelerated depreciation of $4,000, as follows:

Sales	$ 6,000
Depreciation expense	4,000
Taxable income	$ 2,000
Tax rate	× 40%
Tax payable to IRS	$ 800

For 2017, Startup owes $800 of tax to the IRS. This amount is ordinarily recorded as tax payable until the time it is remitted.

What amount should be shown as tax expense on the income statement? Remember that the tax payable amount was calculated using the depreciation method that Startup chose for tax

---

[2] *Deferred Tax* ASC Topic 740 (formerly *Statement of Financial Accounting Standards No. 109*, "Accounting for Income Taxes").

purposes. The income statement must be calculated using the straight-line method, which Startup uses for book purposes. Therefore, Startup's income statement for 2017 appears as follows:

Sales	$6,000
Depreciation expense	2,500
Income before tax	$3,500
Tax expense (40%)	1,400
Net income	$2,100

In Example 10-9, Startup must make an accounting entry to record the amount of tax expense and tax payable for 2017. The effect is as follows:

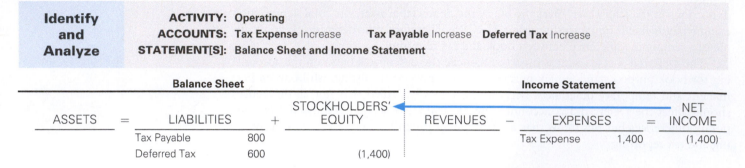

Identify and Analyze	ACTIVITY: Operating
	ACCOUNTS: Tax Expense Increase Tax Payable Increase Deferred Tax Increase
	STATEMENT[S]: Balance Sheet and Income Statement

Balance Sheet					Income Statement			
ASSETS	=	LIABILITIES	+	STOCKHOLDERS' EQUITY	REVENUES	−	EXPENSES	= NET INCOME
		Tax Payable 800					Tax Expense 1,400	(1,400)
		Deferred Tax 600		(1,400)				

The Deferred Tax account is a balance sheet account that is used to reconcile the differences between the accounting for book purposes and tax purposes. A balance in it reflects the fact that Startup has received a tax benefit by recording accelerated depreciation, in effect delaying the ultimate obligation to the IRS. The amount of deferred tax still represents a liability of Startup. The Deferred Tax account balance of $600 represents the amount of the 2017 temporary difference of $1,500 times the tax rate of 40% ($1,500 × 40% = $600).

What can you learn from Startup Firm in Example 10-9?

- **First, when you see a firm's income statement, the amount listed as tax expense does not represent the amount of cash paid to the government for taxes.** Accrual accounting procedures require that the tax expense amount be calculated using the accounting methods chosen for book purposes.

- **Second, when you see a firm's balance sheet, the amount in the Deferred Tax account reflects all of the temporary differences between the accounting methods chosen for tax and book purposes.** The accounting and financial communities are severely divided on whether the Deferred Tax account represents a "true" liability. The FASB has taken the stance that deferred tax is an amount that results in a future obligation and meets the definition of a liability.

MODULE 5 TEST YOURSELF

Review	LO10 Explain deferred taxes and calculate the deferred tax liability.	• Differences arise between the tax treatment of revenue and expense items for financial accounting (book) and tax accounting methods. Deferred taxes are those amounts that reconcile these differences. • Permanent differences occur when an item is included for tax purposes but not book, or vice versa. • Temporary differences occur when there are differences between the time an item is recognized for tax purposes and the time it is recognized for book purposes.

| Question | 1. Why do firms have a Deferred Tax account? Where should that account be shown on the financial statements? |
| | 2. How can you determine whether an item should reflect a permanent or a temporary difference when calculating the deferred tax amount? |

Apply	On January 1, 2017, Deng Company purchased an asset for $100,000. For financial accounting purposes, the asset will be depreciated on a straight-line basis over five years with no residual value at the end of that time. For tax purposes, the asset will be depreciated as follows: 2017, $40,000; 2018, $30,000; 2019, $20,000; 2020, $10,000; and 2021, $0. Assume that the company is subject to a 40% tax rate.
	a. What is the amount of deferred tax at December 31, 2017?
	b. Does the deferred tax represent an asset or a liability?
	c. What is the amount of deferred tax at December 31, 2021?

Answers are located at the end of the chapter.

RATIO REVIEW

$$\text{Debt-to-Equity Ratio} = \frac{\text{Total Liabilities}}{\text{Total Stockholders' Equity}}$$

$$\text{Times Interest Earned Ratio} = \frac{\text{Income Before Interest and Tax}}{\text{Interest Expense}}$$

ACCOUNTS HIGHLIGHTED

Account Title	Where It Appears	In What Section	Page Number
Bonds Payable	Balance Sheet	Long-Term Liabilities	460
Premium on Bonds Payable	Balance Sheet	Long-Term Liabilities	461
Discount on Bonds Payable	Balance Sheet	Long-Term Liabilities as a contra account	464
Gain on Bond Redemption	Income Statement	Other Income/Expense	466
Loss on Bond Redemption	Income Statement	Other Income/Expense	471
Leased Asset	Balance Sheet	Property, Plant, and Equipment	471
Lease Obligation	Balance Sheet	Long-Term Liabilities	472
Deferred Income Tax	Balance Sheet	May be Asset or Liability	480

KEY TERMS QUIZ

Read each definition below and write the number of the definition in the blank beside the appropriate term. The quiz solutions appear at the end of the chapter.

_____ Long-term liability
_____ Face value
_____ Debenture bonds
_____ Serial bonds
_____ Callable bonds
_____ Face rate of interest
_____ Market rate of interest
_____ Bond issue price
_____ Premium
_____ Discount

_____ Effective interest method of amortization
_____ Carrying value
_____ Gain or loss on redemption
_____ Operating lease
_____ Capital lease or finance lease
_____ Deferred tax (Appendix)
_____ Permanent difference (Appendix)
_____ Temporary difference (Appendix)

1. The principal amount of the bond as stated on the bond certificate.
2. Bonds that do not all have the same due date; a portion of the bonds comes due each time period.
3. The rate of interest on the bond certificate.
4. The present value of the annuity of interest payments plus the present value of the principal.
5. An obligation that will not be satisfied within one year or the current operating cycle.
6. The excess of the issue price over the face value of the bonds.
7. Bonds that are not backed by specific collateral.
8. The excess of the face value of bonds over the issue price.
9. Bonds that may be redeemed or retired before their specified due date.
10. The process of transferring a portion of the premium or discount to interest expense; this method results in a constant effective interest rate.
11. The face value of a bond plus the amount of unamortized premium or minus the amount of unamortized discount.
12. The rate that investors could obtain by investing in other bonds that are similar to the issuing firm's bonds.
13. The difference between the carrying value and the redemption price at the time bonds are redeemed.
14. A lease that does not meet any of the criteria and is not recorded as an asset by the lessee.
15. A lease that is recorded as an asset by the lessee.
16. A difference that affects both book and tax records but not in the same time period.
17. The account used to reconcile the difference between the amount recorded as income tax expense and the amount that is payable as income tax.
18. A difference that affects the tax records but not the accounting records, or vice versa.

ALTERNATE TERMS

bond retirement extinguishment of bonds
carrying value book value
effective interest method of amortization interest method
face rate of interest stated rate, nominal rate, contract rate, coupon rate

face value par value
market rate of interest effective rate, bond yield
redemption price reacquisition price
temporary difference timing difference

REVIEW PROBLEM & SOLUTION

The following items pertain to the liabilities of Brent Foods. You may assume that Brent Foods began business on January 1, 2017; therefore, the beginning balance of all accounts was zero.

a. On January 1, 2017, Brent Foods issued bonds with a face value of $50,000. The bonds are due in five years and have a face interest rate of 10%. The market rate on January 1 for similar bonds was 12%. The bonds pay interest annually each December 31. Brent has chosen to use the effective interest method of amortization for any premium or discount on the bonds.
b. On January 1, 2018, Brent redeems its bonds payable at the specified redemption price of 101. Because this item occurs in 2018, it does not affect the balance sheet prepared for year-end 2017.

Required

1. Determine the effect on the accounting equation on December 31, 2017, for the interest adjustment in (a).
2. Develop the Long-Term Liabilities section of Brent Foods' balance sheet as of December 31, 2017. You do not need to consider the notes that accompany the balance sheet.
3. Calculate the gain or loss on the bond redemption for (b).

Solution to Review Problem

1. The issue price of the bonds on January 1 must be calculated at the present value of the interest payments and the present value of the principal, as follows:

$5,000 × 3.60478 $18,024
$50,000 × 0.56743   28,372
        Issue price $46,400   (rounded to the nearest hundred)

The amount of the discount is calculated as follows:

$50,000 − $46,400 = $3,600

The effect of the payment and amortization is as follows:

Identify and Analyze	**ACTIVITY:** Operating **ACCOUNTS:** Interest Expense Increase Discount on Bonds Payable Decrease Cash Decrease **STATEMENT[S]:** Balance Sheet and Income Statement

	Balance Sheet					Income Statement		
ASSETS	=	LIABILITIES	+	STOCKHOLDERS' EQUITY	REVENUES	−	EXPENSES	= NET INCOME
Cash (5,000)		Discount on Bonds Payable* 568		(5,568)			Interest Expense 5,568	(5,568)

*The Discount on Bonds Payable account has decreased. It is shown as an increase in the equation above because it is a contra account and causes total liabilities to increase.

The interest expense is calculated using the effective interest method by multiplying the carrying value of the bonds times the market rate of interest ($46,400 × 12%).

Brent must show two accounts in the Long-Term Liabilities section of the balance sheet: Bonds Payable of $50,000 and Discount on Bonds Payable of $3,032 ($3,600 less $568 amortized).

2. The Long-Term Liabilities section of Brent's balance sheet for December 31, 2017, is as follows:

Brent Foods
Partial Balance Sheet
As of December 31, 2017

Long-term liabilities:		
Bonds payable	$50,000	
Unamortized discount on bonds payable	3,032	$46,968
Lease obligation		9,936
Total long-term liabilities		$56,904

3. Brent must calculate the loss on the bond redemption as the difference between the carrying value of the bonds ($46,968) and the redemption price ($50,000 × 1.01). The amount of the loss is calculated as follows:

$50,500 − $46,968 = $3,532 loss on redemption

EXERCISES

Exercise 10-1 Relationships

The following components are computed annually when a bond is issued for other than its face value:

- Cash interest payment
- Interest expense

LO2
EXAMPLE 10-3, 10-4

Show me how

(Continued)

- Amortization of discount/premium
- Carrying value of bond

Required

State whether each component will increase (I), decrease (D), or remain constant (C) as the bond approaches maturity given the following situations:

1. Issued at a discount
2. Issued at a premium

LO3

EXAMPLE 10-1, 10-2

Exercise 10-2 Issue Price

Youngblood Inc. plans to issue $500,000 face value bonds with a stated interest rate of 8%. They will mature in ten years. Interest will be paid semiannually. At the date of issuance, assume that the market rate is (a) 8%, (b) 6%, and (c) 10%.

Required

For each market interest rate, answer the following questions:

1. What is the amount due at maturity?
2. How much cash interest will be paid every six months?
3. At what price will the bond be issued?

LO3

EXAMPLE 10-1, 10-2

Exercise 10-3 Issue Price

The following terms relate to independent bond issues:

a. 500 bonds; $1,000 face value; 8% stated rate; 5 years; annual interest payments
b. 500 bonds; $1,000 face value; 8% stated rate; 5 years; semiannual interest payments
c. 800 bonds; $1,000 face value; 8% stated rate; 10 years; semiannual interest payments
d. 2,000 bonds; $500 face value; 12% stated rate; 15 years; semiannual interest payments

Required

Assuming the market rate of interest is 10%, calculate the selling price for each bond issue.

LO4

EXAMPLE 10-1, 10-2

Exercise 10-4 Impact of Two Bond Alternatives

Yung Chong Company wants to issue 100 bonds, $1,000 face value, in January. The bonds will have a ten-year life and pay interest annually. The market rate of interest on January 1 will be 9%. Yung Chong is considering two alternative bond issues: (a) bonds with a face rate of 8% and (b) bonds with a face rate of 10%.

Required

1. Could the company save money by issuing bonds with an 8% face rate? If it chooses alternative (a), what would be the interest cost as a percentage?
2. Could the company benefit by issuing bonds with a 10% face rate? If it chooses alternative (b), what would be the interest cost as a percentage?

LO6

EXAMPLE 10-5

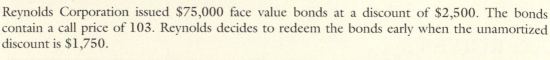

Exercise 10-5 Redemption of Bonds

Reynolds Corporation issued $75,000 face value bonds at a discount of $2,500. The bonds contain a call price of 103. Reynolds decides to redeem the bonds early when the unamortized discount is $1,750.

Required

1. Calculate Reynolds Corporation's gain or loss on the early redemption of the bonds.
2. Describe how the gain or loss would be reported on the income statement and in the notes to the financial statements.

Exercise 10-6 Redemption of a Bond at Maturity

LO6
EXAMPLE 10-5

On March 31, 2017, Sammonds Inc. issued $250,000 face value bonds at a discount of $7,000. The bonds were retired at their maturity date, March 31, 2027.

Required

Assuming that the last interest payment and the amortization of the discount have already been recorded, calculate the gain or loss on the redemption of the bonds on March 31, 2027. Identify and analyze the effect of the redemption of the bonds.

Exercise 10-7 Leased Asset

LO7
EXAMPLE 10-8

Hopper Corporation signed a ten-year capital lease or finance lease on January 1, 2017. The lease requires annual payments of $8,000 every December 31.

Required

1. Assuming an interest rate of 10%, calculate the present value of the minimum lease payments.
2. Explain why the value of the leased asset and the accompanying lease obligation are not reported on the balance sheet initially at $80,000.

Exercise 10-8 Financial Statement Impact of a Lease

LO7
EXAMPLE 10-8

Benjamin's Warehouse signed a six-year capital lease or finance lease on January 1, 2017, with payments due every December 31. Interest is calculated annually at 10%, and the present value of the minimum lease payments is $13,065.

Required

1. Calculate the amount of the annual payment that Benjamin's must make every December 31.
2. Calculate the amount of the lease obligation that would be presented on the December 31, 2019, balance sheet (after two lease payments have been made).

Exercise 10-9 Leased Assets

LO7
EXAMPLE 10-7, 10-8

Koffman and Sons signed a four-year lease for a forklift on January 1, 2017. Annual lease payments of $1,510, based on an interest rate of 8%, are to be made every December 31, beginning with December 31, 2017.

Required

1. Assume that the lease is treated as an operating lease.

    a. Will the value of the forklift appear on Koffman's balance sheet?
    b. What account will indicate that lease payments have been made?

2. Assume that the lease is treated as a capital lease or finance lease.

    a. Identify and analyze the effect when the lease is signed. Explain why the value of the leased asset is not recorded at $6,040 ($1,510 × 4).
    b. Identify and analyze the effect of the first lease payment on December 31, 2017.
    c. Calculate the amount of depreciation expense for the year 2017.
    d. At what amount would the lease obligation be presented on the balance sheet as of December 31, 2017?

Exercise 10-10 Impact of Transactions Involving Bonds on Statement of Cash Flows

LO9

In the following list, identify each item as operating (O), investing (I), financing (F), or not separately reported on the statement of cash flows (N).

_____ Proceeds from issuance of bonds payable
_____ Interest expense
_____ Redemption of bonds payable at maturity

LO9   **Exercise 10-11 Impact of Transactions Involving Capital Leases on Statement of Cash Flows**

Assume that Garnett Corporation signs a lease agreement with Duncan Company to lease a piece of equipment and determines that the lease should be treated as a capital lease. Garnett records a leased asset in the amount of $53,400 and a lease obligation in the same amount on its balance sheet.

Required

1. Indicate how this transaction would be reported on Garnett's statement of cash flows.
2. In the following list of transactions relating to this lease, identify each item as operating (O), investing (I), financing (F), or not separately reported on the statement of cash flows (N).

_____   Reduction of lease obligation (principal portion of lease payment)
_____   Interest expense
_____   Depreciation expense—leased assets

LO9   **Exercise 10-12 Impact of Transactions Involving Tax Liabilities on Statement of Cash Flows**

In the following list, identify each item as operating (O), investing (I), financing (F), or not separately reported on the statement of cash flows (N). For items identified as operating, indicate whether the related amount would be added to or deducted from net income in determining the cash flows from operating activities.

_____   Decrease in taxes payable
_____   Increase in deferred taxes

LO10   **Exercise 10-13 Temporary and Permanent Differences (Appendix)**

EXAMPLE 10-9

Madden Corporation wants to determine the amount of deferred tax that should be reported on its 2017 financial statements. It has compiled a list of differences between the accounting conducted for tax purposes and the accounting used for financial reporting (book) purposes.

Required

For each of the following items, indicate whether the difference should be classified as a permanent or a temporary difference.

1. During 2017, Madden received interest on state bonds purchased as an investment. The interest can be treated as tax-exempt interest for tax purposes.
2. During 2017, Madden paid for a life insurance premium on two key executives. Madden's accountant has indicated that the amount of the premium cannot be deducted for income tax purposes.
3. During December 2017, Madden received money for renting a building to a tenant. Madden must report the rent as income on its 2017 tax form. For book purposes, however, the rent will be considered income on the 2018 income statement.
4. Madden owns several pieces of equipment that it depreciates using the straight-line method for book purposes. An accelerated method of depreciation is used for tax purposes, however.
5. Madden offers a warranty on the product it sells. The corporation records the expense of the warranty repair costs in the year the product is sold (the accrual method) for book purposes. For tax purposes, however, Madden is not allowed to deduct the expense until the period the product is repaired.
6. During 2017, Madden was assessed a large fine by the federal government for polluting the environment. Madden's accountant has indicated that the fine cannot be deducted as an expense for income tax purposes.

LO10   **Exercise 10-14 Deferred Tax (Appendix)**

EXAMPLE 10-9

On January 1, 2017, Kunkel Corporation purchased an asset for $32,000. Assume that this is the only asset owned by the corporation. Kunkel has decided to use the straight-line method to depreciate it. For tax purposes, it will be depreciated over three years. It will be depreciated over five years, however, for the financial statements provided to stockholders. Assume that Kunkel Corporation is subject to a 40% tax rate.

Required

Calculate the balance to be reflected in the Deferred Tax account for Kunkel Corporation for each year 2017 through 2021.

MULTI-CONCEPT EXERCISES

Exercise 10-15 Issuance of a Bond at Face Value

LO4 • 5
EXAMPLE 10-1, 10-2

On January 1, 2017, Whitefeather Industries issued 300, $1,000 face value bonds. The bonds have a five-year life and pay interest at the rate of 10%. Interest is paid semiannually on July 1 and January 1. The market rate of interest on January 1 was 10%.

Required

1. Calculate the issue price of the bonds and record the issuance of the bonds on January 1, 2017.
2. Explain how the issue price would have been affected if the market rate of interest had been higher than 10%.
3. Identify and analyze the effect of the payment of interest on July 1, 2017.
4. Calculate the amount of interest accrued on December 31, 2017.

Exercise 10-16 Impact of a Discount

LO4 • 5
EXAMPLE 10-1, 10-3

Berol Corporation sold 20-year bonds on January 1, 2017. The face value of the bonds was $100,000, and they carry a 9% stated rate of interest, which is paid on December 31 of every year. Berol received $91,526 in return for the issuance of the bonds when the market rate was 10%. Any premium or discount is amortized using the effective interest method.

Required

1. Identify and analyze the effect of the sale of the bonds on January 1, 2017, and the proper balance sheet presentation on this date.
2. Identify and analyze the effect of the payment of interest on December 31, 2017, and indicate the proper balance sheet presentation on this date.
3. Explain why it was necessary for Berol to issue the bonds for only $91,526 rather than $100,000.

Exercise 10-17 Impact of a Premium

LO4 • 5
EXAMPLE 10-2, 10-4

Assume the same set of facts for Berol Corporation as in Exercise 10-16 except that it received $109,862 in return for the issuance of the bonds when the market rate was 8%.

Required

1. Identify and analyze the effect of the sale of the bonds on January 1, 2017, and the proper balance sheet presentation on this date.
2. Identify and analyze the effect of the payment interest on December 31, 2017, and indicate the proper balance sheet presentation on this date.
3. Explain why the company was able to issue the bonds for $109,862 rather than for the face amount.

PROBLEMS

Problem 10-1 Factors That Affect the Bond Issue Price

LO3

Becca Company is considering the issue of $100,000 face value, ten-year term bonds. The bonds will pay 6% interest each December 31. The current market rate is 6%; therefore, the bonds will be issued at face value.

(Continued)

Required

1. For each of the following situations, indicate whether you believe the company will receive a premium on the bonds or will issue them at a discount or at face value. Without using numbers, explain your position.

   a. Interest is paid semiannually instead of annually.
   b. Assume instead that the market rate of interest is 7%; the nominal rate is still 6%.

2. For each situation in part (1), prove your statement by determining the issue price of the bonds given the changes in (a) and (b).

LO5   Problem 10-2 Amortization of Discount

Stacy Company issued five-year, 10% bonds with a face value of $10,000 on January 1, 2017. Interest is paid annually on December 31. The market rate of interest on this date is 12%, and Stacy Company receives proceeds of $9,279 on the bond issuance.

Required

1. Prepare a five-year table (similar to Exhibit 10-4) to amortize the discount using the effective interest method.
2. What is the total interest expense over the life of the bonds? cash interest payment? discount amortization?
3. Identify and analyze the effect of the payment of interest and the amortization of discount on December 31, 2019 (the third year), and determine the balance sheet presentation of the bonds on that date.

LO5   Problem 10-3 Amortization of Premium

Assume the same set of facts for Stacy Company as in Problem 10-2 except that the market rate of interest of January 1, 2017, is 8% and the proceeds from the bond issuance equal $10,799.

Required

1. Prepare a five-year table (similar to Exhibit 10-5) to amortize the premium using the effective interest method.
2. What is the total interest expense over the life of the bonds? cash interest payment? premium amortization?
3. Identify and analyze the effect of the payment of interest and the amortization of premium on December 31, 2019 (the third year), and determine the balance sheet presentation of the bonds on that date.

LO6   Problem 10-4 Redemption of Bonds

McGee Company issued $200,000 face value bonds at a premium of $4,500. The bonds contain a call provision of 101. McGee decides to redeem the bonds due to a significant decline in interest rates. On that date, McGee had amortized only $1,000 of the premium.

Required

1. Calculate the gain or loss on the early redemption of the bonds.
2. Calculate the gain or loss on the redemption assuming that the call provision is 103 instead of 101.
3. Indicate where the gain or loss should be presented on the financial statements.
4. Why do you suppose the call price is normally higher than 100?

LO7   Problem 10-5 Financial Statement Impact of a Lease

On January 1, 2017, Muske Trucking Company leased a semitractor and trailer for five years. Annual payments of $28,300 are to be made every December 31 beginning December 31, 2017. Interest expense is based on a rate of 8%. The present value of the minimum lease payments is $112,994 and has been determined to be greater than 90% of the fair market value of the asset on January 1, 2017. Muske uses straight-line depreciation on all assets.

Required

1. Prepare a table similar to Exhibit 10-7 to show the five-year amortization of the lease obligation.
2. Identify and analyze the effect of the lease transaction on January 1, 2017.
3. Identify and analyze the effect of all transactions on December 31, 2018 (the second year of the lease).
4. Prepare the balance sheet presentation as of December 31, 2018, for the leased asset and the lease obligation.

Problem 10-6 Deferred Tax (Appendix)   LO10

Erinn Corporation has compiled its 2017 financial statements. Included in the Long-Term Liabilities category of the balance sheet are the following amounts:

	2017	2016
Deferred tax	$180	$100

Included in the income statement are the following amounts related to income taxes:

	2017	2016
Income before tax	$500	$400
Tax expense	200	160
Net income	$300	$240

In the notes that accompany the 2017 statement are the following amounts:

	2017
Current provision for tax	$120
Deferred portion	80

Required

1. Identify and analyze the effect of the transaction in 2017 for income tax expense, deferred tax, and income tax payable.
2. Assume that a stockholder has inquired about the meaning of the numbers recorded and disclosed about deferred tax. Explain why the Deferred Tax liability account exists. Also, what do the terms *current provision* and *deferred portion* mean? Why is the deferred amount in the note $80 when the deferred amount on the 2017 balance sheet is $180?

Problem 10-7 Deferred Tax Calculations (Appendix)   LO10

Wyhowski Inc. reported income from operations, before taxes, for 2015–2017 as follows:

2015	$210,000
2016	240,000
2017	280,000

When calculating income, Wyhowski deducted depreciation on plant equipment. The equipment was purchased January 1, 2015, at a cost of $88,000. The equipment is expected to last three years and have an $8,000 salvage value. Wyhowski uses straight-line depreciation for book purposes. For tax purposes, depreciation on the equipment is $50,000 in 2015, $20,000 in 2016, and $10,000 in 2017. Wyhowski's tax rate is 35%.

Required

1. How much did Wyhowski pay in income tax each year?
2. How much income tax expense did Wyhowski record each year?
3. What is the balance in the Deferred Income Tax account at the end of 2015, 2016, and 2017?

MULTI-CONCEPT PROBLEMS

Problem 10-8 Bond Transactions   LO4 • 5

Brand Company issued $1,000,000 face value, eight-year, 12% bonds on April 1, 2017, when the market rate of interest was 12%. Interest payments are due every October 1 and April 1. Brand uses a calendar year-end.

(Continued)

Required

1. Identify and analyze the effect of the issuance of the bonds on April 1, 2017.
2. Identify and analyze the effect of the interest payment on October 1, 2017.
3. Explain why additional interest must be recorded on December 31, 2017. What impact does this have on the amounts paid on April 1, 2018?
4. Determine the total cash inflows and outflows that occurred on the bonds over the eight-year life.

LO1 • 8 • 10   Problem 10-9 Partial Classified Balance Sheet for Walgreens

REAL WORLD

The following items, listed alphabetically, appear on **Walgreens Boots Alliance, Inc** consolidated balance sheet at August 31, 2015 (in millions):

Accrued expenses and other liabilities	$ 5,225
Deferred income taxes (long-term)	3,538
Long-term debt	13,315
Other non-current liabilities	4,072
Short-term borrowings	1,068
Trade accounts payable	10,088
Income taxes	176

Source: Walgreens, 2015 Form 10-K.

Required

1. Prepare the Current Liabilities and Long-Term Liabilities sections of Walgreens' classified balance sheet at August 31, 2015.
2. Walgreens had total liabilities of $16,633 and total shareholders' equity of $20,561 at August 31, 2014. Total shareholders' equity at August 31, 2015, amounted to $31,300. (All amounts are in millions.) Compute Walgreens' debt-to-equity ratio at August 31, 2015 and 2014. As an investor, how would you react to the changes in this ratio?
3. What other related ratios would the company's lenders use to assess the company? What do these ratios measure?

ALTERNATE PROBLEMS

LO3   Problem 10-1A Factors That Affect the Bond Issue Price

Rivera Inc. is considering the issuance of $500,000 face value, ten-year term bonds. The bonds will pay 10% interest each December 31. The current market rate is 10%; therefore, the bonds will be issued at face value.

Required

1. For each of the following situations, indicate whether you believe the company will receive a premium on the bonds or will issue them at a discount or at face value. Without using numbers, explain your position.

   a. Interest is paid semiannually instead of annually.
   b. Assume interest is paid annually but that the market rate of interest is 8%; the nominal rate is still 10%.

2. For each situation in part (1), prove your statement by determining the issue price of the bonds given the changes in (a) and (b).

LO5   Problem 10-2A Amortization of Discount

Ortega Company issued five-year, 5% bonds with a face value of $50,000 on January 1, 2017. Interest is paid annually on December 31. The market rate of interest on this date is 8%, and Ortega Company receives proceeds of $44,011 on the bond issuance.

Required

1. Prepare a five-year table (similar to Exhibit 10-4) to amortize the discount using the effective interest method.
2. What is the total interest expense over the life of the bonds? cash interest payment? discount amortization?
3. Identify and analyze the effect of the payment of interest on December 31, 2019 (the third year), and the balance sheet presentation of the bonds on that date.

Problem 10-3A Amortization of Premium

LO5

Assume the same set of facts for Ortega Company as in Problem 10-2A except that the market rate of interest of January 1, 2017, is 4% and the proceeds from the bond issuance equal $52,227.

Required

1. Prepare a five-year table (similar to Exhibit 10-5) to amortize the premium using the effective interest method.
2. What is the total interest expense over the life of the bonds? cash interest payment? premium amortization?
3. Identify and analyze the effect of the payment of interest on December 31, 2019 (the third year), and the balance sheet presentation of the bonds on that date.

Problem 10-4A Redemption of Bonds

LO6

Elliot Company issued $100,000 face value bonds at a premium of $5,500. The bonds contain a call provision of 101. Elliot decides to redeem the bonds due to a significant decline in interest rates. On that date, Elliot had amortized only $2,000 of the premium.

Required

1. Calculate the gain or loss on the early redemption of the bonds.
2. Calculate the gain or loss on the redemption assuming that the call provision is 104 instead of 101.
3. Indicate how the gain or loss would be reported on the income statement and in the notes to the financial statements.
4. Why do you suppose the call price is normally higher than 100?

Problem 10-5A Financial Statement Impact of a Lease

LO7

On January 1, 2017, Kiger Manufacturing Company leased a factory machine for six years. Annual payments of $21,980 are to be made every December 31 beginning December 31, 2017. Interest expense is based on a rate of 9%. The present value of the minimum lease payments is $98,600 and has been determined to be greater than 90% of the fair market value of the machine on January 1, 2017. Kiger uses straight-line depreciation on all assets.

Required

1. Prepare a table similar to Exhibit 10-7 to show the six-year amortization of the lease obligation.
2. Identify and analyze the effect of the lease transaction on January 1, 2017.
3. Identify and analyze the effect of all transactions on December 31, 2018 (the second year of the lease).
4. Prepare the balance sheet presentation as of December 31, 2018, for the leased asset and the lease obligation.

Problem 10-6A Deferred Tax (Appendix)

LO10

Thad Corporation has compiled its 2017 financial statements. Included in the Long-Term Liabilities category of the balance sheet are the following amounts:

	2017	2016
Deferred tax	$180	$200

(Continued)

Included in the income statement are the following amounts related to income taxes:

	2017	2016
Income before tax	$500	$400
Tax expense	100	150
Net income	$400	$250

Required

1. Determine the effect on the accounting equation in 2017 for income tax expense, deferred tax, and income tax payable.
2. Assume that a stockholder has inquired about the meaning of the numbers recorded and disclosed about deferred tax. Explain why the Deferred Tax liability account exists.

LO10 **Problem 10-7A** **Deferred Tax Calculations (Appendix)**

Clemente Inc. has reported income for book purposes as follows for the past three years:

(In thousands)	Year 1	Year 2	Year 3
Income before taxes	$120	$120	$120

Clemente has identified two items that are treated differently in the financial records and in the tax records. The first one is interest income on municipal bonds, which is recognized on the financial reports to the extent of $5,000 each year but does not show up as a revenue item on the company's tax return. The other item, equipment, is depreciated using the straight-line method at the rate of $20,000 each year for financial accounting but is depreciated for tax purposes at the rate of $30,000 in Year 1, $20,000 in Year 2, and $10,000 in Year 3.

Required

1. Determine the amount of cash that Clemente paid for income taxes each year. Assume that a 40% tax rate applies to all three years.
2. Calculate the balance in the Deferred Tax account at the end of Years 1, 2, and 3. How does this account appear on the balance sheet?

ALTERNATE MULTI-CONCEPT PROBLEMS

LO4 • 6 **Problem 10-8A** **Financial Statement Impact of a Bond**

Worthington Company issued $1,000,000 face value, six-year, 10% bonds on July 1, 2017, when the market rate of interest was 12%. Interest payments are due every July 1 and January 1. Worthington uses a calendar year-end.

Required

1. Identify and analyze the effect of the issuance of the bonds on July 1, 2017.
2. Identify and analyze the effect of the transaction on December 31, 2017, to accrue interest expense.
3. Identify and analyze the effect of the interest payment on January 1, 2018.
4. Calculate the amount of cash that will be paid for the retirement of the bonds on the maturity date.

LO1 • 8 • 10 **Problem 10-9A** **Partial Classified Balance Sheet for Boeing**

REAL WORLD

The following items appear on the consolidated balance sheet of **Boeing Inc.** at December 31, 2014 (in millions). The information in parentheses was added to aid in your understanding.

Accounts payable	$10,667
Accrued retiree health care	6,802
Accrued pension plan liability, net	17,182
Accrued liabilities	13,343
Advances and billings in excess of related costs (current)	23,175
Deferred income taxes and income taxes payable (assume current)	8,603

Short-term debt and current portion of long-term debt	$ 929
Non-current income taxes payable	358
Other long-term liabilities	1,208
Long-term debt	8,141

Source: Boeing, Inc., 2014 Form 10-K.

Required

1. Prepare the Current Liabilities and Long-Term Liabilities sections of Boeing's classified balance sheet at December 31, 2014.
2. Boeing had total liabilities of $77,666 and total shareholders' equity of $14,997 at December 31, 2013. Total shareholders' equity amounted to $6,397 at December 31, 2014. (All amounts are in millions.) Compute Boeing's debt-to-equity ratio at December 31, 2014 and 2013. As an investor, how would you react to the changes in this ratio?
3. What other related ratios would the company's lenders use to assess the company? What do these ratios measure?

DECISION CASES

Reading and Interpreting Financial Statements

Decision Case 10-1 Evaluating the Liabilities of Panera Bread Co.

LO1 • 8

REAL WORLD

Refer to the **Panera Bread**'s financial statements at the end of the text and answer the following questions:
1. What are the items listed as long-term liabilities by Panera Bread? How did those liabilities change from 2014 to 2015?
2. Calculate the debt-to-equity ratio and the times interest earned ratio of the company for 2014 to 2015. What do those ratios reveal about the company and its ability to meet its obligations on its long-term liabilities?

Decision Case 10-2 Making Business Decisions: Comparing Two Companies in the Same Industry: Panera Bread and Chipotle

LO9 • 10

RATIO ANALYSIS
BUSINESS DECISION MODEL

Refer to the financial information at the back of the book for **Panera Bread** and **Chipotle**.

Required

Part A. The Ratio Analysis Model
For each company, determine:

The debt-to-equity ratio

Is the debt-to-equity ratio of either company too high? Have the companies effectively used leverage? Replicate the five steps in the Ratio Analysis Model on pages 474–475 to perform the analysis.
1. Formulate the Question
2. Gather the Information from the Financial Statements
3. Calculate the Ratio
4. Compare the Ratio with Other Ratios
5. Interpret the Ratios

REAL WORLD

Part B. The Business Decision Model
If you were an investor, would you be willing to lend money to either or both companies based on their use of debt?
1. Formulate the Question
2. Gather Information from the Financial Statements and Other Sources
3. Analyze the Information Gathered
4. Make the Decision
5. Monitor Your Decision

LO9 · 10   Decision Case 10-3 Reading PepsiCo's Statement of Cash Flows

A portion of the Financing Activities section of **PepsiCo**'s statement of cash flows for the year ended December 27, 2014, follows (in millions):

	2014
Financing Activities	
Proceeds from issuances of long-term debt	$ 3,855
Payments of long-term debt	(2,189)
Short-term borrowings, by original maturity	
More than three months—proceeds	50
More than three months—payments	(10)
Three months or less, net	(2,037)
Cash dividends paid	(3,730)
Share repurchases—common	(5,012)
Share repurchases—preferred	(10)

Source: PepsiCo, Form 10-K, For the Fiscal Year Ended December 27, 2014.

Required

1. Explain why proceeds from debt is shown as a positive amount and payment of debt is shown as a negative amount.
2. During 2014, interest rates remained at low levels. Explain why the company might have paid off debt during such conditions.
3. What are possible reasons why the company repurchased some of its stock?

Making Financial Decisions

LO1 · 7   Decision Case 10-4 Making a Loan Decision

Assume that you are a loan officer in charge of reviewing loan applications from potential new clients at a major bank. You are considering an application from Molitor Corporation, which is a fairly new company with a limited credit history. It has provided a balance sheet for its most recent fiscal year as follows:

Molitor Corporation
Balance Sheet
December 31, 2017

Assets		Liabilities	
Cash	$ 10,000	Accounts payable	$100,000
Receivables	50,000	Notes payable	200,000
Inventory	100,000		
Equipment	500,000	**Stockholders' Equity**	
		Common stock	80,000
		Retained earnings	280,000
Total assets	$660,000	Total liabilities and stockholders' equity	$660,000

Your bank has established certain guidelines that must be met before it will make a favorable loan recommendation. These include minimum levels for several financial ratios. You are particularly concerned about the bank's policy that loan applicants must have a total-assets-to-debt ratio of at least 2 to 1 to be acceptable. Your initial analysis of Molitor's balance sheet indicates that the firm has met the minimum total-assets-to-debt ratio requirement. On reading the notes that accompany the financial statements, however, you discover the following statement:

> Molitor has engaged in a variety of innovative financial techniques resulting in the acquisition of $200,000 of assets at very favorable rates. The company is obligated to make a series of payments over the next five years to fulfill its commitments in conjunction with

these financial instruments. Current GAAP do not require the assets acquired or the related obligations to be reflected on the financial statements.

Required

1. How should this note affect your evaluation of Molitor's loan application? Calculate a revised total-assets-to-debt ratio for Molitor.
2. Do you believe that the bank's policy concerning a minimum total-assets-to-debt ratio can be modified to consider financing techniques that are not reflected on the financial statements? Write a statement that expresses your position on this issue.

Decision Case 10-5   Bond Redemption Decision   LO6

Armstrong Aero Ace, a flight training school, issued $100,000 of 20-year bonds at face value when the market rate was 10%. The bonds have been outstanding for ten years. The company pays annual interest on January 1. The current rate for similar bonds is 4%. On January 1, the controller would like to retire the bonds at 102 and then issue $100,000 of ten-year bonds to pay 4% annual interest.

Required

Draft a memo to the controller advising him to retire the outstanding bonds and issue new debt. Ignore taxes.

Ethical Decision Making

Decision Case 10-6   Determination of Asset Life   LO7

ETHICAL DECISION MODEL

Jen Latke is an accountant for Hale's Manufacturing Company. Hale's has entered into an agreement to lease a piece of equipment from EZ Leasing. Jen must decide how to report the lease agreement on Hale's financial statements.

Jen has reviewed the lease contract carefully. She also has reviewed the four lease criteria specified in the accounting rules. She has been able to determine that the lease does not meet three of the criteria. However, she is concerned about the criterion that indicates that if the term of the lease is 75% or more of the life of the property, the lease should be classified as a capital lease. Jen is fully aware that Hale's does not want to record the lease agreement as a capital lease, but prefers to show it as a type of off-balance-sheet financing.

Jen's reading of the lease contract indicates that the asset has been leased for seven years. She is unsure of the life of such assets, however, and has consulted two sources to determine it. One of them states that equipment similar to that owned by Hale's is depreciated over nine years. The other, a trade publication of the equipment industry, indicates that equipment of this type will usually last for 12 years.

Required

Use the Ethical Decision Framework in Exhibit 1-9 to complete the following requirements:
1. **Recognize an ethical dilemma:** What ethical dilemma(s) do you face?
2. **Analyze the key elements in the situation:**
   a. Who may benefit from the decision? Who may be harmed?
   b. How are they likely to benefit or be harmed?
   c. What rights or claims may be violated?
   d. What specific interests are in conflict?
   e. What are your responsibilities and obligations?
3. **List alternatives and evaluate the impact of each on those affected:** What are your options in dealing with the ethical dilemma(s) you identified in (1) above?
4. **Select the best alternative:** Among the alternatives, which one would you select?

Answers

MODULE 1 Answers to Questions

1. The issue price of a bond should always be calculated using the market rate of interest. The market rate is used to calculate the present value of the interest payments and the present value of the principal (and therefore the issue price).

2. The tax advantage for bonds is the fact that interest paid on bonds is an expense that is deductible for tax purposes, whereas dividends paid on stock are not deductible.

3. When bonds are issued at a premium, it is an indication that the face rate of interest (also called the stated rate, nominal rate, contract rate, or coupon rate) is higher than the market rate.

MODULE 1 Answers to Apply

1. a.

$100,000 × 0.74409	=	$ 74,409	Table 9-2, $n = 10$, $i = 3\%$
4,000 × 8.53020	=	34,121	Table 9-4, $n = 10$, $i = 3\%$
Issue price		$108,530	

b. If the face rate is equal to the market rate, the bond will be issued at face value, or $100,000.

c.

$100,000 × 0.61391	=	$61,391	Table 9-2, $n = 10$, $i = 5\%$
4,000 × 7.72173	=	30,887	Table 9-4, $n = 10$, $i = 5\%$
Issue price		$92,278	

2. a. If the bond was issued at a discount, then the market rate of interest exceeded the face rate of 7%.

b.

Bonds payable	$10,000
Discount on bonds	(800)
	$ 9,200

c. Since the discount will be amortized, the amount will be higher than $9,200.

MODULE 2 Answers to Questions

1. By basing each period's interest expense on a decreasing or increasing amount, the amount of interest expense is different each period, but the rate of interest remains the same.

2. Amortization of a premium decreases the bond carrying value because it decreases the Premium on Bonds Payable account. Since Discount on Bonds Payable is a contra-liability account, amortization of a discount increases the bond carrying value.

3. Gain or loss on bond redemption will almost always occur when bonds are redeemed or retired before their scheduled due date. The gain or loss is computed as the difference between the bond carrying value and the redemption price at the time the bonds are redeemed.

MODULE 2 Answers to Apply

1. The issue price of the bonds is:

$100,000 × 0.74409	=	$ 74,409	Table 9-2, $n = 10$, $i = 3\%$
4,000 × 8.53020	=	34,121	Table 9-4, $n = 10$, $i = 3\%$
Issue price		$108,530	

Cash	Interest Expense	Amortized	Present Value
			$108,530.00
$4,000.00	$3,255.90*	$744.10	107,785.90
4,000.00	3,233.58	766.42	107,019.48

a. Amount amortized is $744.10.
    Amount of interest expense is $3,255.90.

b. Amount amortized is $766.42.
    Amount of interest expense is $3,233.58.
    *$108,530 × 3% = $3,255.90

2. a. Gain = Carrying Value – Call Price
       Gain = $107,019.48 – $102,000.00
       Gain = $5,019.48

b. Bonds Payable 100,000.00
    Premium on Bonds 7,019.48
        Cash 102,000.00*
        Gain on Bond Redemption 5,019.48
    To record redemption of bonds.
    *$100,000 × 102% = $102,000

MODULE 3 Answers to Questions

Leases are not all accounted for in the same manner because of the variety of provisions that can be found in lease agreements. Some leases are only short-term rental arrangements to use the asset, and others are actually purchases of the asset over a long time period. It may be possible to develop an accounting rule to treat all leases similarly. However, the rule must also be flexible enough to cover the wide variety of financial arrangements that are all called leases.

MODULE 3 Answers to Apply

a. The present value of the lease payments can be calculated as follows:

Present Value = $4,000 × (3.31213) using Table 9-4, where i = 8%, n = 4
= $13,249

b. The effect of the lease agreement is as follows:

Identify and Analyze	**ACTIVITY:** Investing and Financing
	ACCOUNTS: Leased Asset Increase Lease Obligation Increase
	STATEMENT[S]: Balance Sheet and Income Statement

Balance Sheet				Income Statement		
ASSETS	=	LIABILITIES	+	STOCKHOLDERS' EQUITY	REVENUES –	EXPENSES = NET INCOME
Leased Asset 13,249		Lease Obligation 13,249				

c. The amount of interest can be calculated as follows:

Interest = $13,249 × 0.08
= $1,059.92

MODULE 4 Answers to Questions

Increase in long-term liabilities—a positive amount in the Financing category
Decrease in long-term liabilities—a negative amount in the Financing category
Interest expense—when using the indirect method, the interest expense is in the Operating category. It is not shown separately, but is part of the net income amount.

Depreciation expense on leased assets—a positive amount in the Operating category
Increase in deferred tax—a positive amount in the Operating category

MODULE 4 Answers to Apply

Total Liabilities = Current Liabilities, $10,000 + Bonds Payable, $3,000 + Lease Obligations, $4,000 + Notes Payable, $600 = $17,600

Total stockholders' equity was $12,000.
Debt-to-Equity Ratio = $17,600/$12,000 = 1.47
Correct answer is D.

MODULE 5 Answers to Questions

1. Deferred Tax is a balance sheet account that reconciles the differences between the accounting for tax purposes and the accounting for the financial statement prepared for stockholders ("book" purposes). In most cases, this account appears in the Long-Term Liabilities section of the balance sheet.

2. A permanent difference affects only book accounting but not tax accounting, or vice versa, tax accounting but not book accounting. Temporary differences affect both book and tax accounting but in different time periods.

MODULE 5 Answers to Apply

a. Deferred Tax = $8,000 ($40,000 – $20,000*) × 0.4
b. The amount will be a deferred tax liability.

*Depreciation for Financial Accounting = ($100,000 – $0)/5years = $20,000

c. At December 31, 2021, the amount of deferred tax will be $0.

Answers to Connect to the Real World

10-1 (p. 459)

Coca-Cola listed three items as long-term liabilities: Long-Term Debt, Other Liabilities, and Deferred Income Taxes. Long-Term Debt increased from 2014 to 2015, Other Liabilities decreased from 2014 to 2015, and Deferred Income Taxes decreased from 2014 to 2015.

Answers to Key Terms Quiz

5	Long-term liability		10	Effective interest method of amortization
1	Face value		11	Carrying value
7	Debenture bonds		13	Gain or loss on redemption
2	Serial bonds		14	Operating lease
9	Callable bonds		15	Capital lease or finance lease
3	Face rate of interest		17	Deferred tax (Appendix)
12	Market rate of interest		18	Permanent difference (Appendix)
4	Bond issue price		16	Temporary difference (Appendix)
6	Premium			
8	Discount			

11

Stockholders' Equity

MODULES	LEARNING OBJECTIVES	WHY IS THIS CHAPTER IMPORTANT?
1 **Stockholders' Equity, Issuance of Stock, and Treasury Stock**	**LO1** Understand the concept of stockholders' equity and identify the components of the Stockholders' Equity category. **LO2** Show that you understand the characteristics of common and preferred stock and the differences between the classes of stock. **LO3** Determine the financial statement impact when stock is issued for cash or for other consideration. **LO4** Describe the financial statement impact of stock treated as treasury stock.	• You need to know what components are presented in the Stockholders' Equity section of the balance sheet. (See pp. 502–505.) • You need to know the types of stock that companies can issue and the advantages of each class of stock. (See pp. 505–506.) • You need to know the importance and the meaning of treasury stock. (See pp. 507–509.)
2 **Cash Dividends, Stock Dividends, and Stock Splits**	**LO5** Compute the amount of cash dividends when a firm has issued both preferred and common stock. **LO6** Show that you understand the difference between cash and stock dividends and the effect of stock dividends. **LO7** Determine the difference between stock dividends and stock splits.	• You need to know the types of dividends that a company might pay. (See pp. 511–515.)
3 **Analysis and Cash Flow Issues**	**LO8** Show that you understand the statement of stockholders' equity and comprehensive income. **LO9** Understand how investors use ratios to evaluate stockholders' equity. **LO10** Explain the effects that transactions involving stockholders' equity have on the statement of cash flows.	• You need to know what comprehensive income is and how it differs from the net income amount a company may present. (See pp. 516–518.) • You need to understand how stockholders' equity items affect the cash flow statement. (See p. 520.)
4 **Sole Proprietorships and Partnerships**	**LO11** Describe the important differences between the sole proprietorship and partnership forms of organization versus the corporate form (Appendix).	• You need to know how sole proprietorships and partnerships present their equity accounts (Appendix). (See pp. 521–527.)

E.J. Baumeister Jr./Alamy

SOUTHWEST AIRLINES

The airline industry is very volatile and has certainly experienced difficulties over the past few years. With reduced revenues, weak demand, high fixed costs, high fuel costs, and increasing expenses for security and insurance, the results for many of the airline companies have been grim. **United Airlines** and several other airlines declared bankruptcy in order to restructure, but throughout all of the bad times, **Southwest Airlines** has performed fairly well and has become the model for the future of the industry. The other airlines know that they must cut costs and become more efficient in order to compete with Southwest.

How does Southwest do it? Southwest Airlines Company provides short-haul, high-frequency, point-to-point, low-fare air transportation services. The company's operating strategy also permits Southwest to achieve high-asset utilization. Aircraft are scheduled to minimize the amount of time they sit at the gate, pegged at approximately 25 minutes, consequently reducing the number of aircraft and gate facilities that would otherwise be required.

Southwest Airlines has consistently been an innovator in the industry. In January 1995, Southwest introduced a ticketless travel option, eliminating the need to print and then process a paper ticket. Recently, Southwest has resisted the move by other airlines to charge flyers for checking a bag, thereby maintaining its identity for quality, customer-friendly service at a low cost.

All of the company's efforts are consistent with its financial strategy to build shareholder value, which contributes to the Stockholders' Equity portion of the balance sheet shown here.

The company experienced a loss during the economic downturn of 2008 but has recovered and has been consistently profitable. As a result, the stockholders have benefited, and shareholder value will likely continue to grow.

This chapter, and the accompanying financial statements of Southwest Airlines and other companies, will help you to understand the Stockholders' Equity section of the balance sheet.

Southwest Airlines Co. Consolidated Balance Sheet (in millions, except share data)	December 31,	
	2015	**2014**
Stockholders' equity:		
Common stock, $1.00 par value: 2,000,000,000 shares authorized; 807,611,634 shares issued in 2015 and 2014	$ 808	$ 808
Capital in excess of par value	1,374	1,315
Retained earnings	9,409	7,416
Accumulated other comprehensive loss	(1,051)	(738)
Treasury stock, at cost: 160,010,017 and 132,017,550 shares in 2015 and 2014 respectively	(3,182)	(2,026)
Total stockholders' equity	$ 7,358	$ 6,775
	$21,312	$19,723

Source: Southwest Airlines Co., Form 10-K, For the Fiscal Year Ended December 31, 2015.

MODULE 1 STOCKHOLDERS' EQUITY, ISSUANCE OF STOCK, AND TREASURY STOCK

LO1 Understand the concept of stockholders' equity and identify the components of the Stockholders' Equity category.

Financing can be divided into two general categories: debt (borrowing from banks or other creditors) and equity (issuing stock). The company's management must consider the advantages and disadvantages of each alternative. Exhibit 11-1 indicates a few of the factors that must be considered.

Issuing stock is a popular method of financing because of its flexibility. It provides advantages for the issuing company and the investors (stockholders). Investors are primarily concerned with the return on their investment. With stock, the return might be in the form of dividends paid to the investors but might also be the price appreciation of the stock. Stock is popular because it generally provides a higher rate of return (but also a higher degree of risk) than can be obtained by creditors who receive interest from lending money. Stock is popular with issuing companies because higher dividends can be paid when the firm is profitable; lower dividends, when it is not. Interest on debt financing, on the other hand, is generally fixed and is a legal liability that cannot be adjusted when a company experiences lower profitability.

There are several disadvantages in issuing stock. Stock usually has voting rights, and issuing stock allows new investors to vote. Existing investors may not want to share the control of the company with new stockholders. From the issuing company's viewpoint, there is also a serious tax disadvantage to stock versus debt. As indicated in Chapter 10, interest on debt is tax-deductible and results in lower taxes. Dividends on stock, on the other hand, are not tax-deductible and do not result in tax savings to the issuing company. Finally, issuing stock has an impact on the company's financial statements. Issuing stock decreases several important financial ratios, such as earnings per share. Issuing debt does not have a similar effect on the earnings per share ratio.

Management must consider many other factors in deciding between debt and equity financing. The company's goal should be financing the company in a manner that results in the lowest overall cost of capital to the firm. Usually, companies attain that goal by having a reasonable balance of both debt and equity financing.

EXHIBIT 11-1 Advantages and Disadvantages of Stock versus Debt Financing

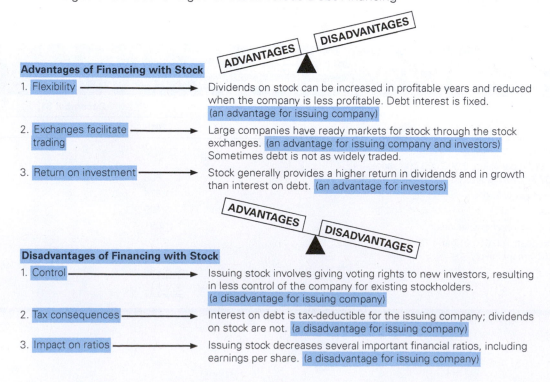

Advantages of Financing with Stock

1. Flexibility ⟶ Dividends on stock can be increased in profitable years and reduced when the company is less profitable. Debt interest is fixed. (an advantage for issuing company)

2. Exchanges facilitate trading ⟶ Large companies have ready markets for stock through the stock exchanges. (an advantage for issuing company and investors) Sometimes debt is not as widely traded.

3. Return on investment ⟶ Stock generally provides a higher return in dividends and in growth than interest on debt. (an advantage for investors)

Disadvantages of Financing with Stock

1. Control ⟶ Issuing stock involves giving voting rights to new investors, resulting in less control of the company for existing stockholders. (a disadvantage for issuing company)

2. Tax consequences ⟶ Interest on debt is tax-deductible for the issuing company; dividends on stock are not. (a disadvantage for issuing company)

3. Impact on ratios ⟶ Issuing stock decreases several important financial ratios, including earnings per share. (a disadvantage for issuing company)

Stockholders' Equity on the Balance Sheet

The basic accounting equation for a corporation is as follows:

Assets = Liabilities + Stockholders' Equity

Stockholders' equity is viewed as a residual amount. That is, the owners of a corporation have a claim to all assets after the claims represented by liabilities to creditors have been satisfied.

The Stockholders' Equity category of all corporations has two major components or subcategories:

Total Stockholders' Equity = Contributed Capital + Retained Earnings

Contributed capital represents the amount the corporation has received from the sale of stock to stockholders. Retained earnings is the amount of net income the corporation has earned but not paid as dividends. Within these two categories, corporations use a variety of accounts that have several different titles.

CONNECT TO THE REAL WORLD

SOUTHWEST AIRLINES
READING THE FINANCIAL STATEMENTS

11-1 Refer to the Retained Earnings account of Southwest Airlines on page 501. Did the account increase or decrease from 2014 to 2015? What factors may cause the account to change? *(See answers on p. 553.)*

How Income and Dividends Affect Retained Earnings

The Retained Earnings account serves as a link between the income statement and the balance sheet. The term *articulated statements* refers to the fact that the information on the income statement is related to the information on the balance sheet. The bridge (or link) between the two statements is the Retained Earnings account. Exhibit 11-2 presents this relationship graphically. As the exhibit indicates, the income statement is used to calculate a company's net income for a given period of time. The amount of the net income is transferred to the statement of retained earnings and is added to the beginning balance of retained earnings (with dividends deducted) to calculate the ending balance of retained earnings. The ending balance of retained earnings is portrayed on the balance sheet in the Stockholders' Equity category. That is why you must prepare the income statement before the balance sheet, as you discovered when developing financial statements in previous chapters of the text.

Identifying Components of the Stockholders' Equity Section of the Balance Sheet

All corporations begin the Stockholders' Equity category with a list of the firm's contributed capital. In some cases, there are two categories of stock: common stock and

EXHIBIT 11-2 Retained Earnings Connects the Income Statement and the Balance Sheet

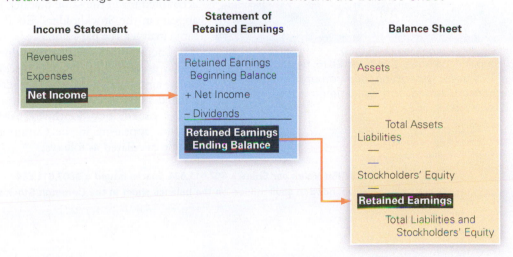

preferred stock. (The latter is discussed later in this chapter.) Common stock normally carries voting rights. The common stockholders elect the corporation's officers and establish its bylaws and governing rules. Corporations often have more than one type of common stock, each with different rights or terms.

Number of Shares   It is important to determine the number of shares of stock for each stock account. Corporate balance sheets report the number of shares in three categories: **authorized**, **issued**, and **outstanding shares**.

To become incorporated, a business must develop articles of incorporation and apply to the proper state authorities for a corporate charter. The corporation must specify the maximum number of shares that it will be allowed to issue. This maximum number of shares is called the *authorized stock*. A corporation applies for authorization to issue many more shares than it will issue immediately to allow for future growth and other events that may occur over its long life. For example, as shown on page 501, Southwest Airlines has 2,000,000,000 shares of common stock authorized, but only 807,611,634 shares had been issued as of December 31, 2015.

The number of shares *issued* indicates the number of shares that have been sold or transferred to stockholders. The number of shares issued does not necessarily mean, however, that those shares are currently outstanding. The term *outstanding* indicates shares actually in the stockholders' hands. Shares that have been issued by the corporation and then repurchased are counted as shares issued but not as shares outstanding. Quite often, corporations repurchase their own stock as treasury stock (explained in more detail later in this chapter). Treasury stock reduces the number of shares outstanding. The number of Southwest Airlines' shares of common stock outstanding at December 31, 2015, could be calculated as follows:

Number of shares issued	807,611,634
Treasury stock	160,010,017
Number of shares outstanding	647,601,617

Par Value: The Firm's "Legal Capital"   The Stockholders' Equity category of many balance sheets refers to an amount as the *par value* of the stock. For example, Southwest Airlines' common stock has a par value of $1 per share. **Par value** is an arbitrary amount stated on the face of the stock certificate and represents the legal capital of the corporation. Most corporations set the par value of the stock at very low amounts because there are legal difficulties if stock is sold at less than par. Therefore, par value does not indicate the stock's value or the amount that is obtained when the stock is sold on the stock exchange; it is simply an arbitrary amount that exists to fulfill legal requirements. A company's legal requirement depends on its state of incorporation. Some states do not require corporations to indicate a par value; other states require corporations to designate the *stated value* of the stock. A stated value is accounted for in the same manner as a par value and appears in the Stockholders' Equity category in the same manner as a par value.

The amount of the par value is the amount that is presented in the stock account. That is, the dollar amount in a firm's stock account can be calculated as its par value per share times number of shares issued. For Southwest Airlines, the dollar amount appearing in the Common Stock account can be calculated as follows:

$1 Par Value per Share × 807,611,634 Shares Issued = $807,611,634

(rounded to $808 million on the balance sheet in the Common Stock account)

Authorized shares
The maximum number of shares a corporation may issue as indicated in the corporate charter.

Issued shares
The number of shares sold or distributed to stockholders.

Outstanding shares
The number of shares issued less the number of shares held as treasury stock.

STUDY TIP

Treasury stock is included in the number of shares issued. It is not part of the number of shares outstanding.

Par value
An arbitrary amount that represents the legal capital of the firm.

CONNECT TO THE REAL WORLD

CHIPOTLE
READING THE FINANCIAL STATEMENTS

11-2 Refer to Chipotle balance sheet for 2015 reproduced at the end of this book. Determine the number of shares of common stock authorized, issued, and outstanding at the balance sheet date. *(See answers on p. 553.)*

Additional Paid-In Capital The dollar amounts of the stock accounts in the Stockholders' Equity category do not indicate the amount that was received when the stock was sold to stockholders. The Common Stock and Preferred Stock accounts indicate only the par value of the stock. When stock is issued for an amount higher than the par value, the excess is reported as **additional paid-in capital**. Several different titles are used for this account, including Capital in Excess of Par Value and Premium on Stock. Regardless of the title, the account represents the amount received in excess of par when stock was issued.

Southwest Airlines' balance sheet (shown on page 501) indicates paid-in capital of $1,374 million at December 31, 2015. The company, like many other corporations, presents only one amount for additional paid-in capital for all stock transactions. Therefore, we are unable to determine whether the amount resulted from the issuance of common stock or other stock transactions.

Additional paid-in capital
The amount received for the issuance of stock in excess of the par value of the stock.

Alternate term: Paid-in capital in excess of par.

Retained Earnings: The Amount Not Paid as Dividends

Retained earnings represents net income that the firm has earned but has *not paid* as dividends. Remember that retained earnings is an amount that is accumulated over the entire life of the corporation and does not represent the income or dividends for a specific year. A balance in retained earnings does not indicate that the company had a net income of this amount in the current year; it simply means that over the life of the corporation, the company has retained more net income than it paid out as dividends to stockholders.

It is also important to remember that the balance of the Retained Earnings account does not mean that liquid assets of that amount are available to the stockholders. Corporations decide to retain income because they have needs other than paying dividends to stockholders. The needs may include the purchase of assets, the retirement of debt, or other financial needs. Money spent for those needs usually benefits the stockholders in the long run, but liquid assets equal to the balance of the Retained Earnings account are not necessarily available to stockholders.

Retained earnings
Net income that has been made by the corporation but not paid out as dividends.

Alternate term: Retained income.

IFRS and Stockholders' Equity

The accounting for stockholders' equity under U.S. accounting rules is similar in most respects to the accounting under international accounting rules. However, there is one important difference regarding items that have characteristics of both debt and equity. For example, a convertible bond (discussed in Chapter 10) is in some ways similar to debt, but because it will become stock if converted, it also has the characteristics of equity. Under international accounting rules, an item such as this must be separated into two parts and one portion shown in the Liability category and another in the Stockholders' Equity category. U.S. accounting standards do not require such an item to be recorded as a separate amount. It is recorded as either a liability or an amount in stockholders' equity.

Preferred Stock

Many companies have a class of stock called *preferred stock*. One of the advantages of preferred stock is the flexibility it provides because its terms and provisions can be tailored to meet the firm's needs. Generally, preferred stock offers holders a preference to dividends declared by the corporation. That is, if dividends are declared, the preferred stockholders must receive dividends first, before the holders of common stock.

The dividend rate on preferred stock may be stated two ways:

1. It may be stated as a percentage of the stock's par value. For example, if a stock is presented on the balance sheet as $100 par, 7% preferred stock, its dividend rate is $7 per share ($100 × 7%).
2. The dividend may be stated as a per-share amount. For example, a stock may appear on the balance sheet as $100 par, $7 preferred stock, meaning that the dividend rate is $7 per share.

LO2 Show that you understand the characteristics of common and preferred stock and the differences between the classes of stock.

Investors in common stock should note the dividend requirements of the preferred shareholder. The greater the obligation to the preferred shareholder, the less desirable the common stock becomes.

In the event that a corporation is liquidated, or dissolved, preferred stockholders have a right to the company's assets before the common stockholders. Following are additional terms and features that may be associated with preferred stock:

- *Convertible* Preferred stock may allow stockholders the right to convert the stock into common stock.
- *Redeemable* Preferred stock may allow stockholders to redeem their stock at a specified price.
- *Callable* Preferred stock may be callable at the option of the company. In this case, the company can choose to pay a specified amount to the stockholders in order to redeem or retire the stock.
- *Cumulative* The dividend on preferred stock may be cumulative. When this is the case, dividends that are not paid are considered to be *in arrears*. Before a dividend on common stock can be declared in a subsequent period, the dividends in arrears as well as the current year's dividend must be paid to the preferred stockholders.
- *Participating* When preferred stock carries a participating feature, it allows the preferred stockholders to receive a dividend in excess of the regular rate when the firm has been particularly profitable and declares an abnormally large dividend.

Preferred stock is attractive to many investors because it offers a return in the form of a dividend at a level of risk that is lower than that of most common stocks. Usually, the dividend available on preferred stock is more stable from year to year; as a result, the market price of the stock is also more stable. In fact, when preferred stock carries certain provisions, the stock is very similar to bonds and notes payable. Management must evaluate whether such securities represent debt and should be presented in the Liability category of the balance sheet or whether they represent equity and should be presented in the Equity category. Such a decision involves the concept of *substance over form*. That is, a company must look not only at the legal form but also at the economic substance of the security to decide whether it is debt or equity.

Issuance of Stock

Stock Issued for Cash

LO3 Determine the financial statement impact when stock is issued for cash or for other consideration.

When stock is issued for cash, the amount of its par value should be reported in the Stock account and the amount in excess of par should be reported in the Additional Paid-In Capital account.

Convertible feature
Allows preferred stock to be exchanged for common stock.

Redeemable feature
Allows stockholders to sell stock back to the company.

Callable feature
Allows the firm to eliminate a class of stock by paying the stockholders a specified amount.

Cumulative feature
The right to dividends in arrears before the current-year dividend is distributed.

Participating feature
Allows preferred stockholders to share on a percentage basis in the distribution of an abnormally large dividend.

EXAMPLE 11-1 Recording Stock Issued for Cash

Assume that on July 1, a firm issued 1,000 shares of $10 par common stock for $15 per share. The effect of the issuance could be identified and analyzed as follows:

Identify and Analyze	ACTIVITY: Financing
	ACCOUNTS: Cash Increase Common Stock Increase
	Additional Paid-In Capital—Common Increase
	STATEMENT(S): Balance Sheet

Balance Sheet				Income Statement		
ASSETS	=	LIABILITIES +	STOCKHOLDERS' EQUITY	REVENUES −	EXPENSES =	NET INCOME
Cash 15,000			Common Stock 10,000			
			Additional Paid-In Capital—Common 5,000			

As noted earlier, the Common Stock account and the Additional Paid-In Capital account are both presented in the Stockholders' Equity category of the balance sheet and represent the contributed capital component of the corporation.

If no-par stock is issued, the corporation does not distinguish between common stock and additional paid-in capital. If the firm in Example 11-1 had issued no-par stock on July 1 for $15 per share, the entire amount of $15,000 would have been presented in the Common Stock account.

Stock Issued for Noncash Consideration

Occasionally, stock is issued in return for something other than cash. For example, a corporation may issue stock to obtain land or buildings. When such a transaction occurs, the company faces the difficult task of deciding what value to place on the transaction. According to the general guideline, the transaction should be reported at fair market value. Market value may be indicated by the value of the consideration given (stock) or the value of the consideration received (property), whichever can be most readily determined.

EXAMPLE 11-2 Recording Stock for Noncash Consideration

Assume that on July 1, a firm issued 500 shares of $10 par preferred stock to acquire a building. The stock is not widely traded, and the current market value of the stock is not evident. The building has recently been appraised by an independent firm as having a market value of $12,000. In this case, the issuance of the stock could be identified and analyzed as follows:

Identify and Analyze		
	ACTIVITY: Financing and Investing	
	ACCOUNTS: Building Increase **Preferred Stock** Increase	
	Additional Paid-In Capital—Preferred Increase	
	STATEMENT(S): Balance Sheet	

Balance Sheet				Income Statement			
ASSETS	= LIABILITIES	+	STOCKHOLDERS' EQUITY	REVENUES	−	EXPENSES	= NET INCOME
Building 12,000			Preferred Stock 5,000				
			Additional Paid-In Capital—Preferred 7,000				

In other situations, the market value of the stock might be more readily determined and should be used as the best measure of the value of the transaction. The company should attempt to develop the best estimate of the market value of the noncash transaction and should neither intentionally overstate nor intentionally understate the assets received by the issuance of stock.

What Is Treasury Stock?

The Stockholders' Equity category of Southwest Airlines' balance sheet in the chapter opener on page 501 includes **treasury stock** in the amount of $3,182 million. The Treasury Stock account is created when a corporation buys its own stock sometime after issuing it. For an amount to be treated as treasury stock:

1. It must be the corporation's own stock.
2. It must have been issued to the stockholders at some point.
3. It must have been repurchased from the stockholders.
4. It must not be retired, but must be held for some purpose. Treasury stock is not considered outstanding stock and does not have voting rights.

LO4 Describe the financial statement impact of stock treated as treasury stock.

Treasury stock
Stock issued by the firm and then repurchased but not retired.

A corporation might repurchase stock as treasury stock for several reasons. The most common reason is to have stock available to distribute to employees for bonuses or to make available as part of an employee benefit plan. Firms also might buy treasury stock to maintain a favorable market price for the stock or to improve the appearance of the firm's financial ratios. More recently, firms have purchased their stock to maintain control of the ownership and to prevent unwanted takeover or buyout attempts. Of course, the lower the stock price, the more likely a company is to buy back its own stock and wait for the shares to rise in value before reissuing them.

The two methods to account for treasury stock transactions are the cost method and the par value method. We will present the more commonly used cost method.

EXAMPLE 11-3 Recording the Purchase of Treasury Stock

Assume that the Stockholders' Equity section of Rezin Company's balance sheet on December 31, 2017, appears as follows:

Common stock, $10 par value,	
1,000 shares issued and outstanding	$10,000
Additional paid-in capital—Common	12,000
Retained earnings	15,000
Total stockholders' equity	$37,000

Assume that on February 1, 2018, Rezin buys 100 of its shares as treasury stock at $25 per share. The effect of the purchase of treasury stock is as follows:

Identify and Analyze	ACTIVITY: **Financing**
	ACCOUNTS: **Treasury Stock** Increase **Cash** Decrease
	STATEMENT(S): **Balance Sheet**

Balance Sheet				Income Statement				
ASSETS	=	LIABILITIES	+	STOCKHOLDERS' EQUITY	←	REVENUES	−	EXPENSES	=	NET INCOME
Cash (2,500)				Treasury Stock (2,500)				

The purchase of treasury stock does not directly affect the Common Stock account. The Treasury Stock account is considered a contra account and is subtracted from the total of contributed capital and retained earnings in the Stockholders' Equity section. Treasury Stock is *not* an asset account. When a company buys its own stock, it is contracting its size and reducing the equity of stockholders. Therefore, Treasury Stock is a *contra-equity* account, not an asset.

The Stockholders' Equity section of Rezin's balance sheet on February 1, 2018, after the purchase of the treasury stock, appears as follows:

Common stock, $10 par value, 1,000 shares issued, 900 outstanding	$10,000
Additional paid-in capital—Common	12,000
Retained earnings	15,000
Total contributed capital and retained earnings	$37,000
Treasury stock, 100 shares at cost	(2,500)
Total stockholders' equity	$34,500

Corporations may choose to reissue stock to investors after it has been held as treasury stock. When treasury stock is resold for more than it cost, the difference between the sales price and the cost appears in the Additional Paid-In Capital—Treasury Stock account. For example, if Rezin resold 100 shares of treasury stock on May 1, 2018, for $30 per share, the Treasury Stock account would be reduced by $2,500 (100 shares times $25 per share) and the Additional Paid-In Capital—Treasury Stock account would be increased by $500 (100 shares times the difference between the purchase price of $25 and the reissue price of $30).

When treasury stock is resold for an amount less than its cost, the difference between the sales price and the cost is deducted from the Additional Paid-In Capital—Treasury Stock account. If that account does not exist, the difference should be deducted from the Retained Earnings account. For example, assume that Rezin Company had resold 100 shares of treasury stock on May 1, 2018, for $20 per share instead of $30 as in the previous example. Since Rezin has had no other treasury stock transactions, no balance existed in the Additional Paid-In Capital—Treasury Stock account. Rezin would then reduce the Treasury Stock account by $2,500 (100 shares times $25 per share) and would reduce Retained Earnings by $500 (100 shares times the difference between the purchase price of $25 and the reissue price of $20 per share). Thus, the Additional Paid-In Capital—Treasury Stock account may have a positive balance, but entries that result in a negative balance in the account should not be made.

Note that income statement accounts are never involved in treasury stock transactions. Regardless of whether treasury stock is reissued for more or less than its cost, the effect is reflected in the Stockholders' Equity accounts. It is simply not possible for a firm to engage in transactions involving its own stock and have the result affect the performance of the firm as reflected on the income statement.

Retirement of Stock

Retirement of stock occurs when a corporation buys back stock after it has been issued to investors and does not intend to reissue the stock. Retirement often occurs because the corporation wants to eliminate a particular class of stock or a particular group of stockholders. When stock is repurchased and retired, the balances of the Stock account and the Paid-In Capital account that were created when the stock was issued must be eliminated. When the original issue price is higher than the repurchase price of the stock, the difference is reflected in the Paid-In Capital from Stock Retirement account. When the repurchase price of the stock is more than the original issue price, the difference reduces the Retained Earnings account. The general principle for retirement of stock is the same as for treasury stock transactions. No income statement accounts are affected by the retirement. The effect is reflected in the Cash account and the Stockholders' Equity accounts.

Retirement of stock
When the stock is repurchased with no intention of reissuing at a later date.

	MODULE 1 TEST YOURSELF	
Review	**LO1** Understand the concept of stockholders' equity and identify the components of the Stockholders' Equity category.	• Stockholders' equity consists of contributed capital from stockholders and retained earnings from the current and prior periods of operation that have not been paid as dividends. • Disclosure for stocks must include the number of shares authorized, issued, and outstanding, along with the par value.

	LO2 Show that you understand the characteristics of common and preferred stock and the differences between the classes of stock.	• The types of stock issued by a firm are common stock and preferred stock.
		  • Preferred stock receives first preference for dividends and generally provides a more stable dividend stream to stockholders than does common stock.
		  • Common stockholders have a claim to the residual interest in a company after all debtors' and preferred stockholders' claims are satisfied. Generally, only common stockholders are allowed voting rights.

	LO3 Determine the financial statement impact when stock is issued for cash or for other consideration.	• When stock is issued for cash or other consideration, the number of outstanding shares is increased and the par value of stock is recorded along with any amount in excess of par being recorded to the Additional Paid-In Capital account. • When stock is sold for cash, the asset Cash is increased. When issued for noncash consideration, other asset accounts are increased.
	LO4 Describe the financial statement impact of stock treated as treasury stock.	• Treasury stock results when a corporation buys back its own stock. • Treasury stock is accounted for as a contra-equity account and is a reduction of stockholders' equity.

Question	1. What are the two major components of stockholders' equity? Which accounts generally appear in each component?
	2. If a firm has a net income for the year, will the balance in the Retained Earnings account equal the net income? What is the meaning of the balance of the account?
	3. What is treasury stock? Where does it appear on a corporation's financial statements?

Apply	1. Nash Company has the following accounts among the items on its balance sheet at December 31, 2017: Common Stock, $10 par, 10,000 shares authorized, 9,000 issued, 8,000 outstanding Preferred Stock, $100 par, 8%, cumulative, 1,000 shares authorized, issued, and outstanding

Cash Dividend Payable	$ 50,000
Additional Paid-In Capital	200,000
Retained Earnings	100,000
Investment in Common Stock of Horton Company	60,000
Treasury Stock, 1,000 shares, common stock	20,000
Accumulated Other Comprehensive Income—Unrealized Gain on Investment Security	5,000

Develop the Stockholders' Equity section of the balance sheet for Nash Company at December 31, 2017.

2. Morris had the following transactions during 2017: (Show me how)

   a. Issued 2,000 shares of $10 par common stock for cash at $17 per share.

   b. Issued 1,000 shares of preferred stock to acquire land. The preferred stock has a par value of $5 per share. The land has been appraised at $7,000.

   c. Issued 5,000 shares of $10 par common stock as payment to a company that provided advertising for the company. The stock was selling on the stock exchange at $12 per share at the time of issuance.

   Record a journal entry for each transaction.

3. Indicate whether the following transactions increase, decrease, or have no effect on (a) total assets and on (b) total stockholders' equity.

   a. _____ Issue 1,000 shares of common stock at $10 per share

   b. _____ Purchase 500 shares of common stock as treasury stock at $15 per share

   c. _____ Reissue 400 shares of treasury stock at $18 per share

   d. _____ Reissue 100 shares of treasury stock at $12 per share

Answers are located at the end of the chapter.

MODULE 2 CASH DIVIDENDS, STOCK DIVIDENDS, AND STOCK SPLITS

Cash Dividends

Corporations may declare and issue several different types of dividends, the most common of which is a cash dividend to stockholders. Cash dividends may be declared quarterly, annually, or at other intervals. Normally, cash dividends are declared on one date, referred to as the *date of declaration,* and are paid out on a later date, referred to as the *payment date.* The dividend is paid to the stockholders who own the stock as of a particular date, the *date of record.*

Generally, two requirements must be met before the board of directors can declare a cash dividend. First, sufficient cash must be available by the payment date to pay to the stockholders. Second, the Retained Earnings account must have a sufficient positive balance, because dividends reduce the balance of the account. Most firms have an established policy concerning the portion of income that will be declared as dividends. The **dividend payout ratio** is calculated as the annual dividend amount divided by the annual net income. The dividend payout ratio for many firms is 50% or 60% and seldom exceeds 70%. Typically, utilities pay a high proportion of their earnings as dividends. In contrast, fast-growing companies in technology often pay nothing to stockholders.

Cash dividends become a liability on the date they are declared. An accounting entry should be recorded on that date to acknowledge the liability and reduce the balance of the Retained Earnings account.

LO5 Compute the amount of cash dividends when a firm has issued both preferred and common stock.

Dividend payout ratio
The annual dividend amount divided by the annual net income.

EXAMPLE 11-4 Recording the Declaration of a Dividend

Assume that on July 1, the board of directors of Grant Company declared a cash dividend of $7,000 to be paid on September 1. The effect of the declaration of the dividend is as follows:

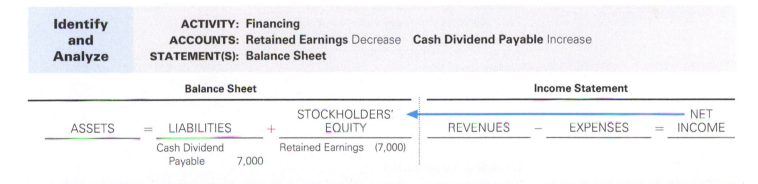

Identify and Analyze	**ACTIVITY:** Financing
	ACCOUNTS: Retained Earnings Decrease Cash Dividend Payable Increase
	STATEMENT(S): Balance Sheet

Balance Sheet

ASSETS	=	LIABILITIES	+	STOCKHOLDERS' EQUITY
		Cash Dividend Payable 7,000		Retained Earnings (7,000)

Income Statement

REVENUES	−	EXPENSES	=	NET INCOME

The Cash Dividend Payable account is a liability and is normally shown in the Current Liabilities section of the balance sheet.

Dividends reduce the amount of retained earnings *when declared.* When dividends are paid, the company reduces the liability to stockholders reflected in the Cash Dividend Payable account.

Cash Dividends for Preferred and Common Stock

When cash dividends involving more than one class of stock are declared, the corporation must determine the proper amount to allocate to each class of stock. As indicated earlier, the amount of dividends to which preferred stockholders have rights depends on the terms and provisions of the preferred stock. The proper allocation of cash dividends is illustrated with an example of a firm that has two classes of stock: preferred and common.

> **STUDY TIP**
>
> A dividend is not an expense on the income statement. It is a reduction of retained earnings and appears on the retained earnings statement. If it is a cash dividend, it also reduces the cash balance when paid.

EXAMPLE 11-5 Computing Dividend Payments for Noncumulative Preferred Stock

Assume that on December 31, 2017, Stricker Company has outstanding 10,000 shares of $10 par, 8% preferred stock and 40,000 shares of $5 par common stock. Stricker was unable to declare a dividend in 2015 or 2016 but wants to declare a $70,000 dividend for 2017.

If the terms of the stock agreement indicate that the preferred stock is not cumulative, the preferred stockholders do not have a right to dividends in arrears. The dividends that were not declared in 2015 and 2016 are simply lost and do not affect the distribution of the dividend in 2017. Therefore, the cash dividend declared in 2017 is allocated between preferred and common stockholders as follows:

	To Preferred	To Common
Step 1: Distribute current-year dividend to preferred (10,000 shares × $10 par × 8% × 1 year)	$8,000	
Step 2: Distribute remaining dividend to common ($70,000 – $8,000)		$62,000
Total allocated	$8,000	$62,000
Dividend per share:		
Preferred: $8,000/10,000 shares	$ 0.80	
Common: $62,000/40,000 shares		$ 1.55

EXAMPLE 11-6 Computing Dividend Payments for Cumulative Preferred Stock

If the terms of the stock agreement in Example 11-5 indicate that the preferred stock is cumulative, the preferred stockholders have a right to dividends in arrears before the current year's dividend is distributed. Therefore, Stricker performs the following steps:

	To Preferred	To Common
Step 1: Distribute dividends in arrears to preferred (10,000 shares × $10 par × 8% × 2 years)	$16,000	
Step 2: Distribute current-year dividend to preferred (10,000 shares × $10 par × 8% × 1 year)	8,000	
Step 3: Distribute remainder to common ($70,000 – $24,000)		$46,000
Total allocated	$24,000	$46,000
Dividend per share:		
Preferred: $24,000/10,000 shares	$ 2.40	
Common: $46,000/40,000 shares		$ 1.15

Stock Dividends

LO6 Show that you understand the difference between cash and stock dividends and the effect of stock dividends.

Cash dividends are the most popular and widely used form of dividend, but at times, corporations may use stock dividends instead of or in addition to cash dividends. A **stock dividend** occurs when a corporation declares and issues additional shares of its own stock to existing stockholders. Firms use stock dividends for several reasons.

Stock dividend
The issuance of additional shares of stock to existing stockholders.

1. Stock dividends do not require the use of cash. A corporation may not have sufficient cash available to declare a cash dividend.
2. Stock dividends reduce the market price of the stock. The lower price may make the stock more attractive to a wider range of investors.
3. Stock dividends do not represent taxable income to recipients and may be attractive to some wealthy investors.

Similar to cash dividends, stock dividends are normally declared by the board of directors on a specific date and the stock is distributed to the stockholders at a later date. The corporation recognizes the stock dividend on the date of declaration.

EXAMPLE 11-7 Recording a Small Stock Dividend

Assume that Shah Company's Stockholders' Equity category of the balance sheet appears as follows as of January 1, 2017:

Common stock, $10 par, 5,000 shares issued and outstanding	$ 50,000
Additional paid-in capital—Common	30,000
Retained earnings	70,000
Total stockholders' equity	$150,000

Assume that on January 2, 2017, Shah declares a 10% stock dividend to common stockholders to be distributed on April 1, 2017. Small stock dividends (usually those of 20% to 25%) normally are recorded at the *market value* of the stock as of the date of declaration. Assume that Shah's common stock is selling at $40 per share on that date. Therefore, the total market value of the stock dividend is $20,000 (10% of 5,000 shares outstanding, or 500 shares, times $40 per share). Shah records the transaction on the date of declaration and the effect is as follows:

Identify and Analyze

ACTIVITY: Financing
ACCOUNTS: Retained Earnings Decrease   Common Stock Dividend Distributable Increase
Additional Paid-In Capital—Common Increase
STATEMENT(S): Balance Sheet

Balance Sheet				Income Statement				
ASSETS	= LIABILITIES	+	STOCKHOLDERS' EQUITY	REVENUES	–	EXPENSES	=	NET INCOME
			Retained Earnings (20,000)					
			Common Stock					
			Dividend Distributable 5,000					
			Additional Paid-In					
			Capital—Common 15,000					

The Common Stock Dividend Distributable account represents shares of stock to be issued; it is not a liability account because no cash or assets are to be distributed to the stockholders. Thus, it should be treated as an account in the Stockholders' Equity section of the balance sheet and is a part of the contributed capital component of equity.

Note that the declaration of a stock dividend does not affect the total stockholders' equity of the corporation, although the retained earnings are reduced. That is, the Stockholders' Equity section of Shah's balance sheet on January 2, 2017, is as follows after the declaration of the dividend:

Common stock, $10 par, 5,000 shares issued and outstanding	$ 50,000
Common stock dividend distributable, 500 shares	5,000
Additional paid-in capital—Common	45,000
Retained earnings	50,000
Total stockholders' equity	$150,000

The account balances are different, but total stockholders' equity is $150,000 both before and after the declaration of the stock dividend. In effect, retained earnings has been capitalized (transferred permanently to the contributed capital accounts). When a corporation actually issues a stock dividend, an amount from the Stock Dividend Distributable account must be transferred to the appropriate stock account.

When a large stock dividend is declared (a stock dividend of more than 20% to 25% of the number of shares of stock outstanding), the stock dividend is reported at *par value* rather than at fair market value. Retained Earnings is decreased in the amount of the par value per share times the number of shares to be distributed.

EXAMPLE 11-8 Recording the Declaration of a Large Stock Dividend

Refer to the Shah Company in Example 11-7. Assume that instead of a 10% dividend, on January 2, 2017, Shah declares a 100% stock dividend to be distributed on April 1, 2017. The stock dividend results in 5,000 additional shares being issued and certainly meets the definition of a large stock dividend. The effect of the declaration of the large stock dividend is as follows:

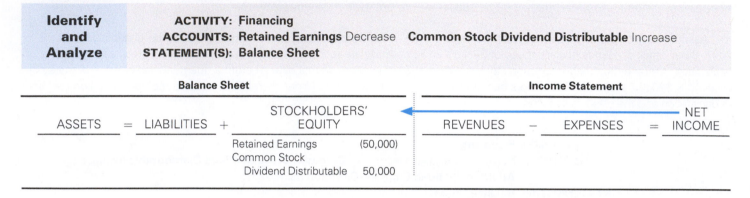

The effect when the stock is actually distributed is as follows:

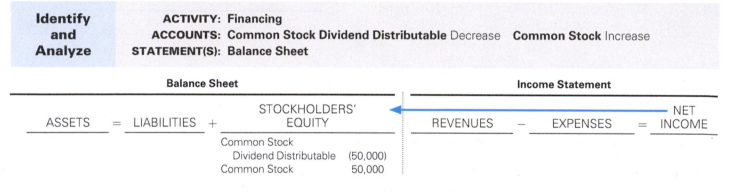

The Stockholders' Equity category of Shah's balance sheet as of April 1 after the stock dividend is as follows:

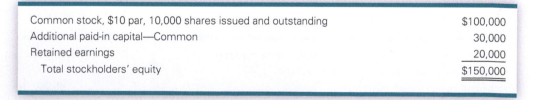

Common stock, $10 par, 10,000 shares issued and outstanding	$100,000
Additional paid-in capital—Common	30,000
Retained earnings	20,000
Total stockholders' equity	$150,000

Again, note that the stock dividend has not affected total stockholders' equity. Shah has $150,000 of stockholders' equity both before and after the stock dividend. The difference between large and small stock dividends is the amount transferred from retained earnings to the Contributed Capital portion of equity.

LO7 Determine the difference between stock dividends and stock splits.

Stock split
The creation of additional shares of stock with a reduction of the par value of the stock.

Stock Splits

A **stock split** is similar to a stock dividend in that it results in additional shares of stock outstanding and is nontaxable. In fact, firms may use a stock split for nearly the same reasons as a stock dividend: to increase the number of shares, reduce the market price per share, and make the stock more accessible to a wider range of investors.

There is an important legal difference, however. Stock dividends do not affect the par value per share of the stock, whereas stock splits reduce the par value per share. There also is an important accounting difference. An accounting transaction is *not recorded* when a corporation declares and executes a stock split. None of the Stockholders' Equity accounts are affected by the split. Rather, the note information accompanying the balance sheet must disclose the additional shares and the reduction of the par value per share.

EXAMPLE 11-9 Reporting a Stock Split

Refer to the Shah Company in Examples 11-7 and 11-8. Assume that on January 2, 2017, Shah issued a 2-for-1 stock split instead of a stock dividend. The split results in an additional 5,000 shares of stock outstanding but is not recorded in a formal accounting transaction. Therefore, the Stockholders' Equity section of Shah Company immediately after the stock split on January 2, 2017, is as follows:

Common stock, $5 par, 10,000 shares issued and outstanding	$ 50,000
Additional paid-in capital—Common	30,000
Retained earnings	70,000
Total stockholders' equity	$150,000

Note in Example 11-9 that the par value per share has been reduced from $10 to $5 per share of stock as a result of the split. Like a stock dividend, the split does not affect total stockholders' equity because no assets have been transferred. Therefore, the split simply results in more shares of stock with claims to the same net assets of the firm.

MODULE 2 TEST YOURSELF

Review	LO5 Compute the amount of cash dividends when a firm has issued both preferred and common stock.	• The amount of a preferred stock dividend depends on the terms of the stock agreement: cumulative, noncumulative, or cumulative and participating.
	LO6 Show that you understand the difference between cash and stock dividends and the effect of stock dividends.	• Stock dividends are given in lieu of cash dividends. Stockholders receive shares of stock, which do not require a current use of cash resources by the corporation. • Stock dividends do not affect total stockholders' equity. They reduce retained earnings and increase the amount of common stock and additional paid-in capital.
	LO7 Determine the difference between stock dividends and stock splits.	• Both stock splits and stock dividends increase the number of shares of stock outstanding although they are fundamentally different transactions. • Stock splits do not require an accounting transaction to be recorded, do not reduce the par value of the stock, and have no effect on retained earnings or additional paid-in capital.

Question	
	1. What is a stock dividend? How should it be recorded?
	2. Would you rather receive a cash dividend or a stock dividend from a company? Explain.
	3. What is the difference between stock dividends and stock splits? How should stock splits be recorded?

Apply

1. At December 31, 2017, White Company has the following:

    Common Stock, $10 par, 10,000 shares authorized, 9,000 issued, 8,000 outstanding

    Indicate whether the following would increase, decrease, or have no effect on (a) assets, (b) retained earnings, and (c) total stockholders' equity.

    a. _____ A company declares and pays a cash dividend of $25,000.

    b. _____ A company declares and issues a 10% stock dividend.

2. At December 31, 2017, Green Company and Blue Company have identical amounts of common stock and retained earnings as follows:

    Common Stock, $10 par, 50,000 shares authorized, 9,000 issued, 9,000 outstanding

    Retained Earnings, $500,000

    At December 31, 2017, Green Company declares and issues a 100% stock dividend, while Blue Company declares and issues a 2-for-1 stock split.

    Determine for each company the following amounts as of January 1, 2018:

    _____ Number of shares of common stock outstanding
    _____ Par value per share of the common stock
    _____ Total amount reported in Common Stock account
    _____ Retained earnings

Answers are located at the end of the chapter.

MODULE 3 ANALYSIS AND CASH FLOW ISSUES

LO8 Show that you understand the statement of stockholders' equity and comprehensive income.

Statement of stockholders' equity
Reflects the differences between beginning and ending balances for all accounts in the Stockholders' Equity category of the balance sheet.

In addition to a balance sheet, an income statement, and a cash flow statement, many annual reports contain a **statement of stockholders' equity**. This statement explains the reasons for the difference between the beginning and ending balance of each account in the Stockholders' Equity category of the balance sheet. Of course, if the only changes are the result of income and dividends, a statement of retained earnings is sufficient. When other changes have occurred in Stockholders' Equity accounts, this more complete statement is necessary.

The statement of stockholders' equity of Fun Fitness, Inc., is presented in Exhibit 11-3 for the year 2017. The statement starts with the beginning balances of each of the accounts as of December 31, 2017.

EXHIBIT 11-3 Fun Fitness's Statement of Stockholders' Equity, 2017

Fun Fitness, Inc. Statement of Stockholders' Equity For the Year Ended December 31, 2017				
(dollar amounts in millions)				
	Common Stock		**Paid-In Capital**	**Retained Earnings**
Stockholders' Equity	**Shares**	**Amount**		
Balance, December 31, 2016	1,000,000	$50.0	$350.0	$400.0
Net earnings				64.0
Cash dividend declared				(25.0)
Issuance of stock	100,000	5.0	39.0	
Balance, December 31, 2017	1,100,000	$55.0	$389.0	$439.0

The statement of stockholders' equity indicates the items or events that affected stockholders' equity during 2017. The items or events were as follows:

Item or Event	Effect on Stockholders' Equity
Net earnings	Increased retained earnings by $64.0 million
Dividends	Decreased retained earnings by $25.0 million
Shares issued	Increased common stock by $5.0 million and Increased paid-in capital by $39.0 million

The last line of the statement of stockholders' equity indicates the ending balances of the stockholders' equity accounts as of the balance sheet date, December 31, 2017. Note that each of the stockholders' equity accounts increased during 2017. The statement of stockholders' equity is useful in explaining the reasons for the changes that occurred.

What Is Comprehensive Income?

There has always been some question about which items or transactions should be shown on the income statement and included in the calculation of net income. Generally, the accounting rule-making bodies have held that the income statement should reflect an *all-inclusive* approach. That is, all events and transactions that affect income should be shown on the income statement. This approach prevents manipulation of the income figure by those who would like to show "good news" on the income statement and "bad news" directly on the retained earnings statement or the statement of stockholders' equity. The result of the all-inclusive approach is that the income statement includes items that are not necessarily under management's control, such as losses from natural disasters, meaning that the income statement may not be a true reflection of a company's future potential.

The FASB has accepted certain exceptions to the all-inclusive approach and has allowed items to be recorded directly to the Stockholders' Equity category. This text discussed one such item: unrealized gains and losses on investment securities. Exhibit 11-4 presents several additional items that are beyond the scope of this text. Items such as these have been excluded from the income statement for various reasons. Quite often, the justification is a concern for the volatility of the net income number.

Comprehensive income is the net assets increase resulting from all transactions during a time period (except for investments by owners and distributions to owners). Exhibit 11-4 presents the statement of comprehensive income and its relationship to the

Comprehensive income
The total change in net assets from all sources except investments by or distributions to the owners.

EXHIBIT 11-4 The Relationship between the Income Statement and the Statement of Comprehensive Income

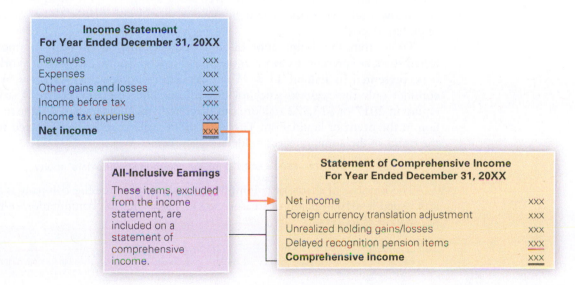

traditional income statement. It illustrates that comprehensive income encompasses all of the revenues and expenses that are presented on the income statement and includes items that are not presented on the income statement but affect total stockholders' equity.[1] The comprehensive income measure is truly all-inclusive because it includes transactions such as unrealized gains that affect stockholders' equity. Firms are required to disclose comprehensive income because it provides a more complete measure of performance.

What Analyzing Stockholders' Equity Reveals About a Firm's Value

LO9 Understand how investors use ratios to evaluate stockholders' equity.

Book value per share
Total stockholders' equity divided by the number of shares of common stock outstanding.

Users of financial statements are often interested in computing the value of a corporation's stock. This is a difficult task because *value* is not a well-defined term and means different things to different users. One measure of value is the book value of the stock. **Book value per share** of common stock represents the rights that each share of common stock has to the net assets of the corporation. The term *net assets* refers to the total assets of the firm minus total liabilities. In other words, net assets equal the total stockholders' equity of the corporation. Therefore, when only common stock is present, book value per share is measured as follows:

$$\text{Book Value per Share} = \frac{\text{Total Stockholders' Equity}}{\text{Numbers of Shares of Stock Outstanding}}$$

The book value per share is the amount per share of net assets to which the company's common stockholders have the rights. Book value per share does not indicate the price that should be paid by those who want to buy or sell the stock on the stock exchange. Book value also is an incomplete measure of value because the corporation's net assets are normally measured on the balance sheet at the original cost, not at the current value of the assets.

Calculating Book Value When Preferred Stock Is Present

The focus of the computation of book value per share is always on the value per share of the *common* stock. Therefore, the computation must be adjusted for corporations that have both preferred and common stock. The numerator of the fraction, total stockholders' equity, should be reduced by the rights that preferred stockholders have to the corporation's net assets. Normally, this can be accomplished by deducting the redemption value or liquidation value of the preferred stock along with any dividends in arrears on cumulative preferred stock. The denominator should not include the number of shares of preferred stock.

To illustrate the computation of book value per share when both common and preferred stock are present, we refer to the Stockholders' Equity category of Workout Wonders, presented in Exhibit 11-5. When calculating book value per share, we want to consider only the *common* stockholders' equity. The company had total stockholders' equity in 2017 of $13,972 million, but preferred stockholders had a right to $500 million in the event of liquidation. Therefore, $500 million must be deducted to calculate the rights of the common stockholders:

$13,972 – $500 = $13,472 million common stockholders' equity

The number of shares of common stock *outstanding* for the company is 1,782 million issued less 103 million of treasury stock. Therefore, the computation of book value per share is as follows:

[1] The format of Exhibit 11-4 is suggested by the FASB. The FASB also allows other possible formats of the statement of comprehensive income.

EXHIBIT 11-5 Workout Wonders' Stockholders' Equity Section

Stockholders' Equity Section of Balance Sheet December 31, 2017, and December 31, 2016		
(in millions)	2017	2016
Preferred stock, no par value (liquidation value, $500)	$ 400	$ 400
Common stock, par value 1 2/3 per share (issued 1,782 shares)	30	30
Capital in excess of par value	618	548
Retained earnings	18,730	15,961
Accumulated other comprehensive loss	(886)	(1,267)
Repurchased common stock, at cost (103 and 77 shares, respectively)	(4,920)	(3,376)
Total shareholders' equity	$13,972	$12,296

$13,472/1,679 = $8.02 Book Value per Share

If the company was liquidated and the assets sold at their recorded values, the common stockholders would receive $8.02 per share. Of course, if the company went bankrupt and had to liquidate assets at distressed values, stockholders would receive something less than book value.

Market Value per Share

The market value of the stock is a more meaningful measure of the value of the stock to those financial statement users interested in buying or selling shares of stock. The **market value per share** is the price at which stock is currently selling. For example, the listing for **Nike Inc.** stock on the Internet may indicate the following:

52-Week			Daily			
High	Low	Sym	High	Low	Last	Change
68.17	39.17	NKE	43.3	42.01	42.93	+0.48 (1.13%)

Market value per share
The selling price of the stock as indicated by the most recent transactions.

The two left-hand columns indicate the stock price for the last 52-week period. Nike Inc. sold as high as $68.17 and as low as $39.17 during that time period. The right-hand portion indicates the high and low for the previous day's trading and the closing price. Nike sold as high as $43.30 per share and as low as $42.01 per share and closed at $42.93. For the day, the stock increased by 1.13%, or $0.48 per share.

The market value of the stock depends on many factors. Stockholders must evaluate a corporation's earnings and liquidity as indicated in the financial statements. They also must consider a variety of economic factors and project all of the factors into the future to determine the proper market value per share of the stock. Many investors use sophisticated investment techniques, including large databases, to identify factors that affect a company's stock price.

How Changes in Stockholders' Equity Affect the Statement of Cash Flows

It is important to determine the effect that the issuance of stock, the repurchase of stock, and the payment of dividends have on the statement of cash flows. Exhibit 11-6 indicates how these stockholders' equity transactions affect cash flow and where the items should be placed on the statement of cash flows.

The issuance of stock is a method to finance business. Therefore, the cash *inflow* from the sale of stock to stockholders should be reflected as an inflow in the Financing Activities section of the statement of cash flows. Generally, companies do not disclose

STUDY TIP

Transactions affecting the Stockholders' Equity category of the balance sheet will appear in the Financing Activities category of the cash flow statement. Dividends are included in the cash flow statement when they are paid rather than when they are declared.

LO10 Explain the effects that transactions involving stockholders' equity have on the statement of cash flows.

EXHIBIT 11-6 The Effect of Stockholders' Equity Items on the Statement of Cash Flows

Item	Statement of Cash Flows	
	Operating Activities	
Net Income		xxx
	Investing Activities	
	Financing Activities	
Issuance of stock ➝		+
Retirement or repurchase of stock ➝		−
Payment of dividends ➝		−

separately the amount received for the par value of the stock and the amount received in excess of par. Rather, one amount is listed to indicate the total inflow of cash.

The repurchase or retirement of stock also represents a financing activity. Therefore, the cash *outflow* should be reflected as a reduction of cash in the Financing Activities section of the statement of cash flows. Again, companies do not distinguish between the amount paid for the par of the stock and the amount paid in excess of par.

How Will I Use ACCOUNTING?

If you are a portfolio manager, you will help clients meet their investing needs.

The income statement and the statement of cash flows are very useful in the analysis of companies because they tell the story of how a company's decisions have affected the value of that company. There is a great deal of information to be gleaned from these two statements—they provide a wealth of information to users of financial statements.

Dividends paid to stockholders represent a cost of financing the business with stock. Therefore, dividends paid should be reflected as a cash *outflow* in the Financing Activities section of the statement of cash flows. It is important to distinguish between the declaration of dividends and the payment of dividends. The cash outflow occurs at the time the dividend is paid and should be reflected on the statement of cash flows in that period.

The 2015 partial statement of cash flows for Southwest Airlines Co. is shown in Exhibit 11-7. During 2015, the company had considerable cash outflows associated with its long-term debt and capital lease obligations of $213 million. The company had additional cash outflows for payments of dividends of $180 million and repurchases of common stock of $1,180 million.

EXHIBIT 11-7 Southwest Airlines Co.'s Partial Statement of Cash Flows

Southwest Airlines Co.			
Consolidated Statement of Cash Flows			
	Year Ended December 31,		
(in millions)	**2015**	**2014**	**2013**
Cash Flows from Financing Activities:			
Proceeds from issuance of long-term debt	500	300	—
Proceeds from Employee stock plans	46	110	96
Reimbursement for assets constructed for others	24	27	—
Proceeds from termination of interest rate derivative instrument	12	—	—
Payments of long-term debt and capital lease obligations	(213)	(561)	(313)
Payments of cash dividends	(180)	(139)	(71)
Repayment of construction obligation	(10)	(11)	(5)
Repurchase of common stock	(1,180)	(955)	(540)
Other, net	(23)	(19)	(18)
Net cash used in financing activities	(1,024)	(1,248)	(851)

Source: Southwest Airlines Co., Form 10-K, For the Fiscal Year Ended December 31, 2015.

MODULE 3 TEST YOURSELF

Review	**LO8** Show that you understand the statement of stockholders' equity and comprehensive income.	• The statement of stockholders' equity shows how all of the equity accounts changed for a particular accounting period or specific periods. • Comprehensive income is based on the notion that the income statement be inclusive of all items affecting the wealth of an entity. The calculation of comprehensive income takes into account the increase in net assets during a time period.

	LO9 Understand how investors use ratios to evaluate stockholders' equity.	• Ratios used to analyze stockholders' equity are designed to measure some aspect of the value of the firm held by stockholders. Some common measures include:
		  • Book value per share—a measure based on balance sheet accounting amounts recorded.
		  • Market value per share—a measure aimed at assessing fair market value based on the current price of stock.

	LO10 Explain the effects that transactions involving stockholders' equity have on the statement of cash flows.	• Transactions involving stockholders' equity accounts are classified as financing activities. Issuing stock produces cash inflows. Dividends and the retirement or repurchase of stock produce cash outflows.

Question	1. How is the book value per share calculated? Does the amount calculated as book value per share mean that stockholders will receive a dividend equal to the book value?
	2. Can the market value per share of stock be determined by the information on the income statement?
	3. What is the difference between a statement of stockholders' equity and a retained earnings statement?

Apply	1. Deer Company has the following amounts in the Stockholders' Equity category of the balance sheet at December 31, 2017:

Preferred Stock, $100 par, 8%, noncumulative (liquidation value of $110 per share)	$100,000
Paid-In Capital—Preferred	50,000
Common Stock, $5 par	400,000
Paid-In Capital—Common	40,000
Retained Earnings	200,000

Determine the book value per share of the Deer Company stock.

2. For each of the following items, indicate (a) in what category of the statement of cash flows the item will be reported and (b) whether it will appear as a cash inflow, cash outflow, or neither.
Issuance of common stock for cash
Purchase of treasury stock
Issuance of a stock dividend
Reissuance of treasury stock
Issuance of common stock to acquire land

Answers are located at the end of the chapter.

MODULE 4 SOLE PROPRIETORSHIPS AND PARTNERSHIPS

The focus of Chapter 11, as with the rest of the text, has been on the corporate form of organization. Most of the large, influential companies in the United States are organized as corporations. They have a legal and economic existence that is separate from that of the owners of the business, the stockholders. Yet many other companies in the

APPENDIX

LO11 Describe the important differences between the sole proprietorship and partnership forms of organization versus the corporate form (Appendix).

economy are organized as sole proprietorships or partnerships. The purpose of this appendix is to show briefly how the characteristics of such organizations affect the accounting, particularly the accounting for the Owners' Equity category of the balance sheet.

Sole Proprietorships

Sole proprietorship
A business with a single owner.

A **sole proprietorship** is a business owned by one person. Most sole proprietorships are small in size, with the owner serving as the operator or manager of the company. The primary advantage of the sole proprietorship form of organization is its simplicity. The Owners' Equity category of the balance sheet consists of one account, the owner's capital account. The owner answers to no one but himself or herself. A disadvantage of the sole proprietorship is that all responsibility for the success or failure of the venture attaches to the owner, who often has limited resources.

There are three important points to remember about this form of organization:

1. A sole proprietorship is not a separate entity for legal purposes. This means that the law does not distinguish between the assets of the business and those of its owner. If an owner loses a lawsuit, for example, the law does not limit an owner's liability to the amount of assets of the business, but extends liability to the owner's personal assets. Thus, the owner is said to have *unlimited liability*.

2. Accountants adhere to the *entity principle* and maintain a distinction between the owner's personal assets and the assets of the sole proprietorship. The balance sheet of a sole proprietorship should reflect only the "business" assets and liabilities, with the difference reflected as owner's capital.

3. A sole proprietorship is not treated as a separate entity for federal income tax purposes. That is, the sole proprietorship does not pay tax on its income. Rather, the business income must be declared as income on the owner's personal tax return, and income tax is assessed at the personal tax rate rather than the rate that applies to companies organized as corporations. This may or may not be advantageous depending on the amount of income involved and the owner's tax situation.

Typical Transactions

When the owners of a corporation, the stockholders, invest in the corporation, they normally do so by purchasing stock. When investing in a sole proprietorship, the owner simply contributes cash or other assets to the business.

EXAMPLE 11-10 Recording Investments in a Sole Proprietorship

Assume that on January 1, 2017, Peter Tom began a new business by investing $10,000 cash. The effect of the investment by the owner is as follows:

Identify and Analyze	**ACTIVITY:** Financing **ACCOUNTS:** Cash Increase Peter Tom, Capital Increase **STATEMENT(S):** Balance Sheet

Balance Sheet			Income Statement		
ASSETS	= LIABILITIES +	STOCKHOLDERS' EQUITY	REVENUES	− EXPENSES	= NET INCOME
Cash 10,000		Peter Tom, Capital 10,000			

The Peter Tom, Capital account is an owner's equity account and reflects the rights of the owner to the business assets.

An owner's withdrawal of assets from the business is recorded as a reduction of owner's equity. Assume that on July 1, 2017, Peter Tom took an auto valued at $6,000 from the business to use as his personal auto. The effect of the withdrawl is as follows:

Identify and Analyze	**ACTIVITY:** Financing and Investing
	ACCOUNTS: Peter Tom, Drawing Increase Equipment Decrease
	STATEMENT(S): Balance Sheet

Balance Sheet					Income Statement			
ASSETS	=	LIABILITIES	+	OWNERS' EQUITY ←	REVENUES	−	EXPENSES	= NET INCOME
Equipment (6,000)				Peter Tom, Drawing (6,000)				

The Peter Tom, Drawing account is a contra-equity account. Sometimes a drawing account is referred to as a *withdrawals account,* as in Peter Tom, Withdrawals. An increase in the account reduces the owner's equity. At the end of the fiscal year, the drawing account should be closed to the capital account and the effect is as follows:

Identify and Analyze	**ACTIVITY:** Operating
	ACCOUNTS: Peter Tom, Capital Decrease Peter Tom, Drawing Decrease
	STATEMENT(S): Balance Sheet

Balance Sheet					Income Statement			
ASSETS	=	LIABILITIES	+	OWNERS' EQUITY ←	REVENUES	−	EXPENSES	= NET INCOME
				Peter Tom, Capital (6,000)				
				Peter Tom, Drawing 6,000				

The amount of the net income of the business also should be reflected in the capital account. Assume that all revenue and expense accounts of Peter Tom Company have been closed to the Income Summary account, resulting in a balance of $4,000, the net income for the year. The Income Summary account is closed to capital and the effect is as follows:

Identify and Analyze	**ACTIVITY:** Operating
	ACCOUNTS: Income Summary Decrease Peter Tom, Capital Increase
	STATEMENT(S): Balance Sheet

Balance Sheet					Income Statement			
ASSETS	=	LIABILITIES	+	OWNERS' EQUITY ←	REVENUES	−	EXPENSES	= NET INCOME
				Income Summary (4,000)				
				Peter Tom, Capital 4,000				

The Owner's Equity section of the balance sheet for Peter Tom Company consists of one account, the capital account, calculated as follows:

Beginning balance, Jan.1, 2017	$ 0
Investments	10,000
Net income	4,000
Withdrawals	(6,000)
Ending balance, Dec. 31, 2017	$ 8,000

Partnerships

A **partnership** is a company owned by two or more people. Like sole proprietorships, most partnerships are fairly small businesses formed when individuals combine their capital and managerial talents for a common business purpose. Other partnerships are

Partnership
A business owned by two or more individuals that has the characteristic of unlimited liability.

large, national organizations. For example, the major public accounting firms are very large, national companies but are organized in most states as partnerships.

Partnerships have characteristics similar to those of sole proprietorships. The following are the most important characteristics of partnerships:

1. Unlimited liability
  - Legally, the assets of the business are not separate from the partners' personal assets.
  - Each partner is personally liable for the debts of the partnership.
  - Creditors have a legal claim first to the assets of the partnership and then to the assets of the individual partners.

2. Limited life
  - Partnerships do not have a separate legal existence and an unlimited life. The life of a partnership exists only so long as the contract between the partners is valid.
  - The partnership ends when a partner withdraws or a new partner is added. A new partnership must be created for the business to continue.

3. Not taxed as a separate entity
  - Partnerships are subject to the same tax features as sole proprietorships.
  - The partnership itself does not pay federal income tax. Rather, the income of the partnership is treated as personal income on each of the partners' individual tax returns and is taxed as personal income.
  - All partnership income is subject to federal income tax on the individual partners' returns even if it is not distributed to the partners.
  - A variety of other factors affects the tax consequences of partnerships versus the corporate form of organization. Those aspects are quite complex and beyond the scope of this text.

Partnership agreement
Specifies how much the owners will invest, what their salaries will be, and how profits will be shared.

A partnership is based on a **partnership agreement**. The agreement should be in writing and should detail items such as how much capital each partner is to invest, how much time each partner is expected to devote to the business, what the salary of each partner is, and how income of the partnership is to be divided. If a partnership agreement is not present, the courts may be forced to settle disputes between partners. Therefore, the partners should develop a partnership agreement when the firm is first established and review the agreement periodically to determine if changes are necessary.

Investments and Withdrawals

In a partnership, it is important to account separately for the capital of each partner. A capital account should be established in the Owners' Equity section of the balance sheet for each partner. Investments into the company should be credited to the partner making the investment.

EXAMPLE 11-11 Recording Investments in a Partnership

Assume that on January 1, 2017, Paige Thoms and Amy Rebec begin a partnership named AP Company. Paige contributes $10,000 cash, and Amy contributes equipment valued at $5,000. The effect of the investment is as follows:

Identify and Analyze	**ACTIVITY:** Financing and Investing **ACCOUNTS:** Cash Increase Equipment Increase Page Thoms, Capital Increase Amy Rebec, Capital Increase **STATEMENT(S):** Balance Sheet

Balance Sheet					Income Statement				
ASSETS		= LIABILITIES +	OWNERS' EQUITY		REVENUES	–	EXPENSES	=	NET INCOME
Cash	10,000		Paige Thoms, Capital	10,000					
Equipment	5,000		Amy Rebec, Capital	5,000					

A drawing account also should be established for each owner of the company to account for withdrawals of assets. Assume that on April 1, 2017, each owner withdraws $2,000 of cash from AP Company. The effect of the withdrawal is as follows:

Identify and Analyze	**ACTIVITY:** Financing
	ACCOUNTS: **Page Thoms, Drawing** Increase **Amy Rebec, Drawing** Increase
	Cash Decrease
	STATEMENT(S): Balance Sheet

Balance Sheet				Income Statement			
ASSETS	= LIABILITIES	+	OWNERS' EQUITY	REVENUES	– EXPENSES	=	NET INCOME
Cash (4,000)			Paige Thoms, Drawing (2,000)				
			Amy Rebec, Drawing (2,000)				

Distribution of Income

The partnership agreement governs the manner in which income should be allocated to partners. The distribution may recognize the partners' relative investment in the business, their time and effort, their expertise and talents, or other factors. Three methods of income allocation will be illustrated, but be aware that partnerships use many other allocation methods.

One way to allocate income is to divide it evenly between the partners. In fact, when a partnership agreement is not present, the courts specify that an equal allocation must be applied regardless of the relative contributions or efforts of the partners. For example, assume that AP Company has $30,000 of net income for the period and has established an agreement that income should be allocated evenly between the two partners, Paige and Amy. Each capital account would be increased by $15,000. The effect of closing the Income Summary account to the capital accounts is as follows:

Identify and Analyze	**ACTIVITY:** Operating
	ACCOUNTS: **Income Summary** Decrease **Page Thoms, Capital** Increase
	Amy Rebec, Capital Increase
	STATEMENT(S): Balance Sheet

Balance Sheet				Income Statement			
ASSETS	= LIABILITIES	+	OWNERS' EQUITY	REVENUES	– EXPENSES	=	NET INCOME
			Income Summary (30,000)				
			Paige Thoms, Capital 15,000				
			Amy Rebec, Capital 15,000				

An equal distribution of income to all partners is easy to apply but is not fair to those partners who have contributed more in money or time to the partnership.

Another way to allocate income is to specify in the partnership agreement that income be allocated according to a *stated ratio*. For example, Paige and Amy may specify that all income of AP Company should be allocated in a 2-to-1 ratio, with Paige receiving the larger portion. If that allocation method is applied to Example 11-11, Paige Thoms, Capital would be increased by $20,000 and Amy Rebec, Capital would be increased by $10,000. If that allocation method is applied to Example 11-11, the effect is as follows:

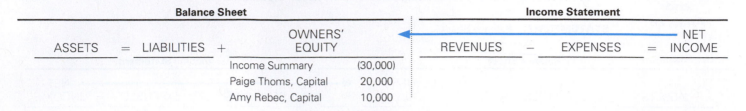

Identify and Analyze	**ACTIVITY:** Operating **ACCOUNTS:** Income Summary Decrease **Page Thoms, Capital** Increase **Amy Rebec, Capital** Increase **STATEMENT(S):** Balance Sheet

Balance Sheet   **Income Statement**

ASSETS	=	LIABILITIES	+	OWNERS' EQUITY		REVENUES	−	EXPENSES	=	NET INCOME
				Income Summary	(30,000)					
				Paige Thoms, Capital	20,000					
				Amy Rebec, Capital	10,000					

Finally, an allocation method that more accurately reflects the partners' input is illustrated. It is based on salaries, interest on invested capital, and a stated ratio. Assume that the partnership agreement of AP Company specifies that Paige and Amy be allowed a salary of $6,000 and $4,000, respectively; that each partner receive 10% on her capital balance; and that any remaining income be allocated equally. Assume that AP Company has been in operation for several years and that the capital balances of the owners at the end of 2017, before the income distribution, are as follows:

Paige Thoms, Capital	$40,000
Amy Rebec, Capital	50,000

If AP Company calculated that its 2017 net income (before partner salaries) was $30,000, income would be allocated between the partners as follows:

	Paige	Amy
Distributed for salaries:	$ 6,000	$ 4,000
Distributed for interest:		
Paige ($40,000 × 10%)	4,000	
Amy ($50,000 × 10%)		5,000
Remainder = $30,000 − $10,000 − $9,000 = $11,000		
Remainder distributed equally:		
Paige ($11,000/2)	5,500	
Amy ($11,000/2)		5,500
Total distributed	$15,500	$14,500

Paige Thoms, Capital would be increased by $15,500, and Amy Rebec, Capital, by $14,500. The effect of closing the Income Summary account to the capital accounts is as follows:

Identify and Analyze	**ACTIVITY:** Operating **ACCOUNTS:** Income Summary Decrease **Paige Thoms, Capital** Increase **Amy Rebec, Capital** Increase **STATEMENT(S):** Balance Sheet

Balance Sheet   **Income Statement**

ASSETS	=	LIABILITIES	+	OWNERS' EQUITY		REVENUES	−	EXPENSES	=	NET INCOME
				Income Summary	(30,000)					
				Paige Thoms, Capital	15,500					
				Amy Rebec, Capital	14,500					

This indicates that the amounts of $15,500 and $14,500 were allocated to Paige and Amy, respectively. It does not indicate the amount actually paid to (or withdrawn by) the partners. However, for tax purposes, the income of the partnership is treated as personal income on the partners' individual tax returns regardless of whether the income is actually paid in cash to the partners.

MODULE 4 TEST YOURSELF

Review	**LO11** Describe the important differences between the sole proprietorship and partnership forms of organization versus the corporate form (Appendix).	• Sole proprietorships are businesses that are not incorporated and are owned by one individual. The business entity and individual are not distinguished from one another for legal and tax purposes. • Partnerships are also unincorporated entities but are owned by two or more individuals. The partners and their respective shares of the business are not distinguished from one another for legal purposes. The partnership itself is not taxed on earnings, but individual partners are taxed for their share. • Corporations, unlike partnerships, have some of the following distinguishing characteristics: they are generally taxable entities and have an unlimited life. The corporate form has been adopted by most larger businesses and is therefore emphasized in this text.
Question	1. What is an advantage of organizing a company as a corporation rather than a partnership? Why don't all companies incorporate? (Appendix)	
	2. What are some ways that partnerships could share income among the partners? (Appendix)	
Apply	Furyk Company opened business as a sole proprietorship on January 1, 2017. The owner contributed $500,000 cash on that date. During the year, the company had a net income of $10,000. The company purchased equipment of $100,000 during the year. The owner also withdrew $60,000 to pay for personal expenses during 2017. Determine the company's owner's equity at December 31, 2017.	

Answers are located at the end of the chapter.

RATIO REVIEW

$$\text{Book Value per Share} = \frac{\text{Total Stockholders' Equity}^*}{\text{Number of Shares of Stock Outstanding}}$$

*When preferred stock is outstanding, the redemption value or liquidation value (disclosed on the preferred stock line or in the notes) of the preferred stock must be subtracted from total stockholders' equity.

ACCOUNTS HIGHLIGHTED

Account Title	Where It Appears	In What Section	Page Number
Common Stock	Balance Sheet	Contributed Capital	506
Preferred Stock	Balance Sheet	Contributed Capital	507
Additional Paid-In Capital	Balance Sheet	Contributed Capital	508
Retained Earnings	Balance Sheet	Retained Earnings	511
Treasury Stock	Balance Sheet	(bottom portion of stockholders' equity as a contra account)	513
Cash Dividend Payable	Balance Sheet	Current Liabilities	514
Stock Dividend Distributable	Balance Sheet	Contributed Capital	514

KEY TERMS QUIZ

Read each definition below and write the number of the definition in the blank beside the appropriate term. The quiz solutions appear at the end of the chapter.

_____ Authorized shares
_____ Issued shares
_____ Outstanding shares
_____ Par value
_____ Additional paid-in capital
_____ Retained earnings
_____ Convertible feature
_____ Callable feature
_____ Cumulative feature
_____ Participating feature
_____ Treasury stock

_____ Retirement of stock
_____ Dividend payout ratio
_____ Stock dividend
_____ Stock split
_____ Statement of stockholders' equity
_____ Comprehensive income
_____ Book value per share
_____ Market value per share
_____ Sole proprietorship (Appendix)
_____ Partnership (Appendix)
_____ Partnership agreement (Appendix)

1. The number of shares sold or distributed to stockholders.
2. An arbitrary amount that represents the legal capital of the firm.
3. Net income that has been made by the corporation but not paid out as dividends.
4. The right to dividends in arrears before the current-year dividend is distributed.
5. Allows preferred stock to be exchanged for common stock.
6. Stock issued by the firm and then repurchased but not retired.
7. The annual dividend amount divided by the annual net income.
8. Reflects the differences between beginning and ending balances for all accounts in the Stockholders' Equity category of the balance sheet.
9. The creation of additional shares of stock with a reduction of the par value of the stock.
10. Total stockholders' equity divided by the number of shares of common stock outstanding.
11. The total change in net assets from all sources except investments by or distributions to the owners.
12. The selling price of the stock as indicated by the most recent transactions.
13. The maximum number of shares a corporation may issue as indicated in the corporate charter.
14. The number of shares issued less the number of shares held as treasury stock.
15. The amount received for the issuance of stock in excess of the par value of the stock.
16. Allows preferred stockholders to share on a percentage basis in the distribution of an abnormally large dividend.
17. Allows the firm to eliminate a class of stock by paying the stockholders a specified amount.
18. When the stock is repurchased with no intention of reissuing at a later date.
19. The issuance of additional shares of stock to existing stockholders.
20. A business owned by two or more individuals that has the characteristic of unlimited liability.
21. Specifies how much the owners will invest, what their salaries will be, and how profits will be shared.
22. A business with a single owner.

ALTERNATE TERMS

additional paid-in capital paid-in capital in excess of par
additional paid-in capital—treasury stock paid-in capital from treasury stock transactions
callable feature redeemable

capital account owners' equity account
contributed capital paid-in capital
retained earnings retained income
small stock dividend stock dividend less than 20%
stockholders' equity owners' equity

REVIEW PROBLEM & SOLUTION

Andrew Company was incorporated on January 1, 2017, under a corporate charter that authorized the issuance of 50,000 shares of $5 par common stock and 20,000 shares of $100 par, 8% preferred stock. The following events occurred during 2017. Andrew wants to record the events and develop financial statements on December 31, 2017.

a. Issued for cash 10,000 shares of common stock at $25 per share and 1,000 shares of preferred stock at $110 per share on January 15, 2017.

b. Acquired a patent on April 1 in exchange for 2,000 shares of common stock. At the time of the exchange, the common stock was selling on the local stock exchange for $30 per share.

c. Repurchased 500 shares of common stock on May 1 at $20 per share. The corporation is holding the stock to be used for an employee bonus plan.

d. Declared a cash dividend of $1 per share to common stockholders and an 8% dividend to preferred stockholders on July 1. The preferred stock is noncumulative, nonparticipating. The dividend will be distributed on August 1.

e. Distributed the cash dividend on August 1.

f. Declared and distributed to preferred stockholders a 10% stock dividend on September 1. At the time of the dividend declaration, preferred stock was valued at $130 per share.

g. On December 31, calculated the annual net income for the year to be $200,000.

Required

1. Identify and analyze the effect of items (a) through (f).
2. Develop the Stockholders' Equity section of Andrew Company's balance sheet at December 31, 2017. You do not need to consider the notes that accompany the balance sheet.
3. Determine the book value per share of the common stock. Assume that the preferred stock can be redeemed at par.

Solution to Review Problem

1. The following entries should be recorded:

   a. The effect of the issuance of stock is as follows:

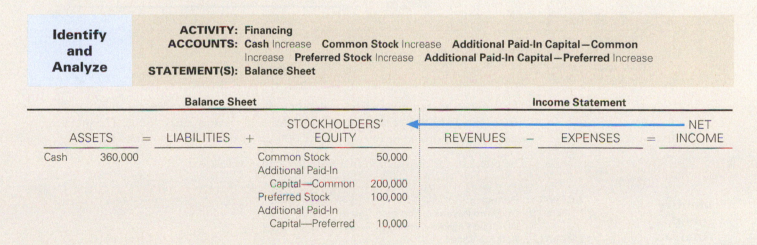

b.   The effect of the issuance of stock for the patent is as follows:

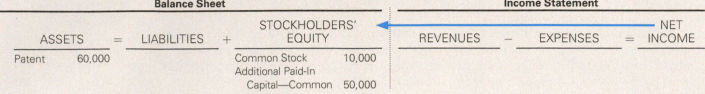

Identify and Analyze	**ACTIVITY:** Financing and Investing
	ACCOUNTS: **Patent** Increase **Common Stock** Increase
	Additional Paid-In Capital—Common Increase
	STATEMENT(S): Balance Sheet

Balance Sheet						Income Statement					
				STOCKHOLDERS'							NET
ASSETS	=	LIABILITIES	+	EQUITY		REVENUES	−	EXPENSES	=		INCOME
Patent 60,000				Common Stock 10,000							
				Additional Paid-In							
				Capital—Common 50,000							

c.   The effect of the stock acquired as treasury stock is as follows:

Identify and Analyze	**ACTIVITY:** Financing
	ACCOUNTS: **Treasury Stock** Increase **Cash** Decrease
	STATEMENT(S): Balance Sheet

Balance Sheet						Income Statement					
				STOCKHOLDERS'							NET
ASSETS	=	LIABILITIES	+	EQUITY		REVENUES	−	EXPENSES	=		INCOME
Cash (10,000)				Treasury Stock (10,000)							

d.   A cash dividend should be declared on the number of shares of stock outstanding as of July 1. The effect is as follows:

Identify and Analyze	**ACTIVITY:** Financing
	ACCOUNTS: **Retained Earnings** Decrease **Dividend Payable—Common** Increase
	Dividend Payable—Preferred Increase
	STATEMENT(S): Balance Sheet

Balance Sheet						Income Statement					
				STOCKHOLDERS'							NET
ASSETS	=	LIABILITIES	+	EQUITY		REVENUES	−	EXPENSES	=		INCOME
		Dividend Payable—		Retained Earnings (19,500)							
		Common 11,500									
		Dividend Payable—									
		Preferred 8,000									

The number of common shares outstanding should be calculated as the number of shares issued (12,000) less the number of shares of treasury stock (500). The preferred stock dividend should be calculated as 1,000 shares times $100 par times 8%.

e.   The effect of the distribution of a cash dividend is as follows:

Identify and Analyze	**ACTIVITY:** Financing
	ACCOUNTS: **Dividend Payable—Common** Decrease
	Dividend Payable—Preferred Decrease **Cash** Decrease
	STATEMENT(S): Balance Sheet

Balance Sheet						Income Statement					
				STOCKHOLDERS'							NET
ASSETS	=	LIABILITIES	+	EQUITY		REVENUES	−	EXPENSES	=		INCOME
Cash (19,500)		Dividend Payable—									
		Common (11,500)									
		Dividend Payable—									
		Preferred (8,000)									

f.   A stock dividend should be based on the number of shares of stock outstanding and should be declared and recorded at the market value of the stock. The effect is as follows:

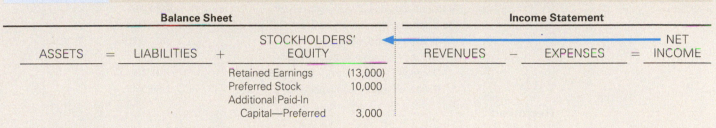

| **Identify and Analyze** | **ACTIVITY:** Financing
ACCOUNTS: Retained Earnings Decrease Preferred Stock Increase
Additional Paid-In Capital—Preferred Increase
STATEMENT(S): Balance Sheet |

	Balance Sheet					Income Statement			
ASSETS	=	LIABILITIES	+	STOCKHOLDERS' EQUITY		REVENUES	−	EXPENSES	= NET INCOME
				Retained Earnings	(13,000)				
				Preferred Stock	10,000				
				Additional Paid-In Capital—Preferred	3,000				

2.   The Stockholders' Equity section for Andrew Company after completing these transactions appears as follows:

Preferred stock, $100 par, 8%, 20,000 shares authorized, 1,100 issued	$110,000
Common stock, $5 par, 50,000 shares authorized, 12,000 issued	60,000
Additional paid-in capital—Preferred	13,000
Additional paid-in capital—Common	250,000
Retained earnings	167,500*
Total contributed capital and retained earnings	$600,500
Treasury stock, 500 shares, common	(10,000)
Total stockholders' equity	$590,500

*$200,000 − $19,500 − $13,000 = $167,500

3.   The book value per share of the common stock is calculated as follows:

($590,500 − $110,000)/11,500 shares = $41.78

EXERCISES

Exercise 11-1 Stockholders' Equity Accounts   LO1

MJ Company has identified the following items. Indicate whether each item is included in an account in the Stockholders' Equity category of the balance sheet and identify the account title. Also, indicate whether the item would increase or decrease stockholders' equity.
1.   Preferred stock issued by MJ
2.   Amount received by MJ in excess of par value when preferred stock was issued
3.   Dividends in arrears on MJ preferred stock
4.   Cash dividend declared but unpaid on MJ stock
5.   Stock dividend declared but unissued by MJ
6.   Treasury stock
7.   Amount received in excess of cost when treasury stock is reissued by MJ
8.   Retained earnings

Exercise 11-2 Solve for Unknowns   LO1

The Stockholders' Equity category of Zache Company's balance sheet appears below.

Common stock, $10 par, 10,000 shares issued, 9,200 outstanding	$?
Additional paid-in capital	?
Total contributed capital	$350,000
Retained earnings	100,000
Treasury stock, ? shares at cost	10,000
Total stockholders' equity	$?

(Continued)

Required

1. Determine the missing values indicated by question marks.
2. What was the cost per share of the treasury stock?

LO1   Exercise 11-3 Solving for Stockholders' Equity Amounts

Assume that the following amounts are known for Miles Company for the current year:

Retained Earnings, beginning balance	$420,000
Retained Earnings, ending balance	500,000
Cash dividends declared	100,000
Fair value of large stock dividend declared	50,000
Dividend Payable, beginning balance	90,000
Dividend Payable, ending balance	80,000

Required

1. Assume that the only other amount that affected Retained Earnings during the year was the net income. Compute the net income for Miles Company for the current year.
2. Compute the amount of cash dividends actually paid in cash to stockholders during the year.

LO1   Exercise 11-4 Solving for Stockholders' Equity Amounts

Assume that the following amounts are known for Colten Company for the current year:

Retained Earnings, beginning balance	$210,000
Retained Earnings, ending balance	250,000
Net income	115,000
Fair value of large stock dividend declared	25,000
Dividend Payable, beginning balance	75,000
Dividend Payable, ending balance	80,000

Required

1. Assume that the only other amount that affected Retained Earnings during the year was a cash dividend that was declared. Compute the amount of the cash dividend declared during the current year.
2. Compute the amount of cash dividends actually paid in cash to stockholders during the year.

LO3   Exercise 11-5 Stock Issuance

EXAMPLE 11-1, 11-2

Horace Company had the following transactions during 2017, its first year of business.

a. Issued 5,000 shares of $5 par common stock for cash at $15 per share.
b. Issued 7,000 shares of common stock on May 1 to acquire a factory building from Barkley Company. Barkley had acquired the building in 2013 at a price of $150,000. Horace estimated that the building was worth $175,000 on May 1, 2017.
c. Issued 2,000 shares of stock on June 1 to acquire a patent. The accountant has been unable to estimate the value of the patent but has determined that Horace's common stock was selling at $25 per share on June 1.

Required

1. Identify and analyze the effect of each transaction.
2. Determine the balance sheet amounts for common stock and additional paid-in capital.

LO3   Exercise 11-6 Stock Issuance

EXAMPLE 11-1

The following transactions are for Weber Corporation in 2017:

a. On March 1, the corporation was organized and received authorization to issue 5,000 shares of 8%, $100 par value preferred stock and 2,000,000 shares of $10 par value common stock.
b. On March 10, Weber issued 5,000 shares of common stock at $35 per share.
c. On March 18, Weber issued 100 shares of preferred stock at $120 per share.
d. On April 12, Weber issued another 10,000 shares of common stock at $45 per share.

Required

1. Identify and analyze the effect of each transaction.
2. Prepare the Stockholders' Equity section of the balance sheet as of December 31, 2017.
3. Does the balance sheet indicate the market value of the stock at year-end? Explain.

Exercise 11-7 Treasury Stock

LO4
EXAMPLE 11-3

The Stockholders' Equity category of Bradford Company's balance sheet on January 1, 2017, appeared as follows:

Common stock, $10 par, 10,000 shares issued and outstanding	$100,000
Additional paid-in capital	50,000
Retained earnings	80,000
Total stockholders' equity	$230,000

The following transactions occurred during 2017:

a. Reacquired 2,000 shares of common stock at $20 per share on July 1.
b. Reacquired 400 shares of common stock at $18 per share on August 1.

Required

1. Identify and analyze the effect of each transaction.
2. Assume that the company resold the shares of treasury stock at $28 per share on October 1. Did the company benefit from the treasury stock transaction? If so, where is the "gain" presented on the balance sheet?

Exercise 11-8 Treasury Stock Transactions

LO4
EXAMPLE 11-3

The Stockholders' Equity category of Little Joe's balance sheet on January 1, 2017, appeared as follows:

Common stock, $5 par, 40,000 shares issued and outstanding	$200,000
Additional paid-in capital	90,000
Retained earnings	100,000
Total stockholders' equity	$390,000

The following transactions occurred during 2017:

a. Reacquired 5,000 shares of common stock at $20 per share on February 1.
b. Reacquired 1,200 shares of common stock at $13 per share on March 1.

Required

1. Identify and analyze the effect of the transactions.
2. Assume that the treasury stock was reissued on October 1 at $12 per share. Did the company benefit from the treasury stock reissuance? Where is the "gain" or "loss" presented on the financial statements?
3. What effect did the two transactions to purchase treasury stock and the later reissuance of that stock have on the Stockholders' Equity section of the balance sheet?

Exercise 11-9 Cash Dividends

LO5
EXAMPLE 11-5, 11-6

Kerry Company has 1,000 shares of $100 par value, 9% preferred stock and 10,000 shares of $10 par value common stock outstanding. The preferred stock is cumulative and nonparticipating. Dividends were paid in 2013. Since 2013, Kerry has declared and paid dividends as follows:

2014	$ 0
2015	10,000
2016	20,000
2017	25,000

(Continued)

Required

1. Determine the amount of the dividends to be allocated to preferred and common stockholders for each year 2015 to 2017.
2. If the preferred stock had been noncumulative, how much would have been allocated to the preferred and common stockholders each year?

LO5 **Exercise 11-10 Cash Dividends**

EXAMPLE 11-5, 11-6

The Stockholders' Equity category of Jackson Company's balance sheet as of January 1, 2017, appeared as follows:

Preferred stock, $100 par, 8%, 2,000 shares issued and outstanding	$200,000
Common stock, $10 par, 5,000 shares issued and outstanding	50,000
Additional paid-in capital	300,000
Total contributed capital	$550,000
Retained earnings	400,000
Total stockholders' equity	$950,000

The notes that accompany the financial statements indicate that Jackson has not paid dividends for the two years prior to 2017. On July 1, 2017, Jackson declares a dividend of $100,000 to be paid to preferred and common stockholders on August 1.

Required

1. Determine the amounts of the dividends to be allocated to preferred and common stockholders assuming that the preferred stock is noncumulative, nonparticipating stock.
2. Identify and analyze the effect of the transactions on July 1 and August 1, 2017.
3. Determine the amounts of the dividends to be allocated to preferred and common stockholders assuming instead that the preferred stock is cumulative, nonparticipating stock.

LO6 **Exercise 11-11 Stock Dividends**

EXAMPLE 11-7

The Stockholders' Equity category of Worthy Company's balance sheet as of January 1, 2017, appeared as follows:

Common stock, $10 par, 40,000 shares issued and outstanding	$400,000
Additional paid-in capital	100,000
Retained earnings	400,000
Total stockholders' equity	$900,000

The following transactions occurred during 2017:

a. Declared a 10% stock dividend to common stockholders on January 15. At the time of the dividend, the common stock was selling for $30 per share. The stock dividend was to be issued to stockholders on January 30, 2017.
b. Distributed the stock dividend to the stockholders on January 30, 2017.

Required

1. Identify and analyze the effect of each transaction.
2. Develop the Stockholders' Equity category of Worthy Company's balance sheet as of January 31, 2017, after the stock dividend was issued. What effect did those transactions have on total stockholders' equity?

LO7 **Exercise 11-12 Stock Dividends versus Stock Splits**

EXAMPLE 11-8, 11-9

Campbell Company wants to increase the number of shares of its common stock outstanding and is considering a stock dividend versus a stock split. The Stockholders' Equity section of the firm's most recent balance sheet appeared as follows:

Show me how

Common stock, $10 par, 50,000 shares issued and outstanding	$ 500,000
Additional paid-in capital	750,000
Retained earnings	880,000
Total stockholders' equity	$2,130,000

If a stock dividend is chosen, the firm wants to declare a 100% stock dividend. Because the stock dividend qualifies as a "large stock dividend," it must be recorded at par value. If a stock split is chosen, Campbell will declare a 2-for-1 split.

Required

1. Compare the effects of the stock dividends and stock splits on the accounting equation.
2. Develop the Stockholders' Equity category of Campbell's balance sheet (a) after the stock dividend and (b) after the stock split.

Exercise 11-13 Stock Dividends and Stock Splits

LO7
EXAMPLE 11-7, 11-9

Whitacre Company's Stockholders' Equity section of the balance sheet on December 31, 2016, was as follows:

Common stock, $10 par value, 60,000 shares issued and outstanding	$ 600,000
Additional paid-in capital	480,000
Retained earnings	1,240,000
Total stockholders' equity	$2,320,000

On May 1, 2017, Whitacre declared and issued a 15% stock dividend, when the stock was selling for $20 per share. Then on November 1, it declared and issued a 2-for-1 stock split.

Required

1. How many shares of stock are outstanding at year-end?
2. What is the par value per share of these shares?
3. Develop the Stockholders' Equity category of Whitacre's balance sheet as of December 31, 2017.

Exercise 11-14 Reporting Changes in Stockholders' Equity Items

LO8

On May 1, 2016, Ryde Inc. had common stock of $345,000, additional paid-in capital of $1,298,000, and retained earnings of $3,013,000. Ryde did not purchase or sell any common stock during the year. The company reported net income of $556,000 and declared dividends in the amount of $78,000 during the year ended April 30, 2017.

Required

Prepare a financial statement that explains the differences between the beginning and ending balances for the accounts in the Stockholders' Equity category of the balance sheet.

Exercise 11-15 Comprehensive Income

LO8

Assume that you are the accountant for Ellis Corporation, which has issued its 2017 annual report. You have received an inquiry from a stockholder who has questions about several items in the annual report, including why Ellis has not shown certain transactions on the income statement. In particular, Ellis's 2017 balance sheet revealed two accounts in Stockholders' Equity (Unrealized Gain/Loss—Available-for-Sale Securities and Loss on Foreign Currency Translation Adjustments) for which the dollar amounts involved were not reported on the income statement.

Required

Draft a written response to the stockholder's inquiry that explains the nature of the two accounts and the reason the amounts involved were not recorded on the 2017 income statement. Do you think that the concept of comprehensive income would be useful to explain the impact of all events for Ellis Corporation? Why or why not?

LO9   **Exercise 11-16 Payout Ratio and Book Value per Share**

Divac Company has developed a statement of stockholders' equity for the year 2017 as follows:

	Preferred Stock	Paid-In Capital— Preferred	Common Stock	Paid-In Capital— Common	Retained Earnings
Balance, Jan. 1	$100,000	$50,000	$400,000	$40,000	$200,000
Stock issued			100,000	10,000	
Net income					80,000
Cash dividend					−45,000
Stock dividend	10,000	5,000			−15,000
Balance, Dec. 31	$110,000	$55,000	$500,000	$50,000	$220,000

Divac's preferred stock is $100 par, 8% stock. If the stock is liquidated or redeemed, stockholders are entitled to $120 per share. There are no dividends in arrears on the stock. The common stock has a par value of $5 per share.

Required

1. Determine the dividend payout ratio for the common stock.
2. Determine the book value per share of Divac's common stock.

LO10   **Exercise 11-17 Impact of Transactions Involving Issuance of Stock on Statement of Cash Flows**

From the following list, identify each item as operating (O), investing (I), financing (F), or not separately reported on the statement of cash flows (N).

_____   Issuance of common stock for cash
_____   Issuance of preferred stock for cash
_____   Issuance of common stock for equipment
_____   Issuance of preferred stock for land and building
_____   Conversion of preferred stock into common stock

LO10   **Exercise 11-18 Impact of Transactions Involving Treasury Stock on Statement of Cash Flows**

From the following list, identify each item as operating (O), investing (I), financing (F), or not separately reported on the statement of cash flows (N).

_____   Repurchase of common stock as treasury stock
_____   Reissuance of common stock (held as treasury stock)
_____   Retirement of treasury stock

LO10   **Exercise 11-19 Impact of Transactions Involving Dividends on Statement of Cash Flows**

From the following list, identify each item as operating (O), investing (I), financing (F), or not separately reported on the statement of cash flows (N).

_____   Payment of cash dividend on common stock
_____   Payment of cash dividend on preferred stock
_____   Distribution of stock dividend
_____   Declaration of stock split

LO10   **Exercise 11-20 Determining Dividends Paid on Statement of Cash Flows**

Clifford Company's comparative balance sheet included dividends payable of $80,000 at December 31, 2016, and $100,000 at December 31, 2017. Dividends declared by Clifford during 2017 amounted to $400,000.

Required

1. Calculate the amount of dividends actually paid to stockholders during 2017.
2. How will Clifford report the dividend payments on its 2017 statement of cash flows?

Exercise 11-21 Sole Proprietorships (Appendix)

LO11
EXAMPLE 11-10

Terry Woods opened Par Golf as a sole proprietor by investing $50,000 cash on January 1, 2017. Because the business was new, it operated at a net loss of $10,000 for 2017. During the year, Terry withdrew $20,000 from the business for living expenses. Terry also had $4,000 of interest income from sources unrelated to the business.

Required

Present the Owner's Equity category of Par Golf's balance sheet as of December 31, 2017.

Exercise 11-22 Partnerships (Appendix)

LO11
EXAMPLE 11-11

Sports Central is a sporting goods store owned by Lewis, Jamal, and Lapin in partnership. On January 1, 2017, their capital balances were as follows:

Lewis, Capital	$20,000
Jamal, Capital	50,000
Lapin, Capital	30,000

During 2017, Lewis withdrew $5,000; Jamal, $12,000; and Lapin, $9,000. Income for the partnership for 2017 was $50,000.

Required

If the partners agreed to allocate income equally, what was the ending balance in each of their capital accounts on December 31, 2017?

PROBLEMS

Problem 11-1 Stockholders' Equity Category

LO1

Peeler Company was incorporated as a new business on January 1, 2017. The corporate charter approved on that date authorized the issuance of 1,000 shares of $100 par, 7% cumulative, non-participating preferred stock and 10,000 shares of $5 par common stock. On January 10, Peeler issued for cash 500 shares of preferred stock at $120 per share and 4,000 shares of common stock at $80 per share. On January 20, it issued 1,000 shares of common stock to acquire a building site at a time when the stock was selling for $70 per share.

During 2017, Peeler established an employee benefit plan and acquired 500 shares of common stock at $60 per share as treasury stock for that purpose. Later in 2017, it resold 100 shares of the stock at $65 per share.

On December 31, 2017, Peeler determined its net income for the year to be $40,000. The firm declared the annual cash dividend to preferred stockholders and a cash dividend of $5 per share to the common stockholders. The dividends will be paid in 2018.

Required

Develop the Stockholders' Equity category of Peeler's balance sheet as of December 31, 2017. Indicate on the statement the number of shares authorized, issued, and outstanding for both preferred and common stock.

Problem 11-2 Evaluating Alternative Investments

LO2

Ellen Hays received a windfall from one of her investments. She would like to invest $100,000 of the money in Linwood Inc., which is offering common stock, preferred stock, and bonds on the open market. The common stock has paid $8 per share in dividends for the past three years, and the company expects to be able to perform as well in the current year. The current market price of the common stock is $100 per share. The preferred stock has an 8% dividend rate, cumulative and nonparticipating. The bonds are selling at par with an 8% stated rate.

Required

1. What are the advantages and disadvantages of each type of investment?
2. Recommend one type of investment over the others to Ellen and justify your reason.

LO5   **Problem 11-3 Dividends for Preferred and Common Stock**

The Stockholders' Equity category of Greenbaum Company's balance sheet as of December 31, 2017, appeared as follows:

Preferred stock, $100 par, 8%, 1,000 shares issued and outstanding	$ 100,000
Common stock, $10 par, 20,000 shares issued and outstanding	200,000
Additional paid-in capital	250,000
Total contributed capital	$ 550,000
Retained earnings	450,000
Total stockholders' equity	$1,000,000

The notes to the financial statements indicate that dividends were not declared or paid for 2015 or 2016. Greenbaum wants to declare a dividend of $59,000 for 2017.

Required

Determine the total and the per-share amounts that should be declared to the preferred and common stockholders under the following assumptions:
1. The preferred stock is noncumulative, nonparticipating.
2. The preferred stock is cumulative, nonparticipating.

LO6   **Problem 11-4 Effect of Stock Dividend**

Favre Company has a history of paying cash dividends on its common stock. However, the firm did not have a particularly profitable year in 2017. At the end of the year, Favre found itself without the necessary cash for a dividend and therefore declared a stock dividend to its common stockholders. A 50% stock dividend was declared to stockholders on December 31, 2017. The board of directors is unclear about a stock dividend's effect on Favre's balance sheet and has requested your assistance.

Required

1. Write a statement to indicate the effect the stock dividend has on the financial statements of Favre Company.
2. A group of common stockholders has contacted the firm to express its concern about the effect of the stock dividend and to question the effect the stock dividend may have on the market price of the stock. Write a statement to address the stockholders' concerns.

LO7   **Problem 11-5 Dividends and Stock Splits**

On January 1, 2017, Frederiksen Inc.'s Stockholders' Equity category appeared as follows:

Preferred stock, $80 par value, 7%, 3,000 shares issued and outstanding	$ 240,000
Common stock, $10 par value, 15,000 shares issued and outstanding	150,000
Additional paid-in capital—Preferred	60,000
Additional paid-in capital—Common	225,000
Total contributed capital	$ 675,000
Retained earnings	2,100,000
Total stockholders' equity	$2,775,000

The preferred stock is noncumulative and nonparticipating. During 2017, the following transactions occurred:

a. On March 1, declared a cash dividend of $16,800 on preferred stock. Paid the dividend on April 1.
b. On June 1, declared a 5% stock dividend on common stock. The current market price of the common stock was $18. The stock was issued on July 1.
c. On September 1, declared a cash dividend of $0.50 per share on the common stock; paid the dividend on October 1.
d. On December 1, issued a 2-for-1 stock split of common stock when the stock was selling for $50 per share.

Required

1. Explain each transaction's effect on the stockholders' equity accounts and the total stockholders' equity.
2. Develop the Stockholders' Equity category of the December 31, 2017, balance sheet. Assume that the net income for the year was $650,000.
3. Write a paragraph that explains the difference between a stock dividend and a stock split.

Problem 11-6 Statement of Stockholders' Equity   LO8

Refer to all of the facts in Problem 11-1.

Required

Develop a statement of stockholders' equity for Peeler Company for 2017. The statement should start with the beginning balance of each stockholders' equity account and explain the changes that occurred in each account to arrive at the 2017 ending balances.

Problem 11-7 Southwest Airlines' Comprehensive Income   LO8

Following is the consolidated statement of comprehensive income for **Southwest Airlines** for the year ended December 31, 2014:

REAL WORLD

Southwest Airlines Co.
Consolidated Statement of Comprehensive Income
(in millions)

	2014	2013
Net Income	$1,136	$754
Unrealized gain (loss) on fuel derivative instruments, net of deferred taxes of ($430), $31, and $74	(727)	52
Unrealized gain (loss) on interest rate derivative instruments, net of deferred taxes of $5, $19, and $0	8	31
Unrealized gain (loss) on defined benefit plan items, net of deferred taxes of ($8), $15, and ($11)	(16)	24
Other, net of deferred taxes of $0, $7, and $3	—	9
Other Comprehensive Income (LOSS)	$ (735)	$116
Comprehensive Income	$ 401	$870

Source: Southwest Airlines Co., Form 10-K, For the Fiscal Year Ended December 31, 2014.

Required

1. Which items were included in comprehensive income? If these items had been included on the income statement as part of net income, what would have been the effect?
2. Would the concept of comprehensive income help to explain to Southwest Airlines' stockholders the impact of all events that took place in 2014? Why or why not?

Problem 11-8 Effects of Stockholders' Equity Transactions on   LO10
Statement of Cash Flows

Refer to all of the facts in Problem 11-1.

(Continued)

Required

Indicate how each transaction affects the cash flow of Peeler Company by preparing the Financing Activities section of the 2017 statement of cash flows. Provide an explanation for the exclusion of any of these transactions from the Financing Activities section of the statement.

LO11   Problem 11-9 Income Distribution of a Partnership (Appendix)

Louise Abbott and Buddie Costello are partners in a comedy club business. The partnership agreement specifies the manner in which income of the business is to be distributed. Louise is to receive a salary of $20,000 for managing the club. Buddie is to receive interest at the rate of 10% on her capital balance of $300,000. Remaining income is to be distributed at a 2-to-1 ratio.

Required

Determine the amount that should be distributed to each partner assuming the following business net incomes:
1. $15,000
2. $50,000
3. $80,000

LO11   Problem 11-10 Sole Proprietorships (Appendix)

On May 1, Chong Yu deposited $120,000 of his own savings in a separate bank account to start a printing business. He purchased copy machines for $42,000. Expenses for the year, including depreciation on the copy machines, were $84,000. Sales for the year, all in cash, were $108,000. Chong withdrew $12,000 during the year.

Required

1. What is the balance in Chong's capital account at the end of the year?
2. Explain why the balance in Chong's capital account is different from the amount of cash on hand.

LO11   Problem 11-11 Partnerships (Appendix)

Kirin Nerise and Milt O'Brien agreed to form a partnership to operate a sandwich shop. Kirin contributed $25,000 cash and will manage the store. Milt contributed computer equipment worth $8,000 and $92,000 cash. Milt will keep the financial records. During the year, sales were $90,000 and expenses (including a salary to Kirin) were $76,000. Kirin withdrew $500 per month. Milt withdrew $4,000 (total). Their partnership agreement specified that Kirin would receive a salary of $7,200 for the year. Milt would receive 6% interest on his initial capital investment. All remaining income or loss would be equally divided.

Required

Calculate the ending balance in each partner's equity account.

MULTI-CONCEPT PROBLEMS

LO1 • 4   Problem 11-12 Analysis of Stockholders' Equity

The Stockholders' Equity section of the December 31, 2017, balance sheet of Eldon Company appeared as follows:

Preferred stock, $30 par value, 5,000 shares authorized, ? shares issued	$120,000
Common stock, ? par, 10,000 shares authorized, 7,000 shares issued	70,000
Additional paid-in capital—Preferred	6,000
Additional paid-in capital—Common	560,000
Additional paid-in capital—Treasury stock	1,000

Total contributed capital	$757,000
Retained earnings	40,000
Treasury stock, preferred, 100 shares	(3,200)
Total stockholders' equity	$?

Required

Determine the following items based on Eldon's balance sheet.
1. The number of shares of preferred stock issued
2. The number of shares of preferred stock outstanding
3. The average per-share sales price of the preferred stock when issued
4. The par value of the common stock
5. The average per-share sales price of the common stock when issued
6. The cost of the treasury stock per share
7. The total stockholders' equity
8. The per-share book value of the common stock assuming that there are no dividends in arrears and that the preferred stock can be redeemed at its par value

Problem 11-13 Effects of Stockholders' Equity Transactions on the Balance Sheet   LO3 • 4 • 7

The following transactions occurred at Horton Inc. during its first year of operation:

a. Issued 100,000 shares of common stock at $5 each; 1,000,000 shares are authorized at $1 par value.
b. Issued 10,000 shares of common stock for a building and land. The building was appraised for $20,000, but the value of the land is undeterminable. The stock is selling for $10 on the open market.
c. Purchased 1,000 shares of its own common stock on the open market for $16 per share.
d. Declared a dividend of $0.10 per share on outstanding common stock. The dividend is to be paid after the end of the first year of operations. Market value of the stock is $26.
e. Declared a 2-for-1 stock split. The market value of the stock was $37 before the stock split.
f. Reported $180,000 of income for the year.

Required

1. Indicate each transaction's effect on the assets, liabilities, and stockholders' equity of Horton Inc.
2. Prepare the Stockholders' Equity section of the balance sheet.
3. Write a paragraph that explains the number of shares of stock issued and outstanding at the end of the year.

Problem 11-14 Stockholders' Equity Section of the Balance Sheet   LO1 • 4

The newly hired accountant at Ives Inc. prepared the following balance sheet:

Assets	
Cash	$ 3,500
Accounts receivable	5,000
Treasury stock	500
Plant, property, and equipment	108,000
Retained earnings	1,000
Total assets	$118,000
Liabilities	
Accounts payable	$ 5,500
Dividends payable	1,500
Stockholders' Equity	
Common stock, $1 par,	
100,000 shares issued	$100,000
Additional paid-in capital	11,000
Total liabilities and stockholders' equity	$118,000

(Continued)

Required

1. Prepare a corrected balance sheet. Write a short explanation for each correction.
2. Why does the Retained Earnings account have a negative balance?

ALTERNATE PROBLEMS

LO1 Problem 11-1A Stockholders' Equity Category

Kebler Company was incorporated as a new business on January 1, 2017. The corporate charter approved on that date authorized the issuance of 2,000 shares of $100 par, 7% cumulative, non-participating preferred stock and 20,000 shares of $5 par common stock. On January 10, Kebler issued for cash 1,000 shares of preferred stock at $120 per share and 8,000 shares of common stock at $80 per share. On January 20, it issued 2,000 shares of common stock to acquire a building site at a time when the stock was selling for $70 per share.

During 2017, Kebler established an employee benefit plan and acquired 1,000 shares of common stock at $60 per share as treasury stock for that purpose. Later in 2017, it resold 100 shares of the stock at $65 per share.

On December 31, 2017, Kebler determined its net income for the year to be $80,000. The firm declared the annual cash dividend to preferred stockholders and a cash dividend of $5 per share to the common stockholders. The dividend will be paid in 2018.

Required

Develop the Stockholders' Equity category of Kebler's balance sheet as of December 31, 2017. Indicate on the statement the number of shares authorized, issued, and outstanding for both preferred and common stock.

LO2 Problem 11-2A Evaluating Alternative Investments

Rob Lowe would like to invest $100,000 in Franklin Inc., which is offering common stock, preferred stock, and bonds on the open market. The common stock has paid $1 per share in dividends for the past three years, and the company expects to be able to double the dividend in the current year. The current market price of the common stock is $10 per share. The preferred stock has an 8% dividend rate. The bonds are selling at par with a 5% stated rate.

Required

1. Explain Franklin's obligation to pay dividends or interest on each instrument.
2. Recommend one type of investment over the others to Rob and justify your reason.

LO5 Problem 11-3A Dividends for Preferred and Common Stock

The Stockholders' Equity category of Rausch Company's balance sheet as of December 31, 2017, appeared as follows:

Preferred stock, $100 par, 8%, 2,000 shares issued and outstanding	$ 200,000
Common stock, $10 par, 40,000 shares issued and outstanding	400,000
Additional paid-in capital	500,000
Total contributed capital	$1,100,000
Retained earnings	900,000
Total stockholders' equity	$2,000,000

The notes to the financial statements indicate that dividends were not declared or paid for 2015 or 2016. Rausch wants to declare a dividend of $118,000 for 2017.

Required

Determine the total and the per-share amounts that should be declared to the preferred and common stockholders under the following assumptions:

1. The preferred stock is noncumulative, nonparticipating.
2. The preferred stock is cumulative, nonparticipating.

Problem 11-4A   Effect of Stock Dividend   LO6

Travanti Company has a history of paying cash dividends on its common stock. Although the firm has been profitable this year, the board of directors is planning construction of a second manufacturing plant. To reduce the amount that they must borrow to finance the expansion, the directors are contemplating replacing their usual cash dividend with a 40% stock dividend. The board is unsure about a stock dividend's effect on the company's balance sheet and has requested your assistance.

Required

1. Write a statement to explain the effect the stock dividend has on the financial statements of Travanti Company.
2. A group of common stockholders has contacted the firm to express its concern about the effect of the stock dividend and to question the effect the stock dividend may have on the market price of the stock. Write a statement to address the stockholders' concerns.

Problem 11-5A   Dividends and Stock Splits   LO7

On January 1, 2017, Svenberg Inc.'s Stockholders' Equity category appeared as follows:

Preferred stock, $80 par value, 8%, 1,000 shares issued and outstanding	$ 80,000
Common stock, $10 par value, 10,000 shares issued and outstanding	100,000
Additional paid-in capital—Preferred	60,000
Additional paid-in capital—Common	225,000
Total contributed capital	$ 465,000
Retained earnings	1,980,000
Total stockholders' equity	$2,445,000

The preferred stock is noncumulative and nonparticipating. During 2017, the following transactions occurred:

a. On March 1, declared a cash dividend of $6,400 on preferred stock. Paid the dividend on April 1.
b. On June 1, declared an 8% stock dividend on common stock. The current market price of the common stock was $26. The stock was issued on July 1.
c. On September 1, declared a cash dividend of $0.70 per share on the common stock; paid the dividend on October 1.
d. On December 1, issued a 3-for-1 stock split of common stock, when the stock was selling for $30 per share.

Required

1. Explain each transaction's effect on the stockholders' equity accounts and the total stockholders' equity.
2. Develop the Stockholders' Equity category of the balance sheet. Assume that the net income for the year was $720,000.
3. Write a paragraph that explains the difference between a stock dividend and a stock split.

Problem 11-6A   Statement of Stockholders' Equity   LO8

Refer to all of the facts in Problem 11-1A.

Required

Develop a statement of Stockholders' Equity for Kebler Company for 2017. The statement should start with the beginning balance of each stockholders' equity account and explain the changes that occurred in each account to arrive at the 2017 ending balances.

REAL WORLD

LO8   Problem 11-7A Costco's Comprehensive Income

Following is the consolidated statement of stockholders' equity of **Costco Wholesale Corporation** for the year ended August 30, 2015:

Costco Wholesale Corporation
Consolidated Statements of Equity
(amounts in millions)

	Additional Paid-in Capital	Accumulated Other Comprehensive Income (Loss)	Retained Earnings	Total Costco Stockholders' Equity
Balance at August 31, 2014	4,919	(76)	7,458	12,303
Net income	—	—	2,377	2,377
Foreign-currency translation adjustment and other, net	—	(1,045)	—	(1,045)
Stock-based compensation	394	—	—	394
Stock options exercised, including tax effects	69	—	—	69
Release of vested RSUs, including tax effects	(122)	—	—	(122)
Repurchases of common stock	(42)	—	(452)	(494)
Cash dividends declared	—	—	(2,865)	(2,865)
Balance at August 30, 2015	$5,218	$(1,121)	$ 6,518	$10,617

Source: Costco Wholesale Corporation, Form 10-K, For the Fiscal Year Ended August 30, 2015.

Required

1. Costco has an item in the statement of stockholders' equity called Accumulated Other Comprehensive Income. What are the possible sources of other comprehensive income as discussed in your text?
2. Besides net income and other comprehensive income, what other items affected stockholders' equity during the period?
3. How do cash dividends affect stockholders' equity? How would a stock dividend affect stockholders' equity?

LO10   Problem 11-8A Effects of Stockholders' Equity Transactions on the Statement of Cash Flows

Refer to all of the facts in Problem 11-1A.

Required

Indicate how each transaction affects the cash flow of Kebler Company by preparing the Financing Activities section of the 2017 statement of cash flows. Provide an explanation for the exclusion of any of these transactions from the Financing Activities section of the statement.

LO11   Problem 11-9A Income Distribution of a Partnership (Appendix)

Kay Katz and Doris Kan are partners in a dry-cleaning business. The partnership agreement specifies the manner in which income of the business is to be distributed. Kay is to receive a salary of $40,000 for managing the business. Doris is to receive interest at the rate of 10% on her capital balance of $600,000. Remaining income is to be distributed at a 2-to-1 ratio.

Required

Determine the amount that should be distributed to each partner assuming the following business net incomes:

1. $30,000
2. $100,000
3. $160,000

Problem 11-10A Sole Proprietorships (Appendix)

On May 1, Chen Chien Lao deposited $150,000 of her own savings in a separate bank account to start a printing business. She purchased copy machines for $52,500. Expenses for the year, including depreciation on the copy machines, were $105,000. Sales for the year, all in cash, were $135,000. Chen withdrew $15,000 during the year.

Required

1. What is the balance in Chen's capital account at the end of the year?
2. Explain why the balance in Chen's capital account is different from the amount of cash on hand.

Problem 11-11A Partnerships (Appendix)

Karen Locke and Gina Keyes agreed to form a partnership to operate a sandwich shop. Karen contributed $35,000 cash and will manage the store. Gina contributed computer equipment worth $11,200 and $128,800 cash. Gina will keep the financial records. During the year, sales were $126,000 and expenses (including a salary for Karen) were $106,400. Karen withdrew $700 per month. Gina withdrew $5,600 (total). Their partnership agreement specified that Karen would receive a salary of $10,800 for the year. Gina would receive 6% interest on her initial capital investment. All remaining income or loss would be equally divided.

Required

Calculate the ending balance in each partner's equity account.

ALTERNATE MULTI-CONCEPT PROBLEMS

Problem 11-12A Analysis of Stockholders' Equity

The Stockholders' Equity section of the December 31, 2017, balance sheet of Carter Company appeared as follows:

Preferred stock, $50 par value, 10,000 shares authorized, ? shares issued	$ 400,000
Common stock, ? par value, 20,000 shares authorized, 14,000 shares issued	280,000
Additional paid-in capital—Preferred	12,000
Additional paid-in capital—Common	980,000
Additional paid-in capital—Treasury stock	2,000
Total contributed capital	$1,674,000
Retained earnings	80,000
Treasury stock, preferred, 200 shares	(12,800)
Total stockholders' equity	$?

Required

Determine the following items based on Carter's balance sheet.
1. The number of shares of preferred stock issued
2. The number of shares of preferred stock outstanding
3. The average per-share sales price of the preferred stock when issued
4. The par value of the common stock
5. The average per-share sales price of the common stock when issued
6. The cost of the treasury stock per share
7. The total stockholders' equity
8. The per-share book value of the common stock assuming that there are no dividends in arrears and that the preferred stock can be redeemed at its par value

Problem 11-13A Effects of Stockholders' Equity Transactions on Balance Sheet

The following transactions occurred at Hilton Inc. during its first year of operation:

a. Issued 10,000 shares of common stock at $10 each; 100,000 shares are authorized at $1 par value.

(Continued)

b. Issued 10,000 shares of common stock for a patent, which is expected to be effective for the next 15 years. The value of the patent is undeterminable. The stock is selling for $10 on the open market.
c. Purchased 1,000 shares of its own common stock on the open market for $10 per share.
d. Declared a dividend of $0.50 per share of outstanding common stock. The dividend is to be paid after the end of the first year of operations. Market value of the stock is $10.
e. Reported $340,000 of income for the year.

Required

1. Indicate each transaction's effect on the assets, liabilities, and stockholders' equity of Hilton Inc.
2. Hilton's president has asked you to explain the difference between contributed capital and retained earnings. Discuss the terms as they relate to Hilton.
3. Determine the book value per share of the stock at the end of the year.

LO1 • 4   Problem 11-14A Stockholders' Equity Section of the Balance Sheet

The newly hired accountant at Grainfield Inc. is considering the following list of accounts as he prepares the balance sheet. All of the accounts have positive balances. The company is authorized to issue 1,000,000 shares of common stock and 10,000 shares of preferred stock. The treasury stock was purchased at $5 per share.

Treasury stock (common)	$ 15,000
Retained earnings	54,900
Dividends payable	1,500
Common stock, $1 par	100,000
Additional paid-in capital	68,400
Preferred stock, $10 par, 5%	50,000

Required

1. Prepare the Stockholders' Equity section of the balance sheet for Grainfield.
2. Explain why some of the listed accounts are not shown in the Stockholders' Equity section.

DECISION CASES

Reading and Interpreting Financial Statements

LO1 • 8   Decision Case 11-1 Comparing Two Companies in the Same Industry: Panera Bread and Chipotle

REAL WORLD

Refer to the Stockholders' Equity section of the balance sheets of **Panera Bread** and **Chipotle** as of December 31, 2015.

Required

1. For each company, what are the numbers of shares of common stock authorized, issued, and outstanding as of the balance sheet date?
2. Did the balance of the Retained Earnings account of each company increase or decrease during the year? What factors can affect the Retained Earnings balance?
3. How does the total stockholders' equity of each company compare to that of the other company? Does the difference mean that one company's stock is more valuable than the other's? Explain your answer.

LO10   Decision Case 11-2 Reading Panera Bread's Statement of Cash Flows

REAL WORLD

Refer to **Panera Bread**'s statement of cash flows for the year ending December 31, 2015.

Required

1. What are the largest sources and uses of cash revealed in the Financing Activities category of the statement of cash flows?

2. What was the amount of dividends paid to stockholders during the period?
3. The Financing Activities section indicates a large negative amount for the repurchase of stock, presumably as treasury stock. When treasury stock is purchased, what is the effect on the accounts of the balance sheet?

Making Financial Decisions

Decision Case 11-3 Debt versus Preferred Stock   LO1 • 2

Assume that you are an analyst attempting to compare the financial structures of two companies. In particular, you must analyze the debt and equity categories of the two firms and calculate a debt-to-equity ratio for each firm. The Liability and Equity categories of First Company at year-end appeared as follows:

Liabilities	
Accounts payable	$ 500,000
Loan payable	800,000
Stockholders' Equity	
Common stock	300,000
Retained earnings	600,000
Total liabilities and equity	$2,200,000

First Company's loan payable bears interest at 8%, which is paid annually. The principal is due in five years.

The Liability and Equity categories of Second Company at year-end appeared as follows:

Liabilities	
Accounts payable	$ 500,000
Stockholders' Equity	
Common stock	300,000
Preferred stock	800,000
Retained earnings	600,000
Total liabilities and equity	$2,200,000

Second Company's preferred stock is 8%, cumulative. A provision of the stock agreement specifies that the stock must be redeemed at face value in five years.

Required

1. It appears that the loan payable of First Company and the preferred stock of Second Company are very similar. What are the differences between the two securities?
2. When calculating the debt-to-equity ratio, do you believe that the Second Company preferred stock should be treated as debt or as stockholders' equity? Write a statement expressing your position on the issue.

Decision Case 11-4 Preferred versus Common Stock   LO2

Rohnan Inc. needs to raise $500,000. It is considering two options:

a. Issue preferred stock, $100 par, 8%, cumulative, nonparticipating, callable at $110. The stock could be issued at par.
b. Issue common stock, $1 par, market $10. Currently, the company has 400,000 shares outstanding distributed equally in the hands of five owners. The company has never paid a dividend.

Required

Rohnan has asked you to consider both options and make a recommendation. It is equally concerned with cash flow and company control. Write your recommendations.

Ethical Decision Making

ETHICAL DECISION MODEL

LO9   Decision Case 11-5 Inside Information

Jim Brock was an accountant with Hubbard Inc., a large corporation with stock that was publicly traded on the New York Stock Exchange. One of Jim's duties was to manage the corporate reporting department, which was responsible for developing and issuing Hubbard's annual report. At the end of 2017, Hubbard closed its accounting records and initial calculations indicated a very profitable year. In fact, the net income exceeded the amount that had been projected during the year by the financial analysts who followed Hubbard's stock.

Jim was pleased with the company's financial performance. In January 2018, he suggested that his father buy Hubbard's stock because he was sure the stock price would increase when the company announced its 2017 results. Jim's father followed that advice and bought a block of stock at $25 per share.

On February 15, 2018, Hubbard announced its 2017 results and issued the annual report. The company received favorable press coverage about its performance, and the stock price on the stock exchange increased to $32 per share.

Required

Use the Ethical Decision Framework in Exhibit 1-9 to complete the following requirements:

1. **Recognize an ethical dilemma:** What ethical dilemma(s) do you face?
2. **Analyze the key elements in the situation:**

    a. Who may benefit from Jim's action? Who may be harmed?
    b. How are they likely to benefit or be harmed?
    c. What rights or claims may be violated?
    d. What specific interests are in conflict?
    e. What are your responsibilities and obligations?

3. **List alternatives and evaluate the impact of each on those affected:** What are your options in dealing with the ethical dilemma(s) you identified in (1) above?
4. **Select the best alternative:** Among the alternatives, which one would you select?

LO5   Decision Case 11-6 Dividend Policy

Hancock Inc. is owned by nearly 100 shareholders. Judith Stitch owns 48% of the stock. She needs cash to fulfill her commitment to donate the funds to construct a new art gallery. Some of her friends have agreed to vote for Hancock to pay a larger-than-normal dividend to shareholders. Judith has asked you to vote for the large dividend because she knows that you also support the arts. When informed that the dividend may create a working capital hardship on Hancock, Judith responded: "There is plenty of money in Retained Earnings. The dividend will not affect the cash of the company." Respond to her comment. What ethical questions do you and Judith face? How would you vote?

INTEGRATIVE PROBLEM

Evaluating financing options for asset acquisition and their impact on financial statements

Following are the financial statements for Griffin Inc. for the year 2017:

Griffin Inc.
Balance Sheet
December 31, 2017
(in millions)

Assets		Liabilities	
Cash	$ 1.6	Other current liabilities	$ 4.0
Other current assets	6.4	Other long-term liabilities	12.0
Equipment (net of accumulated		Total liabilities	$16.0
depreciation)	7.0	**Stockholders' Equity**	
Other long-term assets	45.0	Preferred stock	$ 1.0
		Additional paid-in capital—Preferred	2.0
		Common stock	4.0
		Additional paid-in capital—Common	16.0
		Retained earnings	21.0
		Total stockholders' equity	$44.0
Total assets	$60.0	Total liabilities and stockholders' equity	$60.0

Griffin Inc.
Income Statement
For the Year Ended December 31, 2017
(in millions)

Revenues		$ 50.00
Expenses:		
Depreciation	$ 4.20	
Other expenses	27.90	
Income tax (30% rate)	5.37	
Total expenses		(37.47)
Net income		$ 12.53
EPS		$ 3.10

Additional information:

Griffin Inc. has authorized 500,000 shares of 10%, $10 par value, cumulative preferred stock. There were 100,000 shares issued and outstanding at all times during 2017. The firm also has authorized 5 million shares of $1 par common stock, with 4 million shares issued and outstanding.

On January 1, 2017, Griffin Inc. acquired an asset, a piece of specialized heavy equipment, for $8 million, using cash the company had in the bank. The asset is depreciated using the straight-line method over eight years with zero salvage value.

Required

The management of Griffin Inc. is considering the financial statement impact of methods of financing that could have been used to acquire the equipment. For each alternative (a) and (b), provide the additional entries needed and indicate the effect on the accounting equation, and prepare revised 2017 financial statements.

Assume that the following alternative actions would have taken place on January 1, 2017:

a. Instead of acquiring the equipment with cash on hand, Griffin Inc. issued bonds for $8 million and purchased the equipment with the proceeds of the bond issue. Assume that the bond interest of $0.5 million was accrued and paid on December 31, 2017. A portion of the principal also is paid each year for eight years. On December 31, 2017, the company paid $1 million of principal and anticipated another $1 million of principal to be paid in 2018. Assume that the equipment would have an eight-year life and would be depreciated on a straight-line basis with zero salvage value.

b. Instead of acquiring the equipment with cash on hand, Griffin Inc. issued 200,000 additional shares of 10% preferred stock to raise $8 million and purchased the equipment for $8 million with the proceeds from the stock issue. Dividends on the stock are declared and paid annually. Assume that a dividend payment was made on December 31, 2017. Assume that the equipment would have an eight-year life and would be depreciated on a straight-line basis with zero salvage value.

Answers

MODULE 1 Answers to Questions

1. Stockholders' equity has two major components: contributed capital and retained earnings. Contributed capital represents the amount the corporation received from the sale of stock to the stockholders. Retained earnings is the amount of net income over the life of the company not paid out as dividends. It represents an important link between the income statement and the balance sheet.

2. The balance of the Retained Earnings account is not equal to the firm's net income. The account indicates the amount of income for all previous years that has been earned but has not been paid out as dividends to the stockholders.

3. Treasury stock is created when a company buys back (repurchases) its own stock sometime after issuing it. It represents the corporation's own stock, previously issued to shareholders, repurchased from stockholders and not retired, but held for various purposes. Treasury Stock is a *contra*-equity account and is shown as a reduction of stockholders' equity. When treasury stock is purchased, it reduces the total stockholders' equity.

MODULE 1 Answers to Apply

1.

Nash Company
Partial Balance Sheet
December 31, 2017

Stockholders' Equity	
Common stock, $10 par, 10,000 authorized, 9,000 issued	$ 90,000
Preferred stock $100 par, 8%, cumulative, 1,000 issued and outstanding	100,000
Additional paid-in capital	200,000
Total contributed capital	$390,000
Retained earnings	100,000
Treasury stock	(20,000)
Accumulated other comprehensive income—Unrealized gain	5,000
Total stockholders' equity	$475,000

2. a.

Identify and Analyze	**ACTIVITY:** Financing
	ACCOUNTS: Cash Increase Common Stock Increase
	Additional Paid-In Capital—Common Increase
	STATEMENT(S): Balance Sheet

Balance Sheet					**Income Statement**			
ASSETS	=	LIABILITIES	+	STOCKHOLDERS' EQUITY	REVENUES	−	EXPENSES	= NET INCOME
Cash 34,000				Common Stock 20,000				
				Additional Paid-In Capital—Common 14,000				

Cash = 2,000 shares × $17 = $34,000
Common Stock = 2,000 shares × $10 = $20,000
Additional Paid-In Capital—Common = 2,000 shares × ($17 − $10) = $14,000

b.

Identify and Analyze	**ACTIVITY:** Financing and Investing
	ACCOUNTS: Land Increase Preferred Stock Increase
	Additional Paid-In Capital—Preferred Increase
	STATEMENT(S): Balance Sheet

Balance Sheet					**Income Statement**			
ASSETS	=	LIABILITIES	+	STOCKHOLDERS' EQUITY	REVENUES	−	EXPENSES	= NET INCOME
Land 7,000				Preferred Stock 5,000				
				Additional Paid-In Capital—Preferred 2,000				

c.

Identify and Analyze	**ACTIVITY:** Financing and Operating
	ACCOUNTS: Common Stock Increase
	Additional Paid-In Capital—Common Increase
	Advertising Expense Increase
	STATEMENT(S): Balance Sheet and Income Statement

Balance Sheet					**Income Statement**			
ASSETS	=	LIABILITIES	+	STOCKHOLDERS' EQUITY	REVENUES	−	EXPENSES	= NET INCOME
				(60,000)			Advertising Expense 60,000	(60,000)
				Common Stock 50,000				
				Additional Paid-In Capital—Common 10,000				

Advertising Expense = 5,000 shares × $12 = $60,000
Common Stock = 5,000 shares × $10 = $50,000
Additional Paid-In Capital—Common = 5,000 shares × ($12 − $10) = $10,000

3. a. Increase total assets, increase total stockholders' equity
   b. Decrease total assets, decrease total stockholders' equity
   c. Increase total assets, increase total stockholders' equity
   d. Increase total assets, increase total stockholders' equity

MODULE 2 Answers to Questions

1. A stock dividend occurs when a company issues shares of stock to its existing stockholders instead of paying cash as a dividend. Stock dividends should be recorded as a reduction of Retained Earnings and an increase in Stock Dividend Distributable. Therefore, stock dividends do not affect total stockholders' equity. Normally, retained earnings is reduced by the market value of the stock distributed.

2. It is better to receive a stock dividend when the company is using earnings to expand and reinvest in the business. A cash dividend is preferred by investors who need the cash to meet current needs.

3. Stock dividends do not reduce the par value per share of the stock. Stock splits do reduce the par value per share. Splits do not require any journal entry but should be noted in the notes that accompany the balance sheet.

MODULE 2 Answers to Apply

1. a. Decrease assets
      Decrease retained earnings
      Decrease total stockholders' equity
   b. No change in assets
      Decrease retained earnings
      No change in total stockholders' equity

2. Green Company:

Number of shares outstanding	18,000
Par value per share	$ 10

Common Stock account	$180,000
Retained earnings	$410,000

Blue Company:

Number of shares outstanding	18,000
Par value per share	$ 5
Common Stock account	$ 90,000
Retained earnings	$500,000

MODULE 3 Answers to Questions

1. Book value per share is calculated as the total net assets of the corporation divided by the number of shares of common stock. It is a measure of the rights of the common stockholders to the assets of the firm in the event of liquidation. It does not mean that the common stockholders will receive a dividend equal to the book value per share.

2. The market value per share of the stock is related to the income of the corporation, but many other factors also influence the market value. General economic factors such as inflation, factors related to the particular industry, tax consequences, and the mood of current and potential investors all have an impact on the market value of the stock.

3. The statement of stockholders' equity explains *all* reasons for the difference between the beginning and ending balances of each of the accounts in the Stockholders' Equity category. The retained earnings statement details the changes in only one component of stockholders' equity—retained earnings.

MODULE 3 Answers to Apply

1. Book value per share

Total stockholders' equity	$790,000*
Preferred stock liquidation value	110,000
Rights of common stockholder	$680,000
Divided by number of shares of common stock—80,000 shares	
Book value per share ($680,000/80,000)	$ 8.50

*$100,000 + $50,000 + $400,000 + $40,000 + $200,000 = $790,000

2. Issuance of common stock for cash—Financing category as a cash inflow

Purchase of treasury stock—Financing category as a cash outflow

Issuance of a stock dividend—does not appear on the statement of cash flows

Reissuance of treasury stock—Financing category as a cash inflow

Issuance of common stock to acquire land—does not appear on the statement of cash flows but the company should provide a supplement indicating the transaction

MODULE 4 Answers to Questions

1. The advantages of organizing as a corporation include limited liability and the increased ability to raise funds from a wider group of unrelated investors. Companies choose not to incorporate because it costs to file papers with the state and to issue stock, and corporations must file annual reports, open to public inspection. (Appendix)

2. Partners could share income equally, as a percentage of investment (capital balance), or as a proportion based on the amount of hours each partner works. The partners can share income based on any method that is reasonable, provided that the method has been agreed upon, in writing, by the partners. (Appendix)

MODULE 4 Answers to Apply

Initial investment	$500,000
Net income	10,000
Withdrawal	(60,000)
Owner's equity, December 31, 2017	$450,000

Answers to Connect to the Real World

11-1 (p. 503)

The Retained Earnings account actually increased from $7,416 million to $9,409 million. In most cases, an increase in the account is caused by the company's net income, and a decrease is caused by dividends.

11-2 (p. 504)

Chipotle had 230,000 shares authorized and 35,790 shares issued. There were 5,206 shares of treasury stock so the number of shares outstanding was 35,970 − 5,206 = 30,764.

Answers to Key Terms Quiz

13	Authorized shares
1	Issued shares
14	Outstanding shares
2	Par value
15	Additional paid-in capital
3	Retained earnings
5	Convertible feature
17	Callable feature
4	Cumulative feature
16	Participating feature
6	Treasury stock

18	Retirement of stock
7	Dividend payout ratio
19	Stock dividend
9	Stock split
8	Statement of stockholders' equity
11	Comprehensive income
10	Book value per share
12	Market value per share
22	Sole proprietorship (Appendix)
20	Partnership (Appendix)
21	Partnership agreement (Appendix)

The Statement of Cash Flows

MODULES	LEARNING OBJECTIVES	WHY IS THIS CHAPTER IMPORTANT?
1 **Purpose and Format for the Statement of Cash Flows**	**LO1** Explain the concept of cash flows and accrual accounting and the purpose of a statement of cash flows. **LO2** Explain what cash equivalents are and how they are treated on the statement of cash flows. **LO3** Describe operating, investing, and financing activities and give examples of each. **LO4** Describe the difference between the direct and indirect methods of computing cash flow from operating activities.	• You need to understand why net earnings are not the same as cash provided by operating activities and how accountants reconcile the difference between these two amounts. (See pp. 556–558.) • You need to know what are the various sources and uses of cash in a company's investing and financing activities. (See pp. 559–561.)
2 **Preparing the Statement of Cash Flows Using the Direct Method**	**LO5** Prepare a statement of cash flows using the direct method to determine cash flow from operating activities.	• You need to know how to prepare a statement of cash flows using the direct method in the Operating Activities section. (See pp. 567–578.)
3 **Preparing the Statement of Cash Flows Using the Indirect Method**	**LO6** Prepare a statement of cash flows using the indirect method to determine cash flow from operating activities.	• You need to know how to prepare a statement of cash flows using the indirect method in the Operating Activities section. (See pp. 578–581.)
4 **Cash Flow Analysis**	**LO7** Use cash flow information to help analyze a company.	• You need to know how you can use information about a company's cash flows to analyze its performance. (See pp. 582–584.)
5 **A Work Sheet Approach to Preparing the Statement of Cash Flows**	**LO8** Use a work sheet to prepare a statement of cash flows using the indirect method to determine cash flow from operating activities (Appendix).	• You need to know how a work sheet can be useful to prepare the statement of cash flows using the indirect method in the Operating Activities section. (See pp. 586–588.)

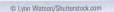

WALGREENS BOOTS ALLIANCE

A statement of cash flows reveals critical information about a company not found on either its income statement or balance sheet. **Walgreens Boots Alliance**'s statement of cash flows shows that in fiscal year 2013, the company borrowed $4,000 million (that is, $4 billion) and two years later another $12,285 million. This is the company that resulted from the merger of U.S. based Walgreen Co. and a large European pharmacy company, Alliance Boots. Note the

$4,461 million paid during 2015 to acquire Alliance Boots. Eventually long-term debt has to be repaid. The statement of cash flows also shows that the company made payments on long-term debt of $4,300 million in 2013 and $10,472 million in 2015.

Much of the recent history of this first global pharmacy company in the world can be gleaned by examining its statement of cash flows!

Walgreens Boots Alliance, Inc. and Subsidiaries
Consolidated Statements of Cash Flows
For the years ended August 31, 2015, 2014 and 2013
(In millions)

	2015	2014	2013
Cash Flows from Operating Activities:			
Net earnings	$ 4,279	$ 2,031	$ 2,548
Adjustments to reconcile net earnings to net cash provided by operating activities -			
Depreciation and amortization	1,742	1,316	1,283
Change in fair value of warrants and related amortization	(779)	(385)	(120)
Loss on exercise of call option	—	866	—
Gain on previously held equity interest	(563)	—	—
Deferred income taxes	(32)	177	202
Stock compensation expense	109	114	104
Equity earnings in Alliance Boots	(315)	(617)	(496)
Other	728	181	113
Changes in operating assets and liabilities -			
Accounts receivable, net	(338)	(616)	(449)
Inventories	719	860	321
Other current assets	22	(10)	18
Trade accounts payable	268	(339)	182
Accrued expenses and other liabilities	170	195	424
Income taxes	(335)	17	103
Other non-current assets and liabilities	(11)	103	68
Net cash provided by operating activities	5,664	3,893	4,301
Cash Flows from Investing Activities:			
Additions to property, plant and equipment	(1,251)	(1,106)	(1,212)
Proceeds from sale leaseback transactions	867	67	115
Proceeds related to the sale of businesses	814	93	20
Proceeds from sale of other assets	184	139	30
Alliance Boots acquisition, net of cash acquired	(4,461)	—	—
Other business and intangible asset acquisitions, net of cash acquired	(371)	(344)	(630)
Purchases of short-term investments held to maturity	(49)	(59)	(66)
Proceeds from short-term investments held to maturity	50	58	16
Investment in AmerisourceBergen	—	(493)	(224)
Other	(59)	(86)	(45)
Net cash used for investing activities	(4,276)	(1,731)	(1,996)
Cash Flows from Financing Activities:			
Payments of short-term borrowings, net	(226)	—	—
Proceeds from issuance of long-term debt	12,285	—	4,000
Payments of long-term debt	(10,472)	(550)	(4,300)
Proceeds from financing leases	—	268	—
Stock purchases	(1,226)	(705)	(615)
Proceeds related to employee stock plans	503	612	486
Cash dividends paid	(1,384)	(1,199)	(1,040)
Other	(395)	(48)	(27)
Net cash used for financing activities	(915)	(1,622)	(1,496)
Effect of exchange rate changes on cash and cash equivalents	(119)	—	—
Changes in Cash and Cash Equivalents:			
Net increase in cash and cash equivalents	354	540	809
Cash and cash equivalents at beginning of period	2,646	2,106	1,297
Cash and cash equivalents at end of period	$ 3,000	$ 2,646	$ 2,106

Nearly $4.5 billion invested to acquire another company

Borrowed about $12.3 billion in 2015 and repaid about $10.5 in 2015

The accompanying Notes to Consolidated Financial Statements are an integral part of these Statements.

Source: Walgreens Boots Alliance, website and Form 10-K, For the Fiscal Year Ended August 31, 2015.

MODULE 1 PURPOSE AND FORMAT FOR THE STATEMENT OF CASH FLOWS

LO1 Explain the concept of cash flows and accrual accounting and the purpose of a statement of cash flows.

All external parties have an interest in a company's cash flows.

- Stockholders need some assurance that enough cash is being generated from operations to pay dividends and to invest in the company's future.
- Creditors want to know if cash from operations is sufficient to repay their loans along with interest.

This chapter will show you how to read, understand, and prepare the statement of cash flows, which is perhaps the key financial statement for the survival of every business.

In recent years, managers, stockholders, creditors, analysts, and other users of financial statements have become more wary of focusing on any one number as an indicator of a company's overall performance. Most experts now agree that there has been a tendency to rely far too heavily on net income and its companion, earnings per share, and in many cases to ignore a company's cash flows.

To understand the difference between a company's net income and its cash flow, consider the case of **Walgreens Boots Alliance** in its 2015 fiscal year. The company reported net earnings (income) of $4,279 million. However, as shown on page 555, during this same time period, its cash increased by only $354 million. Why such a disparity? First, net income is computed on an accrual basis, not a cash basis. Second, the income statement primarily reflects events related to the operating activities of a business, that is, selling products or providing services.

A company's cash position can increase or decrease over a period, and it can report a net profit or a net loss. One of four combinations is possible:

1. **A company can report an increase in cash and a net profit.**
2. **A company can report a decrease in cash and a net profit.**
3. **A company can report an increase in cash and a net loss.**
4. **A company can report a decrease in cash and a net loss.**

To summarize, a company with a profitable year does not necessarily increase its cash position, nor does a company with an unprofitable year always experience a decrease in cash.

Purpose of the Statement of Cash Flows

Statement of cash flows
The financial statement that summarizes an entity's cash receipts and cash payments during the period from operating, investing, and financing activities.

The **statement of cash flows** is an important complement to the other major financial statements. It summarizes the operating, investing, and financing activities of a business over a period of time. The balance sheet summarizes the cash on hand and the balances in other assets, liabilities, and owners' equity accounts, providing a snapshot at a specific point in time. The statement of cash flows reports the changes in cash over a period of time and, most importantly, *explains those changes.*

The income statement summarizes performance on an accrual basis. Income on this basis is a better indicator of *future* cash inflows and outflows than is a statement limited to current cash flows. The statement of cash flows complements the accrual-based income statement by allowing users to assess a company's performance on a cash basis. As you will see in Example 12-1, however, it also goes beyond presenting data related to operating performance and looks at other activities that affect a company's cash position.

Reporting Requirements for a Statement of Cash Flows

Accounting standards specify both the basis for preparing the statement of cash flows and the classification of items on the statement.[1] First, the statement must be prepared on a cash basis. Second, the cash flows must be classified into three categories:

---

[1] *Statement of Cash Flows*, ASC Topic 230 (formerly *Statement of Cash Flows*, Statement of Financial Accounting Standards No. 95, Financial Accounting Standards Board).

- Operating activities
- Investing activities
- Financing activities

EXAMPLE 12-1 Preparing a Statement of Cash Flows

Consider the following discussion between the owner of Fox River Realty and the company accountant. After a successful first year in business in 2016 in which the company earned a profit of $100,000, the owner reviews the income statement for the second year, as presented below.

Fox River Realty Income Statement For the Year Ended December 31, 2017	
Revenues	$400,000
Depreciation expense	$ 50,000
All other expenses	100,000
Total expenses	$150,000
Net income	$250,000

The owner is pleased with the results and asks to see the balance sheet. Comparative balance sheets for the first two years are presented below.

Fox River Realty Comparative Balance Sheets December 31		
	2017	2016
Cash	$ 50,000	$ 150,000
Plant and equipment	600,000	350,000
Accumulated depreciation	(150,000)	(100,000)
Total assets	$ 500,000	$ 400,000
Notes payable	$ 100,000	$ 150,000
Common stock	250,000	200,000
Retained earnings	150,000	50,000
Total equities	$ 500,000	$ 400,000

Where Did the Cash Go? At first glance, the owner is surprised to see the significant decline in the Cash account. Why has cash decreased from $150,000 to $50,000 even though income rose from $100,000 in the first year to $250,000 in the second year?

The accountant points out that income on a cash basis is even higher than the reported $250,000. Because depreciation expense is an expense that does not use cash (cash is used when the plant and equipment are purchased, not when they are depreciated), cash provided from operating activities is calculated as follows:

Net income	$250,000
Depreciation expense	50,000
Cash provided by operating activities	$300,000

Further, the accountant reminds the owner of the additional $50,000 that she invested in the business during the year. Now the owner is even more bewildered: with cash from operations of $300,000 and her own infusion of $50,000, why did cash *decrease* by $100,000? The accountant refreshes the owner's memory about three major outflows of cash during the year. First, even though the business earned $250,000, she withdrew $150,000 in dividends during the year. Second, the comparative balance sheets indicate that notes payable with the bank were reduced from $150,000 to $100,000, requiring the use of $50,000 in cash. Finally, the comparative balance sheets show an increase in plant and equipment for the year from $350,000 to $600,000—a sizable investment of $250,000 in new long-term assets.

Statement of Cash Flows To summarize what happened to the cash, the accountant prepares a statement of cash flows, shown below.

Fox River Realty Statement of Cash Flows For the Year Ended December 31, 2017	
Cash provided (used) by operating activities	
Net income	$ 250,000
Depreciation expense	50,000
Net cash provided (used) by operating activities	$ 300,000
Cash provided (used) by investing activities	
Purchase of new plant and equipment	$(250,000)
Cash provided (used) by financing activities	
Additional investment by owner	$ 50,000
Cash dividends paid to owner	(150,000)
Repayment of notes payable to bank	(50,000)
Net cash provided (used) by financing activities	$(150,000)
Net increase (decrease) in cash	$(100,000)
Cash balance at beginning of year	150,000
Cash balance at end of year	$ 50,000

Although the owner is not particularly happy with the decrease in cash, she is satisfied with the statement as an explanation of where the cash came from and how it was used. The statement summarizes the important cash activities for the year and fills a void created with the presentation of just an income statement and a balance sheet.

The Definition of Cash: Cash and Cash Equivalents

LO2 Explain what cash equivalents are and how they are treated on the statement of cash flows.

The purpose of the statement of cash flows is to provide information about a company's cash inflows and outflows. Thus, it is essential to have a clear understanding of what the definition of *cash* includes. According to accounting standards, certain items are recognized as being equivalent to cash and are combined with cash on the balance sheet and the statement of cash flows.

Cash equivalent
An item readily convertible to a known amount of cash with a maturity to the investor of three months or less.

Commercial paper (short-term notes issued by corporations), money market funds, and Treasury bills are examples of cash equivalents. To be classified as a **cash equivalent**, an item must be readily convertible to a known amount of cash and have a maturity *to the investor* of three months or less. For example, a three-year Treasury note purchased two months before its maturity is classified as a cash equivalent. However, the same note purchased two years before maturity would be classified as an investment.

EXAMPLE 12-2 Determining What Is a Cash Equivalent

To understand why cash equivalents are combined with cash when a statement of cash flows is prepared, assume that a company has a cash balance of $10,000 and no assets that qualify as cash equivalents. Further assume that the $10,000 is used to purchase 90-day Treasury bills. The effect of the transaction can be identified and analyzed as follows:

Identify and Analyze	**ACTIVITY: Operating**
	ACCOUNTS: Investment in Treasury Bills Increase **Cash** Decrease
	STATEMENT(S): Balance Sheet

Balance Sheet				Income Statement		
ASSETS	= LIABILITIES +	STOCKHOLDERS' EQUITY	◄────	REVENUES	− EXPENSES =	NET INCOME
Investment in Treasury Bills 10,000						
Cash (10,000)						

For record-keeping purposes, this transaction is a transfer between cash in the bank and an investment in a government security. In the strictest sense, the investment represents an outflow of cash. However, the purchase of a security with such a short maturity does not involve any significant degree of risk in terms of price changes and thus is not reported on the statement of cash flows as an outflow. Instead, for purposes of classification on the balance sheet and the statement of cash flows, this is merely a transfer *within* the cash and cash equivalents category. The point is that before the purchase of the Treasury bills, the company had $10,000 in cash and cash equivalents and that after the purchase, it still had $10,000 in cash and cash equivalents. *Because nothing changed, the transaction is not reported on the statement of cash flows.*

Consider a different transaction in which a company purchases shares of MG common stock for cash. This transaction can be identified and analyzed as follows:

Identify and Analyze	**ACTIVITY: Investing**
	ACCOUNTS: Investment in MG Common Stock Increase **Cash** Decrease
	STATEMENT(S): Balance Sheet

Balance Sheet				Income Statement		
ASSETS	= LIABILITIES +	STOCKHOLDERS' EQUITY	◄────	REVENUES	− EXPENSES =	NET INCOME
Investment in MG Common Stock 10,000						
Cash (10,000)						

This purchase involves a certain amount of risk for the company making the investment. The MG stock is not convertible to a known amount of cash because its market value is subject to change. Thus, for balance sheet purposes, the investment is not considered a cash equivalent; therefore, it is not combined with cash but is classified as either a short- or long-term investment depending on the company's intent in holding the stock. **The investment in stock of another company is considered a significant activity and thus is reported on the statement of cash flows.**

Classification of Cash Flows

For the statement of cash flows, companies are required to classify activities into three categories: operating, investing, or financing. These categories represent the major functions of an entity, and classifying activities in this way allows users to look at important relationships. For example, one important financing activity for many businesses is borrowing money. Grouping the cash inflows from borrowing money during the period with the cash outflows from repaying loans during the period makes it easier for analysts and other users of the statements to evaluate the company.

LO3 Describe operating, investing, and financing activities and give examples of each.

Each of the three types of activities can result in both cash inflows and cash outflows to the company. Thus, the general format for the statement is shown in Exhibit 12-1. Note the direct tie between the bottom portion of this statement and the balance sheet. The beginning and ending balances in cash and cash equivalents, shown as the last two

EXHIBIT 12-1 Format for the Statement of Cash Flows

Smith Corporation Statement of Cash Flows For the Year Ended December 31, 2017		
Cash flows from operating activities		
Inflows	$ xxx	
Outflows	(xxx)	
Net cash provided (used) by operating activities		$xxx
Cash flows from investing activities		
Inflows	$ xxx	
Outflows	(xxx)	
Net cash provided (used) by investing activities		xxx
Cash flows from financing activities		
Inflows	$ xxx	
Outflows	(xxx)	
Net cash provided (used) by financing activities		xxx
Net increase (decrease) in cash and cash equivalents		$xxx
Cash and cash equivalents at beginning of year		xxx
Cash and cash equivalents at end of year		$xxx

lines on the statement of cash flows, are taken directly from the comparative balance sheets. Some companies end their statement of cash flows with the figure for the net increase or decrease in cash and cash equivalents and do not report the beginning and ending balances in cash and cash equivalents directly on the statement of cash flows.

Operating activities
Activities concerned with the acquisition and sale of products and services.

Operating Activities Operating activities involve acquiring and selling products and services. The specific activities of a business depend on its type. For example, the purchase of raw materials is an important operating activity for a manufacturer. For a retailer, the purchase of inventory from a distributor constitutes an operating activity. For a realty company, the payment of a commission to a salesperson is an operating activity. All three types of businesses sell either products or services, and their sales are important operating activities.

A statement of cash flows reflects the cash effects, inflows or outflows, associated with each of these activities. For example, the manufacturer's payment for purchases of raw materials results in a cash outflow. The receipt of cash from collecting an account receivable results in a cash inflow.

Investing activities
Activities concerned with the acquisition and disposal of long-term assets.

Investing Activities Investing activities involve acquiring and disposing of long-term assets. Replacing worn-out plant and equipment and expanding the existing base of long-term assets are essential to all businesses. Cash is paid for these acquisitions, often called *capital expenditures*. The following excerpt from Walgreens Boots Alliance's 2015 statement of cash flows (also shown in the chapter opener on page 555) indicates that the company spent $1,251 million ❶ for additions to property and equipment during fiscal 2015. (All amounts are in millions of dollars.) As described in the chapter opener, the company spent $4,461 million during 2015 ❷ to complete its acquisition of Alliance Boots.

	Cash Flows from Investing Activities:	
❶	Additions to property, plant and equipment	(1,251)
	Proceeds from sale leaseback transactions	867
	Proceeds related to the sale of businesses	814
	Proceeds from sale of other assets	184
❷	Alliance Boots acquisition, net of cash acquired	(4,461)
	Other business and intangible asset acquisitions, net of cash acquired	(371)
	Purchases of short-term investments held to maturity	(49)

Proceeds from short-term investments held to maturity	50
Investment in AmerisourceBergen	—
Other	(59)
Net cash used for investing activities	(4,276)

Financing Activities

Financing Activities All businesses rely on internal financing, external financing, or a combination of the two in meeting their needs for cash. Initially, a new business must have a certain amount of investment by the owners to begin operations. After this, many companies use notes, bonds, and other forms of debt to provide financing. Issuing stock and various forms of debt results in cash inflows that appear as **financing activities** on the statement of cash flows. On the other side, the repurchase of a company's own stock and the repayment of borrowings are important cash outflows to be reported in the Financing Activities section of the statement. The payment of cash dividends is listed in this section as well. Walgreens Boots Alliance's statement of cash flows (shown on page 555) lists many of the common cash inflows and outflows from financing activities (amounts in millions of dollars):

Financing activities
Activities concerned with the raising and repaying of funds in the form of debt and equity.

	Cash Flows from Financing Activities	
	Payments of short-term borrowings, net	(226)
❶	Proceeds from issuance of long-term debt	12,285
❷	Payments of long-term debt	(10,472)
	Proceeds from financing leases	—
❸	Stock purchases	(1,226)
	Proceeds related to employee stock plans	503
❹	Cash dividends paid	(1,384)
	Other	(395)
	Net cash used for financing activities	(915)

In 2015, Walgreens Boots Alliance received $12,285 million ❶ from the issuance of long-term debt and spent $10,472 million ❷ to pay off long-term debt. The company paid $1,226 million ❸ to buy back stock and another $1,384 million ❹ to pay cash dividends.

Summary of the Three Types of Activities

Summary of the Three Types of Activities To summarize the operating, investing, and financing activities of a business, refer to Exhibit 12-2. The exhibit lists examples of each of the three activities along with the related balance sheet accounts and the account classifications on the balance sheet.

In the exhibit, operating activities center on the acquisition and sale of products and services and related costs, such as wages and taxes. Two important observations can be made about the cash flow effects from the operating activities of a business:

1. **The cash flows from operating activities are the cash effects of transactions that enter into the determination of net income.** For example, the sale of a product enters into the calculation of net income. The cash effect of this transaction—that is, the collection of the account receivable—results in a cash inflow from operating activities.

2. **Cash flows from operating activities usually relate to an increase or decrease in a current asset or in a current liability.** For example, the payment of taxes to the government results in a decrease in taxes payable, which is a current liability on the balance sheet.

Investing activities normally relate to long-term assets on the balance sheet. For example, the purchase of new plant and equipment increases long-term assets, and the sale of those same assets reduces long-term assets on the balance sheet. **Financing activities usually relate to either long-term liabilities or stockholders' equity accounts.**

Noncash Investing and Financing Activities

Occasionally, companies engage in important investing and financing activities that do not affect cash.

STUDY TIP

Later in the chapter, you will learn a technique to use in preparing the statement of cash flows. Recall then the observations made here regarding what types of accounts affect each of the three activities.

EXHIBIT 12-2 Classification of Items on the Statement of Cash Flows

Activity	Examples	Effect on Cash	Related Balance Sheet Account	Classification on Balance Sheet
Operating	Collection of customer accounts	Inflow	Accounts receivable	Current asset
	Payment to suppliers for inventory	Outflow	Accounts payable	Current liability
			Inventory	Current asset
	Payment of wages	Outflow	Wages payable	Current liability
	Payment of taxes	Outflow	Taxes payable	Current liability
Investing	Capital expenditures	Outflow	Plant and equipment	Long-term asset
	Purchase of another company	Outflow	Long-term investment	Long-term asset
	Sale of plant and equipment	Inflow	Plant and equipment	Long-term asset
	Sale of another company	Inflow	Long-term investment	Long-term asset
Financing	Issuance of capital stock	Inflow	Capital stock	Stockholders' equity
	Issuance of bonds	Inflow	Bonds payable	Long-term liability
	Issuance of bank note	Inflow	Notes payable	Long-term liability
	Repurchase of stock	Outflow	Treasury stock	Stockholders' equity
	Retirement of bonds	Outflow	Bonds payable	Long-term liability
	Repayment of notes	Outflow	Notes payable	Long-term liability
	Payment of dividends	Outflow	Retained earnings	Stockholders' equity

EXAMPLE 12-3 Determining Noncash Investing and Financing Activities

Assume that at the end of the year, Wolk Corp. issues capital stock to an inventor in return for the exclusive rights to a patent. Although the patent has no ready market value, the stock could have been sold on the open market for $25,000. The effect of this transaction can be identified and analyzed as follows:

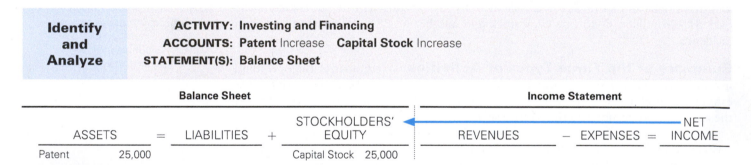

This transaction does not involve cash and therefore is not reported on the statement of cash flows. However, what if the scenario was changed slightly? Assume that Wolk wants the patent but the inventor is not willing to accept stock in return for it. So, instead, Wolk sells stock on the open market for $25,000 and then pays this amount in cash to the inventor for the rights to the patent. Consider the effects of these two transactions. First, the issuance of the stock increases Cash and Stockholders' Equity and can be identified and analyzed as follows:

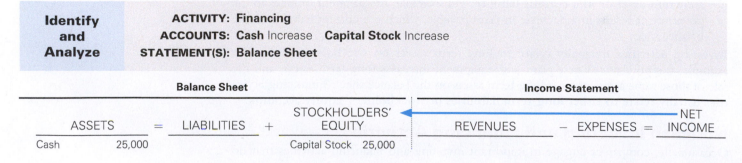

Next, the acquisition of the patent can be identified and analyzed as follows:

Identify and Analyze	**ACTIVITY: Investing** **ACCOUNTS: Patent** Increase **Cash** Decrease **STATEMENT(S): Balance Sheet**

	Balance Sheet					Income Statement			
ASSETS	=	LIABILITIES	+	STOCKHOLDERS' EQUITY		REVENUES	− EXPENSES =	NET INCOME
Patent	25,000							
Cash	(25,000)							

How would these two transactions be reported on a statement of cash flows? The first transaction appears as a cash inflow in the Financing Activities section of the statement; the second is reported as a cash outflow in the Investing Activities section. Even though the *form* of this arrangement (with stock sold for cash and then the cash paid to the inventor) differs from the form of the first arrangement (with stock exchanged directly for the patent), the *substance* of the two arrangements is the same. That is, both involve a significant financing activity, the issuance of stock, and an important investing activity, the acquisition of a patent. Accounting standards require that any significant noncash transactions be reported in a separate schedule or in a note to the financial statements. For the transaction in which stock was issued directly to the inventor, presentation in a schedule is as follows:

Supplemental schedule of noncash investing and financing activities

Acquisition of patent in exchange for capital stock $25,000

Two Methods of Reporting Cash Flow from Operating Activities

Companies use one of two methods to report the amount of cash flow from operating activities. The first approach, called the **direct method**, involves reporting major classes of gross cash receipts and cash payments. For example, cash collected from customers is reported separately from any interest and dividends received. Each of the major types of cash payments related to the company's operations follows, such as cash paid for inventory, for salaries and wages, for interest, and for taxes. Under the **indirect method**, net cash flow from operating activities is computed by adjusting net income to remove the effect of all deferrals of past operating cash receipts and payments and all accruals of future operating cash receipts and payments.

The FASB prefers the direct method, but it is used much less frequently than the indirect method. To compare and contrast the two methods, assume that Boulder Company begins operations as a corporation on January 1, 2017, with the owners' investment of $10,000 in cash. An income statement for 2017 and a balance sheet as of December 31, 2017, are presented in Exhibits 12-3 and 12-4, respectively.

LO4 Describe the difference between the direct and indirect methods of computing cash flow from operating activities.

Direct method
For preparing the Operating Activities section of the statement of cash flows, the approach in which cash receipts and cash payments are reported.

Indirect method
For preparing the Operating Activities section of the statement of cash flows, the approach in which net income is reconciled to net cash flow from operations.

EXHIBIT 12-3 Boulder Company's Income Statement

Boulder Company **Income Statement** **For the Year Ended December 31, 2017**	
Revenues	$80,000
Operating expenses	64,000
Income before tax	$16,000
Income tax expense	4,000
Net income	$12,000

EXHIBIT 12-4 Boulder Company's Balance Sheet

Boulder Company Balance Sheet As of December 31, 2017			
Assets		**Liabilities and Stockholders' Equity**	
Cash	$15,000	Accounts payable	$ 6,000
Accounts receivable	13,000	Capital stock	10,000
		Retained earnings	12,000
Total	$28,000	Total	$28,000

EXAMPLE 12-4 Determining Cash Flows from Operating Activities—Direct Method

To report cash flow from operating activities under the direct method, we look at each of the items on the income statement and determine how much cash each of those activities generated or used. Revenues for the period were $80,000. The balance sheet at the end of the period shows a balance in Accounts Receivable of $13,000; however, Boulder collected only $80,000 – $13,000, or $67,000, from its sales of the period. Thus, the first line on the statement of cash flows in Exhibit 12-5 reports $67,000 in cash collected from customers. Remember that the *net increase* in Accounts Receivable must be deducted from sales to find cash collected. For a new company, this is the same as the ending balance because the company starts the year without a balance in Accounts Receivable.

The same logic can be applied to determine the amount of cash expended for operating purposes. Operating expenses on the income statement are reported at $64,000. According to the balance sheet, however, $6,000 of the expense is unpaid at the end of the period as evidenced by the balance in Accounts Payable. Thus, the amount of cash expended for operating purposes as reported on the statement of cash flows in Exhibit 12-5 is $64,000 – $6,000, or $58,000. The other cash payment in the Operating Activities section of the statement is $4,000 for income taxes. Because no liability for income taxes is reported on the balance sheet, we know that $4,000 represents both the income tax expense of the period and the amount paid to the government. The only other item on the statement of cash flows in Exhibit 12-5 is the cash inflow from financing activities for the amount of cash invested by the owner in return for capital stock.

EXHIBIT 12-5 Statement of Cash Flows Using the Direct Method

Boulder Company Statement of Cash Flows For the Year Ended December 31, 2017	
Cash flows from operating activities	
Cash collected from customers	$ 67,000
Cash payments for operating purposes	(58,000)
Cash payments for taxes	(4,000)
Net cash inflow from operating activities	$ 5,000
Cash flows from financing activities	
Issuance of capital stock	$ 10,000
Net increase in cash	$ 15,000
Cash balance, beginning of period	0
Cash balance, end of period	$ 15,000

EXAMPLE 12-5 Determining Cash Flows from Operating Activities—Indirect Method

When the indirect method is used, the first line in the Operating Activities section of the statement of cash flows as shown in Exhibit 12-6 is the net income of the period. Net income is then adjusted to reconcile it to the amount of cash provided by operating activities. As reported on the income statement, this net income figure includes sales of $80,000 for the period. As we know, however, the amount of cash collected was $13,000 less than this because not all customers paid Boulder the amount due. **The increase in Accounts Receivable for the period is deducted from net income on the statement because the increase indicates that the company sold more during the period than it collected in cash.**

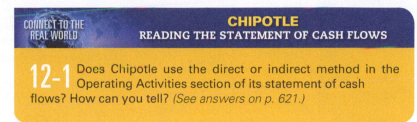

CHIPOTLE
READING THE STATEMENT OF CASH FLOWS

12-1 Does Chipotle use the direct or indirect method in the Operating Activities section of its statement of cash flows? How can you tell? *(See answers on p. 621.)*

The logic for the addition of the increase in Accounts Payable is similar, although the effect is the opposite. The amount of operating expenses deducted on the income statement was $64,000. We know, however, that the amount of cash paid was $6,000 less than this, as the balance in Accounts Payable indicates. **The increase in Accounts Payable for the period is added back to net income on the statement because the increase indicates that the company paid less during the period than it recognized in expense on the income statement.**

EXHIBIT 12-6 Statement of Cash Flows Using the Indirect Method

Boulder Company Statement of Cash Flows For the Year Ended December 31, 2017	
Cash flows from operating activities	
Net income	$ 12,000
Adjustments to reconcile net income to net cash	
from operating activities:	
Increase in accounts receivable	(13,000)
Increase in accounts payable	6,000
Net cash inflow from operating activities	$ 5,000
Cash flows from financing activities	
Issuance of capital stock	$ 10,000
Net increase in cash	$ 15,000
Cash balance, beginning of period	0
Cash balance, end of period	$ 15,000

Two important observations should be made in comparing the two methods illustrated in Examples 12-5 and 12-6:

1. The amount of cash provided by operating activities is the same under the two methods: $5,000; they simply use different computational approaches to arrive at the cash generated from operations.
2. The remainder of the statement of cash flows is the same regardless of which method is used.

MODULE 1 TEST YOURSELF

Review

LO1 Explain the concept of cash flows and accrual accounting and the purpose of a statement of cash flows.

- The statement of cash flows helps investors understand cash inflows and outflows of an entity based on its operating, investing, and financing activities. It provides complementary information to the accrual-based income statement.

LO2 Explain what cash equivalents are and how they are treated on the statement of cash flows.

- Cash equivalents are assets that are readily convertible to a determinable amount of cash, having a maturity date of three months or less.
- The term *cash* in the statement of cash flows includes cash and cash equivalents.

LO3 Describe operating, investing, and financing activities and give examples of each.

- Activities that generate or consume cash are classified into three categories for the statement of cash flows.
  - Operating activities usually involve cash flows related to the production of goods or services for customers.
  - Investing activities relate to acquiring and disposing of long-term assets.
  - Financing activities relate to raising funds through debt and equity securities and making payments related to those securities.

LO4 Describe the difference between the direct and indirect methods of computing cash flow from operating activities.

- The direct method reports cash receipts and cash disbursements related to operations.
- The indirect method derives cash flows from operating activities by starting with net income and then making adjustments for the effects of accruals and deferrals resulting from accrual-based accounting.

Question

1. What is the purpose of the statement of cash flows? Explain how it differs from the income statement.

2. Hansen Inc. made two purchases during December. One was a $10,000 Treasury bill that matures in 60 days from the date of purchase. The other was a $20,000 investment in Motorola common stock that will be held indefinitely. How should each purchase be treated for purposes of preparing a statement of cash flows?

3. Companies are required to classify cash flows as operating, investing, or financing. Which of these three categories do you think will most likely have a net cash outflow over a number of years? Explain your answer.

4. A fellow student says to you: "The statement of cash flows is the easiest of the basic financial statements to prepare because you know the answer before you start. You compare the beginning and ending balances in cash on the balance sheet and compute the net inflow or outflow of cash. What could be easier?" Do you agree? Explain your answer.

Apply

1. For each of the following activities, indicate whether it should appear on the statement of cash flows as an operating (O), investing (I), or financing (F) activity. Assume that the company uses the direct method of reporting in the Operating Activities section.
   _____ a. New equipment is acquired for cash.
   _____ b. Thirty-year bonds are issued.
   _____ c. Cash receipts from the cash register are recorded.
   _____ d. The biweekly payroll is paid.
   _____ e. Common stock is issued for cash.
   _____ f. Land that was being held for future expansion is sold at book value.

2. For each of the following transactions on the statement of cash flows, indicate whether it would appear in the Operating Activities section (O), in the Investing Activities section (I), or in the Financing Activities section (F). Assume the use of the direct method in the Operating Activities section.
   _____ a. Repayment of long-term debt
   _____ b. Purchase of equipment
   _____ c. Collection of customer's account
   _____ d. Issuance of common stock
   _____ e. Purchase of another company
   _____ f. Payment of dividends
   _____ g. Payment of income taxes
   _____ h. Sale of equipment

3. For each of the following items, indicate whether it would appear on a statement of cash flows prepared using the direct method (D) or the indirect method (I).

_____ a. Net income
_____ b. Increase in accounts receivable
_____ c. Collections on accounts receivable
_____ d. Payments on accounts payable
_____ e. Decrease in accounts payable
_____ f. Depreciation expense
_____ g. Gain on early retirement of bonds
_____ h. Cash sales

Answers are located at the end of the chapter.

MODULE 2 PREPARING THE STATEMENT OF CASH FLOWS USING THE DIRECT METHOD

Two interesting observations can be made about the statement of cash flows. First, the "answer" to a statement of cash flows is known before it is prepared. That is, the change in cash for the period is known by comparing two successive balance sheets. Thus, it is not the change in cash that is emphasized on the statement of cash flows but the *explanations* for the change in cash. That is, each item on a statement of cash flows helps to explain why cash changed by the amount it did during the period. The second important observation relates even more specifically to how this statement is prepared. An income statement and a balance sheet are prepared by taking the balances in each of the various accounts in the general ledger and putting them in the right place on the right statement. In preparing the statement of cash flows, the transactions during the period must be analyzed to (1) determine which of them affected cash and (2) classify each of the cash effects into one of the three categories.

So far in this chapter, the statements of cash flows have been prepared without the use of any special tools. In more complex situations, however, some type of methodology is needed. We will review the basic accounting equation and then illustrate a systematic approach for preparing the statement. The chapter appendix presents a work sheet approach to the preparation of the statement of cash flows.

LO5 Prepare a statement of cash flows using the direct method to determine cash flow from operating activities.

The Accounting Equation and the Statement of Cash Flows

The basic accounting equation is as follows:

Assets = Liabilities + Stockholders' Equity

Next, consider this refinement of the equation:

Assets = **Liabilities + Stockholders' Equity**

Cash + Noncash current assets + Long-term assets = Current liabilities + Long-term liabilities + Capital stock + Retained earnings

The equation can be rearranged so that only cash is on the left side and all other items are on the right side:

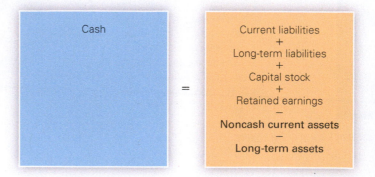

Therefore, any changes in cash must be accompanied by a corresponding change in the right side of the equation. For example, an increase or inflow of cash could result from an increase in long-term liabilities in the form of issuing bonds payable. Or an increase in cash could come from a decrease in long-term assets in the form of a sale of fixed assets. The various possibilities for inflows (+) and outflows (−) of cash can be summarized by activity as follows:

Activity	Left Side	Right Side	Example
Operating			
	+ Cash	− Noncash current assets	Collect accounts receivable
	− Cash	+ Noncash current assets	Prepay insurance
	+ Cash	+ Current liabilities	Collect customer's deposit
	− Cash	− Current liabilities	Pay suppliers
	+ Cash	+ Retained earnings	Make a cash sale
Investing			
	+ Cash	− Long-term assets	Sell equipment
	− Cash	+ Long-term assets	Buy equipment
Financing			
	+ Cash	+ Long-term liabilities	Issue bonds
	− Cash	− Long-term liabilities	Retire bonds
	+ Cash	+ Capital stock	Issue capital stock
	− Cash	− Capital stock	Buy capital stock
	− Cash	− Retained earnings	Pay dividends

Those examples show that inflows and outflows of cash relate to increases and decreases in the various balance sheet accounts. We now turn to analyzing these accounts as a way to assemble a statement of cash flows.

An Approach to Preparing the Statement of Cash Flows: Direct Method

The following steps can be used to prepare a statement of cash flows:

1. Set up three schedules with the following headings:
   a. Cash Flows from Operating Activities
   b. Cash Flows from Investing Activities
   c. Cash Flows from Financing Activities
   As we analyze the transactions that affect each of the noncash balance sheet accounts, any cash effects are entered on the appropriate master schedule. When completed, the three master schedules contain all of the information needed to prepare a statement of cash flows.

2. **Determine the cash flows from operating activities.** Generally, this requires analyzing each item on the *income statement* and in the *Current Asset* and *Current Liability accounts*. As cash flows are identified in this analysis, they are entered on the schedule of cash flows from operating activities.

3. **Determine the cash flows from investing activities.** Generally, this requires analyzing the *Long-Term Asset* accounts and any additional information provided. As cash flows are identified in this analysis, they are entered on the schedule of cash flows from investing activities. Any significant noncash activities are entered on a supplemental schedule.

4. **Determine the cash flows from financing activities.** Generally, this requires analyzing the *Long-Term Liability* and *Stockholders' Equity* accounts and any additional information provided. As cash flows are identified in this analysis, they are entered on the schedule of cash flows from financing activities. Any significant noncash activities are entered on a supplemental schedule.

In general, the cash effects of changes in current accounts are reported in the Operating section; changes relating to long-term asset accounts are reported in the Investing section; and changes relating to long-term liabilities and stockholders' equity are reported in the Financing section.

To illustrate this approach, we will refer to the income statement in Exhibit 12-7 and to the comparative balance sheets and the additional information provided for Julian Corp. in Exhibit 12-8. Assuming we have already set up the three schedules for operating, investing, and financing activities (Step 1), we outline the preparation of the statement of cash flows starting with Step 2.

Step 2: Determine the Cash Flows from Operating Activities

To determine the cash flows from operating activities, consider each of the items on the income statement and any related current assets or liabilities from the balance sheet.

Sales Revenue and Accounts Receivable Sales as reported on the income statement in Exhibit 12-7 amounted to $670,000.

EXHIBIT 12-7 Julian Corp.'s Income Statement

Julian Corp. Income Statement For the Year Ended December 31, 2017		
Revenues and gains:		
Sales revenue	$670,000	
Interest revenue	15,000	
Gain on sale of machine	5,000	
Total revenues and gains		$690,000
Expenses and losses:		
Cost of goods sold	$390,000	
Salaries and wages	60,000	
Depreciation	40,000	
Insurance	12,000	
Interest	15,000	
Income taxes	50,000	
Loss on retirement of bonds	3,000	
Total expenses and losses		570,000
Net income		$120,000

EXHIBIT 12-8 Julian Corp.'s Comparative Balance Sheets

Julian Corp. Comparative Balance Sheets		
	December 31	
	2017	**2016**
Cash	$ 35,000	$ 46,000
Accounts receivable	63,000	57,000
Inventory	84,000	92,000
Prepaid insurance	12,000	18,000
Total current assets	$ 194,000	$ 213,000
Long-term investments	$ 120,000	$ 90,000
Land	150,000	100,000
Property and equipment	320,000	280,000
Accumulated depreciation	(100,000)	(75,000)
Total long-term assets	$ 490,000	$ 395,000
Total assets	$ 684,000	$ 608,000
Accounts payable	$ 38,000	$ 31,000
Salaries and wages payable	7,000	9,000
Income taxes payable	8,000	5,000
Total current liabilities	$ 53,000	$ 45,000
Notes payable	$ 85,000	$ 35,000
Bonds payable	200,000	260,000
Total long-term liabilities	$ 285,000	$ 295,000
Capital stock	$ 100,000	$ 75,000
Retained earnings	246,000	193,000
Total stockholders' equity	$ 346,000	$ 268,000
Total liabilities and stockholders' equity	$ 684,000	$ 608,000

Additional Information

1. Long-term investments were purchased for $30,000.
2. Land was purchased by issuing a $50,000 note payable.
3. Equipment was purchased for $75,000.
4. A machine with an original cost of $35,000 and a book value of $20,000 was sold for $25,000.
5. Bonds with a face value of $60,000 were retired by paying $63,000 in cash.
6. Capital stock was issued in exchange for $25,000 in cash.
7. Dividends of $67,000 were paid.

Based on the beginning and ending balances in Exhibit 12-8, Accounts Receivable increased by $6,000, from $57,000 to $63,000. *This indicates that Julian had $6,000 more in sales to its customers than it collected in cash from them* (assuming that all sales are on credit). Thus, cash collections must have been $670,000 − $6,000, or $664,000. Another way to look at this is as follows:

Beginning accounts receivable	$ 57,000
+ Sales revenue	670,000
− Cash collections	(X)
= Ending accounts receivable	$ 63,000

Solving for X, we can find cash collections:

$$\$57,000 + \$670,000 - X = \$ 63,000$$
$$X = \$664,000$$

At this point, note the inflow of Cash for $664,000 as shown on the Schedule of Cash Flows from Operating Activities in Exhibit 12-9.

EXHIBIT 12-9 Schedule of Cash Flows from Operating Activities

Cash Flows from Operating Activities	
Cash receipts from:	
Sales on account	664,000
Interest	15,000
Cash payments for:	
Inventory purchases	(375,000)
Salaries and wages	(62,000)
Insurance	(6,000)
Interest	(15,000)
Taxes	(47,000)

Interest Revenue Julian reported interest revenue of $15,000 on the income statement. Did the company actually receive that amount of cash, or was it merely an accrual of revenue not yet received? The answer can be found by examining the Current Assets section of the balance sheet. Because there is no Interest Receivable account, the amount of interest recognized was the amount of cash received.

The amount of cash received should be entered on the Schedule of Cash Flows from Operating Activities, as shown in Exhibit 12-9.

Gain on Sale of Machine A gain on the sale of machine of $5,000 is reported as the next line on the income statement. Any cash received from the sale of a long-term asset is reported in the Investing Activities section of the statement of cash flows. Thus, we ignore the gain when reporting cash flows from operating activities under the direct method.

Cost of Goods Sold, Inventory, and Accounts Payable Cost of goods sold, as reported on the income statement, amounts to $390,000. Recall that $390,000 is not the amount of cash expended to pay suppliers of inventory. First, cost of goods sold represents the cost of the inventory sold during the period, not the amount purchased. Thus, we must analyze the Inventory account to determine the purchases of the period. Second, the amount of purchases is not the same as the cash paid to suppliers because purchases are normally on account. Therefore, we must analyze the Accounts Payable account to determine the cash payments.

Based on the beginning and ending balances in Exhibit 12-8, inventory decreased during the year by $8,000, from $92,000 to $84,000. *This means that the cost of inventory sold was $8,000 more than the purchases of the period.* Thus, purchases must have been $390,000 – $8,000, or $382,000. Another way to look at this is as follows:

Beginning inventory	$ 92,000
+ Purchases	X
– Cost of goods sold	(390,000)
= Ending inventory	$ 84,000

Solving for X, we can find purchases:

$$\$92,000 + X - \$390,000 = \$\ 84,000$$
$$X = \$382,000$$

Note from Exhibit 12-8 the $7,000 net increase in Accounts Payable. *This means that Julian's purchases were $7,000 more during the period than its cash payments.* Thus, cash payments must have been $382,000 – $7,000, or $375,000. Another way to look at this is as follows:

Beginning accounts payable	$ 31,000
+ Purchases	382,000
− Cash payments	(X)
= Ending accounts payable	$ 38,000

Solving for X, we can find cash payments:

$$\$31{,}000 + \$382{,}000 - X = \$\ 38{,}000$$
$$X = \underline{\$375{,}000}$$

The amount of cash paid of $375,000 should be entered on the schedule in Exhibit 12-9.

Salaries and Wages Expense and Salaries and Wages Payable The second expense listed on the income statement in Exhibit 12-8 is salaries and wages of $60,000. However, did Julian *pay* this amount to employees during the year? The answer can be found by examining the Salaries and Wages Payable account in the balance sheet in Exhibit 12-8. From the balance sheet, we note that the liability account decreased by $2,000, from $9,000 to $7,000. *This means that the amount of cash paid to employees was $2,000 more than the amount of expense accrued.* Another way to look at the cash payments of $60,000 + $2,000, or $62,000, is as follows:

Beginning salaries and wages payable	$ 9,000
+ Salaries and wages expense	60,000
− Cash payments to employees	(X)
= Ending salaries and wages payable	$ 7,000

Solving for X, we can find cash payments:

$$\$9{,}000 + \$60{,}000 - X = \$\ 7{,}000$$
$$X = \underline{\$62{,}000}$$

As you can see in Exhibit 12-9, the cash paid of $62,000 appears as a cash outflow on the Schedule of Cash Flows from Operating Activities.

Depreciation Expense The next item on the income statement is depreciation of $40,000. Depreciation of tangible long-term assets, amortization of intangible assets, and depletion of natural resources are different from most other expenses in that they have no effect on cash flow. The only related cash flows are from the purchase and sale of these long-term assets, and these are reported in the Investing Activities section of the statement of cash flows. Thus, depreciation is not reported on the Schedule of Cash Flows from Operating Activities when the direct method is used.

Insurance Expense and Prepaid Insurance According to the income statement in Exhibit 12-7, Julian recorded insurance expense of $12,000 during 2017. This amount is not the cash payments for insurance, however, because Julian has a Prepaid Insurance account on the balance sheet. Recall from Chapter 4 that as a company buys insurance, it increases the Prepaid Insurance account. As the insurance expires, this account is reduced and an expense is recognized. Note from the balance sheet in Exhibit 12-8 that the Prepaid Insurance account decreased during the period by $6,000, from $18,000 to $12,000. *This means that the amount of cash paid for insurance was $6,000 less than the amount of expense recognized.* Thus, the cash payments must have been $12,000 – $6,000, or $6,000. Another way to look at the cash payments is as follows:

Beginning prepaid insurance	$ 18,000
+ Cash payments for insurance	X
− Insurance expense	(12,000)
= Ending prepaid insurance	$ 12,000

Solving for X, we can find the amount of cash paid:

$$\$18{,}000 + X - \$12{,}000 = \$12{,}000$$
$$X = \underline{\$\ 6{,}000}$$

Note the cash outflow of $6,000 as entered in Exhibit 12-9 on the Schedule of Cash Flows from Operating Activities.

Interest Expense The amount of interest expense reported on the income statement is $15,000. Because the balance sheet does not report an accrual of interest owed but not yet paid (an Interest Payable account), we know that $15,000 is also the amount of cash paid. The schedule in Exhibit 12-9 reflects the cash outflow of $15,000 for interest.

   Whether interest paid is properly classified as an operating activity is subject to considerable debate. The FASB decided in favor of classification of interest as an operating activity because, unlike dividends, it appears on the income statement. This, it was argued, provides a direct link between the statement of cash flows and the income statement. Many argue, however, that it is inconsistent to classify dividends paid as a financing activity but interest paid as an operating activity. After all, both represent returns paid to providers of capital: interest to creditors and dividends to stockholders.

Income Taxes Expense and Income Taxes Payable The income statement in Exhibit 12-7 reports income tax expense of $50,000. We know, however, that this is not necessarily the amount paid to the government during the year. In fact, note the increase in the Income Taxes Payable account on the balance sheets in Exhibit 12-8. The liability increased by $3,000, from $5,000 to $8,000. *This means that the amount of cash paid to the government in taxes was $3,000 less than the amount of expense accrued.* Another way to look at the cash payments of $50,000 − $3,000, or $47,000, is as follows:

Beginning income taxes payable	$ 5,000
+ Income tax expense	50,000
− Cash payments for taxes	(X)
= Ending income taxes payable	$ 8,000

Solving for X, we can find the amount of cash paid:

$$\$5{,}000 + \$50{,}000 - X = \$\ 8{,}000$$
$$X = \underline{\$47{,}000}$$

As you can see by examining Exhibit 12-9, the cash payment for taxes is the last item on the Schedule for Cash Flows from Operating Activities.

Loss on Retirement of Bonds A $3,000 loss on the retirement of bonds is reported as the last item under expenses and losses on the income statement in Exhibit 12-7. Any cash paid to retire a long-term liability is reported in the Financing Activities section of the statement of cash flows. Thus, we ignore the loss when reporting cash flows from operating activities under the direct method.

Compare Net Income with Net Cash Flow from Operating Activities At this point, all of the items on the income statement have been analyzed, as have all of the current asset and current liability accounts. All of the information needed to prepare the Operating Activities section of the statement of cash flows has been gathered.

   To summarize, **preparation of the Operating Activities section of the statement of cash flows requires the conversion of each item on the income statement to a cash basis. The Current Asset and Current Liability accounts are analyzed to discover the cash effects of each item on the income statement.** Exhibit 12-10 summarizes this conversion process.

EXHIBIT 12-10 Conversion of Income Statement Items to Cash Basis

Income Statement	Amount	Adjustments	Cash Flows
Sales revenue	$670,000		$670,000
		+ Decreases in accounts receivable	0
		– Increases in accounts receivable	(6,000)
		Cash collected from customers	$664,000
Interest revenue	15,000		$ 15,000
		+ Decreases in interest receivable	0
		– Increases in interest receivable	0
		Cash collected in interest	$ 15,000
Gain on sale of machine	5,000	*Not an operating activity*	$ 0
Cost of goods sold	390,000		$390,000
		+ Increases in inventory	0
		– Decreases in inventory	(8,000)
		+ Decreases in accounts payable	0
		– Increases in accounts payable	(7,000)
		Cash paid to suppliers	$375,000
Salaries and wages	60,000		$ 60,000
		+ Decreases in salaries and wages payable	2,000
		– Increases in salaries and wages payable	0
		Cash paid to employees	$ 62,000
Depreciation	40,000	*No cash flow effect*	$ 0
Insurance	12,000		$ 12,000
		+ Increases in prepaid insurance	0
		– Decreases in prepaid insurance	(6,000)
		Cash paid for insurance	$ 6,000
Interest	15,000		$ 15,000
		+ Decreases in interest payable	0
		– Increases in interest payable	0
		Cash paid for interest	$ 15,000
Income taxes	50,000		$ 50,000
		+ Decreases in income taxes payable	0
		– Increases in income taxes payable	(3,000)
		Cash paid for taxes	$ 47,000
Loss on retirement of bonds	3,000	*Not an operating activity*	$ 0
Net income	$120,000	Net cash flow from operating activities	$174,000

Note in the exhibit the various adjustments made to put each income statement item on a cash basis. For example, the $6,000 increase in accounts receivable for the period is deducted from sales revenue of $670,000 to arrive at cash collected from customers. Similar adjustments are made to each of the other income statement items with the exception of depreciation, the gain, and the loss. Depreciation is ignored because it does not have an effect on cash flow. The gain relates to the sale of a long-term asset, and any cash effect is reflected in the Investing Activities section of the statement of cash flows. Similarly, the loss resulted from the retirement of bonds and any cash flow effect is reported in the Financing Activities section. The bottom of the exhibit highlights an important point: Julian reported net income of $120,000, but generated $174,000 in cash from operations.

Step 3: Determine the Cash Flows from Investing Activities

To determine the cash flows from investing activities, we will look at the Long-Term Asset accounts and any additional information available about these accounts. Julian has three long-term assets on its balance sheet: Long-Term Investments, Land, and Property and Equipment.

Long-Term Investments Item 1 in the additional information in Exhibit 12-8 indicates that Julian purchased $30,000 of investments during the year. The $30,000 net increase in the Long-Term Investments account confirms this. (No mention is made of the sale of any investments during 2017.) The purchase of investments requires the use of $30,000 in cash, as indicated on the Schedule of Cash Flows from Investing Activities in Exhibit 12-11.

EXHIBIT 12-11 Schedule of Cash Flows from Investing Activities

Cash Flows from Investing Activities	
Cash inflows from:	
Sale of machine	25,000
Cash outflows for:	
Purchase of investments	(30,000)
Purchase of property and equipment	(75,000)

Land Note the $50,000 net increase in land. Item 2 in the additional information indicates that Julian purchased land by issuing a $50,000 note payable. This transaction obviously does not involve cash. It has an important financing element and an investing component, however. The issuance of the note is a financing activity, and the acquisition of land is an investing activity. Because no cash was involved, the transaction is reported in a separate schedule instead of directly on the statement of cash flows:

Supplemental schedule of noncash investing and financing activities

Acquisition of land in exchange for note payable	$50,000

Property and Equipment Property and equipment increased by $40,000 during 2017. However, Julian acquired equipment and sold a machine (item 3 and item 4, respectively, in the additional information). As was discussed earlier in the chapter, acquisitions of new plant and equipment are important investing activities for most businesses. Thus, the $75,000 expended to acquire new plant and equipment appears on the Schedule of Cash Flows from Investing Activities in Exhibit 12-11 as a cash outflow.

As reported in the balance sheets in Exhibit 12-8, the Property and Equipment account increased during the year by only $40,000, from $280,000 to $320,000. Since Julian *added* to this account $75,000, however, we know that it must have disposed of some assets as well. Item 4 in the additional information in Exhibit 12-8 reports the sale of a machine with an original cost of $35,000. An analysis of the Property and Equipment account confirms this amount:

Beginning property and equipment	$280,000
+ Acquisitions	75,000
− Disposals	(X)
= Ending property and equipment	$320,000

Solving for X, we can find the *cost* of the property and equipment sold during the year:

$$\$280{,}000 + \$75{,}000 - X = \$320{,}000$$
$$X = \$\ 35{,}000$$

The additional information also indicates that the book value of the machine sold was $20,000. This means that if the original cost was $35,000 and the book value was $20,000, the Accumulated Depreciation on the machine sold must have been $35,000 − $20,000, or $15,000. An analysis similar to the one we just looked at for Property and Equipment confirms this amount:

Beginning accumulated depreciation	$ 75,000
+ Depreciation expense	40,000
− Accumulated depreciation on assets sold	(X)
= Ending accumulated depreciation	$100,000

Solving for X, we can find the accumulated depreciation on the assets disposed of during the year:

$$\$75,000 + \$40,000 - X = \$100,000$$
$$X = \$\ \underline{15,000}$$

Finally, we are told in the additional information that the machine was sold for $25,000. *If the selling price was $25,000 and the book value was $20,000, Julian reports a gain on the sale of $5,000, an amount that is confirmed on the income statement in Exhibit 12-7.* To summarize, the machine was sold for $25,000, an amount that exceeded its book value of $20,000, thus generating a gain of $5,000. The cash inflow of $25,000 is entered on the Schedule of Cash Flows from Investing Activities in Exhibit 12-11.

Step 4: Determine the Cash Flows from Financing Activities

Cash flows from financing activities generally involve long-term liabilities and stockholders' equity. First, we consider Julian's two long-term liabilities: Notes Payable and Bonds Payable; then, the two stockholders' equity accounts: Capital Stock and Retained Earnings.

Notes Payable Recall that item 2 in the additional information reported that Julian purchased land in exchange for a $50,000 note payable. This amount is confirmed on the balance sheets, which show an increase in notes payable of $50,000, from $35,000 to $85,000. In the discussion of investing activities, we already entered this transaction on a supplemental schedule of noncash activities because it was a significant financing activity but did not involve cash.

Bonds Payable The balance sheets in Exhibit 12-8 report a decrease in bonds payable of $60,000, from $260,000 to $200,000. Item 5 in the additional information in Exhibit 12-8 indicates that bonds with a face value of $60,000 were retired by paying $63,000 in cash. The book value of the bonds retired is the same as the face value of $60,000 because there is no unamortized discount or premium on the records. *When a company has to pay more in cash ($63,000) to settle a debt than the book value of the debt ($60,000), it reports a loss.* Recall the $3,000 loss reported on the income statement in Exhibit 12-7. For purposes of preparing a statement of cash flows with the direct method, however, the important amount is the $63,000 in cash paid to retire the bonds. This amount appears as a cash outflow on the Schedule of Cash Flows from Financing Activities shown in Exhibit 12-12.

Capital Stock Exhibit 12-8 indicates an increase in capital stock of $25,000, from $75,000 to $100,000. According to item 6 in the additional information in Exhibit 12-8, Julian issued capital stock in exchange for $25,000 in cash. The increase in cash from this issuance is presented as a cash inflow on the Schedule of Cash Flows from Financing Activities shown in Exhibit 12-12.

EXHIBIT 12-12 Schedule of Cash Flows from Financing Activities

Cash Flows from Financing Activities	
Cash inflows from:	
Issuance of stock	25,000
Cash outflows for:	
Retirement of bonds	(63,000)
Payment of cash dividends	(67,000)

Retained Earnings This account increased during the year by $53,000, from $193,000 to $246,000. Because we know from Exhibit 12-7 that net income was $120,000, however, the company must have declared some dividends.

We can determine the amount of cash dividends for 2017 in the following manner:

Beginning retained earnings	$193,000
+ Net income	120,000
− Cash dividends	(X)
= Ending retained earnings	$246,000

Solving for X, we can find the amount of cash dividends paid during the year.[2]

$$\$193{,}000 + \$120{,}000 - X = \$246{,}000$$
$$X = \$\ 67{,}000$$

Item 7 in the additional information confirms that this was in fact the amount of dividends paid during the year. The dividends paid appear on the Schedule of Cash Flows from Financing Activities presented in Exhibit 12-12.

Using the Three Schedules to Prepare a Statement of Cash Flows

All of the information needed to prepare a statement of cash flows is now available in the three schedules, along with the supplemental schedule prepared earlier. From the information gathered in Exhibits 12-9, 12-11, and 12-12, a completed statement of cash flows appears in Exhibit 12-13.

What does Julian's statement of cash flows tell us? Cash flow from operations totaled $174,000. Cash used to acquire investments and equipment amounted to $80,000 after $25,000 was received from the sale of a machine. A net amount of $105,000 was used for financing activities. Thus, Julian used more cash than it generated, which is why the cash balance declined.

EXHIBIT 12-13 Completed Statement of Cash Flows for Julian Corp.

Julian Corp. Statement of Cash Flows For the Year Ended December 31, 2017	
Cash flows from operating activities	
Cash receipts from:	
Sales on account	$ 664,000
Interest	15,000
Total cash receipts	$ 679,000

(Continued)

---

[2] Any decrease in Retained Earnings represents the dividends *declared* during the period rather than the amount paid. If there had been a Dividends Payable account, we would have analyzed it to find the amount of dividends paid. The lack of a balance in such an account at the beginning or end of the period tells us that Julian paid the same amount of dividends that it declared during the period.

Cash payments for:	
Inventory purchases	$(375,000)
Salaries and wages	(62,000)
Insurance	(6,000)
Interest	(15,000)
Taxes	(47,000)
Total cash payments	$(505,000)
Net cash provided by operating activities	$ 174,000
Cash flows from investing activities	
Purchase of investments	$ (30,000)
Purchase of property and equipment	(75,000)
Sale of machine	25,000
Net cash used by investing activities	$ (80,000)
Cash flows from financing activities	
Retirement of bonds	$ (63,000)
Issuance of stock	25,000
Payment of cash dividends	(67,000)
Net cash used by financing activities	$(105,000)
Net decrease in cash	$ (11,000)
Cash balance, December 31, 2016	46,000
Cash balance, December 31, 2017	$ 35,000
Supplemental schedule of noncash investing and financing activities	
Acquisition of land in exchange for note payable	$ 50,000

MODULE 2 TEST YOURSELF

Review	**LO5** Prepare a statement of cash flows using the direct method to determine cash flow from operating activities.	• Using the systematic approach illustrated in this module, it is possible to determine the cash flow from the major operating activities, such as sales, purchases, salaries and wages, and operating expenses, and from investing and financing activities.
Question	1. Why is it necessary to analyze both inventory and accounts payable in trying to determine cash payments to suppliers when the direct method is used?	
	2. Jackson Company prepays the rent on various office facilities. The beginning balance in Prepaid Rent was $9,600, and the ending balance was $7,300. The income statement reports Rent Expense of $45,900. Under the direct method, what amount would appear for cash paid in rent in the Operating Activities section of the statement of cash flows?	
	3. Baxter Inc. buys as treasury stock 2,000 shares of its own common stock at $20 per share. How is this transaction reported on the statement of cash flows?	

Apply

Fill in the blank for each of the following situations.

Balance Sheet	Beginning	Ending	Income Statement	Cash Inflow (Outflow)
a. Accounts receivable	$2,000	$5,000	Sales on account, $15,000	$_____
b. Prepaid insurance	$4,000	$3,000	Insurance expense, $7,000	$_____
c. Income taxes payable	$6,000	$9,000	Income tax expense, $20,000	$_____
d. Wages payable	$5,000	$3,000	Wages expense, $25,000	$_____

Answers are located at the end of the chapter.

MODULE 3 PREPARING THE STATEMENT OF CASH FLOWS USING THE INDIRECT METHOD

The purpose of the Operating Activities section of the statement changes when the indirect method is used. Instead of reporting cash receipts and cash payments, **the objective is to reconcile net income to net cash flow from operating activities.** The other two sections of the completed statement in Exhibit 12-13, the Investing and Financing sections, are unchanged.

An approach similar to that used for the direct method can be used to prepare the Operating Activities section of the statement of cash flows under the indirect method.

LO6 Prepare a statement of cash flows using the indirect method to determine cash flow from operating activities.

Net Income Recall that the first line in the Operating Activities section of the statement under the indirect method is net income. That is, we start with the assumptions that all revenues and gains reported on the income statement increase cash flow and that all expenses and losses decrease cash flow. Julian's net income of $120,000, as reported on its income statement in Exhibit 12-7, is reported as the first item in the Operating Activities section of the statement of cash flows shown in Exhibit 12-14.

Accounts Receivable Recall from the balance sheets in Exhibit 12-8 the net increase in Accounts Receivable of $6,000. Because net income includes sales (as opposed to cash collections), the $6,000 *net increase* must be *deducted* to adjust net income to cash from operations, as shown in Exhibit 12-14.

> **CONNECT TO THE REAL WORLD**
>
> **WALGREENS**
> **READING THE STATEMENT OF CASH FLOWS**
>
> **12-2** Did Walgreens Boots Alliance's Accounts Receivable, net, increase or decrease during the most recent year? Why is the change in this account deducted on the statement of cash flows? *(See answers on p. 621.)*

Gain on Sale of Machine The gain itself did not generate any cash, but the sale of the machine did. As we found earlier, the cash generated by selling the machine was reported in the Investing Activities section of the statement. The cash proceeds included the gain. Because the gain of $5,000 is included in the net income figure, it must be *deducted* to determine cash from operations, as shown in Exhibit 12-14. Also note that the gain is included twice in cash inflows if it is not deducted from the net income figure in the Operating Activities section.

EXHIBIT 12-14 Indirect Method for Reporting Cash Flows from Operating Activities

Julian Corp. Partial Statement of Cash Flows For the Year Ended December 31, 2017	
Net cash flows from operating activities	
Net income	$120,000
Adjustments to reconcile net income to net cash provided by operating activities:	
Increase in accounts receivable	(6,000)
Gain on sale of machine	(5,000)
Decrease in inventory	8,000
Increase in accounts payable	7,000
Decrease in salaries and wages payable	(2,000)
Depreciation expense	40,000
Decrease in prepaid insurance	6,000
Increase in income taxes payable	3,000
Loss on retirement of bonds	3,000
Net cash provided by operating activities	$174,000

Inventory As the $8,000 net decrease in the Inventory account indicates, Julian liquidated a portion of its stock of inventory during the year. A net decrease in this account indicates that the company sold more products than it purchased during the year. As shown in Exhibit 12-14, the *net decrease* of $8,000 is *added back* to net income.

Accounts Payable According to Exhibit 12-8, Julian owed suppliers $31,000 at the start of the year. By the end of the year, the balance had grown to $38,000. Effectively, the company saved cash by delaying the payment of some of its outstanding accounts payable. The *net increase* of $7,000 in this account is *added back* to net income, as shown in Exhibit 12-14.

Salaries and Wages Payable Salaries and Wages Payable decreased during the year by $2,000. The rationale for *deducting* the $2,000 *net decrease* in this liability in Exhibit 12-14 follows from what was just said about an increase in Accounts Payable. The payment to employees of $2,000 more than the amount included in expense on the income statement requires an additional deduction under the indirect method.

Depreciation Expense Depreciation is a noncash expense. Because it was deducted to arrive at net income, we must *add back* $40,000, the amount of depreciation, to find cash from operations. The same holds true for amortization of intangible assets and depletion of natural resources.

Prepaid Insurance This account decreased by $6,000, according to Exhibit 12-8. A decrease in this account indicates that Julian deducted more on the income statement for the insurance expense of the period than it paid in cash for new policies. That is, the cash outlay for insurance protection was not as large as the amount of expense reported on the income statement. Thus, the *net decrease* in the account is *added back* to net income in Exhibit 12-14.

Income Taxes Payable Exhibit 12-8 reports a net increase of $3,000 in Income Taxes Payable. The *net increase* of $3,000 in this liability is *added back* to net income in Exhibit 12-14 because the payments to the government were $3,000 less than the amount included on the income statement.

Loss on Retirement of Bonds The $3,000 loss from retiring bonds was reported on the income statement as a deduction. There are two parts to the explanation for adding back the loss to net income to eliminate its effect in the Operating Activities section of the statement. First, any cash outflow from retiring bonds is properly classified as a financing activity, not an operating activity. Second, the amount of the cash outflow is $63,000, not $3,000. To summarize, to convert net income to a cash basis, the loss is added back in the Operating Activities section to eliminate its effect.

Summary of Adjustments to Net Income under the Indirect Method

Following is a list of the most common adjustments to net income when the indirect method is used to prepare the Operating Activities section of the statement of cash flows:

Additions to Net Income	Deductions from Net Income
Decrease in accounts receivable	Increase in accounts receivable
Decrease in inventory	Increase in inventory
Decrease in prepayments	Increase in prepayments
Increase in accounts payable	Decrease in accounts payable
Increase in accrued liabilities	Decrease in accrued liabilities
Losses on sales of long-term assets	Gains on sales of long-term assets
Losses on retirements of bonds	Gains on retirements of bonds
Depreciation, amortization, and depletion	

Comparison of the Indirect and Direct Methods

The amount of cash provided by operating activities is the same under the direct and indirect methods. The FASB has expressed a strong preference for the direct method but allows companies to use the indirect method.

If a company uses the indirect method, it must separately disclose two important cash payments: income taxes paid and interest paid. Thus, if Julian uses the indirect method, it reports the following at the bottom of the statement of cash flows or in a note to the financial statements:

Income taxes paid	$47,000
Interest paid	15,000

Advocates of the direct method believe that the information provided with this approach is valuable in evaluating a company's operating efficiency. For example, use of the direct method allows the analyst to follow any trends in cash receipts from customers and compare them with cash payments to suppliers. Someone without a technical background in accounting can easily tell where cash came from and where it went during the period.

Advocates of the indirect method argue two major points: (1) The direct method reveals too much to competitors by telling them the amount of cash receipts and cash payments from operations. (2) The indirect method focuses attention on the differences between income on an accrual basis and a cash basis. In fact, this reconciliation of net income and cash provided by operating activities is considered to be important enough that if a company uses the direct method, it must present a separate schedule to reconcile net income to net cash from operating activities. This schedule, in effect, is the same as the Operating Activities section for the indirect method.

MODULE 3 TEST YOURSELF

Review	**LO6** Prepare a statement of cash flows using the indirect method to determine cash flow from operating activities.	• The systematic approach illustrated in this module uses the changes in current asset and liability accounts related to accruals and deferrals to adjust net income to cash flows from operating activities.

Question	1. What is your evaluation of the following statements? Depreciation is responsible for providing some of the highest amounts of cash for capital-intensive businesses. This is obvious by examining the Operating Activities section of the statement of cash flows. Other than the net income of the period, depreciation is often the largest amount reported in this section of the statement.
	2. Assume that a company uses the indirect method to prepare the Operating Activities section of the statement of cash flows. Why would a decrease in accounts receivable during the period be added back to net income?
	3. A company reports a net loss for the year. Is it possible that cash could increase during the year? Explain your answer.
	4. Why do accounting standards require a company to separately disclose income taxes paid and interest paid if it uses the indirect method in the Operating Activities section of the statement of cash flows?

Apply

1. Assume that a company uses the indirect method to prepare the Operating Activities section of the statement of cash flows. For each of the following items, indicate whether it would be added to net income (A), be deducted from net income (D), or not be reported in this section of the statement under the indirect method (NR).

   _____ a. Decrease in accounts payable
   _____ b. Increase in accounts receivable
   _____ c. Decrease in prepaid insurance
   _____ d. Purchase of new factory equipment
   _____ e. Depreciation expense
   _____ f. Gain on retirement of bonds

2. Assume that a company uses the indirect method to prepare the Operating Activities section of the statement of cash flows. For each of the following items, indicate whether it would be added to (A) or deducted from (D) net income to arrive at net cash provided by operating activities.

   _____ a. Decrease in accounts receivable
   _____ b. Increase in prepaid rent
   _____ c. Decrease in inventory
   _____ d. Increase in accounts payable
   _____ e. Decrease in income taxes payable
   _____ f. Depreciation expense
   _____ g. Loss on sale of equipment

3. Duke sold a delivery truck for $9,000. Its original cost was $25,000, and the book value at the time of the sale was $11,000. Explain how the transaction to record the sale appears on a statement of cash flows prepared using the indirect method.

Answers are located at the end of the chapter.

MODULE 4 CASH FLOW ANALYSIS

LO7 Use cash flow information to help analyze a company.

The statement of cash flows is a critical disclosure to a company's investors and creditors. Many investors focus on cash flow from operations rather than net income as their key statistic. Similarly, many bankers are as concerned with cash flow from operations as they are with net income because they care about a company's ability to pay its bills. Accrual accounting can mask cash flow problems. For example, a company with smooth earnings could be building up accounts receivable and inventory. This may not become evident until the company is in deep trouble.

The statement of cash flows provides investors, analysts, bankers, and other users with a valuable starting point as they attempt to evaluate a company's financial health. They pay particular attention to the relationships among various items on the statement, as well as to other financial statement items. In fact, many large banks have their own cash flow models, which typically involve a rearrangement of the items on the statement of cash flows to suit their needs. We now consider two examples of how various groups use cash flow information.

Creditors and Cash Flow Adequacy

Bankers and other creditors are especially concerned with a company's ability to meet its principal and interest obligations. *Cash flow adequacy* is a measure intended to help in this regard.[3] It gauges the cash that a company has available to meet future debt

---

[3] An article appearing in the January 10, 1994, edition of *The Wall Street Journal* reported that **Fitch Investors Service Inc.** has published a rating system to compare the cash flow adequacy of companies that it rates single-A in its credit ratings. The rating system is intended to help corporate bond investors assess the ability of these companies to meet their maturing debt obligations. Lee Berton, ''Investors Have a New Tool for Judging Issuers' Health: 'Cash-Flow Adequacy,''' p. C1.

obligations after paying taxes and interest costs and making capital expenditures. Because capital expenditures on new plant and equipment are a necessity for most companies, analysts are concerned with the cash available to repay debt *after* the company has replaced and updated its existing base of long-term assets.

$$\text{Cash Flow Adequacy} = \frac{\text{Cash Flow from Operating Activities} - \text{Capital Expenditures}}{\text{Average Amount of Debt Maturing over Next Five Years}}$$

How could you use the information in an annual report to measure a company's cash flow adequacy? First, whether a company uses the direct or indirect method to report cash flow from operating activities, this number represents cash flow after interest and taxes are paid. The numerator of the ratio is determined by deducting capital expenditures, as they appear in the Investing Activities section of the statement, from cash flow from operating activities. A disclosure required by the SEC provides the information needed to calculate the denominator of the ratio. This regulatory body requires companies to report the annual amount of long-term debt maturing over each of the next five years.

MAKING BUSINESS DECISIONS
NORDSTROM

Analyzing Cash Flow Adequacy

Managers, investors, and creditors are all interested in a company's cash flows. Use the following models to help you in your role as a banker to decide whether to lend money to **Nordstrom, Inc.**

A. The Ratio Analysis Model

1. Formulate the Question
Did Nordstrom generate enough cash this year from its operations to pay for its capital expenditures and meet its maturing debt obligations?

2. Gather the Information from the Financial Statements
To calculate a company's cash flow adequacy, it is essential to know the amounts of three items:

Net cash from operating activities: From the statement of cash flows
Capital expenditures: From the statement of cash flows
Average debt maturing over the next five years: From the note disclosures

3. Calculate the Ratio

$$\text{Cash Flow Adequacy} = \frac{\text{Net Cash Flow from Operating Activities} - \text{Capital Expenditures}}{\text{Average Amount of Debt Maturing over Next Five Years}}$$

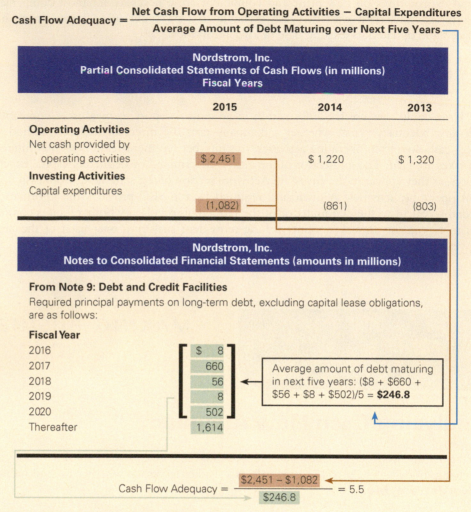

Nordstrom, Inc. Partial Consolidated Statements of Cash Flows (in millions) Fiscal Years			
	2015	**2014**	**2013**
Operating Activities			
Net cash provided by operating activities	$ 2,451	$ 1,220	$ 1,320
Investing Activities			
Capital expenditures	(1,082)	(861)	(803)

Nordstrom, Inc. Notes to Consolidated Financial Statements (amounts in millions)

From Note 9: Debt and Credit Facilities

Required principal payments on long-term debt, excluding capital lease obligations, are as follows:

Fiscal Year

2016	$ 8
2017	660
2018	56
2019	8
2020	502
Thereafter	1,614

Average amount of debt maturing in next five years: ($8 + $660 + $56 + $8 + $502)/5 = **$246.8**

$$\text{Cash Flow Adequacy} = \frac{\$2,451 - \$1,082}{\$246.8} = 5.5$$

4. Compare the Ratio with Other Ratios

Ratios are of no use in a vacuum. It is necessary to compare them with prior years and with competitors.

CASH FLOW ADEQUACY			
Nordstrom, Inc.		Dillard's, Inc.	
Fiscal Years		Fiscal Years	
2015	**2014**	**2015**	**2014**
5.5	1.7	5.7	9.3

5. Interpret the Ratios

Nordstrom's cash flow adequacy ratio in 2015 is very similar to its competitor, Dillard's. Nordstrom's ratio increased from the prior year, while Dillard's ratio decreased. Nordstrom's 2015 ratio of 5.5 is an indication the company generated enough cash from operations to not only make necessary capital expenditures but also to cover its average annual debt maturing over the next five years.

B. The Business Decision Model

1. Formulate the Question

If you were a banker, would you loan money to Nordstrom, Inc.?

2. Gather Information from the Financial Statements and Other Sources

This information will come from a variety of sources, not limited to but including:

- The balance sheet provides information about liquidity, the income statement regarding profitability, and the statement of cash flows on inflows and outflows of cash.
- The outlook for the retail apparel industry, including consumer trends, the competitive landscape, labor issues, and other factors.
- The outlook for the economy in general.
- Alternative uses for the money.

3. Analyze the Information Gathered

- Compare Nordstrom's cash flow adequacy ratio in (A) above with Dillard's as well as with industry averages.
- Look at trends over time in the cash flow adequacy ratios.
- Look at trends in cash provided by operations over time as an indication of the ability to generate enough cash to make necessary capital expenditures and meet debt obligations.
- Review projections for the economy and the industry.

4. Make the Decision

Taking into account all of the various sources of information, decide either to

- Loan money to Nordstrom, Inc., or
- Find an alternative use for the money

5. Monitor Your Decision

If you decide to make the loan, you will need to monitor it periodically. During the time the loan is outstanding, you will want to assess the company's continuing ability to generate cash from operations as well as other factors you considered before making the loan.

Stockholders and Cash Flow per Share

One measure of the relative worth of an investment in a company is the ratio of the stock's market price per share to the company's earnings per share (that is, the price/earnings ratio). Many stockholders and analysts are even more interested in the price of the stock in relation to the company's cash flow per share. Cash flow for purposes of this ratio is normally limited to cash flow from operating activities. These groups have used this ratio to evaluate investments—even though the accounting profession has expressly forbidden the reporting of cash flow per share information in the financial statements. The accounting profession's belief is that this type of information is not an acceptable alternative to earnings per share as an indicator of company performance.

MODULE 4 TEST YOURSELF

Review	LO7 Use cash flow information to help analyze a company.	• Cash flow per share and cash flow adequacy are two measures that investors and creditors can use to evaluate the financial health of an entity.
Question	Explain where to find the information needed to determine a company's cash flow adequacy.	
Apply	A company generated $1,500,000 from its operating activities and spent $900,000 on additions to its plant and equipment during the year. The total amount of debt that matures in the next five years is $750,000. Compute the cash flow adequacy ratio for the year.	

Answers are located at the end of the chapter.

APPENDIX

LO8 Use a work sheet to prepare a statement of cash flows using the indirect method to determine cash flow from operating activities.

MODULE 5 A WORK SHEET APPROACH TO PREPARING THE STATEMENT OF CASH FLOWS

The chapter illustrated a systematic approach to help in analyzing the transactions of the period. We now consider the use of a work sheet as an alternative tool to organize the information needed to prepare the statement of cash flows. We will use the information given in the chapter for Julian Corp. (Refer to Exhibits 12-7 and 12-8 for the income statement and comparative balance sheets, respectively.) Although it is possible to use a work sheet to prepare the statement when the Operating Activities section is prepared under the direct method, we illustrate the use of a work sheet using the more popular indirect method.

A work sheet for Julian Corp. is presented in Exhibit 12-15. The following steps were taken to prepare the work sheet:

Step 1: The balances in each account at the end and the beginning of the period are entered in the first two columns of the work sheet. For Julian, these balances can be found in its comparative balance sheets in Exhibit 12-8. Note that the contra-asset account, accumulated depreciation, as well as the liability and stockholders' equity accounts are shown in parentheses on the work sheet. Because the work sheet lists all balance sheet accounts, the total of the asset balances must equal the total of the liability and stockholders' equity balances; thus, the totals at the bottom for these first two columns equal $0.

Step 2: The additional information listed at the bottom of Exhibit 12-8 is used to record the various investing and financing activities on the work sheet. (The item numbers that follow correspond to the superscript numbers on the work sheet in Exhibit 12-15.)

1. Long-term investments were purchased for $30,000. Because this transaction required the use of cash, it is entered in parentheses in the Investing column and in the Changes column as an addition to the Long-Term Investments account.

2. Land was acquired by issuing a $50,000 note payable. This transaction is entered on two lines on the work sheet. First, $50,000 is added to the Changes column for Land and as a corresponding deduction in the Noncash column (the last column on the work sheet). Likewise, $50,000 is added to the Changes column for Notes Payable and to the Noncash column.

3. Item 3 in the additional information indicates the acquisition of equipment for $75,000. This amount appears on the work sheet as an addition to Property and Equipment in the Changes column and as a deduction (cash outflow) in the Investing column.

EXHIBIT 12-15 Julian Corp. Statement of Cash Flows Work Sheet

	Julian Corp. Statement of Cash Flows Work Sheet (Indirect Method) (all amounts in thousands of dollars)						
	Balances			**Cash Inflows (Outflows)**			**Noncash Activities**
Accounts	**12/31/17**	**12/31/16**	**Changes**	**Operating**	**Investing**	**Financing**	
Cash	35	46	$(11)^{16}$				
Accounts Receivable	63	57	6^{10}	$(6)^{10}$			
Inventory	84	92	$(8)^{11}$	8^{11}			
Prepaid Insurance	12	18	$(6)^{12}$	6^{12}			
Long-Term Investments	120	90	30^1		$(30)^1$		
Land	150	100	50^2				$(50)^2$
Property and Equipment	320	280	75^3		$(75)^3$		
			$(35)^4$		25^4		
Accumulated Depreciation	(100)	(75)	15^4				
			$(40)^9$	40^9			
Accounts Payable	(38)	(31)	$(7)^{13}$	7^{13}			
Salaries and Wages Payable	(7)	(9)	2^{14}	$(2)^{14}$			
Income Taxes Payable	(8)	(5)	$(3)^{15}$	3^{15}			
Notes Payable	(85)	(35)	$(50)^2$				50^2
Bonds Payable	(200)	(260)	$(60)^6$			$(63)^5$	
Capital Stock	(100)	(75)	$(25)^6$			25^6	
Retained Earnings	(246)	(193)	67^7	$(5)^4$		$(67)^7$	
				3^5			
			$(120)^8$	120^8			
Totals	0	0	0	174	(80)	(105)	0
Net decrease in cash				$(11)^{16}$			

Source: The authors are grateful to Jeannie Folk for the development of this work sheet.

4. A machine with an original cost of $35,000 and a book value of $20,000 was sold for $25,000, resulting in four entries on the work sheet. First, the amount of cash received, $25,000, is entered as an addition in the Investing column on the line for property and equipment. On the same line, the cost of the machine, $35,000, is entered as a deduction in the Changes column. The difference between the cost of the machine, $35,000, and its book value, $20,000, is its accumulated depreciation of $15,000. This amount is shown as a deduction from this account in the Changes column. Because the gain of $5,000 is included in net income, it is deducted in the Operating column (on the Retained Earnings line).

5. Bonds with a face value of $60,000 were retired by paying $63,000 in cash, resulting in the entry of three amounts on the work sheet. The face value of the bonds, $60,000, is entered as a reduction of Bonds Payable in the Changes column. The amount paid to retire the bonds, $63,000, is entered on the same line in the Financing column. The loss of $3,000 is added in the Operating column because it was a deduction to arrive at net income.

6. Capital stock was issued for $25,000. This amount is entered on the Capital Stock line under the Changes column (as an increase in the account) and under the Financing column as an inflow.

7. Dividends of $67,000 were paid. This amount is entered as a reduction in Retained Earnings in the Changes column and as a cash outflow in the Financing column.

Step 3: Because the indirect method is being used, net income of $120,000 for the period is entered as an addition to Retained Earnings in the Operating column of the work sheet [entry (8)]. The amount is also entered as an increase (in parentheses) in the Changes column.

Step 4: Any noncash revenues or expenses are entered on the work sheet on the appropriate lines. For Julian, depreciation expense of $40,000 is added (in parentheses) to Accumulated Depreciation in the Changes column and in the Operating column. This entry is identified on the work sheet as entry (9).

Step 5: Each of the changes in the noncash current asset and current liability accounts is entered in the Changes column and in the Operating column. These entries are identified on the work sheet as entries (10) through (15).

Step 6: Totals are determined for the Operating, Investing, and Financing columns and entered at the bottom of the work sheet. The total for the final column, Noncash Activities, of $0, is also entered.

Step 7: The net cash inflow (outflow) for the period is determined by adding the totals of the Operating, Investing, and Financing columns. For Julian, the net cash *outflow* is $11,000, shown as entry (16) at the bottom of the statement. This same amount is then transferred to the line for Cash in the Changes column. Finally, the total of the Changes column at this point should net to $0.

MODULE 5 TEST YOURSELF

Review	**LO8** Use a work sheet to prepare a statement of cash flows using the indirect method to determine cash flow from operating activities.	• A work sheet is an alternative tool to help in the preparation of a statement of cash flows.

Question	Assume the format illustrated in Exhibit 12-15 for a statement of cash flows work sheet. Why will the Changes column of the work sheet total to 0?

Apply

Assume that a company uses a work sheet as illustrated in Exhibit 12-15 to prepare its statement of cash flows and that it uses the indirect method in the Operating Activities section of the statement. For each of the following changes in balance sheet accounts, indicate in one of the three columns whether it is an addition (A) or a deduction (D). Assume that the change in (b) and (f) includes a corresponding change in cash.

	Type of Activity		
Balance Sheet Change	**Operating**	**Investing**	**Financing**
a. Accounts receivable increased	_____	_____	_____
b. Land increased	_____	_____	_____
c. Inventory decreased	_____	_____	_____
d. Accounts payable decreased	_____	_____	_____
e. Income taxes payable increased	_____	_____	_____
f. Capital stock increased	_____	_____	_____

Answers are located at the end of the chapter.

RATIO REVIEW

Cash Flow Adequacy =

$$\text{Cash Flow Adequacy} = \frac{\text{Cash Flow from Operating Activities – Capital Expenditures (Statement of Cash Flows)}}{\text{Average Amount of Debt Maturing over Next Five Years (Notes to the Financial Statements)}}$$

KEY TERMS QUIZ

Read each definition below and write the number of the definition in the blank beside the appropriate term. The quiz solutions appear at the end of the chapter.

_____ Statement of cash flows   _____ Financing activities
_____ Cash equivalent   _____ Direct method
_____ Operating activities   _____ Indirect method
_____ Investing activities

1. Activities concerned with the acquisition and sale of products and services.
2. For preparing the Operating Activities section of the statement of cash flows, the approach in which net income is reconciled to net cash flow from operations.
3. The financial statement that summarizes an entity's cash receipts and cash payments during the period from operating, investing, and financing activities.
4. An item readily convertible to a known amount of cash with a maturity to the investor of three months or less.
5. Activities concerned with the acquisition and disposal of long-term assets.
6. For preparing the Operating Activities section of the statement of cash flows, the approach in which cash receipts and cash payments are reported.
7. Activities concerned with the raising and repaying of funds in the form of debt and equity.

ALTERNATE TERMS

bottom line net income
cash flow from operating activities
   cash flow from operations

statement of cash flows cash flows
   statement

REVIEW PROBLEM & SOLUTION

An income statement and comparative balance sheets for Dexter Company follow.

Dexter Company
Income Statement
For the Year Ended December 31, 2017

Sales revenue	$89,000
Cost of goods sold	57,000
Gross profit	$32,000
Depreciation expense	$ 6,500
Advertising expense	3,200
Salaries expense	12,000
Total operating expenses	$21,700
Operating income	$10,300
Loss on sale of land	2,500
Income before tax	$ 7,800
Income tax expense	2,600
Net income	$ 5,200

Dexter Company
Comparative Balance Sheets
December 31

	December 31	
	2017	**2016**
Cash	$ 12,000	$ 9,500
Accounts receivable	22,000	18,400
Inventory	25,400	20,500
Prepaid advertising	10,000	8,600
Total current assets	$ 69,400	$ 57,000
Land	$120,000	$ 80,000
Equipment	190,000	130,000
Accumulated depreciation	(70,000)	(63,500)
Total long-term assets	$240,000	$146,500
Total assets	$309,400	$203,500
Accounts payable	$ 15,300	$ 12,100
Salaries payable	14,000	16,400
Income taxes payable	1,200	700
Total current liabilities	$ 30,500	$ 29,200
Capital stock	$200,000	$100,000
Retained earnings	78,900	74,300
Total stockholders' equity	$278,900	$174,300
Total liabilities and stockholders' equity	$309,400	$203,500

Additional Information:
1. Land was acquired during the year for $70,000.
2. An unimproved parcel of land was sold during the year for $27,500. Its original cost to Dexter was $30,000.
3. A specialized piece of equipment was acquired in exchange for capital stock in the company. The value of the capital stock was $60,000.
4. In addition to the capital stock issued in (3), stock was sold for $40,000.
5. Dividends of $600 were paid.

Required

Prepare a statement of cash flows for 2017 using the direct method in the Operating Activities section of the statement. Include supplemental schedules to report any noncash investing and financing activities and to reconcile net income to net cash provided by operating activities.

Solution to Review Problem

1.   **Dexter Company**
                           Statement of Cash Flows
                     For the Year Ended December 31, 2017

Cash flows from operating activities	
Cash collections from customers	$ 85,400
Cash payments:	
To suppliers	$(58,700)
For advertising	(4,600)
To employees	(14,400)
For income taxes	(2,100)
Total cash payments	$(79,800)
Net cash provided by operating activities	$ 5,600
Cash flows from investing activities	
Purchase of land	$(70,000)
Sale of land	27,500
Net cash used by investing activities	$(42,500)

Cash flows from financing activities

Issuance of capital stock	$ 40,000
Payment of cash dividends	(600)
Net cash provided by financing activities	$ 39,400
Net increase in cash	$ 2,500
Cash balance, December 31, 2016	9,500
Cash balance, December 31, 2017	$ 12,000

Supplemental schedule of noncash investing and financing activities

Acquisition of specialized equipment in exchange for capital stock	$ 60,000

Reconciliation of net income to net cash provided by operating activities

Net income	$ 5,200
Adjustments to reconcile net income to net cash provided by operating activities:	
Increase in accounts receivable	(3,600)
Increase in inventory	(4,900)
Increase in prepaid advertising	(1,400)
Increase in accounts payable	3,200
Decrease in salaries payable	(2,400)
Increase in income taxes payable	500
Depreciation expense	6,500
Loss on sale of land	2,500
Net cash provided by operating activities	$ 5,600

EXERCISES

Exercise 12-1 Cash Equivalents

Metropolis Industries invested its excess cash in the following instruments during December 2017:

LO2

EXAMPLE 12-2

Certificate of deposit, due January 31, 2018	$ 35,000
Certificate of deposit, due June 30, 2018	95,000
Investment in City of Elm bonds, due May 1, 2019	15,000
Investment in Quantum Data stock	66,000
Money market fund	105,000
90-day Treasury bills	75,000
Treasury note, due December 1, 2018	200,000

Required

Determine the amount of cash equivalents that should be combined with cash on the company's balance sheet at December 31, 2017, and for purposes of preparing a statement of cash flows for the year ended December 31, 2017.

Exercise 12-2 Classification of Activities

For each of the following transactions reported on a statement of cash flows, indicate whether it would appear in the Operating Activities section (O), in the Investing Activities section (I), or in the Financing Activities section (F). Put an S in the blank if the transaction does not affect cash but is reported in a supplemental schedule of noncash activities. Assume that the company uses the direct method in the Operating Activities section.

LO3

EXAMPLE 12-1, 12-3, 12-4

_____ 1. A company purchases its own common stock in the open market and immediately retires it.
_____ 2. A company issues preferred stock in exchange for land.
_____ 3. A six-month bank loan is obtained.
_____ 4. Twenty-year bonds are issued.
_____ 5. A customer's open account is collected.
_____ 6. Income taxes are paid.
_____ 7. Cash sales for the day are recorded.

(Continued)

_____   8.   Cash dividends are declared and paid.
_____   9.   A creditor is given shares of common stock in the company in return for cancellation of a long-term loan.
_____   10.   A new piece of machinery is acquired for cash.
_____   11.   Stock of another company is acquired as an investment.
_____   12.   Interest is paid on a bank loan.
_____   13.   Factory workers are paid.

LO3   Exercise 12-3   Retirement of Bonds Payable on the Statement of Cash Flows—Indirect Method

Redstone Inc. has the following debt outstanding on December 31, 2017:

10% bonds payable, due 12/31/21	$500,000	
Discount on bonds payable	(40,000)	$460,000

On this date, Redstone retired the entire bond issue by paying cash of $510,000.

Required

1.   Identify and analyze the transaction to record the bond retirement.
2.   Describe how the bond retirement would be reported on the statement of cash flows assuming that Redstone uses the indirect method.

LO3   Exercise 12-4   Classification of Activities for Carnival Corporation

EXAMPLE 12-1, 12-5

REAL WORLD

Carnival Corporation & plc is one of the largest cruise companies in the world with such well-known brands as Carnival Cruise Lines, Holland America Line, and Princess Cruises. Classify each of the following items found on the company's 2015 statement of cash flows according to whether it would appear in the Operating Activities section (O), in the Investing Activities section (I), or in the Financing Activities section (F). The company uses the indirect method in the Operating Activities section of its statement.

_____   1.   Dividends paid
_____   2.   Proceeds from issuance of long-term debt
_____   3.   Depreciation and amortization
_____   4.   Additions to property and equipment
_____   5.   Purchases of treasury stock
_____   6.   Net income

LO3   Exercise 12-5   Cash Flows from Investing and Financing Activities and Noncash Activities

EXAMPLE 12-1, 12-3

For each of the following transactions, indicate whether they would be reported in the Investing Activities section of the statement of cash flows (I) or the Financing Activities section (F). Put an *S* in the blank if the transaction does not affect cash but is reported in a supplemental schedule of noncash activities.

_____   1.   Issued capital stock for cash.
_____   2.   Issued a five-year note payable in exchange for a patent.
_____   3.   Acquired land for cash.
_____   4.   Issued bonds payable for cash.
_____   5.   Issued capital stock in exchange for a trademark.
_____   6.   Acquired equipment for cash.

LO5   Exercise 12-6   Cash Collections—Direct Method

Spencer Corp. reported accounts receivable of $28,000 on its December 31, 2016, balance sheet. On December 31, 2017, accounts receivable had decreased to $22,000. Sales for the year amounted to $55,000. What is the amount of cash collections that Spencer will report in the Operating Activities section of its 2017 statement of cash flows assuming that the direct method is used?

Exercise 12-7   Cash Collections—Direct Method   LO5

Stanley Company's comparative balance sheets included accounts receivable of $80,800 at December 31, 2016, and $101,100 at December 31, 2017. Sales reported by Stanley on its 2017 income statement amounted to $1,450,000. What is the amount of cash collections that Stanley will report in the Operating Activities section of its 2017 statement of cash flows assuming that the direct method is used?

Exercise 12-8   Working Backward: Cash Collections—Direct Method   LO5

Butler Corp. reported the following in the Current Assets section of its comparative balance sheets:

	12/31/17	12/31/16
Current Assets:		
Accounts receivable	$12,500	$15,300

The company uses the direct method on its statement of cash flows and reported that it collected $45,200 during 2017 from its customers. Determine sales revenue for 2017.

Exercise 12-9   Cash Payments—Direct Method   LO5

Wolf's comparative balance sheets included inventory of $45,000 at December 31, 2016, and $63,000 at December 31, 2017. The comparative balance sheets also included accounts payable of $33,000 at December 31, 2016, and $39,000 at December 31, 2017. Wolf's accounts payable balances are composed solely of amounts due to suppliers for purchases of inventory on account. Cost of goods sold, as reported on the 2017 income statement, amounted to $120,000. What is the amount of cash payments for inventory that Wolf will report in the Operating Activities section of its 2017 statement of cash flows assuming that the direct method is used?

Exercise 12-10   Cash Payments—Direct Method   LO5

Lester Enterprises' comparative balance sheets included inventory of $90,200 at December 31, 2016, and $70,600 at December 31, 2017. Lester's comparative balance sheets also included accounts payable of $57,700 at December 31, 2016, and $39,200 at December 31, 2017. Lester's accounts payable balances are composed solely of amounts due to suppliers for purchases of inventory on account. Cost of goods sold, as reported by Lester on its 2017 income statement, amounted to $770,900. What is the amount of cash payments for inventory that Lester will report in the Operating Activities section of its 2017 statement of cash flows assuming that the direct method is used?

Exercise 12-11   Working Backward: Cash Payments—Direct Method   LO5

Homeier Heating reported the following amounts on its comparative balance sheets:

	12/31/17	12/31/16
Current Assets:		
Inventories	$66,000	$55,000
Current Liabilities:		
Accounts payable	33,000	24,000

The company uses the direct method on its statement of cash flows and reported that it spent $44,000 during 2017 to acquire inventory. Determine cost of goods sold expense for 2017.

Exercise 12-12   Operating Activities Section—Direct Method   LO5

The following account balances for the noncash current assets and current liabilities of Labrador Company are available:

(Continued)

	December 31	
	2017	**2016**
Accounts receivable	$ 4,000	$ 6,000
Inventory	32,000	25,000
Office supplies	7,000	10,000
Accounts payable	7,500	4,500
Salaries and wages payable	1,500	2,500
Interest payable	500	1,000
Income taxes payable	4,500	3,000

In addition, the income statement for 2017 is as follows:

	2017
Sales revenue	$100,000
Cost of goods sold	75,000
Gross profit	$ 25,000
General and administrative expense	$ 8,000
Depreciation expense	3,000
Total operating expenses	$ 11,000
Income before interest and taxes	$ 14,000
Interest expense	3,000
Income before tax	$ 11,000
Income tax expense	5,000
Net income	$ 6,000

Required

1. Prepare the Operating Activities section of the statement of cash flows using the direct method.
2. What does the use of the direct method reveal about a company that the indirect method does not?

LO5 **Exercise 12-13 Determination of Missing Amounts—Cash Flow from Operating Activities**

The computation of cash provided by operating activities requires analysis of the noncash current asset and current liability accounts. Determine the missing amounts for each of the following independent cases:

Case 1

Accounts receivable, beginning of year	$150,000
Accounts receivable, end of year	100,000
Credit sales for the year	175,000
Cash sales for the year	60,000
Write-offs of uncollectible accounts	35,000
Total cash collections for the year (from cash sales and collections on account)	?

Case 2

Inventory, beginning of year	$ 80,000
Inventory, end of year	55,000
Accounts payable, beginning of year	25,000
Accounts payable, end of year	15,000
Cost of goods sold	175,000
Cash payments for inventory (assume all purchases of inventory are on account)	?

Case 3

Prepaid insurance, beginning of year	$ 17,000
Prepaid insurance, end of year	20,000

Insurance expense	15,000
Cash paid for new insurance policies	?
Case 4	
Income taxes payable, beginning of year	$ 95,000
Income taxes payable, end of year	115,000
Income tax expense	300,000
Cash payments for taxes	?

Exercise 12-14 Dividends on the Statement of Cash Flows   LO5

The following selected account balances are available from the records of Lewistown Company:

	December 31	
	2017	**2016**
Dividends payable	$ 30,000	$ 20,000
Retained earnings	375,000	250,000

Other information available for 2017 is as follows:

a. Lewistown reported net income of $285,000 for the year.
b. It declared and distributed a stock dividend of $50,000 during the year.
c. It declared cash dividends at the end of each quarter and paid them within the next 30 days of the following quarter.

Required

1. Determine the amount of cash dividends *paid* during the year for presentation in the Financing Activities section of the statement of cash flows.
2. Should the stock dividend described in part (b) appear on a statement of cash flows? Explain your answer.

Exercise 12-15 Working Backward: Dividends on the Statement   LO5
of Cash Flows

Stanton Corp. began operations on January 1, 2017. The statement of cash flows for the first year reported dividends paid of $160,000. The balance sheet at the end of the first year reported $40,000 in dividends payable and $580,000 in ending retained earnings. Determine Stanton's net income for its first year of operations.

Exercise 12-16 Cash Payments for Income Taxes—Indirect Method   LO6

Timber Corp. began the year with a balance in its Income Taxes Payable account of $10,000. The year-end balance in the account was $15,000. The company uses the indirect method in the Operating Activities section of the statement of cash flows. Therefore, it presents the amount of income taxes paid at the bottom of the statement as a supplemental disclosure. The amount of taxes paid during the year was $12,000.

What amount of income tax expense will appear on Timber's income statement?

Exercise 12-17 Adjustments to Net Income with the Indirect Method   LO6

EXAMPLE 12-1, 12-5

Assume that a company uses the indirect method to prepare the Operating Activities section of the statement of cash flows. For each of the following items, indicate whether it would be added to net income (A), deducted from net income (D), or not reported in this section of the statement under the indirect method (NR).

_____ 1. Depreciation expense
_____ 2. Gain on sale of used delivery truck
_____ 3. Increase in accounts receivable
_____ 4. Increase in accounts payable
_____ 5. Purchase of new delivery truck

_____   6. Loss on retirement of bonds
_____   7. Increase in prepaid rent
_____   8. Decrease in inventory
_____   9. Issuance of note payable due in three years
_____   10. Amortization of patents

LO6   Exercise 12-18 Operating Activities Section—Indirect Method

Show me how

The following account balances for the noncash current assets and current liabilities of Suffolk Company are available:

	December 31	
	2017	2016
Accounts receivable	$43,000	$35,000
Inventory	30,000	40,000
Prepaid rent	17,000	15,000
Totals	$90,000	$90,000
Accounts payable	$26,000	$19,000
Income taxes payable	6,000	10,000
Interest payable	15,000	12,000
Totals	$47,000	$41,000

Net income for 2017 is $40,000. Depreciation expense is $20,000. Assume that all sales and all purchases are on account.

Required

1. Prepare the Operating Activities section of the statement of cash flows using the indirect method.
2. Provide a brief explanation as to why cash flow from operating activities is more or less than the net income of the period.

LO7   Exercise 12-19 Cash Flow Adequacy

On its most recent statement of cash flows, a company reported net cash provided by operating activities of $12,000,000. Its capital expenditures for the same year were $2,000,000. A note to the financial statements indicated that the total amount of debt that would mature over the next five years was $20,000,000.

Required

1. Compute the company's cash flow adequacy ratio.
2. If you were a banker considering loaning money to this company, why would you be interested in knowing its cash flow adequacy ratio? Would you feel comfortable making a loan based on the ratio you computed in part (1)? Explain your answer.

MULTI-CONCEPT EXERCISES

LO2 • 3   Exercise 12-20 Classification of Activities

EXAMPLE 12-1, 12-2

Use the following legend to indicate how each transaction would be reported on the statement of cash flows. (Assume that the stocks and bonds of other companies are classified as long-term investments.)

II   = Inflow from investing activities
OI = Outflow from investing activities
IF   = Inflow from financing activities
OF = Outflow from financing activities
CE = Classified as a cash equivalent and included with cash for purposes of preparing the statement of cash flows

_____ 1. Purchased a six-month certificate of deposit
_____ 2. Purchased a 60-day Treasury bill
_____ 3. Issued 1,000 shares of common stock
_____ 4. Purchased 1,000 shares of stock in another company
_____ 5. Purchased 1,000 shares of its own stock to be held in the treasury
_____ 6. Invested $1,000 in a money market fund
_____ 7. Sold 500 shares of stock of another company
_____ 8. Purchased 20-year bonds of another company
_____ 9. Issued 30-year bonds
_____ 10. Repaid a six-month bank loan

Exercise 12-21 Classification of Activities

LO3 • 5

EXAMPLE 12-1, 12-3, 12-4

Use the following legend to indicate how each transaction would be reported on the statement of cash flows. (Assume that the company uses the direct method in the Operating Activities section.)

IO = Inflow from operating activities
OO = Outflow from operating activities
II = Inflow from investing activities
OI = Outflow from investing activities
IF = Inflow from financing activities
OF = Outflow from financing activities
NR = Not reported in the body of the statement of cash flows but included in a supplemental schedule

_____ 1. Collected $10,000 in cash from customers' open accounts for the period
_____ 2. Paid one of the company's inventory suppliers $500 in settlement of an open account
_____ 3. Purchased a new copier for $6,000; signed a 90-day note payable
_____ 4. Issued bonds at face value of $100,000
_____ 5. Made $23,200 in cash sales for the week
_____ 6. Purchased an empty lot adjacent to the factory for $50,000; the seller of the land agrees to accept a five-year promissory note as consideration
_____ 7. Renewed the property insurance policy for another six months; cash of $1,000 is paid for the renewal
_____ 8. Purchased a machine for $10,000
_____ 9. Paid cash dividends of $2,500
_____ 10. Reclassified as short-term a long-term note payable of $5,000 that is due within the next year
_____ 11. Purchased 500 shares of the company's own stock on the open market for $4,000
_____ 12. Sold 500 shares of Maple stock for book value of $10,000 (they had been classified as long-term investments)

Exercise 12-22 Long-Term Assets on the Statement of Cash Flows— Indirect Method

LO3 • 6

The following account balances are taken from the records of Martin Corp. for the past two years.

	December 31	
	2017	2016
Plant and equipment	$750,000	$500,000
Accumulated depreciation	160,000	200,000
Patents	92,000	80,000
Retained earnings	825,000	675,000

(Continued)

Other information available for 2017 is as follows:

a. Net income for the year was $200,000.
b. Depreciation expense on plant and equipment was $50,000.
c. Plant and equipment with an original cost of $150,000 were sold for $64,000. (You will need to determine the book value of the assets sold.)
d. Amortization expense on patents was $8,000.
e. Both new plant and equipment and patents were purchased for cash during the year.

Required

Indicate, with amounts, how all items related to these long-term assets would be reported in the 2017 statement of cash flows, including any adjustments in the Operating Activities section of the statement. Assume that Martin uses the indirect method.

LO3 • 6   Exercise 12-23 Working Backward: Investing Activities on the Statement of Cash Flows

The Operating Activities section of Miller Corp.'s statement of cash flows reported an adjustment for depreciation expense of $25,000, as well as another for a loss on the sale of equipment of $5,000 (the equipment was sold on the last day of the year). The equipment was Miller's only long-term asset, and it had a book value of $80,000 at the beginning of the year.

Required

1. Is the depreciation expense added or deducted in the Operating Activities section of the statement of cash flows? Is the loss added or deducted in this section?
2. What other section of the statement of cash flows will be affected by the sale of the equipment? What amount will appear in this section?

LO3 • 6   Exercise 12-24 Working Backward: Financing Activities on the Statement of Cash Flows

The Operating Activities section of Washburn Company's statement of cash flows reported an adjustment for a gain on the retirement of bonds of $5,000. The Financing Activities section of the statement reported a cash outflow of $95,000 from the retirement of the bonds.

Required

1. Is the gain on the retirement of the bonds added or deducted in the Operating Activities section of the statement of cash flows?
2. What was the book value of the bonds retired?

LO1 • 5   Exercise 12-25 Income Statement, Statement of Cash Flows (Direct Method), and Balance Sheet

The following events occurred at Handsome Hounds Grooming Company during its first year of business:

a. To establish the company, the two owners contributed a total of $50,000 in exchange for common stock.
b. Grooming service revenue for the first year amounted to $150,000, of which $40,000 was on account.
c. Customers owe $10,000 at the end of the year from the services provided on account.
d. At the beginning of the year, a storage building was rented. The company was required to sign a three-year lease for $12,000 per year and make a $2,000 refundable security deposit. The first year's lease payment and the security deposit were paid at the beginning of the year.
e. At the beginning of the year, the company purchased a patent at a cost of $100,000 for a revolutionary system to be used for dog grooming. The patent is expected to be useful for ten years. The company paid 20% down in cash and signed a four-year note at the bank for the remainder.
f. Operating expenses, including amortization of the patent and rent on the storage building, totaled $80,000 for the first year. No expenses were accrued or unpaid at the end of the year.
g. The company declared and paid a $20,000 cash dividend at the end of the first year.

Required

1. Prepare an income statement for the first year.
2. Prepare a statement of cash flows for the first year using the direct method in the Operating Activities section.
3. Did the company generate more or less cash flow from operations than it earned in net income? Explain why there is a difference.
4. Prepare a balance sheet as of the end of the first year.

PROBLEMS

Problem 12-1   Statement of Cash Flows—Indirect Method   LO6

The following balances are available for Chrisman Company:

	December 31	
	2017	**2016**
Cash	$ 8,000	$ 10,000
Accounts receivable	20,000	15,000
Inventory	15,000	25,000
Prepaid rent	9,000	6,000
Land	75,000	75,000
Plant and equipment	400,000	300,000
Accumulated depreciation	(65,000)	(30,000)
Totals	$462,000	$401,000
Accounts payable	$ 12,000	$ 10,000
Income taxes payable	3,000	5,000
Short-term notes payable	35,000	25,000
Bonds payable	75,000	100,000
Common stock	200,000	150,000
Retained earnings	137,000	111,000
Totals	$462,000	$401,000

Bonds were retired during 2017 at face value, plant and equipment were acquired for cash, and common stock was issued for cash. Depreciation expense for the year was $35,000. Net income was reported at $26,000.

Required

1. Prepare a statement of cash flows for 2017 using the indirect method in the Operating Activities section.
2. Did Chrisman generate sufficient cash from operations to pay for its investing activities? How did it generate cash other than from operations? Explain your answers.

Problem 12-2   Statement of Cash Flows Using a Work Sheet—Indirect   LO8
Method (Appendix)

Refer to all of the facts in Problem 12-1.

Required

1. Using the format in the chapter's appendix, prepare a statement of cash flows work sheet.
2. Prepare a statement of cash flows for 2017 using the indirect method in the Operating Activities section.
3. Did Chrisman generate sufficient cash from operations to pay for its investing activities? How did it generate cash other than from operations? Explain your answers.

LO5   Problem 12-3   Statement of Cash Flows—Direct Method

Peoria Corp. just completed another successful year, as indicated by the following income statement:

	For the Year Ended December 31, 2017
Sales revenue	$1,250,000
Cost of goods sold	700,000
Gross profit	$ 550,000
Operating expenses	150,000
Income before interest and taxes	$ 400,000
Interest expense	25,000
Income before taxes	$ 375,000
Income tax expense	150,000
Net income	$ 225,000

Presented here are comparative balance sheets:

	December 31	
	2017	2016
Cash	$ 52,000	$ 90,000
Accounts receivable	180,000	130,000
Inventory	230,000	200,000
Prepayments	15,000	25,000
Total current assets	$ 477,000	$ 445,000
Land	$ 750,000	$ 600,000
Plant and equipment	700,000	500,000
Accumulated depreciation	(250,000)	(200,000)
Total long-term assets	$1,200,000	$ 900,000
Total assets	$1,677,000	$1,345,000
Accounts payable	$ 130,000	$ 148,000
Other accrued liabilities	68,000	63,000
Income taxes payable	90,000	110,000
Total current liabilities	$ 288,000	$ 321,000
Long-term bank loan payable	$ 350,000	$ 300,000
Common stock	$ 550,000	$ 400,000
Retained earnings	489,000	324,000
Total stockholders' equity	$1,039,000	$ 724,000
Total liabilities and stockholders' equity	$1,677,000	$1,345,000

Other information is as follows:

a. Dividends of $60,000 were declared and paid during the year.
b. Operating expenses include $50,000 of depreciation.
c. Land and plant and equipment were acquired for cash, and additional stock was issued for cash. Cash also was received from additional bank loans.

The president has asked you some questions about the year's results. She is very impressed with the profit margin of 18% (net income divided by sales revenue). She is bothered, however, by the decline in the company's cash balance during the year. One of the conditions of the existing bank loan is that the company maintain a minimum cash balance of $50,000.

Required

1. Prepare a statement of cash flows for 2017 using the direct method in the Operating Activities section.
2. On the basis of your statement in part (1), draft a brief memo to the president to explain why cash decreased during such a profitable year. Include in your explanation any recommendations for improving the company's cash flow in future years.

Problem 12-4 Statement of Cash Flows—Indirect Method   LO6

Refer to all of the facts in Problem 12-3.

Required

1. Prepare a statement of cash flows for 2017 using the indirect method in the Operating Activities section.
2. On the basis of your statement in part (1), draft a brief memo to the president to explain why cash decreased during such a profitable year. Include in your explanation any recommendations for improving the company's cash flow in future years.

Problem 12-5 Statement of Cash Flows Using a Work Sheet—Indirect   LO8
Method (Appendix)

Refer to all of the facts in Problem 12-3.

Required

1. Using the format in the chapter's appendix, prepare a statement of cash flows work sheet.
2. Prepare a statement of cash flows for 2017 using the indirect method in the Operating Activities section.
3. On the basis of your statement in part (2), draft a brief memo to the president to explain why cash decreased during such a profitable year. Include in your explanation any recommendations for improving the company's cash flow in future years.

Problem 12-6 Statement of Cash Flows—Direct Method   LO5

The income statement for Astro Inc. for 2017 is as follows:

	For the Year Ended December 31, 2017
Sales revenue	$ 500,000
Cost of goods sold	400,000
Gross profit	$ 100,000
Operating expenses	180,000
Loss before interest and taxes	$ (80,000)
Interest expense	20,000
Net loss	$(100,000)

Presented here are comparative balance sheets:

	December 31	
	2017	2016
Cash	$ 95,000	$ 80,000
Accounts receivable	50,000	75,000
Inventory	100,000	150,000
Prepayments	55,000	45,000
Total current assets	$ 300,000	$ 350,000
Land	$ 475,000	$ 400,000
Plant and equipment	870,000	800,000
Accumulated depreciation	(370,000)	(300,000)
Total long-term assets	$ 975,000	$ 900,000
Total assets	$1,275,000	$1,250,000
Accounts payable	$ 125,000	$ 100,000
Other accrued liabilities	35,000	45,000
Interest payable	15,000	10,000
Total current liabilities	$ 175,000	$ 155,000
Long-term bank loan payable	$ 340,000	$ 250,000
Common stock	$ 450,000	$ 400,000
Retained earnings	310,000	445,000
Total stockholders' equity	$ 760,000	$ 845,000
Total liabilities and stockholders' equity	$1,275,000	$1,250,000

(Continued)

Other information is as follows:

a. Dividends of $35,000 were declared and paid during the year.
b. Operating expenses include $70,000 of depreciation.
c. Land and plant and equipment were acquired for cash, and additional stock was issued for cash. Cash also was received from additional bank loans.

The president has asked you some questions about the year's results. He is disturbed with the $100,000 net loss for the year. He notes, however, that the cash position at the end of the year is improved. He is confused about what appear to be conflicting signals: "How could we have possibly added to our bank accounts during such a terrible year of operations?"

Required

1. Prepare a statement of cash flows for 2017 using the direct method in the Operating Activities section.
2. On the basis of your statement in part (1), draft a brief memo to the president to explain why cash increased during such an unprofitable year. Include in your memo your recommendations for improving the company's bottom line.

LO6 **Problem 12-7 Statement of Cash Flows—Indirect Method**

Refer to all of the facts in Problem 12-6.

Required

1. Prepare a statement of cash flows for 2017 using the indirect method in the Operating Activities section.
2. On the basis of your statement in part (1), draft a brief memo to the president to explain why cash increased during such an unprofitable year. Include in your memo your recommendations for improving the company's bottom line.

LO8 **Problem 12-8 Statement of Cash Flows Using a Work Sheet—Indirect Method (Appendix)**

Refer to all of the facts in Problem 12-6.

Required

1. Using the format in the chapter's appendix, prepare a statement of cash flows work sheet.
2. Prepare a statement of cash flows for 2017 using the indirect method in the Operating Activities section.
3. On the basis of your statement in part (2), draft a brief memo to the president to explain why cash increased during such an unprofitable year. Include in your memo your recommendations for improving the company's bottom line.

LO6 **Problem 12-9 Year-End Balance Sheet and Statement of Cash Flows—Indirect Method**

The balance sheet of Terrier Company at the end of 2016 is presented here, along with certain other information for 2017:

	December 31, 2016
Cash	$ 140,000
Accounts receivable	155,000
Total current assets	$ 295,000
Land	$ 300,000
Plant and equipment	500,000
Accumulated depreciation	(150,000)
Investments	100,000
Total long-term assets	$ 750,000
Total assets	$1,045,000

	December 31, 2016
Current liabilities	$ 205,000
Bonds payable	$ 300,000
Common stock	$ 400,000
Retained earnings	140,000
Total stockholders' equity	$ 540,000
Total liabilities and stockholders' equity	$1,045,000

Other information is as follows:

a. Net income for 2017 was $70,000.
b. Included in operating expenses was $20,000 in depreciation.
c. Cash dividends of $25,000 were declared and paid.
d. An additional $150,000 of bonds was issued for cash.
e. Common stock of $50,000 was purchased for cash and retired.
f. Cash purchases of plant and equipment during the year were $200,000.
g. An additional $100,000 of bonds was issued in exchange for land.
h. During the year, sales exceeded cash collections on account by $10,000. All sales are on account.
i. The amount of current liabilities remained unchanged during the year.

Required

1. Prepare a statement of cash flows for 2017 using the indirect method in the Operating Activities section. Include a supplemental schedule for noncash activities.
2. Prepare a balance sheet at December 31, 2017.
3. Provide a possible explanation as to why Terrier decided to issue additional bonds for cash during 2017.

Problem 12-10 Statement of Cash Flows Using a Work Sheet—Indirect Method (Appendix)   LO8

Refer to all of the facts in Problem 12-9.

Required

1. Prepare a balance sheet at December 31, 2017.
2. Using the format in the chapter's appendix, prepare a statement of cash flows work sheet.
3. Prepare a statement of cash flows for 2017 using the indirect method in the Operating Activities section.
4. Provide a possible explanation as to why Terrier decided to issue additional bonds for cash during 2017.

MULTI-CONCEPT PROBLEMS

Problem 12-11 Statement of Cash Flows—Direct Method   LO4 • 5

Glendive Corp. is in the process of preparing its statement of cash flows for the year ended June 30, 2017. An income statement for the year and comparative balance sheets are as follows:

	For the Year Ended June 30, 2017
Sales revenue	$550,000
Cost of goods sold	350,000
Gross profit	$200,000
General and administrative expenses	$ 55,000
Depreciation expense	75,000
Loss on sale of plant assets	5,000

(Continued)

	For the Year Ended June 30, 2017
Total expenses and losses	$135,000
Income before interest and taxes	$ 65,000
Interest expense	15,000
Income before taxes	$ 50,000
Income tax expense	17,000
Net income	$ 33,000

	June 30	
	2017	2016
Cash	$ 31,000	$ 40,000
Accounts receivable	90,000	75,000
Inventory	80,000	95,000
Prepaid rent	12,000	16,000
Total current assets	$ 213,000	$ 226,000
Land	$ 250,000	$ 170,000
Plant and equipment	750,000	600,000
Accumulated depreciation	(310,000)	(250,000)
Total long-term assets	$ 690,000	$ 520,000
Total assets	$ 903,000	$ 746,000
Accounts payable	$ 155,000	$ 148,000
Other accrued liabilities	32,000	26,000
Income taxes payable	8,000	10,000
Total current liabilities	$ 195,000	$ 184,000
Long-term bank loan payable	$ 100,000	$ 130,000
Common stock	$ 350,000	$ 200,000
Retained earnings	258,000	232,000
Total stockholders' equity	$ 608,000	$ 432,000
Total liabilities and stockholders' equity	$ 903,000	$ 746,000

Dividends of $7,000 were declared and paid during the year. New plant assets were purchased during the year for $195,000 in cash. Also, land was purchased for cash. Plant assets were sold during the year for $25,000 in cash. The original cost of the assets sold was $45,000, and their book value was $30,000. Additional stock was issued for cash, and a portion of the bank loan was repaid.

Required

1. Prepare a statement of cash flows for 2017 using the direct method in the Operating Activities section.
2. Evaluate the following statement: Whether a company uses the direct or indirect method to report cash flows from operations is irrelevant because the amount of cash flow from operating activities is the same regardless of which method is used.

LO4 • 6   Problem 12-12 Statement of Cash Flows—Indirect Method

Refer to all of the facts in Problem 12-11.

Required

1. Prepare a statement of cash flows for 2017 using the indirect method in the Operating Activities section.
2. Evaluate the following statement: Whether a company uses the direct or indirect method to report cash flows from operations is irrelevant because the amount of cash flow from operating activities is the same regardless of which method is used.

Problem 12-13 Statement of Cash Flows—Direct Method

LO2 • 5

Lang Company has not yet prepared a formal statement of cash flows for 2017. Following are comparative balance sheets as of December 31, 2017 and 2016, and a statement of income and retained earnings for the year ended December 31, 2017:

Lang Company
Balance Sheet
December 31
(thousands omitted)

Assets	2017	2016
Current assets:		
Cash	$ 60	$ 100
U.S. Treasury bills (six-month)	0	50
Accounts receivable	610	500
Inventory	720	600
Total current assets	$1,390	$1,250
Long-term assets:		
Land	$ 80	$ 70
Buildings and equipment	710	600
Accumulated depreciation	(180)	(120)
Patents (less amortization)	105	130
Total long-term assets	$ 715	$ 680
Total assets	$2,105	$1,930
Liabilities and Owners' Equity		
Current liabilities:		
Accounts payable	$ 360	$ 300
Taxes payable	25	20
Notes payable	400	400
Total current liabilities	$ 785	$ 720
Term notes payable—due 2021	200	200
Total liabilities	$ 985	$ 920
Owners' equity:		
Common stock outstanding	$ 830	$ 700
Retained earnings	290	310
Total owners' equity	$1,120	$1,010
Total liabilities and owners' equity	$2,105	$1,930

Lang Company
Statement of Income and Retained Earnings
For the Year Ended December 31, 2017
(thousands omitted)

Sales		$2,408
Less expenses and interest:		
Cost of goods sold	$1,100	
Salaries and benefits	850	
Heat, light, and power	75	
Depreciation	60	
Property taxes	18	
Patent amortization	25	
Miscellaneous expense	10	
Interest	55	2,193
Net income before income taxes		$ 215

(Continued)

Income taxes	105
Net income	$ 110
Retained earnings—January 1, 2017	310
	$ 420
Stock dividend distributed	130
Retained earnings—December 31, 2017	$ 290

Required

1. For purposes of a statement of cash flows, are the U.S. Treasury bills cash equivalents? If not, how should they be classified? Explain your answers.
2. Prepare a statement of cash flows for 2017 using the direct method in the Operating Activities section.   (CMA adapted)

ALTERNATE PROBLEMS

LO6   **Problem 12-1A** **Statement of Cash Flows—Indirect Method**

The following balances are available for Madison Company:

	December 31	
	2017	**2016**
Cash	$ 12,000	$ 10,000
Accounts receivable	10,000	12,000
Inventory	8,000	7,000
Prepaid rent	1,200	1,000
Land	75,000	75,000
Plant and equipment	200,000	150,000
Accumulated depreciation	(75,000)	(25,000)
Totals	$231,200	$230,000
Accounts payable	$ 15,000	$ 15,000
Income taxes payable	2,500	2,000
Short-term notes payable	20,000	22,500
Bonds payable	75,000	50,000
Common stock	100,000	100,000
Retained earnings	18,700	40,500
Totals	$231,200	$230,000

Bonds were issued during 2017 at face value, and plant and equipment were acquired for cash. Depreciation expense for the year was $50,000. A net loss of $21,800 was reported.

Required

1. Prepare a statement of cash flows for 2017 using the indirect method in the Operating Activities section.
2. Briefly explain how Madison was able to increase its cash balance during a year in which it incurred a net loss.

LO8   **Problem 12-2A** **Statement of Cash Flows Using a Work Sheet—Indirect Method (Appendix)**

Refer to all of the facts in Problem 12-1A.

Required

1. Using the format in the chapter's appendix, prepare a statement of cash flows work sheet.
2. Prepare a statement of cash flows for 2017 using the indirect method in the Operating Activities section.
3. Briefly explain how Madison was able to increase its cash balance during a year in which it incurred a net loss.

Problem 12-3A Statement of Cash Flows—Direct Method   LO5

Wabash Corp. just completed another successful year, as indicated by the following income statement:

	For the Year Ended December 31, 2017
Sales revenue	$2,460,000
Cost of goods sold	1,400,000
Gross profit	$1,060,000
Operating expenses	460,000
Income before interest and taxes	$ 600,000
Interest expense	100,000
Income before taxes	$ 500,000
Income tax expense	150,000
Net income	$ 350,000

Presented here are comparative balance sheets:

	December 31	
	2017	2016
Cash	$ 140,000	$ 210,000
Accounts receivable	60,000	145,000
Inventory	200,000	180,000
Prepayments	15,000	25,000
Total current assets	$ 415,000	$ 560,000
Land	$ 600,000	$ 700,000
Plant and equipment	850,000	600,000
Accumulated depreciation	(225,000)	(200,000)
Total long-term assets	$1,225,000	$1,100,000
Total assets	$1,640,000	$1,660,000
Accounts payable	$ 140,000	$ 120,000
Other accrued liabilities	50,000	55,000
Income taxes payable	80,000	115,000
Total current liabilities	$ 270,000	$ 290,000
Long-term bank loan payable	$ 200,000	$ 250,000
Common stock	$ 450,000	$ 400,000
Retained earnings	720,000	720,000
Total stockholders' equity	$1,170,000	$1,120,000
Total liabilities and stockholders' equity	$1,640,000	$1,660,000

Other information is as follows:

a. Dividends of $350,000 were declared and paid during the year.
b. Operating expenses include $25,000 of depreciation.
c. Land was sold for its book value, and new plant and equipment were acquired for cash.
d. Part of the bank loan was repaid, and additional common stock was issued for cash.

The president has asked you some questions about the year's results. She is very impressed with the profit margin of 14% (net income divided by sales revenue). She is bothered, however, by the decline in the company's cash balance during the year. One of the conditions of the existing bank loan is that the company maintain a minimum cash balance of $100,000.

Required

1. Prepare a statement of cash flows for 2017 using the direct method in the Operating Activities section.
2. On the basis of your statement in part (1), draft a brief memo to the president to explain why cash decreased during such a profitable year. Include in your explanation any recommendations for improving the company's cash flow in future years.

LO6   Problem 12-4A Statement of Cash Flows—Indirect Method

Refer to all of the facts in Problem 12-3A.

Required

1. Prepare a statement of cash flows for 2017 using the indirect method in the Operating Activities section.
2. On the basis of your statement in part (1), draft a brief memo to the president to explain why cash decreased during such a profitable year. Include in your explanation any recommendations for improving the company's cash flow in future years.

LO8   Problem 12-5A Statement of Cash Flows Using a Work Sheet—Indirect Method (Appendix)

Refer to all of the facts in Problem 12-3A.

Required

1. Using the format in the chapter's appendix, prepare a statement of cash flows work sheet.
2. Prepare a statement of cash flows for 2017 using the indirect method in the Operating Activities section.
3. On the basis of your statement in part (2), draft a brief memo to the president to explain why cash decreased during such a profitable year. Include in your explanation any recommendations for improving the company's cash flow in future years.

LO5   Problem 12-6A Statement of Cash Flows—Direct Method

The income statement for Pluto Inc. for 2017 is as follows:

	For the Year Ended December 31, 2017
Sales revenue	$350,000
Cost of goods sold	150,000
Gross profit	$200,000
Operating expenses	250,000
Loss before interest and taxes	$ (50,000)
Interest expense	10,000
Net loss	$ (60,000)

Presented here are comparative balance sheets:

	December 31	
	2017	2016
Cash	$ 25,000	$ 10,000
Accounts receivable	30,000	80,000
Inventory	100,000	100,000
Prepayments	36,000	35,000
Total current assets	$191,000	$225,000
Land	$300,000	$200,000
Plant and equipment	500,000	250,000
Accumulated depreciation	(90,000)	(50,000)
Total long-term assets	$710,000	$400,000
Total assets	$901,000	$625,000
Accounts payable	$ 50,000	$ 10,000
Other accrued liabilities	40,000	20,000
Interest payable	22,000	12,000
Total current liabilities	$112,000	$ 42,000

	December 31	
	2017	**2016**
Long-term bank loan payable	$450,000	$100,000
Common stock	$300,000	$300,000
Retained earnings	39,000	183,000
Total stockholders' equity	$339,000	$483,000
Total liabilities and stockholders' equity	$901,000	$625,000

Other information is as follows:

a. Dividends of $84,000 were declared and paid during the year.
b. Operating expenses include $40,000 of depreciation.
c. Land and plant and equipment were acquired for cash. Cash was received from additional bank loans.

The president has asked you some questions about the year's results. He is disturbed with the net loss of $60,000 for the year. He notes, however, that the cash position at the end of the year is improved. He is confused about what appear to be conflicting signals: "How could we have possibly added to our bank accounts during such a terrible year of operations?"

Required

1. Prepare a statement of cash flows for 2017 using the direct method in the Operating Activities section.
2. On the basis of your statement in part (1), draft a brief memo to the president to explain why cash increased during such an unprofitable year. Include in your memo your recommendations for improving the company's bottom line.

Problem 12-7A Statement of Cash Flows—Indirect Method   LO6

Refer to all of the facts in Problem 12-6A.

Required

1. Prepare a statement of cash flows for 2017 using the indirect method in the Operating Activities section.
2. On the basis of your statement in part (1), draft a brief memo to the president to explain why cash increased during such an unprofitable year. Include in your memo your recommendations for improving the company's bottom line.

Problem 12-8A Statement of Cash Flows Using a Work Sheet—Indirect   LO8
Method (Appendix)

Refer to all of the facts in Problem 12-6A.

Required

1. Using the format in the chapter's appendix, prepare a statement of cash flows work sheet.
2. Prepare a statement of cash flows for 2017 using the indirect method in the Operating Activities section.
3. On the basis of your statement in part (2), draft a brief memo to the president to explain why cash increased during such an unprofitable year. Include in your memo your recommendations for improving the company's bottom line.

Problem 12-9A Year-End Balance Sheet and Statement of Cash   LO6
Flows—Indirect Method

The balance sheet of Poodle Company at the end of 2016 is presented here, along with certain other information for 2017:

(Continued)

	December 31, 2016
Cash	$ 155,000
Accounts receivable	140,000
Total current assets	$ 295,000
Land	$ 100,000
Plant and equipment	700,000
Accumulated depreciation	(175,000)
Investments	125,000
Total long-term assets	$ 750,000
Total assets	$1,045,000
Current liabilities	$ 325,000
Bonds payable	$ 100,000
Common stock	$ 500,000
Retained earnings	120,000
Total stockholders' equity	$ 620,000
Total liabilities and stockholders' equity	$1,045,000

Other information is as follows:

a. Net income for 2017 was $50,000.
b. Included in operating expenses was $25,000 in depreciation.
c. Cash dividends of $40,000 were declared and paid.
d. An additional $50,000 of common stock was issued for cash.
e. Bonds payable of $100,000 were purchased for cash and retired at no gain or loss.
f. Cash purchases of plant and equipment during the year were $60,000.
g. An additional $200,000 of land was acquired in exchange for a long-term note payable.
h. During the year, sales exceeded cash collections on account by $15,000. All sales are on account.
i. The amount of current liabilities decreased by $20,000 during the year.

Required

1. Prepare a statement of cash flows for 2017 using the indirect method in the Operating Activities section. Include a supplemental schedule for noncash activities.
2. Prepare a balance sheet at December 31, 2017.
3. What primary uses did Poodle make of the cash it generated from operating activities?

LO8 Problem 12-10A Statement of Cash Flows Using a Work Sheet—Indirect Method (Appendix)

Refer to all of the facts in Problem 12-9A.

Required

1. Prepare a balance sheet at December 31, 2017.
2. Using the format in the chapter's appendix, prepare a statement of cash flows work sheet.
3. Prepare a statement of cash flows for 2017 using the indirect method in the Operating Activities section.
4. Provide a possible explanation as to why Poodle decided to purchase and retire bonds during 2017.

ALTERNATE MULTI-CONCEPT PROBLEMS

LO4 • 5 Problem 12-11A Statement of Cash Flows—Direct Method

Bannack Corp. is in the process of preparing its statement of cash flows for the year ended June 30, 2017. An income statement for the year and comparative balance sheets are as follows:

	For the Year Ended June 30, 2017
Sales revenue	$400,000
Cost of goods sold	240,000
Gross profit	$160,000
General and administrative expenses	$ 40,000
Depreciation expense	80,000
Loss on sale of plant assets	10,000
Total expenses and losses	$130,000
Income before interest and taxes	$ 30,000
Interest expense	15,000
Income before taxes	$ 15,000
Income tax expense	5,000
Net income	$ 10,000

	June 30	
	2017	2016
Cash	$ 25,000	$ 40,000
Accounts receivable	80,000	69,000
Inventory	75,000	50,000
Prepaid rent	2,000	18,000
Total current assets	$ 182,000	$ 177,000
Land	$ 60,000	$ 150,000
Plant and equipment	575,000	500,000
Accumulated depreciation	(310,000)	(250,000)
Total long-term assets	$ 325,000	$ 400,000
Total assets	$ 507,000	$ 577,000
Accounts payable	$ 145,000	$ 140,000
Other accrued liabilities	50,000	45,000
Income taxes payable	5,000	15,000
Total current liabilities	$ 200,000	$ 200,000
Long-term bank loan payable	$ 75,000	$ 150,000
Common stock	$ 100,000	$ 100,000
Retained earnings	132,000	127,000
Total stockholders' equity	$ 232,000	$ 227,000
Total liabilities and stockholders' equity	$ 507,000	$ 577,000

Dividends of $5,000 were declared and paid during the year. New plant assets were purchased during the year for $125,000 in cash. Also, land was sold for cash at its book value. Plant assets were sold during the year for $20,000 in cash. The original cost of the assets sold was $50,000, and their book value was $30,000. A portion of the bank loan was repaid.

Required

1. Prepare a statement of cash flows for 2017 using the direct method in the Operating Activities section.
2. Evaluate the following statement: Whether a company uses the direct or indirect method to report cash flows from operations is irrelevant because the amount of cash flow from operating activities is the same regardless of which method is used.

LO4 • 6   Problem 12-12A Statement of Cash Flows—Indirect Method

Refer to all of the facts in Problem 12-11A.

Required

1. Prepare a statement of cash flows for 2017 using the indirect method in the Operating Activities section.
2. Evaluate the following statement: Whether a company uses the direct or indirect method to report cash flows from operations is irrelevant because the amount of cash flow from operating activities is the same regardless of which method is used.

LO2 • 5   Problem 12-13A Statement of Cash Flows—Direct Method

Shepard Company has not yet prepared a formal statement of cash flows for 2017. Comparative balance sheets as of December 31, 2017 and 2016, and a statement of income and retained earnings for the year ended December 31, 2017, appear below and on the following page.

Shepard Company
Balance Sheet
December 31
(thousands omitted)

Assets	2017	2016
Current assets:		
Cash	$ 50	$ 75
U.S. Treasury bills (six-month)	25	0
Accounts receivable	125	200
Inventory	525	500
Total current assets	$ 725	$ 775
Long-term assets:		
Land	$ 100	$ 80
Buildings and equipment	510	450
Accumulated depreciation	(190)	(150)
Patents (less amortization)	90	110
Total long-term assets	$ 510	$ 490
Total assets	$1,235	$1,265
Liabilities and Owners' Equity		
Current Liabilities:		
Accounts payable	$ 370	$ 330
Taxes payable	10	20
Notes payable	300	400
Total current liabilities	$ 680	$ 750
Term notes payable—due 2021	200	200
Total liabilities	$ 880	$ 950
Owners' equity:		
Common stock outstanding	$ 220	$ 200
Retained earnings	135	115
Total owners' equity	$ 355	$ 315
Total liabilities and owners' equity	$1,235	$1,265

Shepard Company
Statement of Income and Retained Earnings
For the Year Ended December 31, 2017
(thousands omitted)

Sales		$1,416
Less expenses and interest:		
Cost of goods sold	$990	
Salaries and benefits	195	
Heat, light, and power	70	
Depreciation	40	

Property taxes	2	
Patent amortization	20	
Miscellaneous expense	2	
Interest	45	1,364
Net income before income taxes		$ 52
Income taxes		12
Net income		$ 40
Retained earnings—January 1, 2017		115
		$ 155
Stock dividend distributed		20
Retained earnings—December 31, 2017		$ 135

Required

1. For purposes of a statement of cash flows, are the U.S. Treasury bills cash equivalents? If not, how should they be classified? Explain your answers.
2. Prepare a statement of cash flows for 2017 using the direct method in the Operating Activities section. (CMA adapted)

DECISION CASES

Reading and Interpreting Financial Statements

Decision Case 12-1 Comparing Two Companies in the Same Industry: Chipotle and Panera Bread

LO3 • 4

REAL WORLD

Refer to the statement of cash flows for both **Chipotle** and **Panera Bread** for the most recent year and any other pertinent information reprinted at the back of this book.

Required

1. Which method, direct or indirect, does each company use in preparing the Operating Activities section of their statements of cash flows? Explain.
2. By what amount did net cash provided by operating activities increase or decrease from the prior year for each company? What is the largest adjustment to reconcile net income to net cash provided by operating activities for each company?
3. What amount did each company spend during the most recent year to acquire property and equipment? How does this amount compare with the amount that each company spent in the prior year?
4. Did either or both companies buy back some of their own shares during the most recent year? If so, what might be some reasons for doing this?

Decision Case 12-2 Making Business Decisions: Analyzing Kellogg's Cash Flow Adequacy Ratio

LO7

RATIO ANALYSIS

BUSINESS DECISION MODEL

REAL WORLD

You are considering making a loan to **Kellogg's** (Kellogg Company). The following information is from the statements of cash flows and the notes to the consolidated financial statements included in Form 10-K for fiscal years 2015 and 2014 (in millions of dollars):

	2015	2014
Net cash provided by operating activities	$1,691	$1,793
Additions to properties	(553)	(582)

From the 2015 Form 10-K: Scheduled principal repayments on long-term debt are (in millions): 2016—$1,262; 2017—$627; 2018—$407; 2019—$506; 2020—$851; 2021 and beyond—$2,864.

(Continued)

From the 2014 Form 10-K: Scheduled principal repayments on long-term debt are (in millions): 2015—$607; 2016—$1,256; 2017—$661; 2018—$402; 2019—$501; 2020 and beyond—$3,121.

The following information is from **General Mills'** statements of cash flows and the notes to the consolidated financial statements included in Form 10-K for fiscal years 2015 and 2014 (in millions of dollars):

	2015	2014
Net cash provided by operating activities	$2,542.8	$2,541.0
Purchases of land, buildings, and equipment	(712.4)	(663.5)

From the 2015 Form 10-K: Principal payments due on long-term debt in the next five years based on stated contractual maturities, our intent to redeem, or put rights of certain note holders are $1,000.4 million in fiscal 2016, $1,103.4 million in fiscal 2017, $604.5 million in fiscal 2018, $1,150.2 million in fiscal 2019, and $500.1 million in fiscal 2020.

From the 2014 Form 10-K: Principal payments due on long-term debt in the next five years based on stated contractual maturities, our intent to redeem, or put rights of certain note holders are $1,250.6 million in fiscal 2015, $1,000.6 million in fiscal 2016, $1,000.0 million in fiscal 2017, $100.0 million in fiscal 2018, and $1,150.0 million in fiscal 2019.

Required

Part A. The Ratio Analysis Model

A lender must assess a company's ability to generate sufficient cash from operations to not only invest in property and equipment but also to make scheduled payments on long-term debt. The cash flow adequacy ratio helps a lender make this determination. Replicate the five steps in the Ratio Analysis Model on pages 583–584 to analyze the cash flow adequacy ratios for Kellogg's and General Mills:

1. Formulate the Question
2. Gather the Information from the Financial Statements
3. Calculate the Ratio
4. Compare the Ratio with Other Ratios
5. Interpret the Ratios

Part B. The Business Decision Model

A lender must consider a variety of factors, including financial ratios, before making a loan. Replicate the five steps in the Business Decision Model on page 585 to decide whether to loan money to Kellogg's.

1. Formulate the Question
2. Gather Information from the Financial Statements and Other Sources
3. Analyze the Information Gathered
4. Make the Decision
5. Monitor Your Decision

LO2・3 ## Decision Case 12-3 Reading and Interpreting Walgreens Boots Alliance's Statement of Cash Flows

REAL WORLD

Refer to **Walgreens Boots Alliance's** statement of cash flows shown in the chapter opener on page 555 and answer the following questions for the most recent year.

Required

1. Which method, direct or indirect, does Walgreens Boots Alliance use in preparing the Operating Activities section of its statement of cash flows? Explain how you know which method is being used.
2. By what amount does net cash provided by operating activities differ from net earnings? What is the largest adjustment to reconcile the two numbers? Explain the nature of this adjustment. Why is it added?
3. What is the largest source of cash in the Investing Activities section of the statement? What is the largest use in this section? What is the next largest use of cash in this section?
4. What is the largest source of cash in the Financing Activities section of the statement? What is the largest use of cash in this section?

Making Financial Decisions

Decision Case 12-4 Dividend Decision and the Statement of Cash Flows—Direct Method

LO1 • 5

Bailey Corp. just completed the most profitable year in its 25-year history. Reported earnings of $1,020,000 on sales of $8,000,000 resulted in a very healthy profit margin of 12.75%. Each year before releasing the financial statements, the board of directors meets to decide on the amount of dividends to declare for the year. For each of the past nine years, the company has declared a dividend of $1 per share of common stock, which has been paid on January 15 of the following year.

Presented here are the income statement for the year and the comparative balance sheets as of the end of the last two years.

Additional information follows:

	For the Year Ended December 31, 2017
Sales revenue	$8,000,000
Cost of goods sold	4,500,000
Gross profit	$3,500,000
Operating expenses	1,450,000
Income before interest and taxes	$2,050,000
Interest expense	350,000
Income before taxes	$1,700,000
Income tax expense (40%)	680,000
Net income	$1,020,000

	December 31	
	2017	2016
Cash	$ 480,000	$ 450,000
Accounts receivable	250,000	200,000
Inventory	750,000	600,000
Prepayments	60,000	75,000
Total current assets	$ 1,540,000	$ 1,325,000
Land	$ 3,255,000	$ 2,200,000
Plant and equipment	4,200,000	2,500,000
Accumulated depreciation	(1,250,000)	(1,000,000)
Long-term investments	500,000	900,000
Patents	650,000	750,000
Total long-term assets	$ 7,355,000	$ 5,350,000
Total assets	$ 8,895,000	$ 6,675,000
Accounts payable	$ 350,000	$ 280,000
Other accrued liabilities	285,000	225,000
Income taxes payable	170,000	100,000
Dividends payable	0	200,000
Notes payable due within next year	200,000	0
Total current liabilities	$ 1,005,000	$ 805,000
Long-term notes payable	$ 300,000	$ 500,000
Bonds payable	2,200,000	1,500,000
Total long-term liabilities	$ 2,500,000	$ 2,000,000
Common stock, $10 par	$ 2,500,000	$ 2,000,000
Retained earnings	2,890,000	1,870,000
Total stockholders' equity	$ 5,390,000	$ 3,870,000
Total liabilities and stockholders' equity	$ 8,895,000	$ 6,675,000

(Continued)

Additional information follows:

a. All sales are on account, as are all purchases.

b. Land was purchased through the issuance of bonds. Additional land (beyond the amount purchased through the issuance of bonds) was purchased for cash.

c. New plant and equipment were acquired during the year for cash. No plant assets were retired during the year. Depreciation expense is included in operating expenses.

d. Long-term investments were sold for cash during the year.

e. No new patents were acquired, and none were disposed of during the year. Amortization expense is included in operating expenses.

f. Notes payable due within the next year represents the amount reclassified from long term to short term.

g. Fifty thousand shares of common stock were issued during the year at par value.

As Bailey's controller, you have been asked to recommend to the board whether to declare a dividend this year and, if so, whether the precedent of paying a $1-per-share dividend can be maintained. The president is eager to keep the dividend at $1 in view of the successful year just completed. He is also concerned, however, about the effect of a dividend on the company's cash position. He is particularly concerned about the large amount of notes payable that comes due next year. He further notes the aggressive growth pattern in recent years, as evidenced this year by large increases in land and plant and equipment.

Required

1. Using the format in Exhibit 12-10, convert the income statement from an accrual basis to a cash basis.

2. Prepare a statement of cash flows using the direct method in the Operating Activities section.

3. What do you recommend to the board of directors concerning the declaration of a cash dividend? Should the $1-per-share dividend be declared? Should a smaller amount be declared? Should no dividend be declared? Support your answer with any necessary computations. From a cash flow perspective, include in your response your concerns about the following year.

LO1 • 6 Decision Case 12-5 Equipment Replacement Decision and Cash Flows from Operations

Conrad Company has been in operation for four years. The company is pleased with the continued improvement in net income but is concerned about a lack of cash available to replace existing equipment. Land, buildings, and equipment were purchased at the beginning of Year 1. No subsequent fixed asset purchases have been made, but the president believes that equipment will need to be replaced in the near future. The following information is available. (All amounts are in millions of dollars.)

	Year of Operation			
	Year 1	Year 2	Year 3	Year 4
Net income (loss)	$(10)	$ (2)	$15	$20
Depreciation expense	30	25	15	14
Increase (decrease) in:				
Accounts receivable	32	5	12	20
Inventories	26	8	5	9
Prepayments	0	0	10	5
Accounts payable	15	3	(5)	(4)

Required

1. Compute the cash flow from operations for each of Conrad's first four years of operation.

2. Write a memo to the president explaining why the company is not generating sufficient cash from operations to pay for the replacement of equipment.

Ethical Decision Making

Decision Case 12-6 Loan Decision and the Statement of Cash Flows—Indirect Method

LO1 • 6

ETHICAL DECISION MODEL

Mega Enterprises is in the process of negotiating an extension of its existing loan agreements with a major bank. The bank is particularly concerned with Mega's ability to generate sufficient cash flow from operating activities to meet the periodic principal and interest payments. In conjunction with the negotiations, the controller prepared the following statement of cash flows to present to the bank:

Mega Enterprises
Statement of Cash Flows
For the Year Ended December 31, 2017
(all amounts in millions of dollars)

Cash flows from operating activities	
Net income	$ 65
Adjustments to reconcile net income to net cash provided by operating activities:	
Depreciation and amortization	56
Increase in accounts receivable	(19)
Decrease in inventory	27
Decrease in accounts payable	(42)
Increase in other accrued liabilities	18
Net cash provided by operating activities	$ 105
Cash flows from investing activities	
Acquisitions of other businesses	$(234)
Acquisitions of plant and equipment	(125)
Sale of other businesses	300
Net cash used by investing activities	$ (59)
Cash flows from financing activities	
Additional borrowings	$ 150
Repayments of borrowings	(180)
Cash dividends paid	(50)
Net cash used by financing activities	$ (80)
Net decrease in cash	$ (34)
Cash balance, January 1, 2017	42
Cash balance, December 31, 2017	$ 8

During 2017, Mega sold one of its businesses in California. A gain of $150 million was included in 2017 income as the difference between the proceeds from the sale of $450 million and the book value of the business of $300 million. The effect of the sale can be identified and analyzed as follows (in millions of dollars):

Identify and Analyze

ACTIVITY: Investing
ACCOUNTS: Cash Increase California Properties Decrease Gain on Sale Increase
STATEMENT(S): Balance Sheet and Income Statement

Balance Sheet				Income Statement			
ASSETS		= LIABILITIES +	STOCKHOLDERS' EQUITY	REVENUES		− EXPENSES =	NET INCOME
Cash	450			Gain on Sale	150		150
California Properties	(300)		150				

(Continued)

As assistant controller, one of your assignments is to review the financial statements prior to their release. When you ask your boss for an explanation of the way in which the sale of the business was reported on the statement of cash flows, he explains that "the gain is correctly included in net income and that is all that matters."

Required

Use the Ethical Decision Framework in Exhibit 1-9 to complete the following requirements:

1. **Recognize an ethical dilemma:** What ethical dilemma(s) do you face? Do you agree with the way in which the controller treated the sale of the business on the statement of cash flows? Explain why you agree or disagree.

2. **Analyze the key elements in the situation:**
    a. Who may benefit if the sale of the business is reported on the statement of cash flows in the manner the controller insists it be reported? Who may be harmed?
    b. How are they likely to benefit or be harmed?
    c. What rights or claims may be violated?
    d. What specific interests are in conflict?
    e. What are your responsibilities and obligations?

3. **List alternatives and evaluate the impact of each on those affected:** As assistant controller, what are your options in dealing with the ethical dilemma(s) you identified in (1) above? If the sale of the business is reported on the statement of cash flows as the controller insists, will users have reliable information needed to make decisions? Why or why not?

4. **Select the best alternative:** Among the alternatives, which one would you select?

LO2 • 3   **Decision Case 12-7** **Cash Equivalents and the Statement of Cash Flows**

In December 2017, Rangers Inc. invested $100,000 of idle cash in U.S. Treasury notes. The notes mature on October 1, 2018, at which time Rangers expects to redeem them at face value of $100,000. The treasurer believes that the notes should be classified as cash equivalents because of the plans to hold them to maturity and receive face value. He also wants to avoid presentation of the purchase as an investing activity because the company made sizable capital expenditures during the year. The treasurer realizes that the decision about classification of the Treasury notes rests with you as controller.

Required

1. According to GAAP, how should the investment in U.S. Treasury notes be classified for purposes of preparing a statement of cash flows for the year ended December 31, 2017? Explain your answer.

2. If the purchase of the notes is classified as an operating rather than an investing activity, is the information provided to outside readers free from bias? Explain.

3. As controller for Rangers, what would you do in this situation? What would you tell the treasurer?

Answers

MODULE 1 Answers to Questions

1. The purpose of the statement of cash flows is to summarize an entity's cash flows from operating, investing, and financing activities during a period. Because it is concerned with activity for a specific period of time, the statement is similar to the income statement. However, they differ in two important respects. First, with a few exceptions, the income statement deals only with operating activities. Second, the income statement is on an accrual basis, while the statement of cash flows reports operating activities on a cash basis.

2. A 60-day Treasury bill would be classified as a cash equivalent and combined with cash on the balance sheet. Therefore, the purchase of the Treasury bill would not be reported as an investing activity. However, the purchase of Motorola stock would appear as a cash outflow in the Investing Activities section of the statement of cash flows.

3. Companies cannot continue in business if they do not generate positive cash flows from operating activities. Also, over a period of years, a company cannot continue to borrow more than it repays, nor can it issue capital stock indefinitely. Thus, you would not expect a net cash outflow from financing activities over a sustained period of time. However, many companies regularly experience a net cash outflow from investing activities. A company must at a minimum replace existing assets and in many cases acquire additional plant and equipment to remain competitive. At the same time, disposals of long-term assets may be fairly common, but usually they will not generate significant amounts of cash inflow.

4. The student is correct in that it is simple enough to find the net inflow or outflow of cash during the period. But this is only the starting point in preparing the statement of cash flows. First, all of the balance sheet accounts must be analyzed to find the explanations for the increases and decreases in cash during the period. Second, each of these inflows and outflows must be classified as either operating, investing, or financing activities.

MODULE 1 Answers to Apply

1. a. I b. F c. O d. O e. F f. I
2. a. F b. I c. O d. F e. I f. F g. O h. I
3. a. I b. I c. D d. D e. I f. I g. I h. D

MODULE 2 Answers to Questions

1. Inventory is analyzed to determine the purchases of the period. Cost of goods sold decreases the Inventory account, and purchases increase it. After the purchases of the period are found, they are added to the beginning balance in the Accounts Payable account. The difference between the addition of these amounts and the ending balance in Accounts Payable is the amount of cash payments.

2. An analysis of the Prepaid Rent account can be used to find the amount of cash paid for rent:

Beginning prepaid rent	$ 9,600
Cash payment	X
Rent expense	(45,900)
Ending prepaid rent	$ 7,300

(Continued)

$9,600 + X - \$45,900 = \$7,300$

$X = \underline{\$43,600}$

3. The purchase of 2,000 shares of treasury stock at $20 per share would be reflected on the statement of cash flows as a cash outflow of $40,000 in the Financing Activities section of the statement.

MODULE 2 Answers to Apply

a. $12,000   b. $(6,000)   c. $(17,000)   d. $(27,000)

MODULE 3 Answers to Questions

1. The only accurate part of these statements is that depreciation is often one of the largest items in the Operating Activities section of the statement. However, this is merely a result of using the indirect method to prepare this section. In computing net income, depreciation is deducted. Therefore, under the indirect method, it must be added back to net income because it is a noncash expense. Depreciation does not in any way generate cash.

2. Under the indirect method, net income is reported at the top of the Operating Activities section, and adjustments are made to convert income to a cash basis. Sales revenue is included in net income. However, on a cash basis, we are interested in cash collections from sales, not the sales on an accrual basis. A decrease in accounts receivable indicates that cash collections exceeded sales revenue. Therefore, the excess is added back to the net income of the period.

3. Yes, it is possible to report a net loss and still experience a net increase in cash. First, a company could report large noncash charges against net income, such as depreciation and various types of losses. Thus, it is possible that net cash provided by operating activities is positive even though a net loss is reported. Second, the net loss deals only with operating activities. It is possible that a net cash inflow was provided by either investing or financing activities, or both.

4. The requirement to separately disclose income taxes paid and interest paid when the indirect method is used is a compromise. Accounting standards strongly encourage companies to use the direct method because each major operating cash receipt and payment is reported in the Operating Activities section of the statement. However, if a company chooses to use the indirect approach, it is still required to report separately how much cash was actually paid to the government in taxes and to creditors in interest.

MODULE 3 Answers to Apply

1. a. D   b. D   c. A   d. NR   e. A   f. D
2. a. A   b. D   c. A   d. A   e. D   f. A   g. A
3. The effect of the sale of the truck can be identified and analyzed as follows:

Identify and Analyze	**ACTIVITY:**	Investing
	ACCOUNTS:	**Cash** Increase **Delivery Truck** Decrease
		Accumulated Depreciation Decrease
		Loss on Sale Increase
	STATEMENT[S]:	**Balance Sheet and Income Statement**

Balance Sheet						Income Statement				
ASSETS		=	LIABILITIES	+	STOCKHOLDERS' EQUITY	REVENUES	−	EXPENSES	=	NET INCOME
Cash	9,000				(2,000)			Loss on Sale 2,000***		(2,000)
Accumulated Depreciation*	14,000**									
Delivery Truck	(25,000)									

*The Accumulated Depreciation account has decreased. It is shown as an increase in the equation above because it is a contra account and causes total assets to increase.

**$25,000 − $11,000

***$11,000 − $9,000

Two items would be reported on a statement of cash flows using the indirect method. First, the loss of $2,000 would be added back to net income in the Operating Activities section. Second, the cash received of $9,000 would be reported as a cash inflow in the Investing Activities section.

MODULE 4 Answers to Questions

The numbers in the numerator of the cash flow adequacy ratio, net cash provided by operating activities and capital expenditures, appear on the statement of cash flows. The amount of average annual debt maturing over the next five years in the denominator can be found in a note to the financial statements.

MODULE 4 Answers to Apply

Cash flow adequacy = (Cash from operating activities − Capital expenditures)/Average amount of debt maturing over next five years:

$(\$1,500,000 - \$900,000)/(\$750,000/5) = \$600,000/\$150,000 = \underline{\underline{4.0}}$

MODULE 5 Answers to Questions

The Changes column on the work sheet reports the increase or decrease in each of the balance sheet accounts. Assets equal liabilities plus stockholders' equity in the accounting equation and it is this equality that results in the column totaling to zero.

MODULE 5 Answers to Apply

a. Operating: D   b. Investing: D   c. Operating: A
d. Operating: D   e. Operating: A   f. Financing: A

Answers to Connect to the Real World

12-1 (p. 565)

Chipotle uses the indirect method in the Operating Activities section of the statement of cash flows. The first line on the statement is net income, and the necessary adjustments are made to reconcile net income to net cash provided by operating activities.

12-2 (p. 579)

The deduction of $338 million in Accounts Receivable, net on Walgreens Boots Alliance's statement of cash flows for the year is an indication that Receivables increased during the year. An increase in receivables means that the company sold more during the year than it collected in cash; therefore, the difference is deducted from net earnings in the Operating Activities section of the statement.

Answers to Key Terms Quiz

3	Statement of cash flows
4	Cash equivalent
1	Operating activities
5	Investing activities

7	Financing activities
6	Direct method
2	Indirect method

Financial Statement Analysis

MODULES	LEARNING OBJECTIVES	WHY IS THIS CHAPTER IMPORTANT?
1 Horizontal and Vertical Analysis	**LO1** Explain the various limitations and considerations in financial statement analysis. **LO2** Use comparative financial statements to analyze a company over time (horizontal analysis). **LO3** Use common-size financial statements to compare various financial statement items (vertical analysis).	• You need to understand the limitations in using financial statements to analyze a company. (See p. 624–625.) • You need to know what tools you can use to assess the performance of a company over time. (See pp. 625–628.) • You need to know how you can use common-size financial statements to assess a company's performance in any one period. (See pp. 629–631.)
2 Liquidity Analysis	**LO4** Compute and use various ratios to assess liquidity.	• You need to know what ratios can be used to assess a company's liquidity. (See pp. 632–637.)
3 Solvency Analysis	**LO5** Compute and use various ratios to assess solvency.	• You need to know what ratios can be used to assess a company's solvency. (See pp. 638–641.)
4 Profitability Analysis	**LO6** Compute and use various ratios to assess profitability.	• You need to know what ratios can be used to assess a company's profitability. (See pp. 641–646.)

LULULEMON ATHLETICA INC.

Have you ever made an observation about a growing trend in society and wondered if you could somehow capitalize on it? This is precisely what prompted Dennis "Chip" Wilson to found **lululemon athletica inc.** in 1998. The growing trend was the popularity of yoga classes and what he observed was that cotton clothing was still being used. With this in mind, he started this chic designer and retailer of technical athletic apparel to meet what he considered a void in the market. Since its humble beginnings, this Canadian-based company has broadened both its product line and its targeted customers to include male athletes and female youth.

In its 2015 fiscal year—a mere 17 years since its founding—lululemon's revenues topped $2 billion and net income exceeded $266 million, resulting in a profit margin of nearly 13%.

The three-year comparative income statements for lululemon shown below are not reported in dollars, but rather in percentages, with each line item stated as a percentage of net revenues. As we will see starting in this chapter, these "common-size financial statements" allow the user to focus on the relationships between statement items rather than on absolute dollar amounts. Three years of income statement data also make it possible to detect trends over time, such as the decline in the profit margin from 17.6% to the most recent 12.9%.

In this chapter, we examine in more detail many of the ratios introduced in earlier chapters and also consider other tools you can use to judge the financial health and performance of companies such as lululemon.

lululemon athletica inc. Results of Operations			
	Fiscal Year Ended		
	January 31, 2016	February 1, 2015	February 2, 2014
	(% of net revenue)		
Net revenue	100.0%	100.0%	100.0%
Cost of goods sold	51.6	49.1	47.2
Gross profit	48.4	50.9	52.8
Selling, general and administrative expenses	30.5	30.0	28.2
Income from operations	17.9	20.9	24.6
Other (expense) income, net	—	0.4	0.4
Income before income tax expense	17.9	21.3	25.0
Income tax expense	5.0	8.0	7.4
Net income	12.9 %	13.3%	17.6%

Annotations on table:
- Over 50% of every dollar of sales goes to pay for products. (Cost of goods sold)
- About 30% goes to pay operating costs. (Selling, general and administrative expenses)
- Income from operations is about 18% of sales.
- Net income to sales, called profit margin, was about 13%, after paying taxes. (Net income)

Source: lululemon athletica inc. website and Form 10-K, For the Fiscal Year Ended January 31, 2016.

MODULE 1 HORIZONTAL AND VERTICAL ANALYSIS

LO1 Explain the various limitations and considerations in financial statement analysis.

Various groups have different purposes for analyzing a company's financial statements. For example, a banker is interested primarily in the likelihood that a loan will be repaid. Certain ratios indicate the ability to repay principal and interest. A stockholder, on the other hand, is concerned with a fair return on the amount invested in the company. Again, certain ratios are helpful in assessing the return to the stockholder. The managers of a business also are interested in the tools of financial statement analysis because various outside groups judge managers by using certain key ratios. Fortunately, most financial statements provide information about financial performance. Publicly held corporations are required to include in their annual reports a section that reviews the past year, with management's comments on its performance as measured by selected ratios and other forms of analysis.

Watch for Alternative Accounting Principles

Every set of financial statements is based on various assumptions. For example, a cost-flow method must be assumed in valuing inventory and recognizing cost of goods sold. The accountant chooses FIFO, LIFO, or one of the other acceptable methods. Analysts or other users find this information in the financial statement notes. The selection of a particular inventory valuation method has a significant effect on certain key ratios.

Recognition of the acceptable alternatives is especially important in comparing two or more companies. Changes in accounting methods, such as a change in the depreciation method, also make comparing results for a given company over time more difficult.

Take Care When Making Comparisons

Users of financial statements often place too much emphasis on summary indicators and key ratios such as the current ratio and the earnings per share amount. No single ratio is capable of telling the user everything there is to know about a particular company. Ratios for different periods of time should be compared. Has the ratio gone up or down from last year? What is the percentage of increase or decrease in the ratio over the last five years? Recognizing trends in ratios is important when analyzing any company.

The potential investor also must recognize the need to compare one company with others in the same industry. For example, a particular measure of performance may cause an investor to conclude that the company is not operating efficiently. Comparison with an industry standard, however, might indicate that the ratio is normal for companies in that industry. Various organizations publish summaries of selected ratios organized by industry for a sample of U.S. companies.

Although industry comparisons are useful, caution is necessary in interpreting the results of such analyses. Few companies in today's economy operate in a single industry. Exceptions exist, but most companies cross the boundaries of a single industry. *Conglomerates,* companies operating in more than one industry, present a special challenge to the analyst. Also, it is not unusual to find companies in the same industry using different inventory valuation techniques or depreciation methods.

Finally, many corporate income statements contain nonoperating items such as extraordinary items and gains and losses from discontinued operations. When these items exist, the reader must exercise extra caution in making comparisons. To assess the future prospects of a group of companies, you may want to compare income statements *before* taking into account the effects these items have on income.

Understand the Possible Effects of Inflation

Inflation, or an increase in the level of prices, is another important consideration in analyzing financial statements. The statements, to be used by outsiders, are based on historical costs and are not adjusted for the effects of increasing prices. For example, consider the following trend in a company's sales for the past three years:

	2017	2016	2015
Net sales	$121,000	$110,000	$100,000

As measured by the actual dollars of sales, sales have increased by 10% each year. Is the company better off in each succeeding year because of the increase in sales *dollars*? Assume, for example, that 2015 sales of $100,000 are the result of selling 100,000 units at $1 each. Are 2016 sales of $110,000 the result of selling 110,000 units at $1 each or of selling 100,000 units at $1.10 each? Although on the surface knowing which result accounts for the sales increase may seem unimportant, the answer can have significant ramifications. If the company found it necessary to increase the selling price to $1.10 in the face of increasing costs, it may be no better off than it was in 2015 in terms of gross profit. On the other hand, if the company is able to increase sales revenue by 10% based primarily on growth in unit sales, its performance would be considered stronger than if the increase were due merely to a price increase.

Analysis of Comparative Statements: Horizontal Analysis

We will analyze a set of financial statements by looking at the comparative balance sheets, statements of income and retained earnings, and statements of cash flows of a company for a two-year period. This analysis of the statements over a series of years is often called **horizontal analysis**. We will then see how the statements can be recast in what are referred to as *common-size statements*. The analysis of common-size statements is called **vertical analysis**. Finally, we will consider the use of a variety of ratios to analyze a company.

LO2 Use comparative financial statements to analyze a company over time (horizontal analysis).

Horizontal analysis
A comparison of financial statement items over a period of time.

Vertical analysis
A comparison of various financial statement items within a single period with the use of common-size statements.

EXAMPLE 13-1 Preparing and Reading Comparative Balance Sheets—Horizontal Analysis

Comparative balance sheets for a hypothetical entity, Henderson Company, are presented below.

Read from earlier year to later year. Usually, this is from right to left.

Henderson Company
Comparative Balance Sheets
December 31, 2017 and 2016
(all amounts in thousands of dollars)

The base year is normally on the right.

Dollar change from year to year.

Percentage change from one year to the next year.

In **horizontal analysis**, read right to left to compare one year's results with the next as a dollar amount of change and as a percentage of change from year to year.

| | December 31 | | Increase (Decrease) | |
	2017	2016	Dollars	Percent
Cash	$ 320	$ 1,350	$ (1,030) ❶	(76)%
Accounts receivable	5,500	4,500	1,000	22
Inventory	**4,750**	2,750	2,000 ❷	73
Prepaid insurance	150	200	(50)	(25)
Total current assets	$10,720	$ 8,800	$ 1,920	22
Land	$ 2,000	$ 2,000	$ 0	0
Buildings and equipment	6,000	4,500	1,500	33
Accumulated depreciation	(1,850)	(1,500)	(350)	(23)
Total long-term assets	$ 6,150	$ 5,000	$ 1,150	23
Total assets	$16,870	$13,800	$ 3,070	22
Accounts payable	$ 4,250	$ 2,500	$ 1,750 ❸	70
Taxes payable	2,300	2,100	200	10
Notes payable	600	800	(200)	(25)
Current portion of bonds	100	100	0	0
Total current liabilities	$ 7,250	$ 5,500	$ 1,750	32
Bonds payable	700	800	(100)	(13)
Total liabilities	$ 7,950	$ 6,300	$ 1,650	26
Preferred stock, $5 par	$ 500	$ 500	$ 0	0
Common stock, $1 par	1,000	1,000	0	0
Retained earnings	7,420	6,000	1,420	24
Total stockholders' equity	$ 8,920	$ 7,500	$ 1,420	19
Total liabilities and stockholders' equity	$16,870	$13,800	$ 3,070	22

Note: Referenced amounts are boldfaced for convenience.

The increase or decrease in each of the major accounts on the balance sheet is shown in absolute dollars and as a percentage. The base year for computing the percentage increase or decrease in each account is the first year, 2016, and is normally shown on the right side. By reading across from right to left (thus the term *horizontal analysis*), the analyst can quickly spot any unusual changes in accounts from the previous year. Three accounts stand out: ❶ Cash decreased by 76%, ❷ Inventory increased by 73%, and ❸ Accounts Payable increased by 70%. These changes send the financial statement user the warning that the business may be deteriorating. Each of these large changes should be investigated further.

EXAMPLE 13-2   Preparing and Reading Comparative Statements of Income and Retained Earnings—Horizontal Analysis

Shown below are comparative statements of income and retained earnings for Henderson for 2017 and 2016.

Henderson Company
Comparative Statements of Income and Retained Earnings
For the Years Ended December 31, 2017 and 2016
(all amounts in thousands of dollars)

	December 31 2017	December 31 2016	Increase (Decrease) Dollars	Increase (Decrease) Percent	
Net sales	$24,000	$20,000	$ 4,000	❶ 20%	
Cost of goods sold	18,000	14,000	4,000	❷ 29	These three increases in revenue and expenses resulted in an operating income *decrease* of 25%.
Gross profit	$ 6,000	$ 6,000	$ 0	0	
Selling, general, and administrative expense	3,000	2,000	1,000	❸ 50	
Operating income	$ 3,000	$ 4,000	$(1,000)	❹ (25)	
Interest expense	140	160	(20)	(13)	
Income before tax	$ 2,860	$ 3,840	$ (980)	(26)	
Income tax expense	1,140	1,540	(400)	(26)	
Net income	$ 1,720	$ 2,300	$ (580)	(25)	
Preferred dividends	50	50			
Income available to common	$ 1,670	$ 2,250			
Common dividends	250	250			
To retained earnings	$ 1,420	$ 2,000			
Retained earnings, 1/1	6,000	4,000			
Retained earnings, 12/31	$ 7,420	$ 6,000			

Note: Referenced amounts are boldfaced for convenience.

At first glance, ❶ the 20% increase in sales to $24 million appears promising; but management was not able to limit the increase in ❷ cost of goods sold or ❸ selling, general, and administrative expense to 20%. The analysis indicates that cost of goods sold increased by 29% and selling, general, and administrative expense increased by 50%. The increases in these two expenses more than offset the increase in sales and resulted in a ❹ decrease in operating income of 25%.

Companies that experience sales growth often become lax about controlling expenses. Their managements sometimes forget that the bottom line is what counts, not the top line. Perhaps the salespeople are given incentives to increase sales without considering the costs of the sales. Maybe management is spending too much on overhead, including its own salaries.

Horizontal analysis can be extended to include more than two years of results. At a minimum, publicly held companies are required to include income statements and statements of cash

CONNECT TO THE REAL WORLD

LULULEMON
READING THE INCOME STATEMENT

13-1 Refer to lululemon's financial data in Exhibit 13-1. Compute the company's gross profit ratio for each of the five years. Is there a noticeable upward or downward trend in the ratio over this time period? *(See answers on p. 684.)*

flows for the three most recent years and balance sheets as of the end of the two most recent years. Many annual reports include, as supplementary information, financial summaries of operations for extended periods of time. As illustrated in Exhibit 13-1, **lululemon** includes a five-year summary of selected financial data, such as gross profit, net income, cash and cash equivalents, and total assets. Note the increase in net revenue and gross profit for four consecutive years and in net income in all but the fiscal year ended February 1, 2015. Total assets have also increased significantly over this five-year period to support the company's growing operations, topping $1.3 billion by January 31, 2016.

EXHIBIT 13-1 lululemon Financial Summary

	Fiscal Year Ended				
	January 31, 2016	February 1, 2015	February 2, 2014	February 3, 2013	January 29, 2012
	(In thousands, except per share data)				
Consolidated statement of operations and comprehensive income data:					
Net revenue	$2,060,523	$1,797,213	$1,591,188	$1,370,358	$1,000,839
Cost of goods sold	1,063,357	883,033	751,112	607,532	431,488
Gross profit	997,166	914,180	840,076	762,826	569,351
Selling, general and administrative expenses	628,090	538,147	448,718	386,387	282,393
Income from operations	369,076	376,033	391,358	376,439	286,958
Other (expense) income, net	(581)	7,102	5,768	4,957	2,500
Income before income tax expense	368,495	383,135	397,126	381,396	289,458
Income tax expense	102,448	144,102	117,579	109,965	104,494
Net income	266,047	239,033	279,547	271,431	184,964
Net income attributable to non-controlling interest	—	—	—	875	901
Net income attributable to lululemon athletica inc.	$ 266,047	$ 239,033	$ 279,547	$ 270,556	$ 184,063
Other comprehensive (loss) income:					
Foreign currency translation adjustment	(64,796)	(105,339)	(89,158)	(459)	1,220
Comprehensive income	$ 201,251	$ 133,694	$ 190,389	$ 270,097	$ 185,283
Basic earnings per share	$ 1.90	$ 1.66	$ 1.93	$ 1.88	$ 1.29
Diluted earnings per share	$ 1.89	$ 1.66	$ 1.91	$ 1.85	$ 1.27
Basic weighted-average number of shares outstanding	140,365	143,935	144,913	144,000	143,196
Diluted weighted-average number of shares outstanding	140,610	144,298	146,043	145,806	145,278

> Net revenue and gross profit have both increased each year for four consecutive years.

	As of				
	January 31, 2016	February 1, 2015	February 2, 2014	February 3, 2013	January 29, 2012
	(In thousands)				
Consolidated balance sheet data:					
Cash and cash equivalents	$ 501,482	$ 664,479	$ 698,649	$ 590,179	$409,437
Total assets	1,314,077	1,296,213	1,252,388	1,052,678	736,034
Total stockholders' equity	1,027,482	1,089,568	1,096,682	887,299	606,181
Non-controlling interest	—	—	—	—	4,805

> Assets have been added over the years to support the company's growing operations.

Source: lululemon athletica inc. Form 10-K, For the Fiscal Year Ended January 31, 2016.

Tracking items over a series of years, called *trend analysis*, can be a very powerful tool for the analyst. Advanced statistical techniques are available for analyzing trends in financial data and, most importantly, for projecting those trends to future periods. Some of the techniques, such as time series analysis, have been used extensively in forecasting sales trends.

EXAMPLE 13-3 Preparing and Reading Comparative Statements of Cash Flows—Horizontal Analysis

Comparative statements of cash flows for Henderson are shown below.

Henderson Company
Comparative Statements of Cash Flows
For the Years Ended December 31, 2017 and 2016
(all amounts in thousands of dollars)

	2017	2016	Increase (Decrease) Dollars	Increase (Decrease) Percent
Net Cash Flows from Operating Activities				
❷ Net income	$ 1,720	$ 2,300	$ (580)	(25)%
Adjustments:				
Depreciation expense	350	300		
Changes in:				
❸ Accounts receivable	(1,000)	500		
❹ Inventory	(2,000)	(300)		
Prepaid insurance	50	50		
Accounts payable	1,750	(200)		
Taxes payable	200	300		
Net cash provided by operating activities ❶ Unfavorable	$ 1,070	$ 2,950	$(1,880)	(64)%
Net Cash Flows from Investing Activities				
Purchase of buildings	$(1,500)	$(2,000)	$ (500)	(25)%
Net Cash Flows from Financing Activities				
Repayment of notes	$ (200)	$ (200)	0	0
Retirement of bonds	(100)	(100)	0	0
Cash dividends—preferred	(50)	(50)	0	0
Cash dividends—common	(250)	(250)	0	0
Net cash used by financing activities	$ (600)	$ (600)	0	0
Net increase (decrease) in cash	$ (1,030)	$ 350		
Beginning cash balance	1,350	1,000		
Ending cash balance	$ 320	$ 1,350		
Supplemental Information				
Interest paid	$ 140	$ 160		
Income taxes paid	$ 940	$ 1,440		

Note: Referenced amounts are boldfaced for convenience.

Henderson's financing activities remained constant over the two-year period. Each year, the company paid $200,000 on notes, another $100,000 to retire bonds, and $300,000 to stockholders in dividends. Cash outflow from investing activities slowed down somewhat in 2017 with the purchase of $1.5 million in new buildings compared with $2 million the year before.

The most noticeable difference between Henderson's statements of cash flows for the two years is in the Operating Activities section. Operations ❶ generated almost $2 million less in cash in 2017 than in 2016 ($1.07 million in 2017 versus $2.95 million in 2016). The decrease in ❷ net income was partially responsible for this reduction in cash from operations. However, the increases in ❸ accounts receivable and ❹ inventory in 2017 had a significant impact on the decrease in cash generated from operating activities.

Analysis of Common-Size Statements: Vertical Analysis

Often, it is easier to examine comparative financial statements when they have been standardized. *Common-size statements* recast all items on the statement as a percentage of a selected item on the statement. This excludes size as a relevant variable in the analysis. This type of analysis could be used to compare **Wal-Mart** with the smaller **Target**. It is also a convenient way to compare the same company from year to year.

LO3 Use common-size financial statements to compare various financial statement items (vertical analysis).

EXAMPLE 13-4 Preparing and Reading Common-Size Balance Sheets—Vertical Analysis

Vertical analysis involves looking at the relative size and composition of various items on a particular financial statement. Common-size comparative balance sheets for Henderson Company are presented below.

Henderson Company
Common-Size Comparative Balance Sheets
December 31, 2017 and 2016
(all amounts in thousands of dollars)

	December 31, 2017		December 31, 2016	
	Dollars	Percent	Dollars	Percent
Cash	$ 320	1.9%	$ 1,350	9.8%
Accounts receivable	5,500	32.6	4,500	32.6
Inventory	4,750	28.1	2,750	19.9
Prepaid insurance	150	0.9	200	1.5
Total current assets	$ 10,720	63.5%	$ 8,800	63.8%
Land	$ 2,000	11.9%	$ 2,000	14.5%
Buildings and equipment, net	4,150	24.6	3,000	21.7
Total long-term assets	$ 6,150	36.5%	$ 5,000	36.2%
Total assets	$16,870	100.0%	$13,800	100.0%
Accounts payable	$ 4,250	25.2%	$ 2,500	18.1%
Taxes payable	2,300	13.6	2,100	15.2
Notes payable	600	3.6	800	5.8
Current portion of bonds	100	0.6	100	0.7
Total current liabilities	$ 7,250	43.0%	$ 5,500	39.8%
Bonds payable	700	4.1	800	5.8
Total liabilities	$ 7,950	47.1%	$ 6,300	45.6%
Preferred stock, $5 par	$ 500	3.0%	$ 500	3.6%
Common stock, $1 par	1,000	5.9	1,000	7.3
Retained earnings	7,420	44.0	6,000	43.5
Total stockholders' equity	$ 8,920	52.9%	$ 7,500	54.4%
Total liabilities and stockholders' equity	$16,870	100.0%	$13,800	100.0%

Note: Referenced amounts are boldfaced for convenience.

Compare percentages across years to spot year-to-year trends.

In **vertical analysis**, compare each line item as a percentage of total (100%) to highlight a company's overall condition.

Note that all asset accounts are stated as a percentage of total assets. Similarly, all liability and stockholders' equity accounts are stated as a percentage of total liabilities and stockholders' equity. The combination of the comparative balance sheets for the two years and the common-size feature allows the analyst to spot critical changes in the composition of the assets. We noted in Example 13-1 that cash had decreased by 76% over the two years. The decrease of ❶ cash from 9.8% of total assets to only 1.9% is highlighted here.

You can also observe that ❷ total current assets have continued to represent just under two-thirds (63.5%) of total assets. If cash has decreased significantly in terms of the percentage of total assets, what accounts have increased to maintain current assets at two-thirds of total assets? We can quickly determine from these data that although ❸ inventory represented 19.9% of total assets at the end of 2016, the percentage is up to 28.1% at the end of 2017. This change in the relative composition of current assets between cash and inventory may signal that the company is having trouble selling inventory.

Total ❹ current liabilities represent a slightly higher percentage of total liabilities and stockholders' equity at the end of 2017 than at the end of 2016. The increase is balanced by a slight decrease in the relative percentages of ❺ long-term debt (the bonds) and ❻ stockholders' equity. We will return later to further analysis of the composition of both the current and the noncurrent accounts.

EXAMPLE 13-5 Preparing and Reading Common-Size Income Statements—Vertical Analysis

Common-size comparative income statements for Henderson are presented below.

Henderson Company
Common-Size Comparative Income Statements
For the Years Ended December 31, 2017 and 2016
(all amounts in thousands of dollars)

	2017 Dollars	2017 Percent	2016 Dollars	2016 Percent	
Net sales	$ 24,000	❶ 100.0%	$ 20,000	100.0%	
Cost of goods sold	❸ 18,000	75.0	14,000	70.0	Gross profit as a percentage of sales is the **gross profit ratio**.
Gross profit	$ 6,000	❷ 25.0%	$ 6,000	30.0%	
Selling, general, and administrative expense	3,000	12.5	2,000	10.0	
Operating income	$ 3,000	12.5%	$ 4,000	20.0%	
Interest expense	140	0.6	160	0.8	
Income before tax	$ 2,860	11.9%	$ 3,840	19.2%	
Income tax expense	1,140	4.8	1,540	7.7	The ratio of net income to net sales is the **profit margin ratio**.
Net income	$ 1,720	❹ 7.1%	$ 2,300	11.5%	

Note: Referenced amounts are boldfaced for convenience.

Gross profit ratio
Gross profit to net sales.

Profit margin ratio
Net income to net sales.

The *base*, or benchmark, on which all other items in the income statement are compared is ❶ net sales. Again, observations from the comparative statements alone are further confirmed by examining the common-size statements. Although the **gross profit ratio**—gross profit as a percentage of net sales—was 30.0% in 2016, the same ratio for 2017 is only 25.0% ❷. Recall the earlier observation that although sales increased by 20% from one year to the next, ❸ cost of goods sold increased by 29%.

In addition to the gross profit ratio, an important relationship from this example is the ratio of net income to net sales, or **profit margin ratio**. The ratio, an overall indicator of management's ability to control expenses, reflects the amount of income for each dollar of sales. Some analysts prefer to look at income before tax rather than at final net income

CONNECT TO THE REAL WORLD
CHIPOTLE
READING THE INCOME STATEMENT

13-2 Refer to Chipotle's three-year comparative income statements reprinted in the back of this book. For each of the three years presented, compute the profit margin ratio. Is there a noticeable upward or downward trend in the ratio over this time period? *(See answers on p. 684.)*

because taxes are not typically an expense that can be controlled. Further, if the company does not earn a profit before tax, it will incur no tax expense. Note the decrease in Henderson's ❹ profit margin: from 11.5% in 2016 to 7.1% in 2017 (or from 19.2% to 11.9% on a before-tax basis).

MODULE 1 TEST YOURSELF

Review

LO1 Explain the various limitations and considerations in financial statement analysis.

- Financial statement analysis can be a powerful and useful tool in assessing various characteristics of a firm's operations, but the following factors should be considered when conducting this analysis:
  - Alternative accounting principles may sometimes be used.
  - Comparisons must consider inflation, trends over time, and industry norms.
  - Ratios from financial statements tell only part of the story about a firm's performance.

LO2 Use comparative financial statements to analyze a company over time (horizontal analysis).

- Amounts appearing on comparative financial statements may be used to perform horizontal analysis.

LO3 Use common-size financial statements to compare various financial statement items (vertical analysis).

- Common-size statements recast all items as a percentage of a selected item on the statement, such as sales on the income statement.
- The use of common-size financial statements, also known as vertical analysis, facilitates comparisons between companies in addition to comparisons between different periods for the same company.

Question

1. Two companies are in the same industry. Company A uses the LIFO method of inventory valuation, and Company B uses FIFO. What difficulties does this present when comparing the two companies?

2. Distinguish between horizontal and vertical analyses. Why is the analysis of common-size statements called *vertical* analysis? Why is horizontal analysis sometimes called *trend* analysis?

3. A company experiences a 15% increase in sales over the previous year. However, gross profit actually decreased by 5% from the previous year. What are some of the possible causes for an increase in sales but a decline in gross profit?

4. A company's total current assets have increased by 5% over the prior year. Management is concerned, however, about the composition of the current assets. Why is the composition of current assets important?

Apply

1. A supplier is thinking of extending credit to a company but decides not to because the company's current ratio is only 0.50. Do you agree with the supplier's decision? What other factors need to be considered in drawing any conclusions about a company's liquidity?

2. Fill in the blanks for each of the following statements.
   A comparison of financial statement items within a single period is called _____ analysis.
   A comparison of financial statement items over a period of time is called _____ analysis.

3. Assume that your boss has asked you to prepare common-size financial statements. All accounts on the balance sheet should be stated as a percentage of which number? All accounts on the income statement should be stated as a percentage of which number?

Answers are located at the end of the chapter.

MODULE 2 LIQUIDITY ANALYSIS

LO4 Compute and use various ratios to assess liquidity.

Liquidity
The nearness to cash of the assets and liabilities.

Two ratios were discussed in the last section: the *gross profit ratio* and the *profit margin ratio*. This section considers a wide range of ratios that management, analysts, and others use for a variety of purposes. The ratios are classified in three main categories according to their use in performing (1) liquidity analysis, (2) solvency analysis, and (3) profitability analysis.

Liquidity is a relative measure of the nearness to cash of the assets and liabilities of a company. Nearness to cash deals with the length of time before cash is realized. Various ratios are used to measure liquidity, and they concern basically the company's ability to pay its debts as they come due. Recall the distinction between the current and long-term classifications on the balance sheet. Current assets are assets that will be converted into cash or consumed within one year or within the operating cycle if the cycle is longer than one year. The operating cycle for a manufacturing company is the length of time between the purchase of raw materials and the eventual collection of any outstanding account receivable from the sale of the product. Current liabilities are a company's obligations that require the use of current assets or the creation of other current liabilities to satisfy the obligations.

The nearness to cash of the current assets is indicated by their placement on the balance sheet. Current assets are listed on the balance sheet in descending order of their nearness to cash. Liquidity is, of course, a matter of degree, with cash being the most liquid of all assets. With few exceptions, such as prepaid insurance, most current assets are convertible into cash. However, accounts receivable is closer to being converted into cash than is inventory. An account receivable need only be collected to be converted to cash. An item of inventory must first be sold; then assuming that sales of inventory are on account, the account must be collected before cash is realized.

Working Capital

Working capital
Current assets minus current liabilities.

Working capital is the excess of current assets over current liabilities at a point in time:

Working Capital = Current Assets − Current Liabilities

EXAMPLE 13-6 Computing Working Capital

Henderson's comparative balance sheets in Example 13-1 indicate the following:

	December 31	
	2017	**2016**
Current assets	$10,720,000	$8,800,000
Current liabilities	7,250,000	5,500,000
Working capital	$ 3,470,000	$3,300,000

The management of working capital is an extremely important task for any business. A comparison of Henderson's working capital at the end of each of the two years indicates a slight increase in the degree of protection for short-term creditors of the company. Management must strive for the ideal balance of current assets and current liabilities. However, working capital is limited in its informational value. It reveals nothing about the composition of the current accounts. Also, the dollar amount of working capital may not be useful for comparison with other companies of different sizes in the same industry. Working capital of $3,470,000 may be adequate for Henderson Company, but it might signal impending bankruptcy for a much larger company.

Current Ratio

The **current ratio**, one of the most widely used financial statement ratios, is as follows:

$$\text{Current Ratio} = \frac{\text{Current Assets}}{\text{Current Liabilities}}$$

Current ratio
The ratio of current assets to current liabilities.

EXAMPLE 13-7 Computing and Interpreting the Current Ratio

For Henderson Company, the ratio at each year-end is as follows:

	December 31	
2017		**2016**
$\dfrac{\$10,720,000}{\$7,250,000} = 1.48$ to 1		$\dfrac{\$8,800,000}{\$5,500,000} = 1.60$ to 1

At the end of 2017, Henderson had $1.48 of current assets for every $1 of current liabilities. Is this current ratio adequate, or is it a sign of impending financial difficulties? Some analysts use a general rule of thumb of 2 to 1 for the current ratio as a sign of short-term financial health. However, companies in certain industries have historically operated with current ratios much less than 2 to 1.

Interpreting the current ratio also involves the composition of the current assets. Cash is usually the only acceptable means of payment for most liabilities. Therefore, it is important to consider the makeup, or *composition*, of the current assets. Refer to Example 13-4 and Henderson's common-size balance sheets. Not only did the current ratio decline during 2017, but the proportion of the total current assets made up by inventory also increased, whereas the proportion made up by accounts receivable remained the same. Recall that accounts receivable is only one step removed from cash, whereas inventory requires both sale and collection of the subsequent account.

> ### STUDY TIP
>
> Some of the ratios discussed in this chapter, such as the current ratio, were introduced in earlier chapters. Use the information here as a review of those earlier introductions.

Acid-Test Ratio

The **acid-test or quick ratio** is a stricter test of a company's ability to pay its current debts as they are due. Specifically, it is intended to deal with the composition problem because it *excludes* inventories and prepaid assets from the numerator of the fraction:

$$\text{Acid-Test or Quick Ratio} = \frac{\text{Quick Assets}}{\text{Current Liablities}}$$

Acid-test or quick ratio
A stricter test of liquidity than the current ratio; excludes inventory and prepayments from the numerator.

where

$$\text{Quick Assets} = \text{Cash} + \text{Marketable Securities} + \text{Current Receivables}$$

EXAMPLE 13-8 Computing and Interpreting the Acid-Test Ratio

Henderson's quick assets consist of only cash and accounts receivable, and its quick ratios are as follows:

	December 31	
2017		**2016**
$\dfrac{\$320,000 + \$5,500,000}{\$7,250,000} = 0.80$ to 1		$\dfrac{\$1,350,000 + \$4,500,000}{\$5,500,000} = 1.06$ to 1

Does the quick ratio of less than 1 to 1 at the end of 2017 mean that Henderson will be unable to pay creditors on time? **For many companies, an acid-test ratio below 1 is not desirable because it may signal the need to liquidate marketable securities to pay bills, regardless of the current trading price of the securities**. (Recall that Henderson has no marketable securities.) Although the quick ratio is a better indication of short-term debt-paying ability than the current ratio, it is still not perfect. Henderson's own normal credit terms and the credit terms that it receives from its suppliers would answer this question.

Assume that Henderson requires its customers to pay their accounts within 30 days and that its suppliers allow payment anytime within 60 days. The relatively longer credit terms extended by Henderson's suppliers give the company some cushion in meeting its obligations. The due date of the $2,300,000 in taxes payable also could have a significant effect on the company's ability to remain in business.

Cash Flow from Operations to Current Liabilities

Two limitations exist with either the current ratio or the quick ratio as a measure of liquidity:

1. Almost all debts require the payment of cash. Thus, a ratio that focuses on cash is more useful.
2. Both ratios focus on liquid assets at a *point in time*. Cash flow from operating activities, as reported on the statement of cash flows, can be used to indicate the flow of cash during the year to cover the debts due.

Cash flow from operations to current liabilities ratio
A measure of the ability to pay current debts from operating cash flows.

The **cash flow from operations to current liabilities ratio** is as follows:

$$\text{Cash Flow from Operations to Current Liabilities Ratio} = \frac{\text{Net Cash Provided by Operating Activities}}{\text{Average Current Liabilities}}$$

Note the use of *average* current liabilities in the denominator. Because we need to calculate the *average* current liabilities for both years, Henderson's ending balance sheet on December 31, 2015, is given in Exhibit 13-2.

EXHIBIT 13-2 Henderson Company's Balance Sheet, End of 2015

Henderson Company Balance Sheet December 31, 2015 (all amounts in thousands of dollars)	
Cash	$ 1,000
Accounts receivable	5,000
Inventory	2,450
Prepaid insurance	250
Total current assets	$ 8,700
Land	$ 2,000
Buildings and equipment, net	1,300
Total long-term assets	$ 3,300
Total assets	$12,000
Accounts payable	$ 2,700
Taxes payable	1,800
Notes payable	1,000
Current portion of bonds	100
Total current liabilities	$ 5,600
Bonds payable	900
Total liabilities	$ 6,500
Preferred stock, $5 par	$ 500
Common stock, $1 par	1,000
Retained earnings	4,000
Total stockholders' equity	$ 5,500
Total liabilities and stockholders' equity	$12,000

EXAMPLE 13-9 Computing and Interpreting Cash Flow from Operations to Current Liabilities

Henderson's cash flow from operations to current liabilities ratio each year is as follows:

2017	2016
$\dfrac{\$1,070,000}{(\$7,250,000 + \$5,500,000)/2} = 16.8\%$	$\dfrac{\$2,950,000}{(\$5,500,000 + \$5,600,000)/2} = 53.2\%$

Two factors are responsible for the large decrease in this ratio from 2016 to 2017. First, cash generated from operations during 2017 was less than half what it was during 2016 (the numerator). Second, average current liabilities were smaller in 2016 than in 2017 (the denominator). An analysis of the company's health in terms of its liquidity would concentrate on the reason for these changes.

Accounts Receivable Analysis

The analysis of accounts receivable is an important component in the management of working capital. A company must be willing to extend credit terms that are liberal enough to attract and maintain customers, but at the same time, management must continually monitor the accounts to ensure collection on a timely basis. One measure of the efficiency of the collection process is the **accounts receivable turnover ratio**:

$$\text{Accounts Receivable Turnover Ratio} = \frac{\text{Net Credit Sales}}{\text{Average Accounts Receivable}}$$

Both the current and the quick ratios measure liquidity at a point in time and all numbers come from the balance sheet, but a turnover ratio is an *activity* ratio and consists of an activity (sales in this case) divided by a base to which it is naturally related (accounts receivable). Because an activity such as sales is for a period of time (a year in this case), the base should be stated as an average for that same period of time.

Accounts receivable turnover ratio
A measure of the number of times accounts receivable are collected in a period.

EXAMPLE 13-10 Computing and Interpreting Accounts Receivable Turnover and Number of Days' Sales in Receivables

The accounts receivable turnover ratios for both years for Henderson follow. (We will assume that all sales are on account.)

2017	2016
$\dfrac{\$24,000,000}{(\$5,500,000 + \$4,500,000/2)} = 4.8 \text{ times}$	$\dfrac{\$20,000,000}{(\$4,500,000 + \$5,000,000)/2} = 4.2 \text{ times}$

Accounts turned over, on average, 4.2 times in 2016, compared with 4.8 times in 2017. What does this mean about the average length of time that an account was outstanding? Another way to measure efficiency in the collection process is to calculate the **number of days' sales in receivables**:

$$\text{Number of Days' Sales in Receivables} = \frac{\text{Number of Days in the Period}}{\text{Accounts Receivable Turnover}}$$

Number of days' sales in receivables
A measure of the average age of accounts receivable.

For simplicity, we assume 360 days in a year:

2017	2016
$\dfrac{360 \text{ days}}{4.8 \text{ times}} = 75 \text{ days}$	$\dfrac{360 \text{ days}}{4.2 \text{ times}} = 86 \text{ days}$

The average number of days an account is outstanding, or the average collection period, is 75 days in 2017, down from 86 days in 2016. Is this acceptable? The answer depends on the company's credit policy. If Henderson's normal credit terms require payment within 60 days, further investigation is needed even though the number of days outstanding has decreased from the previous year.

Management needs to be concerned with both the collectibility of an account as it ages and the cost of funds tied up in receivables. For example, a $1 million average receivable balance that requires an additional month to collect suggests that the company is foregoing $10,000 in profits assuming that the money could be reinvested in the business to earn 1% per month, or 12% per year.

Inventory Analysis

Inventory turnover ratio
A measure of the number of times inventory is sold during a period.

A similar set of ratios can be calculated to analyze the efficiency in managing inventory. The **inventory turnover ratio** is as follows:

$$\text{Inventory Turnover Ratio} = \frac{\text{Cost of Goods Sold}}{\text{Average Inventory}}$$

EXAMPLE 13-11 Computing and Interpreting Inventory Turnover and Number of Days' Sales in Inventory

The inventory turnover ratio for each of the two years for Henderson is as follows:

2017	2016
$\dfrac{\$18{,}000{,}000}{(\$4{,}750{,}000 + \$2{,}750{,}000)/2} = 4.8 \text{ times}$	$\dfrac{\$14{,}000{,}000}{(\$2{,}750{,}000 + \$2{,}450{,}000)/2} = 5.4 \text{ times}$

Number of days' sales in inventory
A measure of how long it takes to sell inventory.

Henderson was slightly more efficient in 2016 in moving its inventory. The number of "turns" each year varies widely for different industries. For example, a wholesaler of perishable fruits and vegetables may turn over inventory at least 50 times per year. An airplane manufacturer, however, may turn over its inventory once or twice a year. What does the number of turns per year reveal about the average length of time it takes to sell an item of inventory? The **number of days' sales in inventory** is an alternative measure of the company's efficiency in managing inventory. It is the number of days between the date an item of inventory is purchased and the date it is sold:

$$\text{Number of Days' Sales in Inventory} = \frac{\text{Number of Days in the Period}}{\text{Inventory Turnover}}$$

The number of days' sales in inventory for Henderson is as follows:

2017	2016
$\dfrac{360 \text{ days}}{4.8 \text{ times}} = 75 \text{ days}$	$\dfrac{360 \text{ days}}{5.4 \text{ times}} = 67 \text{ days}$

This measure can reveal a great deal about inventory management. An unusually low turnover (and, of course, a high number of days in inventory) may signal a large amount of obsolete inventory or problems in the sales department, or it may indicate that the company is pricing its products too high and the market is reacting by reducing demand for the company's products.

Cash Operating Cycle

Cash-to-cash operating cycle
The length of time from the purchase of inventory to the collection of any receivable from the sale.

The **cash-to-cash operating cycle** is the length of time between the purchase of merchandise for sale, assuming a retailer or wholesaler, and the eventual collection of the cash from the sale. One method to approximate the number of days in a company's operating cycle involves combining two measures:

$$\text{Cash-to-Cash Operating Cycle} = \text{Number of Days' Sales in Inventory} + \text{Number of Days' Sales in Receivables}$$

EXAMPLE 13-12 **Computing and Interpreting the Cash-to-Cash Operating Cycle**

Henderson's operating cycles for 2017 and 2016 are as follows:

2017	2016
75 days + 75 days = 150 days	67 days + 86 days = 153 days

The average length of time between the purchase of inventory and the collection of cash from sale of the inventory was 150 days in 2017. Although the length of the operating cycle did not change significantly from 2016 to 2017, the composition did change: the increase in the average number of days in inventory was offset by the decrease in the average number of days in receivables.

MODULE 2 TEST YOURSELF

Review	**LO4** Compute and use various ratios to assess liquidity.	• Liquidity is a measure of the relative ease with which assets can be converted to cash. Several ratios may be used to assess different aspects of liquidity, including: • Current, acid-test (quick), cash from operations to current liabilities, accounts receivable turnover, and inventory turnover ratios. • The cash-to-cash operating cycle measures the average length of time between the purchase of inventory and collection of cash after a sale takes place.
Question		1. A company has a current ratio of 1.25 but an acid-test (or quick) ratio of only 0.65. How can this difference in the two ratios be explained? What concerns might you have about this company? 2. Sanders Company's accounts receivable turned over nine times during the year. The credit department extends terms of 2/10, n/30. Does the turnover ratio indicate any problems that management should investigate? Explain. 3. The turnover of inventory for Ace Company has slowed from 6.0 times per year to 4.5. What are some possible explanations for this decrease?
Apply		1. Company A reported sales during the year of $1,000,000. Its average accounts receivable balance during the year was $250,000. Company B reported sales during the same year of $400,000 and had an average accounts receivable balance of $40,000. Compute the accounts receivable turnover for both companies. What is the average length of time each company takes to collect its receivables? 2. For each of the following ratios, fill in the missing numerator.

Ratio

Current: $\dfrac{\rule{2cm}{0.4pt}}{\text{Current Liabilities}}$

Acid-Test: $\dfrac{\rule{2cm}{0.4pt}}{\text{Current Liabilities}}$

Accounts Receivable Turnover: $\dfrac{\rule{2cm}{0.4pt}}{\text{Average Accounts Receivable}}$

Inventory Turnover: $\dfrac{\rule{2cm}{0.4pt}}{\text{Average Inventory}}$

Answers are located at the end of the chapter.

MODULE 3 SOLVENCY ANALYSIS

LO5 Compute and use various ratios to assess solvency.

Solvency
The ability of a company to remain in business over the long term.

Debt-to-equity ratio
The ratio of total liabilities to total stockholders' equity.

Solvency refers to a company's ability to remain in business over the long term. It is related to liquidity but differs in time. Although liquidity relates to the firm's ability to pay next year's debts as they come due, solvency concerns the ability of the firm to stay financially healthy over the period of time that existing debt (short- and long-term) is outstanding.

Debt-to-Equity Ratio

Capital structure—the mix between debt and stockholders' equity—is the focal point in solvency analysis. The composition of debt and equity is an important determinant of the cost of capital to a company. Consider the **debt-to-equity ratio**:

$$\text{Debt-to-Equity Ratio} = \frac{\text{Total Liabilities}}{\text{Total Stockholders' Equity}}$$

EXAMPLE 13-13 Computing and Interpreting the Debt-to-Equity Ratio

Henderson's debt-to-equity ratio at each year-end is as follows:

	December 31	
2017		**2016**
$\frac{\$7,950,000}{\$8,920,000} = 0.89 \text{ to } 1$		$\frac{\$6,300,000}{\$7,500,000} = 0.84 \text{ to } 1$

The 2017 ratio indicates that for every $1.00 of capital that stockholders provided, creditors provided $0.89. Variations of the debt-to-equity ratio are sometimes used to assess solvency. For example, an analyst might calculate the ratio of total liabilities to the sum of total liabilities and stockholders' equity. This results in a ratio that differs from the debt-to-equity ratio, but the objective of the measure is the same—to determine the degree to which the company relies on outsiders for funds.

STUDY TIP

The elements in many ratios are intuitive and should not require memorization. For example, it is logical that the debt-to-equity ratio is computed by dividing total liabilities by total stockholders' equity.

What is an acceptable ratio of debt to equity? As with all ratios, the answer depends on the company, the industry, and many other factors. You should not assume that a lower debt-to-equity ratio is better. Certainly, taking on additional debt is risky. Many companies are able to benefit from borrowing money, however, by putting the cash raised to good use in their businesses. Later in the chapter, we discuss the concept of leverage: using borrowed money to benefit the company and its stockholders.

Times Interest Earned

Times interest earned ratio
An income statement measure of the ability of a company to meet its interest payments.

The debt-to-equity ratio is a measure of the company's overall long-term financial health. Management must also be aware of its ability to meet current interest payments to creditors. The **times interest earned ratio** indicates the company's ability to meet the current year's interest payments out of the current year's earnings:

$$\text{Times Interest Earned Ratio} = \frac{\text{Net Income + Interest Expense + Income Tax Expense}}{\text{Interest Expense}}$$

Both interest expense and income tax expense are added back to net income in the numerator because interest is a deduction in arriving at the amount of income subject to tax. If a company had just enough income to cover the payment of interest, tax expense would be zero. As far as lenders are concerned, the greater the interest coverage, the better. Bankers often place more importance on the times interest earned ratio than on earnings per share.

EXAMPLE 13-14 Computing and Interpreting the Times Interest Earned Ratio

The times interest earned ratio for Henderson for 2017 and 2016 can be computed as follows:

2017	2016
$\dfrac{\$1{,}720{,}000 + \$140{,}000 + \$1{,}140{,}000}{\$140{,}000}$	$\dfrac{\$2{,}300{,}000 + \$160{,}000 + \$1{,}540{,}000}{\$160{,}000}$
= 21.4 to 1	= 25.0 to 1

The ratios for both years indicate that Henderson's earnings are more than ample to cover its interest.

Debt Service Coverage

Two problems exist with the times interest earned ratio as a measure of the ability to pay creditors. First, the denominator of the fraction considers only *interest*. Management must also be concerned with the *principal* amount of loans maturing in the next year. The second problem deals with the difference between the cash and accrual bases of accounting. The numerator of the times interest earned ratio is not a measure of the *cash* available to repay loans. Keep in mind the various noncash adjustments, such as depreciation, that enter into the determination of net income. Also, recall that the denominator of the times interest earned ratio is a measure of interest expense, not interest payments.

The **debt service coverage ratio** is a measure of the amount of cash that is generated from operating activities during the year and that is available to repay interest due and any maturing principal amounts (i.e., the amount available to "service" the debt):

Debt service coverage ratio
A statement of cash flows measure of the ability of a company to meet its interest and principal payments.

$$\text{Debt Service Coverage Ratio} = \frac{\text{Cash Flow from Operations Before Interest and Tax Payments}}{\text{Interest and Principal Payments}}$$

Some analysts use an alternative measure in the numerator of this ratio called EBITDA, which stands for earnings before interest, taxes, depreciation, and amortization. Whether EBITDA is a good substitute for cash flow from operations before interest and tax payments depends on whether there were significant changes in current assets and current liabilities during the period. If significant changes in these accounts occurred during the period, cash flow from operations before interest and tax payments is a better measure of a company's ability to cover interest and debt payments.

EXAMPLE 13-15 Computing and Interpreting the Debt Service Coverage Ratio

Cash flow from operations is available on the comparative statement of cash flows in Example 13-3. As was the case with the times interest earned ratio, the net cash provided by operating activities is adjusted to reflect the amount available before paying interest and taxes.

The income statement in Example 13-2 reflects the *expense* for interest and taxes each year. The amounts of interest and taxes paid each year are shown as supplemental information at the bottom of the statement of cash flows in Example 13-3 and are relevant in computing the debt service coverage ratio.

Any principal payments must be included with interest paid in the denominator of the debt service coverage ratio. According to the Financing Activities section of the statements of cash flows in Example 13-3, Henderson repaid $200,000 each year on the notes payable and $100,000 each year on the bonds. The debt service coverage ratios for the two years are calculated as follows:

2017

$$\frac{\$1{,}070{,}000 + \$140{,}000 + \$940{,}000}{\$140{,}000 + \$200{,}000 + \$100{,}000} = 4.89 \text{ times}$$

$$\frac{\$2{,}950{,}000 + \$160{,}000 + \$1{,}440{,}000}{\$160{,}000 + \$200{,}000 + \$100{,}000} = 9.89 \text{ times}$$

Like Henderson's times interest earned ratio, its debt service coverage ratio decreased during 2017. According to the calculations, however, Henderson still generated almost $5 of cash from operations during 2017 to "cover" every $1 of required interest and principal payments.

Cash Flow from Operations to Capital Expenditures Ratio

Cash flow from operations to capital expenditures ratio
A measure of the ability of a company to finance long-term asset acquisitions with cash from operations.

The **cash flow from operations to capital expenditures ratio** measures a company's ability to use operations to finance its acquisitions of productive assets. To the extent that a company is able to do this, it should rely less on external financing or additional contributions by the owners to replace and add to the existing capital base. The ratio is as follows:

$$\text{Cash Flow from Operations to Capital Expenditures Ratio} = \frac{\text{Cash Flow from Operations} - \text{Total Dividends Paid}}{\text{Cash Paid for Acquisitions}}$$

The numerator of the ratio measures the cash flow *after* all dividend payments are met.[1]

EXAMPLE 13-16 Computing and Interpreting the Cash Flow from Operations to Capital Expenditures Ratio

The calculation of the ratios for Henderson follows:

2017	2016
$\dfrac{\$1{,}070{,}000 - \$300{,}000}{\$1{,}500{,}000} = 51.3\%$	$\dfrac{\$2{,}950{,}000 - \$300{,}000}{\$2{,}000{,}000} = 132.5\%$

Although the amount of capital expenditures was less in 2017 than in 2016, the company generated considerably less cash from operations in 2017 to cover these acquisitions. In fact, the ratio of less than 100% in 2017 indicates that Henderson was not able to finance all of its capital expenditures from operations *and* cover its dividend payments.

MODULE 3 TEST YOURSELF

Review	LO5 Compute and use various ratios to assess solvency.	• Solvency measures a company's ability to maintain its financial health over the long term. Several ratios may be used to assess different aspects of solvency, including: • Debt-to-equity, times interest earned, debt service coverage, and cash flow from operations to capital expenditures ratios.

Question	1. Why is the debt service coverage ratio a better measure of solvency than the times interest earned ratio?
	2. A friend tells you that the best way to assess solvency is by comparing total debt to total assets. Another friend says that solvency is measured by comparing total debt to total stockholders' equity. Which friend is correct?
	3. A company is in the process of negotiating with a bank for an additional loan. Why will the bank be interested in the company's debt service coverage ratio?
	4. What is the rationale for deducting dividends when computing the ratio of cash flow from operations to capital expenditures?

---

[1] Dividends paid are reported on the statement of cash flows in the Financing Activities section. The amount *paid* should be used for this calculation rather than the amount declared, which appears on the statement of retained earnings.

Apply

1. Fill in the blank with the name of the ratio that would be used for each of the following situations.

Ratio	Measures the ability of the company to
_____	Meet its interest and principal payments
_____	Finance long-term asset acquisitions with cash from operations
_____	Meet its interest payments

2. A company's total assets amounted to $300 million at the beginning of the year and $400 million at year-end. The debt-to-equity ratio at the beginning of the year was 2 to 1. The only change in stockholders' equity during the year was the increase in retained earnings for the year's net income of $50 million. Compute the company's debt-to-equity ratio at year-end.

Answers are located at the end of the chapter.

MODULE 4 PROFITABILITY ANALYSIS

Creditors are concerned with a company's profitability because a profitable company is more likely to be able to make principal and interest payments. Of course, stockholders care about a company's profitability because it affects the market price of the stock and the ability of the company to pay dividends. Various measures of **profitability** indicate how well management is using the resources at its disposal to earn a return on the funds invested by various groups. Two frequently used profitability measures, the gross profit ratio and the profit margin ratio, were discussed earlier in the chapter. We now turn to other measures of profitability.

LO6 Compute and use various ratios to assess profitability.

Profitability
How well management is using company resources to earn a return on the funds invested by various groups.

Rate of Return on Assets

Before computing the rate of return, we must answer an important question: *return to whom?* Every return ratio is a measure of the relationship between the income earned by the company and the investment made in the company by various groups. The broadest rate of return ratio is the **return on assets ratio** because it considers the investment made by *all* providers of capital, from short-term creditors to bondholders to stockholders. Therefore, the denominator, or base, for the return on assets ratio is average total liabilities and stockholders' equity—which, of course, is the same as average total assets.

The numerator of a return ratio will be some measure of the company's income for the period. The income selected for the numerator must match the investment or base in the denominator. For example, if average total assets is the base in the denominator, it is necessary to use an income number that is applicable to all providers of capital.

Therefore, the income number used in the rate of return on assets is income *after* interest expense is added back. This adjustment considers creditors as one of the groups that has provided funds to the company. In other words, we want the amount of income before creditors or stockholders have been given any distributions (i.e., interest to creditors or dividends to stockholders). Interest expense must be added back on a net-of-tax basis. Because net income is on an after-tax basis, for consistency purposes, interest must also be placed on a net, or after-tax, basis.

The return on assets ratio is as follows:

Return on assets ratio
A measure of a company's success in earning a return for all providers of capital.

$$\text{Return on Assets Ratio} = \frac{\text{Net Income} + \text{Interest Expense, Net of Tax}}{\text{Average Total Assets}}$$

EXAMPLE 13-17 Computing the Return on Assets Ratio

If we assume a 40% tax rate (which is the actual ratio of income tax expense to income before tax for Henderson), its return on assets ratios will be as follows:

		2017		2016
Net income		$ 1,720,000		$ 2,300,000
Interest expense	$ 140,000		$ 160,000	
× (1 – tax rate)	× 0.6	84,000	× 0.6	96,000
Numerator		$ 1,804,000		$ 2,396,000
Assets, beginning of year		$13,800,000		$12,000,000
Assets, end of year		16,870,000		13,800,000
Total		$30,670,000		$25,800,000
Denominator:				
Average total assets (total above divided by 2)		$15,335,000		$12,900,000
		$ 1,804,000		$ 2,396,000
		$15,335,000		$12,900,000
Return on assets ratio		= 11.76%		= 18.57%

Components of Return on Assets

What caused Henderson's return on assets to decrease so dramatically from the previous year? The answer can be found by considering the two components that make up the return on assets ratio. The first of these components is the **return on sales ratio** and is as follows:

Return on sales ratio
A variation of the profit margin ratio; measures earnings before payments to creditors.

$$\text{Return on Sales Ratio} = \frac{\text{Net Income} + \text{Interest Expense, Net of Tax}}{\text{Net Sales}}$$

EXAMPLE 13-18 Computing and Interpreting the Return on Sales Ratio

The return on sales ratios for Henderson for the two years are as follows:

2017	2016
$\dfrac{\$1,720,000 + \$84,000}{\$24,000,000} = 7.52\%$	$\dfrac{\$2,300,000 + \$96,000}{\$20,000,000} = 11.98\%$

The ratio for 2017 indicates that for every $1.00 of sales, the company was able to earn a profit (before the payment of interest) of between $0.07 and $0.08, as compared with a return of almost $0.12 on the dollar in 2016.

Asset turnover ratio
The relationship between net sales and average total assets.

The other component of the rate of return on assets is the **asset turnover ratio**. The ratio is similar to both the inventory turnover and the accounts receivable turnover ratios because it is a measure of the relationship between some activity (net sales in this case) and some investment base (average total assets):

$$\text{Asset Turnover Ratio} = \frac{\text{Net Sales}}{\text{Average Total Assets}}$$

EXAMPLE 13-19 Computing the Asset Turnover Ratio

For Henderson, the ratio for each of the two years follows:

2017	2016
$\dfrac{\$24,000,000}{\$15,335,000} = 1.57 \text{ times}$	$\dfrac{\$20,000,000}{\$12,900,000} = 1.55 \text{ times}$

The explanation for the decrease in Henderson's return on assets lies in the drop in the return on sales since the asset turnover ratio was almost the same. To summarize, note the relationship among the three ratios:

Return on Assets = Return on Sales × Asset Turnover

For 2017, Henderson's return on assets consists of the following:

$$\frac{\$1,804,000}{\$24,000,000} \times \frac{\$24,000,000}{\$15,335,000} = 7.52\% \times 1.57 = 11.8\%$$

Finally, notice that net sales cancels out of both ratios, leaving the net income adjusted for interest divided by average assets as the return on assets ratio.

Return on Common Stockholders' Equity

Reasoning similar to that used to calculate return on assets can be used to calculate the return on capital provided by the common stockholder. Because we are interested in the return to the common stockholder, our base is no longer average total assets, but average common stockholders' equity. Similarly, the appropriate income figure for the numerator is net income less preferred dividends because we are interested in the return to the common stockholder after all claims have been settled. Income taxes and interest expense have already been deducted in arriving at net income, but preferred dividends have not been because dividends are a distribution of profits, not an expense.

The **return on common stockholders' equity ratio** is as follows:

Return on common stockholders' equity ratio
A measure of a company's success in earning a return for the common stockholders.

$$\text{Return on Common Stockholders' Equity Ratio} = \frac{\text{Net Income} - \text{Preferred Dividends}}{\text{Average Common Stockholders' Equity}}$$

EXAMPLE 13-20 Computing and Interpreting the Return on Common Stockholders' Equity

The average common stockholders' equity for Henderson is calculated using information from Example 13-1 and Exhibit 13-2:

	Account Balances at December 31		
	2017	2016	2015
Common stock, $1 par	$1,000,000	$1,000,000	$1,000,000
Retained earnings	7,420,000	6,000,000	4,000,000
Total common equity	$8,420,000	$7,000,000	$5,000,000

Average common equity:
  2016: ($7,000,000 + $5,000,000)/2 = $6,000,000
  2017: ($8,420,000 + $7,000,000)/2 = $7,710,000

Net income less preferred dividends—or "income available to common" as it is called—can be found by referring to net income on the income statement and to preferred dividends on the statement of retained earnings. The combined statement of income and retained earnings in Example 13-2 gives the relevant amounts for the numerator. Henderson's return on equity for the two years is as follows:

2017	2016
$\dfrac{\$1,720,000 - \$50,000}{\$7,710,000} = 21.66\%$	$\dfrac{\$2,300,000 - \$50,000}{\$6,000,000} = 37.50\%$

Even though Henderson's return on stockholders' equity ratio decreased significantly from one year to the next, most stockholders would be very happy to achieve these returns on their money. Very few investments offer more than 10% return unless substantial risk is involved.

Return on Assets, Return on Equity, and Leverage

The return on assets for 2017 was 11.8%. But the return to the common stockholders was much higher: 21.7%. How do you explain this phenomenon? Why are the stockholders receiving a higher return on their money than all of the providers of money combined are getting? A partial answer to those questions can be found by reviewing the cost of the various sources of capital.

Example 13-1 indicates that notes, bonds, and preferred stock are the primary sources of capital other than common stock. (Accounts payable and taxes payable are *not* included because they represent interest-free loans to the company from suppliers and the government.) These sources and the average amount of each outstanding during 2017 follow:

	Account Balances at December 31		
	2017	2016	Average
Notes payable	$ 600,000	$ 800,000	$ 700,000
Current portion of bonds	100,000	100,000	100,000
Bonds payable—Long-term	700,000	800,000	750,000
Total liabilities	$1,400,000	$1,700,000	$1,550,000
Preferred stock	$ 500,000	$ 500,000	$ 500,000

What was the cost to Henderson of each of these sources? The cost of the money provided by the preferred stockholders is clearly the amount of dividends of $50,000. The cost as a percentage is $50,000/$500,000, or 10%. The average cost of the borrowed money can be approximated by dividing the 2017 interest expense of $140,000 by the average of the notes payable and bonds payable of $1,550,000. The result is an average cost of these two sources of $140,000/$1,550,000, or approximately 9%.

Leverage
The use of borrowed funds and amounts contributed by preferred stockholders to earn an overall return higher than the cost of these funds.

The concept of **leverage** refers to the practice of using borrowed funds and amounts received from preferred stockholders in an attempt to earn an overall return that is higher than the cost of these funds. Recall the rate of return on assets for 2017: 11.8%. Because this return is on an after-tax basis, it is necessary for comparative purposes to convert the average cost of borrowed funds to an after-tax basis. Although we computed an average cost for borrowed money of 9%, the actual cost of the borrowed money is 5.4% [9% × (100% − 40%)] after taxes. Because dividends are *not* tax-deductible, the cost of the money provided by preferred stockholders is 10%, as calculated earlier.

Has Henderson successfully employed favorable leverage? That is, has it been able to earn an overall rate of return on assets that is higher than the amounts that it must pay creditors and preferred stockholders? Henderson has been successful in using outside money: neither of the sources must be paid a rate in excess of the 11.8% overall rate on assets used. Henderson has also been able to borrow some amounts on an interest-free basis. As mentioned earlier, the accounts payable and taxes payable represent interest-free loans from suppliers and the government, although the loans are typically for a short period of time, such as 30 days.

In summary, the excess of the 21.7% return on equity over the 11.8% return on assets indicates that Henderson's management has been successful in employing leverage. Is it possible to be unsuccessful in this pursuit; that is, can there be unfavorable leverage? If the company must pay more for the amounts provided by creditors and preferred stockholders than it can earn overall, as indicated by the return on assets, there will, in fact, be unfavorable leverage. This may occur when interest requirements are high and net income is low. A company would likely have a high debt-to-equity ratio as well when there is unfavorable leverage.

Earnings per Share

Earnings per share (EPS)
A company's bottom line stated on a per-share basis.

Earnings per share (EPS) is one of the most quoted statistics for publicly traded companies. Stockholders and potential investors want to know what their share of profits is, not just the total dollar amount. Presentation of profits on a per-share basis also allows the stockholder to relate earnings to what he or she paid for a share of stock or to the current trading price of a share of stock.

In simple situations, earnings per share is as follows:

$$\text{Earnings per Share} = \frac{\text{Net Income} - \text{Preferred Dividends}}{\text{Weighted Average Number of Common Shares Outstanding}}$$

EXAMPLE 13-21 Computing Earnings per Share

Because Henderson had 1,000,000 shares of common stock outstanding throughout both 2016 and 2017, its EPS for each of the two years is as follows:

2017	2016
$\dfrac{\$1{,}720{,}000 - \$50{,}000}{1{,}000{,}000 \text{ shares}} = \$1.67 \text{ per share}$	$\dfrac{\$2{,}300{,}000 - \$50{,}000}{1{,}000{,}000 \text{ shares}} = \$2.25 \text{ per share}$

A number of complications can arise in the computation of EPS, and the calculations can become exceedingly complex for a company with many different types of securities in its capital structure. These complications are beyond the scope of this book and are discussed in more advanced accounting courses.

Price/Earnings Ratio

Earnings per share is an important ratio for an investor because of its relationship to dividends and market price. Stockholders hope to earn a return by receiving periodic dividends or eventually selling the stock for more than they paid for it or both. Although earnings are related to dividends and market price, the latter two are of primary interest to the stockholder.

Now that we have stated Henderson's earnings on a per-share basis, we can calculate the **price/earnings (P/E) ratio**. What market price is relevant? Should we use the market price that the investor paid for a share of stock, or should we use the current market price? Because earnings are based on the most recent evaluation of the company for accounting purposes, it seems logical to use current market price, which is based on the stock market's current assessment of the company. Therefore, the ratio is as follows:

Price/earnings (P/E) ratio
The relationship between a company's performance according to the income statement and its performance in the stock market.

$$\text{Price/Earnings Ratio} = \frac{\text{Current Market Price}}{\text{Earnings per Share}}$$

EXAMPLE 13-22 Computing the Price/Earnings Ratio

Assume that the current market price for Henderson's common stock is $15 per share at the end of 2017 and $18 per share at the end of 2016. The price/earnings ratio for each of the two years is as follows:

2017	2016
$\dfrac{\$15 \text{ per share}}{\$1.67 \text{ per share}} = 9 \text{ to } 1$	$\dfrac{\$18 \text{ per share}}{\$2.25 \text{ per share}} = 8 \text{ to } 1$

What is normal for a P/E ratio? The P/E ratio compares the stock market's assessment of a company's performance with the company's success as reflected on the income statement. A relatively high P/E ratio may indicate that a stock is overpriced by the market; a P/E ratio that is relatively low could indicate that a stock is underpriced.

The P/E ratio is often thought to indicate the "quality" of a company's earnings. For example, assume that two companies have identical EPS ratios of $2 per share. Why should investors be willing to pay $20 per share (or 10 times earnings) for the stock of one company but only $14 per share (or 7 times earnings) for the stock of the other company? First, we must realize that many factors in addition to the reported earnings of the company affect market prices. General economic conditions, the outlook for the particular industry, and pending lawsuits are just three factors that can affect the trading price of a company's stock. The difference in P/E ratios for the two companies may reflect the market's assessment of the accounting practices of the companies, however. Assume that the company with a market price of $20 per share uses LIFO in valuing inventory and that the company trading at $14 per share uses FIFO. The difference in prices may indicate that investors believe that even though the companies have the same

EPS, the LIFO company is "better off" because it will have a lower amount of taxes to pay. (Recall that in a period of inflation, the use of LIFO results in more cost of goods sold, less income, and therefore lower income taxes.) Finally, also consider that, to a large extent, earnings reflect the use of historical costs, as opposed to fair market values, in assigning values to assets. Investors must consider the extent to which a company's assets are worth more than what was paid for them.

Dividend Ratios

Dividend payout ratio
The percentage of earnings paid out as dividends.

Two ratios are used to evaluate a company's dividend policies: the *dividend payout ratio* and the *dividend yield ratio*. The **dividend payout ratio** is the ratio of the common dividends per share to the earnings per share:

$$\text{Dividend Payout Ratio} = \frac{\text{Common Dividends per Share}}{\text{Earnings per Share}}$$

EXAMPLE 13-23 Computing and Interpreting the Dividend Payout Ratio

Example 13-2 indicates that Henderson paid $250,000 in common dividends each year, or with 1 million shares outstanding, $0.25 per share. The two payout ratios are as follows:

2017	2016
$\frac{\$0.25}{\$1.67} = 15.0\%$	$\frac{\$0.25}{\$2.25} = 11.1\%$

Henderson's management was faced with an important financial policy decision in 2017. Should the company maintain the same dividend of $0.25 per share even though EPS dropped significantly? Many companies prefer to maintain a level dividend pattern, hoping that a drop in earnings is only temporary.

Dividend yield ratio
The relationship between dividends and the market price of a company's stock.

The second dividend ratio of interest to stockholders is the **dividend yield ratio**. It is the ratio of common dividends per share to the market price per share.

$$\text{Dividend Yield Ratio} = \frac{\text{Common Dividends per Share}}{\text{Market Price per Share}}$$

EXAMPLE 13-24 Computing and Interpreting the Dividend Yield Ratio

The yield to Henderson's stockholders would be calculated as follows:

2017	2016
$\frac{\$0.25}{\$15} = 1.7\%$	$\frac{\$0.25}{\$18} = 1.4\%$

As shown, Henderson common stock does not provide a high yield to its investors. The relationship between the dividends and the market price indicates that investors buy the stock for reasons other than the periodic dividend return.

The dividend yield is very important to investors who depend on dividend checks to pay their living expenses. Utility stocks are popular among retirees because these shares have dividend yields as high as 5%. That is considered a good investment with relatively low risk and some opportunity for gains in the stock price. On the other hand, investors who want to put money into growing companies are willing to forego dividends if it means the potential for greater price appreciation.

Summary of Selected Financial Ratios

Exhibit 13-3 summarizes the ratios discussed in this chapter. Keep in mind that this list is not all-inclusive and that certain ratios used by analysts and others may be specific to a particular industry or type of business.

EXHIBIT 13-3 Summary of Selected Financial Ratios

Liquidity Analysis

Working capital

Current Assets − Current Liabilities

Current ratio

$$\frac{\text{Current Assets}}{\text{Current Liabilities}}$$

Acid-test ratio (quick ratio)

$$\frac{\text{Cash + Marketable Securities + Current Receivables}}{\text{Current Liabilities}}$$

Cash flow from operations to current liabilities ratio

$$\frac{\text{Net Cash Provided by Operating Activities}}{\text{Average Current Liabilities}}$$

Accounts receivable turnover ratio

$$\frac{\text{Net Credit Sales}}{\text{Average Accounts Receivable}}$$

Number of days' sales in receivables

$$\frac{\text{Number of Days in the Period}}{\text{Accounts Receivable Turnover}}$$

Inventory turnover ratio

$$\frac{\text{Cost of Goods Sold}}{\text{Average Inventory}}$$

Number of days' sales in inventory

$$\frac{\text{Number of Days in the Period}}{\text{Inventory Turnover}}$$

Cash-to-cash operating cycle

Number of Days' Sales in Inventory + Number of Days' Sales in Receivables

Solvency Analysis

Debt-to-equity ratio

$$\frac{\text{Total Liabilities}}{\text{Total Stockholders' Equity}}$$

Times interest earned ratio

$$\frac{\text{Net Income + Interest Expense + Income Tax Expense}}{\text{Interest Expense}}$$

Debt service coverage ratio

$$\frac{\text{Cash Flow from Operations before Interest and Tax Payments}}{\text{Interest and Principal Payments}}$$

Cash flow from operations to capital expenditures ratio

$$\frac{\text{Cash Flow from Operations − Total Dividends Paid}}{\text{Cash Paid for Acquisitions}}$$

Profitability Analysis

Gross profit ratio

$$\frac{\text{Gross Profit}}{\text{Net Sales}}$$

Profit margin ratio

$$\frac{\text{Net Income}}{\text{Net Sales}}$$

Return on assets ratio

$$\frac{\text{Net Income + Interest Expense, Net of Tax}}{\text{Average Total Assets}}$$

Return on sales ratio

$$\frac{\text{Net Income + Interest Expense, Net of Tax}}{\text{Net Sales}}$$

Asset turnover ratio

$$\frac{\text{Net Sales}}{\text{Average Total Assets}}$$

Return on common stockholders' equity ratio

$$\frac{\text{Net Income − Preferred Dividends}}{\text{Average Common Stockholders' Equity}}$$

Earnings per share

$$\frac{\text{Net Income − Preferred Dividends}}{\text{Weighted Average Number of Common Shares Outstanding}}$$

Price/earnings ratio

$$\frac{\text{Current Market Price}}{\text{Earnings per Share}}$$

Dividend payout ratio

$$\frac{\text{Common Dividends per Share}}{\text{Earnings per Share}}$$

Dividend yield ratio

$$\frac{\text{Common Dividends per Share}}{\text{Market Price per Share}}$$

MODULE 4 TEST YOURSELF

Review	**LO6** Compute and use various ratios to assess profitability.	• Profitability concerns the ability of management to use a company's resources to earn a return on funds invested. Measures of profitability include: • Return on assets, return on common stockholders' equity, earnings per share, price/earnings, dividend payout, and dividend yield ratios.

Question	1. The rate of return on assets ratio is computed by dividing net income and interest expense, net of tax, by average total assets. Why is the numerator net income and interest expense, net of tax, rather than just net income?
	2. A company has a return on assets of 14% and a return on common stockholders' equity of 11%. The president of the company has asked you to explain the reason for this difference. What causes the difference? How is the concept of financial leverage involved?
	3. What is meant by the "quality" of a company's earnings? Explain why the price/earnings ratio for a company may indicate the quality of earnings.

Apply	1. A company reported net income during the year of $90,000 and paid dividends of $15,000 to its common stockholders and $10,000 to its preferred stockholders. During the year, 20,000 shares of common stock were outstanding and 10,000 shares of preferred stock were outstanding. Compute the earnings per share for the year.
	2. For each of the following ratios, indicate what adjustment must be made to net income in the numerator and whether the adjustment is an addition to (A) or a deduction from (D) net income.

Ratio	Adjustment to Net Income in Numerator (A) or (D)
Return on assets	_____
Return on common stockholders' equity	_____
Earnings per share	_____
Return on sales	_____

Answers are located at the end of the chapter.

KEY TERMS QUIZ

Because of the number of terms introduced in this chapter, there are two quizzes on key terms. For each quiz, read each definition below and write the number of that definition in the blank beside the appropriate term. The quiz solutions appear at the end of the chapter.

Quiz 1:

_____	Horizontal analysis	_____	Cash flow from operations to current liabilities ratio
_____	Vertical analysis		
_____	Gross profit ratio	_____	Accounts receivable turnover ratio
_____	Profit margin ratio		
_____	Liquidity	_____	Number of days' sales in receivables
_____	Working capital	_____	Inventory turnover ratio
_____	Current ratio	_____	Number of days' sales in inventory
_____	Acid-test or quick ratio	_____	Cash-to-cash operating cycle

1. A stricter test of liquidity than the current ratio; excludes inventory and prepayments from the numerator.
2. Current assets minus current liabilities.
3. The ratio of current assets to current liabilities.
4. A measure of the average age of accounts receivable.
5. A measure of the ability to pay current debts from operating cash flows.
6. A measure of the number of times accounts receivable are collected in a period.
7. A measure of how long it takes to sell inventory.
8. The length of time from the purchase of inventory to the collection of any receivable from the sale.
9. A measure of the number of times inventory is sold during a period.
10. Gross profit to net sales.
11. A comparison of various financial statement items within a single period with the use of common-size statements.
12. Net income to net sales.
13. The nearness to cash of the assets and liabilities.
14. A comparison of financial statement items over a period of time.

Quiz 2:

_____ Solvency
_____ Debt-to-equity ratio
_____ Times interest earned ratio
_____ Debt service coverage ratio
_____ Cash flow from operations to capital expenditures ratio
_____ Profitability
_____ Return on assets ratio
_____ Return on sales ratio

_____ Asset turnover ratio
_____ Return on common stockholders' equity ratio
_____ Leverage
_____ Earnings per share (EPS)
_____ Price/earnings (P/E) ratio
_____ Dividend payout ratio
_____ Dividend yield ratio

1. A measure of a company's success in earning a return for the common stockholders.
2. The relationship between a company's performance according to the income statement and its performance in the stock market.
3. The ability of a company to remain in business over the long term.
4. A variation of the profit margin ratio; measures earnings before payments to creditors.
5. A company's bottom line stated on a per-share basis.
6. The percentage of earnings paid out as dividends.
7. The ratio of total liabilities to total stockholders' equity.
8. A measure of the ability of a company to finance long-term asset acquisitions with cash from operations.
9. A measure of a company's success in earning a return for all providers of capital.
10. The relationship between net sales and average total assets.
11. The relationship between dividends and the market price of a company's stock.
12. The use of borrowed funds and amounts contributed by preferred stockholders to earn an overall return higher than the cost of these funds.
13. An income statement measure of the ability of a company to meet its interest payments.
14. A statement of cash flows measure of the ability of a company to meet its interest and principal payments.
15. How well management is using company resources to earn a return on the funds invested by various groups.

ALTERNATE TERMS

acid-test ratio quick ratio
horizontal analysis trend analysis

number of days' sales in receivables average collection period
price/earnings ratio P/E ratio

REVIEW PROBLEM

REAL WORLD

On pages 650–652 are three comparative financial statements for **lululemon athletica inc.**, as shown in its 2015 Form 10-K. The 2015 fiscal year ends on January 31, 2016, and the 2014 fiscal year ends on February 1, 2015.

Required

1. Compute the following ratios for the years ended January 31, 2016, and February 1, 2015, or as of the end of those two years, as appropriate. Beginning balances for the year ended February 1, 2015, are not available; that is, you do not have a balance sheet as of February 2, 2014. Therefore, to be consistent, use year-end balances for both years where you would normally use average amounts for the year. Finally, note that the company does not report interest expense separately on its income statement. Ignore any interest expense in computing the return on assets ratio.

    a. Current ratio
    b. Quick ratio
    c. Cash flow from operations to current liabilities ratio
    d. Number of days' sales in receivables
    e. Number of days' sales in inventory
    f. Return on assets ratio
    g. Return on common stockholders' equity ratio

2. Comment on lululemon's liquidity. Has it improved or declined over the two-year period?
3. Comment on lululemon's profitability. Would you buy stock in the company? Why or why not?

lululemon athletica inc.
CONSOLIDATED BALANCE SHEETS
(Amounts in thousands, except per share amounts)

	January 31, 2016	February 1, 2015
ASSETS		
Current assets		
Cash and cash equivalents	$ 501,482	$ 664,479
Accounts receivable	13,108	13,746
Inventories	284,009	208,116
Prepaid and receivable income taxes	91,453	40,547
Other prepaid expenses and other current assets	26,987	24,124
	917,039	951,012
Property and equipment, net	349,605	296,008
Goodwill and intangible assets, net	24,777	26,163
Deferred income tax assets	11,802	16,018
Other non-current assets	10,854	7,012
	$1,314,077	$1,296,213
LIABILITIES AND STOCKHOLDERS' EQUITY		
Current liabilities		
Accounts payable	$ 10,381	$ 9,339
Accrued inventory liabilities	25,451	22,296
Accrued compensation and related expenses	43,524	29,932
Income taxes payable	37,736	20,073
Unredeemed gift card liability	57,736	46,252
Other accrued liabilities	50,676	31,989
	225,504	159,881
Deferred income tax liabilities	10,759	3,633
Other non-current liabilities	50,332	43,131
	286,595	206,645

	January 31, 2016	February 1, 2015
Stockholders' equity		
Undesignated preferred stock, $0.01 par value: 5,000 shares authorized; none issued and outstanding	—	—
Exchangeable stock, no par value: 60,000 shares authorized; 9,804 and 9,833 issued and outstanding	—	—
Special voting stock, $0.000005 par value: 60,000 shares authorized; 9,804 and 9,833 issued and outstanding	—	—
Common stock, $0.005 par value: 400,000 shares authorized; 127,482 and 132,112 issued and outstanding	637	661
Additional paid-in capital	245,533	241,695
Retained earnings	1,019,515	1,020,619
Accumulated other comprehensive loss	(238,203)	(173,407)
	1,027,482	1,089,568
	$1,314,077	$1,296,213

See accompanying notes to the consolidated financial statements

lululemon athletica inc.
CONSOLIDATED STATEMENTS OF OPERATIONS AND COMPREHENSIVE INCOME
(Amounts in thousands, except per share amounts)

	Fiscal Year Ended		
	January 31, 2016	February 1, 2015	February 2, 2014
Net revenue	$2,060,523	$1,797,213	$1,591,188
Cost of goods sold	1,063,357	883,033	751,112
Gross profit	997,166	914,180	840,076
Selling, general and administrative expenses	628,090	538,147	448,718
Income from operations	369,076	376,033	391,358
Other (expense) income, net	(581)	7,102	5,768
Income before income tax expense	368,495	383,135	397,126
Income tax expense	102,448	144,102	117,579
Net income	$ 266,047	$ 239,033	$ 279,547
Other comprehensive loss:			
Foreign currency translation adjustment	(64,796)	(105,339)	(89,158)
Comprehensive income	$ 201,251	$ 133,694	$ 190,389
Basic earnings per share	$ 1.90	$ 1.66	$ 1.93
Diluted earnings per share	$ 1.89	$ 1.66	$ 1.91
Basic weighted-average number of shares outstanding	140,365	143,935	144,913
Diluted weighted-average number of shares outstanding	140,610	144,298	146,043

See accompanying notes to the consolidated financial statements

lululemon athletica inc.
CONSOLIDATED STATEMENTS OF CASH FLOWS
(Amounts in thousands)

	Fiscal Year Ended		
	January 31, 2016	February 1, 2015	February 2, 2014
Cash flows from operating activities			
Net income	$ 266,047	$ 239,033	$ 279,547
Items not affecting cash			
Depreciation and amortization	73,383	58,364	49,068

(Continued)

	Fiscal Year Ended		
	January 31, 2016	February 1, 2015	February 2, 2014
Stock-based compensation expense	10,356	8,269	10,087
Derecognition of unredeemed gift card liability	(3,647)	(1,468)	(4,654)
Deferred income taxes	11,142	2,087	820
Tax benefits from stock-based compensation	1,202	(413)	(6,457)
Changes in operating assets and liabilities			
Inventories	(83,286)	(26,806)	(38,507)
Prepaid and receivable income taxes	(52,110)	(15,234)	3,067
Other prepaid expenses and other current assets	(3,816)	(6,444)	(13,939)
Accounts payable	1,247	(2,198)	11,627
Accrued inventory liabilities	5,198	8,276	6,985
Accrued compensation and related expenses	14,937	11,561	(6,282)
Income taxes payable	19,470	19,304	(35,075)
Unredeemed gift card liability	16,574	11,326	9,306
Other accrued liabilities	19,563	3,788	7,998
Other non-current assets and liabilities	2,480	5,004	4,748
Net cash provided by operating activities	298,740	314,449	278,339
Cash flows from investing activities			
Purchase of property and equipment	(143,487)	(119,733)	(106,408)
Net cash used in investing activities	(143,487)	(119,733)	(106,408)
Cash flows from financing activities			
Proceeds from settlement of stock-based compensation	4,704	2,913	8,171
Tax benefits from stock-based compensation	(1,202)	413	6,457
Taxes paid related to net share settlement of stock-based compensation	(2,857)	(4,972)	(5,721)
Repurchase of common stock	(274,193)	(147,431)	—
Registration fees associated with prospectus supplement	(145)	—	—
Net cash (used in) provided by financing activities	(273,693)	(149,077)	8,907
Effect of exchange rate changes on cash	(44,557)	(79,809)	(72,368)
(Decrease) increase in cash and cash equivalents	(162,997)	(34,170)	108,470
Cash and cash equivalents, beginning of period	$ 664,479	$ 698,649	$ 590,179
Cash and cash equivalents, end of period	$ 501,482	$ 664,479	$ 698,649

See accompanying notes to the consolidated financial statements

Solution to Review Problem

1. Ratios:
    Notes: 2015 is the fiscal year ended January 31, 2016, and 2014 is the fiscal year ended February 1, 2015.

    a. 2015: $917,039/$225,504 = 4.07
        2014: $951,012/$159,881 = 5.95
    b. 2015: ($501,482 + $13,108)/$225,504 = 2.28
        2014: ($664,479 + $13,746)/$159,881 = 4.24
    c. 2015: $298,740/$225,504 = 1.32
        2014: $314,449/$159,881 = 1.97
    d. 2015: 360 days/[($2,060,523/$13,108)] = 2.29 days
        2014: 360 days/[($1,797,213/$13,746)] = 2.75 days
    e. 2015: 360 days/[($1,063,357/$284,009)] = 96.15 days
        2014: 360 days/[($883,033/$208,116)] = 84.85 days

f.   2015: $266,047/$1,314,077 = <u>20.25%</u>

    2014: $239,033/$1,296,213 = <u>18.44%</u>

g.   2015: $266,047/$1,027,482 = <u>25.89%</u>

    2014: $239,033/$1,089,568 = <u>21.94%</u>

2. Both the current ratio and the quick ratio declined over the two-year period, as did cash flow from operations to current liabilities. Even with the declines in these ratios, the company appears to be liquid and able to meet its short-term obligations. The number of days' sales in inventory for 2015 of 96 days means that the company turns its inventory over about every three months.

3. The return on assets for 2015 is over 20%, and the return on common stockholders' equity is nearly 26%. Both ratios improved from the prior year and indicate a high level of profitability. It should be noted that the company did not pay dividends in either of the two years and therefore would not be a good investment for those who want periodic dividend receipts. Lululemon appears to be a very sound investment, but many other factors, including information on the current market price of the stock, should be considered before making a decision.

EXERCISES

Exercise 13-1 Working Backward: Current Ratio

LO4

EXAMPLE 13-7

Cass Corp.'s December 31, 2016, balance sheet reported current assets of $120,000 and current liabilities of $100,000. The current ratio increased by 25% one year later, on December 31, 2017. Current liabilities on this date were $140,000. Determine current assets on December 31, 2017.

Exercise 13-2 Accounts Receivable Analysis

LO4

EXAMPLE 13-10

The following account balances are taken from the records of the Faraway Travel Agency:

	December 31		
	2017	**2016**	**2015**
Accounts receivable	$150,000	$100,000	$80,000

	2017	**2016**
Net credit sales	$600,000	$540,000

Faraway extends credit terms requiring full payment in 60 days, with no discount for early payment.

Required

1. Compute Faraway's accounts receivable turnover ratio for 2017 and 2016.
2. Compute the number of days' sales in receivables for 2017 and 2016. Assume 360 days in a year.
3. Comment on the efficiency of Faraway's collection efforts over the two-year period.

Exercise 13-3 Working Backward: Accounts Receivable Analysis

LO4

EXAMPLE 13-10

Adair Corp. is concerned because the average time to collect its accounts receivable was 15 days longer than its normal credit terms of net 30. Adair reported the following in the Current Assets section of its comparative balance sheets:

	12/31/17	12/31/16
Current Assets:		
Accounts receivable	$115,000	$85,000

Assuming 360 days in a year, determine Adair's net credit sales for 2017.

LO4

EXAMPLE 13-11

Exercise 13-4 Inventory Analysis

The following account balances are taken from the records of Lewis Inc., a wholesaler of fresh fruits and vegetables:

	December 31		
	2017	**2016**	**2015**
Merchandise inventory	$200,000	$150,000	$120,000
	2017	**2016**	
Cost of goods sold	$7,100,000	$8,100,000	

Required

1. Compute Lewis's inventory turnover ratio for 2017 and 2016.
2. Compute the number of days' sales in inventory for 2017 and 2016. Assume 360 days in a year.
3. Comment on your answers in parts (1) and (2) relative to the company's management of inventory over the two years. What problems do you see in its inventory management?

LO4

EXAMPLE 13-10, 13-11, 13-12

REAL WORLD

Show me how

Exercise 13-5 Accounts Receivable and Inventory Analyses for Kellogg's and General Mills

The following information was obtained from the fiscal year 2015 and 2014 financial statements included in Form 10-K of **Kellogg Company and Subsidiaries** and **General Mills, Inc. and Subsidiaries**. (Year-ends for Kellogg's are January 2, 2016, and January 3, 2015, and for General Mills are May 31, 2015, and May 25, 2014.) Assume all sales are on credit for both companies.

(in millions)			Kellogg's	General Mills
Accounts receivable, net[a]	End of	2015	$ 1,344	$ 1,386.7
	End of	2014	1,276	1,483.6
Inventories	End of	2015	1,250	1,540.9
	End of	2014	1,279	1,559.4
Net sales		2015	13,525	17,630.3
		2014	14,580	17,909.6
Cost of goods sold[b]		2015	8,844	11,681.1
		2014	9,517	11,539.8

[a]Described as "receivables" by General Mills.
[b]Described as "cost of sales" by General Mills.

Required

1. Using the information provided, compute the following for each company for 2015:
   a. Accounts receivable turnover ratio
   b. Number of days' sales in receivables
   c. Inventory turnover ratio
   d. Number of days' sales in inventory
   e. Cash-to-cash operating cycle
2. Comment briefly on the liquidity of each of these two companies.

LO4

EXAMPLE 13-7, 13-8, 13-9

REAL WORLD

Exercise 13-6 Liquidity Analyses for Kellogg's and General Mills

The following information was summarized from the balance sheets included in the Form 10-K for the 2015 fiscal year of **Kellogg Company and Subsidiaries** at January 2, 2016, and **General Mills, Inc. and Subsidiaries** at May 31, 2015:

(in millions)	Kellogg's	General Mills
Cash and cash equivalents	$ 251	$ 334.2
Accounts receivable, net*	1,344	1,386.7
Inventories	1,250	1,540.9
Deferred income taxes		100.1

(in millions)	Kellogg's	General Mills
Prepaid expenses and other current assets**	391	423.8
Total current assets	$3,236	$3,785.7
Total current liabilities	$5,739	$4,890.1

*Described as "receivables" by General Mills.
**Described as "other current assets" by Kellogg's.

Required

1. Using the information provided, compute the following for each company at the end of the 2015 fiscal years.

    a. Current ratio
    b. Quick ratio

2. Kellogg's reported net cash provided by operating activities of $1,691 million during 2015. General Mills reported net cash provided by operating activities of $2,542.8 million. Total current liabilities reported by Kellogg's at January 3, 2015, and General Mills at May 25, 2014, were $4,364 million and $5,423.5 million, respectively. Compute the cash flow from operations to current liabilities ratio for each company for 2015.

3. Comment briefly on the liquidity of each of these two companies. Which appears to be more liquid?

4. What other ratios would help you more fully assess the liquidity of these companies?

Exercise 13-7 Liquidity Analyses for McDonald's and Wendy's

LO4
EXAMPLE 13-6, 13-7, 13-8

The following information was summarized from the balance sheets included in Form 10-K of **McDonald's Corporation** at December 31, 2015, and **The Wendy's Company and Subsidiaries** at January 3, 2016.

REAL WORLD

	McDonald's (in millions)	Wendy's (in thousands)
Current Assets:		
Cash and cash equivalents*	$ 7,685.5	$ 327,216
Accounts and notes receivable	1,298.7	104,854
Inventories	100.1	4,312
Prepaid expenses and other current assets	558.7	112,788
Advertising funds restricted assets		67,399
Total current assets	$ 9,643.0	$ 616,569
Total current liabilities	$ 2,950.4	$ 268,774
Total noncurrent liabilities	$27,900.4	$3,087,032
Total shareholders' equity**	$ 7,087.9	$ 752,914

*Described as "Cash and equivalents" by McDonald's.
**Described as "Stockholders' equity" by Wendy's.

Required

1. Using the information provided, compute the following for each company at year-end:

    a. Working capital
    b. Current ratio
    c. Quick ratio

2. Comment briefly on the liquidity of each of these two companies. Which appears to be more liquid?

Exercise 13-8 Solvency Analyses for Nordstrom, Inc.

LO5
EXAMPLE 13-13, 13-14, 13-15, 13-16

The following information was obtained from the comparative financial statements included in **Nordstrom**'s Form 10-K for its 2015 fiscal year. (All amounts are in millions of dollars.)

	January 30, 2016	January 31, 2015
Total assets	$7,698	$9,245
Total shareholders' equity	871	2,440

REAL WORLD

(Continued)

	For the Years Ended	
	January 30, 2016	**January 31, 2015**
Interest expense, net	$ 125	$ 138
Cash paid during the year for interest, net of capitalized interest	136	152
Income tax expense	376	465
Cash paid during the year for income taxes, net of refunds	383	391
Net earnings	600	720
Net cash provided by operating activities	2,451	1,220
Cash dividends paid	1,185	251
Capital expenditures	1,082	861
Principal payments on long-term borrowings	8	7

Required

1. Using the information provided, compute the following for the years ended January 30, 2016, and January 31, 2015:

   a. Debt-to-equity ratio (at each year-end)
   b. Times interest earned ratio
   c. Debt service coverage ratio
   d. Cash flow from operations to capital expenditures ratio

2. Comment briefly on the company's solvency.

LO5   ## Exercise 13-9 Solvency Analysis

EXAMPLE 13-13, 13-14, 13-15

The following information is available from the balance sheets at the ends of the two most recent years and the income statement for the most recent year of Impact Company:

	December 31	
	2017	**2016**
Accounts payable	$ 65,000	$ 50,000
Accrued liabilities	25,000	35,000
Taxes payable	60,000	45,000
Short-term notes payable	0	75,000
Bonds payable due within next year	200,000	200,000
Total current liabilities	$ 350,000	$ 405,000
Bonds payable	$ 600,000	$ 800,000
Common stock, $10 par	$1,000,000	$1,000,000
Retained earnings	650,000	500,000
Total stockholders' equity	$1,650,000	$1,500,000
Total liabilities and stockholders' equity	$2,600,000	$2,705,000

	2017
Sales revenue	$1,600,000
Cost of goods sold	950,000
Gross profit	$ 650,000
Selling and administrative expense	300,000
Operating income	$ 350,000
Interest expense	89,000
Income before tax	$ 261,000
Income tax expense	111,000
Net income	$ 150,000

Other Information

a. Short-term notes payable represents a 12-month loan that matured in November 2017. Interest of 12% was paid at maturity.

b. One million dollars of serial bonds had been issued ten years earlier. The first series of $200,000 matured at the end of 2017, with interest of 8% payable annually.
c. Cash flow from operations was $185,000 in 2017. The amounts of interest and taxes paid during 2017 were $89,000 and $96,000, respectively.

Required

1. Compute the following for Impact Company:

   a. The debt-to-equity ratio at December 31, 2017, and December 31, 2016
   b. The times interest earned ratio for 2017
   c. The debt service coverage ratio for 2017

2. Comment on Impact's solvency at the end of 2017. Do the times interest earned ratio and the debt service coverage ratio differ in their indication of Impact's ability to pay its debts? Explain.

Exercise 13-10 Working Backward: Debt Service Coverage

LO5
EXAMPLE 13-15

Madison Corp. reported the following in the Current Assets section of its comparative balance sheets:

	December 31, 2017	December 31, 2016
Current Liabilities:		
Current portion of notes payable	$400,000	$600,000

Supplemental information at the bottom of Madison's 2017 statement of cash flows was as follows:

	2017	2016
Interest paid	$135,000	$155,000
Income taxes paid	550,000	425,000

Madison's 2017 debt service coverage ratio was 20 to 1. Determine Madison's cash flow from operations for 2017.

Exercise 13-11 Profitability Analysis for Apple, Inc.

LO6
EXAMPLE 13-20

For the year ended September 26, 2015, **Apple, Inc.**, reported net income of $53,394 million. Total shareholders' equity on this date was $119,355 million, and on September 27, 2014, it was $111,547 million. No preferred stock was outstanding in either year.

REAL WORLD

Required

1. Compute Apple's return on common stockholders' equity for the year ended September 26, 2015.
2. What other ratio would you want to compute to decide whether Apple is successfully employing leverage? Explain your answer.

Exercise 13-12 Working Backward: Profitability Analysis

LO6
EXAMPLE 13-19

Murphy Company's total liabilities on December 31, 2017, amounted to $1,500,000. The debt-to-equity ratio on this date was 1.5 to 1. Net income for 2017 was $250,000, and the profit margin was 5%.

Required

1. Determine Murphy's net sales for 2017.
2. Determine Murphy's total assets on December 31, 2017.
3. Determine Murphy's asset turnover ratio for 2017, using year-end total assets, rather than average total assets.

Exercise 13-13 Return on Stockholders' Equity

LO6
EXAMPLE 13-20

Rogers Inc. had 500,000 shares of $2 par common stock outstanding at the end of both 2016 and 2017. Retained earnings at the end of 2016 amounted to $1,800,000. No dividends were paid during 2017, and net income for the year was $400,000. Determine Rogers' return on stockholders' equity for 2017.

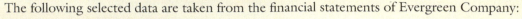

LO6

EXAMPLE 13-17, 13-18, 13-19, 13-20

Exercise 13-14 Return Ratios and Leverage

The following selected data are taken from the financial statements of Evergreen Company:

Sales revenue	$ 650,000
Cost of goods sold	400,000
Gross profit	$ 250,000
Selling and administrative expense	100,000
Operating income	$ 150,000
Interest expense	50,000
Income before tax	$ 100,000
Income tax expense (40%)	40,000
Net income	$ 60,000
Accounts payable	$ 45,000
Accrued liabilities	70,000
Income taxes payable	10,000
Interest payable	25,000
Short-term loans payable	150,000
Total current liabilities	$ 300,000
Long-term bonds payable	$ 500,000
Preferred stock, 10%, $100 par	$ 250,000
Common stock, no par	600,000
Retained earnings	350,000
Total stockholders' equity	$1,200,000
Total liabilities and stockholders' equity	$2,000,000

Required

1. Compute the following ratios for Evergreen Company:

    a. Return on sales

    b. Asset turnover (Assume that total assets at the beginning of the year were $1,600,000.)

    c. Return on assets

    d. Return on common stockholders' equity (Assume that the only changes in stockholders' equity during the year were from the net income for the year and dividends on the preferred stock.)

2. Comment on Evergreen's use of leverage. Has it successfully employed leverage? Explain.

LO6

EXAMPLE 13-17, 13-18, 13-19

Exercise 13-15 Relationships among Return on Assets, Return on Sales, and Asset Turnover

A company's return on assets is a function of its ability to turn over its investment (asset turnover) and earn a profit on each dollar of sales (return on sales). For each of the following independent cases, determine the missing amounts. *(Note:* Assume in each case that the company has no interest expense; that is, net income is used as the definition of income in all calculations.)

Case 1

Net income	$ 10,000
Net sales	$ 80,000
Average total assets	$ 60,000
Return on assets	?

Case 2

Net income	$ 25,000
Average total assets	$ 250,000
Return on sales	2%
Net sales	?

Case 3

Average total assets	$ 80,000
Asset turnover	1.5 times

Return on sales	6%
Return on assets	?
Case 4	
Return on assets	10%
Net sales	$ 50,000
Asset turnover	1.25 times
Net income	?
Case 5	
Return on assets	15%
Net income	$ 20,000
Return on sales	5%
Average total assets	?

Exercise 13-16 EPS, P/E Ratio, and Dividend Ratios

LO6
EXAMPLE 13-21, 13-22,
13-23, 13-24

The Stockholders' Equity section of the balance sheet for Cooperstown Corp. at the end of 2017 appears as follows:

8%, $100 par, cumulative preferred stock, 200,000 shares authorized, 50,000 shares issued and outstanding	$ 5,000,000
Additional paid-in capital on preferred	2,500,000
Common stock, $5 par, 500,000 shares authorized, 400,000 shares issued and outstanding	2,000,000
Additional paid-in capital on common	18,000,000
Retained earnings	37,500,000
Total stockholders' equity	$65,000,000

Net income for the year was $1,300,000. Dividends were declared and paid on the preferred shares during the year, and a quarterly dividend of $0.40 per share was declared and paid each quarter on the common shares. The closing market price for the common shares on December 31, 2017, was $24.75 per share.

Required

1. Compute the following ratios for the common stock:
   a. Earnings per share
   b. Price/earnings ratio
   c. Dividend payout ratio
   d. Dividend yield ratio

2. Assume that you are an investment adviser. What other information would you want to have before advising a client regarding the purchase of Cooperstown stock?

MULTI-CONCEPT EXERCISES

Exercise 13-17 Common-Size Balance Sheets and Horizontal Analysis

LO2 • 3
EXAMPLE 13-1, 13-4

Comparative balance sheets for Farinet Company for the past two years are as follows:

	December 31	
	2017	**2016**
Cash	$ 16,000	$ 20,000
Accounts receivable	40,000	30,000
Inventory	30,000	50,000
Prepaid rent	18,000	12,000
Total current assets	$ 104,000	$112,000

(Continued)

	December 31	
	2017	**2016**
Land	$ 150,000	$150,000
Plant and equipment	800,000	600,000
Accumulated depreciation	(130,000)	(60,000)
Total long-term assets	$ 820,000	$690,000
Total assets	$ 924,000	$802,000
Accounts payable	$ 24,000	$ 20,000
Income taxes payable	6,000	10,000
Short-term notes payable	70,000	50,000
Total current liabilities	$ 100,000	$ 80,000
Bonds payable	$ 150,000	$200,000
Common stock	$ 400,000	$300,000
Retained earnings	274,000	222,000
Total stockholders' equity	$ 674,000	$522,000
Total liabilities and stockholders' equity	$ 924,000	$802,000

Required

1. Using the format in Example 13-4, prepare common-size comparative balance sheets for the two years for Farinet Company.
2. What observations can you make about changes in the relative composition of Farinet's accounts from the common-size balance sheets? List at least five observations.
3. Using the format in Example 13-1, prepare comparative balance sheets for Farinet Company, including columns for the dollars and for the percentage increase or decrease in each item on the statement.
4. Identify the five items on the balance sheet that experienced the largest change from one year to the next. For each of these items, explain where you would look to find additional information about the change.

LO2 • 3
EXAMPLE 13-2, 13-5

Exercise 13-18 Common-Size Income Statements and Horizontal Analysis

Income statements for Mariners Corp. for the past two years are as follows:

	(amounts in thousands of dollars)	
	2017	**2016**
Sales revenue	$60,000	$50,000
Cost of goods sold	42,000	30,000
Gross profit	$18,000	$20,000
Selling and administrative expense	9,000	5,000
Operating income	$ 9,000	$15,000
Interest expense	2,000	2,000
Income before tax	$ 7,000	$13,000
Income tax expense	2,000	4,000
Net income	$ 5,000	$ 9,000

Required

1. Using the format in Example 13-5, prepare common-size comparative income statements for the two years for Mariners Corp.
2. What observations can you make about the common-size statements? List at least four observations.
3. Using the format in Example 13-2, prepare comparative income statements for Mariners Corp., including columns for the dollars and for the percentage increase or decrease in each item on the statement.
4. Identify the two items on the income statement that experienced the largest change from one year to the next. For each of these items, explain where you would look to find additional information about the change.

PROBLEMS

Problem 13-1 Effect of Transactions on Working Capital, Current Ratio, and Quick Ratio

LO4

(*Note:* Consider completing Problem 13-2 after this problem to ensure that you obtain a clear understanding of the effect of various transactions on these measures of liquidity.) The following account balances are taken from the records of Liquiform Inc.:

Cash	$ 70,000
Short-term investments	60,000
Accounts receivable	80,000
Inventory	100,000
Prepaid insurance	10,000
Accounts payable	75,000
Taxes payable	25,000
Salaries and wages payable	40,000
Short-term loans payable	60,000

Required

1. Use the information provided to compute the amount of working capital and Liquiform's current and quick ratios (round to three decimal points).
2. Determine the effect that each of the following transactions will have on Liquiform's working capital, current ratio, and quick ratio by recalculating each and then indicating whether the measure is increased, decreased, or not affected by the transaction. (For the ratios, round to three decimal points.) Consider each transaction independently; that is, assume that it is the *only* transaction that takes place.

Transaction	Effect of Transaction on		
	Working Capital	Current Ratio	Quick Ratio
a. Purchased inventory on account, $20,000			
b. Purchased inventory for cash, $15,000			
c. Paid suppliers on account, $30,000			
d. Received cash on account, $40,000			
e. Paid insurance for next year, $20,000			
f. Made sales on account, $60,000			
g. Repaid short-term loans at bank, $25,000			
h. Borrowed $40,000 at bank for 90 days			
i. Declared and paid $45,000 cash dividend			
j. Purchased $20,000 of short-term investments			
k. Paid $30,000 in salaries			
l. Accrued additional $15,000 in taxes			

Problem 13-2 Effect of Transactions on Working Capital, Current Ratio, and Quick Ratio

LO4

(*Note:* Consider completing this problem after Problem 13-1 to ensure that you obtain a clear understanding of the effect of various transactions on these measures of liquidity.) The following account balances are taken from the records of Veriform Inc.:

Cash	$ 70,000
Short-term investments	60,000
Accounts receivable	80,000
Inventory	100,000
Prepaid insurance	10,000
Accounts payable	75,000
Taxes payable	25,000
Salaries and wages payable	40,000
Short-term loans payable	210,000

(*Continued*)

Required

1. Use the information provided to compute the amount of working capital and Veriform's current and quick ratios (round to three decimal points).
2. Determine the effect that each of the following transactions will have on Veriform's working capital, current ratio, and quick ratio by recalculating each and then indicating whether the measure is increased, decreased, or not affected by the transaction. (For the ratios, round to three decimal points.) Consider each transaction independently; that is, assume that it is the *only* transaction that takes place.

Transaction	Working Capital	Current Ratio	Quick Ratio
	Effect of Transaction on		
a. Purchased inventory on account, $20,000			
b. Purchased inventory for cash, $15,000			
c. Paid suppliers on account, $30,000			
d. Received cash on account, $40,000			
e. Paid insurance for next year, $20,000			
f. Made sales on account, $60,000			
g. Repaid short-term loans at bank, $25,000			
h. Borrowed $40,000 at bank for 90 days			
i. Declared and paid $45,000 cash dividend			
j. Purchased $20,000 of short-term investments			
k. Paid $30,000 in salaries			
l. Accrued additional $15,000 in taxes			

LO6 Problem 13-3 Goals for Sales and Return on Assets

The president of Blue Skies Corp. and his vice presidents are reviewing the operating results of the year just completed. Sales increased by 15% from the previous year to $60,000,000. Average total assets for the year were $40,000,000. Net income, after adding back interest expense, net of tax, was $5,000,000.

The president is happy with the performance over the past year but is never satisfied with the status quo. He has set two specific goals for next year: (1) a 20% growth in sales and (2) a return on assets of 15%.

To achieve the second goal, the president has stated his intention to increase the total asset base by 12.5% over the base for the year just completed.

Required

1. For the year just completed, compute the following ratios:
   a. Return on sales
   b. Asset turnover
   c. Return on assets
2. Compute the necessary asset turnover for next year to achieve the president's goal of a 20% increase in sales.
3. Calculate the income needed next year to achieve the goal of a 15% return on total assets. (*Note:* Assume that *income* is defined as net income plus interest, net of tax.)
4. Based on your answers to parts (2) and (3), comment on the reasonableness of the president's goals. On what must the company focus to attain these goals?

LO6 Problem 13-4 Goals for Sales and Income Growth

Sunrise Corp. is a major regional retailer. The chief executive officer (CEO) is concerned with the slow growth both of sales and of net income and the subsequent effect on the trading price of the common stock. Selected financial data for the past three years follow.

Sunrise Corp.
(in millions)

		2017	2016	2015
1.	Sales	$200.0	$192.5	$187.0
2.	Net income	6.0	5.8	5.6
3.	Dividends declared and paid	2.5	2.5	2.5
December 31 balances:				
4.	Owners' equity	70.0	66.5	63.2
5.	Debt	30.0	29.8	30.3
Selected year-end financial ratios				
	Net income to sales	3.0%	3.0%	3.0%
	Asset turnover	2 times	2 times	2 times
6.	Return on owners' equity*	8.6%	8.7%	8.9%
7.	Debt to total assets	30.0%	30.9%	32.4%

*Based on year-end balances in owners' equity.

The CEO believes that the price of the stock has been adversely affected by the downward trend of the return on equity, the relatively low dividend payout ratio, and the lack of dividend increases. To improve the price of the stock, she wants to improve the return on equity and dividends.

She believes that the company should be able to meet these objectives by (1) increasing sales and net income at an annual rate of 10% a year and (2) establishing a new dividend policy that calls for a dividend payout of 50% of earnings or $3,000,000, whichever is larger.

The 10% annual sales increase will be accomplished through a new promotional program. The president believes that the present net income to sales ratio of 3% will be unchanged by the cost of this new program and any interest paid on new debt. She expects that the company can accomplish this sales and income growth while maintaining the current relationship of total assets to sales. Any capital that is needed to maintain this relationship and that is not generated internally would be acquired through long-term debt financing. The CEO hopes that debt would not exceed 35% of total liabilities and owners' equity.

Required

1. Using the CEO's program, prepare a schedule that shows the appropriate data for the years 2018, 2019, and 2020 for the items numbered 1 through 7 on the preceding schedule.
2. Can the CEO meet all of her requirements if a 10% per-year growth in income and sales is achieved? Explain your answer.
3. What alternative actions should the CEO consider to improve the return on equity and to support increased dividend payments?
4. Explain the reasons that the CEO might have for wanting to limit debt to 35% of total liabilities and owners' equity.

(CMA adapted)

MULTI-CONCEPT PROBLEMS

Problem 13-5 Basic Financial Ratios   LO4 • 5 • 6

The accounting staff of CCB Enterprises has completed the financial statements for the 2017 calendar year. The statement of income for the current year and the comparative statements of financial position for 2017 and 2016 follow.

CCB Enterprises
Statement of Income
For the Year Ended December 31, 2017
(thousands omitted)

Revenue:	
Net sales	$800,000
Other	60,000
Total revenue	$860,000

(Continued)

Expenses:

Cost of goods sold .	$540,000
Research and development	25,000
Selling and administrative	155,000
Interest	20,000
Total expenses	$740,000
Income before income taxes	$120,000
Income taxes	48,000
Net income	$ 72,000

CCB Enterprises
Comparative Statements of Financial Position
December 31, 2017 and 2016
(thousands omitted)

	2017	2016
Assets		
Current assets:		
Cash and short-term investments	$ 26,000	$ 21,000
Receivables, less allowance for doubtful accounts ($1,100 in 2017 and $1,400 in 2016)	48,000	50,000
Inventories, at lower of FIFO cost or market	65,000	62,000
Prepaid items and other current assets	5,000	3,000
Total current assets	$144,000	$136,000
Other assets:		
Investments, at cost	$106,000	$106,000
Deposits	10,000	8,000
Total other assets	$116,000	$114,000
Property, plant, and equipment:		
Land	$ 12,000	$ 12,000
Buildings and equipment, less accumulated depreciation ($126,000 in 2017 and $122,000 in 2016)	268,000	248,000
Total property, plant, and equipment	$280,000	$260,000
Total assets	$540,000	$510,000
Liabilities and Owners' Equity		
Current liabilities:		
Short-term loans	$ 22,000	$ 24,000
Accounts payable	72,000	71,000
Salaries, wages, and other	26,000	27,000
Total current liabilities	$120,000	$122,000
Long-term debt	$160,000	$171,000
Total liabilities	$280,000	$293,000
Owners' equity:		
Common stock, at par	$ 44,000	$ 42,000
Paid-in capital in excess of par	64,000	61,000
Total paid-in capital	$108,000	$103,000
Retained earnings	152,000	114,000
Total owners' equity	$260,000	$217,000
Total liabilities and owners' equity	$540,000	$510,000

Required

1. Calculate the following financial ratios for 2017 for CCB Enterprises:
    a. Times interest earned
    b. Return on total assets

c. Return on common stockholders' equity
d. Debt-to-equity ratio (at December 31, 2017)
e. Current ratio (at December 31, 2017)
f. Quick (acid-test) ratio (at December 31, 2017)
g. Accounts receivable turnover ratio (Assume that all sales are on credit.)
h. Number of days' sales in receivables
i. Inventory turnover ratio (Assume that all purchases are on credit.)
j. Number of days' sales in inventory
k. Number of days in cash operating cycle

2. Prepare a few brief comments on the overall financial health of CCB Enterprises. For each comment, indicate any information that is not provided in the problem that you would need to fully evaluate the company's financial health.

(CMA adapted)

Problem 13-6 Projected Results to Meet Corporate Objectives

LO5 • 6

Tablon Inc. is a wholly owned subsidiary of Marbel Co. The philosophy of Marbel's management is to allow the subsidiaries to operate as independent units. Corporate control is exercised through the establishment of minimum objectives for each subsidiary, accompanied by substantial rewards for success and penalties for failure. The time period for performance review is long enough for competent managers to display their abilities.

Each quarter, the subsidiary is required to submit financial statements. The statements are accompanied by a letter from the subsidiary president explaining the results to date, a forecast for the remainder of the year, and the actions to be taken to achieve the objectives if the forecast indicates that the objectives will not be met.

Marbel management, in conjunction with Tablon management, had set the objectives listed below for the year ending May 31, 2018. These objectives are similar to those set in previous years.

- Sales growth of 20%
- Return on stockholders' equity of 15%
- A long-term debt-to-equity ratio of not more than 1.0
- Payment of a cash dividend of 50% of net income, with a minimum payment of at least $400,000

Tablon's controller has just completed the financial statements for the six months ended November 30, 2017, and the forecast for the year ending May 31, 2018. The statements follow.

After a cursory glance at the financial statements, Tablon's president concluded that not all objectives would be met. At a staff meeting of the Tablon management, the president asked the controller to review the projected results and recommend possible actions that could be taken during the remainder of the year so that Tablon would be more likely to meet the objectives.

Tablon Inc.
Income Statement
(thousands omitted)

	Year Ended May 31, 2017	Six Months Ended November 30, 2017	Forecast for Year Ending May 31, 2018
Sales	$25,000	$15,000	$30,000
Cost of goods sold	$13,000	$ 8,000	$16,000
Selling expenses	5,000	3,500	7,000
Administrative expenses and interest	4,000	2,500	5,000
Income taxes (40%)	1,200	400	800
Total expenses and taxes	$23,200	$14,400	$28,800
Net income	$ 1,800	$ 600	$ 1,200
Dividends declared and paid	600	0	600
Income retained	$ 1,200	$ 600	$ 600

(Continued)

Tablon Inc.
Statement of Financial Position
(thousands omitted)

	May 31, 2017	November 30, 2017	Forecast for May 31, 2018
Assets			
Cash	$ 400	$ 500	$ 500
Accounts receivable (net)	4,100	6,500	7,100
Inventory	7,000	8,500	8,600
Plant and equipment (net)	6,500	7,000	7,300
Total assets	$18,000	$22,500	$23,500
Liabilities and Equities			
Accounts payable	$ 3,000	$ 4,000	$ 4,000
Accrued taxes	300	200	200
Long-term borrowing	6,000	9,000	10,000
Common stock	5,000	5,000	5,000
Retained earnings	3,700	4,300	4,300
Total liabilities and equities	$18,000	$22,500	$23,500

Required

1. Calculate the projected results for each of the four objectives established for Tablon Inc. State which results will not meet the objectives by year-end.
2. From the data presented, identify the factors that seem to contribute to the failure of Tablon Inc. to meet all of its objectives.
3. Explain the possible actions that the controller could recommend in response to the president's request.

(CMA adapted)

LO4 • 5 • 6   Problem 13-7 Comparison with Industry Averages

Heartland Inc. is a medium-size company that has been in business for 20 years. The industry has become very competitive in the last few years, and Heartland has decided that it must grow if it is going to survive. It has approached the bank for a sizable five-year loan, and the bank has requested Heartland's most recent financial statements as part of the loan package.

The industry in which Heartland operates consists of approximately 20 companies relatively equal in size. The trade association to which all of the competitors belong publishes an annual survey of the industry, including industry averages for selected ratios for the competitors. All companies voluntarily submit their statements to the association for this purpose.

Heartland's controller is aware that the bank has access to this survey and is very concerned about how the company fared this past year compared with the rest of the industry. The ratios included in the publication and the averages for the past year are as follows:

Ratio	Industry Average
Current ratio	1.23
Acid-test (quick) ratio	0.75
Accounts receivable turnover	33 times
Inventory turnover	29 times
Debt-to-equity ratio	0.53
Times interest earned	8.65 times
Return on sales	6.57%
Asset turnover	1.95 times
Return on assets	12.81%
Return on common stockholders' equity	17.67%

The financial statements to be submitted to the bank in connection with the loan follow.

Heartland Inc.
Statement of Income and Retained Earnings
For the Year Ended December 31, 2017
(thousands omitted)

Sales revenue	$ 542,750
Cost of goods sold	(435,650)
Gross profit	$ 107,100
Selling, general, and administrative expenses	$ (65,780)
Loss on sales of securities	(220)
Income before interest and taxes	$ 41,100
Interest expense	(9,275)
Income before taxes	$ 31,825
Income tax expense	(12,730)
Net income	$ 19,095
Retained earnings, January 1, 2017	58,485
	$ 77,580
Dividends paid on common stock	(12,000)
Retained earnings, December 31, 2017	$ 65,580

Heartland Inc.
Comparative Statements of Financial Position
(thousands omitted)

	December 31, 2017	December 31, 2016
Assets		
Current assets:		
Cash	$ 1,135	$ 750
Marketable securities	1,250	2,250
Accounts receivable, net of allowances	15,650	12,380
Inventories	12,680	15,870
Prepaid items	385	420
Total current assets	$ 31,100	$ 31,670
Long-term investments	$ 425	$ 425
Property, plant, and equipment:		
Land	$ 32,000	$ 32,000
Buildings and equipment, net of accumulated depreciation	216,000	206,000
Total property, plant, and equipment	$248,000	$238,000
Total assets	$279,525	$270,095
Liabilities and Stockholders' Equity		
Current liabilities:		
Short-term notes	$ 8,750	$ 12,750
Accounts payable	20,090	14,380
Salaries and wages payable	1,975	2,430
Income taxes payable	3,130	2,050
Total current liabilities	$ 33,945	$ 31,610
Long-term bonds payable	$ 80,000	$ 80,000
Stockholders' equity:		
Common stock, no par	$100,000	$100,000
Retained earnings	65,580	58,485
Total stockholders' equity	$165,580	$158,485
Total liabilities and stockholders' equity	$279,525	$270,095

(Continued)

Required

1. Prepare a columnar report for the controller of Heartland Inc. comparing the industry averages for the ratios published by the trade association with the comparable ratios for Heartland. For Heartland, compute the ratios as of December 31, 2017, or for the year ending December 31, 2017, whichever is appropriate.
2. Briefly evaluate Heartland's ratios relative to the industry averages.
3. Do you think that the bank will approve the loan? Explain your answer.

ALTERNATE PROBLEMS

LO5   Problem 13-1A Effect of Transactions on Debt-to-Equity Ratio

(*Note:* Consider completing Problem 13-2A after this problem to ensure that you obtain a clear understanding of the effect of various transactions on this measure of solvency.) The following account balances are taken from the records of Monet's Garden Inc.:

Current liabilities	$150,000
Long-term liabilities	375,000
Stockholders' equity	400,000

Required

1. Use the information provided to compute Monet's debt-to-equity ratio (round to three decimal points).
2. Determine the effect that each of the following transactions will have on Monet's debt-to-equity ratio by recalculating the ratio and then indicating whether the ratio is increased, decreased, or not affected by the transaction. (Round to three decimal points.) Consider each transaction independently; that is, assume that it is the *only* transaction that takes place.

Transaction	Effect of Transaction on Debt-to Equity Ratio
a. Purchased inventory on account, $20,000	
b. Purchased inventory for cash, $15,000	
c. Paid suppliers on account, $30,000	
d. Received cash on account, $40,000	
e. Paid insurance for next year, $20,000	
f. Made sales on account, $60,000	
g. Repaid short-term loans at bank, $25,000	
h. Borrowed $40,000 at bank for 90 days	
i. Declared and paid $45,000 cash dividend	
j. Purchased $20,000 of short-term investments	
k. Paid $30,000 in salaries	
l. Accrued additional $15,000 in taxes	

LO5   Problem 13-2A Effect of Transactions on Debt-to-Equity Ratio

(*Note:* Consider completing this problem after Problem 13-1A to ensure that you obtain a clear understanding of the effect of various transactions on this measure of solvency.) The following account balances are taken from the records of Degas Inc.:

Current liabilities	$ 25,000
Long-term liabilities	125,000
Stockholders' equity	400,000

Required

1. Use the information provided to compute Degas's debt-to-equity ratio (round to three decimal points).

2. Determine the effect that each of the following transactions will have on Degas's debt-to-equity ratio by recalculating the ratio and then indicating whether the ratio is increased, decreased, or not affected by the transaction. (Round to three decimal points.) Consider each transaction independently; that is, assume that it is the *only* transaction that takes place.

Transaction	Effect of Transaction on Debt-to-Equity Ratio
a. Purchased inventory on account, $20,000	
b. Purchased inventory for cash, $15,000	
c. Paid suppliers on account, $30,000	
d. Received cash on account, $40,000	
e. Paid insurance for next year, $20,000	
f. Made sales on account, $60,000	
g. Repaid short-term loans at bank, $25,000	
h. Borrowed $40,000 at bank for 90 days	
i. Declared and paid $45,000 cash dividend	
j. Purchased $20,000 of short-term investments	
k. Paid $30,000 in salaries	
l. Accrued additional $15,000 in taxes	

Problem 13-3A Goals for Sales and Return on Assets   LO6

The president of Blue Moon Corp. and her department managers are reviewing the operating results of the year just completed. Sales increased by 12% from the previous year to $750,000. Average total assets for the year were $400,000. Net income, after adding back interest expense, net of tax, was $60,000.

The president is happy with the performance over the past year but is never satisfied with the status quo. She has set two specific goals for next year: (1) a 15% growth in sales and (2) a return on assets of 20%.

To achieve the second goal, the president has stated her intention to increase the total asset base by 10% over the base for the year just completed.

Required

1. For the year just completed, compute the following ratios:
   a. Return on sales
   b. Asset turnover
   c. Return on assets

2. Compute the necessary asset turnover for next year to achieve the president's goal of a 15% increase in sales.

3. Calculate the income needed next year to achieve the goal of a 20% return on total assets. (*Note:* Assume that *income* is defined as net income plus interest, net of tax.)

4. Based on your answers to parts (2) and (3), comment on the reasonableness of the president's goals. On what must the company focus to attain these goals?

Problem 13-4A Goals for Sales and Income Growth   LO6

Sunset Corp. is a major regional retailer. The chief executive officer (CEO) is concerned with the slow growth both of sales and of net income and the subsequent effect on the trading price of the common stock. Selected financial data for the past three years follow.

Sunset Corp.
(in millions)

	2017	2016	2015
1. Sales	$100.0	$96.7	$93.3
2. Net income	3.0	2.9	2.8
3. Dividends declared and paid	1.2	1.2	1.2

(Continued)

	2017	2016	2015
December 31 balances:			
4. Stockholders' equity	40.0	38.2	36.5
5. Debt	10.0	10.2	10.2
Selected year-end financial ratios			
Net income to sales	3.0%	3.0%	3.0%
Asset turnover	2 times	2 times	2 times
6. Return on stockholders' equity*	7.5%	7.6%	7.7%
7. Debt to total assets	20.0%	21.1%	21.8%

*Based on year-end balances in stockholders' equity.

The CEO believes that the price of the stock has been adversely affected by the downward trend of the return on equity, the relatively low dividend payout ratio, and the lack of dividend increases. To improve the price of the stock, he wants to improve the return on equity and dividends.

He believes that the company should be able to meet these objectives by (1) increasing sales and net income at an annual rate of 10% a year and (2) establishing a new dividend policy that calls for a dividend payout of 60% of earnings or $2,000,000, whichever is larger.

The 10% annual sales increase will be accomplished through a product enhancement program. The president believes that the present net income to sales ratio of 3% will be unchanged by the cost of this new program and any interest paid on new debt. He expects that the company can accomplish this sales and income growth while maintaining the current relationship of total assets to sales. Any capital that is needed to maintain this relationship and that is not generated internally would be acquired through long-term debt financing. The CEO hopes that debt would not exceed 25% of total liabilities and stockholders' equity.

Required

1. Using the CEO's program, prepare a schedule that shows the appropriate data for the years 2018, 2019, and 2020 for the items numbered 1 through 7 on the preceding schedule.
2. Can the CEO meet all of his requirements if a 10% per-year growth in income and sales is achieved? Explain your answers.
3. What alternative actions should the CEO consider to improve the return on equity and to support increased dividend payments?

(CMA adapted)

ALTERNATE MULTI-CONCEPT PROBLEMS

LO4 • 5 • 6 **Problem 13-5A** **Basic Financial Ratios**

The accounting staff of SST Enterprises has completed the financial statements for the 2017 calendar year. The statement of income for the current year and the comparative statements of financial position for 2017 and 2016 follow.

SST Enterprises
Statement of Income
Year Ended December 31, 2017
(thousands omitted)

Revenue:	
Net sales	$600,000
Other	45,000
Total revenue	$645,000
Expenses:	
Cost of goods sold	$405,000
Research and development	18,000
Selling and administrative	120,000
Interest	15,000
Total expenses	$558,000

Income before income taxes	$ 87,000
Income taxes	27,000
Net income	$ 60,000

SST Enterprises
Comparative Statements of Financial Position
December 31, 2017 and 2016
(thousands omitted)

	2017	2016
Assets		
Current assets:		
Cash and short-term investments	$ 27,000	$ 20,000
Receivables, less allowance for doubtful accounts ($1,100 in 2017 and $1,400 in 2016)	36,000	37,000
Inventories, at lower of FIFO cost or market	35,000	42,000
Prepaid items and other current assets	2,000	1,000
Total current assets	$100,000	$100,000
Property, plant, and equipment:		
Land	$ 9,000	$ 9,000
Buildings and equipment, less accumulated depreciation ($74,000 in 2017 and $62,000 in 2016)	191,000	186,000
Total property, plant, and equipment	$200,000	$195,000
Total assets	$300,000	$295,000
Liabilities and Stockholders' Equity		
Current liabilities:		
Short-term loans	$ 20,000	$ 15,000
Accounts payable	80,000	68,000
Salaries, wages, and other	5,000	7,000
Total current liabilities	$105,000	$ 90,000
Long-term debt	15,000	40,000
Total liabilities	$120,000	$130,000
Stockholders' equity:		
Common stock, at par	$ 50,000	$ 50,000
Paid-in capital in excess of par	25,000	25,000
Total paid-in capital	$ 75,000	$ 75,000
Retained earnings	105,000	90,000
Total stockholders' equity	$180,000	$165,000
Total liabilities and stockholders' equity	$300,000	$295,000

Required

1. Calculate the following financial ratios for 2017 for SST Enterprises:

   a. Times interest earned
   b. Return on total assets
   c. Return on common stockholders' equity
   d. Debt-to-equity ratio (at December 31, 2017)
   e. Current ratio (at December 31, 2017)
   f. Quick (acid-test) ratio (at December 31, 2017)
   g. Accounts receivable turnover ratio (Assume that all sales are on credit.)
   h. Number of days' sales in receivables
   i. Inventory turnover ratio (Assume that all purchases are on credit.)
   j. Number of days' sales in inventory
   k. Number of days in cash operating cycle

(Continued)

2. Prepare a few brief comments on the overall financial health of SST Enterprises. For each comment, indicate any information that is not provided in the problem that you would need to fully evaluate the company's financial health.

(CMA adapted)

LO5 • 6   Problem 13-6A Projected Results to Meet Corporate Objectives

Grout Inc. is a wholly owned subsidiary of Slait Co. The philosophy of Slait's management is to allow the subsidiaries to operate as independent units. Corporate control is exercised through the establishment of minimum objectives for each subsidiary, accompanied by substantial rewards for success and penalties for failure. The time period for performance review is long enough for competent managers to display their abilities.

Each quarter, the subsidiary is required to submit financial statements. The statements are accompanied by a letter from the subsidiary president explaining the results to date, a forecast for the remainder of the year, and the actions to be taken to achieve the objectives if the forecast indicates that the objectives will not be met.

Slait management, in conjunction with Grout management, had set the objectives listed below for the year ending September 30, 2018. These objectives are similar to those set in previous years.

- Sales growth of 10%
- Return on stockholders' equity of 20%
- A long-term debt-to-equity ratio of not more than 1.0
- Payment of a cash dividend of 50% of net income, with a minimum payment of at least $500,000

Grout's controller has just completed preparing the financial statements for the six months ended March 31, 2018, and the forecast for the year ending September 30, 2018. The statements are presented below.

After a cursory glance at the financial statements, Grout's president concluded that not all objectives would be met. At a staff meeting of the Grout management, the president asked the controller to review the projected results and recommend possible actions that could be taken during the remainder of the year so that Grout would be more likely to meet the objectives.

Grout Inc.
Income Statement
(thousands omitted)

	Year Ended September 30, 2017	Six Months Ended March 31, 2018	Forecast for Year Ending September 30, 2018
Sales	$10,000	$6,000	$12,000
Cost of goods sold	$ 6,000	$4,000	$ 8,000
Selling expenses	1,500	900	1,800
Administrative expenses and interest	1,000	600	1,200
Income taxes	500	300	600
Total expenses and taxes	$ 9,000	$5,800	$11,600
Net income	$ 1,000	$ 200	$ 400
Dividends declared and paid	500	0	400
Income retained	$ 500	$ 200	$ 0

Grout Inc.
Statement of Financial Position
(thousands omitted)

	September 30, 2017	March 31, 2018	Forecast for September 30, 2018
Assets			
Cash	$ 400	$ 500	$ 500
Accounts receivable (net)	2,100	3,400	2,600
Inventory	7,000	8,500	8,400
Plant and equipment (net)	2,800	2,500	3,200
Total assets	$12,300	$14,900	$14,700

	September 30, 2017	March 31, 2018	Forecast for September 30, 2018
Liabilities and Equities			
Accounts payable	$ 3,000	$ 4,000	$ 4,000
Accrued taxes	300	200	200
Long-term borrowing	4,000	5,500	5,500
Common stock	4,000	4,000	4,000
Retained earnings	1,000	1,200	1,000
Total liabilities and equities	$12,300	$14,900	$14,700

Required

1. Calculate the projected results for each of the four objectives established for Grout Inc. State which results will not meet the objectives by year-end.
2. From the data presented, identify the factors that seem to contribute to the failure of Grout Inc. to meet all of its objectives.
3. Explain the possible actions that the controller could recommend in response to the president's request.

(CMA adapted)

Problem 13-7A Comparison with Industry Averages   LO4 • 5 • 6

Midwest Inc. is a medium-size company that has been in business for 20 years. The industry has become very competitive in the last few years, and Midwest has decided that it must grow if it is going to survive. It has approached the bank for a sizable five-year loan, and the bank has requested Midwest's most recent financial statements as part of the loan package.

The industry in which Midwest operates consists of approximately 20 companies relatively equal in size. The trade association to which all of the competitors belong publishes an annual survey of the industry, including industry averages for selected ratios for the competitors. All companies voluntarily submit their statements to the association for this purpose.

Midwest's controller is aware that the bank has access to this survey and is very concerned about how the company fared this past year compared with the rest of the industry. The ratios included in the publication and the averages for the past year are as follows:

Ratio	Industry Average
Current ratio	1.20
Acid-test (quick) ratio	0.50
Inventory turnover	35 times
Debt-to-equity ratio	0.50
Times interest earned	25 times
Return on sales	3%
Asset turnover	3.50 times
Return on common stockholders' equity	20%

The financial statements to be submitted to the bank in connection with the loan follow.

Midwest Inc.
Comparative Statements of Financial Position
(thousands omitted)

	December 31, 2017	December 31, 2016
Assets		
Current assets:		
Cash	$ 1,790	$ 2,600
Marketable securities	1,200	1,700
Accounts receivable, net of allowances	400	600
Inventories	8,700	7,400
Prepaid items	350	400
Total current assets	$ 12,440	$ 12,700

(Continued)

	December 31, 2017	December 31, 2016
Long-term investments	$ 560	$ 400
Property, plant, and equipment:		
Land	$ 12,000	$ 12,000
Buildings and equipment, net of accumulated depreciation	87,000	82,900
Total property, plant, and equipment	$ 99,000	$ 94,900
Total assets	$112,000	$108,000
Liabilities and Stockholders' Equity		
Current liabilities:		
Short-term notes	$ 800	$ 600
Accounts payable	6,040	6,775
Salaries and wages payable	1,500	1,200
Income taxes payable	1,560	1,025
Total current liabilities	$ 9,900	$ 9,600
Long-term bonds payable	$ 36,000	$ 36,000
Stockholders' equity:		
Common stock, no par	$ 50,000	$ 50,000
Retained earnings	16,100	12,400
Total stockholders' equity	$ 66,100	$ 62,400
Total liabilities and stockholders' equity	$112,000	$108,000

Midwest Inc.
Statement of Income and Retained Earnings
For the Year Ended December 31, 2017
(thousands omitted)

Sales revenue	$ 420,500
Cost of goods sold	(300,000)
Gross profit	$ 120,500
Selling, general, and administrative expenses	(85,000)
Income before interest and taxes	$ 35,500
Interest expense	(8,600)
Income before taxes	$ 26,900
Income tax expense	(12,000)
Net income	$ 14,900
Retained earnings, January 1, 2017	12,400
	$ 27,300
Dividends paid on common stock	(11,200)
Retained earnings, December 31, 2017	$ 16,100

Required

1. Prepare a columnar report for the controller of Midwest Inc. comparing the industry averages for the ratios published by the trade association with the comparable ratios for Midwest. For Midwest, compute the ratios as of December 31, 2017, or for the year ending December 31, 2017, whichever is appropriate.
2. Briefly evaluate Midwest's ratios relative to the industry averages.
3. Do you think that the bank will approve the loan? Explain your answer.

DECISION CASES

Reading and Interpreting Financial Statements

Decision Case 13-1 Horizontal Analysis for Chipotle

LO2

Refer to the financial statement information of **Chipotle** reprinted at the back of the book.

Required

1. Prepare a work sheet with the following headings:

	Increase (Decrease) from			
	2014 to 2015		2013 to 2014	
Income Statement Accounts	**Dollars**	**Percent**	**Dollars**	**Percent**

2. Complete the work sheet using each of the account titles on Chipotle's income statement. Round all percentages to the nearest one-tenth of a percent.
3. What observations can you make from this horizontal analysis? What is your overall analysis of operations? Have the company's operations improved over the three-year period?

Decision Case 13-2 Vertical Analysis for Chipotle

LO3

Refer to the financial statement information of **Chipotle** reprinted at the back of the book.

Required

1. Using the format in Example 13-5, prepare common-size comparative income statements for 2015 and 2014. Round all percentages to the nearest one-tenth of a percent.
2. What changes do you detect in the income statement relationships from 2014 to 2015?
3. Using the format in Example 13-4, prepare common-size comparative balance sheets at the end of 2015 and 2014. Round all percentages to the nearest one-tenth of a percent.
4. What observations can you make about the relative composition of Chipotle's assets from the common-size statements? What observations can be made about the changes in the relative composition of liabilities and stockholders' equity accounts?

Decision Case 13-3 Comparing Two Companies in the Same Industry: Chipotle and Panera Bread

LO3

This case should be completed after responding to the requirements in Decision Case 13-2. Refer to the financial statement information of **Chipotle** and **Panera Bread** reprinted at the back of the book.

Required

1. Using the format in Example 13-5, prepare common-size comparative income statements for 2015 and 2014, for Panera Bread. Use total revenues as the base (i.e., 100%). Round all percentages to the nearest one-tenth of a percent.
2. The common-size comparative income statements indicate the relative importance of items on the statement. Compare the common-size income statements of Panera Bread and Chipotle. What are the most important differences between the two companies' income statements?
3. Using the format in Example 13-4, prepare common-size comparative balance sheets at the end of 2015 and 2014, for Panera Bread. Round all percentages to the nearest one-tenth of a percent.
4. The common-size comparative balance sheets indicate the relative importance of items on the statement. Compare the common-size balance sheets of Panera Bread and Chipotle. What are the most important differences between the two companies' balance sheets?

LO4 • 5 • 6   **Decision Case 13-4 Ratio Analysis for Panera Bread**

REAL WORLD

Refer to the financial statement information of **Panera Bread** reprinted at the back of the book.

Required

1. Compute the following ratios and other amounts for each of the two years, ending December 30, 2015, and December 31, 2014. Because only two years of data are given on the balance sheets, to be consistent, you should use year-end balances for each year in lieu of average balances. Assume 360 days to a year. State any other necessary assumptions in making the calculations. Round all ratios to the nearest one-tenth of a percent.

    a. Working capital
    b. Current ratio
    c. Acid-test ratio
    d. Cash flow from operations to current liabilities
    e. Debt-to-equity ratio
    f. Cash flow from operations to capital expenditures
    g. Asset turnover
    h. Return on sales
    i. Return on assets
    j. Return on common stockholders' equity

2. What is your overall analysis of the financial health of Panera Bread?

Making Financial Decisions

LO4 • 5 • 6 • 7   **Decision Case 13-5 Acquisition Decision**

Diversified Industries is a large conglomerate that is continually in the market for new acquisitions. The company has grown rapidly over the last ten years through buyouts of medium-size companies. Diversified does not limit itself to companies in any one industry, but looks for firms with a sound financial base and the ability to stand on their own financially.

The president of Diversified recently told a meeting of the company's officers: "I want to impress two points on all of you. First, we are not in the business of looking for bargains. Diversified has achieved success in the past by acquiring companies with the ability to be a permanent member of the corporate family. We don't want companies that may appear to be a bargain on paper but can't survive in the long run. Second, a new member of our family must be able to come in and make it on its own—the parent is not organized to be a funding agency for struggling subsidiaries."

Ron Dixon is the vice president of acquisitions for Diversified, a position he has held for five years. He is responsible for making recommendations to the board of directors on potential acquisitions. Because you are one of his assistants, he recently brought you a set of financials for a manufacturer, Heavy Duty Tractors Inc. Dixon believes that Heavy Duty is a "can't-miss" opportunity for Diversified and asks you to confirm his hunch by performing basic financial statement analysis on the company. The most recent comparative balance sheets and income statement for the company follow.

Heavy Duty Tractors Inc.
Comparative Statements of Financial Position
(thousands omitted)

	December 31, 2017	December 31, 2016
Assets		
Current assets:		
Cash	$ 48,500	$ 24,980
Marketable securities	3,750	0
Accounts receivable, net of allowances	128,420	84,120
Inventories	135,850	96,780
Prepaid items	7,600	9,300
Total current assets	$324,120	$215,180
Long-term investments	$ 55,890	$ 55,890

	December 31, 2017	December 31, 2016
Property, plant, and equipment:		
Land	$ 45,000	$ 45,000
Buildings and equipment, less accumulated depreciation of $385,000 in 2017 and $325,000 in 2016	545,000	605,000
Total property, plant, and equipment	$590,000	$650,000
Total assets	$970,010	$921,070
Liabilities and Stockholders' Equity		
Current liabilities:		
Short-term notes	$ 80,000	$ 60,000
Accounts payable	65,350	48,760
Salaries and wages payable	14,360	13,840
Income taxes payable	2,590	3,650
Total current liabilities	$162,300	$126,250
Long-term bonds payable, due 2024	$275,000	$275,000
Stockholders' equity:		
Common stock, no par	$350,000	$350,000
Retained earnings	182,710	169,820
Total stockholders' equity	$532,710	$519,820
Total liabilities and stockholders' equity	$970,010	$921,070

Heavy Duty Tractors Inc.
Statement of Income and Retained Earnings
For the Year Ended December 31, 2017
(thousands omitted)

Sales revenue	$875,250
Cost of goods sold	542,750
Gross profit	$332,500
Selling, general, and administrative expenses	255,360
Operating income	$ 77,140
Interest expense	45,000
Net income before taxes	$ 32,140
Income tax expense	9,250
Net income	$ 22,890
Retained earnings, January 1, 2017	169,820
	$192,710
Dividends paid on common stock	10,000
Retained earnings, December 31, 2017	$182,710

Required

1. How liquid is Heavy Duty Tractors? Support your answer with any ratios that you believe are necessary to justify your conclusion. Also indicate any other information that you would want to have in making a final determination on its liquidity.
2. In light of the president's comments, should you be concerned about the solvency of Heavy Duty Tractors? Support your answer with the necessary ratios. How does the maturity date of the outstanding debt affect your answer?
3. Has Heavy Duty demonstrated the ability to be a profitable member of the Diversified family? Support your answer with the necessary ratios.
4. What will you tell your boss? Should he recommend to the board of directors that Diversified put in a bid for Heavy Duty Tractors?

LO3 ## Decision Case 13-6 Pricing Decision

BPO's management believes the company has been successful at increasing sales because it has not increased the selling price of its products even though its competition has increased prices and costs have increased. Price and cost relationships in Year 1 were established because they represented industry averages. The following income statements are available for BPO's first three years of operation:

	Year 3	Year 2	Year 1
Sales	$125,000	$110,000	$100,000
Cost of goods sold	62,000	49,000	40,000
Gross profit	$ 63,000	$ 61,000	$ 60,000
Operating expenses	53,000	49,000	45,000
Net income	$ 10,000	$ 12,000	$ 15,000

Required

1. Using the format in Example 13-5, prepare common-size comparative income statements for the three years.
2. Explain why net income has decreased while sales have increased.
3. Prepare an income statement for Year 4. Sales volume in units is expected to increase by 10%, and costs are expected to increase by 8%.
4. Do you think BPO should raise its prices or maintain the same selling prices? Explain your answer.

Ethical Decision Making

ETHICAL DECISION MODEL

LO4 • 5 ## Decision Case 13-7 Provisions in a Loan Agreement

As assistant controller of Midwest Construction Company, you are reviewing with your boss, the controller, Dave Jackson, the financial statements for the year just ended. During the review, Jackson reminds you of an existing loan agreement with Southern National Bank. Midwest has agreed to the following conditions:

- The current ratio will be maintained at a minimum level of 1.5 to 1.0 at all times.
- The debt-to-equity ratio will not exceed 0.5 to 1.0 at any time.

Jackson has drawn up the following preliminary condensed balance sheet for the year just ended:

Midwest Construction Company
Balance Sheet
December 31
(in millions of dollars)

Current assets	$16	Current liabilities	$10
Long-term assets	64	Long-term debt	15
		Stockholders' equity	55
Total	$80	Total	$80

Jackson wants to discuss two items with you and make sure you are in agreement with him. First, long-term debt currently includes a $5 million note payable to Eastern State Bank that is due in six months. The plan is to go to Eastern before the note is due and ask it to extend the maturity date of the note for five years. Jackson doesn't believe that Midwest needs to include the $5 million in current liabilities because the plan is to roll over the note.

Second, in December of this year, Midwest received a $2 million deposit from the state for a major road project. The contract calls for the work to be performed over the next 18 months. Jackson recorded the $2 million as revenue this year because the contract is with the state; there shouldn't be any question about being able to collect.

Required

Use the Ethical Decision Framework in Exhibit 1-9 to complete the following requirements:

1. **Recognize an ethical dilemma:** Based on the balance sheet that Jackson prepared, is Midwest in violation of its loan agreement? Support your answer by computing the current and debt-to-equity ratios. Do you see anything wrong with the way Jackson handled these two items? If so, compute revised current and debt-to-equity ratios. What ethical dilemma(s) do you face?

2. **Analyze the key elements in the situation:**

    a. Who may benefit if the two items are handled as suggested by the controller? Who may be harmed?

    b. How are they likely to benefit or be harmed?

    c. What rights or claims may be violated?

    d. What specific interests are in conflict?

    e. What are your responsibilities and obligations?

3. **List alternatives and evaluate the impact of each on those affected:** As assistant controller, what are your options in dealing with the ethical dilemma(s) you identified in (1) above? If the two items are handled as suggested by the controller, will users have reliable information needed to make decisions? Why or why not?

4. **Select the best alternative:** Among the alternatives, which one would you select?

Decision Case 13-8 Inventory Turnover
LO4

Garden Fresh Inc. is a wholesaler of fresh fruits and vegetables. Each year, it submits a set of financial ratios to a trade association. Even though the association doesn't publish the individual ratios for each company, the president of Garden Fresh thinks it is important for public relations that his company look as good as possible. Due to the nature of the fresh fruits and vegetables business, one of the major ratios tracked by the association is inventory turnover. Garden Fresh's inventory stated at FIFO cost was as follows:

	Year Ending December 31	
	2017	**2016**
Fruits	$10,000	$ 9,000
Vegetables	30,000	33,000
Totals	$40,000	$42,000

Sales revenue for the year ending December 31, 2017, is $3,690,000. The company's gross profit ratio is normally 40%.

Based on these data, the president thinks the company should report an inventory turnover ratio of 90 times per year.

Required

1. Using the necessary calculations, explain how the president came up with an inventory turnover ratio of 90 times.

2. Do you think the company should report a turnover ratio of 90 times? If not, explain why you disagree and explain, with calculations, what you think the ratio should be.

3. Assume that you are the controller for Garden Fresh. What will you tell the president?

INTEGRATIVE PROBLEM

Presented here are a statement of income and retained earnings and comparative balance sheets for Gallagher, Inc., which operates a national chain of sporting goods stores.

(Continued)

Gallagher, Inc.
Statement of Income and Retained Earnings
For the Year Ended December 31, 2017
(all amounts in thousands of dollars)

Net sales	$48,000
Cost of goods sold	36,000
Gross profit	$12,000
Selling, general, and administrative expense	6,000
Operating income	$ 6,000
Interest expense	280
Income before tax	$ 5,720
Income tax expense	2,280
Net income	$ 3,440
Preferred dividends	100
Income available to common	$ 3,340
Common dividends	500
To retained earnings	$ 2,840
Retained earnings, 1/1	12,000
Retained earnings, 12/31	$14,840

Gallagher, Inc.
Comparative Balance Sheets
December 31, 2017 and 2016
(all amounts in thousands of dollars)

	December 31	
	2017	**2016**
Cash	$ 840	$ 2,700
Accounts receivable	12,500	9,000
Inventory	8,000	5,500
Prepaid insurance	100	400
Total current assets	$21,440	$17,600
Land	$ 4,000	$ 4,000
Buildings and equipment	12,000	9,000
Accumulated depreciation	(3,700)	(3,000)
Total long-term assets	$12,300	$10,000
Total assets	$33,740	$27,600
Accounts payable	$ 7,300	$ 5,000
Taxes payable	4,600	4,200
Notes payable	2,400	1,600
Current portion of bonds	200	200
Total current liabilities	$14,500	$11,000
Bonds payable	1,400	1,600
Total liabilities	$15,900	$12,600
Preferred stock, $5 par	$ 1,000	$ 1,000
Common stock, $1 par	2,000	2,000
Retained earnings	14,840	12,000
Total stockholders' equity	$17,840	$15,000
Total liabilities and stockholders' equity	$33,740	$27,600

Required

1. Prepare a statement of cash flows for Gallagher, Inc., for the year ended December 31, 2017, using the *indirect* method in the Operating Activities section of the statement.

2. Gallagher's management is concerned with its short-term liquidity and its solvency over the long run. To help management evaluate these, compute the following ratios, rounding all answers to the nearest one-tenth of a percent:

   a. Current ratio
   b. Acid-test ratio
   c. Cash flow from operations to current liabilities ratio
   d. Accounts receivable turnover ratio
   e. Number of days' sales in receivables
   f. Inventory turnover ratio
   g. Number of days' sales in inventory
   h. Debt-to-equity ratio
   i. Debt service coverage ratio
   j. Cash flow from operations to capital expenditures ratio

3. Comment on Gallagher's liquidity and its solvency. What additional information do you need to fully evaluate the company?

Answers

MODULE 1 Answers to Questions

1. Depending on the relative movement of prices, the choice between LIFO and FIFO will result in significantly different amounts reported for inventory. For example, in a period of rising prices, the use of LIFO will reduce inventory (relative to what it would have been under FIFO) and thus reduce the current ratio and the acid-test ratio. The inventory turnover ratio will differ as well, because LIFO will result in more cost of goods sold expense. Thus, all other things being equal, in a period of rising prices, a LIFO company will report a higher turnover of inventory than a FIFO company. The LIFO company's cash flow will be better because it will pay less in taxes. Thus, the various ratios that involve cash from operations will be affected. Finally, the profitability ratios will be affected by the choice of an inventory method. For example, the LIFO company will report lower profits and thus have a lower profit margin.

2. The analysis of financial statements over a series of years is called horizontal analysis. For example, by looking for trends in certain costs over a series of years (thus, the name *trend analysis*), the analyst is able to more accurately predict future costs. Common-size financial statements are statements in which all amounts are stated as a percentage of one selected item on the statement, such as net sales. Thus, vertical analysis of a single year's income statement will help the analyst discern the relative amounts incurred for various costs.

3. Rising costs to either manufacture or purchase inventory could be responsible for a decline in gross profit in the face of an increase in sales. Assume that 1,000 units of a product are sold with a unit cost of $80 and a selling price of $100. Sales total $100,000, and gross profit is $20,000. Assume that in the following year, the company raises the selling price to $115 because of rising costs. If the cost to make a unit goes up to $96 and the company sells another 1,000 units, sales will increase by 15% to $115,000, but gross profit will decrease to 1,000 × ($115 − $96), or $19,000—a decrease in gross profit of 5%.

4. The composition of current assets indicates the relative size of cash, accounts receivable, inventory, and other

short-term assets. A relatively large balance in inventory may indicate that a company is not turning over its products quickly enough. Similarly, a large accounts receivable balance could signal a problem in the collec-

tion department. Finally, a large cash balance may be a sign that the company is not taking advantage of short-term investment opportunities.

MODULE 1 Answers to Apply

1. Although a current ratio of 0.50 is certainly low, other factors need to be considered before making a decision on whether to extend credit. Has the company operated successfully in the past with a low current ratio? How does this ratio compare with other companies in the same industry? What is the composition of the company's current assets?

2. A comparison of financial statement items within a single period is called vertical analysis. A comparison of financial statement items over a period of time is called horizontal analysis.

3. Accounts on the balance sheet should be stated as a percentage of total assets. All accounts on the income statement should be stated as a percentage of net sales.

MODULE 2 Answers to Questions

1. A relatively low acid-test, or quick, ratio compared with the current ratio probably indicates a large inventory balance. Large amounts of inventory may be normal for a company; on the other hand, they could signal problems in moving obsolete items. The inventory turnover ratio for the most recent period should be compared with those of prior periods to determine whether there has been a decrease in the number of turns per year. A less likely explanation for a low quick ratio compared with the current ratio would be large balances in various prepayments, such as supplies and insurance.

2. An accounts receivable turnover of nine times translates to an average number of days in receivables of 40 (360/9). If the credit department extends terms of 2/10, n/30, investigation of the company's actual credit policies is warranted. For example, the department may routinely

give customers up to 40 or 50 days to pay. If this policy does not create any cash flow problems, why have terms of 2/10, n/30? Alternatively, the average time to collect may be an indication that the credit department is extending credit to customers who are not good credit risks.

3. One possible explanation for a decrease in inventory turnover is slow-moving items. Caution must be used, however, because a low inventory turnover may simply be a seasonal phenomenon. For example, the ratio for the third quarter of the year should be compared with that of the third quarter of the prior year. Problems in the sales department may also partially explain a low turnover of inventory. Or, the company may be pricing itself out of the market and need to consider lowering its prices to meet the competition.

MODULE 2 Answers to Apply

1. On average, Company A turns over its accounts receivable four times during the year ($1,000,000/$250,000); Company B, ten times during the year ($400,000/$40,000). Assuming 360 days in a year, Company A takes, on average, 90 days to collect its accounts receivable; Company B takes, on average, 36 days.

2. Current ratio: Current Assets

   Acid-Test ratio: Cash + Marketable Securities + Current Receivables

   Accounts Receivable Turnover ratio: Net Credit Sales

   Inventory Turnover ratio: Cost of Goods Sold

MODULE 3 Answers to Questions

1. The debt service coverage ratio is superior to the times interest earned ratio as a measure of solvency for two reasons. First, the ratio considers the need to pay both interest and principal, whereas the times interest earned ratio deals only with interest. Second, the necessary payments to service debt are compared with the cash

available to pay the debt, while the times interest earned ratio uses an accrual income number in its numerator.

2. Both are right. Many different ratios are used to assess the relative mix of a company's capital structure. The debt-to-equity ratio measures the amount of

outstanding debt relative to the amount of stockholders' equity. An alternative measure is to divide the same debt by the total assets of the company. A different ratio will obviously result, but as long as the same measure is used consistently, either ratio is an indicator of solvency.

3. The debt service coverage ratio measures the amount of cash generated from operating activities that is available to repay the interest and any maturing debt. A loan

officer is primarily concerned with the company's ability to meet interest and principal payments on time and, therefore, would be very interested in this ratio.

4. Dividends are not a legal obligation, but they often become an expectation on the part of stockholders. Therefore, when computing the cash available to make capital acquisitions, it is helpful to take into account the normal dividend requirements.

MODULE 3 Answers to Apply

1. Meet its interest and principal payments: Debt service coverage ratio

   Finance long-term asset acquisitions with cash from operations: Cash flow from operations to capital expenditures ratio

   Meet its interest payments: Times interest earned ratio

2. With total assets at the beginning of year of $300 million and a debt-to-equity ratio of 2 to 1, total stock-

holders' equity was $100 million. The only change in stockholders' equity during the year was the net income of $50 million; thus, ending stockholders' equity was $150 million. Total assets at year-end were $400 million; thus, total liabilities were $250. The year-end debt-to-equity ratio was $250 million/$150 million or 1.67.

MODULE 4 Answers to Questions

1. The numerator in any rate of return ratio must match the investment or base in the denominator. If total assets is the base, the numerator must be a measure of the income available to all providers of capital. Interest expense, net of tax, is added back to net income because the creditors are one of the sources of capital, and we want to consider the income available before any of the sources of funds are given a distribution. Interest must be on a net or after-tax basis to be consistent with net income, which is on an after-tax basis.

2. A return on stockholders' equity that is lower than the return on assets means that the company is not successfully using borrowed funds. Return on assets measures the return to all providers of capital, whereas return on equity is concerned only with common stockholders. The company has not been able to earn an overall return that is as high as what is being paid to creditors and preferred stockholders. Leverage deals with the use

of someone else's money to earn a favorable return. Presently, this company is not successfully employing financial leverage.

3. The price/earnings ratio is sometimes used as an indicator of the quality of a company's earnings because it combines a measure of the company's performance, based on its earnings, and the company's worth as measured by the market price of its stock. The ratio of price to earnings is an indication of the market's assessment of the company's performance. For example, the use of different accounting methods can cause the market to value the price of one company's stock higher than another company's stock, even though they report similar earnings. This could be the case if in a period of rising prices one defers taxes by using LIFO whereas the other uses FIFO. This differing treatment of the two stocks is a statement by the market about the "quality" of the two companies' earnings.

MODULE 4 Answers to Apply

1. Earnings per share: ($90,000 − $10,000)/20,000 shares = $4 per share

2. Return on assets: Interest Expense, Net of Tax (A)

Return on common stockholders' equity: Preferred Dividends (D)

Earnings per share: Preferred Dividends (D)

Return on sales: Interest Expense, Net of Tax (A)

Answers to Connect to the Real World

13-1 (p. 626)

lululemon's gross profit ratio for each year is as follows:

Fiscal year ending:
January 31, 2016: $997,166/$2,060,523 = 48.4%
February 1, 2015: $914,180/$1,797,213 = 50.9%
February 2, 2014: $840,076/$1,591,188 = 52.8%
February 3, 2013: $762,826/$1,370,358 = 55.7%
January 29, 2012: $569,351/$1,000,839 = 56.9%

After reaching nearly 57% in the fiscal year ended January 29, 2012, the gross profit ratio has decreased each year, dropping below 50% in the most recent year.

13-2 (p. 630)

Chipotle's profit margin ratio for each year is as follows:

Fiscal year ending December 31,
2015: $475,602/$4,501,223 = 10.6%
2014: $445,374/$4,108,269 = 10.8%
2013: $327,438/$3,214,591 = 10.2%

The profit margin ratio has remained relatively stable over this three-year period.

Answers to Key Terms Quiz

Quiz 1:

14	Horizontal analysis		5	Cash flow from operations to current liabilities ratio
11	Vertical analysis			
10	Gross profit ratio		6	Accounts receivable turnover ratio
12	Profit margin ratio		4	Number of days' sales in receivables
13	Liquidity		9	Inventory turnover ratio
2	Working capital		7	Number of days' sales in inventory
3	Current ratio		8	Cash-to-cash operating cycle
1	Acid-test or quick ratio			

Quiz 2:

3	Solvency		1	Return on common stockholders' equity ratio
7	Debt-to-equity ratio			
13	Times interest earned ratio		12	Leverage
14	Debt service coverage ratio		5	Earnings per share (EPS)
8	Cash flow from operations to capital expenditures ratio		2	Price/earnings (P/E) ratio
			6	Dividend payout ratio
15	Profitability		11	Dividend yield ratio
9	Return on assets ratio			
4	Return on sales ratio			
10	Asset turnover ratio			

International Financial Reporting Standards

LEARNING OBJECTIVES	WHY IS THIS APPENDIX IMPORTANT?
LO1 Explain why accounting standards currently differ among countries around the world.	• You need to know why accounting standards differ across countries. (See pp. A2–A3.)
LO2 Explain the benefits from a single set of accounting standards.	• You need to know whether accounting standards should be the same in all countries. (See pp. A3–A4.)
LO3 Describe the role of the International Accounting Standards Board in setting accounting standards and be familiar with the time frame for the convergence of U.S. GAAP and IFRS standards.	• You need to know who is responsible for developing a single set of global standards. (See pp. A4–A5.) • You need to know if and when international standards will be adopted in the United States and when it is likely that a single set of standards will be used by all companies. (See p. A5.)
LO4 Describe the most significant differences between U.S. GAAP and IFRS.	• You need to know the *major differences* between IFRS and U.S. GAAP. (See pp. A5–A8.)
LO5 Understand how differences in format and terminology affect the appearance of financial statements in various countries.	• You need to know if there is a standard format and set of terms used on financial statements around the world. (See pp. A8–A10.)

FORD AND DAIMLER

You have $1,000 to invest and are trying to decide between the common shares of two car makers: **Ford Motor Company** in the United States and **Daimler AG** in Germany. As part of your analysis, you read the notes to the financial statements for each company and realize that the accounting standards used by these two companies might not necessarily be the same. Not surprisingly, Ford's statements are prepared in accordance with U.S. generally accepted accounting principles (U.S. GAAP) as determined by the Financial Accounting Standards Board (FASB). On the other hand, Daimler follows a set of international accounting standards that we will describe later in this appendix. When you compare the net income of these companies, can you be assured that you are comparing "apples to apples"? Or could it be that differences in accounting standards are responsible for some of the differences in the earnings of these companies?

The objective of this appendix is to give you an appreciation for the differences in accounting standards around the world and an understanding of efforts to develop a unified set of standards that all companies would use. Regardless of your career path, these issues will be important to your future in business. With the rapid development of global business, your need to understand the movement toward a unified set of accounting standards will only increase in importance.

Why Do Accounting Standards Differ?

No single explanation can be given for the divergence of accounting standards. However, the following are among the most important reasons why they differ:

LO1 Explain why accounting standards currently differ among countries around the world.

1. Legal System

The two primary legal systems used around the world are the *common law system* and the *code law system*. The common law system has its roots in the United Kingdom and, because of historical ties, is also the system used in the United States. In common law countries, there are generally fewer statutes written into the laws and thus more reliance on interpretation by the courts. In code law countries, such as Germany, there are more detailed rules written into the statutes. But what does this difference have to do with accounting standards? Because less detailed laws are written into the statutes of common law countries such as the United States, nongovernmental bodies such as the Financial Accounting Standards Board (FASB) have developed more detailed rules. In contrast, the accounting standards in Germany are much briefer.

2. Taxation

Countries differ in terms of how similar or different the rules are for determining accounting income and taxable income. For example, in the United States significant differences exist between the two because the computation of accounting income is based on the rules of the FASB whereas taxable income is based on the rules as set forth by the Internal Revenue Service. In many other countries, including Japan and much of Europe, fewer differences exist between the amount of income reported to stockholders and that reported to the taxing authorities.

3. Financing

Corporations in the United States receive most of their financing from two sources: creditors and stockholders. Because stockholders and creditors such as bondholders and banks are not privy to the internal records of the corporation, accountability to the public is of paramount importance. In some other countries, more of the financing may come from families, banks, and even the government. In these cases, there has been less need to develop detailed rules for disclosure.

4. Inflation

In some countries, notably those in Latin America and South America, inflation has been much more rampant than in other parts of the world. Because of the instability of the measuring unit that is the currency in those countries, companies have been required to adjust their financial statements to take into account the effects of inflation. At one time, the FASB developed rules for companies in the United States to use to adjust for inflation. As inflation has subsided in this country, U.S. companies no longer present financial information adjusted for the effects of inflation.

5. Relationships Between Countries

Countries that have strong political and economic ties often share similar accounting practices. For example, the roots of accounting systems in Canada and Australia, two former British colonies, can be traced to those found in the United Kingdom.

6. State of Economic Development

At any one time, all countries around the world are at different stages in the development of their economies. For example, the free-market systems used in the United Kingdom and in the United States have been in place for many years. Complex business arrangements such as leases and pension plans necessitate relatively detailed accounting rules to deal with them. In contrast, the economies in some countries, such as those that made up the former Soviet Union, are just beginning to develop and thus so are the accounting standards in those countries.

We have now seen that accounting standards differ around the world for a variety of reasons, some of which are interrelated. For example, the legal system in the United States, coupled with a highly advanced economy, has resulted in a lengthy and complex set of accounting standards. Although the Securities and Exchange Commission has ultimate authority to set accounting standards, it has delegated much of the responsibility to the non-governmental FASB. As a private-sector, independent body, the FASB gathers information from a variety of sources, including the multi-billion-dollar corporations that dominate business in this country. The influence of these companies in setting accounting standards is considerable. In some of the less-developed countries of the world, especially those in which the forces of capitalism are less prevalent, accounting standards have developed at a much slower pace.

Benefits from a Single Set of Standards

LO2 Explain the benefits from a single set of accounting standards.

Consider the case of **General Mills**. According to the company's web site, it sells its products in more than 100 countries and its international business accounted for almost 30 percent of total sales in fiscal 2015. It operates a joint venture with **Nestlé**, a Swiss company, called **Cereal Partners Worldwide**. Like a vast majority of publicly traded U.S. corporations, General Mills truly is a global company. So what would be some of the advantages to General Mills and its stockholders if a single set of accounting standards were used around the world?

1. Save on Accounting Costs

The development of accounting systems, their maintenance, and the eventual preparation of financial statements are major costs to most businesses, especially those with significant international operations. For example, the financial statements of General Mills's foreign subsidiaries must be consolidated with those of the parent corporation. The income from the company's joint venture with Nestlé must be accounted for prior to presenting the company's net income. Both of these tasks are that much more costly to General Mills if accounting principles differ in those other countries. A single set of worldwide accounting standards would save companies considerable money in accounting fees.

2. Make It Easier to Acquire Foreign Companies

According to General Mills's web site, in fiscal 2012 the company acquired a controlling interest in French-based Yoplait. Certainly, General Mills took a close look at the financial statements of this French company prior to acquiring it. But what if those statements were prepared using different standards than those used in the United States? A single set of standards would make it much easier to decide whether to acquire a foreign company.

3. Make It Easier to Access Foreign Capital Markets

Assume that a U.S. company wants to borrow money from a bank in Japan. With the current differences in accounting standards between the two countries, the Japanese bank might require the U.S. borrower to present financial statements prepared in accordance with Japanese standards. Or conversely, consider the case of a Japanese company that wants to list its stock on a stock exchange in the United States. It might need to adjust its financial statements so that they were in conformity with U.S. accounting practices. Both the U.S. company looking to borrow money abroad and the Japanese company wanting to access the U.S. capital markets could save considerable time and money if a single set of standards were used universally.

4. Facilitate Comparisons

Recall the dilemma presented at the beginning of this appendix: you are deciding whether to invest in Ford Motor Company in this country or Daimler AG in Germany. Just as it would be easier for one corporation to evaluate alternative investments if those companies all used the same accounting rules, so would it be easier for analysts and individual investors to compare companies if a single set of standards were used by all of them.

To a large extent, corporations are the primary beneficiaries of a unified set of accounting standards. They save accounting costs and can more easily make acquisition decisions and access foreign capital markets. Thus, stockholders, as the owners of corporations, have a vested interest in the development of common standards. However, not all companies and their stockholders are convinced that unified standards are in their best interests. For example, the argument has been made that U.S. corporations may find themselves more susceptible to lawsuits in a principles-based system that relies on fewer detailed rules. Considerable costs will be incurred in training accountants under a new set of standards. Ultimately, it will be the responsibility of the Securities and Exchange Commission in this country to decide if the advantages outweigh the disadvantages.

Who Is Responsible for Developing Global Accounting Standards?

The IFRS Foundation and the International Accounting Standards Board (IASB) state as their mission:

> to develop IFRS Standards that bring transparency, accountability and efficiency to financial markets around the world.[1]

The International Accounting Standards Committee was established in 1973 to develop worldwide standards and was replaced in 2001 by the IASB. With headquarters in London, the IASB not only issues new accounting standards (called *International Financial Reporting Standards* or *IFRS*), but it also works with national accounting groups such as the FASB towards convergence of standards.

According to the IASB, more than 100 countries now require the use of IFRS by public companies. In fact use of IFRS is now mandatory in all member states of the economic and political organization known as the European Union. Outside Europe, other countries have formally announced their convergence plans. For example, China has substantially reached convergence with IFRS. Beginning in 2011, all Canadian listed companies were required to use IFRS. Companies in Mexico began using IFRS in 2012. Interestingly, Japan had still not made a decision as of mid 2016 about mandatory adoption.[2]

LO3 Describe the role of the International Accounting Standards Board in setting accounting standards and be familiar with the time frame for the convergence of U.S. GAAP and IFRS standards.

---

[1] IFRS Foundation and IASB web site.

[2] Ibid.

Where does this leave the United States? In 2002, the IASB and the FASB formalized their commitment to the union of U.S. and international standards with the Norwalk agreement. Since that time, the two groups have continued their efforts in this regard. For example, in October 2009, the FASB and the IASB reaffirmed their commitment to achieving convergence and since then have continued to work on a number of joint projects.

In 2007, the SEC dropped its long-standing rule that required foreign companies that filed financial statements with it to adjust those statements to conform with U.S. GAAP. The only stipulation is that the statements must follow the standards of the IASB. However, since then the SEC has delayed any final decision on convergence. In the meantime, the FASB and the IASB continue their efforts to eliminate differences between U.S. and international standards.

Throughout this book, we have focused our attention on the fundamental concepts underlying financial reporting and the standards that have been developed in this country to support those concepts. Many of the differences between U.S. GAAP and IFRS deal with complex issues beyond the scope of this book. In the next section, we consider the major differences between the two sets of rules, emphasizing those topics that have been discussed in each of the chapters.

Major Differences Between U.S. GAAP and IFRS

LO4 Describe the most significant differences between U.S. GAAP and IFRS.

Chapter 1: Accounting as a Form of Communication

By July 1, 2009, when the codification of accounting standards took effect, the FASB had issued 168 standards, in addition to various interpretations and other documents that comprise what is considered to be U.S. GAAP. In contrast, during a very similar time period, the IASB and its predecessor body had released only about 50 standards. Additionally, FASB statements are generally much more detailed than those of the IASB. Because there are significantly more standards in the United States and they are more detailed, standard setting in the United States has often been characterized as *rule based,* whereas the approach used by the international body is said to be more *principle based.* Because less-detailed guidance is usually provided in international standards, it stands to reason that more disclosures are warranted. Thus, it is common to see significantly more disclosures in notes to the financial statements of companies that follow IFRS than for those companies following U.S. GAAP. These differences are summarized as follows:

	U.S. GAAP	IFRS
Type of standards	Rule based	Principle based
Number of standards	More	Fewer
Level of detail in standards	More detailed	Less detailed
Level of disclosure required	Less	More

Chapter 2: Financial Statements and the Annual Report

As another indication of the cooperation between the FASB and the IASB, in September 2010, the two groups released a joint statement titled "Conceptual Framework for Financial Reporting." With this statement, both the objectives of financial reporting and the qualitative characteristics that make accounting information useful are the same for the two groups. These concepts are discussed in detail in Chapter 2. Both U.S. GAAP and IFRS require a complete set of financial statements to include a balance sheet, a statement of stockholders' equity, an income statement, and a statement of cash flows.

Chapter 3: Processing Accounting Information

How accounting information is processed is largely a function of the technology available to implement an accounting system rather than the result of any specific accounting standards in a particular country. The technology available in less-developed countries may influence the development of accounting systems in those countries. The double-entry system devised in 15th-century Italy is still used almost universally today.

Chapter 4: Income Measurement and Accrual Accounting

The accrual accounting system is used almost universally and is the basis for financial statements prepared using both U.S. GAAP and IFRS. In 2014, the FASB and the IASB issued a joint revenue recognition standard. To date, this is one of the most important joint efforts of the two groups, resulting in convergence in the way companies recognize revenue for a variety of complex situations.

Chapter 5: Inventories and Cost of Goods Sold

The LIFO inventory method is popular in the United States, to some extent due to the fact that it allows companies to minimize income taxes during a period of rising prices. Recall from Chapter 5 that the LIFO conformity rule requires that a company that wants to use the LIFO method for reporting cost of goods sold on its tax return must also use LIFO on its books. Many countries do not allow LIFO for either tax or financial reporting purposes. In fact, the IASB strictly prohibits the use of LIFO by companies that follow its standards. There has been considerable discussion in the United States about the repeal of LIFO for tax purposes. If this were to happen, it is likely that its use for financial reporting purposes would be eliminated as well, which would then remove one of the most significant differences between U.S. and international accounting standards.

Both U.S. GAAP and IFRS require use of the lower-of-cost-or-market rule to value inventories. However, the two sets of standards differ in two respects. First, U.S. GAAP define market value as *replacement cost,* subject to a maximum and minimum amount. In contrast, IFRS uses *net realizable value* as the measure of the market value of inventory, and no upper or lower limits are imposed. Second, under U.S. GAAP, if inventory is written down to a new, lower market value, this amount becomes the basis for that inventory. Future write-downs of the inventory use this new amount to compare with market value. However, under IFRS, write-downs of inventory can be reversed in later periods. That is, a gain is recognized when the value of the inventory goes back up.

Chapter 6: Cash and Internal Control

The Sarbanes-Oxley Act of 2002 (SOX) placed strict reporting requirements on companies that want to list their securities on U.S. stock exchanges. The initial costs to comply with the act and the annual requirements to maintain an effective system of internal control have been substantial for these companies. No such reporting requirements exist for companies that report using IFRS. Were convergence to be achieved, it remains uncertain whether any additional requirements would be added to international standards similar to those now imposed in this country under SOX.

Chapter 7: Receivables and Investments

No significant differences exist in the accounting for receivables in this country and internationally. U.S. GAAP and IFRS both require that investments be carried at fair value rather than historical cost, although there are minor differences in the rules for application of fair value accounting.

Chapter 8: Operating Assets: Property, Plant, and Equipment, and Intangibles

While the accounting for operating assets is similar under IFRS and U.S. GAAP standards, there are several important differences.

The same depreciation methods are available for long-term assets under both sets of standards, but the estimates of residual values and the depreciable lives of assets may be assessed differently. Under IFRS, estimates of the life of assets and the residual value of assets must be reviewed at least annually, and if the estimates have changed, then the company should treat the change as a change in estimate. U.S. GAAP require companies to assess the estimate of residual value and life only when circumstances have changed and the accountant believes a change in estimate is necessary. Also, the treatment of interest to be capitalized on self-constructed assets varies between IFRS and U.S. GAAP. U.S. GAAP require that a company **must** capitalize interest on such assets, while IFRS permits capitalization but does not require it.

There are also differences in the reporting for particular operating assets. Both IFRS and U.S. GAAP require companies to report an amount for goodwill and record a write-down of the goodwill if the asset has been "impaired." However, the methods of evaluating impairment differ between the two sets of standards. The treatment of research and development (R&D) costs also differs. U.S. GAAP require all internally generated research and development costs to be treated as an expense. IFRS requires research costs to be recognized as an expense but does allow certain development costs to be accounted for as an asset.

Perhaps the most significant difference in the accounting for operating assets concerns the use of fair values. Generally, both sets of standards require operating assets to be carried at their historical cost. However, IFRS allows companies to revalue the assets at fair value (either up or down from historical cost) if reliable measures are available. U.S. GAAP do not allow companies to revalue to fair value except in cases where an impairment of an asset has occurred and the asset must be written down to a lower value.

Chapter 9: Current Liabilities, Contingencies, and the Time Value of Money

You may be surprised to learn that U.S. GAAP do not require companies to present a balance sheet with classifications for current and long-term liabilities, or any other classifications. Many companies do, however, present a classified balance sheet in order to present information that balance sheet readers consider to be important. In contrast to U.S. GAAP, IFRS does require companies to present current and noncurrent classifications of assets and liabilities.

The IFRS and U.S. GAAP standards differ significantly on what we have referred to as contingencies in Chapter 9. For reporting in the United States, liabilities for which the outcome is dependent upon a future event must be recorded if the unfavorable outcome is probable and the amount can be reasonably estimated. If the outcome is at least reasonably possible, then the liability should be disclosed, usually in the notes to the financial statements. For IFRS, the term *contingent liabilities* is used only for items that are not recorded on the financial statements. The liabilities that are considered probable and are recorded are referred to as *provisions*. Also, the two sets of standards differ somewhat on what should be considered as "probable."

Finally, the standards differ on the reporting of liabilities where a range of values is available as a possible outcome. U.S. GAAP require that a company report the low end of the range if the outcome is probable and disclose the upper end of the range in the notes. IFRS, however, requires companies to record the midpoint of the range as a provision if the unfavorable outcome is probable.

Chapter 10: Long-Term Liabilities

There are two issues in Chapter 10 that illustrate the attempts of the rule-making bodies to make the U.S. and international standards more aligned. The FASB has issued a revised standard on leasing. When that standard is implemented, there will still be differences between U.S. and international standards, but the differences will be reduced. Most importantly, the FASB has adopted the terminology of the international standards.

Leases will no longer be classified as operating or capital leases. They will be classified as operating or finance leases, as in the international standards.

Also, both sets of standards address the topics of deferred taxes. While there are still some important technical differences, there is no longer a difference in whether deferred taxes are classified as current or long-term. The FASB has adopted the international standard that indicates deferred taxes should be treated as long-term items.

Chapter 11: Stockholders' Equity

In general, the accounting for stockholders' equity is the same for IFRS and U.S. GAAP. The most significant difference concerns financial instruments that have both debt and equity characteristics (a convertible bond is one example). IFRS requires the portion of the instrument that represents debt to be presented in the Liability category and the portion of the instrument that represents equity to be in stockholders' equity. U.S. GAAP do not always require such instruments to be separately reported as debt and equity.

Also, both IFRS and U.S. GAAP require the presentation of comprehensive income amounts in the Stockholders' Equity category. However, the manner of reporting comprehensive income amounts as income on the income statement or statement of comprehensive income varies between the two sets of standards. These variations are beyond the scope of this textbook.

Chapter 12: The Statement of Cash Flows

Both U.S. GAAP and IFRS require the inclusion of a statement of cash flows in a complete set of financial statements. Each set of standards also mandates that activities be classified into three categories: operating, investing, and financing. Some differences in classification exist. For example, interest (either received or paid) and dividends received are always classified as operating activities under U.S. GAAP. IFRS allows flexibility; cash receipts may be classified as either operating or investing activities and cash payments as either operating or financing. Similarly, dividends paid are always classified as financing activities under U.S. GAAP, but they may be classified as either operating or financing activities under IFRS. Recall from Chapter 12 that significant noncash activities may be presented in either a separate schedule on the face of the statement of cash flows or in the notes to the statements. Under IFRS, these noncash activities must be presented in the notes.

Chapter 13: Financial Statement Analysis

The IASB prohibits the presentation of items on the income statement as extraordinary. Until recently, U.S. GAAP required certain gains and losses to be classified as extraordinary. With a recent change in U.S. GAAP to prohibit any items to be classified as extraordinary, the standards of the two groups are in conformity in this regard.

Both U.S. GAAP and IFRS require separate presentation on the income statement for discontinued operations.

Format and Terminology Differences

Up to this point, the focus has been on the differing accounting standards used in the preparation of financial statements around the world. But what about the *format* for the statements and the *terms* used for the various statement items? It should come as no surprise that significant differences exist in how financial statements are presented and the names given to various accounts. For example, consider the partial *statement of financial position* (balance sheet) for Daimler AG shown in Exhibit A-1. (We show only the first two columns on the statement titled "Consolidated"—the entire statement also displays columns for its divisions: "Industrial Business" and "Daimler Financial Services.")

LO5 Understand how differences in format and terminology affect the appearance of financial statements in various countries.

EXHIBIT A-1 Daimler AG's Consolidated Statement of Financial Position

	Note	Consolidated	
		At December 31,	
		2015	2014
In millions of euros			
Assets			
Intangible assets	10	10,069	9,367
Property, plant and equipment	11	24,322	23,182
Equipment on operating leases	12	38,942	33,050
Equity-method investments	13	3,633	2,294
Receivables from financial services	14	38,359	34,910
Marketable debt securities	15	1,148	1,374
Other financial assets	16	4,908	3,634
Deferred tax assets	9	3,284	4,124
Other assets	17	654	555
Total non-current assets		125,319	112,490
Inventories	18	23,760	20,864
Trade receivables	19	9,054	8,634
Receivables from financial services	14	35,155	26,769
Cash and cash equivalents		9,936	9,667
Marketable debt securities	15	7,125	5,260
Other financial assets	16	2,546	2,353
Other assets	17	4,271	3,598
Total current assets		91,847	77,145
Total assets		217,166	189,635
Equity and liabilities			
Share capital		3,070	3,070
Capital reserve		11,917	11,906
Retained earnings		36,991	28,487
Other reserves		1,583	202
Treasury shares		–	–
Equity attributable to shareholders of Daimler AG		53,561	43,665
Non-controlling interests		1,063	919
Total equity	20	54,624	44,584
Provisions for pensions and similar obligations	22	8,663	12,806
Provisions for income taxes		875	851
Provisions for other risks	23	6,120	6,712
Financing liabilities	24	59,831	50,399
Other financial liabilities	25	2,876	2,644
Deferred tax liabilities	9	2,215	1,070
Deferred income	26	4,851	3,581
Other liabilities	27	30	14
Total non-current liabilities		85,461	78,077
Trade payables		10,548	10,178
Provisions for income taxes		777	757
Provisions for other risks	23	9,710	7,267
Financing liabilities	24	41,311	36,290
Other financial liabilities	25	9,484	8,062
Deferred income	26	2,888	2,413
Other liabilities	27	2,363	2,007
Total current liabilities		77,081	66,974
Total equity and liabilities		217,166	189,635

The accompanying notes are an integral part of these consolidated financial statements.

Source: Daimler AG, Annual Report, 2015.

Annotations (margin callouts):

- The monetary unit is "euros"
- Non-current assets listed before current assets
- Same as Capital Stock
- Same as Additional Paid-In Capital
- Equity listed first
- Non-current liabilities listed before current liabilities

Note that amounts are stated in millions of euros, the common currency for members of the European Union. Also, a vast majority of the statement items are referenced to notes to the financial statements. As mentioned earlier in this appendix, because IFRS is less rules based, it is common to see more disclosures in notes to the financial statements (recall that Daimler AG uses IFRS in preparing its statements).

One of the most striking differences is the *ordering* of both the assets and the equity and liabilities on the statement. For example, long-term assets (non-current) are presented first, followed by current assets. Also, note that three common current assets are listed in reverse order of liquidity: inventories first, followed by trade receivables and then cash and cash equivalents. Similarly, equity items are presented before liabilities, with current liabilities as the last category on the statement. *Essentially, the entire statement of financial position is inverted compared to what is commonly seen in the United States.*

Significant differences in terminology are also evident in looking at Daimler AG's statement. For example, consider the Equity section. *Share Capital* is the name the company uses for what would normally be referred to as Capital Stock by a U.S. company. *Capital Reserve* is the equivalent of Additional Paid-In Capital. Daimler AG's non-current and current liabilities both contain an item called *Provisions for Other Risks*. This is what most U.S. companies would refer to as Contingent Liabilities. Financial statement users need to be aware of these differences in format and terminology. However, these differences should not impede the ability to analyze and make effective use of foreign statements.

TEST YOURSELF

Review		
	LO1 Explain why accounting standards currently differ among countries around the world.	• Accounting standards vary around the world for a variety of reasons, including: • Some countries follow a common law system and others rely more heavily on code law. • In some countries, accounting standards follow the tax law more closely than in other countries. • The source of financing can affect how accounting standards are developed. • Significant inflation may result in accounting rules to adjust the statements for its effects. • The standards in some countries are influenced by those in other countries. • The state of economic development can affect accounting standards.
	LO2 Explain the benefits from a single set of accounting standards.	• Certain benefits would result from a uniform set of accounting standards, including: • Save on accounting costs. • Make it easier to acquire foreign companies. • Make it easier to access foreign capital markets. • Facilitate comparisons.
	LO3 Describe the role of the International Accounting Standards Board in setting accounting standards and be familiar with the time frame for the convergence of U.S. GAAP and IFRS standards.	• The International Accounting Standards Board is the group responsible for the development of a single set of worldwide accounting standards. • The FASB and similar accounting bodies in other countries are currently working with the IASB to achieve the goal of a single set of standards.
	LO4 Describe the most significant differences between U.S. GAAP and IFRS.	• Although U.S. GAAP and IFRS are similar in many respects, significant differences still exist. • U.S. GAAP are much more detailed. • The FASB has issued many more standards than has the IASB. • IFRS requires more disclosures in the notes to the financial statements.

LO5 Understand how differences in format and terminology affect the appearance of financial statements in various countries.

- In some countries, long-term assets are listed before current assets on the balance sheet and long-term liabilities before current liabilities. It is also common to see the stockholders' equity accounts displayed above the liability accounts.
- Users must be alert to differing terms to describe the same items on financial statements.

Question

1. What are at least four reasons that accounting standards currently differ between countries?

2. How have accounting standards developed differently in countries that use a common law system as opposed to those using code law?

3. Why might you expect the accounting standards in Australia to be similar to those in the United Kingdom?

4. What are at least three advantages in all companies around the world using the same accounting standards?

5. How would you describe the current role of the IASB in setting accounting standards?

6. How would you evaluate the following statement: "All of the other major industrialized countries of the world have now adopted IFRS and the United States has set a date for adoption by all companies that currently follow FASB standards"?

7. You are considering investing in the airline industry and are looking specifically at buying shares of either **Southwest Airlines** or **British Airways**. Would you expect the financial statements of these two companies to be prepared using the same accounting principles? Explain your answer.

8. How does the application of the lower-of-cost-or-market rule differ between U.S. GAAP and IFRS?

9. How would you evaluate the following statement: "Both the tax laws in the United States and IFRS allow the use of LIFO for tax purposes but only if the method is also used for financial reporting purposes"?

10. How are research and development costs accounted for differently under U.S. GAAP and IFRS?

11. Do either or both U.S. GAAP and IFRS allow operating assets to be carried on the balance sheet at fair value?

12. How does the meaning of the term *contingent liabilities* differ between U.S. GAAP and IFRS?

13. What differences are there in classification of interest received and interest paid under U.S. GAAP and IFRS?

14. Is there a standard format used in all countries for the statement of financial position? Explain.

Apply

1. Fill in the blanks below with either "more" or "less" to indicate the differences in U.S. GAAP and IFRS:

	U.S. GAAP	IFRS
Number of standards	_____	_____
Level of detail in standards	_____	_____
Level of disclosure required	_____	_____

2. The cost of Baxter's inventory at the end of the year was $50,000. Due to obsolescence, the cost to replace the inventory was only $40,000. Net realizable value—what the inventory could be sold for—is $42,000. Determine the amount Baxter should report on its year-end balance sheet for inventory assuming the company follows (a) U.S. GAAP and (b) IFRS.

3. Maple Corp. owns a building with an original cost of $1,000,000 and accumulated depreciation at the balance sheet date of $200,000. Based on a recent appraisal, the fair value of the building is $850,000.
   a. At what amount will the building be reported on the year-end balance sheet if Maple follows U.S. GAAP?
   b. Does Maple have a choice in the amount to report for the building if instead it follows IFRS? What are those choices?

4. During the most recent year, Butler paid $95,000 in interest to its lenders and $80,000 in dividends to its stockholders.

   a. In which category of the statement of cash flows (operating, investing, or financing) should each of these amounts be shown if Butler follows U.S. GAAP? If more than one category is acceptable, indicate what the choices are.

   b. In which category of the statement of cash flows (operating, investing, or financing) should each of these amounts be shown if Butler follows IFRS? If more than one category is acceptable, indicate what the choices are.

5. Refer to the statement of financial position for **Daimler AG** as shown on page A-9.

   a. What is the currency used in preparing this statement?

   b. Identify at least three differences in the format of the statement compared to what would normally be seen on a statement of financial position for a U.S. company.

   c. Refer to the Equity section of the statement. What account titles would normally be used in the United States for the first two items in this section?

Answers

Answers to Questions

1. Accounting standards currently differ between countries for a variety of reasons, including differences in legal systems, how similar or different the rules are for determining accounting income and taxable income, primary means for financing businesses, the significance of inflation in the country, the extent to which a country has political and economic ties to another country, and the state of economic development.

2. Accounting standards are generally more detailed in common law countries such as the United States because less-detailed laws are written in the statutes provided by the government. In code law countries, more detailed rules are written directly into the statutes.

3. Accounting standards in Australia are similar to those in the United Kingdom due to the strong economic and political ties between the countries. Australia is a former British colony.

4. A number of benefits would result from all companies around the world using the same accounting standards, including savings on accounting costs for companies with international operations, ease in acquiring foreign companies, ease in accessing foreign capital markets, and the facilitation of comparisons by analysts and investors.

5. The IASB is the leader in the development of international accounting standards. The group both issues new pronouncements and works closely with accounting bodies in other countries, such as the FASB in the United States, towards the convergence of standards.

6. Although over 100 countries around the world now require public companies to use IFRS, not all of the major industrialized countries are currently on board. Companies in Mexico and Canada now use IFRS. Japan has not yet made a final decision about mandatory adoption. The FASB has worked on convergence with the IASB but the SEC in the United States has delayed any final decision on adoption of IFRS.

7. No, the airlines do not use the same accounting principles in preparing their financial statements. Southwest Airlines would follow U.S. GAAP while British Airways would report using IFRS. The lack of a common set of standards makes comparisons more difficult, but not impossible.

8. The lower-of-cost-or-market rule differs in two respects between U.S. GAAP and IFRS. First, U.S. GAAP define market value as replacement cost, subject to a maximum and minimum amount. IFRS uses net realizable value with no upper or lower limits. Second, under U.S. GAAP, if inventory is written down to a new, lower market value, this amount becomes the basis for that inventory. In contrast, under IFRS, write-downs of inventory can be reversed in later periods.

9. The IASB expressly prohibits the use of LIFO by companies that follow IFRS. However, the Internal Revenue Service in the United States does allow the use of LIFO for tax purposes if the method is also used for financial reporting purposes.

10. U.S. GAAP require all internally generated research and development costs to be recognized as expense as they are incurred. Although IFRS requires research costs to be treated in the same manner, certain development costs may be accounted for initially as an asset.

11. U.S. GAAP require operating assets to be carried at historical cost, unless an impairment in value has occurred. Conversely, IFRS does allow companies to revalue operating assets at fair value if reliable measures are available.

12. Under U.S. GAAP, a contingent liability is accrued and presented on the balance sheet if it is probable and the amount can be reasonably estimated. IFRS reserves the term *contingent liabilities* for those items that are *not* recorded on the balance sheet. Those liabilities that are probable and are recorded are called *provisions*.

13. U.S. GAAP require both interest received and interest paid to be classified as operating activities on the statement of cash flows. Conversely, IFRS allows interest received to be classified as either an operating or an investing activity. Similarly, interest paid may be classified as either operating or financing under IFRS.

14. No, there is no standard format in various countries for the statement of financial position. In some countries, it is common to present long-term assets before current assets. Also, stockholders' equity may appear before liabilities, which is the opposite of the presentation used in the United States.

Answers to Apply

1.

	U.S. GAAP	IFRS
Number of standards	More	Less
Level of detail in standards	More	Less
Level of disclosure required	Less	More

2. Amount to be reported on year-end balance sheet for inventory assuming:
   a. U.S. GAAP: $40,000
   b. IFRS: $42,000

3. a. $1,000,000 − $200,000 = $800,000.
   b. Under IFRS, Maple has a choice to present the building at either historical cost less accumulated depreciation ($1,000,000 − $200,000) = $800,000 or fair value of $850,000.

4. a. Under U.S. GAAP, the interest paid of $95,000 must be classified as an operating activity, and the dividends paid of $80,000 must be classified as a financing activity.
   b. Under IFRS, the interest paid of $95,000 may be classified as either an operating activity or a financing activity. Dividends paid of $80,000 may also be classified as either an operating activity or a financing activity.

5. a. Daimler AG reports amounts in millions of euros, the common currency for members of the European Union.
   b. Differences in format from a balance sheet for a U.S. company include: (1) non-current assets listed before current assets; (2) equity presented before liabilities; (3) non-current liabilities listed before current liabilities; and (4) inventories, receivables, and cash reported in reverse order of liquidity.
   c. Share Capital is the same as Capital Stock for a U.S. company. Capital Reserve is the equivalent of the Additional Paid-In Capital account.

B

Excerpts from Chipotle Mexican Grill, Inc. Form 10-K for the Fiscal Year Ended December 31, 2015

UNITED STATES
SECURITIES AND EXCHANGE COMMISSION
WASHINGTON, D.C. 20549
FORM 10-K

☒ ANNUAL REPORT PURSUANT TO SECTION 13 OR 15(d) OF THE SECURITIES EXCHANGE ACT OF 1934
For the fiscal year ended December 31, 2015

or

☐ TRANSITION REPORT PURSUANT TO SECTION 13 OR 15(d) OF THE SECURITIES EXCHANGE ACT OF 1934
For the transition period from   to
Commission File Number: 1-32731

CHIPOTLE MEXICAN GRILL, INC.
(Exact name of registrant as specified in its charter)

Delaware	84-1219301
(State or other jurisdiction of incorporation or organization)	(IRS Employer Identification No.)
1401 Wynkoop Street, Suite 500 Denver, CO	80202
(Address of Principal Executive Offices)	(Zip Code)

Registrant's telephone number, including area code: (303) 595-4000

Securities registered pursuant to Section 12(b) of the Act:

Title of each class	Name of each exchange on which registered
Common stock, par value $0.01 per share	New York Stock Exchange

Securities registered pursuant to Section 12(g) of the Act: None

Indicate by check mark if the registrant is a well-known seasoned issuer, as defined in Rule 405 of the Securities Act.   Yes ☒   No ☐

Indicate by check mark if the registrant is not required to file reports pursuant to Section 13 or Section 15(d) of the Act.   Yes ☐   No ☒

Indicate by check mark whether the registrant: (1) has filed all reports required to be filed by Section 13 or 15(d) of the Securities Exchange Act of 1934 during the preceding 12 months (or for such shorter period that the registrant was required to file such reports), and (2) has been subject to such filing requirements for the past 90 days.   Yes ☒   No ☐

Indicate by check mark whether the registrant has submitted electronically and posted on its corporate Web site, if any, every Interactive Data File required to be submitted and posted pursuant to Rule 405 of Regulation S-T (§232.405 of this chapter) during the preceding 12 months (or for such shorter period that the registrant was required to submit and post such files).   ☒ Yes   ☐ No

Indicate by check mark if disclosure of delinquent filers pursuant to Item 405 of Regulation S-K (§229.405 of this chapter) is not contained herein, and will not be contained, to the best of registrant's knowledge, in definitive proxy or information statements incorporated by reference in Part III of this Form 10-K or any amendment to this Form 10-K. ☐

Indicate by check mark whether the registrant is a large accelerated filer, an accelerated filer, a non-accelerated filer, or a smaller reporting company. See the definitions of "large accelerated filer," "accelerated filer," and "smaller reporting company" in Rule 12b-2 of the Exchange Act (check one):

☒ Large accelerated filer   ☐ Accelerated filer   ☐ Non-accelerated filer (do not check if a smaller reporting company)   ☐ Smaller reporting company

Indicate by check mark whether the registrant is a shell company (as defined in Rule 12b-2 of the Act).   Yes ☐   No ☒

As of June 30, 2015, the aggregate market value of the registrant's outstanding common equity held by non-affiliates was $11.2 billion, based on the closing price of the registrant's common stock on such date, the last trading day of the registrant's most recently completed second fiscal quarter. For purposes of this calculation, shares of common stock held by each executive officer and director and by holders of 5% or more of the outstanding common stock have been excluded since those persons may under certain circumstances be deemed to be affiliates. This determination of affiliate status is not necessarily a conclusive determination for other purposes.

As of January 29, 2016, there were 30,044,250 shares of the registrant's common stock, par value of $0.01 per share outstanding.

DOCUMENTS INCORPORATED BY REFERENCE

Part III incorporates certain information by reference from the registrant's definitive proxy statement for the 2016 annual meeting of shareholders, which will be filed no later than 120 days after the close of the registrant's fiscal year ended December 31, 2015.

ITEM 6. SELECTED FINANCIAL DATA

Our selected consolidated financial data shown below should be read together with Item 7. "Management's Discussion and Analysis of Financial Condition and Results of Operations" and our consolidated financial statements and respective notes included in Item 8 "Financial Statements and Supplementary Data." The data shown below are not necessarily indicative of results to be expected for any future period (in thousands, except per share data).

	Year ended December 31,				
	2015	**2014**	**2013**	**2012**	**2011**
Statement of Income:					
Revenue	$ 4,501,223	$ 4,108,269	$ 3,214,591	$ 2,731,224	$ 2,269,548
Food, beverage and packaging costs	1,503,835	1,420,994	1,073,514	891,003	738,720
Labor costs	1,045,726	904,407	739,800	641,836	543,119
Occupancy costs	262,412	230,868	199,107	171,435	147,274
Other operating costs	514,963	434,244	347,401	286,610	251,208
General and administrative expenses	250,214	273,897	203,733	183,409	149,426
Depreciation and amortization	130,368	110,474	96,054	84,130	74,938
Pre-opening costs	16,922	15,609	15,511	11,909	8,495
Loss on disposal of assets	13,194	6,976	6,751	5,027	5,806
Total operating expenses	3,737,634	3,397,469	2,681,871	2,275,359	1,918,986
Income from operations	763,589	710,800	532,720	455,865	350,562
Interest and other income (expense), net	6,278	3,503	1,751	1,820	(857)
Income before income taxes	769,867	714,303	534,471	457,685	349,705
Provision for income taxes	(294,265)	(268,929)	(207,033)	(179,685)	(134,760)
Net income	$ 475,602	$ 445,374	$ 327,438	$ 278,000	$ 214,945
Earnings per share					
Basic	$ 15.30	$ 14.35	$ 10.58	$ 8.82	$ 6.89
Diluted	$ 15.10	$ 14.13	$ 10.47	$ 8.75	$ 6.76
Weighted average common shares outstanding					
Basic	31,092	31,038	30,957	31,513	31,217
Diluted	31,494	31,512	31,281	31,783	31,775

	December 31,				
	2015	**2014**[1]	**2013**[1]	**2012**[1]	**2011**[1]
Balance Sheet Data:					
Total current assets	$ 814,647	$ 859,511	$ 653,095	$ 537,745	$ 494,954
Total assets	$ 2,725,066	$ 2,527,317	$ 1,996,068	$ 1,659,805	$ 1,419,070
Total current liabilities	$ 279,942	$ 245,710	$ 199,228	$ 186,852	$ 157,453
Total liabilities	$ 597,092	$ 514,948	$ 457,780	$ 413,879	$ 374,844
Total shareholders' equity	$ 2,127,974	$ 2,012,369	$ 1,538,288	$ 1,245,926	$ 1,044,226

———

(1) Balances were adjusted because we adopted Financial Accounting Standards Board Accounting Standards Update No. 2015-17, "Income Taxes" which requires that deferred tax liabilities and assets be classified as noncurrent in a classified balance sheet, as discussed in further detail in Note 1. "Description of the Business and Summary of Significant Accounting Policies" in our consolidated financial statements included in Item 8. "Financial Statements and Supplementary Data."

ITEM 8. FINANCIAL STATEMENTS AND SUPPLEMENTARY DATA

INDEX TO CONSOLIDATED FINANCIAL STATEMENTS

Report of Independent Registered Public Accounting Firm

The Board of Directors and Shareholders of
Chipotle Mexican Grill, Inc.

We have audited the accompanying consolidated balance sheets of Chipotle Mexican Grill, Inc. (the "Company") as of December 31, 2015 and 2014, and the related consolidated statements of income and comprehensive income, shareholders' equity and cash flows for each of the three years in the period ended December 31, 2015. These financial statements are the responsibility of the Company's management. Our responsibility is to express an opinion on these financial statements based on our audits.

We conducted our audits in accordance with the standards of the Public Company Accounting Oversight Board (United States). Those standards require that we plan and perform the audit to obtain reasonable assurance about whether the financial statements are free of material misstatement. An audit includes examining, on a test basis, evidence supporting the amounts and disclosures in the financial statements. An audit also includes assessing the accounting principles used and significant estimates made by management, as well as evaluating the overall financial statement presentation. We believe that our audits provide a reasonable basis for our opinion.

In our opinion, the financial statements referred to above present fairly, in all material respects, the consolidated financial position of Chipotle Mexican Grill, Inc. at December 31, 2015 and 2014, and the consolidated results of its operations and its cash flows for each of the three years in the period ended December 31, 2015, in conformity with U.S. generally accepted accounting principles.

We also have audited, in accordance with the standards of the Public Company Accounting Oversight Board (United States), Chipotle Mexican Grill, Inc.'s internal control over financial reporting as of December 31, 2015, based on criteria established in Internal Control-Integrated Framework issued by the Committee of Sponsoring Organizations of the Treadway Commission (2013 framework) and our report dated February 4, 2016 expressed an unqualified opinion thereon.

/s/ Ernst & Young LLP

Denver, Colorado
February 4, 2016

CHIPOTLE MEXICAN GRILL, INC.

CONSOLIDATED BALANCE SHEET
(in thousands, except per share data)

	December 31,	
	2015	**2014**
		(as adjusted)
Assets		
Current assets:		
Cash and cash equivalents	$ 248,005	$ 419,465
Accounts receivable, net of allowance for doubtful accounts of $1,176 and $1,199 as of December 31, 2015 and December 31, 2014, respectively	38,283	34,839
Inventory	15,043	15,332
Prepaid expenses and other current assets	39,965	34,795
Income tax receivable	58,152	16,488
Investments	415,199	338,592
Total current assets	814,647	859,511
Leasehold improvements, property and equipment, net	1,217,220	1,106,984
Long term investments	622,939	496,106
Other assets	48,321	42,777
Goodwill	21,939	21,939
Total assets	$ 2,725,066	$ 2,527,317
Liabilities and shareholders' equity		
Current liabilities:		
Accounts payable	$ 85,709	$ 69,613
Accrued payroll and benefits	64,958	73,894
Accrued liabilities	129,275	102,203
Total current liabilities	279,942	245,710
Deferred rent	251,962	219,414
Deferred income tax liability	32,305	21,561
Other liabilities	32,883	28,263
Total liabilities	597,092	514,948
Shareholders' equity:		
Preferred stock, $0.01 par value, 600,000 shares authorized, no shares issued as of December 31, 2015 and December 31, 2014, respectively	-	-
Common stock $0.01 par value, 230,000 shares authorized, and 35,790 and 35,394 shares issued as of December 31, 2015 and December 31, 2014, respectively	358	354
Additional paid-in capital	1,172,628	1,038,932
Treasury stock, at cost, 5,206 and 4,367 common shares at December 31, 2015 and December 31, 2014, respectively	(1,234,612)	(748,759)
Accumulated other comprehensive income (loss)	(8,273)	(429)
Retained earnings	2,197,873	1,722,271
Total shareholders' equity	2,127,974	2,012,369
Total liabilities and shareholders' equity	$ 2,725,066	$ 2,527,317

See accompanying notes to consolidated financial statements.

CHIPOTLE MEXICAN GRILL, INC.

CONSOLIDATED STATEMENT OF INCOME AND COMPREHENSIVE INCOME
(in thousands, except per share data)

	Year ended December 31,		
	2015	2014	2013
Revenue	$ 4,501,223	$ 4,108,269	$ 3,214,591
Restaurant operating costs (exclusive of depreciation and amortization shown separately below):			
Food, beverage and packaging	1,503,835	1,420,994	1,073,514
Labor	1,045,726	904,407	739,800
Occupancy	262,412	230,868	199,107
Other operating costs	514,963	434,244	347,401
General and administrative expenses	250,214	273,897	203,733
Depreciation and amortization	130,368	110,474	96,054
Pre-opening costs	16,922	15,609	15,511
Loss on disposal of assets	13,194	6,976	6,751
Total operating expenses	3,737,634	3,397,469	2,681,871
Income from operations	763,589	710,800	532,720
Interest and other income (expense), net	6,278	3,503	1,751
Income before income taxes	769,867	714,303	534,471
Provision for income taxes	(294,265)	(268,929)	(207,033)
Net income	$ 475,602	$ 445,374	$ 327,438
Other comprehensive income (loss), net of income taxes:			
Foreign currency translation adjustments	(6,322)	(2,049)	596
Unrealized loss on investments, net of income taxes of $946, $0, and $0	(1,522)	-	-
Other comprehensive income (loss), net of income taxes	(7,844)	(2,049)	596
Comprehensive income	$ 467,758	$ 443,325	$ 328,034
Earnings per share:			
Basic	$ 15.30	$ 14.35	$ 10.58
Diluted	$ 15.10	$ 14.13	$ 10.47
Weighted average common shares outstanding:			
Basic	31,092	31,038	30,957
Diluted	31,494	31,512	31,281

See accompanying notes to consolidated financial statements.

CHIPOTLE MEXICAN GRILL, INC.
CONSOLIDATED STATEMENT OF SHAREHOLDERS' EQUITY
(in thousands)

	Common Stock		Additional Paid-In Capital	Treasury Stock		Retained Earnings	Accumulated Other Comprehensive Income (Loss)	Total
	Shares	Amount		Shares	Amount			
Balance, December 31, 2012	34,912	$ 349	$ 816,612	3,819	$ (521,518)	$ 949,459	$ 1,024	$ 1,245,926
Stock-based compensation			64,781					64,781
Stock plan transactions and other	333	3	97					100
Excess tax benefit on stock-based compensation, net of utilization of $29			38,350					38,350
Acquisition of treasury stock				393	(138,903)			(138,903)
Net income						327,438		327,438
Other comprehensive income (loss), net of income tax							596	596
Balance, December 31, 2013	35,245	$ 352	$ 919,840	4,212	$ (660,421)	$ 1,276,897	$ 1,620	$ 1,538,288
Stock-based compensation			97,618					97,618
Stock plan transactions and other	149	2	(193)					(191)
Excess tax benefit on stock-based compensation			21,667					21,667
Acquisition of treasury stock				155	(88,338)			(88,338)
Net income						445,374		445,374
Other comprehensive income (loss), net of income tax							(2,049)	(2,049)
Balance, December 31, 2014	35,394	$ 354	$ 1,038,932	4,367	$ (748,759)	$ 1,722,271	$ (429)	$ 2,012,369
Stock-based compensation			59,465					59,465
Stock plan transactions and other	396	4	(211)					(207)
Excess tax benefit on stock-based compensation			74,442					74,442
Acquisition of treasury stock				839	(485,853)			(485,853)
Net income						475,602		475,602
Other comprehensive income (loss), net of income tax							(7,844)	(7,844)
Balance, December 31, 2015	35,790	$ 358	$ 1,172,628	5,206	$ (1,234,612)	$ 2,197,873	$ (8,273)	$ 2,127,974

CHIPOTLE MEXICAN GRILL, INC.

CONSOLIDATED STATEMENT OF CASH FLOWS
(in thousands)

	Year ended December 31,		
	2015	2014	2013
Operating activities			
Net income	$ 475,602	$ 445,374	$ 327,438
Adjustments to reconcile net income to net cash provided by operating activities:			
Depreciation and amortization	130,368	110,474	96,054
Deferred income tax (benefit) provision	11,666	(20,671)	2,103
Loss on disposal of assets	13,194	6,976	6,751
Bad debt allowance	(23)	9	19
Stock-based compensation expense	57,911	96,440	63,657
Excess tax benefit on stock-based compensation	(74,442)	(21,667)	(38,379)
Other	582	104	507
Changes in operating assets and liabilities:			
Accounts receivable	(3,504)	(10,966)	(7,238)
Inventory	262	(2,307)	(1,950)
Prepaid expenses and other current assets	(5,259)	(658)	(6,806)
Other assets	(5,619)	1,071	(1,354)
Accounts payable	19,525	2,168	2,052
Accrued liabilities	(7,440)	35,019	12,020
Income tax payable/receivable	32,756	8,831	44,334
Deferred rent	32,911	27,025	25,715
Other long-term liabilities	4,826	4,845	3,857
Net cash provided by operating activities	683,316	682,067	528,780
Investing activities			
Purchases of leasehold improvements, property and equipment	(257,418)	(252,590)	(199,926)
Purchases of investments	(559,372)	(521,004)	(387,639)
Maturities of investments	352,650	254,750	159,250
Net cash used in investing activities	(464,140)	(518,844)	(428,315)
Financing activities			
Acquisition of treasury stock	(460,675)	(88,338)	(138,903)
Excess tax benefit on stock-based compensation	74,442	21,667	38,379
Stock plan transactions and other financing activities	(207)	(66)	173
Net cash used in financing activities	(386,440)	(66,737)	(100,351)
Effect of exchange rate changes on cash and cash equivalents	(4,196)	(224)	536
Net change in cash and cash equivalents	(171,460)	96,262	650
Cash and cash equivalents at beginning of year	419,465	323,203	322,553
Cash and cash equivalents at end of year	$ 248,005	$ 419,465	$ 323,203
Supplemental disclosures of cash flow information			
Income taxes paid	$ 248,547	$ 280,687	$ 160,973
Increase (decrease) in purchases of leasehold improvements, property and equipment accrued in accounts payable and accrued liabilities	$ (2,870)	$ 9,424	$ (1,736)
Increase in acquisition of treasury stock accrued in accrued liabilities	$ 25,178	$ -	$ -

See accompanying notes to consolidated financial statements.

CHIPOTLE MEXICAN GRILL, INC.

NOTES TO CONSOLIDATED FINANCIAL STATEMENTS

(dollar and share amounts in thousands, unless otherwise specified)

1. Description of Business and Summary of Significant Accounting Policies

Chipotle Mexican Grill, Inc., a Delaware corporation, together with its subsidiaries (collectively the "Company") develops and operates fast-casual, fresh Mexican food restaurants. As of December 31, 2015, the Company operated 1,971 Chipotle restaurants throughout the United States. The Company also has 11 restaurants in Canada, seven in England, four in France, and one in Germany. Further, the Company operated 13 ShopHouse Southeast Asian Kitchen restaurants, serving fast-casual, Asian inspired cuisine, as well as is an investor in a consolidated entity that owned and operated three Pizzeria Locale restaurants, a fast casual pizza concept. The Company manages its operations based on nine regions and has aggregated its operations to one reportable segment.

Principles of Consolidation and Basis of Presentation

The consolidated financial statements include the accounts of the Company, including wholly and majority owned subsidiaries. All intercompany balances and transactions have been eliminated.

Management Estimates

The preparation of financial statements in conformity with U.S. generally accepted accounting principles requires management to make estimates and assumptions that affect the reported amounts of assets and liabilities and disclosure of contingent assets and liabilities as of the date of the financial statements and the reported amounts of revenue and expenses during the reporting period. Actual results could differ from those estimates under different assumptions or conditions.

Revenue Recognition

Revenue from restaurant sales is recognized when payment is tendered at the point of sale. The Company reports revenue net of sales and use taxes collected from customers and remitted to governmental taxing authorities.

The Company sells gift cards which do not have an expiration date and it does not deduct non-usage fees from outstanding gift card balances. The Company recognizes revenue from gift cards when: (i) the gift card is redeemed by the customer; or (ii) the Company determines the likelihood of the gift card being redeemed by the customer is remote (gift card breakage) and there is not a legal obligation to remit the unredeemed gift cards to the relevant jurisdiction. The determination of the gift card breakage rate is based upon Company-specific historical redemption patterns. Gift card breakage is recognized in revenue as the gift cards are used on a pro rata basis over a six month period beginning at the date of the gift card sale and is included in revenue in the consolidated statement of income and comprehensive income. The Company has determined that 4% of gift card sales will not be redeemed and will be retained by the Company. Breakage recognized during the years ended December 31, 2015, 2014 and 2013 was $4,226, $3,146 and $1,976, respectively.

Cash and Cash Equivalents

The Company considers all highly liquid investment instruments purchased with an initial maturity of three months or less to be cash equivalents. The Company maintains cash and cash equivalent balances with financial institutions that exceed federally-insured limits. The Company has not experienced any losses related to these balances and believes the risk to be minimal.

Accounts Receivable

Accounts receivable primarily consists of receivables from third party gift card distributors, tenant improvement receivables, payroll-related tax receivables, vendor rebates, and receivables arising from the normal course of business. The allowance for doubtful accounts is the Company's best estimate of the amount of probable credit losses in the Company's existing accounts receivable based on a specific review of account balances. Account balances are charged off against the allowance after all means of collection have been exhausted and the potential for recoverability is considered remote.

Inventory

Inventory, consisting principally of food, beverages, and supplies, is valued at the lower of first-in, first-out cost or market. Certain key ingredients (beef, pork, chicken, beans, rice, sour cream, cheese, and tortillas) are purchased from a small number of suppliers.

Investments

Investments classified as "trading" securities are carried at fair value with any unrealized gain or loss being recorded in the consolidated statement of income and comprehensive income. Investments classified as "available-for-sale" are carried at fair market value with unrealized gains and losses, net of tax, included as a component of other comprehensive income (loss). Held-to-maturity securities are carried at amortized cost. The Company recognizes impairment charges on its investments in the consolidated statement of income and comprehensive income when management believes the decline in the fair value of the investment is other-than-temporary.

Leasehold Improvements, Property and Equipment

Leasehold improvements, property and equipment are recorded at cost. Internal costs directly associated with the acquisition, development and construction of a restaurant are capitalized and were $9,554, $7,756 and $9,024 for the years ended December 31, 2015, 2014 and 2013, respectively. Expenditures for major renewals and improvements are capitalized while expenditures for minor replacements, maintenance and repairs are expensed as incurred. Depreciation is calculated using the straight-line method over the estimated useful lives of the assets. Leasehold improvements are amortized over the shorter of the lease term, which generally includes reasonably assured option periods, or the estimated useful lives of the assets. Upon retirement or disposal of assets, the accounts are relieved of cost and accumulated depreciation and the related gain or loss, if any, is reflected in loss on disposal of assets in the consolidated statement of income and comprehensive income.

At least annually, the Company evaluates, and adjusts when necessary, the estimated useful lives of leasehold improvements, property and equipment. The changes in estimated useful lives did not have a material impact on depreciation in any period. The estimated useful lives are:

Leasehold improvements and buildings	3-20 years
Furniture and fixtures	4-7 years
Equipment	3-10 years

Goodwill

Goodwill represents the excess of cost over fair value of net assets of the business acquired. Goodwill is not subject to amortization, but instead is tested for impairment at least annually, and the Company is required to record any necessary impairment adjustments. Impairment is measured as the excess of the carrying value over the fair value of the goodwill. Based on the Company's analysis, no impairment charges were recognized on goodwill for the years ended December 31, 2015, 2014 and 2013.

Other Assets

Other assets consist primarily of restricted cash assets of $22,572 and $19,889 as of December 31, 2015 and 2014, respectively, a rabbi trust as described further in Note 7, "Employee Benefit Plans," transferable liquor licenses which are carried at the lower of fair value or cost, and rental deposits related to leased properties. Restricted cash assets are primarily insurance related restricted trust assets.

Impairment of Long-Lived Assets

Long-lived assets are reviewed for impairment whenever events or changes in circumstances indicate that the carrying amount of an asset may not be recoverable. For the purpose of reviewing restaurant assets to be held and used for potential impairment, assets are grouped together at the market level, or in the case of a potential relocation or closure, at the restaurant level. The Company manages its restaurants as a group with significant common costs and promotional activities; as such, an individual restaurant's cash flows are not generally independent of the cash flows of others in a market. Recoverability of assets to be held and used is measured by a comparison of the carrying amount of an asset to the estimated undiscounted future cash flows expected to be generated by the asset. If the carrying amount of an asset exceeds its estimated future cash flows, an impairment charge is recognized as the amount by which the carrying amount of the asset exceeds the fair value of the asset. During the years ended December 31, 2015, 2014 and 2013, an aggregate impairment charge of $6,675, $0 and $1,220, respectively, was recognized in loss on disposal of assets in the consolidated statement of income and comprehensive income. During the year ended December 31, 2015, the impairment charges resulted from an internally developed software program that the Company chose not to implement and the related hardware, the discontinued use of certain kitchen equipment from the Company's restaurants, as well as restaurant relocations. Impairment charges for software and equipment write-offs were equal to the net book value of assets on the balance sheet. Fair value of relocated restaurants was determined using Level 3 inputs (as described below under "Fair Value Measurements") based on a discounted cash flows method through the estimated date of closure.

Income Taxes

The Company recognizes deferred tax assets and liabilities at enacted income tax rates for the temporary differences between the financial reporting bases and the tax bases of its assets and liabilities. Any effects of changes in income tax rates or tax laws are included in the provision for income taxes in the period of enactment. The deferred income tax impacts of investment tax credits are recognized as an immediate adjustment to income tax expense. When it is more likely than not that a portion or all of a deferred tax asset will not be realized in the future, the Company provides a corresponding valuation allowance against the deferred tax asset. When it is more likely than not that a position will be sustained upon examination by a tax authority that has full knowledge of all relevant information, the Company measures the amount of tax benefit from the position and records the largest amount of tax benefit that is greater than 50% likely of being realized after settlement with a tax authority. The Company's policy is to recognize interest to be paid on an underpayment of income taxes in interest expense and any related statutory penalties in the provision for income taxes in the consolidated statement of income and comprehensive income.

Restaurant Pre-Opening Costs

Pre-opening costs, including rent, wages, benefits and travel for the training and opening teams, food and other restaurant operating costs, are expensed as incurred prior to a restaurant opening for business.

Insurance Liability

The Company maintains various insurance policies including workers' compensation, employee health, general liability, automobile, and property damage. Pursuant to these policies, the Company is responsible for losses up to certain limits and is required to estimate a liability that represents the ultimate exposure for aggregate losses below those limits. This liability is based on management's estimates of the ultimate costs to be incurred to settle known claims and, where applicable, claims not reported as of the balance sheet date. The estimated liability is not discounted and is based on a number of assumptions and factors, including historical trends, actuarial assumptions, and economic conditions. If actual trends differ from the estimates, the financial results could be impacted. As of December 31, 2015 and 2014, $28,391 and $25,596, respectively, of the estimated liability was included in accrued payroll and benefits and $11,898 and $8,359, respectively, was included in accrued liabilities in the consolidated balance sheet.

Advertising and Marketing Costs

Advertising and marketing costs are expensed as incurred and totaled $69,257, $57,290 and $44,389 for the years ended December 31, 2015, 2014 and 2013, respectively. Advertising and marketing costs are included in other operating costs in the consolidated statement of income and comprehensive income.

Rent

Rent expense for the Company's leases, which generally have escalating rentals over the term of the lease, is recorded on a straight-line basis over the lease term. The lease term is the lesser of 20 years inclusive of reasonably assured renewal periods, or the lease term. The lease term begins when the Company has the right to control the use of the property, which is typically before rent payments are due under the lease. The difference between the rent expense and rent paid is recorded as deferred rent in the consolidated balance sheet. Pre-opening rent is included in pre-opening costs in the consolidated income statement. Tenant incentives used to fund leasehold improvements are recorded in deferred rent and amortized as reductions of rent expense over the term of the lease.

Additionally, certain of the Company's operating leases contain clauses that provide additional contingent rent based on a percentage of sales greater than certain specified target amounts. The Company recognizes contingent rent expense provided the achievement of that target is considered probable.

Fair Value of Financial Instruments

The carrying value of the Company's cash and cash equivalents, accounts receivable and accounts payable approximate fair value because of their short-term nature.

Fair Value Measurements

Fair value is the price the Company would receive to sell an asset or pay to transfer a liability (exit price) in an orderly transaction between market participants. For assets and liabilities recorded or disclosed at fair value on a recurring basis, the Company determines fair value based on the following:

Level 1: Quoted prices in active markets for identical assets or liabilities that the entity has the ability to access.

Level 2: Observable inputs other than prices included in Level 1, such as quoted prices for similar assets and liabilities in active markets; quoted prices for identical or similar assets and liabilities in markets that are not active; or other inputs that are observable or can be corroborated with observable market data.

Level 3: Unobservable inputs that are supported by little or no market activity and that are significant to the fair value of the assets and liabilities. This includes certain pricing models, discounted cash flow methodologies and similar techniques that use significant unobservable inputs.

Foreign Currency Translation

The Company's international operations generally use the local currency as the functional currency. Assets and liabilities are translated at exchange rates in effect as of the balance sheet date. Income and expense accounts are translated at the average monthly exchange rates during the year. Resulting translation adjustments are recorded as a separate component of other comprehensive income (loss) in the consolidated statement of income and comprehensive income.

Recently Issued Accounting Standards

In May 2014, the FASB issued Accounting Standards Update ("ASU") No. 2014-09, "Revenue from Contracts with Customers (Topic 606)." The pronouncement was issued to clarify the principles for recognizing revenue and to develop a common revenue standard and disclosure requirements for U.S. GAAP and IFRS. The pronouncement is effective for reporting periods beginning after December 15, 2017. The expected adoption method of ASU 2014-09 is being evaluated by the Company and the adoption is not expected to have a significant impact on the Company's consolidated financial position or results of operations.

In June 2014, the FASB issued ASU No. 2014-12, "Compensation – Stock Compensation (Topic 718)." The pronouncement was issued to clarify the accounting for share-based payments when the terms of an award provide that a performance target could be achieved after the requisite service period. The pronouncement is effective for reporting periods beginning after December 15, 2015. The adoption of ASU 2014-12 is not expected to have a significant impact on the Company's consolidated financial position or results of operations.

In April 2015, the FASB issued ASU No. 2015-05, "Intangibles – Goodwill and Other – Internal-Use Software (Subtopic 350-40)." The pronouncement was issued to provide guidance concerning accounting for fees in a cloud computing arrangement. The pronouncement is effective for reporting periods beginning after December 15, 2015. The adoption of ASU 2015-05 is not expected to have a significant impact on the Company's consolidated financial position or results of operations.

In July 2015, the FASB issued ASU No. 2015-11, "Inventory (Topic 330)." The pronouncement was issued to simplify the measurement of inventory and changes the measurement from lower of cost or market to lower of cost and net realizable value. This pronouncement is effective for reporting periods beginning after December 15, 2016. The adoption of ASU 2015-11 is not expected to have a significant impact on the Company's consolidated financial position or results of operations.

In January 2016, the FASB issued ASU 2016-01, "Financial Instruments – Overall: Recognition and Measurement of Financial Assets and Financial Liabilities." The pronouncement requires equity investments (except those accounted for under the equity method of accounting, or those that result in consolidation of the investee) to be measured at fair value with changes in fair value recognized in net income, requires public business entities to use the exit price notion when measuring the fair value of financial instruments for disclosure purposes, requires separate presentation of financial assets and financial liabilities by measurement category and form of financial asset, and eliminates the requirement for public business entities to disclose the method(s) and significant assumptions used to estimate the fair value that is required to be disclosed for financial instruments measured at amortized cost. These changes become effective for the Company's fiscal year beginning January 1, 2018. The expected adoption method of ASU 2016-01 is being evaluated by the Company and the adoption is not expected to have a significant impact on the Company's consolidated financial position or results of operations.

Recently Adopted Accounting Standard

In November 2015, the FASB issued ASU No. 2015-17, "Income Taxes" which requires that deferred tax liabilities and assets be classified as noncurrent in a classified balance sheet. Prior to the issuance of the standard, deferred tax liabilities and assets were required to be separately classified into a current amount and a noncurrent amount in the balance sheet. The new accounting guidance represents a change in accounting principle and the standard is required to be adopted in annual periods beginning after December 15, 2016. Early adoption is permitted and the Company elected to early adopt this guidance as of December 31, 2015 and to apply the guidance retrospectively to all periods presented. Accordingly, the Company reclassified the prior period amount of $18,968 related to its deferred tax asset from current to noncurrent, resulting in an offset to the noncurrent deferred income tax liability for the same amount for that period, according to the requirement to offset and present as a single amount. Because the application of this guidance affects classification only, such reclassifications did not have a material effect on the Company's consolidated financial position or results of operations.

2. Supplemental Financial Information

Leasehold improvements, property and equipment were as follows:

	December 31,	
	2015	2014
Land	$ 13,052	$ 11,062
Leasehold improvements and buildings	1,419,418	1,267,108
Furniture and fixtures	142,825	127,260
Equipment	362,800	315,230
	1,938,095	1,720,660
Accumulated depreciation	(720,875)	(613,676)
	$ 1,217,220	$ 1,106,984

Accrued liabilities were as follows:

	December 31,	
	2015	2014
Gift card liability	$ 51,055	$ 48,105
Transaction tax payable	15,634	22,929
Treasury stock liability	25,178	0
Other accrued expenses	37,408	31,169
	$ 129,275	$ 102,203

3. Investments

As of December 31, 2015, the Company's investments, consisting of U.S. treasury notes with maturities up to approximately two years, were classified as available-for-sale. As of December 31, 2014, the Company's investments consisted of U.S. treasury notes and CDARS, certificates of deposit placed through an account registry service, with maturities up to approximately two years, and were classified as held-to-maturity. Fair market value of U.S. treasury notes is measured on a recurring basis based on Level 1 inputs and fair market value of CDARS is measured on a recurring basis based on Level 2 inputs (level inputs are described in Note 1 under "Fair Value Measurements").

The Company designates the appropriate classification of its investments at the time of purchase based upon the intended holding period. During the year ended December 31, 2015, the Company transferred the classification of its investments from held-to-maturity to available-for-sale due to anticipated liquidity needs related to increased repurchases of shares of the Company's common stock. The carrying value of held-to-maturity securities transferred to available-for-sale during the year ended December 31, 2015 was $1,040,850 and the fair market value of those securities was determined to be $1,038,138, resulting in an unrealized holding loss of $2,712. As a result, the Company recorded $2,468 ($1,522, net of tax) of unrealized holding losses in other comprehensive income (loss), and an other-than-temporary impairment charge of $244 in interest and other income (expense), in the consolidated statement of income and comprehensive income. The Company determined its investments approximated fair value as of December 31, 2014, and no impairment charges were recognized on the Company's investments for the years ended December 31, 2014 and 2013.

The Company has elected to fund certain deferred compensation obligations through a rabbi trust, the assets of which are designated as trading securities, as described further in Note 7. "Employee Benefit Plans."

4. Income Taxes

The components of the provision for income taxes are as follows:

	Year ended December 31,		
	2015	2014	2013
Current tax:			
U.S. Federal	$ 244,470	$ 248,219	$ 165,731
U.S. State	37,957	41,225	39,136
Foreign	172	156	63
	282,599	289,600	204,930
Deferred tax:			
U.S. Federal	11,000	(13,890)	5,238
U.S. State	699	(6,740)	(3,105)
Foreign	(2,288)	(3,075)	(1,330)
	9,411	(23,705)	803
Valuation allowance	2,255	3,034	1,300
Provision for income taxes	$ 294,265	$ 268,929	$ 207,033

Actual taxes paid for each tax period were less than the current tax expense due to the excess tax benefit on stock-based compensation of $74,442, $21,667, and $38,379 during the years ended December 31, 2015, 2014, and 2013, respectively.

The effective tax rate differs from the statutory tax rates as follows:

	Year ended December 31,		
	2015	2014	2013
Statutory U.S. federal income tax rate	35.0 %	35.0 %	35.0 %
State income tax, net of related federal income tax benefit	3.6	3.7	4.2
Other	(0.4)	(1.1)	(0.5)
Effective income tax rate	38.2 %	37.6 %	38.7 %

In 2015 and 2014, the effective tax rate was lower than 2013 because there was a decrease in the state tax rate. Additionally, 2014 included a benefit from filing the 2013 tax returns, which included a non-recurring change in the estimate of usable employer credits.

Deferred income tax liabilities are taxes the Company expects to pay in future periods. Similarly, deferred income tax assets are recorded for expected reductions in taxes payable in future periods. Deferred income taxes arise because of the differences in the book and tax bases of certain assets and liabilities. Deferred income tax liabilities and assets consist of the following:

	December 31,	
	2015	2014
		(as adjusted)
Long-term deferred income tax liability:		
Leasehold improvements, property and equipment	$ 192,125	$ 175,808
Goodwill and other assets	1,696	1,519
Prepaid assets and other	8,297	6,091
Total long-term deferred income tax liability	202,118	183,418
Long-term deferred income tax asset:		
Deferred rent	57,716	52,147
Gift card liability	3,171	1,451
Capitalized transaction costs	502	503
Stock-based compensation and other employee benefits	83,058	87,713
Foreign net operating loss carry-forwards	11,407	8,618
State credits	4,783	4,281
Allowances, reserves and other	18,577	14,656
Valuation allowance	(9,401)	(7,512)
Total long-term deferred income tax asset	169,813	161,857
Net long-term deferred income tax liability	$ 32,305	$ 21,561

As described in Note 1, the Company elected to early adopt FASB guidance ASU 2015-17 "Income Taxes" as of December 31, 2015 and to apply the guidance retrospectively to all periods presented related to the classification of current and noncurrent deferred tax assets and liabilities. Accordingly, the Company reclassified the prior period amount of $18,968 related to its net deferred tax asset from current to noncurrent, resulting in an offset to the noncurrent deferred income tax liability for the same amount for that period.

The unrecognized tax benefits are as follows:

	2015	2014	2013
Beginning of year	1,342	-	-
Increase resulting from prior year tax position	402	-	-
Increase resulting from current year tax position	2,032	1,342	-
End of year	$ 3,776	$ 1,342	$ -

The Company is open to federal and state tax audits until the applicable statutes of limitations expire. Tax audits by their very nature are often complex and can require several years to complete. The Company is no longer subject to U.S. federal tax examinations by tax authorities for tax years before 2012. For the majority of states where the Company has a significant presence, it is no longer subject to tax examinations by tax authorities for tax years before 2012. Some of the Company's foreign net operating losses began expiring in 2015.

5. Shareholders' Equity

Through December 31, 2015, the Company announced authorizations by its Board of Directors of the expenditure of an aggregate of up to $1,300,000 to repurchase shares of the Company's common stock. The Company announced that its Board of Directors authorized the expenditure of up to an additional $300,000 on January 6, 2016 and $300,000 on February 2, 2016 to repurchase shares of its common stock. Under the remaining repurchase authorization, shares may be purchased from time to time in open market transactions, subject to market conditions.

The shares of common stock repurchased under authorized programs were 839, 154 and 336 for a total cost of $485,841, $87,996 and $109,987 during 2015, 2014 and 2013, respectively. As of December 31, 2015, $116,394 was available to be repurchased under the authorized programs. The Company repurchased 609 shares of common stock for a total cost of $270,013 from January 1, 2016 through February 3, 2016 under programs announced on December 4, 2015 and January 6, 2016. The shares repurchased are being held in treasury until such time as they are reissued or retired, at the discretion of the Board of Directors.

During 2015, 2014, and 2013, shares of common stock were netted and surrendered as payment for minimum statutory tax withholding obligations in connection with the exercise and vesting of outstanding stock awards. Shares surrendered by the participants in accordance with the applicable award agreements and plan are deemed repurchased by the Company but are not part of publicly announced share repurchase programs. For the years ended December 31, 2015, 2014, and 2013, the Company's repurchases in connection with such netting and surrender were less than 1 share, 1 share, and 57 shares for a total cost of $12, $342, and $28,916 respectively.

6. Stock Based Compensation

The Company issues shares pursuant to the Amended and Restated Chipotle Mexican Grill, Inc. 2011 Stock Incentive Plan (the "2011 Incentive Plan"), approved at the annual shareholders' meeting on May 13, 2015. Shares issued pursuant to awards granted prior to the 2011 Incentive Plan were issued subject to previous stock plans. For purposes of counting the shares remaining available under the 2011 Incentive Plan, each share issuable pursuant to outstanding full value awards, such as restricted stock units and performance shares, will count as two shares used, whereas each share underlying a stock appreciation right or stock option will count as one share used. Under the 2011 Incentive Plan, 5,560 shares of common stock have been authorized and reserved for issuance to eligible participants, of which 2,988 represent shares that were authorized for issuance but not issued or subject to outstanding awards at December 31, 2015. The 2011 Incentive Plan is administered by the Compensation Committee of the Board of Directors, which has the authority to select the individuals to whom awards will be granted or to delegate its authority under the plan to the Company's executive officers to make grants to non-executive officer level employees, to determine the type of awards and when the awards are to be granted, the number of shares to be covered by each award, the vesting schedule and all other terms and conditions of the awards. The exercise price for stock awards granted under the 2011 Incentive Plan cannot be less than fair market value at the date of grant.

Stock only stock appreciation rights ("SOSARs") generally vest equally over two and three years and expire after seven years. Stock-based compensation expense is generally recognized on a straight-line basis for each separate vesting portion. Compensation expense related to employees eligible to retire and retain full rights to the awards is recognized over six months which coincides with the notice period. The Company has also granted SOSARs and stock awards with performance vesting conditions and/or market vesting conditions. Compensation expense on SOSARs subject to performance conditions is recognized over the longer of the estimated performance goal attainment period or time vesting period. Compensation expense on stock awards subject to performance conditions, which is based on the quantity of awards the Company has determined are probable of vesting, is recognized over the longer of the estimated performance goal attainment period or time vesting period. Compensation expense is recognized ratably for awards subject to market conditions regardless of whether the market condition is satisfied, provided that the requisite service has been provided.

Stock-based compensation recognized as capitalized development is included in leasehold improvements, property and equipment in the consolidated balance sheet. The following table sets forth stock-based compensation expense, including SOSARs and stock awards:

	Year ended December 31,		
	2015	2014	2013
Stock-based compensation expense	$ 59,465	$ 97,618	$ 64,781
Stock-based compensation expense, net of tax	36,666	60,084	39,465
Stock-based compensation expense recognized as capitalized development	1,554	1,178	1,124

The tables below summarize the option and SOSAR activity under the stock incentive plans (in thousands, except years and per share data):

| | 2015 | | 2014 | | 2013 | |
	Shares	Weighted-Average Exercise Price Per Share	Shares	Weighted-Average Exercise Price Per Share	Shares	Weighted-Average Exercise Price Per Share
Outstanding, beginning of year	2,087	$ 395.46	1,690	$ 312.44	1,449	$ 274.92
Granted	379	$ 659.12	764	$ 545.66	672	$ 320.21
Exercised	(716)	$ 297.25	(315)	$ 310.32	(369)	$ 176.23
Forfeited	(56)	$ 554.73	(52)	$ 419.74	(62)	$ 329.76
Outstanding, end of year	1,694	$ 490.70	2,087	$ 395.46	1,690	$ 312.44

	Shares	Weighted-Average Exercise Price Per Share	Weighted-Average Remaining Years of Contractual Life	Aggregate Intrinsic Value
Outstanding as of December 31, 2015	1,694	$ 490.70	4.9	$ 92,773
Vested and expected to vest as of December 31, 2015	1,640	$ 486.10	4.8	$ 92,622
Exercisable as of December 31, 2015	321	$ 339.72	3.5	$ 45,112

During the years ended December 31, 2014, and 2013, the Company granted SOSARs that include performance conditions, in amounts totaling 220 and 191 shares, respectively. No SOSARs that include performance conditions were granted during 2015. As of December 31, 2015, 426 SOSARs that include performance conditions were outstanding, of which 316 awards had met the performance conditions. In addition to time vesting described above, the shares vest upon achieving a targeted cumulative cash flow from operations. The total intrinsic value of options and SOSARs exercised during the years ended December 31, 2015, 2014 and 2013 was $260,466, $88,245 and $91,178. Unearned compensation as of December 31, 2015 was $40,298 for SOSAR awards, and is expected to be recognized over a weighted average period of 1.5 years.

The following table reflects the average assumptions utilized in the Black-Scholes option-pricing model to value SOSAR awards granted for each year:

	2015	2014	2013
Risk-free interest rate	1.1 %	0.8 %	0.5 %
Expected life (years)	3.4	3.4	3.4
Expected dividend yield	0.0 %	0.0 %	0.0 %
Volatility	30.8 %	33.3 %	35.4 %
Weighted-average Black-Scholes fair value per share at date of grant	$ 156.32	$ 136.18	$ 82.51

The Company has not paid dividends to date and does not plan to pay dividends in the near future. The risk-free interest rate is based upon U.S. Treasury rates for instruments with similar terms. The volatility assumption was based on the Company's historical data and implied volatility, and the expected life assumptions were based on the Company's historical data.

A summary of non-vested stock award activity under the stock incentive plans is as follows (in thousands, except per share data):

	2015		2014		2013	
	Shares	Grant Date Fair Value Per Share	Shares	Grant Date Fair Value Per Share	Shares	Grant Date Fair Value Per Share
Outstanding, beginning of year	70	$ 525.60	71	$ 520.27	120	$ 218.34
Granted	47	$ 785.32	2	$ 495.92	68	$ 527.45
Vested	(1)	$ 413.07	(2)	$ 284.11	(117)	$ 215.76
Forfeited	-	$ 534.55	(1)	$ 410.55	—	$ —
Outstanding, end of year	116	$ 511.88	70	$ 525.60	71	$ 520.27

At December 31, 2015, 106 of the outstanding non-vested stock awards were subject to performance and/or market conditions, in addition to service vesting conditions. During the year ended December 31, 2013, the Company granted 66 stock awards that were subject to both service and performance vesting conditions ("the 2013 stock awards"). The quantity of shares that ultimately vest is determined based on the cumulative cash flow from operations reached during the three year period ending on September 30, 2016. The quantity of shares awarded ranges from 0% to 100% based on the level of achievement of the performance conditions. If the cumulative cash flow from operations during the three year period does not reach a specified level, no shares will vest. During the year ended December 31, 2015, the Company reduced its estimate of the number of the 2013 stock awards that it expects will vest, which resulted in a cumulative adjustment to expense of $10,851 ($6,691 net of tax as well as $.22 to basic and $.21 diluted earnings per share).

During the year ended December 31, 2015, the Company awarded 40 performance shares that were subject to service, performance, and market vesting conditions ("the 2015 stock awards"). The quantity of shares that will ultimately vest is determined based on Chipotle's relative performance versus a restaurant industry peer group in the annual average of: revenue growth, net income growth, and total shareholder return. The quantity of shares awarded ranges from 0% to 200% based on the level of achievement of the performance and market conditions. If minimum targets are not met, then no shares will vest. Each performance and market measure will be weighted equally, and performance is calculated over a three year period beginning January 1, 2015 through December 31, 2017. During the year ended December 31, 2015, the Company reduced its estimate of the number of the 2015 stock awards that it expects will vest, which resulted in a cumulative adjustment to expense of $1,344 ($829 net of tax and $.03 to basic and diluted earnings per share).

The Company's measurement of the grant date fair value of the 2015 stock awards included using a Monte Carlo simulation model, which incorporates into the fair-value determination the possibility that the market condition may not be satisfied, using the following assumptions:

	2015
Risk-free interest rate	1.0 %
Expected life (years)	2.9
Expected dividend yield	0.0 %
Volatility	33.7 %

Unearned compensation as of December 31, 2015 was $19,511 for non-vested stock awards the Company has determined are probable of vesting, and is expected to be recognized over a weighted average period of 1.6 years. The fair value of shares earned as of the vesting date during the year ended December 31, 2015, 2014, and 2013 was $634, $783, and $58,941, respectively.

7. Employee Benefit Plans

The Company maintains the Chipotle Mexican Grill 401(k) Plan (the "401(k) Plan"). The Company matches 100% of the first 3% of pay contributed by each eligible employee and 50% on the next 2% of pay contributed. Employees become eligible to receive matching contributions after one year of service with the Company. For the years ended December 31, 2015, 2014, and 2013, Company matching contributions totaled approximately $4,995, $3,881 and $2,644, respectively.

The Company also offers an employee stock purchase plan ("ESPP"). Employees become eligible to contribute after one year of service with the Company and may contribute up to 15% of their base earnings, subject to an annual maximum dollar amount, toward the monthly purchase of the Company's common stock. Under the ESPP, 250 shares of common stock have been authorized and reserved for issuances to eligible employees, of which 248 represent shares that were authorized for issuance but not issued at December 31, 2015. For each of the years ended December 31, 2015, 2014, and 2013, the number of shares issued under the ESPP were less than 1.

The Company also maintains the Chipotle Mexican Grill, Inc. Supplemental Deferred Investment Plan (the "Deferred Plan") which covers eligible employees of the Company. The Deferred Plan is a non-qualified plan that allows participants to make tax-deferred contributions that cannot be made under the 401(k) Plan because of Internal Revenue Service limitations. Participants' earnings on contributions made to the Deferred Plan fluctuate with the actual earnings and losses of a variety of available investment choices selected by the participant. Total liabilities under the Deferred Plan as of December 31, 2015 and 2014 were $18,331 and $16,147, respectively, and are included in other long-term liabilities in the consolidated balance sheet. The Company matches 100% of the first 3% of pay contributed by each eligible employee and 50% on the next 2% of pay contributed once the 401(k) contribution limits are reached. For the years ended December 31, 2015, 2014, and 2013, the Company made deferred compensation matches of $617, $536 and $201 respectively, to the Deferred Plan.

The Company has elected to fund its deferred compensation obligations through a rabbi trust. The rabbi trust is subject to creditor claims in the event of insolvency, but the assets held in the rabbi trust are not available for general corporate purposes. Amounts in the rabbi trust are invested in mutual funds, as selected by participants, which are designated as trading securities and carried at fair value, and are included in other assets in the consolidated balance sheet. Fair value of mutual funds is measured using Level 1 inputs (quoted prices for identical assets in active markets), and the fair values of the investments in the rabbi trust were $18,331 and $16,147 as of December 31, 2015 and 2014, respectively. The Company records trading gains and losses in general and administrative expenses in the consolidated statement of income and comprehensive income, along with the offsetting amount related to the increase or decrease in deferred compensation to reflect its exposure of the Deferred Plan liability. The following table sets forth unrealized gains and losses on investments held in the rabbi trust:

	Year ended December 31,		
	2015	2014	2013
Unrealized gains (losses) on investments held in rabbi trust	$ (571)	$ 184	$ 722

8. Leases

The Company generally operates its restaurants in leased premises. Lease terms for traditional shopping center or building leases generally include combined initial and option terms of 20-25 years. Ground leases generally include combined initial and option terms of 30-40 years. The option terms in each of these leases are typically in five-year increments. Typically, the lease includes rent escalation terms every five years including fixed rent escalations, escalations based on inflation indexes, and fair market value adjustments. Certain leases contain contingent rental provisions based upon the sales of the underlying restaurants. The leases generally provide for the payment of common area maintenance, property taxes, insurance and various other use and occupancy costs by the Company. In addition, the Company is the lessee under non-cancelable leases covering certain offices.

Future minimum lease payments required under existing operating leases as of December 31, 2015 are as follows:

2016	$ 239,683
2017	241,366
2018	244,698
2019	245,251
2020	239,933
Thereafter	2,257,081
Total minimum lease payments	$ 3,468,012

Minimum lease payments have not been reduced by minimum sublease rentals of $6,217 due in the future under non-cancelable subleases.

Rental expense consists of the following:

	Year ended December 31,		
	2015	2014	2013
Minimum rentals	$ 227,602	$ 200,575	$ 178,395
Contingent rentals	$ 4,542	$ 4,616	$ 2,719
Sublease rental income	$ (1,879)	$ (1,838)	$ (1,726)

The Company has six sales and leaseback transactions. These transactions do not qualify for sale leaseback accounting because of the Company's deemed continuing involvement with the buyer-lessor due to fixed price renewal options, which results in the transaction being recorded under the financing method. Under the financing method, the assets remain on the consolidated balance sheet and the proceeds from the transactions are recorded as a financing liability. A portion of lease payments are applied as payments of deemed principal and imputed interest. The deemed landlord financing liability was $3,060 and $3,233 as of December 31, 2015, and 2014, respectively, with the current portion of the liability included in accrued liabilities, and the remaining portion included in other liabilities in the consolidated balance sheet.

9. Earnings Per Share

Basic earnings per share is calculated by dividing income available to common shareholders by the weighted-average number of shares of common stock outstanding during each period. Diluted earnings per share ("diluted EPS") is calculated using income available to common shareholders divided by diluted weighted-average shares of common stock outstanding during each period. Potentially dilutive securities include shares of common stock underlying SOSARs and non-vested stock awards (collectively "stock awards"). Diluted EPS considers the impact of potentially dilutive securities except in periods in which there is a loss because the inclusion of the potential common shares would have an anti-dilutive effect. Stock awards are excluded from the calculation of diluted EPS in the event they are subject to performance conditions or antidilutive. The following stock awards were excluded from the calculation of diluted EPS:

	Year ended December 31,		
	2015	2014	2013
Stock awards subject to performance conditions	266	385	381
Stock awards that were antidilutive	289	232	393
Total stock awards excluded from diluted earnings per share	555	617	774

The following table sets forth the computations of basic and diluted earnings per share:

	Year ended December 31,		
	2015	2014	2013
Net income	$ 475,602	$ 445,374	$ 327,438
Shares:			
Weighted average number of common shares outstanding	31,092	31,038	30,957
Dilutive stock awards	402	474	324
Diluted weighted average number of common shares outstanding	31,494	31,512	31,281
Basic earnings per share	$ 15.30	$ 14.35	$ 10.58
Diluted earnings per share	$ 15.10	$ 14.13	$ 10.47

10. Commitments and Contingencies

Purchase Obligations

The Company enters into various purchase obligations in the ordinary course of business, generally of short term nature. Those that are binding primarily relate to commitments for food purchases and supplies, amounts owed under contractor and subcontractor agreements, orders submitted for equipment for restaurants under construction, and marketing initiatives and corporate sponsorships.

Litigation

Receipt of Grand Jury Subpoenas

In December 2015, the Company was served with a Federal Grand Jury Subpoena from the U.S. District Court for the Central District of California in connection with an official criminal investigation being conducted by the U.S. Attorney's Office for the Central District of California, in conjunction with the U.S. Food and Drug Administration's Office of Criminal Investigations. The subpoena required the Company to produce a broad range of documents related to a Chipotle restaurant in Simi Valley, California, that experienced an isolated norovirus incident during August 2015. On January 28, 2016, the Company was served with an additional subpoena broadening the investigation and requiring the production of documents and information related to company-wide food safety matters dating back to January 1, 2013. The Company has been informed that this subpoena supersedes the subpoena served in December 2015, which has been withdrawn. The Company intends to fully cooperate in the investigation. It is not possible at this time to determine whether the Company will incur, or to reasonably estimate the amount of, any fines or penalties in connection with the investigation pursuant to which the subpoena was issued.

Shareholder Class Action

On January 8, 2016, Susie Ong filed a complaint in the U.S. District Court for the Southern District of New York on behalf of a purported class of purchasers of shares of the Company's common stock between February 4, 2015 and January 5, 2016. The complaint purports to state claims against the Company, each of its co-Chief Executive Officers and its Chief Financial Officer under Sections 10(b) and 20(a) of the Exchange Act and related rules, based on the Company's alleged failure during the claimed class period to disclose material information about the Company's quality controls and safeguards in relation to consumer and employee health. The complaint asserts that those failures and related public statements were false and misleading and that, as a result, the market price of the Company's stock was artificially inflated during the claimed class period. The complaint seeks damages on behalf of the purported class in an unspecified amount, interest, and an award of reasonable attorneys' fees, expert fees and other costs. The Company intends to defend this case vigorously, but it is not possible at this time to reasonably estimate the outcome of or any potential liability from the case.

Notices of Inspection of Work Authorization Documents and Related Civil and Criminal Investigations

Following an inspection during 2010 by the U.S. Department of Homeland Security, or DHS, of the work authorization documents of the Company's restaurant employees in Minnesota, the Immigration and Customs Enforcement arm of DHS, or ICE, issued to the Company a Notice of Suspect Documents identifying a large number of employees who, according to ICE and notwithstanding the Company's review of work authorization documents for each employee at the time they were hired, appeared not to be authorized to work in the U.S. The Company approached each of the named employees to explain ICE's determination and afforded each employee an opportunity to confirm the validity of their original work eligibility documents, or provide valid work eligibility documents. Employees who were unable to provide valid work eligibility documents were terminated in accordance with the law. In December 2010, the Company was also requested by DHS to provide the work authorization documents of restaurant employees in the District of Columbia and Virginia, and the Company provided the requested documents in January 2011. The Company subsequently received requests from the office of the U.S. Attorney for the District of Columbia for work authorization documents covering all of the Company's employees since 2007, plus employee lists and other documents concerning work authorization. The Company believes its practices with regard to the work authorization of its employees, including the review and retention of work authorization documents, are in compliance with applicable law. However, the termination of large numbers of employees in a short period of time does disrupt restaurant operations and results in a temporary increase in labor costs as new employees are trained.

In May 2012, the U.S. Securities and Exchange Commission notified the Company that it is conducting a civil investigation of the Company's compliance with employee work authorization verification requirements and its related disclosures and statements, and the office of the U.S. Attorney for the District of Columbia advised the Company that its investigation has broadened to include a parallel criminal and civil investigation of the Company's compliance with federal securities laws. The Company intends to continue to fully cooperate in the government's investigations. It is not possible at this time to determine whether the Company will incur, or to reasonably estimate the amount of, any fines, penalties or further liabilities in connection with these matters.

Miscellaneous

The Company is involved in various other claims and legal actions that arise in the ordinary course of business. The Company does not believe that the ultimate resolution of these actions will have a material adverse effect on the Company's financial position, results of operations, liquidity or capital resources. However, a significant increase in the number of these claims, or one or more successful claims under which the Company incurs greater liabilities than the Company currently anticipates, could materially and adversely affect the Company's business, financial condition, results of operations and cash flows.

11. Quarterly Financial Data (Unaudited)

Summarized unaudited quarterly financial data:

	2015			
	March 31	June 30	September 30	December 31
Revenue	$ 1,089,043	$ 1,197,783	$ 1,216,890	$ 997,507
Operating income	$ 197,801	$ 227,416	$ 234,759	$ 103,613
Net income	$ 122,641	$ 140,204	$ 144,883	$ 67,874
Basic earnings per share	$ 3.95	$ 4.51	$ 4.65	$ 2.19
Diluted earnings per share	$ 3.88	$ 4.45	$ 4.59	$ 2.17

	2014			
	March 31	June 30	September 30	December 31
Revenue	$ 904,163	$ 1,050,073	$ 1,084,222	$ 1,069,811
Operating income	$ 135,650	$ 179,842	$ 207,436	$ 187,872
Net income	$ 83,069	$ 110,270	$ 130,801	$ 121,234
Basic earnings per share	$ 2.67	$ 3.55	$ 4.22	$ 3.91
Diluted earnings per share	$ 2.64	$ 3.50	$ 4.15	$ 3.84

ITEM 9. CHANGES IN AND DISAGREEMENTS WITH ACCOUNTANTS ON ACCOUNTING AND FINANCIAL DISCLOSURE

None.

ITEM 9A. CONTROLS AND PROCEDURES

We maintain disclosure controls and procedures (as defined in Rule 13a-15(e) promulgated under the Securities Exchange Act of 1934, as amended (the "Exchange Act")) that are designed to ensure that information required to be disclosed in Exchange Act reports is recorded, processed, summarized and reported within the time periods specified in the Securities and Exchange Commission's rules and forms, and that such information is accumulated and communicated to our management, including our co-Chief Executive Officers and Chief Financial Officer, as appropriate, to allow timely decisions regarding required disclosure.

Evaluation of Disclosure Controls and Procedures

As of December 31, 2015, we carried out an evaluation, under the supervision and with the participation of our management, including our co-Chief Executive Officers and Chief Financial Officer, of the effectiveness of the design and operation of our disclosure controls and procedures. Based on the foregoing, our co-Chief Executive Officers and Chief Financial Officer concluded that our disclosure controls and procedures were effective as of the end of the period covered by this annual report.

Changes in Internal Control over Financial Reporting

During the quarter ended March 31, 2015, we implemented a new human resource information and payroll system. We continued to integrate the software with our processes, systems, and controls in the quarter ended December 31, 2015. There were no other changes during the fiscal quarter ended December 31, 2015 in our internal control over financial reporting (as defined in Rule 13a-15(f) under the Exchange Act) that have materially affected or are reasonably likely to materially affect our internal control over financial reporting.

Management's Annual Report on Internal Control over Financial Reporting

The management of Chipotle Mexican Grill, Inc. is responsible for establishing and maintaining adequate internal control over financial reporting. Our internal control over financial reporting is a process designed to provide reasonable assurance regarding the reliability of financial reporting and the preparation of financial statements for external purposes in accordance with accounting principles generally accepted in the United States of America. Our internal control over financial reporting includes those policies and procedures that (i) pertain to the maintenance of records that, in reasonable detail, accurately and fairly reflect the transactions and dispositions of our assets; (ii) provide reasonable assurance that transactions are recorded as necessary to permit preparation of financial statements in accordance with accounting principles generally accepted in the United States of America, and that our receipts and expenditures are being made only in accordance with authorizations of our management and directors; and (iii) provide reasonable assurance regarding prevention or timely detection of unauthorized acquisition, use, or disposition of assets that could have a material effect on our financial statements.

Because of its inherent limitations, internal control over financial reporting may not prevent or detect misstatements. Also, projections of any evaluation of effectiveness to future periods are subject to the risk that controls may become inadequate because of changes in conditions, or that the degree of compliance with the policies or procedures may deteriorate.

Management assessed the effectiveness of our internal control over financial reporting as of December 31, 2015, based on the framework set forth by the Committee of Sponsoring Organizations of the Treadway Commission in Internal Control—Integrated Framework (the "2013 framework"). Based on that assessment, management concluded that, as of December 31, 2015, our internal control over financial reporting was effective based on the criteria established in the 2013 framework.

Our independent registered public accounting firm, Ernst & Young LLP, has issued an attestation report on the effectiveness of our internal control over financial reporting as of December 31, 2015. This report follows.

Report of Independent Registered Public Accounting Firm

The Board of Directors and Shareholders of
Chipotle Mexican Grill, Inc.

We have audited Chipotle Mexican Grill, Inc.'s internal control over financial reporting as of December 31, 2015, based on criteria established in Internal Control-Integrated Framework issued by the Committee of Sponsoring Organizations of the Treadway Commission (2013 framework) (the COSO criteria). Chipotle Mexican Grill, Inc.'s management is responsible for maintaining effective internal control over financial reporting, and for its assessment of the effectiveness of internal control over financial reporting included in the accompanying Management's Annual Report on Internal Control over Financial Reporting. Our responsibility is to express an opinion on the company's internal control over financial reporting based on our audit.

We conducted our audit in accordance with the standards of the Public Company Accounting Oversight Board (United States). Those standards require that we plan and perform the audit to obtain reasonable assurance about whether effective internal control over financial reporting was maintained in all material respects. Our audit included obtaining an understanding of internal control over financial reporting, assessing the risk that a material weakness exists, testing and evaluating the design and operating effectiveness of internal control based on the assessed risk, and performing such other procedures as we considered necessary in the circumstances. We believe that our audit provides a reasonable basis for our opinion.

A company's internal control over financial reporting is a process designed to provide reasonable assurance regarding the reliability of financial reporting and the preparation of financial statements for external purposes in accordance with generally accepted accounting principles. A company's internal control over financial reporting includes those policies and procedures that (1) pertain to the maintenance of records that, in reasonable detail, accurately and fairly reflect the transactions and dispositions of the assets of the company; (2) provide reasonable assurance that transactions are recorded as necessary to permit preparation of financial statements in accordance with generally accepted accounting principles, and that receipts and expenditures of the company are being made only in accordance with authorizations of management and directors of the company; and (3) provide reasonable assurance regarding prevention or timely detection of unauthorized acquisition, use, or disposition of the company's assets that could have a material effect on the financial statements.

Because of its inherent limitations, internal control over financial reporting may not prevent or detect misstatements. Also, projections of any evaluation of effectiveness to future periods are subject to the risk that controls may become inadequate because of changes in conditions, or that the degree of compliance with the policies or procedures may deteriorate.

In our opinion, Chipotle Mexican Grill, Inc. maintained, in all material respects, effective internal control over financial reporting as of December 31, 2015, based on the COSO criteria.

We also have audited, in accordance with the standards of the Public Company Accounting Oversight Board (United States), the consolidated balance sheets of Chipotle Mexican Grill, Inc. as of December 31, 2015 and 2014, and the related consolidated statements of income and comprehensive income, shareholders' equity and cash flows for each of the three years in the period ended December 31, 2015 and our report dated February 4, 2016 expressed an unqualified opinion thereon.

/s/ Ernst & Young LLP

Denver, Colorado
February 4, 2016

Excerpts from Panera Bread Company Form 10-K for the Fiscal Year Ended December 29, 2015

UNITED STATES SECURITIES AND EXCHANGE COMMISSION
WASHINGTON D.C. 20549

Form 10-K

(Mark One)

☑ **ANNUAL REPORT PURSUANT TO SECTION 13 OR 15(d) OF THE SECURITIES EXCHANGE ACT OF 1934**

For the fiscal year ended December 29, 2015

or

☐ **TRANSACTION REPORT PURSUANT TO SECTION 13 OR 15(d) OF THE SECURITIES EXCHANGE ACT OF 1934**

For the transition period from _____ to _____

Commission file number 0-19253

Panera Bread Company
(Exact Name of Registrant as Specified in Its Charter)

Delaware	04-2723701
(State or Other Jurisdiction of Incorporation or Organization)	*(I.R.S. Employer Identification No.)*
3630 South Geyer Road, Suite 100, St. Louis, MO	**63127**
(Address of Principal Executive Offices)	*(Zip Code)*

(314) 984-1000
(Registrant's telephone number, including area code)

Securities registered pursuant to Section 12(b) of the Act:

Title of Each Class	Name of Exchange on Which Registered
Class A Common Stock, $.0001 par value per share	The NASDAQ Global Select Market

Securities registered pursuant to Section 12(g) of the Act:
None.

Indicate by check mark if the registrant is a well-known seasoned issuer, as defined in Rule 405 of the Securities Act. Yes ☑ No ☐

Indicate by check mark if the registrant is not required to file reports pursuant to Section 13 or Section 15(d) of the Act. Yes ☐ No ☑

Indicate by check mark whether the registrant: (1) has filed all reports required to be filed by Section 13 and 15(d) of the Securities Exchange Act of 1934 during the preceding 12 months (or for such shorter period that the registrant was required to file such reports), and (2) has been subject to such filing requirements for the past 90 days. Yes ☑ No ☐

Indicate by check mark whether the registrant has submitted electronically and posted on its corporate Web site, if any, every Interactive Data File required to be submitted and posted pursuant to Rule 405 of Regulation S-T (§232.405 of this chapter) during the preceding 12 months (or for such shorter period that the registrant was required to submit and post such files). Yes ☑ No ☐

Indicate by check mark if disclosure of delinquent filers pursuant to Item 405 of Regulation S-K is not contained herein, and will not be contained, to the best of the registrant's knowledge, in definitive proxy or information statements incorporated by reference in Part III of this Form 10-K or any amendment to this Form 10-K. ☐

Indicate by check mark whether the registrant is a large accelerated filer, an accelerated filer, a non-accelerated filer, or a smaller reporting company. See the definitions of "large accelerated filer," "accelerated filer" and "smaller reporting company" in Rule 12b-2 of the Exchange Act. (Check one):

Large accelerated filer ☑   Accelerated filer ☐   Non-accelerated filer ☐   Smaller reporting company ☐

(Do not check if a smaller reporting company)

Indicate by check mark whether the registrant is a shell company (as defined in Rule 12b-2 of the Act). Yes ☐ No ☑

The aggregate market value of the registrant's voting common equity held by non-affiliates of the registrant, based on the last sale price of the registrant's Class A Common Stock at the close of business on June 30, 2015, was $2,725,304,483.

As of February 17, 2016, the registrant had 22,995,342 shares of Class A Common Stock ($.0001 par value per share) and 1,381,730 shares of Class B Common Stock ($.0001 par value per share) outstanding.

Part III of this Annual Report incorporates by reference certain information from the registrant's definitive proxy statement for the 2016 annual meeting of shareholders, which the registrant intends to file pursuant to Regulation 14A with the Securities and Exchange Commission not later than 120 days after the registrant's fiscal year end of December 29, 2015.

ITEM 6. SELECTED FINANCIAL DATA

The following selected financial data has been derived from our consolidated financial statements. The data set forth below should be read in conjunction with "Management's Discussion and Analysis of Consolidated Financial Condition and Results of Operations" and our consolidated financial statements and notes thereto.

| | For the fiscal year ended (1) | | | | |
	(in thousands, except per share and percentage information)				
	December 29, 2015	December 30, 2014	December 31, 2013	December 25, 2012	December 27, 2011
Revenues:					
Bakery-cafe sales, net	$ 2,358,794	$ 2,230,370	$ 2,108,908	$ 1,879,280	$ 1,592,951
Franchise royalties and fees	138,563	123,686	112,641	102,076	92,793
Fresh dough and other product sales to franchisees	184,223	175,139	163,453	148,701	136,288
Total revenues	2,681,580	2,529,195	2,385,002	2,130,057	1,822,032
Costs and expenses:					
Bakery-cafe expenses:					
Cost of food and paper products	$ 715,502	$ 669,860	$ 625,622	$ 552,580	$ 470,398
Labor	754,646	685,576	625,457	559,446	484,014
Occupancy	169,998	159,794	148,816	130,793	115,290
Other operating expenses	334,635	314,879	295,539	256,029	216,237
Total bakery-cafe expenses	1,974,781	1,830,109	1,695,434	1,498,848	1,285,939
Fresh dough and other product cost of sales to franchisees	160,706	152,267	142,160	131,006	116,267
Depreciation and amortization	135,398	124,109	106,523	90,939	79,899
General and administrative expenses	142,904	138,060	123,335	117,932	113,083
Pre-opening expenses	9,089	8,707	7,794	8,462	6,585
Refranchising loss	17,108	—	—	—	—
Total costs and expenses	2,439,986	2,253,252	2,075,246	1,847,187	1,601,773
Operating profit	241,594	275,943	309,756	282,870	220,259
Interest expense	3,830	1,824	1,053	1,082	822
Other (income) expense, net	1,192	(3,175)	(4,017)	(1,208)	(466)
Income before income taxes	236,572	277,294	312,720	282,996	219,903
Income taxes	87,247	98,001	116,551	109,548	83,951
Net income	149,325	179,293	196,169	173,448	135,952
Less: Net loss attributable to noncontrolling interest	(17)	—	—	—	—
Net income attributable to Panera Bread Company	$ 149,342	$ 179,293	$ 196,169	$ 173,448	$ 135,952
Earnings per common share attributable to Panera Bread Company:					
Basic	$ 5.81	$ 6.67	$ 6.85	$ 5.94	$ 4.59
Diluted	$ 5.79	$ 6.64	$ 6.81	$ 5.89	$ 4.55
Weighted average shares of common and common equivalent shares outstanding:					
Basic	25,685	26,881	28,629	29,217	29,601
Diluted	25,788	26,999	28,794	29,455	29,903

For the fiscal year ended (1)
(in thousands, except per share and percentage information)

	December 29, 2015	December 30, 2014	December 31, 2013	December 25, 2012	December 27, 2011
Consolidated balance sheet data:					
Cash and cash equivalents	$ 241,886	$ 196,493	$ 125,245	$ 297,141	$ 222,640
Trade and other accounts receivable	115,786	106,653	84,602	86,262	54,709
Property and equipment, net	776,248	787,294	669,409	571,754	492,022
Total assets	1,475,318	1,390,686	1,180,862	1,268,163	1,027,322
Current liabilities	399,443	352,712	303,325	277,540	238,334
Long-term liabilities	574,594	301,790	177,645	168,704	133,912
Redeemable noncontrolling interest	3,981	—	—	—	—
Stockholders' equity	497,300	736,184	699,892	821,919	655,076
Franchisee revenues (2)	$ 2,477,963	$ 2,281,755	$ 2,175,155	$ 1,981,674	$ 1,828,188
Comparable net bakery-cafe sales percentage for (2)(3):					
Company-owned bakery-cafes	3.0%	1.4%	2.6%	6.5%	4.9%
Franchise-operated bakery-cafes	1.0%	0.9%	2.0%	5.0%	3.4%
Bakery-cafe data:					
Company-owned bakery-cafes open	901	925	867	809	740
Franchise-operated bakery-cafes open	1,071	955	910	843	801
Total bakery-cafes open	1,972	1,880	1,777	1,652	1,541

(1) The fiscal year ended December 31, 2013, or fiscal 2013, was a 53 week year consisting of 371 days. All other fiscal years presented contained 52 weeks consisting of 364 days.

(2) We do not record franchise-operated net bakery-cafe sales as revenues. However, royalty revenues are calculated based on a percentage of franchise-operated net bakery-cafe sales, as reported by franchisees. We use franchise-operated and system-wide sales information internally in connection with store development decisions, planning, and budgeting analyses. We believe franchise-operated and system-wide sales information is useful in assessing consumer acceptance of our brand, facilitates an understanding of financial performance and the overall direction and trends of sales and operating income, helps us appreciate the effectiveness of our advertising and marketing initiatives to which our franchisees also contribute based on a percentage of their sales, and provides information that is relevant for comparison within the industry.

(3) Comparable net bakery-cafe sales information above for the fiscal year ended December 30, 2014, or fiscal 2014, reflects a calendar basis comparison. We believe that calendar basis comparable net bakery-cafe sales percentages better reflects the performance of the business as it eliminates the impact of the extra week in fiscal 2013 and compares consistent calendar weeks. Comparable net bakery-cafe sales information above for fiscal 2013 reflects a comparative 53 week period in fiscal 2012 (52 weeks in fiscal 2012 plus week one of fiscal 2013).

ITEM 8. FINANCIAL STATEMENTS AND SUPPLEMENTARY DATA

The following consolidated financial statements are included in response to this item:

Report of Independent Registered Public Accounting Firm

Consolidated Balance Sheets

Consolidated Statements of Income

Consolidated Statements of Comprehensive Income

Consolidated Statements of Cash Flows

Consolidated Statements of Changes in Equity and Redeemable Noncontrolling Interest

Notes to the Consolidated Financial Statements

Report of Independent Registered Public Accounting Firm

To Board of Directors and Stockholders of Panera Bread Company:

In our opinion, the accompanying consolidated balance sheets and the related consolidated statements of income, comprehensive income, of changes in equity and redeemable noncontrolling interest, and of cash flows present fairly, in all material respects, the financial position of Panera Bread Company and its subsidiaries at December 29, 2015 and December 30, 2014, and the results of their operations and their cash flows for each of the three years in the period ended December 29, 2015 in conformity with accounting principles generally accepted in the United States of America. In addition, in our opinion, the financial statement schedule listed in the accompanying index appearing under Item 15(a)(2) presents fairly, in all material respects, the information set forth therein when read in conjunction with the related consolidated financial statements. Also in our opinion, the Company maintained, in all material respects, effective internal control over financial reporting as of December 29, 2015, based on criteria established in *Internal Control - Integrated Framework (2013)* issued by the Committee of Sponsoring Organizations of the Treadway Commission (COSO). The Company's management is responsible for these financial statements and financial statement schedule, for maintaining effective internal control over financial reporting and for its assessment of the effectiveness of internal control over financial reporting, included in Management's Report on Internal Control over Financial Reporting under Item 9A. Our responsibility is to express opinions on these financial statements, on the financial statement schedule, and on the Company's internal control over financial reporting based on our integrated audits. We conducted our audits in accordance with the standards of the Public Company Accounting Oversight Board (United States). Those standards require that we plan and perform the audits to obtain reasonable assurance about whether the financial statements are free of material misstatement and whether effective internal control over financial reporting was maintained in all material respects. Our audits of the financial statements included examining, on a test basis, evidence supporting the amounts and disclosures in the financial statements, assessing the accounting principles used and significant estimates made by management, and evaluating the overall financial statement presentation. Our audit of internal control over financial reporting included obtaining an understanding of internal control over financial reporting, assessing the risk that a material weakness exists, and testing and evaluating the design and operating effectiveness of internal control based on the assessed risk. Our audits also included performing such other procedures as we considered necessary in the circumstances. We believe that our audits provide a reasonable basis for our opinions.

A company's internal control over financial reporting is a process designed to provide reasonable assurance regarding the reliability of financial reporting and the preparation of financial statements for external purposes in accordance with generally accepted accounting principles. A company's internal control over financial reporting includes those policies and procedures that (i) pertain to the maintenance of records that, in reasonable detail, accurately and fairly reflect the transactions and dispositions of the assets of the company; (ii) provide reasonable assurance that transactions are recorded as necessary to permit preparation of financial statements in accordance with generally accepted accounting principles, and that receipts and expenditures of the company are being made only in accordance with authorizations of management and directors of the company; and (iii) provide reasonable assurance regarding prevention or timely detection of unauthorized acquisition, use, or disposition of the company's assets that could have a material effect on the financial statements.

Because of its inherent limitations, internal control over financial reporting may not prevent or detect misstatements. Also, projections of any evaluation of effectiveness to future periods are subject to the risk that controls may become inadequate because of changes in conditions, or that the degree of compliance with the policies or procedures may deteriorate.

/s/ PricewaterhouseCoopers LLP
St. Louis, Missouri
February 18, 2016

PANERA BREAD COMPANY
CONSOLIDATED BALANCE SHEETS
(in thousands, except share and per share information)

	December 29, 2015	December 30, 2014
Assets		
Current assets:		
Cash and cash equivalents	$ 241,886	$ 196,493
Trade accounts receivable, net	38,211	36,584
Other accounts receivable	77,575	70,069
Inventories	22,482	22,811
Prepaid expenses and other	59,457	51,588
Deferred income taxes	34,479	28,621
Assets held for sale	28,699	—
Total current assets	502,789	406,166
Property and equipment, net	776,248	787,294
Other assets:		
Goodwill	121,791	120,778
Other intangible assets, net	63,877	70,940
Deposits and other	10,613	5,508
Total other assets	196,281	197,226
Total assets	$ 1,475,318	$ 1,390,686
Liabilities, Redeemable Noncontrolling Interest, and Stockholders' Equity		
Current liabilities:		
Accounts payable	$ 19,805	$ 19,511
Accrued expenses	359,464	333,201
Current portion of long-term debt	17,229	—
Liabilities associated with assets held for sale	2,945	—
Total current liabilities	399,443	352,712
Long-term debt	388,971	99,784
Deferred rent	62,610	67,390
Deferred income taxes	70,447	76,589
Other long-term liabilities	52,566	58,027
Total liabilities	974,037	654,502
Commitments and contingencies (Note 14)		
Redeemable noncontrolling interest	3,981	—
Stockholders' equity:		
Common stock, $.0001 par value per share:		
Class A, 112,500,000 shares authorized; 30,836,669 shares issued and 23,346,188 shares outstanding at December 29, 2015 and 30,703,472 shares issued and 25,442,728 shares outstanding at December 30, 2014	3	3
Class B, 10,000,000 shares authorized; 1,381,730 shares issued and outstanding at December 29, 2015 and 1,381,865 shares issued and outstanding at December 30, 2014	—	—
Treasury stock, carried at cost; 7,490,481 shares at December 29, 2015 and 5,260,744 shares at December 30, 2014	(1,111,586)	(706,073)
Preferred stock, $.0001 par value per share; 2,000,000 shares authorized and no shares issued or outstanding at December 29, 2015 and December 30, 2014	—	—
Additional paid-in capital	235,393	214,437
Accumulated other comprehensive income (loss)	(5,029)	(1,360)
Retained earnings	1,378,519	1,229,177
Total stockholders' equity	497,300	736,184
Total liabilities, redeemable noncontrolling interest, and stockholders' equity	$ 1,475,318	$ 1,390,686

The accompanying notes are an integral part of the consolidated financial statements.

PANERA BREAD COMPANY
CONSOLIDATED STATEMENTS OF INCOME
(in thousands, except per share information)

	For the fiscal year ended		
	December 29, 2015	December 30, 2014	December 31, 2013
Revenues:			
Bakery-cafe sales, net	$ 2,358,794	$ 2,230,370	$ 2,108,908
Franchise royalties and fees	138,563	123,686	112,641
Fresh dough and other product sales to franchisees	184,223	175,139	163,453
Total revenues	$ 2,681,580	$ 2,529,195	$ 2,385,002
Costs and expenses:			
Bakery-cafe expenses:			
Cost of food and paper products	$ 715,502	$ 669,860	$ 625,622
Labor	754,646	685,576	625,457
Occupancy	169,998	159,794	148,816
Other operating expenses	334,635	314,879	295,539
Total bakery-cafe expenses	1,974,781	1,830,109	1,695,434
Fresh dough and other product cost of sales to franchisees	160,706	152,267	142,160
Depreciation and amortization	135,398	124,109	106,523
General and administrative expenses	142,904	138,060	123,335
Pre-opening expenses	9,089	8,707	7,794
Refranchising loss	17,108	—	—
Total costs and expenses	2,439,986	2,253,252	2,075,246
Operating profit	241,594	275,943	309,756
Interest expense	3,830	1,824	1,053
Other (income) expense, net	1,192	(3,175)	(4,017)
Income before income taxes	236,572	277,294	312,720
Income taxes	87,247	98,001	116,551
Net income	$ 149,325	$ 179,293	$ 196,169
Less: Net loss attributable to noncontrolling interest	(17)	—	—
Net income attributable to Panera Bread Company	$ 149,342	$ 179,293	$ 196,169
Earnings per common share:			
Basic	$ 5.81	$ 6.67	$ 6.85
Diluted	$ 5.79	$ 6.64	$ 6.81
Weighted average shares of common and common equivalent shares outstanding:			
Basic	25,685	26,881	28,629
Diluted	25,788	26,999	28,794

The accompanying notes are an integral part of the consolidated financial statements.

PANERA BREAD COMPANY
CONSOLIDATED STATEMENTS OF COMPREHENSIVE INCOME
(in thousands)

	For the fiscal year ended		
	December 29, 2015	December 30, 2014	December 31, 2013
Net income	$ 149,325	$ 179,293	$ 196,169
Less: Net loss attributable to noncontrolling interest	(17)	—	—
Net income attributable to Panera Bread Company	$ 149,342	$ 179,293	$ 196,169
Other comprehensive income (loss), net of tax:			
Unrealized gains (losses) on cash flow hedging instruments	(2,552)	—	—
Tax (expense) benefit	1,009	—	—
Foreign currency translation adjustment	(2,126)	(1,027)	(1,005)
Other comprehensive income (loss) attributable to Panera Bread Company	(3,669)	(1,027)	(1,005)
Comprehensive income attributable to Panera Bread Company	$ 145,673	$ 178,266	$ 195,164

The accompanying notes are an integral part of the consolidated financial statements.

PANERA BREAD COMPANY
CONSOLIDATED STATEMENTS OF CASH FLOWS
(in thousands)

	December 29, 2015	December 30, 2014	December 31, 2013
Cash flows from operating activities:			
Net income	$ 149,325	$ 179,293	$ 196,169
Adjustments to reconcile net income to net cash provided by operating activities:			
Depreciation and amortization	135,398	124,109	106,523
Stock-based compensation expense	15,086	10,077	10,703
Tax benefit from stock-based compensation	(2,057)	(3,089)	(8,100)
Deferred income taxes	(10,991)	10,459	10,356
Refranchising loss	12,942	—	—
Other	3,505	4,617	6,353
Changes in operating assets and liabilities, excluding the effect of acquisitions and dispositions:			
Trade and other accounts receivable, net	(3,605)	(22,139)	3,021
Inventories	(1,698)	(895)	(2,186)
Prepaid expenses and other	(7,191)	(8,524)	(841)
Deposits and other	(455)	239	1,449
Accounts payable	(183)	1,978	8,162
Accrued expenses	31,169	35,288	13,372
Deferred rent	3,751	1,067	5,868
Other long-term liabilities	(6,951)	2,599	(2,432)
Net cash provided by operating activities	318,045	335,079	348,417
Cash flows from investing activities:			
Additions to property and equipment	(223,932)	(224,217)	(192,010)
Acquisitions, net of cash acquired	—	—	(2,446)
Purchase of investments	—	—	(97,919)
Proceeds from sale of investments	—	—	97,936
Proceeds from refranchising	46,869	—	—
Proceeds from sale of property and equipment	1,553	—	—
Proceeds from sale-leaseback transactions	10,095	12,900	6,132
Net cash used in investing activities	(165,415)	(211,317)	(188,307)
Cash flows from financing activities:			
Proceeds from issuance of long-term debt	299,070	100,000	—
Repayments of long-term debt	(6,301)	—	—
Capitalized debt issuance costs	(363)	(193)	—
Payment of deferred acquisition holdback	—	(270)	(4,112)
Repurchase of common stock	(405,513)	(159,503)	(339,409)
Exercise of employee stock options	288	1,116	573
Tax benefit from stock-based compensation	2,057	3,089	8,100
Proceeds from issuance of common stock under employee benefit plans	3,525	3,247	2,842
Net cash used in financing activities	(107,237)	(52,514)	(332,006)
Net increase (decrease) in cash and cash equivalents	45,393	71,248	(171,896)
Cash and cash equivalents at beginning of period	196,493	125,245	297,141
Cash and cash equivalents at end of period	$ 241,886	$ 196,493	$ 125,245

The accompanying notes are an integral part of the consolidated financial statements.

PANERA BREAD COMPANY
CONSOLIDATED STATEMENTS OF CHANGES IN EQUITY AND REDEEMABLE NONCONTROLLING INTEREST
(in thousands)

| | Common Stock Class A | | Common Stock Class B | | Treasury Stock | | Additional Paid-in Capital | Retained Earnings | Accumulated Other Comprehensive Income (Loss) | Total | Redeemable Noncontrolling Interest |
	Shares	Amount	Shares	Amount	Shares	Amount					
Balance, December 25, 2012	28,209	$ 3	1,384	$ —	2,250	$ (207,161)	$ 174,690	$ 853,715	$ 672	$821,919	$ —
Net income	—	—	—	—	—	—	—	196,169	—	196,169	—
Other comprehensive income (loss)	—	—	—	—	—	—	—	—	(1,005)	(1,005)	—
Issuance of common stock	20	—	—	—	—	—	2,841	—	—	2,841	—
Stock-based compensation expense	—	—	—	—	—	—	10,703	—	—	10,703	—
Repurchase of common stock	(2,033)	—	—	—	2,033	(339,409)	—	—	—	(339,409)	—
Tax benefit from exercise of stock options	—	—	—	—	—	—	8,100	—	—	8,100	—
Other	94	—	(2)	—	—	—	574	—	—	574	—
Balance, December 31, 2013	26,290	$ 3	1,382	$ —	4,283	$ (546,570)	$ 196,908	$ 1,049,884	$ (333)	$699,892	$ —
Net income	—	—	—	—	—	—	—	179,293	—	179,293	—
Other comprehensive income (loss)	—	—	—	—	—	—	—	—	(1,027)	(1,027)	—
Issuance of common stock	23	—	—	—	—	—	3,247	—	—	3,247	—
Stock-based compensation expense	—	—	—	—	—	—	10,077	—	—	10,077	—
Repurchase of common stock	(978)	—	—	—	978	(159,503)	—	—	—	(159,503)	—
Tax benefit from exercise of stock options	—	—	—	—	—	—	3,089	—	—	3,089	—
Other	108	—	—	—	—	—	1,116	—	—	1,116	—
Balance, December 30, 2014	25,443	$ 3	1,382	$ —	5,261	$ (706,073)	$ 214,437	$ 1,229,177	$ (1,360)	$736,184	$ —
Net income (loss)	—	—	—	—	—	—	—	149,342	—	149,342	(17)
Other comprehensive income (loss)	—	—	—	—	—	—	—	—	(3,669)	(3,669)	—
Issuance of common stock	23	—	—	—	—	—	3,527	—	—	3,527	—
Stock-based compensation expense	—	—	—	—	—	—	15,086	—	—	15,086	—
Repurchase of common stock	(2,229)	—	—	—	2,229	(405,513)	—	—	—	(405,513)	—
Tax benefit from exercise of stock options	—	—	—	—	—	—	2,057	—	—	2,057	—
Redeemable noncontrolling interest resulting from acquisition	—	—	—	—	—	—	—	—	—	—	3,998
Other	109	—	—	—	—	—	286	—	—	286	—
Balance, December 29, 2015	23,346	$ 3	1,382	$ —	7,490	$ (1,111,586)	$ 235,393	$ 1,378,519	$ (5,029)	$497,300	$ 3,981

The accompanying notes are an integral part of the consolidated financial statements.

PANERA BREAD COMPANY
NOTES TO THE CONSOLIDATED FINANCIAL STATEMENTS

1. Nature of Business

Panera Bread Company and its subsidiaries (the "Company") operate a retail bakery-cafe business and franchising business under the concept names Panera Bread®, Saint Louis Bread Co.®, and Paradise Bakery & Café®. As of December 29, 2015, retail operations consisted of 901 Company-owned bakery-cafes and 1,071 franchise-operated bakery-cafes. The Company specializes in meeting consumer dining needs by providing high-quality food, including the following: fresh baked goods, made-to-order sandwiches on freshly baked breads, soups, pasta dishes, salads, and cafe beverages, and targets urban and suburban dwellers and workers by offering a premium specialty bakery-cafe experience with a neighborhood emphasis. Bakery-cafes are located in urban, suburban, strip mall and regional mall locations and currently operate in the United States and Canada. Bakery-cafes use fresh dough for their artisan and sourdough breads and bagels. In addition to the in-bakery-cafe dining experience, the Company offers Panera Catering, a nation-wide catering service that provides breakfast assortments, sandwiches, salads, soups, pasta dishes, drinks, and bakery items using the same high-quality, fresh ingredients enjoyed in bakery-cafes. As of December 29, 2015, the Company's fresh dough and other product operations, which supply fresh dough, produce, tuna, and cream cheese items daily to most Company-owned and franchise-operated bakery-cafes, consisted of 22 Company-owned and two franchise-operated fresh dough facilities.

2. Summary of Significant Accounting Policies

Basis of Presentation and Principles of Consolidation

The consolidated financial statements of the Company have been prepared in accordance with generally accepted accounting principles in the United States ("GAAP") and under the rules and regulations of the Securities and Exchange Commission (the "SEC"). The consolidated financial statements consist of the accounts of Panera Bread Company, its wholly owned direct and indirect subsidiaries and investees it controls. All intercompany balances and transactions have been eliminated in consolidation. Certain reclassifications have been made to prior year amounts to conform to the fiscal 2015 presentation.

Fiscal Year

The Company's fiscal year ends on the last Tuesday in December. The fiscal years ended December 29, 2015 ("fiscal 2015") and December 30, 2014 ("fiscal 2014") each had 52 weeks. The fiscal year ended December 31, 2013 ("fiscal 2013") had 53 weeks with the fourth quarter comprising 14 weeks.

Use of Estimates

The preparation of financial statements in conformity with GAAP requires management to make estimates and assumptions that affect the reported amounts of assets and liabilities and disclosure of contingent assets and liabilities at the date of the financial statements and the reported amounts of revenues and expenses during the reporting period. Actual results could differ from those estimates.

Cash and Cash Equivalents

The Company considers all highly liquid investments with an original maturity at the time of purchase of three months or less to be cash equivalents. The Company maintains cash balances with financial institutions that exceed federally insured limits. The Company has not experienced any losses related to these balances and believes credit risk to be minimal.

Investments

Management designates the classification of its investments at the time of purchase based upon its intended holding period. See Note 4 and Note 5 for further information with respect to the Company's investments.

Trade Accounts Receivable, net and Other Accounts Receivable

Trade accounts receivable, net consists primarily of amounts due to the Company from its franchisees for purchases of fresh dough and other products from the Company's fresh dough facilities, royalties due to the Company from franchisee sales, and receivables from credit card and catering on-account sales.

As of December 29, 2015, other accounts receivable consisted primarily of $29.8 million due from income tax refunds, $29.5 million due from wholesalers of the Company's gift cards, and tenant allowances due from landlords of $11.8 million. As of December 30, 2014, other accounts receivable consisted primarily of $33.4 million due from income tax refunds, $24.5 million due from wholesalers of the Company's gift cards, and tenant allowances due from landlords of $7.0 million.

PANERA BREAD COMPANY
NOTES TO THE CONSOLIDATED FINANCIAL STATEMENTS (continued)

The Company does not require collateral and maintains reserves for potential uncollectible accounts based on historical losses and existing economic conditions, when relevant. The allowance for doubtful accounts at December 29, 2015 and December 30, 2014 was $0.1 million, respectively.

Inventories

Inventories, which consist of food products, paper goods, and supplies, are valued at the lower of cost or market, with cost determined under the first-in, first-out method.

Property and Equipment, net

Property, equipment, leasehold improvements, and land are stated at cost less accumulated depreciation. Depreciation is provided using the straight-line method over the estimated useful lives of the assets. Leasehold improvements are depreciated using the straight-line method over the shorter of their estimated useful lives or the related reasonably assured lease term. Costs incurred in connection with the development of internal-use software are capitalized in accordance with the accounting standard for internal-use software, and are amortized over the expected useful life of the software. The estimated useful lives used for financial statement purposes are:

Leasehold improvements	15 - 20 years
Machinery and equipment	3 - 15 years
Furniture and fixtures	2 - 7 years
Computer hardware and software	3 - 5 years

Interest, to the extent it is incurred in connection with the construction of new locations or facilities, is capitalized. The capitalized interest is recorded as part of the asset to which it relates and is amortized over the asset's estimated useful life. Interest incurred for such purposes was $0.2 million and $0.1 million for fiscal 2015 and fiscal 2014, respectively. No interest was incurred for such purposes during fiscal 2013.

Upon retirement or sale, the cost of assets disposed and their related accumulated depreciation are removed from the Company's accounts. Any resulting gain or loss is credited or charged to operations. Maintenance and repairs are charged to expense when incurred, while certain improvements are capitalized. The total amounts expensed for maintenance and repairs was $67.3 million, $62.0 million, and $56.6 million, for fiscal 2015, fiscal 2014, and fiscal 2013, respectively.

Goodwill

The Company evaluates goodwill for impairment on an annual basis during our fourth quarter, or more frequently if circumstances indicate impairment might exist. Goodwill is evaluated for impairment through the comparison of fair value of our reporting units to their carrying values. When evaluating goodwill for impairment, the Company may first perform an assessment of qualitative factors to determine if the fair value of the reporting unit is more-likely-than-not greater than its carrying amount. If, based on the review of the qualitative factors, the Company determines it is not more-likely-than-not that the fair value of a reporting unit is less than its carrying value, the Company bypasses the required two-step impairment test. If the Company does not perform a qualitative assessment or if the fair value of the reporting unit is not more-likely- than-not greater than its carrying value, the Company performs a quantitative assessment and calculates the estimated fair value of the reporting unit. If the carrying value of the reporting unit exceeds the estimated fair value, there is an indication that impairment may exist. The amount of impairment is determined by comparing the implied fair value of the reporting unit goodwill to the carrying value of the goodwill in the same manner as if the reporting unit was being acquired in a business combination. If the implied fair value of goodwill is less than the recorded goodwill, the Company would record an impairment loss for the difference.

The fair value of a reporting unit is the price a willing buyer would pay for the reporting unit and is estimated using a discounted cash flow model. The discounted cash flow estimate is based upon, among other things, certain assumptions about expected future operating performance, such as revenue growth rates, operating margins, risk-adjusted discount rates, and future economic and market conditions.

No goodwill impairment charges were recorded during fiscal 2015 and fiscal 2013. The Company recorded a goodwill impairment charge of $2.1 million during fiscal 2014. This charge was recorded in other (income) expense, net in the Consolidated Statements of Income.

PANERA BREAD COMPANY
NOTES TO THE CONSOLIDATED FINANCIAL STATEMENTS (continued)

Other Intangible Assets, net

Other intangible assets, net consist primarily of favorable lease agreements, re-acquired territory rights, and trademarks. The Company amortizes the fair value of favorable lease agreements over the remaining related lease terms at the time of the acquisition, which ranged from approximately four years to 19 years as of December 29, 2015. The fair value of re-acquired territory rights was based on the present value of the acquired bakery-cafe cash flows. The Company amortizes the fair value of re-acquired territory rights over the remaining contractual terms of the re-acquired territory rights at the time of the acquisition, which ranged from approximately five years to 20 years as of December 29, 2015. The fair value of trade names and trademarks is amortized over their estimated useful life of eight years and 22 years, respectively.

The Company reviews intangible assets with finite lives for impairment when events or circumstances indicate these assets might be impaired. When warranted, the Company tests intangible assets with finite lives for impairment using historical cash flows and other relevant facts and circumstances as the primary basis for an estimate of future cash flows. There were no other intangible asset impairment charges recorded during fiscal 2015, fiscal 2014, and fiscal 2013. There can be no assurance that future intangible asset impairment tests will not result in a charge to earnings.

Impairment of Long-Lived Assets

The Company evaluates whether events and circumstances have occurred that indicate the remaining estimated useful life of long-lived assets may warrant revision or that the remaining balance of an asset may not be recoverable. The Company compares anticipated undiscounted cash flows from the related long-lived assets of a bakery-cafe or fresh dough facility with their respective carrying values to determine if the long-lived assets are recoverable. If the sum of the anticipated undiscounted cash flows for the long-lived assets is less than their carrying value, an impairment loss is recognized for the difference between the anticipated discounted cash flows, which approximates fair value, and the carrying value of the long-lived assets. In performing this analysis, management estimates cash flows based upon, among other things, certain assumptions about expected future operating performance, such as revenue growth rates, operating margins, risk-adjusted discount rates, and future economic and market conditions. Estimates of cash flow may differ from actual cash flow due to, among other things, economic conditions, changes to the Company's business model or changes in operating performance. The long-term financial forecasts that management utilizes represent the best estimate that management has at this time and management believes that the underlying assumptions are reasonable.

The Company recognized impairment losses of $3.8 million, $0.9 million, and $0.8 million during fiscal 2015, fiscal 2014, and fiscal 2013, respectively, related to distinct, underperforming Company-owned bakery-cafes. For fiscal 2015, the impairment loss was recorded in refranchising loss in the Consolidated Statements of Income. For fiscal 2014 and fiscal 2013, these impairment losses were recorded in other operating expenses in the Consolidated Statements of Income.

Self-Insurance Reserves

The Company is self-insured for a significant portion of its workers' compensation, group health, and general, auto, and property liability insurance with varying deductibles of as much as $0.8 million for individual claims, depending on the type of claim. The Company also purchases aggregate stop-loss and/or layers of loss insurance in many categories of loss. The Company utilizes third party actuarial experts' estimates of expected losses based on statistical analyses of the Company's actual historical data and historical industry data to determine required self-insurance reserves. The assumptions are closely reviewed, monitored, and adjusted when warranted by changing circumstances. The estimated accruals for these liabilities could be affected if actual experience related to the number of claims and cost per claim differs from these assumptions and historical trends. Based on information known at December 29, 2015, the Company believes it has provided adequate reserves for its self-insurance exposure. As of December 29, 2015 and December 30, 2014, self-insurance reserves were $37.2 million and $32.6 million, respectively, and were included in accrued expenses in the Consolidated Balance Sheets. The total amounts expensed for self-insurance were $54.3 million, $50.7 million, and $46.9 million for fiscal 2015, fiscal 2014, and fiscal 2013, respectively.

Income Taxes

The Company recognizes deferred tax assets and liabilities for the future tax consequences attributable to differences between the financial statement carrying amounts of existing assets and liabilities and their respective tax basis. Deferred tax assets and liabilities are measured using enacted income tax rates expected to apply to taxable income in the years in which those temporary differences are expected to be recovered or settled. Any effect on deferred tax assets and liabilities from a change in tax rates is recognized in income in the period that includes the enactment date. A valuation allowance is recognized if the Company determines it is more likely than not that all or some portion of the deferred tax asset will not be recognized. As of December 29, 2015 and December 30, 2014 the Company had recorded a valuation allowance related to deferred tax assets of the Company's Canadian operations of $5.3 million and $4.6 million, respectively.

PANERA BREAD COMPANY
NOTES TO THE CONSOLIDATED FINANCIAL STATEMENTS (continued)

In accordance with the authoritative guidance on income taxes, the Company establishes additional provisions for income taxes when, despite the belief that tax positions are fully supportable, there remain certain positions that do not meet the minimum probability threshold, which is a tax position that is more likely than not to be sustained upon ultimate settlement with tax authorities assuming full knowledge of the position and all relevant facts. In the normal course of business, the Company and its subsidiaries are examined by various federal, state, foreign, and other tax authorities. The Company regularly assesses the potential outcomes of these examinations and any future examinations for the current or prior years in determining the adequacy of its provision for income taxes. The Company routinely assesses the likelihood and amount of potential adjustments and adjusts the income tax provision, the current tax liability and deferred taxes in the period in which the facts that give rise to a revision become known. The Company classifies estimated interest and penalties related to the unrecognized tax benefits as a component of income taxes in the Consolidated Statements of Income.

Capitalization of Certain Development Costs

The Company has elected to account for construction costs in accordance with the accounting standard for real estate in the Company's consolidated financial statements. The Company capitalizes direct costs clearly associated with the acquisition, development, design, and construction of bakery-cafe locations and fresh dough facilities as these costs have a future benefit to the Company. The types of specifically identifiable costs capitalized by the Company include primarily payroll and payroll related taxes and benefit costs incurred by those individuals directly involved in development activities, including the acquisition, development, design, and construction of bakery-cafes and fresh dough facilities. The Company does not consider for capitalization payroll or payroll-related costs incurred by individuals that do not directly support the acquisition, development, design, and construction of bakery-cafes and fresh dough facilities. The Company uses an activity-based methodology to determine the amount of costs incurred for Company-owned projects, which are capitalized, and those for franchise-operated projects and general and administrative activities, which both are expensed as incurred. If the Company subsequently makes a determination that sites for which development costs have been capitalized will not be acquired or developed, any previously capitalized development costs are expensed and included in general and administrative expenses in the Consolidated Statements of Income.

The Company capitalized $9.8 million, $10.4 million, and $9.6 million of direct costs related to the development of Company-owned bakery-cafes during fiscal 2015, fiscal 2014, and fiscal 2013, respectively. The Company amortizes capitalized development costs for each bakery-cafe and fresh dough facility using the straight-line method over the shorter of their estimated useful lives or the related reasonably assured lease term and includes such amounts in depreciation and amortization in the Consolidated Statements of Income. In addition, the Company assesses the recoverability of capitalized costs through the performance of impairment analyses on an individual bakery-cafe and fresh dough facility basis pursuant to the accounting standard for property and equipment, net specifically related to the accounting for the impairment or disposal of long-lived assets.

Deferred Financing Costs

Debt issuance costs incurred in connection with the issuance of long-term debt are capitalized and amortized to interest expense based on the related debt agreement using the straight-line method, which approximates the effective interest method.

Revenue Recognition

The Company records revenues from bakery-cafe sales upon delivery of the related food and other products to the customer. Revenues from fresh dough and other product sales to franchisees are recorded upon delivery to the franchisees. Sales of soup and other branded products outside of the Company's bakery-cafes are recognized upon delivery to customers.

Franchise royalties are generally paid weekly based on the percentage of franchisee sales specified in each Area Development Agreement ("ADA") (generally five percent of net sales). Royalties are recognized as revenue in the period in which the sales are reported to have occurred based on contractual royalty rates applied to the net franchise sales. Royalties were $134.6 million, $120.1 million, and $110.5 million for fiscal 2015, fiscal 2014, and fiscal 2013, respectively. Franchise fees are the result of the sale of area development rights and the sale of individual franchise locations to third parties. The initial franchise fee is generally $35,000 per bakery-cafe to be developed under the ADA. Of this fee, $5,000 is generally paid at the time of the signing of the ADA and is recognized as revenue when it is received as it is non-refundable and the Company has to perform no other service to earn this fee. The remainder of the fee is paid at the time an individual franchise agreement is signed and is recognized as revenue upon the opening of the bakery-cafe. Franchise fees also include information technology-related fees for access to and the usage of proprietary systems. Franchise fees were $4.0 million, $3.6 million, and $2.2 million for fiscal 2015, fiscal 2014, and fiscal 2013, respectively.

The Company sells gift cards that do not have an expiration date and from which the Company does not deduct non-usage fees from outstanding gift card balances. Gift cards are redeemable at both Company-owned and franchise-operated bakery-cafes. Gift cards sold by either Company-owned bakery-cafes or through wholesalers and redeemed at franchise-operated bakery-cafes

PANERA BREAD COMPANY
NOTES TO THE CONSOLIDATED FINANCIAL STATEMENTS (continued)

reduce the Company's gift card liability but do not result in the recognition of revenue. When gift cards are redeemed at Company-owned bakery-cafes, the Company recognizes revenue and reduces the gift card liability. When the Company determines the likelihood of the gift card being redeemed by the customer is remote ("gift card breakage"), based upon Company-specific historical redemption patterns, and there is no legal obligation to remit the unredeemed gift card balance in the relevant jurisdiction, gift card breakage is recorded as a reduction of general and administrative expenses in the Consolidated Statements of Income; however, such gift cards will continue to be honored. During fiscal 2015, fiscal 2014, and fiscal 2013, the Company recognized gift card breakage as a reduction of general and administrative expenses of $6.9 million, $4.9 million, and $2.8 million, respectively. Incremental direct costs related to the sale of gift cards are deferred until the associated gift card is redeemed or breakage is deemed appropriate. These deferred incremental direct costs are reflected as a reduction of the unredeemed gift card liability, net which is a component of accrued expenses in the Consolidated Balance Sheets and, when recognized, as a reduction of bakery-cafe sales, net in the Consolidated Statements of Income.

The Company maintains a customer loyalty program referred to as MyPanera in which customers earn rewards based on registration in the program and purchases within Panera Bread bakery-cafes. The Company records the full retail value of loyalty program rewards as a reduction of net bakery-cafe sales and a liability is established within accrued expenses in the Consolidated Balance Sheets as rewards are earned while considering historical redemption rates. Fully earned rewards generally expire if unredeemed after 60 days. Partially earned awards generally expire if inactive for a period of one year. The accrued liability related to the Company's loyalty program was $2.7 million and $2.5 million as of December 29, 2015 and December 30, 2014, respectively. Costs associated with coupons are classified as a reduction of net bakery-cafe sales in the period in which the coupon is redeemed.

Advertising Costs

National advertising fund and marketing administration contributions received from franchise-operated bakery-cafes are consolidated with those from the Company in the Company's consolidated financial statements. Liabilities for unexpended funds received from franchisees are included in accrued expenses in the Consolidated Balance Sheets. The Company's contributions to the national advertising and marketing administration funds are recorded as part of general and administrative expenses in the Consolidated Statements of Income, while the Company's own local bakery-cafe media costs are recorded as part of other operating expenses in the Consolidated Statements of Income. The Company's policy is to record advertising costs as expense in the period in which the costs are incurred. The Company's advertising costs include national, regional, and local expenditures utilizing primarily radio, billboards, social networking, Internet, television, and print. The total amounts recorded as advertising expense were $68.5 million, $65.5 million, and $55.6 million for fiscal 2015, fiscal 2014, and fiscal 2013, respectively.

Pre-Opening Expenses

Pre-opening expenses directly associated with the opening of new bakery-cafe locations, which consists primarily of pre-opening rent expense, labor, and food costs incurred during in-store training and preparation for opening, but exclude manager training costs which are included in labor expense in the Consolidated Statements of Income, are expensed when incurred.

Rent Expense

The Company recognizes rent expense on a straight-line basis over the reasonably assured lease term as defined in the accounting standard for leases. The reasonably assured lease term for most bakery-cafe leases is the initial non-cancelable lease term plus one renewal option period, which generally equates to an aggregate of 15 years. The reasonably assured lease term on most fresh dough facility leases is the initial non-cancelable lease term plus one to two renewal option periods, which generally equates to an aggregate of 20 years. In addition, certain of the Company's lease agreements provide for scheduled rent increases during the lease terms or for rental payments commencing at a date other than the date of initial occupancy. The Company includes any rent escalations and construction period and other rent holidays in its determination of straight-line rent expense. Therefore, rent expense for new locations is charged to expense beginning on the date at which the Company has the right to control the use of the property. Many of the Company's lease agreements also contain provisions that require additional rental payments based upon net bakery-cafe sales volume, which the Company refers to as contingent rent. Contingent rent is accrued each period as the liability is incurred, in addition to the straight-line rent expense noted above. This results in variability in occupancy expense over the term of the lease in bakery-cafes where the Company pays contingent rent.

The Company records landlord allowances and incentives received as deferred rent in the Consolidated Balance Sheets based on their short-term or long-term nature. This deferred rent is amortized on a straight-line basis over the reasonably assured lease term as a reduction of rent expense. Additionally, payments made by the Company and reimbursed by the landlord for improvements deemed to be lessor assets have no impact on the Consolidated Statements of Income. The Company considers improvements to be a lessor asset if all of the following criteria are met:

- the lease specifically requires the lessee to make the improvement;

PANERA BREAD COMPANY
NOTES TO THE CONSOLIDATED FINANCIAL STATEMENTS (continued)

- the improvement is fairly generic;

- the improvement increases the fair value of the property to the lessor; and

- the useful life of the improvement is longer than the lease term.

The Company reports the period to period change in the landlord receivable within the operating activities section of its Consolidated Statements of Cash Flows.

Earnings Per Share

Basic earnings per share is computed by dividing net income by the weighted-average number of shares of common stock outstanding during the fiscal year. Diluted earnings per common share is computed by dividing net income by the weighted-average number of shares of common stock outstanding and dilutive securities outstanding during the year.

Foreign Currency Translation

The Company has 11 Company-owned bakery-cafes, one Company-owned fresh dough facility, and six franchise-operated bakery-cafes in Canada which use the Canadian Dollar as their functional currency. Assets and liabilities are translated into U.S. dollars using the current exchange rate in effect at the balance sheet date, while revenues and expenses are translated at the weighted-average exchange rate during the fiscal period. The resulting translation adjustments are recorded as a separate component of accumulated other comprehensive income in the Consolidated Balance Sheets and Consolidated Statements of Changes in Equity and Redeemable Noncontrolling Interest. Gains and losses resulting from foreign currency transactions have not historically been significant and are included in other (income) expense, net in the Consolidated Statements of Income.

Derivative Instruments

The Company records all derivatives in the Consolidated Balance Sheets at fair value. The Company does not enter into derivative instruments for trading purposes. For derivative instruments that are designated and qualify as cash flow hedges, the effective portion of the derivative's gain or loss is reported as component of other comprehensive income and recorded in accumulated other comprehensive income, net of tax in the Consolidated Balance Sheets. The gain or loss is subsequently reclassified into earnings when the hedged exposure affects earnings. To the extent that the change in the fair value of the contract corresponds to the change in the value of the anticipated transaction, the hedge is considered effective. The remaining change in fair value of the contract represents the ineffective portion, which is immediately recorded in interest expense in the Consolidated Statements of Income. Once established, cash flow hedges generally remain designated as such until the hedged item impacts earnings, or the anticipated transaction is no longer likely to occur.

Fair Value of Financial Instruments

The carrying amounts of cash, accounts receivable, accounts payable, and other accrued expenses approximate their fair values due to the short-term nature of these assets and liabilities. The fair value of the Company's interest rate swaps are determined based on a discounted cash flow analysis on the expected future cash flows of each derivative. This analysis reflects the contractual terms of the derivatives and uses observable market-based inputs, including interest rate curves and credit spreads.

Stock-Based Compensation

The Company accounts for stock-based compensation in accordance with the accounting standard for stock-based compensation, which requires the Company to measure and record compensation expense in the Company's consolidated financial statements for all stock-based compensation awards using a fair value method. The Company maintains several stock-based incentive plans under which the Company may grant incentive stock options, non-statutory stock options and stock settled appreciation rights (collectively, "option awards") and restricted stock and restricted stock units to certain directors, officers, employees and consultants. The Company also offers a stock purchase plan where employees may purchase the Company's common stock each calendar quarter through payroll deductions at 85 percent of market value on the purchase date and the Company recognizes compensation expense on the 15 percent discount.

For option awards, fair value is determined using the Black-Scholes option pricing model, while restricted stock is valued using the closing stock price on the date of grant. The Black-Scholes option pricing model requires the input of subjective assumptions. These assumptions include estimating the expected term until the option awards are either exercised or canceled; the expected volatility of the Company's stock price, for a period approximating the expected term; the risk-free interest rate with a maturity that approximates the option awards expected term; and the dividend yield based on the Company's anticipated dividend payout over the expected term of the option awards. These assumptions are evaluated and revised, as necessary, to reflect market conditions

PANERA BREAD COMPANY
NOTES TO THE CONSOLIDATED FINANCIAL STATEMENTS (continued)

and historical experience. Stock-based compensation expense is recognized only for those awards expected to vest, with forfeitures estimated at the date of grant based on historical experience. The fair value of the awards expected to vest is amortized over the vesting period. Options and restricted stock generally vest 25 percent after two years and thereafter 25 percent each year for the next three years and options generally have a six-year term. Stock-based compensation expense is included in general and administrative expenses in the Consolidated Statements of Income.

Asset Retirement Obligations

The Company recognizes the future cost to comply with lease obligations at the end of a lease as it relates to tangible long-lived assets in accordance with the accounting standard for the asset retirement and environmental obligations ("ARO") in the Company's consolidated financial statements. Most lease agreements require the Company to restore the leased property to its original condition, including removal of certain long-lived assets the Company has installed, at the end of the lease. A liability for the fair value of an asset retirement obligation along with a corresponding increase to the carrying value of the related long-lived asset is recorded at the time a lease agreement is executed. The Company amortizes the amount added to property and equipment, net and recognizes accretion expense in connection with the discounted liability over the reasonably assured lease term. The estimated liability is based on the Company's historical experience in closing bakery-cafes, fresh dough facilities, and support centers and the related external cost associated with these activities. Revisions to the liability could occur due to changes in estimated retirement costs or changes in lease terms. As of December 29, 2015 and December 30, 2014, the Company's net ARO asset included in property and equipment, net was $10.3 million and $13.3 million, respectively, and its net ARO liability included in other long-term liabilities was $19.5 million and $19.8 million, respectively. ARO accretion expense was $1.0 million, $0.6 million, and $0.6 million for fiscal 2015, fiscal 2014, and fiscal 2013, respectively.

Variable Interest Entities

The Company applies relevant accounting standards for variable interest entities ("VIE"), which defines the process for how an enterprise determines which party consolidates a VIE. The enterprise that consolidates the VIE (the primary beneficiary) is defined as the enterprise with (1) the power to direct activities of the VIE that most significantly affect the VIE's economic performance and (2) the obligation to absorb losses of the VIE or the right to receive benefits from the VIE. The Company does not possess any ownership interests in franchise entities or other affiliates. The franchise agreements are designed to provide the franchisee with key decision-making ability to enable it to oversee its operations and to have a significant impact on the success of the franchise, while the Company's decision-making rights are related to protecting its brand. Based upon its analysis of all the relevant facts and considerations of the franchise entities and other affiliates, the Company has concluded that these entities are not variable interest entities and they have not been consolidated as of December 29, 2015. As discussed further at Note 3, the Company also evaluated all of the applicable criteria for an entity subject to consolidation and concluded its interest in a certain bakery-cafe concept is a VIE requiring consolidation.

Recent Accounting Pronouncements

In November 2015, the Financial Accounting Standards Board ("FASB") issued Accounting Standards Update ("ASU") 2015-17, "Balance Sheet Classification of Deferred Taxes". This update requires that deferred tax liabilities and assets be classified as noncurrent in a classified statement of financial position. This update is effective for annual and interim reporting periods beginning after December 15, 2016. Early adoption is permitted. The Company plans on adopting this guidance in the first quarter of fiscal 2016.

In September 2015, the FASB issued ASU 2015-16, "Business Combinations (Topic 805): Simplifying the Accounting for Measurement-Period Adjustments". This update eliminates the requirement for an acquirer in a business combination to account for measurement-period adjustments retrospectively. Acquirers would now recognize measurement-period adjustments during the period in which they determine the amount of the adjustment. This update is effective for annual and interim reporting periods beginning after December 15, 2015, including interim periods within those fiscal years, and should be applied prospectively to adjustments for provisional amounts that occur after the effective date with early adoption permitted for financial statements that have not been issued. The adoption of this guidance is not expected to have a material effect on the Company's consolidated financial statements.

In July 2015, the FASB issued ASU 2015-11, "Inventory (Topic 330): Simplifying the Measurement of Inventory". This update provides guidance on the subsequent measurement of inventory, which changes the measurement from lower of cost or market to lower of cost and net realizable value. This update is effective for annual and interim periods beginning after December 15, 2016. The adoption of this guidance is not expected to have a material effect on the Company's consolidated financial statements.

In April 2015, the FASB issued ASU 2015-03, "Interest – Imputation of Interest (Subtopic 835-30): Simplifying the Presentation of Debt Issuance Costs". This update requires debt issuance costs related to a recognized debt liability to be presented in the

PANERA BREAD COMPANY
NOTES TO THE CONSOLIDATED FINANCIAL STATEMENTS (continued)

balance sheet as a direct deduction from the carrying value of that debt liability, consistent with debt discounts. The recognition and measurement guidance for debt issuance costs were not affected by this update. The Company early adopted ASU 2015-03 during the thirteen weeks ended June 30, 2015. As a result of the retrospective adoption, the Company reclassified unamortized debt issuance costs of $0.2 million as of December 30, 2014 from Deposits and other to Long-term debt in the Consolidated Balance Sheets. Adoption of this standard did not impact the Company's results of operations or cash flows in either the current or previous interim and annual reporting periods.

In August 2014, the FASB issued ASU 2014-15, "Presentation of Financial Statements - Going Concern (Subtopic 205-40): Disclosure of Uncertainties about an Entity's Ability to Continue as a Going Concern". This update requires management of the Company to evaluate whether there is substantial doubt about the Company's ability to continue as a going concern. This update is effective for the annual period ending after December 15, 2016, and for annual and interim periods thereafter. Early adoption is permitted. The Company is currently evaluating the effect of the standard but its adoption is not expected to have an impact on the Company's consolidated financial statements.

In May 2014, the FASB issued ASU 2014-09, "Revenue from Contracts with Customers (Topic 606)". This update provides a comprehensive new revenue recognition model that requires a company to recognize revenue to depict the transfer of goods or services to a customer at an amount that reflects the consideration it expects to receive in exchange for those goods or services. The guidance also requires additional disclosure about the nature, amount, timing, and uncertainty of revenue and cash flows arising from customer contracts. In August 2015, the FASB issued ASU 2015-14 delaying the effective date for adoption. The update is now effective for interim and annual reporting periods beginning after December 15, 2017. Early adoption is permitted. The update permits the use of either the retrospective or cumulative effect transition method. The Company is evaluating the effect this guidance will have on the Company's consolidated financial statements and related disclosures. The Company has not yet selected a transition method nor has it determined the effect of the standard on its ongoing financial reporting.

In April 2014, the FASB issued ASU 2014-08, "Presentation of Financial Statements (Topic 205) and Property, Plant, and Equipment (Topic 360)". This update was issued to clarify the reporting for discontinued operations and disclosures for disposals of components of an entity. This update is effective for annual and interim periods beginning after December 15, 2014. The adoption of this update did not have a material effect on the Company's consolidated financial statements or related disclosures; however, it may impact the reporting of future discontinued operations if and when they occur.

3. Business Combinations and Divestitures

Refranchising Initiative

In February 2015, the Company announced a plan to refranchise approximately 50 to 150 Company-owned bakery-cafes by the end of fiscal 2015.

On March 3, 2015, the Company sold substantially all of the assets of one bakery-cafe to an existing franchisee for cash proceeds of approximately $3.2 million, which resulted in a gain on sale of approximately $2.6 million.

The Company recognized impairment losses of $3.8 million during the thirteen weeks ended March 31, 2015 related to certain under-performing bakery-cafes in one of the refranchised markets for which the Company had signed letters of intent, which were excluded from the proposed sale.

On July 14, 2015, the Company sold substantially all of the assets of 29 bakery-cafes in the Boston market to an existing franchisee for a purchase price of approximately $19.6 million, including $0.5 million for inventory on hand, with $2.0 million held in escrow for certain holdbacks, and recognized a loss on sale of $0.6 million. The holdback amount is primarily to satisfy any indemnification obligations of the Company and will be held in escrow until July 14, 2017, the two-year anniversary of the transaction closing date, with the remaining balance of the holdback amount reverting to the Company.

On October 7, 2015, the Company sold substantially all of the assets of 45 bakery-cafes in the Seattle and Northern California markets to a new franchisee for a purchase price of approximately $26.8 million, including $0.9 million for inventory on hand, and recognized a loss on sale of $1.6 million.

During the thirteen weeks ended December 29, 2015, eight Company-owned bakery-cafes that the Company concluded no longer met all of the criteria required to be classified as held for sale were reclassified to held and used at their depreciated carrying value, assuming depreciation had not ceased while classified as held for sale.

PANERA BREAD COMPANY
NOTES TO THE CONSOLIDATED FINANCIAL STATEMENTS (continued)

As of December 29, 2015, the Company classified as held for sale the assets and certain liabilities of 35 Company-owned bakery-cafes the Company expects to sell during the next 12 months. During fiscal 2015, the Company recorded losses on assets held for sale of $11.0 million. The Company classifies assets as held for sale and ceases depreciation of the assets when those assets meet the held for sale criteria, as defined in GAAP. The following summarizes the financial statement carrying amounts of assets and liabilities associated with the bakery-cafes classified as held for sale (in thousands):

	December 29, 2015
Inventories	$ 738
Property and equipment, net	26,462
Goodwill	1,499
Assets held for sale	$ 28,699
Deferred rent	$ 2,410
Asset retirement obligation	535
Liabilities associated with assets held for sale	$ 2,945

Assets held for sale were valued using Level 3 inputs, primarily representing information obtained from signed letters of intent. Costs to sell are considered in the estimates of fair value for those assets included in assets held for sale in the Company's Consolidated Balance Sheets.

The following summarizes activity associated with the refranchising initiative recorded in the caption entitled refranchising loss in the Consolidated Statements of Income (in thousands):

	For the fiscal year ended December 29, 2015
Loss on assets held for sale	$ 10,999
Impairment of long-lived assets and lease termination costs	5,461
Professional fees and severance	1,088
Gain on sale of bakery-cafes	(440)
Refranchising loss (1)	$ 17,108

(1) The caption entitled refranchising loss in the Consolidated Statements of Cash Flows as a non-cash adjustment to reconcile net income to net cash provided by operating activities includes only non-cash refranchising amounts.

Tatte Acquisition

On December 7, 2015, the Company acquired a 50.01% interest in Tatte Holdings, LLC ("Tatte"), for a cash contribution of $4.0 million (the "Tatte Acquisition"). Tatte is a bakery-cafe concept with five locations in the Boston area. The Company has evaluated all of the applicable criteria for an entity subject to consolidation under the provisions of the variable interest model and has concluded that Tatte is a VIE requiring consolidation.

The following summarizes the consolidated assets and liabilities of Tatte as of December 7, 2015, including the Company's investment in Tatte, which is eliminated in consolidation (in thousands):

PANERA BREAD COMPANY
NOTES TO THE CONSOLIDATED FINANCIAL STATEMENTS (continued)

Current assets, including cash	$	4,136
Property and equipment		1,757
Goodwill		2,512
Intangible assets		1,657
Deposits and other		87
Total assets	$	10,149
Current liabilities	$	777
Long-term debt		1,237
Other long-term liabilities		137
Total liabilities		2,151
Redeemable noncontrolling interest		3,998
Panera Bread Company investment in Tatte		4,000
Total liabilities, redeemable noncontrolling interest, and stockholders' equity	$	10,149

Redeemable noncontrolling interest reflects that the noncontrolling interest holder holds a written put option, which will allow them to sell their noncontrolling interest to the Company at any time after the end of the third year after the Tatte Acquisition. In addition to the written put option, the Company holds a call option to acquire the noncontrolling interest after 42 months after the Tatte Acquisition. Under each of these alternatives, the exercise price will be based on a contractually defined multiple of cash flows, subject to certain limitations (the "redemption value"), which is not a fair value measurement and is payable in cash. As the written put option is redeemable at the option of the noncontrolling interest holder, and not solely within the Company's control, the noncontrolling interest in Tatte is classified as temporary equity and reflected in redeemable noncontrolling interest between the Liabilities and Stockholders' Equity sections of the Company's Consolidated Balance Sheets. The initial carrying amount of the noncontrolling interest is the fair value of the noncontrolling interest as of the acquisition date.

The noncontrolling interest is adjusted each period for comprehensive income attributable to the noncontrolling interest and changes in the Company's ownership interest in Tatte, if any. An additional adjustment to the carrying value of the noncontrolling interest may be required if the redemption value exceeds the current carrying value. Changes in the carrying value of the noncontrolling interest related to a change in the redemption value will be recorded against permanent equity and will not affect net income. While there is no impact on net income, the redeemable noncontrolling interest will impact the Company's calculation of earnings per share. Utilizing the two-class method, the Company will adjust the numerator of the earnings per share calculation to reflect the changes in the excess, if any, of the noncontrolling interest's redemption value over the noncontrolling interest carrying amount. The Company did not record any such adjustments as of December 29, 2015.

The pro-forma impact of the Tatte Acquisition on prior periods is not presented, as the impact is not material to reported results. All of the recorded goodwill is included in the Company Bakery-Cafe Operations segment.

Florida Bakery-cafe Acquisition

On April 9, 2013, the Company acquired substantially all the assets of one bakery-cafe from its Hallandale, Florida franchisee for a purchase price of $2.7 million. The Company paid approximately $2.4 million of the purchase price on April 9, 2013 and paid the remaining $0.3 million with interest during fiscal 2014. The Consolidated Statements of Income include the results of operations for the bakery-cafe from the date of its acquisition. The pro-forma impact of the acquisition on prior periods is not presented, as the impact is not material to reported results.

4. Investments Held to Maturity

During fiscal 2013, the Company purchased and sold seven zero-coupon discount notes that were classified as held-to-maturity. The amortized cost of the investments sold was $97.9 million. The Company realized a loss on the sale of less than $0.1 million. The Company sold the investments prior to maturity during fiscal 2013 as a result of higher than anticipated liquidity needs.

PANERA BREAD COMPANY
NOTES TO THE CONSOLIDATED FINANCIAL STATEMENTS (continued)

5. Fair Value Measurements

The following summarizes assets and liabilities measured at fair value on a recurring basis (in thousands):

	Total	Quoted Prices in Active Markets for Identical Assets (Level 1)	Significant Other Observable Inputs (Level 2)	Significant Unobservable Inputs (Level 3)
December 29, 2015:				
Cash equivalents	$ 2	$ 2	$ —	$ —
Total assets	$ 2	$ 2	$ —	$ —
Interest rate swap liability	$ 2,552	$ —	$ 2,552	$ —
Total liabilities	$ 2,552	$ —	$ 2,552	$ —
December 30, 2014:				
Cash equivalents	$ 92,316	$ 92,316	$ —	$ —
Total assets	$ 92,316	$ 92,316	$ —	$ —

The fair value of the Company's cash equivalents is based on quoted market prices for identical securities. The fair value of the Company's interest rate swaps are determined based on a discounted cash flow analysis on the expected future cash flows of each derivative. This analysis reflects the contractual terms of the derivatives and uses observable market-based inputs, including interest rate curves and credit spreads.

6. Inventories

Inventories consisted of the following (in thousands):

	December 29, 2015	December 30, 2014
Food:		
Fresh dough facilities:		
Raw materials	$ 3,561	$ 3,413
Finished goods	446	460
Bakery-cafes:		
Raw materials	14,819	15,152
Paper goods	3,656	3,786
Total	$ 22,482	$ 22,811

PANERA BREAD COMPANY
NOTES TO THE CONSOLIDATED FINANCIAL STATEMENTS (continued)

7. Property and Equipment, net

Major classes of property and equipment consisted of the following (in thousands):

	December 29, 2015	December 30, 2014
Leasehold improvements	$ 683,296	$ 693,503
Machinery and equipment	338,500	340,854
Computer hardware and software	192,521	137,663
Furniture and fixtures	159,653	167,383
Construction in progress	97,416	99,255
Smallwares	29,056	29,841
Land	1,604	2,060
	1,502,046	1,470,559
Less: accumulated depreciation	(725,798)	(683,265)
Property and equipment, net	$ 776,248	$ 787,294

The Company recorded depreciation expense related to these assets of $126.7 million, $115.4 million, and $97.2 million during fiscal 2015, fiscal 2014, and fiscal 2013, respectively.

8. Goodwill

The following is a reconciliation of the beginning and ending balances of the Company's goodwill by reportable segment at December 29, 2015 and December 30, 2014 (in thousands):

	Company Bakery-Cafe Operations	Franchise Operations	Fresh Dough and Other Product Operations	Total
Balance as of December 31, 2013	$ 119,384	$ 1,934	$ 1,695	$ 123,013
Impairment charge	(2,057)	—	—	(2,057)
Currency translation	(178)	—	—	(178)
Balance as of December 30, 2014	$ 117,149	$ 1,934	$ 1,695	$ 120,778
Acquisition of Tatte	2,512	—	—	2,512
Goodwill classified as held for sale	(1,499)	—	—	(1,499)
Balance as of December 29, 2015	$ 118,162	$ 1,934	$ 1,695	$ 121,791

The Company did not record a goodwill impairment charge in either fiscal 2015 or fiscal 2013. The Company recorded a $2.1 million full impairment charge of goodwill for the Canadian bakery-cafe operations reporting unit during fiscal 2014.

9. Other Intangible Assets

Other intangible assets consisted of the following (in thousands):

	December 29, 2015			December 30, 2014		
	Gross Carrying Value	Accumulated Amortization	Net Carrying Value	Gross Carrying Value	Accumulated Amortization	Net Carrying Value
Trademark	$ 7,080	$ (2,283)	$ 4,797	$ 5,610	$ (2,017)	$ 3,593
Re-acquired territory rights	97,865	(40,432)	57,433	97,865	(32,369)	65,496
Favorable leases	5,012	(3,365)	1,647	4,825	(2,974)	1,851
Total other intangible assets	$ 109,957	$ (46,080)	$ 63,877	$ 108,300	$ (37,360)	$ 70,940

Amortization expense on these intangible assets for fiscal 2015, fiscal 2014, and fiscal 2013, was approximately $8.7 million, $8.7 million, and $9.3 million, respectively. Future amortization expense on these intangible assets as of December 29, 2015 is

PANERA BREAD COMPANY
NOTES TO THE CONSOLIDATED FINANCIAL STATEMENTS (continued)

estimated to be approximately: $8.8 million in fiscal 2016, $8.8 million in fiscal 2017, $8.7 million in fiscal 2018, $8.3 million in fiscal 2019, $7.2 million in fiscal 2020 and $22.1 million thereafter.

10. Accrued Expenses

Accrued expenses consisted of the following (in thousands):

	December 29, 2015	December 30, 2014
Unredeemed gift cards, net	$ 123,363	$ 105,576
Compensation and related employment taxes	64,882	59,442
Capital expenditures	53,914	56,808
Insurance	37,208	32,559
Taxes, other than income tax	20,206	21,068
Fresh dough and other product operations	10,854	6,812
Occupancy costs	8,594	7,263
Deferred revenue	5,690	5,291
Advertising	5,242	10,147
Utilities	4,581	5,527
Loyalty program	2,653	2,525
Other	22,277	20,183
Total	$ 359,464	$ 333,201

11. Debt

Long-term debt consisted of the following (in thousands):

	December 29, 2015	December 30, 2014
2014 Term Loan	$ 100,000	$ 100,000
2015 Term Loan	296,250	—
2015 Note Payable	10,144	—
Debt assumed in Tatte acquisition	1,147	—
Aggregate unamortized lender fees and issuance costs	(1,341)	(216)
Total carrying amount	406,200	99,784
Current portion of long-term debt	17,229	—
Long-term debt	$ 388,971	$ 99,784

Term Loans

On June 11, 2014, the Company entered into a term loan agreement (the "2014 Term Loan Agreement"), by and among the Company, as borrower, Bank of America, N.A., as administrative agent, and other lenders party thereto. The 2014 Term Loan Agreement provides for an unsecured term loan in the amount of $100 million (the "2014 Term Loan"). The 2014 Term Loan is scheduled to mature on July 11, 2019, subject to acceleration upon certain specified events of default, including breaches of representations or covenants, failure to pay other material indebtedness or a change of control of the Company, as defined in the 2014 Term Loan Agreement. The Company incurred lender fees and issuance costs totaling $0.2 million in connection with the issuance of the 2014 Term Loan. The lender fees and issuance costs are being amortized to expense over the term of the 2014 Term Loan.

On July 16, 2015, the Company entered into a term loan agreement (the "2015 Term Loan Agreement"), with Bank of America, N.A., as administrative agent, and other lenders party thereto. The 2015 Term Loan Agreement provides for an unsecured term loan in the amount of $300 million (the "2015 Term Loan"). The 2015 Term Loan is scheduled to mature on July 16, 2020, subject to acceleration upon certain specified events of default, including breaches of representations or covenants, failure to pay other material indebtedness or a change of control of the Company, as defined in the 2015 Term Loan Agreement, and is amortized in equal quarterly installments in an amount equal to 1.25 percent of the original principal amount of the 2015 Term Loan. The Company incurred lender fees and issuance costs totaling $1.4 million in connection with the issuance of the 2015 Term Loan. The lender fees and issuance costs are being amortized to expense over the term of the 2015 Term Loan. As of December 29,

PANERA BREAD COMPANY
NOTES TO THE CONSOLIDATED FINANCIAL STATEMENTS (continued)

2015, $14.7 million of the 2015 Term Loan's carrying amount is presented as the Current portion of long-term debt in the Consolidated Balance Sheets.

Each of the 2014 Term Loan and 2015 Term Loan bears interest at a rate equal to, at the Company's option, (1) the Eurodollar rate plus a margin ranging from 1.00 percent to 1.50 percent depending on the Company's consolidated leverage ratio or (2) the highest of (a) the Bank of America prime rate, (b) the Federal funds rate plus 0.50 percent or (c) the Eurodollar rate plus 1.00 percent, plus a margin ranging from 0.00 percent to 0.50 percent depending on the Company's consolidated leverage ratio. The Company's obligations under the 2014 Term Loan Agreement and 2015 Term Loan Agreement are guaranteed by certain of its direct and indirect subsidiaries.

The weighted-average interest rate for the 2014 Term Loan, excluding the amortization of issuance costs, was 1.21 percent and 1.15 percent for fiscal 2015 and fiscal 2014, respectively. The weighted-average interest rate for the 2015 Term Loan, excluding the amortization of lender fees and issuance costs, was 1.33 percent for fiscal 2015. As of December 29, 2015, the carrying amounts of the 2014 Term Loan and 2015 Term Loan approximate fair value as the interest rates approximate current market rates (Level 2 inputs).

On July 16, 2015, in order to hedge the variability in cash flows from changes in benchmark interest rates, the Company entered into two forward-starting interest rate swap agreements with an aggregate initial notional value of $242.5 million. The forward-starting interest rate swaps have been designated as cash flow hedging instruments. See Note 12 for information on the Company's interest rate swaps.

Installment Payment Agreement

On September 15, 2015, the Company entered into a Master Installment Payment Agreement (the "Master IPA") with PNC Equipment Finance, LLC ("PNC") pursuant to which PNC financed the Company's purchase of hardware, software, and services associated with new storage virtualization and disaster recovery systems. The Master IPA provides for a secured note payable in the amount of $12.7 million (the "2015 Note Payable"), payable in five annual installments beginning November 1, 2015 and each September 1st thereafter. As of December 29, 2015, there was $10.1 million outstanding under the Master IPA, and $2.5 million of the Master IPA is presented as the Current portion of long-term debt in the Consolidated Balance Sheets.

Revolving Credit Agreements

On November 30, 2012, the Company entered into a credit agreement (the "2012 Credit Agreement") with Bank of America, N.A. and other lenders party thereto. The 2012 Credit Agreement provided for an unsecured revolving credit facility of $250 million that would have become due on November 30, 2017. As of December 30, 2014, the Company had no loans outstanding under the 2012 Credit Agreement.

On July 16, 2015, the Company terminated the 2012 Credit Agreement and entered into a new credit agreement (the "2015 Credit Agreement"), with Bank of America, N.A., as administrative agent, swing line lender and L/C issuer, and each lender from time to time party thereto. The 2015 Credit Agreement provides for an unsecured revolving credit facility of $250 million that will become due on July 16, 2020, subject to acceleration upon certain specified events of default, including breaches of representations or covenants, failure to pay other material indebtedness or a change of control of the Company, as defined in the 2015 Credit Agreement. The 2015 Credit Agreement provides that the Company may select interest rates under the credit facility equal to, at the Company's option, (1) the Eurodollar rate plus a margin ranging from 1.00 percent to 1.50 percent depending on the Company's consolidated leverage ratio or (2) the highest of (a) the Bank of America prime rate, (b) the Federal funds rate plus 0.50 percent or (c) the Eurodollar rate plus 1.00 percent, plus a margin ranging from 0.00 percent to 0.50 percent depending on the Company's consolidated leverage ratio. As of December 29, 2015, the Company had no loans outstanding under the 2015 Credit Agreement.

The 2014 Term Loan Agreement, 2015 Term Loan Agreement and 2015 Credit Agreement contain customary affirmative and negative covenants, including covenants limiting liens, dispositions, fundamental changes, investments, indebtedness, and certain transactions and payments. In addition, such term loan and credit agreements contain various financial covenants that, among other things, require the Company to satisfy two financial covenants at the end of each fiscal quarter: (1) a consolidated leverage ratio less than or equal to 3.00 to 1.00, and (2) a consolidated fixed charge coverage ratio of greater than or equal to 2.00 to 1.00. As of December 29, 2015, the Company was in compliance with all covenant requirements.

12. Derivative Financial Instruments

The Company enters into derivative instruments solely for risk management purposes. To the extent the Company's cash-flow hedging instruments are effective in offsetting the variability in the hedged cash flows, and otherwise meet the cash flow hedge accounting criteria, changes in the derivatives' fair value are not included in current earnings but are included in accumulated other

PANERA BREAD COMPANY
NOTES TO THE CONSOLIDATED FINANCIAL STATEMENTS (continued)

comprehensive income (loss), net of tax in the Consolidated Balance Sheets. These changes in fair value will be reclassified into earnings at the time of the forecasted transaction. By using these instruments, the Company exposes itself, from time to time, to credit risk and market risk. Credit risk is the failure of the counterparty to perform under the terms of the derivative contract. The Company minimizes this credit risk by entering into transactions with high-quality counterparties. Market risk is the adverse effect on the value of a financial instrument that results from changes in interest rates. The Company minimizes this market risk by establishing and monitoring parameters that limit the types and degree of market risk that may be undertaken.

On July 16, 2015, the Company entered into two forward-starting interest rate swap agreements with an aggregate initial notional value of $242.5 million to hedge a portion of the cash flows of its term loan borrowings. For each of the swaps, the Company has agreed to exchange with a counterparty the difference between fixed and variable interest amounts calculated by reference to an agreed-upon principal amount.

The following table summarizes the Company's interest rate swaps as of December 29, 2015:

Trade Date	Effective Date	Term (in Years)	Notional Amount (in thousands)	Fixed Rate
July 16, 2015	July 11, 2016	4	$ 100,000	1.75%
July 16, 2015	July 18, 2016	5	142,500	1.97%

The notional amount for the interest rate swap with an effective date of July 18, 2016 decreases quarterly by $1.9 million over the five-year term of the interest rate swap beginning in September 2016.

The interest rate swaps, which have been designated and qualify as cash flow hedges, are recorded at fair value in other long-term liabilities in the Consolidated Balance Sheets. The fair value of the interest rate swaps was approximately $2.6 million as of December 29, 2015. The change in fair value of the interest rate swaps resulted in an after-tax loss of approximately $1.5 million as of December 29, 2015, which is recorded in accumulated other comprehensive income (loss). A net of tax loss of approximately $0.7 million is expected to be reclassified from accumulated other comprehensive income (loss) to earnings within the next twelve months. The Company did not recognize a gain or loss due to hedge ineffectiveness during fiscal 2015.

The Company does not hold or use derivative instruments for trading purposes. The Company also does not have any derivatives not designated as hedging instruments and has not designated any non-derivatives as hedging instruments.

13. Share Repurchase Authorization

On August 23, 2012, the Company's Board of Directors approved a three year share repurchase authorization of up to $600 million of the Company's Class A common stock (the "2012 repurchase authorization"), pursuant to which the Company repurchased shares on the open market under a Rule 10b5-1 plan. During fiscal 2014, the Company repurchased 514,357 shares under the 2012 share repurchase authorization, at an average price of $170.15 per share, for an aggregate purchase price of approximately $87.5 million. During fiscal 2013, the Company repurchased 1,992,250 shares under the 2012 repurchase authorization, at an average price of $166.73 per share, for an aggregate purchase price of approximately $332.1 million. On June 5, 2014, the Company's Board of Directors terminated the 2012 repurchase authorization.

On June 5, 2014, the Company's Board of Directors approved a new three year share repurchase authorization of up to $600 million of the Company's Class A common stock (the "2014 repurchase authorization"), pursuant to which the Company may repurchase shares from time to time on the open market or in privately negotiated transactions and which may be made under a Rule 10b5-1 plan. Repurchased shares may be retired immediately and resume the status of authorized but unissued shares or may be held by the Company as treasury stock. The 2014 repurchase authorization may be modified, suspended, or discontinued by the Company's Board of Directors at any time. During fiscal 2014, the Company repurchased 427,521 shares under the 2014 repurchase authorization, at an average price of $155.78 per share, for an aggregate purchase price of approximately $66.6 million. In total, during fiscal 2014, the Company repurchased 941,878 shares under the 2012 and 2014 repurchase authorizations, at an average price of $163.62 per share, for an aggregate purchase price of approximately $154.1 million.

On April 15, 2015, our Board of Directors approved an increase of the 2014 repurchase authorization to $750 million. During fiscal 2015, the Company repurchased 2,201,719 shares under the 2014 repurchase authorization, at an average price of $181.65 per share, for an aggregate purchase price of approximately $399.9 million. There was approximately $283.5 million available under the 2014 repurchase authorization as of December 29, 2015.

PANERA BREAD COMPANY
NOTES TO THE CONSOLIDATED FINANCIAL STATEMENTS (continued)

In addition, the Company has repurchased shares of its Class A common stock through a share repurchase authorization approved by its Board of Directors from participants of the Panera Bread 2006 Stock Incentive Plan and the Panera Bread 2015 Stock Incentive Plan, which are netted and surrendered as payment for applicable tax withholding on the vesting of their restricted stock. Shares surrendered by the participants are repurchased by the Company pursuant to the terms of those plans and the applicable award agreements and not pursuant to publicly announced share repurchase authorizations. See Note 16 for further information with respect to the Company's repurchase of the shares.

14. Commitments and Contingencies

Lease Commitments

The Company is obligated under operating leases for its bakery-cafes, fresh dough facilities and trucks, and support centers. Lease terms for its trucks are generally for five to seven years. The reasonably assured lease term for most bakery-cafe and support center leases is the initial non-cancelable lease term plus one renewal option period, which generally equates to an aggregate of 15 years. The reasonably assured lease term for most fresh dough facility leases is the initial non-cancelable lease term plus one to two renewal periods, which generally equates to an aggregate of 20 years. Lease terms generally require the Company to pay a proportionate share of real estate taxes, insurance, common area, and other operating costs. Certain bakery-cafe leases provide for contingent rental (i.e., percentage rent) payments based on sales in excess of specified amounts, scheduled rent increases during the lease terms, and/or rental payments commencing at a date other than the date of initial occupancy.

Aggregate minimum requirements under non-cancelable operating leases, excluding contingent payments, as of December 29, 2015, were as follows (in thousands):

Fiscal Years						
2016	2017	2018	2019	2020	Thereafter	Total
$ 149,882	148,430	145,041	138,941	130,083	659,087	$ 1,371,464

Rental expense under operating leases was approximately $146.6 million, $138.0 million, and $130.0 million in fiscal 2015, fiscal 2014, and fiscal 2013, respectively, which included contingent (i.e., percentage rent) expense of $2.0 million, $1.5 million, and $2.2 million, respectively.

The Company complies with lease obligations at the end of a lease as it relates to tangible long-lived assets, in accordance with the accounting guidance for asset retirement obligations. The liability as of December 29, 2015 and December 30, 2014 was $19.5 million and $19.8 million, respectively, and is included in other long-term liabilities in the Consolidated Balance Sheets.

In connection with the Company's relocation of its St. Louis, Missouri support center in fiscal 2010, it simultaneously entered into a capital lease for certain personal property and purchased municipal industrial revenue bonds of a similar amount from St. Louis County, Missouri. As of December 29, 2015 and December 30, 2014, the Company held industrial revenue bonds and had recorded a capital lease of $0.9 million and $1.1 million in the Consolidated Balance Sheets, respectively.

The following table summarizes sale-leaseback transactions for the periods indicated (dollars in thousands):

	For the fiscal year ended		
	December 29, 2015	December 30, 2014	December 31, 2013
Number of bakery-cafes sold and leased back	4	6	3
Proceeds from sale-leaseback transactions	$ 10,095	$ 12,900	$ 6,132

The leases have been classified as either capital or operating leases, depending on the substance of the transaction, and have initial terms of 15 years, with renewal options of up to 20 years. The Company realized gains on these sales totaling $0.4 million, $0.3 million, and $0.3 million during fiscal 2015, fiscal 2014, and fiscal 2013, respectively, which have been deferred and are being recognized on a straight-line basis over the reasonably assured lease term for the leases.

Lease Guarantees

As of December 29, 2015, the Company has guaranteed the operating leases of 75 franchisee locations, which the Company accounted for in accordance with the accounting requirements for guarantees. These guarantees are primarily a result of the Company's sales of Company-owned bakery-cafes to franchisees, pursuant to which the Company exercised its right to assign the

PANERA BREAD COMPANY
NOTES TO THE CONSOLIDATED FINANCIAL STATEMENTS (continued)

lease for the bakery-cafe but remain liable to the landlord in the event of a default by the assignee. These guarantees expire on various dates from July 15, 2020 to February 28, 2049, with a maximum potential amount of future rental payments of approximately $244.4 million as of December 29, 2015. The obligation from these leases will decrease over time as these operating leases expire. The Company has not recorded a liability for these guarantees because the fair value of these lease guarantees was determined by the Company to be insignificant individually, and in the aggregate, based on an analysis of the facts and circumstances of each such lease and each such assignee's performance, and the Company did not believe it was probable that it would be required to perform under any guarantees at the time the guarantees were issued. The Company has not had to make any payments related to any of these guaranteed leases. Applicable assignees continue to have primary liability for these operating leases. As of December 29, 2015, future commitments under these leases were as follows (in thousands):

Fiscal Years						
2,016	**2017**	**2018**	**2019**	**2020**	**Thereafter**	**Total**
$ 11,832	12,092	12,409	12,549	12,623	182,907	$ 244,412

Employee Commitments

The Company has executed confidential and proprietary information and non-competition agreements ("non-compete agreements") with certain employees. These non-compete agreements contain a provision whereby employees would be due a certain number of weeks of their salary if their employment was terminated by the Company as specified in the non-compete agreement. The Company has not recorded a liability for these amounts potentially due employees. Rather, the Company will record a liability for these amounts when an amount becomes due to an employee in accordance with the appropriate authoritative literature. As of December 29, 2015, the total amount potentially owed employees under these non-compete agreements was $24.8 million.

Legal Proceedings

On July 2, 2014, a purported class action lawsuit was filed against one of the Company's subsidiaries by Jason Lofstedt, a former employee of one of the Company's subsidiaries. The lawsuit was filed in the California Superior Court, County of Riverside. The complaint alleges, among other things, violations of the California Labor Code, failure to pay overtime, failure to provide meal and rest periods, and violations of California's Unfair Competition Law. The complaint seeks, among other relief, collective and class certification of the lawsuit, unspecified damages, costs and expenses, including attorneys' fees, and such other relief as the Court might find just and proper. In addition, more recently, several other purported class action lawsuits based on similar claims and seeking similar damages were filed against the subsidiary: on October 30, 2015 in the California Superior Court, County of San Bernardino by Jazmin Dabney, a former subsidiary employee; on November 3, 2015, in the United States District Court, Eastern District of California by Clara Manchester, a former subsidiary employee; and on November 30, 2015 in the California Superior Court, County of Yolo by Tanner Maginnis, a current subsidiary assistant manager. The Company believes its subsidiary has meritorious defenses to each of the claims in these lawsuits and is prepared to vigorously defend the allegations therein. There can be no assurance, however, that the Company's subsidiary will be successful, and an adverse resolution of any one of these lawsuits could have a material adverse effect on the Company's consolidated financial position and results of operations in the period in which one or all of these lawsuits are resolved. The Company is not presently able to reasonably estimate potential losses, if any, related to the lawsuits.

In addition to the legal matters described above, the Company is subject to various legal proceedings, claims, and litigation that arise in the ordinary course of its business. Defending lawsuits requires significant management attention and financial resources and the outcome of any litigation, including the matter described above, is inherently uncertain. The Company does not believe the ultimate resolution of these actions will have a material adverse effect on its consolidated financial statements. However, a significant increase in the number of these claims, or one or more successful claims under which the Company incurs greater liabilities than is currently anticipated, could materially and adversely affect its consolidated financial statements.

Other

The Company is subject to on-going federal and state income tax audits and sales and use tax audits. The Company does not believe the ultimate resolution of these actions will have a material adverse effect on its consolidated financial statements. However, a significant increase in the number of these audits, or one or more audits under which the Company incurs greater liabilities than is currently anticipated, could materially and adversely affect its consolidated financial statements. The Company believes reserves for these matters are adequately provided for in its consolidated financial statements.

PANERA BREAD COMPANY
NOTES TO THE CONSOLIDATED FINANCIAL STATEMENTS (continued)

15. Income Taxes

The components of income (loss) before income taxes, by tax jurisdiction, were as follows for the periods indicated (in thousands):

	For the fiscal year ended		
	December 29, 2015	December 30, 2014	December 31, 2013
United States	$ 242,860	$ 285,564	$ 317,479
Canada	(6,288)	(8,270)	(4,759)
Income before income taxes	$ 236,572	$ 277,294	$ 312,720

The provision for income taxes consisted of the following for the periods indicated (in thousands):

	For the fiscal year ended		
	December 29, 2015	December 30, 2014	December 31, 2013
Current taxes:			
U.S. federal	$ 83,005	$ 73,234	$ 87,548
U.S. state and local	16,242	14,306	18,638
Total current taxes	99,247	87,540	106,186
Deferred taxes:			
U.S. federal	(9,737)	9,609	8,547
U.S. state and local	(2,263)	950	1,804
Foreign	—	(98)	14
Total deferred taxes	$ (12,000)	$ 10,461	$ 10,365
Total provision for income taxes	$ 87,247	$ 98,001	$ 116,551

A reconciliation of the statutory U.S. federal income tax rate to the Company's effective tax rate is as follows for the periods indicated:

	For the fiscal year ended		
	December 29, 2015	December 30, 2014	December 31, 2013
Statutory U.S. federal rate	35.0%	35.0%	35.0%
U.S. state and local income taxes, net of federal tax benefit	4.1	4.1	4.5
U.S. federal tax credits	(1.8)	(1.4)	(0.8)
Other, including discrete tax items	(0.4)	(2.4)	(1.4)
Effective tax rate	36.9%	35.3%	37.3%

The Company's higher effective tax rate for fiscal 2015 as compared to fiscal 2014 was primarily due to the discrete income tax benefits reported during fiscal 2014 related to additional federal and state tax credits and an increased deduction for domestic production activities.

PANERA BREAD COMPANY
NOTES TO THE CONSOLIDATED FINANCIAL STATEMENTS (continued)

The tax effects of the significant temporary differences which comprise the deferred tax assets and liabilities were as follows for the periods indicated (in thousands):

	December 29, 2015	December 30, 2014
Deferred tax assets:		
Accrued expenses	$ 75,360	$ 72,891
Foreign net operating loss carryforward	4,938	4,178
Stock-based compensation	4,705	3,125
Other	2,160	1,701
Less: valuation allowance	(5,299)	(4,625)
Total deferred tax assets	$ 81,864	$ 77,270
Deferred tax liabilities:		
Property and equipment	$ (92,580)	$ (101,533)
Goodwill and other intangibles	(25,252)	(23,705)
Total deferred tax liabilities	$ (117,832)	$ (125,238)
Net deferred tax liability	$ (35,968)	$ (47,968)
Current deferred income tax assets	$ 34,479	$ 28,621
Long-term deferred income tax liabilities	$ (70,447)	$ (76,589)

In assessing the realization of deferred tax assets, the Company considers the generation of future taxable income and utilizes a more likely than not standard to determine if deferred tax assets will be realized. Based on this assessment, the Company has recorded a valuation allowance of $5.3 million and $4.6 million as of December 29, 2015 and December 30, 2014, respectively, as a full valuation allowance against all Canadian deferred tax assets, including the net operating loss carryforwards of the Company's Canadian operations. The Company's Canadian net operating loss carryforwards begin expiring in 2027.

As of both December 29, 2015 and December 30, 2014, the amount of unrecognized tax benefits that, if recognized in full, would be recorded as a reduction of income tax expense was $6.1 million, inclusive of applicable interest and penalties and net of federal tax benefits, respectively. Estimated interest and penalties related to the underpayment of income taxes are classified as a component of income tax expense in the Consolidated Statements of Income. These amounts were income of $0.2 million, expense of $0.3 million, and income of $0.1 million during fiscal 2015, fiscal 2014, and fiscal 2013, respectively. Accrued interest and penalties were $0.9 million and $1.4 million as of December 29, 2015 and December 30, 2014, respectively.

The following is a rollforward of the Company's liability for unrecognized tax benefits for the periods indicated (in thousands):

	December 29, 2015	December 30, 2014	December 31, 2013
Beginning balance	$ 6,455	$ 2,999	$ 3,051
Tax positions related to the current year:			
Additions	1,339	1,536	653
Tax positions related to prior years:			
Additions	—	2,671	256
Reductions	(483)	—	(49)
Settlements	(200)	(131)	(425)
Expiration of statutes of limitations	(443)	(620)	(487)
Ending balance	$ 6,668	$ 6,455	$ 2,999

The U.S. Internal Revenue Service has completed exams of the Company's U.S. federal tax returns for fiscal years 2012 and prior. While certain state returns in fiscal years 2002 through 2011 may be subject to future assessment by taxing authorities, the Company is no longer subject to examination in Canada and most states in fiscal years prior to 2012.

PANERA BREAD COMPANY
NOTES TO THE CONSOLIDATED FINANCIAL STATEMENTS (continued)

It is reasonably possible that the Company's liability for unrecognized tax benefits with respect to the Company's uncertain tax positions will increase or decrease during the next twelve months; however, an estimate of the amount or range of the change cannot be made at this time.

16. Stockholders' Equity

Common Stock

The holders of Class A common stock are entitled to one vote for each share owned. The holders of Class B common stock are entitled to three votes for each share owned. Each share of Class B common stock has the same dividend and liquidation rights as each share of Class A common stock. Each share of Class B common stock is convertible, at the stockholder's option, into Class A common stock on a one-for-one basis. At December 29, 2015, the Company had reserved 3,041,295 shares of its Class A common stock for issuance upon exercise of awards granted under the Company's 1992 Equity Incentive Plan, 2001 Employee, Director, and Consultant Stock Option Plan, the 2006 Stock Incentive Plan, and the 2015 Stock Incentive Plan, and upon conversion of Class B common stock.

Registration Rights

At December 29, 2015, 94.9 percent of the outstanding Class B common stock was owned by the Company's Chairman of the Board and Chief Executive Officer (the "Chairman"). Pursuant to stock subscription agreements, certain holders of Class B common stock, including the Chairman, can require the Company under certain circumstances to register their shares under the Securities Act of 1933, or have included in certain registrations all or part of such shares at the Company's expense.

Preferred Stock

The Company is authorized to issue 2,000,000 shares of Class B preferred stock with a par value of $0.0001. The voting, redemption, dividend, liquidation rights, and other terms and conditions are determined by the Board of Directors upon approval of issuance. There were no shares issued or outstanding in fiscal 2015 and 2014.

Treasury Stock

Pursuant to the terms of the Panera Bread 2006 Stock Incentive Plan and the Panera Bread 2015 Stock Incentive Plan, and the applicable award agreements, the Company repurchased 28,018 shares of Class A common stock at a weighted-average cost of $196.78 per share during fiscal 2015, 35,461 shares of Class A common stock at a weighted-average cost of $151.17 per share during fiscal 2014, and 41,601 shares of Class A common stock at a weighted-average cost of $172.79 per share during fiscal 2013, as were surrendered by participants as payment of applicable tax withholdings on the vesting of restricted stock and SSARs. Shares so surrendered by the participants are repurchased by the Company at fair market value pursuant to the terms of those plans and the applicable award agreements and not pursuant to publicly announced share repurchase authorizations. The shares surrendered to the Company by participants and repurchased by the Company are currently held by the Company as treasury stock.

Share Repurchase Authorization

During fiscal 2015, fiscal 2014, and fiscal 2013, the Company purchased shares of Class A common stock under authorized share repurchase authorizations. Repurchased shares may be retired immediately and resume the status of authorized but unissued shares or may be held by the Company as treasury stock. See Note 13 for further information with respect to the Company's share repurchase authorizations.

Accumulated Other Comprehensive Income (Loss)

Accumulated other comprehensive income reported on the Company's Consolidated Balance Sheets consists of foreign currency translation adjustments and the unrealized gains and losses, net of applicable taxes, on derivative instruments designated and qualifying as cash flow hedges.

PANERA BREAD COMPANY
NOTES TO THE CONSOLIDATED FINANCIAL STATEMENTS (continued)

The following tables summarize changes in accumulated other comprehensive income (loss), net of tax, for fiscal 2015 and fiscal 2014 (in thousands):

	Foreign Currency Translation Adjustment	Cash Flow Hedging Instruments	Total
December 29, 2015			
Net gains (losses), beginning of period	$ (1,360)	$ —	$ (1,360)
Net gains (losses) recognized before reclassification	(2,126)	(1,543)	(3,669)
Net gains (losses) reclassified to earnings	—	—	—
Other comprehensive income (loss), net of tax	(2,126)	(1,543)	(3,669)
Net gains (losses), end of period	$ (3,486)	$ (1,543)	$ (5,029)
December 30, 2014			
Net gains (losses), beginning of period	$ (333)	$ —	$ (333)
Net gains (losses) recognized before reclassification	(1,027)	—	(1,027)
Net gains (losses) reclassified to earnings	—	—	—
Other comprehensive income (loss), net of tax	(1,027)	—	(1,027)
Net gains (losses), end of period	$ (1,360)	$ —	$ (1,360)

17. Stock-Based Compensation

As of December 29, 2015, the Company had one active stock-based compensation plan, the 2015 Stock Incentive Plan (the "2015 Plan"), and had incentive stock options, non-statutory stock options and stock settled appreciation rights (collectively "option awards") and restricted stock outstanding (but can make no future grants) under three other stock-based compensation plans, the 1992 Equity Incentive Plan (the "1992 Plan"), the 2006 Stock Incentive plan (the "2006 Plan"), and the 2001 Employee, Director, and Consultant Stock Option Plan (the "2001 Plan").

2015 Stock Incentive Plan

In fiscal 2015, the Company's Board of Directors adopted the 2015 Plan, which was approved by the Company's stockholders in May 2015. The 2015 Plan provides for the grant of up to 1,750,000 shares of the Company's Class A common stock (subject to adjustment in the event of stock splits or other similar events) as option awards, restricted stock, restricted stock units, and other stock-based awards. As a result of stockholder approval of the 2015 Plan, effective as of May 21, 2015, the Company will grant no further stock options, restricted stock or other awards under the 2006 Plan. The Company's Board of Directors administers the 2015 Plan and has sole discretion to grant awards under the 2015 Plan. The Company's Board of Directors has delegated the authority to grant awards under the 2015 Plan, other than to the Company's Chairman of the Board and Chief Executive Officer, to the Company's Compensation and Management Development Committee (the "Compensation Committee").

Long-Term Incentive Program

In fiscal 2005, the Company adopted the 2005 Long Term Incentive Plan (the "2005 LTIP") as a sub-plan under the 2001 Employee, Director, and Consultant Stock Option Plan (the "2001 Plan") and the 1992 Equity Incentive Plan (the "1992 Plan"). In May 2006, the Company amended the 2005 LTIP to provide that the 2005 LTIP is a sub-plan under the 2006 Plan. In August 2015, the Company further amended the 2005 LTIP to provide that the 2005 LTIP is a sub-plan under the 2015 Plan. Under the amended 2005 LTIP, certain directors, officers, employees, and consultants, subject to approval by the Compensation Committee, may be selected as participants eligible to receive a percentage of their annual salary in future years, subject to the terms of the 2006 Plan. This percentage is based on the participant's level in the Company. In addition, the payment of this incentive can be made in several forms based on the participant's level including performance awards (payable in cash or common stock or some combination of cash and common stock as determined by the Compensation Committee), restricted stock, choice awards of restricted stock and/or stock settled appreciation rights ("SSARs") (or, if determined by the Compensation Committee, stock options), or deferred annual bonus match awards. The Compensation Committee may consider the Company's performance relative to the performance of its peers in determining the payout of performance awards, as further discussed below.

For fiscal 2015, fiscal 2014 and fiscal 2013, compensation expense related to performance awards, restricted stock, options, SSARs, and deferred annual bonus match was $16.4 million, $11.1 million, and $16.0 million, net of capitalized compensation expense of $1.5 million, $1.1 million, and $0.9 million, respectively.

PANERA BREAD COMPANY
NOTES TO THE CONSOLIDATED FINANCIAL STATEMENTS (continued)

Performance awards under the 2005 LTIP are earned by participants based on achievement of performance goals established by the Compensation Committee. The performance period relating to the performance awards is a three-fiscal-year period. The performance goals, including each performance metric, weighting of each metric, and award levels for each metric, for such awards are communicated to each participant and are based on various predetermined earnings metrics. The performance awards are earned based on achievement of predetermined earnings performance metrics at the end of the three-fiscal-year performance period, assuming continued employment, and after the Compensation Committee's consideration of the Company's performance relative to the performance of its peers. The performance awards range from 0 percent to 300 percent of the participant's salary based on their level in the Company and the level of achievement of each performance metric. However, the actual award payment will be adjusted, based on the Company's performance over a three-consecutive fiscal year measurement period, and any other factors as determined by the Compensation Committee. The actual award payment for the performance award component could double the individual's targeted award payment, if the Company achieves maximum performance in all of its performance metrics, subject to any adjustments as determined by the Compensation Committee. The performance awards have generally been paid 100 percent in cash but may be paid in some other combination of cash and common stock as determined by the Compensation Committee. In fiscal 2015, in lieu of a performance award, the Compensation Committee granted a restricted stock award and a choice award, each which will vest in full on the third anniversary of the grant date in an aggregate amount having a value at the time of grant equal to the participant's targeted performance award payment. For fiscal 2015, fiscal 2014, and fiscal 2013, compensation expense related to the performance awards was $2.0 million, $1.2 million, and $4.3 million, net of capitalized compensation expense of less than $0.1 million, $0.1 million, and $0.2 million, respectively.

Restricted stock of the Company under the 2005 LTIP is granted at no cost to participants. While participants are generally entitled to voting rights with respect to their respective shares of restricted stock, participants are generally not entitled to receive accrued cash dividends, if any, on restricted stock unless and until such shares have vested. The Company does not currently pay a dividend, and has no current plans to do so. For awards of restricted stock granted to date under the 2005 LTIP, restrictions generally limit the sale or transfer of these shares during a five year period whereby the restrictions lapse on 25 percent of these shares after two years and thereafter 25 percent each year for the next three years, subject to continued employment with the Company. In the event a participant is no longer employed by the Company, any unvested shares of restricted stock held by that participant will be forfeited. Upon issuance of restricted stock under the 2005 LTIP, unearned compensation is recorded at fair value on the date of grant to stockholders' equity and subsequently amortized to expense over the five year restriction period. The fair value of restricted stock is based on the market value of the Company's stock on the grant date. As of December 29, 2015, there was $46.5 million of total unrecognized compensation cost related to restricted stock included in additional paid-in capital in the Consolidated Balance Sheets. This unrecognized compensation cost is expected to be recognized over a weighted-average period of approximately 3.4 years. For fiscal 2015, fiscal 2014, and fiscal 2013, restricted stock expense was $12.6 million, $8.3 million, and $9.2 million, net of capitalized compensation expense of $1.3 million, $0.9 million, and $0.6 million, respectively. For fiscal 2015, fiscal 2014, and fiscal 2013, the income tax benefit related to restricted stock expense was $5.0 million, $3.3 million, and $3.4 million, respectively.

A summary of the status of the Company's restricted stock activity is set forth below:

	Restricted Stock (in thousands)	Weighted Average Grant-Date Fair Value
Non-vested at December 30, 2014	325	$ 142.41
Granted	154	187.76
Vested	(82)	121.46
Forfeited	(49)	151.05
Non-vested at December 29, 2015	348	$ 166.15

Under the deferred annual bonus match award portion of the 2005 LTIP, eligible participants received an additional 50 percent of their annual bonus, which was to be paid three years after the date of the original bonus payment provided the participant was still employed by the Company. For fiscal 2015, fiscal 2014, and fiscal 2013, compensation expense related to deferred annual bonus match awards was $1.1 million, $1.3 million, and $2.1 million, net of capitalized compensation expense of $0.1 million, $0.1 million, and $0.1 million, respectively, and was included in general and administrative expenses in the Consolidated Statements of Income. The Company determined that it would no longer grant the deferred annual bonus match award portion under the 2005 LTIP beginning with the 2014 measurement year. Compensation expense related to deferred annual bonus match awards for years prior to fiscal 2014 will continue to be recognized through fiscal 2016.

PANERA BREAD COMPANY
NOTES TO THE CONSOLIDATED FINANCIAL STATEMENTS (continued)

Stock options under the 2005 LTIP are granted with an exercise price equal to the quoted market value of the Company's common stock on the date of grant. In addition, stock options generally vest 25 percent after two years from the date of grant and thereafter 25 percent each year for the next three years and have a six-year term. The Company uses historical data to estimate pre-vesting forfeiture rates. As of December 29, 2015, there was no unrecognized compensation cost related to non-vested options. For fiscal 2015, fiscal 2014, and fiscal 2013, stock-based compensation expense related to stock options charged to general and administrative expenses was $0.2 million, $0.1 million, and $0.2 million, respectively.

The following table summarizes the Company's stock option activity under its stock-based compensation plans during fiscal 2015:

	Shares (in thousands)	Weighted Average Exercise Price	Weighted Average Contractual Term Remaining (Years)	Aggregate Intrinsic Value (1) (in thousands)
Outstanding at December 30, 2014	16	$ 120.97		
Granted	3	174.80		
Exercised	(4)	67.94		470
Cancelled	—	—		
Outstanding at December 29, 2015	15	$ 146.79	2.9	726
Exercisable at December 29, 2015	15	$ 146.79	2.9 $	726

(1) Intrinsic value for activities other than exercises is defined as the difference between the grant price and the market value on the last day of fiscal 2015 of $197.08 for those stock options where the market value is greater than the exercise price. For exercises, intrinsic value is defined as the difference between the grant price and the market value on the date of exercise.

Cash received from the exercise of stock options in fiscal 2015, fiscal 2014, and fiscal 2013 was $0.3 million, $1.1 million, and $0.6 million, respectively. Windfall tax benefits realized from exercised stock options in fiscal 2015, fiscal 2014, and fiscal 2013 were $2.1 million, $3.1 million, and $8.1 million, respectively, and were included as cash flows from financing activities in the Consolidated Statements of Cash Flows.

A SSAR is an award that allows the recipient to receive common stock equal to the appreciation in the fair market value of the Company's Class A common stock between the date the award was granted and the conversion date for the number of shares vested. SSARs under the 2005 LTIP are granted with an exercise price equal to the quoted market value of the Company's common stock on the date of grant. In addition, SSARs generally vest 25 percent after two years from the date of grant and thereafter 25 percent each year for the next three years and have a six-year term. As of December 29, 2015, the total unrecognized compensation cost related to non-vested SSARs was $1.9 million, and is expected to be recognized over a weighted-average period of approximately 2.8 years. The Company uses historical data to estimate pre-vesting forfeiture rates. For fiscal 2015, fiscal 2014, and fiscal 2013, stock-based compensation expense related to SSARs was $0.5 million, $0.2 million, and $0.2 million, respectively, and was charged to general and administrative expenses in the Consolidated Statements of Income.

The following table summarizes the Company's SSAR activity under its stock-based compensation plan during fiscal 2015:

	Shares (in thousands)	Weighted Average Conversion Price (1)	Weighted Average Contractual Term Remaining (Years)	Aggregate Intrinsic Value (2) (in thousands)
Outstanding at December 30, 2014	29	$ 144.63	4.0 $	885
Granted	33	174.25		
Converted	(4)	89.71		
Cancelled	(1)	152.14		
Outstanding at December 29, 2015	57	$ 165.54	4.5 $	1,814
Convertible at December 29, 2015	7	$ 141.04	2.7 $	399

(1) Conversion price is defined as the price from which SSARs are measured and is equal to the market value on the date of issuance.

PANERA BREAD COMPANY
NOTES TO THE CONSOLIDATED FINANCIAL STATEMENTS (continued)

(2) Intrinsic value for activities other than conversions is defined as the difference between the grant price and the market value on the last day of fiscal 2015 of $197.08 for those SSARs where the market value is greater than the conversion price. For conversions, intrinsic value is defined as the difference between the grant price and the market value on the date of conversion.

All SSARs outstanding at December 29, 2015 have a conversion price ranging from $99.30 to $202.52 and are expected to be recognized over a weighted-average period of approximately 4.5 years.

The fair value for both stock options and SSARs (collectively "option awards") is estimated on the grant date using the Black-Scholes option pricing model. The assumptions used to calculate the fair value of option awards are evaluated and revised, as necessary, to reflect market conditions and historical experience.

The weighted-average fair value of option awards granted and assumptions used for the Black-Scholes option pricing model were as follows for the periods indicated:

	For the fiscal year ended		
	December 29, 2015	December 30, 2014	December 31, 2013
Fair value per option awards	$ 47.56	$ 46.01	$ 55.63
Assumptions:			
Expected term (years)	5	5	5
Expected volatility	27.6%	28.8%	36.5%
Risk-free interest rate	1.6%	1.6%	1.3%
Dividend yield	0.0%	0.0%	0.0%

- *Expected term* — The expected term of the option awards represents the period of time between the grant date of the option awards and the date the option awards are either exercised or canceled, including an estimate for those option awards still outstanding, and is derived from historical terms and other factors.

- *Expected volatility* — The expected volatility is based on an average of the historical volatility of the Company's stock price, for a period approximating the expected term, and the implied volatility of externally traded options of the Company's stock that were entered into during the period.

- *Risk-free interest rate* — The risk-free interest rate is based on the U.S. Treasury yield curve in effect at the time of grant and with a maturity that approximates the option awards expected term.

- *Dividend yield* — The dividend yield is based on the Company's anticipated dividend payout over the expected term of the option awards.

The amounts presented for the weighted-average fair value of option awards granted are before the estimated effect of forfeitures, which reduce the amount of stock-based compensation expense recorded in the Consolidated Statements of Income.

1992 Equity Incentive Plan

The Company adopted the 1992 Plan in May 1992. A total of 8,600,000 shares of Class A common stock were authorized for issuance under the 1992 Plan as awards, which could have been in the form of stock options (both qualified and non-qualified), stock appreciation rights, performance shares, restricted stock, or stock units, to employees and consultants. As a result of stockholder approval of the 2006 Plan, effective as of May 25, 2006, the Company will grant no further stock options, restricted stock, or other awards under the 1992 Plan.

2001 Employee, Director, and Consultant Stock Option Plan

The Company adopted the 2001 Plan in June 2001. A total of 3,000,000 shares of Class A common stock were authorized for issuance under the 2001 Plan as awards, which could have been in the form of stock options to employees, directors, and consultants. As a result of stockholder approval of the 2006 Plan, effective as of May 25, 2006, the Company will grant no further stock options under the 2001 Plan.

1992 Employee Stock Purchase Plan

In May 1992, the Company adopted the 1992 Employee Stock Purchase Plan (the "ESPP"). The ESPP was subsequently amended in years prior to fiscal 2014 to increase the number of shares of the Company's Class A common stock authorized for issuance to

PANERA BREAD COMPANY
NOTES TO THE CONSOLIDATED FINANCIAL STATEMENTS (continued)

950,000. The ESPP gives eligible employees the option to purchase Class A common stock (total purchases in a year may not exceed 10 percent of an employee's current year compensation) at 85 percent of the fair market value of the Class A common stock at the end of each calendar quarter. There were approximately 24,000, 23,000, and 20,000 shares purchased with a weighted-average fair value of purchase rights of $26.21, $24.71, and $25.01 during fiscal 2015, fiscal 2014, and fiscal 2013, respectively. For fiscal 2015, fiscal 2014, and fiscal 2013, the Company recognized expense of approximately $0.6 million, $0.6 million, and $0.5 million in each of the respective years related to stock purchase plan discounts. Effective June 5, 2014, the Plan was amended to further increase the number of the Company's Class A common stock shares authorized for issuance to 1,050,000. Cumulatively, there were approximately 925,000 shares issued under this plan as of December 29, 2015, 901,000 shares issued under this plan as of December 30, 2014, and 878,000 shares issued under this plan as of December 31, 2013.

18. Defined Contribution Benefit Plan

The Panera Bread Company 401(k) Savings Plan (the "Plan") was formed under Section 401(k) of the Internal Revenue Code ("the Code"). The Plan covers substantially all employees who meet certain service requirements. Participating employees may elect to defer a percentage of his or her salary on a pre-tax basis, subject to the limitations imposed by the Plan and the Code. The Plan provides for a matching contribution by the Company equal to 50 percent of the first three percent of the participant's eligible pay. All employee contributions vest immediately. Company matching contributions vest beginning in the second year of employment at 25 percent per year, and are fully vested after five years. The Company contributed $2.3 million, $2.2 million, and $2.0 million to the Plan in fiscal 2015, fiscal 2014, and fiscal 2013, respectively.

19. Business Segment Information

The Company operates three business segments. The Company Bakery-Cafe Operations segment is comprised of the operating activities of the bakery-cafes owned directly and indirectly by the Company. The Company-owned bakery-cafes conduct business under the Panera Bread®, Saint Louis Bread Co.® or Paradise Bakery & Café® names. These bakery-cafes offer some or all of the following: fresh baked goods, made-to-order sandwiches on freshly baked breads, soups, salads, pasta dishes, custom roasted coffees, and other complementary products through on-premise sales, as well as catering.

The Franchise Operations segment is comprised of the operating activities of the franchise business unit, which licenses qualified operators to conduct business under the Panera Bread or Paradise Bakery & Café names and also monitors the operations of these bakery-cafes. Under the terms of most of the agreements, the licensed operators pay royalties and fees to the Company in return for the use of the Panera Bread or Paradise Bakery & Café names.

The Fresh Dough and Other Product Operations segment supplies fresh dough, produce, tuna, cream cheese, and indirectly supplies proprietary sweet goods items through a contract manufacturing arrangement, to Company-owned and franchise-operated bakery-cafes. The fresh dough is sold to a number of both Company-owned and franchise-operated bakery-cafes at a delivered cost generally not to exceed 27 percent of the retail value of the end product. The sales and related costs to the franchise-operated bakery-cafes are separately stated line items in the Consolidated Statements of Income. The sales, costs, and operating profit related to the sales to Company-owned bakery-cafes are eliminated in consolidation in the Consolidated Statements of Income.

PANERA BREAD COMPANY
NOTES TO THE CONSOLIDATED FINANCIAL STATEMENTS (continued)

The accounting policies applicable to each segment are consistent with those described in Note 2, "Summary of Significant Accounting Policies." Segment information related to the Company's three business segments is as follows (in thousands):

		For the fiscal year ended				
		December 29, 2015		December 30, 2014		December 31, 2013
Revenues:						
Company bakery-cafe operations	$	2,358,794	$	2,230,370	$	2,108,908
Franchise operations		138,563		123,686		112,641
Fresh dough and other product operations		382,110		370,004		347,922
Intercompany sales eliminations		(197,887)		(194,865)		(184,469)
Total revenues	$	2,681,580	$	2,529,195	$	2,385,002
Segment profit:						
Company bakery-cafe operations (1)	$	366,905	$	400,261	$	413,474
Franchise operations		133,449		117,770		106,395
Fresh dough and other product operations		23,517		22,872		21,293
Total segment profit	$	523,871	$	540,903	$	541,162
Depreciation and amortization	$	135,398	$	124,109	$	106,523
Unallocated general and administrative expenses		137,790		132,144		117,089
Pre-opening expenses		9,089		8,707		7,794
Interest expense		3,830		1,824		1,053
Other (income) expense, net		1,192		(3,175)		(4,017)
Income before income taxes	$	236,572	$	277,294	$	312,720
Depreciation and amortization:						
Company bakery-cafe operations	$	105,535	$	103,239	$	90,872
Fresh dough and other product operations		9,367		8,613		8,239
Corporate administration		20,496		12,257		7,412
Total depreciation and amortization	$	135,398	$	124,109	$	106,523
Capital expenditures:						
Company bakery-cafe operations	$	174,633	$	167,856	$	153,584
Fresh dough and other product operations		12,175		12,178		11,461
Corporate administration		37,124		44,183		26,965
Total capital expenditures	$	223,932	$	224,217	$	192,010

(1) Includes refranchising losses of $17.1 million for the fiscal year ended December 29, 2015.

		December 29, 2015		December 30, 2014
Segment assets:				
Company bakery-cafe operations	$	953,717	$	953,896
Franchise operations		13,049		13,145
Fresh dough and other product operations		75,634		65,219
Total segment assets	$	1,042,400	$	1,032,260
Unallocated cash and cash equivalents	$	241,886	$	196,493
Unallocated trade and other accounts receivable		2,968		3,104
Unallocated property and equipment		107,333		84,224
Unallocated deposits and other		6,660		3,575
Other unallocated assets		74,071		71,030
Total assets	$	1,475,318	$	1,390,686

PANERA BREAD COMPANY
NOTES TO THE CONSOLIDATED FINANCIAL STATEMENTS (continued)

"Unallocated cash and cash equivalents" relates primarily to corporate cash and cash equivalents, "unallocated trade and other accounts receivable" relates primarily to rebates and interest receivable, "unallocated property and equipment" relates primarily to corporate fixed assets, "unallocated deposits and other" relates primarily to insurance deposits, and "other unallocated assets" relates primarily to current and deferred income taxes.

20. Earnings Per Share

The following table sets forth the computation of basic and diluted earnings per share (in thousands, except for per share data):

	For the fiscal year ended		
	December 29, 2015	December 30, 2014	December 31, 2013
Amounts used for basic and diluted per share calculations:			
Net income attributable to Panera Bread Company	$ 149,342	$ 179,293	$ 196,169
Weighted average number of shares outstanding — basic	25,685	26,881	28,629
Effect of dilutive stock-based employee compensation awards	103	118	165
Weighted average number of shares outstanding — diluted	25,788	26,999	28,794
Earnings per common share:			
Basic	$ 5.81	$ 6.67	$ 6.85
Diluted	$ 5.79	$ 6.64	$ 6.81

For each of fiscal 2015, fiscal 2014, and fiscal 2013, weighted-average outstanding stock options, restricted stock, and stock-settled appreciation rights of less than 0.1 million shares were excluded in calculating diluted earnings per share as the exercise price exceeded fair market value and the inclusion of such shares would have been antidilutive.

21. Supplemental Cash Flow Information

The following table sets forth supplemental cash flow information for the periods indicated (in thousands):

	For the fiscal year ended		
	December 29, 2015	December 30, 2014	December 31, 2013
Cash paid during the year for:			
Interest	$ 3,073	$ 773	$ 253
Income taxes	92,964	91,187	104,072
Non-cash investing and financing activities:			
Change in accrued property and equipment purchases	$ (2,894)	$ 15,479	$ 16,194
Financed property and equipment purchases	12,680	—	—
Accrued purchase price of Florida acquisition	—	—	270
Investment in municipal industrial revenue bonds	(186)	(186)	(186)
Asset retirement obligations	635	9,341	664

PANERA BREAD COMPANY
NOTES TO THE CONSOLIDATED FINANCIAL STATEMENTS (continued)

22. Selected Quarterly Financial Data (unaudited)

The following table presents selected unaudited quarterly financial data for the periods indicated (in thousands, except per share data):

	Fiscal 2015 - quarters ended (1)			
	March 31	June 30	September 29	December 29
Revenues	$ 648,504	$ 676,657	$ 664,654	$ 691,765
Operating profit	51,197	68,412	52,102	69,883
Net income attributable to Panera Bread Company	31,860	41,929	32,393	43,160
Earnings per common share:				
Basic	$ 1.20	$ 1.60	$ 1.28	$ 1.75
Diluted	$ 1.20	$ 1.60	$ 1.27	$ 1.74

	Fiscal 2014 - quarters ended (1)			
	April 1	July 1	September 30	December 30
Revenues	$ 605,753	$ 631,055	$ 619,890	$ 672,497
Operating profit	67,005	73,942	57,959	77,037
Net income attributable to Panera Bread Company	42,395	49,192	39,214	48,492
Earnings per common share:				
Basic	$ 1.55	$ 1.83	$ 1.47	$ 1.82
Diluted	$ 1.55	$ 1.82	$ 1.46	$ 1.82

(1) Fiscal quarters may not sum to the fiscal year reported amounts due to rounding.

ITEM 9. CHANGES IN AND DISAGREEMENTS WITH ACCOUNTANTS ON ACCOUNTING AND FINANCIAL DISCLOSURE

None.

ITEM 9A. CONTROLS AND PROCEDURES

Disclosure Controls and Procedures and Changes in Internal Control Over Financial Reporting

The Company's management, with the participation of the Company's Chief Executive Officer and Chief Financial Officer, evaluated the effectiveness of the Company's disclosure controls and procedures as of December 29, 2015. The term "disclosure controls and procedures," as defined in Rules 13a-15(e) and 15d-15(e) under the Exchange Act, means controls and other procedures of a company that are designed to ensure that information required to be disclosed by a company in the reports that it files or submits under the Exchange Act is recorded, processed, summarized and reported, within the time periods specified in the Securities and Exchange Commission's rules and forms. Disclosure controls and procedures include, without limitation, controls and procedures designed to ensure that information required to be disclosed by a company in the reports that it files or submits under the Exchange Act is accumulated and communicated to the company's management, including its principal executive and principal financial officers, as appropriate to allow timely decisions regarding required disclosure. Management recognizes that any controls and procedures, no matter how well designed and operated, can provide only reasonable assurance of achieving their objectives and management necessarily applies its judgment in evaluating the cost-benefit relationship of possible controls and procedures. Based on the evaluation of the Company's disclosure controls and procedures as of December 29, 2015, the Company's Chief Executive Officer and Chief Financial Officer concluded that, as of such date, the Company's disclosure controls and procedures were effective at the reasonable assurance level.

No change in the Company's internal control over financial reporting occurred during the fiscal quarter ended December 29, 2015 that has materially affected, or is reasonably likely to materially affect, the Company's internal control over financial reporting.

Management's Report on Internal Control Over Financial Reporting

The Company's management is responsible for establishing and maintaining adequate internal control over financial reporting. Internal control over financial reporting is defined in Rule 13a-15(f) under the Exchange Act as a process designed by, or under the supervision of, the company's principal executive and principal financial officers and effected by the company's board of directors, management and other associates, to provide reasonable assurance regarding the reliability of financial reporting and the preparation of financial statements for external purposes in accordance with generally accepted accounting principles and those policies and procedures that:

(1) Pertain to the maintenance of records that in reasonable detail accurately and fairly reflect the transactions and dispositions of the assets of the company;

(2) Provide reasonable assurance that transactions are recorded as necessary to permit preparation of financial statements in accordance with generally accepted accounting principles, and that receipts and expenditures of the company are being made only in accordance with authorizations of management and directors of the company; and

(3) Provide reasonable assurance regarding prevention or timely detection of unauthorized acquisition, use or disposition of the company's assets that could have a material effect on the financial statements.

Because of its inherent limitations, internal control over financial reporting may not prevent or detect misstatements. Projections of any evaluation of effectiveness to future periods are subject to the risk that controls may become inadequate because of changes in conditions, or that the degree of compliance with the policies or procedures may deteriorate.

The Company's management assessed the effectiveness of the Company's internal control over financial reporting as of December 29, 2015. In making this assessment, the Company's management used the criteria established in *Internal Control - Integrated Framework* (2013), issued by the Committee of Sponsoring Organizations of the Treadway Commission. Based on its assessment, management has concluded that, as of December 29, 2015, the Company's internal control over financial reporting was effective to provide reasonable assurance based on those criteria. The scope of management's assessment of the effectiveness of internal control over financial reporting includes all of the Company's consolidated operations.

The Company's independent registered public accounting firm audited the financial statements included in this Annual Report on Form 10-K and has audited the effectiveness of the Company's internal control over financial reporting. Their report is included in Part II, Item 8 of this Annual Report on Form 10-K.

Glossary

A

Accelerated depreciation A higher amount of depreciation is recorded in the early years and a lower amount in the later years. (p. 363)

Account A record used to accumulate amounts for each individual asset, liability, revenue, expense, and component of stockholders' equity. (p. 107)

Accounting The process of identifying, measuring, and communicating economic information to various users. (p. 9)

Accounting controls Procedures concerned with safeguarding the assets or the reliability of the financial statements. (p. 287)

Accounting cycle A series of steps performed each period and culminating with the preparation of a set of financial statements. (p. 172)

Accounting system Methods and records used to accurately report an entity's transactions and to maintain accountability for its assets and liabilities. (p. 287)

Accounts payable Amounts owed for inventory, goods, or services acquired in the normal course of business. (p. 404)

Accounts receivable A receivable arising from the sale of goods or services with a verbal promise to pay. (p. 312)

Accounts receivable turnover ratio A measure of the number of times accounts receivable are collected during the period. (pp. 319, 635)

Accrual Cash has not yet been paid or received but expense has been incurred or revenue recognized. (p. 166)

Accrual basis A system of accounting in which revenues are recognized when a performance obligation is satisfied and expenses are recognized when incurred. (p. 153)

Accrued asset An asset resulting from the recognition of a revenue before the receipt of cash. (p. 166)

Accrued liability A liability that has been incurred but has not yet been paid. (pp. 166, 408)

Acid-test or quick ratio A stricter test of liquidity than the current ratio; excludes inventory and prepayments from the numerator. (p. 633)

Acid-test ratio Quick ratio. (p. 650)

Acquisition cost The amount that includes all of the cost normally necessary to acquire an asset and prepare it for its intended use. (p. 358)

Additional paid-in capital The amount received for the issuance of stock in excess of the par value of the stock. (p. 505)

Adjusting entries Journal entries made at the end of a period by a company using the accrual basis of accounting. (p. 158)

Administrative controls Procedures concerned with efficient operation of the business and adherence to managerial policies. (p. 287)

Aging schedule A form used to categorize the various individual accounts receivable according to the length of time each has been outstanding. (p. 317)

Allowance for doubtful accounts A contra-asset account used to reduce accounts receivable to its net realizable value. (p. 315)

Allowance method A method of estimating bad debts on the basis of either the net credit sales of the period or the accounts receivable at the end of the period. (p. 314)

American Institute of Certified Public Accountants (AICPA) The professional organization of certified public accountants. (p. 21)

Annuity A series of payments of equal amounts. (p. 420)

Asset A future economic benefit. (p. 7)

Asset turnover ratio The relationship between net sales and average total assets. (p. 642)

Audit committee A board of directors subset that acts as a direct contact between the stockholders and the independent accounting firm. (p. 285)

Auditing The process of examining the financial statements and the underlying records of a company to render an opinion as to whether the statements are fairly presented. (p. 22)

Auditors' report The opinion rendered by a public accounting firm concerning the fairness of the presentation of the financial statements. (p. 76)

Authorized shares The maximum number of shares a corporation may issue as indicated in the corporate charter. (p. 504)

B

Balance sheet The financial statement that summarizes the assets, liabilities, and owners' equity at a specific point in time. (p. 12)

Bank reconciliation A form used by the accountant to reconcile or resolve any differences between the balance shown on the bank statement for a particular account with the balance shown in the accounting records. (p. 281)

Bank statement A detailed list, provided by the bank, of all activity for a particular account during the month. (p. 279)

Blind receiving report A form used by the receiving department to account for the quantity and condition of merchandise received from a supplier. (p. 294)

Board of directors A group composed of key officers of a corporation and outside members responsible for general oversight of the affairs of the entity. (p. 285)

Bond A certificate that represents a corporation's promise to repay a certain amount of money and interest in the future. (p. 6)

Bond issue price The present value of the annuity of interest payments plus the present value of the principal. (p. 459)

Book value The original cost of an asset minus the amount of accumulated depreciation. (p. 362)

Book value per share Total stockholders' equity divided by the number of shares of common stock outstanding. (p. 518)

Bottom line Net income. (p. 589)

Business All of the activities necessary to provide the members of an economic system with goods and services. (p. 4)

Business entity An organization operated to earn a profit. (p. 5)

C

Callable feature Allows the firm to eliminate a class of stock by paying the stockholders a specified amount. (p. 506)

Callable bonds Bonds that may be redeemed or retired before their specified due date. (p. 458)

Capital expenditure A cost that improves the asset and is added to the asset account. (p. 367)

Capital lease A lease that is recorded as an asset by the lessee. (p. 469)

Capital stock Indicates the owners' contributions to a corporation. (p. 7)

Capitalization of interest Interest on constructed assets is added to the asset account. (p. 359)

Carrying value The face value of a bond plus the amount of unamortized premium or minus the amount of unamortized discount. (p. 463)

Cash basis A system of accounting in which revenues are recognized when cash is received and expenses are recognized when cash is paid. (p. 152)

Cash equivalent An investment that is readily convertible to a known amount of cash and has an original maturity to the investor of three months or less. (pp. 278, 558)

Cash flow from operations to capital expenditures ratio A measure of the ability of a company to finance long-term asset acquisitions with cash from operations. (p. 640)

Cash flow from operations to current liabilities ratio A measure of the ability to pay current debts from operating cash flows. (p. 634)

Cash-to-cash operating cycle The length of time from the purchase of inventory to the collection of any receivable from the sale. (p. 636)

Certified Public Accountant (CPA) The designation for an individual who has passed a uniform exam administered by the AICPA and has met other requirements as determined by individual states. (p. 21)

Change in estimate A change in the life of the asset or in its residual value. (p. 365)

Chart of accounts A numerical list of all accounts used by a company. (p. 107)

Closing entries Journal entries made at the end of the period to return the balance in all nominal accounts to zero and transfer the net income or loss and the dividends to Retained Earnings. (p. 174)

Comparability For accounting information, the quality that allows a user to analyze two or more companies and look for similarities and differences. (p. 54)

Compound interest Interest calculated on the principal plus previous amounts of interest. (p. 416)

Comprehensive income The total change in net assets from all sources except investments by or distributions to the owners. (p. 517)

Conservatism The practice of using the least optimistic estimate when two estimates of amounts are about equally likely. (p. 55)

Consistency For accounting information, the quality that allows a user to compare two or more accounting periods for a single company. (p. 54)

Contingent assets An existing condition for which the outcome is not known but by which the company stands to gain. (p. 414)

Contingent liability An existing condition for which the outcome is not known but depends on some future event. (p. 411)

Contra account An account with a balance that is opposite that of a related account. (p. 160)

Control account The general ledger account that is supported by a subsidiary ledger. (p. 312)

Convertible feature Allows preferred stock to be exchanged for common stock. (p. 506)

Corporation A form of entity organized under the laws of a particular state; ownership evidenced by shares of stock. (p. 5)

Cost of goods available for sale Beginning inventory plus cost of goods purchased. (p. 213)

Cost of goods sold Cost of goods available for sale minus ending inventory. (p. 213)

Cost principle Assets are recorded at the cost to acquire them. (p. 20)

Credit An entry on the right side of an account. (p. 112)

Credit memoranda Additions on a bank statement for such items as interest paid on the account and notes collected by the bank for the customer. (p. 281)

Creditor Someone to whom a company or person has a debt. (p. 7)

Cumulative feature The right to dividends in arrears before the current-year dividend is distributed. (p. 506)

Current assets An asset that is expected to be realized in cash or sold or consumed during the operating cycle or within one year if the cycle is shorter than one year. (p. 58)

Current liability An obligation that will be satisfied within the next operating cycle or within one year if the cycle is shorter than one year. (pp. 59, 404)

Current maturities of long-term debt The portion of a long-term liability that will be paid within one year. (p. 407)

Current ratio The ratio of current assets to current liabilities. (pp. 62, 633)

Current value The amount of cash or its equivalent that could be received by selling an asset currently. (p. 151)

D

Debenture bonds Bonds that are not backed by specific collateral. (p. 458)

Debit An entry on the left side of an account. (p. 112)

Debit memoranda Deductions on a bank statement for items such as NSF checks and various service charges. (p. 281)

Debt securities Securities issued by corporations and governmental bodies as a form of borrowing. (p. 327)

Debt service coverage ratio A statement of cash flows measure of the ability of a company to meet its interest and principal payments. (p. 639)

Debt-to-equity ratio The ratio of total liabilities to total stockholders' equity. (p. 638)

Deferral Cash has been paid or received but expense or revenue has not yet been recognized. (p. 166)

Deferred expense An asset resulting from the payment of cash before the incurrence of expense. (p. 166)

Deferred revenue A liability resulting from the receipt of cash before the recognition of revenue. (p. 166)

Deferred tax The account used to reconcile the difference between the amount recorded as income tax expense and the amount that is payable as income tax. (p. 478)

Deposit in transit A deposit recorded on the books but not yet reflected on the bank statement. (p. 280)

Depreciation The process of allocating the cost of a long-term tangible asset over its useful life. (pp. 54, 361)

Direct method For preparing the Operating Activities section of the statement of cash flows, the approach in which cash receipts and cash payments are reported. (p. 563)

Direct write-off method The recognition of bad debts expense at the point an account is written off as uncollectible. (p. 314)

Discount The excess of the face value of bonds over the issue price. (p. 460)

Discount on notes payable A contra-liability that represents interest deducted from a loan in advance. (p. 406)

Discounting The process of selling a promissory note. (p. 326)

Dividend payout ratio The annual dividend amount divided by the annual net income; the percentage of earnings paid out as dividends. (pp. 511, 646)

Dividend yield ratio The relationship between dividends and the market price of a company's stock. (p. 646)

Dividends A distribution of the net income of a business to its stockholders. (p. 14)

Double-declining-balance method Depreciation is recorded at twice the straight-line rate, but the balance is reduced each period. (p. 363)

Double-entry system A system of accounting in which every transaction is recorded with equal debits and credits, and the accounting equation is kept in balance. (p. 114)

E

Earnings per share (EPS) A company's bottom line stated on a per-share basis. (p. 644)

Economic entity concept The assumption that a single, identifiable unit must be accounted for in all situations. (p. 5)

Effective interest method of amortization The process of transferring a portion of the premium or discount to interest expense; this method results in a constant effective interest rate. (p. 463)

Equity securities Securities issued by corporations as a form of ownership in the business. (p. 327)

Estimated liability A contingent liability that is accrued and reflected on the balance sheet. (p. 412)

Event A happening of consequence to an entity. (p. 102)

Expenses Outflows of assets or incurrences of liabilities resulting from delivering goods, rendering services, or carrying out other activities. (pp. 7, 157)

External event An event involving interaction between an entity and its environment. (p. 102)

F

Face rate of interest The rate of interest on the bond certificate. (p. 458)

Face value The principal amount of the bond as stated on the bond certificate. (p. 457)

Faithful representation The quality of information that makes it complete, neutral, and free from error. (p. 54)

FIFO method An inventory costing method that assigns the most recent costs to ending inventory. (p. 226)

Financial accounting The branch of accounting concerned with the preparation of financial statements for outsider use. (p. 9)

Financial Accounting Standards Board (FASB) The group in the private sector with authority to set accounting standards. (p. 21)

Financing activities Activities concerned with the raising and repaying of funds in the form of debt and equity. (p. 561)

Finished goods A manufacturer's inventory that is complete and ready for sale. (p. 211)

FOB destination point Terms that require the seller to pay for the cost of shipping the merchandise to the buyer. (p. 217)

FOB shipping point Terms that require the buyer to pay for the shipping costs. (p. 217)

Future value of a single amount Amount accumulated at a future time from a single payment or investment. (p. 417)

Future value of an annuity The amount accumulated in the future when a series of payments is invested and accrues interest. (p. 420)

G

Gain on Sale of Asset The excess of the selling price over the asset's book value. (p. 370)

Gain or loss on redemption The difference between the carrying value and the redemption price at the time bonds are redeemed. (p. 467)

General journal The journal used in place of a specialized journal. (p. 118)

General ledger A book, a file, a hard drive, or another device containing all of the accounts. (p. 107)

Generally accepted accounting principles (GAAP) The various methods, rules, practices, and other procedures that have evolved over time in response to the need to regulate the preparation of financial statements. (p. 21)

Going concern The assumption that an entity is not in the process of liquidation and that it will continue indefinitely. (p. 20)

Goodwill The excess of the purchase price to acquire a business over the value of the individual net assets acquired. (p. 372)

Gross profit Net sales less cost of goods sold. (pp. 65, 211)

Gross profit ratio Gross profit divided by net sales. (pp. 218, 630)

H

Historical cost The amount paid for an asset and used as a basis for recognizing it on the balance sheet and carrying it on later balance sheets. (p. 150)

Horizontal analysis A comparison of financial statement items over a period of time. (p. 625)

I

Income statement A statement that summarizes revenues and expenses. (p. 13)

Indirect method For preparing the Operating Activities section of the statement of cash flows, the approach in which net income is reconciled to net cash flow from operations. (p. 563)

Intangible assets Assets with no physical properties. (p. 372)

Interim statements Financial statements prepared monthly, quarterly, or at other intervals less than a year in duration. (p. 174)

Internal audit staff The department responsible for monitoring and evaluating the internal control system. (p. 288)

Internal control report A report required by Section 404 of the Sarbanes-Oxley Act to be included in a company's annual report in which management assesses the effectiveness of the internal control structure. (p. 285)

Internal control system Policies and procedures necessary to ensure the safeguarding of an entity's assets, the reliability of its accounting records, and the accomplishment of overall company objectives. (p. 284)

Internal event An event occurring entirely within an entity. (p. 102)

International Accounting Standards Board (IASB) The organization formed to develop worldwide accounting standards. (p. 21)

Inventory profit The portion of the gross profit that results from holding inventory during a period of rising prices. (p. 230)

Inventory turnover ratio A measure of the number of times inventory is sold during a period. (pp. 238, 636)

Investing activities Activities concerned with the acquisition and disposal of long-term assets. (p. 560)

Invoice A form sent by the seller to the buyer as evidence of a sale. (p. 292)

Invoice approval form A form the accounting department uses before making payment to document the accuracy of all information about a purchase. (p. 294)

Issued shares The number of shares sold or distributed to stockholders. (p. 504)

J

Journal A chronological record of transactions. (p. 117)

Journalizing The act of recording journal entries. (p. 117)

K

Key terms for promissory notes These terms, with their definitions in the text, are important for your understanding. (p. 323)

L

Land improvements Costs that are related to land but that have a limited life. (p. 360)

Leverage The use of borrowed funds and amounts contributed by preferred stockholders to earn an overall return higher than the cost of these funds. (p. 644)

Liability An obligation of a business. (p. 6)

LIFO conformity rule The IRS requirement that when LIFO is used on a tax return, it must also be used in reporting income to stockholders. (p. 229)

LIFO liquidation The result of selling more units than are purchased during the period, which can have negative tax consequences if a company is using LIFO. (p. 228)

LIFO method An inventory costing method that assigns the most recent costs to cost of goods sold. (p. 227)

LIFO reserve The excess of the value of a company's inventory stated at FIFO over the value stated at LIFO. (p. 229)

Liquidity The ability of a company to pay its debts as they come due; the nearness to cash of the assets and liabilities. (pp. 62, 632)

Long-term liability An obligation that will not be satisfied within one year or the current operating cycle. (p. 456)

Loss on Sale of Asset The amount by which selling price is less than book value. (p. 370)

Lower-of-cost-or-market (LCM) rule A conservative inventory valuation approach that is an attempt to anticipate declines in the value of inventory before its actual sale. (p. 235)

M

Maker The party that agrees to repay the money for a promissory note at some future date. (p. 322)

Management accounting The branch of accounting concerned with providing management with information to facilitate planning and control. (p. 9)

Market rate of interest The rate that investors could obtain by investing in other bonds that are similar to the issuing firm's bonds. (p. 458)

Market value per share The selling price of the stock as indicated by the most recent transactions. (p. 519)

Matching principle The association of revenue of a period with all of the costs necessary to generate that revenue. (p. 156)

Materiality The magnitude of an accounting information omission or misstatement that will affect the judgment of someone relying on the information. (p. 55)

Merchandise Inventory The account wholesalers and retailers use to report inventory held for resale. (p. 210)

Monetary unit The yardstick used to measure amounts in financial statements; the dollar in the United States. (p. 20)

Moving average The name given to an average cost method when a weighted average cost assumption is used with a perpetual inventory system. (p. 244)

Multiple-step income statement An income statement that shows classifications of revenues and expenses as well as important subtotals. (p. 65)

N

Net income The excess of revenues over expenses. (p. 13)

Net realizable value The amount a company expects to collect on an account receivable. (p. 313)

Net sales Sales revenue less sales returns and allowances and sales discounts. (p. 212)

Nominal accounts The name given to revenue, expense, and dividend accounts because they are temporary and are closed at the end of the period. (p. 174)

Nonbusiness entity An organization operated for some purpose other than to earn a profit. (p. 6)

Note payable A liability resulting from the signing of a promissory note. (pp. 323, 405)

Note receivable An asset resulting from the acceptance of a promissory note from another company. (p. 323)

Number of days' sales in inventory A measure of how long it takes to sell inventory. (pp. 239, 636)

Number of days' sales in receivables A measure of the average age of accounts receivable. (pp. 321, 635)

O

Operating activities Activities concerned with the acquisition and sale of products and services. (p. 560)

Operating cycle The period of time between the purchase of inventory and the collection of any receivable from the sale of the inventory. (p. 57)

Operating lease A lease that does not meet any of the four criteria and is not recorded as an asset by the lessee. (p. 469)

Outstanding check A check written by a company but not yet presented to the bank for payment. (p. 279)

Outstanding shares The number of shares issued less the number of shares held as treasury stock. (p. 504)

Owners' equity The owners' claims on the assets of an entity. (p. 11)

P

Par value An arbitrary amount that represents the legal capital of the firm. (p. 504)

Participating feature Allows preferred stockholders to share on a percentage basis in the distribution of an abnormally large dividend. (p. 506)

Partnership A business owned by two or more individuals that has the characteristic of unlimited liability; the organization form often used by accounting firms and law firms. (pp. 5, 523)

Partnership agreement Specifies how much the owners will invest, what their salaries will be, and how profits will be shared. (p. 524)

Payee The party that will receive the money from a promissory note at some future date. (p. 322)

Periodic system A system in which the Inventory account is updated only at the end of the period. (p. 214)

Permanent difference A difference that affects the tax records but not the accounting records, or vice versa. (p. 478)

Perpetual system A system in which the Inventory account is increased at the time of each purchase and decreased at the time of each sale. (p. 214)

Petty cash fund Money kept on hand for making minor disbursements in coin and currency rather than by writing checks. (p. 283)

Posting The process of transferring amounts from a journal to the ledger accounts. (p. 117)

Premium The excess of the issue price over the face value of the bonds. (p. 460)

Present value of a single amount The amount at a present time that is equivalent to a payment or an investment at a future time. (p. 419)

Present value of an annuity The amount at a present time that is equivalent to a series of payments and interest in the future. (p. 421)

Price/earnings (P/E) ratio The relationship between a company's performance according to the income statement and its performance in the stock market. (pp. 645, 650)

Profit margin Net income divided by sales. (p. 66)

Profit margin ratio Net income to net sales. (p. 630)

Profitability How well management is using company resources to earn a return on the funds invested by various groups. (p. 641)

Promissory note A written promise to repay a definite sum of money on demand or at a fixed or determinable date in the future. (p. 322)

Public Company Accounting Oversight Board (PCAOB) The five-member body created by the Sarbanes-Oxley Act that was given the authority to set auditing standards in the United States. (pp. 21, 285)

Purchase order A form sent by the purchasing department to the supplier. (p. 292)

Purchase requisition form A form a department uses to initiate a request to order merchandise. (p. 292)

Purchases An account used in a periodic inventory system to record acquisitions of merchandise. (p. 216)

R

Raw materials The inventory of a manufacturer before the addition of any direct labor or manufacturing overhead. (p. 210)

Real accounts The name given to balance sheet accounts because they are permanent and are not closed at the end of the period. (p. 174)

Recognition The process of recording an item in the financial statements as an asset, a liability, a revenue, an expense, or the like. (p. 150)

Redeemable feature Allows stockholders to sell stock back to the company. (p. 506)

Relevance The capacity of information to make a difference in a decision. (p. 54)

Replacement cost The current cost of a unit of inventory. (p. 230)

Research and development costs Costs incurred in the discovery of new knowledge. (p. 372)

Retained earnings The part of stockholders' equity that represents the income earned less dividends paid over the life of an entity. (pp. 12, 505)

Retirement of stock When the stock is repurchased with no intention of reissuing at a later date. (p. 509)

Return on assets ratio A measure of a company's success in earning a return for all providers of capital. (p. 641)

Return on common stockholders' equity ratio A measure of a company's success in earning a return for the common stockholders. (p. 643)

Return on sales ratio A variation of the profit margin ratio; measures earnings before payments to creditors. (p. 642)

Revenue An inflow of assets resulting from the sale of goods and services. (p. 7)

Revenue expenditure A cost that keeps an asset in its normal operating condition and is treated as an expense. (p. 367)

Revenue recognition principle Revenues are recognized when a performance obligation is satisfied. (p. 155)

Revenues Inflows of assets or settlements of liabilities from delivering or producing goods, rendering services, or conducting other activities. (p. 155)

S

Sales revenue A representation of the inflow of assets from the sale of a product. (p. 211)

Sarbanes-Oxley Act An act of Congress in 2002 intended to bring reform to corporate accountability and stewardship in the wake of a number of major corporate scandals. (pp. 25, 284)

Securities and Exchange Commission (SEC) The federal agency with ultimate authority to determine the rules for preparing statements for companies whose stock is sold to the public. (p. 21)

Serial bonds Bonds that do not all have the same due date; a portion of the bonds comes due each time period. (p. 458)

Share of stock A certificate that acts as evidence of ownership in a corporation. (p. 5)

Simple interest Interest is calculated on the principal amount only. (p. 416)

Single-step income statement An income statement in which all expenses are added together and subtracted from all revenues. (p. 64)

Sole proprietorships A form of organization with a single owner. (pp. 5, 522)

Solvency The ability of a company to remain in business over the long term. (p. 638)

Source document A piece of paper that is used as evidence to record a transaction. (p. 102)

Specific identification method An inventory costing method that relies on matching unit costs with the actual units sold. (p. 224)

Statement of cash flows The financial statement that summarizes a company's cash receipts and cash payments during the period from operating, investing, and financing activities. (pp. 14, 556)

Statement of retained earnings The statement that summarizes the income earned and dividends paid over the life of a business. (p. 14)

Statement of stockholders' equity Reflects the differences between beginning and ending balances for all accounts in the Stockholders' Equity category of the balance sheet. (p. 516)

Stock dividend The issuance of additional shares of stock to existing stockholders. (p. 512)

Stock split The creation of additional shares of stock with a reduction of the par value of the stock. (p. 514)

Stockholder One of the owners of a corporation. (p. 7)

Stockholders' equity The owners' equity in a corporation. (p. 12)

Straight-line method A method by which the same dollar amount of depreciation is recorded in each year of asset use. (pp. 160, 362)

Subsidiary ledger The detail for a number of individual items that collectively make up a single general ledger account. (p. 312)

T

Temporary differences A difference that affects both book and tax records but not in the same time period. (p. 479)

Time period An artificial segment on the calendar used as the basis for preparing financial statements. (p. 21)

Time value of money An immediate amount should be preferred over an amount in the future. (p. 415)

Times interest earned ratio An income statement measure of the ability of a company to meet its interest payments. (p. 638)

Transaction Any event that is recognized in a set of financial statements. (p. 102)

Transportation-In An adjunct account used to record freight costs paid by the buyer. (p. 216)

Treasury stock Stock issued by the firm and then repurchased but not retired. (p. 507)

Trial balance A list of each account and its balance; used to prove equality of debits and credits. (p. 119)

U

Understandability The quality of accounting information that makes it comprehensible to those willing to spend the necessary time. (p. 53)

Units-of-production method Depreciation is determined as a function of the number of units the asset produces. (p. 362)

V

Vertical analysis A comparison of various financial statement items within a single period with the use of common-size statements. (p. 625)

W

Weighted average cost method An inventory costing method that assigns the same unit cost to all units available for sale during the period. (p. 225)

Work in process The cost of unfinished products in a manufacturing company. (p. 211)

Work sheet A device used at the end of the period to gather the information needed to prepare financial statements without actually recording and posting adjustments. (p. 173)

Working capital Current assets minus current liabilities. (pp. 62, 632)

Index

Real company names, individuals, and key terms appear in boldfaced type, and any page numbers where definitions appear are also in bold.

Ethics and Accounting: A Decision-Making Model

IDENTIFICATION

1. **Recognize an ethical dilemma.**

   - Conflicting accounting rules.
   - No GAAP to follow.
   - Fraud or other questionable actions have occurred.

ANALYSIS

2. **Analyze the key elements in the situation.**

   - Who benefits?
   - Who is harmed?
   - What are their rights and claims?
   - What are the conflicting interests?
   - What are the accountant's responsibilities?

3. **List alternatives and evaluate the impact on each of those affected.**

   - Most useful and timely information for decisions?
   - Most complete, relevant and a faithful representation for decision makers?
   - Most accurate information?
   - Is the information free from bias?
   - Most likely impact on those affected?

RESOLUTION

4. **Select the best alternative.**

   - Which alternative is most relevant, most complete, most neutral, and most free from error?

Making Business Decisions

RATIO ANALYSIS MODEL

1. Formulate the Question.
2. Gather the Information from the Financial Statements.
3. Calculate the Ratio.
4. Compare the Ratio with Other Ratios.
5. Interpret the Ratios.

BUSINESS DECISION MODEL

1. Formulate the Question.
2. Gather the Information from the Financial Statements and Other Sources.
3. Analyze the Information Gathered.
4. Make the Decision.
5. Monitor Your Decision.

SUMMARY OF SELECTED FINANCIAL RATIOS

RATIO NAME	FORMULA	PAGE REFERENCE*
Liquidity Analysis		
Working capital	Current Assets − Current Liabilities	62, 632
Current ratio	$\dfrac{\text{Current Assets}}{\text{Current Liabilities}}$	**73–74**, 633, 647
Acid-test ratio (quick ratio)	$\dfrac{\text{Cash + Marketable Securities + Current Receivables}}{\text{Current Liabilities}}$	633, 647
Cash flow from operations to current liabilities ratio	$\dfrac{\text{Net Cash Provided by Operating Activities}}{\text{Average Current Liablities}}$	634, 647
Accounts receivable turnover ratio	$\dfrac{\text{Net Credit Sales}}{\text{Average Accounts Receivable}}$	**319–321**, 635, 647
Number of days' sales in receivables	$\dfrac{\text{Number of Days in the Period}}{\text{Accounts Receivable Turnover}}$	**321**, 635, 647
Inventory turnover ratio	$\dfrac{\text{Cost of Goods Sold}}{\text{Average Inventory}}$	**238–239**, 636, 647
Number of days' sales in inventory	$\dfrac{\text{Number of Days in the Period}}{\text{Inventory Turnover}}$	**239**, 636, 647
Cash-to-cash operating cycle	Number of Days' Sales in Inventory + Number of Days' Sales in Receivables	636, 647
Solvency Analysis		
Debt-to-equity ratio	$\dfrac{\text{Total Liabilities}}{\text{Total Stockholders' Equity}}$	473, **474–476**, 638, 647
Times interest earned ratio	$\dfrac{\text{Net Income + Interest Expense + Income Tax Expense}}{\text{Interest Expense}}$	473, **474–476**, 638, 647
Debt service coverage ratio	$\dfrac{\text{Cash Flow from Operations before Interest and Tax Payments}}{\text{Interest and Principal Payments}}$	639, 647
Cash flow from operations to capital expenditures ratio	$\dfrac{\text{Cash Flow from Operations − Total Dividends Paid}}{\text{Cash Paid for Acquisitions}}$	640, 647
Profitability Analysis		
Gross profit ratio	$\dfrac{\text{Gross Profit}}{\text{Net Sales}}$	**219–220**, 647
Profit margin ratio	$\dfrac{\text{Net Income}}{\text{Net Sales}}$	75, 647
Return on assets ratio	$\dfrac{\text{Net Income + Interest Expense, Net of Tax}}{\text{Average Total Assets}}$	641, 647
Return on sales ratio	$\dfrac{\text{Net Income + Interest Expense, Net of Tax}}{\text{Net Sales}}$	642, 647
Asset turnover ratio	$\dfrac{\text{Net Sales}}{\text{Average Total Assets}}$	642, 647
Return on common stockholders' equity ratio	$\dfrac{\text{Net Income − Preferred Dividends}}{\text{Average Common Stockholders' Equity}}$	643, 647
Earnings per share	$\dfrac{\text{Net Income − Preferred Dividends}}{\text{Weighted Average Number of Common Shares Outstanding}}$	644, 647
Price/earnings ratio	$\dfrac{\text{Current Market Price}}{\text{Earnings per Share}}$	645, 647
Dividend payout ratio	$\dfrac{\text{Common Dividends per Share}}{\text{Earnings per Share}}$	646, 647
Dividend yield ratio	$\dfrac{\text{Common Dividends per Share}}{\text{Market Price per Share}}$	646, 647
Cash flow adequacy	$\dfrac{\text{Cash Flow from Operating Activities − Capital Expenditures}}{\text{Average Amount of Debt Maturing over Next Five Years}}$	**583–585**, 589

*boldface = Ratio Analysis Model

The Accounting Equation

The accounting equation is the foundation for the entire accounting system:

Assets = Liabilities + Owners' Equity

or

Assets = Liabilities + Stockholders' Equity

Accounting Equation and the Balance Sheet

Assets = Liabilities + Stockholders' Equity

Economic resources
Examples:
• Cash
• Accounts receivable
• Land

Creditors' claims to the assets
Examples:
• Accounts payable
• Notes payable

Owners' claims to the assets
Examples:
• Capital stock
• Retained earnings

The Financial Statements

Balance Sheet *shows* assets, liabilities, and stockholders' equity at a certain date.

Income Statement *shows* revenues and expenses for the period.

Statement of Retained Earnings *shows* changes in retained earnings during the period.

Statement of Cash Flows *shows* cash flow effects of operating, investing, and financing activities for the period.

Relationships among the Financial Statements

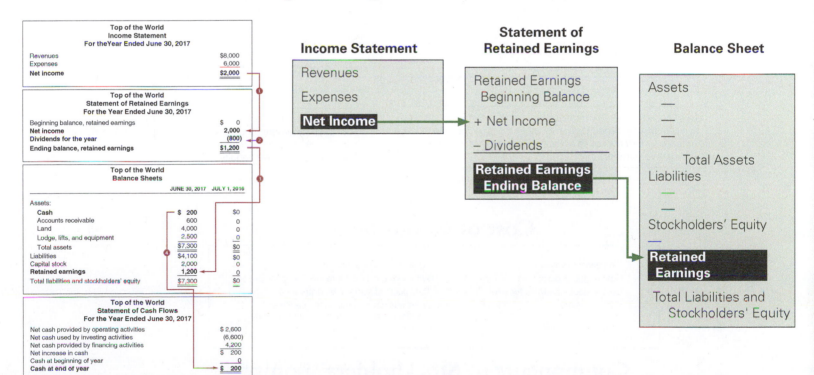

Transaction Analysis*

	Assets					=	Liabilities		+	Stockholders' Equity	
Transaction Number	Cash	Accounts Receivable	Equipment	Building	Land		Accounts Payable	Notes Payable		Capital Stock	Retained Earnings

*The accounts shown here are one possible set of accounts.

EXHIBIT 3-5 Introducing the Identify and Analyze Transaction Format

> Example: Transaction 4, p. 104 : Sale of monthly memberships on account:

Transaction Analysis Format (used in **Ch. 3**)

- Shows how transactions are analyzed in account names (**Cash, Accounts Receivable**, etc., as shown below) and accounting equation categories (**Assets, Liabilities, Stockholders' Equity**). (Amounts are eventually reflected in the financial statements.)

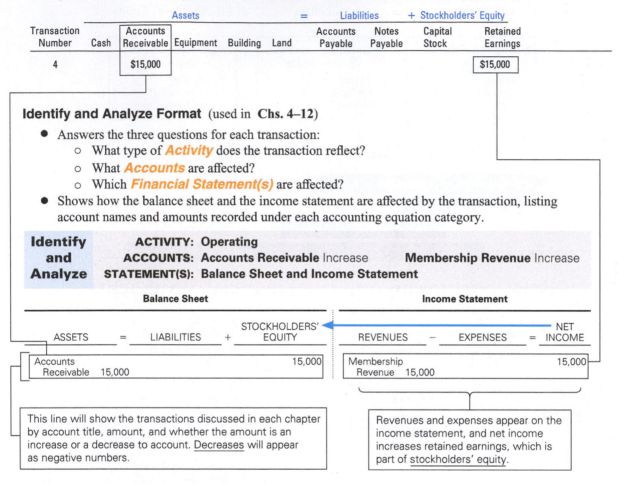

		Assets				=	Liabilities		+	Stockholders' Equity	
Transaction Number	Cash	Accounts Receivable	Equipment	Building	Land		Accounts Payable	Notes Payable		Capital Stock	Retained Earnings
4		$15,000									$15,000

Identify and Analyze Format (used in **Chs. 4–12**)

- Answers the three questions for each transaction:
  - What type of *Activity* does the transaction reflect?
  - What *Accounts* are affected?
  - Which *Financial Statement(s)* are affected?
- Shows how the balance sheet and the income statement are affected by the transaction, listing account names and amounts recorded under each accounting equation category.

Identify and Analyze	**ACTIVITY:** Operating	
	ACCOUNTS: Accounts Receivable Increase	**Membership Revenue** Increase
	STATEMENT(S): Balance Sheet and Income Statement	

Balance Sheet			Income Statement		
ASSETS	= LIABILITIES	+ STOCKHOLDERS' EQUITY	REVENUES	− EXPENSES	= NET INCOME
Accounts Receivable 15,000		15,000	Membership Revenue 15,000		15,000

This line will show the transactions discussed in each chapter by account title, amount, and whether the amount is an increase or a decrease to account. Decreases will appear as negative numbers.

Revenues and expenses appear on the income statement, and net income increases retained earnings, which is part of stockholders' equity.

Cost of Goods Sold

	Beginning inventory	What is on hand to start the period
+	Cost of goods purchased	What was acquired for resale during the period
=	Cost of goods available for sale	The "pool" of costs to be distributed
−	Ending inventory	What was not sold during the period and therefore is on hand to start the next period
=	Cost of goods sold	What was sold during the period

Components of Stockholders' Equity

Assets = Liabilities + Stockholders' Equity

Total Stockholders' Equity = Contributed Capital
+
Retained Earnings